THE THIRD REICH

THE THIRD REICH

HOWARD FERTIG

NEW YORK   1975

First published in Great Britain in 1955
by George Weidenfeld & Nicolson Ltd.
Howard Fertig, Inc. Edition 1975
Published by arrangement with
George Weidenfeld & Nicolson Ltd.

Library of Congress Cataloging in Publication Data
International Council for Philosophy and Humanistic
Studies
   The Third Reich.
   Reprint of the 1955 ed. published by Weidenfeld and
Nicolson, London.
   Essays,
   Includes bibliographical references.
   1.   National socialism—Addresses, essays, lectures.
2.   Germany—Politics and government—1933-1945—
Addresses, essays, lectures.   3.   Nationalism—Germany
—Addresses, essays, lectures.   I.   Title.
DD256.5.I58   1975   320.5'33   74-19383

Printed in the United States of America

This volume is published under the auspices of the International Council for Philosophy and Humanistic Studies and with the assistance of UNESCO

CONTENTS

INTRODUCTION
Jacques Rueff

INTRODUCTION
Jacques Rueff

THE present inquiry into the methods and procedure of Fascism and Nazism was first agreed to in principle by the General Conference of UNESCO, held at Beirut in November–December 1948.

The resolution, which was proposed by Mr McKeon, the United States delegate, and seconded by Mme Saunte, the Danish delegate, was adopted in the following terms:

> 4.33 'A conference of leading authorities on the subject ought to be held, in order to draw up a report on the methods and procedure used to propagate Fascism and Nazism in the period preceeding the Second World War: this should help to make possible the identification of similar movements in the future, from the first moment of their appearance. The conclusions reached in this report ought to be made known as widely as possible.'

In the course of a conversation which took place soon after this, Dr Torres Bodet, Director-General of UNESCO, asked me if the International Council for Philosophy and Humanistic Studies would be willing to undertake the supervision of the proposed report.

This request raised a serious problem for the Council. It had only been in existence a year as an institution, and showed the inexperience of youth, as well as natural enthusiasm, in the way it tackled the multitude of tasks which faced it.

After an introductory memorandum by M. Klineberg, head of the Social Science Division of UNESCO, the Standing Committee of the Council settled down to an exhaustive discussion of the whole question, during its session of the 3rd–5th May 1949. Finally it accepted the responsibility of the proposed inquiry, and set up, under its supervision, a special committee to carry it out.

This Committee was composed of MM. Robert Fawtier, Carsten Hoeg, H. J. Pos, Paul Rivet, Jacques Rueff, and Alf. Sommerfelt.

After a preliminary examination of the task before it, the Committee invited a number of leading authorities on the subject to collaborate in the development of the project, in the course of a meeting from 15th to 18th November 1949. Those who took part, in addition to members of the Committee of the Council already named, were as follows:

Professor Kurt Latte, Germany
Professor G. Ritter, Germany
Canon Gregoire, Belgium
Professor Troels Fink, Denmark
Professor Hammerich, Denmark
M. Maurice Baumont, France
M. S. Grumbach, France
Dr Minkowsky, France
M. Poliakoff, France

M. E. Vermeil, France
M. Henri Wallon, France
Mrs Eva Reichmann, Great Britain
Mr A. J. P. Taylor, Great Britain
M. L. de Jong, Holland
Dr John Fried, U.S.A.
Dr O. Klineberg, U.S.A.

UNESCO was represented by Dr Thompson and Dr Klineberg. The Committee recognised that the terms of the Beirut resolution limited the proposed report to the methods and procedure used to propagate Fascism and Nazism in Italy and Germany, and gave it a definite aim: the quickest possible identification of any similar movements which might appear in the future. It was thought that this limitation, which gave the proposed report a descriptive, rather than an explanatory character, greatly reduced both its usefulness and interest. The Committee was unanimous in thinking that, without in any way detracting from the importance of the facts, it was essential to trace both movements to their underlying causes, and place them in the historical setting from which they had emerged.

The Committee also decided, provided the appropriate authorities approved, to divide the task which had been entrusted to it into three sub-commissions.

The first, of which M. H. J. Pos was to be president and M. Vermeil *rapporteur*, was commissioned to study the philosophic origins of Fascism amd Nazism; the second, presided over by M. Jacques Rueff, with M. Baumont as *rapporteur*, was to study the circumstances which made possible the transformation of an ideology into a political programme; and the third, over which Dr O. Klineberg presided and of which Dr Fried was *rapporteur*, was to devote itself to a detailed study of the techniques and methods of Fascism and Nazism.

The collective nature of the work that has been accomplished makes it necessary for the Committee to emphasise that each author was given the entire responsibility for his contribution. No attempt was made to determine the scope of the studies which have been commissioned, and only their subject was fixed beforehand. The Committee preferred a certain amount of overlapping to an over-strict regimentation which would have interfered with the creative freedom of the authors.

The Committee has not shrunk from including clearly expressed opinions, even in the political sphere. Many of the subjects discussed demanded that the author should make his own attitude clear, and each author has been allowed perfect freedom to adopt his point of view. The Committee prefers sincerity and plain speaking to the impersonal neutrality of a lifeless report. But it goes without saying that in publishing the individual contributions which have been given to them, the Committee has been careful to leave with the authors the entire responsibility for the ideas which they have expressed.

Originally this book was intended to deal equally fully with Fascism and Nazism. But owing to unforeseen circumstances, a number of contributors who had been asked for works on Fascism found it impossible to complete their work within the allotted time. In order to avoid a delay in the publication of the work, the Council decided, with the approval of the Director-General of UNESCO, to divide the publication of the book into two distinct parts. Only the section on Nazism is given here.

In my capacity as President of the Council for Philosophy and Humanistic Studies, I take this opportunity to express my gratitude to the Presidents of the Commissions, the secretaries, and the other contributors, who did not hesitate to add to their ordinary work the heavy weight of additional research, in a relatively short time.

I ought also to record the trouble which the Council has taken over this work, and the doubts and difficulties it has experienced with regard to it.

The inquiry into Fascism and Nazism has been a notable experience for our Council. However excellent the contributions we have collected, we are conscious that our inquiry is not complete. We have discovered the many difficulties which an institution like ours undergoes in selecting contributors and obtaining their co-operation in good time. We have done our best to solve these problems. We await the verdict of enlightened opinion on the result of our work and the place the Council should reserve for research in its work in the future.

Jacques Rueff

President of the International Council
for Philosophy and Humanistic Studies
Membre de l'Institut de France

PART ONE

I

THE ORIGIN, NATURE AND DEVELOPMENT OF GERMAN NATIONALIST IDEOLOGY IN THE 19TH AND 20TH CENTURIES

Edmond Vermeil

I. WHAT IS MEANT BY 'NATIONAL REVOLUTION'?

MANY Germans, who have studied National-Socialism, have been all too ready to deny the existence of an ideology peculiar to it, or, if they admit of its existence, they separate it from the traditions which go to make up their national cultural heritage.[1]

In 1935, for example, historians who had come from Germany to hold discussions with their French colleagues in Paris suggested that we attached too much importance to Pangermanism.[2] Hjalmar Schacht states quite dogmatically in his memoirs that it is impossible to find in the Hitler movement an ideology in which the movement's principles are clearly formulated.[3] Then Karl Jaspers, in his forceful study of responsibility, seems to place the racial theories and the mass mysticism of the Third Reich outside German culture as such.[4]

This is a complex but also a vital question. It will be dealt with

---

[1] For the whole of this essay I have drawn both on my own works and also on the four volumes which Charles Andler, with the help of many collaborators, devoted to Pangermanism at the time of the First World War.

These volumes appeared under the following titles:

> Les Origines du Pangermanisme (1800–88) (L. Conard, Paris, 1915).
> Le Pangermanisme continental sous Guillaume II (L. Conard, Paris, 1915).
> Le Pangermanisme colonial sous Guillaume II (L. Conard, Paris, 1916).
> Le Pangermanisme philosophique (1800–1914) (L. Conard, Paris, 1917).

They give an extremely full documentation, but in the form of individual monographs, biographical notes, and texts carefully edited and translated from German. This abundance of material, unique in the world, is presented here in summarised form and arranged chronologically. In fact the four volumes themselves can be arranged chronologically in the following order: Les Origines du Pangermanisme, le Pangermanisme philosophique, le Pangermanisme continental, le Pangermanisme colonial. We shall refer to them in this order as: C.A.I, C.A.II, C.A.III, C.A.IV.

Abbé Laberthonnière, 'Pangermanisme et Christianisme' in Oeuvres de Laberthonnière published by Louis Canet (I. Vrin, Paris, 1945).

Other collections of texts have appeared in French and English, but they add nothing of note to the works cited above.

[2] See Probleme der deutschfranzösischen Geschichtsschreibung (Baden-Baden, 1949).

[3] Hjalmar Schacht, Abrechnung mit Hitler. English translation: Account Settled (Weidenfeld & Nicolson, London).   [4] Karl Jaspers, Die Schuldfrage.

3

here objectively, *sine ira et studio*; only thus can, and must, the investigations instigated by Unesco bear full fruit.

Why this strange conjunction (in Germany) of such terms as 'national' and 'social'? Why this peculiar bracketing of 'Socialism' and 'nationalism'? And, above all, why should the term 'revolution' be applied to the unusual historical phenomenon we have just witnessed? [1]

Jakob Burckhardt, the famous Swiss historian, was the first to realise the meaning and complexity of this phenomenon. His prophetic gaze had fallen on the example previously set to the world by France when she passed suddenly from democracy to cæsarism. Instead of the healthy, productive compromise which the Western revolutions had achieved between the passion for individual freedom and the collective institutions which mass impetus had made indispensable, came the despotism of 'terrible simplifiers'. It was on military force that they relied to bend the masses to their will and force them to repudiate the elementary freedoms so recently acquired.

This explains the second revolutionary wave, which is so fundamentally different from the first. It is a revolution of *bourgeois* nationalism, sustained and inspired by grandiose colonial ambitions. It has nothing in common with the social revolution which should logically have taken place in 1789 and only broke out much later; this is a so-called 'national' revolution which moves inexorably towards a goal of power and expansion. It does not presuppose the destruction of an outworn collective order. It comes to terms with what remains of the old aristocracies, who are joined by the upper middle-class of the business world. It professes to protect and conserve the privileges of wealth and culture. It defends the interests of a class which threatens Socialism. The difference between this *bourgeois* national imperialism and the socialist conception of a world proletarian revolution could not be more fundamental.

The historian, when he comes to study these two varieties of revolution, is immediately confronted with perfectly legitimate claims. If Socialism is concerned with guaranteeing the working masses a reasonable existence and regards this as inevitably bound up with a struggle for political power, *bourgeois* imperialism aims at economic success, from which all classes of the nation should profit, and which may therefore with some justice be called 'social', if not 'socialist'.

In other words, in a young nation like Germany, only recently united by Bismarck, the thesis 'justice between nations' either goes together with or is opposed to the thesis 'justice between classes'.

---

[1] See Fr. Meinecke, *Die deutsche Katastrophe* (1946) for excellent passages on the union of Nationalism and Socialism in Germany and the origins of German Fascism.

Here, and here only, lies the very core of the German enigma. In the nineteenth century, Germany, through Karl Marx, formulated a programme of world social revolution. But she was caught up in an industrial revolution of unprecedented magnitude and speed, carried away, after centuries of internal disruption, by a sudden upsurge of nationalism, and her *bourgeoisie*, shrinking from the menace of Socialism, voluntarily abandoned Liberalism and, together with the middle-class, joined forces with those who until recently had been the ruling class, the heirs of absolute rule. Their imperial dream, which owes nothing to either East or West, is adequately represented by Pangermanism.

To the experienced historian Bismarck's Germany takes two distinct forms: that of a centralised national state under the hegemony of Prussia and that of a super-nation, of a greater Germany, which regards itself as the mother of the European nations, and therefore as called upon to dominate and rule them—in other words to transform them, too, into a 'projection of Prussia'.

With the outbreak of the First World War, this German *bourgeois* imperialism succeeded in enlisting the support of a section of the Social Democrats, whose Socialism had been tainted by opportunism and who had been won over some time before to the colonial ambitions of the *bourgeoisie*. From then on, the idea of a revolution that was both 'national' and 'social' or, more precisely perhaps, of a total irruption (*Durchbruch*) of Germanism in Europe and the world completely overshadowed the idea of a socialist revolution. The German proletariat, which has already been partly won over before 1914, succumbs a second time, after the 1918 defeat and the unfortunate Weimar Republic that follows, and falls victim to the fanatical nationalism of the Third Reich. The Third Reich also believes itself justified in assuming the title 'National-Socialist'. It can only do so by vulgarising and bringing within reach of the disillusioned masses the programme which the *élite* had drawn up in the nineteenth century, which had been considerably expanded under Wilhelm II, and then resuscitated under the ægis of the Republic.

In a work entitled *Die Deutsche Katastrophe*, which appeared in 1946, Fr. Meinecke, the greatest of contemporary German historians, attributes the breach which seems to have appeared between the advanced cosmopolitan culture of the past and the *bourgeois* imperialism of the last 200 years, to the spread of Prussian militarism and disciplinarianism throughout all classes of society, to the psychological insecurity that appears to have seized the Germans as a result of repeated crises, and finally to the failure to reconcile *bourgeois* nationalism and socialist aspirations. Hardly had Bismarck's dominating personality left the political stage in 1890, when these latent incongruities asserted themselves and the Germans *en masse* seemed to run amok until, in the fateful years 1933–45, the country was subjected to the arbitrary power of leaders who were no longer worthy of its confidence.

II. THE HISTORICAL FOUNDATIONS OF GERMAN NATIONALISM

At various periods of their history, and particularly in the nineteenth century, the Germans have believed with a desperate conviction, born either of their internal divisions and weaknesses or, on the contrary, of the idea of a sovereign and invincible power, that they have a divine mission, that Germany has been singled out by Providence. By virtue of a superior right and sustained by Prussian arms, the Germanic community, they have thought, must prevail over its neighbours as it prevails over its own members, over their many activities, and over the means by which its pre-eminence can be assured.

1. Origins up to the Fourteenth Century

This irrational and fervent faith is the outcome of a historical development which, throughout the centuries, gives the German imagination, with its combination of fanatical nationalism and pre-occupation with internal cohesion, precedents which it can never forget and on which it builds up limitless aspirations.

Hence the constant references to the struggles between the Teutons and the Romans, to the legendary fame of Arminius, and above all to the migrations. The Germans dislike the word 'barbarian' as applied to the great invasions. Herder launched a violent attack on Voltaire for describing the invaders as 'savages'. Long before the Romantics he saw in them the saviours of medieval Europe. It was Herder who evolved the thesis that the Teutons brought youth and virility to a declining and corrupt world. Herder believed that the Teutons had a divine mission. He naturally linked up their emergence with that of Christianity. Klopstock, and later on the Romantics, confidently followed the same line of argument. One need only read Fichte or Fr. Schlegel to find confirmation of this.[1]

Under the influence of J. J. Rousseau, the famous antithesis between nature and civilisation was frequently exploited in Germany to elaborate these phenomena of history which were easy to elaborate because they were difficult to establish. A number of historians stressed the contrast between the civilisation of Rome, with its selfish individualism, its abuse of legal contracts, its cult of private property, its state absolutism, and its highly-developed culture, and the Germanic world with its sentiment (*Gefühl*) and dynamic drive

[1] See Vermeil, *L'Allemagne, Essai d'explication* (Gallimard, Paris, 1945), pp. 46 ff.

(*Wucht*), its spontaneous instinct and its burning passion, and its link between religious ritual and military discipline. Such old clichés were constantly revived and led to grave misunderstandings.

It will always be a subject of speculation to what extent the dynasties, which attempted between 450 and 1050 to unify those parts of Europe represented today by Germany, France, Spain, and Italy, actually succeeded in blending the Germanic tradition with the contributions made by the ancient and Christian civilisations of the Mediterranean. The view of a historian like Adolf Bartels is typical. He considers that 'a Germanic culture, pagan and warlike, a true culture endowed with a proud, moral virility such as one finds in a highly-developed poetic tradition, came into conflict with Latin and Christian "pacifism",' and he adds: 'It was the peace-loving culture that gained the ascendancy over the war-like culture'. He deplores the destruction of Aryanism as a mortal blow to Germanic development. The polished civilisation of the Latin countries undermined the healthy and virile customs of the people.

Others argue, however, that the Carolingian renaissance and the renaissance under the Ottos, far from achieving their aim, which was to preserve the Germanic tradition but at the same time imbue it with the Christian spirit, were not motivated solely by a Germanic ideal. Karl Lamprecht asserts quite positively that the victory of the Church imposed on Germany during that remote period a culture which was contrary to her own heroic traditions.

Underlying all the German literary outpourings between 1150 and the end of the thirteenth century there is, as we know, a constant struggle between ideas of ancestral paganism, memories of Greco-Roman antiquity, and a Christian teaching adapted to contemporary requirements. It is reflected in poems, such as the 'Nibelungen' and 'Gudrun', in the 'Round Table' stories, and in Gottfried's 'Tristan', in the poems of Hartmann von Aue and Walter von der Vogelweide. No one seems to have captured the spirit of that time more vividly than Wolfram von Eschenbach. In his 'Parzival', a mixture of aggressive paganism, of rustic enthusiasm, and aristocratic fervour, which has remained a characteristic feature of the German soul, is offset by the moderation and restraint of a Christian-cum-Hellenist. His Community of the Grail is a tolerant Church with strong Germanic leanings, independent of Rome, a secret society which obeys the eternal laws of nature and claims to have discovered spiritual values in the world which are more universal than the doctrines preached by the popes. The eternal dualism among the Children of God has disappeared. True religion leads us from a primitive confusion to a growing clarity and perfection, which man achieves by his own efforts and according to his own deserts. Here, one might say, is the forerunner of Leibnitz and Goethe, for here pantheism, unashamed and inspired by worldly beauty, tries to come to terms with orthodoxy and Christian asceticism.[1]

The logical outcome is a vision of a German Empire, a national community which is both political and religious. Wilhelm Scherer, the well-known German literary historian, draws the legitimate conclusion that this literature laid the foundations of German 'nationality' in the Middle Ages just as Dante's *Divine Comedy* laid the foundations of Italian nationality. The moment the temporal Empire crumbles, the spiritual Empire takes over and asserts its claim to universality.

So up to the fourteenth century three historical images or mirages gradually materialised, which were to haunt the German imagination. The Holy Roman Empire, the new Prussia that inherited the Teutonic Order, and the first beginnings of the Hanseatic League embody all the essential elements.

The popular legends which sprang up throughout the German territories to preserve the memory and the cult of a once-great Empire are all too well known. There is no need to recall the legend of Frederick Barbarossa, holding eternal vigil at Kyffhäuscr, surrounded by his sleeping warriors. It is such legends that have kept alive the dream of a Reich which would transcend the political frontiers laid down by history, reunite all German-speaking peoples under a great Leader or Monarch, and conquer the world by force of arms.[2]

Well before the fourteenth century, however, the fame of Prussia had grown on more solid foundations. The history of the Teutonic Order has never been forgotten. What it symbolises is the victory of the Germanic over the Slav, a victory which Spengler and Hitler acclaim once again in the twentieth century. It took the three centuries before the fourteenth to complete this costly and ruthless conquest. The victors gave their name to the conquered peoples, and the lofty Marienburg still epitomises that sombre and tragic turn of history.

The Hansa was founded in 1241. It represents the achievement of medieval Germany's *bourgeoisie*, most of them traders, without whose civic federations such prodigious victories would have been impossible. The colonies of the Hanseatic League spread like mushrooms along the Baltic coast right up to Riga. Here were the beginnings of that world policy (*Weltpolitik*) which was to become Wilhelm II's dream. How often the ambitious Emperor recalled the dazzling achievements of the Hansa!

---

[1] See Vermeil, op. cit., pp. 62 ff.
[2] See C.A.I, Preface, pp. xii ff.

2. THE FOURTEENTH AND FIFTEENTH CENTURIES

In the fourteenth and fifteenth centuries the relationship between Prussia and the Reich has already begun to dominate the historical development of the German peoples. On the one hand, the structure of Prussian militarism is taking shape, and the part it is to play in Germany's territorial development is already dimly apparent, in particular the hold it is to gain on Germany after the Reformation. But it is during this same period that the towns and the Hansa reach the summit of their prosperity.

While the various territories of Germany are moving inexorably towards a hegemony, Germany is also opening her gates to the outside world. In these two crucial centuries, Germany's *bourgeois* culture blossoms out into a mysticism which already divides it from Roman Catholicism, into a humanism which draws it back to national origins, and into a literature which, ably supported by the plastic arts, never tires of preaching the values that are German.

While the powers of the King-Emperor and the Roman Papacy are gradually declining, the nobility, too, is falling into decay. As the lot of the peasantry remains hard and precarious, life is concentrated in the towns and the small principalities. The history of the medieval towns, of their fabulous rise and their ultimate fall, cannot be dissociated, in the fourteenth and fifteenth centuries, from the history of the Hansa. To the *bourgeoisie* of the nineteenth century, with its ardent nationalism, it served as a magnificent pointer. Was it not the first example of a dual expansion, continental on the one hand, global on the other? Did it not provide the precedent of a Germany enriched and made prosperous by its *bourgeoisie*?

Flourishing internal trade and the development of primitive capitalism; the emergence of a new sense of independence and personal freedom, of the rule of law and elementary rights made accessible to all; remarkable achievements in the political, administrative, and military fields; these are all impressive evidence of a spirit of municipal enterprise which neither the Empire nor the growing principalities did anything to discourage. By 1300 the Hansa had already been functioning for half a century. Much later, in the middle of the eighteenth century, Justus Moser in his *Patriotic Fantasies* recalled with pride the eighty-five federated northern towns and the mighty commercial empire they had built up. As late as the end of the fifteenth century they are still strong enough to state their terms to France and England, and German historians in the nineteenth century are constantly asking why only Holland and Great Britain profited by so much prosperity.

Today we know why the towns in the interior and the Hansa, cut off from the central power and exposed by their very autonomy to the whims and appetites of petty princes greedy for power, fell into decay on the eve of the Reformation. Among the principalities which lay firm foundations in the midst of the general confusion, Prussia takes a leading place. She has been making steady progress since the twelfth century. Soon she will be the most modern of all the small monarchies, with an administration and an army superior to any of the others. In the fifteenth century Frederick I establishes a dynasty which is fully conscious of its power and which perpetuates the achievements of the Teutonic Order in its military conquests.

This *bourgeois* Germany has also developed a rich culture, of which coming centuries are to be justly proud.[1]

German mysticism, like the Hansa, first sees the light of day towards the middle of the fourteenth century. It reaches its peak in the first half of the fourteenth century with the preachings and works of Master Eckhart, Tauler, and Suso, and later, in the fifteenth century, of Dietrich of Fribourg, Rulman Merswin, and, above all, Thomas à Kempis. It is a predominantly *bourgeois* mysticism, which subsequently leads to an upsurge of Pietism. It takes the place of knightly love, but claims to embrace all men by seeking that divine presence which slumbers in the depths of every human soul and by meditating on the mysterious communication that arises between the human mind and its innermost essence. It brings out the fundamental traits of German religious feeling and evolves a vocabulary which ultimately finds its way into the most advanced German religious and philosophical works. It comes as no surprise to find the Nazi A. Rosenberg giving it pride of place in his *Myth of the Twentieth Century*.

Side by side with this *bourgeois* mysticism emerges the scientific spirit. In Germany, as elsewhere, humanism is not content to retrace its steps through centuries of Christianity to antiquity. Roughly between 1350 and 1500 universities sprang up in all parts of the country. Just as mysticism was an emotional reaction against the Scholastics, so the New Science is a bold protest against the pure transcendentalism of medieval dogma. Pandynamic and monist in character, it sets out to study the universe and the earth. Under the inspiration of Campanella and Giordano Bruno, it profits by the progress already made by the natural sciences. Nicolas de Cuse is a kind of Faust who tries to penetrate all the mysteries of nature. From its beginnings in Western Germany the movement spreads rapidly to the colonised territories.

Humanism, too, in Germany quickly assumes a markedly national character. As soon as the Empire loses its authority and sinks to the level of the other principalities, the salient features of the future German nation begin to emerge. Contemporary historians are

[1] See Vermeil, op. cit., pp. 66 ff.

already delving into the remote past, reviving the legendary figure of Arminius, and claiming that over the mosaic of principalities hovers the Idea of the Empire, of the Eternal Reich. Forceful personalities appear whose patriotic enthusiasm evokes dreams of a rebirth of the Empire. Among the nobility there is Ulrich von Hutten, among the *bourgeoisie* Celtes. They conjure up visions of a great Reich to come. Later, in the nineteenth and twentieth centuries, the nationalists, more particularly Spengler, stress the 'German' character of this renaissance.

As for the popular reality of the time, it is revealed forcibly in literature and the arts. The literature of that period remains close to the masses, whose aspirations it voices. It attacks all institutions in which the remaining power of the Empire and the Church is vested. Lyricism draws its inspiration from the fresh springs of poetry. Satire flourishes on the vast social, political, and moral canvas of the centuries before the Reformation. Hugo von Trimberg, Heinrich der Teichner, and Sachsenwirt find their targets in Rome and the high clergy, the ideal of chivalry that is still cherished by the aristocracy, the corruption of medieval society, the avarice of the *bourgeois* as they grow fat on capitalism. Chroniclers and orators bring the life and past of the nation to the knowledge of the people. Prose becomes German, in protest against abuses or in the effort to remind the people of their glorious history. The plastic arts also take a natural turn towards a democratic ideal. Everywhere, in the building of churches, the *bourgeois* is taking over from the clergy, at a time when civil architecture is vying with religious architecture, while sculpture and painting are abandoning abstract mysticism for a virile naturalism.

From these fifteen centuries of German history two motifs emerge: on the one hand, a sort of national religion, a communal sense which seems to find inspiration in the decay of the Holy Roman Empire itself, and, on the other hand, a sort of Republic of Principalities and towns in the midst of which Prussia rises like the lodestar of future unity. Even in this chaos one can already discern the deepseated antagonism, which has persisted ever since in Germany, between the professional man or the technician and the thinker or philosopher. Dreams of unlimited grandeur inspired by visions of the Reich and an iron militarism forged by Prussia in her arduous rise to fame, these are the two partners in the incongruous alliance which never ceases to torment Pangermanists in the nineteenth and twentieth centuries.

3. FROM 1500 TO 1648

In the course of the three centuries—roughly from 1500 to 1800—which lie between the Reformation and modern Pangermanism, the problem not only grows clearer but also grows. One begins to understand why the *bourgeois* nationalist in the nineteenth and twentieth centuries was so obsessed with the question whether Prussian militarism could produce a cultural revival or not.[1]

No historic figure ever gave these nationalists so much food for thought as Luther. In so far as the great reformer, after partially liberating the Germans from the influence of Rome, imbued them with a religious impulse in keeping with their secret aspirations, he is the great national hero. It was held against him, of course, especially in the Third Reich, that he had kept this religious impulse within the bounds of Pauline Christianity and had shown a humility which presupposes the basic corruption of human nature and cannot admit of any praise for a vitality born of heroism, however well-merited. Modern imperialism has criticised the Lutheran doctrine for that exclusive worship of the inner life, which appeared to militate against great economic achievements, and for its conception of the invisible Church which is still formally subject to the state: in short, the existence of that confessional dualism which the Treaties of Westphalia ratified in 1648 and which was to keep pace with Germany's territorial disruption.

With all such reservations, however, Nietzsche's words are still true: 'The outstanding event of our history is still Luther' (*'Unser Ereignis ist immer noch Luther'*). In a troubled age, when the principalities were the sole guardians of order, Luther's appeal rang throughout central Germany and echoed and re-echoed in the north. From a spiritual point of view, Luther's reform was doubly national, for it was a protest against Rome and a protest against the Western Reformation. Exhausted by a scrupulous observance of traditional rites, the young monk turns his back on the complex mechanism of Catholic piety and, in a flash of intuition, lays his finger directly on the mystery of the soul, that domain where divine grace acts and pardons with absolute sovereignty. This, in its earliest form, is the tragedy of the tormented conscience which has continued in Germany right up to modern existentialism.

Fortified by this experience, Luther goes on to reject the heroic humanism of Zwingli, which links the salvation of the soul with the democratic reorganisation of the Church and civil society, Calvinist predestination, the first germ of Western individualism with its anxiety to transform the world 'for the honour of God', and finally the tolerance and internationalism of Erasmus. Against this Western world, which is preparing to conquer the universe and which glorifies the practical energy of the *bourgeois*, Luther creates his own tragic and pessimistic conception of a world divided between the active or authoritative heroism of the ruling minority and the un-

[1] See Vermeil, op. cit., pp. 72 ff.

questioning obedience of the masses whom that minority is chosen by Providence to lead.

But is it possible to understand Germany at that period if one studies only the Reformation and ignores the Renaissance, if one neglects to study Copernicus as well as Luther? Towards 1770, when the young *élite*, led by Goethe, looked back upon the sixteenth century in search of the living sources of a genuinely national culture, they were to find not only Luther and the Reformation but also the dazzling miracle of the Renaissance. A new vision of the universe burst upon them, a vision radically opposed to Christian teaching.

At that moment the great problem of the relationship between Christianity and modern science arises. In Germany it becomes a particularly acute problem. It means, in effect, bringing these two spiritual powers face to face, but this juxtaposition is fully achieved only in the nineteenth century, when Nietzsche formulates his views on Christianity and launches a violent attack on Western humanism and its influence on the formation of a *bourgeois* nationalism which is not only ardent but cynical in its realism.

From the sixteenth century up to Leibnitz the juxtaposition of Christianity and science continues in Germany till it culminates, after Schwenkfeld and Sebastian Franck, in Valentin Weigel and, above all, in the theosophy of Jakob Boehme. These theosophists, forerunners of the romantic philosophers, regard God as creative energy and active goodness, universally and permanently revealed. For them the fall and the redemption are original and eternal facts. Good and evil, light and shade exist, according to Boehme, outside and beyond the divine essence. They are proper to man, who is compelled to live between the infernal kingdom of anger and the celestial kingdom of goodness and love. Our mission consists in assuring the victory of the latter over the former, both within ourselves and around us.

It might perhaps be worth while reviewing briefly the political features of the Reformation, the Republic of Princes, the formation of territorialism, and Luther's conception of the relations between Church and state. In the century following Luther's death the dominant factor is the tragic collision between Reformation and Counter-Reformation and, above all, the Thirty Years War, with its endless devastation. In this welter of disaster and suffering, Prussia still stands out, the same Prussia which in 1525 and during the Peasants' War had taken over the heritage of the Teutonic knights. It is, in fact, at this time that the Order was dissolved and that a great master, Albert von Hohenzollern-Anspach, became Prince of Prussia and vassal of the King of Poland. Later, when the Hohenzollern-Anspach branch dies out, there is war between the Hohenzollerns of Prussia and their Polish sovereign. Strengthened by alliances, at one time with the Swedes, at another with the Russians, Prussia invades Poland to enlarge her own territory and enhance her prestige. Then by degrees she welds the parts into a cohesive unity, pushing back the Swedish invader, who, starting with Gustavus Adolphus, has crushed all his neighbours and set up a bridgehead on the shores of the Baltic and in Pomerania.[1]

There is nothing more intriguing, nothing more suggestive than the prophecy made immediately after the Thirty Years War by Grimmelshausen, the outstanding writer in Germany at that time. That war should play a crucial part in his *Simplicissimus* is not surprising. Grimmelshausen has described the appalling misery and incalculable damage it brought in its train. It meant for Germany a grave setback in her civilisation, a return to semi-barbarism. War had become a sort of national industry, the soldier's life a trade, a business enterprise which brought its returns and which certain people had every interest in prolonging. It combined the most shameless organised robbery with the traditions of a pillaging and criminal nobility. Grimmelshausen had studied Machiavelli's 'Prince'. He knew that sovereignty is achieved by means of crime, by using war for personal enrichment.

This does not mean that Grimmelshausen turns his back on the monarchy. He believes, long before Frederick II, in a prince who is the first servant of the state. He desires a strong central authority, the abolition of small principalities, and a complete reorganisation of the Imperial régime.

What is at stake for him, as later for the romantic thinkers after the wars of the Revolution and the Empire, is the nation's honour, the future greatness and supremacy of a nation that has been reconstituted. He is buoyed up by a confidence and hope such as inspired the *Discourses* of Fichte after the disaster of Jena. His is a vision of future happiness, when the star of a new Germany will rise to dazzle not only Europe but the world. The Holy Roman Empire, clad in a new dignity, will be the guarantor of the *Pax Germanica*. The Saviour approaches. The Messiah has come, the German Hero who will transform the world! Stronger than Hercules, more beautiful than Narcissus, and more intelligent than Mercury, he will embody all the qualities, enjoy incredible repute, and need no outside aid. How could the Muses fail to settle in a Garden of Eden so admirably organised and governed?

Then follows a programme of conquests which might have served as model for the Third Reich. It is from the German nation, we are assured, that the kings of Europe will receive their crowns. Are not England, Sweden, and Denmark countries of German origin and blood? Were not France, Spain, and Portugal at one time con-

[1] See Vermeil, op cit., pp. 96 ff.

quered and governed by Germanic rulers? Why should the *Pax Germanica* not take the place of the *Pax Romana*?

It will be a religious peace. The war broke out because the Protestants of Bohemia revolted against the fanaticism of the heir to the Imperial throne. The country of Luther has been thrown off balance. Everyone is wondering where true faith can be found! Why, then, attach oneself to any particular religious party? Why look for salvation in one religion rather than another? It is better to reflect and to reserve judgment. And Grimmelshausen then conjures up before us a vision of the new religion Germany will create, a religion which is both national and universal and which will resolve all differences. The same conception is taken up later by Leibnitz in his religious reorganisation of the earth, to say nothing of Paul de Lagarde or Constantin Franz in the nineteenth century. Grimmelshausen leaves no problem untouched, including that of the Jews, whom he reproaches for their usury and their financial power, but whose intellectual superiority he also admits.[1]

At this point one might recall, with M. Colleville, the words of Droysen, the well-known historian, who saw in the Thirty Years War 'the great German Revolution', from which all future revolutions would stem.

4. THE CLASSICAL AND COSMOPOLITAN SPIRIT (1648–1800)

Grimmelshausen's prediction was not sheer madness. With the insight of genius he glimpsed at the end of the seventeenth century the cultural revival that was to come so soon in Germany. Everything seems in place in this strange picture. Roughly between 1650 and 1800 German culture did, as Grimmelshausen foretold, become genuinely European. If one considers how universal was the appeal of the music, philosophy, and later the literature of that splendid era, within the framework of classical cosmopolitanism, then why not speak of a sort of *Pax Germanica* in the truest sense of the word? What must be eradicated for all time from Grimmelshausen's predictions is the vision, the hope of a sovereignty and a hegemony exercised by Germany over the old Continent, the idea of a physical domination through the medium of a leader.

But who would not bow before the universal genius of a Leibnitz and the essentially European compositions of a J. S. Bach or a Handel in the century from 1650 to 1750 which followed immediately on the Thirty Years War? And, in the later period from the middle of the eighteenth century to the death of Goethe, who would deny that Goethe was the most European, the most universal of minds, the one German to whom, right up to the end of his glorious

[1] See M. Colleville, 'La Pangermanisme de Grimmelshausen' in *L'Univers Français*, No. 3, 1945, pp. 242 ff.

career, nationalism was completely alien, even as a means to his own personal aggrandisement? [1]

The first of these periods bears all the hallmarks of transition.

Once the war is over, leaving its wake of devastation, the *bourgeoisie* look round for new openings, for any promise of better times. They set about reconstructing what the religious strife of their own time had destroyed. They seize upon the material advantages to be gained from modern scientific invention and the spiritual riches which Christian culture had still left untapped. The sudden influx of so much that is novel strains the old habits of thought and action to breaking-point. As Goethe himself said, time-honoured safeguards were discarded; there was a new surge of self-confidence and realism, a new sense of working with what was known. 'Physician, heal thyself' was the advice Goethe gave his contemporaries.

Antiquity and Christianity, the twin pillars of the humanist tradition, had established strong links between nature and reason, between the 'physical' and the 'logical'. The wisdom of the ancient Greeks and the moral teachings of Christianity had been brought together and a model of human conduct set up, an 'Order of Salvation', embodied in a clearly formulated set of dogmas which had assumed a different shape in each of the three post-Reformation Churches. But now a new and more comprehensive form of Christianity is under way. Towards the end of the seventeenth century the philosophy of enlightenment (*Aufklärung*) and pietism burst upon Germany's reviving culture. A double attack is launched on the traditional order of salvation. It is launched from two directions: (1) on behalf of a rationalism, which will give free rein to utilitarian individualism, to the exact sciences, and to the development of more severe standards of conduct; (2) on behalf of 'irrationalism', of an obscure, undetermined reality, of primitive instincts and instinctive reality. The old orthodoxy of the Lutheran and Catholic Churches comes under fire. The old problem of the relationship between emotion and reason, licence and constraint, emerges from the battle in an entirely new form. The order of salvation is to be replaced by 'salvation through order', both for society and for the individual.

One is not surprised to encounter Leibnitz at the climax of this development. He died in 1716, but his *New Essays on Understanding* were only published towards the middle of the eighteenth century. In this work he propounds a theory of knowledge which was nothing more nor less than a magnificent attempt to reconcile the apparently irreconcilable in the problem confronting him, the two conflicting elements in German culture. Leibnitz distinguished, in fact, between the obscure, spontaneous, so-called 'inferior' knowledge and the 'superior' knowledge which we acquire by applying the ex-

[1] See Vermeil, op. cit., pp. 83 ff.

perience of our senses to the discovery of incontrovertible and eternal truths. Is not the complete man he who combines experience and intelligence, feeling and reason, enthusiastic fervour and technical precision?

Now, if the monads achieve perfection only in attaining such a union, they rise by degrees up the human ladder to share finally in the clarity and power of God. This is a natural hierarchy, based on living syntheses which mount one above the other.

Here lies the explanation of that all-embracing and more optimistic religious feeling, which places its own interpretation on the dogma of the fall and the redemption, and so leads the traditional Christian dualism towards a more elastic, and indeed more universal, conception of the opposition between the decline and the regeneration of humanity. The Lutheran doctrine, whose astringency has already been modified by Melanchthon, undergoes yet another change. There is a genuine religious enthusiasm at the root of Leibnitz's ideas on the religious reorganisation of the earth and the suppression of confessional differences or conflicts. These ideas really lay the foundation of German cosmopolitanism. They re-echo the prophetic views of Grimmelshausen and are at the same time the forerunners of that German national religion which, in the nineteenth century, is to be the dream of Paul de Lagarde, Constantin Franz, and certain Pangermanists such as H. S. Chamberlain.

What could be more European than the German music of that era? True, J. S. Bach throughout his immense work expresses all the depth and mystery of Lutheranism. Handel, who lived in England, evokes all the grandeur and heroism of the Western Reformation. But what could be more complete than this art, in which an unprecedented formal discipline is so admirably wedded to feelings and emotions which cannot always be expressed in words? This century and a half of German culture, in which the genius of a renascent nation finds its finest expression in philosophy and music, was an admirable preparation for classicism.

The secret of this classicism as it blossoms forth in the forty years before the French Revolution has never been better defined than by Fichte in the eighth of his *Discourses to the German Nation*, delivered immediately after the disaster of Jena. How can one account for such a wealth of spiritual freedom, for such grandiose conceptions, for so much disinterestedness in the cosmopolitanism of Goethe and Schiller which, in the name of 'world literature' (*Weltliteratur*), appeals to the nations, to Europe, and to the world, and at the same time remains, particularly in Goethe, deaf to the appeals of the new spirit of nationalism which the wars of the Revolution and the Empire are to kindle? The answer is that the great minds of this time lived in a sort of providential no man's land between the small principality, the small regional state, which took good care not to confine them to its own narrow limits, and, on the other hand, an empire, which had lost all substance and authority. In other words, there was no room in Germany at the close of the eighteenth century for a narrow patriotism, for a national obsession. Hence the striking contrast, which is so difficult to explain, between the unbridled cosmopolitanism of some and the ardent nationalism of others; hence this startling change of course, which was conceivable only in Germany, from a perfectly genuine lack of interest in things national to a fanatical Pangermanism. The German passion for the universal finds its outlet through both these channels simultaneously. But in and through Pangermanism it will achieve universalism, and thereby profit the nation.[1]

The years 1750–1830, throughout which the classical spirit continued in full spate right up to the death of Goethe in 1832, witnessed a third phase of Christian secularisation, very different from the one in France which marked a transition from Catholicism and the monarchy to free thinking and democracy, very different, too, from the one in England, where the authoritarianism of the High Church was challenged by the modern principle of free religious association and free religious thought. The philosophy of enlightenment, which reached its peak in Kant, and the pantheism, in which the senses and passions awakened by pietism were to find fulfilment, have their roots in that form of religious feeling known to the Germans as 'world piety' (*Weltfrömmigkeit*), a sort of earthly religion which excludes neither transcendence and the losing of oneself nor the profound and vibrant emotional appeal which religion makes. It is through *Weltfrömmigkeit*, according to Schleiermacher's famous formula, that the German learns to act always 'with religion'. Disillusioned by ecclesiastical and orthodox territorialism, the *élite* devote all their attention once more to philosophy, music, and, for the first time, to literature.

Rationalism and mysticism, mastery of the emotions, bold and impressive æsthetic doctrines which profess to organise the life of the individual and determine the fate of societies, a new humanism, more troubled but also more comprehensive than that of the Western nations—these are all present in classical Germany. The nation still does not believe that God has entrusted it with a divine mission, but it does believe that this God, this divine Energy, works in us, and is at the heart of genius and of its creative manifestations. German culture, enormously enriched by the influence of Shakespeare and of Rousseau, magnifies in man the exercise of those virtues which restore to him his absolute and essential purity.

[1] See Vermeil, op. cit., pp. 109 ff.

This brings us beyond the French Revolution, the Napoleonic Empire, and the wars provoked by them to the period when the preoccupation with personal culture, which had haunted the soul of the *bourgeois* until then, is joined by cares of a social nature. Goethe said once, in criticising Kant and his scepticism, that if man was no longer the centre of the universe, as was generally assumed before Copernicus, he nevertheless had the power to know the eternal laws which govern the universe and let himself be guided by them. The latter works of this great European all centre around the problem of decline and regeneration. Individual and society both decline when they sin against the eternal laws; they rise again by conforming to them. Like Shakespeare and Rousseau, Goethe believes in the existence of a moral order which is not static and which is based on the laws of change and growth. A counsel of peace, certainly, but based on the notion of tireless effort which individual and society must make to maintain order by perpetually renewing it. Grimmelshausen, and later Leibnitz, had spoken of a German peace. We find it again in Goethe in the conception, the profound conviction, of a harmony which men can and must realise, but which is constantly threatened, and must therefore be ruthlessly defended.

The Lutheran Reformation had laid the foundations of the future German nation, which one day would be called upon to take over a crumbling Holy Roman Empire. From this point of view it had not been one whit less 'national' than the humanism of the Renaissance. If Ulrich von Hutten had Europe very much in mind and urged the German nobles to make the nation completely independent of Rome, if the humanists of Erfurt endeavoured to give a real purpose once again to the historical development of the German territories, Luther, the disciple of fourteenth- and fifteenth-century mysticism, reader of *Theologie deutsch* and of Gabriel Biel—Luther, too, makes his final appeal to the nobles, to the *élite* of the German nation.

Here he compares the re-established honour of the Gospel to that of Germania. He claims that he is obeying the voice 'of his beloved Germany'. His dream is the spiritual and moral unity of his compatriots. 'We Germans are Germans and we shall remain German.' The Germany whose future he predicts will be 'the best country, the nation *par excellence*'. Is he not evoking its spiritual supremacy when he draws the bold outlines of an educational reform, of a school which will be both 'Christian' and 'national', capable of providing Germany with men and women worthy of her?

Above all, he believes he has discovered what separates Roman and Western religious feeling, obsessed as it is with reason and surrounded by legal restrictions, from German religious feeling, which gives pride of place to emotion, to a trusting faith, to the spontaneous appeal of the heart, and which refuses to submit to what it already calls 'the slavery' of a clerical hierarchy that has been firmly established for centuries. Not that Luther rejects Christian ecumenism and its transcendent character. When he invites the Princes to reform the Church, he declares: 'It is for you Germans that I seek salvation and sanctity'. He converts the Imperial ambitions of the past, particularly those of an Otto I and a Frederick Barbarossa, into terms of Protestant faith and the politico-social order it implies. Through his Word translated into German, God turns towards Germany and, through Germany, towards all men.

'The Word came down to the Jews. Saint Paul brought it to the Greeks. Rome and the Latin countries received it in their turn. But Germany has been visited, illuminated by its grace to an imcomparably greater extent than any other nation.'

This national consciousness, with its after-taste of spiritual imperialism, seemed to float somewhere between the reality of the Holy Roman Empire and the idea, still remote, of a national state, of a Reich equipped with a real central power. Could it be reconciled with territorialism? It is here that the tragic paradox of the German Reformation becomes apparent. While the nation's culture grows and blossoms over 300 years, and more particularly after 1648, on a superior plane of its own, culminating in the cosmopolitanism we have just described, Germany herself remains divided into aristocrats, patricians, *bourgeois*, and peasants, and, more tragic still, she is divided by innumerable territorial barriers within that same 'Republic of Princes' which the Reformation had created and in which the Treaties of Westphalia had ratified confessional dualism.[1]

It is out of this territorial mosaic that Prussia emerges towards 1650. She is by far the most powerful of the German states. Already she is pushing out her feelers towards the Rhine provinces. Essentially a Lutheran state, she is at daggers' drawn with Austria from 1650 to 1750. Between 1640 and 1688 she had become a military monarchy. In the wars against Poland and Sweden between 1688 and 1700 the monarchy had strengthened its hold. While Austria was struggling to absorb the most heterogeneous possessions, Brandenburg was quietly digesting its successive conquests. The state's interests were supreme. It had 80,000 soldiers against France's 160,000.

We know what use Frederick II made of this army from 1740 onwards. And there were undeniable qualities of mind and character in his creation of the most powerful and most efficient military state of the pre-1789 era. These qualities are well known, as are the institutions to which they gave birth. Here was the mentality of

[1] See Vermeil, op. cit., pp. 145 ff.

military battalions accustomed to clearing the most difficult terrain and to laying the foundations of a prosperity based on ascetic renunciation. Compared with the cosmopolitan culture which we have traced back to its origins, Prussia is another world with quite different habits of mind and principles of action. It is in this respect that Frederick II is, and remains, a 'national hero'. He turns the army into an instrument of aggression, and the echo of its cannons has not yet died away in Germany. He combines a ruthless realism with the spirit of a revolutionary; no one could be more conservative when the internal security of the state of nation is at stake, no one more revolutionary when it comes to overturning the old-established order to his own advantage. Everything that could be said on this question has been said. And the events of the years 1787–1815 in a decadent Prussia or, during the same period, in a crumbling Reich are well known.

When the nineteenth century opens, Germany will find herself faced with two great currents, two great traditions: a culture that goes back three centuries and has now become cosmopolitan, a Prussian chrysalis which, after a brief decline, has undergone a prodigious revival. In opposition to this culture, which has achieved the spiritual unification of the Reich, is Romanticism. In opposition to Prussia, conqueror of Napoleon, is a growing agglomeration of military aspirations. In the first half of the nineteenth century it is the problem of relations between Prussia and the Reich that the new Pangermanism will have to grapple with.

III. FIRST THESES AND FIRST DEVELOPMENTS
(1790–1850)

In the half-century between the revolution of 1789 and that of 1848, romanticism established the key positions which, in modern times, were to be those of the German spirit. The link with classicism is clear. The two movements have the same ideal of social organisation and personal salvation. But they differ in that in classicism this ideal is enveloped in Western humanism, whereas in romanticism it is given the dominant position which its national, and particularly German, character entitles it to, in the sense given to the word by the new Germany when it reacts against the French Revolution and the Napoleonic system.

1. PROPHETS AND REVOLUTIONARIES

This means, in effect, that Germany undergoes a revolution of her own in opposition to the French Revolution. This historic development is clearly marked out by a series of highly significant prophecies, which serve as starting-points.

B

In 1799—ten years, that is, after 1789—the poet Novalis, in a small work entitled *Christianity or Europe*, warns us that 1789 will not be the only revolution in the old Continent. Why should the inevitable revival only be French? Germany, says Novalis, is moving slowly but surely towards a position of assured supremacy. And the same year, in the preface to the first edition of his *Discourse on Religion*, Schleiermacher was hinting that the time had come for Germany, deprived of her necessary living-space, to defend herself against the greed of her neighbours.[1]

After the 1830 revolution, again a French one, Heinrich Heine, then a refugee in Paris, reveals the true meaning of this German revolution in a fascinating and famous work which appeared in 1834. He describes it in sombre, tragic terms quite different from those of Novalis. If the Germans, says Heine with some solemnity, hark back to their mythology and brandish the hammer of their God Thor to burst open the old Continent's Christian armour, then the surrounding nations will witness dreadful struggles in the heart of the arena and will have to take their own precautions.[2]

It is from 1848 to 1849, at the same time as France, that Germany ventures on revolution. At least, she drafts it out on paper for Prussia subsequently to break the seal. Was this revolution as 'liberal' as it has been made out to be? The historian S. A. Kähler, Professor of History at the University of Göttingen, shows that the revolution of 1848 was only an episode in that revolutionary wave which broke in the beginning of 1848 and dashed itself against the political régimes of that time. Led, as far as the German Confederation is concerned, by a cultured and wealthy minority, by a flourishing *bourgeoisie*, this revolution proclaims the demands of the new class. In Germany, liberal nationalism gains the upper hand over social problems. A few enlightened spirits talk of a republic, one and indivisible, but they are outnumbered by those who still feel the old imperial nostalgia. No one could fail to see that the Frankfurt Parliament laid the foundations of a policy of domination in Central Europe. Doubtless in response to the Communist Manifesto of Marx and Engels![3]

This *bourgeois* liberalism, therefore, had no other aim but to save Germany's separatist monarchies. It has stepped into the shoes of the old aristocracy. Through these monarchies it hopes to achieve national unity. In other words, it dreams of squaring a circle. How can one hope to arrive at a 'general will' with so many Parliaments, great and small? And how would the neighbouring Powers react if

[1] See Novalis, *Werke*, Ed. H. Friedemann, Part 4, Essay 'Die Christenheit oder Europa,' pp. 132–47.
[2] See Heine, *Zur Geschichte der Religion und Philosophie in Deutschland*, Ed. Elster, Vol. IV, pp. 161 ff.
[3] See S. A. Kähler, *Etudes historiques*.

a state of 70,000,000 inhabitants should one day rise in the centre of Europe? What the enthusiasts of that period did not realise was that this was a European affair, that Europe's very existence was threatened by this revolutionary nationalism. What was to become of that right of peoples which is limited by the power of other peoples? S. A. Kähler reminds us that as early as the summer of 1848 the Schleswig problem had already determined the future of the Frankfurt Assembly. In fact, Europe had no desire for a German revolution. To understand why, it is enough to refer back to Heinrich von Gagern. He makes no bones about Austria's mission to carry German culture into the Danube states and to expand eastwards. The Catholic Reichensperger, the Austrian Beust, and many others, foreseeing the Russian menace, talk of establishing a gigantic Central European state capable of fighting simultaneously against Latins and Slavs. Rash prophecies which are soon to be hastily abandoned. S. A. Kähler summarises the adverse judgment of Namier, the English historian, on such dreams of the future.

A study of the doctrines involved throws a revealing light on these three prophecies. At the end of the eighteenth century one can already dimly perceive what later will be the nationalists' aspirations. They are beginning to appear in the works of Herder and Schiller, and indeed of Klopstock, too, in his later writings. From 1800 to 1830 we see it emerging in religion and philosophy, with views on Germany's dominant position in Europe and its military implications already taking shape. Then, between 1830 and 1850, come the first signs of a new 'realism'. Heine may still stress the philosophical and religious origins, but Friedrich List, for one, can already see what economic developments will take place in the next few years, and his predictions, coupled with the stirring appeals of the Frankfurt Parliament, make a highly impressive picture.

Here, then, is what we have to consider now: (1) the root causes of the impending schism between German thought and Western humanism; (2) the emergence of a new brand of nationalism between 1790 and 1830; (3) finally, the birth, between 1830 and 1850, of a Pangermanism which is as realistic as it is ambitious.

2. THE ORIGINS OF THE SCHISM BETWEEN GERMAN ROMANTICISM AND WESTERN THOUGHT

The French Revolution was the political and social outcome of previous trends in Western humanism. German romanticism sets up an opposing ideology, out of which the nationalist movement comes with which we are about to deal.

In his *Manual of French Literature*, F. Brunetière gave a precise definition of the problem when he wrote of romanticism:

'The universality at which it (romanticism) aims is a universality not of abstraction and generalisation but of *composition*, which determines that each element, far from sacrificing anything of its originality, must develop it by the very fact of its contrast with the others.'

Like Goethe before him, the German romanticist goes beyond the scepticism of Kant and idolises the living organism. In opposition to the ideal of collective organisation set up by the Western revolutionaries, he creates his own ideal, which he applies to Germany in order to guarantee her a position of absolute supremacy.[1]

Not that Germany has never known Western humanism. She has been much too exposed to the influence of England and France to be able to repudiate it. But in the early nineteenth century she tends to break away from it. Soon there is an unbridgeable gulf between German thought and that of the West. More and more, in the nineteenth and twentieth centuries, Germany moves towards a sort of intellectual and moral autarky.

National right and humanism are the terms that best characterise the Western European conception. They have their origin in antiquity and Christianity. The Western world as a whole believes in an eternal order established by divine reason on the religious plane and by reason on the earthly plane. On this order it bases morality and universal right. Humanity as a whole has one, and only one destiny. All races, peoples, and nations must conform to the same common standards.[2]

This implies a tremendous belief in oneself, but one which is demonstrably threatened from two sides: on the one hand, there is the threat of abstract nationalism, which may give rise to egalitarian atomism, selfish individualism, and a facile superficiality; on the other hand, there is also the danger of a hypocritical phariseeism, if democracy and Socialism fail to solve the proletarian problem and, out of despair, take refuge in a *bourgeois* order which is past its prime.

The cosmopolis of the ancient world, Christian universalism, the Christian natural right based on the antithesis between original sin and the ways to redemption offered by the Churches: out of these emerged the modern natural right, which, from its first beginnings in the seventeenth century, was finally accepted and established in the middle of the eighteenth century. After moving towards monarchical absolutism it veered round in the opposite direction, towards revolutionary liberalism, and finally found its home in the doctrines and institutions that rest on the

---

[1] See Brunetière, *Manuel de l'histoire de la Littérature Française*, pp. 412–13.
[2] For the split between Western thought and German Romanticism see Ernst Troeltsch, *Naturrecht und Humanität in der Welpolitik*.

sovereignty of the people. There is no room here to discuss the differences which exist between the American or English world and the French nation. It is none the less true that in 1789 the Rights of Man and the citizen completed this process, and on a grandiose scale.

This humanism, which is essentially a cult of the classical humanities, Christianity in all its many forms, parliamentary democracy, and international Socialism, was condemned out of hand by Nietzsche, who compared it to a 'disease' that had been gnawing at humanity for 2,000 years. Such a radical attack was clearly unjustified. But this does not mean that humanism is without its grave weaknesses. It did not succeed in solving the social problem. Its outstanding contemporary achievement, the League of Nations at Geneva, failed between the wars, and its successor, the United Nations Organisation, cannot be said to have met with much more success. At the present moment, the Churches that issued from the Reformation represent the order of salvation. But salvation through order, through individual and social order, is still not within the grasp of human communities.

We know the paths that Germany has followed since the Thirty Years War and the Treaties of Westphalia, at a time when England was reaping the harvest of her 'glorious revolution' of 1688 and France was preparing for hers a century later. The paths that Germany followed led to romanticism, to a romanticism pure and simple, which is not to be confused with the movement that went by the same name in the West.

When Germany steps on to the stage some years after 1789, she has: (1) a widespread and powerful cosmopolitan spirit that is evident in her philosophy, her music, and her literature; (2) a great state in her midst, Prussia, whose political and military armour had been forged and strengthened throughout the centuries.

It has been said, not without reason, that the most original, the most 'natural' elements in German thought are romantic in origin. It is even claimed that German romanticism was virtually a revolution in the sense that, through it, the cosmopolitan universalism of the past was canalised into a nationalism which was both jealous and zealous and which turned the German nation, in the centre of Europe, into not only a 'national state' with a strong centralised authority, but also a kind of 'super-nation' with dreams of conquest.

Germany, regarding herself as a self-sufficient organic whole, is soon claiming that her new phase of development will be in accordance with the laws governing the universe, and that she therefore has the right to exercise sovereign sway over Europe, after she has extended her own European frontiers. After the collapse of Napoleon, she shows a growing tendency to substitute this principle, by fair means or foul, for that of a United States of Europe.

Moreover, as opposed to Western humanism, German romanticism rejects the idea of an eternal order founded on reason and takes the view that the divine Spirit manifests itself in history through successive creations, which are constantly renewed, in other words, through collective 'individualities'. The spirit of the people or *Volksgeist*, national genius, and total culture are some of the phrases bandied about. The rights possessed by any one group are in exact proportion to its potential strength: a mystical conception, which can lead to almost any act of brute force.

So from the womb of German romanticism is born the religion of the organic and organised nation, and this religion is irreconcilable with Western humanism. It condemns moral equality and universality, any science which is too rational and based on pure mathematics, any political creed founded on a general will which could find expression only through counting votes and a parliamentary majority. It also rebels against *bourgeois* respectability and natural rights. The Lutheran Reformation had already joined issue with the West. Romanticism takes up the cudgels again, but its attack goes still farther and still deeper. It sets out to purge Germany of the philosophy of enlightenment, the *Aufklärung*, which had exercised such a beneficent influence, but which had fallen into discredit through its intransigence and its excesses. The anti-West campaign overshot its mark, however, and ultimately pushed the German nation to the opposite extreme of an absurd irrationalism.

The German romantic ideology was more recent and less mature than the Western conceptions and, for that reason, remained incomplete. It had not yet proved its worth. All it could offer in reply to humanism was a vision, both æsthetic and religious, of the national community, a vision born of necessity and destined to replace the internal disruption of the past by an internal cohesion which until then had been impossible. There was no real spirit of conservatism or of revolution here. The Western revolutions had become conservative. If Germany was revolutionary, it was only in order to acquire a new unity and cohesion which would make mass action possible and enable her to overthrow a European system which, she claimed, had failed to give her a 'place in the sun'. Some conservative authority was needed within, to provide the necessary discipline. The desire for a revolution was directed outwards, towards Europe's periphery. So, at the same time as she is entertaining aggressive designs, Germany describes her alleged democracy as the integration of popular and national forces in the totality that is the Reich.

In fact, the German vision was that of a nation condemned not only to federalism but to the hegemony of a great state such as Prussia. Any potentialities it had were relative. It served its purpose for German science and politics. Having shaken off both the scepticism of Kant and the moderation of Goethe, romanticism regarded the idea of a living organism as the key to the secret of the universe. Nothing in human history had such a fatal fascination for the German romantics as the vast collective creations which they looked upon as original and elemental phenomena. The human Cosmos was revealed to them as an agglomeration of living and acting collectivities, which, however, were doomed to an eternal rivalry, of impersonal Powers dominating the individual and forcing him to execute their will.

This implied, of course, a revival of the notion of humanity. Reason was no longer the sole guarantor of human dignity. In the context of history nations emerged in all their rich and diverse complexity. There seemed little doubt that a living nation could not be built up solely on the Social Contract, on more or less artifical conventions or for purely rational ends. No one would deny the stimulus that the romantic ideology gave to the science of history in Germany and later in the neighbouring countries.

But no one could fail to see the dangers inherent in such a vision of the world. Was it necessary, in order to have done with the limited methods of the *Aufklärung*, to break finally with the idea of humanity's indefinite progress and the belief that certain standards must be applicable to all nations? Was this not tantamount to the acceptance of war for the sake of war, of cohesion for the sake of cohesion? Was this not preparing the ground for the leader who commands and is obeyed, for an ominous revival of myths and primitive customs? Very soon the idea of the 'master-people' (*Herrenvolk*) will germinate in the German imagination. Germany turns full circle. From a sense of impotence she switches suddenly to visions of unprecedented greatness. The cosmopolitanism of the eighteenth century is primarily preoccupied in nineteenth-century Germany with a Reich that is backward, but alone possesses, so it is claimed, fresh reserves of strength and is the sole power in Europe which can regenerate the old Continent.

That is why the German romantics finally shattered the time-honoured vision of universal history. They introduced into the study of history a menacing undertone of anarchy, of extreme relativism, of specialisation hostile to any spirit of synthesis. Above all, they stimulated in the Germans that national egocentricity, that parochial universalism which was to have such disastrous consequences for them. For this conception of life aims at dissociating right from morality, at creating a fatal gulf between personal morality, whether Christian or lay, and public or collective morality. A remote result, no doubt, of Luther's ideas on the relations between Church and state. At all events, human rights are turned into positive realities that are bound and associated with a human group, which makes its own rules from them, to be defended by its own instruments of power and boosted to its own advantage. Enveloped in such a communal mysticism, the rights of man lose all universal value. And morality suffers a similar fate.

The self-appointed mission of romantic Germany is to deify the empirical state, to turn it into a spiritual and religious entity and invest it with individuality. Sincere and clear-sighted Germans, while they insist on the relative fertility of this romanticism, have argued that fate did not allow it to formulate its ideas impartially, to base them on experimental research, or to keep them free from nationalist fanaticism. The years 1790–1815 brought a series of humiliating disasters, which were followed, during the wars of independence, by an unprecedented explosion of patriotism. Between 1815 and 1835 the new trend of thought is closely bound up with the reactionary absolutism of the Holy Alliance, then, towards 1848, emerges into the open with dreams of Continental greatness conjured up by the Frankfurt Assembly. In Bismarck's time, pangermanism, though opposed to it in principle, still maintains its tradition, while Wagner airs it again in the 'Meistersinger' and still more in 'Parsifal', and Nietzsche produces his ruthless criticism of Western humanism. So it comes as no surprise when, under Wilhelm II, this dangerous, romantic megalomania blossoms out into the visions of Oswald Spengler just when Germany suffers her first defeat, only to take a new lease of life, however, in 1919, in the doctrine of the Party which is to lead the German nation and with it the whole of Europe to disaster.

3. The Beginning of Pangermanism (1790–1830)

The death of Goethe in 1832 marked the end of the great classical tradition. Thanks to the extraordinary influence of Shakespeare and J. J. Rousseau, this great literary movement had penetrated into the whole of Western culture and thought. When the historian compares the work of Goethe with that of Rousseau and finds the surprising analogies that exist between the citizen of Geneva and the poet of Weimar, he at once perceives that both arrive at a doctrine concerning the decline and regeneration of individuals and societies, a doctrine which, on the one hand, claims to be completely independent of Christianity and, on the other hand, is firmly established on an unshakeable faith, on the carefully reasoned belief in a moral order, which is divine in origin and which does not allow men to transgress against its laws without expiating their sins and their errors in suffering. [1]

But in Germany between 1790 and 1830 minds were not open to

[1] See Vermeil, 'J. J. Rousseau et Goethe' in *Annales de la Société J. J. Rousseau*, 1949.

such a generous and disinterested cosmopolitanism, even although Goethe, in his later works between 1815 and 1830, gave it final expression. At that time there is thought for nothing but Germany. Lutherans and Catholics take up again the theme of decadence and regeneration, reintroduce it in its confessional framework, and this time ascribe the regeneration to Germany, the decadence to the Western nations. One can hardly imagine a more startling change of mind. It was soon to bear fruit.

A peculiar mixture of philosophy and religion is the salient feature of the outstanding productions during this first epoch. Philosophy harks back to a religious devotion which tries to understand itself and to make itself understood. It imagines that all the realities of daily life, whether individual or collective, are creations of what is called 'the Divine'; on this one premiss it bases all its interpretations of the elements that go to make up the external world and the human groups that go to make up organised societies.

Every Western religion, after its own fashion, preaches predestination. Every human life and every nation, originating as it does in God, is charged with a message, a mission, which alone gives it its meaning. From that moment between the disaster of 1806 and the victory of 1814, when Prussia and Germany drew closer together, the two great forces of the past, Lutheranism and Catholicism, arouse a wave of devotion and are reborn. A similar and no less striking revival had taken place in France in 1789 and the years that followed.

Germany feels threatened by the convulsions that are shaking the West to its foundations, and she, too, takes refuge in the eternal. Her reply to the Rights of Man and the Citizen is a national revival, a new national consciousness, a communal mysticism. On the Jewish model, she declares herself a chosen people. She launches violent attacks on England, where she sees only a desire for gold, and on France, which, she considers, is committed irrevocably to a purely abstract rationalism. She seems suddenly to ignore all the passion and sensitiveness and fervour in the England of Young's *Nights* or in the France of J. J. Rousseau. She believes that she alone possesses the mental equipment to reconstruct Europe and the world. She ascribes to herself, following Goethe, a wisdom that is cosmic in its magnitude and peculiar only to herself. She is convinced that she alone envisages the world 'as it must be envisaged', that she is endowed with a sort of intrinsic supremacy, which fills her with inordinate pride. The neighbouring nations, which have known greatness, are dismissed as exhausted and decadent. But a Germanic hour is coming, an hour that Germany has been waiting for with such nostalgic impatience and that will reveal her in all her regenerative greatness to a decaying Europe, particularly to the Latins.

As was to be expected, Lutherans like Fichte and Hegel and more or less converted Catholics like Novalis, Fr. Schlegel, and J. Görres also take up, in a new atmosphere, this theme of decline and regeneration which Rousseau and Goethe had dealt with, and which, in the last analysis, can be traced back to the Christian dogma of the fall and the redemption.

Take Fichte for example, that visionary who draws so much from Luther. No one had a more profound belief in Germany's predestination. Reared in the school of Leibnitz, Kant, and Herder, he proclaims his faith in the famous *Discourses*. Where does he find decadence? In the world of the Jews and the Latins. He builds up his case on linguistic arguments, finding only in Germany a truly living language born of an essentially 'natural' evolution. The Latin tongues he regards as useless instruments forged from dead languages and from a habit of thought imprisoned in its own immutable concepts. As for French, what value can be attached to such glittering virtuosity? Can one juggle with a nation's language as with dice? No prophecy was ever more false. Unlike that of Ezekiel, it condemns to decay a reality which had just given proof of tremendous virility and creative power.[1]

Nowhere is the Pangermanic illusion, and its dangers, so fully exposed as in the *Discourses* and the writings of this philosopher whose self-avowed conviction it is that the Latin race invariably reduces all things to a mere mechanical game and sees in its culture nothing more than the peace of a churchyard. The political thought of the Latins, and particularly of the French, we are told, is a mere question of 'mechanics', and therefore incapable of creating true nations welded together by bonds of love. He sees in them nothing but the ashes of individuals, living each in isolation, and of petrified souls, which can be fanned into a sudden flame of revolution, but are equally capable of sinking into a craven conformity which is the first step to dictatorship.

As against such decadence, there is one country that possesses the spirit of regeneration: Germany. In Fichte's famous theory of the 'original language' one can see the first glimmerings of later racial theories, a pure creation of the mind. Bathed in a glow of idealism, the people and the language which Fichte calls 'original' emerge in immaculate purity. We have not yet come to the point where H. S. Chamberlain imposes on the German people the duty of racial segregation. It is of Rousseau—however misinterpreted—that we are reminded by this so-called primitive purity. But it was not sufficient. What still remained to be established was that the German people, by taking up with Luther the great problem of salvation, had regenerated Christianity itself, after Latin Rome had

[1] See C.A.II, pp. 5–34.

corrupted and distorted it. For Luther it is the inner life that is the source of a profound religious sense. His Reformation is acclaimed as eminently popular, a universal priesthood accessible to all, to the lowest and to the highest. It is this Reformation that guarantees the Germans hegemony and legitimate domination, founded in God. The Germans restored spiritual freedom. They are now, after centuries of anarchy, to reap the harvest! The German Reformation, looking to the past, demolished a medieval order that was fossilised in an impotent scholasticism. Looking to the future, Luther's thunderings, echoed by Fichte, his successor, will demolish the Latin order, the France that had just collapsed under the weight of the Napoleonic system.

As far as philosophy is concerned, Fichte places Leibnitz midway between Luther and himself, the same Leibnitz he claims to emulate. He appears completely unaware of the profoundly European character of Leibnitz's philosophy, so strong is his conviction that true philosophy must be German. Racialism was never taken more literally. Does not Fichte make the life of the mind dependent on purely material conditions of origin and race? A monstrous preconception, which, as we know today, can have dreadful consequences.

Inevitably this line of reasoning culminated in an apologia for Germany's future political development. Fichte, it must be admitted, was not insensible to Germany's retarded growth. But he made a virtue of it, seeing in it a guarantee that, under German stimulus, a new era in the history of the universe was about to break. Nor did Fichte hesitate to describe in advance the perfection his fatherland would attain. He, too, maintained that it would reflect the order of the cosmos, an argument which Hitler was to develop in *Mein Kampf*. It only remained to show, as Fichte did, that the life of a nation pre-exists and outlives ephemeral individual existences, which have meaning only in so far as they are bound up with the life of the nation. It follows, if that is 'individuality' and 'living organism', that the relation between the whole and the parts, between the head and the limbs is a mystery which can only be revealed, not to the intelligence, but to the emotions.

Germany has her roots in the irrational, and here Fichte joins hands again with her romantics.

Once this ideal image of the Fatherland of the future has taken shape, past misfortunes and shortcomings fade magically away. The mirage is complete. Fichte invests the *élite* of the future, the governing minority of tomorrow with all the simple, elementary virtues of which the Germans so readily boast. As he believes that any real education for freedom, for collective and, of course, for national freedom, begins with constraint, this theory leads ultimately to a dictatorship. And we know how Fichte quotes Machiavelli to urge the liberation of a future monarchy from any moral obligation of a so-called 'private' nature.

Hegel is also concerned with the problem of decline and regeneration, but his reasoning takes quite a different course from that of Fichte.[1]

To begin with, he appreciates the sterling merits and qualities of the Latin nations. He knows that they created the sceptical and critical spirit. In his *Phenomenology* he does not hesitate to praise the *Aufklärung* and the French Revolution. What he finds in Kant, his master, and in the French revolutionaries is that freedom of the will which, from purely formal beginnings, comes more and more to life as it embraces reality. Where can this free will be found save in the individual? It, and it alone, will attack the old régime, knowing its privileges and abuses. But why such a short-lived enthusiasm? Why should corruption have gained the upper hand? Because France killed her own religious Reformation. She made the mistake of emancipating the rights of man before liberating his conscience.

Penetrating views, which combine praise and just blame. More important still is Hegel's description of the decline and misfortunes of Germany, a subject Fichte barely mentions. He sees the reverse side of the Lutheran revolution. In this respect he is the prototype of those Germans who, disgusted and disillusioned by a political reality that never reaches fruition, that is incoherent and incomplete, set up for their guidance an ideal state which is an absolute necessity rather than a consoling dream. He, too, will be a prophet, but what he will dimly foresee will be the Bismarckian state.

While he was in Berne, Hegel had seen something of the decadence and tyranny of the Swiss patriarchal system, and he shows just as little indulgence for the territorial states of the dying Holy Roman Empire. His attack on the régime in Württemberg is well known. It is uncompromising. But how much harsher, and at the same time more impressive, is his criticism of the Holy Roman Empire itself! The French Revolution of 1789 and Napoleon completed its downfall. It was an edifice of 'rounded stones' that were mutually incompatible, a pyramid constantly on the verge of collapse. It is Germany's eternal problem, in 1830 as in 1802: 'Are we really a political people, or merely a collection of individuals defending their own interests?' For Hegel, Germany in 1802 is no more than an agglomeration of private rights, of cynical egoisms, in which each man is concerned only to do himself justice. Had Goethe not said the same in his *Götz von Berlichingen*? Hegel goes so far as to make

---

[1] See C.A.II, pp. 35–58, and Vermeil, 'Les idées politiques de Hegel' in *Revue de Métaphysique et de Morale*, 1931.

the Lutheran Reformation, the '*Corpus Evangelicum*', responsible for this general state of anarchy. And he looks with admiration at France, where nationality and state finally banished the threat of internal decay.

Does this mean that he will apply the French methods to his own country? The republican idea, egalitarian democracy, the rights of man, all this remains alien to him. And later, in 1821, he attacks Western conceptions in his *Philosophy of Right*. He speaks of French 'abstractions' and of their 'stultifying atomism', and in so doing comes very close to some of Fichte's more derogatory theses. But shortly before his death, in 1831, he voices his admiration of England's electoral reform.

His over-riding idea is that Germany must be regenerated by methods adapted to her genius and that, in this way, Europe and the world will also be regenerated. His system emanates from romanticism, and has never received formal recognition in any actual institutions. He recognises the relative merits of the *Aufklärung*, but rejects it as monotonous and uninspired. He finds Kant and Fichte too rationalistic. And, brushing aside the emotional traits of romanticism, he arrives at what he considers a complete synthesis of emotion and reason. Abandoning the Western idea of natural right, he formulates a new right and a new 'German style' of morality. He refuses to admit *a priori* principles. Right, according to him, cannot be universal, common to all people. What is needed is a 'positive' knowledge of moral right and moral duty. What is suitable for countries such as England and France, with their stress on the citizen as individual, is quite unsuitable for such a patchwork of territories as Germany. If she hopes to become a true nation, Germany must think in terms of a 'moral totality', a 'supreme morality', embodied in, and realised through, the state.

In short, Germany must re-discover her national genius, created by God and alone capable of revealing her mission in the world. Her right will depend upon her power of cohesion and of collective conviction, upon her internal coherence, from which the highest morality springs, for the duty of each individual will be linked with the superior aims of the community. A nation is 'divine' only in so far as it is a whole and organically alive. This is what Fichte said, though in other words and another context, in the *Discourses* of 1806. The *Phenomenology* and the *Philosophy of Right* merely develop this basic conception of the organised community.

In this way, German thought becomes committed to and confined in the rational state. The really fruitful political idea, it is argued, is a creation not of abstract understanding, but of divine, eternal reason, and in his *Philosophy of History* Hegel makes the prophetic announcement that 'Germany's hour' will come. For the

Germany of the future the hour is already striking in the clock-tower of history.

As one can see, Hegelian Pangermanism is basically religious in character. Fichte ends with Machiavellism; Hegel starts out from it. At a very early stage he had refuted Frederick II's arguments against Machiavelli. It is his firm conviction that a personal morality has no place in the history of peoples, of their rivalries and struggles. So for Germany, despite her past mistakes, he can conceive of a particular predestination. Apart from individual life there is social life, and, above all, the historical development of the people. These forms of collective life imply a higher truth, a scale of values ascending towards a collective form of liberty. For the world is directed by thought, and German thought is best adapted to this sovereign mission. Here again Hegel joins forces with Fichte.

When the Germans have become so enlightened as to will themselves into a nation of their own, then they will be competent to lead Europe and the world to higher things, for there is no greater task than 'to extend the reign of thought throughout the world', a thought that is divine in essence. What is the state but one great complex and total liberty, which takes legitimate possession of its means of existence? One begins to realise to what abuses and distortions a statement of this kind can lead!

History, being man-made, is by no means devoid of reason. The peoples who control its development are 'collective individualities' which find expression in carefully deliberated actions. It is only by making a rational effort that one triumphs over irrational realities. There comes a moment, which is unique in itself, when a certain people emerges as the most mature. The Israelites, the Greeks, and the Romans had their hour, so why not the Germans? Hegel is influenced by the epic period of Napoleon. He aims to recreate it for his own country. He mingles Latin imperialism with the German dream of a Holy Empire. And he, too, ends up by producing an apologia for the Lutheran Reformation. Christ's great discovery, of which Greece and Rome remained ignorant, is that freedom means a natural identity of absolute Spirit with individual conscience. This discovery makes all men 'sons of God'. Luther understood that better than anyone else in Europe.

Hegel naturally rejects the Fichtian theory of an original people, and even more so the apologia for sacerdotalism of a Catholic like Görres. It is enough for him to show that the Germans, 'barbarians' though they may have been, have an undivided, virgin will, which is entirely selfless and pursues neither wealth nor glory. They are pure desire, ready for anything. Hegel draws a parallel between the Carolingian Empire and the Persian royalty. He compares the Middle Ages in Europe to disrupted Greece, almost justifying the piece-meal territorialism on which he had formerly poured scorn. He believes that the Reformation and the Renaissance started an evolution which must of necessity culminate in German supremacy. Luther's Reformation was a total revelation of the Spirit. Every true culture must from now on embody the social realities of the past purified by the spirit of Luther. From now on, right, morality, government, and constitution will be no more than an 'externalised religion'. And, describing the Germany of the future as he visualises her, Hegel gravitates unconsciously towards a system similar to that of Bismarck. He seeks a strong man who, like Richelieu in France, will prove immune to all hatred, who will shatter 'particularism' and noxious egoism.

Hegel, however, does not envisage for Germany the French type of centralisation. He attaches importance only to the total political power which will arise somewhere in a concentrated form. In other words, he hopes for a great all-powerful state among the German states. The more solid and stable this centre of political action is, the more autonomy it will allow other member-states. Hegel knows that in the territorial mosaic two poles of power and of magnetism have appeared: Austria and Prussia. Believing that Prussia is self-sufficient, he turns his attention to Austria. He regards Austrian supremacy as, in the long run, more tolerable than that of Prussia. Hegel even vaguely foresees the three fundamental compromises that are to be an integral part of Bismarck's constitution of 1871: union between the great state and the Reich, conciliation between central and federal institutions, and healthy, fruitful relations between monarchy and Parliament. It is not a 'state in the clouds' that he is trying to set up. There is a certain disparity between his romantic conceptions of the organic state and his views on the future, which are impregnated with the realism one notices in his early works. It is none the less true that Hegel, in his way, has evolved a theory of the decline and regeneration of Germany.

One can easily find in Schleiermacher, the great Lutheran theologian, views on the future of German religion which, though not Hegelian in tone, nevertheless emanate from the purest romanticism. But the time has come to contrast with the Lutherian trio, Fichte, Hegel, and Schleiermacher, the Catholic trio, Novalis, Fr. Schlegel, and J. Görres. The second trio have also elaborated a doctrine of decline and regeneration.[1]

In his remarkable work *Christianity or Europe*, Novalis begins with an idealised picture of the Catholic Middle Ages, then goes on to condemn the Lutheran Reformation and its consequences, gives high praise to the Jesuit Order, passes judgment on modern science and criticism, and finally, as we have seen, predicts the German

[1] See C.A.II, pp. 59–85.

revolution. Let it never be said that the only Church Reformation was that of Luther or that the sole political revolution was in 1789! Novalis hopes that 'other' European nations will experience this religious renovation and will find their preoccupation with mundane things swallowed up in a new Church. But he allots Germany a special mission, an exalted destiny. While various other countries are preoccupied with party politics, financial speculation, or war, the German is meditating, slowly finding himself, maturing with all the necessary deliberation and becoming a model for a superior culture which will be the culture of a new Europe. He will, therefore, soon hold a dominant position. He will be the Messiah of the New Age. He will bring the world the Catholic peace of which the Continent is so much in need.

Fr. Schlegel, for his part, is the spokesman of Austrian Catholicism. The Roman world has decayed and its withered roots have lost all fertility. Human relations are now governed by abstract reason and empty words, on which the new republic has been designed that is to be imposed on Europe. So there must be an end to: (1) the Lutheran Reformation, which has engendered a sterile criticism fatal to the religious spirit; (2) the spirit of profanity with the taste for a mode of living that rebels against the most sacred traditions. Protestantism has given rise to modern absolutism, to individual freedom of belief, to the growing secularisation of institutions and of education, to the Treaties of Westphalia, which arbitrarily split up the Holy Roman Empire and capped this deliberate disruption with confessional dualism.

So for Novalis, the Catholic convert, Luther's Reformation is the root cause of Germany's decline. But history is made not by Fichte's liberty, with its facile appetite, but by a divine Providence soon to be incarnate in the new Germany, a divinely protected people, both sound and strong, which has kept its blood and race pure and which, at the time of the Barbarian invasions, for which Fr. Schlegel now makes out a case, grafted its aristocratic heroism on a decaying Roman and Latin reality.

Thus Germania, which had to be led to Christianity and antiquity by force, became a regenerating influence throughout the entire Western world. The German Empire, charged with the protection of Christianity, fulfilled its task. The German monarchs never became despots. They ruled by virtue of the spontaneous loyalty of their subjects. They knew only that noble brand of freedom which is inextricably bound up with honour, the cultivation of natural genius, the horror any man must feel for those treaties and legal contracts which crush and paralyse their authors.

Fr. Schlegel favours the idea of a Germanic Federation, which will have to be subordinated to the Empire and extended throughout the world. The *Concordantia catholica* will bring peace to the old Continent after so many wars. From its birthplace, Germany will reorganise Europe and the world. Germany's privilege is none other than to possess the living truth. Basically, Schlegel's ideas on this all-important point are the same as Fichte's.

J. Görres draws a similar conclusion. He, too, has his ideas on the decline of the Holy Roman Empire, which, in 1806, is crumbling before his eyes. Exploiting the arguments of Novalis and Schlegel, he launches his main attack on the French Revolution, which he compares to a hollow mountain crushed by the Napoleonic régime, an image that also appears in the classic 'Walpurgis Night' in the second *Faust*. Görres, like all the Romantics of his persuasion, protests against the tragic swing of the pendulum that threw revolutionary France into the Napoleonic dictatorship. And here, he points out, we have Germany caught between the barbaric immobility of the Russians and the crazy mobility of the English, and particularly the French! Let her be on her guard both to right and to left of her!

According to Görres, Germany is the nation marked out by destiny for regeneration. The leader she needs is in Rome. It is the Pope. She would be well-advised to renew her alliance with him, for the union of the temporal and the spiritual, the Empire and the Papacy, must be renewed. Like Schlegel, Görres borrows extensively from the authentic Lutheran, Fichte, for the advancement of German Catholicism. He believes that one must not abuse spiritual freedom and become lost in the universe. On the other hand, one must not become confined within such narrow limits that one is condemned to suffocation. A lesson learned not only from Fichte but also from Goethe! Keep faith with the nation and its exalted traditions. See to it that its full vitality spreads throughout the world. What must be revived is both the race and its thought—that is, the living community.

Germany alone in Europe can ensure this revival. Just as the barbarians of a past epoch watered the arid plains of Western Europe with their life-giving blood, so now on the ruined states of Europe ideas must rain down through channels of German thought to bring order into chaos. Divine ideas, like a new cloud of fire which will lead those who have been called by destiny to the succession of superior peoples. In a federated Europe under German domination, state and Church will be more closely united than ever. By this union they will overcome the terrible mechanisation that threatens modern society. The Reformation and Renaissance of the sixteenth century are over and done with. They suffered a disastrous defeat. In resisting Napoleon as she is doing, Germany is getting ready to replace him. Let France lose her Lorraine and let Latin corruption be wiped out with her defeat.

E. M. Arndt and F. L. Jahn are not, strictly speaking, philosophers and are not so closely tied to the confessionalism of their period, but they are more strongly committed to the geniune restoration brought about by the recovery of Prussia and the wars of independence. Both are popular prophets, representing a new offshoot of primitive Pangermanism, which established itself in Germany in the first years of the nineteenth century. Their works were written between 1806 and 1830, although Arndt only published his *Pro populo germanico* in 1854. From 1810 onwards Jahn founded his gymnastic societies with the object not only of building up a strong race but also of surmounting class barriers and preparing the ground for a popular resistance movement.[1]

The ideas which these two choir-leaders of patriotism propound on Germany's predestined mission are not particularly original when compared with those of the Lutheran philosophers or Catholic publicists. What they hold against the Treaties of Westphalia is that they cut off Germany from the Low Countries and the Swiss Confederation. The result is that neither the source nor the mouth of the Rhine is in Germany. Yet this German people, which was so badly treated in 1648, is the most direct heir of Hellenism and primitive Christianity. At this point a hint of paganism creeps in, for we are told that it is German nationality that comes closest to the Greek. Mention is even made of certain affinities with the Persians and the Hindus. Jahn anticipates the Nazi Rosenberg and his 'Myth of the Twentieth Century'. As for primitive Christianity, it is the natural, human purity of the Germans that binds them to it. If the Lutheran Reformation shook the entire world, it was because it rediscovered its secret. So the 'holy race' is an idea that permeates these strange lucubrations, which draw largely on Romantic sources. What Germany represents is the unity and 'transcendent' totality of human nature.

Hence the antagonism between this pre-eminently revitalising nation and the decadent nations surrounding it. Our patriots guarantee it a brilliant future. If a wise Power rules over the moral world, as a wise reason governs the physical world, then Germany need not be too downcast by her misfortunes. For the time is coming when she will rule Europe and the world by her own wisdom, in accordance with the eternal laws of an organised Cosmos. Jahn also hopes that one day the 'book of Pangermanism' will be written, in which its virtues and its model culture will be described.

There is, of course, nothing new in this fiery sermonising. Arndt and Jahn differ from their predecessors in one thing: they allot Germany a precise place in the Europe of their time. Arndt defines it in greatest detail. When the Reich has achieved a solid foundation,

[1] See C.A.I, pp. 83–116.

it will be allowed to develop as 'chance and its own nature' dictate. Has a state not the right to make its demands of neighbouring nations who are unjustly robbing it of air and light? But Arndt talks of future German supremacy and in the same breath protests against the dictatorship of Napoleon! He visualises his country ravaging France and England and seizing small neighbouring states, all in order to become a 'people of masters'. He regards Holland as the most outrageous blow struck at Germany's 'natural' frontiers. Describing these frontiers precisely, he shows the whole of southern Germany pushing, by means of her rivers, towards the sea, the great instrument of culture and activity. He pities such nations as Poland and Hungary, which have neglected this access to the sea. The Somme appears to him the natural northern frontier between France and Germany. To the east the frontier would run along the Ardennes, the Jura, and the Vosges. This does not prevent Arndt, however, from branding those parts of France which Germany would acquire as 'nests of corruption'!

In 1809, Jahn, in his *Deutsches Volkstum*, raises the question of Austria, freed of the 'heavy burden' of Silesia and Bavaria by Frederick II. The Danube basin depends naturally on Habsburg domination. Jahn has the idea of a military Germany federated round Prussia. With Austria included, she would be a new Holy Roman Empire resuscitated by the state of Prussia. It was up to the Habsburgs to realise the situation and to allow Prussia to seize all the territories within her sphere of military action.

Here, then, we have a complete programme of continental Pangermanism. In ten years of peace, declares Arndt, Germany, France, and Italy will be grossly over-populated. What is to be done with the surplus population? They should be sent not west to America but east to the real cradle of European civilisation. A fine task for the Holy Alliance, to mobilise a European wave towards Asia and Africa in order to rejuvenate these continents with Christianity and human culture!

So far, thinkers and publicists have thought of Germany from a global point of view. Their preoccupation with Prussia has been purely incidental. But the Prussian problem and the military problems relating to it have been dealt with in a highly pertinent and prophetic way by Dietrich von Bülow, a career soldier born in 1757, who died in 1807, soon after the disaster of Jena.[1]

He, too, considers what position Germany should have in Europe. In his view, wars are inevitable so long as great Powers seek to expand quite spontaneously towards their natural frontiers. The thing most vital to a state is neither its nationality nor its language, but the central military core, within which it subjects everything to

[1] See C.A.I, pp. 59–82.

its domination. That is why, in particular, the Rhine can never be the natural frontier between France and Germany. Its left bank is part of the aforementioned core. Holland should be in German hands, but not Belgium, where the opposing armies would inevitably clash. A remarkable forecast of 1940!

In the south it is Austria that interests von Bülow. He, too, allots it the Danube basin with the specific function of keeping Russia and Turkey apart and guaranteeing the independence of Greece. Austria may, of course, attack, but it will not be Russia, whose military core lies to the north of the Carpathians. It will be Prussia herself, and the attack may come from four different directions. Prussia's sole protection would seem to be Bohemia.

Von Bülow considers that Prussia is in an impregnable position. He is convinced that she can make up for the possible loss of the Vistula by occupying northern Germany and invading Holland. What obviously interests von Bülow in drawing up the geographical balance-sheet of a changing Europe is Prussian North Germany. In this he is the forerunner of Bismarck. When one recalls the attempts made by Frederick II's minister, Hertzberg, to have Holland invaded and Austria pushed back to the Danube delta, one begins to understand what Dietrich von Bülow is really after. In fact, Hertzberg and von Bülow both visualise Prussia: (1) occupying the whole of northern Germany and Holland and threatening French territory at its nearest point; (2) seizing Denmark; (3) annexing an Austria which has expanded towards the Balkans and Bavaria. This programme foreshadows the three wars between 1864 and 1871, and from there to the visions of 1848–9 is but a short step.

What shape, then, will the war of the future take? Von Bülow's admiration for Frederick II is by no means boundless. He considers that the great King did not conquer enough. He was a philosopher who loved leisure and lucid thinking and for that reason missed his best opportunities. He sees things differently from Mirabeau, who hoped that atheist Prussia would triumph over Catholic Austria. Weakened by Prussia, Austria proves incapable of resisting Napoleon. But can Prussia hold out by herself, without the help of Austria? And if she perishes, will Frederick II not be at fault?

Frederick II was, in the last resort, a mere amateur in aggression. He omitted to conquer Westphalia and Austria. To put it bluntly, he was incapable of conquering the whole of Germany, although he had it in his power to do so. It is too late to retrieve the past, but the idea is there: the reunification of Germany and Austria by force. Not surprisingly, Bülow, like many another, was jealous of Napoleon. He realises that the end-result of Frederick II's policy was to separate

Austria from Germany. Prussia at that time was bankrupt, and she paid dearly for it between 1786 and 1806. She failed in her mission because, in the person of Frederick II, she neglected to unify Germany at one stroke. As for the great King's internal policy, the less said the better, for no serious attempt was made to improve the living conditions of the Prussian people. Frederick II only gathered enlightened men about him for his own personal amusement. He left Napoleon and Bismarck to do what was really necessary.

When it comes to the 'strong' Germany of tomorrow, von Bülow is a reliable prophet. He has his own way of dealing with the problem of a possible capital. Without a capital there can be no unity and no true culture. Who will unite Germany? Prussia. She will begin in the north, which she will force into submission in preparation for war against France. The small princes of the great plain will be easly dispossessed. Then the Prussian monarchy, having become national and German, will have to make good the mistake it has always made in the past of separating the north from the south. But has Frederick William III the necessary boldness for such a venture? The impending conflict will call for the utmost speed, the utmost possible weight, a lightning attack on the nearest enemy states and a strangle-hold on them before the others can come to their assistance. Only a politico-military strategy such as this establishes, for an indefinite time, empires that enjoy lasting prestige. In the offensive war of the future, numbers will be decisive. Everything will depend on amassing fighting men and material. Small states can do nothing against their powerful neighbours, and what Europe needs is one great state, which alone is capable of subduing all the others and of establishing a continental monarchy. One can hardly imagine a more accurate prediction of the eventual Prussification of the old Continent of Europe!

So this early nationalism is both German and Prussian. If it finds its inspiration in a doctrine which condemns the Western nations to decadence and reserves for Germany the mission of revival, it believes that this revival is possible only under the aegis of Prussia. Fr. Schlegel would undoubtedly opt for Austria. But for most of them Prussia remains the only great state, which, thanks to her military strength, is capable of achieving the new unity.

4. THE REALISTS (1830–50)

Between 1830 and 1850 the fulminations of the Romantics continue in the final appeals of a patriot like Arndt or in the early writings and operas of R. Wagner, who in his great theoretical work of 1850–51, *Opera and Drama*, once more expresses his messianic hopes. A new factor appears with Friedrich List's economic realism and the visions of a Greater Germany which, you will remember, played such a part in the deliberations of the Frankfurt Assembly.

From 1820 to 1840, Arndt, condemned for 'Jacobinism' because he was too deeply concerned with German unity, had been forgotten. He makes a sudden reappearance towards 1840 as Professor of History at Bonn University. He is to remain in the public eye until 1860, when he withdraws covered in glory and heaped with honours. His *Pro Populo Germanico*, published in 1854, was the fruit of his silent meditation. Does he add much to what he had written before 1830? [1]

He takes up again the familiar theme of Germany's divine mission, the final echo of the romantic fanfares. The German philosophers, the Fichtes, Hegels, and Schellings, have been attacked, but, he asks, is it realised that any impurities in German thought could only have come from abroad? Let the French run towards Socialism and the life of Paris sink into disrepute. The active intellectual life of the German people is evidence of its outstanding merit. It is the surest guarantee for the future. 'Never', cries Arndt, 'could a people as courageous and intelligent as ours fall victim to inferior neighbours.'

The German people's warlike spirit will lead it to a legitimate position of supremacy. It gave proof of that between 1807 and 1814. The same courage in the political and social spheres will enable it to carve out its destiny in the contemporary world, to thrust its way forward through the whirlpools of present-day life. It will crush the French and Russians and will become the only rival to British power.

After Olmütz, this fervent patriot is troubled by the Austrian danger. He describes the attempt made by Schwarzenberg after 1849 to repair the damage. Does this foolhardy Austrian imagine that he can coax the German people into his pot-pourri of nationalities? On the contrary, everything that is noble in Germany dreams only of unity, supreme power, complete restoration of national honour. Can one really envisage uniting Germans with the most barbaric of foreign races? Arndt will have nothing to do with a '*Mitteleuropa*' administered by Austria. He hopes rather that Austria will help Italy to put her house in order. If she knows what is best for herself, she will handle Italy skilfully, and occupy the 'strongest and finest' rear position in the world. For from her Alpine heights she can see the whole of European politics in one glance. If she wishes to expand, let it be on the Danube, with one eye on the Levant. If she had done this earlier, the Russians would not be the masters in Bucharest and Jassy. Let Austria, therefore, watch over Turkey and keep her clear of the Slav influence.

Arndt, moreover, brings his dream of German greatness up to

[1] See C.A.I, pp. 92–7, 100–4.

date. Everywhere, he writes, the Germans are becoming involved in industrial activities, political undertakings, and social innovations. They are setting up colonial agencies, improving their navigation, extending their commerce without, at the same time, neglecting their agriculture. They are everywhere: in the Mediterranean, in North and South America, in the Scandinavian countries, and in Russia. They are working alongside the English; tomorrow they will be their successful rivals. How crushing is the superiority of the Germans over the Latins! As is well known, 'the German, belligerent, enterprising and resolute, was created to collaborate in the domination of the world, but above all else to establish a strong national unity inside his own frontiers'.

That is the over-riding, unique conception: internal cohesion as a stepping-stone to external expansion. At a time when the Customs Union is being set up under the patent and determined direction of Prussia, does such a conception not prepare the way for Friedrich List? [1]

Born in 1789, List is Professor of Commercial Law at Tübingen University from 1817 onwards. Germany is still broken up into the thirty-nine states of the German Confederation. List secures election to the Landtag of Württemberg and flings himself into the Liberal movement with four specific aims: (1) a wider national sovereignty; (2) abolition of internal customs barriers; (3) a postal union; (4) a common system of protective tariffs.

Why does he reject free trade? Because this solution would call for the creation of a 'universal republic' which could only be oppressive to a nation as backward as Germany. Germany's young industry can develop only if it is protected against foreign competition. List, like Arndt a too-fervent champion of unity, is compelled to emigrate to America, where he is able to study a highly developed industry at close quarters and to nourish his hatred for free trade. One year after his return to Europe in 1839 he publishes his *National System of Political Economy*. Other works follow till his death in 1846. In his work is concentrated all the realistic and effective nationalism of these twenty years, which were to prove so decisive for the future of Germany.

Protectionism, for List, was no more than the logical consequence of his views on the internal unity and external expansion of the nation. Arndt had the same idea, but List presented his argument differently, with a wealth of reasoning based on sound information. One can confidently say that List was the first theorist of national economics. Though very different from Bülow, he yet complements him. On his notion of a military core, the Prussian officer had built up a rigid theory, according to which every nation must take

[1] See C.A.I, pp. 117–46.

possession of territories that come within its sphere of military activity. List believes that nations must do the same for their economic sphere of activity. We pass from the military domain to the economic and vice versa. So the science of the future will be the science of national growth. Figures, statistics, and curves will all be pressed into service.

Seen from this angle, the race problem seems to List to be closely linked with the problem of German supremacy. In the most cavalier fashion he ignores the Latins in the west and the Slavs in the east. He is interested only in the Anglo-German sphere.

List, who goes no farther than Napoleon in France, considers that the Latins, even under French leadership, are not made for sovereign domination. Behind their progress in war are no agricultural and industrial specialists, who are to be found nowhere in the west except in Alsace and Flanders. They have virtually no maritime sense, no urge to expand. France, suspecting this, would like to have a frontier on the Rhine in order to absorb an element of stability from Germany. Will she be allowed to exploit Germany for her own ends of Asiatic expansion?

Russia can only be compared to a wild beast. One moment she is in a deep sleep, the next leaping about madly. We must keep an eye on her, for she aims to dominate Asia and the Balkans. We must follow her growing strength very closely. The Russian state is, in effect, essentially interested in conquest, and List is careful to treat her with respect. It is a vast military colony, which doubles its power every half-century. Everything in Russia is meticulously designed with aggression in view. Whereas France now only desires tranquillity, in the east, next door to a weakened Turkey, Russian ambition and Russian strength are growing, and with them the desire to lay hands on Turkey and act as arbiter between Austria and Hungary.

The future lies with the Germans. List knows the Anglo-American world too well to imagine that Germany will find it easy to assert her supremacy over it. But, as he includes Americans, English, and Germans in the vague concept 'Germanic race', he, too, ascribes to this predestined race a providential mission. He sees it directing the affairs of the entire world, civilising the barbarians in the east, disciplining the Latins in the west, populating territories that are still uninhabited. All the requisite qualities are there: pacific energy, industrial capacity, a sense of order and discipline, a taste for autonomy, a passion for communal efficiency.

The conclusion List reaches is that Germany must at all costs supplant England at the heart of this vast reservoir of energy and ambition.

Her first duty, then, is to be strong as a nation, with a dense population and an efficient army. Her first lesson should be learnt from the Hanseatic League, which, by concentrating on the acquisition of material wealth, neglected its political interests. It drew away from the Holy Roman Empire in order to play at ruling the seas, instead of joining forces with the towns of Upper Germany, founding a powerful House of Commons, struggling against the decrepit nobility, and ensuring German supremacy by realising the unity of the nation. It failed to achieve mastery of the seas. The Princes toyed with it as with the cities of the interior. A history of failure, yet an example to be borne constantly in mind.

Germany must become what England is today: a real empire, a federation of powerful cities, both industrial centres and ports, protected by a strong national army which guards its foreign markets right out to the heart of the Tropics. Modern science will enable her to regain what she lost so pitifully in the Middle Ages.

She must expand inside Europe itself; that is where she must begin. The Low Countries and Switzerland are Germanic territory, prosperous countries which were greatly influenced by the Carolingian culture. No country has developed its river and sea traffic as Holland has done. On the other hand, why not colonise in Hungary and cast an eye on Turkey? Germany can afford a tremendous expansion of her agriculture, still more of her industry and commerce. She would off-load her surplus population towards the south-east and not overseas. She must follow the Danube. What are Hungarians and Magyars without Germany?

A colonial empire? Yes, to be sure, but the means to this end must be prepared: factories, foreign trade, a commercial fleet and a navy, enterprise and tenacity! The Mediterranean routes to the Persian Gulf must not remain the exclusive property of England. Austria must be exploited. And the Germans, following the example set by the French, must gain a footing in the most remote of England's colonies.

Once Central Europe has been reorganised along these lines, it will serve as intermediary between East and West, which will be compelled to submit to its superior power. So long as Germany remains in a state of disruption, East and West will fight over it. Why should she not begin by allying herself with England? But List regards peace in Europe as precarious. While the power of the United States grows steadily, England is hurriedly rearming, and France and Russia ask nothing more than to fight for the expansion of their respective spheres of action. How could the Turkish spoils possibly be divided between these three nations? Has the time not come for an Anglo-German partnership with a view to pushing forward into Africa and Asia? But this can happen only if Germany is as united as her eventual ally. With Holland and

Belgium in her possession, what a partner she would be in the competitive wars of the future! This alliance is the sole means of staving off the Franco-Russian menace and the American threat. A Germany united in herself and allied with England would have nothing to fear from France and Russia, both of which are opposed to her unification. And what could England have to gain from weakening Germany?

The Anglo-German alliance occurs to List only on the eve of his death, by which time he has come to regard the Franco-Russian danger as something more to be feared than English rivalry. His great idea, his sole idea is German unity, on the presupposition that the '*Zollverein*' will succeed and that new means of communication will be developed. This idea is a logical outcome of the idea of German superiority, a superiority which implies a tremendous effort on Germany's part to expand both in Europe and overseas. List's aim is to organise Europe around Germany. He is haunted by Napoleon in so far as Napoleon envisaged economic domination.

So List visualises the old Continent organised in one closed commercial unit, the moving force and the heart of which will be, not France this time, but Germany. He thinks in terms of a common Parliament and a common fleet. Such a Europe on a German axis would be able easily to exploit the Near and Far East. A drive to the Persian Gulf, a fighting navy, colonies in Australia and New Zealand, a vast Germano-Magyar Empire, which would include France and would keep England and Russia at arm's length: this strange prophet sees all these visions. And they will go on living in the imagination of the Germans during Bismarck's Empire.

Von Moltke, whose studies appear simultaneously with List's principal work, has views on the Turkish problem and the East which complement List's ideas. Von Moltke is seriously troubled by the possible break-up of Turkey, for he fears that England, France, and Russia all have designs on her. Is Germany to be denied her share? Why is no mention ever made in Turkey of Austria looking to the West instead of following her natural course eastwards? Has she not claims on the Gardens of the Hesperides? It is she who should bar the Russians' way into the Balkans.[1]

But it is now, between 1830 and 1850, that a new historiography appears in Germany. Pertz, Ranke, Dunker, and Droysen are mature. In 1830 Pertz and Ranke are thirty-five, Dunker and Droysen some fifteen years younger. They form the romantic school of the Renaissance. It is naturally hostile to the philosophy of enlightenment and violently opposed to Jacobinism-turned-Bonapartist in France. It revives the old ideas in support of clerical legitimism and the divine right of kings. Somewhat later, when the

[1] See C.A.I, pp. 147–64.

economic and social problems of the Biedermeier period appear, *bourgeois* nationalism rears its head, producing not only the philological and critical methods, but also the ideas of Humbold on history, the school of Savigny and the conservatism of the landed gentry, an impassioned apologia for Prussia and the expansionist liberalism which indulges in the same dreams of national greatness that cast their illusory halo round the movement of 1848–9.

So German history is modelling itself either on the conservatism that is a characteristic feature of the German Confederation and later Little Germany, or on the ambitious liberalism that becomes enamoured of Greater Germany.

Landed gentry and *bourgeois* are pursuing the same ideal. Both are irretrievably committed to the feudal, monarchic state. So no attempt is even made between 1830 and 1850 to write history on broad, generous, original lines. The historians, intoxicated by the exploits of the new Prussia, present the national state to Germany's *bourgeoisie* not as the result of a typically Western evolution in the direction of democratic freedom, but as a phenomenon peculiar to the Germans and designed to guarantee that internal unity which is indispensable for their future expansion on the Continent or in the world as a whole. In other words, the historians of this period prepare the ground for a 'national' revolution which will establish not the elementary, basic freedoms within the nation, but a collective freedom, a freedom of movement for Germany, so that she can gain more living-space.

IV. THE NEW IMPERIALISM (1850–1918)

We now see the Bismarckian Empire emerging. Its roots lie in the 1848 Revolution, when Bismarck made his début as a political orator, in a speech praising Prussia's traditions and attacking Western conceptions. In this chapter, as in the last, two periods stand out. The first is between 1850 and 1890, when Bismarck's personality dominates everything else. The second, from 1890 to the armistice in 1918, has been called the 'Wilhelmian' period. When Bismarck unites Germany in accordance with the Prussian prescription, all eyes are on the principal actors. Fervent nationalism remains in the background, frequently hostile to the man who is forging the nation's new destiny. Bismarck subdues rather than encourages chauvinism. But barely has he left the political stage after breaking with Wilhelm II than Pangermanism is let loose. It widens and develops its programme, calls on contemporary science to support it, and draws up its plan of expansion.

1. The Bismarck Period (1850–90)

In 1885 Bismarck declared in the *Reichstag* that Bulgaria was of no interest to Germany. In his last year of political power, on the 28 April 1890, he said: 'We have no further demands to make. Germany does not need the three million Dutchmen who have no desire to be absorbed by us, nor the Baltic countries, nor Poland, nor any other territory. We have enough annexed populations.'

The gulf that separates Bismarck from the Wilhelmian nationalists emerges clearly from his political strategy. While they dream of the unattainable, Bismarck's method is to bring his ideas into line with what he achieves, and vice versa. He is careful not to make the mistake that the Wilhelmian diplomats are to make between 1900 and 1914 of forcing into existence a European coalition which directly threatens the Triple Alliance. The dualism inherent in the German problem, the strange fact that Germany is at one and the same time a national state and a super-nation, is the work of Bismarck, but he surmounts it by his moderation and prudence.[1]

One must not forget that in 1854 the continental ambitions of the Frankfurt Assembly could have been realised. If they were not, it was because Prussia and Austria hesitated. In 1859 Austria had the opportunity of a lifetime to acquire the Danube principalities. If Prussia and Austria felt frustrated, they had only themselves to blame. At that turning-point in the history of nineteenth-century Germany, Bismarck was pursuing his Prussian policy with single-minded ruthlessness. His main objective was to bring down Austria and break up the German Confederation. Yet what he, in fact, was doing was reverting to the policy that Dietrich von Bülow reproached Frederick II with having pursued. Bismarck was separating Prussia from Austria, a policy fatal for a Greater Germany, but not for Prussia herself, who was to wage three victorious wars between 1864 and 1871. Bismarck could not visualise a united Germany and a resuscitated Empire except under the aegis of Prussia. In other words, he never yielded to the temptation of a Pangermanism under Austrian leadership.

The political course he steered for Prussia from 1852 onwards is well known. His plan is for a Greater Prussia to take over control of Germany and turn her into the dominant Power in Europe. Any continental Pangermanism will be Prussian in tone and in trend. Europe will become 'a projection of Prussia', as the new Germany herself will be.

When Bismarck follows up the military victories of 1864–71 with his Triple Alliance, he appears to revert to the dreams of 1848. While he postpones the Customs Union with Austria, he still has

[1] See C.A.I, pp. 165–96.

clear views on Central Europe and on the brilliant future of the Germanic race, which he, too, asserts is physically and morally supreme. He is skilful enough, however, to keep the opposition quiet. The Franco-Russian alliance does not take shape till 1891, after he has left the political stage. But there is ample evidence that he believed in the decadence of the Latins, whom he describes, like Fichte before him, as past their prime and on the decline. He is equally confident that the Slavs cannot do without German competition. In his view, only the Germans are and remain young in spirit, powerful, stable, and charged with a mission that is indispensable to humanity. The old Chancellor endows the Germans with qualities that are preponderantly masculine and virile. Individually, the Germans give their governments ample trouble, but, where the national idea is concerned, they have the faith that moves mountains.

That is why Bismarck, in his conservative peace policy, intends to lean on a conquered Austria, to which he believes Germany can be of use. Once England has welcomed the Austro-German Entente, Bismarck remains faithful to it. It is a thinly disguised revival of the Holy Roman Empire under Prussian aegis. As for Austria, she finds her salvation in 'Germanising' her institutions. The economic differences are obvious, however, and Austria does not become a full member of the Customs Union. The aim is not to annex Austria, but to win her over as a safe ally.

Bismarck realised that Germany's greatest weakness lay in her enormous defence front. That is why he worked tirelessly to prevent or, at least, to delay the outbreak of war. Bismarck appreciated the widespread anxiety in Europe. While he firmly believed, in his heart, in German supremacy, he took great pains to make it palatable, and even desirable, to others. He had to win their confidence. If he wants a well-armed Germany, then it is primarily in order to discourage any potential aggressor from attacking. Realising that Germany could be beaten, Bismarck, with prophetic clarity, assesses the damage in advance. As she has two fronts to defend, those who watch over her destiny can never be too vigilant.

In the Bismarck era it is Germany's historians who are the most consistent worshippers at his shrine.

We have already seen how the traditions of German historiography grew out of romanticism. The ideas of Fichte and Hegel are aired again and presented in every imaginable form. The German historian begins with the assumption that Germany knows the secret whereby peoples achieve greatness. Germany's privilege consists in the fact that, arriving late on the scene, she is called upon to synthesise the experiences of other peoples. The aim of the new historiography is to draw from the past positive conclusions on which faith in the future can be established. These historians still believe in Germany's mission, but under the influence of Bismarckian realism they abandon the metaphysical arguments. For writers like Pertz, Ranke, Dunker, and Droysen the gulf between decline and regeneration loses its religious significance. They prefer to study the laws which govern the fall or survival of nations, and they will show that the only political forms that can last are those of a reorganised Germany led by Prussia.

Ranke has described in detail the bond created between the old landed aristocracy and the new *bourgeois* intelligentsia by the national idea and the prestige it enjoyed. In fact, he led the whole of Germany's science of history into a sort of blind alley. He felt impelled to declare, towards the end of his life, that the events of his lifetime meant the ruin of revolutionary principles. Completely blind to the real moving forces in human society, Ranke could only project his narrow conservatism on the past. It seemed to him that the creation of Bismarck's Reich was equivalent to a decisive victory for the counterrevolution. He found his inspiration in a sort of secularised theology, according to which a divine Providence controls Germany's destiny and harmonises spirit with power. As he had neither the genius nor the sincerity of Nietzsche, he imagined that there was present in power, and in Prussian power, a presiding genius that protected Germany's culture. And finally it was he who first conceived the idea of 'justice among nations', the real meaning of which has already been explained. It was he who cultivated that hothouse plant, the sacred union, which permits and justifies an aggressive policy of expansion and conquest. Ranke, in short, personified the capitulation of progressive liberalism in Germany.

Side by side with Ranke one finds historians like Ernst Curtius and Mommsen attempting to prove in their main works that the German people is the legitimate heir of Greece and Rome.[1] In a collection of essays which was published between 1876 and 1882, Curtius states the conclusions he reached in the course of his historical research. He compares the Holy Roman Empire to the federation of states in Greece which fell apart when faced with the barbarians and on the eve of the Medean wars. Is it possible to progress from such a state of weakness and decadence to unity and power? The Greek problem? The German problem? It can be solved only by heroism. Themistocles has his modern counterpart in the Great Elector of Prussia; Salamis, in the victory of Fehrbellin. It is easy to unite around a dominant military state the vassal states it has subdued. For Prussia, with her arid soil, is reminiscent of Attica. Prussia, like Athens, will attract many talents and intellectual currents. The state of ancient times, which Athens revived as a

[1] See C.A.II, Preface, lx–lxvi.

concept, comes to life again, with all its essential attributes, in Prussia. The Prussian state will demand the absolute Pericles, who, whenever necessary, will place democratic rights in abeyance. The Aegean League will find its modern counterpart in Bismarck's Federal State. Are there not 'eternal values' that are handed down from one great civilisation to another?

The most cogent reply to this naïve display of arrogance is Nietzsche's forceful and brilliant warning of the barrenness that threatens Bismarck's Germany after her military triumphs. We shall consider this later, when we come to Bismarck's opponents and critics.

Greece was crushed by Rome. Mommsen takes up the case where Curtius left off and compares the German Empire's military strength to that of the Roman Empire. Was Augustus not the predecessor of Wilhelm I? Was his Imperial status not a compromise 'à la Bismarck' between monarchy and republic? The Prussian régime, like Rome, has succeeded in combining military command with public administration. In Berlin, in accordance with the Hegelian formula, authority and liberty go hand in hand. The monarch is responsible before the public conscience. The standing army cements the whole structure. While the Augustan state lacked the touch of genius that one finds under Caesar, at least it survived for five centuries, thanks to patience and prudence, which are also so clearly evident in Prussia today. Moreover, the Prussian kings do not make the mistake that Augustus made of failing to keep the army adequately equipped or to provide heirs for the ruling dynasty. Prussia commands the same people that defeated the legions of Varus; it will last longer than Rome!

Inevitably, Rome must have 'her' historian. It is Heinrich von Treitschke. His conception of history is almost as elementary and naïve as that of Sybel the other high priest of the master-state. Sybel was a disciple of Ranke, adopting his idea that all governments must be liberal above and absolute below, for otherwise it is impossible to protect those in power. But Treitschke goes farther. He wants the Government to be firm in its dealings with the liberals themselves. Treitschke rejects constitutionalism and parliamentary democracy and considers that a national culture can be preserved only if the state is protected against the outside world by its dynasty, its bureaucracy, and its armed forces. What he foresees is ruthless competition between the great European imperialist systems. He is shrewd enough to realise that Social Democracy in Germany represents a real historic force, capable of carrying Germany beyond the Bismarckian idea and its narrow conservatism.[1]

He is convinced, on the other hand, that only a Germanic people could convert a confederation like that of 1815 into a federation à la

[1] See C.A.I, pp. 197–230.

Bismarck. In Switzerland, the Low Countries, and the United States it would have been impossible. They had no room for hegemony. But in Germany the difference between Prussia and the other states is the difference between power and impotence—that is the secret of the German enigma. Prussia is strong enough to mould the Reich into a federation by taking on herself the central power which is entrusted to a dynasty that ceases to be Prussian only to become 'Imperial'. Prussia's strength, Treitschke adds, fosters the very liberties it protects and controls. So we are back again with Hegel.

In describing Prussia's guiding motives and institutions, Treitschke cannot be accused of lack of moderation. But his aim is to make Prussia the embryo of German unity. He believes in a Germany which is 'a projection of Prussia', a conception which can only be interpreted by Germany's neighbours as a grave menace. Like his master Bismarck, Treitschke is entirely committed to this Prussian conception. He is more Prussian than Pangermanist.

His idea of the state, of the social discipline on which it is based and the activities it implies, is derived, in part, from other countries: imitation of Sparta and Rome, imitation of Machiavellism from the Renaissance, ideas borrowed from the soldier-monarch, Gustavus Adolphus, and above all perhaps from Slav history. But here the state is mere power (*Macht*). Its right is limited only by its might. On this extremely important point, Treitschke is a follower of von Bülow and F. List. A state is as great, or small, as the means at its disposal, and this applies to all spheres of activity. Large states devour small states in self-defence. Treitschke could hardly be thinking still of the two great Powers to the west and east of the old continent of Europe.

He arrives, therefore, at a very clear definition of war, which he regards as inevitable, moral, and sacred. There can be no judgment passed on states. They are motivated by impersonal considerations. They cannot be bound by any contract. War, and war alone, governs relations between peoples. Every nation is bound to conquer. Every citizen is bound, by implication, to sacrifice his life. A nation's strength is the strength of its army and industry. So, in Treitschke's view, Frederick II was right to ensure Prussian supremacy in Germany. From this dominant position she can keep an eye on Alsace and on the Danube at the same time.

Treitschke believes that in the nineteenth century Germans will dominate political science. Not all peoples, said Herder, have the same right to happiness. Treitschke knows Savigny and Niebuhr, the romantic historians and their teachings. He will have nothing to do with natural and universal right, for which he substitutes diversity of political forms and wealth of experience analysed by the historical scientist. Frederick II acted in accordance with Prussia's 'historic right', although he was familiar with natural right.

It is by following this clearly marked path that Prussianism will become an integral part of Imperialist nationalism. Prussia is careful, Treitschke declares, not to confuse politics and ethics. All that counts is bold action which is not bogged down by the consideration of favourable and unfavourable elements.

It is a known fact that, if Frederick II had not seized western Prussia, eastern Europe would have sunk into subjection. Frederick II re-established what internal dissension and weakness in Germany had destroyed.

Finally, Treitschke applies to Germany, with Prussia as intermediary, the Hegelian conception of the state. The state in its totality is free and sovereign, which does not by any means imply that its members, too, are free and sovereign, or even that the people is sovereign in relation to the monarchy. For Treitschke, a political community which is unarmed has no right to exist. As soon as war breaks out, international treaties lose their validity.

Who, in the middle of the nineteenth century, could stand in Prussia's way? She will introduce compulsory military service, because the other states refuse to undertake military reforms. She will then annex Hanover and the Electorate of Hesse to form a state under one head. There is thus a 'natural boundary midway between the Rhine province and Pomerania'. And Prussia emerges as a Great Power. Shame upon the particularists, who are blind to Prussia's great destiny, blind to the fact that it is Germany's destiny that is at stake! Prussia will also have to deal firmly with Austria and put her in her place. And the final task will be to prepare for the absorption into the Prussian state of all that will constitute a future greater Germany. Treitschke suggests to his compatriots the example set by Cavour in Italy.

There is no question of Germany becoming imbued by the Prussian spirit, but only of the so-called 'national' party becoming 'more Prussian than ever'. Let Prussia expand to the northern plain and the other states will join up with her. She will inspire them with 'a tough national pride'. Treitschke then passes on to Holland and, as far as Austria is concerned, to the Balkans. It is not surprising, for the Dutch will open up the entire Rhine to Germany, and Austria will have to watch over 'sub-Germanic Europe'!

We must be ruthless, cries Treitschke, with German states that show signs of revolting against the re-establishment of the Empire! For this Empire will be 'the German monarchy in full flight'. This appeal was made in 1869. No sentiment—war is an unavoidable necessity. 'No genuine political idealism is conceivable without

c

aggressive idealism.' That is the motto of this fanatical champion of Prussia. He is one of those who believe the Reich must be absorbed by Prussia. He repudiated the suggestion made in 1848-9 that Prussia should be absorbed by the Reich but that the Prussian King should be offered the Imperial Crown. He sides neither with Fichte nor with Stein. Nor does he accept, as Pfizer does, the idea of a liberal Prussia. Dimly perceptible on his political horizon there is even a vision of Europe too becoming a projection of Prussia.

Does such fanatical support for Bismarck's policy allow of any opposition? [1]

As we know, Bismarck's plans are not destined to progress farther than 1871 and the results achieved by three victorious wars. Is he, too, like Frederick II, to be accused of building up Germany's military strength but weakening her politically? After Sadowa, who could still cherish the dream of a Greater Germany? And yet this dream was still cherished. The thorough-going Pangermanist could not be content with a little Germany. During Bismarck's lifetime, Paul de Lagarde and Constantin Franz produced the pre-eminently religious conception of a genuine Holy Roman Empire, and, as spokesmen of the super-nation, they accused Bismarck of having failed to fulfil Germany's true mission. Bismarck, the great realist, could have had little to fear from them and must have paid them scant attention, and yet these writers did express a thought which was inherent in the whole German idea, a thought that could not die.

Paul de Lagarde comes of Lutheran stock; he grew up in a Pietist atmosphere. He studies religion as a scholar, not a romantic philosopher. Professor at the University of Göttingen from 1866 to 1891, he is one of the German historians of the Bismarck period. He is a disciple of Fichte, the Fichte of the *Discourses*.

Being himself deeply religious, he becomes increasingly intent upon creating a religious revival in Germany, a national revival this time, which can become identified with Germany's destiny, even confused with it, to the point where it finally triumphs over confessional dualism. That, he feels, is the only way to repair the damage done in 1648. When he attempts to disentangle religious feeling from the dogmas and rites which emerge and evolve out of the centuries to make Germany the motive power and the centre of a universal religious revival, he is in fact merely resuscitating the time-honoured doctrine which was first propounded after the Reformation, which had been taken up by the theosophists of the sixteenth and seventeenth centuries, in the vision of Grimmelshausen and in Leibnitz's plan for a reorganisation of religion throughout the world.

[1] See C.A.I, pp. 231-330.

He naturally sees religion in the same way as Luther did. Above all, he believes in an inner life, a free, unfettered reaching-out for God, an individual and collective regeneration which can remove the stains of decadence and sin. He believes the self can be transcended and that each person and each people on this earth has a mission. In every nation worthy of the name, he sees a moral personality. He does not place it, from this point of view, beneath individual conscience and its infinite value. Individuals and nations both have their origin in God. In other words, a variety of Christian Pantheism, that has been latent in Germany for centuries, now attempts to embrace the positive features and the apparently irreconcilable contradictions of various confessions or sects in a Christianity that is essentially German, and therefore national.

So it is not surprising to find Paul de Lagarde expressing the view that the three main religions of the West are dead: Protestantism, Catholicism, and Judaism. Protestantism has revived nothing, but merely accepted the essential dogmas handed down to it. Lutheranism is not really dominated by justification through faith; it is only there to put an end to abuse of Holy Writ. The Protestant Churches in Germany and their theology have long since lost such original thought as they once had. As for Pietism, what has it awakened? The original Catholicism has disappeared and its place has been taken by Jesuitism and Papal decrees, sworn enemies of modern nationalities, of science, and of history.

It is on primitive pre-Pauline Christianity that Paul de Lagarde concentrates. He mistrusts St Paul. He accuses him of having sullied the water in the well of life. And he rejects the claims of contemporary Jews that their religion is universal. For true religion is not confined to faith. It is not limited to a belief in facts which are both outworn and dubious.

True religion is a 'life'. The Gospels revealed to man the conditions in which a life of the spirit can be lived. They led him to meditate on sin, salvation, eternal life, and the Kingdom of God, realities as universal as the cosmic laws. Each man is unique in his fashion, and therefore deserves to be 'cultivated' by an education worthy of the name. A living community can be such only if it brings together men of this kind. While Lagarde realises how widespread and how deep-rooted is sin, he devotes all his attention to redemption, which comes only to those who 'love God in man'. This is the price Germany must pay to become a nation. It is clear, then, why Paul de Lagarde calls for a 'German religion'. It is the sole aim of theology, in his view: to discover the German religion.

Lagarde urged the Germans to relive the Gospels in their own way. In a sense, he is a strange forerunner of the *Deutsche Christen* of

Hitler's time. Paul de Lagarde, like the Romantics, thought this Germanic religion would regenerate other peoples by its example. At the same time, he considers that every nation has the right to create its own religion, that no one can prevent it from working out its own salvation or arrest it in its growth and natural development.

And here we come to the heart of Lagarde's beliefs. Every spiritual development, particularly if it has some degree of universalism in view, must have a material basis. There is no spiritual power without temporal power. Once Europe is rid of France and Russia—military nations which must be crushed—Germany will be able to fulfil her sovereign mission in the Old World. She must be freed of her malevolent and uncomprehending neighbours. Which brings Paul Lagarde into direct line with von Bülow, Fr. List, and Treitschke. He adds to the spheres of military, economic, and political action a sphere of religious activity. What he can never forgive Bismarck is that he neglected the latter.

Paul de Lagarde's reproach of religious bankruptcy is not his only one. If he condemns Bismarck, it is because he failed to conquer either Luxemburg, the Vosges, or Belfort, and that he proved just as timid on the Vistula and the Pregel, near Memel. He also failed to occupy the Vilna–Grodno and Brest–Litovsk line. He simply forgot that Prussia once extended as far as Warsaw. Lagarde has the same criticisms to make of Bismarck as von Bülow of Frederick II.

He also accuses him of maintaining not unfriendly relations with the Russians instead of driving them out of Poland and away from the Black Sea. The same mistakes as Frederick II made with Austria which prevented him from annexing Bavaria and from pushing forward to the Rhine. What Lagarde would like is the complete Germanisation of the Balkans, a Hohenzollern–Habsburg union and a Germanic central Europe.

There follows, inevitably, an apologia for war. A people and a race, according to Lagarde, rise to greater heights in proportion to the greatness of the mission they are charged with. A nation can express its natural qualities only in war. Was Germany's true history not made in the frontier areas where she was almost constantly at war? It is in the east that Germany's destiny will be realised. In these famous marches the German character has asserted itself against the Slavs, while at the same time appropriating some of their virtues. In this way northern Germany took shape with a virility and a tireless aggressiveness which made it superior to the south. What has Austria to offer by comparison? Her rulers could only pay homage to the northerners and admit that their most urgent need was for union with a dominant race. Paul de Lagarde, moreover, frankly recognises the dangers threatening Prussia from every direction, the hazards of war on two fronts, the poverty of her soil, even the artificial character of her industrialisation, which is likely to collapse as soon as the political barometer drops, and finally the ruthless competition German exports are bound to encounter. What can Germany do to acquire foreign currency, apart from selling the English Russian goods and the Russians English goods? Only the commercial class in Germany is growing rich. The majority of the population remain poor. If the Germans wish to 'fly on their own', they must expand their Empire. If not, they will be mere brokers.

Paul de Lagarde criticises Austria severely. The praise he heaps on Prussia is crushing for Austria. Towards 1875 he regards Austria-Hungary as no longer viable. He sees no hope for her, and indeed believes the only remedy lies in a German emigration towards Austria and the Balkans. From this point of view, Greater Germany seems to him an absolute necessity. He even regards war as inevitable if Central Europe is to be reorganised in the grand style. For at all costs the Slavs must be prevented from joining up with France and the Danes.

What could be more curious, or more characteristic, than this mixture of religious intensity and thoughts of national greatness, which foresees a ruthless struggle between Germany with her self-imposed evangelical mission and the nations of west or east, ranking with military states. A frightening Messianic vision, which is destined to lead Germany, and Europe, to disaster!

That strange self-taught man, Constantin Frantz, was fifty-three when Bismarck unified Germany. While Paul de Lagarde follows in Fichte's footsteps, Frantz is closer to Hegel. Later, when his nationalism takes a Christian and Conservative turn, he discovers an affinity with Schelling. His main interest is in the relationship between Christian reality and world history. He sees the religion of Christ hovering over all civilisation, and this he and Lagarde have in common. He has little liking for Stahl, the pseudo-philosopher on whom Bismarck was reared and who, to Germany's cost, confused Christianity and the totalitarian organisation of the state—the Prussian state naturally—which Stahl treated as a separate entity outside its international context.

Frantz's idea of the Christian state is something quite different. It will be essentially universalist. What intrigues him is Schelling's idea of a Christian League of Nations, a faint echo of Leibnitz's views on the religious organisation of the world. Seen thus, political Christianity envisages neither a monarchy nor a republic. It does not commit itself to any particular form or to any preconceived system.

Was the Middle Ages truly Christian? Frantz does not think so. The barbarian invasions were followed by a wild despotism. Out of it emerged a feudal system in which the Church was established in order to give the system an appearance of Christianity, to sanction scrfdom, brigandage, and widespread misery. What horrors were committed in the name of the Gospels!

Frantz sharply defines the area in which the new world religion will take root. How, he asks, did Austria and Prussia come into being? The Austrian monarchy he regards as a species of international institution thrown up by the dubious Middle Ages we have just discussed. The German monarchy escaped this development. The House of Austria owed its greatness to its liaison with Rome. It struck roots deep into German soil. But it is anything but German, and the colonisation of the East is a phenomenon of only secondary importance for it. It is in this colonised area that Prussia began to take shape. The East was Christianised. The Duchy of Prussia was set up there, grew rich on Swedish and Polish spoils, and was destined to become the hard core of a military Germany.

What are Prussia's political ideas? Does she not hark back to the Renaissance and to Machiavellism? Does she not represent a clean break with the Christian idea, with the same Church that Machiavelli so bitterly fought? Where did Hegel's theories originate if not with Machiavelli? These are only a few of the many questions that flow from Frantz's pen. What he is trying to establish is the authentic origin of Bismarck's system.

Prussia's power, isolated in the north-east, was never brought under control, although at an early stage Prussia and Austria should have been united to form a true Germanic confederation. This would have averted the decomposition and appalling paralysis which fell on the Holy Roman Empire in its death-throes. Once Austria was detached from Germany, a true Federal state was impossible. What did Bismarck do? He entrusted the central power to Prussia alone. Frantz sees the problem clearly. Anyone thinking in terms of the old Duchy of Prussia must always assume that 'self-extinction is too high a price to pay for the honour of dominating the German Empire'.

Frantz is far from denying the greatness of Prussia and of the colonisation in the east. What he disputes is the claim that the Mark of Brandenburg can be made the German 'core' *par excellence*. He admits that Prussia has a part to play, but she will play it 'in her place'. A true German Empire is possible only if one bears in mind: (1) the medieval Holy Roman Empire, which floated midway between constitutional and international law; (2) the modern nations in which the idea of the state dominates; (3) the period ahead and the need to pass from the present confederation to a wider federation —that is, to a great Central European Federation.

Instead of this solution, we have that of the new German Empire, which automatically implies the separation of Austria and Germany. Now, Austria 'could' remain united with Germany, Hungary 'could' follow suit, Prussia and Poland 'could' join in. The real German line passes north-east and south-east. There was no need for Prussian Lutheranism to oppress Polish Catholicism. According to Frantz, a Christian western Germany was possible, carried north-eastwards by the Prussian Empire and south-eastwards by the Austrian Empire, both forming an impregnable barrier against Russia.

Constantin Frantz's ideas are on a grand scale. He deals with the demographic growth of Germany and her rapid industrial progress. What will happen if she fails to gain a footing in foreign markets? Germany must reckon not only with France, to say nothing of England, in the west, but also with Russia and Austria in the east. And here she is, forced to gravitate towards the pole of Prussian militarism, thereby running the risk of losing her soul. Frantz seems to forget that his greater Germany was also a popular dream in 1848–9 and that Europe then would not tolerate it! It is pointless for him to sing the praises of federalism, of the latitude he allows states for their own development, of the possibility of continued expansion he provides for. It will convince no one. For it is continued expansion that the Continent most fears.

He insists, of course, on the need to substitute continental colonialism for colonialism proper. Frantz is not interested in seizing the Dutch East Indies, acquiring territory in the Pacific, or setting up an overseas empire. He is obsessed by a continental dream, has his eye on Holland and in 1871 advocates a harsh policy towards France. He is no less severe towards Russia in the east. Enamoured of the Holy Roman Empire, hostile to any policy that is specifically Prussian, he sees only one means of reviving his country, by forming a Greater Germany which, he believes, would not crush Europe, but on the contrary would ensure a brilliant future for it. The Germany of Wilhelm II was to remember his dream, but to exploit it for Prussian ends.

The third of Bismarck's great adversaries was Nietzsche. In his *Untimely Studies* he shows remarkable fervour and clear-sightedness in his approach to the problem of the new German culture, to the relationship between the bureaucracy of a completely militarised state and the spiritual life of the nation imprisoned in it. But Nietzsche was no fanatical nationalist! Shortly after writing his *Untimely Studies* he was preaching European union, warning the Europeans against the monstrous state that was establishing itself in the heart of the Continent, and finally, in his last works, broaching the tragic question of a possible world government. Most of his work does not fall within this brief outline.

2. IMPERIALIST IDEOLOGY UNDER WILHELM II (1890–1914)

No sooner has Bismarck disappeared than the wave grows, breaks, and spreads to carry along with it the whole of what is called the *bourgeoise élite*. Imperialist nationalism takes every imaginable form. It exploits anti-Semitism and draws upon the universities for their research into geography, German history, and biology. Racialism appears and, towards 1900, H. S. Chamberlain gives it shape. A sort of philosophy of war creeps into military writings. Even literature falls victim to a patriotic megalomania. The outcome of this vast agitation is a continental plan and a colonial plan. Germany becomes the most restless nation in Europe, directly threatening its immediate neighbours not merely on the Continent, but in the entire world.[1]

In Germany around 1890 anti-Semitism was nothing new. It was a long time since skilfully organised propaganda had first created the Jewish–Aryan antithesis. Not that it was inspired as yet by a blind, unquenchable hatred, but a distinction was drawn between the Germanic element, recognised as genuinely national, and the Israelite element, which was regarded as foreign. Since 1850, and particularly after the Emancipation Law in 1869, the Jewish minority had increased as a result of the tremendous growth of urban population. Germany, then undergoing a rapid industrialisation, was a *terra nova* with great prospects. In fact, as Nietzsche had realised, industrial Germany needed Jewish intelligence. On the eve of the famous Crash of 1873–5, the landed aristocracy and the Lutheran Church had come out in favour of emancipating the Jews, though naturally it would be in the nature of a 'concession'. The Jews were granted free access to politics, journalism, science, and publishing, to the world of business, the arts, and literature.

The Jews and the middle and proletarian classes obviously had much in common. The latter were in full development. Quite a number of Jews with Marxist leanings had joined the ranks of the Social Democrats. Had Marx not declared that only Socialism could achieve the total emancipation of the Jews? But Marxism was also out to destroy the big capitalist, particularly the liberal pro-Semite capitalist.

Judaism, in effect, remained close to Liberalism and to Socialism according as the two movements fought against capitalism and against the reaction which was gaining more and more ground among the middle class. This reaction was a direct threat to the Jews, to their freedom, and to their activities. Anti-Semitism could not have served better the ends it was supposed to serve. After the Crash, in which the Jews had played a leading part, two things were

[1] On anti-Semitism under Wilhelm II see the remarkable study by Paul W. Massing, *Rehearsal for Destruction* (Harper and Brothers, New York, 1949).

apparent: (1) German Socialism turned on Jewish capitalism and (2) the middle class protested against methods for which Jews were held responsible. Catholics and Lutherans condemned them in the name of Christianity.

In 1873 the German Marr produced a pamphlet, the purpose of which was to show the fundamental distinction between German and Jew. Quoting a recent crisis, Marr insisted that the Jews, as an international Power, were opposed to the Germans, who were genuine descendants of the 'German nation' and were represented in particular by the various Christian confessions. Like Paul de Lagarde and Constantin Frantz, Marr accused Bismarck of favouring capitalist and free-trade liberalism, of 'Judaising' the Reich. Nationalism, in other words, is being defended against invasion by its opposite, internationalism. This is the self-imposed task of the famous *Gartenlaube*, a semi-popular review read by the working-class.

Bismarck's conversion to protectionism brought a profound change. From 1873 to 1878 social unrest grows and working-class agitation increases correspondingly. Alarmed by so much hostility among the workers, the middle-class appeal to the state and the Church for help. They take the same steps as they are to take on a very much bigger scale from 1929 to 1933. The Churches, for their part, try to grapple with the social question. They are prepared to risk conciliating the *bourgeois* middle-class and the working-class masses. They will thus succeed: (1) in mobilising the middle-classes and Socialists against Jewish high finance; (2) in mobilising these same middle-classes against proletarian Marxism. And here we see the beginnings of that particular social *milieu* in which, later, the Nazi movement is to flourish so tragically.

Only against this background can one appreciate the part played, from about 1880 onwards, by the Court Chaplain, Pastor Stöcker. Clerical authoritarianism is rising up against economic Liberalism, which it accuses of having given a free run to Jewish capitalism and Socialism. Christian speculators are only too ready to take shelter behind this cassock. From 1880 to 1890 Stöcker, acting on behalf of the Government and the governing minority, goes about his work of anti-Socialist social conciliation. The poison of revolution must be drawn out. Marxism is accused of alienating the working-masses from the nation, an argument which is taken up later by the National Socialists. The middle-classes are mobilised, in the name of Christianity, against Jewish intellectualism and against the liberal and socialist press. It even seemed possible that the Conservatives in their fury against Jewish wealth would also attack Christian wealth. Even Bismarck himself might find himself involved. The Iron Chancellor took steps to dam the wave. He knew that he needed Jewish big business!

The Stöcker movement also collapsed under Caprivi, between 1890 and 1894. Stöcker had been mistaken in his belief that he could rekindle the flame of Christianity in the middle-classes by means of anti-Semitism. He had merely exacerbated their bitterness and resentment. Jewish financiers had not failed to point out to the Government how dangerous the Imperial Chaplain's social agitation was. In spite of Stöcker, Bismarck had stood by the pro-Jewish laws. The fact remained, however, that anti-Semitism had taken root in the 'Mittelstand'.

In a glow of enthusiasm for social welfare, Wilhelm II abandons Stöcker. The Social Democrats suddenly increase their votes from 437,000 to 1,472,000. The middle-classes see themselves faced with emigration. And anti-Semitism grows. It achieves official status, becomes respectable, set up as champion of the divine right of the monarchy. It filters into the country and the small towns. The 1893 elections guarantee its success. The most virulent racialism is knocking at Germany's gates. It revives the old romantic racial theories of Jahn and makes full play with Gobineau. Then comes the 'Anti-Semitic Catechism' by Fritsch, which brands Judaism as a decadent element in Germany. The middle-classes are in a state of psychological uncertainty, which is to remain with them and to turn them into ardent followers of pangermanic nationalism such as is reflected in the continental plan and the colonial plan.

The geographical and historical theses are soon to be followed by biological and racial theses. Ratzel and Arthur Dix provide the neo-imperialist propagandists with weighty arguments drawn from geography. Ratzel, who is forty-six years old in 1890, sets out to prove Germany's predestined mission from anthropo-geographical evidence. He had a considerable influence. What he aims to do is to revivify the philosophy of history by a study of the geographical foundations on which human groups formed and developed. He is mainly interested in the psychology of war. It is through war that he sees humanity and, in particular, Germany. The international balance seems to him precarious, for he believes it to be based on 'an abnormal distribution of political spheres of influence and of the instruments of power inherent in them'. Germany must prepare a general upheaval which will turn her from an 'anvil' into a 'hammer'.

Ratzel's pupil, Arthur Dix, develops this when he asserts that peoples expand on the line of least resistance, that only means of communication are really important, and that political systems are, in fact, conditioned by economic developments. And he expresses the conviction that, from this viewpoint, Germany can stand up to the shock of a European war.[1]

Ratzel and Dix compare peoples to living organisms, which

[1] See C.A.II, pp. 86–125.

develop on a soil that feeds them. They are bound to it by ties of an intellectual and moral nature. The majority of historical events can be explained by the interchange of large and small areas traversed by economic or intellectual streams. Every state tends to spread over an increasing area. But, as every such modification affects adjacent areas, the least change in Europe is of interest to the entire world. Every people, therefore, feels the need to strengthen its position. All history is movement, and nothing could be more erroneous than the idea that peoples are closely confined within immutable frontiers. Politics is the art of exploiting this natural movement in order to increase the jurisdiction of the state. The nations of West and Central Europe are grotesquely packed together. Every spot on the globe has its intrinsic value, which may be unlimited. This is true, for example, of Trieste and Fiume.

Seen from this angle, war becomes a sudden mass-movement from one country to another. In time of peace, states remain stationary. In time of war, the territories of the belligerents merge into one, which is termed 'the theatre of war'. War in the true sense of the word is designed to gain possession of a specific territory, whether economic, national, or colonial. That is why expansionist forces are meeting with more and more resistance. The European Powers are no longer in sole control of world politics. A central situation like that of Germany and Austria is as formidable as it is perilous. Germany can exist and continue to exist only if she is strong— that is, fully armed. It is the eternal problem of internal unity as a prerequisite of limitless expansion.

Any progressive policy which is worthy of the name must, therefore, be both a continental and a maritime policy. A nation with one continental front and one seaboard front can exert pressure on either side at will. Germany will have to establish a balance between her land forces and her fleet, so that each reinforces the other. One day Britain's maritime policy will beat a retreat in Asia before the continental policy of the Russians, and in America before that of the United States. The relations between Germany and France are of secondary importance. How can there be a just balance, if the Russian Empire is forty-five times larger than Germany and France together, or if Germany, with her colonies, represents only one-eighth of the British Empire? The prevailing unrest of our time demands that a real balance should be worked out.

Hence the crying need for solidarity among the Central European states in face of the fast-growing world empires which are becoming commercially inaccessible. It is essential that Europe herself should know the situation outside Europe. Europe is living from day to day, from hand to mouth. While everything around her is in a state of ferment, she is chary of change. Would it not be folly for a people to imagine that its own past has already shaped its destiny? As there will always be peoples that give orders and peoples that take them, Germany must endeavour to be among the former. Germany's first duty must be: (1) to establish good relations with the Orient through Austro-Hungary; (2) to embark upon an active policy in the Balkans, in conjunction with Austria; (3) to pave a way for herself to the Persian Gulf. But most important of all is Anglo-German rivalry. There is, as one can see, nothing very new in these conclusions.

Ratzel and Dix are clearly inspired by Lamarck. They believe that a people is strong and likely to endure only if it adjusts its aims to its territory. Germany, they say, must not make the mistake, made by the great commercial Powers, of building up a world policy on trade. What she needs is fresh territory. Man's education comes from a combination of space, land or sea, ambition and boldness. An idea that surely originated with Hegel? If geography has made Germany 'a sort of medieval Greece torn by petty rivalries', the Marches colonised by her have become the nursery of her governing minority. Prussia and Germany together can embark upon a great territorial and maritime policy.

The historians come now to the support of the geographers. Karl Lamprecht sets out to be a 'modern' historian in line with his times and with its needs. His method is that of a man trying to reconstruct the progress and future development of an entire national civilisation. He applies this method in his *History of Germany*. He owes a great deal to Ratzel. The latter used history to revivify geography; Lamprecht does the opposite. It is not the ideas and actions of individuals that make history, but the customs, institutions, and movements of multitudes. Genius is nothing without the influence it exerts on the public. Following the example of Marx, for whom he does not conceal his admiration, Lamprecht studies the soul, the social 'psyche' as it changes under the influence of economic factors. Here we see again the collective individuality which romantics like Novalis, Savigny, and so many others had exalted, the pessimism of G. Hauptmann, who shows the importance of material situations for moral strength or weakness, and finally the cult of emotion, of impressionistic disquiet conditioned by the industrial revolution. The space-idea reappears in this vision of history. It amounts, in fact, to nothing more than the means employed by men to organise steadily growing masses in larger areas. A nation is no longer limited to its own territory. It spreads throughout the globe. The modern state thus becomes 'tentacular'.[1]

Industrial activity accumulates armies and fleets for purposes of expansion, but this can be done only by nations of sterling quality.

[1] See C.A.II, pp. 126–86.

Neither the Latins nor the Slavs are equal to it. And here again we see the old theme reappearing: the future lies with the Germanic peoples—that is, with the Americans, the English, and the Germans. Lamprecht is not such a sound prophet as Tocqueville or Constantin Frantz.

And if Albert Wirth, another disciple of Ratzel, works along the same lines, he ends up with a theory of the German race and culture, following in the footsteps of Gobineau and linking up the historian-geographers and the racialists. Wirth urges the Germans to blend, in their national blood, Celtic and Slav elements with the ancestral virtues of Germanism. Once this blend has been made, Germany will need a soil which is in accordance with its legitimate ambitions. For the ambition of a people is by way of being a kind of free resolution which 'does not submit to the law of any fatality'. Germany's demands, therefore, need know no bounds. Internal unity is the first prerequisite of external expansion. Carving out for Germany and maintaining a vital niche in the world of today is something that will call for steady nerves. Every means, both material and intellectual, must be employed in this tremendous task.

Why not Americanise Germany? Germany fears the United States less than do the South Americans. Germanism has a great mission to fulfil. Nor should one forget the migration which brought an infusion of Germanic blood to the Celto-Romans. Has Germany not dispersed her culture, philosophy, poetry, and music, her Socialism, and her spirit of discipline literally to the world at large? Wirth places Germany between Russia and the United States, between Panslavism and Anglo-Saxon Imperialism. In his megalomania he makes her the Middle Empire, destined to rule the world. But how could such a future ever come to fruition without war? National individualism must take precedence over international egalitarianism. This is an idea that history will one day turn into a popular slogan.

This means that any imperialism worthy of its name is racial, a race being a combination of corporal and spiritual qualities. In its pure and undiluted original state, a race is a primary phenomenon. And culture is as much part of a race as lightning of a storm. This is Fichte's thesis in the *Discourses*, with a touch of Nietzsche added.

In the eighteenth century, when Leibnitz's idea of harmony was in vogue, racialism hardly existed. In the nineteenth century the doctrines of Malthus and Darwin popularised the idea of natural selection and the struggle for existence. The extraordinary development of the natural sciences gradually stimulated the idea of race in the minds of the Germans and made them conscious of themselves as a race. In other words, they became convinced that they belonged to a specific and a superior race, or alternatively that they could, if they wished, establish that superiority by exploiting their native soil, their psychological qualities, and their moral virtues. We have seen how familiar the idea of a 'holy race', religious in origin, was to the Romantics and how they applied it to Germany. It does not go beyond an apologia for ancestral virtues. Bismarck's contempt for the Latins and the theories of Curtius and Mommsen are in the same catagory.[1]

The works of Gobineau, which appear at intervals between 1850 and 1880, exercised an influence in Germany only at the beginning of the Wilhelmian era, at a time when biology, anthropology, and sociology were flourishing in the universities. Equally bound up with doctrinaire anti-Semitism, the idea gains ground that religion and culture depend on virtues of the blood, on physiological and racial qualities. These are the first steps towards what is later called 'authoritarian biology', a new version of the national idea, endorsed by all dictatorships and every form of violence. Before or behind history, pseudo-values are sought which seem to derive from the dynamism peculiar to unconscious, instinctive, and primitive life. It is quite simply a return to primitive barbarism. This fanatical racial mysticism is undoubtedly the compensation for the industrial and military discipline which weighs so heavily on the German people. How easy it proved to resolve all difficulties by means of racialism, by reducing them to simple terms of vitality! There is something frightening about this defence of existence for its own sake, of the people for the people's sake, and of the masses for the specific purpose of coercing them into militarised nations in preparation for the struggle that will bring final supremacy. This nihilism of violence and destruction had shocked Kierkegaard, Nietzsche, and Marx. Once Gobineau had announced that only the whites had produced superior civilisations, and this because of their 'aryan' blood, the new variety of Pangermanic nationalism took it for gospel. Anti-Semitism, which was latent everywhere, seized upon it to oppose the Aryan or Germanic to the Jewish, to elaborate the theme Marr had already outlined. The superior elements in all civilisations are of Nordic blood, apart from which there is only 'degermanisation' and 'decadence'.

The first German racialists are Wilser, Woltmann, and Driesmans. The first two arrive by different routes at the same conclusion, that the blond dolichocephalic man, who represents the northern European race, is the cream of humanity and is physiologically present in all superior peoples. Rosenberg takes up the theory later in his *Myth of the Twentieth Century*. These racialists go farther, and believe that 'pure-blooded' Germans should be forbidden to marry into inferior races. Here we have the famous idea of the master-

[1] See for all this development, C.A.II, pp. 187–377.

race. By falsifying Nietzsche it is then argued that only the blond man is strong, either because of his chastity or because he is endowed with unrivalled will-power. They are hunters, shepherds, migrants, capable of bringing down and setting up empires. Germanic man is the most fertile, the most inventive, the most audacious. Was it not men of Germanic stock who built the French cathedrals? And how the Italian nobility of the Renaissance period swarms with Germanic names! Here, surely, is scholarly *naïveté* running wild!

Another racialist, Driesmans, stresses the relationship between power and culture in Germany. It is the great enigma. The Germans now are regarded as more capable of a 'profound culture' because they are 'less civilised' than their Western neighbours and 'less barbaric' than the Russians. Being iconoclasts by nature, they have no qualms about breaking the old idols. Is not true culture a return to the uninhibited vigour of primitive life, to the wellhead of creative power? Then comes the eternal cliché, the contrast between Greeks and Semites, between the Germanic and the Latin, between the capacity for regeneration and incurable decadence. From here, following in the footsteps of Fichte, it is only a step to an impassioned eulogy of the Lutheran Reformation. Driesmans, like Nietzsche before him, refuses to believe that Prussianism threatens German culture. The essential thing, in his view, is the integrity of the race, which must, of course, include the Anglo-Saxons.

Towards 1900 this line of development reaches its peak in the work of H. S. Chamberlain, *Foundations of the Nineteenth Century*. Its resounding success alone indicates to what an extent racialism had already gained ground among the German *bourgeoisie*. Chamberlain, the son of an English admiral, and later the son-in-law of R. Wagner, became converted to Germanism in its most exalted form. A great admirer of Carlyle, he believed he had discovered in Germany the superior brand of heroism which Carlyle had so eloquently praised. But he differs from the preceding racialists in one respect: knowing that it is impossible for every nation to be racially pure, he asserts that a nation is superior when it gives priority to the healthiest and most authentic racial element in its own make-up. A nation that wishes to dominate others must achieve this racial synthesis. It will then possess the greatest number of geniuses, and its cultural qualities will pass from generation to generation.

This is an important doctrine, for H. S. Chamberlain was the best known of the Nazi doctrinaires. For him, the Empire and the universal priesthood directed the normal evolution of the Germanic peoples into false channels. To the Empire's over-centralisation the nation responded with the victory of the territorial Powers, to the aspirations of the Vatican with Luther's Reformation. It was the great reformer who laid the foundations of real Germanisation at the very time when France was being 'degermanised', destroying its aristocracy and lapsing into the abstractions of 1789.

The original contribution made by the Germanic races was as important as it was beneficial. They provided science, civilisation, and culture with a great idea: organisation. They managed to reconcile the forces of concentration and expansion, and thus to realise Goethe's dream. They (1) purged science by turning knowledge into a disinterested passion, (2) purged civilisation by creating co-operative life and setting it up as a model for society, and (3) purged culture by liberating it from its yoke of verbiage and from the artifices of Western rationalism.

As a result, they succeeded in putting genius in its place, establishing the rule of wisdom, and establishing themselves triumphantly between West and East. Germany is and must remain the leading Power in the world, the true Middle Empire. Right up to 1916, two years before the German collapse in 1918, H. S. Chamberlain was still hawking his shoddy ideas on the European market.

Nationalist imperialism in the Wilhelmian era was faced by a vital problem: was it conceivable to blend Prussian militarism and culture? From 1870 to 1888 Nietzsche had denied it. And, although some of his ideas were twisted or removed from their context to flatter Pangermanism, his formal denial was a real stumbling-block for many enthusiastic publicists.

That Germany must be militarily strong no one doubted. Now, a thorough-going definition of Prussian militarism as it had spread throughout Germany since the triumph of Bismarck's policy, led to the conclusion aired first by Fr. Meinecke that militarism is not merely a question of 'soldiers' as such, but also of the attitude one finds in all forms of national activity in Germany, a spirit, a way of life, and above all a perpetual oscillation between the rigid discipline of daily toil and the compensation offered by dreams, megalomania, nostalgia for wider horizons, and metaphysical reflection.

It is none the less true, however, that where specifically military needs were concerned, quite a number of leading thinkers insisted that war was something inevitable and drew the most alarming conclusions.

Although he was not a professional writer, Klaus Wagner could wield a pen to considerable effect and produce a marked, lasting impression on the public. The famous General von Bernhardi, who was a great admirer of Treitschke, had a gift for co-ordinating the ideas of others and for communicating to his readers a kind of impassioned vitality that has always had a great appeal in Germany. Convinced that Germany must ultimately dominate Europe, intellectually, morally, economically, and militarily, he works out a philosophy of war. He draws up the same plans for territorial conquest as the Hasses, Naumanns, and Rohrbachs, whom we will meet again as champions of Continental Pangermanism.[1]

According to General von Bernhardi, war is a result of economic necessity. The growth of population in a healthy country creates the need for more and more space. This space is acquired by emigration (provided that the emigrants do not lose their nationality), by conquering neighbouring territories, and finally, if necessary, by distant colonies. The burning question is that of exports and the closing of vast foreign markets to them. But Bernhardi also falls back on the biological argument. War, the struggle for life and power, is an essential part of evolution. It is even a kind of moral obligation. Without it, there can be no civilisation worthy of the name. Militarism and culture go together. Bernhardi has no difficulty in resolving the contradiction.

Klaus Wagner bases his argument on the so-called 'Germanoid', 'mongoloid', and 'negroid' races, old distinctions which crop up in the works of Hegel and Max Stirner. 'We Germanoids will have the strength to break and crush the power and future of the other races. German blood must no longer mingle with foreign, bastard, weak elements.'

So for these amateur biologists war is a matter of natural selection. Klaus Wagner even talks of the 'justice' that selection by war implies and establishes between peoples. His argument could not be more elementary and crude. The world must make way for the superior Germanic race and bow before it. For nature and culture are based on inequality. Equality of rights is no more than a vain nightmare of the human brain. Behind such facile assertions there is a hint of Darwinism, but distorted and reduced to puerility. In the eyes of these naïve soldiers, German history proves that the most robust vitality always asserts itself in the end and that the enemy, however united they may be, court disaster by abusing their temporary victory. The German people will profit by its recent victories, and is in a position to establish a great culture in the heart of Europe. Wagner, in fact, adopts exactly the opposite approach to Nietzsche. The species can progress only through war.

The people capable of the highest culture, then, will be the people which proves capable of acquiring *manu militari* the living space it needs. In other words, war, if well conducted and well exploited, guarantees a healthy race the unity, freedom of movement, and isolation that it requires. Which brings us to the aggressive and autarkic totalitarian state. The Germans, we are told further, will have to push back their conquered rivals and organise forced migrations. For the nation is above the individual and humanity. True social transformism presupposes an eternal state of war between

[1] See C.A.II, pp. 378–92.

national groups. If the individual cultivates his 'I' before all else, the state works only for its own power. It protects and multiplies all that is most noble and precious. There will be no more treaties and contracts, no more cosy pacifism. Jurists and pacifists provoke war instead of preventing it. For the sharing-out of the globe every nation must rely on its sword. There is no law or rule that can arbitrate between rival nations.

The appalling *naïveté* of this conception is a clear indication of what we must understand by militarism, the mobilisation of the entire labour force for the purposes of war. In a country like Germany, where industry and the army were closely linked, the idea of 'culture' as opposed to militarism in this sense has a special meaning. There is no question of individual culture (*Bildung*), but only of collective culture (*Kultur*), of various institutions on which the social and political edifice rests. Nietzsche realised full well that *Kultur* and *Bildung* were hard to reconcile.[1]

1890 saw the appearance in Germany of Julius Langbehn's famous book: *Rembrandt as Teacher*. The title was borrowed from the third of Nietzsche's *Untimely Studies* which was called *Schopenhauer as Teacher*. The book ran to forty-two editions. Criticism and praise were heaped on it. Langbehn appeared as the representative of a young generation that was prepared to make the Dutch painter a sort of national hero, a symbol of the chiaroscuro and of a line of thought which, wrongly inspired by Leibnitz, set out to plumb the hidden depths of the unconscious and cull from it lucid ideas. It was, undoubtedly, a sign of the times. While Nietzsche had not hesitated to attack Bismarck, Langbehn led the cohorts of idolators. He contrasted the strong personality of Bismarck with the new Imperial Government.

Langbehn, who had read P. de Lagarde with great care, feared, as Nietzsche had done, a decline of German culture. But he did not hold the Bismarckian state responsible. Primed with Carlyle, he looked round for a model hero and found him in Rembrandt. The latter, whom he appropriated for Germany, seemed to him to represent the 'integral' culture which was menaced by so-called 'Americanism'. Langbehn, incidentally, drew a flattering parallel between Germany and Greece. He posed the question whether his country, like Hellas, would not provide the world with 'the spectacle of a forceful political power which would protect with its rough bark the delicate fruit of high culture'. One could cite Winckelmann, Carsten, Goethe, and Hölderlin as products of the Bismarckian régime to confirm the combination of artistic sensibility and virile hardness in the two peoples. These 'glacial rocks', Stein, Scharnhorst, Bismarck, and von Moltke, thus joined the classics. The gulf between a great past and modern times had been bridged.

[1] See C.A.II, pp. 187–257.

It was a particularly frail and treacherous bridge! Langbehn placed Germany midway between the United States and Russia, he was perhaps not unfamiliar with Constantin Frantz. Prussia had many features reminiscent of America and big business, but other features that suggested the Slavs and the world behind the Elbe. West and East were intermingled in this Middle State of the northern plain. Was it not ruled over by a strong and disciplinarian monarchy which was sure of its subjects' loyalty and which, enthroned by the grace of God, embodied rare virtues? In fact, Langbehn defined the Nordics—the race of Lower Germany—as 'Aryan *par excellence* and destined to dominate the world, a race of soldier-peasants made for colonisation'. The same theme was to be taken up and exploited *ad nauseam* by the Nazis.

It was also, to some extent, a definition of Prussian militarism. Prussia, reduced to her essentials, was the 'cup'. All that was needed was the 'wine', the great culture of Upper Germany. Could the nation not become 'militarised' and 'cultured' at the same time? The 'myrtle' could surely be combined with the 'sword'? Was there not a secret link between war and art? Soldierly courage was compared to artistic sincerity. And if Bismarck, like Luther, had his faults, these two personalities alone symbolised Germany's destiny and her incomparable greatness. The Greater Germany of to-morrow would govern Europe and, transcending Europe's borders, would achieve a kind of universal domination. Her true religion, says Langbehn, is Aryanism, not Christianity. There was no one, including Shakespeare, whom Langbehn was not prepared to appropriate. But how typical was this whole mental conjuring trick, this dream of childish megalomania!

There is little to be said of a publicist such as F. Lange, except that he was the most mediocre of philosophers. He was, however, a 'liberal', and his presence among the fanatical nationalists of this period shows how right Fr. Meinecke was in his claim that the pompous nationalism of the Wilhelmian era did not derive from purely Conservative sources. Its main following was among the semi-cultured element in the *bourgeoisie* which later took to National-Socialism. F. Lange too spoke of a Christian decline and of a new religion, a new Protestantism. He, too, was a disciple of Paul de Lagarde. He nevertheless used biological and transformist arguments in favour of an aggressive Germanism destined to impose its will on so-called 'inferior' races. He formulated 'laws' of pure Germanism and detailed its genuine virtues. There was no childish cliché he did not employ in depicting the sound, healthy German people surrounded by over-mature peoples ready to drop from the tree of life like rotten fruit. His *naïveté* was crushing.

From this point of view, the work of the poet Stefan George

acquired a very real significance. The better known of Stefan George's lyrical works reveal, subtly but unmistakably, a vibrant patriotism and an enthusiastic fervour which will reappear a few years later when Germany has suffered the first of her defeats, in the ranks of the young Nazis. Nothing could be more cogent than this literary episode for anyone trying to prove that the salient features of National-Socialist mass-mysticism are already apparent in the culture of the Wilhelmian period, not forgetting, of course, Wagner or Nietzsche, who are distorted at will by many a publicist.[1]

It is indubitably a Hellenic dream of beauty that George, a convert to Pangermanism, sets out to reveal to contemporary youth when, towards 1900, at the end of the group of poems entitled *The Tapestry of Life*, he draws a rapid pen-portrait of young Maximin. Somewhat later, around 1903, he summons Wotan, the dead god, to whom harvesters made sacrifice in olden times at the ripening of the corn. He also cherishes the memory, not of Goethe, but of Hölderlin, the poet who, long before Nietzsche, rediscovered Dionysus and Orpheus. Who is the new god who lurks behind these names, taken from the Greek or borrowed from Germanic mythology, waiting to be announced to Germany's youth? It is the young warrior, who achieves distinction by his unflagging resolution and by the sovereign arrogance with which he gazes already over the battlefields of the future. The poet suggests that a Christian upbringing has somewhat softened him, casting a veil of melancholy over his brow, but he will be master of the future Germany. He will lead her to victory. Nietzsche prophesied the appearance of new gods, but only to destroy them later. He felt the ground shifting under his feet. Stefan George's young god, who combines divine body and god incarnate, who predicts a union of delicious intoxication and implacable clarity, this young god, healthy in body and in mind and ready to fight for a greater Germany, is the Nazi of tomorrow. George also proposes an oath which will bind together the members of the new community. Between mass enthusiasm, revived from ancient Greece, and a rational mobilisation of popular energy a fundamental harmony is envisaged, which is reflected in the title of George's 1914 volume, *The Star of the Covenant*.

3. The Continental and Colonial Plan

From these premisses emerged the continental and colonial plan of action.[2]

Jealousy and resentment played a predominant part, which was, of course, strengthened by the success of the Customs Union. Under

---

[1] On Stefan George, see the essay in this volume by Claude David, pp. 287-315.
[2] On continental and colonial Pangermanism see C.A.III and IV.

Wilhelm II plans are revived which are already outdated, particularly for Europe, and which might have been thought abandoned for ever.

Since 1890 general discontent had grown. But it should not be confused with the political protests made by the progressive Liberals on the one hand and the Social Democrats on the other. In fact, it is Bismarck who encourages and stimulates it from his retirement. Whereas the young Emperor had dismissed the old Chancellor for urging brutal repression of the demonstrators, new factors are now emerging which force Wilhelm II's hand.

When France and England were in conflict, Bismarck, as we know, had allowed the Western nations to settle their own differences. It is from Caprivi that ruling circles demanded a more aggressive policy. On the Continent difficulties were increasing. After having treated Russia severely in 1878, Bismarck had concluded a treaty with her which Caprivi was not to renew.

In effect, the new Chancellor intended to support Austria against Russia and defend the Polish peasants against Russian demands. He also had the colonialists against him, who, on the contrary, would gladly have allied themselves with Russia in a policy hostile to the Western nations. In reality, continental plans and colonial ambitions clashed in sterile conflict.

This is the moment when the Imperial Government turns to Julius von Eckardt, a German Russophobe of Baltic origin, who urged the formation of a Central European Customs Union which would push Russia out of the Balkans. Germany would get a firm footing in Turkey, break with the pro-Russian policy which Prussia was pursuing, and impose her culture on Europe by cutting off Europe from the Czars. Central Europe would take its place between the Anglo-Saxon world and the East. The same ideas were put forward by Bismarck's opponents. Caprivi's resignation put an end to this episode in 1894.

Hohenlohe renews relations with the Russians. He announces his support for the Colonial policy, favours the campaign on behalf of the Boers, tries to gain a foothold in China, and from then on becomes an implacable enemy of England. In the meanwhile, the Franco-Russian Alliance is taking shape, while Delcassé is making overtures to England. Hohenlohe antagonises both Russia and Britain at the same time.

From 1895 to 1908 von Bülow's main preoccupation is to assemble the necessary forces to launch a foreign policy of world dimensions. A naval programme, maritime aspirations, confused visions, and high-sounding speeches, a union of all Germans throughout the world, a rally of nationalities in Europe of German origin, and finally a share-out of territories still unclaimed in favour of

Germany, all these claims are noisily and openly confirmed. To weaken Russia by pushing her into a conflict with Japan will be child's play. That is to be the pretext for the Anglo-Russian *rapprochement* and, following Algeciras, we see the first steps taken towards the Triple Entente. Under Bethmann-Hollweg and from the time Bosnia and Herzegovina are annexed by Austria, events move quickly towards disaster.

Throughout this quarter-century the favourite theme of continental Pangermanists has been the European Customs Union. Public opinion, very much on the alert, returns to the ideas of Fr. List. There is talk of a European tariff which would be equivalent to the American tariff. The idea appealed at that time to the English, who were anxious about American competition. German industry is pushing forward for the defence of Europe and has no hesitation in profiting from the crisis at the expense of England and France. The Triple Alliance and the Customs Union are twin visions. Germany's sole interest is in gaining economic and military supremacy on the Continent.

Publicists like Julius Wolf, Paul Dehn, and many others are obsessed by this dream. They hope to see the Central European states linked together by a coherent system of commercial treaties and customs agreements. They conjure up the grim spectre of a vast empire, a powerful economic, political, and military organism directed primarily against Britain.

Towards 1905 a work called *A Pangermanic Germany* by Reimer, a pupil of H. S. Chamberlain, is published. Reimer demands: (1) an all-out struggle against the French, a decadent people, the remains of whom will be herded into the area round the Massif Central, thus allowing the Germans to reach the Mediterranean; (2) a struggle between Prussia and Austria in order to clear the ground for the reorganisation of Central Europe; (3) the union of the Scandinavian, Dutch, Swiss, and Balkan states with Germany. This will be the 'Empire of the Germanic Race and Humanity'. Here we certainly have the German super-nation, the monster-state predicted by Nietzsche, not very far removed from the New Order to be proclaimed by the Nazis.

Reduced to a system, the specifically continental views of the Pangermanists form a very impressive whole. Their feelers go out to the four points of the compass.

The theme of German emigration towards the East reappears now, in particular in the works of F. Lange, who calls for a new colonisation, the breaking-up of big rural properties, the creation of model farms, of peasant syndicates, and other organisations in Poland and Silesia, all as part of Germany's historic mission. Poles would be transferred to the interior of Germany and authentic

Germans sent out to people the frontier areas. A linguistic drive to the East has long since been under way. Germany must actively prolong this spontaneous movement. Poland and Ruthenia will have to enter the future Customs Union.

The Germanisation of Poland is the subject of a great many studies. Ernst Hasse maintains that the whole of Poland's culture comes from Germany, even her Catholicism, which, we are assured, was brought to Poland during the Counter-Reformation by German Jesuits. So industrialisation in the East should be slowed down in order to make full use of the rural population and prepare the way for their emigration. It will be Austria's task, declares A. Wirth, to defend Germanism in the East, while Germany mounts guard in the West.

As for Russia, she proposes to become a national state, instead of remaining a territorial state. She must have one, and only one, faith, one, and only one, language, one and the same Czar! The great mass of Russians are gaining in homogeneity, but on the Polish-Baltic front Russia is failing. She will, therefore, be denied access to it, and Central Europe, under German leadership, will control the situation. It is P. de Lagarde's doctrine of a bulwark against the muscovite giant and of the advantages to be gained by withdrawing from the Anglo-French quarrel. Germany knows that she must mount guard against the Slavs.

In the West, the Dutch theme crops up again. Some believe it will not be necessary to coerce the Low Countries and Belgium into a Greater German Confederation. Will these peoples themselves not ask to be admitted, as soon as their present independence has become untenable? Are they not Low German populations? The French-speaking Walloons will have to limit their claims, and the Flemish will be reminded of their duty to maintain the link with Germany as a whole. If there is a schism or a catastrophe, then Germany will intervene. Antwerp will be ceded to her and will be linked with the Rhine, then with Berlin. Flanders and Holland will administer the Belgian Congo for the benefit of Germany!

How many other well-intended publicists take up the same slogan! They speak of the new Low Germany thus created as if it were a Fountain of Youth, but close to the sea. They accuse the Belgians of 'particularism'. Have not the Belgians, like the population of the Pas-de-Calais and the North, pronounced Germanic traits? They should be granted rights analogous to those of Bavaria, says Ernst Hasse. Does Holland believe she can defend her colonies?

Luxemburg and Switzerland are not lost sight of. An anonymous brochure, which caused quite a sensation, declares that the natural frontier of these two countries is their linguistic boundary, which runs from the Ardennes to the Vosges, the Jura, and Mont Blanc. One day Switzerland will have to abandon Tessin to Italy, her French-speaking part to Germany, who will naturally also acquire her German areas. Luxemburg will become part of the Reich.

According to Fr. Lange, Germany, in annexing Alsace-Lorraine, was only recovering her own property. Also her behaviour is that of a policeman who, having tightened the prisoner's shackles, loosens them little by little to see if he is still prepared to resist. A policy of total expropriation will restore Alsace-Lorraine to the Reich. This is the price of integration. The authentic Germans will be settled along the frontiers, and the 'Francillons' will be severely dealt with. Ernst Hasse insists on the Germanisation of Lorraine. He suggests it be colonised by German rural population, after the land that was owned by the French has been regained. In the west military 'Margravates' should be established. Ernst Hasse complains, incidentally, of the 'shortcomings' of the Treaty of Frankfurt, Alsace-Lorraine remains untouchable, and the problem can be solved only by a 'marriage of reason' between Germany and France.

France is to be invited either to turn against England or to ask Germany for help. In such a case she would serve as Germany's supply base while the Germans drove the English out of Egypt and annexed the Walloon country or French-speaking Switzerland. If, on the other hand, she resists, if she shows signs of attacking the Triple Alliance, she will pay dearly. All of which anticipates the policy outlined by Maximilan Harden in 1913–14 in his *Zukunft*. If France does not respond to the summons of this 'male', Germany, 'her flame will be quenched in blood'!

The anti-British polemics are given free rein in most of these publications. Fritz Bley sees in perfidious Albion the power which denies Germany the advantages she earned at Sadowa and Sedan, and which prevents Germany from annexing Holland. Count Reventlow stresses the anti-British side of the Greater Germany of the future. All this documentation makes it easy to understand why the Anglo-German rivalry has quite another importance than that of the Franco-German rivalry.

In the north the problem is Schleswig, the Kiel Canal, and the new Germany's maritime future. F. Lange feels obliged to admit that the assimilation of Schleswig ended in failure. Germany possesses the necessary warlike vigour, but not the tact or the skill. Why not settle Germans on the frontiers and push the recalcitrant Nordics southwards? E. Hasse indulges in similar speculations. He would like to see the 'Northern Marches' re-established. An anonymous brochure that appeared in 1893 emphasises the signal importance of the Kiel Canal and hints that the Danes will one day have to become part of the German Empire.

It is towards the south that German aspirations are mainly directed. The Nationalists of the Wilhelmian period are haunted by the Austrian problem. F. Lange is aware of the fact that Austria-Hungary is 'a political monstrosity'. How, then, could she become the urgently needed bulwark against Slavism? Is she not, on the contrary, the most forward bastion of Slavism? From the point of view of German emigration, Austria-Hungary can be regarded as 'a German colony half-lost'. Is such a thing permissible? Should not everything possible be done to save Germanism in the southeast? Are the Austrians to be allowed to go on 'prostituting themselves' to the Czechs, Slovenes, Hungarians, or Italians? Will the Imperial Government continue to tolerate the Slavonisation of Austria-Hungary? Will it be necessary to sacrifice the Triple Alliance? The Germans must act with determination, in the name of justice among peoples, and consolidate Austrian Germanism. The Danubian monarchy would collapse quickly, once its bonds with Germany were broken. If the German Government is conscious of its mission, Germany will enjoy such 'an hour of repletion and of strength . . . as she has never experienced before in her history'.

Relations between Austria and Italy must be put in order. But the nationalists are more interested in the Balkans. Who will help Austria in her present state of disruption to prevent Russia from intervening in Bohemia or in Hungary? Who will reorganise the Austrian state, with the incorporation of Rumania in the future Customs Union? Would it not be wise to take the advice of P. de Lagarde and replace the moribund Habsburgs by a new dynasty? In 1899 a new anonymous brochure asserts that Austria is now in a state of complete helplessness and demands that Austria, with Trieste and Cattaro, be annexed by the Reich and that Germanism be established between the Baltic and the Adriatic. Plans of this kind appear almost uninterruptedly, all following the lines laid down by P. de Lagarde and C. Frantz. There is talk of a Central Europe of 1950, which will crown Bismarck's work! In the event of a victory over Russia, why not divide up Bessarabia between Rumania and Austria? Then at last one would have a Greater Germany independent of England and Russia. That would merely mean resuming the work of colonisation where the Ottos, the Saxons of Transylvania, the Teutonic Order, and the early Prussian kings left off.

All these views betray not only anxiety over the position of Austria-Hungary but also the hopes that German *bourgeois* nationalists nourish, should Austria-Hungary collapse. Diplomatic documents will also reveal, though somewhat later, the same anxiety and the same ambition.

Out of this plethora of complaints and dreams emerges the vision of a Greater Germany, of a dominant super-nation. Paul Dehn and Ernst Hasse are its leading prophets.

Nothing could be more typical than Ernst Hasse's predictions. He visualises all German-speaking countries united in one German national state. From this centre Germanic democracy, an integration of all the nation's energies, will radiate throughout Europe and the world, in a south-easterly direction. Is Germany not the 'Mother of peoples'? The same dream reappears in the anonymous brochure of 1899, which insists that Germany, before thinking of her colonial Empire, must remedy the enormous extension of her continental front by regrouping her forces and pulling them together. Here already one glimpses the idea of an organised Europe, ready to meet the possible dual threat from west and east, from America and Russia. The most important thing is to Americanise agriculture and develop industry, without, of course, neglecting the social question and the conciliation between *bourgeoisie* and proletariat! One must also have done with 'international baubles'. That can mean only one thing: the 'national revolution' is looming up on the horizon.

In this respect, Ernst Hasse draws an apt distinction between the terms 'all-German' and 'Pangermanic'. The first only covers the solidarity that unites High and Low Germany; the second is confused with racial ideas, for which this particular nationalist does not hold out much of a future. But they are to reappear soon with Hitler, immediately after the first of Germany's defeats.

It is, moreover, well known that the notorious 'All-German Association' brought considerable pressure to bear on the von Bülow Government between 1899 and 1908. In fact, Germany was regrouping the whole of her forces on the Continent, the first step towards Hitler's New Autarchic Order. 'In thus abandoning all idea of dominating other great peoples', declared E. Hasse, 'we are abandoning the plan for a universal Empire, a dream which we no longer cherish but which we will not tolerate in others!' German imperialism, we are assured, is anything but 'caesarian'; it is rather 'federative' and 'democratic'! As for the anti-British barb, it crops up everywhere—in Hasse, in Count Reventlow, in A. Wirth, and many others. The aim is to get Russia and England out of Europe and govern the Old Continent undisturbed. The British Empire is believed to be ripe for collapse. Why not a sudden attack? Is this not one of the possibilities that must be considered at this time?

There was no shortage of publicists and prophets in Wilhelm II's reign to remind the Government that continental problems must take priority over colonial dreams. In fact, continental colonisation, which goes back almost a thousand years, was at one time the greatest hindrance to German colonialism. This is an established fact. Germany never outgrew her particularism. Austria and Brandenburg were constantly at one another's throats. As soon as Germany left the Empire of Charles V, her colonial ambitions lapsed into inertia.

One must not forget that the Frankfurt Parliament took note of this state of bankruptcy, and even created a fleet, which was scattered immediately after the setback of 1848–9. During this period the first colonial plans to be produced are by no means niggardly, and in 1871 colonial literature is in full swing. There is already some talk of depriving France of her very desirable colonies. But all these dreams were quickly and firmly dispelled by Bismarck, who knew better than anyone else why Germany could not afford the luxury of a colonial Empire so soon after her triumph on the Continent. Nevertheless, between 1871 and 1890 colonial ambitions are given free play and, with Bismarck yielding more and more ground on this point, the outcome is clear. France and Britain are all the more threatened as they themselves have an age-old quarrel to settle over the same subject.

Under Wilhelm II the various political parties remained divided on this question. The Progressives and the Catholic Centre favoured wise moderation. The Socialists saw in colonial rivalries little more than the death-throes of capitalism. On the Right, only the National-Liberals were interested in a future colonial Empire.

For Caprivi, the colonies Germany had already acquired were mere pawns to be used if necessary to bargain for advantages on the Continent. He sacrifices Zanzibar for Heligoland. Furthermore, he is constantly engaged in petty quarrels with the clan of colonialists, who refuse to recognise the wrong methods and inept brutality of the Germans in their African colonies.

In fact, the administrative machinery set up by Bismarck was well equipped for action on the Continent but not for enterprises farther afield. The first serious clash between Germany and Britain arises over the Transvaal. Not till von Bülow comes to power does Germany embark on a colonial enterprise of any magnitude. In 1898 there is Kiao-Chow, a deal arranged by Hohenlohe; in 1898 Wilhelm II's visit to Palestine; in 1899 and 1900 the Philippines and Samoa. These seem modest conquests, but they are carried through in style. In 1900 comes the campaign for a fleet and a world policy, then Germany is stung by a mad jealousy and demands 'a place in the sun'; a series of diplomatic storms blow up between 1900 and 1914, on which everything that could be said has been said.

Why did Germany want colonies?

Did she formulate any doctrine on this point?

There were some Englishmen like Gladstone and some Frenchmen like Paul Leroy-Beaulieu, who understood Germany's longing.

There was no lack of sentiment and prestige behind it. If colonies were demonstrably necessary, then propaganda was essential to rouse public opinion and the Government. Where should the colonies be? In what parts of the globe? And how were they to be acquired?

Germany in Wilhelm II's time did not forget either her settlements during the Renaissance or the more recent attempts made with the support of the Bismarck régime.

In 1897 we find a publicist like Wohltmann quoting the demographic argument and the fact that emigration had deprived the homeland of its finest German citizens. He also reminded his public of the lack of fixed and reliable markets, of the need, in the interest of the nation's new maritime power, to gain experience of overseas territories, and finally of Germany's right, as a highly cultured country, to spread her civilisation through the world.

There was evidently a certain amount of indifference in Germany to colonies. Again in 1897 von Werner complains of it, and accuses in particular the Hanseatic Towns and big business. This indifference seemed to arise from the lack of national feeling among the Germans, who were no sooner abroad than they were quickly absorbed by their new *milieu*, particularly in British or American territories. The conversion of the political parties to colonialism seems, however, to have taken place about 1904. It just precedes, as we see, the formation of the Triple Entente. The colonialists are naturally thinking of territories that are still unoccupied. Will Germany allow herself to be outpaced by older colonial nations with their superior equipment? The Germans are ambitious, but at the same time have a certain inferiority complex. They live on frustrated dreams and imaginary sufferings. Hence a state of anxiety, which from now on is to increase, provoked by the jealousy which had become traditional in the course of the nineteenth century. Germany's foreign policy was one of commercial expansion to every corner of the earth. The official machinery set up by the Government is soon supplemented by Colonial Societies and the Pangermanic League. The inevitable propaganda is made through periodicals, brochures, and a vast literature which draws on scientific research of every kind and description. In German universities some fifty institutes are established, which are admirably equipped and which undertake prospecting work of the greatest value throughout the world.

The conclusion is quickly reached that Germany has a special mission to fulfil in South America, if necessary in the teeth of North American opposition; that the large number of German-Americans in the United States can play a vital part in such an area; that a crisis is blowing up in the British and French Empires, and that

Germany must be on the spot 'in full strength'; that Germanism can colonise the globe and still maintain its home population intact; that colonial settlements will undoubtedly be possible on the flank of British India, particularly after the Crown Prince's visit to India; that the break up of Turkey opens up tremendous possibilities and new perspectives in the Orient; that North Africa, and especially Morocco, is within easy reach and ready for the taking. The imagination of the Germans is aglow with so many wonderful opportunities!

The true theorist of colonialism is Paul Rohrbach. In his work *The German Idea in the World* he describes in detail the particular qualities which the Reich must bring to bear everywhere 'for humanity'. The theme of natural selection reappears. Rome, the Latins, and the British having exhausted their potentialities, it is the turn of the German idea, which means Germanism (*Deutschtum*), to assert itself. It will either dominate the world or come to nothing. Like his colleagues, Rohrbach places Germany between the Anglo-American world and a Russia that is still in a state of barbarism. German dynamism will have to make an all-out effort, without pause or respite. This fact alone implies that the colonies will have a most beneficial influence on the national character. Africa lies wide open to continental Europe and therefore to Germany. It is fortunate that, since Bismarck, the nation has abandoned its purely continental policy for a 'world' policy.

This does not mean, of course, that the Government should adopt these suggestions blindly. Like Bismarck, Wilhelm II and his Chancellors, with all their shortcomings, and perhaps even because of them, will show considerable caution. It is generally thought that colonies ripe for exploitation should be given priority over colonies to be settled. The latter seemed more important at a time when emigration was scattering thousands of Germans all over the globe. But, since emigration ceased and national industry seems to be absorbing more than enough labour, colonial exploitation appears to be essential. Hence the idea of a virtual Colonial Empire, F. List's idea, the idea of a totality that would be self-sufficient. Such a scheme was well worth publicising!

Even the Social Democrats, and particularly their young leaders, revelled in this prediction of forceful expansion. Although they were believed in France to be opposed to war, well-informed observers discovered that the German Socialists, afraid that Wilhelm II's Empire was facing an imminent crisis, also had drawn up a colonial programme and that they, too, in their way, were Pangermanists. This was to become abundantly clear in 1912, when they voted for the famous war budget!

When, in 1913, on the eve of the First World War, an anonymous brochure appeared which seemed to inform the world at large that from now on German imperialism would be a policy of peace, people wondered who had inspired it and what its object was. There seemed no doubt that the anonymous author was a person of some note in higher government circles. He gave encouragement, on the one hand, to colonial Pangermanism, but, on the other hand, stressed the importance of avoiding any danger of a world war. He condemned any aggressive colonisation that might provoke both England and Russia. At all costs, therefore, claims on Morocco and Mesopotamia must be abandoned. The author pointed to Central Africa as the only reasonable objective. It could also be interpreted as a sort of veiled warning to the Triple Entente that they would have to renounce all interest in Portugal and Belgium in Germany's favour.

At all events, the brochure made the following points: (1) that Germany was in no sense over-populated and had not the same density of population as England or Belgium; (2) that she could not afford to settle peasants in her colonies; (3) that the present mood of unrest was due to the overcrowding of the liberal professions; (4) that colonies should be sought which would provide Germany with certain raw materials she badly needed. Hence the obvious importance of Central Africa—and the threat to Portugal and Belgium, both small nations cheek by jowl with the Great Reich!

As for the method to be adopted, Germany, in her nostalgia for colonies, turned to England as the country that had set the best example. Colonialists like Rohrbach and Dernburg had a fine opportunity to describe the best lines to adopt, but they could not rid themselves of unpleasant memories, especially of the repression of the Herrero rebellion! And they made no secret of their conviction that war was closely linked with colonial activity.

Prudent as the 1913 brochure had been, the German colonialists under Wilhelm II had, nevertheless, carried their dream into every corner of the globe. They had lavished it particularly on North America and still more on South America, where they conjured up every incident from past history that seemed to strengthen their case. Albert Schaeffle had investigated the prospects in Central Africa with painstaking care. Emil Jung had made a close study of German infiltration in the South Pacific.

Heinrich Class, one of the most ardent Pangermanists, had given all his attention to Morocco and proved that western Morocco must belong to Germany. And Joachim von Bülow, the Prince-Chancellor's paper, the *Conservative Correspondence*, Harden, and other publicists had played up the journey to Tangier and the Agadir incident in their articles and arguments. Not forgetting, of course, the break-up of Turkey and the Oriental aspirations! Even Fr.

Naumann stressed in 1913 the speech that Wilhelm II had recently made in Damascus. As for Paul Rohrbach, he had indulged in so many suggestive speculations about Baghdad, China, and India!

We have seen how, under Wilhelm II, anti-Semitism had gained its first real footing in Germany and how, thanks to shrewd propaganda, it had infiltrated into the middle-classes. But it still has not made common cause with the imperialist nationalism of the period. Religious Pangermanism, for its part, seems to have sought refuge among the opponents of Bismarck and of the Little Germany policy with its flavour of Lutheranism, as in P. de Lagarde, and its Catholic flavour, as in C. Frantz. The current that comes out on top, first of all in the Bismarck era and subsequently in the reign of Wilhelm II, is Pangermanism with scientific pretensions. It makes full use of geography, history, and, above all, the natural sciences, to end up with the racial theories of H. S. Chamberlain, the spiritual father of National-Socialist ideology. He also outlines a philosophy of war and militarism in an attempt to determine the high-water marks of German culture. But running through all these theories and dreams is the main stream of German romantic thought, never losing its influence, especially in the course prepared for it by Fichte and Hegel. This time a plan of action is emerging with striking clarity. It is both continental and colonial. In a nation that has considerable difficulty in establishing internal unity and that has a less stable government than is generally believed, this plan of action expresses a violent urge to move outwards, a longing for immediate expansion which causes Germany's neighbours considerable alarm, and will lead to a series of diplomatic embarrassments culminating in the first world war. The ultimate result is the catastrophe of 1918.

V. TOWARDS THE THIRD REICH (1914–45)

National-Socialist ideology took shape in Germany almost as soon as the armistice was signed. Its first programme appears in 1920. But between it and the nationalist ideology of the Wilhelmian era there is a transitional period of neo-nationalism, which finds it supporters mainly among the defeated and disillusioned *bourgeois élite*. It is important to consider this first.

1. THE NEO-NATIONALISM OF THE INTELLECTUAL ÉLITE (1917–32)

Some writers of note, more or less belated prophets of a spiritual revival in Germany, have tried to define their country's mission after the armistice and at a time when the Treaty of Versailles is about to be signed.

It is not an easy task. Germany under Wilhelm II had placed her dreams of greatness at the service of her industrial and military power. Four years of prodigious effort had shaken the Bismarckian edifice to its foundations. A tremendous task of reconstruction now had to be done on what remained of sound and relatively stable foundations.[1]

The new ideology, which deals harshly with the pseudo-revolution of November 1918 and the régime that followed it in 1919, proclaims a true revolution, a national revolution. Writers like W. Rathenau, Th. Mann, and Count Keyserling, born between 1867 and 1880 and heirs to the great classical and romantic traditions, had already published their first works between 1900 and 1914. The war had stimulated and matured their writing. By 1925 anything new in their prophecies has been said. What they demand of Germany is a spiritual purge that will rid her of false intellectualism and a brutal mechanisation which they regard as fatal to the future evolution of her civilisation. In this they are, and remain, the disciples of Nietzsche, particularly of the early Nietzsche. But they still talk with an arrogance that makes little impact on the lesser minds of the *bourgeoisie* and is, of course, far above the heads of the toiling and suffering masses.

These well-meaning prophets hope for a humanist revival in Germany. Rathenau dreams of an organic, just order of things which will restore the 'kingdom of the soul', an ardent, enthusiastic, spiritual life which he contrasts so admirably with the world of conscious aims, of national calculation, and utilitarian intelligence. The pre-1914 nationalists used to speak of combining militarism and true culture. Rathenau visualises a kind of synthesis, which is incidentally impracticable, between the most brutal industrialism and the most refined culture, between technical and spiritual achievement. For he himself is both an industrialist and a reader of H. Bergson. So he arrives at a kind of compromise, based on the idea that the world would be much better off if the wealth it amasses were handled and controlled, in the interest of all, by a highly-cultured and technically trained *élite*. Germany would then become a national community that was both spontaneous and conscious of itself, profoundly religious, and strongly disciplined in its aspirations and its institutions.

Rathenau prescribes the terrain for the new revolution. One must revolt and protest, he feels, not against a particular social class or a particular political system, but against mechanisation as such and all that is excessive and crushing in it. This would mean returning to true Germanism, the duty of which is to replace present society by a community that is based on the mind, realising 'a German Socialism' and bringing together the governing *bourgeoisie* and the mass of the governed.

[1] On the neo-nationalism of 1918–32 see Vermeil, *Doctrinaires de la révolution allemande* (Sorlot, Paris, 1938).

This was, in the last resort, a National-Socialist conception, to link Germany's future with a true Socialism of Germanic origin. Naturally, Rathenau did not confine himself to Germany. He also ranged over Europe. He insisted that the Western spirit must bear its share of responsibility for the World War, accused it of having started mechanisation and feared that Versailles prepared the way for a violent upsurge of capitalism in its crassest form. In fact, Rathenau likes neither the democracy of the West nor the Soviet system of Russia. In his view, Germany is on the right path in trying to integrate the proletariat in the nation. The future lies with her, because she is the 'middle country' that is destined to set Europe an example. So the old idea of Germanic predestination has survived the defeat of 1918.

Rathenau had, however, realised the risk Germany was running before the outbreak of war. He saw her in the position of a farmer, who, in order to improve his land, spends more than he has earned from the harvest. After indulging in grandiose speculations, the German spirit had worked wonders in science and technics. That might well be its downfall if it lost itself in such achievements. Defeat had taken Rathenau unawares, and he found himself wondering whether Germany was a nation. He had noticed the gulf that had appeared again between the ruling minority and the masses deprived of moral and political education. Never before in Germany had there been so much besotted, collective pride and false glory. Did this ardent Pangermanism of the Wilhelmian era, Rathenau wonders, not swallow up and destroy the nation's cultural tradition? This was a grave accusation, of which Rathenau himself was to be the first victim, when he was assassinated in 1922.

As against a small aristocratic and *bourgeois élite*, we have the urban masses, who, in the large industrial centres, have felt the full impact of mechanisation. Simple-minded and barely conscious of themselves, they have only one ambition: organised labour. With real culture threatened, the middle and working classes have become outrageously rationalised by industrialisation. No one appreciated better than Rathenau how extremely vulnerable Germany was to the industrial revolution of the nineteenth century. Beyond the Rhine, he cries, there is neither form nor style nor a desire for freedom. Everywhere lack of will-power, a permanent state of confusion between loyalty and slavery, between autonomy and anarchy. The masses bow down before whichever party or faction is in power. A mere handful of genuine Germans are faced with a wave of Slavonic atavism. Was Germany's defeat not the result of her 'degeneration'? The humanism of the past, still conserved in England and France, has given way to authoritarianism for some and slavery for others.

D

Before the outbreak of war there had been no more penetrating criticism of the Kaiser's régime than that of Rathenau. His pessimism was reminiscent of Harden. He accused the *bourgeoisie* of narrow-minded Prussianism and lack of intelligence. For him the war was a kind of last judgment. Wars break out, he says, where peoples offer least resistance. Prussia and Russia were the weak spots in Europe. So the German people learned to its cost what it means to take over a semi-Slav inheritance. It obeyed blindly the mad dictates of its masters.

Rathenau knows that the Weimar Republic is not cured of this danger. He puts forward a theory of the new state. He would like to restore the *civis germanicus* of tomorrow and integrate it in a national community in which the economic and the spiritual would be perfectly balanced, a nation which would be the core of a true League of Nations. This revolution would be both German and universal. Europe would find its cure in a reborn Germany. Which brings us right back to the Pangermanic dream! The suffering, defeated Germany of today is restored, to become a model people!

A model which would presumably appeal to everyone, since Rathenau imagines, before Hitler has created his Third Reich, a sort of Utopian National-Socialism which would produce not bloodless mechanised careerists, but strong, healthy personalities capable of material asceticism, or renouncing personal profit and the selfish ownership of the means of production. Property would be limited, as Goethe had said, to objects that fall within the socially useful orbit of activity of each person. The desire for power, the instinct to dominate, the spirit of ruthless competition that corrupts modern societies must be destroyed. In an economic system directed by an *élite* of carefully selected leaders, of which the proletariat would form an integral part, Germany would become the ideal corporate state, which would make all Germans workers with equal rights and duties, divide them into professional classes, and grade them according to their specific value. And the foreign policy of the new Reich would aim at the reconstruction of Europe. Nothing at all in common with Wilson. In the world of this engineer-philosopher a real League of Nations would guarantee an equitable redistribution of world raw materials, of foreign markets and of financial means among continents and nations.

Rathenau paid with his life for this generous dream of an Israelite prophet. The ideas of Count Keyserling and Th. Mann are on similar lines. They add nothing of interest to the serious student. Rathenau's words carried particular weight because of his dual capacity as a highly competent industrialist and a philosopher able to collate his experience. But once again, as in the time of Fichte and Hegel, Germany was setting herself up as a model to Europe at a time when her defeat made a terrible mockery of such a claim.

The work of Oswald Spengler, a contemporary of Rathenau, marked a step nearer to the brutality of the totalitarian, Caesarean state. This historian-philosopher moved in the vast spaces of universal history, delighting in fascinating syntheses which started with humanity and ended with a privileged nation, which returned in short to the eternal theme of German predestination.

Spengler's point of departure was a deliberate and uncompromising irrationalism, the irreducible opposition between the unconscious and the conscious life, between a spontaneous life that shapes its own destiny and a state of sleeplessness or of reflection which attempts to explain life and the world as best it can. A curse upon the intellect that turns upon life and paralyses it in all its members! The mind can grasp the rhythm and creative originality of facts only by intuition. Spengler cites Goethe in support of this, and then goes on to assert that universal history has an organic structure and can be reduced to certain elementary phenomena which recur in all great cultures. Only the birth, development, and death of individual or group organisms are eternal. Here Spengler reveals the influence both of German romanticism and of the German historiographers. He is the successor, in more than one respect, to Lamprecht, Meyer, and Lindner. He revives historical Pangermanism.

From this point of view, the strength of peoples lies in their acceptance of a coherent destiny. Primitive peoples are far removed from us. The distinction that interests Spengler is the one between decadent and cultured peoples. The decadent peoples are those which are cut off from their own soil and hover between nationalism and internationalism, love of war and love of peace, because they tend to substitute reason for destiny. The cultured and progressive peoples are those in which the individuals, bound by a common destiny, form part of clearly defined cultures and live within them. History is the state in motion, and the state is a living organism which, existing and asserting itself in relation to other states, defends itself or attacks with the knowledge that struggle and war alone are creative.

So a nation worthy of the name must have authority and discipline within, before it can undertake any determined action without. The state is being turned, and the Nazis are soon to say the same, into a kind of 'sportive' entity which is 'in form', an attempt by the ruling clique to offset class and party anarchy. The state is finished when a city-bred *bourgeoisie*, riddled with intellectualism, is in power and pretends to administer justice and to maintain the rights of man and economic freedom. As the masses remain apart from the *bourgeoisie*, the latter take fright and have recourse to dictatorial caesarism. Beware of casearism, of the sword that will conquer money! For this modern variety of caesarism with its mass-mystique is intent upon wreaking the vengeance of its blood and race on the victory of cosmic existence over artificial life and civilisation. There is no known cliché that Spengler does not make use of.

Spengler reduces world history as we know it to a certain number of 'cultures'. But what interests him particularly is the so-called 'Western' culture to which Germany belongs. This is a 'Faustian' culture; in other words, its ruling principle and its centre are in Germany. Now, the Faustian idea is essentially that of progression, of an effort which never ceases and which never balks at any change that may be necessary. The symbol of this culture is limitless space, as limitless as the effort to which man is condemned in order to mould his destiny. The Western Christian needs a forceful and active God, who creates and recreates the world uninterruptedly. For this reason, Spengler prefers the Renaissance to the Reformation as a precedent to follow, for he considers that Luther, with all his greatness, lacked a practical sense.

The map of Europe that Spengler draws, following upon Rathenau, Th. Mann, and Count Keyserling, places England and Germany in the centre of the Continent as the highest expression of the Faustian culture. Spengler finds no difficulty in reducing English history to the antithesis between Capitalism and Socialism, between the wealthy satisfied with their work and the poor demanding their rights. With this England he contrasts Prussia in a famous brochure of about a hundred pages entitled *Prussianism and Socialism*, which had an enormous success. Here again we have a forerunner of 'National-Socialism'—in other words, a Prussian definition of Socialism, which excludes all *bourgeois* liberalism, this much-despised German Liberalism which was infected with so many foreign germs: Catholicism faithful to the idea of Rome, the plutocratic democracy of France and Britain, Marxist Socialism, international Judaism. For the Germans Liberalism can never be anything but a source of weakness and decadence.

So in Germany there can be no regeneration without a revival of the sound Prussian tradition. The Prussian nation was the last to arise in the west, the Hohenzollerns were the embodiment of the Faustian culture. Prussianism, with its spirit of disciplined solidarity, is an agglomeration of physical properties and of intellectual and moral qualities. What was of real consequence in Prussia during her colonising period was the work done as a community. Commanding and obeying are the two poles of this solidarity. Which brings us very close to the *Führer* and the *Gefolgschaft*, the favourite slogans of the Nazis. In Spengler's view, by restoring this great tradition, the German revolution, the true revolution will be made. This revolution implies a political restoration, the creation of a ruling minority capable of *leading* the nation. All Spengler's proposed reforms hinge on this basic condition, which the Nazis are to revive later in their demand for a new aristocracy and the restoration of the nobility.

Spengler himself is interested in the Third Reich, in the Hitler era which he can already see dawning. But he expects it to materialise at the real turning-points, when an effective victory has been gained outside the Reich. He dimly foresees and fears that the Hitler régime may merely engulf the masses in a 'passing wave of mad intoxication'.

Another impassioned apostle of Prussianism follows Spengler, but only to disappear from the scene before him by committing suicide. 'German nationalism,' writes Moeller van den Bruck, 'wants to maintain Germany intact because, as the "middle country", she represents the only solid foundation for a balanced Europe.' In fact, Rathenau, Count Keyserling, Thomas Mann, and Spengler himself had said much the same thing.

Moeller protested vehemently against Spengler's pessimism. He considered that every people possesses inexhaustible vitality and can renew all its activities after making mistakes and suffering defeats. That is his message to the Germans at a time when they are confronted with a crumbling Weimar Republic. It is his mission to open up new vistas that will reawaken the nation's energy. He believes that Germany is much too amenable to Western and Eastern influence. Like his predecessors and like the Nazis after him, he would want to see Germany withdrawing into a kind of glorious isolation, of economic and intellectual autarky, in preparation for a 'national' revolution on lines that are familiar to us. Moeller states his case with an ardent simplicity that contrasts sharply with Spengler's weighty compactness.

He abhors the liberal democracy of the West as he does the Soviet system in Russia. To right and to left of Germany he sees nothing but mad egalitarianism, which is reducing the international situation to absurdity. For, while he sees the Western nations and Russia in terms of a pure, abstract universalism, either *bourgeois* or proletarian, he also sees behind this façade the realities of national life. Whether democratic or communist, the nations nonetheless go on with their daily lives. For Moeller there are only peoples and nations. But by refusing to admit the possibility of an international order of things, of a common standard, is he not preparing the ground for Hitlerism?

When he comes to consider the history of Germany, he does not conceal his implacable hatred for Rome. Germany is for him the Mother of Peoples. She owes it to herself to restore her European

unity by leading the nations that have strayed, back to the Germanic
fold. The ancient Germanic race lives on only in the German nation.
So the German nation must, by analogy, embody once again the
Nordic race. German unity was shattered by the struggles between
Papacy and Empire. The romanised nations prevented the Germans
from founding a complete Germanic Empire, the Roman Papacy
and the Russian Church prevented them from creating a universal
Church. Moeller dreams of a new union between the spiritual and
the temporal to be brought about by the Germanic religion, a religion which the Germans could have established in Europe, thanks
to Aryanism, but they became converted to Christianity. Hence the
ruin of the first Reich.

The future lies entirely in a union between Prussia and Germany.
Like Penelope's spinning, the work must be constantly resumed.
Moeller's sole interest in the Westphalian Treaties at the Congress
of Vienna lies in the rise of Prussia. He describes it lovingly and with
feeling. Influenced by the works of Fr. Meinecke, he interprets the
fusion of the Prussian with the German spirit as the great mystery
of this historical development. It is a blend of concrete Prussianism
and ardent Germanism. The natural hero of this drama is Frederick
II. Moeller is also intensely moved by Herder, who points out the
true path that Germanism must follow, and Stein, whom he regards
as the most genuine statesman. But Moeller admits that he cannot
explain the extraordinary territorial contraction imposed on Germany by Napoleon.

Moeller's basic idea—and he undoubtedly owes it to Fr. Meinecke
—is that in the fusion of Prussia and the Reich the latter can emerge
triumphant by 'romanticising' Prussia. Prussia runs the risk of losing
her traditional mode of life, if she cannot hold out against a technical
development inspired by a remarkable spirit of adventure and becomes 'economic romanticism' in action, exposed to every disaster.
Here Moeller is both making a prophecy and issuing a warning.
He condemns Wilhelmian Germany and the Germany of Weimar
with the same desperate vehemence.

His dream is a 'true German revolution'. What form will it take?
It will restore the values of the eternal Reich, of the Germany that
is the Mother of Peoples. The Third Reich that Moeller dreams of
before Hitler is a relapse to the normal primitive and classical
Germany, a protest against Western rationalism, a protest which
Luther made in its most profound and significant form. Hence
Moeller's favourite formula: 'to win the revolution'. What Moeller
preaches, after Rathenau and after Spengler, is a National-Socialism
based on a complete spiritual regeneration. There must be an
absolute identification with the living *Volkstum*, a mystical totality in
which each German is intent upon sensing the nation's rhythm and

upon entering into her natural evolution. In fact, Moeller seems to have adopted a modern brand of Hegelianism, that is prophetic and practical at one and the same time. His lesson to the youth is one of obedience to the call of Germany's genius. But this means nothing, for Moeller carefully avoids defining the 'call'. As Hitler was to do later, Moeller unleashes a sort of violent dynamism, a fervour that has no precise aims, a taste for risks for their own sake and for conquest for its own sake. As Hitler said, action for its own sake.

Moeller arrives in this way at his idea of 'soldiership'. On this basis, Moeller van den Bruck, forerunner of the Nazis, yet at the same time a distinguished, refined aristocrat, takes up once more the three familiar themes: the idea of an over-populated nation, the idea that the war to be declared is a Holy War, and finally the idea that it is Germany's mission to rule Europe and to rule it in the framework of a planned economy—that is, of National-Socialism. Then, we are assured, Germany will have 'her' democracy, her *Volkstaat*, and complete social, economic, political, and spiritual integration. There will be a true renaissance when Germany identifies her Socialism with that of the people as a whole. Her revolution will be the concern of the entire people. The Third Reich, reconstituted within, internally coherent and stable, will exert a powerful influence beyond its frontiers by reason of the super-national mission it is called upon to fulfil. For that reason, true German nationalism aims at a united Europe as well as a united Germany. Such is the specific destiny of Germany where 'justice among nations' is concerned.

Between all these prophets of a new future for Germany, who despite her first major defeat seem to have rejected none of the essential claims made by the imperialist nationalists, and Hitlerism, there is a flurry of professors, publicists, and journalists whose ideas gravitate round those of Rathenau and Moeller, though with some modifications, or round those of Spengler, though with considerably more vehemence.

Internally, an authoritarian state, complete state-control and a planned economy in a framework of national autarky, the revenge of the Protestant spirit and the Lutheran tradition. Externally, a clear break with the economic Liberalism of the West, a new relationship envisaged with Russia, and an expansionist drive in Central Europe. Continental Pangermanism is gaining ground everywhere, supported, moreover, and to a greater extent than is generally supposed, by Stresemann's skilful diplomacy. Few, if any, of these intellectuals between 1930 and 1932 believe that Hitler's star is in the ascendant. Their spiritual and religious ideas and also their *bourgeois* aristocratism make it impossible for them to accept either Communism or Hitlerism—in other words, demagogy.

But they have no clear conception of the popular dynamism that is produced in 1929 and after by the most appalling social crisis Germany has known since 1918.

2. THE NATIONAL-SOCIALIST RACIAL IDEOLOGY: RELIGIOUS AND PHILOSOPHICAL IDEAS

There is obviously an appearance of kinship between the preceding ideology and what one can call the National-Socialist doctrine. The original source common to both is the romanticism which became traditional in the nineteenth and twentieth centuries, closely blended with a growing Prussianism. The old, ineradicable opposition between irrationalism and rationalism is fundamental. On the one hand, we have an impassioned plea for natural, spontaneous life; on the other hand, constant criticism of intellectualism which poisons life at its source. The 'Hitlerian' revolution can be said to have been a 'revolution against reason'.[1]

That is why all the elements of the old philosophical and religious Pangermanism recur in the ideology of Hitler's Third Reich. But the spirit, the general inspiration, and the presentation are different, because they correspond to the needs of the masses. In Hitlerism everything seems larger than life, horribly vulgarised, reduced to the simple terms that guarantee the success of a propaganda backed by powerful material means. From one intellectual plane to the other there is a kind of all-engulfing landslide. Lenin had said that the masses were entering politics. They were entering it, in Germany, for the first time, not to take part in a well-conceived, democratically conducted political action, but to bolster up with their fanaticism a totalitarian, dictatorial government. It was to be a sharp drop to this lower level where brute-force prevails and where violence breaks out in its crudest forms. The middle classes, until then disorganised, suddenly grouped together and rushed in compact groups on to the public stage. They were dominated and led by a younger generation without any real critical faculty, which, having suffered cruelly, was carried away by simple ideas and apparent political novelty. A good portion of the proletariat followed on behind, impressed by the solidarity of a mass movement which it was all too easy to confuse with socialism.

In the eighteenth century and at the beginning of the nineteenth the movement of protest against Western intellectualism had been philosophical and religious. Then, under Bismarck and Wilhelm II, it became the action of a people made extremely vulnerable by

---

[1] On National-Socialist ideology see Vermeil, *Doctrinaires de la révolution allemande* and *L'Allemagne, Essai d'explication.*

an excess of industrialisation, which had emptied its fields and crowded its workers into enormous improvised cities, of a people of factory-hands, whose living institutions and most cherished traditions, and, not least, whose love of work, were being undermined by the inevitable mechanisation of technical ideas and activities. Nazism, heir to an imperialist Nationalism, whose ambitions and megalomania had been shattered by the defeat of 1918, set up the national myth, the people, as people and as race, the totalitarian *Volkstum* against the European statute embodied in the Treaty of Versailles, which had balkanised the old Continent of Europe.

In fact, pre-world-war Pangermanism and the ideology of the Republic of Weimar were the work of a certain *bourgeois*, intellectual *élite*. The Nazi ideology was worked out by mediocre men to meet the needs of mediocre men. The more cultured ideologists regarded the Nazi chiefs as gross iconoclasts. The lowering of the intellectual standard corresponded to a change in the social structure. And that is the real reason why the old antithesis between vitalism and intellectualism, between irrationalism and rationalism, between culture and civilisation, between healthy enthusiasm and decadent indifference is replaced in undeveloped, inmature minds by the antithesis between Nordic Aryans and Semitic Jews.

Let there be no mistake, mass-mysticism remains. But in the Nazi system it is wrapped up in a degenerate, decadent version of the great intellectual, moral, and religious tradition which German thinkers had built up under the influence of the Reformation, classicism, and romanticism. The German mind had fallen into a trap of its own setting. It accused nations as alive, as closely bound to their native soil, their traditions, and their varied and resilient culture as were England and France of being content with a synthetic intellectualism. What it did not realise was that in Germany herself it was creating an intellectualism *sui generis*, as superficial and as dangerous in its way as that of the West.

In his study *Idea and Existence*, published in 1935, the Nazi Hans Heyse tries to make comprehensible what he calls his really Nordic conception, a high-sounding metaphysical argument which distinguishes between chaos and an organised 'Cosmos', between Christian transcendence, which admits a 'Beyond', and what Heyse calls 'existence in truth'—that is, a sort of transcendence inherent in earthly reality or, if you like, a 'life on earth' that implies, both for man and for society, a certain 'surpassing'. This is plain existentialism, and one is not surprised to find the Nazi Heyse coming very close to Heidegger and tying up the latter's fairly pronounced individualism to the group-mysticism we have already discussed. To know one's destiny, he tells us, is worth more than believing, like the Christians, in dogmas. Salvation comes not from Christian humility, but from a courageous, heroic will that shapes its own destiny because it is fully conscious of it.[1]

Heyse also accepts Heidegger's conception of anguish. He naturally prefers it to that of the Christian Kierkegaard. Anguish is a subjective state which reveals in the existence of men and societies a transcendent element. Was it not Luther's main idea in his early youth, and does Heidegger not come back to it? Is it not our supreme duty to be ready for, to expose ourselves to, anguish? And, still more, is not this the way to separate Luther from the Jew St Paul and from Christianity, a humiliating religion for the Germans? That, then, is the true courage of life. There is no contradiction between anguish and courage, for it is in anguish that courage is born. The reality that Heidegger is confronted with is that of a hunted man driven towards nothingness, towards the abyss of death. Only such a man exists essentially, gains possession of his real 'I' and of himself. And the Nazi notes the analogy with the god Wotan, chief god of Germanic mythology, the god of storms and war, above all the omniscient god who knows the implacable Fates, the god who is concerned with all things because he foresees them.

Heyse also tries to correct Heidegger on the meaning of the collective dictatorship that the Hitler régime is establishing in Germany. The 'Cosmos' as opposed to chaos is the Germany of the post-1918 years, a Germany which intends to rebuild itself. And he delves into her history to unearth the Vikings, the peasant spirit of the Bronze Age, this curious mixture of aggressive spirit and placid calm that is authentically Nordic. If, therefore, Heidegger considers man among his fellows, he remains, according to Heyse, an individualist, in that he is particularly concerned with man condemned to solitude and advancing alone towards inevitable death. For Nazism, the essential form of existence in truth is the state, the Reich, communal life. The cosmic order, as opposed to chaos, is realised in and through the Third Reich. So there is in Heidegger an individualism that is very near to Nihilism, the isolated form of anguish which the warrior knows. He fights for his country in a limited space, while Heidegger's man has no space, but only time. In other words, man only finds a place, a lodging, and relative security in his race. For the Christian refuge of the past Nazism substitutes a racial refuge, which derives from the substance, form, and entire heritage of one's ancestors. That is the truth embodied in the Nordicism, which A. Rosenberg in his *Myth of the Twentieth Century* makes the origin and principle of all superior civilisations, and of which Germany alone holds the secret.

It is a strange discussion, which makes clear the difference to be

[1] On Heidegger and the Nazi Heyse see *Races et Racisme*, No. 7. January–March 1938, pp. 7 ff.

maintained between Nazism and Christianity, between Nazism and the existentialism of the philosophers of anguish. It is a modernised Hegelianism, a new way of reviving the cult of the organic and sacred community, which romanticism had already mapped out.

Philosophy and religion intermingle here, as they already did in the romantic conception. How can one doubt that National-Socialism is the direct heir of religious Pangermanism? The American idea of a Nazi 'conspiracy', on which the report of Judge Jackson for the Nuremberg Trial is based, is false. We are dealing not with a mere conspiracy, but with a conception of life, with a *Weltanschauung* which is to be imposed on the whole of Germany, then on Europe and the world.

We have seen how, from Fichte and Hegel to the Wilhelmian Pangermanists, more particularly in Paul de Lagarde and Constantin Frantz, the idea of a German national religion took shape in the nineteenth and twentieth centuries. A curious paradox, for on the one hand there is the confused diversity and the many aspects of a confessionalism attached to its local traditions, on the other hand the assertion of national unity and greatness on a religious level. The Third Reich, equipped with a unique religion of its own, had haunted the German mind for centuries. Under Wilhelm II a number of nationalists deplore the fact that Aryanism has not replaced Christianity. In fact, the Nazi German seeks to identify his personal religion with his membership of the Reich, with a Reich that is never completed and eternally in process of creation. Historical evolution has led to a fundamental disagreement between nationalism and Christianity. While the latter splits up into two confessions, which in turn branch out into territorial Churches, nationalism keeps alive the dream of absolute unity, religious and political. The Germany of tomorrow will be not only a religious community, but also a racial and biological one.

In the Nazi Party's original programme, Article 4 promised the confessions equality of treatment. They would be, it was said, free and respected so long as they threatened neither the morale of the Germanic race nor the existence of the state. This promise contained a thinly veiled but very real threat. The Party, without binding itself to any specific dogma, admitted 'positive Christianity'. It proposed to subordinate all religious life to the interests of the state and to fight against what it called 'Jewish materialism'.[1]

Hitler is not very explicit on this point. He states that he has no intention of substituting for Christianity a conception of the world or a religion. He simply declares in *Mein Kampf* that he will demand from the Churches a 'positive' and 'national' Christianity, absolute

[1] On the religious aspects of National-Socialism see Vermeil, *Hitler et le Christianisme* (Gallimard, Paris, 1940).

unity of the nation with a view to satisfying its most legitimate desires. As the German people has never had a general will, coherence, or stability, the two Christian confessions would be well advised to cease their age-old quarrels, which the Jews do their utmost to aggravate for their own advantage. So Hitler demands from them an implacable anti-Semitism, repudiation of the Old Testament and of every tradition of Israelite origin, and complete devotion to the national movement, which cannot do without them. For the masses, says the *Führer*, will become integrated in the Reich only if they are inspired by a new faith and make a true religion of their national consciousness. Hitler was picking up again, though in a peculiarly brutal and crude form, the line of thought which P. de Lagarde and C. Frantz had followed on a higher level.

Hitler was obviously treating Catholicism with respect, partly because he admitted its strong discipline. The decisive and hazardous assault was to be made by A. Rosenberg in his *Myth of the Twentieth Century*. He nourished an undying hatred for the black international, Roman Catholicism. A disciple of Nietzsche, Wagner, and H. S. Chamberlain, he was no less hostile to Rome than to Judaism. He was convinced that Catholic Christianity had corrupted the entire German people, from the early period of conversion up to the Reformation, then from Luther to the contemporary era, both through Lutheranism remaining faithful to the Old Testament and ecumenical Christianity, and because of the key positions that the Counter-Reformation gained for Roman Catholicism in German territory. Rosenberg invented nothing. He contented himself with reviving and rearranging the arguments the Pangermanists had produced in their time against the Roman idea and its role in history, against Catholic institutions and certain aspects of Lutheranism.

The first and the most important charge he makes is that St Paul judaised primitive Christianity by diverting it from its natural course. St Paul replaced the true Christ, the Aryan, heroic Christ whose existence was admitted by H. S. Chamberlain, the model of all the warrior virtues, of all sacrifices to a great communal Idea, by the weak Christ whom God is alleged to have sent down to the earth as a mediator charged with bringing man, the victim of original sin, eternal salvation—namely, humility, love, brotherhood, and everlasting peace. True Christianity, according to Rosenberg, must lead men, if necessary by violence, to heroic superhumanity. A thoroughly 'Nordic' ideal, which has been abandoned by semitised Christianity, thereby reducing the whole of Western humanity to little better than animals. If universal history has any meaning at all, it owes it solely to the North, the centre of creation and original light that emanated from a mysterious Atlantis, the source of all great cultures and the origin of this Galilean world in which the true Christ lived and suffered.

Seen from this point of view, Rome—ancient Rome—could be represented as a creation of the Nordic spirit. But disastrous race-mixtures took place there. A sense of sin is a sign of racial bastardisation. That is why the genuine Greco-Latin culture, a Nordic product, like the Indian and Persian cultures, gave way to a decadent Christianity which was later to soften, corrupt, and undermine the German world.

Rosenberg comes to the conclusion that Catholicism and Protestantism in his time are worm-eaten and ready to collapse. Only Hitler's 'positive' Christianity—in other words 'Germanic' Christianity—will restore to the German and European world its lost virtues and vitality. Rosenberg makes no secret of his sources, particularly the writings of H. S. Chamberlain, who, as we have seen, spent most of his life trying to prove that only the Germans are capable of regenerating and rebuilding Europe. Thus the Nazi leaders take up the old theme of decline and regeneration. Their attitude is in some ways analogous to that of the romantics, regeneration being a Germanic and German privilege, decadence the work of the Latin world. It was a single step from this to branding the Papacy as the main enemy of the German Empire, to setting up against Charlemagne the heroes of national resistance, and to rewriting the whole of German history. That this criticism was also directed against the Catholic Centre, pivot of the Weimar democracy, there could be little doubt.

The Lutheran problem was more complex. As was done by the pre-war nationalists, so again now the Reformation was represented as a return to Germanism. It was a strange phenomenon, Luther and Calvin sharing a sort of halo of prestige bestowed on them by Rosenberg, who had no hesitation in associating with them the Albigenses, the Catharists, the Valaisans, the Huguenots, and even the free-thinkers of the French laity as representatives of the eternal struggle of the German spirit against Rome. Luther's Germany, slipping into Paulinism, offended, through lack of vigilance, against her own blood. She even furthered the doctrine of original sin, which Luther admits to be consubstantial to man. She also maintained contact with the Old Testament and Judaism. Why not, therefore, restore Lutheranism to its true origins, to its genuine course? Why not make it a national religion, completely Germanic—in other words, 'positive', imbued with combatant heroism, with Nordic aggressiveness, a religion capable of satisfying the demands of national honour? Luther's real importance lies in the revolution that he prepared when, defying the priesthood, he struck at the heart of the Church of Rome, the cause of universal bastardisation.

German Catholicism in its entirety resisted this attack, with the exception of a very small minority, which fought in vain to defend the ideal of a Catholic 'germanism'.

Nazi paganism produced two curious movements: the 'German Christians' in the Lutheran Evangelical Church and the doctrine 'of the German Faith' of Professors Hauer and Bergmann—a doctrine very similar to the ideas of Rosenberg.

The 'German Christians' were first organised in 1932 in an attempt to establish a Church of the Reich, to define positive Christianity, which consists in believing in Christ 'in the German manner' and in accordance with Lutheran heroism, to combat the Centre and Marxism by every possible means, to put an end to race-mixture by breaking with Judaism and the Old Testament, and at the same time with Christian ecumenicism or Freemasonry, and finally to declare, as all Pangermanists had done before, that the German people is entrusted with a providential mission blessed by God.

The German Faith movement was more pantheistic and mystical. It drew its inspiration from medieval mysticism, proposed to substitute for static Christianity a dynamic religion, which was based on the idea and the reality of a perpetual human progression, was adapted to the deepest aspirations of the Nordic peoples, and could not be expressed in immutable dogmas. It drew its sustenance from personal intuition, for the divine in man manifests itself in an infinite variety of ways. God, it was argued, is in no sense distinct from man, who creates his own God in making himself more and more divine. Hauer regarded Christ as human nature that had 'become divine' and was destined to show us that every man can follow this sublime example. Redemption is a process that is both present and eternal, the true Redeemer, whether individual or people, being a good anthropologist who from his knowledge of race-eugenics will create the strong and pure individual as heroic as he is sincere. 'National' shrines will be built in which the German people will glorify its great men. Here was a mixture of many influences: Nietzsche, Gobineau and Vacher de Lapouge, H. S. Chamberlain and Ed. von Hartmann, the philosopher of the Unconscious.

Apart from these religious parties, a minority rejected Christianity out of hand and returned to the primitive Germanic religion, the cult of Wotan, the authentic Aryan Jesus, to a Galilee alleged to have been colonised by the Nordics. Why not go straight back to the myths of the Teutons, to their thought and heroic virtues as recorded in the Gospels?

Hitler and the other Nazi leaders wanted, and hoped, to eradicate confessional Christianity completely. But, far from destroying the Churches at one blow, as they were doing with the synagogues, they were talking rather of winning them over, of gradually discrediting them. On 24 February 1934 Hitler stressed the exclusive, totalitarian character of the Third Reich and added that universalism was about to pass over from the Christian religion to that of the Nazis. On the 19 March, Goebbels reminded the German people that National-Socialism was a revolutionary movement because it created a radical transformation, the Christian confessions not excepted. As we know, the Nazis did not stop at mere words, but attempted to establish one Church side by side with the one party and school. We also know how the Churches resisted.

3. Anti-Semitism and Racialism

It is not difficult to see how Nazism revives the philosophical and religious Pangermanism of the nineteenth and early twentieth centuries and adds to it anti-Semitism and racialism. Under Wilhelm II both these currents had already made their appearance. On this crucial point the Nazis once again invent nothing. They vulgarise. They bring their communal mysticism within reach of the masses.

Immediately after the armistice, anti-Semitism reappears in conquered Germany with increased virulence, due to the fact that the ruling minority exploits it to create the notorious 'stab-in-the-back' legend, which is designed to place the responsibility for the war and the defeat on the Jews and their propaganda, as well as on the democrats and socialists who are influenced by Jewish doctrines.

The strange story of the 'Protocols of the Elders of Zion', which appears simultaneously in the north and the south of a war-shattered Germany, is abundant proof of the tremendous part anti-Semitism played after the defeat. We are all of us familiar with the story today, and the whole world knows what practical results it was to have. What we have to determine here is what part anti-Semitism played in Nazi doctrine.[1]

The Nazi doctrine, if there is such a thing, takes the negative form of criticism directed against the Jewish spirit in all its manifestations, whether in the international sphere or in Germany herself, then the positive form of racial reconstruction on a purely national basis. Rosenberg, after reviewing fifteen centuries of European history, was able to reach the conclusion that this period shows how

[1] The Protocols of the Elders of Sion have a long history. Consult Henry Rollin, *Apocalypse de notre temps*. The basis for this publication is *Entretiens de Machiavel et de Montesquieu aux Enfers* by M. Joly, a French lawyer. This book, translated and altered for the purposes of Czarist propaganda, was brought to Germany from Russia about 1919. See *L'Allemagne, Essai d'explication*, pp. 302 ff. It is essential to realise that M. Joly's book was a violent criticism of the régime which Napoleon III installed in France after the Coup d'État of 2 Dec. and that it was used, after alteration, as an outline of Fascist procedures and methods and as a source of anti-Semitic arguments.

'all nations have . . . moved in the orbit of a universalist conception of the world. . . . Religious Universalism in Roman Catholicism and Protestant dogma; universalism of a moral and social
nature in . . . liberalism such as was produced by the French
Revolution; finally nihilist universalism in the latest representation of Marxism, in a world Communism that no longer recognises
national States. . . . Now, each of these values, in one form or
another, is embodied in a political party, principally in Germany.
Medieval universalism is represented by the Centre, the dynastic
Idea by the Conversatives, the republican and economic Idea by
the Democrats, the class Idea by the groups that have emerged
from Marxism. . . . Faced by all these groups in Germany, the
National-Socialist Movement proclaims a supreme value that is
both new and old, namely, National Honour. . . .'

This meant—for this declaration is of crucial importance—that
the nations of the Continent would from then on evolve in an
atmosphere of nationalism. This is the aim of Germany's Third
Reich, with its craving for continental hegemony. Rosenberg, who
gives a very exact interpretation of the tragedy of Weimar, explains
it in terms of the insoluble conflict between the European Internationals. These Internationals, as symbolised by the political
parties, became involved in a mortal struggle in the German parliamentary arena after the federalised monarchies of Bismarck's
Reich had disappeared. As the Jews are accused of being present
and active at the heart of all these Internationals, anti-Semitism
becomes a fundamental doctrine, which is to serve as a lever for
racialism, for the so-called 'Aryan' community.

From 1914 to 1918 Jews had poured into Germany from the east.
At the time of defeat and humiliation, the German Jews had proved
providential scapegoats. Then the Weimar régime had allowed the
Jews to occupy a more and more important place in business,
politics, the press, and the liberal professions, by virtue of the outstanding qualities that gave them a very real advantage over the
native German. By such means as the 'Protocols of the Elders of
Zion', complete responsibility both for the war and for the defeat
that followed could be placed on their shoulders. The general
public accepted all these fantastic charges with lamentable credulity. The Jews, it was said, had hatched a plot to achieve world
domination by ruining the various peoples with democracy, Communism, or anarchy. It was no coincidence that Rosenberg first
made contact with Hitler through a notorious anti-Semite, Dietrich
Eckart.

On this point, too, Hitler proved to have more elementary, less
subtle ideas than Rosenberg. In *Mein Kampf* he recalls his experience of Judaism in Vienna. The Jews, he declares, are a 'people by
themselves', an existential collectivity, a clearly defined race, which

places its own interests above all else. Their example must, therefore, be followed on a national basis, for the good of Germany alone. It is up to the Germans to exploit the inheritance of Jewish racialism. Although it seems to be up-to-date, the study of racial biology takes the Old Testament as its jumping-off ground. Hitler accuses the Jews of every imaginable physical, intellectual, and moral taint. He condemns them for their egalitarian leanings, their predilection for homogeneous international masses: high finance, a socialist proletariat, and even a humanistic culture. The Jew is made the originator of large-scale Capitalism, then of democratic Liberalism, then again of Marxist Socialism. He is accused of being behind the Manchester School, Franco-British plutocracy, Western Freemasonry, and parliamentarianism, and even the excessive industrialisation to which Germany has fallen victim. 'The Jew', cried Hitler, 'has always known how to unite princes, aristocrats, and *bourgeois* on a national basis.' He also managed to invent 'Workers of the world, unite!' The Jew uses the small people to rob the great, the great to rob the small. It is he who, in the cultural sphere, encourages a corrosive intellectualism. He lacks idealism, exploits the inventions of others, ignores culture that emanates from blood and soil, and only practises an earthly religion.

Rosenberg's anti-Semitism is more of a doctrine. But he deals with analogous themes. Judaism, which incidentally is confused with Semitism, is the essence of root-evil and original sin—in short, of intellectualism. It separates the natural, instinctive elements of blood and race closely bound up with native soil from the mind and the soul, from our thoughts and our actions. The Jew is essentially uprooted, a non-existential Being, an accursed wanderer. He corrupts all superior Nordic cultures. The Jewish spirit has remained the same for centuries. The Talmudic tradition has produced all the combatant organisations that the Jews have employed for the conquest of the world. Liberal and socialist Jews divert the Germans from their national duty by preaching reconciliation between peoples. In addition, they acquire privileged positions in the Reich, without, however, becoming an integral part of the nation.

It is mere child's play for the Nazis to discover that Christianity originated with the Jews.

Hitler is not exactly an adept at this subject. Rosenberg's views on Roman Catholicism are well known. He believes that Catholicism allowed itself to be led astray, and thus lost sight of its origins, of Nordic Hellenism, by a bastardised Asiaticism and Semitism. Christ was an authentic Aryan, but St Paul compromised his teaching by introducing corruptive elements. Socratic Hellenism contributed its particular poison. Rome with its dogma of sin undermined the resistance of entire peoples and diverted the stream of

the German will. In this way, Aryanism, Germany's natural religion, was eliminated. Germany's sole debt to Rome is Mediterranean and Semitic corruption. The German Catholics also are
wrong not to break with Judaism. Hitler, however, seems to demand
anti-Semitism only of the Lutherans. Some of them, the 'German
Christians', were prepared to follow him. But in any case the tactics
of the Nazi leaders are well known. They consist in directing the
Chrisian confessions towards anti-Semitic racialism in order to turn
them against ecumenism and fetter them to the national state, to the
Third Reich.

The same manoeuvre is employed with Western liberalism. On
this point Hitler is more violent than Rosenberg. He is so offensive
as to defeat his own purpose. According to him, the Jews take
advantage of the weaknesses of democracy to establish a plutocracy
together with its opposite, Marxist Socialism. In short, they burn
the candle at both ends.

Rosenberg regards Liberalism as an eighteenth-century invention,
the chief result of German and European urbanisation. Like the
Jew, the Liberal has no roots and is the inferior of both peasant and
artisan. He has allowed himself to be completely mechanised.
It is a weak analysis which is no more than a distortion of Nietzsche
that attempts to explain decadence by an excess of conscious deliberation peculiar to the Jewish mentality. In Rosenberg's view
the French Revolution was no more than a sterile disaster.

Still worse is the denunciation of Marxism and Communism.
Marxism and Communism, which are linked with Judaism through
their theorists and their leaders, who are very close to the plutocratic democracy that exploits the urban proletariat, and who are
out to replace the Celestial City of the Christian International by
the earthly city of the worker's International, are the corruptive
force that combines the worst features of all the others. They are
the most dangerous foe. Hitler once again quotes his Viennese experiences. The Jew, he declares, speaks to the worker of his misery
in order to stifle his racial and national loyalty. Nothing could be
more hostile to a Germanic aristocracy than the doctrines of the Jew,
Marx. The Jewish press works upon the working masses as freemasonry has worked on the *bourgeoisie* of the West. The egoism of
employers and strikes by the workers, both stimulated by Jews, help
them in their sinister work. The skilfulness of the Jews takes Hitler's
breath away. He cannot help admiring them as he also admires the
Catholic orders. He studies their methods of organisation. He urges
German nationalism to learn from them!

Rosenberg's case is less crude and better presented. He, too, pours
invective on what he calls Judeo-Communism. He draws the following conclusions about Marx's doctrines: (1) they devitalise and up-

root the workers by proclaiming their international solidarity; (2) they maintain the class-struggle by promising employers and proletariat alike that the nation's ills will be cured; (3) they preach pacifism instead of demanding 'justice among nations'; (4) they deny true property, which is each man's source of creative power. Jews were the life and soul of the 1917 revolution in Russia, and it is they who are striking most openly at the colonial empires. They are the sworn enemies of a European culture which is based on the irrefutable diversity of nations.

This, cries Rosenberg, is the process which for centuries past has been installing the Jewish parasite in the very heart of Europe. This parasite has gained possession of the agrarian country that Russia once was. There it met with no resistance. In the west the Jews are achieving their ends by means of Bolshevism, which is spreading from Europe towards Asia and even towards America. Jerusalem is quickly becoming 'the axis of the world'. Only Germany understands and resists. Her soldiers and students are building the National-Socialist barricades. It is the last bulwark, the final defence!

Nazism thus supplements the philosophical and religious Pangermanism from which it derives with a basic anti-Semitism which conditions its entire approach to Western humanism and international affairs.

On this revised basis, made more comprehensive and above all more comprehensible to the masses, the Nazis in their own way revive the scientific argument, which is both historical and biological. Thus they oppose the Jew with the Aryan, this so-called 'Nordic' German type, who embodies all the virtues of the sovereign race.

It is Rosenberg who draws up the new schedule to which German history is to be adapted. He deals at great length with the First Reich, with the resistance which Witikind put up to Charlemagne and which Germanic culture has always maintained against the ancient civilisation and the Christianity that came from the southwest. Rosenberg, as a Balt, feels compelled to remind his readers that the Vikings once conquered Russia and brought the blessings of their civilisation to the Russian steppes. Is Bolshevism anything other than a 'mongoloid' revolt against the Nordics?

German history, viewed now from the racial point of view, again becomes similar to that of Greece. It was not Charlemagne but Witikind who founded the German Reich, by defending German *Volkstum* against a universal Germano-Christian monarchy. After the first Thirty Years War, the Francs were swallowed up by the Gauls, and France, whose upper strata are of German origin, broke away from the Mother of Peoples. Then came the struggles between Arminius and the Romans, between Witikind and Charlemagne, and between Henry the Lion and Barbarossa, the offensive by the Hansa and German mysticism against Rome, the Lutheran Reformation, and the creation of Nordic science by Copernicus—all these themes thread their way through the argument.

The Nazi leaders do not spare Bismarck's Empire, but they retain their admiration for Prussia, for her monarchy, her bureaucracy, and her army. Hitler and Rosenberg have only one fault to find with her, but it is a vital one: she left the popular masses to themselves, with the result that they sank gradually into a state of decadence for which foreign internationals and their principal agents, the Jews, were responsible. Nothing could be more discreditable to the German people than this charge-sheet that clears the former rulers of the Bismarckian and Wilhelmian Reich of any responsibility for the catastrophe and seems to indicate that the only corruption in Germany between 1871 and 1914 was among the middle and working classes! It was easy to say, and keep on saying, that Jewish internationalism was responsible for all misfortune. As one can well imagine, the Nazi leaders blame their defeat on the Weimar Republic and on the two parties that were its creators and beneficiaries, the Catholic Centre and the Social Democrats. The latter serve, in their turn, as scapegoats. They, we are told, in collaboration with international high finance, would have dragged Germany down into a purely material way of life, fighting at the same time against any truly national economic policy—an attack that was all the more treacherous because it cleared the German industrialists and bankers of all blame.

This is a subject which it would be superfluous to emphasise. The consequence of, and at the same time the real commentary on, those views of history is to be found in the instructions issued by Minister Rust on the German history curriculum for high schools in the Reich. As we know, the Nazi historians were planning to 'rewrite' the history of the Reich to their own pattern.

The biological argument applied to race is much more important. Hitler, Rosenberg, and H. F. K. Günther, the leading Nazi race theorist, all have practically the same conception of what they call 'the racial soul'. They differ only in their presentation.[1]

Hitler contents himself with opposing the Aryan to the Jew, the Aryan being the symbol of the German type, an authentic member of the national community. There is nothing more appalling than these abstractions, which are destined to create utter confusion in the minds of the uninitiated and to provoke the most bitter hatreds. Hitler is mainly concerned to draw the distinction between his brand of nationalism and that of the Bismarck era. Yet he is nonetheless

[1] Hitler, *Mein Kampf*, and A. Rosenberg, *Der Mythus des 20 Jahrhunderts* should be studied.

the disciple and heir of the Woltmanns, the Driesmans, the H. S. Chamberlains, and the Reimers. Like them he underlines the inequality of races, the notion of the *Herrenvolk* and the *Volkstum*—an ideology as crude as it is famous, thanks to the propaganda about it and to the *Führer*'s speeches at the Nuremberg Rallies. It is enough to say that, according to Hitler, the German *Volkstum* must attune itself to the rhythm of the universe and to the 'first meaning of things' (*Ursinn der Dinge*).

Once more Rosenberg's thesis is more subtle, while that of H. F. K. Günther is more scholarly. Rosenberg compares the discovery of race to Copernicus's discovery. The state no longer revolves round the individuals within it; it is they who gravitate round the *Volk*. The people, in order to achieve true unity, must move round a 'racial dominant'. This is H. S. Chamberlain's theory. The German becomes the normal Aryan. More of a mystic than Hitler, Rosenberg simplifies and uses the old idea of the Body of Christ, the dream of the nineteenth and twentieth centuries in Germany, that of a community which is both organic and religious and which, by comparison with the absolutist or individualist state of the West and with Communism, would be a kind of national Church, a Nation-Church pre-existent to its members, and by that very fact entitled to demand from them the complete sacrifice of their liberty, activities, and life.

Rosenberg has elaborated in some detail the idea of blood, that of pure continuity, and finally that of the part to be played by symbolic insignia. The blood is that portion of the unconscious, spontaneous life which determines the race. The conscious, rational life tends to separate us from this obscure source of existence and to alienate us from the national community. The mystery is how this blood circulates through the national and racial body. When the individual plunges into the depths of his being, the commandments of the blood are revealed to him, a supreme height which the leader attains symbolically by his thought and actions. Hence that continuity of action which is the opposite of the pure discontinuity that is clear consciousness. Hence the fact that Nordic Germany, like Greece, personifies its national symbolism in the form of superior men and women, and that the insignia and the uniforms are designed to reveal her, in all her existential and racial reality, to the eyes of the masses. For race is the great womb of the German people which, proceeding from it, lives and develops as an organised body, represented in its essence by the one Party.

From this point of view, the leader is not only the strong man but also the dreamer and visionary, the inventor of myths, and the interpreter of the old mythological representations of the race. That is the male's function *par excellence*, the woman's being to perpetuate the physiological continuity of the race. The next stage is the organisation of the leaders in an order which is reminiscent of the Teutonic Order and of the order of 'soldiership', every member of the community, whatever his sphere of activity, being a 'soldier' of the régime.

Apart from this historical and biological thesis which is a vulgarised version of the thesis elaborated in the nineteenth and early twentieth centuries, there is an upsurge of cultural neo-Pangermanism. For, to employ a pseudo-philosophical term, the Nazi state is a 'phenomenon', as compared with the 'noumenon' that is the racial soul. It is the doctrine that is totalitarian, not the state. Or, if you like, the state is totalitarian because the doctrine is. We are dealing with a general conception of life which follows upon, having triumphed over, another, that is regarded as decadent and outdated. This state is a 'culture' in the German sense of the world. Controlled by a new *élite* that is closely linked with the masses, it has the law, the administration, and the army on its side. In the economic sphere, Capitalism is at its beck and call, and, with it, the mass of the workers, who this time have become docile. In factories and barracks Germany sets out to educate both bodies and minds. She does it by propaganda. In 1933 at Nuremberg Hitler hazards a picture of the new culture, an eminently Aryan culture that is geared for war. This is the famous comparison between the 'soldier' and the 'artist'. It recalls the myrtle and the sword of the Wilhelmian Pangermanists.

4. FOREIGN POLICY AND DESTRUCTION OF INTERNATIONAL ORDER— SUPREMACY OR COLLABORATION?

What place will Germany take among the nations? In other words, are we to see a revival, in modern dress, of the continental and colonial programmes of the Wilhelmian era?

What will Germany's relations be with her neighbours, one of German pre-eminence or one of collaboration? German pre-eminence followed logically from the régime's doctrinal synthesis and methods. When Nazism comes out in support of collaboration, it will always be with the object of lulling the other nations into a sense of false security. Hitler, who inherited, though unconsciously, the ideas of Curtius and Mommsen, likes to stress the racial solidarity that creates a bond between Germany on the one hand and Greece and Rome on the other, the Rome of the Empire. Everything in the world that bears the stamp of genius is Aryan. It is right that there should be inferior men and peoples to carry out the wishes of the superior race. The world is moving towards a great revolution. The crucial question is to know whether it will benefit Judaism or Germanism. Hitler's speeches from 1922 to 1933 are all couched in the same language. When Hitler comes to power, he is to make three demands: (1) the same rights and the same degree of sovereignty as other nations; (2) a natural balance between nations having equal sovereignty; (3) the need for German hegemony in Europe. In 1933 at the Nuremberg Rally he begins by drawing a distinction between peoples that 'rise' and peoples that 'decline'. Both nature and reason recognise the right of the stronger. When Hitler speaks to the world on behalf of Germany, he talks of justice and collaboration. But when he speaks to Germany of the outside world, he talks of racial supremacy—a contradiction that is all the more unacceptable because Germany refuses Russia equality of rights. In theory, the world is divided into victors and vanquished, but in practice it is an injustice to treat Germany as a vanquished country.

So there is in the minds of the Nazi leaders a certain vacillation, which is undoubtedly deliberate. When addressing the Germans, they proclaim Germany to be the Mother of Peoples, with the right, therefore, to the supremacy that is inherent in her Nordic supremacy. When addressing the other nations, they recall violations of juridical equality in the past and urge collaboration between nations in the future.

The Nazi leaders claimed they could do better than their predecessors of the Wilhelmian period. It is impossible, they said, to feed a starving people and at the same time curb its pride of birth or expect it to be content with colonisation at home. Yet excessive exporting to stimulate excessive importing is also no solution, for then the Germans are condemned to purely industrial and commercial activities. The Wilhelmian Reich, says Hitler, should, in the first place, have launched a policy of territorial conquest in Europe, then taken up again in the east the traditional policy of the Teutonic Order, which has been quiescent since the fifteenth century. This would have meant falling into line deliberately with the British, who offered Germany an alliance against Russia in 1900. On the whole, and not without justification, the Nazi leaders reproach Wilhelmian Germany with obstinately pursuing a colonial dream before it had made its position in Europe safe.

Apart from this reservation, which is not unimportant, as it concerns Germany's pre-1914 foreign policy as a whole, there is nothing in the Nazi foreign programme that was not contained already in the demands and plans of Continental Pangermanism.

This programme, like the Nazi doctrine itself, comprises a negative and a positive section.

As regards the first, we are given to understand at an early stage, as Reimer announced in 1905, that the Third Reich must take action against France and Russia to isolate them from each other and then crush them, for these two nations are breeding-grounds for the

most loathsome forms of universalism: Judaism, Catholicism, liberal
and Marxist Socialist-Democracy. The new factor, by comparison
with the pre-1914 period, is the hope that this enormous task of
liquidation will be made possible by a policy of benevolent neutrality
on the part of England and the northern countries, thus enabling
Germany, together with Italy, to set up a '*Mitteleuropa*' and, together with Japan, to form an Axis, that can also be regarded as
something new. So the primary aim is to isolate France and Russia
from Britain, Spain, and Italy, as well as from the Balkans and
Poland, and thus prevent them from offering any joint opposition
to the dynamic urge of the Germanic people to expand nort-east-
wards in the direction of Poland and the Baltic, but above all to
cross the mountain barrier in the south and thus be free to move down
the 2,000-kilometre land isthmuses: the one in the south-west that
leads to the western Mediterranean, and the one in the south-east
that can give Germany access to the Mediterranean by way of the
Balkans and to the Black Sea by way of Rumania and Turkey.

 If one studies the text of *Mein Kampf*, the famous pages on France,
which were written immediately after Locarno and were never dis-
avowed by the *Führer*, although he had the French translated
versions cleverly pruned to make them palatable to French public
opinion, reveal both an undying hate and the most blatant injustice.
It was a quite deliberate, propaganda hate, backed up by grotesque
assertions which are a hopeless mixture of truth and falsehood.
France, Hitler declares, is well-protected on all her frontiers and
counts upon the friendliness of the Weimar Republic. Dominated by
Jews, who have succeeded admirably in marrying a policy of the
purse with chauvinism, France is an Empire which, with the help
of the Jews, is 'negrifying' the old Continent of Europe. But above
all, in Hitler's eyes, she is the country who defends the 1919 treaties,
the League of Nations, and the collective security pacts. Hitler
proposes, in his own way and by her defeat, to liquidate her historic
tradition, all her political principles, and, with her, the entire
tradition of the West, of Versailles or of Geneva.

 His case against Russia overlaps with his case against Communism.
The two together provide admirable ammunition for the campaign
designed to show the people of the West that Germany is the rampart
erected by Providence against Bolshevism. Hitler talks of conquering
Russia and of the reward he will get, above all from her territory
and her boundless wealth. He reproaches Wilhelmian Germany
with not having pursued this policy before 1914. In his view, as in
Rosenberg's, Russia will be conquered because, like her former ally,
France, she has become degermanised, replacing with Jews the
ruling class of Baltic barons who did so much for her and brought
her so much success.

The object of these diatribes is clear. Hitler is not content merely to say that Germany cannot tolerate two great military states on either side of her. His dual anti-French and anti-Russian campaign is intended to mollify the German middle classes by combating Western plutocracy on the one hand and Communism on the other. The small *bourgeoisie* nourishes two simultaneous hates: one of Capitalism, that condemns it to the degradation of proletarianisation, the other of Socialism, that aims to merge *bourgeoisie* and poletariat into one. And, at the same time, Hitler is able to persuade the old ruling caste in Germany that he is saving it from a social revolution.

This dual offensive, based on a dual diagnosis of the situation, calls for a constructive programme—a programme of Continental hegemony that revives, embraces, and popularises the claims which have been voiced uninterruptedly in Germany since 1871.

German diplomacy, in order to achieve its aims, has to abandon the methods of the past and, in particular, the absence of a specific plan of action which Hitler so bitterly deplored. On the contrary, prudence is essential. Instead of beginning with expansion, as was foreseen in Wilhelm II's '*Weltpolitik*', in order to capture world markets which have eluded the Germans, instead of wasting so much energy in remote parts of the globe, the Germans will be better advised to confine themselves to Europe at first and to organise '*Mitteleuropa*'—that is, the space that is necessary for the free, spontaneous development of their legitimate ambitions. They will form a formidable wedge between East and West. A view that is quite correct if seen in relation to Wilhelmian imperialism, but that presupposes something the Germans take for granted: the decadence of the Western Powers and the complete impotence of the U.S.S.R. Not to mention the fact that any reliance on a benevolent neutrality by England was a fatal mistake. On this point Hitler pours out the most specious arguments, recalling the 'racial kinship' of the two countries and quoting, as Ludendorff did in 1918, the 'balance-of-power' theory. England, Hitler thinks, is anxious to put an end to France's dominating position on the Continent. She will not have won the war till this domination has been destroyed. So much the better! Germany will help her!

But the urge of the Germans to push southwards and westwards and the Italo-German Fascist alliance should not be taken too literally. The real drive is to be eastwards. And here Hitler looks towards Austria, Czechoslovakia, Poland, and the Balkans. The Teutonic Order's task of colonising the East must be resumed. After sharply criticising pre-war colonial policy, Hitler states that he disapproves of vast colonial undertakings. Germany's destiny lies in her natural living-space, Europe.

While Hitler prefers to confine himself to Europe, Rosenberg surveys a much wider horizon. Like Spengler, he discusses the problem of the rebellious lower classes and also that of coloured races. The situation in the Far East alarms him, particularly the Nationalist China of Sun Yat Sen and the Communist China of the Kuomintang. But Rosenberg goes farther than Spengler. He does not leave the task of saving Europe from Bolshevism, invasion, and white decadence to Prussia alone. He would like to see America quickly converted to racialism, so that she can support Germany in her European struggle on behalf of the Whites. And, when Germany has more than 100,000,000 inhabitants, the American-German-Italian-Japanese bloc will be invincible. It will rule the world. Such are the first 'planetary' hopes of National-Socialism. While the British Empire ruled the waves and Italy dominated the Mediterranean, the German Third Reich would have as its preserve 'Eurasia', or, as Mackensen later calls it, 'the heartland'.

In fact, the old Wilhelmian programmes are now melted down into geopolitics, which draws virtually no distinction between a continental and a colonial programme. What the Nazis call 'imperial growth' clearly implies a perspective that is limitless and planetary. This is not the place to compare the conceptions of General Haushofer with those of the Nazis, but there is no doubt that the geopoliticans exercised a considerable influence on the Nazi leaders. They had one thing in common: a narrow, egotistical nationalism that blossoms out into a phony universalism. Karl Troll, the German geographer, drew attention to this in 1948 in a study of the science of geography in Germany from 1938 to 1945. General Haushofer, like Hitler, lacked the necessary culture for such a vast undertaking.

That brings my survey to an end. It has confined itself strictly to the ideological aspect. I think one can safely say that, from the early days of German romanticism to the eve of the First World War, an imperialist doctrine *sui generis* has developed in Germany, a form of elated nationalism which one can rightly call 'Pangermanism' by virtue of its undisguised pretensions to a certain hegemonic universalism.

This tradition seems to me to have arisen from four sources, from four basic components which, in the nineteenth and twentieth centuries, develop and expand, particularly under Wilhelm II, with growing clarity and force: (1) a philosophical and religious type of Pangermanism, which insists on Germany's predestination and divine mission; (2) a coherent series of pseudo-scientific arguments culled from geography, history, biology, or anthropology, which attempt to define the so-called 'living-space' that the Reich needs and the so-called 'racial cohesion' that it must acquire; (3) a plan of continental conquest and expansion; (4) finally a so-called 'world' political programme, the final aim of which is the creation of a colonial Empire that will supplement or replace colonial Empires already existing.

One may well wonder, of course, to what extent this vast symposium can be—or even must be—identified with the mentality of the German public throughout the two centuries in question. Ideas are born, more often than not, in the minds of individual thinkers. But, when they are stimulated by social upheavals, widespread collective crises, or sudden, far-reaching changes, they rapidly filter down to the masses. Even a historian of the eminence of Fr. Meinnecke was not afraid to admit in his recent work *The German Catastrophe* (1946) that fanatical nationalism in the pre-1914 years wrought havoc in the ranks of the German *bourgeoisie*, an aggressive, ambitious nationalism that treated Socialism and the demands of the workers with scorn and gravitated more and more towards the 'national revolution' I have tried to define. The term *alldeutsch*, which applies only to fairly small groups, cannot by itself explain away the importance of this aggressive imperialism and the terrible consequences it had for Europe.

But one can, in all fairness, admit that up to 1914 the popular masses had not been entirely won over to Pangermanism, although its most natural and most effective breeding-grounds were the primary Confessional schools, the high schools, the universities, and, above all, the barracks. Pangermanism, as it developed under Wilhelm II from 1890 to 1914, became a mass-movement with Hitler in 1919 only when the single Party was first set up. The neo-nationalism of the intellectuals in the Weimar period had an importance all of its own.

But, from 1929 and the great social crisis onwards, the Nazi tidal wave carries everything before it. The Nazi doctrine, with the help of anti-Semitism, revives and popularises the current themes of the Pangermanic tradition. If it is guilty of any originality at all, it is in using anti-Semitism as a jumping-off ground for its attack on Western humanism and for its active policy in Germany, and also in giving the continental programme priority over the colonial programme.

Hitler could never have established the totalitarian dictatorship he did establish in January 1933 if his Party, so to speak under the mantle of the Weimar Republic, had not revived the essential themes of Pangermanic imperialism, reinforcing them with an extremely powerful propaganda machine, and if, on the other hand, the Schachts, von Seeckts, and Stresemanns had not reorganised industry and the banking system, the army and foreign policy. This dual effort is the really significant feature of the Weimar episode, and throws a revealing light not only on the past, but also on the future of the German Reich.

2

THE POLITICAL THOUGHT OF CONSTANTIN FRANTZ

Louis Sauzin

Constantin Frantz belongs to the generation which still heard the great voices of romanticism vibrating and was just reaching manhood at the time of that great uprush of hope in 1848 and of the disillusion brought by 1849. That generation saw Bismarck lay hold of its most generous dreams, in order to give them the hard and narrow reality they have in the constitutions of 1866 and 1871. That generation felt the appeals of discordant sentiments, between which it was difficult to strike the balance. On the one hand, unity had been realised, and it was thrilling to see the German fatherland promoted to the rank of a Great Power, entering the concert of nations, playing a first-class part in the economic life of the world. The victory over France, the milliards pouring in to revive commerce and industry, brought Bismarck many conversions. On the other hand, certain Germans regretted that the Iron Chancellor should offer them only a disappointing caricature of their dreams, that the unity of Germany such as he had made it should remain incomplete, and that this Reich, which was, after all, only an aggrandised Prussia, should have failed, through contempt for data inscribed in history and in the very configuration of Europe, to protect itself against a morrow which might prove formidable. Constantin Frantz was one of those Germans whose dreams 1866 and 1871 could not satisfy, and who quickly felt the rising bitterness of disappointment.

Like so many of those who wanted to knead and model that plastic mass, the Germany of the nineteenth century, Frantz was the son of a Protestant priest. His father's parish was not far from Halberstadt, at Börneke, and there young Gustav Adolf Constantin was born on 12 September 1817. He was the Benjamin of the family. His mother was descended from Huguenot refugees and was related to the Berlin family of the Catels, which has left a name in theology, literary criticism, and art criticism. The child went to school at the Halberstadt *Domgymnasium*. At Easter 1836 he left it with a 'certificate of maturity' and went up to the University of Halle. There he first read mathematics and physics, at the same time attending the philosophy courses. After three years he went to complete his studies in Berlin, where he tried to live by teaching algebra and geometry. This teaching career did not hold him for long. His head was busy with a study on the philosophy of mathematics, which appeared in 1842, followed by another on the philosophy of Hegel, whose disciple he then proclaimed himself, only to break away almost at once. He then threw himself into philosophical criticism and attracted attention by two short works, one against Friedrich Strauss, the other against Ludwig Feuerbach. He declared war on atheism and laid down the principles of what he called 'the true idealism'.

He began to travel as secretary to various politicians or diplomats. He journeyed through East Germany, Posnania, Russian Poland—he learnt Polish for the purpose—Austria and the Balkans. He went as far as the Turkish frontier. In company with the Russian diplomat von Meyendorff, he turns up at Gastein, where he makes the acquaintance of Count Prokesch-Osten, Prince Schwarzenberg, and even Metternich. A study on *The Present and Future of the Prussian Constitution* (1846) was followed in 1850 by a pamphlet, *Our Policy*, which aroused the attention of Manteuffel, then Prussian Prime Minister. Manteuffel suggested that he should join the Foreign Affairs administration and offered him a post at the Ministry as technical councillor. Frantz accepted. In the autumn of 1851 a mission takes him to Paris, *via* Switzerland. In June 1852 he is back in Berlin, where he receives the title of *Geheimer expedierender Sekretär* —which does not prevent a pamphlet just published by him, under the title *The Sickness of our State*, from being seized and pulped. In the summer of 1853 he is appointed head of chancery to the Prussian Consulate-General at Barcelona. In the years that followed he was to make use of his new situation to travel all through Spain and Portugal and as far as North Africa. He was, indeed, convinced that the study of a political question must be pursued *in situ* and that the sciences of the state would gain by taking their inspiration from the methods of natural history. At the end of 1856 he is recalled to Berlin. For a few months more he continues to work at the Ministry, then, rather suddenly, resigns. His chiefs are sorry that office life in Berlin should have cut him off from a career and, by way of compensation, they offer him the Consulate-General at Smyrna, which he refuses, then that of Galatz, which he does not accept either. Almost at the same time he declines the flattering offer of a chair at the University of Breslau, then one at the University of Riga. Having decided to live by his pen, he settles in Berlin and remains there till 1873. Then, stifled in that capital of the new Reich, where heads that seemed solid enough have been made giddy by the French milliards, he prefers to withdraw to the immediate

suburbs of Dresden, to Blasewitz, in a part of the country traditionally hostile to Prussia. He continues to write, and it is at Blasewitz
that death comes to look for him on 2 May 1891.

The work of Frantz is copious. The list of his publications contains no fewer than sixty items, running from a thirty-page brochure
to treatises in three volumes.[1]

Starting with the philosphy of mathematics and with a study on
Hegel, all his life long he kept, in the fashion of the romantics, the
taste for vast speculations. Did he not, in 1873, undertake to expose
'to enlightened persons', as the title of his *magnum opus* puts it, 'the
contents and significance of the positive philosophy of Schelling, in
order to stimulate a complete revision of opinions which still prevail
today'?

Frantz has, at the same time, a combative temperament. He lacks
neither courage nor tenacity. He needed to possess both these
qualities in order to attack as stubbornly as he did an adversary
so formidable and so haloed with success as Bismarck. Frantz did
not lack consistency of doctrine either. His theories make their
appearance early and are maintained without flinching. The last
works—*Die Weltpolitik*, for instance—take up again themes already
developed, but treat them now with a masterly amplitude. It is
inevitable, when one reads the work of Frantz from end to end, that
one should suffer from a feeling of monotony. He always attacked
the same weaknesses, the same people. He always preached the
same remedies, the same solutions. Some will reproach his work for
abounding in repetitions. Yet it should be conceded that these are
in large part redeemed by the alacrity, indeed petulance, of the
polemical writer, for that is what Frantz was and remained; and

---

[1] In 1917, for the centenary of Frantz, one of his disciples, Professor Heldmann
of Halle, published a catalogue of his works in the *Thüringisch-Sächsische Zeitschrift für Geschichte und Kunst*. This bibliography was republished as an appendix
to his extracts from *Der Föderalismus* by Walter Ferber (Coblenz, 1948). The most
important of these works are:

   Untersuchungen über das Europäische Gleichgewicht, Anon. (Berlin, 1859).
   Die Wiederherstellung Deutschlands (Berlin, 1865).
   Die Naturlehre des Staates als Grundlage aller Staatswissenschaft (Leipzig and Heidel-
berg, 1870).
   Das Neue Deutschland, beleuchtet in Briefen an einen preussischen Staatsmann (Leipzig,
1871).
   *Literarisch-politische Aufsätze, nebst einem Vorwort über die Verdienste des Fürsten
Bismarck und einem Vorwort über die deutsche Politik* (Munich, 1876).
   *Der Föderalismus als leitendes Prinzip für die soziale, staatliche und internationale
Organisation* (Mainz, 1879).
   Die Weltpolitik unter besonderer Bezugname auf Deutschland (Chemnitz, 1882),
3 vols.

In the following notes we shall use these abbreviations:—

   LPA   (*Literarisch-politische Aufsätze*);
   Föd   (*Der Föderalismus*);
   WP   (*Die Weltpolitik*).

though always aiming at the same targets, he did manage to vary infinitely the manner of his attacks. It must also be recognised that in his polemics he does not lack finesse and uses humour adroitly.

When, in the years which followed 1945, the Allies attempted, in each zone, to bring some sort of German public opinion to life again and to revive the critical sense, some people, certainly not evilly disposed, made use of Constantin Frantz. Had he not, at a moment when his fellow-citizens had lost their heads and were inclined to see in the work of Bismarck the fulfilment of the designs of Providence, protested with vigour against the statements of the official pundits and applied a pitiless criterion to the principles which were guiding the Chancellor? It was fortunate to have, in the person of Frantz, a German who had not even believed in the Second Reich. There appeared, therefore, under the stamp of the official censorship, some very well chosen extracts from *Der Föderalismus* which, precisely because they had been most cleverly extracted and presented, were in danger of showing Frantz in a misleading light.[1] If he was a stubborn adversary of the Reich of 1871, this did not mean that he was a democrat, or even in favour of a constitutional monarchy. If he was a federalist, he was so not altogether in the same spirit as the Americans of 1786. Frantz was not merely a negative critic, a great voice refusing to accept the changes which had come about between the Rhine and the Niemen from 1866 to 1871. He had in mind a theory of his own, well formed from the beginning, and it is because Bismarck was brutally smashing to pieces his proposals that Frantz set to work indefatigably to explain what lines the Chancellor ought to have followed, if he had had a clear vision of the mission entrusted by God to Germany.

Frantz remains full of respect for Bismarck the man. He does not take up the complaints of the military and of the old nobility against 'a certain General of Cuirassiers from the Reserve'. Let us pay Frantz the homage due to him: he was a punctilious adversary. Keen as was the tone of his polemics, he always abstained from descending to arguments of the kind that hurt but do not hit in the right place.

The Bismarckian principles are what he attacks so tirelessly. Bismarck, he tells us, is suffering from the same sickness which he denounces in his liberal and socialist opponents. These, soaked in Lassalle and Marx, have pushed Hegelianism to its extreme consequences. Their socialism is a work of pure intellect and of nothing else. Similarly the Germany of 1866 and then that of 1871 were born of an excess of rationalism, Hegelian rationalism.[2] Only a

---

[1] Constantin Frantz, *Der Föderalismus, in Auszügen herausgegeben und mit einem Vorwort und Anhang versehen von Walter Ferber* (Coblenz. Preface dated 24 Dec. 1947).
[2] *Der Bankrott der herrschenden Staatsweisheit* (Munich, 1874), p. 30.

reason reasoning in the void can exclude with cold disdain all historical values and all living sentiment of the past; it alone can imagine that one can construct by fire and the sword and in the course of a fratricidal war[1] this state which is usurping the fair name of Federation or Empire and to which all that is lacking is to have been born viable.[2] One has to be blind not to see how unfortunately the Northern Confederation or the 1871 Reich recall the fable of the sheep and the goat who went out hunting with the lion.[3] With fine courage Frantz goes for the National Liberals, who think only of acclaiming successes without examining how these were come by. He asserts uncompromisingly that right comes before might and not, as had been claimed, the other way round.[4] Instead of the Germany at once unified and diverse which he might have built up if he had not been mad on centralisation, Herr von Bismarck has constructed a Reich in which he has given Prussia a dangerous preponderance. Certainly, in German history we constantly witness the same phenomenon: the colonial provinces of the East, those which were conquered, beyond the Elbe, by soldier-monks and peopled by colonists from western Germany, from the old Romanised and Christian Germany—these provinces, as time passed, have weighed more and more on German policy. But, says Frantz, this preponderance can be preserved for the eastern provinces without necessarily ignoring historical differences, without forcing into the mould of the Prussian army and administration a population which was accustomed to living in accordance with a different way of life worthy of respect. The Prussification of Germany may involve dangerous consequences.[5] Even if no more than the conflict which will arise from the unification of law. Law is not a play of concepts which the intellect sets going logically, once some initial axiom has been accepted. Law grows, develops like a living being. The customary law of the eastern provinces, which issued from the urban law brought by the German colonists from the West, the law codified on Roman lines which still governs the states neighbouring the Rhine and the Rhenish province, are going to be supplanted by an arbitrary creation derived from the thought of a few National Liberal doctrinaires. Herr von Bismarck is being unfaithful to the old Prussian tradition which thought it important to safeguard the principle of regional autonomy. Instead of seeking unity in diversity which is the very principle of life and of every living creation, he is aiming only at centralisation and uniformity.[6] Herr von Bismarck, who so often proclaimed his aversion to the political system of the West,

---

[1] *Bankrott*, p. 1.
[2] *Die nationale Rechtseinheit, und das Reichsgericht* (Augsburg, 1873). Cf. p. 20.
[3] *Rechtseinheit*, p. 2.   [4] ibid., p. 36.
[5] *WP*, Vol. II, p. 6.   [6] *Rechtseinheit*, pp. 4–5.

who so often made the speech for the prosecution against the revolutionary spirit incarnate in France, finds himself, two years after an
unprecedented military victory, vanquished by this very France.
What a revenge for Paris to see Germany abandoning the juridical
principles which had at one time governed the French monarchy,
like the Prussian monarchy, and had given them the cohesion of a
living organism, to see yesterday's victor applying the Code Napo-
léon and also the centralised hierarchy of tribunals placed under the
authority of a Court of Appeal, which will not fail to establish a
jurisprudence in conformity with the desires of the Government.
Prussia and the Reich are becoming an eastern replica of France—
ein östliches Frankreich: what a mockery![1]

It is already difficult enough to accept the unification under
Prussia of the federal army. The special rights reserved to the king-
doms of Saxony, Bavaria, and Württemberg remain on the whole
somewhat slender. The Berlin General Staff rules over the whole
military organisation. In the same way a juridical General Staff is
going to rule over the juridical organisation. Justice and law, those
sacred principles, are going to be militarised at the same time as they
are unified.[2]

The proof is easily supplied. Only look at what is happening in
the *Reichsland*, in that arbitrary assemblage of an Alsace and a
Lorraine which were unified by decree in spite of their fundamental
divergences, and which it is proposed to submit *ex abrupto* to a
foreign and arbitrarily created law. It can be seen from this example
how little our military care about law. The General Staff sees only
the necessities of a frontier to be defended; it pronounces; let the
jurists submit.[3]

Frantz does not fear to denounce the General Staff and its insatiable demands as the abettor of a situation which might bring the
new Reich to catastrophe. He is never tired of deploring the fruitless
expenditure involved by the armed peace. The militarisation of
Germany, which is the direct result of Prussian hegemony, imposes
on the peoples financial burdens under which they gasp and gain
nothing.

'The honeymoon of the new Europe is over, and so is that
drunken joy caused by the victory and the French milliards. All
that is left to the nation is a frightful headache. . . . And so the
nectar Herr von Bismarck promised us turns to gall. Did you
think that military unification would bring with it a diminution
of the burdens? What an illusion! They are half as much again.
Before 1866, frankly, was Germany threatened? Now look how,
since that fatal year, the whole people has remained armed to the

[1] *Rechtseinheit*, pp. 2, 7.   [2] ibid., p. 6.   [3] *WP*, Vol. II, p. 47.

E

teeth, perpetually mounting guard. The danger of war has become permanent since 1866. Let us not say *post hoc*, but *propter hoc*. The German people imagined that, along with unity, it had won liberty. As for liberty, all it is experiencing is the tyranny of the military. The fine fruit promised by Herr von Bismarck has rotted before ripening.' [1]

It would be impossible to tire of quoting those vengeful pages in which Frantz opposes to Bismarck's policy and to Treitschke's hypocritical approval of it the radiant principles laid down by Kant in his *Perpetual Peace*. Since in a peace treaty no germ of war should be allowed to subsist, no part of what Herr von Bismarck created by fire and sword is solid. A genuine federation cannot be constructed by cementing it with the blood of brothers,[2] and since it was desired to win the heart of the Alsacians, letting the Baden artillery bombard Strasbourg, damaging the cathedral, and reducing the library to ashes was a strange method to use. The law of annexation itself contradicts the Kantian principles;[3] as for Hegel's theory of the state, it constitutes a real return to barbarism, for politics should know no other rules than those of morality. Politics should mean the treatment of other people as an end, not as a means, and the cynical system of Machiavelli amounts to a total contempt for wisdom and justice.[4]

Frantz likewise deplores the attitude adopted by the Reich towards the ethnic minorities which it has incorporated. If the bombardment of Strasbourg was an irreparable folly, Frantz regrets quite as much that Alsace and Lorraine—whose return into the German community he rejoices to see—should remain subject to an exceptional régime which will end by setting against Germany this *Reichsland* made up of disparate pieces. The supreme danger, according to him, would be to make the *Reichsland* a new Prussian province.[5]

Likewise Berlin's policy with regard to the Polish provinces arouses, in the highest degree, Frantz's combative ardour. It was an absurdity, a real crime against Germany, to destroy the Polish state. The Poles were quite naturally offering themselves as allies against the common enemy, Russia. The error of the Berlin policy ever since Wilhelm I was to turn to Russia for support, now against Sweden, now against the sister-nation Austria, or against those of the Slavs who had the least reason to relish the proximity and policy of Russia, the Poles. The Prussian diplomats have played the game of sawing the branch on which they were sitting.[6] The out-and-out

---

[1] *Föd*, pp. 235–7.   [2] *Rechtseinheit*, p. 20.   [3] ibid., p. 22.
[4] *WP*, Vol. III, pp. 75–6.
[5] *Was soll aus Elsass-Lothringen werden?* (Munich, 1873). Cf. pp. 12–15.
[6] *Gefahr aus dem Osten*, unpublished, later published by O. Schuchhardt, in *Die Deutsche Politik der Zukunft* (Celle, 1899–1900), 2 vols. Cf. Vol. I, p. 74.

Germanisation of Posnania is given a facile explanation by the
Prussian conservatives: in replacing the Slav peasants by German
colonists the Berlin Government is continuing the work of slow
conquest begun in the tenth century in the provinces east of the
Elbe by the great monastic or military orders. The explanation,
retorts Frantz, is historically justified: yet the fact remains that the
Berlin policy is setting against Prussia the Slav people which most
deeply detests the Russians and which would have sought in Berlin
its natural support, while at the same time providing Germany
with an ally against the only enemy Europe has to fear—namely,
Asia.

Herr von Bismarck, says Frantz again, is glad to display in his
speeches that he is a Christian. We are agreed on the principle: a
German monarchy can only be Christian, and likewise its whole
policy. Some have also taken pride in Herr von Bismarck's moderation when the social question had to be dealt with; they have discovered in his conduct the praiseworthy determination to conciliate
two points of view which seemed to confront one another in a
struggle without issue.

Such is not the opinion of Frantz. He reproaches the Chancellor,
the National Liberal Party, and the *Kreuz-Zeitung* with not estimating
correctly the problem raised by the multiplication of the proletariat. An attempt is being made to stabilise the present state of
affairs, to prevent it from growing worse. Very good. But is anyone
thinking of the danger of too pronounced social inequalities? There
is a peasant proletariat as poverty-stricken as the urban proletariat.
Is there any help for it if it should want to acquire land? Again, is
the help they deserve accorded to the artisan's co-operatives, which
make it possible for the worker to be no longer a machine delivering
to the owner, for a fixed wage, a set quantity of work? The error of
Marx was to reduce everything to a quantity of work. What are the
great German industrialists doing to take the wind out of Marxism's
sails by helping the worker to free himself from so degrading a
condition?

German industrialists remain narrow-minded. They are unable to
rise above their most immediate interests. A proof of this lies in the
extravagant development of the German sugar industry, which, by
ruining certain countries producing sugar-cane, is closing to German
industry a once-flourishing market. Herr von Bismarck's Government raises protective tariffs before the factories of the 'Beetroot
Barons' and does not hesitate to make the spinners and weavers
starve. A short-sighted social and commercial policy which dares,
what is more, to adorn itself with the sign of the Cross! [1]

[1] *WP*, Vol. I, p. 31.

Are not the industrialists and Herr von Bismarck practising rather the cult of the golden calf? This can scarcely be doubted when one sees the speculation which is rife about the railway plans.[1] And in this connection Frantz takes up once more formulas made familiar to us by the political romanticism of an Adam Heinrich Müller: *Beruf ist kein Geldverdienen.* A profession is above all a vocation, and involves a partial renunciation for the benefit of the community. Property imposes more duties than it grants rights, and the increase in value of certain goods, due to mere circumstances, independent of the owner's work—Frantz quotes as example the rise in the price of land in Berlin, where a few acres of sand are worth as much as a gold-mine—should in all justice accrue to the community, in other words to the Treasury.[2] The indirect taxes to which governments have recourse in order to avoid attacking frontally the lucky owners constitute in fact a bonus to celibacy, a sanction against large families, a mockery of the Gospels.[3] Frantz is not afraid to subject the right of property to a severe criticism: in its origin the crudest sort of seizure, it was able to find justification for itself through the community's approval which was due to the good use made of it. It seems clear that, for Frantz, it has not the primordial character of certain rights which we enjoy by virtue of our birth and of our baptism, and that it is no more than a usufruct agreed to by our equals and sanctioned by habit.[4]

It is an undiminishing pleasure to read the pages in which Frantz riddles with his arrows the Christianity of the high ecclesiastics, intent on establishing that the social hierarchy, aristocratic or economic, corresponds to an especial concern of the Creator's and to His immutable will. A gay revolutionary breath animates the attacks which he delivers without any mercy at all against ministers' offices bent above all on increasing the lustre of a dynasty; against the career diplomats, that caste which admits you only after a long probation, whereas the example of Herr von Bismarck himself shows that there is not the slightest need of some particular aptitude reinforced by a special training which is given as though under confidential seal;[5] or again, against those diplomats who profess empiricism but remain prisoners of the few principles which have shaped their brains.[6]

This holy anger, which goes side by side with his open enthusiasm for Kant or for the pacifism of the Abbé de Saint Pierre,[7] leads Frantz towards a positive doctrine. It seems necessary to renounce

---

[1] *Föd*, 2, p. 76.
[2] *Föd*, Chap. VI (Positive Vorschläge zu Sozial-reformen), in particular pp. 186-7.
[3] *Föd*, p. 181.   [4] ibid., pp. 24, 187.
[5] *WP*, Vol. III, pp. 20-6.   [6] ibid., pp. 3-4.   [7] ibid., pp. 72-6.

the pagan principles of Machiavelli, even if they be supported by Roman law—which upholds, whenever wanted, the legitimacy of conquest.[1] It is time to make the peace of Christ reign between states as between men. It is absurd that sects professing one and the same Saviour, Him who desired His sheep to form but one flock, should tear one another to pieces. It is absurd that, even in the name of the principle of nationalities, a pagan principle which places the gods of the city above Christ, nations which once composed one single and same community, bearing the truly fine name of *Corpus Christianum*, should murder one another.

The remedy? It is simple and infallible. Two examples offer themselves to our eyes (those wilfully blind things): Switzerland and the United States. Let federalism come, then, and all our ills will be cured, for it has as its support and motive power love of one's neighbour. If people are willing to form a federation with others, without injury to the partner's individual character, their agreement can only be fruitful and all differences will be *ipso facto* smoothed over.

Is it logical, asks Frantz, to see Europe still crumbling itself up into nations separated by frontiers guarded by police and customs officials? Economics claims its due, and it was a merit in Marxist socialism to have shown that the economic situation of a country can influence the mentality and political opinions of its inhabitants. Now it is a need of the modern world, industrialised as it is, to go in search of markets for its activity all over the world. In the era of the press and rapid communications it has been necessary to create the world-wide Postal Union and Telegraphic Union, organisations which would have seemed fantastic when the system of special couriers still prevailed. The nations can no longer live in closed receptacles: whether they like it or not, they have to take account of what is happening outside their frontiers. The export of German grain made the fortune of Dantzig and Lübeck. It will be no good protecting Prussian barley and wheat by strengthening tariff barriers, the world market will still be closed to German grain because they are dearer than those of Russia, America, or even Australia. In economic affairs nationalism looks old-fashioned, if not monstrous. When it is a matter of selling grain, timber, wool, or iron, it is no use now thinking on the scale of one's own country, but looking at the whole world. A world economy is taking the place of national economy. Just as the customs union brings with it the unification of Germany, the economic unification first of Europe, then of the whole world, can only bring the masters of this world towards a policy expanded to the scale of the planet, *eine Welt-politik*.[2] The conditions being such, the nations will, whether of

[1] *WP*, Vol. III, p. 13.   [2] ibid., Vol. I, pp. 4–9.

their own free will or driven by economic necessities, be obliged to give up living each for itself. But as none of them will consent—and quite rightly—to give up its personality, they will have to have recourse to the only possible solution, federalism.

The term recurs untiringly from the pen of Constantin Frantz. Without fear of wearying the reader, he praises the merits of his system. As though under the influence of some magic word, all difficulties will be smoothed away, for federalism is the only system basing itself on the natural history of nations. It has indeed been too often forgotten that the nations were not creations of the intellect, but in some sort living beings.

To the rivalry of nations Roman law imagines only one solution: conquest pure and simple. The victor absorbs the vanquished. The ultimate issue of national conflicts would thus be the universal monarchy which would cover, as once Rome covered the Mediterranean world, all the lands that are known. But this solution, though it may flatter the mind, suffers from a fatal vice: it holds for nought the diversity of races, climates, languages. It reduces man to a mere concept, makes of him a creature everywhere identical and interchangeable. Living reality loses its rights. We are no longer dealing with men of flesh and blood, but with diagrams, with human beings in the abstract.

Federalism will not slip into so grave a fault, for it is, by definition, organic. Frantz, who never ceases to insist that there should be applied to politics the methods of biology,[1] declares without beating about the bush that federalism is the principle which, in politics, presides over evolution everywhere.[2] It is indeed because he has neglected this principle that Herr von Bismarck has manufactured a doomed Germany: sooner or later outraged nature will take its revenge.[3] A universal monarchy, or even confederations like the North Germany of 1866, or the Empire of 1871, suffer from an irremediable vice: they are arbitrary creations which have systematically disdained precious heritages. Bismarck has not acted differently from his sworn enemies the socialists, who would like to make of the past a *tabula rasa*. Conservatism wants only to look back. Socialism wants to abolish the past. Federalism avoids these one-sided policies and resolves to preserve the organic link which joins the generations together: it will take it as its over-riding duty to transmit to the sons what their fathers have bequeathed. Federalism sees in history the continuous growth of one single body, which is humanity; and humanity is one in the sequence of times.

And it is one at every moment. If we cannot disinterest ourselves in those who came before us, nor in those who will come after us, neither can we neglect those who inhabit the planet at the same time

---

[1] Cf. especially *Naturlehre des Staates*.   [2] *Föd*, Preface.   [3] ibid., p. 303.

as we. A well-conducted policy looks at the facts 'in the organic whole which they form', and at all questions 'in their reciprocal action upon one another and in their relations with the whole'. Continuity of evolution, action of the parts on the whole and of the whole on the parts—these are ideas which have, so to speak, slipped from the field of biology into that of politics.

Federalism is above all a marriage. It does not consist in adding together creatures who are alike in being abstract—those theoretical men dear to the French revolutionaries. But just as marriage is the indissoluble union of two dissimilar beings, though of the same species, so federalism will be the marriage of states which, in their union, will keep each its individual character. Look at the Swiss cantons, or the states of the American Union. Lucerne has not abdicated in favour of Berne, nor have the Pacific states before those of the East. Neither liberalism, which sees in marriage no more than a contract that can be revoked, nor socialism, which is busy trying to dissolve the bonds of marriage—only think, says Frantz, of those reformers who dare to advocate women being held in common—is able to look at the problem lucidly, for neither the one nor the other grants the family its true value, which is that of being the initial cell of every society, of every nation as of every union of nations.

Marriage is in fact the will of the Creator. *Et creavit eos marem et feminam.* Frantz does not quote this text of Scripture, but one can feel that he has it on the point of his pen. Without giving it a sacramental value—which would be catholic—Frantz concedes to marriage a religious value. Such is the nature of the family that those régimes which refuse it a primordial place and do not protect it deserve to be rejected; such unhealthy states will not be able to reach the federalist paradise. The monarchy which gives the sovereign couple the fair names of *Landesvater* and *Landesmutter* is far superior to the republican régime from which all respect for the initial cell has disappeared.

Federalism, which has just asserted its essentially religious character, will take good care not to banish the observances of religion from the life of the state. Religious facts have no less value than the other facts of our life, and the state that is unwilling to recognise them and grant them their legitimate place is on a false track.[1]

Based as it is on the family and religion, federalism cannot but be pacific. Otherwise it would be denying its Christian inspiration. What is more, it is evident that the two federations which exist in this wicked world threaten nobody. The Helvetic or American militias do not create, in Berne or in Washington, this stifling barracks atmosphere one is forced to breathe in Berlin or in Potsdam,

[1] *Föd*, pp. 141–9.

where the concentration of troops is such that it would lead one
to suppose that the King of Prussia reigns by force over a hostile
population.[1] One need only compare the Swiss budget and the
German budget to see at the first glance what relief a well-conceived federalism would bring the German tax-payer. It could not
fail to kill, once for all, militarism and the armed peace, to replace
them by a militia system, and to set up in schools a compulsory
physical training which would shorten considerably the length of the
period in barracks.[2]

If it is asked what is the nature of the bond which will attach the
federated states one to another, if it is desired to seek out the origin
of this *religio* which welds them together so closely and yet allows
their personalities to be maintained, Frantz's answer will be seen
to be tinged with an evangelical gentleness: it is that same sentiment
of brotherhood which already united the members of the *Corpus
Christianum*, before the Pagan spirit of the Renaissance and the
selfish interests of the nations tore it to pieces, or, in short, the love
of one's neighbour, that charity without which the most ardent
faith remains vain. Even material interest, however powerful it may
be, will not have the strength of charity.[3]

At the mere name of this federalism founded on charity, difficulties can but solve themselves. One would be tempted to say, when
one reads Frantz, 'as by enchantment'. No more the disastrous
opposition of great and small powers, no more that system of balance
which makes some states the masters of Europe and of the world and
obliges the small, willy nilly, to move in the wake of the stronger.
It will at last be possible in the name of federalism, to create a
comity of nations which shall not be the camouflaged hegemony of
a few great ones, or of one of them alone. It will at last be possible,
as it was for Byron or Goethe, to feel oneself European.[4] A truly
federal Germany would not be a Prussia raised a step higher. In
such a Germany the Berlin Government would remember that
Prussia has two million Slavs among its subjects, that its role is not
to dictate its law to states situated west of the Elbe and themselves
of purely Germanic race. The 'pagan' system of balance of power or
hegemony would give place to a Christian fraternity. Better still:
it would be possible to cultivate a nationalism without aggressiveness at the same time as the most generous internationalism.

'In the eyes of Christianity, no nationality has particular value,
because, on the contrary, Christianity aims at reuniting in one
body the peoples which have in the past come from a humanity
originally one. In this connection, how pregnant is that story in the
Bible which tells of the founding of the first Christian community

[1] *Föd*, p. 138.   [2] *WP*, Vol. III, p. 82.
[3] *Föd*, pp. 374, 387.   [4] ibid., p. 378.

—that moment at which the diversity of languages, the diversity which separates the peoples, ceased for an instant! The Fathers were indeed right when they saw in Pentecost the counterpart of the confusion of Babel.'

Federalism is capable of every miracle: of not abolishing Babel and yet making a lasting Pentecost. The man who is born German, or English, or French, will never forget the linguistic or political community in which his birth placed him, but he will constantly endeavour to overcome his narrow nationalism within the federalist ideal, in order to feel himself truly a man and truly a Christian.[1]

For a federalism capable of such miracles it will be mere child's-play to end the antinomy which opposes liberalism and socialism, free trade and protection, capital and proletariat, agriculture and industry, manual workers and intellectual workers. Finally, religious pacification will come about of its own accord. Frantz gives as proof and as model the United States, where the confessions live side by side without coming into conflict. The rise of the sciences, also, must lead to complete confessional freedom, and it is painful, Frantz adds, to see Germany, the cradle of reform and the promised land of scientific research, still writing into its codes the obligation to baptism and to religious marriage.[2] Through federalism, science and faith will live in peace.

Federalism, the peacemaker, will everywhere restore harmony between opposed principles. It has the same aim as the philosophy of Heraclitus. But when one reads Frantz—and this is where our uneasiness begins—one cannot avoid finding in his federalist ideal a terrible after-taste of romanticism. What a lot of old acquaintances we have been able to recognise on our way through! Edmund Burke had already reproached the French revolutionaries with reducing the citizen to an abstract, uniform, and empty concept which ignored the living diversity of men; upon which A. H. Müller and de Bonald had gone one better, proclaiming that *homo* does not exist, but only *vir* and *femina*. The apologia for the family as the original cell of every society, leading up to the apotheosis of the royal couple, we have already read in Novalis; but Novalis tried to reconcile the monarchy-republic antinomy, and did not banish democracy, the daughter of the Revolution, from the future Europe. A. H. Müller had already criticised the 'Roman' theory of property, its definition as *jus utendi et abutendi*, and he had already laid it down as a principle that property is by nature precarious, always subject to supervision by the community, and that it involved duties towards the community. The living state, the organic state, is the

[1] *WP*, Vol. III, pp. 85–6.   [2] ibid., p. 84.

old warhorse of Burke, of Bonald, of A. H. Müller, already mentioned. The old preoccupation with the whole antecedent to its parts, with the state antecedent to the citizen, with Europe antecedent to the nationalities, is the old answer given to the social or international contract theory and to Rousseau. The insistence on observing states in their reciprocal relations—*in ihrer Wechselwirkung*—seems to have escaped straight out of the *Elemente der Staatskunst* of A. H. Müller, whose vocabulary Frantz has faithfully reproduced.[1] As for Frantz's 'positive' Christianity, it recalls strangely that of Schelling, whom he was anxious to bring within the reach of all sound minds.[2]

Frantz seems to us to be a prisoner to the same obsession as the majority of the Romantics. Armed with Goethe's saying that an irreconcilable antinomy is a logical impossibility, a real absurdity; armed also with the tradition which, ever since the beginnings of Fichte and Hegel, has been absolutely determined to put an end to the Kantian dualism, to reconcile experience and intuition, the phenomenal world and the absolute: they have sought, and Frantz with them, that Third Term, that *tertium quid*, to use the Scholastics' language, *das höhere Dritte*, to employ the vocabulary of A. H. Müller—in short, that term in which all contradictions come to be paid off and to be harmonised. Just like Novalis, just like A. H. Müller, Frantz wants to make *die Liebe*—that term of many meanings which is at the same time the most material love and the purest charity, the only motive and the only guarantee of conciliation. In Frantz we are dealing with a belated Romantic, with the descendant of generous but often imprudent minds which sought, without bothering about the risks such a combination might cause to be run, to marry democracy and absolute power, the conquests of the Revolution and the principles of just the régime this Revolution had overthrown.

The same method is not, in Frantz, above criticism. He first of all followed Hegel, then, shocked at the mere formalism evident in Hegel's picture of the world, reproached him with resolving everything into triads, with wanting to force everything into his dialectical scheme. Does not Frantz suffer from the same defect? Like A. H. Müller in *Die Lehre vom Gegensatz* or in *Elemente der Staatskunst*, he reduces the world to a series of antinomic couples which federalism, successor in this to Mueller's living state, will come at the appointed moment to reconcile.

What does federalism tend to do, if not to promote Germany to

[1] *WP*, Vol. III, 207. 'Betrachtet die Dinge in ihrem organischen Zusammenhange wonach die einzelnen Fragen nur in ihrer Wechselwirkung miteinander, wie nach ihrem Verhältnis zum Ganzen zu beurtheilen sind.'

[2] Cf.: *Schellings positive Philosophie . . . in ihrem Inhalt dargestellt* (Cöthen, 1880), 3 vols.

being that ideal political state which Frantz, like Fichte, calls *das Reich*? Does not Frantz reproach Bismarck with having misused this splendid term, with having debased it, tarnished it, soiled it by attaching it, as label, to his 1871 creation? Is not this Reich for Frantz rather like a New Jerusalem? To a dialectic in the style of an impenitent romantic is joined an unavowed millenarianism.

Let us suppose the problem solved. A federation has been organised on Frantz's lines. How will it live? What will be its internal régime?

It will not be liberal, we already know. Liberalism lives in fact on a false idea—that of the always identical and interchangeable citizen. It bases everything merely on human intelligence and will, and it takes no account, except to note them, of natural conditions. For it, society is an aggregate, a sum of individuals in no way distinguishable and it gives equal rank in the city to the farm hand and the big industrialist, the factory hand and the artist. To it, it suffices that they are all called 'citizen'. The theory leads us in the end to what Frantz calls the absurdities of universal suffrage. There he is in agreement with his adversary Bismarck in condemning the Western method, which consists in adding votes together—*Kopfzahlwahlsystem*—like a grocer counting the herrings in a barrel. What is even more dangerous: since liberalism takes no account of differences of social position, why should it take account of sex? Logically it leads on to women's suffrage. But nothing is more absurd in the eyes of Frantz than tearing woman away from her hearth and her children to make her a working woman or a citizeness. Or, even worse, to give her a place in the magistracy, in Parliament, or in the Civil Service, the repositories of the authority of the state.[1]

The ideal federation will not be socialist either. It will not slip into the errors of Marx, who reduces everything to hours of work—and of work thought of as uniform. He adds to the mistakes of liberalism his own weaknesses, the chief of which is that he tends towards protectionism and autarky, if not to a universal state. Frantz includes in one and the same reproof Marx's *Das Kapital* and Fichte's *Closed Commercial State*.[2]

What will the federation be if it is neither liberal nor socialist? How will the magic word 'federalism' be transcribed on to the political plane and the economic plane? Frantz defines it chiefly by what he rejects.

The federation will not be republican. Frantz has already made no secret of his aversion to a régime which claims to do without the royal couple, 'one and indivisible'; it is incompatible with the

[1] *Föd*, pp. 54–7, 114–17.   [2] *WP*, Vol. I.

principle of federalism. Frantz could be met with this objection:
you cite as references, if not as models, Switzerland and the United
States; are not these federations the oldest republics there are in
the world? Was a line of their constitution altered, even temporarily, during the grave crises they went through—the Sonder-
bund, or the War of Secession? Why this ostracism directed at the
republican régime when it has managed to supply such proofs of its
compatibility with a federal structure of the state?

Because clearly whoever says republic will soon be saying democracy, and democracy rests on the principle that the majority decides. On this point Frantz is categorical. *Autorität nicht Majorität*.
The federation will be monarchical, authoritarian, and it will not
be parliamentary.

There, too, Frantz is sailing in the wake of his adversary Bismarck, who consented that the monarchy should be constitutional—
the aristocracy had to be given its say in the running of the country—
but always energetically rejected parliamentarianism, that English
or French invention. Never would he agree to a government
responsible to elected representatives. We shall see what Frantz
thinks of England and France and their capacity to enter a European federation. In Germany the first attempt at a parliament was
unfortunate. At Frankfurt, in 1848, too many lawyers, above all
too many professors, were seen and heard. The Republic of the
professors, what nonsense! [1]

If it is not parliamentary, would the federalist monarchy be absolute? Not at all, replies Frantz. At the sovereign's side will sit a
body representing the population. But it will not be composed of
elected deputies. Choice by ballot is a fiction whose untenableness
has been amply demonstrated by experience. No mind capable of
thinking is any longer willing to believe in the ballot.[2] In that case,
if the citizen does not elect his deputies, if he is no longer represented
as citizen, of what will the council which is to assist the monarch be
composed? Of delegates from the big organisations and the large
bodies in the state, for they alone are *vertretungsfähig*, qualified to be
represented. Frantz does not give us—and it is a pity—the list of
these organisations. Does he include in them, alongside economic
organisations, the trade unions? His thought was left undefined.
He confines himself to saying that the *Körperschaften* and the
Landschaften will be qualified to be represented. In addition to an
economic and social representation of the big organisations and the
large bodies in the state, there will be some regional representation.
The only concrete indication given by Frantz is his absolute refusal
to admit to representation the intellectual class—that *Lehrstand*
which, since the time of Luther, had had its place alongside the

---

[1] *Bankrott*, p. 1.　　　　　　　　　　[2] *Föd*, p. 2.

Wehrstand and the *Nährstand*, the army and the economic world. Out of hatred for the professor, Frantz denies to the universities the right to be represented before the sovereign.[1]

Representation of regional interests will oblige the Government to respect individual customs rooted in history. But Frantz does not tell us how the appointment of the members of this council is to work. Will they be chosen by the corporations or regions, and if so how? Or will the choice be made from above? What exactly will be the line drawn between historic rights and the rights of the federation? There will have to be a federal constitution fixing, as in Switzerland or the United States, the point at which regional law stops and federal law begins. Finally, Frantz does not tell us what the function of this representative body will be in its dealings with the monarch. Will it have the power to initiate legislation? That is not very likely, seeing that authority is the principle of the régime. What will happen if, for example, this body of representatives rejects a clause of the budget? The love of one's neighbour, charity, will smoothe everything down. Granted, but we should like to know by what procedure. Frantz blamed Bismarck for having created the National Liberal Party, ever ready to acclaim with enthusiasm the Chancellor's least gesture, ever ready to confirm with its vote his least demand for expenditure. But who guarantees us that this body of representatives under a régime founded on authority and not on a majority, will be anything other than an accommodating assembly chosen by the man in power or in accordance with his wishes, in order to register automatically, and with acclamations, his every decision?

Still graver difficulties are destined to arise when Frantz marks out on the map the successive federations required to bring the peoples a lasting peace.

Frantz resolutely detests Bismarck; it is rare for him to find himself in agreement with the policy of the Berlin Cabinet. We have noted the liveliness of his reactions on the question of Alsace. Certainly he advocates more liberality and more comprehension with regard to the people of Alsace and of Lorraine, but it is not long before suspicious signs become visible. We shall not be unduly severe on him for the joy *he* feels at seeing the provinces 'ravished by Louis XIV' return to the German community. It is quite certain that, for him, as for all Germans, the so-called Bordeaux Protest is null and void, and yet it emanates from the representation of a region. But if Frantz advocates better treatment for Alsace, and that it should cease to be considered as a minor, this is because, in his projects, it is destined to become the nucleus of a primary federation of

[1] *Föd*, pp. 116–17, 124.

Alemanic states with Strasbourg as capital. This federation would also include the Bavarian Palatinate and probably Rhenish Hesse together with Mainz, plus the part of the Grand-Duchy of Baden situated to the west of the Black Forest. This federation would be raised to a kingdom—the German dynasties would offer plenty of candidates for this crown—and the army would be commanded by a Bavarian prince. Lorraine, augmented by Luxembourg, would form the Grand-Duchy of Metz, to be left perhaps to the Luxembourg branch of the Orange–Nassau family.[1] The Alemanic federation will serve as model to other primary territorial groupings which, by federating in their turn, will make it possible to constitute the new Germany, and then the new Europe.

Frantz reproaches Bismarck with having solved the problem of unity in too narrow a manner. He himself is *grossdeutsch* and could never be satisfied with a Reich from which Austria is excluded. Rather than the single-headed eagle, transferred from the coats-of-arms of the Hohenzollerns to those of the Reich, Bismarck ought to have adopted the two-headed eagle of Sigismund. It symbolised admirably the mission of Germany, keeping watch both towards the East and towards the West, of Germany predestined by her situation in the midst of Europe—*das Reich der Mitte*, as A. H. Müller had already put it—to become the nucleus around which the future Europe will constitute itself.[2] Europe should not, however, be taken in the sense to which the geography taught in schools has accustomed us. For Frantz, who blames Bismarck for having excluded Austria from the German federation, there are a certain number of countries which he has no desire to enrol in his European federation, although they believe and profess themselves European.

In the first place, England. The British Empire is no longer a European power. Certainly England is still there, moored as it were to the west of our Continent, but she is no more a part of it than is a ship at anchor, and her interests are on the seas or in her colonies. The British Empire could never pass for an organic state. It is an artificial creation, born of the will of the London merchants, with its disparate pieces held together only by a thin and fragile thread: the fleet. What is more, England's mission pulls her away from Europe. Of the two great countries of Germanic blood, England has orientated herself towards the New World; the influx of Norman blood has rendered her travel-struck and enterprising. Her aims and her future lie outside the Continent, while Germany, formed of peoples faithful to the soil of Europe, must expand between the Baltic and the Mediterranean, between the Meuse and the Slav world. Likewise France represents the stable

[1] *Els-Lothr.*, p. 28; *WP*, Vol. II, pp. 48–9.
[2] *Föd*, p. 248.

element among the Roman peoples, Spain the migrating and conquering element orientated towards South America.[1]

France, too, will only with difficulty find a place in the federation imagined by Frantz. She is doctrinaire to excess and would infuse into the new state an obsession with rationalism which would disturb its leaders. It is enough that French rationalism should have taken its revenge in the matter of the federal law and the new German codes. If, when only just vanquished, France is capable of winning such a spiritual victory, what preponderance would she not exercise if she were allowed to enter the federation on an equal footing and with equal rights? No doubt, under Louis XIV, France was a European power—and even the European power *par excellence.* Trafalgar, and then the campaign in Russia, put an end to this primacy, and since 1815 France has been only one of the European powers. Napoleon III had some big ideas. He took a wrong turning in basing his European policy on the principle of nationalities, a principle which federalism goes beyond. But if the Mexican campaign had succeeded, France would have played a role of the first order in Latin America; she would have awakened all that sleeping continent from its lethargy. Not that the French are good colonisers. Still it is best not to oppose their efforts in North Africa and their claims on Syria. They will expend there the warlike ardour which they possess in abundance. Occupied as they will be with their Moslem empire, they will turn their eyes away from Alsace and Lorraine. They will be only too glad to give reality to the celebrated saying of Leibnitz, that France had been placed in this world by God to supply Christendom with arms and with leaders like Baudoin, Godefroi de Bouillon, or Saint Louis. Let us encourage them also in their peaceful undertakings. The cutting of the isthmus of Suez and other successes will distract them from thoughts of revenge. If we do not urge them along this way, we shall have to prepare ourselves for a new war which, to establish a lasting peace, will incorporate Belgium into Germany and carry the German frontiers up to the Meuse and the Saone.[2]

Dug in behind her Pyrenees, and deprived of a vast empire which she proved unable to keep, Spain is living on the memory of her splendour, in an isolation where it is best to leave her. She will not come into the European federation. Nor will Italy, who has no 'organic' past and, instead of arming and claiming her place in Europe, would do better to drain the Pontine Marshes and the Maremma.[3]

There remains Russia. Is she really European, except by an abuse

[1] *WP*, Vol. I, p. 107; Vol. II, p. 126.
[2] ibid., Vol. I, pp. 108, 110, 132.
[3] ibid., p. 133.

of nomenclature, a habit of colouring over atlases in a certain way, and an error of Prussian politics? Frantz cannot forgive Friedrich Wilhelm I for having concluded an alliance with Russia merely to seize from Sweden a little piece of Pomerania. Just as in 1815 Prussia made the mistake, in order to make sure of the aid of the Russians, of granting them as a frontier the course of the Prosna, three days' march from Breslau. An irremediable mistake! Every time, since Peter the Great, that the Russians have made a step westwards, one can be sure that they will not retrace it. It is by a narrow margin, if at all, that their defeat in the Crimea has made them lose that control which, after 1849 and 1850, after their intervention in Hungary, they claimed to exercise over the affairs of Central Europe. Russia was at one time an Eastern march of Europe, the rampart of Europe against the Tartars. But here she is now, conquering a place in world economy, and here are her corn exports supplanting the grain of Germany on the market. Her growth is disquieting. Her riches in farmland and forests are beyond all estimating. Just try to reckon up what Transcaucasia, Turkestan, and even the distant valley of the Amur would produce, once they were exploited scientifically! Russia's mineral riches also have incalculable surprises in store. Certainly Russia is less well distributed than America and has outlets only on a hostile sea and on the Caspian. But she forms a continent by herself. Her population is growing rapidly. Her demographic coefficient is the best in Europe. Russia, whatever people may say, is not bad at work. An industry can be created there. Her instinct for expansion is equal to that of the North Americans. The latter, however, have an empty continent in which to spread themselves. Russia, unless she pushes back Asia, which is already over-populated and is difficult of access, can only spill out her surplus towards the west, once she has filled the little space remaining to her in Siberia and Turkestan. Instead of remaining Europe's eastern march, she will become, unless good care is taken, the mass which by its weight will drag Europe in its wake. As the Russian does not adapt himself and is essentially a conqueror, he would want to russify Europe, and that would be the end of the federal ideal.[1] Russia can already be seen pushing out her pawns towards all the squares of the chess-board. She claims her place in all diplomatic negotiations. She has developed her representation in Germany to the extreme limit: an embassy, six ministers, ten consuls. What can Russia be seeking at Fiume or at Ancona, if not to trouble the waters of the Adriatic? For Russian policy allies the Norman boldness of the Wareges to the cunning of the Mongols and the Western *savoir-faire*. The hermetic closing of her frontiers leaves Europe in the presence of a disquieting enigma, a dangerous un-

[1] *WP*, Vol. I, pp. 67, 92; Vol. II, p. 55.

known. A system which would admit Russia into the Europe of tomorrow would be *ein Unsystem*.[1]

The conclusion is clear: the European federation can only be constituted around Germany. The geographical situation predestines her to it, as also does the fact that, with the exception of Constantinople, she has supplied the whole of Europe with sovereigns by marriage or by choice. Sometimes by somewhat irregular unions: it is no secret to anyone that there is perhaps more German blood, legitimate or not, than Russian blood in the veins of the Romanoffs. The stability of the thrones of Europe rests on Germany, that nursery of dynasties, where the dynastic sentiment has indeed thrust out deeper roots than anywhere else. Germany and her princely families constitute the surest rampart against the revolutionary spirit and republicanism.[2]

What is more, German history offers as the example of a European federation the Germanic Holy Roman Empire, which contrived to unite divine right and election in one and the same monarchy. The future federation will be able to use this model as its inspiration. Above the princes, who will be irremovable by divine right, would reign a head to be chosen, if need be by the sovereign people, and responsible. Let no one, like Sybel, come attacking the Holy Empire, accusing it of a congenital weakness. Frantz's reply would be that the Holy Empire was not born of the lucubrations of politicians and jurists, and that it must indeed have answered to a profound organic need, since it managed to give the peoples who composed it a thousand years of relative tranquillity, and thus to assure a continuity of tradition between the Roman Empire and modern times. The Holy Empire was not, like the Reich of 1871, 'a raising of the realm of Germany a step higher'. The title *Kaiser*, which is Latin and not German, alone marked its international character. As for the spiritual unity formed by Pope and Emperor, it was made plain to the eyes of all—Frantz states this without a smile—by the fact that all the cathedrals built at the time when the Holy Empire was shining at its brightest had two towers. Within the unity of the Christian unity the diversity of the powers was safeguarded.[3]

It would be dangerous to enrol France in the federation, because Paris would at once become a pole of attraction and would rapidly concentrate all the forces of Europe. Germany offers us the advantage of being absolutely apart in the world, *sui generis*, and not being reducible to any classical concept. She can very well have two capitals, and it is regrettable that no one thought, in 1848, of offering to Prussia and Austria the alternating presidency of the empire. In any case Germany will never be a state in the classic sense of the

---

[1] *WP*, Vol. II, pp. 128–31.   [2] ibid., pp. 126 seq.   [3] ibid., pp. 128–31.

term, but, literally, an entity 'going beyond the concepts of nation and state'.[1]

That is indeed what the term *Reich* really means—an ideal state in which the contrasts of language, nationality, or law die harmoniously away. The Reich, that *tertium quid*, answers to a requirement of reason. But also, Frantz confesses, the ring of it makes our whole being vibrate, and the intoning of it is like that of a magic formula. The Germans will always follow that supernatural guide, the idea of a Reich, just as once the Hebrews, as they wandered in the desert, marched towards the pillar of fire which God made shine in the darkness.[2]

Thus, born of a German initiative, the federation will group the states of Middle Europe together, in the first place around an Austria and a Germany reconciled—we shall soon see how. But whatever may be thought of the magic virtues of federalism, the problems will not all turn out to be solved as soon as the federation is concluded. Peace will not yet be established in Europe or in the world. The world is moving, because of the unlimited growth of two nations, towards a disquieting situation, a future heavy with dangers.

The United States are, of course, far from Europe. But they are not lacking either in the spirit of enterprise or in material resources. Thanks to the influx of Europeans attracted by wide horizons, their population is growing very fast, and it is clear enough that they too claim a place in the concert of nations. Wide as it is, the ocean will not prevent the United States from meddling in the affairs of Europe, though at the same time invoking the Monroe Doctrine to forbid Europe to mix in American affairs. Up to now Europe has guided and aided the New World. The time is near when the power of the United States will be such that they will decide the fate of Europe. It would not be difficult to calculate at what date, given the speed at which it is growing, the population of the United States will equal England, France, and Prussia put together. The immensity of American resources will dominate the world market. All the more so since the two immense ocean seaboards of the United States abound in excellent ports. Certainly America is not without defects. Corruption ravages its governing class, the emancipation of women is ruining the family. Finally, the contempt for coloured people will sooner or later raise a grave social problem. However, popular culture is very widespread. The American respects other people's thought. Legislation is humane and the

---

[1] *WP*, Vol. III, p. 32. 'Kein geschlossener Nationalkörper auch kein blosser Staat. Deutschland, im buchstäblichen Sinne, ist ein ebenso übernationales als überstaatliches Wesen.'
[2] *WP*, Vol. III, pp. 32–5.

absence of militarism allows a youth which does not waste its time in barracks to benefit from what the state does not expend on arms and fortifications. The American likes work, and it would be miraculous if America did not grow rich as Europe grew poor. They have not been afraid over there, to spend millions of dollars on equipping Oregon or California, on making San Francisco a centre radiating towards China and Japan. Without a doubt Mexico will be obliged to get into step with the United States, which will, Frantz claims, in in the end absorb Canada, where the French minority will before long be absorbed by the Anglo-Saxon elements. An unlucky prophecy. Yet Frantz sees more clearly when he notes—as early as 1882—that although the Panama Canal is a European idea (he does not say, a French idea), financed by European capital, and although the affair interests all the maritime nations and should by rights remain under international control, the United States will seize the first occasion to become the sole masters of the canal. Anyway, the hour is approaching when their colossal strength will make its weight felt as far as Europe.[1]

During this time Russia is growing too, and is pushing out her antennae ever further. She is hastily building those railways of which the Crimean War and the War of 1871 showed her the vital necessity. During the siege of Sebastopol, the Russian regiments coming from the provinces of the centre and the north lost more men in their interminable marches than from the fire of the enemy. The Russians are not the people to forget such a lesson. They have just, moreover, invented panslavism and set themselves up as protectors of the Balkan Slavs. They are claiming a say in the affairs of Herzegovina. That is where the policy of Berlin has brought Europe. Is Europe going to find itself caught between two colossi of growing strength?

Germany, God be thanked, has always had the advantage of an excess of population. She exported in the past, and still exports, men to America. The United States are indeed a tempting field. It is regrettable, however, that the departure of these colonists should mean for Germany a sterile loss of substance. Between two dangers, one has always to run to meet the more pressing. The federation of Middle Europe is going to be short of men when Germany makes ready to carry out her mission.

This mission is not to swarm towards distant lands. If the German-Americans had even concentrated in a single state of the Union, Germany would have been able to enjoy there a quasi-colony. Likewise if they had all massed in the Rio Grande do Sul around Sao Paulo. In less than a hundred years they would have

[1] WP, Vol. I, pp. 71–86, 152.

created there a new Germany. There is no longer any opening in the direction of Abyssinia, Madagascar, or the Sunda Islands. As for the German establishments in Oceania, they are only expensive toys, and when he pays the bill the taxpayer has the right to ask himself whether 'the sauce is not dearer than the meat'. To say 'colonies' is to say 'navy'. Germany has much more need of cargo-boats than of cruisers. Besides, the time for naval strategy has gone by. No naval battle, since Navarino or even Trafalgar, has been able any longer to decide a war. War fleets are a costly survival of an out-worn idea. In short, to dream of a German colonial empire is absurd. It would be more sensible to look for colonies on the moon than on this planet.

And yet, says Frantz, we could, if we wanted, have ready-made colonies. It would not be necessary to go far, since they are there, staring us in the face, within reach—since we have already possessed them, as in the case of Livonia, or they are still attached to us by a very loose and dangerously threatened link, as in the case of Transylvania. And to be frank, who would not give all these Samoas, Borneos, and New Guineas for Livonia? And Bosnia? And Herzegovina? It would be child's-play to eliminate the beys: they would be open to the highest bidder. The property of the mosques and Moslem fraternities would be secularised and German peasants settled on it.[1]

Overseas colonies are outrageously expensive. They also threaten to become a formidable centre of infection for the mother country. Look at Cuba and Spain. Spain would have done better to let the Antilles go and occupy Morocco, which is its natural extension, just as England would have done better to let the French wear themselves out in Canada and to colonise Ireland. 'The future belongs to free and peaceful immigration.'[2] All that is needed is to find where to direct it. And that is the mission to which it is high time for Germany to give thought.

In his *Föderalismus*, as in his *Weltpolitik* or his unpublished *Danger to the East*, Frantz returns untiringly to this heaven-sent task allotted to the Federation of Middle Europe. Bismarck's mistake lies in not seeing the Eastern question in its true light, and in believing that it is merely a matter of a bargain between Austria and Turkey over 'a little bit of Herzegovina'. The Eastern question ought rather to be called the Russian question. It is essentially a matter of barring against Russia the road to Constantinople. If Russia were to instal herself on the Straits, Europe might as well renounce all influence over the East. The essential mission of Germany, or of the Federation of Middle Europe, is to hold Russia in check. To execute the testa-

[1] *WP*, Vol. II, pp. 73 seq., 94 seq., 106–23. [2] ibid., p. 101.

ment of Peter the Great the more easily, Russia is seeking to disrupt the organisation of the European peoples. The first essential is to avoid making the mistake of Friedrich Wilhelm I a second time and treating that barbarian country as a genuine European power. Better still, she should be driven out of the Balkans, where she has no place.

What opportunities have been missed through the fault of Berlin! If only, at the moment of the Crimean War, Prussia and Austria had seized the occasion prepared for them by Napoleon III! The Russian question would have been settled quite cheaply.

'Austria would have advanced her troops in the direction of Kiev, Prussia entered Poland and Lithuania. At one stroke, Russia would have been swept back behind the Dniester and the Duna. A little firmness, and she would have let go of Finland. . . . Never will such a chance be offered again.'

Unfortunately, in the eyes of the Prussian conservatives, Russia was the citadel of the sacred principles, the monarchy and nobility based on divine right. By remaining passive when the French and English were drawing to Sebastopol the best of the Russian troops, Prussia betrayed her mission. She even went so far as to condole with beaten Russia and to fear lest France should reap too much glory in the Crimea.

'Let us cease, then, to mouth the worn-out formula "Holy Russia" and let us send all this russophilia to the Devil! The reality is this: our hereditary friend to the East may one fine day give us more trouble than our hereditary enemy to the West.'

Similarly in 1866, instead of hurling ourselves into a criminal war against Austria, we would have done better to march with three armies on Riga, Warsaw, and Kiev. The occasion was let slip. At least the principle remains:

'If Berlin's pro-Russian were to change to an anti-Russian policy, the event would have repercussions all over Europe, and of the most salutary kind. *There would only be need to strike one big blow,* and then we should see the end of these perpetual preparations for war. We should see them succeeded by that disarmament which it is impossible to think of as long as Russia is installed in Poland and Lithuania. For it is on the entry of these countries to the East into the German Federation that the future of Germany depends.'[1]

There we have, expressed with circumlocution, the programme of expansion to the East which the Pangermanists with their *Drang nach Osten* took up again—those Pangermanists whom Frantz professed

---

[1] *Föd*, pp. 248, 388–9; *WP*, Vol. II, pp. 57–61, 149–52.

to hate along with all system-mongers; taken up again, also, by the men of the Third Reich, with Rosenberg and the Commissariat for the Territories to the East.

The drive to the East, Frantz reminds us, does not date from the nineteenth century. At the end of the Middle Ages, colonists were already settling on the shores of Lake Peipus, and German municipal law was already governing all the urban communities as far as Dunaburg, Smolensk, and Kiev. A new Germany was developing beyond the Vistula, closely united to the mother country by the ties of blood, language, and law. It is this new Germany that must be reconstituted, in order to kick 'Asiatic barbarism' once for all out of Europe. Prussia and Austria, reconciled, will share the task.

Once cured of its pernicious russophilia, Prussia will seek to germanise as much as possible of the lands stretching beyond the Niemen. She will first settle the Polish question to her benefit. Instead of exciting Polish patriotism by operating the brutal policy of expropriations and expulsions in her eastern provinces, the statesmen of Berlin will use to their advantage the Poles' natural hatred towards the Russians. This is an essential trump card which we must have in hand, for if the Russians and the Poles came to an agreement and threw themselves on the territories once Polish and now Prussian, it is hard to say where their appetite would stop. In any case, it would be the end of Prussia for ever. Let us tame the Poles by conceding them some rights, by allowing Polish to be taught in the secondary schools, by flattering if need be their russophobe instincts. Are we to go so far as to resuscitate the old Polish kingdom? That would be useless, says Frantz. It is dead, well and truly dead. It would be better to unite to Prussia by federal ties the Poland of the Congress and Lithuania.

'Not by making them Prussian provinces, as was done, alas! with the Grand Duchy of Warsaw, but by preserving for them their status as individual territories, with their own constitution and administration, Poland governed by a Viceroy, Lithuania by a Lieutenant-General, a *Statthalter*. This Viceroy, if taken from the family of the Hohenzollerns, will not be misplaced on the throne of Poland. The marriage of the black eagle and the white eagle is inscribed, as though by predestination, in Prussia's national colours, and on the female side the present Hohenzollerns have some of the blood of the Jagellons.'

To get over the confessional difficulties, this Viceroy would be chosen from the Catholic, Sigmaringen branch of the Hohenzollerns, and the King of Prussia would then be styled Emperor of Prussia, King of Poland, and Grand Duke of Lithuania.

Already in 1848 Frantz was publishing a pamphlet called *Poland*,

Prussia, Germany : a Contribution to the Reorganisation of Europe; and declaring in it flatly that Prussia departed from the mission traced out for her by Providence on the day when she decided to go beyond Magdeburg to the west. Thirty-five years later he returns indefatigably to the charge. Prussia is not specifically German. Pomeranians, Brandenburgers, and Prussians are late-comers to the German community. They have not experienced the German Middle Ages. Their tradition is recent. None of the great emperors ever set foot in Pomerania. At most, margraves, Teutonic knights, and captains of the Hanseatic League went there. Certainly their exists a Prussian people. It affirmed its existence magnificently in 1814 and 1815, but it must be said that it is less German than Prussian. This country, which looks towards the north-east, has received a different mission from that of prussifying the Germany of the west and south. 'If the Reich of 1871 were to disappear, that would not be so great a misfortune.' It is only an episode in German history, and not an organic consequence of that history. On the other hand, what marvels might not one expect from a Prusso-Polish-Lithuanian empire, which all the Baltic provinces, Lithuania first of all, would join of their own accord? It would make a harmonious pendant to the Austro-Hungarian Empire, which likewise has its mission marked out for it.[1]

Prussia drives back Slavism—'Asiatic barbarism'—to the north-east, Austria will drive it back out of the Balkans and the approaches to the Mediterranean. At the time of the Crimean War the Vienna Government was as blind—wilfully blind—as that of Berlin. The Austrian army, if it had marched on Kiev, would have assured itself of the control of the Balkans, Romania, Podolia, and Bessarabia. Even if they had had to be paid for at the price of Milan, these bases would have not been too dear, for, starting from them, it would have been possible to 'work' the Ukraine and the Black-Earth country and thrust in peaceful colonists. Established at the mouths of the Danube, Austria would oblige Russia to renounce the straits. Under her protection the Greeks, as on their side the Latin countries, would have pushed back the Arab or Arabised peoples, would have helped to make of the Mediterranean a European lake. Better still, the Austrian influence would have been extended to the northern part of Asia Minor. And woe to Austria if she does not undertake this programme: it alone will enable her to restore to the German elements of which she is made up their preponderance over the Magyar and Slav elements.[2]

To prevent Russia from gaining ground in the Balkans, a Danubian Union has been proposed. Neither the Magyars nor the

[1] *Föd*, p. 248; *WP*, Vol. II, p. 62 seq.
[2] *WP*, Vol. II, pp. 66–71, 143, 147–8; Vol. III, p. 71.

Romanians will accept it, for it would contain a Slav majority too easily permeated by the insinuations of St Petersburg. For this antinomian situation to be reconciled it is absolutely essential that this Danubian federation be organised by Austria and under her. Is not German the common language which makes it possible for these heterogeneous populations to understand one another? Is it not through Germany that they trade with the rest of the world? Austria's mission is as clearly defined as that of Prussia. The two together will make the German people what it aspires to become— *ein Weltvolk*, a people without which the world would have neither sense nor cohesion.[1]

Frantz advocates peaceful colonisation, penetration without violence. But Russia will not stand still without reacting in face of this Federation of Middle Europe which seeks to add to itself Russian territory.

And so Frantz, in spite of the praises he awards to Kant and the *Perpetual Peace*, resigns himself to the use of violent means. 'It will be enough to strike one big blow . . .' The Russian frontiers are hermetically sealed. Not a colonist has a chance of passing. The only remedy that remains is force.

'Let me make my meaning clear: it is necessary, *quite simply*, that Russia be driven back behind the Duna. Then only shall we be able to found that imperial Prussian monarchy of which I have been giving you an idea. . . . We shall not manage to create the community of European peoples as long as Prussia and Austria walk in the footsteps of Russia. To cease to be bound to her, it is necessary that we should separate the Polish territories from her, sword in hand. . . . The man who dealt this Caesarian stroke would well deserve the title of Caesar.'

He would at the same time have assured the western frontiers of the empire, for France is only watching for a Russian drive in order to seize the occasion for a revenge.

Frantz does not hide from himself the difficulties of a war against Russia. Even if Tsarism collapsed and the Nihilists proclaimed a republic, the military organisation would remain intact, the moral resistance of the Russian people would not be so easily destroyed, the material resources would not be exhausted in a few months. A war against a Russian republic would consolidate in that country the democratic régime which, in peace-time, has an unfortunate tendency to let authority crumble. Russia would be able to make play with her railways, whether in attack or in retreat. She would have in her rear an infinite expanse for manœuvre. Three or four

[1] *WP*, Vol. II, pp. 147–56.

battles won brilliantly would not bring the Russian army to its knees, and it would allow its adversary to wade deep into hostile territory denuded of resources, obliging him to lengthen endlessly his lines of communications, which would be more and more dangerously threatened by guerillas.

If it had been attempted at the moment of the Crimean War, this war could not have failed to be victorious and would not have cost a tenth of what the 1870 campaign required. Whatever the difficulties inherent in any campaign in the Russian space, the solution can only be a brutal one. May all the European peoples, therefore— even those that will not form part of Middle Europe—aid the latter in its crusade, and then persuade Russia that her mission lies in Asia, where, by pushing constantly further forward, she will be giving European civilisation security from the Mongol menace.[1]

Let us suppose now that Russia has been rendered inoffensive and persuaded that her task is to face eastwards. What will then be the configuration of Europe?

Frantz cannot resist the temptation to redraw the map. Being a federalist, he will not allow himself to shift frontier posts. Nor will he follow the principle of nationalities. This principle is a dangerous, double-edged weapon. Frantz imagines a regrouping of the ethnic entities which make up Europe by forming *Territories*. We accepted, he says, the *Reichshauptschluss* of 1803, which reduced the number of sovereign states in Germany from three hundred to fifty: we shall be even better able to accept the federalist revision which will allow individual characteristics and a certain autonomy to survive. The federation of Middle Europe will comprise, then, two Empires, the Prussian and the Austrian. To these empires will be added the federation of the southern German states, the Alemanic federation augmented by the Grand-Duchy of Metz-Luxembourg. All these states will form the German Federation, or Middle Europe. Switzerland, Belgium, and Holland are hardly tempted to enter the empire of 1871. It is beyond doubt that, if only for economic reasons, they will sooner or later ask for admittance to Middle Europe. A vast empire will be constituted once more, running from Antwerp to the Danube delta, from Denmark to Trieste, and from Riga to Salonica. Holland would bring to this federation the maritime tradition which it lacks.

To the north, the Scandinavian states could form a *Territorium*, a sub-federation if one may call it so. But England, Spain, France, and Italy will remain outside, at most admitted to benevolent neighbourly relations. It would, though, be as well, the better to establish peace in the Mediterranean world, that England should

[1] *WP*, Vol. I, pp. 123-7.

return Gibraltar to Spain—she would have already restored Heligoland to Germany—keeping Malta, however; and that France should restore Nice to Italy in exchange for Sardinia. And Prussia, in imitation, would return Northern Schleswig to Denmark.

We shall be reminded, says Frantz, that formerly Burgundy and Italy were part of Europe, and that the federation would nonetheless have some rights over these countries. It gives them up, willingly. The old Empire had its reasons for attaching importance to the frontier of the Meuse, Saone, and Rhone. These reasons are no longer valid. The economic interest of Europe has moved eastwards. The error of the Pangermanists, as of all system-mongers, is in not taking account of economic realities, which shift with time.

Russia having been faced towards the east and placed on guard against the Tartars, the Eastern Question is *ipso facto* resolved, to the great relief of the diplomats and the taxpayers. To settle religious peace once for all, the Holy See will be transferred to Jerusalem. The thorny question of Rome would be faced. The Papacy, the one power that held out against Bismarck, the only one that did not compromise with the Rothschilds, would cease to be Italian and would become once more catholic, in the full sense of the word. It would gain by its transfer to the Holy Places; and Catholicism, now more free in relation to temporal powers, would find itself consolidated thereby.

For more than a thousand years peace would extend its beneficent wings over Europe. And the nations would be able to devote their activity to labours which would have rejoiced old Goethe—the very labours of Faust: the isthmus of Panama would be cut, then the base of Jutland, and then, by means of a third canal, the waters of the Mediterranean would be brought into the Shott el Jerid depression, to create that Saharan inland sea which would restore areas of desert to agriculture and civilisation.[1]

Pacified Europe would live in a growing prosperity. Armaments and protective tariffs would disappear together with their budgetary incidence. Just as Germany had already given the world the Reformation of the faith, so it will have given it the Reformation of politics. At one stroke it would set the world on the road to salvation; war being struck out from among its preoccupations, the world would live and think in Christian fashion. Just as she has managed to go beyond the frame of nationality, so Germany would contrive to go beyond that of confessions and, strong in the theory of revelation as expounded by Schelling, would make straight towards a new conquest: a deep, intense, authentic Christianity, freed from every confessional tie.

[1] *Föd*, p. 312; *WP*, Vol. I, pp. 141–62; Vol. II, pp. 68–9, 138–9, 143–4, 161–9; Vol. III, pp. 71–4.

'It is somewhat strange that it should not yet have been re-marked that the public conflict between the religious confessions has imposed on the German people, more than on any other, an aim which is among the loftiest. It is deplorable that Germany as a nation should have suffered from this conflict. . . . We reject all thought of putting the clock back. All returns to the past, except those that are the fruit of a real progress, lead to ruin and perdi-tion. With its whole being the German nation aspires to become religious, but in the proper way; it tends towards a religion that would be closely united to exact knowledge and based on science. . . . Recognition of religion by the firmest science. . . .'

While affirming that the Reformation was to Christianity a spiritual leaven, Frantz deplores the fanaticism of Luther and advocates a 'super-confessional' Christianity. This would be no longer that 'narrow, outlandish, stunted, shrunken religion of our dogmatic schools', still less 'that poor personal Christianity which contains itself as best it can in a formalism that is afraid of the light', but, at last, 'a genuine public religion—not an official, state religion, not a "High Church", but a religion of mankind in posses-sion of the supreme knowledge'.

The absurdity of Caesaropapism would be left to the Russians, and in the end it would be perceived that the true Church is that which establishes itself above the diversities of confessions. This Church will not be able to wear the features of an administrative entity; it will remain the Invisible Church. However, a Federation of the particular Churches must not be rejected from the list of Utopias. Their alliance is required by the primary truth that Christianity is essentially alliance, an alliance between God and man. Thus Europe will move towards the Kingdom of God at the same time as towards earthly happiness. The Evangelist well says: 'Fear not, little flock, for it is your father's desire that I should give you *das Reich*'. St Luke's saying shall be accomplished, as also—if the juxtaposition may be excused—that of Friedrich Gentz: 'Europe which fell through Germany's fault, shall rise up again through Germany.' [1]

Thus Germany will make her way towards radiant morrows if only, while honouring Kant, the Abbé de St Pierre, and the 'Per-petual Peace', she has the sense to federate and, if need be by striking one great blow, to compel Russia to look towards the East. Frantz may well advocate the reconciliation of contradictories—all he offers us in place of the crushing armed peace is an aggressive pacifism which is as like it as a twin brother. Where Bossuet and Leibnitz failed, he offers us, to conciliate the confessional antinomies,

[1] *WP*, Vol. II, pp. 164–9; Vol. III, pp. 134–74; *Föd*, p. 437.

an invisible Christianity pacifying the divergencies by allowing them to subsist—a strange operation which confounds our logic and leaves in the reader of *Weltpolitik* an obstinate uneasiness. Behind these pacific smoke-clouds which envelop federalism, underneath this Christianity which haloes it, what exactly lies hidden?

Frantz again and again exalts scientific knowledge, that pillar, along with faith, of the new religion. But he never misses an opportunity of attacking humanism, classical rationalism, and the spirit of the Renaissance. These are so many tools of paganism. Nationalism and, through it, classical humanism bear the responsibility for the evils from which humanity is suffering, and in the first place for Machiavellian politics. They have allowed the pernicious theory of contract to destroy legitimate monarchy and the old hierarchical society. They have spread Roman law and abstractions: they have turned jurists into people who reason in the void, they have driven out Christ from everywhere. Finally, through Hegelianism, they have opened the doors to socialism. They have set in motion the conflict of state and Church and irremediably set against one another the world of faith and that of science. Rationalism and humanism, those last convulsions of paganism, have no place in the federation according to Frantz.[1]

Frantz condemns in categorical terms Pangermanism, which merely kindles the hatreds between people and people: *Deutschtuerei*, that aggressive form of Teutonomania, sets Germany's neighbours against her—and, first of all, Poland. A hatred between races is quite as absurd as a hatred between confessions. Frantz defends himself from the charge of being an obscurantist, and denounces categorically that conservatism—*laudator temporis acti*—which would like to resuscitate a past now done with once and for all. And yet this apostle of evangelical peace between nations and between creeds lets himself slide heavily into anti-Semitism.

On occasion he praises the Jews. The institution of the sabbatical year ought to be restored. For the land ceased to bear fruits, then it was redistributed. This made it plain to the most wilfully blind eyes that the right of property is not eternal, but simply a precarious right of usufruct dependent on the consent of the community. The offering of the first-fruits, a religious homage to the Creator, was a form of that public observance which Frantz would like to set up in his ideal city.

The Old Testament may contain excellent principles, but this does not make Frantz detest the Jews any the less. That people, on which the Spirit once breathed, is clearly abandoned by God. It thinks now only of material riches, of Mammon. The proof? Karl Marx, who is incapable of considering society and economy except

[1] *Bankrott*, pp. 31–5.

from the angle of output, of equivalence between labour and money. Berlin is getting more and more judaised, thanks to Herr von Bismarck and his friends the Bleichröders, and the whole Israelite banking system. The Jews have been left to invade the upper reaches of trade, the stock exchange, the press, the theatre, the universities, the Berlin municipal council and mayor's office, and finally the *Reichstag*. The Tiergarten district ought to be called the New Jerusalem. These Jews form a state within the state, a society within society. They are unproductive and live by being parasites. One never sees any of them as factory workers or farm workers, or even domestic servants: they are always employers. Frantz goes one better than Richard Wagner when he sees in the emancipation of the Jews the most hateful folly that could have been committed by governments besotted with rationalism. Let no one speak to him of compassion or humanity: the Jews remain unassimilable; they will always form a nation apart, sealed by a religion which consists less in the strict observance of the Mosaic law than in the need to aid one another, push one another, invade and disrupt. The Jews laugh when federalism is mentioned, because they want the world to suffer from its divisions. And besides, they are rationalists to the point of mania. The hollow dialectic of a Hegel has enchanted them, for they adore vain controversies. It would certainly have taken more than that poor Schleiermacher 'with his Christian lemonade poured out in dirty Spinozist glasses and served up on Platonic trays' to counterbalance the influence of Moses Mendelssohn and his dissolving rationalism.[1]

The Jews will never become genuine citizens, and rather than put into force that *Kanzelparagraph* which places Christian preachers under police supervision—those who do not consider Christ as a prisoner of state—we should have done better to vote a law to curb the efforts of the synagogue. The Judaised circles even dare to claim that the state should be laicised. It would at once become impossible to administer any oath. And who that has lived at all in diplomatic circles has not a hundred times seen Jews practising political espionage, hawking gossip, and trying to influence secretly the gravest decisions? They are the sole instigators of the armed peace: in a conflict they have nothing to lose, everything to gain. It is urgent to settle the Jewish question—without that the European renewal will remain a dead letter. To this question there are no two solutions. Short of beheading the lot of them and giving them fresh heads in which there is not a memory of the Talmud left, let Europe reconquer the Holy Land—in which Frantz has already installed the Pope—and let them be packed off to their Palestine.

[1] *Bankrott*, p. 13; *Föd*, pp. 33, 268–9, 352. See especially the pamphlet *Der Nationalliberalismus und die Judenherrschaft* (Munich, 1874).

Do not come telling us that Disraeli was a great Englishman. The fact that he was needed as Prime Minister proves the decadence of the British aristocracy and nothing more. The real Jew is Ahasuerus, the Wandering Jew, hateful to all men.

In *Weltpolitik*, ten years after writing his *Jewish Domination*, Frantz declares: a new Exodus must be brought about, all the Jews must leave Europe, they must become wanderers again, *peregrini*. The people's hatred, a sacred hatred, is not mistaken. 'One fine day the rope will have to break. And the enraged people will not let either the army or the police protect the Jews.' The appeal to the pogrom is scarcely veiled.[1]

By reducing Frantz's theses to their simplest expression, by stripping them of the brilliant adornments with which their author had clothed them, we have brought out with a crudity absent from the original a certain number of contradictory and dangerous aspects.

It is possible, it is even probable, that Frantz wrote every word in good faith. That is just the tragedy. Hell itself is paved with good intentions. He had no thought of hoodwinking his public, but was confessing his most settled conviction, when he promised in the name of federalism a thousand years of peace in a brotherly Europe. He would have protested with the utmost vigour if he had been suspected of a shadow of hypocrisy when he professed his desire to re-Christianise Europe. We are touching, here, on a painful spot: he is not conscious of going back on his principles of Christian charity and peace when he admits that federalism will not be established without recourse to violence, without striking a great blow against Russia, without driving, in the name of Christ, the Jews back to Palestine—reconquered, no doubt, at the cost of bloodshed. It would be cruel to ask Frantz if the contradiction in which he is imprisoned is among those which his federalist ardour resolves.

Let us retain in his favour the pleasing, ingenious, bold turn he manages, more often than not, to give to his polemics. Let us rejoice at seeing him deal Bismarck, the 1871 Reich, the Prussian and Austrian conservatives, and the diplomats of the Wilhelmstrasse and the Ballplatz blows which strike where they should. Let us be fair: he could discern, as early as 1874, the qualities and potentialities of two great nations, the United States and Russia. It was not easy at that time to foresee their rapid growth. If, on certain points, his prophecies fall flat, on others, more numerous, events proved them true.

This far-seeing empiricist who wanted politics to become the natural history of states falls, when he dreams of reconstituting the planet, into the very defect which he denounces. He remains

[1] *Föd*, p. 352; *WP*, Vol. III, pp. 108, 115–18, 124.

prisoner of certain Romantic dreams. He goes through life filled with nostalgia for the *Corpus christianum*, for a Holy Empire which he adorns with all the virtues, for a Europe which has become confused with Christendom. He dreams of a Germany that shall be 'the median and mediatrix of Europe', called to knead Europe according to a new plan. He detests the rationalism of the Renaissance, the ideas of 1789, and, still more, socialism. Above all, he retains the taste for bringing extremes together at any price—even that of an explosion.

If he had contented himself with dreamily caressing a pure theory, with deciding his political principles almost in a void, like A. H. Müller, there would have been less harm done. Frantz wanted to work on the map, and his concern for Christian pacifism was not strong enough to resist. Frantz ceases then to be the peace-making preacher of love between mankind in the name of Christ. He replaces the armed peace, which he condemns, by the violent action of a conquering Middle Europe. In the blue-print which he traces of the *Mitteleuropäischer Bund*, that federation which is to extend from Antwerp to Galatz, from Riga to Fiume, and is to thrust its antennae as far as the Russian lakes, the gates of Odessa and towards Trebizond, in that federation in which authority is to replace the majority principle, which is to banish from the real Europe the Latins and the English and to drive the Jews brutally away, one discovers the prefiguration of Pangermanist Germany and—alas!— of that Third Reich which Hitler tried to set up by fire and sword over a bloodstained Europe.

Doubtless Constantin Frantz is of a different spiritual and intellectual stuff from the chorus-leaders of National-Socialism, from an Alfred Rosenberg. His work has a more honest ring. Nonetheless Frantz remains an important witness in that evolution of ideas which leads from the reveries of the Romantics to the bloody frenzies with which we are all too familiar. A psychological witness in the first place, since in him the insistence on reconciling all opposites comes dangerously near to abolishing the sense of logic. And then a historical witness: in him we see how certain Romantic dreams, which managed to seem legitimate and to adorn themselves with attractive and inoffensive colours (after all, they were only soap-bubbles), proved capable, as soon as people began trying to endow them with reality, of stirring up, for lack of any logical curb, political systems which had latent in them an arbitrary brutality and which could, in the name of a millenarist and vaguely Christian mirage, trample underfoot the most sacred human rights and plunge the world into a conflict from which it has not yet recovered.

3
PAUL DE LAGARDE
Jean-Jacques Anstett

'We worship strange gods; that is our misfortune.' [1]
'The Christian religion is not a genus, but only an example of a species.' [2]

1827–1891: these two dates, one of the birth, the other of the death, of Paul de Lagarde, mark a particularly exciting phase in German history.

In this space of approximately sixty years Germany achieves a measure of unity which, for centuries past, she has not known. She becomes a State wielding and enjoying a high degree of diplomatic and military power. Her economy, which for a long time has been backward and largely agricultural, is modernised, becomes more and more industrialised, and gains a firm footing in the world markets. Political and social laws are passed, which seem to give the nation reason to hope that, should it so desire, it can take a more active part in public affairs than has for so long been the case. Like her thinkers and artists, Germany's scholars and technicians reflect the excellence of her universities and schools. In short, the world witnesses the birth, the organisation, and the consolidation of a great state, and there seems little likelihood of this edifice crumbling when, in 1890, the experienced and determined man who presided over its construction, Bismarck, is brusquely dismissed.

Such an achievement, of course, was not carried through without violence and resentment; there were fratricidal struggles; not all the wounds are healed; there are still some painful scars; this over-rapid evolution brings with it grave economic crises; political, social, and religious dissensions indicate that internal unity is far from complete; abroad, the anxious question is being asked when and where this meteoric rise will stop. But must one conclude from this that everything still remains to be done or that everything must be done all over again?

Lagarde is one of those who think it must. It is possible that in his frequently harsh criticism there is something of the discontent of a scholar whose standing in the field of orientalism and religious

[1] P. de Lagarde to his wife: 8 Aug. 1871.
[2] P. de Lagarde: *Über die gegenwärtige Lage des deutschen Reichs.*

148

history is recognised abroad but who has not received the consideration and recognition in his own country that are his just due.
It is possible, more generally, that Lagarde, the man, bears the marks
of the struggle he had during his childhood and adolescence to assert
his personality in a gloomy family circle, from which the mother disappeared too early and in which the father imposed a pietism as
melancholy as it was strict. Yet it is not entirely from a kind of resentment that he makes so many attacks on his contemporaries and
expresses so much disapproval of their ideas, customs, and actions.

Seldom, in fact, does Lagarde take a negative stand without reference to a positive ideal and without making a constructive suggestion; he seldom criticises without, at the same time, appealing for an
effort of will so that necessary reforms can at last be realised in spite
of the shortcomings and lapses of the time. Lagarde's disillusionment
may have been protracted and profound, but one must also bear in
mind the tireless energy with which he urges his compatriots to re-
pent and to embark on a new life. So much tenacity and consistency
—his thought, which has been justly described as rhapsodic, hardly
varies from his first to his last publication—can only be based on,
explained, and inspired by faith in a certain ideal.

Like every genuine faith, Lagarde's idealism is not a flight from
reality, a search for some refuge in unreality. This philologist, who
is a specialist in Oriental languages, this theologian who, throughout
his life, cherishes the hope of publishing a definitive edition of the
Bible, becomes just as passionately interested in the immediate
problems of every kind that beset his country and his period. His
Deutsche Schriften are untimely not because they tend in any way to
move in a rarefied atmosphere far above that of contemporary life,
but because they shock that contemporary life by urging it not to remain as it is, but to assume a new form and a new substance.
Lagarde shares the frustration which frequently gives an idealist the
appearance of a sterile pessimist; he can write, in 1885: 'I hope that
no one will ever see a satisfied German.'[1] But one must see in this
hope not so much a tired and disillusioned confession of the gulf that
cannot but separate ideal and reality, as an affirmation of the will to
continue indefinitely the effort which is at the root of all religious
thought and life. 'Our grievances', declares Lagarde in the closing
years of his life, 'are the clearest proof that we are alive, life consists
in growing and in penetrating into the future out of dissatisfaction
with the present.'[2]

We must, then, begin by establishing the nature and meaning of

---

[1] Unless otherwise stated, we quote P. de Lagarde from *Deutsche Schriften* (K. A.
Fischer, Munich, 1937), and *Ausgewählte Schriften* (P. Fischer, Munich, 1934),
referred to as *D.S.* and *A.S.* respectively.

[2] *D.S.*, p. 442.

F

the criticisms which Lagarde directs against contemporary Germany, since it is an analysis of her material and spiritual condition that is his starting-point in all his writings. We shall thus be in a position to say what is the state of greater perfection towards which he aims to lead his people and how he proposes to attain it; and we shall then be able to pass judgment on it.

'In all essential things we are dependent on the outside world, i.e. we are not our own masters.' [1]

As early as 1853, well before the economic crisis in Germany that followed France's payment of a 5 milliard war indemnity after her defeat in 1871, Lagarde, in *Über die gegenwärtigen Aufgaben der deutschen Politik*, is concerned by the trend of his country's economy towards steadily increasing industrialisation; in his view it shows a dangerous misconception of Germany's natural potentialities.

The doubts he expresses about this development are dictated by economic considerations. The German subsoil is, in his opinion, deficient in rich ores; the additional supplies industry requires must therefore be imported, while the products that are urgently needed for daily consumption (wheat, livestock, and textiles) are lacking. So industry is developing quite artificially; it creates wealth only by accepting dependence on other countries. This wealth, moreover, is illusory and ephemeral: illusory, because it consists merely in a transfer of wealth to the profit of a few and at the expense of the greater number, and, whatever claims one may make, this transfer cannot be regarded as the creation of really new wealth; ephemeral, because the sale of these products is at the mercy both of foreign competition, which works on lower wage-rates than in Germany and can strangle any exports, and fluctuation in the taste of the clientele. Unemployment and slump are dangers inherent in this transformation, both fraught with suffering and, in consequence, revolt. Germany would do better to build up an entrepôt, or so to speak transit, industry: she would satisfy the needs of other countries, while contenting herself with small profits; multiplied and assured, they would bring fresh currency across her frontiers.

But Lagarde's grievances are of a moral even more than an economic nature. Industry, in order to prosper, creates a demand for the superfluous and the luxurious; these fresh, vain needs undermine the whole of healthy living. Mechanisation, which inevitably goes with it, kills any joy in work; it robs man of his sense of dignity or irritates him to the point of despair. Division of labour leads, on the one hand, to the formation of a class of slaves of the machine and of capital, and, on the other hand, to the concentration of wealth in the hands of 'sugar-beet, coal, and alcohol barons' or 'kings of the

[1] P. de Legarde: *Über die gegenwärtige Lage des deutschen Reichs.*

Stock Exchange', who stifle their scruples, when they have any, by establishing benefit or holiday funds. Industrialisation, therefore, is ruining the soul of the Germans and runs counter to the realisation of a closer social unity in Germany.

A poor country, barely able to support herself, Germany is yielding to the temptation to live beyond her means; disillusionment, crises, and crashes lie ahead. Yet she could easily improve her position—by the commerce to which, in spite of her lack of ocean ports, she is predestined by virtue of her situation in the centre of Europe, and, equally, by improved exploitation of a none-too-rich soil. But, still more important, she must come to realise that a nation's happiness does not lie where so many states in the nineteenth century seek it. For Lagarde, a nation enjoys well being when its members receive, for an amount of work that is both physically and morally tolerable, a wage sufficient to enable them to live with their families on a plot of land that belongs to them, to bring up their children, and to accumulate a nest-egg for their declining years.[1]

These conceptions might well be an echo of the Fichtean ideal of the closed commercial state; but Lagarde mentions at no point, to my knowledge, the corresponding treaty of 1800 and, above all, he is far from expressing his views in the minute detail of Fichte. They might equally be regarded as forerunners of recent autarkist theories; but Lagarde does not have in mind at all an organisation of Germany for a future war. We are dealing rather with a scholar who is ill-equipped to understand the meaning of material development, is appalled by the upheavals it causes, and takes refuge in a kind of ancient economic and social wisdom, which is somewhat narrow.

But while Lagarde, deploring his country's inadequate resistance to the modern worship of money and machines, adopts, in the sphere that concerns us here, an attitude almost of conservatism and acceptance, I hasten to add that this moderation is compensated for, and even cancelled out by, his constant assertion that the territory then occupied by the Germans is of a smaller area than that which destiny has singled out for them; and this reminder can only act as an incitement to keep constantly in mind the need for extending Germany's frontiers. But if the Germans are more at ease in a more expansive living-space, will they remain faithful to the economic ideal that Lagarde contrasts with their present trends? Or will they at last be able, and indeed be obliged, to go through the same evolution as the other great nations, though now without risk? This is a question that Lagarde does not answer in so many words. We must therefore content ourselves with noting that territorial expansion is, in any case, urgently necessary for Germany.

[1] *D.S.*, p. 122.

The problem, then, becomes a twofold one: it is a simple ethnical and demographical problem if one thinks primarily in terms of the Germans populating areas in which they are sparsely represented, of a mass-emigration; it is a political problem if this process of settling on foreign soil leads, of necessity, to changes in the frontiers of the area in question.

'Germanism is not rooted in the blood, but in sentiment.' [1]

Like his economic ideas, Lagarde's conception of race is devoid of any materialist principle. He does not, in fact, link up with the presence in man of certain physical and biological characteristic the existence of certain intellectual qualities or certain moral virtues. He is too much of a scholar not to know to what an extent whole peoples have become intermingled throughout the centuries and, in consequence, he does not indulge in any fantastic lucubrations on the pure blood of this one or that one. In particular, he makes no secret of the fact that his compatriots have in their veins Germanic, Celtic, Latin, Slav, and even Hun blood, and he has no hesitation in stating:

'Purity of blood is now of little consequence: no one hesitates to regard Leibnitz and Lessing as true Germans, although their names indicate their Slav origin. Kant's father was a Scottish immigrant: does that mean he is not a German?' [2]

The adherents of racial determinism, the believers in Nazi racialism, the worshippers of the pure Aryan cannot, therefore, claim Lagarde as one of themselves:

'We Germans know that we are of Indo-Germanic origin. Yet we do not feel ourselves to be Indo-Germans or Aryans but Germans, as distinct from Romans or Slavs, who also belong to the Indo-European Stock, as distinct even from non-German Germanic people.' [3]

But, while Largarde does not profess to any racialism in the strict sense of the word, if only because he has no doubt of the efficacy of education in its influence on individuals and human communities, he is still far from regarding all peoples as equal. The passage I have just quoted is impregnated with an indisputable German pride, which is also by no means absent from the judgments he passes on Germany's neighbours.

In these judgments he has recourse not to physiological criteria but to the qualities certain peoples have displayed throughout

[1] P. de Lagarde: *Über die gegenwärtigen Aufgaben der deutschen Politik.*
[2] *D.S.*, p. 143.
[3] We are ignoring P. de Lagarde's anti-Semitism here: it is not of a racialist order, as we shall see when we deal with his religious thought.

history; from past and present he draws conclusions for the future. Theoretically, for him there are no peoples mysteriously predestined to remain or to become inferior peoples and, in certain given circumstances, a people can always, to some extent, forge its destiny by first forging its character. But certain peoples sink into apathy and resign themselves to their condition; the horizontality of their history, as well as their ultimate decadance, shows that they are inferior peoples, and they deserve to be treated as such.

Towards the Slavs, Lagarde is particularly severe. The Czechs owe their survival entirely to the mountains that protect them; they have no future. The Poles, who pushed ignorance to the point of suicide, are worth even less. As for the Russians, they count only in so far as they represent, by their very mass, a docile political instrument in the hands of the Czars; the messianic expansionism of these monarchs is a constant threat to the Germans which one must never tire of exposing, even when the Russian potentate and princes and the emperor of Germany are bound by friendship or alliance. One fact remains, at all events, beyond doubt for Lagarde: the Russian people has failed to make the most of its soil and its territory, and this fatalistic negligence gives a less-favoured but more active neighbour the right to demand that a portion be made available, and even entrusted to it. The inveterate hostility of the Teuton towards the Slav, the immemorial *Drang nach Osten*, and the drawing power of unlimited lands and wealth are combined, in Lagarde's view of the Slavs, with more substantial and valuable appreciations.

The Hungarians, too, merit only contempt; their past shows them to be incapable of any political achievement whatsoever, a prey to megalomania, and with a taste for wastefulness; the potential force they once represented and exercised has petered out, and, for Lagarde, it is incomprehensible that Bismarck should have advised Austria to turn towards Budapest, which, whatever one may say, will never be capable of becoming the real centre of the Austro-Hungarian monarchy, although it is its geographical centre.

Thus, to the east, the Germans come head-on against populations of inferior worth. But for Lagarde there is no question of a standard superiority which places all German *Stämme* on the same level. Seen globally, they tower above their neighbours, but they themselves are of different degrees. Nothing could be more wounding and more bitter than certain remarks Lagarde makes, for example, about the Austrians, who are 'capable of ordering a lamb *escalope à la Viennoise* in six languages', but 'incapable of contributing to history', who are merely 'raw material for fresh Germanic creations', 'devoid of political value'.[1] And yet, how easily this German borderland in the East could have acquired energy and vigour, and gained

[1] *D.S.*, pp. 129 seq.

strength in daily conflict against external enemies! But—and the fault lies, to some extent, with her rulers—she failed to become for South Germany what Prussia became for North Germany, in the hard school of necessity.

Remote maternal ancestors, Huguenots who emigrated from France for religious reasons, may well have handed down their name to Paul Boetticher, who adopted the name of Paul de Lagarde; it is paternal heredity from the Old Mark that predominates and gives him a Prussianism that is not exclusive but nonetheless proud and constant. The sovereign and the people of Prussia have achieved a sort of miracle which he always contemplates with wonderment and would like to see extended to the remainder of Germany.

This internal hierarchy of the German *Stämme*, however, does not in practice impair in any way the general superiority of the German character over that of their neighbours, a superiority which carries with it a right and a duty. In the same way, as the Germans, particularly the Prussians, have succeeded in playing, or wished to play, their part in history, they must and can exploit the talents which others, from impotence or from negligence, have left undeveloped, either by taking their place or by compelling them to take on their historic role under German control—in other words, by colonising them.

Lagarde does not by any means scorn the material advantages of such colonisation (expansion of living-space, acquisition of richer territories, improvement of living standards, access to the sea or to more open ports, etc.), yet they are neither predominant in, nor crucial to, his thought. When he first suggests this policy in 1853, he visualises it as a means of unifying Germany by calling forth all her energy to achieve a common national aim. This communal effort would help to develop the sense of national unity, and the German community would no longer see so many of its sons emigrating out of despair, and the consequent drain on its human and moral resources would cease.

These colonists would be, in the first instance, volunteers leaving of their own free will; others would be sent more or less officially, for example the poor and the unemployed—which would be the solution of certain social questions—or those who, for financial reasons, cannot be incorporated in the army to complete their period of service; others would receive a piece of property once their contracts had expired, as a reward for their devotion to the state.

This settlement area in which the Germans would prove their worth must stretch far to the east, beyond the Austro-Hungarian Empire to the Black Sea, and even into Asia Minor.

It is understandable that Lagarde should envisage some kind of systematically organised emigration to solve certain problems confronting Germany as a result of her somewhat restricted territory and none-too-fruitful soil with, at the same time, a surplus population that keeps on growing; it is even understandable that he should regard it as a sort of moral sin that national wealth be left unexploited when it might be helping to improve the general living conditions of humanity. But where will this emigration end? For it cannot fail to set up an ethnic, cultural, and economic zone of influence in the interest of the mother-country. Will it be able to avoid the temptation of becoming mere colonial exploitation and political annexation?

'If only we were able to establish the natural frontiers of Germany, i.e. to delimit Middle Europe in such a way as to enable its inhabitants to feed and defend themselves. . . .' [1]

Whether spontaneous or inspired, individual or national, this urge of the Germans to retrace eastwards the road taken by the great invasions in the past is in danger of meeting with a rebuff at a given moment, when certain states refuse to open their doors, particularly those states which have no ethnic affinity with the emigrants, as well as those which dream of an expansion in the other direction. Such a rebuff would lead, at the very least, to diplomatic difficulties.

Turkey is sinking too far for Lagarde even to consider the possibility of any eventual resistance by 'the sick man'.

The same cannot be said of Russia, which is closely involved in German affairs and is a next-door neighbour. True, she made an important contribution to the defeat of Napoleon and the liberation of Germany. But more recently, in 1850 at Olmütz, she intervened in German affairs on the side of Austria and at the expense of Prussia; it seems, then, that a strong Germany is not to her liking, and there is no doubt that she would not readily agree to cede territories in Poland, Ukraine, or on the shores of the Black Sea in order to allow Germans to settle there with a fair degree of autonomy. If peaceful arguments proved unavailing, should one envisage annexation by means of a victorious war? However bellicose Lagarde may be by temperament, he is not a war-monger. Nevertheless, as it is Germany's future that is at stake for him, he has no hesitation in declaring that, if necessary, armed force should be employed: 'You cannot make an omelette without breaking eggs.' [2] But he does not underestimate the future adversary, at least as far as Russia's material power is concerned.

Moreover, before taking such a step, the territories already inhabited or possessed by Germans, the Habsburg domains, should first be dealt with. These rulers have neglected their vocation as

---

[1] P. de Lagarde: *Über die gegenwärtigen Aufgaben der deutschen Politik.*
[2] *D.S.*, p. 211.

Germans; they have not understood the mission and achievement of the Hohenzollerns; they have always opposed, and continue to oppose, the establishment of a Greater Germany, being more concerned to satisfy their dynastic egoism than to promote the reunion of all Germans in one state. The charges Lagarde prefers against these unfaithful servants of the German cause are severe ones, and Sadowa, when it comes, is not without its sweetness. All the more so as, once this account is settled, Bismarck is shrewd enough to win over the one-time enemy, and on this point Lagarde disagrees with the future Chancellor of the German Empire; he, in fact, would like to see a fusion of the two Empires, which, after 1871, the Germans would share out among themselves.

This fusion would be Austria's salvation, for 'Austria has for a long time had no basic principle to her existence . . .; anyone who wishes to maintain Austria must find her some function that is worth accomplishing; . . . there can be only one function for Austria, to become a colonising State for Germany'.[1] She is a body devoid of thought, who 'must quite definitely pursue a reasonable policy, that is to say, a policy that takes account of Prussia, a German policy, for, without Germany, she is doomed to moral collapse by virtue of her disorientated "austriacism", and moral shipwreck leads inevitably to material shipwreck'.[2] Austria, in her death-throes, would be galvanised into new life by Germany, which would give her an aim in life in keeping with her inherent qualities.

This fusion would also benefit Germany herself. The economic and demographic advantages we know; but there would also be military advantages! The *Ostmark* would form a protective belt against Slavism, and might also serve as a jumping-off ground.

This unification should be preceded by a revision of the political map in view of the reduced number of states at present incorporated in the German and Austro-Hungarian Empires. This continuation of the work begun by Napoleon will deprive certain sovereign princes of their territories: but in many cases they would find it hard to prove that their claims were based on heredity or on merit, and, besides, some indemnity could eventually be offered them in the eastern colonies; any German prince really worthy of the name should at once realise where his duty lies and should bow to the interests of the German community.

Lagarde would like this simplification to lead to a division that is not so much political and administrative as ethnic, based on the *Stämme*. Each of these territories, as homogeneous as possible from the ethnic point of view, would have at its head a prince who would

[1] *D.S.*, p. 129.
[2] ibid., p. 43. Lagarde plays on the derivation of the word *Österreich* and on the situation of an Austria whose influence in Eastern Europe is dwindling.

be not only the natural representative of his compatriots but also the representative of the emperor in this sort of *Gau*, in much the same way as the Dukes were originally. These territories, in their entirety, would therefore correspond to a confederation of free *Stämme* under the authority of the Emperor.

Bearing in mind the differences of every kind and description between the Germans of the south and those of the north, and bearing in mind, too, that an Austro-Hungarian Empire exists which must somehow be taken over, this confederation—if it is to be a practical proposition and not a utopia—might in this nineteenth century, comprise two large groups of secondary states whose demarcation line would be the Main and the Erzgebirge. In the south the predominant influence would be that of the Habsburgs and Austria, in the north of the Hohenzollerns and Prussia; a pact of 'hereditary brotherhood' would bind the two dynasties and cement the unity of their populations. This treaty would establish some kind of equality between the two sovereigns; but, as the emperor of this Greater Germany would be a Hohenzollern, it would, in fact, set the seal on North German supremacy over South Germany.

The frontiers of this Greater Germany, as Lagarde visualises them, cannot be clearly defined, for they vary from one publication to another. By and large, they should enclose a territory so constituted that it can feed its population and at the same time present natural obstacles to any potential invader. In the east, the natural and military frontiers of this future empire cannot be laid down till one has considered the implications of the plans for colonising territories which may not be under the immediate control of the metropolis. In the west, Lagarde is satisfied with the frontier laid down by the Treaty of Frankfurt, although, at the same time, he deplores the retention of Belfort by France.

Greater Germany, so conceived, would therefore be a state in the heart of Europe that united all the German populations in one single political community. Not only the Germans, however, for the non-German population of the Austro-Hungarian Empire, for example, are to be included; not all of them, on the other hand, for the Germans of Switzerland, for instance, are neither to be invited nor compelled to join.

With these few reservations, this *Mitteleuropa* would be, in effect, *Grossdeutschland*. However ambitious it may seem as a plan, it cannot be called Pangermanic in the true sense of the word: as we have just seen, populations of Germanic origin would remain outside its frontiers. Nor are we confronted by a revival of the Germanic Holy Roman Empire. Lagarde does, admittedly, speak with profound admiration of the achievements of that institution, but he is nonetheless conscious of its faults and defects. Moreover, he knows that, if a people can, to some extent, shape its own history, history, which is life, cannot be remade. Possessed, and even obsessed, as he is by the idea of uniting Germany in a strong state, he does not yield to the megalomaniac and anachronistic temptation, as so many Germans ever since the romantics and even earlier have done up to recent times, of longing for a revival of the Holy Roman Empire of their dreams.[1] Although his colonisation plans are ambitious, Lagarde would, I think, have been content to have witnessed the *Anschluss* of the Austro-Hungarian Empire of 1914 to Bismarck's Germany of 1871.

> 'No nation can do without an organic structure; the mechanical division which the State effects and requires does not replace the structure that comes from natural evolution and growth.'[2]

Without overlooking the need for unity in political control as an inevitable part of German unification and unity, Lagarde is primarily concerned with the fusion of the Germans into one single corporate state, because it is mainly to them that he looks for support in his crusade, and, for the furtherance of his work, he knows he must count more on the nation than on its monarchs. History teaches him, in fact, that opposition to the creation of a genuine Greater Germany came chiefly from the separatist princes and from various governments, not only because their subjects had virtually no say in the matter, but still more because the individual dynasties and their ministers cherished illusions of grandeur and power, which the *Kleinstaaterei* encouraged, and, out of vanity and egoism, took pains to maintain them against the aspirations of the nation, however vague they may have been.

The objections and the opposition raised by the ruling monarchs, which Lagarde comes up against so often, may occasionally have a certain validity, but, as he writes,

> 'The head surely takes cognisance of many things which the heart cannot accept; and yet, in politics, the head alone is never efficacious; the head is only efficacious when it goes hand-in-hand with the heart'.[3]

In other words, even if, to present things in the best possible light, the princes cease to be hostile or deaf to the obligations of their German mission, they cannot by themselves promote German unity; they must collaborate with the nation, which has been kept too long out of public affairs by their autocratism. National unity can only be a national achievement.

---

[1] Lagarde refused, for example, to approve the claiming of states which, having once belonged to the Holy Roman Empire, are now completely incorporated in other states, as, for instance, the Franche-Comté.

[2] P. de Lagarde : *Die Reorganisation des Adels*.

[3] P. de Lagarde : *Schriften für Deutschland* (A. Messer, Leipzig, 1933), p. 190.

The problem now arises of the relationship between state and nation: the solution, on which any eventual unification of Germany must depend, will clearly have to be one that allows the national will to be expressed and that implies the acceptance by the state, frequently embodied in a single monarch and his ministers, of this life-giving inspiration. The state, in other words, must be national.

'The State is simply the agglomeration of organisms necessary to the life of a nation when its existence is not developed or assured either by individual members of the nation or by associations of individual members. The State is not the epitome but, in so far as it is not an expedient, merely the form of the nation's life. The State is not sovereign.[1]
The State exists only for the people and not the people for it.'[2]

The government, a concrete manifestation of the state, 'is not the master, nor is it the father of the people, but its servant'.[3] While one can, by and large, admit that state control arises when the state takes precedence over the nation, the extracts I have just quoted show clearly that nothing is farther from Lagarde's mind than state control and the invariable consequence of it, the cult of the state.

In his view, this deification of the state is completely at variance with the German character and, if it exists in Germany, it is because Roman law introduced it; it is one of Lagarde's major grievances against the Lutheran Reformation that, in fact if not in principle, it favoured the development of the state cult and autocracy by Caesaro-Papism.

But it is Hegel in particular that he singles out for attack in this sphere—with what fury! and sometimes with what zest too! The 'Hegelian deluge',[4] whatever form it takes, is really, for him, a mortal danger that threatens Germany; the Encyclopaedia of this pernicious philosopher is a nightmarish and impossible effort; his theory of religion is so stupid that it makes one doubt if humanity has made any progress: 'Where Hegel is esteemed, the human soul remains imprisoned in the case of the world, while the most heartfelt longing of the Christian is to escape from it';[5] this 'chameleon'[6] nibbles at everything and knows nothing; his is the unattractive character of a 'flunkey of power';[6] in his lectures and in his works 'the young students heard the dry rattle of chick-peas in a skull and believed they were apprehending the thoughts of a living being'.[5] And Hegel is not alone; there are all the *Hegelinge* too.[7] It would be a mistake to dismiss this as merely the feeling of a somewhat unappreciated scholar for a colleague who, as an official philosopher, had a vast audience and had been recognised and honoured; one must also allow for the basic incompatibility of two minds, one of

[1] *Schriften für Deutschland*, p. 192.   [2] *D.S.*, p. 479.   [3] ibid., p. 480.
[4] ibid., p. 184.   [5] *A.S.*, p. 69.   [6] ibid., p. 67.   [7] *D.S.*, p. 185.

which makes the state, the state as it is and functions at the time, an incarnation of the Idea, and which therefore runs the risk of evoking a sense of satisfaction so self-assured that Germany will remain as she is at present, which is precisely what the other, Lagarde, does not want.

But even if state control does not take this extreme, almost religious form, it is still anathema to Lagarde. The state must be impersonal; there must therefore always be the danger that it will quickly stifle any individual existence which, by the exorbitance of its standards, hampers it. A certain fixity and a certain rigidity are essential to it and, to a large extent, it ignores the changing conditions of actual life. Experience shows, furthermore, that if the state can or must intervene, it is because the life of the nation has grown sluggish.

This cautious attitude towards the state in general and any excessive state-intervention in particular, which might harm the national development of the nation and the individual, is neither new nor unique in the history of German political thought. Classicism—the essay, for example, in which W. von Humboldt defines the limits of the state's activities—and even Romanticism in its early stage, in certain aphorisms by Novalis or Fr. Schlegel, had voiced similar criticisms, and behind their political theories there was a certain republicanism. For each of them, in fact, the ideal state is one in which concern for public welfare as a whole predominates and in which, thanks to a sound economy and national effort, independently of any specific constitutional stipulation, the individual can, according to his own bent, devote his entire energies to the greatest well-being of all and achieve an orderly and spontaneous harmony with his compatriots for the greatest good of the community. The *Unstaat*, on the other hand, to employ Lagarde's term, is one which, to quote Novalis's description of Prussia under Frederick, is a 'machine', or, in other words, one in which laws and regulations weigh incessantly upon the individual with a view to controlling and canalising his energies.

It would be difficult to exaggerate Lagarde's loathing for this state-machine[1] and, in this sense, political liberalism and individualism are not so remote from his thought as one might suppose. But he is far from accepting the ideas of the classicists, or even of the romanticists before they rapidly lapsed into nationalism.

The eighteenth century in its closing years dreams, in fact, of a humanity in which individual perfection makes the presence and

---

[1] It is easy to find evidence of Lagarde's influence in Nietzsche's criticism of the state. Only whereas Nietzsche made it apply beyond the contemporary state to all states, Lagarde applied it only to certain corrupt forms of the state; Nietzsche's aristocratic anarchism is the reverse of Lagarde's national state.

intervention of the state superfluous and which blossoms out into a harmonious cosmopolitan anarchy. There is nothing of this kind in Lagarde.

His political liberalism and individualism simply serve to rule out conceptions and practices that would be harmful to the unity and power of the nation, and envisage the establishment of a political régime which favours its development and its unity. If the state ceases to be a sort of futile, stifling *cangue* and really becomes the flexible basis and expression of national life that it should be, then its existence and activity are justified; no one need have cause to rue it. In fact, every one of those who are subordinated to it in the essential awareness of belonging to a national community can develop his individuality without the least sense of constraint; he will even find in it conditions favourable to the development of his particular energies and to his personal enrichment by contact with others. So the national life, which is sovereign power both for the state and for the individual, guarantees perfect communion in organic liberty. But Lagarde clearly breaks here with classicism and its basic individualism and joins forces with romanticism, accepting the priority it gives to the national community and granting the state absolute powers.

This commonwealth, and the state that gives it shape, cannot, according to Lagarde, dispense with the presence at its head of a hereditary monarch. This may arise from a long-standing admiration for the British republican monarchy, which he was able to see at work during a long visit to London in 1852 and afterwards on journeys connected with scientific research. It may equally arise from a desire to guarantee to the life of the nation at least an appearance of continuity and to give it some form of living representation. Or is it merely out of respect for a particular need in the Germans, who, he claims, are monarchists by nature?[1] It is of no great consequence.

But how many qualities Lagarde requires of his prince! At least as many as the enthusiastic Novalis ascribes to Frederick-William III of Prussia in his short work *Glauben und Liebe*. This monarch must be etymologically the *Fürst*, the first, the prince. A man possessing the nation's confidence, he senses its will, he foresees its needs, or, still better, by some mysterious intuition, he educates the nation in its needs, he brings its aims into line with its capacity and its density, the nature of which is intuitively revealed to him. In this way the entire life of the nation culminates in him and he becomes its hypostasis. It is hardly necessary to point out the abuses which such a leader-mystique can provoke.[2]

[1] *D.S.*, p. 20.
[2] Is it too far-fetched to suppose that such a *Fürst* is not far from a *Führer*? *D.S.*, p. 141.

There is also no occasion to think of limiting the authority of such a head of state, as it is always exercised in the interest of the nation; nor is it necessary, in principle, to concern oneself with enlightening him on the position of the nation and its demands. At most one might consider providing the prince with administrative councils or assemblies such as a Council of State or a Chancery. A free, constructive press should be sufficient to ventilate the people's criticisms or wishes, and a Supreme Court would deal with all grievances, would administer the law impartially, and would see that justice was done without respect of persons.

In all these general conceptions, which, incidentally, never reached the stage of a detailed constitutional plan, there is undoubtedly an underlying anxiety to respect and promote the life of the nation. But can they be described as republican and democratic? To do so would be to use these adjectives in a very special sense that has nothing in common with the sense in which they are used in western European democracies. The criticisms Lagarde has to make of the characteristic features and machinery of these democracies, of parliamentarism, general elections, and of the party system, bring out certain divergences and even a clear contradiction.

These democracies are based on the parliamentary system, which, in its turn, implies recourse to electoral consultation and to the electoral system in order to enable the nation to express its will and to appoint its representatives and leaders. Now, for Lagarde, 'the people's voice is not heard at all when the voices of isolated individuals are heard. The people speaks only when the soul of the people (*Volkheit*)—I am happy to employ this very apposite word of Goethe's, which has unhappily fallen out of use—succeeds in making itself heard through the individual, that is to say, when the consciousness of common roots and a common stock is awakened and perceives clearly its relationship to the great events of history.'[1] In other words, the electoral system of the democracies is a congress of individuals but not of the national community; instead of ensuring and safeguarding the latter's integrity, it undermines it. This *Stimmviehgetreibe*, which is essentially arithmetical and egalitarian, gives every vote the same weight and takes no account of the value of the voter to the nation or of his sense of belonging to the nation. This mathematical process certainly produces a majority, but one that is only numerically superior and may suppress a minority that is numerically important, or what is even worse, qualitatively important, since strong and judicious men are inclined to dislike large groups. Moreover, there are very few problems on which the electorate can express an informed opinion, and to consult it by means of universal suffrage is too often like 'observing flies on the

[1] *D.S.*, p. 136.

walls of a room through an astronomer's telescope';[1] it can only give
its considered opinion on very wide questions like peace or war or,
alternatively, on local questions. Stein, in Lagarde's view, was fully
aware of this when he introduced his reforms in 1807–8.

The constitution and activities of political parties increase still
more this disintegration of national unity; they implement their
partisan programmes and their biased claims; they are, inevitably,
intermediaries who favour the average man, and he, in his turn, from
personal ambition or lack of initiative, accepts their instructions.

Parliament, in consequence, does not represent the real nation.
It talks a great deal; it makes things difficult for the government in
order to assert itself; it whittles down the responsibilities of public
authorities without itself accepting any responsibility; any consistent, positive work is made impossible by these deputies who are
not genuine representatives of the nation. 'We are really glutted
with parliamentarianism,'[2] Lagarde asserts in 1875; he has had
enough of 'professional parliamentarianism' which scorns the nation
and paralyses it.

Whether they are justified or not, these criticisms of Western
democracy, which Lagarde has picked up from the political thinkers
of German Romanticism and which are repeated *ad nauseam* after
his time, are part and parcel of an attempt to offer the German
people a doctrine which, it is thought, will be more in keeping with
their character than the principles and institutions of Western democracy. That is also Lagarde's aim.

The fact that he declares: 'Below, the people, then a large gap
with nothing at all, and finally, right at the top a Dalai-lama in uniform—this is not the sort of monarchy we envisage; the Germans are
colonisers because the best of them are capable, without further ado,
of exercising princely functions,'[3] the fact that he makes such a statement does not entitle us to regard him as a partisan of the conception of the origins of political power underlying the Western democracies: for him, the authority of the head of state is not derived from
the nation as a collective body and transferred to him by a sort of
contract, it is the privilege of the head of state, who enjoys and exercises it because he is mystically infused with it. What moves Lagarde
to make statements like the one I have just quoted is his regret that
too many German rulers should have proved unworthy of their
privilege, not any suggestion that, in view of these shortcomings, the
people should be allowed again to elect its governors or to supervise
them. There are times—though they are few and far between—
when Lagarde speaks of the monarchy of his dreams as if it were a
republic and a democracy: but it is surely a misuse of these words,
when one considers his idea of the principle of power in the state.

[1] *D.S.*, p. 137.   [2] ibid., p. 141.   [3] ibid., p. 416.

The fact that 'the best of the Germans are, without more ado, capable of exercising princely functions' does not mean that they are to enjoy a greater degree of the liberty and equality to which the Western democracies attach so much importance. This liberty and equality, which, in the last analysis, are based on the sanctity of the individual, have, for Lagarde, a functional basis and an organic meaning, which limits them infinitely more than mere respect for the liberty of others. In Lagarde's national state community I am free only in and for an action which this community is ordered to carry out, and its members are equal only in so far as parts of the body are equally essential to life. But, just as this liberty is more that of the whole than of the individual, so this equality implies the recognition of a hierarchy and of its commands. So the *Bürger*, 'a member organically incorporated in the public community',[1] differs fundamentally from the citizen.

It is true that, for Lagarde, a state that is genuinely concerned with the existence of the nation must not favour its more important or superior members with privileges; it can only enable them to exploit their capacities to the full for the greatest good of all. How is this possible in the political sphere? The question is of little importance to Lagarde, who is quite prepared to commit himself to an aristocracy in his organically hierarchical conception of the nation and the state.

The aristocracy in question, however, is an open one which should not be allowed to remain or become a rigid, hereditary social class. And one can see at once that Lagarde is far from being a conservative in the accepted party sense of the word. Should there be any doubt, it is enough to read the criticisms he directs at the squirearchy and the 'camarilla' to be at once convinced of his lack of consideration for the castes. Furthermore, in 1881 he publishes a short work with a title that is in itself indicative: *Die Reorganisation des Adels* ('*The Reorganisation of the Nobility*'): it would be sufficient, according to him, to observe certain very far-reaching claims of merit in order to establish the real functions of the nobility, whose constitution and substance would thus be subject to constant modification and revivification, as is the case for the landed gentry in England.

It now becomes understandable that Lagarde should like repeating that he is a 'radical conservative'. His main concern is to see to it that none of the nation's energies, whatever they may be and wherever they may originate, should be wasted; it is all-important to conserve, to their very roots, the living, creative forces that give birth to forms which vary with the times, which pass, and must pass, to make way for new and younger forces. In this radical conservatism it is made abundantly clear to what an extent Lagarde is haunted by

[1] *D.S.*, p. 135.

the fear of hampering life and history, and once again one realises how his historical studies, which first bring home to him the exigencies and the beauty of historical development, dovetail with his experiences in England, where the 'conservative progress' recommended by Burke has been put into practice. But, one must add, from the life of the Anglo-Saxon monarchical democracy, Lagarde will abandon many other conditions which are no less essential to it.

Thus, although the very development of national life may lead to a revolution and justify it organically, as the history of England proves, Lagarde, like Burke also, still condemns revolution as such. For him revolution marks a break in historical continuity in so far as it is an attempt to apply abstract principles, and, even if it does not degenerate into a state of chaos which finally ends in a dictatorship, it leads, as in 1518, 1789, and 1849, to a mere transference of fortunes, often very unjustly and always out of proportion to the sufferings caused.

But this condemnation of revolution must not be interpreted as a defence of stagnation:

'The state (*status*) is, in all cases, a *status quo* and, for this reason, the enemy of all progress, the enemy of all that does not subserve, in one way or another, the *status quo*, in other words its egoism. . . . The more a State gives way regularly to another State, the happier is the nation it serves; States with century-old or even thousand-year-old governmental traditions have their place in the burial chambers of the pyramids.' [1]

So we come back again to the distinction already made between the state and the nation and its life.

From this distinction, which sounds here almost like a contradiction, it follows that, for Lagarde, the state must be flexible enough to adapt itself at any given moment to the ever-changing demands of the nation in its continual evolution: so there is no further need for revolution.

Could any policy in the nineteenth century have been more geared to the life of the nation than that of Bismarck? Surely Lagarde must regard his great contemporary as the statesman who translates into reality the same principles that he himself expounds in his writings? And yet, there is no trace in these writings of any enthusiastic tribute to the man who, after all, was responsible for uniting the German territories. Lagarde doubtless sent him a copy of his *Deutsche Schriften* with a suitable dedication: he acknowledges the Chancellors's forceful personality, his energy, his exalted views, his spirit of self-sacrifice, and his eloquence. But, if one were to summarise his overall judgment, it would be that he does not find him

[1] *D.S.*, p. 378.

German enough. In internal policy, Bismarck realises the programme of Gotha and the *Nationalverein*; he favours ideas tinged with a certain Western liberalism, and the National-Liberal Party is never to find favour with Lagarde; more than that, the campaign against the press and socialism should have been conducted with other than material weapons. In foreign policy, after the triumphs of 1864, 1866, and 1871, Bismarck should have adopted a less conciliatory policy towards Russia and, in the *Kulturkampf*, which is also a diplomatic conflict, less hesitancy and less caution would have avoided a repetition of the pilgrimage to Canossa. It is clear that Lagarde, by temperament and by virtue of his confidence as a scholar in the omnipotence of ideas, was ill-equipped to appreciate the series of compromises which, on principle, out of shrewdness or out of sheer necessity, Bismarck made during the long years in which he controlled the political life of the German nation and state.

These judgments on Bismarck's policy, both as planned and as implemented, are confirmed by Lagarde's assessment of other German politicians of his time, who are like dwarfs in the presence of the one giant. One can understand, when one considers the political situation in Germany towards the end of his life, why Lagarde, in a fit of momentary disillusionment yet still with hope for the future, should have come to the conclusion that 'there has never yet been a German state' and that 'we (the Germans) are still not a nation but a collection of nomads eliminating one another'.[1]

'We must break with humanitarianism; for we owe no obligation to that which is common to all men, but only to that which is our own! Humanitarianism is our duty, individualism our task.' [2]

If a German state does not yet exist that unites the German nation in one territory capable of maintaining and protecting it, the fault lies, to some extent, with the rulers; but they are not alone at fault. If the soul of the German nation itself were not dead or dying, it would be strong enough to vitalise its body.

The Germans have doubtless excuses to offer for this spiritual weakness. Fate, as Lagarde points out, was not always very kind to them: Rome imposed upon them a foreign system of law, then a foreign religion, the Reformation divided them, the Thirty Years' War ravaged them and exposed them to foreign influences, the *Aufklärung* spread rationalism and cosmopolitanism among them, and Napoleon used them for his own ends. Moreover, their soul is by nature fraught with contradictions: they love liberty, but are often servile, *wandern* is essential and frequently a source of joy to them, yet they have a deep attachment to hearth and homestead, they are

[1] *D.S.*, p. 470.
[2] P. de Lagarde: *Programm für die Konservative Partei Preussens.*

dreamers yet with an urge to act. These external obstacles and internal difficulties have proved insurmountable; their soul, amorphous and flabby, sinks into a lethargy that troubles and angers Lagarde all the more because, as a historian, he knows the lot which ultimately awaits a people that abandons the struggle, and he realises what judgment will be passed on it by later generations.

The disease which threatens the German soul in the second half of the nineteenth century is, according to Lagarde, liberalism, in other words a tendency to welcome ideas and sentiments from other countries rather than to take stock of its own specific ideas and sentiments and establish their authenticity; the German is becoming the *Literat*[1] that Thomas Mann caricatures and stigmatises in his *Betrachtungen eines Unpolitischen* without, however, going as far as Lagarde does and calling it symbolically an aquatic weed, a 'water pest'. Its evil influence makes itself felt in many directions.

'The German language no longer talks, it shouts; it does not say what it has to say beautifully, but provocatively, not with respect for greatness, but with admiration for anything big; it no longer finds the right word because the word as such has ceased to designate a thing and has become merely the echo of some idle chatter about the thing; it has lost all power of representation because those who speak it have ceased to observe and to draw conclusions from their observation; instead, they give a hasty outline of their impressions, not for listeners but for people who are simply there, silent and undisturbed, out of politeness.'[2]

But if Lagarde, like Herder and Fichte before him, insists that a language is the expression of a soul, then the German soul must indeed have degenerated to make do with such a cheap instrument or, at least, to have allowed the instrument to be so debased!

In literature there is a craze for biography: the industry and enthusiasm devoted in this way to a few notable personalities are hailed hypocritically as creative work when, in fact, they merely amount to living on the substance of others; sentiments and judgments have become stereotyped.

The museums are crammed with works which would be more at home in picture-books.

To witness a performance of *Iphigenia* is an anomaly: if one wanted to do so, it would be difficult, for Sardou is being played everywhere, while on the lyrical stage Offenbach is King.[3]

---

[1] *D.S.*, p. 276.   [2] ibid., p. 201.

[3] Here we do no more than repeat Lagarde's judgments. We would only point out further, that lover of music though he was, he seldom mentions R. Wagner in his correspondence. In the study set at the head of the edition of the works of Giordano Bruno (1888), he sees, however, in him an artist who 'educates through aesthetic emotions', and regrets that 'the people can't go to Bayreuth so as to become better' (II, p. 198). He was an admirer of Schütz, Palestrina, Bach, Mozart,

So much mediocrity, lack of originality and of creative energy is a source of even graver concern to Lagarde, because Germany is unaware of the danger. How is it possible for her to be so rich as she is in ideal and ideals and yet at the same time in a decline? Because she has become a 'harem of ideals';[1] her ideals are mere 'sweepings';[2] they do not spring from the depths of the German soul; they are so numerous that, without committing oneself to any of them, one is yet complacently conscious of having an ideal; *Gemütlichkeit* has taken the place of the *Gemüt* which was at one time an active source of inspiration and originality; a 'culture by the dozen'[3] is spreading rapidly to everything, that is unacknowledged materialism; 'we are being suffocated with the culture and liberalism of privy counsellors' and the nation is covered with the 'glories' of a *Bildungsbarbarei*.[4] People read their newspaper in the happy knowledge that they need form no personal opinions. They spend their evenings in beer-shops, in an atmosphere of tobacco-smoke and stale beer; they are being eaten away by an insidious poison, for which Lagarde coins a pseudo-chemical alkaloid named 'gregarine'.[5]

What remains of the independent spirit, the love of solitude, and the originality which, according to Mme de Staël, went to make up German superiority? Where is the old Germany, 'the country of mountains with eternal snows, of deep chasms, of green meadows, of dark forests and torrents gushing down from glaciers'?[6] This Germany is now a land of *Bildungsphilister*: Nietzsche may be more scathing than Lagarde, but he has nothing to say on this subject that has not already been said in the *Deutsche Schriften*. Individually or collectively, the Germans have lost that moral and psychological energy which Lagarde calls *Ethos*.

This deficiency does not, however, afflict them all equally. The people, despised by its governments, ignored by foreigners, is not affected by this dissolute liberalism; the peasants have remained close to the soil and their local customs, and have thus retained a certain measure of purity and force of character. Both, as the Rousseauist *Sturm und Drang* and subsequently nationalist romanticism had proclaimed, have remained healthy on the whole: 'What will be thrown into the molten metal in order to make the bell of the future ring has nothing in common with newspapers, least of all with government newspapers; it is to be found behind the plough and in the woods, near the anvil in a lonely smithy; it fights our

and Beethoven, but the musical aesthetic of R. Wagner seems to have remained somewhat foreign to him, the more so as he had few opportunities at Göttingen of hearing his operas. It at least remains true, however, that the composer and he had this much in common, that they both tried to make Germany conscious of herself.
[1] *D.S.*, p. 438.   [2] ibid., p. 434.   [3] ibid., p. 281.
[4] ibid., p. 109.   [5] ibid., p. 256.   [6] ibid., p. 202.

battles and grows our corn.'[1] Lagarde warns against 'placing an
apparent centre of gravity where there is none, among educated
people',[2] and one understands why he makes a point of expressing his
gratitude and admitting his indebtedness to J. Grimm, the champion
of popular traditions. So much for the present.

But what of the future? There is Germany's youth which is too
often decried; people forget that, if the young have their faults, the
preceding generation is responsible, for it should have educated them
differently and set them other examples. But even as it is, German
youth has shown itself capable of a spirit of sacrifice and idealism;
it is hungry for purity and authenticity; it has faith and fire, it is the
future. And Lagarde confesses in a burst of lyricism:

> 'I believe in our youth, I believe in the future of our country;
> but I do not believe in the competence of the present ruling system,
> I do not believe in the mission of the men who think they can fulfil
> the ambitions and needs of their children and grandchildren by
> offering them their bric-à-brac, the remnants of what they, the
> old, once possessed.'[3]

So the people, not the depersonalised *Asphaltmensch*, but the artisans,
the people of the fields, the peasantry that watches over the soil, and
the youth, have not betrayed their German soul. With them and
through them, the laborious task of national regeneration can be
started: it will mean education rather than instruction, pedagogy
rather than teaching.

Lagarde, who was a high-school teacher before he took a chair at
Göttingen University, has expert knowledge of German schools.
He realises that they develop in their pupils certain general moral
qualities such as respect for efficiency and integrity, and a sense of
gravity. But they are too intent upon instilling knowledge and not
sufficiently concerned with ethical discipline.

The German school provides part of what is called general culture.
Based on the Greek and Latin humanities, it is fundamentally alien
to the German soul, which cannot assimilate it in any live and en-
livening form and which, in these conditions, merely acquires a superficial layer or practises a lifeless mimicry. Based on the humanism
of antiquity, it cannot possibly meet the needs of nineteenth-
century man with its bloodless pedantry. As this culture is
general, it cannot strike any deep roots in the individual, it tends to
mould all those entrusted to it on the one pattern instead of trying to
cultivate the germ of personality in each one, and the result is a
levelling-down and stultifying of individual energies; as teaching is
general, it is diffuse and badly co-ordinated in overcrowded classes,
it becomes mere cramming, and, as nothing is digested, neither understanding nor knowledge is improved. Would it not therefore be

[1] *D.S.*, p. 276.   [2] ibid., p. 284.   [3] ibid., p. 442.

wiser to abandon such bookish, fruitless efforts, except for a small *élite*, and to create so to speak professional schools in which the children would be trained for the life they will lead tomorrow?

Is higher education, at least, not free from these defects? Lagarde is far from certain. Neither during their University career nor later do the products of higher education—a minority, if not a caste—show signs of any distinguishing qualities;[1] students' customs have hardly changed since Fichte attacked them at Jena and speculated anxiously on the kind of men these coarse, vulgar adolescents would grow up to be. One might object, of course, that Lagarde frequently paints a gloomy picture: that is true; but it does not alter the fact that the universities show few signs of producing new men or even of trying to produce them. But that is by no means all.

The German universities, which are undisputed centres of learning, do not, and cannot, make any serious contribution to the task that lies ahead. It is not that Lagarde, a scholar of international repute, professes any contempt for learning or for the qualities it requires and develops. But, on the one hand, the average student has not the time to embark on true learning and to acquire the discipline it imposes, he remains at university too short a time and is too intent on quickly obtaining a diploma which will allow him to take up a profession, for *Brotstudium* and learning to be compatible. And, on the other hand, Lagarde finds a basic inconsistency between learning and existence: learning, with its positivism, its systematic doubt, its universalism, not only brakes any urge to move beyond what is factual, but also imbues research with a sort of mistrust or, at least, aloofness towards what is. It does not produce that absolute, almost fanatical, enthusiasm which is essential to prophets and reformers if they want to wrest their people out of their present condition and lead them on to a new life. It is no exaggeration to say that, for Lagarde, the complete purity and truth that are essential to learning are a danger to existence, which, for him, is of primary importance: 'Chemically pure water is harmful to the health; chemically pure knowledge is fatal,' he writes in 1874.[2] Impartiality, which is a condition of any approximation to truth, is no spur to action or aid to life, for one comes to the point of desiring knowledge for its own sake and not in order to live. Just as Lagarde only makes his very stringent and detailed philological investigation in order to appreciate the spirit of the texts he is studying and get behind it, so he attacks intellectualism as a fatal germ inherent in all indiscriminate learning. He very nearly anticipated Nietzsche's statement in *Wir*

---

[1] As an example of the mentality of German students and of its permanence, Largarde tells how Bismarck himself accepted, as a souvenir of his years as a student at Göttingen, a diploma in which there appeared onions and herrings, classic cures of *Katzenjammer*: at the time of this gift, he was already Chancellor!

[2] *D.S.*, p. 110.

Philologen: 'We are not made for knowledge, it is knowledge that is made for us.'

So the nation is 'enervated by its schools and universities';[1] at best they give it instruction, but not that power, not that fire and ardour, without which the ideas and ideals that are essential for a revival of Germany cannot be realised; education neither reaches nor reforms the innermost soul of its pupils—can one talk of disciples? —who leave it exactly as they came to it.

Lagarde, who returns again and again to this problem, the importance of which for a revival of Germany he fully realises, goes so far as to suggest, as Fichte does in his *Reden an die deutsche Nation*, that in Germany's present state of sin it would be worth while cutting the country's youth off entirely from the influence of their social environment and of the older, corrupt generations; children and adolescents would be kept in establishments not unlike the cadet training-schools and anticipating to some extent the Nazi *Ordensburgen*.[2] Their will would be moulded there, for 'the essence of man is not the intellect but the will', and, 'like anything that is good, knowledge also comes to us through the will';[3] they would be kept free of any liberal influence which, in the guise of universal humanity, has, in fact, no ties of any kind; armed with a single-minded devotion, they would then set out across Germany; their ardent, forceful personalities would gain them, little by little, new followers who, in their turn, would join this militia that would be able to lift Germany out of her mediocrity and alienation.

When Lagarde speaks of *Bildungsanstalten*, he is thinking, not as one might expect, of teaching establishments but of real educational institutions, in which men would be formed (*bilden*). Their function would be to instil, not in the intellect but in the soul, an image (*Bild*) which becomes the centre, the focal point of our being and our existence, to such an extent that, if deprived of its warmth and light, we die, and this vital bond creates in us the will to give, both to ourselves and to the world, the shape it prescribes. Through it, what is in us and outside us acquires meaning, becomes self-explanatory and, thanks to a myth, takes shape as it develops.

The pedagogy which Lagarde would like to see applied is, then, in the first instance, individual and individualistic. Each man accepts this image according to his own particular capacity and leanings, organises himself and his world round it, in accordance with his peculiar gifts and inclinations. But, at the same time as this effort of stabilisation reveals and qualifies the individuality, it

[1] *D.S.*, p. 72.
[2] Lagarde devotes several pages to reforms in secondary and primary education: we do not deal with them in detail here.
[3] *D.S.*, p. 82.

unifies and strengthens it, so that it becomes a dynamic and distinct moral entity, a character.

Now, 'character is the mark of the eternal on a receptive soul; in the fullest sense of the word, character can only be acquired by piety; in it, and in it alone, can it endure'.[1] To have a character or, still better, to be a character is not to display ostentatiously some vain, capricious originality; it is the will to realise the fragment of the plan God has entrusted to us for the world and its history, a plan we have perceived, either spontaneously or with the help of teachers, in the depths of our being, and to make ourselves its executors, without looking back but with faith in the divine intention of which we are the repositories. So there cannot be a pedagogy that is not religious, for a genuine pedagogy is constantly referring back to a divine image. But if, as we have seen, politics presupposes a pedagogy to provide it with properly qualified men, it appears that politics, too, must be basically religious. We must pause for a moment to consider in more detail this religious element in Lagarde's pedagogy and politics.

Characters express, each in its own way, their divine image, but they are not isolated from one another in water-tight compartments. These images, in effect, are details of one and the same vast work, which alone gives them complete meaning; they are fashioned by the same master-imagist, and the energies with which they are variously charged emanate from one and the same source. These individual characters and the individual piety that inhabits them converge upon a common centre and thereby achieve a communion which unites them in one community. Turned as they are towards God, they are bound together in and by a common religion.

Economically, politically, and psychologically the Germans are, for the present, an amorphous mass in process of dissolution: Lagarde is constantly making this observation and is painfully, tragically aware of it. The reason, he remarks, continuing his analysis, is that each man, and the entire nation, lacks a strong soul, one that would be capable of creating unity and then giving life to a body. To awaken this spirit is the mission he believes he has been entrusted with: 'I have no interest in theoretical reasoning . . . I wish to bind together and liberate my people,' he declares on one occasion.[2]

To bind together and liberate: that could mean enabling Germany to acquire moral and material cohesion, and thus making her strong enough to become independent of any foreign intervention in her affairs.

But, if genuine liberty is possible only by fulfilling the destiny God has mapped out for us, and if the only true and durable bond is in communion with the will that decides each destiny, then binding

[1] *D.S.*, p. 98.   [2] *A.S.*, p. 159.

and liberating means more than ever that Germany must be made aware of her true character, of her eternal being, of her divine image and form, so that she has only one aim: to realise them in one unanimous effort. Once she accepts this mission, she will know the perfect liberty of those who accomplish God's designs; bound to her essence, united in and through it, she will anticipate the liberty that is the glorious attribute of essences.

But from which religion will education borrow this dynamic scheme, this idea-force, this myth of our being and our divine destiny which it must implant or awaken?

'One nation cannot support three souls.' [1]

As far as religion is concerned, the Germans can be divided into Jews and Christians, the latter falling into two main subdivisions, Catholicism and the Churches that emerged from the Reformation. This division makes it clear that Lagarde can hardly look to one of these spiritual families to counteract the disorganisation of the German soul.

'They (the Jews) have either got to be right in or right out.' [1]

P. de Lagarde may well have been the inventor of the word *judain*,[2] the alleged poison which the Jews are supposed to secrete and pass on to others: in other words, he is another anti-semitic German.

His contempt and his hatred are practically indistinguishable in this respect from those of so many others, and his compatriots have by no means the monopoly. Behind a historico-scientific mask one finds the familiar treachery and tenacity of purpose in denouncing the Jewish danger in every hole and corner and in envisaging only one remedy, apart from the possibility of a few individual cases of assimilation: mass-expulsion either to the colonised territories in the East or to their country of origin unless an even more radical and brutal remedy is suggested, the 'Assyrian' method. The Jews, who are foreigners in and to Germany, who intend to remain foreigners and succeed in doing so, must be treated as such, and one must not forget that these foreigners violate the laws of the hospitality they receive and that the prophylactic measures cannot therefore be too ruthless.

It would not be worth while spending any more time on Lagarde's anti-Semitism if it were not accompanied by an explanation of the power and permanence of the Jewish people and character in spite of the diaspora, past and present. This explanation throws a revealing light on Lagarde's ideas on national education. When he

[1] P. de Lagarde: *Über die gegenwärtigen Aufgaben der deutschen Politik.*
[2] *A.S.*, p. 68.

speaks of the Jews, Lagarde is thinking above all of Israel as it developed, particularly after the Babylonian captivity, under the external and internal discipline imposed by its leaders. Whether they
belonged to the tribe of Judah or were members of the sect of
Pharisees, these leaders succeeded in instilling in Israel the faith that
it constituted a separate people—that is, as we know, the meaning of
the word 'pharisee'—a people apart, chosen by God; it must not
therefore become fused with other peoples, but must jealously conserve and proudly display its particular virtues and characteristics by
remaining faithful to its selection by God and by showing gratitude
to God. It is this faith in their own genius and their mission that
gives the Jewish people a unity sufficiently exclusive and sufficiently
powerful for them to survive dispersal and persecution. This national
cohesion is a product not of their race but of their religion, of their
faith in what God does for Israel and expects from her. 'Here you
have a proof of the advantage a people derives from a national religion,'[1] Lagarde points out to his compatriots.

I think we have placed our finger on the original source of Lagarde's anti-Semitism.[2] He is not anti-semitic out of common
jealousy of anyone more richly endowed, who has met with more
success in everyday life, nor is he motivated by a misguided Christianity, for he knows that the Jews were despised before Christ's
crucifixion, nor even by intolerant xenophobia. He is anti-semitic
out of resentment: the Jewish people has succeeded by virtue of its
national religion in being what the German people has not yet succeeded in being: a nation. While Lagarde is made constantly and
depressingly aware of the difficulties that must be surmounted in
order to awaken a national consciousness in the Germans, he is
constantly encountering men in that same Germany who live only by
such a consciousness. Lagarde, who knows better than most the
efficacy of Jewish prophecies, finds his own prophetic power suffering
setbacks of this kind, and he makes no secret of his ill-feeling towards
those who are the cause of them or who remind him of them.
Hatred and contempt are therefore a form of compensation for a
deep-seated sense of inferiority; he counters one messianism—
whether it is inspired by God or is only national does not concern us
here—with another messianism.

So Lagarde is closer to these dishonoured Jews than he thinks or
is prepared to admit. But brothers make the worst enemies, and
here perhaps lies the real source of German anti-Semitism in general.

'To overcome the spirit of Rome by Catholicism is like expelling
one devil by another.'[3]

[1] *D.S.*, p. 30.
[2] To be exact, one should speak of anti-Israelism, rather than anti-Semitism.
[3] P. de Lagarde: *Diagnose*.

Lagarde's attitude to Catholicism, to its ecclesiology if not to its entire dogma, is coloured by the same kind of animosity. The *Kulturkampf* only aggravates the *Anti-Rom-Affekt*, which he displays well before the events of 1875.

The Roman Catholic Church, being Catholic and therefore universalist—in other words, endeavouring to reduce all nationalities to one common denominator ; or being Roman and therefore foreign—in other words, alienating men from their native land and their state—is never holy for Lagarde, and from the moral, cultural, and political viewpoint its activities are heinous.

From the moral viewpoint, the infallibility of the Pope, for example, which in fact antedates the decisions of the Vatican Council and goes back to the appropriation in the name of the Bishop of Rome of Chapter XVI, verse 18, of the Gospel of St Matthew, permits every imaginable change of front and excuses any act of duplicity.

From the cultural viewpoint, the magisterium of the Church hampers the development of the exact sciences, which must submit to its prescriptions or are reduced to an inorganic mass of knowledge; nature and spirit are thereby split, a process which, paradoxically enough, favours materialism; history and evolution are pronounced valueless, thereby encouraging obscurantism. Grievances that are so elementary, so rudimentary that one hesitates to look for any connection with modernism.

From the political viewpoint, even after its defeat in 1870, Rome does not give up its theologically-inspired political activities and still less its attempts to set up inside each state a super-state, a heterogeneous political body with a foreign sovereign, its own subjects, newspapers, and party (the Centre does not really come into being until after 1870). The Vatican divides each nation in order to rule it more easily, pretending to be democratic in order to play off the peoples against their sovereigns and their governments, after they have played off both of these against each other. This interference by the state secretariat—in Lagarde's view, a symptomatic and significant name—is an intolerable intervention by a foreign power in German affairs, which are thereby taken under the protection of a state whose internationalism, different as it may be from that of liberalism, is no better, and, from this point of view, Lagarde lumps together the red international of the workers, the grey international of liberalism, and the black internationalism of Roman Catholicism, for each is a threat to the life and independence of the nations, particularly of Germany over whom the Curia has had its designs ever since the defeat of France and the capture of Rome by the Piedmontese troops.

Indulgence and tolerance are therefore out of place where this political Catholicism is concerned, and Lagarde urges more than once that priests should be made to understand that they must cease to play an active part in politics. If it were necessary, such an injunction would show that a national religion must practise ostracism, must be prepared to bring under the heading of politics anything it does not like!

Lagarde does not think that the battle will be an easy one. As a pedagogue, he does not under-estimate the power and quality of this Roman army of priests and monks, particularly the Society of Jesus, which has never lacked soldierly courage and endurance in its campaign to bring the world into the orbit of the Vatican; he feels the same jealous, admiring bitterness towards the Jesuit training[1] as he does towards the applied pedagogy of Israel, for the theological seminaries form characters which are immunised against all temptation and all abandonment, whereas there are frequent cases of Protestant divinity students turning their backs on the Church as a calling after they have completed their studies at a university.

It even seems at times as if Lagarde's admiration proves stronger than his hostility, so anxious is he that his compatriots should achieve what the Roman Church obtains from its children. He pays a sort of servile homage to the Virgin, perhaps out of nostalgia for the mother he barely knew, but more probably because he expressly urged that virginity must be the basis of all education and of marriage. He is in favour of proclaiming certain men saints as a concrete manifestation of elements of ideal life which remained hidden in Christ. He gives his virtual approval to the Catholic doctrine of the Mass, because this sacrifice, being repeated daily, recalls to mind the eternally recurrent power of life, whereas in the reformed doctrine the faithful are committed solely to inner contemplation of a fact, an accomplished fact.[2] Apart from the two sacraments of the reformed Churches (baptism and communion), he recognises four other, specifically Catholic sacraments (confirmation, marriage, the ordination of priests, and, if not penitence itself, at least the confession that precedes and conditions it).

On the other hand, if Lagarde admits that there is some virtue in certain elements or trends of Catholic dogma, this does not mean he proposes their adoption, but only their adaptation; he always places upon them an interpretation that is based on individual or social psychology, and at most he is prepared to regard them as a spiritual aid to life on earth. But, just as he denies that the Church alone is qualified to administer the sacraments, so he denies the sacraments their divine origin and robs them of all supernatural substance or significance. The recognition of a certain measure of success by Catholic educationalists does not imply for Lagarde any need to

[1] *D.S.*, p. 181.   [2] ibid., pp. 270 seq.; p. 73.

accept their first principles or final aims. He takes such a heterodox stand on this that, as far as he is concerned, a *rapprochement* with Catholicism, which he never ceased to regard as anything but ultramontanism, is out of the question.

Furthermore, not only does Lagarde look upon the Roman Church as a foreign power but, more generally—and this applies also to the Reformed Churches—he believes that any Church which does not make for German unity helps to divide and disorganise the Germans, and should therefore not be recognised by the state. He demands the complete separation of any such Church from the state and, once this separation is enforced, a permanent control by the state over the religious communities—incidentally, every community within the nation must be subject to similar control— which would be dependent for their continued existence on the zeal and sacrifices of their adherents. A Church which is not entirely national should not be recognised or subsidised by the state, for the state is the instrument of the entire nation. It comes therefore as no surprise to find Lagarde reproaching Bismarck with lack of thoroughness in the *Kulturkampf*, which he would have liked to end with a complete *los von Rom*.[1]

[1] Lagarde devoted two works specially to the question of Church and State: *Über das Verhältnis des deutschen Staates zu Theologie, Kirche und Religion* (1875), and *Die Stellung der Religionsgesellschaften im Staate* (1881).
These are his main conclusions:
The State, the living embodiment of the interests of all its members, and directed solely towards the general good, need not concern itself with the fate of the churches, if they are merely private bodies, fragments of the totality of the nation; it allows them to live, guarantees them freedom and justice like any other private corporation, ignores their doctrines, recognises none as holding a privileged position, watches their activities, and forbids any political activity that might be harmful to itself. It guarantees no stipend to priests; but it must return to the Churches the endowments which were taken from them either in 1648, or in 1843, after deducting, however, enough to cover their non-ecclesiastical obligations, which were previously their duty and now devolve on the civil power. It will not interfere in the organisation or the nomination of priests, but these must have received German education and training, because of their potential influence in other fields. The Churches must advertise the denominations from which they originated. The State authorises confessional schools, since parents have a right to educate their children at their own expense; but they must not be indoctrinated with principles contrary to law or dangerous to the national life. The Churches shall be allowed to admit and expel whom they please without interference from the State. This régime of toleration towards ignorance will last only until there exists a national religion in Germany, embracing in a national Church the whole community of the nation. This Church would be officially recognised by the State.
In his struggle against Roman Catholicism, Lagarde did not, it should be added, count upon the Old Catholics and their schismatic opposition to Rome. Though men of honour, in his eyes they were simply Catholics without a pope; they wanted to return from the nineteenth to the second century, which is contrary to history and to life; such strength as they still have they owe to their youth spent inside the Church; like all cut-off members they are bound to wither, and attempts by the state to give them new life are so much wasted effort. (*D.S.*, pp. 166 seq.)

But government measures, however necessary they may be, however severely they must be enforced, are merely preventive, and in consequence negative. One religion can only be combated by another religion, and all attempts to destroy a Church externally will be fruitless if naturally religious souls are not provided with the resources they need and have indeed sought elsewhere. So 'Romanism and Catholicism will be overcome in Germany by means not of an abstract religion but of a national religion'.[1]

'Protestantism must be thrown overboard, and the sooner the better.'[2]

Do the Reformed Churches not represent the religion that is to unite and liberate the Germans by giving them a soul, its soul? The Reformation is, admittedly, not an exclusively German phenomenon, but is it not true to say that it developed with particular vigour in Germany? Can one imagine a more German religious genius than Luther? All that may be true, but Lagarde still does not believe that Protestantism can be relied upon to save Germany.

It may seem surprising that Lagarde, whose French ancestors had emigrated on religious grounds, should have criticised, both violently and sometimes shrewdly, not only Protestantism in general but also its role in Germany. One must, however, bear in mind the impressions left by childhood and adolescence, which were spent in an atmosphere of bigoted pietism; it is also important to remember that Lagarde, as an orientalist and a religious historian who intended also to become a theologian, had more than once a bone to pick with colleagues in the Protestant Theological Faculties, not only because he felt considerable scorn for them but also because, on points of dogma, he was given to a certain laxity. But his hostility—we must use this word, for he went so far as to protest publicly against the organisation by Göttingen University of a ceremony to commemorate the 400th anniversary of Luther's birth in 1883—is more than a mere sentimental reaction or animosity on the part of one scholar towards others.

Lagarde is certainly not so blinded as not to realise that a reform of the Roman Church had become necessary at the beginning of the 16th century, or to think that that work of reformation was undertaken for purely earthly and material motives. It was undoubtedly a religious experience that impelled Luther to denounce the errors and abuses of a Church in which such an experience remained isolated. Lagarde could hardly have failed to understand the depth and meaning of Luther's crisis and behaviour, for the reformer and himself had many psychological traits in common: religious fervour, even mysticism, a prophetic sense, a strong Germanic strain, conservatism,

[1] *D.S.*, p. 113.   [2] P. de Lagarde: *Konservativ?*

pugnaciousness, and a mixture of pride and humility. For Lagarde, however, Luther is no more than an agglomeration of qualities which a certain hagiography tends to retain, and he insists that the former monk must be taken in his entirety: not only the man who comes under the influence of humanism but also the man who curses it, not only the soul that is capable of elation and refinement but also the 'coarse side of him that knows no self-control' and bawls, not only the frank and open mind but also the other Luther, 'whose vision does not go beyond the tips of his hobnailed boots'.[1] This lightning-sketch with its light and shade and even its fidelity are, to Lagarde, a sufficient indication that the idolatrous admiration of so many Germans for Luther was not unlimited. Moreover, there is more than simply Luther the man, there is his work and the influence it had.

If it is permissible to talk of principles in connection with a religious experience, then the principle behind the Lutheran Reformation was salvation through faith with one sole authority, the Bible. Now, for Lagarde, salvation through faith was conceived, if not invented, by St Paul; it was therefore a purely Jewish idea of which the Evangelists and the first Apostles knew nothing. To admit this conception means, in short, replacing the Evangelists' doctrine with Paulinism, reverting to a religion that Christ came to abolish. At most one can credit this view with a certain polemical value: a weapon was needed with which to combat the Roman Church, in which good works and deserts had fallen into abuse. But it is a mistake to try to make a principle of something that has merely passing value.

The exclusive authority of the Bible? But first an authoritative text must be obtained: Lagarde spends his whole life trying to establish it on a scientific basis, and fails. Readers of the Bible should also be in a position to understand it in its various contexts. Can one expect the faithful to possess the necessary knowledge for such a precise understanding of the Scriptures?

Furthermore, who still reads the Bible in its entirety? Most people are content with extracts in instructional handbooks: in other words, hardly anybody even chooses his own anthology of sacred texts, and these excerpts, being incomplete, superficial, and incapable of arousing any genuine response in the soul of the reader, are in danger of being completely ineffectual. So Lagarde deals some hard though shrewd blows at what is sometimes called Protestant bibliocracy and bibliolatry—forgetting that this priority given to the letter over the spirit is, in good doctrine, regarded as infidelity. But Lagarde goes still further.

The Bible, as we know it today, was composed by the primitive

[1] *A.S.*, p. 78.

Church. It was a Catholic Church. Acceptance of this version, and particularly of the New Testament, should imply an obligation to remain in, or return to, the Catholic fold: an argument which is so specious in its simplicity that it does not warrant closer examination. Nor does Lagarde argue with any greater validity when he asserts in a sudden polemical outburst that the Protestant theologians accept the definitions and decisions of the Councils of Nicea and Ephesus just as readily as do the Roman Catholic theologians and that, in consequence, nothing remains for them but to join forces; at least, they should stop airing their fidelity. A surprising confusion of the spirit and the letter, it must be admitted! It is all the more surprising because Lagarde himself reproaches the Reformation with its biblicism, which, for him, finally makes the spirit—that is, life and evolution—subordinate to the letter—that is, death.

So the achievement of the Reformation was a frail and ephemeral one. This is abundantly clear from the fact that, after the sixteenth century, it produced no great theologians. Critical, polemical, and therefore purely negative in character, it believed that merely by borrowing certain elements of Roman Catholicism it would achieve a positive result. Although it was necessary at a given moment, it lost its meaning the moment it was recognised—namely, in 1648; it was a historical phenomenon which was justified at the time but failed to acquire any permanence by continuing to evolve. But there was more against it than the fact that it remained, from the theological point of view, exactly where it was at the beginning, instead of developing a creative vitality. There were also other points of view from which it is open to criticism and condemnation.

It gave birth not to one Church but to a multitude of churches and sects. Lagarde takes obvious pleasure in pointing out how prolific and how varied they were, but his irony is not unmixed with sorrow. All these religious divisions increase the splits in the German national community, whereas if it was really a German church, it would be bound to draw the Germans together into one body animated by one and the same spirit.

Freedom of thought in the religious sphere has degenerated into emancipation of the individual and so into individualism; ideals and obligations have lost their compelling and constraining power; a sort of scepticism is creeping unconsciously into men's souls and taking root there; faith has ceased to exercise to the full its power to inspire and exalt. Lagarde comes very near to seeing in the Reformation the source of liberalism, which in its turn, like so many others before and after it, distorts the original thought of the reformers in a way that is hardly justified by the predominant trends in Protestant theology in the twentieth century.

As the Reformation, by force of circumstance or as a result of the political ineptitude of its prime movers, joined forces with certain princes in its initial stages, it could not dominate and direct the political evolution of Germany. It left that to the dynasties. Whatever some people may think, it was therefore not the Reformation that helped to reshape Germany. The credit for this must go to the Hohenzollerns, who set to work before the Reformation and, when the time came, used it skilfully for their own ends. The Caesaro-Papism that emerged from the Reformation proved an extremely serious handicap to the political unification of the German nation. If the Germans failed to achieve a greater Germany, that was a remote yet none the less certain consequence of the events in the sixteenth century.

The abolition of celibacy among priests and the idea of a universal priesthood did not lead to any improvement in the general state of society in Germany. The sons of influential families turned their backs on high-ranking positions in the Church, in which they could obtain a working knowledge of their duties. The pastoral body became a 'proletariat', which produced highly suspect men of letters and was recruited from the dregs of the people. Where and how was a German *élite* to be formed?

Finally, from the cultural point of view, it would be difficult to argue that the Reformation made Germany richer. Who would dare claim that Lessing, Winckelmann, Herder, and Goethe—Lagarde refrains, not surprisingly, from adding Schiller's name, but he does, curiously enough, add Kant's—were indebted in any way to the Protestant Church? And, whatever may be generally held, the same is true of music as of literature: the Lutheran chorales, even *Ein feste Burg*, are borrowed from plainsong, from popular or religious melodies dating back to the Middle Ages.

Whether the picture is accurate or not is a question we shall not discuss here. But it is certainly a black one, bold in its lines and brutal in its design. Lagarde, moreover, has no intention of confining himself to abstractions; he has concrete observations to make. What is German Protestantism now? Is it still a force to be reckoned with? Does the *Protestantenverein* not maintain that, to be a Protestant, it is enough to have one's children baptised and to join them in Holy Communion on the day of their confirmation?[1] A clergyman, who reads the confession of faith every Sunday, is surely free to withhold his own beliefs and simply to read aloud? How can the official Lutheran Church feel anything but moribund and remote from true Lutheranism, when it persecutes pietist conventicles, which, it is true, are the last refuge of the simple faith, but are also serious obstacles to complete unity of all Protestants in Germany? Is an authentic reformed Church made more so by the fact that the

---

[1] *D.S.*, p. 176.

Gospel is refracted through liberalism? Only a very few pastors still have enough piety and devotion to rescue what is left of the religious heritage handed down from the sixteenth century. Confronted with this spectacle, Lagarde cannot restrain himself: Protestantism is just another 'gangue like Judaism', so much 'hotchpotch' and 'lumber'.[1]

What was once, in spite of everything, a living dynamic religious force has become, like so many others, worn and lifeless; what was once a shattering Christian experience has become a mere name and a memory.

And what has survived is not so much the Christian experience as a German experience. With all his reservations, Lagarde still grants Luther one achievement, that of having realised the Germans' need of a national religion, of a Christianity that would be neither universal nor Roman but a refraction of the Gospel message through the German soul and character, which could gain new life from it and give it new life.

'The religious concept of Christianity is wrong.'[2]

Whether they are directed against Roman Catholicism or against Protestantism, the criticisms we have just analysed barely touch upon the problem which, in fact, seems a crucial one: the validity of the transcription which these Churches and their theologians offer their adherents from the original common fund of Christian doctrine. This question of fidelity is not of primary importance for Lagarde, because Christianity as such implies for him infidelity to the Gospel as preached by Jesus.

Lagarde does not contest either the historical truth of Jesus's existence or the sublime nature of his message. In none of his voluminous writings as an orientalist, theologian, or polemicist is there the slightest suggestion that Jesus might be a mythical character, a product of man's desire for perfection. For him, the very fact that we have so little documentary evidence of, and so few historical references to, the Galilean is a proof of his existence and of his glorious career. When a man, indeed, by his words, his ideas, and his actions, arouses enormous enthusiasm among his contemporaries, the latter cannot be expected, in their exaltation, to be normal objective observers, and their accounts of what they saw and heard cannot but be coloured and transfigured by their wonderment. If the life and death of Jesus had not inspired poetry—in the widest sense of the term—he would not have been a religious genius. Jesus was too far above and beyond the men of his time for their accounts of him to be

---

[1] *D.S.*, pp. 30, 55.
[2] P. de Lagarde: *Über das Verhältnis des deutschen Staates zu Theologie, Kirche und Religion.*

judged by the standards of the conventional chronicler and to fit into the normal framework of human history.[1]

But does this superhuman greatness, which affects Lagarde just as profoundly as it did those who actually witnessed it, mean that Jesus was the Son of God in human form? To answer in the affirmative is to accept the basic dogma of every confession's Christian faith: it is plain logic. But, for Lagarde, that would be evading the obligations of historical criticism and its scientific conclusions.

According to Lagarde, Jesus himself merely stated that he was the child of God. He made no claim to be either the Saviour whom the world had been awaiting since the Creation or the Messiah hoped for by Israel; for, apart from the fact that the word Messiah is not of Hebrew but of Assyrian or Babylonian origin, faith in such a Messiah is not inherent in the Old Testament: it is a Judaic idea. On the one hand, it dates back to a period when, after the Exodus, the tribe of Judah and, more particularly, the sect of the Pharisees, play a predominant part in events and theories, and, on the other hand, it is current not in Israel as a whole, but particularly in the circles which produced the apocalyptic scriptures. So neither in Jesus's preaching nor in the authentic religious tradition of his people is there any mention of the Christ.

And yet, some twelve years after the Crucifixion, Jesus's followers in Antioch are calling themselves Christians, followers of the Christ. Then the Gospels, the apostolic scriptures, speak of the Nazarene as the only Son of God, the Saviour, the Messiah, the Anointed, the Christ. The enthusiasm Jesus had aroused in certain people had done its work.

Jesus is felt to have been a supreme religious genius, who lived in a constant and complete spiritual and active communion with God: he therefore becomes the only Son of God.

Jesus preached an ideal, the beauty of which was fully appreciated not only by his first disciples but by others. Yet he was put to death. Either for reasons of tribal power, or because this judicial error has to be explained and wiped out, he is made a suffering Messiah, then the Son of the Virgin conceived of the Holy Spirit, which frees him from national bonds without taking away from his nation any of the glory of having given him birth; his message becomes applicable to all men, whose Saviour he must be.

Jesus, who proclaims eternal life in God, dies: with the aid of ancient myths he is brought back from the dead, and, as he had

<hr />

[1] D.S., p. 66. We content ourselves here, as in what follows, with an account of the broad outlines of Lagarde's dialectics: to determine or even to discuss their theological and scientific value, would call for an expert knowledge of the history of religions, and of oriental and biblical philology, to which we do not pretend.

manifested an infinite power, his death must have been voluntary, a willing sacrifice, a deliberate prelude to the ascension.

This is how, in brief, Lagarde sees the transition from the religion preached by Jesus to the religion of Christ, from the Gospel to Christianity. The substance of his case Lagarde takes from Lessing's short work *Die Religion Christi* (1780); he develops and illustrates it. As for his conclusions or his method, it would be easy to trace them back, in large measure, to L. Feuerbach, D. F. Strauss, and E. Renan. Without going so far as to be an atheist or a materialist, Lagarde comes to the conclusion that Jesus was not the incarnate Son of God but an outstanding religious teacher, an initiate, and greatly inspired. His admiration and respect for the person and precepts of Jesus obviously do not amount to Christian faith and do not entitle him to take cover in liberalism, which he elsewhere treat with contempt.

Throughout the ages, under a variety of influences these primitive Christian beliefs and dogmas took shape, multiplied, and hardened. The main architect of this dogmatic edifice, which was gradually erected, was, according to Lagarde, St Paul.

St Paul, more than anyone else, is responsible for the bowdlerisation of the Gospel of Jesus into Christianity. St Paul, who never knew Jesus and who saw little of those who did know him, is a Jew and a Pharisee by origin:[1] he has all the pride of his nation, looks upon the outstanding dates in his people's history as landmarks in the salvation of the world, likes exegetical and philosophical sophistry, is not afraid to introduce an idea surreptitiously only to unearth it later, and is obsessed by the talmudic conceptions of law, sin, and sacrifice, which the humble contemporaries of Jesus, who loved him and were loved by him, did not know.

St Paul must also be held largely responsible for another and still more far-reaching alteration in the Gospel. Dogma, which for Lagarde is primarily a conceptual and intellectual transcription of religious experience, tends to become an essential feature of Christian life, although the teaching of Jesus is only the expression of a religious experience. The spontaneous urge that transports the believer towards God with all the ardour of his soul is in danger of being hampered, perhaps even inhibited, by it. When it has passed through this sieve, it is no longer the pure expression of the believer's soul. The danger is all the graver because dogma claims to be universal and unchangeable; even if it has to undergo a subsequent evolution before it is complete, it refuses to admit such a transformation. How,

---

[1] This is one of many inconsistencies to be found in Lagarde; that he should deny that Paul is no longer Saul, while at the same time admitting, as we shall see, the idea of a second birth for individuals and races, and judging them according to their effort directed towards this conversion.

then, can a religion, which has been dogmatised in this way—to say nothing of the strong element of Judaism that has been inherent in these dogmas since the time of St Paul—make any powerful appeal to German hearts? Surely it is clear that nothing of this kind will happen, if, instead of adopting Christianity, people are content with the Gospel of Jesus, the only religion that was really his, a living personal relationship with the God of life.

It is significant that Christianity should lay down and impose as a fundamental belief and dogma a relationship with a historical personality—who is therefore mortal—and with his death. In other words, according to Lagarde it establishes, as obligatory, the fetishist cult of a man, who rejected it, and of an event, which marks the end of his existence. Christianity achieves the paradoxical result that he, in whom the fullness and eternity of life in and through God are manifest, becomes the source and centre of a religion which brings all life to an end on the day of his death on the cross.[1] Can one regard a life turned constantly towards a certain event in the past as anything but a form of lethargy or even of death? What sort of mind is it that allows itself to be harnessed to certain events, ignoring the simple truth that what is of value in any event is the element of eternal energy and external life that produces it? There is something in this contemplation of a death and this meditation over a date that must appeal to certain sentimental pietists, but it has no appeal for Lagarde, who regards Christianity, or at least his interpretation of it, as a gross and sinful perversion of the true teaching and the true life of Jesus.

This criticism of the substance of Christianity is, of course, accompanied by a criticism of the Christian conception of the Church. It comes as no surprise to find Lagarde going out of his way to show and condemn how much Christianity borrowed structurally from the Jewish priesthood.[2] One suspects that Lagarde's purpose is to deplore the fact that the ancient Germans did not make a stronger impression. But he also has in mind the gulf that separates this hierarchised and hieratical edifice from the community that gathered round Jesus and later round the apostles to do works of charity and form a mourning fraternity. So the Church, for Lagarde, cannot be regarded as a divine institution: it is the psychological and sociological outcome of the magnetism of a strong and beautiful personality: Schleiermacher would have agreed. Then why did it not vary in conception and constitution from nation to nation and from age

---

[1] It is not impossible that if Lagarde, instead of tying together Good Friday and Easter Sunday, the death and resurrection of Jesus, puts the main accent on the crucifixion, we have here a relic of his pietist childhood. But it may be that this sort of wilful forgetting of the resurrection is the defiance of a savant in the face of the supernatural; only the second birth is a moral conception.

[2] He exposes Greco-oriental, African, Celtic, and, above all, Roman influences.

to age, instead of adhering, as if to an ideal, to one rigid type that dates back to the distant Orient?

Although Lagarde, in his rejection of Christianity, seems to have Roman Catholicism most in mind, his criticisms have nothing in common with the efforts and aims of the Reformation, for the Reformation never for one moment believed that Jesus was not the Christ, whereas there is not the slightest trace of this faith in Jesus Christ in Lagarde.

For him, Jesus remains simply one of several religious geniuses. At certain moments in certain circumstances, sometimes in agreement, sometimes in disagreement with one or another, he has a sudden, blinding awareness that 'the idea of humanity is an immediate thought of the Creator'.[1] Just as his own life revolved round this experience, so he wanted to imbue the lives of his fellow-men with this sense of the divinity and eternity of life, with its power and its beauty.

If he is a redeemer, it is not in the sense in which Christianity understands it. Not that men are by any means perfect: but, to begin with, no one can take upon himself the faults of others, and it is up to each one of us to fight a constant moral struggle against the evil that is in him and around him, and finally—most important of all—our sinfulness is not irredeemable: each of us can, and must, be born a second time.

If Jesus is a redeemer, then only in so far as he called upon men to be born a second time; in his preaching and in his life he set them an example of this conversion, whereby we break the bonds laid upon us by our first birth and by nature and rise above our original imperfection. Through this second birth, which is within the power of any person who looks to God and is strong, each one is in touch with God and sets out to realise the image of the divine element within him; far from allowing the image to fade, he wants to establish it.

In this struggle to become what we are, we find in Jesus the succour that every superior and exemplary being offers to those willing to follow him, but nothing more and nothing less. So Lagarde has in mind not the Christian presence of the Holy Spirit, but only the renewed strength that comes from communion with heroes or saints, who have devoted themselves, with all their hearts and in all their deeds, to living up to their ideal and to spreading it abroad.

Nor does Lagarde envisage a kingdom, which would be, in his own words, some kind of synagogue-state or would lie in some other world. His community is here on earth, a human community, whose members have realised the need for rising above the present and living above it, and who will then make others aware of this new existence that is always divinely inspired, will exercise a regenerating

[1] *D.S.*, p. 274.

influence on their nation and on history and finally mould them to God's wishes.

Whatever may be said about the validity of these interpretations, Lagarde does not intend them to detract in any way from the value of what he regards as the authentic teaching of Jesus, and he is unshaken in his confidence that the Gospel contains the eternal law of spiritual life.[1]

This confession, however, which is noticeably vague, is not a return to the earlier criticisms of Christianity. It does not amount to a modification of them, but it does imply a measure of attenuation: Christianity is merely the Gospel as proclaimed by men who, like each of us, are subject to conditions and resolutions which give rise, in fact, either involuntarily or intentionally, to limitations and distortions. In so far as Christianity, despite this relativity, is still in keeping with the true message of Jesus, Lagarde feels bound to state that 'we have not the right to lag behind it'; but, where this relativity is tainted with infidelity, he feels bound to add that 'we have the right to move ahead of Christianity'.[2]

This is what Lagarde aims to do, in order to rouse the German nation from its lethargy, when he proclaims the true religion of life.

'My longing for eternal life I explain, by my enjoyment of this life.'[3]

Lagarde distinguishes[4] between two types of religion: the religions of primitive times, which are the result of a collective effort by entire peoples, and the religions of the historical era, which, if not actually created, were at least occasioned by certain individuals known to us by name. But this distinction, which would involve the admission that there is a kind of religious function inherent in the *Volksgeist* at a certain stage in its mysterious existence, was modified by Lagarde almost as soon as he had formulated it: the so-called primitive peoples, he declared, had reached 'a much higher level than a society of heroes in our time'. Leaving aside for the moment the question of the relationship of these heroes with their people, I think it is not misrepresenting Lagarde to say that, for him, every religion is rooted in some experience by an individual consciousness, that of a prophet or of a disciple.

The word 'experience', in this context, must be given something of the mystical significance of the German noun *Erlebnis* or the English verb *to experience*. It describes a condition of the soul, a certain feeling; one is moved to the very depths of one's being and, from that moment, launched on a new and unsuspected path. The quality and content of this moment and this movement cannot be described or

---

[1] *D.S.*, p. 69.
[3] P. de Lagarde: *Über einige Berliner Theológen.*
[2] op. cit., note 11, p. 152.
[4] *D.S.*, p. 256.

analysed in precise terms; but Lagarde attempts to evoke them in a
page which is worth quoting:

'There are moments in the life of every man, when he becomes
aware of a plan that runs through his entire existence, a plan that
he himself has not drafted, that he himself does not execute, yet
the idea of it delights him as much as if he had conceived it himself
and the execution of it seems to him a very great blessing and encouragement, although his hands are not engaged in it. He is as
free as the chess-player is free to make each move; yet he is not his
own master, just as the chess-player is subject to the constraint
of a superior opponent; he realises that the game will not end with
a checkmate for him but that, in defeat, it will bring victory. As
the end approaches, he becomes more and more impatient to
taste the joy of that unshakeable will which compels the free man
to go where supreme freedom awaits him: given this supreme
freedom, his innermost being can manifest itself and find unlimited
expression. The scalpel hurts as it cuts into the sensitive block and
finds the god; but as the steel penetrates, the marble grows calm,
feeling joy in this spiritual form that is being conceived of nature.
As a bird, at night, when its dreams are shot by the first gleams
of a new day, utters in its sleep a few joyous, plaintive cries towards
the warm light, then, head under wing, continues sleeping, so,
in the same way, man in his earthly life sometimes feels a presentiment of the joys of eternity and the delight that wells up unconsciously in his heart speaks more convincingly for this eternity than
the long silence, which he only breaks with great difficulty, speaks
against life on earth. Yet the true proof of the eternity of the soul
lies not in presentiments but in the plan that appears in the life of
every man who is advancing along the path of goodness.
'To recognise this plan, to reflect upon it and devote oneself to
its realisation, that is piety and the guarantee of eternal life. All
else, even the Church and the sacraments, is merely a means towards the execution of this plan made by God with individual
souls, a means whereby knowledge of it may become both possible
and easier. . . . What awaits souls educated by life is the secret
of God: even after death there is a life, and eternity lasts a long
time.'[1]

The clumsy lyricism of this passage leaves no room for doubt that
the author himself had a similar experience. It is not surprising in a
man who, whatever one may say, had acquired at least one thing
from pietism: a deep sensibility and a profound confidence in
emotional impulses. But it is surprising in a theologian from whom
one might expect a more precise and profound dogmatic approach;
Lagarde, however, is not so much a theologian as a religious historian, and his primary aim is to determine, by means of historical

[1] *D.S.*, p. 272.

and psychological comparisons, the basic element of religion, and then to apply his conclusions to his own people.

This basic element, as we are beginning to realise, does not lie in any intellectual acceptance of theological principles or of an event represented as sufficient in itself; these are at best merely a preparation for an experience or an emotion which affects our entire being, filling it with an obscure but irresistible urge. Till this experience occurs, we feel a sort of disquiet, even anguish; our fragile, fugitive existence seems meaningless and aimless; we are plunged in darkness. But suddenly some kind of light appears; we feel caught up in a plan that is beyond our control; we are no longer mere straws tossed hither and thither without any real *raison d'être*. This clear, irrefutable conviction of dependence and integration puts an end to our solitude; it also gives us the freedom of the children of God; it both binds and liberates us; we are no longer victims of the world around us but, through knowing and recognising a superior order of things, we have become masters of all things in and through God.

This birth, like every birth, is painful: the mediocrity of a vegetative, materialist existence is not without its charm; habit has its appeal and facility its power. But it is a euphoria that precedes and heralds death. One cannot live unless one breaks with this slavery, for only by making such a break do we become conscious of our own personality, or, as Fichte put it, of the destination allotted to us in God's plan. When we are fully what we are called upon to be, we are free.

So the organic quality that is characteristic of Lagarde's political thought reappears in his religious thought. Whether he is dealing with a political or a religious subject, it is through being integrated in a living whole that his individual finds fulfilment. As Schleiermacher, one of the few theologians who finds any favour with Lagarde, had already asserted, the religious experience is one of intensification of life through dependence.

Dependence on whom? On God. But on what God? This is the crucial question in Lagarde's theology as in any theology based on feeling: the religious person, with all the delight and exaltation he feels, does not seek knowledge beyond this experience, which raises him above his limited condition to an eternal life. When feeling is all, the remainder counts for little, so to speak. So let us not demand of Lagarde any precise definition of his God; let us content ourselves with what light we can gather from comparisons and differences.

His God is obviously not the divinity who is manifest to the Christian in the Old Testament and whose incarnation is Jesus Christ: this God is too entirely remote as is evident from the fact that he could only become known through an incarnation. A being who bears no essential relation to humanity and lives in a state of transcendence, which he alone can end, cannot be of any conceivable interest to men. If they must strive to rise above themselves there is no need for self-abnegation. This comes as no surprise if one remembers that Lagarde rejects the idea of original sin and if one recalls that he is, by character, inclined to attach more importance to an effort of will than to the grace of love through which transcendence becomes immanent.

Although he described himself as having the soul of a pantheist, and although in his prose writings and his poems there are traces of naturalism, Lagarde does not teach naturalistic immanentism:[1] his moral idealism will not allow him to believe that God is to be found in the diffusion of elementary cosmic forces.

But this does not mean that he is entirely free of pantheism. To qualify God he frequently makes use of rather vague terms like Father and Creator. It is impossible to establish whether these attributes imply that God is for him a personal God. But they do imply that God is the source of life and guides its evolution. So one could speak of a pantheism which is not only vitalist but historical: God makes and controls history, he is present in it and, though he may not be immanent in it, it does, on the other hand, represent a revelation of his power.

The divinity is either eternally forbidden to us or escapes us in our present condition, and therefore cannot dwell in us. There we must leave dogmatic definitions and theological speculations. We must recognise God in our own religious experiences or in those of religious geniuses, in the great moments of individual life that are each man's only authentic history, just as, applied to humanity, they are the only dates that count in its history. What matters is not a knowledge of theology but experience of God, religion.

'Religion is born wherever human hearts are capable of catching a glimpse of God's life. God is not revealed, but our eyes are dazzled by a glimpse of his existence, and it is so because men are facing in the very direction in which it can be seen. The world and history are a source of joy to the pious man, because he perceives in both something that is neither world nor history.'[2]

So we feel God 'above us, besides us and in us';[3] he is not some miraculous past, but a presence, an ever-present being whose whole power is in most intimate contact with us, giving us the strength and peace that come from the certainty of a living purpose.

We experience a reality which is beyond and above us, and of

---

[1] Although Spinoza certainly does not profess a natural pantheism, we should note that, in spite of his anti-Semitism, Lagarde respects the author of the *Ethics*, possibly because he was excommunicated by his co-religionists.
[2] *D.S.*, p. 182.   [3] *A.S.*, p. 58.

which we know nothing more. Although we lack any criterion by which this feeling can be verified and authenticated, it is not, for that reason, a case of auto-suggestion, for, once a man has had this experience, he is a different being. Far from being content with a sterile, perennial revival of this emotion, piety demands that the force engendered through and in this communion should be employed; the ardour of one's faith stimulates action.

'Religion is to be found wherever superhuman powers, indeed wherever extra-human powers, exert an influence on the hearts of men, where real powers exert a real influence, that is, an influence which produces in the person affected thoughts and actions that he would never otherwise have thought or committed.'[1]

The fruit proves the reality of the tree just as conclusively as it proves its value, and, if only because of the will to act that it engenders, Lagarde's conception of religious truth is distinctly pragmatic; it is by the life it develops in individuals or in peoples that the truth and value of religion must be measured. Once more pragmatism is combined with relativism.

After this experience, this second birth, the pious man is faced with an inner conflict that is the real act of worship. Lagarde does not underrate the importance of ceremonial, ritual, and liturgy as a means whereby a community can find unanimous expression. But, just as he gave an interpretation of the Catholic sacraments which was almost entirely based on their efficacy here on earth, so he believes in only one true worship of God, that which gives concrete evidence of faith in life, which facilitates the development of life and makes it more beautiful and less difficult for others. Divine worship is not only a cult but also a cultivation of life, a service to one's neighbour by helping him to know, in soul and in body, the fulness and splendour of life. Every human existence can, from then on, assume the significance of a cult.[2]

Moral action therefore takes precedence over contemplation, which runs the risk of becoming a form of escape from the world, which, far from being destroyed, must be given life, far from being despised, must be converted, in order that it may model itself on the image we have acquired of present and future eternity. A constant effort of will must be made; it is not enough to abandon oneself to some pious emotion once a week or on particular occasions. It is Martha, rather than Mary, who, in Lagarde's view, leads the exemplary religious life.

This positive, worldly work in the service of God implies an incessant conflict not only with oneself but still more with the greater part of the human race. The prophet must force it, in spite of itself,

[1] *D.S.*, p. 80.   [2] ibid., p. 420.

out of its mediocrity and its nonchalance. Lagarde made a close
study of the history of the *nabi* of Israel and himself knew too well
the hostility that must inevitably come to anyone who, after his second
birth, attempts to induce his contemporaries to follow him, to believe
that victory would come either quickly or easily.[1] But communion
with the power of the eternal life-force keeps his eyes turned towards
the future and makes present difficulties seem insignificant; he is
too actively involved in eternity to doubt or to pause; the very impulse of life and the ideal makes it impossible for him to abandon
the struggle. In fact, such resistance as he meets with is salutary,
because it strengthens and deepens his faith, and, in the ethic-religious
sphere as in others, good is not given but conquered.[2]

So the prophet, by virtue of his religious experience and his will,
is a man apart. Prophetic activity is inconceivable without individualism. 'The source of historical progress is the individual,'
states Lagarde clearly,[3] and adds:

> 'Man can commit only one sin, not to be himself, for, by not
> being himself, he rebels against him who willed his existence and
> who willed it on a predetermined pattern; it is not the existence
> born of the flesh we are concerned with, but the existence that
> begins with the second birth, that has become ethical; we are
> concerned with the sacrament which every man must be when,
> spirit and body indissolubly united, he makes his pilgrimage
> through the world.'[4]

But these assertions, which have an unmistakable ring of individualism, do not mean that the individual, however strong he
may have to be in his divinely-willed originality, can or must retire
into himself.

The very diversity of elements that make up the community in
which he lives is a challenge to the religious man to find inspiration
in some and to rise above others: 'The ideal is a product of an immediate vision and cannot therefore emerge from solitude.'[5] Moreover,
God's intention with regard to an inspired person is of immediate
concern to him as an individual, but also as a member of a community which has a destination of its own in God's Kingdom on
earth. If the religious genius knows the tribulation of solitude or
persecution, it is chiefly because he is more cruelly alive than most to
this double aim that binds individuality and community.

The power of an individual lies, to a large extent, in his more
penetrating comprehension and more exacting appreciation of the
task confronting his community; the spirit of the community—
Lagarde, on the basis of his Old Testament studies claims that it is
the Holy Spirit—becomes in this way the foundation of individual

[1] *D.S.*, pp. 258 seq.   [2] ibid., p. 280.   [3] ibid., p. 138.
[4] ibid., p. 423.   [5] ibid., p. 252.

genius, whose function it is to reveal it to his fellow-men in his divine being and energy.

Individual religion and the religion of a national community are therefore inseparable, bound together by a mutual determination.

'It is clear that peoples play the greatest part in the formation of particular religions, for, on every occasion, the founder of a religion . . . is far from being a mere monad, who had not yet existed and who is flung from heaven upon earth, but he too has grown up among the people and in the age for which he works; his work consists, on the one hand, in taking an active part in the life of vital elements scattered about him, and, on the other hand, in recognising and removing the germs of death, the putrefying, fossilising formations in the world about him which fill it with instinctive hate.'[1]

'Thus each conscious mind acquires its determination from its relationship to the moral conceptions of a community.'[2]

People, surroundings, environment, time: these words in themselves make it clear that the community concerned is not the shapeless human community, but one that is determined and distinct in the human sphere, in other words, a nation; so the ideal to be attained and served is not a universal but a national one.

For Lagarde, a nation is not characterised essentially by its language or race, by political or geographical conditions; it is a physical entity, but one that is alive only because it is animated by a soul, and it is this soul that makes a nation. Like every soul, the soul of a nation can only be the will and gift of God.

'Nations are born not by a physical process but of historical events; historical events are subject to the government of Providence, which maps out their course and aims; that is why nations are divine institutions, divine creations. If this is the case, if they come into existence neither in the regular course of nature nor by accident, then their creator created them with a purpose and this purpose is their vital principle; to recognise this purpose means to recognise the divine will that wishes this purpose to be fulfilled; neither the life of a nation nor a nation is conceivable without this recognition. To recognise anew and always the mission of a nation is to plunge it into the fountain of eternal youth; to be always engaged in this mission is to achieve higher things and, with them, a higher life.'[3]

In so far, therefore, as a man works to promote the individualised personality of a nation—in other words, the image God has made of it and offers it as its goal—he not only enriches himself with everything this collective soul comprises that is not present in his own, but he

[1] *D.S.*, p. 256.   [2] ibid., p. 48.   [3] ibid., p. 79.

fulfils a strictly religious duty: in effect, therefore, he obeys a divine commandment and strengthens the bonds between himself and his nation on the one hand and God on the other.

Before Lagarde's time, Herder and, to go no farther back, the romantics, Fichte and Arndt had suggested or developed this religious conception of the nation and of one's duties towards it, but, like them, Lagarde cannot explain how the individualised personality of a nation, its divinely-inspired *Ethos*, is known; one must allow him a sort of illumination by the spirit of the nation, and we can now understand better why Lagarde should consider this spirit, which creates and animates a community established by God, the Holy Spirit.

Like his predecessors again, Lagarde, when he speaks of a nation, is not thinking of it in present, concrete terms; he is thinking of the ideal reality of a nation, of the nation as God sees it and wills it, and of a destiny that is not only indefinite but infinite. 'This German national religion,' says Lagarde,[1] 'corresponds to the essence, willed by God, of the German nation, but not to the manifestation of that essence as it appears at a particular period . . .; it never corresponds, therefore, to the spirit of the time but is in opposition to this spirit.' This image of a nation which God carries in himself is, for men, a myth. But a myth is never fully realised, if only because, in form and in content, it is inevitably vague and mobile. A religion based on a myth can, in consequence, only be a religion of the future.[2]

The individual members of a nation can only become what they are destined to be if they become conscious of this myth and use it for their own advantage and that of those around them. In this way all of them, each one independently, achieve what one might call, by a misuse of Christian terminology, a communion with the same species. Spiritual bonds grow up among them which have all the strength of a common will and give their community its unanimity. This unanimity cannot fail to influence the concrete existence of their nation; it is continually fed by one single force, full and undiminished, which will inevitably and incessantly be abreast of the times.

Incessantly. This raises a particularly serious question. This spiritual force, with all its inexhaustible energy, tends to give body to a myth which is not circumscribed or limited by any clear-cut feature. During its growth, this body will, sooner or later, clash with other bodies which also claim to give life to a myth that is, for its particular adherents, divinely inspired. What is to prevent this clash from becoming a conflict or even a war? Unless one or other of these

---

[1] *D.S.*, p. 113.
[2] *Die Religion der Zukunft* (1878) is the title of Lagarde's work which contains the essence of his religious thought.

two myths is prepared to deny its divine origin and the commandments it implies, neither can admit that it is inferior to the other or be
otherwise than imperialist and hegemonist. So material force will
have to decide between these two wills to power, both equally
founded in God. This material force may derive part of its power
from the spiritual energy of those applying and wielding it; but, one
must agree, it does not imply any lack of faith in the ideal if one considers that part reduced and, even if one cannot agree to this, if one
thinks that material defeat is not synonymous with moral defeat, the
fact still remains that a conflict has arisen which the spiritual force
of the ideal was not strong enough to prevent or to settle. It appears
therefore, to say the least of it, that national religion leads to
divisions.

In order to avoid such schisms and conflicts, Lagarde, who,
though not opposed in principle to war, is no warmonger, preaches a
polyphonic conception of humanity. Each nation must naturally
pursue its own particular myth with all the power of its Ethos and
must strive to realise it as fully as possible, but it must not reach out
towards some common universal ideal established by deduction on
the basis of particular national characteristics. The more each
nation perseveres in this way in its own being, the more varied and
rich the world becomes; this would not be the case if each nation
sought to model itself on one and the same image, however perfect
it might be.

'Any particular nation is superior to humanity and each particular member of a nation is more—one might even say, must be
more—than merely national, more than what, as such, each com-
patriot is; in nationality a very precious x is added to humanity,
and in individuality a still more precious y is added to this x;
humanity, nationality, tribal identity, family character and individuality form a pyramid, the peak of which is nearer to heaven
than the base.'[1]

And yet, however reassuring and attractive such variety may seem,
however fascinating this 'systematised anarchy'[2] may be, it is difficult to see what higher, if not supreme instance will systematise it
and will prevent the emulation it may produce from becoming open
conflict. 'When the rose adorns herself, she also adorns the garden,'
Lagarde once wrote to his wife: true, but, apart from the fact that
comparison is no argument, there are other things besides roses, plants
that are too luxuriant and can only grow by thrusting other plants
into the shade or suffocating them.

Conceiving the universal by composition instead of by abstraction,
stressing what distinguishes and not what unites inevitably leads one

[1] *D.S.*, p. 164. [2] ibid., p. 423.

into a blind alley. An organically inclined thought can avoid it to
some extent in questions of internal policy, because the state can exercise arbitrary and authoritative power; it is even conceivable that
various states might agree to their international relations being
governed by international laws and an international court. But in
things of the spirit and the soul, as Lagarde envisages them, such a
superior univeral authority seems to be unavoidably absent.

But, one might object, there is God, to whose will the various
nations are subject. Would it not be more correct to say that, for
Lagarde, there are gods? His pietist upbringing from which, it is as
well to remember, he acquired the habit of attaching more value to
the intimate sense of the immediate presence of God than to a dogmatic knowledge of him, his study of religious history, which brought
home to him the great diversity of beliefs and theologies, led Lagarde
not to deny the transcendence and absoluteness of God in themselves
but to think, on the whole, and to act as if they were not tenable, since
they are not disclosed to all men in a single, complete revelation.
From then on, there are only reflections of God through the prism of
the ages and the individual national temperaments.

The religious experience may gain in fervour thereby, for God is
brought closer. On the other hand the unity of God is shattered,
his absoluteness becomes relativised in a multiplicity of different
manifestations, which are in no way comparable to genuine revelations. 'The arrogant belief that children of God could not have lived
as well on the Ganges as on the Hwang-Ho, the Kherka or the Amur
revolts me,' Lagarde states.[1] But, though one cannot and must not
deny that the peoples on these distant shores have been and are children of God and that they have worshipped and still worship God in
complete sincerity and to the best of their knowledge of Him, it still
remains to be seen whether their worship is in accordance with his
truth and his Spirit. The love of the Creator goes out to all his
creatures, but that does not imply that all forms of worship have
equal validity. Lagarde, in his pragmatism, confuses life with truth
and places a rather slipshod interpretation on the assurance that in
the Father's house there are many mansions.

To safeguard to some small extent the unity and singleness of God,
Lagarde has recourse, once again, to the notion of composition. For
to him 'it is clear that the human species will take cognisance of
different aspects of the ideal, depending upon what functions are
imposed on it; in the prehistoric era they are different from the
historic era, different in Rome from in Germany. The result is,
undoubtedly, a plurality of religions, which can only become a unity
in the course of history; men will recognise that, apart from their
own mode of life, there are also many other modes of life, which are

[1] *D.S.*, p. 252.

just as justified and must be studied. True monotheism, born merely of negation and rationality, as, for example, that of modern Judaism and modern culture, is idolatry'.[1] If one remembers what a nation's religion means to it at every stage of its evolution, and if one remembers further that, for Lagarde, who keeps returning to this point,[2] a religion is inevitably regarded as exclusive truth, and is therefore essentially intolerant and aggressive, then it is difficult to see how this passage can ever be put into effect, how multiplicity can ever be converted into unity, the gods into God.

Every nation will maintain not only that its religion is the only true one, but that its god is the only god. We have then something more than just a religious or ecclesiastical pluralism, which, in the last resort, does not necessarily threaten the unity of God; we have, in fact, polytheism. We are certainly not confronted with such a pullulation of divinities as emerged in primitive mythology;[3] but the fact remains that there will be no single, eternal truth or absolute to guide us in our thoughts and actions. This is not altogether surprising, for, in Lagarde's view, 'religion does not aim to give truth'.[4]

It is, in these circumstances, almost miraculous that Lagarde, as we have seen, should still look upon religion, whether of individuals or of nations, as a sense of being caught up in a predetermined and controlled universal evolution. God speaks and acts in history, but it is very much to be feared that, in Lagarde's conception, each man will interpret these words and actions in his own way or according to his own specific needs, unless he can be given some immutable criterion, which allows him to distinguish between events inspired by God and those that are man-made. Lagarde is agreed on one thing, that God is the master of history. And yet he allows God to become involved in history and engulfed by it. For, although Lagarde does not admit it, transcendence, in his doctrine, does not stand up to the buffetings and fluctuations of immanence. In Hegelian monism, historical pantheism still gives history a meaning; in Lagarde, no such possibility exists. Life, which is divine by virtue of its origin in God and which remains divine so long as it remains faithful to its creator's intentions, is in danger of being regarded as divine in itself. Lagarde, who is a religious historian rather than a theologian, whatever he may say, for he is more concerned with the subject, than with the object of religion, although it is in the latter that its sole value lies—

[1] D.S., p. 252.
[2] ibid., pp. 88, 318, 366, 438, where the criticism and rejection of liberalism and of indiscriminate universalism reappears.
[3] Thus Lagarde never contemplates a return, on the lines of Deutsche Glaubensbewegung, to the Germanic Deities, if only because this mythology is historically exhausted, and consequently worthless.
[4] Cf. F. Krog, Lagarde und der deutsche Staat (Munich, 1930), pp. 15 seq. D.S., pp. 81 seq.

Lagarde allows the changing diversity of life to gain the ascendancy over the eternal unity of truth; existence triumphs over essence.

Religion thus becomes an instrument of human ends, whereas, by accepting the divine yoke, it should give men the freedom of the children of God, which alone is glorious and eternal; as, in spite of its pretensions, it establishes no link of any kind with the eternal, it cannot bring true freedom. The national religion which Lagarde proposes to establish, without pausing to consider the latent contradiction between the noun and the adjective, only creates a link with the god engendered by the nation. Each nation will produce its own; the result, to say the least, will be disorder. No judgment based either on right or on grace will be possible, and where there is neither judgment nor judge, there is neither true order nor true freedom.

The idea which this religion puts before the nation is its own existence and the intensification of it; it is an ideal rooted in the moral and physical vitality of the nation. Religion, in fact, is merely one form of the will to power. It enlists the energy of every individual in blind obedience to this will; it welds that energy into a solid mass by giving it work to do which is allegedly willed by God, and it appeals to something, in individuals as well as in communities, that is least capable of discernment, the vague and elementary life-instinct both of conservation and of aggression.

It may be that the sad state of his nation and his own determination to remedy this situation made it impossible for Lagarde to realise the full implications and consequences of his conception of religion; it may be that he was so sensitive to the impulses of national instinct that he paid too little attention to clarity of exposition—in this sphere, at least—and that he allowed his preoccupation with the impending struggle to cloud his idealism and his reflection. But that is not important. Once more he gives the nation not only a divine mission—that is inherent in everything that is called into existence— but a divine value: the absolute that once was God is now the nation.

Normally therefore the national community will be the true Church, an assembly of those who from birth are conscious of their people's origin and mission, who share the same feelings and the same thoughts, and who therefore see their salvation in the realisation of the people's aims. Taking an active part in the life of the nation means leading the religious life par excellence, for it is the fruition of that eternity, of which the people is both the instrument and the repository. As the Nation-Church is militant,[1] it clearly cannot will anything but victory.

[1] Here we deliberately avoid the term 'National Church'. By the uncouth compound 'Nation-Church', we mean that by national religion the whole nation will be transformed into a Church in the accepted sense of the word, this being the only

But this victory, which every religion promises its adherents, does not in this case consist in rising to a purer form of humanity, inspired and guided by an absolute ideal; it means stabilisation, the sanctification of national habits and customs,[1] of the individual institutions and the appetites of the nation. The second birth will be not so much a transformation of the essential nature of the nation as a more penetrating and more intense awareness of that nature. The sapling, which has been neither grafted nor pruned, will perhaps grow to be more luxuriant and more sturdy: it remains to be seen whether it will bear better fruit, whether its trunk will be more upright, its stature greater.

'The Germanic peoples must correlate their religion and their nationality.' [2]

It is with his own nation constantly in mind that Lagarde develops the conception of religion we have just analysed and it is the salvation of his people that he hopes to achieve by it. So we have the right to deplore the fact that, after having criticised with an impulsive vehemence that frequently amounts to a complete condemnation of the present, and after having praised the forces of regeneration with an ardent faith that rises to a prophetic fervour, he should finally present an image of the new Germany that is little more than a mere vision. We have had occasion to notice here and there a rather less vague note, which, moreover, was frequently introduced

---

institution in which the nation will be able to satisfy its religious needs in the future; outside it, there is no salvation.

Without wishing to use a hackneyed expression, we would also point out that, for Lagarde, the question of national Churches does not arise; the question that is of Churches, which either for dogmatic or disciplinary reasons, have separated from a Church, which is universalist either in its hierarchy, or spiritual claims. All churches, for Lagarde, are essentially national, and we know that he rejects the idea of a true universalism, and that all reference to a normative oecumenicism is banished from his thought. If, to take another case, Herder, with whom Lagarde has much in common, although he never acknowledged it, declares himself, in *Adrastea* opposed to national Churches, it is simply because there survives in him a humanist and altogether Christian universalism such as cannot be found in the *Deutsche Schriften*.

We would add that it is not possible to regard Lagarde as a forerunner of the *deutsche Christen*. More honest than they, he did, in fact, break with Christianity. As for his pretence that he was clinging to the teaching of Jesus alone, without being willing to commit himself as to whether this could be discovered in the New Testament, we have some doubt whether this pretended pure Gospel may not be mutilated and perverted in his work. 'Paul de Lagarde', writes Ch. Andler (*La Jeunesse de Nietzsche*, Paris, 1921, p. 360), 'is a pioneer of that courageous school of free-thinkers who aim at reaching the Christian life through an extreme scepticism towards tradition.' Is it in fact only towards tradition that this liberty and scepticism is manifested?

[1] It would be easy to show that with Lagarde, as with Hegel, there exists between *Sitte* and *Sittlichkeit* more than an etymological affinity.

[2] P. de Lagarde: *Die Religion der Zukunft*.

only by way of contrast. But, in general, our search for signs of lucidity is in vain.

This is particularly true of the German national religion. We would like to know what are the characteristic features of the Germans' authentic nature, to which they are to return and in which they are then to persevere; we would like to know the divine image, of which they are to become conscious, and the myth, which will inspire them to vitalise their nation. In fact, however, we only learn that all this is the opposite of what nineteenth-century Germany has to offer.

But in our search we have forgotten that national religion and genius are not, in principle, human in origin. In other words, we can no more define them than we can produce them;[1] we can only remove the obstacles of habit and of false or outdated conceptions and prepare men's souls to hear and listen to the call of God.

Now, the tenor of this appeal, which, because of its origin alone, is difficult if not impossible to formulate, varies, for one and the same nation, in the course of history according to the unfathomable intentions of God. There is, of course, a certain continuity in evolution, but not sufficient to enable us to deduce the future accurately from the past and the present. And it is the future that really counts, for the ideal is always inextricably bound up with the future. To specify, at any given moment, what are the essence and religion of the German nation implies, on the one hand, a pretension to be able to fathom and foresee the plans of God and so to determine them, and, on the other hand, a risk that the German nation might regard this image as final, cling to it, and so take no further active part in life. We have seen that one must not be content with the life and death of Jesus; similarly, one must not immobilise Germany in one specific aspect of her nationality. The religion of which Lagarde is the prophet is not a religion of the past—although it contains some salutary precedents—nor is it a religion of the present—although it urges a constant incarnation of the ideal—but, unmistakably, a religion of the future.

All that Lagarde can tell his compatriots in particular is that, as they are born into the new life, they must remain faithful to it, or, in other words, must adopt an attitude of constant, confident preparedness for life. Without this submission to its inspiration, there can be no evolution and no future, either for the individual or for the nation. Life becomes manifest only through its intensification and its acceleration. Just as the divine image that the national religion offers Germany has no clear outlines, so this movement, which seems boundless, can know no end. So once more the German nation is allotted the goal and characteristic of being the nation of infinite desire and

[1] *D.S.*, p. 268.

progression; her own religious duty is to reveal through her history
the eternal fertility of life and its metamorphoses.

But while, in the past, this eternal quest for infinite being had
often brought this nation to a state of concrete impotence, all that
will change from now on: the national state, strong in the unity and
the religious fervour of a unanimous nation, will leave imprinted on
the earth those forms of the development of the idea, which the
nation develops out of its own nationality, and, as it evolves and progresses, it will constantly reaffirm, in terms of the present, its own
development.

As we have pointed out, Lagarde does not envisage this continued expansion under the pressure of the nation's faith in the future
as something entirely without limits, as far as Germany's territory is
concerned, although, particularly towards the East, he does not lay
down the limits at all clearly, and what might otherwise be no more
than an influence can often become, in a powerful State, a disguised
form of annexation.

While Germany, with a new-born consciousness of her true being,
will, and must, pursue a policy of territorial expansion, she may, if
only out of realism, be able to avoid excesses; but, in the spiritual
sphere, it does not seem to be expected of her that she should observe
a certain moderation, and, even if it were, it seems unlikely that she
would observe it. If, instead of sinking into a drunken sleep after her
recent victories, Germany awakens, she will realise how much she
can expect to gain from a national religion; but this religion was
made known to her before it was made known to any other nation,
and it was a German who first hit upon it. Why should this priority
in the divine plan not give rise to a certain sense of pride? And if,
faithful to her mission or for some other, less noble motive, she proposes to teach the other nations, how could this self-allotted role of
teacher fail to give her a sense of supremacy and hegemony, both *de
jure* and *de facto*? 'The Germans are a peaceful people', says Lagarde solemnly,[1] 'and they are convinced that they have the right to
live according to their own nature, that is, as Germans.' It would
serve no useful purpose to point out how much better it might be to
rise above nationality, without serving one's country any the less,
in order to strive for humanity. But the statement continues: 'and
they are convinced that they have a mission towards all the nations
on earth'. It seems pointless to comment on such a declaration of
faith in the messianic mission of the German nation.

Let us just remember, in conclusion, that the same contradiction
that underlies the whole of Lagarde's work appears once again. As
a student of religious history and psychology he is entitled to talk of
national religions in the sense that religious life assumes different

[1] *D.S.*, p. 449.

forms with every nation and every age. But is he entitled, by the same token, to ignore the fact that, beneath this historical diversity, there is a deeper unity, that of a common spiritual and moral reaching-out towards an absolute, universal and eternal power, towards God? As a result of this oversight, the national religion must degenerate into a religion of the nation and, more restrictively and more precisely, into a religion of the German nation.

In the same way, after he has rightly sensed how faith can vitalise life and guarantee the community of the faithful its unity, Lagarde loses sight of the fact that this fervour, instead of being resolvable into intensity alone, must also include purity, and that this purity depends not on the believer but on the goal towards which he is striving. There are religions of every kind and description, but the fervent and sincere piety of their adherents is no criterion of their value; the value of a religion lies in its God.

So Lagarde's attempt, however fruitful it may have been, either in intention or in achievement, shows once again the mistake and the danger of not distinguishing between psychology and theology, between history and intrinsic value, in short, in forgetting that it is not for man to put himself in God's place; by attempting to raise himself towards God instead of allowing himself to be raised up by God, man, in the end, always sinks into self-idolatry.

4

NIETZSCHE AND NATIONAL-SOCIALISM

Wilhelm Grenzmann

THE military and political disaster of 1945, which deprived the German people of the sovereignty it had usurped and plunged it in ruin, had at least one salutary effect: it gave the nation an opportunity to examine its conscience and turned its thoughts to the spiritual interpretation of the dreadful fate that had struck it down. For this was more than a lost war or the collapse of a criminal régime—in National-Socialism and Fascism an entire philosophy and way of life had been judged and condemned. And the judgment covered more than a few irresponsible ringleaders. This much is true: hundreds of thousands of people abandoned their dreams of power and world-domination only when they saw the political system collapse in ruins about them. For many, it seemed, the hard lesson of events was needed to teach them once again how to distinguish between truth and falsehood, between justice and injustice. Germany's guilt in the eyes of the world was mainly that of her *Führer* and his disciples, but countless others were accomplices, even if, for the most part, unconsciously. In the preceding fifteen years, the entire structure of normal life had been upset. People had been deprived of their freedom, persecuted and dishonoured, executed and massacred, left to die of hunger or privation. A war of unparalleled ferocity had been launched, bringing untold misery and suffering, tyranny and devastation to other countries. A superman had been invented and then made into a demi-god. Crimes had been committed and divine laws invoked to justify them. It is impossible to imagine what more might have happened if National-Socialism had been victorious.

How was all this possible? Such a relapse into barbarism would have been impossible if moral and spiritual values had not already been undermined over a period not of years but of decades. National-Socialism was only the final link in a chain of disastrous events, which originated in the sphere of ideas and theories. We all carry the burden of the past. The poison had been creeping through the organism for a long time. The Germans, of course, were not the only people to be contaminated. If we hope to achieve a spiritual revival in the world; if we want to restore normal human relations on earth, we must trace the malady to its source. And, when we

begin our own investigation, we are bound to search into history.
Values are beginning to change. Historical factors, which once
were thought highly of, are now branded as instruments of decadence. A few prominent figures seem to stand out as having
contributed more than most to the disaster. One of these—and he
takes a very high place—is Friedrich Nietzsche.

No other philosopher in modern German history has claimed so
much attention from those seeking the spiritual origin of National-
Socialism. It is recalled that he loved combat and the aggressive,
acquisitive instincts that go with it. His motto was: will to power.
He was a fervent believer in vitality, recommended the elimination
of the sick and the weak, preached moral abandonment, urged the
extermination of the unfit, and sang the praises of the 'Great Man',
whose outstanding virtues were injustice and violence. His fight
against Christianity, against the idea of humanity, and against democracy is not forgotten, and it is stressed that National-Socialism
has taken over his more resounding pronouncements, some of them
literally. The following are borrowed from Nietzsche's writings and
were actually implemented by the National-Socialists:

> 'What is good? Everything that increases man's sense of power,
> his will to power, power itself. What is bad? Everything that
> derives from weakness . . . the weak and the infirm must perish:
> that is the first principle of *our* charity. And we must even actively
> help them.' [1]

> 'What does living mean?—Living means constantly rejecting
> anything that wishes to die; living means being cruel and ruthless
> towards everything that is weak and old in ourselves, but not only
> in ourselves. So living means being without pity for the dying,
> the destitute and the old? Being constantly a murderer? . . .'

> 'You must love peace as a means toward fresh wars. And a
> short rather than a long peace. . . . You say that a good cause
> justifies even war? I say to you: a good war is one that justifies
> all causes. War and courage have done greater things than love
> of one's neighbour. Up till now it is not pity but bravery that has
> saved men in distress.' [2]

> 'Life is *essentially* acquisition, violation, domination of all that is
> alien and weaker; it is oppression, hardness, regimentation,
> annexation or at least, at its mildest, exploitation . . .' [3]

> The strong men, the masters, '*regain* the pure conscience of a beast
> of prey; monsters filled with joy, they can return from a fearful
> succession of murder, arson, rape and torture with the same joy
> in their hearts, the same contentment in their souls as if they had
> indulged in some students' rag. . . . How can one fail to perceive,
> deep down in all noble races, rapacity, the splendid blond beast

---

[1] *Der Antichrist*, no. 1.
[2] *Also sprach Zarathustra*, Vol. I, 'Vom Krieg und Kriegsvolke'.
[3] *Jenseits von Gut und Böse*, no. 259.

that stalks its prey and prowls in search of victory? From time to time this latent urge must reappear, the animal must emerge and return to the jungle:—Roman, Arab, Germanic and Japanese nobles, Homeric heroes, Scandinavian Vikings—all have the same urge in common.' [1]

'I employ the word "State": it is easy to see what I mean—a band of blond beasts, a race of conquerors and masters organised for war and strong enough to organise in their turn, seizing without qualms in their terrible grip a population that is perhaps enormously superior in numbers but that still lacks cohesion. . . . When a man is capable of commanding, when he is by nature a "Master", when he is violent in act and gesture, of what importance are treaties to him?' [2]

'There exists a *Master Morality* and a *Slave Morality*. . . . Noble men as a species feel they have been called upon to stabilise values; they do not look for approval; they believe: "What harms me is harmful in itself". . . . It is quite otherwise with the *Slave Morality*. Suppose the victims, the oppressed, the slaves, the men who suffer, those who are tired or uncertain of themselves, begin to moralise: What will their moral judgments have in common? . . . Scepticism and mistrust, a *refinement* of mistrust towards everything "good". . . . The morality of the slave is essentially one of utility. Here we have the source of the famous distinction between "good and evil".' [3]

'I hold we must say NO to all that weakens, to all that drains energy. I hold we must say YES to all that strengthens, to all that conserves energy, to all that justifies a feeling of strength. . . . We must give *fate* the place of honour, the fate which says to the weak: Perish.' [4]

'To judge morality properly, it must be replaced by two concepts borrowed from zoology: the *taming* of a beast and the *breeding* of a specific species. . . . Breeding, as I understand it, is an incomparable means of conserving humanity's energy, in such a way that succeeding generations can continue to build on the work of their ancestors. . . . The object of breeding can only be, in each particular case, the birth of a *stronger* man.' [5]

It is with the Jews that the moral revolt of the slaves begins, 'the revolt which has a history of two thousand years behind it and which we have only ceased to be aware of today because it has triumphed'.[6]

Phrases of this kind could be quoted indefinitely. Fifty years later the State is urging its scholars, professors, and writers not only to express such precepts, but also to put them into effect. Nietzsche is freely quoted. Goebbels for instance, takes the phrase from Zarathustra: 'Anything that does not weaken me strengthens me!' and he stigmatises *bourgeois* virtue as 'female morality'.[7] Mussolini

[1] *Zur Genealogie der Moral*, Vol. I, no. 11.   [2] ibid., Vol. II, no. 17.
[3] *Jenseits von Gut und Böse*, no. 260.   [4] *Der Wille zur Macht*, Vol. I.
[5] ibid., Vol. II.   [6] *Zur Genealogie der Moral*, Vol. I, no. 7.
[7] *Der Antichrist*, no. 1.

takes his war-cry *'vivere pericolosamente'* from *Die Fröhliche Wissenschaft*. Hitler sends his friend the Duce a specially printed copy of Nietzsche's works in a de luxe edition, and he himself, while on a visit to the archives at Weimar, is presented with the philosopher's walking-stick by Nietzsche's sister. This precious relic is handed over to him because he is destined to realise Nietzsche's prophecies. Nietzsche, we are told, was the philosopher and even the idol of the Third Reich; [1] there can be no doubt he was responsible, in part, for the horrors of the Hitler era (Flake). It is impossible, in the view of Heinrich Scholz, to pass final judgment on the Third Reich without also calling Nietzsche to account. [2]

These are revealing statements. They express the conviction that Nietzsche's ideas and the actions of National-Socialism are closely linked—they suggest that it is necessary to abandon the line of thought associated with Nietzsche, if the political unrest of the present time is to be overcome. But it is equally important to realise what Nietzsche and National-Socialism do not have in common. 'There is no doubt that the prophet of Zarathustra for many reasons would today be the first to condemn many of those who claim to be his followers', writes de Lubac; [3] and many Germans share this view. Thomas Mann declares that Nietzsche 'would have been sickened by the very sight of this revolting band of *petits bourgeois* with their megalomania', and Gottfried Benn considers that Nietzsche cannot be held responsible if a few politicians 'belatedly commissioned their portraits in his studio'. [4]

It is certainly impossible to judge Nietzsche justly if the problem is over-simplified. That is why students of Nietzsche in Germany do not confine themselves simply to stating the case for the prosecution. Nietzsche is much less the creator of a historic destiny than the man who gave that destiny visible form. In his work and in his thought, ideas from the past are developed right to their ultimate conclusions; the turmoil of the future is already perceptible in him. His work is conceived in terms of the great periods of history, but the actions of politicians do not measure up to his prophecies. He was so much in advance of his time that Thomas Mann ventures the paradoxical remark, that it was not Nietzsche who made Fascism but Fascism that made Nietzsche. Ernst Jünger compares him to a seismograph that records the abysmal depths immediately beneath. [5] Whatever the succeeding generation may have thought

---

[1] Fritz Strich, 'Wagner und Nietzsche', in *Der Dichter und die Zeit* (Berne, 1947), p. 331.
[2] Heinrich Scholz, *Begegnungen mit Nietzsche* (Tübingen, 1948), p. 6.
[3] Henri de Lubac, *Le Drame de l'Humanisme Athée* (Paris, 1950), p. 64.
[4] Gottfried Benn, 'Nietzsche—nach 50 Jahren', in *Frühe Prosa und Reden* (Wiesbaden, 1950), p. 254.
[5] Ernst Jünger, *Strahlungen* (1949), p. 9.

and turned over in its mind, it is all there in dangerously concentrated form in Nietzsche. He is inexhaustible. Our present era cannot be fully understood if he is overlooked, any more than if Kierkegaard or Marx is overlooked. For one thing is certain: he made an enormous contribution to the making of history, whether as an initiator or as a prophet.

II

To anyone investigating Nietzsche's *immediate* impact or influence on National-Socialism, a study of the relevant literature is disappointing. The name of Nietzsche plays only a minor role. In the writings of Hitler himself, it occurs very seldom. It does not appear at all in *Mein Kampf* or in Rauschning's *Conversations with Hitler*, or in the recently published *Hitler's Table Talk*. Every time one studies Hitler's written works or re-reads his speeches, one is struck by the *Führer's* primitiveness. He was astonishingly ignorant on all intellectual questions, past or present. Despite his determined efforts to give National-Socialism a groundwork of theory, he was himself quite out of touch with the so-called National-Socialist 'philosophy' which he was instrumental in disseminating. His discussions at table, his apodictical assertions which brooked no contradiction and no dialogue, covered an astonishing variety of subjects: sometimes they were concerned with immediate and important plans, but at another time with the remote, fantastic projects of a quite unpredictable future. The only remarks he ever made on Nietzsche in conversation were mere words and gestures; they were completely uninformed and without any conviction. It is possible that all he knew of Nietzsche was a few expressions like 'will to power', 'reversal of values', 'superman', or 'Anti-Christ'. As a result of his long-standing relationship with the 'Wahnfrieds', he probably had some idea of Wagner's opinions and of Nietzsche's early views, in the 'Birth of Tragedy' period, on the renaissance of a Germanic myth; it is quite likely also that, through his relations with Goebbels, Himmler, and Mussolini, he got to know the theories of Sorel and Pareto on the meaning of violence and the justification of revolutionary movements.[1] But any such knowledge gave him neither a complete mental picture nor a complete conviction. On the contrary, not only was there no spiritual field in which Hitler felt at home, but he resented any attempt by someone else to create a spiritual sphere of his own. On his own evidence, he had only read a very small part of Rosenberg's *Der Mythus des 20*

[1] Hermann Rauschning, *Die Révolution des Nihilismus* (Zürich–New York, 1938), 2nd edn., p. 78.

Jahrhunderts,[1] and he refused to allow such a myth to be created. He reproached Houston Stewart Chamberlain with having persistently regarded Christianity as a spiritual world.[2] No comment has yet been made on his beliefs and philosophical convictions which is of any importance or would warrant closer attention, if it were not that this man was for a time the German 'leader', who plunged the entire world into disaster. What he had to say about Christianity he had acquired from a rapid, superficial perusal of quite elementary sources of information [3] and from his own confused and embittered thoughts. Any attempt to unearth the general outline of his views on the world brings to light a coarser version of Nietzsche. For him the struggle for life is a natural law; he believes in a 'Creative power', of which we are the 'passive instruments'. Any revolt against the laws is senseless; man's sole task is to know them and accept them unconditionally. After death, man 'returns to nature, both as matter and as soul or spirit. A toad does not know what it was in the past; we know no more.' [4] Little value is to be attached to the individual existence. 'A fly lays millions of eggs, all of which perish. But the fly as a species survives. . . . If I have to believe in a divine commandment, then it can only be: preserve the species.' It is wrong to pity people whom fate has condemned to die. In any case, no man should be pitied who lacks the necessary endurance. In the field of selection, as indeed in all other fields, our best guide is nature. One cannot imagine a more perfect work of nature than the evolution of living beings as ordained by nature: endless struggle is its only law.[5] Might is always right. It is with such remarks that Hitler defended his own actions: at the time he was most successful he regarded himself as the favourite child of 'Providence', and his decisions, even if they were cruel and inhuman, seemed to have been ordained by fate and to be in accordance with its laws.

But all this is far from being a 'philosophy': it was nothing more than a lamentable intellectual argument in support of a dreadful policy of brute force. Rauschning stresses again and again that no great importance can be attached to these theories, whatever the circumstances in which they were produced. The only significance Hitler's pronouncements have, both in the early stages and towards the end of the Nazi period, is that they were 'an extremely effective and indispensable aid to the revolutionary disruption of the old order'.[6] Philosophy for him was a sideshow; his *élite* learned, like him, to despise every belief, even the synthetic products he himself offered them; he led them into a nihilism that was both unprincipled

---

[1] Henry Picker, *Hitlers Tischgespräche im Führerhauptquartier*, 1941–42 (Bonn, 1951), no. 145. English Trans. *Hitler's Table Talk* (London, 1953).
[2] *Tischgespräche*, no. 187.   [3] Ritter, Introduction to *Tischgespräche*, p. 15.
[4] *Tischgespräche*, no. 186.   [5] ibid., no. 120.
[6] Rauschning, *Die Revolution des Nihilismus*, p. 79.

and aimless. These intellectual sideshows and masquerades, shrouded in a deliberate obscurity, were important for mass-propaganda. Ideas were at best decorative: the essential thing, the only thing that mattered, was the goal to be attained.[1] It is a characteristic feature of Hitler's personality to pour scorn on everything that belonged to the realm of 'ideas', even where the National-Socialist ideology is concerned. Thus the idea of the community, which was constantly being preached to the German people, was for him devoid of sense. 'He could only smile at these everlasting speeches on the community. A community can only be created and maintained by force.'[2] Hitler is the nihilist of politics. All that was stable, all that had been conserved, was reduced to ruins; National-Socialism became the 'movement' in itself. Devoid of faith and devoid of love, it throws itself into the arms of a destiny whose 'mission' it accepts and fulfils. Senselessness becomes an *a priori* of its every thought and action. The essential thing is that it should remain on top of this ruined world. It is hard to imagine anything more horribly ironical than that there were many who belonged to this movement from real conviction. What connection is there between such an attitude and Nietzsche? Let us leave the question open.

What for Hitler was only a play was for others a reality which they took extremely seriously. The man whom the general public always regarded as the first theorist of the National-Socialist philosophy—wrongly, as was later to become clear—was Alfred Rosenberg. Rauschning describes him as a complete *bourgeois*, who played a special part among the mercenaries of the régime. It is reported that, when he was made responsible for the administration of the recently conquered Eastern territories, he proved much too gentle, almost feminine, in character, for him to have any authority over unprincipled officials. His *Der Mythus des 20 Jahrhunderts*, though devoid of any scientific value, represents the only even approximately coherent philosophical system that emerged from National-Socialism. If Rosenberg had been a mere private individual, his book would have attracted no more attention than countless other volumes that were written at that time only to be consigned to oblivion. It is to Hitler's deliberate dishonesty that one must attribute the sensation made by this book: he rejected it in private conversation, but appointed its author chief controller of National-Socialist thought and education; he never gave this book an official Party Stamp, yet, by virtue of the political protection he gave Rosenberg, he also protected his philosophy. The Christian Churches were alarmed and felt themselves threatened, but by combating the work they unwittingly gave it added publicity.

[1] Alfred von Martin, *Der heroische Nihilismus und seine Überwindung* (Krefeld, 1948), p. 12. [2] *Tischgespräche*, no. 21.

This voluminous work also reveals no important link with Nietzsche. The infrequent mention of his name is, on the contrary, an indication that Nietzsche had no immediate influence on the 'myth'. Only once when his name is brought into an involved argument against Marxist interpretation, does Nietzsche appear as the precursor of a form of life that led Rosenberg to introduce into his education programme the Nietzschean phrase: 'rectangular in body and soul'.[1] But Rosenberg's affinity to Nietzsche is shown in his attempt to replace the image of Dionysus by another myth, which can clearly be traced back to Nietzsche: his panegyric of Nordic man, of the Aryan (to whom Langbehn was also to devote so much attention later), his juggling with ideas of race and blood, the first outlines of a Nordic myth, the new interest shown in the 'Sagas' in which Nietzsche recognised a type of thought similar to his own— all this is revived with an avid enthusiasm by Rosenberg. He follows up these ideas and gives them a new interpretation. The starting-point of Rosenberg's myth is a biological conception of existence in all its forms. There is a suspicion of Darwinian evolutionism behind it, to which Nietzsche had already paid tribute. But the 'renewal of values', a process embarked upon by Nietzsche, is continued here: clinging to life is no longer enough; the idea of race makes it possible to see and judge the phenomena of life from new angles. Rosenberg reveals himself as a direct disciple of Houston Stewart Chamberlain, who, with his predecessor Gobineau, developed the racial theory and hailed the Aryan race as the creator and representative of all superior cultures. Like Chamberlain, Rosenberg postulates a racial conception of God and a racial theology: religion is merely a function of race. Ideas, philosophy, science, and ethics have value only in so far as they can justify themselves before the tribunal of the Nordic race. The apollonic cosmic principle, which Nietzsche had contrasted with the dionysiac principle, is identified by Rosenberg with the Germanic spirit: from it alone emanate all great exploits, all clarity and light in the world. Everything obscure and ugly is produced by inferior races and race-mixtures. Nietzsche's thoughts, which are fundamentally directed to earthly things, are reflected, in modified form, in Rosenberg:

> 'A new image of the World, rich and colourful, is today beginning to appear, at a time when we are making the breathtaking discovery that the conflict between blood and its environment, between blood and blood, is the ultimate phenomenon to which we have access; we are not permitted to search further.' [2]

[1] Afred Rosenberg, Der Mythus des 20 Jahrhunderts (Munich, 1934), p. 530.
[2] ibid., p. 23.

Like Nietzsche, he professes a dynamic conception of historical development, in which there is nothing permanent. That is why he defends forces that rebel against forces that conserve, those that undermine order against those that maintain it; the ideal line of German history runs from Witikind to Henry the Lion and from him to the Great Elector of Brandenburg, to Frederick the Great and to Bismarck. All, consciously or unconsciously, are in the forefront of the fight for Germanic values, which today are confronted with an unprecedented struggle against a thousand-year-old tradition. Rosenberg shares with Nietzsche this dangerous conviction that the Germanic spirit is essentially a dynamic one, and he carries it to its final conclusions. What Zarathustra meant to Nietzsche, Siegfried represents in the new thought; both are representatives of a dionysiac paganism. Christianity is the major obstacle on the road to 'renewal of values'. Rosenberg preached a hate as blind as did the author of *Der Antichrist* and *Der Wille zur Macht*.

These ideas which, in Rosenberg, profess to be scientific, assume religious form in the *Deutsche Glaubensbewegung*. This was the rendezvous for all who hoped to satisfy a religious need by preaching a pious attitude towards the immanent cosmic forces, life, blood, and race. Abandonment of Christianity, and hostility towards it, played a great part in the *Deutsche Glaubensbewegung*—to such purpose that one wonders to whom this movement was designed to appeal: to those who were looking for a wider public in their anti-Christian campaign, or to those who were seeking a new form of religious community. In any case, however, it is certain that many saw in the adoption of a pious attitude to the world the possibility of a new religion. Ever since the end of the nineteenth century, the 'search for God' has occupied an important place in German thought and poetry, which shows how, since the destruction of Christian organisations, men's thoughts have been turned to the search for new religious bonds. As they had cut themselves off from every approach to a transcendent, personal God, the only course left open to them was to worship the unknown forces that act within and about us. Spranger has taken a phrase from Goethe to describe this new religious feeling: 'piety towards the world', and uses it in particular to define Rilke's existential attitude, his withdrawal into an 'inner cosmic space'. In so far as a strong religious feeling was really manifest in the *Glaubensbewegung*, it could only be a basically analogous phenomenon. But the movement completely failed; it never achieved the slightest importance. Only the individual, in humble meditation, can regain a lost God. But man in the group, particularly when he remains so near to political power, is not equipped to build a new world. On the contrary, he only helps to destroy the old world. This German religion was not a religious revival, even if the individuals who took part in it were impelled by serious motives.

Hauer and his friends adopt an intellectual attitude that is similar to Rosenberg's: their faith is in earthly things, the world for them is in constant motion. The theory of a God 'in transformation', who lives and can only manifest himself on earth, plays, as one might expect, an important part in the *Deutscher Glauben*. This 'faith' does not rest on any one truth: it consists in participating in 'life', in 'force', in the 'security of the inner self'. Nothing could be more remote from the *Deutscher Glauben* than a dogma. 'The religious emotion of the German soul' is the sensation man feels in the very depths of his being when he comes face to face with the sacred and terrible spectacle (*Numinosum* and *Tremendum*) of the universe. Faith, according to Hauer, means 'self-abandonment to the will of this reality', 'creating and struggling within the confines of its necessity', 'being certain of victory. It means having confidence in the force that inhabits our hearts, where the creative God unites with sincere souls that are ready to sacrifice themselves. Faith allows us to accomplish the task that divine authority demands of us. With faith, we stand on bedrock; we draw from it an energy that is blessed in the midst of the most arduous struggles'. The unwieldy, awkward, groping language of the founder of the *Deutsche Glaubensbewegung*, who was extremely well-versed in questions of religion and theology, seems to show that he is trying to express something which it is virtually impossible to put into words. This can be interpreted as a sign of the authenticity of his religious devotion. Hauer establishes a link with the political movements of his time, by making this new form of religious feeling out to be something the Germans and related people specifically need: these peoples are, by their very nature, engrossed in earthly things, and religion for them is nothing more than the sense of piety they experience towards the world. 'This great idea, that everything created has developed organically from a germ of the eternal, corresponds to the Germanic vision of God.' [1] The entire world, according to the German faith, is animated by God. For the ancestors of the Germans, who 'invented the myth of the Tree of the World', the world was a great organism permeated by one eternal life. 'All living beings are an integral part of this organism; nothing exists that does not take part in this divine totality. . . .' What Hauer, like Rosenberg, looks for in history is an expression of this religious consciousness; he finds it less in political rebellions and schismatic revolts than in the 'German' mysticism of Meister Eckhart, and his comments on it, like those of Rosenberg

---

[1] Wilhelm Hauer, *Deutsche Gottschau, Grundzüge eines deutschen Glaubens* (1935), 4th ed., p. 68.

and the other National-Socialist 'scholars' (and they are not alone!), contain some impressive paradoxes. There is no need for us to go back so far. Nietzsche's influence is apparent everywhere. We find this virtuoso of quotations lifting numerous passages from *Zarathustra*. According to Nietzsche we take a tragic view of the world because we know its enigmas and contradictions, but at the same time find it 'good' as it is. We have no need to torment ourselves about the meaning and purpose of existence; 'life well-lived' reveals itself to us on every side. The meaning of this life is inherent in it. In the *Deutscher Glauben* we find Nietzsche's moral laws. Hauer demands veracity in the sense of 'respect for what is real'. The law of sacrifice is implicit in the biological world; it is its fundamental law. Man has a duty to respect and preserve life; he must conserve the force of procreation like a sacred birthright: he must protect what is right. This is the other side of Nietzsche, which National-Socialism usually glossed over. 'Duty and honour' are picked out as the fundamental concepts of Germanic morality. There is no room in a panvitalism of this kind for the Christian idea of guilt and sin. Both belong to human nature. Man discovers his guilt to be an inescapable fact. It is clear that this conglomeration of romantic reveries was not potent enough to unite men in a new Confession. But it was a welcome ally for the political rulers in their struggle against the old order, which was inherently opposed to National-Socialism.

There is one other phenomenon of National-Socialism which must be mentioned in connection with the influence of Nietzsche. It is what is called the 'second generation'. Rauschning devoted particular attention to it in his book *Die Revolution des Nihilismus*, undoubtedly with good reason. Anyone who has studied the evolution of National-Socialism about 1935 knows that a new note was suddenly sounded, very different from the intoxication of the first few years. It was particularly noticeable among the leaders of the Hitler Youth and in the SS ranks and press. Ideas and dreams are no longer all-powerful: the stress is on action. Without too much preliminary talk, preparations are made for ambitious ventures. No attempt is made to defend an ideology in which faith has been lost and which can no longer draw convinced believers. In these circles, says Rauschning in his analysis of that period—

'judgment is passed rather on actions than on words. . . . The dynamism is no longer ecstacy but work. . . . Important new forces, which are destined to play a decisive part, have already appeared . . .; a small, silent circle is working grimly. . . . This second phase of the revolution passes quietly, confined to solving technical problems. . . . In the younger generation there appears, as part of an irresistible evolution, a new feeling which is as

H

different from the style of the Third Reich thus far as from the old traditions of the Prussian officers.' [1]

This movement of the younger generation went well beyond Hitler's nihilism, for it had rid itself of all the 'sideshows' and 'masquerades'. There were no half-measures, no illusions, but also no traces of faith in its preparations for a great political coup, nothing less than the foundation of a world empire which would be, at the same time, the most important symptom of a new age. There was nothing in all this that would stand up to rational examination; it was merely the external sign of a secret, irrational will that was preparing the ground for monstrous exploits.

The individual was carried along by the current, without finding the energy, or even the will, to resist. He had been told often enough that he had ceased to exist as an individual. 'You are nothing, and your people is everything.' Collective man is born; he has lost his 'I'; he is engulfed by a gigantic movement that is alone in the field and embraces everything. He is a soldier and a worker; he marches and works the machines. Ernst Jünger's book, *The Worker*, began to exercise a belated but unfortunate influence. The author had long since changed his views and become openly hostile to the régime. Nietzsche wanted all man's potentialities to be given free play. This idea is now completely reversed: man gives everything he has, even his identity as a person, to fulfil a great supra-individual function. The superman is no longer expected to appear in individual form, but as a sort of *'Super-I'*, like the Leviathan of the totalitarian state. This attitude had arisen, over a long period, from certain characteristic experiences of the modern era. The present-day soldier knows that he plays virtually no part in the gigantic modern battles: technical evolution brings home to each of us the fact that powers, which we ourselves create, have reduced us to a state of impotence. For the Jünger of this particular period personal experience no longer existed; nor was there such a thing as a personal destiny. The individual had been replaced by a type, whose existence was already apparent in a noticeable facial uniformity: in the miner, the factory worker, the scholar, Evolution was destroying individuality. Man was becoming a function; individuals were interchangeable. To be free meant no more than to be confined to the place one was allotted; freedom was synonymous with obedience and service.

Ideas of this kind were conceived and expressed quite independently of National-Socialism; but they exerted an influence among the intellectuals of the younger generation. Rauschning illustrates it in a number of ways. Something to be welcomed, of course, was the fact that the intellectual and moral laxity of the

[1] Hermann Rauschning, loc. cit., p. 103.

early leaders had been replaced by the honesty and humane sense of justice of the younger generation, but to those who were concerned about the ultimate outcome the new symptoms were horrifying. It was only with them that all links between the movement and the Western world were broken and thereby all links with history.

'The very stuff of the nation itself, the most elementary human values, were at stake now. Everyone outbid his neighbour and soon it was impossible to withdraw and regain the peaceful satisfaction of daily work. . . . Something is swallowed up now in a pragmatic collectivism, which had survived the National-Socialist phase of the German revolution, in spite of its brutalities. . . . Now, for the first time, man is swept along by an absolutely controlled evolution; he strips humanity of any meaning and value it possessed till then. . . . The danger is that, in this movement, the productive energies of the nation will become so spent as to be totally exhausted. . . . It is no longer a *Weltanschauung* but a reality. It is a consistent dynamism, the form in which the German revolution becomes serious and really dangerous.'

This generation was getting ready to enter the final stage of evolution known as 'heroic nihilism': a life without content, without conviction, unrelated to any permanent value. Nietzsche's name does not appear any more frequently in these circles; but his spirit is always present. For this young generation, life had meaning only when it was dangerous; there was only one duty—to seize power; the means was violence, and the goal a world empire. These young people, unhampered by tradition and inherited values, saw in the movement itself the meaning of life; they created for the sheer joy of it; they were content 'to abandon themselves to the revolutionary movement for its own sake'.[1] The 'reversal of values' that Nietzsche had preached and urged became self-abandonment to the movement for its own sake; they have even reached the point of believing that a complete revolution was inevitable if life was to be rejuvenated. The doctrinaire side of the movement consisted in rejecting all doctrine, in denying all problems so far discussed, whether national, social, or racial. Political nihilism seems to have entered upon its most extreme phase in Germany with this generation that took account only of impulses of the will and acknowledged no values apart from power, domination, and force.

I shall conclude this general survey with a few observations on the ideological basis of Italian Fascism. By contrast with National-Socialism, on which Nietzsche seems to have had only an indirect influence, Fascism shows the marked influence of Nietzsche. Mussolini was much more interested than Hitler in intellectual matters and

[1] loc. cit., p. 90.

had taken a much more serious interest in the theoretical side of his movement. He was a disciple of Nietzsche and appears to have given a great deal of thought to Nietzsche's philosophical ideas. It is reported that at the age of twenty he was keenly interested in the ideas of Schopenhauer, Nietzsche, Stirner, the Eleatics, and Machiavelli.[1] It was *Der Wille zur Macht* that attracted him most. In a study of 'the philosophy of violence' (published in the republican journal *Il Pensiero romagnolo*) he gives his own personal views on the ideas of the philosopher of Sils-Maria; he extracts from the whole what to him seems usable. The main purpose of this study is to show the man of the future, having rid himself of the burden of the past and of moral scruples, dedicating himself entirely to the great task of world domination.

'To attain this new ideal, a new species of "free minds" must be born, fortified by war, by solitude and by grave dangers; these minds will know storms, peaks, and glaciers and will plumb with calm, untroubled eyes the depths of the abysses; they will be endowed with a kind of sublime perversity, they will deliver us from charity and from a desire for oblivion; they will give the world purpose again and restore men's hopes.'[2]

It is not difficult to recognise the hand of Nietzsche in phrases of this kind. But even more direct and more profound was the influence of George Sorel and Vilfredo Pareto. During his period of exile in Lausanne, Mussolini, then a socialist, attended lectures by Pareto. From both these thinkers he learned the theory of violence and revolution. Sorel preached the overthrow of the state by violence; war, force, and the class-struggle were the most rapid means of acquiring freedom. He also stressed the practical value of a myth. Mussolini followed his advice when he gave himself the title of 'Duce' (and Hitler too when he called his régime the 'Third Reich'). But it was undoubtedly Pareto who exerted the strongest influence on him.[3] Inspired by Nietzsche's idea of eternal return, Pareto 'visualises political history as a cycle of the *élite*; he believes that *élites* reappear in our time to shore up the order and culture which they themselves had formerly created but which had fallen into unworthy hands and begun to decay.'[4] Mussolini is no no more a theorist than Hitler. One can almost hear Nietzsche's voice in the words: 'Fascism is not an arsenal of theoretical doctrines, for every philosophy is a deception and every theory a prison.'[5]   And

---

[1] Margherita G. Sarfatti, *Mussolini*, German translation by Alfred M. Balte (Leipzig, 1926), p. 101.
[2] ibid., p. 115.
[3] ibid., p. 73.
[4] H. Meyer, *Geschichte der abendländischen Weltanschauung* (Würzburg, 1949), Vol. V, p. 412.
[5] Sarfatti, loc. cit., p. 74.

Nietzsche is also behind Mussolini when he cries: 'We are establishing in Italy dionysian humanity'.[1] For Giovanni Gentile, the
philosopher of Fascism, Mussolini's movement was based on 'a
philosophy of pure action'.

III

All the evidence we have given justifies the conclusion that Nietzsche
can hardly be said to have exercised a direct influence on National-
Socialism, either in its early formative stage or during its period
of development. His name is never quoted in any of the countless
speeches and only rarely in the books setting out the Party's programme. He hardly appears in the numerous volumes of National-
Socialist reviews. This fact is specifically confirmed by Baeumler,
the only interpretor of Nietzsche of any importance among the
National-Socialists: National-Socialism, he writes, did not think or
Nietzsche.[2] Hitler and his friends are their own apostles. But, with
all their differences, they have a common source: National-Socialism
is nihilism in politics in its extreme form. But nihilism means the
overthrow of all established systems, the rejection of metaphysics,
the abandonment of every metaphysical link and criterion. Nihilism, finally, is the world without God. Man has failed to achieve
autonomy. National-Socialism was one of the last phases of this
evolution. It paid for its presumption with unparalleled disaster.

The destruction of *all* established régimes, the abandonment of *all*
human dignity, appalling acts of brutality perpetrated on hundreds
of thousands of people, and finally a completely crazy war of
destruction—all these were regarded throughout the civilised world
as signs of man's ultimate degradation. That is why so many
attempts were made afterwards to establish the real causes of the
evil and to induce mankind to change course. It is generally accepted
today that we are in a blind alley; it is hard to imagine how the
world can continue on its present course. National-Socialism is
only one of the phenomena of this world-evolution, though a more
terrifying phenomenon than the others. Views of this kind are
expressed in almost every sphere of spiritual life. The Protestant
theologian Helmut Thielicke [3] believes that we are living in a unique
era. Are we moving towards a super-death, a super-catastrophe, or
towards a new dawn, he asks, without finding an answer. There
is no way of knowing if the era of catastrophes is over. But one
thing at least is certain: the first half of the twentieth century
witnessed a complete collapse of all known realities, a collapse which
was extremely rapid yet which had been brewing for centuries.

[1] Meyer, loc. cit., p. 414.
[2] *Nationalsozialistiche Monatshefte*, April 1934, Vol. 49, p. 289.
[3] Helmut Thielicke, *Der Nihilismus* (Tübingen, 1950), p. 158.

From about 1920 onwards, we were in an unprecedented state of crisis, 'beyond which it was difficult to visualise anything except either total disaster or some kind of renaissance'.[1]

The figure of Friedrich Nietzsche looms up in the first phase of this evolution. From the moment this volcano first erupts and showers its sparks on the world, we feel the ground shuddering and shifting under our feet. It is only with Nietzsche that the spiritual history of the twentieth century really begins. He revealed its state of mind when he expressed what no one else dared to say. Both in his own personality and in his teachings he laid bare a situation which is unparalleled in world history. That is one aspect of his work. The other is this: far from braking humanity's plunge to destruction, he deliberately hastened it.

Alfred Baeumler in an essay entitled *Nietzsche der Philosoph und Politiker*, which appeared in Leipzig in 1931 before the advent to power of National-Socialism, has given an admirable definition of Nietzsche's thought in relation to history. The philosopher begins with the basic assumption that contemporary man has no roots and no country, that he lives in a purely fictitious world.

'For centuries Europe has been living under pressure. It is as if, since the end of the Middle Ages, she had been looking for something but could not find it: a form of life, a lost unity, a certainty in existence. This Europe calls herself Christian. But she is also a thousand-and-one other things: Greek and Roman, Indian and Chinese, philosophical and aesthetic, scientific and technical, warlike and mercantile. All in all, she does not know herself what she really is, and that is why, in her unrest and anxiety, she seeks clearly-defined forms and ideas in every period and in every culture. The inhabitants of this Europe live in the midst of countless uncertainties and countless contradictions. Each man tries to work out his own solution: one kneels before the sacraments as mediaeval men did, another attempts to infuse something of the vitality of modern ideas into Protestantism, while a third seeks refuge in art or in scientific asceticism. Political and social "problems" appear; no one is capable of mastering them; no one knows what course to steer.'[2]

Stumbling humanity finds its escape more and more in 'un-reality' (*ins Uneigentliche*); it lives on expedients and substitutes; it refuses to realise that it is suspended in a void. This is the humanity that Nietzsche seizes in his merciless grip; in order to force it into self-awareness, he confronts it with its lack of faith. We are living in an age of nihilism, whether we are aware of it or not. That is all that is meant by the phrase: 'God is dead'. This famous passage

[1] Sedlmayr, *Verlust der Mitte* (Salzburg, 1948), p. 204.
[2] Baeumler, *Nietzsche der Philosoph und Politiker* (Leipzig, 1931), p. 10.

occurs in *Die Fröliche Wissenschaft*.[1] Nietzsche shows the 'madman' walking in the market-place in full daylight with a lantern in his hand, crying: 'I am searching for God! I am searching for God!' The *petits bourgeois*, who have long since ceased to believe in God, laugh at him and ridicule him.

'The madman [Nietzsche continues] suddenly leapt among them and held them spellbound with his piercing eyes. "Where has God gone?" he cried. "I will tell you. We have killed him— you and I. We are all murderers. Ah! What have we done? How did we drink the whole Ocean? Who gave us the sponge to wipe out the whole horizon? What did we do when we detached this earth from its sun? And now where is it going? Where are we going? Away from every sun? Are we not constantly slipping into an abyss? Behind us, beside us, before us, all around us? Is there still an Above and a Below? Are we not wandering aimlessly in an infinite void? Do we not feel the cold touch of emptiness? Has it not grown colder? Is night not falling ceaselessly and ever darker? . . . Where shall we find solace, we, the most murderous of murderers? The most sacred and most powerful being the world has ever known has perished by our knives. Who will wipe the blood from our hands?" '

Such cries of despair are the confession of a man who makes the sudden horrible discovery that he is an atheist. He feels the ground give way under his feet and the sky shudder over his head; he falls into a bottomless abyss.

The God whose death Nietzsche announces is the God of Christianity, Christ Himself. The Christian world died with Him. When Christ left the hearts of men all the wealth of Christianity was lost, leaving in its place a mere void. For when the Christian attitude was abandoned the entire Western system was abandoned with it. Apart from Christianity, Nietzsche recognised no greater adversary than Socrates, whose name he uses as a symbol of the whole of ancient thought.

The problem of nihilism, therefore, with which Nietzsche found himself confronted at a time when the great crisis of our modern era was taking shape arises from the destruction of the Christian world. In other words, nihilism arises from the abandonment of all metaphysical obligations and the loss of all metaphysical certainty. We no longer believe in a changeless being who makes our laws and imposes our obligations. Man sees himself suspended in a void, detached from all reality and detached from space. As soon as man made this discovery, at the very moment when the Spirit of History seemed, as it were, to examine its conscience, two things were possible. Man might have freely confessed his mistakes and then

[1] *Die Fröliche Wissenschaft*, no. 18.

returned to the previous order and salvation; the indisputable state of chaos in the world could have been averted by the action of one missionary, great or small, taking no counsel but his own. It was the task of Dostoievsky, for whom there was no parallel, in his time, in the Western world. But the alternative was something almost unimaginable: to do exactly the opposite, to deny a centuries-old tradition, to put man's whole condition to the test, to remove the pillars of life; it was an experiment that was quite unprecedented in world history. It was the task that Nietzsche undertook. He believes he can conquer nihilism by linking men to a new reality which has so far been neglected, by establishing them in a new truth. When he turns his back not only on Christ but also on the Christian world of salvation, not only on Socrates, Plato, and Aristotle, but also on the ancient world order, he declares that the world is chaos and man committed to chaos. His philosophy is based on lack of faith in the orderly world-structure of the Creation, on the refusal to allow a higher dignity to the idea, the type, or the species. He denies the duality of Above and Below: he admits only pure dynamism, flux, amorphism, a 'life' that is without limitation and without law, an incongruity that alone, according to him, constitutes and determines existence. The individual is integrated in a world conceived on dionysiac and heraclitean proportions; this world rejects him, then absorbs him anew; an eternal *panta rhei* first pushes him to the surface, then engulfs him. Existence becomes an absolute. On all sides the curtains are drawn. Man belongs to the earth, and to the earth alone. Nietzsche found adequate compensation in the theory of the 'eternal return', which, for him, replaced the sojourn in a transcendant absolute.

Nietzsche, who described himself as a nihilist, believed he would establish a form of existence which would take account of the conditions in a shattered world. In professing to have discovered a side of humanity that had hitherto been overlooked and had remained completely latent, he believed he had unearthed new foundations on which we could build. 'The Thousand-year Empire' of Zarathustra is placed under the sign of Dionysus.

But for all practical purposes the solution is this: man bound to God is replaced, in Nietzsche's mind, by *autonomous* man. Having deserted the divine tables, man becomes his own law-giver. He becomes, in every sense of the word, his own source. 'Superman' is the ultimate form of man abandoned to himself. 'Formerly one spoke of God when contemplating distant seas. But today I enjoin you to say: superman. . . .' Nietzsche, by rejecting the authority of any transcendent power over conscience, reduces man to himself. He no longer mourns God's absence, as did the 'madman'. Man wishes to be alone, without confessor. It is to guarantee the autonomy of the conscience, which cannot tolerate the all-seeing eye, that God does not exist. Indeed, he cannot exist. 'If there were a God, how could I bear not to be God? So, there are no gods!'

The essential fact, which was to dominate the evolution of humanity for several decades, is that *the Western world, through its ruling classes, attempted the same experiment as Nietzsche*. The general spiritual trend, philosophical thought, literature and the plastic arts, and political developments, all, in their various ways, reflect one and the same attitude to the world. The opposite alternative, it seems, was not possible. The forces which confronted Nietzsche were already set on the course which he opened up before them. Far from turning them back, he removed every obstacle from their path. So the stream became a torrent, and the torrent a raging waterfall. The political catastrophe of National-Socialism, which, at least for Germans, seemed like an apocalyptic judgment, would not have been so terrible and so frightening if it had not, of necessity, assumed the vast proportions of the error that produced it. Nietzsche was convinced that he had conquered nihilism; but historical evolution, far from bearing out this conviction, proved him abysmally wrong. Unwittingly and unwillingly he hastened humanity's downward rush to destruction.

But let us return to Nietzsche himself. There are two features of the new thought which must be clearly distinguished, not only in relation to National-Socialism, but also in relation to all trends of the evolution that leads from Nietzsche to final disaster. Between these two aspects there is a very necessary connection. They are still closely connected in Nietzsche, but subsequently they become for the most part sharply divided. Nietzsche, who feels obliged to regard this world as man's sole habitat and to make him familiar with it, is then confronted with another question: Is man to live in harmony or in conflict with this world? Is he to abandon himself to the amorous embrace of omnipotent life, or should he look upon chaos as a challenge, measure up to it, and perhaps only find himself and realise himself in this conflict? Is he to sacrifice his Self to a transcendent All, to find happiness in the suppression of the individual and a mystical harmony with the world, to forget himself in an intimate union with the flux of life? Or must he impose his will on the anarchic and the amorphous, leave his stamp on it, assert and inflate his ego in the struggle, in resistance and hostility, show his contempt, by heroic action and stoical suffering, for the power that is crushing him, trust in himself and his strength, and live as he pleases? Nietzsche preached both doctrines. He was 'shaken and buffeted by the storms of life' (Flake); he demanded of man that he should learn to free himself from his soi-disant Self and live 'cosmically'. But he also preached Superman and the Will to Power.

Chaos and *Superman* are the two poles of modern nihilism; the one balances the other. We must belong to the earth and the earth alone; we must revere life and life alone. But from another side chaos calls forth the superman to master it: this is the doctrine which, for half a century, dominated poetry, the fine arts, and politics. The ground trembles under our feet; it is no superficial, temporary tremor, but a movement emanating from dark depths which are inherent in the world and—in this sense—transcendent. We must therefore be prepared to defend ourselves. The world knows no order; it is absurd and contradictory. We must therefore oppose its pretentions by redoubling our strength and heightening all our powers. Man can hold out against the power of the chaos that threatens our existence on every side only by making an immense effort to resist it, by straining every nerve and summoning all his reserves. He must hold out against the world; he is the enemy of a monster; he is born to hate and violence. Such is the tragic larger-than-life picture of man which Nietzsche had to impress upon all those who took their stand on the same ground. The acts of violence we saw committed, first of all in the spiritual world, then in the physical world, do not arise only from a fundamental lack of respect for the world. They were committed because man mistrusts the world and its structure, because he fears, from one moment to the next, that an unknown power, which threatens him, will strike, because he strives to protect his own Self against all the things surrounding it. And here National-Socialism as a whole shows a marked affinity with the world of Nietzsche; it brings out with perfect clarity the elements of Nietzsche's thought. It certainly went to great lengths to keep man close to life and to teach him to respect the laws of biology. But the leaders of the régime poured ridicule on things that a few credulous people venerated; they committed insane acts of destruction. Both groups realised all too rarely that they were essentially of the same stock.

We must analyse Nietzsche's doctrines one by one. The first, fundamental thesis proclaims the *absolute character of progression* and movement. The conception makes its first appearance in the work on *Die Geburt der Tragödie aus dem Geiste der Musik*. He succeeds in this book in showing the dionysiac character of Hellenism by defining it in relation to its opposite, the apollonian spirit. At that time he met with lively opposition from the scholars; but in the long run they came to understand that he was right. There was more to this book than his contemporaries realised. Since it appeared, it has become impossible to see the Greeks solely through the eyes of Winckelmann. 'There is no mistaking it: here was a new thought, a new knowledge of the Greeks finding expression.' [1]

[1] Friedrich Georg Jünger, *Nietzsche* (Frankfurt, 1949), p. 1.

But this purely æsthetic interpretation, which made the world a focal point of dionysiac forces, was not sufficient. Nietzsche's next step was to apply this concept of 'dionysism' to the understanding of the inner life. He refused to distinguish between an 'Above and Below' in the world; according to him there was only a homogeneous whole; and, as he had rejected the notion of 'a beyond', he could no longer even refer to the world 'here below'. So Nietzsche was left with pure immanence. He conceived of it as a progression, as life, as 'pure' nature, and implicit in this conception was a complete absence of stability, an eternal fluidity, an uninterrupted, incessant movement. As against philosophers who attempted to find an element of permanence in phenomena and who regarded ephemeral things as symbolic 'figures' expressing the imperishable, Nietzsche postulates an absolute progression which, for him, is the only real 'being', while the 'ideas' and systems of philosophers are mere fictions. According to Nietzsche, he who lives by being finds himself in a void; only he who lives by becoming lives in truth. Nietzsche is against immobility, which is mere thought; he is against escape into a beyond, which is a mere void; he is on the side of life.

It is partly under the influence of Darwin's scientific theories that Nietzsche forms this *concept of life*. As we know, transformism (taken as a whole and in radical form) made a profound impression on him. It is true that at the time he was writing *Der Wille zur Macht* he included a few passages against Darwinism. But it is not what separated him from it, but what brought him closer to it that really matters: the conviction that life, in the biological sense, is a universal and indivisible force. At the same time, of course, he had moral implications in view: he thought that what is best suited to the structure of the world is not stability but abandonment, not certainty but risk and sacrifice.

At all events, Nietzsche regarded himself as a disciple of Heraclitus, whom he considered the philosopher of *panta rhei* and eternal struggle. He condemned as fictitious all that is invariable in the world, and he set out to expose as false, if not escapist, all belief in stability. Opposed to the Platonic theory of Ideas and the Aristotelian doctrine of the 'general', he goes back to the pre-Socratic conception of universal flux and of a constantly changing world. Man never places his foot twice in the same river. All pillars crumble. The ground begins to move under our feet. Nowhere is there stability, nowhere truth, nowhere established value. All that remains is the necessity for progression; the nature of the world is to be 'chaos for all eternity '.[1]

Such a conception of the world leads to almost unimaginable conclusions. The world of 'becoming' is completely irrational and

[1] *Die Fröhliche Wissenschaft*, no. 109.

immeasurable. The man who hopes to apprehend it with his intelligence is doomed to failure. And, in any case, it can only be apprehended approximately: it would be better for us to move out of our own confines, to rid ourselves of intelligence, and to enter into a sort of mystical union with the world. For in the world of progression there is neither truth nor science. Man is caught up in a constant modification of values. In place of truth we have 'interpretation'; we form an 'image' of the world which we 'imagine'. Science is merely 'the repugnance felt by the intellect in face of chaos'.

Man's abandonment to chthonian forces leads to yet another result: the pre-eminence of the irrational over the rational. The spirit will no longer dominate life, but life the spirit. As man is reduced to the body, it is impossible to place the spirit higher than life. The spirit, like everything else, is merely a consequence of life; it is driven back to biological phenomena. Nietzsche argues logically: thinking and acting man is more than consciousness; he represents a whole composed of sensibility, will and thought. The spirit is merely a 'symbolic language of the body'.

This theory of Nietzsche's contains a fair measure of truth. It brought out the dubious nature of pure intellectualism and absolute spirituality. Since Descartes, the mind has run the risk of being regarded merely as a faculty of abstraction, as abstract thought capable of grasping only the complexities of mathematics. But Nietzsche, in preaching the opposite doctrine, was on just as dangerous, if not more dangerous, ground. In considering reality from a biological viewpoint, in pressing the claims of the life force, the obscure and the unconscious, all out of reach of the mind, he was to lay himself open to even graver consequences.

The image man forms of himself is conditioned by the way in which he visualises his origin. As Christian convictions had lost their validity in Nietzsche's eyes and, moreover, no longer found favour with the philosophers, scholars, and people as a whole, the time seemed ripe to establish a new doctrine of humanity. The changes that had taken place in the world of astronomy and biology had a decisive influence on the conception of man. Nietzsche's view of man as a pure child of nature excludes any consideration of man as a superior being in view of his supernatural vocation. The fact of belonging to nature deprives man of all value as an individual. He sees the vast universe and finds himself frighteningly insignificant by comparison.

'Ever since Copernicus man seems committed to a downward path. He rolls more and more quickly away from the centre. Where will it lead him? Into nothingness? Into a *poignant* sense of his own nothingness?' [1]

----

[1] *Zur Genealogie der Moral*, Vol. III, no. 25.

'Life on earth—an instant, an incident, an inconsequential exception, something without any importance for the nature of the earth as a whole; the earth itself and all the stars—a hiatus between two voids, an event without purpose, without reason, without will, without consciousness, the worst form of necessity, animal necessity. Something in us rebels against these thoughts: the serpent vanity whispers in our ear: all this must be false, for it is revolting. . . . Is it not possible that all this is a mere illusion?' [1]

'We would be unique in the world! ah! it is really too improbable! Astronomers, whose gaze sometimes does succeed in penetrating further than the earth, give us to understand that the drop of *life* in the universe is of no importance to the total character of the vast ocean in which all becomes and perishes; they tell us that countless stars have the same conditions necessary for life as the earth; a large number of stars, therefore—and yet a mere handful by comparison with the infinite number that have either escaped this eruption or have been long since cured of it; they tell us that life on each of these astral bodies, measured in relation to its existence, is but an instant, a flash after a long, long space of time—so it is in no sense the ultimate aim and object of their existence.' [2]

Faced with this infinite universe, Nietzsche attempts a paradox: he makes the *inorganic* world into real being. It is by finding this world again that man will attain perfection. One can consider it something worth celebrating, Nietzsche wrote once, when one is free of life and returns to the state of inanimate nature. We would thus become reconciled with reality, that is, with the inanimate world.

Biological reasons are also quoted. If man is mere nature, he belongs to the animal world. But he is not even an animal; he has not the sure instincts of the animal, he is in every sense an animal '*manqué*'; his species is not yet determined.

'We have learnt a great deal. We have become, in every respect, much more modest. We no longer trace man back to "spirit", we have placed him once more among the animals. We regard him as the strongest animal because he is the most cunning: hence, amongst other things, his "spirituality". We also resist our vanity which tries to infiltrate here too and to claim that man is the greatest idea . . . of all animal evolution. Man is by no means the peak of creation: all other living beings have an equal measure of perfection with him. . . . And in stating this, we are overstating: man is relatively the most "*manqué*" and the most weakly of animals, who has lost sight of his instincts—and yet, in spite of that, he is the most interesting of all! . . . At one

---

[1] *Der Wille zur Macht*, no. 303.
[2] *Menschliches Allzumenschliches*, no. 14.

time, man was credited with a "free will", like a birthright he brought with him from a higher world: today, we have even deprived him of his will, in the sense that this word no longer represents a faculty. . . . Formerly man's consciousness, his mind, was regarded as proof of his superior origin, of his divinity. . . . In this respect too, we have come to think better: consciousness or "mind" is for us a symptom of a relative organic imperfection; the mind endeavours, it gropes, it errs, it strives and calls for a useless expenditure of nervous energy.' [1]

It is only so that he can subsist in the world about him that man has produced in himself a consciousness and a language.[2] But man, unfitted for life and suffering from inadequate vitality, is no more than 'the earth's skin-disease'. Only the nature of wild beasts can reconcile us with man; Nietzsche honours them with the name 'savage beasts'.

Nietzsche likes hard, brutal propositions of this kind. The frontier that separates the human from the sub-human has been long since crossed. The tremendous danger inherent in such a doctrine becomes clear when little minds come to base their actions on it and to translate it into fact. For Nietzsche, even the most monstrous arguments were never more than an intellectual exercise; he remained anxious about the fate of man, who, in spite of everything, is not an animal; he pursued it to the ultimate limits of existence.

That is one of the characteristic features of his philosophy. The other, which, far from contradicting it, is a necessary complement of the first, is the doctrine of the 'Superman'. This doctrine reaches its culminating point in his book on Der Wille zur Macht. Though unfinished, this is his greatest work. It had an influence on political life; it became the text-book of Italian Fascism; there is no doubt it exercised an indirect influence on National-Socialism. Nietzsche, in fact, does not shrink from any formula, however terrifying.

It is to Schopenhauer, of whom he was a faithful disciple for a time, that he owes his conception of a philosophy of will. His encounter with Schopenhauer's voluntarism was one of the decisive events of his life. The disciple accepted this theory of the will without qualification; he embraced the whole of the master's highly comprehensive exposé. But he changed the stress, and thereby changed everything. The two philosophers differed in the value they attached to suffering. Schopenhauer rejected suffering and demanded the suppression of the human will and a return to nothingness. Nietzsche did the opposite: he regarded suffering as the essential condition of a courageous life; suffering incites men to heroic deeds and to a tragic end.

---

[1] Der Antichrist, no. 9.   [2] Die Fröhliche Wissenschaft, no. 354.

Statements of this kind lead to fresh conclusions. In the first place, they express the will not to abandon oneself to nothingness through weakness, but to face up to it with courage. I experience my own being in my resistance to non-being. Every man who feels he is a victim of absurd circumstances must realise what this means. He has been confronted with this dilemma a hundred times: should he perish or hold out as long as he can? This theory of Nietzsche's had the most profound and far-reaching results. It is only when he comes face to face with nothingness that man's creative powers come to life: the same conclusion has been reached in our day by Gottfried Benn. And the poetry of Stefan George can only be psychologically understood as a determined, deliberate attempt to seek shelter from the terrors of the 'other world'. The National-Socialist leaders thought to profit from such propensities: only he who found an adversary worthy of him could hope to be a true hero and find a hero's death.

Der Wille zur Macht is a confession of faith in '*immoralism*'; Nietzsche attacks 'Moralism'. His first attacks on morality were made in *Jeuseits von Gut und Böse* and *Zur Genealogie der Moral*. In these works he tried to prove that the distinction between Good and Evil could be explained only by the resistance offered by 'the common man' to all that is great and strong. But right on earth lies with active, forceful, spontaneous, aggressive natures.[1] In *Der Wille zur Macht* he praises energetic and skilful men wherever he finds them, and in stronger and stronger terms. They are the world's legislators. They do not find Right ready made: it is they who make Right, by virtue of their superiority. The individual is something absolutely new and creative. Nietzsche envisages him as an absolute regarding all his acts as his exclusive property and assuming sole responsibility for them. Not only do great exploits occur without any thought for the so-called precepts of morality, but they expressly contravene its rules. All important figures in world history ignored morality, ridiculed its claims, and, by a sovereign act of will, established a new law. Every man who considers how best to raise the human species to its supreme splendour and power will realise at once that he must have no truck with morality. For it has always been the fundamental aim of morality to hinder or destroy every ambitious impulse. The great man, whether in the history of thought, in politics, or in war, must be judged according to other precepts than those of morality. Impervious to contradictions and full of that resilient energy that despises all convictions and all doctrines; such is, according to Nietzsche, the typical good German. He finds him not only in Bismarck but also in Handel, Leibnitz, and Goethe. For him, Napoleon is the finest example of the great man of history, who

[1] *Zur Genealogie der Moral*, Vol. II, no. 11.

ignores moral laws and imposes his own law on the world, by virtue of his arbitrary, unlimited power.[1] Everything described as crime must be closely investigated; for a criminal has his own peculiar virtues; he is a man of courage, who risks his life, his honour, and his liberty. A rebel may be punished, but there is nothing despicable in rebellion. Nietzsche, who hates calm and moderation, boldly coins phrases. His models of humanity are the brutal 'geniuses' of the Renaissance, who refused to recognise moral obligations. He was no historian, and his thought consequently shies away from reality and becomes lost in a world of fancy. Caesar Borgia, clad in pontifical dignity, seems to him the highest form humanity can assume. *Der Wille zur Macht* becomes more and more violent in tone; the thought becomes unequivocal but also more absurd.

'The positive passions: pride, joy, health, sexual love, enmity and war, fine gestures, good manners, strong will, mental discipline, will to power and gratitude to the earth and to life—all that is rich and willing to give of its richness, all that showers presents and gold upon life, all that makes it eternal and divine, all the power of virtues that *transfigure*, all that approves and affirms in word and deed.' [2]

Such extravagant language robs the injunction to annihilate the individual and to become fused in the All of its entire meaning. Nietzsche's ideas revolve round 'the great man', the 'master of the masses', the 'future master of the earth'. It is for him that he prepares the 'inversion of valuations'. He writes for a human species that does not yet exist: for the 'masters of the earth'. 'In Plato's Theages are the words: "Each of us would like to be master, if possible of all men, and what we would like still more is to be *God*! This feeling must be revived." ' It is only logical, then, for him to write:

'We must remove supreme goodness from our idea of God: it is unworthy of a God. We must also remove supreme wisdom: it is to the vanity of philosophers that we owe this senseless image of a God who is a monster of wisdom: they wanted God to resemble them! No! Let God have *supreme power*—and that is enough! From this all things are derived, from this "the world" is derived.' [3]

And a few paragraphs later the same idea is expressed in other words:

'Man is a monstrous and superior animal; superior man is inhuman and superhuman: it all holds together. Whenever man grows and betters himself, he gains both in depth and in terror; one cannot will one without the other—or rather: it is sufficient to will the one deliberately in order at once to acquire the other.' [4]

---

[1] *Der Wille zur Macht*, Vol. IV, no. 466.   [2] ibid., no. 479.
[3] ibid., no. 462.   [4] ibid., no. 470.

Nietzsche is not thinking of anything commonplace; as his theory of the hierarchy shows, he is searching for nobility, value, and greatness. He turns to the 'aristocrats'; he appeals to their 'true goodness', to their greatness of soul. These, then, are all his fine doctrines: the wise man must know how to be silent and to bear long periods of hostility; he feels nothing but disgust for demagogy and the familiarity of the populace; he respects honour and manly purity. But this theory, which is incontestably Nietzschean and quite inseparable from his thought as a whole, already marks a departure from the sphere of life and dionysism; it takes us back to an eternal order, 'to a granite-like fidelity of being, which is manifested to us in the shape of moderation and limitation'.[1]

Praise of the great man: the next generation was not to forget these words. It understood the dangerous exigencies of life more readily than the moral hierarchies which, in Nietzsche, go with them. Nietzsche laid himself open to such misunderstandings. The superman, whom Zarathustra was already prophesying, appears again in the war cries and aphorisms of *Der Wille zur Macht*. Nietzsche regards it as an essential phenomenon of life that a large number of individuals should be sacrificed for the benefit of a few, in order to ensure the existence of their betters. He is not afraid to contradict himself: at one point he sacrifices the individual to the species; at another he asserts that the individual must never consider the interests of the species, his own posterity excluded, to the detriment of his own person. He wants unequivocal choice: say no to everything that weakens, say yes to everything that strengthens, to everything that gathers strength, to everything that justifies a feeling of strength. That is why he worships war and the warrior. After demanding strong individuals, he widens his field and demands strong peoples. The idea of race appears: the race is the 'body' that must produce individuals of value, who, in their turn, will continue the evolution. He defends the idea of 'breeding and selection'.[2] But he is thinking not only of the schoolmaster but also of the doctor, who, in certain circumstances, has the right to resort to castration. He is the sworn enemy of Socialism and democracy: he regards them as the tyranny of the little man and the mediocrity. Nothing is more odious to him than the idea that the voices of great men and those of mediocrities can carry the same weight. The Christian doctrine of equality of all men before God he holds responsible for the democratic claims of modern states. This doctrine, he believes, destroys all natural order and prevents the establishment of a 'hierarchy of forces', in which he who commands is given the right to command and he who must obey accepts obedience. Democracy

[1] Friedrich Georg Jünger, loc. cit., p. 83.
[2] *Der Wille zur Macht*, Vol. IV., 312, 333.

is a fatal doctrine that strikes at the roots of all stability. It is a temporal relic of Christianity, the dregs of the religious doctrine after faith has gone. We must put up with them for some time yet.

The future is in the hands of the masters. Nietzsche's entire political thought is summed up in his definition of these new masters.[1] Not only will they be impious (in the Christian sense of the word) but they must succeed, 'without believing in God and without soliciting his guidance, in making their decisions with a sense of responsibility as strong as that formerly acquired from belief in God'.[2] Everything will proceed smoothly: the weak will themselves ask to be guided by the strong, who lead them through perils and darkness and free them of all concern for their responsibility. The path will be more difficult than it was in the eras when one leant on God. The new masters must now replace God and win the profound, absolute confidence of those they dominate. In the future, Nietzsche prophesies, we shall be guided by an intrepid master-race, which will rule over a human flock that has achieved an extremely high degree of intelligence.

It is not unreasonable to conclude that Nietzsche combined the high hopes he vested in those leaders, who are capable of gazing fearlessly into the darkest depths of the universe, with his expectations of a *Germanic neo-paganism*. Most students of Nietzsche attach little importance to this line of thought, which appeared in the last years of Nietzsche's life, and frequently they do not even mention it. Jaspers, to whom we owe the most important modern work on Nietzsche, considers that, compared with the many and extremely profound problems that Nietzsche ventilates, this one does not even merit discussion. Baeumler, on the other hand, devotes his whole attention to it. There is no doubt that a grave misunderstanding has always existed between Nietzsche and Germany. Baeumler attributes it to the fact that the philosopher had succeeded in unearthing the Germanic foundations of the German nature with much more assurance and forcefulness than anyone before him. And, in fact, there are thoughts of this kind in his work. They complete our image of him. The letters written to his friends contain much important information on this point. Just as Nietzsche, at the beginning of his career, had discovered the dionysiac elements of the Hellenic nature, so now he thought he could penetrate beyond Christianity to the Germanic roots, and thus liberate the forces of paganism, which had been neutralised in the past but not conquered. Siegfried steps out against Parsifal. Out of the vast, sombre landscape of Nordic paganism comes the bold warrior to fight Christian Europe. Towards the end of his life he seems to make an effort to become more familiar with the Nordic world. The Sagas play their

[1] K. Jaspers, *Nietzsche und das Christentum*, p. 272.   [2] ibid., p. 273.

part in his thought. In them he found man 'master of himself, knowing when to speak and when to be silent, treating himself with severity and hardness and finding joy in it, and respecting all that is severe and hard'.[1] These thoughts fit quite logically into the general scheme of Nietzsche's ideas. At the same time, they are not so important as they are frequently made out to be. National-Socialism undoubtedly knew what it was doing when it tried to popularise in Germany not only the Germanic spirit but also the figure of Siegfried. It was not only out of love of the country's historic origins. It was a question of crossing the border-line between Christianity and Germanic paganism; and mythical characters helped to re-establish contact with the ancient forms of thought. Nietzsche devoted his entire life to this same attempt.

If we look more closely at Nietzsche's judgments on Christianity we at once perceive the note of violence. It was the most formidable of his adversaries. He never ceases to attack it throughout his entire work, but the attack is concentrated and concerted in one of his later works, *Der Antichrist*. This book would be nothing more than a monstrous blasphemy if one did not discern, behind the cries of fury, a profound reproach. It is impossible to separate Nietzsche's hostility to Christianity from his attachment to the Christian world. It held him captive, even when he was condemning it, as he did right up to his last lucid moment. He felt compelled to reject Christianity because it set up against the dionysiac chaos he wanted to introduce a quite different world—the organised world of the Creation, governed by moderation, the majority and the law. Nietzsche retaliated by accusing Christianity of having caused the 'death of God' by substituting for the tragic truth of life, which was that of the pre-Socratic Greeks, such fictions as a personal God, a moral world-order, a belief in immortality, sin, grace, and redemption. The moment this world of fictions collapses, man is flung into an abyss without precedent in history.[2]

Nietzsche's condemnation of Christianity rests, then, on a pre-philosophical conception of the nature of the world. Nietzsche, in consequence, passed the essentials of Christianity completely by. There has never been any existential encounter between Nietzsche and Christianity, although he was born in a parsonage and spent his youth in an atmosphere that seems to have been saturated with Christianity. It must be admitted that his image of Christianity was distorted at a very early stage either by pietism or by biblical criticism. He became very familiar with the latter thanks to Overbeck and, less directly, to Renan and Strauss, whose influence he acknowledged. It has frequently been stressed that his later work

[1] *Jenseits von Gut und Böse*, no. 260.
[2] K. Jaspers, op. cit., p. 16.

draws on certain elements of Protestantism: his belief in the absurdity of the world and in chaos is another form of the conviction that the world is a prey to demons. Nietzsche was violently opposed to the practices of contemporary Christians, the 'all too many', *die allzuvielen*, who paraded Christian convictions, came to terms, in the name of Christianity, with all men and all doctrines, and separated their lives from their beliefs to such an extent that no trace of Christianity was left. If one also bears in mind that Nietzsche was not a man to reflect calmly and objectively and that he usually jumped, in a sort of feverish exaltation, from his premises to the most remote and the least feasible conclusions, then his impassioned fight against Christianity does not seem to present any psychological problem.

Nietzsche, following the liberal interpretation of the Bible, saw in Jesus the propagator of a religion of love. This, he believed, had been changed by the first Christian community into a religion of faith. St Paul is the chief culprit. These ideas were still sufficiently alive a generation later for Rosenberg to take them up again with his usual naïve temerity. Nietzsche's attitude to Jesus is a twofold one: while he admired the fighter in Him, he condemned His pity for the weak. But he rejected emphatically the Christianity of the apostles. The acts of the apostles seemed to him the best confirmation of his theory of resentment. Christianity, according to him, owed its birth and its success solely to the revolt of slaves against their superiors, against the powerful, against healthy and aristocratic natures that knew when to say Yes to life. His whole criticism of Christianity is based on thoughts of this kind. For him, the sickly ideals of confidence, candour, modesty, patience, love of one's neighbour, and oneness with God were merely a kind of 'resignation and abdication of man in his entirety', which finally gained possession even of strong and noble souls.

> 'What are we combatting in Christianity? Its will to break the strong, to rob them of their courage, to exploit their weak moments and their moments of fatigue, to change their proud assurance into disquiet and scruples of conscience: its gift for poisoning and weakening their aristocratic instincts, till their strength, their will to power changes course and turns against them, till the strong succumb to their excesses and perish from having despised and maltreated themselves: a horrible end, of which Pascal is the most famous example.'

And as Christianity could draw upon the 'pre-existent Christianity' of Socrates and Plato, this is also attacked.

> 'We depend far too much on antiquity, in all the vices from which we suffer, for us to be able to treat it much longer with

indulgence. If the greatest penalty ever exacted of humanity was possible, if Christianity has been able to exist as it has in fact existed, it is the fault of antiquity. Antiquity will be swept away with Christianity.'[1]

IV

Nietzsche, in his last weeks of sanity, was able to see the first effects of his writings. After having complained for so long that no one took account of him, he wrote triumphant letters in the winter of 1888 to his mother, his sister and a few friends: notice was being taken of him in the world. At Copenhagen a series of lectures on him by Georg Brandes attracted large audiences; from France he received friendly letters from Taine; he was expecting lectures on his works to be given in New York and a translation of his works into English; his appeals were finding an echo in Russian high society. He thought his ideas would be particularly well received in the Nordic countries, for there the ground had been prepared 'for his theory of the "morality of the masters" by the detailed and widespread knowledge of the Icelandic Sagas, which offer the richest material in this respect'. As for the Germans, he judged them unsparingly. He was not understood in Germany and it would be a long time before he was.

'My personal conviction is that all my problems, my whole "immoralist" position is much too premature today and too unprepared. Any idea of propaganda is alien to me; I have not so much as lifted a finger on this subject.' [2]

He had no need of propaganda: his compatriots came to him as often as he could have wished. The time was ripe for his ideas. He gave free rein to the tendencies of his period and even gave them a philosophical justification.

He confirmed the will of his epoch to confine itself to earthly things. When he mourned the death of God, he affirmed the fact, to him irrefutable, that man had turned his back on all transcendence. But, in turning towards the dionysiac world, he directed the attention of his time still more exclusively to the inner space of this world, from which there is no escape.

He found appreciation among the military and political circles of the German Empire. In Imperial Germany one heard phrases which bore a strong resemblance to sentences from Zarathustra, phrases like 'blood and iron', hegemony and imperialist aims. The German *bourgeois* with virtually no bent for metaphysics was

---

[1] *Der Philologe der Zukunft*, no. 258 (Vol. X, pp. 403 ff. of the 1901 edition).
[2] *Nietzsche in seinen Briefen und Berichten der Zeitgenossen*, ed. Alfred Baeumler (Stuttgart, 1932), p. 469.

thinking of machines, factories, commerce, banking, and speculation, and was devoting his whole ambition and zeal to rivalling the
dominant position held by the British. 'Imperialism and militarism
were no longer far away, and all these phenomena provided
unanimous evidence that man had turned earthwards towards a
new vitality'.[1] It was only necessary to step outside one's own door
to encounter the will to power. 'Friedrich Nietzsche was neither so
original, nor so unheard-of, nor so untimely nor so un-German;
to say the very least, the milieu which was later to acclaim him
already existed.'[2] In the political and military spheres the sense of
moral responsibility was seen to be crumbling and the 'will to power'
was appearing in its place. The victory of the Prussian over the
German spirit, the programme of the Pangermanists, Treitschke's
science of history—these are different expressions of the same basic
phenomenon. We are concerned here only with events in Germany,
and what happened in other countries is outside our scope. But it
would not be a difficult task to find corresponding movements in
other parts of Europe. It is, however, remarkable that Nietzsche
remained apart from all the forces of his time. Bismarck, despite his
lack of scruples, was, in his view, much too Christian. Although he
himself had been hostile to the Jews, who had furthered the victory
of the slave morality, anti-Semites were anathema to him, probably
because of their noisy attitude. But it is striking that his criticism did
not cover the Prussian spirit. He had a presentiment of future
developments which would reflect his political ideas.

Nietzsche's relations with the thinking world around him can be
summarised by saying that there was no essential opposition between
him and his period.

'All that he demanded—a will directed to the things of this
world, the development of force, the acceptance of a situation
without metaphysics, life-energy—all this was under way, independently of him, in the spheres of politics, economics, the army
and social evolution.'[3]

For some time past not only accepted conventions had been
exposed (Ibsen) but laws had been abrogated and weakness and
decadence had been counteracted by battalions. All that was still
lacking was a lightning-conductor, a philosophy, a theory to illuminate an already established practice, a language in which the
period could find expression. Nietzsche gave his period the arms it
needed. He himself did not know what he was unleashing. For it
is one thing to talk within four walls of the morality of the masters
and the morality of the slaves, of the will to power and the misdeeds

---

[1] O. Flake, *Nietzsche* (Baden-Baden, 1948), p. 176.
[2] ibid., p. 164.   [3] ibid., p. 178.

of Christianity, and to compose personal declarations of war at a writing-desk. But it is another thing to bring the same precept into public discussion. Nietzsche thought without taking into account political reality and without considering the consequences. When these consequences became apparent, they contributed to a world-disaster. Before long the German taste for the immoderate felt itself unhampered; from that moment no movement was strong enough to oppose it with any prospect of success. It was pointless to wonder, then, if these consequences were intended by Nietzsche or not.

It is therefore far from true to say that Nietzsche, the spiritual father of all the major movements of the twentieth century, was, at the time of his death, 'defeated and discredited'.[1] On the contrary, already-existent movements had acquired a direction from him, and he had brought others into being. The currents of political and military life found support in literature, where fresh forces were appearing. One has the impression of a circular movement. The elements common to all these different styles, which follow very rapidly on one another, are the rejection of transcendence, adhesion to the earth, biologism in the sense of Darwinian evolutionism, determination of life by mundane forces. Nietzsche's basic experience repeats itself: the world is chaotic and demands a superman to master it; but the superman, in his turn, can exist only in a chaotic world. The one conditions the other; and this 'eternal return' of the anarchical life forces and the 'saviours' is the curse of the post-Nietzsche epoch, the price it pays for an existence dedicated to pure immanence. The German, who is so prone to become lost in subterranean labyrinths and is 'always on the march towards chaos through disorder and hidden passages',[2] finally invents the forces capable of restoring order, the men capable of controlling anarchy. But he cannot find salvation; in the end he falls victim to both, anarchy and the new order. The speed of interchange quickens, lack of tradition and continuity are constantly compelling new attempts, breathing becomes harder, one idea chases the other. And the sole compensation is that at each step man has a little less to lose.

About 1900 the plot becomes clearly visible. The 'Superman' appears in the shape of Renaissance man, particularly in the historical drama. Nietzsche's admiration for the Renaissance emerges here; but the ideas of Gobineau and Burckhardt on the Renaissance also have an obvious influence, as well as the works of Conrad Ferdinand Meyer. Particular stress is laid on uninhibited egoism, especially in erotic life. 'Beyond Good and Evil' has become a mere formula for moral corruption: Nietzsche's conception could

[1] Gottfried Benn, *Frühe Prosa und Reden* (Wiesbaden, 1950), p. 215.
[2] ibid., p. 218.

not have been more radically misinterpreted. Naturally these Renaissance characters, these 'men of action', are conceived in the image of modern men; but, inversely, modern man can also be invested with the features of Renaissance man. Heinrich Mann, in the novels he wrote at the beginning of the century, is one of the chief exponents of this 'immoralism', as much of the sixteenth-century Renaissance as of the modern Renaissance (*The Duchess of Assy, In the Cockaigne Country*). In them we find all the aspirations of the period: beauty, power, a taste for the superhuman, the sweetness of living, sensual ardour, exuberance, wealth, palaces and thrones, the primitive and the luxurious, the will to destruction, and scandal. Man throws off all moral bonds. The strong man prospers in a world of nihilism.

By contrast there is Gerhart Hauptmann after his naturalist period. This poet of pity does not like the superman, but he is in love with the earth and dionysiac forces. He is sensitive to power and to the richness of germinating life, to the elementary, obscure forces of intoxication; he evokes the appeals and benedictions of the demons of the earth, Dionysos and Demeter. During his tour of Greece in 1907, when he visited Olympia, Delphi, Athens, and Sparta, it was not the relics of ancient art that impressed him most, but nature, the landscape, and the primitive population. He felt himself to be in touch with the secret forces of existence, drinking from the very fountain-head of being. For him the earth was the Mother who dispenses life; and the god Eros shared out good and evil among men.

This hostile juxtaposition between the dionysiac and the Apollonic spirit, between movement and form, the amorphous and the plastic will, diffusion and systematic violence is characteristic of the evolution during the decades following Nietzsche's death.

As soon as a poet appears he finds himself committed to nihilism. In his way, he tries to conquer it, but without ever succeeding in escaping from the vicious circle.

This is clearly indicated in the case of Rilke and George. Rilke thinks that man will find his salvation by breaking away from himself. He attempts to escape from his unbalanced existence by turning towards 'the inner cosmic space': when man, by a mystical act, succeeds in passing 'beyond' being, he is free from his self. Rilke has described many personal experiences of his own to support this. On the other hand, he makes enormous demands on the artist: he expects him to liberate the living creature from itself. Most characteristic of George, from the psychological point of view, is his hostility to chaos; he refuses to abandon himself. War is declared between the I and the non-I; everything retrieved from chaos is a gain for the circle of human relations. The hidden world which, half in terror, half in scorn, he calls 'the other world', drives the I into a conflict in which the whole of life is involved. George professed a deep veneration for Nietzsche, not, however, for the follower of Dionysos, but for the author of *Der Wille zur Macht*. Like Nietzsche, he thought his own creations would enable him to face up to nothingness.

The picture can be reproduced *ad nauseam*. What all these thoughts have in common is a lack of faith in a world order. Since Nietzsche, the evolution has assumed the proportions of a landslide. The essential thing is always the total loss of reality. Gottfried Benn, perhaps the most interesting German thinker in this open discussion with nihilism, still confesses: [1]

'My generation was still left with a few literary relics from preceding generations, to which it could cling: the problems of father and son, antiquity, adventure, travel, social questions, a *fin de siècle* melancholy, the problems of marriage, love-themes. The present generation has nothing left, no substance, no style, neither culture nor knowledge, neither feelings nor formal demands; it has no foundation—and it will be a long time before it finds one again.'

No thinker, in Germany at least, has reproduced so clearly Nietzsche's spiritual condition. All that we see 'at the bottom of things is an uncertain flux, an ambivalence of shape and shapelessness, gods of an hour that destroy and construct. . . . It is this void that we perceive behind all the great figures, behind all the turning-points of history, behind all things.' But it is precisely this situation, Benn believes, that induces man to strain away from the void. It is not true, according to him, that we have reached a turning-point: the world has always been as it is today. The human mind has never known any other atmosphere than this ambivalence of construction and destruction; it has never become conscious of itself except as an arbiter between the formal and the void. Reality is in a constant state of flux.

On the face of it, all these problems have no connection with National-Socialism. But they show how in the mortal conflict between the I and chaos all that has kept men alive for centuries, all that they have died for has been lost: faith in order and in values, the certainty that the world has a meaning and that there exist certain 'good things' which bind us together, which are given to man and do not have to be 'created' by him. All of us, who suffer from the problems of the twentieth century and who strive to exorcise the nihilist peril, must agree that National-Socialism could emerge only at the end of this process of world exhaustion. The man

[1] Gottfried Benn, *Doppelleben* (Wiesbaden, 1950), p. 188.

who no longer believes that values and ideas exist which dominate us
will no longer risk his life for them. When, for over a generation,
men have prayed for the 'superman', whatever meaning they may
have given the word, one must not be surprised if he appears one
day in his most powerful and most cruel form. In thirty years
Nietzsche, from his solitary room at Sils-Maria, had succeeded in
capturing the hearts of millions of people; he had completely undermined their former faith; he had brought them all face to face with
nothingness. No one had now the strength left to hold out against
the monstrous claims of the 'superman' or to rebel against them.
Not only Germany but the whole world will be in mortal peril so
long as normal relations with the world have not been restored in
the conscience of man, in place of chaos and the superman. We shall
never conquer nihilism unless we manage to escape from the clutches
of chaos and the superman. To say, in fact, that man has lost the
'world' in which he lived is, in the end, simply to say that he no
longer possesses anything, that he has no more convictions and ideas
to defend, no conscience to guide him, no sense of responsibility to
direct him. He has lost all continuity, all cohesion, all links. Instead of methodical work, of patient but reasoned action, he is left
with movement for its own sake, with action for its own sake.
National-Socialist Germany practised a nihilism of this kind.
Anyone wishing to live in these conditions only has a choice between
one of two solutions: a pessimistic return to the dark source of things,
or the abandonment of his own I to another more powerful, and if
possible collective, I. The man who has so abandoned himself
frequently adopts both solutions simultaneously: there is no contradiction in this; on the contrary, it is the result of an inner logic.

The destiny of the superman weighs heavily on us. As we well
know today, when the superman comes on the scene, there is no
longer any room for man. The complementary idea of the superhuman is the 'subhuman'. But the superhuman, whatever form it
may take, is always inhuman. How could the superman, the
autonomous man, who has ignored God's commandments, proclaim laws and precepts which were not impious? How could one
expect of him that he should fail to stamp underfoot the dignity of
man and his liberty? He proclaims his will and demands arbitrarily
and expects absolute obedience. There is nothing more odious to
him than to hear men calling upon their conscience or divine
precepts. Every man who accepts the idea of the superman must
abandon all moral order; he condemns himself to act as an auto-
maton and must allow himself to be treated as such. And it has
frequently been demonstrated that he did not even find it unpleasant to be set in motion like an automoton. It is quite logical
that nothing in a dictatorship should carry less weight than respect

for man. Hitler left his friends in no doubt on this point. The 'superman' is always surrounded by creatures without personality, like marionettes or robots.

The 'superman' of modern times is the political dictator, the tyrant who rules over the will of millions, imposes his organisations and institutions on them, and keeps guard over them. But his partner, the individual who has long since been deprived of all personality, is a grey, faceless being, without any spiritual features or an existence of its own. He is a mere fragment of the general chaos, the material that the 'superman' moulds and masters. He has even ceased to know what man's condition is; not only has he forgotten the part he played in the kingdom of salvation, but also his specific function as a thinking being destined to understand and dominate the world. An arbitrary and superior will has confined him in a prison of forces hostile to life, in the kingdom of the machine, of automatism, of technics. He must let himself be persuaded, on the other hand, that his true place is below humanity, that he is descended from the animal, and that he is part of an inanimate life. National-Socialism, with its race theory, did everything possible to reduce man to a biological level. It professed to teach respect for life, to encourage the family sense and veneration for ancestors. But, in reality, it practised a biological materialism, the purpose of which was to make each man understand that, as an individual, he was nothing but 'as a people everything'. This is the very thought Nietzsche expresses when he writes that history is not concerned with the conservation of the individual, but only with that of the species. Man's origin is in the dark forces of the earth; he is bound to the lesser beings; he is dependent on dionysiac powers and, in consequence, on a meaningless power. All these doctrines could not fail to destroy in him the feeling of belonging to a unique species, for which the world had been created, and to develop the gloomy presentiment of his nothingness. Thomàs Mann once wrote: 'All transcendence is animal, all that is animal transcends.' And Gottfried Benn, who quotes this as one of the classic formulæ of the post-Nietzsche period, adds: 'If transcendence . . . still exists, it can only be animal; if man is still able to find support in any element outside the individual, it can only be in the organic world.' [1] It is absurd to give this interpretation of existence a sort of religious consecration, as all the forms of 'German' religion have done: it is all too clear and all too distressing that the only conclusion to be drawn from such a conception is a return to chaos.

Nietzsche's prophecy of the 'superman', his dionysiac faith, the history of the consequences of his philosophy, all the subsequent deviations, the political catastrophes, the punishment humanity

[1] Gottfried Benn, *Frühe Prosa und Reden*, p. 231.

has had to suffer, the horrible, inhuman penalties: all this is the
effect of one sole cause—namely, that man has lost sight of himself.
Nietzsche's historical importance lies in having opened the eyes of
the world to the disaster. He also knew the root of the disease.
He formulated his diagnosis in one crystalline phrase: 'God is dead!'
In going astray himself, he prepared the destiny of humanity in the
following generation and became partly guilty of the general disaster.
He himself was rooted in the traditions of his time, owed much more
to the ideas of his century than he was prepared to admit, and he
was much less of an innovator than he claimed to be. But ever since
he had first raised his voice, ever since 1880 or thereabouts, the
shadows had thickened round man, nothingness had crept in more
and more upon thought, poetry, and—as Sedlmayr has shown so
strikingly in his *Verlust der Mitte* (1948)—still more the fine arts.
It cannot be denied, however, that this situation developed only
gradually. 'The former resources of the humanist tradition have
only drained away slowly.' [1] Research into the main historical
origins of the terrible upheavals of our century has only just begun.
Only when it is completed will we be able to think of solving the
vast problem of the spiritual foundations of our age. The currents
go right back, well beyond Nietzsche and through romanticism, to
the century of Rousseau. Wherever the 'Return of Dionysos'
(*Rossteutscher*) manifests itself, we can be sure that Nietzsche, and at
the same time our own destiny, is emerging.

Nietzsche's doctrine is a terrible one, and it had devastating
results; there can be no doubt of that today. But in the same
judgment one may condemn his ideas, but spare his person. He
was a carrier of messages which often seem merely to have made use
of him as of an instrument. He was the representative of impersonal
powers, which were much stronger than he. Thomas Mann, with his
customary penetration and artistic skill, has described the dispro-
portion between this frail man and his gigantic task, in a way that
can only arouse pity for him.

'His soul, overburdened and crushed by its mission, had been
marked out for knowledge without being prepared for it by birth
and, like that of Hamlet, it succumbed under the load. . . . A
mind, that was originally pious, prone to veneration, attached to
religious traditions, was, so to speak, seized by the hair by destiny
and flung into the intoxication and frenzy of a prophecy, which,
rejecting all piety and raging against itself, sang the praises of
luxuriant and barbaric force, of hardness of heart and of evil.
One must know the springs of this mind . . . to understand the
improbable, adventurous, unforeseeable curve of his life. . . .
We perceive a great and noble talent, according to accepted

[1] Sedlmayr, loc. cit., p. 156.

standards, which seems to promise a most forthright and eminent career. Instead of that, to what unexplored lands did his destiny not drive him! To what fatal peaks he climbed!' [1]

Langbehn, who remained with Nietzsche for some time during his madness and who, in the course of his walks, still heard some highly reasonable observations from the philosopher, passes the following judgment:

> 'Nietzsche's derangement . . . recalls in a striking way the present suicides of overworked students. One must have pity on him and not condemn him. He played with traditional truths like a child with a house of bricks and one day, for his amusement, he demolished everything. It was a criminal act and he was punished. . . . But it must be said to his credit, that he personally never showed the slightest trace of pride. . . . I have never known, among cultured men, a more innocent and more candid creature than he. . . . In Nietzsche I lose a brother. May God have pity on his poor soul! May I beg you to recommend him to God's mercy—*because he was my brother?*' (To Bishop Keppler, Autumn 1900.) [2]

On the other hand, there is no denying that it is possible, even in his very early work, to find the same spirit of negation, of contradiction, of refusal, of denial. Like Lichtenberg in this respect, he felt impelled at one time to deny all things and to make a clear break with all habits of thought. More than one of his biting observations can be understood only if one bears in mind that his primary aim was to irritate and defy his friends. It is undoubtedly the only way to explain the incredible tone of *Ecce Homo*. Nietzsche wanted to destroy everything, root and branch; but his impassioned thought blinded him to such an extent that he could not see the foundations of the edifice. Visitors (like Paneth) had the impression of a man who thought with all his being, like someone possessed, and not merely in a rational or intellectual way. He took no account of contradictions; he ignored system; he yielded to the impulses of his thought, which carried him now one way, now another. The complete absorption of his whole self in his thought, without ever achieving a measure of detachment, and the dependence of his thought upon the world of instinct, unknown and intangible, these are traits which Nietzsche himself frequently underlined, particularly in his letters to his friends, with a mixture of voluptuousness and terror.

---

[1] Thomas Mann 'Nietzsches Philosophie im Lichte unserer Erfahrung' in *Neue Studien* (Frankfurt, 1948), p. 114.
[2] Benedikt Momme Nissen, *Der Rembrandtdeutsche* (Freiburg, 1927), p. 132.

'It is as if I had once again staked my whole being.' [1]

'Good, I have a second nature; but it is not there to destroy the first, it is there to support it. My first nature would have ruined me—it has almost ruined me as it is.' [2]

'Ah! my friend, the idea sometimes crosses my mind that I really lead a madly dangerous life, for I am one of those machines that can *burst*! The intensity of my feelings makes me shudder and laugh . . .' [3]

The whole of *Zarathustra*, of course, is the explosion of forces that have been accumulating for decades: it is not the first time that the author of an explosion of this kind has himself perished in the catastrophe. '. . . You have a terribly dangerous friend, and the worst in him is all that he can retain in himself.'

Nietzsche advised others to mistrust him and his destiny.[4] But thousands have succumbed to his spell. His cries of despair went unnoted, but not his indignation and his war-cries. His moving language caught on; the formulæ he had found stuck in people's minds. With a steadily rising passion, Nietzsche marks the beginning of the crisis. In their torrential speeches, Hitler and Goebbels undertook to bring the whole edifice down in ruins.

It is not difficult now to see where our salvation lies. It will be granted us if we succeed in freeing ourselves from the world of Nietzsche, in rejecting the autonomy of man and restoring the divine laws among men.

---

[1] Nietzsche, *Briefe*, loc. cit., p. 186.   [2] ibid., p. 280.
[3] ibid., p. 249.   [4] ibid., p. 263.

5

THE RELIGIOUS CONCEPTION OF RACE: HOUSTON STEWART CHAMBERLAIN AND GERMANIC CHRISTIANITY

Jean Réal

I. HIS LIFE AND THE GROWTH OF HIS THOUGHT

H. S. CHAMBERLAIN was born in Portsmouth in 1855. Early on he lost his mother. His father, an English admiral, had him brought up at Versailles by a grandmother. But the child's delicate health soon called for the air of the Midi, where he moved from one retreat to another, receiving an intermittent and quite desultory education. What was striking about the child was his unusually emotional temperament. He was the plaything of hidden spirits, of dreams and immoderate enthusiasms. Music or the sight of nature plunged him into ecstasies.[1]

But soon his pathetic loneliness drove this expatriate to look for his homeland within himself and to shut himself up in an imaginary world of heroes.[2] In later life the books that he was to write with passion and in a state of permanent fever would also evoke this inner world where he had cloistered himself in the company of great genius.

Is it, then, surprising under these circumstances, that the first deep and lasting impressions were to leave their impact upon him? From 1870 to 1874 he was in the hands of one remarkable tutor (a real Prussian, Otto Kuntze), who introduced him to an heroic and victorious Germany and to the Germany of the poets and thinkers—William I, Beethoven, Schiller, Wagner. Then in 1874 he fell wildly in love with a Prussian girl called Anna Horst, another true neurotic. It was Germany that attracted and fascinated this Englishman living in France. Under the double influence of his tutor and his fiancée, Chamberlain had soon chosen as his country the fatherland of music and sentimental mysticism. From Seville, in May 1876, he wrote his fiancée an ecstatic letter, his first apologia

[1] H. S. Chamberlain, *Lebenswege meines Denkens* (Bruckmann, Munich, 2nd imp., 1922), pp. 39, 84–7, 169, 170, 172, 174, 184 seq.
H. S. Chamberlain, *Briefe* (1928), II, p. 59. (All Chamberlain's works are published by Bruckmann.)
[2] *Lebenswege*, p. 31.

243

for Germany, showing already all the major themes of his future work.[1]

Let us note well that this letter was written by a hypersensitive, a neurotic, who could be thrown off his balance merely by one vivid impression and launched into ecstasies from which he emerged with sudden resolutions that upset the course of his life.[2] He was a man who, under a robust exterior, was almost always ill and passed from one nervous collapse to another.

From 1879 to 1884 at Geneva, he studied enthusiastically in natural history, physics, chemistry, and even medicine. He undertook a thesis on *The Rising of Sap*, but at the same time he considerably widened his literary, philosophical, and artistic reading. Music thrilled him more than ever. From 1882 to 1884 he went to the festival at Bayreuth. Immortal days! He quickly became an apostle of the new ideals, and, in 1885, with Edouard Dujardin he founded the *Revue Wagnérienne*. In the autumn of 1884, a particularly serious nervous breakdown stopped completely—and for good—his researches into botany. Because abstract thinking tired him less, he turned towards the philosophy of science and to aesthetics—Kant, Schopenhauer, Plato, and Goethe.

At Dresden, where he lived from 1885 to 1889, he was absorbed by his enthusiasm for Bayreuth. In 1888, a landmark, he made the acquaintance of Cosima, to whom he devoted an almost mystical attachment.

But he spent the most active and rewarding years of his life in Vienna between 1889 and 1909.

In Vienna he still followed the botany lectures of Wiesner. But on 19th January 1892 precisely,[3] a demon, which was never to leave him, descended on him and forced him to write. From that day his vocation began: he would fight with his pen and make known to a degenerate humanity what his years of meditation on nature and the work of Wagner had revealed to him: Wagner, the climax of the authentic tradition of Germanic culture.

Nature and Wagner are in effect the two poles of a single philosophy in Chamberlain and the main themes of all his writing. Until 1896, certainly, all his activity seemed to be consecrated to Wagner: helping Cosima, conferences at the Wagner Society, a host of articles, two good books, *The Theatre of Richard Wagner* (1892), and in particular, his moderately well-known *Richard Wagner* (1896).

[1] *Lebenswege*, p. 59.
[2] His first evening in Florence, where he went in 1878, with the firm intention of studying biology, shattered his plans. *Lebenswege*, p. 85. He immediately decided to abandon biology in favour of the fine arts. Six months later, another vision produced another crisis. He left Florence at once; eight days later he was already making his first attempts at histology in Geneva. *Lebenswege*, p. 86.
[3] ibid., pp. 123–5. *Der Schreibdämon*.

But at the same time as he meditated on the externals of living beings, he was trying to penetrate the mystery of life. Suddenly in 1896 his preoccupation as a biologist came to the fore and seemed to arrest all his work for Bayreuth. In the train coming back from Italy, the thoughts which had been so long suppressed, surged upon him so forcefully that he stopped at Gardone and shut himself up for eight days in a hotel, and feverishly set down what he was to call his *Lebenslehre*, thirty pages outlining the essentials of his biological thesis —*Leben ist Gestalt*—with some reference to the tangents shooting off from this basic principle that was to illumine all his work and his analysis of races, civilisations, history, and its heroes.

At this point he was able to look forward to his later books, to see them in relation to each other and allow them to arrange their own order of writing. In the course of this year 1896, he polished his earlier notes on *The Rising of Sap*, set rapidly down on paper the outline and general introduction of his *Foundations of the Nineteenth Century*, and he considered a book on Goethe and another on Kant. An engagement towards his publisher assured to the *Foundations* a quite fortuitous priority, but he had hardly finished this enormous labour and restarted his *Goethe*, when in April 1900 a new demon[1] assailed him and restored the prior claims of the *Kant* for some years. Nevertheless, in the summer of 1900, he edited as well certain important appendices to his *Lebenslehre*, and in the *Kant* some enormous chapters were given to Goethe and to the problem of living beings. Other chapters were devoted to the subject of scientific knowledge; some were reports on art and religion, or Germanic Christianity—all problems which Chamberlain had already tackled in his earlier works.

But the book on Kant was hardly finished when his demon attacked again and he restarted the *Goethe*.[2] This *Goethe*, on which Chamberlain had pondered for twenty years, benefited now from the long meditations on the philosophy of Kant. Obedient to a 'mysterious necessity', this book was a labour of love until 1912. In reality, under the cover of Goethe, whom he interpreted in his own way and in whom he saw reflected the ideas of Plato, Kant, and Wagner, Chamberlain was giving to his own artistic, scientific, and religious ideas their most complete exposition.

After this monumental *Goethe*, Chamberlain returned yet again from 1913 to 1921 to the critical study of Christianity and tried to give a new impression of Germanic Christianity whose development had haunted him for so long; this was to be his last book, *Man and God* (1921), in which the old themes would be treated: chapters on race and religion, on art and religion.

But nothing could be more false than to represent Chamberlain as an author playing successively with every subject or as a wandering

[1] *Lebenswege*, p. 141. [2] ibid., p. 142.

I

biologist studying problems of art and religion. There was a profound unity of inspiration in all his writing; the original design was lasting and all his efforts had a remarkable coherence. These books were primarily the works of a naturalist.[1] One could repeat about them all what Chamberlain had written to Cosima about the *Foundations*: 'dass es ein Stück "Bayreuther Arbeit" werden soll'.[2] Clearly there was always the same inspiration and always the same conflict in all this work, subject to the demoniacal enthusiams of an author who was almost always ill, a poor neurotic whose fine intelligence was dominated by his abnormal sensitivity.

Each of his books was like a terrible fever and a prodigious enthusiasm gripped him;[3] but he would forget this later and then become almost uninterested. Cut off from the world, cloistered with his consuming intoxication, driven into immense labours and sustained by a feeling of sacred duty, he wrote in a state of lucent trance or of split personality so that the results surpassed his own expectations and he was unable to recognise them as his own work.[4] He concentrated entirely on the particular moment, and often bursts of enthusiasm or anger lit up briefly austere points which should have been treated serenely and objectively.[5]

Such was the character of Chamberlain throughout. But the Viennese period, when he conceived and carried through almost the entirety of his work, was, moreover, noteworthy at its apogee—between 1900 and 1906—for the long and terrible crisis of his divorce. The woman whom he had loved passionately, his senior by ten years, even more ill and nervous than himself, had aged prematurely but remained very exacting. The mysterious rupture of a mystical friendship which had linked him to a 'beautiful soul', the Countess of Zichy, made the position all the more pitiful. The writer spent months of anxiety and feared that he would become mad. But fame called: William II was interested in the *Foundations* and invited him to Potsdam. At Bayreuth, Cosima and her daughter Eva (whom he married in 1908 after his divorce) attracted him towards the kingdom of sacred art and pure happiness. But Anna Horst was sixty, and her physical and mental health was disquieting. In a bitter upheaval that one hesitates to judge, Chamberlain, thirsty for life and wanting to work in peace, separated in 1905 from the woman who had been his idolised wife and the partner in all his work.[6]

[1] *Lebenswege*, p. 143.
[2] *Cosima Wagner und H. S. Chamberlain im Briefwechsel* (Leipzig, 1934), p. 500.
[3] Letter of 10 Feb. 1901, to his friend Adolphe Appia (Unpublished Correspondence, Chamberlain-Archiv, Bayreuth).
[4] *Lebenswege*, p. 3.
[5] e.g. H. S. Chamberlain, *Die Grundlagen des XIX. Jahrhunderts* (9th imp., 1909), p. 448.
[6] Anna Chamberlain, *Meine Erinnerungen an H. S. Chamberlain* (Munich, 1923).

Three years later he married Eva Wagner, the Maestro's youngest daughter, and went to live in Bayreuth, near Wahnfried, and Cosima who had fascinated him for twenty years.

One could hardly underestimate the importance of this terrible crisis in the life of a man as sensitive as Chamberlain.

But his new happiness could not last. The war of 1914 obliged this Englishman who had made himself the champion of Imperial Germany to break with his country. Moreover, he certainly did not hesitate before this 'war of annihilation that the bandit peoples have unleashed against Germany, the hearth of peace'.[1] He joined wholeheartedly in the fray. Forgetting all that he owed to France and England, he published absurdly chauvinist pamphlets against them. In April 1915 the Emperor decorated Chamberlain with the Iron Cross, for, from 1901 onwards, after reading the *Foundations*, he had hailed Chamberlain as 'a friend in battle and an ally' sent by God.[2] In April 1916 Chamberlain became a naturalised German.

The defeat in 1918 ruined his hopes but did not break his faith. He remained faithful to the fallen emperor. He was gradually overcome by an incurable paralysis. He withstood the blows of fate with fine courage, and continued, half successfully, to fight his own battles. His lips dictated painfully to his attentive wife his last work *Man and God* and also his last articles.

Meanwhile, one hope lit up the evening of his life: Hitler. From the time of a congress at Bayreuth, the future dictator came to recognise in the old man the prophet of the master race, the clairvoyant of the Third Reich. Characteristically, this emotional giant, on the brink of the grave, allowed himself to be seduced by Hitler's magnetic personality, abandoned himself to him and warmly embraced the new cause. His intuition could see his next step without realising into what depths the theory of race, that theory which he himself had launched and of which Hitler would work out the inevitable conclusions, was going to plunge Germany.

Imprisoned within his idealism, with his faith in the future of Germany, Chamberlain gradually declined and died on 9 January 1927.

It is important to note that the two decisive influences to which Chamberlain remained subject during his life—those of nature and Wagner—acted on him in a parallel way, and both drove him towards an irrationalism to which his temperament had already only too great a tendency.

[1] *Lebenswege*, p. 153.
[2] *Briefe*, II, p. 143. Letter from the Emperor to Chamberlain, 31 Dec. 1901.

What had he learnt from the contemplation of nature, from the ecstasies that bowled him over on the arrival of spring or the 'religious ecstasies', such as that on Monte Generoso when he was seventeen?[1]

He appreciated with certainty that 'experience' was for him the highest and most reliable form of knowledge, defying all logical analysis. He felt that the artist understood the mysteries of life better and interpreted them more exactly than the scholar. Otherwise, his meditations on living forms showed him that living meant to persevere in being, maintaining in face of and against all things a specifically organic form (*Gestalt*), and remaining unresponsive to all forms of evolution.

It is also clear that music exerted considerable effect on his sensitivity and influenced him remarkably. In listening to Beethoven he forgot his physical existence to such a point, that he felt himself disembodied.[2] Wagner, on the contrary, 'electrified him'. His music was for Chamberlain 'like an appeal to action and to battle and made his whole body tremble'.[3] At Dresden he no longer went to concerts, because the music gave him dangerous palpitations.

Since 1875 he knew that Wagner was above argument.[4] His faith in him was total. In 1882 he met him in Bayreuth, and Wagner became and remained 'the sun of his life'. This image, he said, should be taken in its quite literal sense: he was no more himself than a planet gravitating round the heavenly body that provided light and heat.[5] And when, in 1888, he had made the acquaintance of Cosima, he was definitely bewitched; his independence disappeared: he espoused all the causes of the woman to whom he was now devoted, and he went so far as to contradict certain of his previous statements so as to remain orthodox.[6]

But what Chamberlain discovered through Wagner was the exaltation of life and of the intuition, an apologia for Art as an indispensable ancillary to a mystical religion, and the affirmation of the theory of race: the noxiousness of the Jew; and the Germans as the chosen people, the salvation of a decadent humanity.

Besides these two decisive influences, the importance of Kant was evident as the true master of his thinking[7] and the basic source of his metaphysics. We should also mention Schopenhauer, who attracted his attention to the unrestrained *élan* of the will to live and to the liberating function of Art. But from 1896 onwards, Schopenhauer became less important in Chamberlain's view then Kant, and to-

[1] *Lebenswege*, pp. 75, 79, 184; *Briefe*, II, p. 53.   [2] ibid., pp. 197–8.
[3] ibid., pp. 196–7.   [4] ibid., p. 165.   [5] ibid., pp. 159–60.
[6] Nothing is more typical in this respect, than the two contradictory versions that Chamberlain gives of the birth of Tristan: 'Notes sur Tristan et Isolde' in *Revue Wagnérienne* (Nov.–Dec. 1887), and H. S. Chamberlain, *Richard Wagner* (1896).
[7] *Lebenswege*, p. 161.

wards 1905 Kant diminished before Goethe in whom Chamberlain saw as much an anti-evolution naturalist as an artist of genius. Finally, besides Schiller—the Scheller of the *Letters on Education*— besides Plato and Homer, in whom he saw the unexampled creator of an aesthetic religion, it was the India of ancient times, the days of the Vedas and Upanishads, that exercised an important influence on Chamberlain's philosophy and religious ideas.

This was the spiritual background of Chamberlain's development; it was to drag him fatally into the paths of irrationalism, intuitive reasoning, and agnosticism.

II. CHAMBERLAIN'S MAIN IDEAS

NEO-KANTISM

CHAMBERLAIN's whole philosophy ran in a Kantian mould. His theories of knowledge and life, or religion and morals, rest on the first principles of Kant.

One problem preoccupied Chamberlain from youth to death: he was attempting to explain the life and form of living beings. But, like Kant, Chamberlain realised that the human spirit imposed its own laws on all observed phenomena. One could not therefore construct a theory of biology without first positing a theory of metaphysics and aesthetics.[1] In fact, in his *Lebenslehre*, published in 1896, just as later in his *Kant* and in his *Goethe*, Chamberlain only approached the problems of biology—of species, of race, of *Gestalt*—after having carefully analysed the specific activity of the mind. In one apothegm that was inspired by Goethe he summed up this analysis: 'Das Höchste wäre zu begreifen, dass alle Erscheinung schon Idee ist.'[2]

But this basic dualism in man, at the same time responsive and reasoning, natural but free, was full of dangers. The most frequent led man to take for objective reality what was only an artifact of the mind. Following from this came the hypostases and finite dogma, for science as for religion, which could in fact only legitimately be explained in symbolic terms. Some, such as the doctrinaires of the theory of evolution, reduced man to a simple organism and denied his liberty; whilst others, blinded by their religious superstitions, subjected nature to the arbitrary will of an unattainable God, and constructed a historical type of religion. Haphazard materialism, said Chamberlain, and absurd and dreary monotheism! Basing himself on Kant, Chamberlain affirmed the unique legitimacy of a strictly mechanistic science allied to a type of religion that was

[1] H. S. Chamberlain, *Natur und Leben* (1928), p. 115.
[2] H. S. Chamberlain, *Immanuel Kant* (4th imp., 1921), p. 567.

purely 'ideal',[1] that is to say, forbearing from all explanations about natural phenomena in order to remain strictly spiritual.

THE CRITICISM OF 'EXACT SCIENCE'

Chamberlain, who had had a scientific education, never ceased to proclaim his respect for science. However, his outlook on science revealed where his deepest sympathies lay.

Certainly it is only normal to see him attack, around 1900, the abuses of a narrowly scientific outlook or again to underline with remarkable perspicuity the limitations of 'exact science', that is to say, the sciences based on mathematics. He admitted the unarguable success of 'exact science', but took pleasure, as if with secret happiness, in showing its implicit inadequacies and considerable risks.[2]

Exact science only reached the periphery of things. It reduced everything to figures and abstractions. Its ideal was 'a continual movement in an empty void'.[3] It was rich in knowledge but poor in ideas; it dominated nature without understanding her. It finally became inhuman and finished as what Chamberlain called 'eine wissenschaftliche Bildungsbarbarei'.[4] It was exhausted by a sterile —and dangerous—search into first causes, desperately determined to explain the nature of Becoming without being able to grasp the nature of Being. Undoubtedly from this sprang Chamberlain's profound objection to 'exact science' and also the violent invective that he launched against it, for he himself wanted to work out a philosophy and a science of Being.[5] For, besides this, he was too passionately interested in the irrational strands of life and art, and had too mystical an idea of nature for him to accept without question the dryness of the scientific method, when something dear to him was at stake. In fact, he used science, as we shall see, just so long as it was of use to him and threw it aside when it became an embarrassment.[6] With his often good intentions, his often sound ideas, Chamberlain made on this point highly equivocal statements from which he drew the greatest possible profit.

'THE WORLD OF THE EYE'

In order to overcome the difficulties of 'exact science', Chamberlain hoped to build by its side a quite different but complementary

---

[1] *Grundlagen*, p. 924–5; *Kant*, p. 172.
[2] Cf. the striking argument in which he contrasts the mathematical optics of Helmholtz with Goethe's theory of colour (*Kant*, pp. 119 62).
[3] *Kant*, pp. 116, 151.   [4] ibid., p. 137.
[5] See, for example, *Kant*, pp. 135–9, and *Goethe* (Munich, 1932), pp. 395–6, 688.
[6] See, below, III and IV, and *Grundlagen*, Foreword to First Impression, p. xiii.

science which would be that 'world of the eye' of Goethe's dreams.[1] This would involve abandoning all rationalism and anthropomorphism and giving primacy to the intuition of the senses (of which the eye was here the symbol) and to the creative imagination. Renouncing the explanation of processes by causality, it would become necessary to elaborate Ideas, to organise them in one structure that would represent nature, timeless and eternal, and then to plunge into the centre of things instead of remaining at their periphery. One would then try, in the light of Ideas, to see into nature by a sort of transparency. This would be 'diaphysics'.[2]

Goethe had provided a prototype of this kind of thinking with his *Metamorphosis of Plants* and his *Theory of Colours*. Chamberlain also attempted this line of country:[3] the *Foundations of the Nineteenth Century* was an attempt to represent the phenomena studied by anthropology. But he thought that Leonardo da Vinci, both a mechanistic physicist and a painter of the ineffable, showed us more about nature by his works of art than many learned treatises.[4] For art and action were the highest reaches of knowledge. *Experience* was the supreme *understanding*.

Here again one sees Chamberlain embark upon an irrationality which can lead to many unscientific wanderings if one does not take heed.

CHAMBERLAIN'S BIOLOGY

Setting out from this general philosophy, therefore, Chamberlain attacked the theory of evolution and built in its place his personal theory of life.

Darwin, according to Chamberlain, was a remarkable observer but an inferior thinker. His observations were dangerous if, lacking a critique of fundamental knowledge, the materialist theorists of evolution did not take into account the precise meaning of the themes and concepts they were using. The notion of *species* was a a mental construction not to be found in nature. What stupidity to hypostatise this or conclude that there was any relationship between individuals of neighbouring species when this relationship only existed between the species in the limited way that our own mind could understand! In practice the theorists of evolution reasoned falsely about a quite artificial nature. Moreover, preoccupied with Becoming, they were obliged, in order to explain their first

[1] *Natur und Leben*, p. 105.
[2] *Goethe, Linné, und die exakte Naturwissenschaft* (1907), in H. S. Chamberlain, *Rasse und Persönlichkeit* (1928, 2nd imp.), p. 125.
[3] See the pages on astronomy in *Natur und Leben* (pp. 73–83).
[4] *Kant*, pp. 173–4.

beginnings, to resort to a vain *regressus ad infinitum*. Finally, where they had stated that there was an evolution, they interpreted it, mistakenly, as a lasting change and as a step forward. Whereas it was only a sign of degeneration in the individual; nature had no regard for 'simple' or 'complex' forms of for 'decadence' or 'progress'.

Chamberlain's biology was opposed at every point to the theory of evolution and was based from the start on one fundamental principle: 'Leben ist Gestalt'.[1]

The *Gestalt* which characterised living beings and, according to Chamberlain, living beings only, was a specifically organic form— an autonomous unity of one whole, composed of different parts, of which each conditioned the whole as much as it was in turn conditioned by the unity in reciprocal correlation. This was its physical and concrete aspect.

But the *Gestalt* had also an invisible and spiritual aspect. It was the cause of life. This was certainly not the sense in which the physical sciences used this word, but in a final sense, a sort of formative law, an organisation with one end in view (*Zweckmässigkeit*). And this aspect of the *Gestalt* was only accessible to thought.[2]

Between these two aspects of the *Gestalt* there existed no logical but only a transcendental connection (in the Kantian sense of the term), and only living enabled one to establish their identity without understanding it.[3] Chamberlain went further. The method of thinking for a man (or his ideal) was the inner aspect of the *Gestalt* of which the outward sign was the race: and to like physical structure corresponded like mental structure. The whole racial analysis of the *Foundations of the Nineteenth Century* rested on this equipoise, this fundamental correlation.[4]

Lastly, the *Gestalt* was timeless. A formative law escaped all time. It did not evolve. Observation proved that the forms of living beings were remarkably stable. The only limited variations evident internally in a species, proved that the *Gestalt* was elastic and moved like a sort of pendulum around an immovable centre of gravity.[5] And if sometimes the *Gestalt* 'evolved' truly and did definitely move away from its centre, this showed a disquieting sign of unbalance, for evolution, far from being 'a progress' was only 'a step towards death'.[6]

Life submitted both matter and energy to its own ends. Life was

---

[1] *Natur und Leben*, pp. 128, 136, 161, 163; *Kant*, p. 484. We retain the word *Gestalt*, which is difficult to render in English, strictly in the sense that Chamberlain gave to it.

[2] *Kant*, pp. 511–12.   [3] ibid., p. 545.

[4] *Natur und Leben*, p. 164; *Kant*, pp. 606–7.

[5] *Natur und Leben*, pp. 140–9; *Kant*, p. 538.

[6] *Natur und Leben*, pp. 169–70.

the unique conserving principle in all nature and the incarnation of the notion of Being.[1]
These were the essentials of Chamberlain's *Lebenslehre*.

Setting out from this hypothesis, however, Chamberlain attempted even more ambitious additions.

The analysis of the phenomena of symbiosis led him to think that there was an interdependence between all living beings and that Life altogether was a single *Gestalt*, that there was, briefly, in a concrete sense and not only mystically, a 'unity of life' in the universe.[2]

And as the law concerning the structure of beings was 'certainly cosmic', he imagined that there was a 'law for conserving the *Gestalt*' which could be the foundation of a scientific biology worthy to rank beside physics and modern chemistry, founded on the laws of conserving energy and mass.[3] There ought also to exist, he thought, a precise relationship between the size and the complexity of a living being, with an optimal $S \times C = 1$ representing 'a maximum of life' for the living being.[4]

And if there existed in the universe a constant quantity of building energy (*Gestaltungskraft*), then when the construction of one type absorbed more than another any complication in developing one organism would provoke an inverse reaction in another.[5] This would clarify the phenomena of interdependence and of the struggle for existence.

These were indeed bold hypotheses. Chamberlain realised this, but his lyrical ecstasies mastered him when he imagined the vast perspectives that he could open for biology and human thinking.[6] Hypotheses? Undoubtedly Chamberlain only mentioned them in his private letters, and one could find no precise formula for them in his main works published in his lifetime. But the manuscript (which remained unedited until his death) of his *Lebenslehre* threw a very vivid light on the *Foundations*, which Chamberlain wrote immediately afterwards, and made clear exactly why he exalted the racial and national outlook (of the *Gestalten*) and fought against all internationalism (which showed only an absence of *Gestalt*, a bastard type moving towards its destined extinction).

However, do not let us forget that the last paragraph of this *Lebenslehre* modestly entitled *Einiges zur Ergänzung*[7] showed even in 1896 the extraordinary developments that Chamberlain would

[1] *Kant*, p. 542.   [2] *Natur und Leben*, pp. 150, 161, 163; *Kant*, p. 520.
[3] *Natur und Leben*, p. 182; *Kant*, p. 520.   [4] *Natur und Leben*, p. 177.
[5] ibid., pp. 182–3.   [6] ibid., pp. 172–3, 178.   [7] ibid., p. 136.

later make in his theory of life: the anti-evolution biology would transfer all its validity to his metaphysics, form the basis of a sound philosophy of Being and of an idealism which would be the best auxiliary to Sacred Art (that is to say, to Bayreuthean art) and finally promote a new politics and sociology—anti-democratic and 'reacting against the chimera of progress and the spectre of decadence'.

III. A RACIAL VIEW OF HISTORY:
THE FOUNDATIONS OF THE NINETEENTH CENTURY

It was simply chance—an offer by his publisher Bruckmann— which led Chamberlain to write his most important work: *The Foundations of the Nineteenth Century*.[1] The writer wanted at first to refuse, but his 'demon' inspired him to undertake this rather vague project of a book on the nineteenth century, and within a few days he had drawn up a detailed plan (three parts, sixteen chapters, sixty-six paragraphs) which was later hardly changed at all.

Chamberlain was certainly not prepared for this task. But he was intelligent, already endowed with a wide culture, and he knew how to work so that he threw himself into fabulous reading. His book would be filled with the most comprehensive documentation.

Chamberlain at any rate already knew exactly what he wanted to prove; his book would be the work of an intransigent germanophile, an able contribution to the Bayreuthean movement, and above all the expression of his convictions as a biologist.[2]

Let us note also that this enormous work of twelve hundred pages was finished in nineteen months, between 1st April 1897 and 31st October 1898—a powerful improvisation indeed.[3]

THE METHOD: 'DILETTANTISM'

To dare, with so little preparation, to attempt this analysis of history, the author needed to master his newly acquired learning with some light-heartedness. Chamberlain contrived to do this thanks to his method called 'dilettantism', explained in the prefaces to the first and especially—in order to reply to attacks—to the fourth edition of the *Foundations*.

The position of the specialist was, according to him, nowadays

---

[1] The word 'Foundations' has been chosen to translate *Grundlagen* since it expresses Chamberlain's static conception of history.
[2] Chamberlain dedicated the *Foundations* to his master, the physiologist, J. Wiesner (*Grundlagen*, p. viii).
[3] *Lebenswege*, p. 141.

very disquieting. He acquired his mastery only by severely limiting his field and so paralysing certain of his faculties. He was incapable of large-scale syntheses. However, only by contact with different specialist branches of learning was true knowledge possible—the knowledge needed in life. True science called for a mediator between two opposed specialisations: this mediator, that is to say the 'dilettante', the 'non-specialist scholar endowed with a scientific upbringing', would respect facts, but maintain freedom to judge them without letting himself be overwhelmed by their great mass.[1]

Chamberlain claimed to be such a dilettante, and pinned to this, at one and the same time, his humility, his incompetence, and his superb arrogance in the face of specialists' conclusions. Vitalising 'dilettantism' against stifling specialisation? Clearly this was a good cause. But Chamberlain defended it badly and—misled by his irrationalism—he finally betrayed it.

The *Foundations* a 'Work of Art'

We should note that from the outset Chamberlain conceived of his book as an 'organic unity', a '*Gestalt*' of which each part ought to be regarded and judged only in the perspective of the whole. He wrote not as a scholar piling up concrete data, but as an artist wanting to simplify and bring order out of chaos and to create a striking image so that he could, at will, heighten its lights and shades. And in the same way that one should judge a painting with one glance, he wanted to write this book so that it could be read in three or four days, with, as he admitted, some flaws but a generally correct perspective which would not be falsified by errors of detail. Devil take the scholar's objectivity, a source of grandeur, but also of weakness. The artist and the man of action defending a sacred cause had the right to be openly 'subjective'.[2]

For only the artist was capable of giving form and sense to history 'by impressing on the chaos of events the seal of the *Gestalt*'. This could not be done without some violence, and the history should be, according to Byron's formula, only a 'poem imitating truth'.[3] However, it was by unclothing peoples and great men of the vestments which history happened to have given them, that Chamberlain thought he would be able to understand them in their real aspect as natural phenomena, timeless *Gestalten*. By this bias he thought that he could restore a scientific value to this work of art, that history chiefly is.[4]

[1] H. S. Chamberlain, *Dilettantismus, Rasse, Monotheismus, Rom.* Foreword to the 4th ed. of the *Grundlagen* (1903), p. 8.
[2] On this aspect of the *Foundations*, see *Grundlagen*, pp. 1–3, and H. S. Chamberlain, 'Christus ein Germane' in *Die Zukunft* (23 Jan., 1904, pp. 139, 142).
[3] *Lebenswege*, p. 144.   [4] ibid., pp. 146, 223; *Grundlagen*, p. 54.

GENERAL PLAN OF THE BOOK

Chamberlain had envisaged three parts for this work intended to analyse the nineteenth century. He was only able to write the first, a monumental introduction, inquiring into the foundations on which the nineteenth century reposed.

The design of the *Foundations* was simple and clear:

The first part would explain the 'origins of a new world', born at the beginning of the nineteenth century.

The ancient world had left to posterity a triple heritage: Greek art and philosophy, Roman law, and the personality of Christ. There were three *legatees*: two pure races, the Jews and the Germans, and the whole racial confusion of the half-breed Mediterranean peoples, called by Chamberlain the *Völkerchaos*.

Only the Germans were worthy of this splendid ancient heritage. But they came too late into world history to inherit directly. Their heritage was handed down to them, disfigured and spoiled, through the Jews, who were congenitally incapable of understanding the message of Christ, and through the chaos of the peoples of mixed blood, who contaminated everything they touched.

So it was at the price of a long racial war that the Germans succeeded gradually from the fifth century to the thirteenth century in wresting their barely recognisable heritage from usurpers. This battle was engaged on the double plane of religion and the state. To the shallow universal tyranny of the Roman Church's Christianity, the Germans opposed their own religious and political separatism. This triumphed towards the sixteenth century with the constitution of national states and the affirmation—as yet vague—of a Germanic Christianity, that from the Reformation onwards was ridding itself of Jewish elements.

The second part of the *Foundations* described the 'birth of a new world': abandoning the misleading ideas of the 'Middle Ages' and the 'Renaissance', Chamberlain showed that from the year 1200, a new race began to make itself felt in history. The Teutons, at last becoming self-conscious, created a new civilisation which in all the fields successively reviewed by Chamberlain (discovery, science, industry, economics, politics, religion, art) was replacing the bastard and mean conceptions elaborated and vainly upheld by the less gifted races.

Within the limited scope of this study, we must only attempt to examine the most important and characteristic statements in this enormous work, which set out everything ably and often in the most attractive manner, so that, as has been said, nothing was completely false and nothing completely true.

1. History as a Battle of the Races

Chamberlain thought that the word 'humanity' referred only to a datum that could not be completely defined.[1] The hypothesis that men were of common origin was invalid. History showed in reality only distinct and isolated groups of men, races, peoples, nations, or individuals. History resulted from the action of nameless collective forces, compared with which the actions of great men were of no importance.[2] The sole exception to this rule was 'genius', which was 'specifically different' from ordinary mortals if one understood by genius men 'who have lastingly enriched our spiritual heritage by the creations of their imagination'[3] and whose work was therefore indestructible.

The ideas of progress, evolution, and decadence were themselves quite without meaning.[4] Geographical or economic background explained nothing.[5] Races, and only races, subject to a racial discipline could create or destroy civilisations and cultures.[6] But the races were always in ceaseless conflict, either in savage combat on the battlefield, or latent in the blood and heart of individuals, but 'always in battles for life or death'.[7]

WHAT IS A RACE?

What was a race? While stating the contradictions which baffled the anthropologists, Chamberlain adopted a strictly practical point of view.

Strictly speaking, he failed to give even a fairly precise definition to race. One could not, he said, define a biological reality. He also refused to research into origins, to find out if pure races had ever existed. This was a vain and doubtless insoluble problem.[8] The scholars could wait; but life itself never waited.[9] Knowledge paralysed life. But one had only to open one's eyes to find that race was an evident fact of experience.[10] Drawing his inspiration here from Darwin and cattle-raisers, Chamberlain gave to the word race a purely empirical sense: here was a tangible situation in which the essential characteristics of a group of individuals, subject to determined conditions of life, developed with the consistency of natural

---

[1] *Grundlagen*, pp. 837–47: *die angebliche 'Menschkeit'*.
[2] ibid., pp. 8, 23–8; *Anonyme Kräfte*. [3] ibid., pp. 28–9; *Das Genie*.
[4] ibid., pp. 850–8; *Fortschritt und Entartung*. [5] ibid., pp. 840–1.
[6] H. S. Chamberlain, 'Die Rassenfrage', in *Rasse und Persönlichkeit*, p. 75. This article, written by Chamberlain in 1900, and published in several reviews, finally in the *Völkische Beobachter* (24 and 31 May, 1925), sets forth in a succinct manner his ideas on this important point.
[7] *Grundlagen*, pp. 7, 17, 617, 632, 638, 714, 1189. [8] ibid., pp. 837–8.
[9] Foreword to the 4th ed. of *Grundlagen*, p. 21. [10] *Grundlagen*, p. 322.

laws.[1] It was a *Gestalt* in its clearest form.[2] It could exist at any point in history whenever certain conditions, of which we shall speak later, are combined. 'Even if it were proved that there had never been an Aryan race in the past, we will have one in the future; for men of action this is the decisive point of view'.[3]

One sees here the originality of Chamberlain's thought. But he did not limit himself to encouraging 'the Teutons' to fashion or safeguard their race; which is all that this pragmatic approach would warrant. Striding out, as usual, from his point of departure, he claimed as well, with so vague a definition, to be able to use the term 'races' for ethnic groups, as varied as the Jews, the Greeks, the Romans, the Slavs, the Celts, the Teutons, the English, the Prussians,[4] and to be able to judge on the basis of very fragile criteria, the actions of these races in history.

Certainly one could understand his protests when the critics accused him—somewhat lightly—of borrowing his theories from Gobineau. To Gobineau, who knew nothing at all about biology, to his pessimism and his fantasies, he could contrast his own knowledge as a naturalist, his optimism and his empiricism.[5] Moreover, to the School of Scientific Anthropology, to Wilsner or Woltman, or to so many others who denounced his mistakes and superficiality, he also replied—or thought he replied—without difficulty: to their contradictions and to their incapacity he opposed the pragmatism which allowed him the widest liberties. But his point of view, however convenient, still left, as we shall see, very great difficulties.

THE CONDITIONS FOR THE BIRTH OF A RACE

Chamberlain did not fail to define the necessary and required conditions for the birth and expansion of a race: he stated the five 'fundamental laws'.[6]

The first demanded the 'presence of excellent material', that is to say of course, human material. The following laws called for a prolonged endogamy, controlled selection and cross-breeding between peoples of different but compatible types. The fifth law limited the conditions for this cross-breeding, which, if repeated too often, would efface instead of accentuating the racial characteristics.

Chamberlain considered that these laws, deduced from the breeding of animals, also applied to man, since the laws of life

---

[1] *Die Rassenfrage* (op. cit., p. 74).   [2] *Natur und Leben*, p. 152.
[3] *Grundlagen*, p. 317 (end of note 4, p. 316).
[4] For example, *Grundlagen*, pp. 323, 352, and *Die Rassenfrage* (op. cit., pp. 74-5, 81).
[5] *Grundlagen*, pp. 313-14, and 'Letter to M. Edouard Dujardin' in *Mercure de France*, Feb. 1904, p. 570.   [6] *Grundlagen*, pp. 326-40.

concerned all living beings.[1] And history showed, if we believe him, that the remarkable human races always developed under such conditions. However, despite Chamberlain, one ought to point out that these laws are utopian.

It happened, none the less, that his optimistic pragmatism, in contrast to truly scientific researches, was calculated to awake in Germany a facile enthusiasm for eugenics and racial laws such as was later conceived under the Third Reich.

Chamberlain's optimism emboldened him even to state that humanity was moving quite naturally towards a progressive racial differentiation.[2] In his opinion there were everywhere individualised groups capable of becoming races. For this reason the *nations* played for him a decisive role in favouring the cross-breeding followed by endogamy.[3] Certainly, national states succeeded to the universalism of the Holy Roman Empire and the Church after the Reformation. But this great movement, whose analysis occupied the whole of the second part of the *Foundations*, led Chamberlain to overlook the fact that modern life has seen a multiplication of exchanges between nations and the beginning of the end for the national states. He even forgot at this stage in his argument one main point, whose gravity he demonstrated a little earlier: the 'inferior races' and the mixed peoples had a much greater power of reproduction and absorption than the 'master' races.[4] In fact Chamberlain recognised (*Grundlagen*, pp. 631–32) that the adulteration of the Teuton had increased during the nineteenth century. But he never saw in that anything resembling a contradiction.

THE CRITERIA OF RACE

Chamberlain's efforts in trying to work out the distinguishing marks of a race were equally quite contradictory.

The *Foundations* developed the doctrine of the *Lebenslehre*: race had, like *Gestalt*, a physical and visible aspect to which there was, by virtue of a biological correlation, a corresponding spiritual aspect, that is to say, a determined way of thinking. Racial determinism enabled one to recognise a race either by its physical characteristics or by its ideals,[5] which both reacted on it as 'causes'.

In point of fact—and this was symptomatic—Chamberlain thought the best criteria were purely subjective: the individual belonging to a definite race 'feels' his race, and the good observer could recognise it by a 'hundred details which defied all analysis',[6]

[1] *Grundlagen*, pp. 332, 342, note 1. [2] ibid., p. 347.
[3] ibid., p. 347, and all § 11 *Die Nation*, pp. 343–8, 373–7, 412.
[4] ibid., p. 341. [5] ibid., pp. 255, 412, 588–90, 543.
[6] ibid., p. 320. Idem., pp. 319–20, 343, 590.

such as 'firmness of character', or 'simple grandeur', or 'super-abundant vitality'. The race was also recognisable by what it produced.

By 'physical' characteristics Chamberlain referred principally to the shape of the head, the colour of the hair and eyes, and the inheritance of the blood. Among the 'moral' indications he included religion, which was for him the decisive criterion. He also attached great importance to ideology, to qualities and defects, to popular poetry, and to legal usages.[1]

But Chamberlain held very undecided opinions on the value of these varied indications. In general, he thought that for the masses (nations and races) the physical indications were most important. The individual, on the other hand, escaped from the law of the greatest number; for him, moral indications would prevail over the influence of the blood.[2]

Such a position—corresponding to the methods of statistics and to a general determinism tempered by 'uncertainties' for particular cases—would be admissible only if one did not feel that Chamberlain's major concern was to use all these criteria successively, according to the needs, even if provisional, of his argument, without taking into account the logical contradictions that he accumulated. What is most serious is that Chamberlain ultimately destroys, without realising it, the basic proposition of the whole theory of *Gestalt* and race, by which, as we have seen, the physical and moral structure, the blood and the ideal, were the obverse and reverse of one and the same living reality, linked one to the other by the determinism of race.

For Chamberlain himself showed on several occasions the absurdity of this proposition, without which his theory collapsed—when the enthusiastic flow of his imprudent dialectics made him feel the truth of some other statement that was temporarily necessary for him.[3]

---

[1] *Grundlagen*, p. 580 (skull), 437, 577 (hair), 575 (inheritance). Moral indications: pp. 18, 258–61, 544–5, 556, 561, 563, 588, 596–601, 892–3, and *die Preussische Rasse* (*Rasse und Persönlichkeit*, p. 85) where protestantism is treated as a sure sign of germanism. [2] *Grundlagen*, p. 574.
[3] ibid., p. 255. 'That's what they called science in the year of grace 1896! At the end of the nineteenth century scientists still did not know that the shape of the head and the brain structure have a decisive influence on the shape and structure of thoughts; so that the influence of environment, however strong it may be, is linked to definite capabilities and potentialities, in other words, to definite courses, by just this basic factor of physical disposition. . . . When will we emerge from the dark ignorance of the Middle Ages? When will people understand that the physical form is not a matter of chance, but an expression of the innermost being? That it represents the point of contact between the internal and the external, the visible and the invisible?'
But cf. pp. 544–5, 514. 'A man may soon become a Jew without being an Israelite. Some only need to have intensive dealings with Jews, to read Jewish newspapers, and to accustom themselves to the Jewish way of life and Jewish literature and art. On the other hand it is pointless to call the purest bred Israelite a Jew, if he has succeeded in throwing off the shackles of Ezra and Nehemiah, and no longer acknowledges the law of Moses in his mind or despises others in his heart.'

In reality Chamberlain wanted to persuade his reader gradually that science was impotent and that scientific tests mattered little; it was more important to heed intuition and instinct in order to practice what he audaciously entitled 'rational anthropology'—as opposed to the too disappointing technique of scientific anthropology.[1] One has the right to feel uneasy on realising that, on final analysis, it was merely on the intuition of an extreme neurotic, of a passionate Germanophile, that Chamberlain relied when he was confidently weighing the imponderables of history in far-away centuries. Let us recall that in order to safeguard Cosima's prestige he did not hesitate to deny in 1896 what he had written in 1887 about Tristan's birth, although he knew his affirmation of 1887 to be true.

Many other important objections could be made against Chamberlain's thinking on the subject of race. To consider the human races as animal types bred by a breeder was less simple than he contended. How were we to recognise and assemble the 'excellent material' called for by his first 'law'? And how were we to overlook that the breeder could be motivated by very special and often purely commercial intentions, and so develop certain particular qualities to the great detriment of others? But these are only a few points. Chamberlain's greatest weakness was, to reiterate, the quite inconsequential method with which he claimed to judge races. We will now be able to assess better, with some precise problems, how unscientific this method could be.

2. Christ is not a Jew, He Belongs to the Aryans

Apart from Greek art and philosophy and Roman law, the richest treasure handed down to us from the ancient world was the personality of Christ. The third chapter of the *Foundations* aimed to disengage this great figure from historical dogma so that we could revisualise him more exactly.

Breaking with the ascetic puritan tradition, Chamberlain showed us in Jesus primarily a hero overflowing with life, attending banquets, condoning the sins of the flesh, proud and combative, with a few Nietzschean traits [2] added, which—a curious coincidence—happened, like his mysticism, to be specifically Aryan.[3]

Chamberlain then attempted to analyse by his methods Jesus's physical and moral race. By examining his physical characteristics

[1] See among other things *Grundlagen*, pp. 309–19, § entitled *Wissenschaftliche Wirrnis;* pp. 585–6, condemnation of skull-measurement; p. 588, of anatomical anthropology; and on the contrary, p. 562, an appeal to 'the innocent eye', p. 590, to 'intuition', pp. 591–2, to 'innocent eye', to 'childish instinct', or 'the glances of the cattle-breeder'.

[2] *Grundlagen*, pp. 233–45.   [3] ibid., p. 259.

—his Galilean origins, his inability to pronounce correctly the gutturals of Aramaic—Chamberlain was able to show in Jesus 'clear signs of having a large proportion of non-semitic blood', for all Jews pronounce their gutturals with facility.[1] 'Whoever claimed that Jesus was a Jew was either being stupid or telling a lie.'[2] Physical characteristics allowed Chamberlain at least one negative conclusion: 'Jesus was not a Jew'—this was 'almost a certainty'.[3]

From what race, then, did Jesus spring? The ascendancy in his blood of semitic elements was 'likely'. However, the particular country concerned, apart from the pure Jewish race, was lost in such an ethnic confusion that anything further remained a mere hypothesis.[4]

But the moral criteria—they were clear. Comparison of the Jewish religion—materialism and abstract formalism—with Aryan religions founded on myth and sentiment proved that Jesus, far from being a Jew, was more probably an Aryan.

It was clear however that Jesus belonged to a Jewish background. How and why was this?

The main lines of his thought and his life were Jewish. It was only among the Jews that Jesus was able to find—by contrast—favourable ground for the entirely new religious ideal that he brought. For the Jewish people's spiritual barrenness and 'abstract materialism', severely proscribing any graphic representation of the divinity, left Jesus a clear field.[5] Among the Aryans the idealism of Jesus would have been stifled by their luxuriant mythologies.

Moreover, Jesus benefited from the Jews' implacable belief in the coming of a temporal Messiah. He cruelly deceived them in their belief, so the Jews crucified him. It was only among the Jews that this death—this splendid example, so much more eloquent than any doctrine—could have been inflicted on Jesus. In Athens or Rome one would have simply honoured Jesus as a saintly man.[6] If therefore Jesus truly belonged 'morally' to the Jewish background, it was only in so far as he exploited that background and its religious outlook (an all-powerful God, providence, Messiah, free will, strength of will); but he exploited them by radically changing them, since he preached the Fatherhood of God, the conversion of the will and the world of the soul.[7]

Consequently, although not a Jew by blood, this Christ, of no certain race but so nearly related to the Aryans by his attitude and religious thinking, was to become 'the God of the young Indo-

---

[1] *Grundlagen*, p. 254.
[2] ibid., this is the text of the 1st ed., p. 218: 'eine Dummheit oder eine Lüge'. Later, Chamberlain moderated this harsh verdict, writing '. . . ist entweder unwissend, oder unwahr' (9th ed., p. 256).
[3] ibid., p. 256. [4] ibid., p. 257. [5] ibid., p. 272.
[6] ibid., pp. 281–2. [7] ibid., p. 292.

European peoples overflowing with life'[1] and especially of the Teutons, because, according to Chamberlain, 'no other being was so well equipped as the Teutonic to hear this divine voice'.[2]

In fact, the Jewish people, called the 'chosen' people, were only acting as 'a foil' for the Teutonic God.

Wagner had already stated that 'he was more than doubtful whether Jesus was a Jew'.[3] Chamberlain went further. But what ingenuity there was in his argument! He was only categorical on one point: Jesus was not a Jew. For the rest he conceded at first that Jesus was linked with the fundamental ideas of Judaism. This was a tactical and provisional concession, since it led him to conclude that this was the only method at Christ's disposal for effectively launching an ideal quite the reverse of the Jewish one.[4]

Innumerable readers of the *Foundations* thought that 'Jesus was a Teuton'. Chamberlain complained bitterly about this caricature of his thought and of the 'myths' surrounding his name. He protested in the *Zukunft* and the *Mercure de France*.[5] Alas! there, as elsewhere, the readers only came to conclusions to which Chamberlain, conscientiously but quite imprudently, had led them.

3. THE JEW

In Chamberlain's view, European history was the result of the conflict of three racial forces: two pure races, the Jews and Teutons, and an ethnical milieu made up of bastards, the 'chaos of peoples' (*Völkerchaos*), were the contestants.

The *Chaos of Peoples* began at the beginning of the first century, under the dominion of the Roman Empire, with much crossbreeding between Semites and Indo-Europeans. Chamberlain gave two very different examples of these physical, moral, and intellectual half-breeds. One was the Greek writer Lucien, a brilliant mind, but superficial and unstable, not capable of really understanding the philosophy and religion which he expounded.[6] St Augustine was the other example, tragically suspended between sublime Aryan inspiration and the grossest Semitic superstition. With both men the racial balance was disturbed; Lucien, a man of uncontrolled intellect and weak character; St Augustine, a gifted moralist who bridles his disordered thinking.[7]

To have no race was more disastrous even than belonging to an inferior race. However, the heritage of the ancient world was

---

[1] *Grundlagen*, p. 245.   [2] ibid., p. 893.
[3] R. Wagner, *Religion und Kunst* (1880), Werke, Vol. X, p. 232.
[4] *Grundlagen*, p. 293.
[5] H. S. Chamberlain, 'Christus ein Germane' in *die Zukunft* (23 Jan. 1904) and 'Letter to Ed. Dujardin' in *Mercure de France*, Feb. 1904, pp. 571–2.
[6] *Grundlagen*, p. 358.   [7] ibid., p. 363.

handed down through the intermediary of these Chaos half-breeds to the Germanic race—but in what an adulterated form! The Chaos of Peoples was largely responsible for the decadence of the western hemisphere.

Chamberlain devoted the longest chapter in the *Foundations* to the Jews, analysing their emergence in history and defining who they were.

The Jewish race was, according to Chamberlain, a typical example of a pure race, evolving progressively and even 'artificially', as indicated by the 'five laws', through cross-breeding, selection, and endogamy.

THE FORMATION OF THE ISRAELITE

The 'human material' (first law) was, as it happened, mediocre enough.

The Semite (*Homo Arabicus*) or Bedouin of the Desert was a first element 'deprived of all grandeur'.[1] With him the over-mighty will over-rode the intelligence and the feelings. Incapable of any creative work, marked by the poverty-stricken life of the desert, he looked only for concrete and immediate satisfaction. His influence on the Jewish religion was to be considerable, since he combined the 'maximum of the fanatical faith' with the 'minimum of religion'.[2] His narrowly materialist outlook, completely uninterested in all symbolism, turned the myths that he had borrowed into mere historical tales, and the intimate relationship between man and God into a vulgar contract.[3]

The second element of cross-breeding, the Syrian (*Homo Syriacus*), the roundhead Hittite with a 'Jewish' nose, was distinguished by his great physical strength and his moral and intellectual inferiority. He gave the Jew his business sense and was not without influence from the religious point of view.

But the Semite and the Syrian were too disparate as ethnic types for them to be 'crossed' in any beneficial way. Between them there was only 'bastardy' (*Bastardierung*),[4] and in the Hebrew, the corrupted half-breed sprung from this bastardy, the awareness of this 'crime against the blood' eventually fostered the notion of 'original sin' and 'national' sin. The Jewish people was to react against adulteration of the blood through its rigid marriage laws.

The third element (the later crossing of which with the Hebrew gives the Israelite) was an Aryan, the Amorite (*Homo Europaeus*), a

---

[1] *Grundlagen*, pp. 420–3, *der echte Semit*; p. 449–60, *Homo Arabicus*; p. 462–93, *Exkurs über semitische Religion*.
[2] ibid., p. 476.   [3] ibid., pp. 473, 517.   [4] ibid., p. 441.

tall, dolichocephalic blond, a magnificent being. But the tardy addition of noble blood to the corrupt Hebrew strain, far from producing happy results, could be no more than a source of endless fermentation between the irreconcilable natures.[1] The inferior elements, as was normal in such cases, predominated: the Amorite was absorbed and disappeared.[2]

At least this point about 'aryan ferment' in the blood of the Israelites allowed Chamberlain to explain away without difficulty the 'brilliant episodes' in Israel's history, such as the apparition of David and Solomon.[3]

THE FORMATION OF THE JEW

It was through natural selection (the third law) that the Kingdom of Judea was separated in 721 from Israel and abandoned to very great dangers. Clearly, in one sense, selection favoured the inferior, for Israel (with predominantly Syrian blood, from which came all the creative strains of the Jewish inheritance) was superior to Judea.[4] But the greatness of Judea was real enough: it was able to withstand a doubly difficult situation. Aware of the bastardy flowing in its blood, Judea chose the tragic course, and compensated for its racial downfall by a rigid endogamy, which, from the fourth century B.C., maintained the purity of the race.

Moreover, in this little people, surrounded by powerful enemies, the very excess of external dangers induced a decisive religious reaction, quite in character, to which it owed its survival; it clung to the Israelite tradition of Amos and Hosea and, interpreting this in a materialistic sense, it supposed itself the chosen people—never abandoned by Jehovah. The miraculous raising of the siege of Jerusalem by Sennacherib in 701 B.C. allowed this 'fixed idea'[5] to take root so strongly that, a century later, neither the conquest of Jerusalem nor exile could disrupt it. Exile cut the Jews off from their traditions; it allowed an arbitrary priesthood artificially to impose its religious dogma. As a result of a skilful manipulation of the holy books, a new religion was codified in the Law. The Torah formed the basis of a caricatured monotheism: Jehovah was the only God, but the God of Jews alone, to whom, if they obeyed his commandments, he promised dominion over the earth. A contract existed between Jehovah and his people: this contract formed the whole of the Jewish religion, rigid, complicated, formalised.

Sin appeared there, not as a bad intention (this was the Aryan

[1] *Grundlagen*, p. 441.   [2] ibid., p. 448.
[3] ibid., pp. 437–8: David is blond, and his character proves that he is 'half or three-quarters Amorite'. As for Solomon, 'one could hardly call him an Israelite', he is 'a stranger in the midst of his people'.
[4] ibid., pp. 461–2, 497.   [5] ibid., p. 504.

idea!), but merely as a mistake in carrying out an external ritual. With Nehemiah and Ezra, who 'imposed judaism on the Jews',[1] the work was finished: the race's national religion was established. In this way a pure race came into being, distinguishing itself and being maintained in essentials by its religion.[2]

There were, of course, prophets and certain psalmists whose noble ideal was to simplify religion and instil piety into the heart. But in the long run Chamberlain attributed little importance to them. They were not understood by their people, for they had nothing in common with them. Judaism was founded in their despite.[3]

This was the Judaism handed down to us through Christianity, a Semitic Christianity, where Christ was seen as the son of the Jewish Jehovah, where the fanatical Jewish faith, with its materialist ends, prevailed over the inner feelings of grace, and where all the Aryan myths were pitilessly hypostatised and rationalised.[4]

SOME CRITICAL REMARKS

At first glance Chamberlain seemed in this important chapter to be particularly discreet, liberal, and even generous.

He set himself energetically against a certain 'stupid and revolting' anti-Semitism which he condemned. According to him, the Jew was not 'inferior' to the Teuton, but simply 'different' from him.[5] He had his own undeniable grandeur: he knew how to guard the purity of his race—a sacred duty for man—and how to conserve for all men those precious values which would otherwise have been lost amidst the *Chaos of the Peoples*.[6] And if a 'Jewish peril' did exist, this was because the Aryans had too often betrayed their blood and ideals; to attribute this danger primarily to the intrigues of the Jews themselves was mere stupidity.[7]

Moreover, Chamberlain stated that in the best interests of his study he would make use only of pro-Jewish authors,[8] and he made in advance several prudent reservations about the somewhat shaky statistics that he was going to use.[9]

But Chamberlain's prudence did not last. Almost throughout a strong anti-Semitism (which he held back—and condemned in other people—when he was calm) appeared, colouring his style, and sometimes even leading him to make shameful statements, whose

---

[1] *Grundlagen*, p. 516.
[2] ibid., p. 387. *Cosima Wagner und H. S. Chamberlain im Briefwechsel*, p. 639.
[3] *Grundlagen*, pp. 519–25, and Foreword to the 4th ed. of *Grundlagen*, p. 58.
[4] See *Grundlagen*, all Chap. VII, *Religion*, and notably pp. 651–6, 661 seq., 675–83, 684–7.
[5] *Grundlagen*, p. 384.   [6] ibid., pp. 301–3.   [7] ibid., p. 19.
[8] ibid., p. 408.   [9] ibid., pp. 440, 461.

meanness could not be disguised by the most erudite assessment;[1] they also prefigured the heartless caricatures of Julius Streicher's *Stürmer*.

The most serious contradiction in Chamberlain's work was, as we have seen, his statement that Judaism was more a race with a biologically linked anatomical and mental structure, from which the individual could not escape, than simply a way of thinking and feeling, springing from environment. He stated that sometimes the Jew was 'eternally a stranger' to the Teuton.[2] At other times, if his hatred of the Roman Catholics induced him to cite St Ignatius Loyola as the 'type of the anti-Teuton', his tactical skill could suddenly demonstrate that the Jew himself was only separated from the Teuton by an abyss that could be quite easily crossed.[3]

Chamberlain praised the Jews for the purity of their race, but we should note that in the growth of this pure race Chamberlain's laws had been more or less turned upside down; ethnically very inferior 'material', an irremediable 'bastardy' instead of beneficial intermarriage, and lastly an angry 'Aryan ferment'. If Western history had seen the two pure races of the Germans and the Jews, the Jewish race was, on final analysis, the caricature of a pure race or, as Chamberlain insinuated, the 'negative' race; humanity was enriched only in taking a stand against Israel and 'denying' her.[4]

The Jewish people were great only because the Aryans had given them 'a halo of false glory'.[5] And Chamberlain, who considered that nobody before him had been able to interpret the Jews exactly, took it upon himself to remove this religious halo, since it had been won so undeservedly.

What of the Jews' religious instinct? The Jew was of all human creatures the most 'lamentably lacking in true religion'.[6] What of his monotheism? This was fictitious and, what was more, a negative monotheism, proof of spiritual poverty, with nothing in common with true monotheism, such as that of the Aryans, with the organic unity of a superabundant religious richness.[7] What of David and Solomon? This was merely a brilliant 'episode' arising from the strain of Indo-European blood. What of the prophets and the psalmists? These were simple 'moralists', strangers to their own people. What even of Jesus Christ? He was not a Jew, and had only established true religion by taking up arms against the Jewish ideal.

In Chamberlain's view the Old Testament was a 'work of art' (in the special sense which he gave to this phrase): composed of

---

[1] For example, *Grundlagen*, pp. 51–2, 550.
[2] *Grundlagen*, pp. 18, 389.
[3] ibid., p. 625.
[4] ibid., pp. 51, 52–3.
[5] ibid., p. 391.
[6] ibid., p. 19.
[7] ibid., pp. 477 seq., 658 seq.

heterogeneous elements, this book nonetheless gave the impression of being 'whole' and took a remarkably balanced view of the Jewish people. This work of art, an eternal source of life, had alone prevented the Jewish people, so badly endowed in every way, from passing into oblivion. But, in fact, the Old Testament was 'the triumph of the materialist conception of the world'.[1]

One realises that Chamberlain spared nothing. But all this unfortunately showed rather his tactical skill than his scientific objectivity. Numerous critics have given abundant proof of this.[2] We shall simply mention here two points.

Chamberlain gave a quite personal definition of religion, as based on feeling, the imagination, and mythology. And it was by virtue of this subjective and 'Teutonic' definition, that he claimed to judge the Jewish religion. Taking everything into consideration, he finally managed to prove that the Jews were lacking in 'teutonic' religiosity!

But Chamberlain committed a most serious error in method: he only took into account the inferior strands in the Jewish tradition, and ignored or minimised the noblest: the Book of Job, the Psalms, and the Prophets, the writings after the Exile and the literature of Greco-Jewish circles. He gave an arbitrary analysis of the growth of Judaism without any feeling for its subtleties or its various religious currents and their development. It was not astonishing, therefore, that he should discover only a wide gap between Judaism and Christianity.

But on the contrary—as we shall see later—he only judged Germanic religion by its highest achievements. Is it surprising that he was able to prove that a wide gap separated the poorest Jewish tradition, among others the popular tradition, from the most sublime German heritage, Meister Eckhart, Luther, and Kant? Using such methods of comparison you can prove everything.

So that, despite all the good intentions to which he clung, Chamberlain was swayed by an initial bias and, far from analysing the facts objectively, he remained guided by tactical considerations and dominated by his feelings.

4. THE TEUTON

Chamberlain made a definite though hardly convincing attempt, to interpret the Teutons, especially in his Chapter 6, 'The Entry of the Teuton into World History', a model of his fantastic dialectics.

In a first part (pp. 549–72) Chamberlain showed that it was

[1] *Grundlagen*, p. 541.
[2] See among other things, the criticism of Prof. Baentsch: 'H. St. Chamberlain Vorstellung über die Religion der Semiten spez. der in Israeliten' (*Pädegogisches Magazin*, 246th Volume, 1905).

necessary to widen the conception of a Teuton and to comprehend by this term the Celts and Slavs as well: Slavs, Celts, and Teutons had, in fact, common physical and, more especially, common moral traits. In this 'Slavo-Celto-Teuton' group the Teuton was the prime and central element; that was why his name could legitimately be used to cover the whole group.[1]

PHYSICAL OR MORAL CRITERIA

With this reservation made, Chamberlain aimed in the second part of this chapter (pp. 572–605) to limit this conception and work out exactly what physical and moral criteria distinguished the Teuton.

But from the start he encountered serious difficulties which he tried to avoid by acrobatic arguments.

He first of all stated that the physical criteria were so important that 'there is perhaps not a single anatomical detail of the body without the hallmark of race' (A).[2] Consequently he laid down this fundamental limiting rule: 'Whoever does not possess these physical traits, even if he was born in the heart of Germany and has spoken German from infancy, can not be considered as a Teuton' (B).[3]

However, this rule, valid as it was for the masses, could be applied only with difficulty to individuals who remained subject to the omnipotence of ideas. With Paul de Lagarde, Chamberlain accepted this limited notion: 'Das Deutschtum liegt nicht im Geblüte, sondern im Gemüte' (C); and he laid down a further limitation, which contradicted the first rule, at least in so far as the individual was concerned: 'Whoever behaves as a Teuton is a Teuton whatever his racial origin' (D).[4]

But, returning to the original theme, he reiterated the first rule (B) and made it even more rigid by contending that the idea was subject to biological determinism: 'The richer the spirit the more varied and reliable are the links connecting it with the predetermined foundations' (E),[4] thus contradicting Rules C and D.

From this contradiction, Chamberlain concluded 'that Teutonism is shown in the blood not in the sense that the blood provides the outlook and aptitude of the Teutons, but that it makes them possible' (F).[5] This led him to reformulate his first limiting Rule (B): 'Nobody can be a Teuton, generally speaking, who is not born of Teuton parents (G),[5] clearly a general rule, but impossible to reconcile with rules C and D, which he wanted to use for particular cases.

---

[1] *Grundlagen*, pp. 304–5.
[2] ibid., p. 572. For greater clarity, each stage in Chamberlain's argument is marked with a letter.
[3] ibid., p. 573.   [4] ibid., p. 574.   [5] ibid., p. 575.

WORTHLESSNESS OF PHYSICAL CRITERIA

With these subtle distinctions made, Chamberlain analysed the physical criteria which he had said everybody should possess if they were to be considered as Teutons (A and B).

The examination of hair was deceptive: fair hair allowed one 'always to infer the presence of the Teutonic race'. (David the Israelite was blond—ergo!) But Teutons of the best class, however, often had dark hair.[1] Could the scrutiny of the head be better proof? Undoubtedly the Teuton was usually long-headed; but Chamberlain admitted that there had been a 'degermanisation'[2] which had confused the types. Furthermore, the results of contemporary phrenology excited the scorn and anger of the author of the *Foundations*.

Having, therefore, shown the inadequacy of anatomical anthropology, Chamberlain demonstrated that one could not expect anything useful from it and that it might even prove to be a fanciful conception. 'Under a scientific pretext' this recent school had only been able to 'fly the flag of Chaos'.[3] So the author was drawn into pleading a good brief in favour of what he called 'rational anthropology'.[4]

Anthropology showed, said Chamberlain, that 'among races who achieved determined actions there was a predominant and determined physical structure'.[4] Here was the principle of correlation linking the two aspects of the *Gestalt*. Chamberlain came back to this very vague formula (what actions? what 'determined' structures?), but only to beg the question, since this was precisely what he needed to prove before going on to discuss racialism. So the author of the *Foundations*, having failed from the outset with physical tests, proposed a more 'rational' method: 'We ought to establish from the first what groups exist effectively as individualised races, recognisable by moral and intellectual signs, and then to see if there are any anatomical characteristics which are useful in categorising them.'[5]

Furthermore, since measurement, compasses, and logic are powerless before the infinitely varied possibilities of a single *Gestalt*, we should appeal to intuition and instinct. They will recognise, without difficulty, the evidence and the obvious paradoxes and be able to make order of an apparent chaos. With lyrical enthusiasm Chamberlain was blazing a trail, overgrown by science. His 'digression' into the realms of anatomy would not have been useless. For it allowed him to come out into a field more attractive to him: the definition of the

---

[1] *Grundlagen*, p. 577.   [2] ibid., p. 583.   [3] ibid., p. 585.
[4] ibid., p. 588.   [5] ibid., pp. 587–8.

Teuton by the moral criteria alone to which physical characteristics were subordinate.[1]

It was therefore, on final analysis, the spirit which enabled one to recognise a particular race. What was originally admitted—though with reservations [2]—only for the isolated individual (Rules C and D) was now to be equally valid for the masses, whilst the physical criteria at first declared essential (Rules A, B, and G) were now discounted, if not forgotten. Moreover, in place of objective criteria, Chamberlain was now making his personal intuition into the supreme judge. We are already far from the doctrine of the *Lebenslehre*, from the inner determinism of the *Gestalt* and the warranted correlation between physical and mental structures. The postulate about race has not stood up even to Chamberlain's superficial scrutiny.

THE MORAL CRITERIA OF THE TEUTON

Moreover, his attempt to define a Teuton by moral criteria led him, as we shall see, to extravagant enough conclusions.

Chamberlain, first of all, analysed the Teuton's face. Much could be said of his choice of Dante's and Luther's faces as typically Teutonic, whereas the two heads are dissimilar in every feature. But Chamberlain's intuition recognised 'just in this contrast their intimate relationship'.[3] His description was either epic or idyllic; it was never precise; the whole story was reconstructed in the light of what history has later taught us about these two great men.

After these definitions, 'live' doubtless but also vague, Chamberlain analysed the 'depths of the soul'. According to him, three moral and spiritual criteria distinguished the Teuton: the sense of freedom, loyalty, and the union of great idealism with a robust practical sense. This, however, seems little enough by which to define a race.

---

[1] *Grundlagen*, p. 592. [2] ibid., p. 573.

[3] ibid., p. 595. The choice of Dante as a Germanic type says much for the power of Chamberlain's theories. Dante is a Teuton, he says, because he is of Teutonic descent (ibid., p. 592, note 1). It is rule G, subordinated by what follows from mentality. Now moral criteria are, for Dante, very contradictory: he is a Teuton in so far as he subordinated the spiritual power of the Pope to the temporal powers (p. 731). But his religion, the usual deciding factor for Chamberlain, marks him as a son of Chaos. '. . . ein aristotelisches, aus lauter abstraktem Spinngewebe errichtetes Vernunftgerüst, wie wir das bei Dante sahen' (p. 1134); he follows blindly the rationalism and materialism of St Thomas (p. 741 n.), misunderstands Christ (p. 1135), is 'scarcely a Christian' (p. 741), and is inspired by the worst superstitions in his *Inferno* (p. 713 n.), while the refusal to believe in hell is, for so many others, the touchstone of their Teutonic or Chaotic connections (for example, p. 620 for St Ignatius, p. 683 for Tertullian, p. 712 for St Augustin, pp. 744–5 for the Goths; see also particularly p. 1047). If Chamberlain had needed to make Dante an Anti-teuton, the thing would soon have been fixed!

Certainly Chamberlain furnished certain precise notions in line
with contemporary German tradition. This freedom was a harmonious balance between individualism and the sense of community;
it enabled Teutons to establish well-ordered states. As its complement, there was the loyalty of the free man able to choose his ideal
and his leader. This was essentially, therefore, loyalty towards the
self, an autonomy of personality. This was 'the most important
trait in the Teuton's character; it allowed him to ensure whether or
not pure Teuton blood flowed in his veins'.[1] Lastly, the living union
in himself of idealism and practical sense showed that the Teuton's
ideal was not merely theoretical but—in a Kantian sense—'a
practical Idea' capable of being carried into action.[2]

THE TEUTONS' APPEARANCE IN HISTORY

In the last part of the chapter (pp. 606–32) Chamberlain, whilst
examining how the Teutons entered into history, became more
precise about their moral traits. These showed that, in fact, the
'characteristic' traits were very fragile; and Chamberlain only made
use of them at the price of a thousand contradictory quibbles, designed to help his dialectical manœuvres.

In fact, the Teuton 'entered universal history with its contours
already fixed and previously unknown to him'.[3] But this Teuton
idealist, this great innocent, defenceless 'child', was easy to lead
astray. He had an unfortunate tendency towards over-estimating
foreign values and an astonishing—and disquieting—gift for assimilation[4] that his wary enemies quickly exploited to their own
profit. This explained why so many Teutons were attracted by the
tinsel of a foreign ideal and became servants of anti-Germanism,
traitors to their own ideals. For example, there were Charlemagne
and Dante,[5] at once so faithful by their 'will' and so faithless by their
'non-will'. Or again, their was Thomas Aquinas, a Teuton genius
who sold his services completely to Rome![6]

For the Teuton's fidelity to a freely chosen ideal made his unconscious betrayals lasting and even final. It was a cruel paradox that
anti-Teuton ideologies found their most striking expression among
Teutons themselves. Could it be that the Teutons were not the
source of all greatness?[7]

One realises how difficult it is to recognise the Teuton: the physical
criteria had little validity, and the most reliable of the moral criteria

[1] *Grundlagen.*, p. 599.   [2] ibid., pp. 604–5.   [3] ibid., p. 606.
[4] ibid., p. 607. This picture of the Teuton, dear child of Nature, easily led astray,
beset with inferior but cunning enemies, is of Wagnerian origin; it is Siegfried before
Mima, 'der reine Thor'.   [5] ibid., pp. 609–10, 819.
[6] ibid., p. 614, note 1, and p. 1034.   [7] ibid., p. 614, note 1.

—loyalty to the Teuton ideals—often existed under the purely negative form of betraying this ideal! [1]

For the needs of his historical analysis in terms of race, Chamberlain was finally reduced to admitting tacitly the influence of environment. He proposed in fact a new principle of discrimination (Rule H); distinguishing between the results of pure nature (that is, of race) and other things forced on personality. [2]

Chamberlain had moved progressively further, not only from the theory of the *Lebenslehre* and its apparent scientific clarity, but also from the rules of discrimination set out at the beginning of this chapter: in the last resort a man could be a Teuton whether or not he possessed the specified physical (Rules A, B, E, F, G) or mental (Rule C) characteristics.

Chamberlain's meandering dialectics came to an end. The way was free for his 'intuition' or his fantasy. In fact, the idealised picture of the Teuton in the following chapters was skilfully embellished by Chamberlain with traits that were entirely fanciful.

We need to note two points to see clearly the results to which Chamberlain's ideas led. Chamberlain, thinking himself objective, emphasised several times the Teuton's faults: greed, cruelty, scorn for the rights of others, treason, etc., etc. [3] According to him, Germanic history was almost as violent as Jewish history, but—and this is the point—the Teutons had the 'particular gift' of making the best of their defects. Chamberlain saw in this the proof of their 'great cultural talents'. [4]

Since, moreover, Teutonism was in itself the supreme ideal on which the Teuton, even in times of massacre and robbery, ultimately based a superior civilisation, [5] a unique criterion should be applied in judging men in history: the greatest man and the finest act would be those most useful to Teutonism. [6]

Accordingly, Chamberlain enclosed himself in his faith and blind subjectivism. He was so convinced of the excellence of his arguments that he rarely took the trouble to adduce any remotely conclusive evidence. He judged authoritatively, often with absurd self-sufficiency and sometimes without realising that his arguments could easily be turned against himself. [7]

[1] Fr. Hertz calls this 'fidelity' with irony, but some justice: 'eine Anlage zum Aufgeben aller anderer Anlagen' (*Rasse und Kultur, eine kritische Untersuchung der Rassentheorien*, 3rd imp. (1925), p. 217).
[2] *Grundlagen*, p. 617.   [3] ibid., pp. 864, 899, 901.
[4] ibid., p. 901.   [5] ibid., p. 864.   [6] ibid., p. 859.
[7] For example, *Grundlagen*, p. 831, note 1. 'In establishing racial origin, Raphael's passionate veneration of Savonarola . . . is nearly as significant as the fact that Michelangelo never mentioned the Madonna and only once referred jokingly to a saint.' A flimsy proof, specially if one remembers that Chamberlain shows the Teuton, easily induced to admire his enemies and false values; besides, one might

So that, when the Teutons performed great feats, this was attributed to the pre-eminence of their race. If, however, greatness appeared among the adversaries of Teutonism, this would be caused by some German traitor who had betrayed it, and if he had betrayed it, it is because he was sensitive to the influence of environment.

There was nothing astonishing about Chamberlain coming round to 'prove' by this biased method that all greatness in history sprang from the Teutons.[1] Such a conclusion was imposed on Chamberlain not by an objective scrutiny of the facts, but by his initial prejudices arbitrarily twisting all the data of history.

5. THE RACIAL STRUGGLE FOR RELIGION AND THE STATE

After indicating the values at stake and the races fighting for them, Chamberlain went on to analyse the evolution of history in the light of the principles which he had laid down.

Until the thirteenth century, the Teuton's entry into the arena provoked a very confused racial dispute fought on two fronts.

In the world of religion a hybrid Christianity gradually appeared with the Aryan myths nationalised and materialised by the mixed peoples and the Jews. But the authentic Teutons opposed this deplorable development instinctively, though maladroitly. And it was symptomatic that they did not react against the differences in dogma; but they wanted to safeguard their racial and national unity, and this pitted them against the political domination and the universalism of the Roman Church.[2]

This religious war finished with the victory of Rome and Chaos. The Lutheran Reformation itself, so effective in politics, was a partial failure from the religious point of view; for the fatal link between Christianity and the Old Testament, and therefore Judaism, had not been broken. Luther had not been logical with himself.[3]

What the Teutons had to do was defend their *Gestalt*. The chapter devoted to the fight for the State was entirely constructed round one

---

also say that Raphael painted the Madonna more than anything else, and that Dante devoted many fine verses to the Virgin.

[1] Chamberlain was often indignant that his thought should be thus interpreted as it was, among others, by L. Woltmann (*Briefe*, I, p. 178). Now, quite apart from the fact that the entire work of Chamberlain implied such an affirmation, there are a number of passages which state this explicitly (referred to above). See *Grundlagen*, p. 614, note 1; ibid., p. 593, note. It is known that he accounts for the greatness of David and Solomon by an influx of Aryan blood. The peoples of the Chaos, and the Jews, would have achieved nothing without the Aryans; the Chinese and the Arabs are incapable of 'culture' (ibid., pp. 897, 881, 883, and note 1; p. 465, note 3). Chamberlain exalts the virtues of the Sumerians (ibid., p. 473), principally to belittle their debtors, the Semites.

[2] *Grundlagen*, pp. 616, 563, 763, 807, 1007.

[3] ibid., pp. 769, 893, 1037, 1064. *Mensch und Gott*, p. 228.

idea borrowed by Chamberlain from Goethe—that the living individual should be 'externally limited but internally boundless'.[1] On this fundamental theme, Chamberlain embroidered long and often quite artificial arguments.

The Teuton and the Teutonic peoples were 'personalities who, at the expense of a voluntary limitation of their field of external action, had acquired infinite scope in their inner world'.

On the contrary, Roman Catholicism, made Semitic and rational, uninterested by spiritual riches, worked only to extend its exterior grasp over the whole world. There was no liberty of thought, merely dogmas imposed on the conscience; a brutal intolerance and a faith based on dull ritualism.

Certainly, Chamberlain also acknowledges the grandeur of 'specifically Catholic thought',[2] but this was simply a fine distinction enabling him to point the contrast all the more clearly with the thought of the Roman Church as mere political imperialism.[3] The law of correlation, implicit in Goethe's phrase quoted above, imposed the need to choose between a superficial universality and the boundless wealth of the inner world.

The battle for the State was, therefore, engaged between the internationalism of the Roman Church and Teutonic nationalism. But here the Teutons were victorious. The Reformation was above all a political success, since Catholic unity was shattered; and the Teutons were able to build powerful national states which, as we have seen, allowed them to perfect the Teutonic race.

These, therefore, were the main lines of the racial battle stretching from the fifth to the thirteenth centuries. Chamberlain's debt to German romanticism, and especially to Savigny, is clear.

His anti-Roman obsession and his blind prejudice in favour of the Teutons dominated the analysis given in the eleventh and last chapter of the *Foundations*: 'The Birth of a New World'.

On reading the first part, devoted to the great discoveries [4] on how to judge men, the very simple design leaves the impression of a moral tale or a nursery picture. The Teutons stood, on the one side, an unequalled race, thirsty for knowledge; and on the other side stood Rome, the incarnation of anti-Teutonism, claiming omniscience and opposed to all experiments.[5] But Rome needed gold, and in order

---

[1] See the treatment of this 'Gesetz der Begrenzung' in the *Grundlagen*, pp. 791–7, and the highly dubious uses which Chamberlain made of it, especially at the end of the Chapter *Der Staat*, pp. 797–820. Here we have a systematic and abusive application of the formula: $S \times C = 1$, which he saw only as a hypothesis (see above, p. 253).

[2] *Grundlagen*, pp. 375–6.   [3] ibid., p. 1007.

[4] ibid., pp. 895–927, *Entdeckung*, and notably pp. 922 ff.

[5] ibid., p. 909.

to obtain gold, she left one way open to experiment: the route to geographical discovery.[1] The Teuton also hurried into this, equally tempted by the gold. But he at least knew how to draw good from bad. His geographical discoveries would gradually upset Roman dogma and finally provoke the intellectual and religious emancipation of the Teutons.

The Teuton, in fact, was not only the hero of history, but also created the fundamental *foundations* of the world, according to Chamberlain,[2] who made a significant use even of the title of his book to praise the race who had fashioned the modern world.

CONCLUSIONS ON THE *FOUNDATIONS*

Such, then, was the *Foundations of the Nineteenth Century*. Should we attempt here to assess the complete work, having earlier pointed out the serious criticisms to which the author's essential ideas could be subjected?

The book is never boring and is often attractive, for it was written with ability. He opened new perspectives that appeared to uncritical readers to be profound. The author, packed as he was with erudition, knew how to display his humility so adroitly that he could captivate as much by his learning as by his modesty. The innocent reader was sometimes charmed into thinking that vexed points or insurmountable difficulties were resolved as if by magic with the intervention of Chamberlain's intuition and enthusiasm.

The *Foundations* was a pseudo-scientific work. In reality, behind a façade of erudition, it was a poem in the Teuton's glory, a 'work of art' in the sense given to that phrase by Chamberlain in speaking about the Old Testament,[3] and skilful arrangements of the parts of the subject allowed him to put one essential characteristic into better perspective: the Teuton's pre-eminent dignity.[4] By taking the Jew (or even the Greek and the Hindu) as a 'foil', Chamberlain effectively contrived to define the Teuton according to his own subjective views—the ego showing itself in contrast with itself—and also to propose the *partikuläre Gemeinschaft* which, with its messianism and imperialism, characterised all the racialist theories. Erich Voegelin has provided a clear analysis of the stages in this development.[5]

[1] *Grundlagen*, p. 922.   [2] ibid., p. 865.
[3] ibid., p. 1191, note 3. Chamberlain shows that he conceived a work of art (and his books, as we saw, were for him works of art in this sense) as Taine defined it in his *Philosophie de L'art*, I, Chap. 5, p. 51.
In a letter of 23 March, 1897, to his friend A. Appia, Chamberlain wrote significantly something of the kind about his book on Wagner.
[4] Cosima, full of good sense, charged Chamberlain with under-estimating the Greeks. For his reply see *Cosima Wagner und H. S. Chamberlain im Briefwechsel*, pp. 566-7.
[5] Erich Voegelin, *Rasse und Staat* (Tübingen, 1933), Chaps. 3, 4.

IV. THE WAY OF SALVATION
TEUTONIC CULTURE

The *Foundations* showed us the Teutons entering late on to the stage of history and in the course of a long struggle, laying the foundations of a new culture.

But, with the dawn of the twentieth century, although they had imposed their mastery throughout the world, they were very far from triumphing over all their difficulties or from accomplishing their aims.

MODERN DANGERS

They still faced considerable dangers. The emancipation of the Jews corrupted the race. Their ideals risked contamination from contemporary materialism in a thousand forms. In this respect the dogmas of abstract science, particularly of the theory of evolution, were as pernicious as those of the Roman–Jewish church. Protestantism lacked vigour and was itself contaminated.[1] Large-scale capitalism had separated the proletariat from nature and brutalised the masses. The question had become how to safeguard the freedom and dignity of man in a society where thought was declining in quality and losing its sway.[2]

Moreover, a further menace came from the yellow, black, and even Slav races. For the Slavs had been degenerating for a long time. France had, since the wars of religion and the Revolution, liquidated its Nordic *élite*. England was being undermined by Jewishness and democracy.[3] In the face of these mounting dangers, the true Teutons were therefore much less numerous than a few centuries ago.

TEUTONS OR GERMANS?

Of the great Slav-Celtic-Teuton family tree only the central branch still continued to flourish. Only the Teutons in the narrow sense of the term—that was to say, principally the Germans—

[1] *Grundlagen*, p. 769. In matters of catholicism, Chamberlain condemns ultramontanism as essentially anti-Teutonic. But, setting aside Roman influence, he considered catholicism to be less dangerously 'infected' by the Old Testament, than protestantism. It is also nearer to nature, and its liturgy gives a greater place to myth. Chamberlain placed great hope, about 1900, in the *Los von Rom-Bewegung*, which he supported as much as he could. See, for example, the article, 'Katholische Universitäten' (in *Rasse und Persönlichkeit*, pp. 41–65, and especially pp. 54, 55, 63), which ends with a call for the union of Catholics and Protestants against Rome and Anti-Christ.

[2] See the discussion of modern dangers in *Kant*, pp. 712–21.

[3] *Grundlagen*, pp. 559, 560, 835; *Kant*, p. 715 (degeneration of the Slavs, black, and yellow menace); *Grundlagen*, pp. 1011–12 (degeneration of France).

K

remained the truly qualified representatives of this ancient family. Fortunately, the Germans were in essentials the best endowed of them all.[1] Although they were not without faults, they were nevertheless a human type combining in a harmonious balance the qualities of the Greeks and of the Indo-Aryans of former times.[2] Their superiority gave them the right of being masters of the world.[3] In future the salvation of humanity rested with them and with them alone.[4]

Undoubtedly Chamberlain contended throughout his polemical writing that he had never assimilated the Germans to his 'Slavo-Celto-Teuton'.[5] This was true. But he showed in many parts of his work that the Celts and the Slavs had been eliminated or disqualified in the battle of history. What would this mean but that the Teutons in the narrow sense of that term—that was, above all, the Germans—were nowadays the only people to possess the qualities of the great Slavo-Celto-Teuton race, the only people legitimately able to vindicate the heritage and glorious mission to which history had dedicated them. And moreover, he considered it no fault to glorify this high mission of Germany and the German. His work as a whole, his letters to William II (to whom he spoke with an open heart)—without mentioning his absurdly patriotic wartime pamphlets—proved this conclusion to be the inevitable end to all his dialectics.

However, the Teuton could carry out his destiny only by safeguarding Teuton culture and by fostering, in accordance with the genius of his race, all the rich potential latent in it.

Science, religion, and Teuton art were the triple foundations and the triple expression of this 'culture', a conception of the world drawing its strength from the indefatigable and faithful observation of nature, on which art conferred order and form.[6]

A NEW HUMANISM (a) SCIENCE

We have already referred to Chamberlain's conception of what was meant by science. He was very boastful about the remarkable successes that experimental science owed to the Teutons.[7] But—as we know—he was greatly afraid that it would become dogmatic, materialist, and intolerant, and also undermine religion. To avoid this danger and keep the three elements of Teutonic culture homogenous, a new humanism had to be established. That inherited

---

[1] *Grundlagen*, p. 866.   [2] ibid., pp. 890, 937.   [3] ibid., pp. 597, 820.
[4] *Briefe*, Vol. II, p. 138. 'Deutsche Weltanschauung' (April 1917) in *Rasse und Persönlichkeit*, p. 29.
[5] H. S. Chamberlain, 'Letter to M. Dujardin' in *Mercure de France*, Feb. 1904, p. 572.
[6] *Grundlagen*, p. 1195.   [7] ibid., Chap. IX, B, 2: *Wissenschaft*.

from Aristotle, the Romans, and the medieval Church was narrow and out of date. Man would now have to be restored to his place in nature, return to the school of nature, and interpret it in the same way as Goethe.[1] For, in Chamberlain's view, science ought, from a strictly mechanistic point of view, to be a method for 'considering' and not for 'explaining' the external phenomena of the world. Science ought not to encroach on the domain of religion, which, strictly spiritual as it was among the Teutons, would take account only of the inner world free from the relativity of time and space.

(b) RELIGION

What therefore in fact was 'Teuton religion'? According to Chamberlain,[2] the Aryan was moved by his desire to unravel the mysteries of the world and his own heart; between these he feels some relationship. Religion consisted in looking into the depths of oneself. It is a 'state of sensitivity'. Moreover, in the course of exploring a transrational world, man was trying to give form to the invisible and ineffable. Symbols and myths helped him with this task. This again was religion. It had nothing in common with ethics or the chronicles of history. The Aryan would find God within himself and religion to be merely the expression of a respect felt primarily for himself.

Who was God? Since Kant, 'the first complete Teuton personality totally emancipated from Roman dogmatism',[3] the Teuton knew that God was only an empty conception. It was, therefore, useless to attempt any scrutiny of what could not be known.

But Christ lived; his life was a concrete and luminous example. Chamberlain was less interested in the historical facts about Christ than in the experience which the existence of Christ can give us the opportunity to know. Since Christ, religion can only be the 'religion of experience'.[4] God, until then inaccessible, an empty and meaningless framework for the human reason, had become a living reality in the personality of Christ; the framework was enriched by a symbol. Instead of saying 'Christ is God', the gnostic formula of a Semitic and anti-scientific faith, the Teuton was now saying 'God is Christ', the formula of a living faith.[5]

The 'divinity' revealed in Christ, moreover, continually showed itself in the race. 'Germanic Christianity' was still in its infancy, and had hardly emerged from the first crises of its upbringing.[6] The

---

[1] 'Die Natur als Lehrmeisterin' in *Rasse und Persönlichkeit*, pp. 102–11.
[2] *Grundlagen*, pp. 259–60.
[3] ibid., p. 1127.
[4] On this essential concept of *Religion der Erfahrung*, see *Briefe*, Vol. I, pp. 75, 112–13; Vol. II, pp. 183–4, 208–9; *Grundlagen*, pp. 229, 1133–4; and *Kant*, pp. 782–3.
[5] *Briefe*, Vol. II, p. 209, Vol. I, p. 113.   [6] *Grundlagen*, p. 223.

Reformation had been unable radically to cut the sinister link between Christianity and Judaism. It was thus necessary to revive and pursue the Reformation's aims. The most urgent and important of the tasks nowadays facing the Teutons was to foster a specifically religious renaissance.

For religion should be a continuing creation. The revelation was never finished, but was prolonged in each great genius. God had clearly arranged for such men to appear in great numbers among the Teutons and for the last century 'exclusively among the German people'.[1] Were not Schiller, Goethe, Beethoven, Kant, Wagner, and the Hohenzollerns as many 'revelations of God's presence clearer before our eyes than the bush on Sinai'?[2] For the last hundred years Germanic philology through exploiting the mythology and literature of the ancient Indian world and of medieval Europe, showed the Teutons that they possessed holy books finer and nobler than the Old Testament.[3]

Kant knew how to take up where the Reformation left off. Thanks to him, the Teutons have at last renewed connections with ancient Indian metaphysics and religion; at last they are in possession of a purely 'idealistic' religion with no link with an historical chronicle and based solely on subjective experience. This was no longer the half-materialist and anti-scientific outlook of Christians subject to Jewish influence, for whom an anthropomorphic God interfered arbitrarily with the laws of nature.

The Teutons must go yet further. They were still the prisoners of misleading beliefs and misguided priesthoods. Kant's religious ideas were too abstract for them ever to become the living religion of a whole people. Chamberlain, moreover, sketched the main lines of a religion with no church, no priests, and no dogma.[4] As among the Indo-Aryans of old (from whom, under the influence of Paul Deussen and Leopold von Schroeder, Chamberlain borrowed freely), this religion cherished a mythology compatible with the most diverse beliefs and the greatest liberty of thought. This mythology would be inspired by Teutonic art with intense vitality and given the indispensable qualities of a great plasticity and power of suggestion.

(c) ART

In practice, among the Teutons art was closely related to religion. Through art the invisible became visible and the inconceivable capable of expression.

For art alone, and then only the naturalism and symbolism of

---

[1] *Briefe*, Vol. II, p. 171.   [2] ibid., pp. 170–4.
[3] *Grundlagen*, p. 32.   [4] *Mensch und Gott*, pp. 267–77.

true Germanic art, is capable of bringing continually before our eyes and hearts the personality of Christ. Without art this extraordinary and essential figure remains an abstraction or becomes an idol.[1]

This type of art is the mediator between the heterogeneous worlds of nature and liberty. German artists—and particularly Schiller and Wagner—had all acclaimed the highest ends for art. Bayreuth had witnessed the startling rebirth of the old Aryan tradition of sacred mysteries, inexplicable mysteries which man could interpret only through the intimate association of poetry and music.[2]

Chamberlain also drew up a project for a religious community of the liberal protestant type, with a 'cult' where the formal and impressionable elements, centred round the person of Christ, were more important than the intellectual, rational, and ethical elements.[3] In brief, this would be a religion with hazy outlines that contrived by avoiding the hardening effects of logic, to interpret the unknown through the medium of man's senses, heart, and imagination.

This, therefore, was the direction in which the Teutons ought to move. To sum up, the essence of the metaphysical and religious ideas of Kantian idealism should be accessible to everybody—by using the trappings of Wagnerian art.[4] This was the way of salvation which Chamberlain traced for the Germans, that they might escape the perils that beset them and keep their right and power of mastering the world. The rest of mankind could be saved only in so far as they perceived—or could perceive—the revelation of Germanic civilisation.[5]

These philosophic, religious, and aesthetic considerations, combined in Chamberlain with his political thinking, were in turn affected by the principles of the *Gestalt* and racialism. In reality only slightly original, Chamberlain's political thinking merely restated the romantic conception of the organic state and reiterated the old German reproaches against the ideals of Western democracy.

Indeed, the reproaches became more violent as the theory of the organic state, founded on the assumption of racial and individual inequality, became more exacting. Chamberlain insisted that the Jews and ultramontane Catholics should be supervised and even

---

[1] *Mensch und Gott*, pp. 277–90; *Grundlagen*, pp. 1133–8.
[2] *Grundlagen*, pp. 1138–46, 1168.
[3] *Mensch und Gott*, pp. 267–72 (Möglichkeit einer neuen Gemeinschaftsbildung), and pp. 282, 287–96.
[4] See the end of *Kant*, p. 788.
[5] H. S. Chamberlain, *Ideal und Macht*, p. 35. See also Chamberlain's article on Hermann Levi in *Bayreuther Blätter*, 1901.

excluded from common law, for he regarded them as foreigners, and even traitors to Germany.[1]

V. THE INFLUENCE OF H. S. CHAMBERLAIN

Chamberlain has never been very well known in Germany. However, at certain times he played a part that ought not to be under-estimated among Pangerman and Wagnerian groups—for example at Court, where William II's friendship won him many readers. If his books, which are not easy reading, for the most part reached only a limited public of cultivated people, his *Foundations of the Nineteenth Century* and his wartime pamphlets enjoyed some considerable success.[2]

On its publication the *Foundations* created a sensation, and a lively controversy ensued. But this book attracted, in particular, one reader of note—the Emperor. From 1900 onwards William II was reading and being greatly impressed by the *Foundations*. He distributed the book among his entourage and wanted to meet the author. On 28th and 29th October he met Chamberlain at the castle of Liebenberg, the home of Prince Eulenberg. The Emperor was captivated by Chamberlain, whom he invited the following day to Potsdam for an intimate evening—this odd, German-loving Englishman, writing with the authority of a scholar and the charm of a mystic, and opening before the head of the German race noble and exalted horizons.

A fairly sizeable correspondence ensued: from 1901 to 1923 Chamberlain wrote forty-three letters to William II, and some of these amounted to positive dissertations, twenty large-sized pages long. The Emperor replied twenty-three times. Chamberlain's influence on him, especially in religious affairs, was apparent from the outset; in the Aix-la-Chapelle, Posen, and Görlitz speeches, William II obviously drew his inspiration from the *Foundations*.[3] Even for the famous public letter sent by the Emperor to Admiral Hollman on 19th February 1903, which provoked a lively reaction throughout Germany, William II took the essentials, both in matter and in many points even of style, from the letter just addressed to him by Chamberlain on 4th February.[4] When he came to pronounce on the divine inspiration of the Old Testament and on the religious

---

[1] See in H. S. Chamberlain, *Politische Ideale* (1915), the key political ideas of the author.
[2] The 100,000th copy of the *Foundations* came out in 1915; the 24th edition in 1938.
[3] For the Emperor's use of Chamberlain in his Görlitz speech, see, for instance, William's own comment in his letter of 21 Dec. 1902 (*Briefe*, Vol. II, pp. 165–6).
[4] See the letter sent by the Emperor to Chamberlain, on 16 Feb., apologising for having borrowed from him (*Briefe*, Vol. II, pp. 188–9).

revelations of history, it was to Chamberlain that William II turned for guidance. This was symptomatic of a type of Christianity sliding towards racialism.

But in 1915 Chamberlain realised that William II was not the enlightened and resolute leader of his earlier belief. His pamphlets became more violent; he advocated unrestricted submarine warfare and sided with von Tirpitz.

After the defeat, William II at Doorn was still influenced by Chamberlain. He read and made lengthy notes on his last book, *Man and God*. The last exchanges of letters showed that the fallen Prince came finally to accept almost all Chamberlain's religious ideas.

However, it was on racialism proper that Chamberlain exerted his deepest influence; and if an exact assessment of his effect on National-Socialism would be difficult to make, the connection is obvious. It is clear that between 1900 and 1920, Chamberlain was one of the principal agents in popularising and developing the ideology of race.

Let us, first of all, recall certain facts.

On 6th October 1925 Hitler, attending a convention in Bayreuth, paid his respects to Chamberlain on behalf of his party. What resemblances there were between the two men! Both were the slaves of their subconscious, both were often the prey of peculiar trances, both were fervent admirers of Wagner's irrationalism and Pangerman mysticism. On the other hand, what contrasts there were! Chamberlain had a mind stored with a wide and refined culture, and even his excesses and mistakes showed the marks of a generous indiscretion. Hitler was a man warped by resentment, with no true culture; a brutal and terrifying realist.

However, it was Chamberlain, the great, half-paralysed neurotic, who at that meeting fell for the magnetic personality of Hitler. On the following day Chamberlain wrote him an enthusiastic letter; the writer had renewed his hopes, for while Hitler lived and acted, there would be life in the Fatherland.[1]

Chamberlain joined the Nazi Party and contributed to its publications as often as his strength would allow him. On Hitler's thirty-fifth birthday, while the *Führer* was in prison after the failure of his *coup d'état*, Chamberlain sang his praises, and on 24th April 1924 published a long profession of faith in him.[2] Like William II before him, Hitler had been sent by God to the German people; they must rest their faith in him and follow his leadership. The NSDAP's enthusiasm and recognition became obvious.

[1] *Briefe*, Vol. II, p. 126.
[2] G. Schott, *H. S. Chamberlain der Seher des dritten Reiches* (1934), pp. 15–18.

Undoubtedly Hitler would have heard about Chamberlain in Vienna before 1912, in the anti-semitic groups centring round Schoenerer. During the war he must have read and brooded over the *Kriegsaufsätze*. In *Mein Kampf* (Vol. I, p. 296) he quoted Chamberlain as a prophet whom the Germans had wronged by turning a deaf ear.

As to Rosenberg, the party's philosopher, he certainly owed much to Chamberlain. From 1926 onward, moreover, he acknowledged Chamberlain by devoting to him a slim volume of 128 pages, with the significant title: *H. S. Chamberlain, the Pioneer and Founder of a German Future*. And the first volume of his main work, the *Myth of the Twentieth Century*, betrayed in its analysis—even if this was more violent and smouldering—and its arrangement, the influence of the *Foundations* now appropriated by Rosenberg as a theory of racialism that had culminated thirty years ago.

The official tributes paid by the Party to Chamberlain were fervent and frequent. On 5th September 1925 the *Völkischer Beobachter* celebrated Chamberlain's seventieth birthday in five columns and, after recalling that until about 1900 anti-Semitism had been only an instinctive movement, with no ideological backing, it wrote: ' so wurden uns *Die Grundlagen des XIX. Jahrhunderts* das Evangelium der völkischen Bewegung '.

At Chamberlain's funeral Hitler was the only notable personality present, apart from a prince representing the exiled Emperor.

After 1933 the triumphant Nazi state faithfully guarded the memory of Chamberlain, who was, furthermore, given such official titles as Seer, Prophet, Founder. Articles, conferences, books, university theses were devoted to him.[1] There were editions of selected extracts from his work—with significant omissions—and his writings were adapted for radio. In 1938 the French Gymnasium in Berlin included his last book, *Man and God*, in the religious curriculum of its top class, by the side of Eckhart, Lessing, Herder, Goethe, Schleiermacher, Lagarde, and Rosenberg. His more or less unproved hypotheses, his religious and ethical ideas, became 'the common property' of the German people. In practice, they had long been exceeded by the Party.

Those are the facts. It is impossible within the limited scope of this study to show in detail the influence of Chamberlain on Nazism. Let us simply isolate the main points.

Chamberlain was the first to present a clear, attractive, and appar-

---

[1] Three books by W. Vollrath, professor at the University of Erlangen, two by G. Schott, two theses: W. Nielsen, *Der Lebens- und Gestaltbegriff bei H. S. Chamberlain* (Kiel, 1939), and Gepräge, *Germanentum und Christentum bei H. S. Chamberlain* (Tübingen, 1938).

ently durable synthesis of the prime aspirations of a Germanic racialism that around 1900 was still appealing confusedly to several different circles.

Moreover, this synthesis contrived to appear as a compromise between Pangerman Wagnerianism and Gobinism, on the one hand, and scientific anthropology, on the other. Chamberlain claimed to combine the scientific austerity of the second with the troubled mysticism of the former.

Men of Hitler's and Rosenberg's generation borrowed from Chamberlain this radiant formula of a faith awaiting the revelation. Rosenberg acknowledged this specifically: it was, he said, thanks to Chamberlain that he came 'to see clearly'.[1]

It was also especially to the influence of Chamberlain that Nazism owed, in a general way, the pseudo-scientific appearance of so many of its manifestations, which in fact rested only on the lava-like thrust of instinct, and could not be measured by any objective criteria, only admitting anywhere in practice the unique test of the racial community's selfish interest. Service to Germanism was a duty and the supreme trial, said Chamberlain. Nazism was to say, similarly, 'What the race need is right', and would take pleasure, like him, in a convenient but disquieting, shifting philosophy. Like him, it would play the double game of using science so long as it could be of service, and leaving it unceremoniously when it worked against it, to take refuge in a more pliable irrationalism. Like him, Nazism would hesitate between physical and moral methods for defining race and, in the last resort, adopt methods that left the escape-clauses most play.[2] Nazism also owed basically to Chamberlain the first coherent exposition of some of its fundamental premises: the German as the creator of culture, and the Jew as the negative element in history, recognisable by his blood and religion; the complementary ideas of *Race* and *Leader* (or 'Genius'), the attempt to show that religion was linked to race, etc. . . .

On the other hand, there were quite clearly perceptible differences between Chamberlain and Nazism. Chamberlain would have been frightened by the front eventually shown to the world by Nazism and would undoubtedly have condemned it. In December 1938, a few days after the pogroms had broken across Germany, Mrs. Chamberlain remarked to me: 'My husband would not have liked this!' No doubt. But it was he who had given racialism its warhead. The *Völkischer Beobachter* had written in the article reporting

---

[1] A. Rosenberg, *H. S. Chamberlain als Verkünder und Begründer einer deutschen Zukunft*, Foreword, p. 7.

[2] See, for example, the definition of a *Reichsbürger*, according to the *Reichsbürgergesetz* of 15 Sept. 1935, § 2, I. See also Hitler's speech of 7 Feb. 1934, and Göring's on 19 June 1934.

his death on 11th January 1927 that the German people had lost in him 'one of the great blacksmiths whose weapons have not yet found in our day their fullest use'.

The terrible responsibility of this worthy and often generous man was that, like so many others who have indiscriminately exalted unknown forces, he sowed the wind without realising that one day it would be necessary to reap the whirlwind.

6

STEFAN GEORGE: AESTHETES OR TERRORISTS?

Claude David

THOSE who become known to posterity as the forerunners of a revolution are not revolutionaries. They are often the first victims of a movement that they unwittingly fostered. Even when the combatants pay tribute to them, for a time, as ancestors and as guides, it may well be that they refuse this homage, that they do not recognise their thought in the acts they are witnessing, and that they consider themselves dupes of history.

If Stefan George's name figures here among the 'forerunners' of National-Socialism, it is in that sense of the word. Hitler's advent to power scattered the poet's disciples throughout the globe. He himself died outside Germany, and today, almost twenty years later, his remains have still not been brought back to·his native Rhine: he himself is said to have wished it so. Amongst his followers, only a few took an active part in the Nazi ranks; the others either remained silent or fled; a few were among the leaders of the plot of 20th July 1944 which almost succeeded.

And yet the discredit into which George has fallen since the war, and which has thrust into oblivion, quite unjustly, one of Germany's greatest poets, doubtless arises from the fact that public opinion links his name with a past which it prefers to forget. A disciple of George, Friedrich Wolters, in a biography of the poet which he published in 1930, chose as a sub-title: 'History of the German Mind since 1890'. It is an arrogant claim, which is hard to substantiate. But, by stressing the part played by the poet in the history of ideas, it affirms that his name must be quoted when the time comes to assess the influence of thought and the acts that follow from it. Any inquiry into the intellectual origins of National-Socialism soon leads to the conclusion that the pure and the impure in Germany's history cannot be separated. Thoughts interlace and contaminate one another. The ideas which a cunning despotism invoked and which the Germans used, in a given historical crisis, to justify their acts in their own eyes and in the eyes of the world had been prepared long before. Who in Germany, then, can be certain that he has not been affected by the contagion?

I

A poet's audience is usually restricted. George, a difficult and for a long time an unknown poet, had for many years and through no wish of his own found himself performing the function of spiritual guide and counsellor to an important section of the German intellectual public.

George's most abstract work, *The Star of the Covenant*, which appeared in 1914, on the eve of the war, was for many intellectuals a sort of bible, which they carried with them on the battlefields. That was the time when George's influence was at its height. For ten years or so he was a guide.

This influence made itself felt in three ways. Firstly, through his published poems themselves. Secondly, and above all, through his activity as an educator. George gathered disciples round him, mostly young people, whose minds he shaped and whose lives he directed. The Circle, as the society of George and his followers was called, had, to those outside it, all the appearance of a closed sect. In various towns in Germany—Heidelberg, Munich, Kiel, Berlin—small chapels sprang up around an important disciple. George, who had no fixed domicile during the first years of the century, made unexpected visits to his churches. He met the young people, almost all of them poets, who had placed themselves under his wing. He asked them about the books they were reading, about their tastes, their life. For a few days the poet shared his friends' lives. At these family gatherings, in the course of a frugal meal or a short walk, he imparted his teaching in the form of discussions, in which precepts were drawn from day-to-day life. Despite the apparent freedom of this life, the rules were strict. George was familiar with each one's actions; quite unknown to the disciple, he controlled his relations and his friendships. Anyone wishing to remain in the community had to renounce all private life and accept the Master's direction as the only true liberty. In this way a closely-knit society was gradually formed, about which absurd legends grew up. It staged no mysteries and no orgies. But it imitated, in the twentieth century, a community of monks. One can discern fairly easily a hierarchy, a rule, a dogma, and rites. The novice at least takes a vow of obedience; the life he chooses is, if not ascetic, at least frugal, without luxury or indulgence; if chastity is not imposed, at least celibacy is for a long time, for the disciples are only allowed to marry late. As for ritual, it consists of the reading of poems: a public ceremony, in which the individual loses sight of himself, surrenders himself to the community, and which, for the disciples, represents the 'final act of worship'. As to the dogma, it will be explained in detail later.

The Circle of George was conceived by its founder as a new priest-hood. A number of disciples rebelled. Others were expelled from the community by George. But no Master ever had so strict and so pro-found an influence on his followers: not only did the Circle develop a morality and a philosophy of its own, but the disciples adopted a special style of writing, and even came to resemble one another facially. Seldom, writes R. Kassner, 'has such a phenomenon appeared in the history of thought'.

The number of direct disciples or, as they were called, 'direct no-bility' was never very high. But each one attracted other disciples, so that gradually the poet's influence spread.

The doctrine had a third channel of propagation. A few disciples, particularly after the war, occupied University chairs: Professors of Literature, History, or Economics, who passed on the dogmas of the Circle to a wide audience. They also contributed some outstanding works of literary criticism: Gundolf's *Goethe*, Ernst Bertram's *Nietzsche*, Max Kommerell's *The Poets as Guides*, and historical works like Ernst Kantorowicz's *Frederick II* bear the hallmarks of the Georgian Circle.

In this way George became for a certain time one of the centres of German thought; in this way his influence was felt much more beyond the Circle itself. The doctrine that was spread by these means is to be found in George's last collections of poems, *The Star of the Covenant* and *The Kingdom Come*. In fact, it is not until about 1897 that George's name first appears in literary reviews, and only shortly before the outbreak of war does he begin to mean anything to the general public. But a full appreciation of his thought in the later years is possible only if one has some picture, however sketchy, of his formative years. The key to the doctrine lies perhaps in the aesthetic pessimism of George's early poems.

On the face of it there is an unbridgeable gulf between the begin-ning and the end of the poet's career. To begin with, an art that prides itself on being abstract; later, a poetry that aims to change the world and to establish a new order. To begin with, a rhetoric that borrows its precepts from abroad and appears to dream of a European literary community; later, a lyricism with Germany as its theme, Germany as the guide and leader of a rejuvenated Europe.

But if one looks closer one can discern in the first collections of poems very marked analogies with the last collections and see the germ of an ideology running through them all.

It is in France that George finds his first masters. He has fled from naturalist Germany, carrying with him some immature poems, when he discovers, in Paris, the existence of symbolism. He is in time to meet Villiers de l'Isle-Adam; he pays several visits to Mallarmé in the rue de Rome; he catches glimpses of Verlaine.

The lesson he learns from these masters is, to begin with, simply art for art's sake. It is the first precept laid down in 1892 in the Poetry Review that George founds with Hugo von Hofmannsthal: *Blätter für die Kunst*. Poetry must sever all links with society. It is consciously obscure in order to frighten off the uninitiated. It wants to ignore all social or moral values: the only values that count are aesthetic. This aesthetic poetry reduces content virtually to nothing: it is deliberately futile, it records only insignificant occurrences, and it shies away from feelings and ideas as dangerously important. Its form is precious. It looks upon itself as an 'askesis': it is a refuge, it demands from its disciples renunciation of ordinary life. Only the artificial has meaning: life is banal and can give pleasure only to gross natures. The poet despises it: he cultivates the arrogant elegance of the dandy.

I may appear to have wandered from the subject, but only superficially. It is true that George is not the only one in Europe at that time who defends art for art's sake and aestheticism. Shortly before, Mallarmé has written that everything in the world exists to end up in a Book: Oscar Wilde thinks, like George, that artificial flowers are better than natural flowers. But George goes farther, and carries to their logical conclusion ideas which, for the great majority of poets, remain implicit: he uncovers the secret thought that inspires this aestheticism and reveals its consequences.

The philosophy that animates this lyricism is one of pessimism: art is the sole refuge, because life has no meaning. One of George's early poems condemns 'the falsity of being and the world': like the French Parnassus poets, he employs the image of an exotic animal, of a parakeet imprisoned in the cage of a garden, whose white-and-yellow foliage the poet describes with mocking meticulousness.

Just as the aesthete turns his back on the world, he turns his back on society. The futility of the poet in the state is not taken for granted by the writers of this period; their attitude is a voluntary break, which has always something of a challenge to it, abnegation carries a vague hint of condemnation. They have no interest in reformation; they wash their hands of it. They feel themselves to be the inheritors of a dead past and the opponents of a present that can give them no satisfaction and that they have no wish to serve. They are all, in a way, '*bourgeois*', but have reached a point where the *bourgeoisie* condemns itself and destroys itself.

But aestheticism does not remain long iu this first phase. Very soon it is no longer content to affirm the independence of art as against morality: aesthetic values take up the fight against all the others.

Art becomes a form of subversion. Its function is to deny and destroy a world that is abject or merely deceitful. It is the highest expression of misanthropy, pessimism, and nihilism.

This second phase of aestheticism inspired the most important of George's early works, *Algabal*. The choice of theme is, in itself, significant: it is Heliogabalus, the Roman emperor to whom history has given the most evil reputation, the very symbol of 'decadence'. George does not sing the praises of 'decadence' in order to rehabilitate a bygone age that has been misunderstood: what he likes in the Lower Empire is its corruption, its cruelty, its 'Evil'. Aesthetic values are born where all others collapse; the progress of art is completely at variance with civilisation and power. Nothing is more beautiful than the fall of empires. The poet of the later nineteenth century believes he is living in an age like that of the fall of Rome. In a world of ruined values he sees the man of his time faced with only one prospect—to see himself die: art, which has remained 'apart', finds its *raison d'être* in its very futility.

The Algabal whom George depicts is obviously the symbol of the artist as the poet conceives him in such circumstances. But at the same time he is what one could call nihilist man.

Algabal, like the artist, rules over a universe of stone. He has built subterranean palaces in which he lives alone, a complete world of metals and jewels in which he has settled down to defy nature. His life's desire is to create a black rose, more beautiful than any garden rose; his sphere is that of artifice. It is the sole power he considers worthy of interest. He has renounced court intrigues; he has been disillusioned by love.

But, however solitary he wishes to be, he cannot wish other men out of existence; he must come face to face with them. For him, however, they are no more than parts of the landscape; he looks at them from afar, without sympathy, like a show. If a slave dies to enhance his imperial glory, he finds the red blood makes a pleasing contrast with the green meadows. He is detached and contemptuous; he looks with disdain on the works of men. And soon he who should have been 'the salvation and the beloved of peoples' becomes an agent of extermination. He flogs the common people as a punishment for being alive. Aestheticism culminates in terror. Finally the emperor leads his people to destruction on the battlefield, thinking that, in a moment of horror, men may shed their falsity. Despair assumes a barbaric shape, impotence finds expression in cruelty. For the *blasé* emperor it is a mere game, like the orgies which he has stripped of all illusion but in which he still indulges, coldly, in his search for escape and death.

In this early masterpiece of George's the same deep-rooted pessimism is revealed that later becomes a permanent ingredient of all his poems, and that inspires the apocalpytic visions and awe-inspiring disasters in which a tired world gains new strength.

The Year of the Soul and *The Tapestry of Life* mark the beginning of a second phase in George's work. In the first place, the sarcastic pessimism, which had inspired him to create the character of Algabal, mellows into melancholy. In his first books George has already attached a moral significance to the artistic profession. Art is not the statement of a faith but the counterpart of atheism and despair; by constructing stable forms, it is the sole weapon one has against the surrender and abandonment of the soul; it is the lucid attitude that maintains some form of dignity in the midst of nihilism. And now, throughout a personal crisis in which George has grave doubts about his future, perhaps about his talent, and, in any case, despairs of his happiness, it is still for him the sole weapon. At one time, when he is thinking of taking his life, he writes the elegiac verses of *The Year of the Soul:* art is the last bastion.

The Tapestry of Life marks a crucial turning-point. For George, the function of the poet seems to have changed. He becomes the educator of an *élite*, the initiator of a new era. In reality this metamorphosis has already begun in the extreme attitudes of the *Algabal* period. Aestheticism, as George conceived it then, seemed to carry the doctrine of art for art's sake as far as it could go; but, at the same time, he was moving away from his starting-point and was soon disavowing his first premises.

When art no longer claims merely to ignore morality but aims at opposing it and at setting up values against values, before long, in its wish to be 'immoral', it is establishing a new morality in spite of itself. The artist is confronted with a corrupt world; he alone is not impure; he alone, as one of the elect, rediscovers the essential values which the crowd has either lost sight of or debased. Aesthetics continues to produce all its own precepts; but it assumes an ethical value. Not only is art, for some, a genuine way of life but it can— and it is its essential mission to do so—guide others through life.

It should be added that, among the artists, the poet holds a special position, for he creates out of nothing, he evokes worlds out of nothingness. So he is the predestined creator; he can, by decree, change the whole course of the times. His freedom and his power are infinite.

Paradoxically, poetry now regains the pedagogic function which the German classicists had previously given it. It must lay the foundations of what *The Tapestry of Life* called 'the beautiful life'. Life and art are united by a double bond: art will be born only from a change of life, away from the venal activities of the common people; art, once regenerated, will make life richer and fuller. It is both evidence and instrument of progress.

On the one hand, the 'Beautiful Life', as George describes it, is distinguished by its harmony and balance. Of the precepts that guide it, the most important enjoin rejection of all that is sick and corrupted, flight from violence and noise, love of all that furthers the expansion of the soul without threatening its repose, and a choice of the beauty that warms without burning. The subversive note of *Algabal* seems to have gone. But, at the same time, the immoralism of the first years is still there beneath the surface. *The Tapestry of Life* maintains the gulf between the poet and the common people; the latter remain, as in the past, part of the landscape. The good is acquired spontaneously by a chosen few, with more nobly-endowed instincts, like thoroughbred animals; right is embodied in a few in whom nature and mind are reconciled; it is the inheritance of an aristocracy of blood. This aristocracy may ignore common morality: customs are no more than precarious supports for the impure, and there is no reason why the pure should conform to them. 'Love' excludes neither hate nor vengeance; the sense of sin is merely a paralysing obsession, of which the good man rids himself, even if it means comitting a crime or an act condemned by custom.

In the period of *The Tapestry of Life*, George has no other object in mind than to propagate inside Germany a culture which, in his view, she still does not possess. He hopes, by a slow progression, and by education, to create an *élite* of the mind. So he is both patient and optimistic. He intends to establish a tradition; the thinkers of the present must be 'discoverers of beauty'; it is their function, as Nietzsche said, 'to deliver history', to restore life to a frozen past. He wants to create 'a school', which means for him a hierarchical circle, from which a succession of waves radiate that produce a steadily growing culture. The mind must be organised, for the individual by himself is weak; 'it is of the greatest importance to educate and guide weaker minds, so that they may provide the atmosphere without which great thoughts cannot prosper'. It is this hearth of culture that the Circle of his disciples is to form.

During the same period, when George aims to give Germany the culture she lacks, he ceases to look beyond her frontiers. He has found abroad precepts and models which he does not deny. But his task, for the moment, is confined to Germany: from now on, in his own eyes, he is a German poet, till somewhat later he becomes a poet of Germany. And, as he now regards his art as performing a function and an action, he is compelled, in spite of himself, to take a stand among the parties. By condemning '*bourgeois* and popular' literature he is already reaching beyond a literature that has gone astray to the social classes which it expresses or feeds. He takes up a position halfway between the socialists and the military, hostile to 'general culture' and to 'dreams of universal happiness' and also to 'the outdated

barbarism of the mercenaries'. He rejects simultaneously Prussian
rigidity, *bourgeois* taste, and what he calls the hateful humility of the
proletariat.

At this time George is a conservative, a traditionalist, and an op-
timist at one and the same time. In some poems he eulogises representatives of great princely races such as Elizabeth of Austria and
great prelates like Pope Leo XIII who preserve an element of nobility in a corrupt century. But soon his thought is drawn in an apparently opposite direction: it sinks back into pessimism and subversion, while his art loses the classical strain that characterised *The
Tapestry of Life*: instead we have the violence and harsh colours of *The
Seventh Ring*. In the interval the influence of those men normally
called the 'Cosmics' had crept in.

At the beginning of the new century Munich, or rather Schwabing,
a district of Munich, was the scene of certain events, which have
remained obscure because the people involved in them liked to surround themselves with mystery and because subsequent accounts
of them were distorted by legends and absurd interpretations.
But, as far as one can accurately judge, nothing seems to have reflected more vividly the confused state of certain minds during this
period than the intellectual fever, the unconventionality, the violence
and hatred that were displayed in connection with Stefan George in
the midst of the Carnaval and the semi-Bohemian life in Munich.

The men who took part in this 'cosmic movement' were very
different from one another, and they cannot be said to have developed
a common doctrine. At most they all believed that the present world
is corrupt, that the intellect has usurped a power which did not belong to it, and that it is consuming day by day the last remaining
dregs of energy. Man has betrayed his vocation, he has committed
sacrilege, he has angered the Gods. He must appease them, he must
redeem himself. The 'cosmic' thought, drawing on religious history
and the first researches into sociology, goes back to the primitive forms
of cult, to magic. It no longer believes that there is any slow cure for
the world; it relies entirely on a sudden, miraculous salvation, which
might take the form of an expiatory sacrifice. In these predictions of
the 'Cosmics' the blood plays both an important and an obscure part.
It is the 'substance' *par excellence*, the refuge of spent forces, which is
sometimes debased but sometimes strong enough to provoke another dynamic 'demonism'. In any case, to regain spent forces, the
obstacles which Christianity and civilisation have created round man
must first be swept aside. There must be a return to primitive forces,
to instincts which, with further delay, will become completely sterile.
Social bans must be broken, if need be by outrageous behaviour.
Now at least the relics of former festivals remain, through which, in

one brief paroxysm, 'the order of the world' was upset and rejuvenated: for example, there is the Carnaval, which had remained a live tradition at Munich. The 'Cosmics' organise masked balls, which they try to turn into bacchanalia. In fact, they were a mixture of licentiousness and pedantry, of ritual and horseplay, in which drunkenness seems always to have been kept within bounds by the deliberation with which it was induced.

Moreover, each of the 'Cosmics' had a solution of his own to offer. Karl Wolfskehl, who was nearest to George and who always remained faithful to him, propounded his own form of messianism and managed to combine 'cosmic' thought with Zionist plans. Ludwig Klages, on the other hand, who has since become notorious, was more inclined towards a sort of intoxication or ecstasy. But two in particular, both still very little known, may be quoted as examples of these aberrations. One, Alfred Schuler, found his inspiration in J. J. Bachofen's rather unscientific archaeology, and found in ancient Rome, especially in the moral abandonment of imperial Rome, the forces he longed to resuscitate. He taught a sort of paganism. He appeared at these festivals in the costume of a *Magna Mater* and indulged in a form of necromancy, clutching a fragment of a vase or an antique coin in his hand. At one time he planned to cure Nietzsche of his madness by means of a *corybantiasis*. He corresponded with the Empress Elizabeth of Austria, who, he suspected, possessed a 'cosmic substance' which he proposed to exploit. The other, Ludwig Derleth, remained somewhat apart from the 'Cosmics', for he claimed to be a Catholic and disapproved of the 'paganism' of Schwabing. But his thought is closely linked with theirs. He invents a new trinity, in which Dionysus stands side by side with Christ. The latter, who is given the title of *Imperator Maximus*, gives the signal for universal war. In his *Proclamations*, written in 1904, Derleth 'flings his glove' in the face of Christianity.

'I, Ludwig Derleth, I stand alone; I have banded all men together against me and I declare war in the name of Jesus of Nazareth . . . We shall decimate . . . Soldiers, I deliver the world over to you: plunder it!'

The part that George played in such extravagances is open to question. He certainly never committed himself to them wholeheartedly. But the ideas of the 'Cosmics' were too much in line with his pessimism and flattered his aesthetic sense and his desire for action too much for him to be able to remain entirely apart. There is no doubt that Schuler and Klages thought at one time of using him for their nebulous subversive plans. And there is also no doubt that the 'cosmic' thought had a profound influence on such poems as *The Seventh Ring*.

George's relations with the 'Cosmics' came to a violent end. The racialism of Schuler and Klages found a ready target in Karl Wolfskehl, who was a Jew and stood in the closest relationship with George. It is also possible that George was afraid that the various activities of the 'Cosmics' might interfere with his career as a poet. From now on all the myths he invents are designed to counteract the dreams of the 'Cosmics'. But, while he takes issue with them, he still remains akin to them in spirit. Just as behind the aestheticism of his early period there was a thinly veiled resentment and misanthropy, so the messianic nihilism of the 'Cosmics', their desire for subversion, their taste for violence, and their blood-mystique permeate George's poems right to the end.

When George finally breaks with Schuler and Klages in 1904, he enters on what one may call the last phase of his evolution. He resembles the image that the subsequent history of literature and of thought, forms of him. Young disciples gather round him; the 'Circle', as we have already described it, is formed.

George's reply to the 'Cosmics' is, by and large, that the miracle they were seeking in vain dreams or expecting to materialise by some vague magic is in fact constantly being performed, and that it depends, in the last resort, on ourselves. As he puts it in *The Star of the Covenant*, the granaries are full of grain, the cellars full of wine; only one overlooks them, and these treasures remain buried. The poet's function is to make them bear fruit; he is an educator. He must gather round him an aristocracy, an elect. The Word must pave the way for future actions.

This is the real meaning of the myth that dominates the whole of George's later work, the myth of Maximin. To begin with, Maximin is a young poet, for whom George felt a deep affection and who died when hardly seventeen. After the first brief phase, when the myth has a purely personal meaning, it begins to assume a wider significance: Maximin becomes a 'God'; a 'beautiful and good' Ephebe, he is like the 'representative' of heroic youth, a perfect human being. As a Maximin has actually lived, nostalgia and despair are futile. It is up to us alone to evoke 'gods' like him. George set himself up as the prophet of a new 'faith'. But the word 'faith' is deceptive. The sky is empty and there are no other gods than these divinely beautiful men; there is no other law than the one they dictate. If one is prepared to use a rather ambiguous word, one would say that George was a pioneer of 'humanism'. It only remains to consider what man he hopes to form and what dogma he teaches.

II

George begins with a violent attack on the present time. True as it is that the treasures are not far away and can be unearthed and exploited by anyone who is enlightened, it is also certain that no one today is on the right path.

George makes the same reproaches against Wilhelmian Germany as Wagner against the pre-1870 princes or Fichte against Napoleon's contemporaries; venality, cupidity, lust for money and position, a mercenary people with unseeing eyes, wretched in its wealth, blind to spiritual values, and infatuated with its false opulence. The world has grown ugly, ignoble, noisy, and coarse. Power builds extravagant cities, which are out of all human proportion. Then, in our cheerless age, the love of adventure has gone; life has become shabby and shirks danger; all it seeks is a miserable security. Scholars and technicians profess to be establishing new values. In fact, they have merely enslaved men. Man no longer controls his destiny; in his blindness, he is being dragged willy-nilly towards cataclysms that he can no longer foresee. That is the progress people boast of. The mind, which believes it has broken its chains, has merely lost contact with life; deprived of nourishment, it is gradually withering away.

George criticises all classes of society with the same vehemence. The people, in the first place, refuses to recognise merit and rejects a hierarchical system, is obsessed with equality, confuses learning and culture, and distorts in its own image all those who rise above the average. Then there is the *bourgeoisie*, venal and greedy. Above them is the nobility, which has betrayed its mission and sunk to another *bourgeoisie*. And finally, at the very top, is a braggart emperor, whom George compares unfavourably with past rulers.

George's attacks are directed, in the first instance, against democratic institutions: parliaments, which he regards as merely talkative and cowardly; newspapers, which he holds responsible for the mental deterioration of his age; and universal education, which has stifled judgment with knowledge. But he is almost as bitter in his attacks on the conservative parties, and in a famous epigram he expresses the hope that the Rhine will carry down to the ocean, the ruddle, chalk, and tar, the colours of the Second Reich's flag.

He accuses Socialism of being a spineless doctrine, which, if it were realised, would establish such comfort for all as to sap every ounce of energy. But he attacks capitalism equally, stigmatising it as the rule of money with a culpable improvidence that exploits the earth without a thought for the future and paves the way for poverty; he condemns a short-sighted will to power that stimulates a higher birth-rate instead of creating *élites*.

Faced with such sweeping criticism, one wonders if there can

possibly be for George any political solution to the problems of his
age. He spares no class of contemporary society. His condemnation
is so general that it overlooks all the problems and is in danger of
losing all efficacy. He undoubtedly visualises a radical reform in
thinking, not a change of system. For the evil has no apparent
limits: it is the *bourgeoisie*, but it is also the entire population; it is
Prussia with her militarism and her arrogance, but it is also Germany; and beyond that, it is the whole of civilisation; it is the state,
but it is also customs in general and the human mind as a whole.

Although George's thought is not, properly speaking, political,
it does have certain political implications. Its very severity gives
satisfaction to the discontented. It is intended to irritate; it stimulates
a desire for something new at any cost. Behind the policy of greed
that it condemns, there are the outlines of a generous or visionary
policy, which is nothing if not violent. It is based on the ever-present
idea that there exists an inner core that is still sound, that is like a
'real country' which need only be liberated or 'awakened'. He substitutes for the abstract people of the politicians, which shatters any
national community and 'unravels the threads of gold', a peasant,
patriarchal, feudal conception; a people is a concrete reality, inseparable from the soil, and destined always to be misunderstood by
a *bourgeoisie* corrupted by ideas.

George proposed to recruit his disciples from all classes of society.
And, at least, he demanded of those who followed him that they
should forget what he calls 'the place of their cradle'. They came,
however, for the most part from certain very clearly defined milieux:
either from the lesser aristocracy or from the Jewish intelligentsia.
It is the combination of these two groups, hitherto so very much
apart, that gives the Circle its peculiar character. Although George,
like all the others, refused to recognise the prerogatives of a hereditary
aristocracy, it is not improbable that what the aristocrats liked in
him was his dream of re-establishing a governing caste; in him they
found a master completely free from *bourgeois* ideas, a knightly
morality, a predilection for tradition, the virtues of a warrior, and
finally a doctrine that led to some form of feudalism. As for the Jews,
they were doubtless attracted by the messianic side of the dogma;
but also, while their position in an anti-semitic Germany was in-
secure, they found in a group without any Christian attachments the
possibility of rehabilitation, of establishing themselves in a traditionalist *élite* and at the same time of condemning the 'modern' world,
in which they no longer wished to appear as initiators and beneficiaries; George's Circle, in Germany, was a meeting-place for conservative Jewish intellectuals.

While it is easy to see what George condemns, it is difficult, on the other hand, to visualise the world he has in mind. He forbids the poet to take an active part in contemporary events; he places him on such a high pedestal that everyday problems seem remote and politics appears to be no more than futile excitement. Apart from his taunting condemnation of an entire age and an entire civilisation, there is no known writing of George's in which he could be said to pass open judgment on the régimes he saw around him, the Second Reich, the Weimar Republic, and, at the very end, the first phase of Hitlerism. But at the same time George denies that poetry is a mere play with ideas or words; it acquires meaning only if it leads to some form of action. It teaches a morality, it prepares a new state. George has no 'policy'; but running through his precepts as a poet there are temptations and tendencies.

Perhaps the most characteristic feature of George is his rejection of individualism. The development of history has gradually detached the individual from all social structures. This is the source of all misfortune, for a detached individual is no more than a formal justification; an impersonal representative of the species. The sufferings, doubts, and aberrations of the modern consciousness are symptoms of one single malady: solitude. Man acquires meaning, becomes a person only when he is integrated in a group, when he is placed where he belongs by virtue of his birth and his deserts.

Now, what still survives of ancient 'collectivities' is today quite incapable of absorbing any vital energy. The state has become commercialised, the Church corrupted by the protestant spirit, and the family merely teaches the mediocre virtues of the *bourgeoisie*. A new order, a new social cell must be created. But, on the other hand, this new society can only arise spontaneously, otherwise a world already encumbered with false structures will merely acquire another empty form. Only a great man, a Master, can give birth to a new society. He is the hearth round which others congregate spontaneously, organically.

The group that gathers round George is, in the eyes of his disciples, a parent-cell of this kind. And this is implicit in the name 'Circle': the Circle allows not one iota of energy to escape; the energy of each member increases, is communicated to the others and enriched by that of the others. The whole is more than the sum of the parts; the state is superior to all its individual members. As Wolters puts it, 'Creative man is someone strengthened by the constraint of the community, by a closer union of freedom and authority'. The only law is that dictated by the vital force that is dominant at the heart of the Group. As Wolters again puts it, the universal rules worked out by intelligence are sterile and deceptive. It is 'sovereign men' who make the law, the men who 'are the state'. So we see what régime is compatible with these views. The entire state is the result, by a sort of radiation, of one sole will, which is the sovereign judge. There is a rigid hierarchy with a leader at each successive stage, whose power is only limited by the will of the Masters who are superior to him. It is a state based on personal fidelity and loyalty; it is a feudal state. Very soon the duality of Master and disciple gives way in the literature of the Circle to that of Master and servant. The people acquires meaning only through the sovereign man of which it is the instrument. Wolters, who has a striking way of formulating such ideas, because he either exaggerates or simplifies George's thought, expressed it like this: 'The Head is the flame that is fed by the people; the flame is creative in nature and is fed by sacrifice; without flame, the people dies; without people, the flame is extinguished'.

As the law is nothing but the expression of a society, and as, on the other hand, there is no reason why the hierarchy should be confined within national boundaries, one may conclude with Wolters:

'There must exist, in the state, men who dominate, and not merely functionaries and equals; there must exist, in the world, peoples that dominate and not merely representatives of stability . . . A vital neighbour does well to destroy the degenerate and to subjugate what is left of them.'

There is no doubt that Friedrich Wolters, Berthold Vallentin, and several other disciples go well beyond what George had in mind. There is also no doubt, however, that the doctrine defended by the poet is a warlike one.

He continues to believe, like the 'Cosmics', that blood has a magical quality or, to put it more simply, that the only values are those for which one risks one's life. Every conflict of ideas must some day become a real conflict, and what the human mind has started is finally achieved by human hands.

As we have seen, the poet's main reproach against his period is that all energy has been swallowed up in comfort. The mind dies of inanition; great exploits are no longer conceivable. Rather violence, murder, cruelty, and madness than the lassitude that stifles all spirit of adventure. The last Western hero, whom the disciples vie with each other to honour, is Napoleon, 'the last great star at the turning point of our times'. Only conquerors of this calibre can restore to man the qualities of virility. George, too, teaches his disciples to 'live dangerously'. The society he envisages is led by knightly adventurers; the new age must be glorious, and conquerors dangerous.

It is true that George also believes that dangers cannot be dispelled simply by being ignored. This age, that seeks only comfort and speaks only of peace, is unwittingly preparing cataclysms which it will have to face up to, without being equipped for such trials. Ever since *The Seventh Ring* George has been predicting a war of extermination. He thinks it will seem all the more absurd to those who are its instruments and its victims, because it will strike blinded men, who will accept it as an incomprehensible blow of fate.

War, as George visualises it, is an adventure and disinterested. In the remoteness of history, past wars seem to him to have been launched purely from a desire for greatness; in his eyes, the true sovereign has the hall-marks of a poet. Certain periods in history, ancient Rome, the Middle Ages of the Hohenstaufens, are golden ages: warlike ages undoubtedly, but ages in which war was still a sign of 'vitality' and noble blood.

It is not difficult to understand how George can condemn the horse-dealing policy of the Hohenzollerns and, at the same time, imagine the future warlike civilisation that would be in keeping with his ideals. Moreover, he soon comes to believe that the impending trials, which are the punishment an errant civilisation must suffer, are also an essential transition towards a new age in history. So they, too, are salutary. The advent of the Saviours, as the poet visualises them, has all the features of a last judgment: it is a terrible awakening of the earth's powers, a mutiny of healthy forces, a flood of bitterness and vengeance; amidst the impotent cries of the possessed, the Heroes' armies, burning all, instruments of God's wisdom, sow the seeds of a new spring. The League that is formed to wage these battles is recruited, like the founders of Rome, from desperadoes and outcasts; a barbarian army in which each man's blood mingles with that of his companions and each man drinks the blood that gushes from their wounds, an army inspired by an all-powerful leader. This hero is ingenuous and brutal as Siegfried; his eyes are blue, but his body is hardened by bathing in glacial torrents; he sings to the accompaniment of shepherds' pipes, but takes the vulture in its nest; he is a hunter and a warrior. He is a ruthless conqueror, at whose feet the multitudes kneel.

Here we see the fundamental ambiguity of George's attitude, the contradiction that is characteristic of him and that prescribes his place in the history of ideas. The disasters he predicts and of which he apparently warns his disciples and his readers are not only inevitable but, for that reason, salutary. The same poet who attempts to save a world from ruin also believes that the fall must be hastened. There is a *volte-face*: the conservative becomes subversive. The same collection of verses which contains the poems in praise of Leo XIII and the last of the Habsburgs announces that 'the man' whom everyone is awaiting, 'in the great councils' and among the people, will not emerge from the higher ranks or, as Nietzsche said, from among the 'good', but from the deepest dungeons, from among the assassins. There must be a reversal of values; something better can come only from an excess of evil; the best policy is that of the worst.

George also places side by side the new God, the new incarnation, Maximin, on the one hand, and, on the other, the Antichrist. In the end the two are indistinguishable. George thinks that, if he musters a phalanx of the pure, it may still move the world, either by conquest or gradual contagion. But he frequently comes to the conclusion that it is too late and that a zone of flames must first be traversed before a genuine humanity can be found. If this is so, if all the trials of war, violence, and cruelty are essential, only bad masters will order their disciples to make a stand for the conservation of values that are doomed. 'Let the old men rejoice over the possessions they have acquired', we read in *The Star of the Covenant*. The new youth has better things to do than to defend worthless treasures. Maximin will reign not beside the Antichrist but beyond him. The Antichrist is indistinguishable today from the true nobility; he is himself one of the pure, and the function of superior man is to support him.

It comes as no surprise to find George lauding Napoleon, the conqueror of Jena; 'thy heel upon our necks means more to us than many a poor triumph.' Or when he contrasts the spineless Germany that he condemns with those paragons of humanity, the young Germans of Treves who prostituted themselves to Caesar's mercenaries. Just as formerly, at the beginning of his career as a poet, George evoked, in contrast to a pharisaic and spiritless epoch, the cynical, cruel figure of Algabal, so he now demanded the return of the Jesuits to point the contrast between democratic moderation and more vital times when 'dagger and poison' were still in use. One of his last pieces shows a charitable passer-by taking a body from the gallows: the criminal, despising the good people who condemn him, prophesies his own triumph; the future belongs to him; evil, so long as it is forceful, is the motive-power of the world. A Nietzschean type of morality has replaced the aesthetic immoralism of the early years, but it expresses the same will to destroy, and perhaps the same resentment.

Another of George's poems, which appeared in 1919, under the title 'The Burning of the Temple', shows a country in the last stages of exhaustion, which is finally invaded and laid waste by the Huns. The victorious sovereign is a warrior who knows neither pity nor hate. He turns a deaf ear to the entreaties of the merchants and clerics. He is even incapable of weakness towards those he loves: he kills with his own hand the friend who betrayed him and banishes to a convent the woman who nursed him. He prays before a bare stone.

As a child he was fed on the blood of a she-wolf, and when the last surviving Princess of the old dynasty, who bears the evocative name Pamfilia, begs him at least to spare the holy places, he replies:

> 'I have been sent with torch and steel that you
> Grow hard and not that I grow soft. You cannot
> Appraise your needs. If, in your fall, you will not
> Give up what saps you more and more, then I
> Must wrest you from its grip. This is the law.' [1]

It is in this way that the traditional conservatism has gradually become subversive. It is no longer necessary merely to protect, but to destroy first, so that others can build. George, who had hoped to give Germany a culture which, according to him, she was still awaiting, now denounces such optimistic views. The works of the mind are sterile, they are even criminal, so long as the world has not been rejuvenated, so long as the earth has not been turned over: the elect have better things to do than to drug themselves with music and dance on the edge of the abyss. Culture will be saved only if it is first compromised. It must go through the fire; only what emerges from the ruins will be worthy of survival. Let us not be afraid of scars and wounds; the storms that are brewing, the wars that are threatening to destroy all we love are necessary and healthy; they are God's judgment, which will destroy the impure and the half-hearted; when they have passed, a culture, rejuvenated in blood and revitalised, will grow and prosper. A 'holy madness' must strike thousands of men and the 'holy war' must claim even more as its victims. Not one stone must remain untouched.

If one asks which city George is building, Athens or Sparta, the disciples are divided. The last of them to write about the poet tried to remove any political implications from his work, and they reply unhesitatingly: Athens. But others, like Wolters, would undoubtedly have said Sparta, the warlike city before the city of the arts. And they would have found their arguments in George's last works. The Ephebe he depicts there no longer has the effeminate features of the former Eros; he is burning to fight; he is ready for action, and the poet sees him carrying hidden under his laurels the dagger of Harmodius. Athens seems a very remote reward; the new Empire must first be built in the image of Sparta.

It only remains to consider what part Germany is to play in this new era and what part the Circle is to play in Germany.

No harsher picture of Germany has ever been painted than that in George's works. He treats his compatriots with all the severity of Nietzsche. For a long time he denounced them as a barbarian people. Then he represents them as prisoners of themselves, paralysed by

---

[1] Trans. Olga Marx and E. Morwitz.

their dreams, fleeing from happiness, ignorant of grace. They think too much to act, they destroy themselves; it is their disquiet, their lack of self-confidence that make them seem rough and barbaric.

This picture makes George's task clear; he must exorcise the German soul, free it from its inhibitions. He must bring it out of its solitude and direct outwards, towards action, the impulses which, finding no outlet, devour each other and create disquiet.

Dreams, romanticism, and a preference for the amorphous are, in George's view, the legacy of Northern Germany, the contribution made by the great plains of Prussia. This is what he detests and contrasts with the civilisation of the Rhine provinces. It is here, in the land that still preserves the tradition of Rome, that German culture flourished under the Hohenstaufen, in the Renaissance, and in the period of Goethe and Hölderlin. It is a culture that has both balance and proportion and that Prussia has never ceased to threaten with its iconoclasts and puritans. It is by the clear hills of the Rhine, and only there, that a miracle similar to the Greek miracle can take place. George's Germany does not include the Northern plains, but it extends southwards—in spirit—towards the plains and mountains of Italy. For it would not be itself without the nostalgia for the South to save it from dreams. Italy attracted the emperors of olden times; in the races of the Danube and the Rhine George recognises the blood of the sovereigns who controlled Germany's destinies in her hour of greatness; it is in these races that the princely love of adventure can be reborn.

These thoughts are soon joined by another idea, which has since suffered an all-too-familiar fate: France and England have both a glorious past behind them; they are 'finished'; only Germany, still unformed, has not yet been able to blossom forth. Her impotence becomes an argument for her future greatness. Thus Gundolf says, for example:

> 'Only Germany is not yet "finished"—how often this incompletion has tormented and intimidated us, faced with the form, the sureness, the perfection of the Latins and the Celts. Round all the German figures there seemed to hover a chaos of indeterminate forces. But our people, the only people in possession of a wealth that is still intact and formless and, at the same time, of a creative force to mould that wealth, the only people, in short, which is still young, is thereby entitled and in duty bound to regenerate Europe. . . .'

Germany, then, is the only young force, and the Germans are surely destined to become an eternal reservoir of youth; the Germanic blood must, from age to age, revivify the sluggish blood of other peoples.

George's 'spiritual kingdom' gradually acquires more and more concrete frontiers which become indistinguishable from those of Germany. In one part of *The Kingdom Come*, which was doubtless composed during the war, George describes with visionary clarity the future he predicts for his people; the song of the poets rings out beyond the Alps, following the route of the emperors. And when it penetrates northwards, it mingles with the shouting of the warriors; it immortalises new, bloody, and joyous exploits; Germany has regained her former splendour.

Faced with a France which in one poem of *The Star of the Covenant* is compared to a pack of bastards, a rejuvenated Germany must become the centre of Europe. Germany, federated round the Rhine territory, will become the germ of an Empire, of a new world. George, who draws farther and farther away from the Christian attitude and toys with 'pagan' images to the point of choosing as an emblem the solar symbol of the *swastika*, clings at the same time to a kind of romantic catholicism. His poetry insinuates itself into the German tradition of the Counter-Reformation. The revival of the Holy Roman Empire that he visualises, on the same lines as Novalis, is yet another of the methods he employs to condemn the Prussians and their *Kulturkampf*. His thought, which is certainly warlike and undoubtedly imperialist, is part of the continuation of nationalist opposition which men like Paul de Lagarde and Constantin Frantz had organised against Bismarck. Like Lagarde, he can only conceive a political rejuvenation coming with the birth of a new religion, and he tries to stir up a new Jesuitism against liberal internationalism; like Constantin Frantz, he hopes for a renaissance of the Roman spirit, and in his eyes Germany is the West's bastion against the 'infantile or senile' Slavs.

George, in fact, finishes by taking part, in his doctrine, in a 'defence of the West'. In statements ascribed to him during the war, such as, 'If the yellow monkeys arrive, I shall take a gun myself', he is doubtless thinking of the Japanese. But he probably regards the Russians as being among those who threaten Western values. He gives Attila in *The Burning of the Temple* the name of Jli, which, if I am not mistaken, comes from the Slav root meaning 'evil'; and this poem appeared in 1919, two years after the Bolshevik revolution. Later, if he considers that Tannenberg was the only battle in the entire war to have 'lasting significance', it is undoubtedly because Hindenburg held up the Russian advance there. The sole accusation George makes against France is that she perpetrated what he calls 'profanation of the blood'. Commentators are all agreed about the meaning of this phrase: he is referring to the coloured troops that France used against Germany. It is almost a racialist expression; at all events, very soon after, as we know, it becomes part of the racialists' vocabulary. George, in defending Europe, is defending what he calls 'the white race'. He tries to preserve the European domain and in it the values of the past. Like so many other conservatives, he attempts a 'Defence of the West'. It is in this context that he proposes to give Germany the role of guide.

Finally, what part is to be played in these impending struggles by the Cenacle of the poets? Is it merely the model of an ideal state? Or is it the germ of the future state? In other words, must it wait until, as a result of a slow evolution or sudden disasters, the eyes of all are opened? Or must it, from now on, play an active part and hasten the downfall of an evil régime?

The disciples are divided on this point. Wolters, who has done much to form the image posterity has of George, stresses the political aspect of his doctrines, so much so that it frequently appears as if George's work had no other function than to effect the transformation of the German state. Another disciple, Kurt Hildebrandt, likewise considers that art can justify itself only by becoming involved in contemporary struggles, and he reproaches Wagner with having wasted his time composing operas while he had the opportunity, with Ludwig II of Bavaria, of fulfilling 'the noblest of tasks', of exercising an immediate influence on the state and 'effecting a great reform'.

On the other hand, the last works published by the disciples soft-pedal the political ambitions of George's works. To judge by them, George had no other aim than to establish, 'perhaps only for a short time, a certain level of humanity'. The future belongs to the Gods, and what more could a man desire once he has achieved 'an eternal moment' comparable to the Greek miracle? To the impatient who wanted to act without delay and change the state, the master is said to have replied that he had little faith in action, that 'the spiritual realm was beautiful enough in itself', and that every man should be content to cultivate his own garden.

That the realm of the spirit is sufficient to itself is not, however, the lesson of *The Star of the Covenant*: all true thought is active. George's society could hardly fail to become, or at least be tempted to become, a sort of freemasonry. Would the Circle replace the Jesuits, whose disappearance was deplored in *The Seventh Ring*?

But what form of action should be taken? The simpler minds believed that George, or one of the appointed, would take over power when the time came. This belief was particularly current among the disciples at the outbreak of the 1914 war and after the collapse of 1919; Norbert von Hellingrath, for example, the editor of Hölderlin, drew up a plan for a Rhine League, which was to be headed by the poet, and which would have joined a German Federation that was no longer dominated by Prussia. And Hellingrath was not the only one to cherish dreams of this kind. George, we are told, had to warn his disciples against such futile hopes and damp their enthusiasm for action.

But, on the other hand, did it not demand too much patience and forbearance merely to act by precept or to allow the Circle to expand gradually? Moreover, would the minority succeed in imposing their will? And what was it to do in the troubled and violent period ahead, when no one presumably would be allowed not to choose?

George himself seems to have adopted an intermediate position; a state must be established within the state, like the Templars or the Jesuits: a spiritual power which, far from turning its back on the city, would ultimately guide it, but in secret, and which, during the years of conflict, would build up a formidable resistance.

III

It only remains for us to see this doctrine in action: what was the attitude of George and his immediate disciples to the events of his time?

Firstly, the war. In December 1906 George said to Hofmannsthal, who had asked him to put his name to a pacifist petition: 'If this petition did not come from a man for whose intelligence I have the highest admiration, I would take it for a joke. But *we* are not among those who play a game of this kind with the things of the spirit or the affairs of the world. How does this concern us? Furthermore, the situation is not so simple as these printed pages would have us believe. War is merely the final consequence of a mad policy, which has been conducted on both sides for many years past and which makes it necessary. This miserable expedient of a few individuals cannot, it seems to me, have the slightest effect.'

George stood firmly by this view: war was not avoidable. It was even desirable in so far as it was necessary. There seems no doubt that George thought for a time that the conflict, which everyone foresaw, could radically change the world. In one of the poems of *The Star of the Covenant*, addressed in all probability to his former French friends, George cries that 'the day of judgment is approaching' between the two peoples. When, in another poem in the same collection, he speaks of the 'next conflict' for which his faithful followers must be prepared, it was assumed that he was referring to contemporary political events. 'Pacifism', in George's eyes, is a mere trick: vain words that cannot possibly stem the torrent, and would be still more dangerous, if they were to have any effect, for strife is part of man's vocation.

George's opinion, in the first months of the war, is supported by his disciples. Wolfskehl, replying to Romain Rolland in an open letter in the *Frankfurter Zeitung*, writes:

> 'This war, which we did not wish, which was imposed on us, is nevertheless a necessity; for Germany's sake and for the sake of European humanity, in the interest of this world, it had to break out. We did not wish it, but it is sent by God. Our poet knew it. He saw and foretold this war, with all its miseries and its virtues, long before an evil presentment was even dimly felt, before the slightest rustling of the leaves. *The Star of the Covenant* is the work of prophecy . . .'

And after reproaching France for letting loose the hordes of Asia on civilisation, he explains that the Germans, by fighting the Muscovite bands, are fighting for the survival of France herself.

The attitude of the Circle is even better characterised in an article by Gundolf. He criticises the German Nationalists for their logomachy and, like George in *The Seventh Ring*, condemns all power-politics; but he justifies the war by depicting Germany as the sole qualified representative of the Idea, the master-people. Having described the enemies of the Reich as 'mediocre braggarts' and 'blinded mobs', he writes: 'The culture of the future, that is, the new era of European values, is destined to be created by the German mind.' In his view it is 'a unique occasion in the centuries' which must this time change not only frontiers but also men. And the stake seems to him high enough to warrant all destruction: the new world can be built only on the ruins of the old:

> 'We are not fighting to preserve the past but to affirm imperishable values, not for things, however precious they may be, but for the dignity of man. As against what may be, all accumulated treasures are of no importance. That is why all the weeping and shouting over works of art that have been destroyed (in so far as these protests are sincere) are merely expressions of an outdated romanticism and arise from a false and superficial idea of culture, which is reduced to nothing more than the task of a collector and the piety of a contemplator. Culture is no chattel nor enjoyment; it consists in being, in acting, in changing; it is creation, destruction, metamorphosis, and Attila is nearer to culture than all the Shaws, Maeterlincks, d'Annunzios, and their like . . .'

A third disciple, Ernst Bertram: 'Out of this war will emerge . . . a clear and essential idea of Germany, as Germany in her body will emerge great and dazzling from this struggle she is waging for her life.' And again: 'There are forces at work which must rejuvenate our people and which will also produce . . . the great men who dominate centuries.'

But soon George becomes irritated by the constant use of *The Star of the Covenant* as a 'breviary of war'. The struggle now going on is not of the kind to change men. He says to one of his disciples: 'What does your attitude mean, if you can believe that a few sublime moments can change a corrupted people? Is the *bourgeois* of today any different from the *bourgeois* before 1914? Do you believe that the war will produce a new man? What has happened that is of lasting significance? Tannenberg perhaps? But where can one find an image pregnant with meaning (a symbol) when armed masses are fighting without an aim?'

From the spring of 1916 onwards he is one of those who hope that the war, now futile, may soon end. And, in the first months of 1918, he repeats again that the wisest thing would be not to persist with a hopeless struggle: 'If Germany had the strength to renounce her claims to Alsace-Lorraine, it would still not be too late; we should have peace and Germany would be greater than ever.'

The same ideas are expressed in the long poem *War*, which was published in 1917. Everyone holds the enemy responsible for all misfortunes, without realising that every man, on both sides of the firing-line, is equally guilty. The fault lies with a greedy and passive *bourgeoisie*, with a senile and timorous policy. In Germany, the sole object is gain; everyone envies his neighbour and cultivates in secret the vices which he condemns in others. France glories in her past power and civilisation; but these are mere dead memories; she too is in the clutches of the merchants.

And now, from both sides, insults have replaced assurances of brotherly love; and the international spokesmen have become Chauvinists. The prosperity that was everyone's boast has been paid for today by the bloodiest of wars. And all in vain: these mean struggles, in which man burrows into the ground like an animal and is the impotent victim of the very machines he has created, will change nothing. Those who believe they are fighting 'the war to end war' are mistaken: other and still more terrible wars will come. Those who went out to fight in a spirit of senility, will not come back rejuvenated. Those who think they will return, with peace, to a peaceful or glorious past, those who revel in stories of heroism, all those are blind. An idea is lacking and, with it, a man to embody it.

From now on it must be admitted that this war is not 'the holy war' prophesied in *The Star of the Covenant*: that will come later, after many trials and tribulations. Will the men of today ever witness the festival of victory at which 'the sacred dithyramb' will be sung?

On George's post-war attitude it is difficult to do more than conjecture, for he almost entirely ceases to write; at least, only some

L

four or five poems written after Germany's defeat have so far been
published.

In these poems George repeats that the war was a false test and
that, as soon as the fighting was over, the same men were again committing the same mistakes. Salvation is to be hoped for only after a
'third assault', in which the Germans 'purify themselves from shame'
and 'cast off the chains of bondage'.

He condemns the servility of the conquered, who, after heaping
insults on the enemy, are now selling themselves to him, for a few
crumbs of bread, while others are plunged in debauchery.

It is known that in the advice he gave his disciples he departed
from the rule he had laid down during the war never to defame or
even judge the enemy. He now gives vent to a violent and unrestrained hatred of the French: they should be exterminated to the
last man.

There is no doubt that the occupation hurt his feelings as a German and a Rhinelander; the Weimar Republic, and all the unrest of
the first post-war years, increased his feeling of hostility towards
democracy. He may have thought that, with Germany's defeat,
Prussia had ceased to be a threat, and even that the small army Germany was allowed under the treaties was the only effective weapon
of defence against all the dangers he foresaw.

Then came a development that shook the Circle to its foundations:
Gundolf was expelled. From that moment on it was Wolters whose
influence became predominant. He was regarded as one of the most
vehement and most 'reactionary' of the disciples. In his books,
pamphlets, and anthologies he preached a very violent form of
nationalism. In a lecture on Goethe he has no hesitation in asserting that if Goethe had adopted the indifferent attitude during the
Napoleonic wars that is generally ascribed to him, 'despite his poetic
glory, his works should be destroyed and his action forgotten'. In
1923 Wolters published an anthology of writings on the Rhine, which
becomes a propaganda pamphlet against France. He harks back
quite specifically to the tradition of E. M. Arndt and Fichte. In
fact, he returns to the most banal form of nationalism, even to the
point of departing now and then from George's orthodox doctrine.
Catholicism remains one of the basic elements of the German nature,
but Rome again becomes what it was for H. S. Chamberlain, the
eternal enemy. Prussia, previously treated with contempt, now becomes in the general débâcle, the last refuge of such effective national
forces as have survived. Bismarck is among the great heroes; he
realised that the Reich cannot be built up by speeches but only 'on
the down-to-earth level of blood and iron'. The time has come for
Germany to take stock of herself, if she wants to avoid the mistakes
of the second Reich and not 'to survive for a few centuries among the

peoples merely by virtue of her art and her science'. As for France, with her greed, she is no more than a dead civilisation. The hate that she feels is deep-rooted in this people of

'barbaric Gauls; their true nature had been masked by the Roman influence, then dominated and quelled after the great invasions by the Franks and the Visigoths; but, for some centuries now, the Roman and Germanic elements have been absorbed, they have crumbled in a succession of revolutions and now, with all the resentment of inferior and subject races, with the bloodthirsty appetite of Celts reduced once more to barbarism, they fling themselves on their prosperous neighbours and seek to dull their own awareness of their inevitable degradation by uncontrolled cruelty.'

Ernst Bertram in works like *Rheingenius and Génie du Rhin* expresses similar views. And there is no doubt that after the war new elements appeared in the Circle, for whom political action was more important than intellectual commitments or, at least, for whom the mind was a mere vehicle for political action.

On the other hand, George cannot be held responsible for the influence of youth movements like the *Wandervögel*. They too wanted to break with *bourgeois* traditions and to 'liberate the body'; they, too, like George and his disciples, saw in friendship a means of revitalisation. But George always detested these group-movements, which subsequently increased and degenerated: they lacked something that he regarded as essential in his disciples, namely, thought; they were caricatures of his Circle, and produced false disciples who were a much more serious threat to his thought than were his open opponents.

George let his disciples go their own way. He himself kept silent. It is certain that, even in his later years, 'politics' never occupied a predominant place in his mind. It is also certain that he forbade his followers, as in the past, to play an active part in public life. Nevertheless it is perhaps too much to say, as R. Boehringer does, that in his view the 'Right' and the 'Left' were of equal value. He remained as aloof from the 'national' parties as he did from all parties; his attitude was dictated by precepts quite different from theirs. But the writings of the Circle, from the historian's viewpoint, are ranked among the documents of the Conservative and Nationalist opposition to the Weimar Republic. It is virtually impossible to take independent and uncompromising action.

Just under a year before George's death, Hitler came to power. In 1933 the new régime offered George the Presidency of the German Academy. George communicated his refusal to the Minister, Rust, through his disciple, Ernst Morwitz, a Jew. That was the beginning and end of the poet's relations with the Nazi movement. George died in Switzerland in December 1933.

When Hitler became Chancellor, some of George's principal disciples were already dead: Friedrich Wolters, Friedrich Gundolf, Berthold Vallentin. Of the others, the Jewish disciples went into voluntary exile and are still scattered throughout the world. Wolfskehl, who was blind, left Germany to die, almost an octagenarian, in New Zealand. Others, who had no particular reason to fear the concentration camp or death, left from conviction.

A small minority, however, accepted the new régime and, in some cases, gave their support to it. This applied to not more than five or six among the better-known disciples.

But these facts at least prove that the Master's thought was not unambiguous, since the disciples could differ widely on a fundamental point. They also prove that outside the Circle it was regarded as being fairly close to National-Socialist positions, since the Hitler Government wished to honour George and make use of him. On this second point official opinion rapidly changed. To begin with, George was considered one of the forerunners of the new state. Gottfried Benn, in a speech of National-Socialist inspiration, does not hesitate to declare that 'the art of Stefan George and the marching rhythm of the brown battalions are animated by the same motive principles'. George was one of the first to have 'racial vision' and to denounce 'profanation of blood'.

An article, which appeared in a propaganda work designed for Japan, condemns the early George, but hails the author of *The Kingdom Come* as a pioneer of Hitlerism: 'It is, in the true sense of the word, a prophecy, and it paves the way for the birth of a new people, the first moments of which we are conscious of witnessing today.' Finally, an article by Hans Naumann, more daring than the others:

'George established a secret Germany, which is at last appearing today and which, for some time past, had chosen for its insignia the swastika. . . . When the man of action appeared, the poet immediately took his side. . . . He expressly blessed the new Germany. His coffin is still in Switzerland but he awaits his real burial at Bamberg or near the River he loved so much. George felt at ease among the men of the Reich's brown guard and welcomed every opportunity of inviting them to his table. . . . He found the road that leads back, far from the Roman myth, to the Nordic myth. If the world had known the poet better, it would have been less surprised by events in Germany: it would have found them foreshadowed in him.'

For Naumann, George ranks among the Germanic heroes together with the 'Knights of the Sword', Florian Geyer and Schlageter. He is the poet of the Third Reich, as Walther von der Vogelweide was the poet of the Holy Roman Empire.

But soon, when the régime was more firmly established and was less concerned to find mouthpieces among the poets and artists, George was considered heretical and dangerous. In 1938, a work of 400 pages[1] appeared which anathematises George. He and his disciples are now merely exponents of a threadbare humanism; they look for salvation in art rather than in the state, and behind the pronouncements of the last poems the aestheticism of the early period is clearly apparent. George ignores the virtues of race, and that is why he gathers round him the 'civilised and polished representatives of Judaic culture'. 'Any approach to the Germanic world, to the ethical values of the Prussian mind, is denied him.' The cult of the heroic which he inaugurates takes no account of duty and sacrifice and is merely a 'substitute for religion', much closer to 'the Catholic adoration of the Saints' than to 'the Germanic conception of the hero'. The salvation offered by Maximin is no more than 'an aesthetic illusion embroidered with homosexual sensuality'.

It is easy to see how little George and National-Socialism have in common. Firstly, the Jews he gathers round him, who are among his most faithful followers. The parades, which meant for him the Prussia he detested. The plebeian character of this mass movement, diametrically opposed to the aristocracy he had dreamt of. The poet could not accept a policy that professed to despise the values of the mind. In the end, George had to forbid his disciples to serve two masters at the same time. The Circle's only cohesion came from the personal bond between disciple and master. It was George who educated, directed, and ordered. When, in *The Kingdom Come*, he prophesies the coming of a providential Man who will save Germany, it is clearly stated that he will emerge from the secret Germany. If salvation could come from outside, the Circle would have no further *raison d'être* in the present nor justification in the past.

And yet, if certain disciples erred in good faith, how could one expect the readers from 'outside' to avoid misunderstanding? When one enumerates, not the National-Socialists, but those who paved the way for them, either by design or unwittingly, one has to include George's name.

George was a poet, and only a poet, according to him, could re-create the world. He regarded it as one of Germany's misfortunes that it had been a people of philosophers. The solutions he offers are a poet's solutions: if he had envisaged his Circle becoming a Platonic Academy, he was at variance with Plato on this all-important point.

At the time when Max Weber was choosing the word 'demystification '(*Entzauberung*) as a motto, George replied that, on the contrary, it was necessary to 'mystify'. He never thought, as has been so foolishly held against him, of creating a new faith, but at least he

[1] Hans Rössner, *Georgekreis und Litteraturwissenschaft*.

wanted to be an inventor of myths. He was not so much concerned
to convince as to train: he hoped to educate an enthusiastic youth,
or, in current present-day parlance, to create a 'mystique' for the
few.

The morality he preaches is a morality of fine gestures. The society
he aims to establish is built on honour. It is led by an aristocracy,
by knightly adventurers. The legend of Maximin has become
gradually simpler, till the young man symbolises a 'heroic', athletic,
valiant youth, eager for action. The poet's god has 'the sure, firm
step of a young fighter', 'the authority of a war-leader'. Through the
virile society which he gathers round him and which is as fanatical
as any exclusive sect, he hopes, to quote a phrase from Alain, to prepare the youth 'for the twin games of love and war'.

In his thought the idea of justice has lost its meaning. He expects
the creation of a hierarchy to enrich life. In the last resort he believes
only in order. The good he finds nowhere, except possibly in the
will of better men; the cardinal virtue is fidelity, the bond that links
servant and master.

When George condemns the period in which he lives, it is for its
lassitude rather than its lack of wisdom. He wants to restore modern
man to a vitality he has lost. The term is a vague one: he permits
noble acts of violence and appeals to the instincts. George never
entirely rejected the 'paganism' of the 'Cosmics', and it was not pure
coincidence that the Nazi Party and the Georgian Circle both chose
the same symbol, the solar wheel of the ancient Germans.

The idea of a sudden, miraculous regeneration of the world is also
a poetic conception: all poetry is part magic and scorns colourless,
slow action. If there is any reproach to be made against George and
his disciples, it is not that they attached too much importance to
politics, but, on the contrary, that they did not take it seriously
enough. They thought to destroy, by decree or by a miracle, what
in fact cannot be changed by an act of will: the conditions that prevail in present-day life. It was these traces of romantic politics which
made George's thought ambiguous and even dangerous. They conjured up visions and grandiose projects of subversion. George at one
point had said that salvation was near; then, disillusioned by the war,
he had relegated it to an indefinite future. But when the more hot-
headed saw a new régime that promised to change the world overnight, they were prepared to believe that the new age prophesied by
the poet was about to break.

The poet's thought, then, with its love of courtly gestures, of
generosity and sacrifice, is both traditionalist and warlike. Among
the powers of the past that might have satisfied it, the great monarchies have gone, and the Church seems to him a spent force. He
seeks a régime that offers him order and a hierarchy that meets his

demand for adventure and greatness. The aristocracy he longs for is a thing of the past. Today the only political form that could satisfy a belief of this kind, placing honour before justice, is Caesarism.

This doctrine, conservative in origin, soon despairs of saving the values of the past. It comes round to the belief that they can be restored only by first destroying the entire present. It sees no hope of salvation except in great cataclysms and an excess of evil. Were not the barbarism and cruelty of the Hitler régime foreshadowed in George's works? Was not Hitler, the Jli of the 'Burning of the Temple', destined to ruin culture for 500 years so that it might reappear stronger than ever?

Apart from this feature, apart from the will to subversion, the taste for the apocalyptic, George's doctrine and Hitlerism probably have little in common. It was not our purpose to disguise George as a Nazi, however, but to show what part he plays in the movement of thought which made National-Socialism possible. Moreover, is it not doing the latter too much honour to regard it as a doctrine? The characteristic feature of Hitlerism is not its thought, which it borrows freely and adapts to the requirements of the moment, but a certain 'tone': virulent, trivial, sarcastic, destructive, immediately recognisable. Of course this tone is not heard in George's poems, though it appears sometimes in statements ascribed to him and it dominates the *Jahrbuch für die geistige Bewegung*, the review published by the Circle from 1910 to 1912 and strongly influenced by Wolters; it is certainly representative of a small section of the disciples. But it is unfair to blame all for the arrogance of a few.

The true disciples could not accept Hitlerism for long. Klaus and Berthold von Stauffenberg, two of the leaders of 20th July conspiracy, were both former members of the George Circle; other followers were involved in the attempt on Hitler's life or fell victim to the wave of repression that followed. This was a gesture that put George's thought in its true perspective: in the ranks of a Conservative and traditionalist opposition, destined in all probability to be disillusioned by every régime and to combat all of them.

7
REVOLUTIONARY CONSERVATISM: MOELLER VAN DEN BRUCK
Roy Pascal

HITLER came to power in 1933 as the head of a composite government of National-Socialists and Conservatives. Within a few months he had abolished, along with other parties, the main conservative party, the *Deutsch-Nationale Partei*. Its leaders were driven into obscurity, like Hugenberg, or became his henchmen, like Papen. In the following years Hitler dealt ruthlessly with any resistance from the conservative side, in particular where it consolidated in army circles, and it was reduced on the whole to a silent and often contemptuous resentment, like that of the writer Ernst Jünger, which often provoked the wrath of the Nazi authorities. In the latter part of the war the conflict between these conservatives, or nationalists as they are better called, and National-Socialists became ever tenser until it burst in the conspiracy of the generals and the slaughter of 1944, when many of the leaders, from Rommel downwards, were destroyed.

Naturally enough, German nationalists now insist on the sharpness of their conflict with Hitler, and assert that German nationalism is something in its essence different from Nazism. Recently Armin Mohler, a member of the Jünger circle, has devoted a learned and acute book to the purpose of establishing the independent identity of radical nationalism (what he calls 'revolutionary conservatism') and distinguishing it from National-Socialism. He recognises that frontiers cannot be drawn sharply, that at several points this modern nationalism shades into Nazism, just as its members often became, at least for a time, adherents of Hitler. But he asserts that there is a fundamental contrast.[1] He thus challenges the opinion of Vermeil, R. D'O Butler, and many other foreign historians, who see an organic relationship between the tradition of German nationalism and the rise of Nazism. Mohler does, however, recognise that the ideas of conservative nationalism were exploited by the Nazis, and asks in the last sentence of his book whether the Nationalists were not responsible for the misuse of their ideas; but he leaves this question

[1] Armin Mohler, *Die konservative Revolution in Deutschland 1918–32*, pp. 11–18 66.

unanswered.[1] It is a question of a similar order to that of 'War Guilt' after World War I; and, also, not an 'academic' question, since on the answer to this question depends the moral right of conservative nationalists to seek to take the destinies of Germany into their hands once more.

The present study is intended to be a contribution to this problem. With Oswald Spengler and the Thomas Mann of the *Betrachtungen eines Unpolitischen,* Moeller van den Bruck is named by Mohler as a patriarch of 'young conservatism', 'revolutionary conservatism' as Moeller and Mann called it.[2] Moeller van den Bruck was the populariser of the term 'the Third Reich'. Like the groups with whom he was in touch, and like so many of his disciples later on, particularly those of the *Tat* circle, he shows contacts with Nazism and at the same time conflict. One runs in no danger of confounding him with the Nazis, since he died in 1925, before the movement reached any size and significance, and himself had no direct dealing with them. But this study will show, I believe, that distinct as his thought is from that of the Nazis, it made a powerful contribution to Nazi ideology, both in a negative and positive sense; and that he, like other nationalists, shared the fate of the Sorcerer's Apprentice, raising spirits they could not exorcise.[3]

No single person can stand as representative of all revolutionary conservatism. Armin Mohler distinguishes as components of this wide movement four groups—the racists (*Völkische*); the young conservatives; the national-revolutionary groups (Jünger, Ernst von Salomon, E. von Reventlow); and the vaguer groupings among the youth and the peasantry. Moeller van den Bruck he associates particularly with the second group, though he recognises that he is not confined to it. We shall see, indeed, that Moeller van den Bruck himself joined issue with the racists, and that he was lacking in the emotive experience of the Front-Line soldiers (Jünger) and of the Youth movements. He was hardly touched at all by the peasant question, and remained hostile to sentimental backward-looking folklorism. He was an intellectual and wrote for the intelligentsia, unable to find the words that would move the masses. He was a man of politics and culture, a man of the great cities and the modern State, a man who recognised in the industrial proletariat the decisive problem of his times. Despite his limitations, he was in essential ways a central figure of his times, a man who forged or popularised many of the slogans of modern German nationalism, whose work made a

---

[1] Armin Mohler, *Die konservative Revolution in Deutschland 1918–32,* p. 210.
[2] ibid., p. 83.
[3] Moeller's main works, and selections from his articles, were re-issued in very large editions between 1931 and 1933 by his literary executor Hans Schwarz. Unfortunately Schwarz found it necessary to 'touch up' some of the articles in order to bring them up to date, and it is always advisable to consult the original text.

deep imprint on the young intelligentsia and was responsible for bringing many of them to support Hitler: not only through particular political slogans and principles, but even more significantly by teaching them his way of thinking, his *Weltanschauung*—a type of thinking which undermined the belief in rational and scientific thought and ushered in the Nazi ideology.

Two powerful streams meet in the concept of 'revolutionary conservatism', as is apparent from the paradoxical association of 'revolution' and 'conservatism', concepts as a rule diametrically opposed. From one side comes the stream of traditionalism, which continues the nationalist authoritarianism of the nineteenth century, and seeks to sweep away all democratic, liberal, socialist, internationalist ideas and movements. From the other side comes a reckless revolutionism, the challenge to all fixed forms and ancient shibboleths, a 'revolution of nihilism', as Rauschning called it, which condemned old-fashioned conservatism, the conservatism of 'throne and altar', as reaction, and which was ready to overthrow, along with ancient authorities and idols, also all absolutes in morality and thinking. This strange and potent combination of conservatism and revolutionism found its first formulation in Nietzsche, who is the source of so much perilous modern German thought. It is Moeller van den Bruck's chief title to significance that he most completely fuses the two trends, and in a far more precise political form than Nietzsche, his master; and in so doing he became the most important single focus of all pre-Nazi trends.

II

Moeller came from a family of Prussian officials and officers. In his character he embodied that dualism which Georg Lukács has signalled as being specifically Prussian: [1] a rigid devotion to the idea of duty and discipline, and at the same time a temperamental restlessness and irritableness which made it impossible for him to cooperate with anyone for long—the characteristics of the Junker poet Heinrich von Kleist, whom Moeller himself so much admired as 'a mystery of race and soil'.[2] Born in 1876, Moeller was taken with deep disgust at the Wilhelmian age, its cheap patriotism and optimism, its vulgar ostentation and boasting, its rapidly growing luxury, and the misery of its slum and industrial proletariat. He turned with dissatisfaction from the routine of academic studies and linked up with the writers and artists of the 1890s, who in many forms were in revolt against their time. His first book, *Die Moderne Literatur* (1899–1902), was a series of studies of contemporary writers and artists, and

---

[1] G. Lukács, 'Über Preussentum,' in *Schicksalswende* (Berlin, 1948), pp. 68–94.
[2] Moeller van den Bruck, *Der Preussische Stil* (Munich, 1916), p. 161.

shows his sympathy with every revolt against the banal and traditional.

As often happens, the revolt of the young generation of this decade brought together men of widely differing social views, in a broadside attack on the mediocre, the Philistine. Moeller shows a sympathy with the radical group of the Naturalists, like Holz, Schlaf, and Gerhart Hauptmann, whose artistic endeavour was related to socialist ideas; with Dehmel and Wedekind, individualists and anarchists; with Stefan George, the aristocratic formalist. He welcomes all attempts at renewing the language of poetry, whether through the use of real contemporary speech and themes from real contemporary life, or through the invention of new, stylised poetic forms. He evaluates works largely by the measure of protest within them, and he recognises as valuable evidence of a new, growing culture every symptom of revolt—even satanism, sexual licence, anarchism, and every sort of experimental form. Profoundly convinced that he lives in a time of transition, that the future is great and wondrous, he welcomes anything novel and startling. What the future holds, he does not know and cannot define; but it is above all else necessary, he writes, to be 'free of the past'.[1]

This feeling of crisis, of movement towards a great future, is not at this time related to any precise social or political problems. It is essentially cultural, spiritual, even aesthetic, in character. Moeller insists that the consciousness of new aims is instinctive in origin; they arise 'from the depth of the soul' through the organ of the poetic imagination, which itself responds to the stirring of the 'world soul' towards a new self-realisation. The great unknown, the new, must be ushered in by great individuals, great rebels, who act according to their imperious intuitions.[2] The 'idea of the future', he insists, is not to be related to social conditions or forms, but must take shape in the soul of the great man, whose duty it is to realise himself, to be ruthlessly egoistic and despise all altruism.[3]

The Nietzschean origins of his thought are clear and avowed. Like many disciples of Nietzsche, he builds his outlook upon a philosophy of culture. In an essay devoted to Nietzsche, he praises the latter for having revealed that literature is a vital function, an expression of social life; that the artist is the expression of his times, the revelation of the secret life-stream of a period.[4] He praises Nietzsche for his consciousness of living in a time of transition, for his search for a new vital principle that will inspire the movement towards a new world. To Nietzsche he owes his belief that what is to come is

---

[1] *Die moderne Literatur in Gruppen- und Einzeldarstellungen* (Berlin, 1899–1902), Vol. IV, pp. 27, 41.
[2] ibid., Vol. V, pp. 12–23.　　　　　　　　　[3] ibid., Vol. VII, pp. 24–5.
[4] The essay on Nietzsche, ibid., I.

unprecedented, revolutionary, and cannot be judged by the standards of the past—that the future is 'beyond good and evil'. Nietzschean, too, is his emotive attitude, his intoxication with the coming Unknown, with the pathos of struggle and tragedy, his feeling of destiny. He feels himself, like Nietzsche, an agent of mystical forces, a prophet and seer.

He adds, however, a significant criticism of Nietzsche. The individualism of Nietzsche obviously inspires his own emphasis on the role of the great man in the unfolding of the future. But Moeller considers the 'Superman' of Nietzsche to be too vague a concept to be helpful, and dismisses it as utopian. The idea that the future is to be realised in a new type of being, the Superman, seems to him to be merely evidence of Nietzsche's own frustration and impotence. On the contrary, Moeller links the future with Germany's political power. For him, the foundation of the German Empire in 1871 was an event of decisive importance, and he is convinced (in starker contrast to Nietzsche than he allows his readers to see) that Germany is destined to be the leader of the new civilisation he anticipates.[1] Into Nietzsche's thought he infuses a strong dose of vulgar German nationalism of the Treitschke brand. Germany is an 'unspent people', full of vigour and energy, and all the artistic innovations and experiments of his time, its problems and failures, its restlessness and excesses, are symptoms of vitality and of a groping towards a new and higher art. By contrast, the perfection of foreign poetry is condemned as a proof of its completedness, its deadness. This Germanism becomes arrogance when he treats of contemporary Austrian literature. He attacks Hofmannsthal and Schnitzler with great violence as decadent and frivolous, in contrast to the 'young' problematical literature of the Reich. He suggests his real meaning when he drops a hint that some politicians are already thinking of the time when Austria will be a German province.[2]

In general, the book reveals a cultural rebel who is, however, profoundly convinced of the great destiny of his nation; and though the emphasis is mainly on a vital urge towards the new, he refers often enough to the national character, to 'Deutschtum', as a principle linking past and present. He shows himself uneasy with Stefan George's formalism, his misinterpretation of 'racial values', his remoteness from the effort and enthusiasm which inherently belong to 'Deutschtum'.[3] These two elements of Moeller's thought, revolutionism and traditionalism, were to be present in all his future work, in which he combines, in formulations corresponding to the changing social and political situation, Nietzschean dynamism with the idea of

[1] *Die moderne Literatur in Gruppen- und Einzeldarstellungen* (Berlin, 1899–1902, Vol. IX, p. 60, X, pp. 9–10).
[2] ibid., Vol. X, pp. 7–8.   [3] ibid., Vol. IX, pp. 60, 65–8.

fixed national characteristics in the manner of H. S. Chamberlain and J. Langbehn (*Rembrandt als Erzieher*).

For some years, however, Moeller's sense of unease in Wilhelmian Germany drove him along the path of aesthetic anarchism. From 1902 to 1906 he lived an uprooted Bohemian life in Paris, occupying himself in the main with a German edition of Dostoevsky, and till 1914 he travelled a great deal, visiting Italy, England, Russia, and Scandinavia. But already in France the nemesis of aesthetic revolt asserted itself. He began to feel a militant faith in his native land, expressed at first in a crude hostility to French culture; and his later travels were essentially a search for the 'national character' of foreign peoples with the purpose of thereby defining the peculiar character and 'mission' of the Germans.

Between 1904 and 1910 Moeller wrote a series of cultural studies of historic German personalities which shows his movement towards a more political nationalism.[1] The underlying theme of these studies is summed up in *Die Zeitgenossen* of 1906, the opening section of which is an exposition of his general theory of culture. The first pages give a highly characteristic statement of the subjectivist origins of his type of thought. We live in a great time, he writes, a time of destiny and opportunity. Life can become meaningful if we grasp the character of the time, see its purpose and destiny, understand the immediate objectives it sets us, and submit to them. This is the real meaning of freedom; we become active, creative, if we submit to the metaphysical law of our being, of our times.[2] Thus Moeller picks up again the Hegelian conception of freedom as the understanding of necessity; but 'necessity' becomes highly subjective, an intuitive, prophetic surmise of the future, as with Nietzsche. Activity, freedom is possible, he continues later in the book, only when we are set a goal; even further, only when we embrace a dogma, an unquestioned belief—he refers to the dogma of Germanism as enunciated by Fichte a hundred years before, which had such a galvanising effect on Fichte's contemporaries. Only through a prescribed goal and a dogma can man become free.[3] In many forms Moeller later reiterates this view. The idea of Destiny pervades his work, for only through a sense of Mission, of subservience to an irrational, super-personal purpose, can man unfold his energies and become free; an idea which underlies the ideology of National-Socialism.

Destiny is, however, conceived not as a personal fate, but as a national reality; at no point does Moeller discuss the individual personality as a distinct entity. His thought is entirely engrossed with general notions, about the national species or human destiny in

---

[1] *Die Deutschen* (8 vols., Minden, 1904–10). Reprinted by Schwarz as *Das Ewige Reich* (3 vols., Breslau, 1932–34–35).
[2] *Die Zeitgenossen* (Minden, 1906), pp. 3–5.   [3] ibid., p. 46.

general. History interests him only as the history of nations, which are for him the supreme reality. Personal predestination, personal morality is never discussed by him. Just as freedom for him wins meaning and substance only when the individual surrenders himself to the destiny of the nation, so also morality is conceived entirely in terms of the nation. Again his formulations derive from Nietzsche. Goodness is vitality, energy; the most vital, energetic nation is moral; all that serves such a nation is good. He does not fall into such a view as Treitschke's, that 'might is right', for very obvious reasons: such a definition would justify in moral terms the practices of the most powerful nations. But Germany is not yet the most powerful nation, it has to win this place; therefore Moeller has to find a definition that will justify German aims in distinction from those of rival nations. Hence goodness is made identical with effort, struggle, change. He rejects Christianity because it does not embody this notion of perpetually changing standards, which he considers to be proved by Darwinism—it is characteristic that he is critical of Christianity not on rationalistic grounds, but on the grounds that its values (humanitarianism, pity, love, and the like) are static, undynamic. His defence of capitalism and imperialism follows the same pattern. He does not argue in economic or sociological terms. Capitalism is good because it creates tools of power. Imperialism is good because it releases the vital energies of a nation in their highest power. Similarly he is contemptuous of all sated classes, of the *bourgeois*, who merely wish to enjoy their possessions. The best nation is the most vital, the most energetic; and it thereby has the moral right to the leading position.[1]

Moeller's work is therefore essentially a description of national characteristics, of national psychology, in the tradition of Herder; a description which is made with the intention of defining the destiny of a nation, its claim on the future. Through the analysis of the culture of a people he seeks to reveal its spirit, its 'vitality', and thereby to judge it. Thus his arguments in favour of the vitality of Germany are based very little on political or economic facts; he asserts that Germany's political power and unity are the outcome of the spiritual revival of Lessing and Goethe, not of political combinations and power.[2] So he judges England by means of a rapid (and excessively superficial) review of the state of English culture, which he considers to be dead—he devotes a chapter to Oscar Wilde to prove the nation's decadence, its deadness of soul. His most ruthless criticism is reserved for France, whose culture he can never mention without disparagement. In a crudely malevolent little book he wrote on French drama he shows a malicious refusal to admit anything good in the history of the French drama; and he comes to the real point when,

[1] *Die Zeitgenossen*, pp. 21–5, 51–7.   [2] ibid., pp. 73–4.

reviewing the poverty of the French stage in the nineteenth century, he advances to the characteristic generalisation that there is lacking in France 'the precondition of any new development'.[1] That is, the past is considered only to find support for his view of the 'destiny' of the future. It is a typical case of the use of the 'philosophy of culture' for polemical, nationalistic ends.

Moeller's theories of *Kultur*, of 'young peoples', of 'race', give a general form to his pragmatic purpose. In the second section of *Die Zeitgenossen* he launches into a discussion of the terms *Kultur* and *Zivilisation*, the theme so often discussed in nationalist polemics. Following Nietzsche, he sees the cultural products of a nation as the expression of a homogeneous national style: 'Culture is above all the unity of artistic style in all the vital expressions of a people'.[2] He pays a grudging tribute to the perfection of national style in the culture of England and France, and contrasts with the unity of their national art and character the contradictions, imperfections, experimentation of German life and art. But he makes the perfection of French and British national style the proof of their decadence. They have achieved 'civilisation', but thereby are completed, moribund or dead. Germany on the other hand has *Kultur*, it is incomplete, surging forward towards the unknown, but for that very reason is vital, pregnant with the future.

In order to give this contrast of *Kultur* and civilisation a tangible and popular form, Moeller introduces the distinction of 'young' and 'old' peoples, to which he clung to the end of his life.[3] The nations that have achieved a unified national style are old; those who have not, like Germany, are young. The biological metaphor is extremely convenient, for it introduces subtly the notion of a natural death, the notion that the 'young' peoples are naturally the heirs of the past and the claimants on the future: it introduces the notion of an overriding biological law which transcends reason and dominates our being.

The concepts of *Kultur* and 'civilisation' are therefore partly biological in origin. They are associated with the evolutionary theory of Darwin, the importance of which Moeller stresses. But, like Spengler after him, he associates a biological law with a metaphysical power. Such a law means that national destiny on the one hand is subject to a process which is in no sense rational and cannot be guided by human will; on the other hand, that it can be recognised only by intuition and fulfilled through the instinctive energy that resides in the members of the nation. *Kultur* is therefore borne

[1] *Das Théâtre français* (1905), p. 78.
[2] Nietzsche, *Unzeitgemässe Betrachtungen* (Leipzig, 1893), Vol. I, p. 5 (*D. F. Strauss*).
[3] *Die Zeitgenossen*, pp. 48–51, 59–68.

along by metaphysical urges; it is a belief, a religion; it is characterised and justified not by its works, but by its inner energy, its dynamism. Its leaders are 'demi-gods, priests and heroes, Prometheans'.
All civilisations go through a formative period of *Kultur*, which is
always individualistic, aristocratic, swept forward by the 'metaphysical' confidence of great men; but for the English and French
this period is past, and they have reached the end-period. Germany
is now in the stage of *Kultur*, it is now the chief representative of the
creative spirit, and therefore destined to lead the world at its present
stage of evolution.[1] Thus Moeller establishes Germany's claims to
predominance in the modern world, and his argument is all the more
powerful for being cultural, intangible. Instead of making claims for
territory, for power, in precise economic or political terms, he creates
a general cultural and historical theory, based on subjective convictions of energy and subjective judgments of cultural values,
which persuades men that Germany's purposes are linked with
metaphysical forces. This is a fundamental characteristic of Nazi-
type thinking, in which the crude and positive aims of politics are
given a fanatical potency through an intoxicating belief in a metaphysical purpose.

Houston Stewart Chamberlain, who was chiefly responsible for
creating a general theory of culture to support the claims of German
nationalism, had underpinned his Germanism with his theory of
race. Moeller van den Bruck, avowing his great debt to Chamberlain, made a characteristic correction of Chamberlain's racial
theory. He does not question the reality of race in the earlier history
of man. But, he asserts, in modern history the race 'disintegrates' as
the nation emerges; and modern history, modern culture, is essentially a matter of nations; it is in and through nations that Destiny is
fulfilled.[2] The pragmatic, realistic intention behind his theory is
evident. If we speak only about the Aryan race, the identity of Germany is lost among all other 'Aryan' nations. But the future belongs
to the German people, the German nation, not to the vaguer Aryan
race. His continued insistence on the specific identity of national
cultures, of the nation as the 'bearer of culture', brings his readers
back, without ambiguity, to the national destiny of Germany itself.
Notable in this book, as in later writings of Moeller, is his admission
that the Russians have also a great cultural role to play. They, he
considers, are as yet in an earlier cultural stage; the 'race' here has
not yet developed into the form of the 'nation', but will one day do
so. Here again the pragmatic intention is at work; for Moeller, now
as later, was reluctant to abandon the idea of an alliance between
Germany and Russia, and was aware of the advisability of securing
Germany's rear in its conflict with the West.[3]

[1] *Die Zeitgenossen*, pp. 6–11, 36–47.   [2] ibid., pp. 56–7.   [3] ibid., pp. 108–11.

In spite of his repudiation of racism, Moeller recognises the power of the concept of race as a stimulus to confidence and action. We therefore find him using such terms as 'bond of blood', 'race', and accepting some biological basis for nationhood; though his use of such terms is necessarily ambiguous. In his study of Italian art, *Die Italienische Schönheit*, he was to insist that the homogeneity of Italian style, from the Etruscans to the Renaissance, was determined by the character of soil and landscape, and that its excellence corresponded to the degree in which the various races that entered Italy absorbed the heritage of the land. The nation is thus shaped primarily by the land—he was, in fact, to interpret Fascism as the recapture of this physically conditioned nationhood.[1]

In many respects Moeller's views in *Die Zeitgenossen* reflect, as they were always to do, the outlook of normal German nationalism, Pangermanism. The peculiar note seems to be, in the main, his Nietzschean 'realism', his ruthless immoralism, his reckless surrender to the idea of destiny. But there are distinctive elements in his thought which amount to a conflict with the dominant nationalism which thought in terms of mere continuity, of the expansion of Germany's political power overseas, its increasing wealth and profits. As in his first writings on literature, he is savagely contemptuous of the *bourgeois*, the class which thought in terms of wealth and the preservation of social form and privilege. He spurns the culture of his time, 'Wilhelmism'. His earlier attention to the naturalistic literature which reproduced the actual reality of working-class misery now takes a more political form. In Social Democracy, despite his fundamental anti-socialism, he recognises something dynamic, a movement, in this respect, infinitely preferable to the static conservatism of the capitalistic *bourgeoisie*. The main task, he considers, is the organisation of this socialist movement within great national objectives, the unity of socialism and nationalism, and this can be achieved, he believes, only if the nation captures a sense of destiny. The 'social question' is a product of a frustrated nation; it can be solved if the nation can win room for its energies.

At this stage of Moeller's life this idea is vague and general. As we shall see, it was to gain in urgency and precision and to become the main theme of his writings after the First World War, as it was to be the outstanding preoccupation of the National-Socialist movement.

III

The most important of Moeller's works under the Empire is *Der Preussische Stil* (1916), which he was writing when war broke out. It

---

[1] *Die Italienische Schönheit* (2nd ed., 1913), pp. 5–11; *Italia Docet*, 1922 (reprinted in *Das Recht der jungen Völker*, ed. Schwarz 1932).

is most important because it is his simplest, least ambiguous work; because, though it is still a 'cultural' work, its political message is clear. In it he seeks to define the principles of past and future German greatness—it was written in the thick of much public argument about war-aims and peace-aims. Some nationalists were content with universalistic dreams of conquest, democrats hoped for a widening of the basis of government in the future Germany, liberals wrote about the necessity of deepening traditional German culture, and socialists saw the war as the defence of a popular cause. Moeller (like Spengler at the same time) here gives his interpretation and view.

Der Preussische Stil is on the surface an analysis of architectural style. But architecture is for him, as for Nietzsche, the supreme expression of a nation's soul, and the underlying theme is the definition of the character of Prussia. Moeller writes of the beginnings of the Prussian State, of the slow and pertinacious conquest and settlement of the Eastern borders of Germany. Almost polemically he insists that this nation is of a mixed race, in which Slavs and Germans are mingled; that the Prussian character is a product of the Prussian State, not of a race. He describes how its rulers and kings soberly pursued, century by century, a realistic policy of expansion and consolidation, never distracted by romantic dreams of the restoration of the medieval empire, forced even to split and oppose the old empire in the interests of the Prussian mission. In the style of its medieval monuments, in the Prussian baroque and rococo, and then above all in the Prussian classicism of Schinkel and Schadow, Prussia found its full expression, massive, severe, sober. Finally it fulfilled its mission: 'Prussia was that Germany might be';[1] the new Reich was founded. But then a tragic error occurred. Instead of imposing its own sobriety and discipline on Germany, Prussia succumbed under weak leadership to Germany. The consciousness of state was lost in dreams of the Reich; realism was replaced by romanticism. Prussian architecture lost style; Berlin became 'the ugliest city in the world'. It can find a new glory only if the Prussian mission is again understood.

The work is a study of national character, undertaken with the intention of displaying a national mission or destiny: the mission of Prussia as the creator of Germany, and the present mission of Germany, of which Moeller is the prophet. Moeller's whole historical construction is therefore highly subjective, a piece of political special pleading. The historian, or any scrupulous reader, could point out the errors and distortions in Moeller's account of Prussia. He is silent on matters which would contradict his interpretation; the 'errors' of Frederick William III or Frederick William IV are passed

[1] *Der Preussische Stil* (Munich, 1916), p. 170. Ed. Schwarz (1931, reprint of 2nd edition of 1922), p. 196.

over with an indulgent excuse. The characteristically Prussian Christian-conservative tradition of Savigny and Gerlach is ignored. He includes the Königsberg of Kant and Hamann because of the glamour of these names, though these men and their native city were deeply hostile to the Prussian State and king. Heinrich von Kleist, this torn and tragic figure, is deemed to embody Prussianism as much as Frederick the Great or Bismarck. Moeller's aesthetic taste is essentially determined by his Prussian patriotism, which leads him to admire the pretentious designs of Gilly. But such criticisms are, for Moeller, beside the point. He is not concerned with history in the recognised sense; like Nietzsche, he despises the belief that there can be objective standards for the historian. He is concerned with creating a myth, a Prussian myth, a 'principle', as he calls it, which will inspire modern Germans; whether it is true in relation to the past is of only minor importance; what is important is, will it provoke response in appropriate actions? As such the book belongs to the new type of pseudo-historical writing that was to flourish in the Nazi movement: its truth is its expediency, its effectiveness. One might apply to it the words from Schiller's *Wallenstein*:

> Entworfen bloss, ist's ein gemeiner Frevel,
> Vollführt, ist's ein unsterblich Unternehmen.[1]

Moeller's criticism of Wilhelmism was bound to be veiled, in a book which appeared at the height of the war. It is clear, however, that his Prussianism is different from the sentimental admiration for the great past of Prussia in which many Germans indulged. Moeller expresses with urgency his belief that the great tradition is lost, that Germany is floundering about without a sense of direction. In the second edition of 1922 he re-wrote the last chapters in order to sharpen the political criticism of Wilhelmism (and of Wilhelm II himself), and to ascribe to its faults the disasters which had overcome Germany.[2] But, in spite of the acrid taste and outspokenness of the new material, it only develops implications that were present in the first edition. Naturally enough, it was the more explicit second edition that was widely read in the post-war period.

Moeller enlisted in the army in 1916, and was attached to the Foreign Bureau of Supreme Army Headquarters. He continued writing articles for the Press, nearly all of them concerned with foreign policy, and all closely connected with official Army policy, particularly as regards the victories over the Tsarist armies and the German push eastwards. In agreement with the general thesis of *Der Preussische Stil*, Moeller shows little interest in the German

---

[1] 'Merely planned, it is a vulgar crime; but if accomplished, it is an immortal enterprise.'
[2] *Der Preussische Stil*, ed. Schwarz (1931), pp. 179–83, 189–93, 198–9.

overseas empire or the Western Front. He imagines a Germany consolidated in the West through the acquisition of Flanders, but sees its essential mission in the East. It will establish its sovereignty over the Baltic countries and, with Bulgaria and Turkey, will press forward through Central Europe into the Near East. He adopts Friedrich Naumann's conception of Germany as the 'Middle Land', impregnably dominating central Europe and the Western portions of the Russian empire.

These practical aims are characteristically enveloped in general cultural theory. 'West' and 'East' are not mere geographical terms. 'West' stands for age, for civilisation, material power, necessary as an instrument but not a principle of energy; 'East' for youth, for the unformed creative spirit that lives in agricultural peoples who have not yet found a final national form. Germany's drive to the East is a symbol of its creative potentialities, and as the 'Middle Land' it is the means to combine creative dynamism with national form, thus serving a universal metaphysical purpose. Russia is to lose her Western territories, the Baltic countries, the Ukraine. But this should not be understood in terms of vulgar power-politics. The Russian empire was a false 'Western' conception; Russia's expansion westwards has been a spiritual error. It is Russia's destiny to turn eastwards, into Siberia and Asia; Germany is thus helping Russia to discover her true self. 'The Baltic has never belonged to the Slavs. . . . A Russian sailor is a contradiction in itself. . . . The sea will not have the Russians.' [1]

In the winter of 1918–19 Moeller put his views in a book, *Das Recht der jüngen Völker*,[2] in a desperate attempt to win President Wilson for his programme of German expansion. He tries to appeal to the representative of a 'young nation' through his thesis that the war arose out of the envy of the 'old' peoples for the 'young'. The young peoples are those with a high birth-rate, with bursting vitality, those which are united in their need to change the shape of political frontiers. Some, he admits, fought on the side of the old nations, particularly of course Japan and Italy; but this was an error, and the victory of the Allies has been the victory of the old peoples. A satisfactory settlement can only be one which provides for the needs of the 'young' peoples; any other will simply prepare the way for new wars, in which Germany, Japan, Italy, Finland, and Bulgaria will have identical interests: a significant forecast of the Axis.

Moeller is well aware that the concept of 'young peoples' may seem as unacceptable to a rational politician or historian as it does to the

[1] See articles collected under the title 'Baltikum' in *Das Recht der jungen Völker*, ed. Schwarz (1932), pp. 175–89; and 'Abkehr vom Westen' and 'Der Aufbruch nach Osten' in *Der politische Mensch*, ed. Schwarz, 1933.

[2] *Das Recht der jüngen Völker* (Munich, 1919). This work should not be confused with the collection of his articles published by Schwarz in 1932 under the same title.

racist. He sweeps away, however, any scruples as to its validity. In itself, he writes, no people is young or old. The age of a people cannot be ascertained by historical or biological tests. Youth is a question of 'the effect that the people concerned has on the world'; it is demonstrated by the restlessness and vigour a nation shows, by its 'mission not to let the world settle down'.[1] His mode of argument, as well as his political purpose, anticipate Nazi thought. For he uses the stirring slogan of 'youth' as an expedient, a means to a faith and a policy, and troubles himself little about its scientific validity. In this same work he can summarily despatch the claims of Poland to nationality, simply because a Polish state would stand in the way of German expansion. He covers over German aims in Eastern Europe and the Near East with high-sounding generalities like 'moulding (*Durcharbeitung*) of the Near East according to broad principles'; and he justifies the ousting of Russian power on the plea that Russia is a 'young race', not yet a 'people'. Now, as later, he shows a sneaking sympathy with the 'anti-Western' potentialities of the Soviet Revolution.[2] As with Nazi thought in general, it is difficult to decide how much in Moeller's argument is calculated to deceive, and how much is sheer self-deception.

Before we proceed to examine the last period of Moeller's work—the most significant period from the point of view of National-Socialism—it is advisable to consider the relationship of his thought up to 1918 with that of his contemporaries. Little need be said on the anti-socialist and anti-liberal character of his writings, for the main lines of distinction are evident. In making the nation the supreme historical fact he opposes all socialist thought, and the strong executive he advocates would protect 'creative capitalism'. In his advocacy of the Prussian ideal of authoritarianism he consistently attacks all liberal-democratic notions, all humanitarianism, which he despises as a sign of weakness of the national will. This was common ground for all conservatives. What is significant is his divergence from other forms of conservatism. He is aware of the profound reality of the 'social problem', and has a closer kinship with 'National-Socialists' like Stoecker than with the old-fashioned authoritarian Christian conservatism of the Junker party and the *Kreuzzeitung*. His spiritual forebears, to whom he often refers, are men like the Freiherr vom Stein, Friedrich List, and Rodbertus, men who sought to make a strong executive responsible for a national policy which would curb and direct capitalism and protect the working class. He is equally distinct from conservatives like Prince von Bülow, who

[1] *Das Recht der jüngen Völker* (1919), pp. 24-5; similarly in an article of November 1918, and another of 1923, published in *Das Recht der jüngen Völker*, ed. Schwarz, pp. 155-7 and 103.
[2] *Das Recht der jüngen Völker* (1919), pp. 103-6.

believed that the Reich was the legitimate and loyal heir of Prussia, and who shut their eyes to the inner weaknesses of Wilhelmian Germany. Compared with such, Moeller is a revolutionary, who condemns the shoddy thought and easy-going optimism of self-confident Germanism.

Moeller has often been associated with the more acute and disturbed minds, like Keyserling and Thomas Mann and Rathenau, as a founder of modern German nationalism,[1] but here again distinctions are important. The theme of Thomas Mann's *Betrachtungen eines Unpolitischen* is the old contrast of *Kultur* and *civilisation*, one of the key-slogans of Moeller. But Thomas Mann, identifying *Kultur* with Germany, sets it in opposition to political organisation, just as he contrasts the Germanic idea of *Volk* to the Western idea of *nation*, the idea of German 'inwardness' to that of Western 'form'. The German state, the power of an 'organic' authoritarian leadership, is justified by him essentially as the strong armour protecting *Kultur*, which is the product and realm of the middle class—cf. his definition of the German national character as 'inwardness protected by power' (*machtgeschützte Innerlichkeit*). The connection between these ideas and Moeller's should not obscure the difference between the two men. For Moeller, the authoritarian State is not the protective framework of *Kultur*, it is its formative principle, as he shows in *Der Preussische Stil*. His dynamism is completely opposed to the idealisation of a non-political inwardness as the permanent characteristic of Germany; rather he would educate Germans to assume the responsibilities of a great nation, to throw aside their political passivity and acquire a new national consciousness and a new culture.

Like Moeller, Keyserling and Rathenau both deplored the undermining of German transcendentalism by rationalistic intellectualism, which was the cause, in their view, of the ousting of the mystique of leadership and authoritarianism by democratic and humanitarian notions. But their continual feud against the mechanisation of labour processes and the consequent disruption of 'organic' society and 'inward' culture was far too romantic for Moeller. However much he inveighs against the political pretensions of the capitalistic *bourgeoisie*, the plutocracy, he always rejoices in the power that capitalism had developed and that could be utilised by the state. He was totally opposed to Rathenau's opinion that Frederick the Great had struck a blow at the mystique of kingship in proclaiming himself 'the first servant of the state'; for Moeller, the nation is the supreme reality, not the king or a particular form of state. He was to look forward to a new type of *élite*, a new type of leader, and resolutely to

---

[1] e.g. in E. Vermeil, *Doctrinaires de la Révolution Allemande* (1939); R. D'O. Butler, *The Roots of National Socialism* (1941). Armin Mohler (op. cit.) associates him with Thomas Mann and Spengler.

put behind him any romantic hankering after the old sort of king, the old sort of supernatural sanction, and the old culture.[1]

Of all conservatives, Spengler is closest to Moeller. But Spengler's *Decline of the West* appeared only in 1918, and Moeller's relationship with Spengler must properly be discussed in the post-war setting.

IV

The Revolution of 1918 was, in Moeller's view, a disaster. Germany's defeat was remediable; but the Revolution was in his view a complete failure. 'A war can be lost. A luckless war is never irremediable. The worst peace is never final. But a revolution must be won.'[2] The Revolution was lost because it was inspired by disastrous ideas, because in it Germans abandoned a national purpose, and gave themselves up to preoccupations with social reform, socialism or democracy, peace and internationalism; because it was not a 'national' revolution, but an abdication from national political purpose.

From the moment of the Revolution, Moeller devoted himself to a clear and exclusive political aim: the reconstruction of German national power. His immediate purpose was the recalling of Germans to a consciousness of nationhood, of national mission, beyond all parties, all programmes of social reform. He wrote to Heinrich von Gleichen, his closest collaborator, that from the first day after the Revolution they realised that all Germany's misfortune came from the 'parties', from the democratic constitution itself, and that they were united in opposing the whole system of Weimar.[3] He knew it was necessary, of course, to work through the parliamentary parties, and he remained in touch with many of their leaders, particularly those of the conservative-nationalist parties, the *Deutsch-Nationale* and the *Volkspartei*, from whom he and his friends received subsidies from time to time. His sympathies were clearly with the Right, in his opposition to the Revolution, to the Treaty of Versailles, the occupation of the Ruhr, the policy of Fulfilment, his advocacy of a Great Germany, and so forth. But his public utterances deal as it were only incidentally with these themes, and he kept apart from party programmes and party campaigns. His aim was to construct a new political outlook, a new political philosophy, 'to smash the parties from the side of *Weltanschauung*'.[4]

In June 1919 he and a few friends founded the *Juniklub* in Berlin,

---

[1] See the concluding chapter of *Der Preussische Stil*, ed. of 1922.
[2] *Das Dritte Reich*, ed. Schwarz (1931), p. 15.
[3] ibid., *Vorwort* (1922).
[4] ibid., *Vorwort*. See also his article 'Der Aussenseiter' (1919), in *Der Politische Mensch*, ed. Schwarz (1933), pp. 65–75.

of which he was to be the presiding genius and Heinrich von Gleichen the moving spirit.[1] From 1920, when it moved to the Motzstrasse, it was an important headquarters for a host of Right-wing groupings, playing a significant part in the troubles of 1923. The economic and political stabilisation of 1924 brought a fatal decline in the Club's fortunes. Moeller himself suffered a nervous collapse in the middle of 1924, and put an end to his life in June 1925.

The Club was a meeting place for the many nationalistic splinter-groups that came into being after the war. Here came men from the Free Corps, from the Defence units in the lost border regions, from Alsace, Poland, the Sudetenland, the Baltic littoral; men of the Anti-Bolshevik League, retired generals and admirals, editors of nationalist newspapers from all over Germany; here came ideologues of 'leadership' and of the corporative state. The building housed various associations, like the Greater Germany Youth and the Club for Germans Abroad (*Volksdeutsche*), and it was the centre of academic nationalist groupings. Many uprooted and *déclassé* officers found their way there. Club-meetings proper were addressed by a variety of nationalist leaders, including Hitler. A manifesto of the new conservatism for which the club stood, *Die neue Front* (1922), edited by Moeller van den Bruck, Heinrich von Gleichen, and M. H. Boehm, included among its contributors Hans Grimm, Paul Ernst, August Winnig, Ernst Krieck, Wilhelm Stapel, Ernst Stadtler, some of them names well known in the Nazi movement.

It was the aim of the *Juniklub* to provide a meeting-place for trends and personalities which, in the confusion of the new post-war situation, were often at variance. Moeller's task was above all that of mediator, and his influence, acknowledged by men of different groups, contributed greatly towards welding the splinters into a homogeneous movement. He achieved this partly by maintaining a wide network of personal relationships, and partly through the weekly, *Das Gewissen*, of which he was the effective editor: a paper which was described by Radek, the communist leader, as 'the only thinking organ of the nationalistic circles of Germany'.[2] His articles, and his chief work of this period, *Das Dritte Reich*, reflect the discussions in the Club, not least in the emphasis of his epigrams, which seem to have been hammered out in repeated argument. The book itself presents the main themes of his articles. After its re-publica-

[1] The character and ramifications of the influence of the *Juniklub* cannot as yet be accurately assessed, as the biographical material is lacking. Information drawn from personal experience is contained in the following works: several publications of Hans Schwarz; M. H. Boehm, *Ruf der Jungen* (Freiburg/Breisgau, 1933); P. Fechter, *Moeller van den Bruck* (Berlin, 1934); August Winnig, *Aus zwanzig Jahren* (Hamburg, 1949); Armin Mohler, *Die Konservative Revolution*, pp. 92–3.
[2] June 1923—reprinted in a pamphlet, *Schlageter*, issued by *Vereinigung Internationaler Verlags-Anstalten*.

tion in 1931 it was a major influence on the Nazi and near-Nazi intelligentsia.

Moeller's political philosophy in the post-war period found its most general formulation in his refutation of Spengler; and since Spengler, too, though remaining in a superior position above political party associations, made a deep impression on nationalistic thought, it is profitable to consider his main work of this period, the *Decline of the West*. In his admiration of Prussianism, his authoritarianism, his recognition of the significance of the workers' movement (Spengler had a great admiration for Bebel, the builder of the Social-Democratic Party), his attitude to Russia, and in several other respects, Spengler is very close to Moeller. His somewhat snobbish and patronising approval of Hitler, after the latter's accession to power, suggests what might have been Moeller's attitude had he lived to see the victory of National-Socialism. Their disagreement illustrates the difference between Spengler's universalistic theorising and Moeller's desperate and daily struggle for adherents.

Spengler's *Decline of the West* is a philosophy of history. In its methodology it is an attack on the view that the process of history can be analysed scientifically as a system of cause and effect, that the determinants of events can be revealed, and therefore that men may be able in the future to determine social purposes rationally and control the social process. On the contrary, Spengler insists, the history of mankind goes in a series of vast cultural cycles, all showing a similar pattern of birth, growth, maturity, and decay. Whence they arise escapes analysis. They are born from 'cosmic forces', just as their growth and decay follow a principle which is comparable with the life-cycle of any biological organism, and proceed along a preordained path which no efforts of man can alter. The historian cannot understand and analyse this process, since the cosmic principle of the life-process defies analysis; he can only describe it by means of the 'morphological' method, which can establish the identity of the vital process as it recurs in the cyclical process of each great culture. But, if we cannot understand the past rationally or scientifically, we can grasp it intuitively; men can feel the cosmic force within them, the metaphysical 'mission' which carries them along. History is, then, for Spengler 'the logic of Destiny'. We understand it through 'an intuitive life-experience'. The rationalist speaks of a 'purpose' of life; the man of profound vitality, through whom cosmic forces speak, knows only of a 'mission', a 'destiny' which 'is the word for an indescribable inward certainty'. This feeling of destiny gives life its value. Freedom is an illusory concept and deprives man of power; man can act greatly only if he feels himself borne along on the stream of destiny, recognises the specific form of the mission of his time, and accomplishes what is inevitable.[1] The closing words of the book echo Wallenstein's words:

Wir handeln wie wir müssen.
So lass uns das Notwendige mit Würde,
Mit festem Schritte tun.[2]

We do not need to concern ourselves here with the very questionable concept of 'culture' in Spengler's sense, with the distinctions Spengler makes between the 'spirit' of each great culture, nor with the dazzling parallels he draws in order to demonstrate the uniformity of the life-process in each culture. The faults of his method and his generalisations have been pointed out recently by P. A. Sorokin.[3] We are more concerned with the practical applications of this pretentious system. Its conclusions about his own time are that Western Civilisation, the latest of the great cultures, is approaching its end and that this 'end' must be, like the end of all past cultures, 'Caesarism', a period of military imperialism in which the only significant form that human energy can take is that of conquest and ruthless violence, when man shows himself nakedly as the 'beast of prey' he is. This is the 'destiny' and 'mission' of modern man; only by accepting this mission can he achieve anything memorable and great. By evading this mission he dooms himself to futility. And in the Prefaces of 1917 and 1922 Spengler addresses himself particularly, as a German philosopher, to the Germans, expressing the hope that his book may stand beside the achievements of the German armies in the field. His malevolent description of the decay of England and France makes it clear that he believes that the Germans are called to be the Caesarean *élite* in this final stage of civilisation; and in smaller works, such as *Prussianism and Socialism* and *The Hour of Decision*, he calls Germans to this task: 'Germany is the decisive country in the world'.

A great deal of Spengler's thought is built on elements we have already observed in Moeller, though given a systematic and universalistic form and supported by a vast amount of learning. Their joint debt to Nietzsche is evident in the theme of the relativity of morals, the call to abandon the values of earlier social and cultural stages—though with Spengler the idealisation of the 'beast of prey', of power and brutality, is more naked, more ecstatic than in Moeller. Both share Nietzsche's hatred of democracy, free capitalism, and the sated *bourgeoisie*, and are enraptured by the thought of a privileged and despotic *élite* which is moved entirely by ambitions of political power. Both idealise Prussianism as a combination of Caesarean

---

[1] The quotations will be found in Oswald Spengler, *Der Untergang des Abendlandes* (1927), Vol. I, *Vorwort*, pp. 153, 157; Vol. II, pp. 35–8, 56, 630.
[2] 'We act as we must: therefore let us accomplish the inevitable with dignity, with a firm step.'
[3] P. A. Sorokin, *Social Philosophies of an Age of Crisis* (Boston, 1950).

autocracy and popular will, and envisage a leadership that will express the will of a nation, produce a *Volksführer* in whom the masses find themselves mystically embodied. Both see history as a biological process, urged on by an irrational, metaphysical force; and Spengler uses Moeller's distinction of *Kultur* and 'civilisation' to distinguish the earlier, artistically and spiritually creative phase of every cultural cycle from the last one, which is great only in techniques, in political power. Both see history as destiny and mission. And in spite of Spengler's insistence that the supreme realities of history are the super-national cultures (to which he attributes a distinct and specific character, such as 'Magian', 'Faustian', etc.), he is at one with Moeller in attributing to nationalities, to states, a vital reality and role within the general process of the cultural entity to which they belong. Why, then, did Moeller find it necessary to attack Spengler's philosophy of history?

Moeller's criticism is in fact more pertinent than most of the numerous attacks that Spengler's book provoked.[1] He praises Spengler for having 'spoken again of destiny', for 'restoring to man his dignity and attaching his fate to the stars'. But he is repelled by Spengler's too rigid determinism; and he very shrewdly points out the reason for this determinism, which is the very reason why Moeller himself must reject or modify it. Spengler had conceived and written his book during the war (the first volume was completed in 1917), under the impact of the great German military achievements of those years. It was written in anticipation of a German victory. His essential concern was, therefore, to prepare the Germans for the destiny (which was to be theirs) of dominating the world, to persuade them that they must abandon their old ways of life, their old culture, their weakness for humanitarian ideals; they must cease being 'a people of thinkers and poets' and become steeled to rule. But, Moeller points out, things have turned out otherwise. Germany has been defeated. The Caesarean mantle might seem to have fallen to other nations, the victors. The determination of Germans to rise again, the inner conviction of energy, of destiny, needs some other basis than the 'logic', the determinism of Spengler. Moeller's preoccupation is practical and immediate. How can the Germans come to believe that they can break through the shell of events and impose a new course on history?

They can do so, in Moeller's opinion, if they believe they can, if they believe it is their mission to do so. His criticism of Spengler, his whole political philosophy, is built on this principle. Spengler's philosophy of destiny is, he says, still too rationalistic, too mechanical, for it asserts a regularity in the succession of historical (cultural)

---

[1] His article on *Der Untergang des Abendlandes* appeared in *Deutsche Rundschau*, July 1920; reprinted in *Das Recht der jungen Völker*, ed. Schwarz, pp. 11, 39.

phases which binds men to an inescapable future. But, for Moeller, destiny is incalculable; it arises, as he repeats over and over again, from metaphysical sources which are perpetually creative. 'There is always a beginning'; 'history is the story of the incalculable'. There are no parallelisms between the great cultures; every event is unique, unprecedented. Each nation has its unique destiny; and though there is no linear progress in history, no 'advance' in the liberal or moral sense, and though the nation always renews itself from its past, its development goes not in cycles, but in spirals, always developing something new and unforeseen. And, accepting for the sake of argument Spengler's definition of the specific characteristics of each great culture, Moeller cries, why, then, should a 'Faustian' culture end like the others?

At every moment in his argumentation Moeller's practical political preoccupation is apparent. For instance, he asserts that the idea of the progress of mankind towards democracy and internationalism is disproved by the policies of the 'democratic' nations, England and France, towards Germany. It is on pragmatic grounds that he insists that the Germans must break away from any belief in a rigid necessity or destiny. They (like other 'young' peoples, Italy and Japan) must break through the dominant 'civilisation', must assert the rights of their millions. The fundamental condition is that they should be seized by a conviction of obeying a metaphysical destiny in this sense, an inward conviction which need have no rational proof or test, but is the expression of the vital urge which shows itself in the growth of their population, and is justified by its own reality and power. This is the meaning of the term 'metaphysical' as Moeller always uses it—it defines a belief that runs counter to all reason, rests entirely on instinctive conviction, and cannot be contained within any bounds. Often expressed with a grim and almost desperate fanaticism, this type of belief is essentially that of the Nazi movement; and here already, in Moeller, we find such terms as *Aufbruch*, a key-word and slogan of the Nazis, meaning 'departure', 'breaking camp', a resolute break with the past and passionate departure for an unknown future, towards 'a new historic age'. The idea of destiny and mission loses the passivity of the idea of 'fate', and is freed from the limitation of any precise aim; it acquires fully the boundless and fanatical energy which the Nazis gave it.

Moeller's interpretation of history (or better, of destiny) derives directly from his political purpose. In these last years of his life he was engaged in clarifying his conception of race, with a similar practical purpose, and it is convenient to sum up at this point his views on race, which were close to those of Spengler and many other nationalists.

From his earliest work he had used the concept of race, but at the same time had derided the racists' belief that national or personal greatness was a consequence of pure race. He recognises that all the European peoples are of mixed race, including the Prussian people. He is ready to believe that in the dim past, in pre-historical times, race played a large part in the foundation of civilisation; he is even ready to concede that the leading European peoples, though mixed, were the product of a mixture of racial *élites*. At all times he is ready to admit that there was a 'biological basis' to great nations, and that myth arose from this biological past. But these are only concessions. The idea of race is meaningful, for him, not because of its truth, but because of its usefulness. It is necessary to a nation. 'Race is a power. He who feels it in himself, possesses power and exercises it. The racial world-view rests on faith in this power, faith in man, confidence that man is not a slave of circumstance but master of his forces.' [1] Mastery, in this sense, belongs to nations, the creators and bearers of history; and therefore the conviction of race is merged in the conviction of nationality. It is ridiculous to look for biological or ethnological proof of purity of race in the modern nations, as he brought out in *Der Preussische Stil*. His only interest in the idea of race is its value in strengthening national consciousness. Spengler made the same point when he asserted that the 'men of race' who will be the new conquerors of the world are not men who belong biologically to a particular race, but men who 'feel themselves born and called to be masters'; [2] i.e. as opposed to the 'zoological' view, about which Spengler always speaks with great contempt, race is not an objective fact but a subjective conviction.

In an article of 1924 Moeller makes his view clear. He stresses the importance of belief in race: it is a question of 'To be or not to be', a question of the faith without which Germany will succumb into insignificance. But race is a mission, not history; it belongs to the future, not the past. The need is 'unity of race', not 'purity of race' (*Rasseeinheit*, not *Rassereinheit*). Race is, in his normal use of the term, a 'metaphysical' concept—that is, an idea which is not experimentally or rationally demonstrable, but an irrational conviction which is a source of energy and power. Germans must have this conviction for the sake of their national mission.[3]

Such views brought Moeller into conflict with the racists with whom he was closely allied in a common onslaught on the democratic Republic. It is characteristic of his concern for the younger generation that he published in *Das Gewissen* a letter from a young nationalist protesting against his views. The author complained that Moeller's scepticism about racial purity weakened the will to

---

[1] 'Rasseanschauung' (1908), in *Das Recht der jüngen Völker*, ed. Schwarz, pp. 193–6.
[2] *Jahre der Entscheidung* (1933), transl. as *The Hour of Decision*, p. 59.
[3] 'Rasse' (1924), in *Das Recht der jüngen Völker*, ed. Schwarz, pp. 202–6.

national renewal; the conquest of power depended in his view on a sure faith in a 'pure-blooded master-class'. Moeller answered once again that what was needed was not a faith about the past, but a faith in the future; that racist thinking led to vague dreams of domination, to the romanticism he had condemned in *Der Preussische Stil*. What was needed was thinking in 'historical-political' terms, in terms of the nation, of what was realisable. Race is important as a myth, as a faith that can renew and inspire the nation, but racialism must not engulf the nation and supplant with its wild dreams a realistic policy.[1]

Moeller's use of the concept of race, as of that of 'young peoples', shows to the end the influence of Nietzsche's immoralism, his philosophical scepticism and nihilism. Nietzsche had written that the importance of a belief does not rest on its truth; a false belief may be equally or more important. The 'will to illusion' is as justifiable as the 'will to truth'. The only pertinent question is: 'Does a judgment further and preserve life, does it preserve, does it breed our kind?'[2] Moeller adopts this principle, interpreting 'life', 'our kind', in terms of the nation and national power. He is quite conscious of the subjective, expediential nature of this type of thought, and calls it 'metaphysical' in order to distinguish it from rational or scientific or objective thought. Such a term as 'race' is used deliberately for its demagogic effect; it may be used quite cynically. Efforts to disprove its validity by biologists or ethnologists miss the target, for it is founded on a fundamental repudiation of the whole method of rational and scientific thinking. In this respect, and not merely in his political objectives, Moeller gives the lead to much Nazi and near-Nazi thought.

V

Moeller's post-war experience and thought are summed up in his chief work, *Das Dritte Reich*. It was published in 1923, the year of inflation and the French occupation of the Ruhr, and its mood is sombre and bitter. It did not receive much attention at the time, for after 1923 the temporary economic recovery of Germany, with the Dawes Plan and Stresemann's policy of Fulfilment of the economic clauses of the Treaty of Versailles, weakened the nationalistic anti-democratic movement. But with the radicalisation of opinion after the slump of 1929, the growth of a revolutionary mood in face of a complete breakdown of Germany's economic and political system, Moeller's book came into its own. It was republished in 1931 in a

[1] The letter and Moeller's reply, both of 1924, are reproduced in *Das Recht der jüngen Völker*, ed. Schwarz, pp. 207–13.
[2] Nietzsche, *Jenseits von Gut und Böse* (Leipzig, 1896), pp. 12–13.

very large edition and had a 'decisive influence' on the young nationalist intelligentsia who baulked at the crude methods and crude propaganda of the Nazis and yet swelled the anti-democratic, anti-socialist stream. For the crucial years between 1931 and 1933 Moeller's ideas bridged the gap between 'revolutionary conservatism'—or what one might call radical nationalism—and National-Socialism itself. His ideas appear ever-repeated in the writings of those groups who hesitated on the brink of Nazism, some eventually taking the plunge, some holding back, but all contributing to the victory of Nazism, which later paid them such scant respect. The focus of the Moeller influence was the monthly, *Die Tat*, which propagated a radical, anti-capitalistic nationalism among wide circles of the academically trained classes. The periodical was wound up in 1933. Some of its leading contributors, like the editor, Hans Zehrer, threw in their lot with the disappointed nationalists; others, like Giselher Wirsing, became prominent Nazi journalists and ideologues.

The style in which *Das Dritte Reich* is written reflects the ardour and bitterness with which Moeller advocated his cause. It is a mixture of sceptical realism and romantic mysticism, of cynicism and dogma, of precise accusation and far-fetched theory. Difficult to grasp rationally, and elusive to criticism, it is like much Nazi thought, and is the counterpart of the desperate determination, *Draufgängertum*, that was cultivated as a moral ideal by the Nazis. Its weakness is its power. Despair takes on the form of strength and confidence, insecurity turns into fanatical faith, emotive passion disguises itself as sceptical realism, arbitrary judgments are given the standing of metaphysical truths, revolt against past and present appears in the form of a philosophy of history, adventurism clothes itself in the robes of Destiny.

But, at the same time, the book faces up to the reality of the German situation and touches at all points the issues with which Germans were faced. In his opening chapter, entitled 'Revolutionary', Moeller makes clear the attitude of the 'conservative revolutionary', as he now calls himself. The German Revolution of 1918 is a major fact, which cannot be cancelled out; the man of 1918 is different from the man of 1914. Wilhelmism has shown itself to be bankrupt, and a 'restoration' would be a disaster. On Right and on Left there is a new revolutionary spirit; the Revolution must be made the beginning of a new phase of the nation's history. But the Revolution has so far failed. It is in the ban of liberal or socialistic ideas, ideas of the past and of foreign nations, and quite logically its true basis is, not the Weimar Constitution, but the Treaty of Versailles and the policy of Fulfilment. The Revolution has made Germans into serfs. If the Wilhelmian period failed to create a national idea and succumbed to the West, the Revolution has done no better; as a consequence the Revolution has not solved any of the problems that caused it, and Germans are still unable to live, to gain their bread, and are still in the throes of over-population. The problem is to create through and out of the Revolution a new German national idea, a new principle, a new nation. In spite of the failure of ruling circles and the rottenness of certain sections of society, there is a new spirit abroad. From the experience in the front line, from the bitterness of defeat and humiliation, men of all ranks are experiencing 'a feeling of being bound in a common fate' (*ein schicksalsmässiges Verbundenheitsgefühl*). They are sober and realistic, and throw aside all dreams and ancient idols which are no use to them; they are preparing for the future in a matter-of-fact, sceptical, ruthless fashion.

This combination of national principle and Revolution, this determination to reform Germany for a great future on the basis of new authorities, new ideas, distinguishes the new man, who combines conservativism with revolutionary aims, the 'conservative revolutionary', the nationalist. It is Moeller's aim to make the German people, so full of unspent energies, conscious of its 'political ego', to shape it into a new national form—or rather, to shape a new national spirit out of which a new form will arise. With this end in view he criticises the three main groups of political opinion—liberal democracy, Communism, and conservatism—and as he proceeds he adumbrates the new principles of political life, to which the last chapters are devoted.

Under the rubric 'democratic' or 'liberal' Moeller includes all those groups that subscribe to the principles of the Weimar Constitution and consider it provides the framework for German development. It is characteristic of his thought that he contemptuously dismisses Social Democracy as having lost all its peculiar, pre-War significance, since it accepts the principles of 'freedom' and 'democracy' which are the product of free capitalism. Liberalism is 'the principle of having no principle'; it stands for individual freedom and cares not a rap for the *Volk*; it is the rule of groups of interest which deny the idea of national community. It sets no national purpose or task, and confines itself at best to ideals of inner social reform. It therefore fails to grapple with the prime needs of the nation.

Moeller's attitude to liberalism or democracy is somewhat ambiguous. He rejects it for Germany, but does not deny its value to the victorious nations, and his most effective criticism applies to its invalidity for Germany at the present time. Germans have borrowed the conception from England and France. But in these two countries democracy has always been associated with a powerful national spirit, and has been the inspiration of national expansion: they fought the war for 'liberty'. In Germany democracy is the abnegation of national expansion, it is pacifist and acquiescent, it is the spirit of the Treaty of Versailles, a betrayal of the people. General ideas are merely the expression of the will of a people, their meaning changes in another nation; the adoption by one nation of the ideas of another must necessarily mean enslavement to this other nation.

Naïvely and foolishly the Germans have taken 'democracy' at its face-value. They have created the democratic Constitution, which places effective power in the hands of parliamentary groups. But in England and France government works quite differently from the postulates of the theorists. In England the Cabinet is the real repository of power, not the Party; in France the reins are held by extra-Parliamentary groups and interests. The democracy which Germans have constructed is not compatible with national strength, with vigorous government.

All international principles are similarly decried by Moeller as merely a means by which the dominant nations may retain their hegemony. The League of Nations is for him, of course, merely the guarantee of the existing power-relations. And, turning to the socialist movement with its ideal of the international solidarity of the workers, Moeller asserts that such ideas are entertained by British and French workers merely as a means to maintain their privileged position. If he had lived, Moeller would have triumphantly joined the chorus of criticism and disillusion which followed the Hague Conference of 1929–30, when a British Labour Government showed itself as unrelenting to a German Social-Democratic Government as any Imperialist group. He would have considered that it was quite consistent that British Labour should adopt an imperialistic policy towards the German people, under whatever leadership the latter might be.

The tone of contempt disappears from Moeller's phrases when he turns to the problem of Communism. In his earliest works he had shown how sensitive he was to the transformation of German life through the emergence of the industrial proletariat, and he had recognised the need to find a way in which the proletarian masses could be enlisted behind the nationalist movement. He saw that the Revolution of 1918 was the work of the masses, and that it failed to answer their needs. More than most nationalists, he learned from the Revolution; and, to a large extent, the significance of *Das Dritte Reich* is due to his squarely facing the issue of the new problem brought into being by the class-conscious proletariat. 'The problem of the masses approaches from below.' [1] He read Marx, Engels, and Lenin with some care, and entered into direct controversy with leading communists. In *Das Dritte Reich* there are several long arguments with communist theories.

These arguments range from general theory to practical questions.

[1] *Das Dritte Reich*, ed. Schwarz, p. 125.

M

Just as he had attacked the determinism of Spengler, so he attacks
historical materialism. He quotes Marx's statement: 'Mankind only
sets itself problems that it can solve'; and comments: 'No. Mankind
has always set itself only the problems it cannot solve. Here lies its
greatness. Here is the genius that guides it. Here is the daemon that
urges it on.' [1] That is, the immediate objectives of a society cannot be
defined in terms of an actual situation, in terms of scientific observation and rational calculation; men can break through to an unknown unforeseeable future—'Mankind has always been a new
departure (*Aufbruch*), to which it made up its mind without being
sure of the way, let alone the goal'. The spiritual values of a people
do not arise logically from the past, as effects of causes; they are
suddenly there, 'spontaneous and daemonic'.[2] Marxism, says Moeller,
enchains men to circumstances; but he would free them to assert
themselves, to assert the spiritual energy within them. Marx he
thought rightly defined the class-character of the liberal nineteenth
century, and rightly criticised the hollowness of *bourgeois* ideology;
but he failed to rise above the class-conception, failed to understand
the *Volk* and failed to recognise the meaning of 'nation' and 'national
conflict'. These are for Moeller, however, the whole basis of history,
and the source of gigantic, unpredictable energy.

Similarly with a more practical argument, which found many
echoes in Germany. Marx, says Moeller, understood that a proletariat may be oppressed by its *bourgeoisie*; but he failed to understand
that a whole nation may be oppressed and exploited by another
nation. The Germans are a 'proletarian nation'; they, the 'over-
populated' nation, are exploited by the 'under-populated' nations.
The main enemy is abroad; the Germans are united in common
suffering. The workers, said Marx, have no fatherland; but, Moeller
answers, the German workers have nothing but their fatherland to
call their own.[3] Therefore Moeller builds up his doctrine that the
German proletariat can only liberate itself within the framework of a
nationalistic movement, in alliance with other classes of society. It
can form the body, the substance, and power of a national movement; but it must accept the leadership of the upper social strata, the
sensitive brain of the nation, which feels instinctively the character
and destiny of the nation.

These arguments had a great appeal in his time, based as they were
on the real impoverishment of Germany, the loss of colonies and
overseas markets, the payment of Reparations. But Moeller was
wrong in asserting that Marxism ignored the national question, for
before and since that time Marxism has recognised the reality of
imperialistic exploitation and the importance of national resistance

[1] *Das Dritte Reich*, ed. Schwarz, p. 35.   [2] ibid., pp. 37, 189.
[3] ibid., pp. 40-1, 56-60, 160 *passim*.

to foreign exploitation. In his own time there was no lack of opinion in Marxist circles that Germany was, since the war, to be reckoned as an exploited, 'semi-colonial' people, and efforts were made to establish the Communist Party as a national leadership against Western imperialism and the Treaty of Versailles. This tendency became stronger still after 1929, but it also came to a head in 1923, over a matter in which Moeller engaged himself in argument with Radek, the spokesman of the Third (Communist) International. We can conveniently deal with this controversy at this point, though it occurred after the publication of *Das Dritte Reich*.

In 1923, owing to the failure of Reparations deliveries, the French occupied the Ruhr. The protests of the German government and of German industrialists were turned into a real movement of resistance through the strikes and demonstrations of the factory workers. Many radical nationalists went into the Ruhr to take part in anti-French actions. Among them was Schlageter, a former 'Frei-Corps' man, who was executed by the French for sabotage.

At a session of the Third International, Radek spoke sympathetically of the Ruhr struggle as a national rising against Western imperialism, and paid tribute to the patriotism of men like Schlageter. But Schlageter was 'a wanderer into the void', his struggle for freedom was in the service of German imperialists who would not liberate Germany, but subject it to their yoke. The only true movement of liberation must be directed against both home and foreign capitalism; and Radek spoke of the Communist Party as the leader of this national, popular struggle.

Radek's speech resounded through Germany. There was in it the idea of a combination of Soviet Russia and Germany against Western Powers which lingered on in the minds of many Germans. More significantly, it proposed a broad front within Germany against the foreigner, and seemed to engage the German Communist Party in this wider movement. For Moeller and his like this was both attractive and repellent. Moeller went so far as to reprint Radek's speech in his weekly, *Das Gewissen*, and to write an answer. On the Communist side, a pamphlet was issued in which these two items were published, together with an article by Graf E. Reventlow, another radical nationalist, and further contributions by Radek and P. Froelich, the German Communist leader.[1]

Moeller welcomed Radek's speech and the ensuing public discussion. 'There is no more pressing need', he wrote, 'than that the proletariat should concern itself with the motives of nationalism as

---

[1] Radek's speech and Moeller's answer are printed in *Das Recht der jüngen Völker*, ed. Schwarz, pp. 81–100; re-publication at this time, 1932, indicates how important the question remained right up to Hitler's accession to power. The Communist pamphlet was issued, without date, by *Vereinigung Internationaler Verlags-Anstalten*.

THE THIRD REICH

much as nationalism with the problems of communism.' But Radek, he says, misinterprets German nationalism. It is not fascist, which is 'counter-revolutionary', but is conservative and revolutionary at the same time. There is no revolutionary proletarian tradition in Germany; the workers have been perverted by the *petit-bourgeois* revisionism of Social Democracy and are not prepared for the catastrophes and suffering that a revolution demands. On the other hand, the nationalist tradition in Germany is revolutionary (Moeller thinks of Frederick the Great, the War of Liberation against Napoleon, Bismarck); the workers need to ally themselves with the revolutionary force in nationalism, just as the Bolsheviks needed the Russian peasants. The speeches of Radek indicate a recognition that he is abandoning a doctrinaire class-ideology; but why, on doctrinaire grounds, still refuse in this 'proletarian nation' the alliance of the entrepreneur? Moeller agrees that the parasite, the profiteer, the rentier is no ally; but the entrepreneur is a 'creator of values', his inventiveness and energy are needed. The German entrepreneur is quite different from the capitalist of the West, the 'exploiter'. He proves his national worth by his readiness to struggle, to make sacrifices in the cause. A 'war of defence' against the French imperialists is at present impossible; but if the new spirit of solidarity shown in the Ruhr prospers, who knows what will become possible? The struggle will continue, 'as national as it is bolshevistic'. Radek is, he says, confined too mechanistically in his class-analysis; the synthesis of the two opposites, capitalist and proletarian, lies in the concept and service of the nation.[1]

That Moeller was willing to enter into public argument with Radek was significant in itself; but this fact, and the radicalism of his statements, are characteristic of his whole position. He was not alarmed at a revolution which destroyed 'throne and altar', for he knew that Germany itself could not return to such outworn forms. He was aware of the value of Russia, whatever its social structure, as a possible ally of Germany. He recognised that the Russian Revolution was at least in part 'a revolt against the parasitic society of the West'. Writing in the period of the New Economic Policy, he could persuade himself that the Soviet leaders were less concerned for socialist doctrine than for national strength, and so he could interpret the Soviet system as a National-Socialism peculiarly suited to Russia and admit its theoretical validity—'Every land has its own socialism'.[2] He was ready to tolerate Russian Communism providing the Russian communists recognised that 'German socialism' must be of its own special, national character, on a nationalist not a class

[1] Articles of Jul. 1923 in *Das Gewissen. Das Recht der jungen Völker*, ed. Schwarz, pp. 87–100.
[2] *Das Dritte Reich*, pp. 65–68, 162, 173–4.

basis; that is, providing the German communists abandoned Marxism.

It is easy to be misled by the apparent tolerance of these views. But Moeller was closely associated with men engaged in most violent anti-Bolshevik propaganda, men who were anxious to renew the battles in the East that they had been forced to break off. In an article of 1920 he himself had threatened war if the Russians did not change their attitude.[1] It must be remembered what underlies Moeller's conception of a national German mission. The 'German socialism' of which he writes is not primarily a social form; it is a movement of national expansion, directed essentially towards Eastern Europe, the Russian borderlands, the Near East. The recognition he was ready to offer the Soviet Union was based on his 'metaphysical' principle that the Russian mission was in Asia, and that Russia must condone the German mission. The policy was that of his nationalist friends, and not essentially different from that of Hitler. But it was his particular gift to dress it in a new manner, to present it as something radical, even revolutionary, and thus to make it more palatable to an age which was suspicious of the old nationalist slogans.

This radicalism appears in *Das Dritte Reich* wherever Moeller discusses traditional conservatism. In his chapter entitled 'Reactionary' he attacks the conservative parties precisely because they fail to recognise that pre-war principles are meaningless in modern Germany, and above all because they fail to realise that effective nationalism must be built on the proletariat. They hinder the struggle for a unified people; 'they stand between nation and proletariat'. The reactionary does not see that 'the proletariat is destined to be in the van of the struggle for freedom, to lead it as a social struggle and at the same time as a national struggle'.[2] Everyone is a reactionary who would restore life as it was before 1914, and who thinks in terms of the old monarchy.

In contrast to 'reactionary conservatism' stands 'revolutionary conservatism', to the definition of which Moeller devotes his last chapters, 'Conservatism' and 'The Third Reich'. Its principle is 'conservation', the preservation of the spirit of the past; but it does not preserve outworn forms. Its goal is the nation, whose unique character and mission it feels by instinct. The state changes; the principles of 'throne and altar', which belonged to the old state, must now be done away with. Thus 'nationalism' is the true name for revolutionary conservatism, whose aim is to win all the people for the nation, to make a system in which all 'participate in the national destiny'—earlier in the book Moeller had defined true

[1] Reprinted in *Sozialismus und Aussenpolitik*, ed. Schwarz (1933), pp. 77–84.
[2] *Das Dritte Reich*, p. 185.

democracy as 'participation of a people in the state'.[1] Today this national state must be socialistic, a state rooted in and serving the masses. It must be led 'from above', by the 'consciousness of the nation'. But without a movement 'from below' consciousness cannot come into being.

Moeller never gives very precise indications as to the social organisation and the policy of this new 'national socialistic' state, but what he says is significant in view of the nature of Hitler's Germany. He refers to the principle of leadership in ancient Germanic times, to the authoritarianism of Frederick the Great. The Third Reich will be a hierarchical state, in which all classes have a prescribed function. Moeller proclaims his sympathy with List and Rodbertus and their idea of a nationally directed economy; several times he mentions with approval the Freiherr vom Stein's ideas of a corporative organisation of national life. Above the corporative groupings of particular regional and economic interests will rise the national, political leadership, the representatives of the consciousness of the nation, in whose hands political power will lie. But inner organisation is only important, for Moeller, in view of national foreign policy. The various conflicting interests in the state can be reconciled only if they are absorbed in great tasks of national expansion. In the year 1922 one could not write with great confidence of German expansion; but here we find again the notion of Germany's 'super-national mission', its mission to become Greater Germany, 'the central land' which must carry forward the traditional tasks of Prussia and Austria towards the East.

These suggestions are not left as mere practical political tasks. They are given a metaphysical flavour. Germany is a 'principle' necessary to the world, a principle of growth, a principle of rejuvenation and life; the German is an idealist, a mystic. Thus, as always, Moeller summons to his aid an intoxicating conviction of destiny and mission, of mystical urges and metaphysical purpose; an intoxication which swept Germans into Nazism and its catastrophic adventures. Though his political aims are confined to the establishment of a strong Germany as the nucleus of Central Europe, and though his programme of social organisation is sketched in very general terms, Moeller's proposals would assure to Germany a structure and position of such power that no limits would be put on its further expansion. Vermeil can close his study of Moeller with the reasoned conclusion: 'Ici, point d'affirmations belliqueuses, point de menaces guerrières. Mais où est la différence réelle entre le plan extérieur de Moeller van den Bruck et celui de Mein Kampf?'.[2]

Widely admired as Moeller was in some Nazi circles, the criti-

[1] *Das Dritte Reich*, p. 107.
[2] E. Vermeil, *Doctrinaires de la Révolution allemande* (2nd ed. 1939), p. 173.

cism to which his work was subjected brings out important points of difference between 'revolutionary conservatism' and National-Socialism. In a sharply critical study, a National-Socialist condemns Moeller's scepticism about race, points out the contradictions in his concept of 'young peoples', derides him for having misinterpreted Soviet Communism and having argued with Radek, and condemns him as 'an unpractical ideologue', that is, as a man who failed to understand the methods of mass political struggle.[1] This last point may be considered to be the root of all other differences.

It is most noticeable that Moeller rarely, if ever, broaches the question of what form of political organisation or party is needed to ensure his aims. He writes of 'leadership from above', of the 'national consciousness' which resides in the political *élite*, but never does he indicate how this *élite* is chosen, how it acquires power. He kept apart from parties and confined himself to ideological work directed to intellectuals. In this respect he is far from Nazism. Hitler built his party for actual struggle, in Parliament and on the streets, using any means to smash his rivals and the constitution. Within his Party he constructed the instruments of dictatorial control, the SA and the SS, through which his power was absolute, and could be extended over the whole nation as soon as his party came to office. Moeller's thought does not reach so far.

Similarly, Moeller could not conceive of the function of this new Party in stirring and mobilising the masses. For all his recognition of the decisive importance of the proletariat in modern society, he could not find a way to it. Thus he partly despised, partly feared the reckless demagogy of the racists and National-Socialists. We have seen his ambiguous attitude towards racism and Soviet Russia. Hitler and his henchmen, on the other hand, adopted a fanatical racism and anti-Communism not simply because they believed in them (though belief of this kind contributes to the peculiar power of *Mein Kampf*), but because they needed to rouse fanatical belief and fanatical hatred in the masses. Moeller saw the danger in such fanaticism, for it might infect the leaders themselves and lead Germany into extravagant 'romantic' adventures; but the Nazis needed it in order to release sufficient energy to sweep away the old and prepare the new—and in the dictatorial organisation of their Party and State the leaders held a guarantee that the passions they aroused would not sweep them, too, off their feet. We can see, indeed, that Moeller's idea of social revolution was much more traditionalist than that of the Nazis, and that he believed that effective power would and should remain in the hands of the traditional ruling circles of Germany. How typical his attitude was is evident from the

[1] H. Rödel, *Moeller van den Bruck* (Berlin, 1939).

bewildered impotence of the nationalists, once Hitler had been admitted to a position of power.

If the building of a mass-party, with its authoritarian structure and demagogic propaganda, is a distinctive feature of Nazism (and, above all, the child of Hitler himself), in other respects the ideology of National-Socialism is the offspring of the radical nationalism of which Moeller van den Bruck is the central representative. His conception of an expansionist national policy and of an authoritarian political structure links the older nationalism with that of the Nazis; and his sensitive appreciation of the fundamental importance of the proletarian masses, his grim radicalism in face of the post-1918 situation, make him the particular prophet of National-Socialism. His importance as a precursor lies, however, as much in the mode of thinking with which he supported his political aims. His aim was to inculcate a new *Weltanschauung*; and in this he was successful. He called it 'metaphysical'; it is irrational, full of potent and vague suggestion, slippery and expediential, a perfect instrument for any nationalistic power-group.

In his thinking, all definitions and aims are linked to a universalistic purpose, and thus acquire a powerful emotive appeal. The 'nation' is not merely an actual, definable political entity. It is the very substance and purpose of all history. In being associated with ideas like *Volkstum* it acquires a biological character that enables Moeller to assert that national purpose must be instinctively appreciated, through the 'blood', through a feeling of 'race'. The nation is conceived as a means to *Kultur*; it is not an end in itself, but a means to intangible and mysterious cultural values which evoke the intoxication of dedication and self-sacrifice. It is the instrument of the 'World Spirit', the supreme metaphysical reality. As we have seen, Moeller employs universalistic terms even when his intention is most clearly pragmatic. The appeal of ideas like 'race' and 'young peoples' was so great that he uses them even though he recognises that they have no scientific justification. Political concepts are thus removed from the sphere of rational understanding and criticism and are given a sort of religious sanction; the loss of individual freedom is made good by the exaltation and energy which are engendered in service to an irrational purpose.

Hence, in place of verifiable statements about the past or present, in place of 'history', dogma and prophecy are the characteristics of Moeller's political thought. What he and his fellows consider to be politically desirable is clothed in the garb of Destiny and Mission, which lend an appearance of metaphysical purpose to subjective interests, and which would tear men out of the involved pettiness of daily life into a realm of transcendent value and purpose. In a people so bitterly defeated after such high hopes, so dogged by crisis, so much at the mercy of victors and the world-market, such an appeal could scarcely fail to strike home. And this mysticism was given substance by Moeller's shrewd blows at the actual policy and moral pretensions of his antagonists, within and without Germany, so that it could seem to be as realistic as it was transcendental. The new nationalist, he wrote, should be both a mystic and a sceptic; a combination characteristic of National-Socialism.

Moeller was born into a generation of intellectuals in revolt, the generation that fed on Nietzsche. He remained a votary of 'Faustian' energy, but merged Nietzsche's mystical individualism with a dynamic nationalism. His conservatism looked backward to the old Prussian form of the leadership of an *élite*; his radicalism, particularly after 1918, led him to create the ideology of a new *élite* in a new revolutionised society. Ideas are always for him a means to serve power, to unleash power, and under his guidance Germans began to learn the bliss of a passionate blind adherence to a movement, an *Aufbruch*, in which personal responsibility and rational thought were submerged, and whose direction was determined by uncontrollable leaders. Armin Mohler asks whether nationalists like Moeller van den Bruck were responsible for the 'misuse of themselves' by the Nazis. But was there any 'misuse'? Moeller's thought introduces the mental corruption of National-Socialism, and leads to the very threshold of Hitler's Germany.

8

THE POLITICAL IDEAS OF ADOLF HITLER

Alan Bullock

To spend time discussing Hitler's political ideas at first sight appears perverse. The character of Hitler's leadership, with its emphasis upon irrational and emotional motives in politics, and the character of the Nazi movement, with its insistence upon force and its contempt for ideas, both suggest that it is to Nazi tactics and technique that one should turn for an explanation of their success in securing and maintaining power. Moreover, the unoriginality of Hitler's ideas, borrowed from earlier writers (frequently unconsciously and always without acknowledgement) or simply picked up from the current shibboleths of radical and anti-Semitic talk in Central Europe, has led most students of Nazism either to dismiss them as not worth serious attention or to spend their time in tracing the sources from which they were taken.[1]

There is much force in these arguments. But it is worth recalling that Hitler himself always laid great stress upon what he called the *weltanschaulich* element in Nazism. 'The victory of a party is a change of government. The victory of a *Weltanschauung* is a revolution.'[2] It was in terms of the second that Hitler always described the Nazis' coming to power in 1933, and throughout his speeches it is to this National-Socialist *Weltanschauung* that he persistently refers as the essential characteristic both of the Nazi Party and the Nazi revolution. If it is objected that this Nazi *Weltanschauung* was in fact no more than propaganda, it is fair to reply that, even if this is true, it was propaganda of a distinctive type, and that its success in Germany was such as to place Hitler among the greatest masters of political propaganda in history. In analysing his success as a propagandist it is a mistake to concentrate all our intention on the techniques he employed and to ignore the specific content of the appeal which drew more than a third of the German people to vote for Hitler in a free and contested election. Even as propaganda,

---

[1] cf. such studies as Rohan d'O. Butler, *The Roots of National Socialism, 1783–1933* (London, 1941), and E. Vermeil, *Doctrinaires de la revolution allemande, 1914–38* (Paris, 1938).
[2] Hitler at Munich, 19 Mar. 1934. *The Speeches of Adolf Hitler*, translated and edited by Norman H. Baynes, 2 vols. (Oxford, 1942), p. 211. This edition, which I have used throughout this article, is referred to hereafter as Baynes.

Hitler's ideas would be well worth examination, if only because of the uncanny success they enjoyed.

In fact, however, there is no reason to suppose that Hitler was insincere in the ideas to which he gave expression in *Mein Kampf* and his many speeches. Hitler was, after all, an intellectual, in the double sense that he lived intensely in the world of his own thoughts and that words and ideas were the instruments of his power. In striking contrast to the remarkable opportunism of his political tactics and the variability of his political programme, he showed considerable consistency in adhering to certain ideas and conceptions throughout twenty-five years of political activity. In *Mein Kampf* Hitler wrote: 'When a man has reached his thirtieth year he has still a great deal to learn. That is obvious. But henceforward what he learns will principally be an amplification of his basic ideas.' [1] Broadly speaking, this is true of Hitler himself, and it is with the discovery of these basic ideas that this article is concerned.

Without some such understanding of the ideas that lay behind Nazism, it is impossible to appreciate the extent to which this was not only a movement for the seizure of power, but also a conscious and violent revolt against the values and institutions of Western European tradition, both in its Christian and liberal aspects. This is so clear from every page that Hitler ever wrote and every speech he ever made, that I have preferred not to labour the obvious, but to economise in expressions of indignation and confine myself to expounding Hitler's ideas, expressed as far as possible in his own words. At the same time, I have deliberately excluded references to the sources from which he may have borrowed, or by which he may have been influenced, in order to leave the impression of his own thoughts and assumptions as clear as possible.

The material upon which this account is based is, first, *Mein Kampf*, and second, Hitler's speeches. I have made practically no use of other Nazi writers, in the belief that Hitler's was the authentic view of National-Socialism, enjoying an authority shared by no other leader, and certainly not by such peripheral figures as Rosenberg, Gottfried Feder, Darré, or even Goebbels. The only other source on which I have drawn is Hermann Rauschning's account of certain conversations with Hitler between 1932 and 1934 published in his book, *Hitler Speaks*.[2]

---

[1] *Mein Kampf*, p. 68. Throughout this article all quotations from *Mein Kampf* are taken from the unexpurgated English translation by James Murphy (Hurst & Blackett, London, 1939).

[2] *Hitler's Table Talk* (London, 1953) appeared after this article had been written. It supplies valuable confirmation of the extent to which Hitler's ideas remained unaltered.

I

The basis of Hitler's political beliefs was a crude Darwinism.

'Man has become great through struggle. The first fundamental of any rational *Weltanschauung* is the fact that on earth and in the universe force alone is decisive. Whatever goal man has reached is due to his originality plus his brutality. The basis for all development is the creative urge of the individual, not the vote of majorities. The genius of the individual is decisive, not the spirit of the masses. All life is bound up in three theses: Struggle is the father of all things, virtue lies in blood, leadership is primary and decisive. . . . There will never be a solution of the German problem until we return to the three fundamental principles which control the existence of every nation: The concept of struggle, the purity of blood, and the ingenuity of the individual.' [1]

These three principles provide a key not only to Hitler's own beliefs, but also to what he most disliked in other people's views.

'Unfortunately, the contemporary world stresses internationalism instead of the innate values of race, democracy, and the majority instead of the worth of the great leader. Instead of everlasting struggle the world preaches cowardly pacifism and everlasting peace. These three things are the causes of the downfall of all humanity.' [2]

The easiest way to approach Hitler's political ideas is by the closer examination of each of these three antitheses—struggle *v.* pacifism; race *v.* internationalism; inequality and individuality *v.* democracy.

No word occurs more frequently in Hitler's speeches than 'struggle'.

'What is politics? One of the great men of our nation once said: Politics is struggle.' [3]
'The whole work of Nature is a mighty struggle between strength and weakness—an eternal victory of the strong over the weak. There would be nothing but decay in the whole of Nature if this were not so. States which offend against this elementary law fall into decay.' [4]

---

[1] Hitler at Chemnitz, 2 Apr. 1928, quoted in *Hitler's Words (1923–43)*, edited by Gordon W. Prange (American Council on Public Affairs, Washington, 1944) from the *Völkischer Beobachter*, 7 Apr. 1928, pp. 8–9. This selection of Hitler's speeches is referred to throughout the article as Prange.
[2] Hitler at Essen, 22 Nov. 1926; Prange, p. 4, quoting the *V.B.* for 26 Nov. 1926.
[3] Hitler at Vilsbiburg, 6 Mar. 1927; Prange, p. 4, quoting the *V.B.* for 8 Mar. 1927.
[4] Hitler at Munich, 13 Apr. 1923; Baynes, pp. 45–6, quoting *Adolf Hitlers Reden* (1933 edn.), pp. 43–4.

One of the clearest statements of this view is in a speech which he made at Kulmbach in 1928:

'The idea of struggle is as old as life itself, for life is only preserved because other living things perish through struggle. The two most powerful drives of man, those of hunger and love, presuppose for their satisfaction an unending struggle. In this struggle, the stronger, the more able, win, while the less able, the weak, lose. Struggle is the father of all things. Only through struggle has man raised himself above the animal world. Even today it is not by the principles of humanity that man lives or is able to preserve himself above the animal world, but only by means of the most brutal struggle. As it is with the individual, so it is in the destiny of nations. Only by struggle are the strong able to raise themselves above the weak. And every people that loses out in this eternally shifting struggle has, according to the laws of nature, received its just desert. A *Weltanschauung* that denies the idea of struggle is contrary to nature and will breed a people that is guided by it to destruction. . . . For if you do not fight for life, then life will never be won.' [1]

Struggle is not only the sole condition upon which man preserves his life, it is also the basis of all his achievement. 'Only through struggle has man raised himself *above* the animal world.' Or in the words of *Mein Kampf*: 'Man must realise that a fundamental law of necessity reigns throughout the whole realm of Nature, and that his existence is subject to the law of eternal struggle and strife.' [2] For all man's noblest virtues, the heroic virtues—loyalty, self-sacrifice, endurance, faith—and his greatest achievements in art, the sciences, politics, and economics arise from and are nourished by this unremitting competition. Without this goad, without the difficulties which he is forced to overcome in order to survive, man would sink back to the level of the herd and achieve nothing. 'Man has become great through perpetual struggle.' [3] The corollary is valid too. Humanitarianism, pacifism, non-resistance to evil, the Christian virtues of love and humility are so many disguises for weakness, cowardice, and irresolution. 'In perpetual peace man's greatness must decline.' [4]

It follows from this, obviously, that 'through all the centuries force and power are the determining factors. . . . Only force rules. Force is the first law.' [5] Force, however, is more than the decisive fact in any situation; it is force which also creates right. 'Always before God and the world, the stronger has the right to carry through what he wills. History proves: He who has not the strength—him the "right

---

[1] Hitler at Kulmbach, 5 Feb. 1928; Prange, p. 8, quoting the *V.B.* for 9 Feb. 1928.
[2] *Mein Kampf*, p. 208.
[3] ibid., p. 124.   [4] ibid., p. 124.
[5] Hitler at Essen, 22 Nov. 1926; Prange, p. 4, quoting the *V.B.* for 26 Nov. 1926.

in itself" profits not a whit.' [1] The practical application of such a view is not difficult to see.

'There is no historical injustice where soil is concerned, just as there is no historical injustice in possession. Possession must be gained by work and then it exists by right. Space must be fought for and maintained. People who are lazy have no right to the soil. Soil is for him who tills it and protects it. . . . There is no higher justice that decrees that people must starve. There is only power, which creates justice.' [2]

Where is such power to be found? Hitler's answer not only reflects his own experience, but also shows a brilliant psychological appreciation of the state of mind of many Germans who had lived through the era of the Treaty of Versailles, inflation, reparations, and the economic depression. The lesson to be learned, he answers, is self-reliance. It is no use bemoaning one's fate, looking for help from others, or appealing to man's natural right. 'Justice (*Recht*) lies not without, but within us. It can be in our own strength alone. Only strength is at any time justified in raising claims, never weakness. Only strength can wake justice into life.' [3] This is true not only for the individual, but also for the nation.

'Above us all stands the motto "No one in the world will help us if we do not help ourselves". This programme of self-help is a proud and manly programme. It is a different programme from that of my predecessors who continually ran round, going a-begging now in Versailles, now in Geneva, now in Lausanne or at some conference or other elsewhere.' [4]

'A people must understand that its future lies only in its own capacity, its own industry and its own courage. The world gives no help: a people must help itself.' [5]

This, Hitler argues, is in accord with Divine justice.

'For there can be no miracle—whether it comes from above or from without—which gives to man anything he has not himself earned. Heaven at all times has helped only the man who has exerted himself, who has not built upon the help of others, but has set his confidence on his own strength.' [6]

[1] Hitler at Munich, 13 Apr. 1923; Baynes, p. 45, quoting *Adolf Hitlers Reden* (1933 edn.), pp. 43–4.
[2] Hitler in Berlin, 5 May 1930; Prange, pp. 28–9, quoting the *V.B.* for 7 May 1930.
[3] Hitler to the SA and SS at the *Sportspalast* in Berlin, 8 Apr. 1933; Baynes, p. 178, quoting the *V.B.* for 11 Apr. 1933.
[4] Hitler at the opening of the Winter-Help campaign in Berlin, 5 Oct. 1938; Baynes, p. 1531, quoting the *V.B.* for 7 Oct. 1938.
[5] Hitler at Königsberg, 4 Mar. 1933; Baynes, p. 116, quoting *Dokumente der deutschen Politik*, Vol. I (1935), pp. 14–15.
[6] Hitler to workers on the new motor road at Unterhaching, 21 Mar. 1934; Baynes, pp. 882–3, quoting the *V.B.* for 22 Mar. 1934.

'Build on your own strength; hope not for the help of others; for if you do, you do not deserve it. You must be anchored in yourself, set yourself with steadfast feet on this shifting earth. Only then can you raise yourself to your God and pray Him to support and bless your courage, your work, your endurance, your strength, your resolution, and with these your claim to life in this world.' [1]

II

The insistence upon race, perhaps the most characteristic feature of the Nazi *Weltanschauung*, represents one of Hitler's most deep-seated beliefs. Race, as Hitler uses the word, has little to do with biological science, although he frequently claims scientific authority for what he says. Its real role is that of a myth, as Hitler later admitted in a conversation with Hermann Rauschning which is quoted below. And it is by its power to induce men to act as if it were true, not by the canons of historical criticism, that one should judge Hitler's description of the Aryans in *Mein Kampf*.

'Every manifestation of human culture, every product of art, science and technical skill, which we see before our eyes today, is almost exclusively the product of the Aryan creative power. This very fact fully justifies the conclusion that it was the Aryan alone who founded a superior type of humanity; therefore he represents the archetype of what we understand by the term, MAN. He is the Prometheus of mankind, from whose shining brow the divine spark of genius has at all times flashed forth. . . . If we divided mankind into three categories—founders of culture, bearers of culture, and destroyers of culture—the Aryan alone can be considered as representing the first category. It was he who laid the groundwork and erected the walls of every great structure in human culture.' [2]

According to Hitler's version of history, the Aryans subjugated inferior races (Who, When, Where are questions brushed aside) and treated them virtually as slaves.

'While he ruthlessly maintained his position as their master, the Aryan not only remained master but he also maintained and advanced civilisation. For this depended exclusively on his inborn abilities, and therefore, on his preservation of the Aryan race as such. As soon, however, as his subjects began to rise and approach the level of their conqueror, a phase of which ascension was probably the use of his language, the barriers that had distinguished master from servant broke down. The Aryan neglected to maintain his own racial stock unmixed and therewith

[1] Hitler at Frankfurt, 16 Mar. 1936; Baynes, p. 1310, quoting the *V.B.* for 18 Mar. 1936.
[2] *Mein Kampf*, p. 243.

lost the right to live in the paradise which he himself had created. He became submerged in the racial mixture and gradually lost his cultural creativeness. . . . That is how cultures and empires decline and yield their places to new formations. The adulteration of the blood and the racial deterioration conditioned thereby are the only causes that account for the decline of ancient civilisations. For it is never by war that nations are ruined, but by the loss of their powers of resistance, which are exclusively a characteristic of pure racial blood. In this world everything that is not of sound racial stock is like chaff.' [1]

But who are the Aryans? Although Hitler frequently talked as if he regarded the whole German nation as pure Aryan in stock (whatever that may mean), his real view was rather different. In his eyes only a part of any nation (even the German nation) can be regarded as Aryan. This constitutes an *élite* within the nation (represented by the Nazi Party and, later, especially by the SS) stamping its ideas upon the development of the whole nation, and by its leadership giving to this racial agglomeration an Aryan character which in origin belonged only to a section of the whole. Hitler described the process in a speech at Nuremberg in 1933:

'It is first necessary to understand how a people is built up. Almost all the peoples of the world are composed today of different racial primary elements. . . . The higher race subjects to itself a lower race and thus constitutes a relationship which now embraces races of unequal value. Thus there results the subjection of a number of people under the will often of only a few persons, a subjection based simply on the right of the stronger, a right which, as we see it in Nature, can be regarded as the sole conceivable right because founded on reason. . . . But despite this, in the course of a long development, this compulsion has very often been converted into a blessing for all parties. . . . And thus it is that a great and significant Aryan civilisation did not arise when Aryans alone were living in racial purity, but always when they found a vital association with races otherwise constituted, an association founded not on mixture of blood, but on the basis of an organic community of purpose.' [2]

Thus Hitler's views on race are used to justify both the right of the German people to ride rough-shod over such inferior peoples as the uncouth Slavs and the degenerate French, and the right of the Nazis, representing an *élite* sifted and tested by the struggle for power, to rule over the German people. This explains how it is that Hitler can refer to the Nazi seizure of power in Germany as a *racial* revolution, because it represents the replacement of one ruling caste by

---

[1] *Mein Kampf*, p. 248.
[2] Hitler's closing speech at the Nuremberg *Parteitag*, 3 Sep. 1933; Baynes, pp. 464–6, quoting the *V.B.* for 5 Sep. 1933.

another. This also explains Hitler's argument in his discussion with Otto Strasser in May 1930. Hitler dismissed the idea of a radical socialist movement with working-class support:

'We want to make a selection from the new dominating caste which is not moved, as you are, by any ethic of pity, but is quite clear in its own mind that it has the right to dominate others because it represents a better race; this caste ruthlessly maintains and assures its domination over the masses.' [1]

Later in the same discussion, Hitler said explicitly:

'The German people itself is a conglomerate composed of basic elements of differing races. . . . Although the master-race with its capacity for forming a state may have so fused itself with its subjects as to create a new people, yet the process is not always so complete that a relapse into the original elements can simply be regarded as an impossibility.' [2]

The idea of such a racial *élite* played a big part in Hitler's and Himmler's schemes for the SS, recruitment for which was not limited to those who were Germans. The Aryans of other nations were also eligible. What lay at the back of Hitler's mind is clear from one of the conversations recorded by Hermann Rauschning.

'The conception of the nation has become meaningless [Hitler told Rauschning]. We have to get rid of this false conception and set in its place the conception of race. The new order cannot be conceived in terms of the national boundaries of the peoples with an historic past, but in terms of race that transcend those boundaries. . . . I know perfectly well that in the scientific sense there is no such thing as race, but you, as a farmer, cannot get your breeding successfully achieved without the conception of race. And I as a politician need a conception which enables the order which has hitherto existed on historic bases to be abolished and an entirely new and anti-historic order enforced and given an intellectual basis. . . . And for this purpose the conception of race serves me well. . . . France carried her great revolution beyond her borders with the conception of the nation. With the conception of race, National-Socialism will carry its revolution abroad and re-cast the world.

'Just as the conception of the nation was a revolutionary change for the purely dynastic feudal states, and just as it introduced a biological conception, that of the people, so our own revolution is a further step in the rejection of the historic order and the recognition of purely biological values. And I shall bring into operation throughout all Europe and the whole world this process of selection which we have carried out through National-Socialism in

[1] Hitler's conversation with Otto Strasser on 21 May 1930; Baynes, p. 988, quoting Otto Strasser, *Ministersessel oder Revolution?*, pp. 12–14.
[2] ibid., p. 990.

Germany. . . . The active section in the nations, the militant, Nordic section, will rise again and become the ruling element over these shopkeepers and pacifists, these puritans and speculators and busybodies. This revolution of ours is the exact counterpart of the great French Revolution. . . . There will not be much left then of the clichés of nationalism, and precious little among us Germans. Instead there will be an understanding between the various language elements of the one good ruling race.' [1]

This is Hitler at his most flamboyant, and is not to be taken too literally. Hitler was a master of nationalist appeal, and old-fashioned nationalism was very far from being played out in Europe. His foreign policy was nationalist in character, and nationalism, both that of the occupied countries, and that of the Germans, cut across and wrecked the attempt to turn the Quislings and the SS into an international Nazi *élite*, just as it proved too strong in the end for the Jacobins outside of France in the 1790s.

But inside Germany the idea of a racial *élite* played a considerable role in Hitler's view of the function of the Party and the SS. What amounted to a straightforward claim to unlimited power in the state was wrapped up in the myth of a pure race. Hitler characteristically delighted to give it a Wagnerian colouring. What he wanted to do, so he told Rauschning, was to found an Order, and this he claimed was the true interpretation of Wagner's 'Parsifal', in which the Order of the Knights protected the Holy Grail of pure blood and the King, Amfortas, was suffering from the incurable ailment of corrupted blood.

The essential relationship which Hitler expressed in his use of the word 'race' was inequality.

'The differences between individual races, both externally and in their inner natures, can be enormous and in fact are so. The gulf between the lowest creature which can still be styled man and our highest races is greater than that between the lowest type of man and the highest ape.' [2]

This inequality between races and between individuals is for Hitler another of the iron laws of nature. Upon this, he told the *Industrie klub* at Düsseldorf,[3] is founded the sole right to private property. It is equally the basis of all colonisation and imperialism.

'England did not conquer India by the way of justice and of law: she conquered India without regard to the wishes, to the views of the natives, or to their formulations of justice, and when

[1] Hermann Rauschning, *Hitler Speaks* (London, 1939), pp. 229–30.
[2] Hitler at Nuremberg, 3 Sep. 1933; Baynes, p. 464, quoting the *V.B.* for 5 Sep. 1933.
[3] Hitler at Düsseldorf, 27 Jan. 1932; Baynes, pp. 786–7, quoting from the pamphlet version of the speech published by Eher Verlag (Munich, 1932).

necessary, she has upheld this supremacy with the most brutal ruthlessness. . . . The settlement of the North American continent is just as little the consequence of any claim of superior right in any democratic or international sense; it was the consequence of a consciousness of right which was rooted solely in the conviction of the superiority and therefore of the right of the white race.' [1]

'The white race is destined to rule. This is its unconscious urge which arises from an heroic conception of life. . . . By what right do nations possess colonies? By the right of taking them. . . . After all, what a great statesman said is true, the British Empire was built up by adventurers. Today American professors dispute the justification of this conception, but when the white race abandons the foundations of its rule over the world it will lose that rule.' [2]

The fact that democracy and such international institutions as the League of Nations were founded upon the denial of this view and the assertion of equality between men and nations was sufficient to condemn them in Hitler's eyes.

'There are [he said in his speech at Düsseldorf] two closely related factors which we can time and again trace in periods of national decline: one is that, for the conception of the value of personality, there is substituted a levelling idea of the supremacy of mere numbers—democracy—and the other is the negation of the value of a people, the denial of any difference in the inborn capacity, the achievement of individual peoples. . . . International- ism and democracy are inseparable conceptions. It is but logical that democracy, which within a people denies the special value of the individual . . . should proceed in precisely the same way in the life of peoples and should in that sphere result in internationalism.' [3]

To Hitler, such principles could lead only to the denial and the decay of all those values which make a people great.

III

It will be necessary to return to this insistence upon inequality and individuality later, for there is an apparent contradiction between these and that exaltation of the *Volk* [4] which is the corollary of Hitler's belief in race, and to which as the central point of Hitler's political ideas we must now turn.

[1] Hitler at Düsseldorf, 27 Jan. 1932; Baynes, pp. 792-7, quoting from the pamphlet version of the speech published by Eher Verlag (Munich, 1932).
[2] Hitler, speaking to 6,000 students at Munich, 26 Jan. 1936; Baynes, pp. 1258-9, quoting the *Financial News* of 27 Jan. 1936.
[3] Hitler at Düsseldorf, 27 Jan. 1932; Baynes, p. 783.
[4] The German word *Volk* is usually translated as people or nation, and has been so translated here, but these English equivalents do not convey the suggestion of the primitive, instinctive tribal community of blood and soil—by comparison with such modern and artificial constructions as the state—which Hitler's use of the word carries with it in German.

'In the forefront [Hitler said in 1930] stands a fundamental principle: Men do not exist for the state, but the state exists for men. First and far above all else stands the idea of the *Volk*: the state is a form of organisation of this *Volk*, and the meaning and purpose of the state are through this form of organisation to assure the life of the *Volk*. . . . Today our whole official political outlook is rooted in the view that the state must be maintained because the state is the essential thing; we, on the other hand, maintain that the state in its form has a definite purpose to fulfil and the moment that it fails to fulfil its purpose, the form stands condemned. Above everything stands the purpose to maintain the nation's life—that is the essential thing—and one should speak of a law not for the protection of the state but for the protection of the nation.' [1]

Hitler returned to this idea at Nuremberg in 1935:

'It is a great mistake to suppose that the nation exists to defend any formal institution, and that if an institution is not capable of solving the tasks set for its solution the nation must therefore capitulate before these tasks. On the contrary, that which can be solved by the state will be solved through the state, but any problem which the state through its essential character is unable to solve will be solved by means of the Movement. For the state itself is but one of the forms of the organisation of the *Volk*'s life; it is set in motion and dominated by the immediate expression of the *Volk*'s vital will, the Party. . . . Party, State, Army, Economics, Administration, are all but means to an end, and that end is the safeguarding of the nation.' [2]

Again:

'The meaning and purpose of human organisations as well as of all functions can be measured only by their usefulness for the maintenance of the people as a permanent unity. Therefore the primary thing is the *Volk*. Party, state, army, the economic structure, the administration of justice are of secondary importance, they are but a means to the preservation of the *Volk*. In so far as they fulfil this task they are right and useful. When they prove unequal to this task they are harmful and must either be reformed or set aside or replaced by better means.' [3]

The conclusions which Hitler drew from this premiss were considerable. In the first place, here was the justification in Hitler's eyes for the unscrupulous campaign with which the Nazis and the other *völkisch* groups hoped from the beginning to overthrow the

---

[1] Hitler at Munich, Baynes, pp. 187–8, quoting the *V.B.* for 18 Sep. 1930.
[2] Hitler's *Parteitag* Proclamation, 11 Sep. 1935; Baynes, p. 450, quoting the *Frankfurter Zeitung* for 12 Sep. 1935.
[3] Hitler to the *Reichstag*, 30 Jan. 1937; Baynes, p. 525, quoting *Dokumente der deutschen Politik*, Vol. V, (1938), pp. 32–4.

hated Weimar Republic. It was not they who were committing treason, but the 'November criminals of 1918' and the republican government who had committed treason against the German people. Their loyalty was not to the republican state, but to the *Volk*, for betraying the interests of which men like Erzberger and Rathenau were assassinated.

Secondly, the view expressed by Hitler on the relationship between the state and the *Volk* points to the important role to be played by the Party, which he describes as 'the immediate expression of the people's vital will', setting in motion and dominating the state. It will be best to examine this more fully later when discussing the other functions of the Party.

Thirdly, we are brought up sharply against the characteristic Nazi view of the relationship between the individual and the community, the *Volk*, to which he belongs.

'The National-Socialist state has once more planted in the minds of the German people the thought that there is something higher than the freedom of the individual, that is the freedom of the life of all.' [1]

'So long as each individual sees only himself, he lives his life only in the limited sphere of acting his own personality. It is essential to awaken in each individual the living conviction: Mightier than your own will is the will of all those who now stand here. Through this community, problems will be solved before which you would give up hope. . . . It was necessary to give to the German people that great feeling of community; through it, suddenly out of the weak will of sixty million individuals, there springs a mighty compressed will of all.' [2]

'National-Socialism takes as the starting point of its views, its decisions, neither the individual nor humanity. It puts consciously into the central point of its whole thinking the *Volk*. This *Volk* is for it a blood-conditioned entity in which it sees the God-willed building stone of human society. The individual is transitory, the people is permanent. If the liberal *Weltanschauung* in its deification of the single individual must lead to the destruction of the people, National-Socialism, on the other hand, desires to safe-guard the people as such, if necessary even at the expense of the individual. It is essential that the individual should slowly come to realise that his own ego is unimportant when compared with the existence of the whole people . . . above all, he must realise that the freedom of the mind and will of a nation are to be valued more highly than the individual's freedom of mind and will, and that the higher vital interests of the community as a whole must

[1] Hitler on *Stahlhelm* Day, 23 Sep. 1933; Baynes, p. 555, quoting the *F.Z.* for 24 Sep. 1933.
[2] Hitler in the Berlin *Lustgarten*, on May Day, 1936; Baynes, pp. 261-2, quoting the *F.Z.* for 3 May 1936.

here set limits to the interests of the individual and lay duties upon him.' [1]

In an interview with the *New York Times*, Hitler summed up his view in the phrase: 'The underlying idea is to do away with egoism and to lead people into the sacred collective egoism which is the nation.' [2]

In such subordination of his own will to that of the community the individual must see not frustration, but the satisfaction of his longing for a sense of purpose.

'In a word, that state of things will return, which we Germans perhaps dimly saw before the war, when individuals can once more live with joy in their hearts because life has a meaning and purpose, because the close of life is then not in itself the end, since there will be an endless chain of generations to follow: man will know that what we create will not sink into Orcus, but will pass to his children and to his children's children.' [3]

It is this mystical sense of community which unites the Party and binds it to the people.

'To others it seems a riddle, a mystery—this force that ever unites these hundreds of thousands, that gives them the strength to endure distress, pain, and privation. They can conceive of this only as the result of an order issued by the state. They are wrong! It is not the state which has created us; we fashioned for ourselves our state. For to one we may appear to be a party; to another an organisation; to a third something else, but in truth we are the German people. . . . Even if we must pass away, Germany must remain. Even if Fate should strike us individuals, Germany must live. Even if we have to take upon us distress and care, Germany must exist in spite of cares and distress. So, on this evening let us pledge ourselves at every hour, on every day, only to think of Germany, of *Volk* and *Reich*, of our great nation. Our German *Volk*, *Sieg-Heil*!' [4]

Finally, this setting up, not of the state, but of the *Volk* as a moral absolute overrides all other values.

'The right to criticise [Hitler told the foreign press in 1933] must be recognised as an obligation to truth, and truth can only be found within the framework of the task of maintaining a people's life. Never must criticism be an end in itself.' [5]

[1] Hitler in the Harvest Thanksgiving Celebration on the *Bückeberg*, 7 Oct. 1933; Baynes, pp. 871–2.
[2] Interview with Anne O'Hare McCormick, published in the *New York Times* of 10 Jul. 1933, quoted by Baynes, p. 866.
[3] Hitler at Munich; Baynes, p. 190, quoting the *V.B.* for 18 Sep. 1930.
[4] Hitler to the Party political leaders at the Nuremberg *Parteitag*, 7 Sep. 1934; Baynes, pp. 663–4, quoting the *V.B.* for 9 Sep. 1934.
[5] Hitler addressing foreign press representatives, 6 Apr. 1933; Baynes, p. 500, quoting *Dokumente der deutschen Politik*, Vol. I (1935), pp. 252–5.

The same criterion was applied to justice as to truth.

'The task of the Government is the maintenance of the people, the protection of the race and care for the race; all its other tasks are conditioned by this primary duty. It is only within the framework of this fixed *Weltanschauung* that justice can be, or can be allowed to be, independent.' [1]

In March 1933 Hitler told the *Reichstag*:

'Theoretical equality in the eyes of the law cannot be extended to the toleration on an equal basis of those who scorn the laws on principle. . . . But the Government will accord equality in the eyes of the law to all those who take their stand on the line adopted by our nation and behind the national interests and who do not deny their support to the Government. . . . Our legal institutions must serve above all for the maintenance of this national community. . . . Not the individual, but the nation as a whole alone can be the centre of legislative solicitude.' [2]

As Frick, the Minister of the Interior, summed up: '*Recht* is what benefits the German people, *Unrecht* is that which harms it.' [3] Or, to quote two of Hitler's remarks to Rauschning: 'Justice is a means of ruling. Conscience is a Jewish invention. It is a blemish, like circumcision.' [4]

Not only truth and justice had to be subordinated to the overriding claims of the *Volk* and its preservation, but also economics. 'It is not economics which saves people, but the people must control its economic life.' [5] 'In the sphere of economic life', Hitler told the *Reichstag*, 'all action must be governed by one law: the people does not live for business, and business does not exist for capital, but capital serves business and business serves the people.' [6]

How far such a principle involved a socialist organisation of the national economy was much disputed in the Nazi Party, both before they came to power and for the first year or two afterwards. Hitler's views on this vexed question of private enterprise or the state—as Otto Strasser, Gottfried Feder, and many others discovered—were entirely opportunist. Talking to the German Labour Party Front on May Day, or the *Industrie Klub* in Düsseldorf, Hitler would vary his tune to suit his audience with cynical virtuosity. For Hitler was

---

[1] Hitler at the *Tagung* of German jurists, 3 Oct. 1933; Baynes, p. 523, quoting the *F.Z.* for 5 Oct. 1933.
[2] Hitler to the *Reichstag*, 23 Mar. 1933; Baynes, pp. 522–3, quoting *Dokumente der deutschen Politik*, Vol. I (1935), pp. 28–30.
[3] Frick at the meeting of German jurists, 30 Sep. 1933; Baynes, p. 515.
[4] Hermann Rauschning, *Hitler Speaks* (London, 1939), pp. 201, 220.
[5] Hitler at Schwalenberg in the Lippe-Detmold election campaign of Jan. 1933; Baynes, p. 194, quoting the *V.B.* for 10 Jan. 1933.
[6] Hitler to the *Reichstag*, 23 Mar. 1933; Baynes, p. 830, quoting *Dokumente der deutschen Politik*, Vol. I (1935), pp. 30–2.

not interested in economics, and his ideas on the subject were those of an illiterate.

The reason for this indifference is interesting. Hitler had grasped that the greatest hoax of Marxism (in striking contrast to Communist practice) is to assert the supremacy of economics over politics. Unlike the Communists, who practise, but do not preach, the primacy of politics, Hitler found no embarrassment in preaching as well as practising it. It is indeed a familiar theme both in *Mein Kampf* and in many of his speeches. In *Mein Kampf*, Hitler wrote:

> 'The state in itself has nothing whatsoever to do with any definite economic concept. . . . The state is a racial organism, and not an economic organisation. . . . The history of Prussia shows that it is out of the moral virtues of the people and not from this economic circumstance that a state is formed. . . . Wherever the political power of Germany was specially strong the economic situation also improved. But wherever economic interests alone occupied the foremost place in the life of the people . . . the state collapsed and economic ruin followed readily.' [1]

The same argument—that it was not economics, but power, that was decisive—met with great success in the Germany of 1918–33, suffering both from defeat (with the accompanying sense of national humiliation and loss of power) and from such economic evils as inflation, trade depression, and mass unemployment, with the accompanying sense of helplessness. At the time of the inflation, Hitler declared: 'Economics is a secondary matter. World-history teaches us that no people became great through economics.' [2] He used the French occupation of the Ruhr to drive home the same point:

> 'No economic policy is possible without a sword, no industrialisation without power. Today we have no longer any sword grasped in our fist—how can we have a successful economic policy? . . . Three years ago I declared that the collapse of the German national consciousness must carry with it into the abyss the economic life of Germany as well. For liberation something more is necessary than an economic policy. . . . If a people is to become free it needs pride and will-power, defiance, hate, hate, and once again hate.' [3]

Germany will not solve her problems 'until the German people understands that one can conduct politics only when one has the support of power—and again power. Only so is reconstruction possible. . . . It is not an economic question which now faces the German

---

[1] *Mein Kampf*, pp. 136–8.
[2] Hitler at Munich, 18 Sep. 1922; Baynes, p. 42, quoting *Adolf Hitlers Reden* (1933 edn.), pp. 36–9.
[3] Hitler at Munich, 10 Apr. 1923; Baynes, pp. 43–4, quoting *Reden*, pp. 40–2.

people, it is a political question: how shall the nation's resolution be recovered?' [1]

Nine years later, when the German unemployment figures were rising to more than six million and the whole economic life of the country appeared to be in danger of coming to a standstill, Hitler hammered the same point home before an audience of Rhineland industrialists:

'It was not German business which conquered the world and then came the development of German power, but it was the power-state which created for the business world the conditions for its subsequent prosperity. In my view it is putting the cart before the horse when today people believe that by business methods they can recover Germany's power-position instead of realising that the power-position is also the condition for the improvement of the economic situation.' [2]

'Economic progress can never be separated from political development. Power has ever been the path-finder for economic progress.' [3]

IV

It was one of Hitler's most persistent criticisms of the *bourgeois* Weimar Republic and its middle-class parties that they had neglected these truths and had substituted economic for heroic and racial values. The lack of leadership which Hitler—and not only Hitler— regarded as characteristic of the republican government and its parties 'is due to the fact that in the last century political leadership was more and more entrusted to a class which had arisen from purely economic success'. [4]

'Since economic life has for the most part more un-heroic than heroic features, the German bourgeoisie had very little heroic about it: it was rather "economic". And the bourgeois parties were a true reflection of this cast of soul—associations of hucksters, void of any capacity for a real leadership of the people. . . . And this serves also to explain how it was that a bourgeoisie which was not in the least destined for political leadership sought to transfer to the political sphere the methods and usages of economic life. For with the anonymous share in a limited liability company corresponds the anonymous voting-paper, and with the majority of shareholders the parliamentary coalition.' [5]

[1] Hitler at Munich, 4 May 1923; Baynes, pp. 70–1, quoting *Reden*, pp. 64–7.
[2] Hitler at the *Industrie Klub* in Düsseldorf, 27 Jan. 1932; Baynes, pp. 804–5, quoting the German text published by Eher Verlag (Munich, 1932).
[3] Hitler to the *Generalrat der Wirtschaft* in Berlin, 20 Sep. 1933; Baynes, pp. 869–70, quoting the *F.Z.* for 22 Sep. 1933.
[4] Hitler at the *Führertagung*, held in June, 1933; Baynes, p. 481, quoting the *V.B.* for 19/20 Jun. 1933.
[5] Hitler's closing speech at the Nuremberg *Parteitag*, 3 Sep. 1933; Baynes, p. 472–4, quoting the *V.B.* for 5th Sep. 1933.

Hitler's most constant criticism of democracy is that it breeds irresponsibility. Democratic government in Germany meant coalition government, and coalitions meant party bargaining, intrigue, compromise, and the avoidance of any decisive measures for fear of losing votes. To Hitler the anonymity of many democratic processes—not only the secret ballot, but also the majority decisions of party and government committees—was an offence against the principle of individual responsibility. In *Mein Kampf* he writes:

'Parliament passes some act or decree which may have the most devastating consequences, yet nobody bears the responsibility for it. Nobody can be called to account. For surely one cannot say that a cabinet discharges its responsibility when it retires after having brought about a catastrophe. Or are we to say that the responsibility is fully discharged when a new coalition is formed or parliament dissolved? Can the principle of responsibility mean anything else than the responsibility of a definite person? . . . Must not every genuine leader renounce the idea of degrading himself to the level of a political jobber? Must not our parliamentary principle of government by numerical majority necessarily lead to the destruction of the principle of leadership?' [1]

Hitler's dislike of democracy, however, goes deeper than a criticism of the actual working of parliamentary institutions in Germany and Central Europe. It is rooted in the belief that freedom of thought and expression, indeed all discussion, endanger the unity and strength of a nation. From this springs his hatred of a free press and of all criticism.

'In my eyes criticism in itself is not an important function. The world can live without critics. . . . Men whose sole activity is to express an opinion on the activity of others and to paint it in the darkest colours without ever themselves undertaking any practical responsibility—such men I will not tolerate. . . . In this state there can be no right to carp, but only the right to do the thing better.' [2]

Discussion, far from representing a source of strength, is evil because it is corrosive in its effects, undermining the will to action and unity of purpose.

'It is important that the self-assurance of the leaders in their decisions should arouse in the members of the Party an untroubled confidence. It is conceivable that even wise men, in questions of special difficulty, should not be able to reach complete clarity. But it means a capitulation of all leadership if it hands over pre-

---

[1] *Mein Kampf*, pp. 78–9. cf. the whole of this passage, pp. 75–88, for Hitler's criticisms of the parliamentary system as he saw it working in Vienna before 1914. How far the parliamentary institutions of the Habsburg Empire could be accurately described as democratic is a question with which Hitler does not bother himself.

[2] Hitler at Hamburg, 17 Aug. 1934; Baynes, pp. 509–10, quoting the *F.Z.* for 19 Aug. 1934.

cisely these questions to public discussion and allows the public to state its views.' [1]

'Germany is not a hen-roost where everything is in confusion, and everyone cackles and crows, but we are a people which from its infancy learns to be disciplined.' [2]

The metaphor which dominates all Hitler's political thought is that of an army. He sees the state always as an instrument of power. Whatever conduces to discipline, unity, strength, action is good; whatever threatens to weaken these attributes is evil. It is to the Army, therefore, that he looks for the pattern of political organisation, and here that he finds the origin of the *Führerprinzip*—the leadership principle—upon which the National-Socialist state was to be built up. It was upon this basis that Hitler refounded the Nazi Party after his release from prison at the end of 1924. An explanation of his ideas is to be found in a speech he delivered at Weimar in 1936, in which he discussed the reasons that had led him to take this step.

Hitler began his speech by explaining the character he had given to the *Parteitag* (the first of which had been held at Weimar ten years before).

'We freed the statement of the general lines of our policy and the rendering of an account of the work of the Movement from all corrosive discussion; we freed it, in particular, from any discussion depending on a vote—all this led to an unexampled encouragement of those who took part in these demonstrations. All those comrades who once in the year came from their little towns to attend a *Reichsparteitag* were not filled with the doubts and uncertainties which might have arisen from listening to the objections of an opposition, to discussions and so on; on the contrary, they turned homewards filled with a new, blind trust.'

In addition to the Party's Congress, however, certain special sessions for the discussion of particular issues were held.

'Here too the ruling principle is: Never must a resolution be passed by a majority decision. Never! The official in charge of the special session listens to the various expressions of opinion, and then on his side gives his decision. There is no decision possible for which one man does not assume responsibility. That is the ruling principle of our Movement.'

On another occasion Hitler remarked: 'The question of fallibility or infallibility is not under discussion: the individual has as little

---

[1] Hitler's proclamation to the Nuremberg *Parteitag*, 1 Sep. 1933; Baynes, pp. 505–6, quoting the *F.Z.* for 2 Sep. 1933.
[2] Hitler at the Nuremberg *Parteitag*, 14 Sep. 1935; Baynes, p. 544, quoting the *V.B.* for 15 Sep. 1935.

right to question the action of the political leaders as the soldier to question the orders of his military superiors.'[1]

Once the Nazis came to power, the *Führerprinzip*, originally worked out in the organisation of the Party, was applied, not without much confusion, to the political leadership of the nation. From the state of weakness and dissension which was characteristic of democratic Germany 'we have to learn our lesson: one will must dominate us, we must form a single unity; our discipline must weld us together; one obedience, one subordination must fill us all, for above us stands the nation'.[2] 'Our constitution', wrote Nazi Germany's leading lawyer, 'is the will of the *Führer*.'[3] No rational justification of this is provided either by Hitler himself or by other Nazi writers. It is simply stated in the baldest terms that the *Führer* is the incarnation of the unity of the *Volk*, and that he is 'responsible' solely to the German people, without any suggestion of how this assertion is to be tested or the responsibility enforced. As Professor Baynes says in his edition of Hitler's *Speeches*:

'The essential link which in the National-Socialist theory of the state unites the people with the *Führer* is a mystical conception. The people on a basis of common blood creates a community and as such possesses a spirit—a *Volksgeist*—which is rooted in national history and national character. That spirit of the people may indeed be falsified and misled; it remains however anchored in the subconsciousness of the people until the time when a Leader arises who is profoundly inspired by a realisation of the uncorrupted *Volksgeist* which he can then evoke once more from the people's subconsciousness; by this power of evocation he demonstrates his autonomous immediate title to Leadership. . . . He is no representative to whom the people has given a mandate; he is the incarnation of the Spirit of the People, and it is only through his interpretation that the People is led to a full realisation of itself.'[4]

This is a faithful summary not of Nazi propaganda, but of sober constitutional and legal opinion as it was expressed in the standard text-books of the Third Reich. That it was not just a piece of sublime mysticism and nonsense (as Castlereagh described the Holy Alliance) is demonstrated by the sort of claim Hitler was able to make as early as July 1934, when, after the purge of Roehm and the other SA leaders, he declared:

'If anybody reproaches me and asks why I did not resort to the regular courts of justice for conviction of the offenders, then all

---

[1] Hitler at the Nuremberg *Parteitag*, 16 Sep. 1935; Baynes, p. 447, quoting the *V.B.* for 18 Sep. 1935.

[2] Hitler to the *Hitler-Jugend* at Nuremberg, 2 Sep. 1933; Baynes, p. 538, quoting the *V.B.* for 5 Sep. 1933.

[3] Dr Hans Frank in the *V.B.* for 20 May 1936.

[4] Baynes, op. cit., p. 414.

that I can say to him is this: in this hour I was responsible for the fate of the German people, and thereby I became the Supreme Justiciar (*oberster Gerichtsherr*) of the German people.'[1]

Hitler's justification of his own autocratic power is always phrased in terms of this same mystical sense of mission, yet he is always careful to claim that it is rooted in the people. Speaking to the *Reichstag* at the end of his first year of office, Hitler told them:

'Since that historic hour, I have never for a moment regarded the task that became mine otherwise than as a commission entrusted to me by the whole of the German people, even if millions, whether consciously or unconsciously, were not then clear about this fact or if they did not wish to accept it as the truth.'[2]

Two years later, in the election campaign which followed the denunciation of the Locarno Pact and the reoccupation of the Rhineland, Hitler declared that this election would show that

'in Germany bayonets do not terrorise a people, but that here a government is supported by the confidence of the entire people. I care for the people. In fifteen years I have slowly worked my way up together with this Movement. I have not been imposed by anyone upon this people. For the people I have grown up, in the people I have remained, to the people I return. My pride is that I know no statesman in the world who with greater right than I can say that he is the representative of his people.'[3]

Here was something that distinguished the Third Reich from the old Imperial Germany: 'Then the leaders had no roots in the people: it was a class state.'[4] Such statements may be taken for what they are worth, yet it is obvious that Hitler felt—not without justification —that his power, despite the Gestapo and the concentration camps, was founded upon popular support to a degree which few people cared, or still care, to admit.

The *Führerprinzip*, of course, fitted in perfectly with Hitler's view of history. 'All human civilisation', he wrote in *Mein Kampf*, 'has resulted exclusively from the creative activity of the individual.'[5]

'World history, like all events of historical significance, is the result of the activity of single individuals, it is not the fruit of majority decisions.'[6]

---

[1] Hitler to the *Reichstag*, 13 Jul. 1934; Baynes, p. 321, quoting the *F.Z.* for 15 Jul. 1934.
[2] Hitler to the *Reichstag*, 30 Jan. 1934; Baynes, p. 425, quoting the authorised English translation.
[3] Hitler at Hamburg, 20 Mar. 1936; Baynes, pp. 1312–13, quoting the *V.B.* for 22 Mar. 1936.
[4] Hitler at Munich, 8 Nov. 1944; Prange, p. 117, quoting the B.B.C. Monitoring Report.
[5] *Mein Kampf*, p. 373.
[6] Hitler at the *Reichsparteitag* of 1926; Baynes, p. 196, quoting the Nazi periodica *Wille und Macht*, V, 1937, Heft 17.

'I see two diametrically opposed principles: the principle of democracy which is the principle of destruction; and the principle of the authority of the personality which I would call the principle of achievement, because whatever man has achieved in the past— all human civilisations—is conceivable only if the supremacy of this principle is admitted.' [1]

Hitler sometimes broadens this theme into what he calls the aristocratic principle: world history is made by minorities and *élites*. There is no contradiction, however, between this view of the creative role of minorities and the principle of personality, since both are illustrations of the same law of inequality. Nor is there any contradiction between either and the exaltation of the *Volk*, that 'sacred collective egoism' of the nation to which the egoism of the individual must be sacrificed. For the *Volk* is founded upon a racial, not a democratic, basis, and the inequality not only of peoples, but of individuals and groups within each *Volk*, is the fundamental law of race.

'If we admit the significance of blood [Hitler says in *Mein Kampf*] if we recognise the race as the fundamental element on which all life is based, we shall have to apply to the individual the logical consequences of this principle. In general, I must estimate the worth of nations differently, on the basis of the different races from which they spring, and I must also differentiate in estimating the worth of the individual within his own race. . . . The first consequence of this fact is comparatively simple. It demands that those elements within the folk-community which show the best racial qualities ought to be encouraged more than the others and especially they should be encouraged to increase and multiply. . . . A *Weltanschauung* which repudiates the democratic principle of the rule of the masses and aims at giving this world to the best, the highest quality of mankind, must also apply that same aristocratic postulate to the individuals within the folk-community. It must take care that the positions of leadership are given to the best men.' [2]

V

It is here that the role of the Nazi Party, as the corollary of the *Führerprinzip*, fits into place. It is the primary function of the Party to recruit this *élite* and provide the leadership of the state. Party is a misleading word to describe such a function, and Hitler himself rightly insisted that the Nazis were not a party in the ordinary sense of the word, any more than the Communists are. For this reason he often refers to the Party as a Movement (*Bewegung*).

[1] Hitler to the *Industrie Klub* at Düsseldorf, 27 Jan. 1932; Baynes, p. 790.
[2] *Mein Kampf*, pp. 369-70.

'The National-Socialist Party must secure in the political leadership of the nation that selection which takes place in nearly all spheres of life. . . . With the German Army as its model, the Party must see as its task the collection and advancement in its organisation of those elements in the nation which are most capable of political leadership.' [1]

'The Party will for all time form the picked body of the leaders of the German people. It will develop a state of political apostles and combatants who then as obedient officers, true to their duty, will serve the Movement. . . . In it there will develop a tradition in the art of leading a people. . . . It will be in its teaching unalterable, in its organisation hard as steel, in its tactics supple and adaptable, in its whole appearance it will resemble an Order.' [2]

In Hitler's view it was useless to look to the German middle classes for such leadership. Both under the Empire and under the Republic they had shown their incapacity for leading the nation; their talents were economic not political, their values materialistic, not heroic. 'The stratum of society which claimed for itself the leadership has failed us in every hour of crisis, and in the nation's hour of supreme difficulty it collapsed miserably.' [3] Like all revolutionary movements National-Socialism proposed a new *carrière ouverte aux talents*, a new leadership drawn from all classes.

'The fundamental conception of this work was to break with all traditional privileges, and in all spheres of life and in especial in the political sphere to place the leadership of the nation in the hands of hand-picked men, who should be sought and found without regard to descent, to birth, or to social or religious associations —men chosen solely on the basis of their personal gifts and of their character.' [4]

The fourteen years of the Party's struggle for power served as a valuable process of natural selection.

'In these years, just as a magnet draws to itself the steel splinters so did our Movement gather together from all classes and callings and walks of life the forces in the German people which can form and also maintain states. Once more it was proved that one may well be able to control a great business—yet be incapable of leading even a group of eight men. And on the other hand it was shown that from peasants' rooms and workmen's huts came the born leaders.' [5]

[1] Hitler at the Nuremberg *Parteitag*, 16 Sep. 1935; Baynes, p. 442, quoting the *V.B.* for 18 Sep. 1935.

[2] Hitler at the Nuremberg *Parteitag*, 10 Sep. 1934; Baynes, p. 625, quoting the *F.Z.* for 12 Sep. 1934.

[3] Hitler at the First Congress of German Workers, 10 May 1933; Baynes, p. 853, quoting *Dokumente der deutschen Politik*, Vol. I (1935), pp. 154–69.

[4] Hitler's Proclamation to the Nuremberg *Parteitag*, 7 Sep. 1937; Baynes, pp. 684–5, quoting the *V.B.* for 8 Sep. 1937.

[5] Hitler at the Nuremberg *Parteitag*, 3 Sep. 1933; Baynes, pp. 477–8, quoting the *V.B.* for 5 Sep. 1933.

In this way the Party, even before coming to power, had created the cadres of leadership which could take over the state. Once in power, the Party remained the guarantee of the National-Socialist character of the state and of its racial foundations. 'Our Government is supported by two organisations: politically by the community of the *Volk* organised in the National-Socialist Movement, and in the military sphere by the army.'[1] These are 'the two pillars in the state: the undying National-Socialist Party sustaining the political life of the state and the German Army'.[2]

> 'From this sure foundation there will grow up the constitution of the new German Reich. The Party as *weltanschaulich* moulder and as political guide of the destiny of Germany has to give the Leader to the nation and therefore to the Reich. . . . The Army as the representative and organiser of the military forces of our people must ever maintain the organised military force of the Reich entrusted to it and in loyalty and obedience must place it at the disposal of the Leader who has been given to the nation by the Party.'[3]

In his Proclamation to the Nuremberg *Parteitag* in 1935, Hitler made it clear that whenever the state failed to safeguard the interests of the *Volk*, the Party was a power always held in reserve.

> 'It is a great mistake to suppose . . . that if an institution is not capable of solving the tasks set for its solution, the nation must therefore capitulate before these tasks. On the contrary, that which can be solved by the state will be solved through the state, but any problem which the state through its essential character is unable to solve, will be solved by means of the Movement. For the state itself is but one of the forms of the organisation of the People's life; it is set in motion and dominated by the immediate expression of the People's vital will, the Party, the National-Socialist Movement.'[4]

Apart from this primary role of providing the leadership for the Nazi state and guaranteeing its particular character, the Party had two other functions to perform, both logically derived from the first. One was to serve as the link between the *Führer* and the *Volk*. In the speech at Weimar, already quoted, in which he explained the *Führerprinzip*, Hitler ended by an unexpected denial of the charge of dictatorship:

---

[1] Hitler at Hamburg, 17 Aug. 1934; Baynes, pp. 556, quoting the *Berliner Tageblatt* for 19 Aug. 1934.
[2] Hitler at Stettin, 12 Jun. 1938; Baynes, p. 451, quoting the *F.Z.* for 14 Jun. 1938.
[3] Hitler at the Nuremberg *Parteitag*, 16 Sep. 1938; Baynes, pp. 447–8, quoting the *V.B.* for 18 Sep. 1935.
[4] Hitler's proclamation to the Nuremberg *Parteitag*, 11 Sep. 1935; Baynes, p. 450, quoting the *F.Z.* for 12 Sep. 1935.

'But still it may be objected: "Anyhow that is after all a government without a people". No! That would be so if any individual man should have the presumption to put himself at the head of the nation and to declare: "I rule". Then one could justifiably say: "Why do you rule? and by what right? Anybody could come and make the same declaration." No! The Party stands as a living organism of the people behind this leadership. The Party is the people. . . . In it are concentrated all those who from amongst the people are naturally qualified for political life, all those who in any way have the inner conviction that they must perforce devote themselves to politics. . . . The Party as an organisation of picked men thus fulfils all the conditions necessary for a government closely bound up with the people, for the whole personnel which determines the action of the state and of the Reich runs from base to summit through this Movement. . . . If ever it could be maintained of a Movement that it was not built on a single personality, then that is true of our Movement.' [1]

Once again, the characteristic ambiguity in Hitler's use of the word *Volk*, or people, is noticeable. Sometimes he uses it to refer to the whole German nation without distinction, at other times he limits it to the *élite* who by virtue of their 'racial' superiority represent the true '*völkisch*' element in the nation.

The second of the additional functions to be performed by the Party was that of educating the people in the Nazi *Weltanschauung*. 'Revolutions in the past', Hitler said in 1933, 'have with very few exceptions failed because their leaders have not realised that the essential thing is not the assumption of power, but the education of men.' [2]

'The political party must not be content merely to exist as the body which supplies the nation with its political leadership; it must further continuously educate the people in the spirit of its own military conception of its mission and draft into its ranks those who are destined by Providence for leadership.' [3]

Education is one word for what Hitler had in mind: others are compulsion, conscription, the full-time claims of a totalitarian state and a totalitarian party demanding the sacrifice of all individual liberty and privacy to the 'sacred collective egoism' of the nation. How it was done mattered little: the aim 'was to stamp upon Germany the new *Weltanschauung* so durably that it would become the element of cohesion in the German people'. [4]

[1] Hitler at Weimar, 3 Jul. 1936; Baynes, pp. 203-4, quoting the *F.Z.* for 5 Jul. 1936.
[2] Hitler at Reichenhall, 1 Jul. 1933; Baynes, p. 483, quoting the *V.B.* for 3 Jul. 1933.
[3] Hitler at the Nuremberg *Parteitag*, 16 Sep. 1935; Baynes, p. 443, quoting the *V.B.* for 18 Sep. 1935.
[4] Hitler at Godesberg, 19 Aug. 1933; Baynes, p. 485, quoting the *V.B.* for 22 Aug. 1933.

N

It follows from all this that there is room in the state for only one party, and in fact it was made an offence to attempt to organise any other party in Germany after 14 July 1933. Toleration of other points of view was, on Hitler's reasoning, not only unnecessary, but dangerous.

'National-Socialism as a *Weltanschauung* is bound, if it will not betray itself, to be intolerant, that means to champion or maintain the rightness of its views and of its decisions in all circumstances. . . . When a nation is already bewildered by the fact that it is composed of elements which are not completely homogeneous, it is only the harshest principles and an iron resolution which can unite it into a single body capable of resistance—and thereby able to be led successfully in politics.' [1]

VI

'The main plank in the National Socialist programme', Hitler declared in 1937, 'is to abolish the liberalistic concept of the individual and the Marxist concept of humanity and to substitute for them the *Volk* community, rooted in the soil and bound together by the bond of its common blood.' [2] While Hitler's attitude towards liberalism was one of contempt, towards Marxism he showed an implacable hostility. The difference is significant. Liberalism he no longer regarded as a serious threat; its values had lost their attraction in the age of mass-politics, especially in Germany, where liberalism had never taken deep roots. Marxism, however, whether represented by revisionist Social-Democracy or revolutionary Communism, was a rival *Weltanschauung* able to exert a powerful attractive force over the masses comparable with that of Nazism. Ignoring the profound differences between Communism and Social Democracy in practice and the bitter hostility between the rival working-class parties, he saw in their common ideology the embodiment of all that he detested—mass democracy and a levelling egalitarianism as opposed to the authoritarian state and the aristocratic rule of an *élite*; equality and friendship among peoples as opposed to racial inequality and the domination of the strong; class solidarity *v.* national unity; internationalism *v.* nationalism.

With Marxism there could be no compromise.

'The chalk-line which *Weltanschauungungen* have drawn for peoples in the history of the world already more than once has proved to be the death-line. . . . I beg you not to think when a people has once come under the sway of these conflicts of *Weltanschauungen* that one

[1] Hitler at the Nuremberg *Parteitag*, 16 Sep. 1935; Baynes, p. 445, quoting the *V.B.* for 18 Sep. 1935.
[2] Hitler to the *Reichstag*, 30 Jan. 1937; Prange, p. 80, quoting the *V.B.* for 31 Jan. 1937.

can circumvent them. . . . It is quite conceivable to turn Germany into a Bolshevik state—it would be a catastrophe, but it is conceivable. It is also conceivable to build Germany up as a national state. But it is inconceivable that one should create a strong and sound Germany if fifty per cent of its citizens are Bolshevist and fifty per cent nationally-minded. From the solution of this problem we cannot escape. . . . Marxism itself as conception and idea knows no German nation, knows no national state, but knows only the International. . . . Unless Germany can master this internal division in *Weltanschauungen*, no measures of the legislature can stop the decline of the German nation. . . . When people cast in our teeth our intolerance, we proudly acknowledge it—yes, we have formed the inexorable decision to destroy Marxism in Germany down to its very last root.' [1]

This was said in 1932, at a time when Hitler saw in the unbroken organisation of the Social Democratic Party and the trade unions the most solid obstacle to his ambitions, and in the German Communist Party rival extremists, the only other German party whose votes mounted with his own.

Hitler regarded the Marxist conception of the class war and of class solidarity cutting across frontiers as a particular threat to his own exaltation of national unity founded on the community of the *Volk*.

'The splitting up of the nation into groups with irreconcileable views, systematically brought about by the false doctrines of Marxism, means the destruction of the basis of a possible communal life. The disintegration attacks all the foundations of social order. The completely irreconcileable views of the terms state, sovereignty, morals, family and economy gives rise to differences that lead to internecine war.'

By contrast, 'It is only the creation of a real national community, rising above the interests and differences of rank and class, that can permanently remove the source of nourishment of these aberrations.' [2]

The object of National-Socialist policy was to create a truly classless society.

'The slogan: "The dictatorship of the bourgeoisie must make way for the dictatorship of the proletariat ", is simply a question of a change from the dictatorship of one class to that of another, while we wish for the dictatorship of the nation, that is, the dictatorship of the whole community. We do not regard any one

[1] Hitler to the *Industrie Klub* at Düsseldorf, 27 Jan. 1932; Baynes, pp. 825, 809–10, 813, 823.
[2] Hitler to the *Reichstag*, 23 Mar. 1933; Baynes, p. 264, quoting *Dokumente der deutschen Politik*, Vol. I (1935), pp. 25–6.

class as being of paramount importance; such distinctions disappear during the course of centuries, they come and go. What remains is the substance, a substance of flesh and blood, our nation. That is what is permanent, and to that alone should we feel ourselves responsible. . . . Only then shall we be able to restore to the millions of our people the conviction that the state does not represent the interest of a single group or class, and that the government is there to manage the concerns of the entire community.' [1]

This single-minded concept of the national interest was to be embodied in, and guaranteed by, the absolutism of the state, as it had been in the time of Frederick the Great and in the Prussian tradition of the state glorified by Hegel.

Long ago in Vienna, however, Hitler had 'discovered the relations existing between the destructive teaching of Marxism and the specific character of a people, who up to that time had been almost unknown to me. Knowledge of the Jews is the only key whereby one may understand the inner nature and the real aims of Social Democracy.' [2]

For Hitler, the Jew was a mythical figure, evil incarnate, the figure into which he projected all that he hated and feared. Like all obsessions, it was not a partial but a total explanation. The Jew is everywhere, he is responsible for everything. An interesting example of this is to be found in an early speech of 1922.

'The master stroke of the Jew was to claim the leadership of the fourth estate; he founded the Movement both of the Social Democrats and of the Communists. His policy was two-fold and he had his apostles in both camps. Amongst the parties of the Right he encouraged those features which were most repugnant to the people—the passion for money, unscrupulous methods in trade which were employed so ruthlessly as to give rise to the proverb: "Business, too, marches over corpses." And the Jew attacked the parties of the Right through the blood of their members. It was from the Jews that the upper classes took their wives. The result was that in a short time it was precisely the ruling class which became in its attitude completely estranged from its own people.

'And this fact gave the Jew his opportunity with the parties of the Left. Here he played the part of the common demagogue. . . . And one can see constantly how wonderfully the stock exchange Jew and the leader of the workers cooperate. They both pursue one common policy and one single aim. Moses Kohn on the one side encourages his association to resist the workers' demands, while his brother Isaac in the factory incites the masses. . . . The stock exchange organ seeks without intermission to encourage

[1] Hitler to the Labour Front, in Berlin, 10 May 1933, Baynes, p. 455, quoting the *Deutsche Allgemeine Zeitung* for 12 May, 1933.
[2] *Mein Kampf*, p. 55.

fevered speculation and unparalleled "corners" in grain and the people's food, while the workman's newspaper lets off all its guns on the masses, telling them that bread is dearer and this, that and the other is dearer: Up Proletarians, endure it no longer!

'This process means the utter destruction not only of economic life, but of the people. . . . The backbone of its independence, its own national economic life is to be destroyed, that it may the more surely relapse into the golden fetters of the interest slavery of the Jewish race.' [1]

Hitler's anti-Semitism is the master-idea which embraces the whole span of his thought. In whatever direction one follows Hitler's train of thought, sooner or later one encounters the satanic figure of the Jew. Democracy is Jewish—the secret domination of the Jew. Bolshevism and Social-Democracy, capitalism and the 'interest-slavery' of the moneylender; parliamentarianism and the freedom of the press; liberalism and internationalism; anti-militarism and the class war; modernism in art ('*Kultur-Bolschevismus*'), prostitution and miscegenation—all are instruments devised by the Jew to subdue the Aryan peoples to his rule. One of Hitler's favourite phrases, which he claimed to have taken from Mommsen, was: 'The Jew is the ferment of decomposition in peoples'. This points to the fundamental fact about the Jew in Hitler's eyes: unlike the Aryan, the Jew is incapable of founding a state, and so incapable of anything creative. He can only imitate and steal—or destroy in the spirit of envy.

'The Jew has never founded any civilisation, though he has destroyed hundreds. He possesses nothing of his own creation to which he can point. Everything he has is stolen. Foreign peoples, foreign workmen build him his temples; it is foreigners who shed their blood for him. He has no art of his own; bit by bit he has stolen it all from other peoples. He does not even know how to preserve the precious things others have created. . . . In the last resort it was the Aryan alone who could form states and set them on their path to future greatness. All this the Jew cannot do. And because he cannot do it, therefore all his revolutions must be international. They must spread as a pestilence spreads. Already he has destroyed Russia; now it is the turn of Germany and with his envious instinct for destruction he seeks to disintegrate the national spirit of the Germans and to pollute their blood.' [2]

One could pursue this theme for a long time and illustrate it with a thousand quotations. But here clearly one passes out of the realm of rational ideas into that of the mythological and the fantastic, never far below the surface in Hitler's thought. So we come back to the same point from which we began—race and blood, struggle and

---

[1] Hitler at Munich, 28 Jul. 1922; Baynes, pp. 26–9, quoting *Adolf Hitlers Reden*, pp. 21–36.
[2] Speech at Munich, 28 Jul. 1922; Baynes, pp. 21–41.

domination, the Aryan *v.* the Jew, the *Herrenmenschen* v. the *Untermenschen*. It is a crude and ugly picture of the world, but it is one which—as the history of the past quarter-century shows—has more attraction than we like to admit, 'so much less', as Mill pointed out, 'do the majority of mankind prefer liberty than power'.

PART TWO

9

THE HISTORICAL FOUNDATIONS OF THE
RISE OF NATIONAL-SOCIALISM[1]
Gerhard Ritter

THE Germans themselves were more surprised than anyone else by
the rapid rise of the National-Socialist Party to a position in which
overall power in the state was at its disposal. Up to 1930 the vast
majority of educated Germans thought Hitler's disciples to be a
group of loud-mouthed extremists and super-patriots without any
practical importance. The theatricality of their processions and
meetings, the strangeness of their uniforms and of their bright red
banners might awaken the curiosity of a tasteless crowd or seduce
the more vulgar lower-middle-class members of the large towns; but
it all seemed absurd to educated people, who were horrified by the
brutality of the Brown Shirts, by the disturbances which they made at
meetings, and by their nocturnal thuggery in the streets.

The November 1923 *putsch* was generally considered to be a
typical Munich disturbance; in spite of its gory consequences, it
seemed a scene from light opera, much the same as the popular insurrection (*Volksaufstand*) in Munich in 1848, which took place to
drive out Lola Montez, the King's mistress. From his behaviour
Hitler seemed to know nothing about life and to be scarcely less
eccentric than Kurt Eisner, the bearded revolutionary who proposed
a sort of bolshevist republic in Bavaria in 1919. General Ludendorff's participation in the theatrical march on the *Feldherrnhalle* injured his political authority much more seriously than his political
oversights in 1918 (or even than the failure of his strategy, since no
one was prepared to admit that it had been a failure). After this
he was regarded as a man who had had his day (*erledigt*); indeed,

---

[1] This essay does not claim to provide a solution to the problem, either more or
less complete, from the historical point of view. It should be regarded merely as a
contribution to the discussion—hence its form. The moment for a definitive
historical study of the question has not yet, in the opinion of the author, arrived.
I am forced to add the remark that in the time between this essay's composition
(1950) and its publication many new sources have come to light and that my own
research work in this time has altered my views to a certain degree. See also my
essays: 'Le origini storiche del nazional-socialismo' in *Questioni di Storia Contem-
poranea*, Vol. III, p. 2 (Milan, 1953), and 'Vom Ursprung des Einparteienstaates in
Europa' in *Historisches Jahrbuch* (1954). A more detailed discussion of the problem
is given in my book *Carl Goerdeler und die deutsche Widerstands-bewegung*.

many people wondered if he was quite sane, and their wonderings were doubtless encouraged by his association with the racialist (*völkisch*) absurdities of his wife Mathilde in the review 'The Holy Source of German Strength' (*Am heiligen Quell deutscher Kraft*).

After 1923 the Hitlerian movement, too, seemed to have had its day (*erledigt*). At the elections to the fourth *Reichstag* of the Republic in 1928 it gained only 2·6 per cent of the total votes; there were only twelve National-Socialist deputies out of a total of 491. No one would have thought the sudden increase to 18·3 per cent in the September 1930 elections possible—and no one thought so less than the Brüning Government when it pronounced the dissolution of the fourth *Reichstag* a short time earlier.

It was only from this time on that Hitler's movement was taken seriously.

National-Socialist books began to be read widely, although at first their impact was mainly negative. Rosenberg's *Mythus der 20 Jahrhunderts* was not well received and was thought to be the pedantic, muddled, and indeed grotesque work of an amateur in the philosophy of history; later Hitler himself admitted that he had always found it boring and had never read the whole work; the first edition, he was assured, did not sell very well, and its success was the result of the Catholic Church's attacks on it.[1] Hitler's own book, *Mein Kampf*, scared people by its brutality and by the fanaticism of its racial doctrines; I can remember many people, even those who were impressed by Hitler's political successes, saying that they were quite alarmed at it.

Political successes have always an extremely powerful propaganda effect. The speed and unexpectedness of the rise of the National-Socialists were very suggestive, and the masses began to be drawn towards the Party; educated people began, at least, to discuss with animation the causes of this phenomenon.

Some thought it a merely temporary success brought about by the grave economic crisis with its six million unemployed. They could not believe that these eccentric politicians could ever become important in the affairs of the German state. If the National-Socialists ever did come to power for a time, it would not be to stay; the hollowness of their nationalist phraseology and their amateurish approach to their so-called culture would soon be clear to all. Even in 1932 the anecdote about President Hindenburg's remark on first seeing Hitler, 'This man would never be able to have a higher position than Minister for the Posts', was still going around. In this

[1] *Hitler's Table Talk* (London, 1953), No. 190. In *Hitler and I* (London, 1941), p. 107, Otto Strasser reports that Hitler had completely different views on the subject.

way the phenomenon was belittled, its importance ignored, and the will to resist weakened.

Others thought that to prevent this opposition movement from doing any harm it should be approached in the normal way of the parliamentary state, and given public responsibility through participation in government business. The parties of the right, and, in the summer of 1932, certain members of the centre, tried to group the less radical parties together with the Nazis in such a way as to make their control of the cabinet certain, as a safeguard against Hitler. By this means they thought that it would be possible to weave a web of parliamentary and political threads in which Hitler, the bogeyman, would be caught—an idea which deceived men like Schleicher, Papen, Hugenberg, Schacht, and indeed also Hindenburg, to Germany's cost.[1]

Other sections of public opinion, including intellectuals, were seduced by the new, young, contemporary, and optimistic aspects of the popular movement inspired by Hitler's great energy. This was true above all of the independent minds who liked intellectual audacity and despised banal and traditional ideas. In April 1933 one of them told me (to my horror) that even the commonplaces set forth by this popular orator seemed to become words of genius. We must risk all, they said, in order to get rid of the paralysing triviality of parliamentary debates; we must support this Party, which will achieve so much because there are no really wise men in its ranks, because only thus can we become influential and help to control its headlong rush, harness its destructive power, and divert its energy towards healthy constructive ends.

All agreed, however, that the actual Hitlerian movement was not yet ripe, and that it must be regarded as the result of the effervescence of troubled times—all agreed not to take its leaders and its programme quite seriously. Even after the seizure of power on 30th January 1933 it was thought that the new régime could not last long. Many Germans were unwilling to believe that so civilised a people would let themselves be governed for long by such 'barbarian' and eccentric men, or that they would bear with Adolf Hitler's dictatorship for more than a short time.

It was a fact, however, that there were dictatorships and one-party-states elsewhere in Europe, a worrying symptom of a transformed age, one might think. In nearby Russia the bolshevist 'dictatorship of the proletariat' had been in force for over fifteen years, and there were as yet no signs of internal dissolution. But

---

[1] See *Hitler's Table Talk*, No. 225. Also H. Schacht, *Abrechnung mit Hitler* (1948), published by Rowohlt; the depositions of Schacht, Papen, and Meissner before the Nuremberg tribunal. Papen, *Der Wahrheit eine Gasse* (1952); O. Meissner, *Staatssekretär unter Ebert, Hindenburg, Hitler* (1950); H. R. Berndorff, *General zwischen Ost und West* (Schleicher) (1951).

Russians (many Germans thought) had always been more or less slaves of the state, and they were, anyhow, a nation of mystical dreamers whose religion was the patient subjection described by Dostoievsky and Tolstoy—'one should not resist evil'.

The Italians had been living under the orders of their Mussolini for eleven years; but then the Italians were thought to be particularly susceptible to pompous rhetoric, to be more unstable than the Germans in the north, to be too prone to political barn-storming, and to be dangerously fond of anarchy, so that they needed to be forcibly controlled.

In Spain, Portugal, in the Southern and Central American states the danger of anarchy was even greater, and a military dictatorship was therefore essential. The German army had never attempted to set up such a dictatorship because in Germany there was no need of one.

The Poles, too, had a dictator, Pilsudski; but then they were a people of peasants who were incapable of dealing with their internal and external problems by way of normal parliamentary government. The same was true of the Serbs and Croats. That democratic maturity which is essential to parliamentary government could not be expected of such peoples.

Had not the Asiatic peasants in Turkey, under the dictatorial rule of Kemal Pasha, always been the fearful subjects of tyrannical sovereigns? How, then, could they revolt against their national liberator who had founded their state?

It was thought, or rather hoped, that none of these countries provided a comparison with conditions in Germany. It was only slowly and painfully learnt that collective judgments of this kind are useless in estimating political realities, and that the too simple explanations of political phenomena so favoured today of 'mass psychology' and sociology are dangerous because they tend to omit too much. It was only little by little that we learnt that in Germany, also, there were political conditions favouring the establishment of a long-lived dictatorship, in the form of one single party which is the state. It is important for anyone examining these conditions to realise how unprepared internally Germany was for the political events of 1932–33—the sudden rise to power of the Hitlerian party.

There is no doubt that the majority of educated Germans—that part of the nation which was consciously aware of its historical traditions—was very distrustful of the Hitler propaganda, which assured them that his movement was continuing and fulfilling the best traditions and hopes of German history; very many felt at the time of Hitler's victory that his political system was foreign to them; it did not represent the culmination, but rather a contradiction, of tradition, particularly of the Germano-Prussian and Bismarckian tradition.

This was true even of many officers of the *Reichswehr*, in spite of their liking for the distinctly military nature of the movement and for its struggle against the armaments restrictions imposed by the Treaty of Versailles, and in spite of their hopes of future rearmament. All this was not enough to stop the senior officers of the *Reichswehr*, who thought themselves the most distinguished representatives of the Prussian tradition, from despising, distrusting, and failing to understand Hitler's proletarian movement, with its semi-military squads of combatants at political meetings. Except for General von Reichenau, who was regarded as a careerist, there was no other convinced National-Socialist general before 1933.[1] Hitler was very much aware and afraid of the hostile attitude of the generals, and it was for this reason that he was anxious to arrive at power by 'legal' means, with a majority at the elections, and not to undertake the second *putsch* which his more radical supporters such as Röhm and Stennes desired.[2]

The famous Potsdam day (21st March 1933), with the solemn sight of Hindenburg standing near the tomb of Frederick the Great, was organised for the same reason. Its purpose was to convince the *Reichswehr* and the upper middle classes that Hitler's new Reich was nothing but the consequence of the old Prussian tradition, and thus to help them swallow the shock of 30th January. This purpose was ultimately reached both in Germany and abroad, but only with the help of a vast campaign of literary propaganda which naturally was assisted in good faith by many people at the universities. Soon a new Frederick legend was built up.[3] Genuine patriots began to be disillusioned in the summer of 1933, when Hermann Göring and his SA set up a completely new reign of terror.

Why are all these facts mentioned as an introduction? In my opinion they do not in any respect alter the German nation's responsibility for the events of 1933; rather the contrary. But they do warn the historian against over-simplification of the historical situation at the time of the rise of the National-Socialists. Up till the present there has been a strong tendency to seek the sources of National-Socialism in the dim past of German history. Attempts to do this were started in the Vansittart group's propaganda in the Second World War, when they tried to show that National-Socialist methods of violence existed among the Cimbri and the Teutons.

More serious are the efforts of various foreign and German experts

[1] Detailed information is available in H. Foertsch's book on the Fritsch crisis in the spring of 1938 (*Schuld und Verhängnis. Die Fritsch-Krise im Frühjahr* (1938) Stuttgart, 1951).

[2] See *Hitler's Table Talk*, No. 225, etc.

[3] I myself tried to fight this movement as much as was possible at that time by giving lectures on Frederick the Great; these lectures were published in 1936, and were greatly approved by numerous enemies of the Hitlerian Reich. (Third edition 1953.)

to explain the distinctly militarist nature of German nationalism by its origins at the time of the wars of liberation, and the glorification of war throughout the nineteenth century, which is shown by quotations from all kinds of authors.[1] Others trace the pre-history of National-Socialism back to Frederick the Great, or even to the Reformation.

Attempts of this kind may be useful in illustrating the historical characteristics of German views on the state, even in Hitler's time.[2] But they become sterile if they are used to explain the rapid decline of the Weimar Republic and the triumphal ascent of the Hitlerian Party from 1930 to 1933. It is true that, through conscription, war-like nationalism and military discipline had affected many of the people. When Germany's power was at its height there had been a group of fanatical and imperialist 'Pangermanists' whose hopes did not die completely in 1918, and could easily be revived; there was a great deal of distrust of parliaments, of criticism of the democratic system of government, and much monarchist sentiment among the aristocracy, the officer class, and the upper middle class, while there was much anti-Jewish feeling among the people; and there was every kind of racial theory to be found in the literature of the period.

But was all this peculiar to Germany? It is surprising how many expressions of nationalist ambitions, of militarist mentality, of racial pride, and anti-democratic criticism are to be found in the literature of ideas, especially political literature, of any European country. There are, of course, national differences in feeling and in the combination of these elements, and the militant nature of German nationalism makes its expression seem particularly dangerous. But history can never be written by means of quotations from literature, since it is almost always possible to find such quotations contradicted elsewhere. This is especially the case as regards Germany, where literature of ideas is often used merely as a means of personal expression, often abstruse and not representative of real tendencies alive in the people.[3] The historical mind is least benefited by endeavours to justify general psychological judgments by this kind of

---

[1] The most striking examples of such literature are to be found in Rohan d'O. Butler, *The Roots of National Socialism, 1783–1933* (London, 1941), and S. D. Stirk, *The Prussian Spirit*, as well as in various works of Edmond Vermeil.

[2] See my book *Europa und die deutsche Frage. Betrachtungen über die geschichtliche Eigenart des deutschen Staatsdenkens* (Munich, 1948). Chapter 4 examines the development of nationalism in the new Germany up to 1914. See also my essay: 'Das Problem des Militarismus in Deutschland', *Histor Zeitschrift*, 177, 1954, and my book: *Statskunst und Kriegshandwerk. Das Problem des Militarismus in Preussen-Deutschland.* Vol. I, *Die altpreussische Tradition* (1740–1890), 1954.

[3] This is true, above all, of the main works published at the time of Weimar which are so often mentioned in books on National-Socialism. Neither Oswald Spengler, Moeller van den Bruck, nor Ernst Jünger have any real connection with National-Socialism, and I do not think that their works had any effect on it, although their anti-liberalism influenced certain educated members of the younger

quotation. For the political psychology of a people is always as equivocal as it is changeable.

How much ink has been spilt on the subject of the romantic characteristics of 'the German', on his propensity for taking risks and for daring speculations, as contrasted with the rational clarity and classical discipline of Latin, and particularly French, literature! It is not all meaningless. German political literature has always had its romantic dreamers, from Adam Miller to Moeller van den Bruck, Ernst Jünger and Oswald Spengler; there have always been political writers who steeped themselves in daring analyses of their times and made prophecies, and with Frederick Nietzsche the adventures of the mind became a philosophical manner.

But what does this prove? Was all political literature in Germany romantic, and were there not comparable phenomena in France? Had there not been in France, too, intellectual adventures into the domain of politics, from Jean-Jacques Rousseau through the first socialists to Georges Sorel? Literary influences can explain National-Socialism much less than they explain the triumph of revolutionary ideas in France in 1789.

Hitler's victories in the elections were the result of the success of rational mass propaganda, applied with a highly developed technique; those who voted for him had no wish to live adventurously, but, on the contrary, they hoped that under his leadership they would finally leave behind them the chaos which had lasted since the war. In general the German people did not like political adventurers. At the height of the 1918 revolution the Communist adventurers of the extreme left were opposed by the most adventurous elements of the German people, the soldiers in revolt, heavily armed, beaten in battle, and soon to be disbanded, who

---

generation. They were rather isolated thinkers. The arrogant and frequently obscure style of Moeller van den Bruck and Jünger made them comprehensible only to the literary gourmet—they were completely incomprehensible to the average reader. Jünger's romantic transfiguration of modern industrial society (with its new type of man, the 'worker') and of total mobilisation in the First World War was more an analysis of the period than a political programme. His conception of the world was not due to a fundamental realism, but was the vision of a highly strung aesthete. Jünger's declaration of war on the liberal *bourgeois* world becomes in Moeller van den Bruck quite hysterical. The effect which his muddled book *Das Dritte Reich* had on many of its readers was due solely to its expressive title, and his *Preussischer Stil*, with its very romantic idealisation of Prussian traditions which is most un-Prussian.

Oswald Spengler's works are much more important, since he was a true authority on history. His book *Preussentum und Sozialismus* foresees the regeneration of Germany through Prussianism, but hopes that Caesarism will be avoided (in the form that Hitler later brought in); there is much that is impracticable in his programme. The pamphlet *Jahre der Entscheidung* was not published until 1933; its intention was to warn against the easy triumphs of National-Socialism, and it looked forward to a dark epoch in which the bestiality of mankind would be plainly shown. This was the most confusing of Spengler's works because of its assurance of a convulsive heroism (*Heroismus*).

demanded the setting up of a new and stable order. In December 1918, at a national conference of workers and soldiers, a great majority demanded the convocation of a freely-elected national assembly. Would an event of this nature have been probable in St Petersburg, Moscow, Rome, Madrid, or even Paris? The adventure of the Kapp *putsch* failed as miserably as Hitler's *putsch* at Munich in 1923, and as miserably as all the other attempted *putsches* of the left and right, notwithstanding the situation of chaos which existed in the state and in economic life; this failure was not caused by the resistance of the army alone.

Should one speak rather of 'the German's' sense of order, of his native or inculcated servility, of his inability to take up a revolutionary stand, or even to organise democratic self-administration? This theory has also been put forward; according to it, the Germans came beneath Adolf Hitler's rule because they had no natural or acquired sense of liberty, because, like the Russians, they were used to more or less autocratic forms of government.

But what about the Italians, who had come under a similar rule eleven years previously? Had they, too, no natural sense of liberty? Did they, too, suffer from native or inculcated servility, and did they not suffer rather from anarchic tendencies? Only a completely superficial study of German history can ignore the thousands of examples of a true sense of freedom, examples which are numerous since the early Middle Ages, and which frequently made the rulers of the German people think them unruly and difficult to govern. It is true that there was never a great revolution in Germany of the kind which occurred in England and France, when the monarch was executed and all the institutions of the past were overthrown. In Germany the system of constitutional monarchy continued until 1918, whereas in France the same system, which was set up by the restoration of 1815, collapsed in 1830; in France, too, there was the monarchical rule of Napoleon III. But in Germany there were many elements which had contributed to the political education of the German people and which make it impossible to speak of a traditional despotism over German life, and of the blind subjection of the people:[1] the enlightened despotism of the German princes, their

---

[1] There is no point in discussing at length the popular theory that the Lutheran preaching of obedience created a tradition of unreasoning subjection in Germany. Reference can be made to the first chapter of my book *Europa und die deutsche Frage*. All that need be said here is that (1) Passive obedience, even as regards 'unjust authority', was preached by *all* reformers. (2) The State Lutheran Church never interfered anywhere with modern constitutional developments, not even in Scandinavia, where the position of this Church in the state was especially powerful. (3) Hitler's movement was born in Catholic Bavaria, and only reached the Protestant districts of Germany later. (4) It appealed to the less religious or unbelieving urban populations much more than to the rural population which had remained faithful to the Church—in the same way as Italian Fascism found its main support in secular *milieux*, and thus continued the tradition of the *Risorgimento*.

progressive administrations, the great liberal movement of the nineteenth century, and the energetic and successful establishment of constitutional institutions, the highly developed municipal and regional autonomy which extended from municipalities to the province and the confederation, and finally the Weimar republic.

It is true that the monarchical form of government in Germany enjoyed a stronger authority even in the nineteenth century than in the Western European countries, and that, in general, confidence in it was more widely spread in the German people than distrust. Furthermore, it is true that the democratic constitution of the Weimar Republic, with the preponderant place held in it by the parliament, had been felt to be an innovation, devoid of tradition and imposed from outside, and an imitation of foreign models, if not an instrument of the will of foreign Powers, and that consequently it was resented by wide circles of conservative opinion. The Weimar Republic failed because it did not succeed in winning general confidence, in becoming genuinely popular through successes which could be appreciated from a distance. So the rejection of Democratic slogans became one of the essential conditions for the rise of Hitler's Party. But to attribute this rejection simply to 'the Germans' lack of a sense of liberty' explains nothing; it only disguises with a grand phrase the true historical problem: the reasons why the chances of liberals have much diminished in this century, particularly in Germany after the First World War.

The desire to replace the unsettled parliamentary coalition governments with a strong and lasting authority certainly played a very large part in Hitler's rise to power. In his propaganda for such an authority Hitler never ceased to praise, as an ideal model for the constitution of the state, the army, with its definite orders and clear responsibility derived from above, not from below, from those who lead, and not from those who are led; and this won the approval of many old soldiers of the First World War, just as Mussolini did when with his Blackshirts he appealed to the instincts of the old 'front-line soldiers' and 'fighting men'. These instincts were certainly much more developed in Germany than in Italy. Perhaps, too, the pedantic eagerness to serve with which the subalterns carried out their *Führer*'s orders and plans after the establishment of the dictatorship was greater in Germany.

The great electoral successes of Hitler since 1930, however, cannot be explained by the Germans' wish to find in political life a military discipline, by a desire to be given orders and to be able to obey them. The masses who rallied to him did not at all believe that they were helping a dictator to seize power; they supported a man of the people who had their confidence and from whom they expected the fulfilment of their wishes—of a thousand vast hopes.

The same thing had already occurred in Italy, and its repetition after so few years is a striking proof of the fact that ordinary men never learn anything from history. Hitler had clearly copied from Mussolini the technique of setting up, without a *coup d'état* as such and without violating the constitution, a one party state.[1]

In any case, the German dictatorship was not the first, but the last to be established in Europe, and it became by far the most dangerous (if the Russian Bolshevist dictatorship is ignored).

The conclusion is, therefore, that in order to examine the historical foundations of National-Socialism, one must first of all see what it was in twentieth-century Europe that gave the totalitarian state, composed of one single party, such a good opportunity of taking the place of the constitutional liberal parliamentary state. For the totalitarian state, composed of one single party, is a European, and not solely a German phenomenon.

A great deal could be written about the various causes of the decline of liberal ideas in social and political affairs. I can give only a few brief hints:

(1) First, the *changes in social and economic structure* which took place in the nineteenth and twentieth centuries must be borne in mind. Modern industrial society, a mass society of innumerable individuals united by common needs, has taken the place of the former *bourgeois* society, consisting of a layer of economically independent notables who were the great landowners and *bourgeois*.

The First World War accelerated and intensified the process of economic and social levelling, by removing differences during wartime, especially in Germany. The whole of society was ground down into a uniform mass, grey as the soldiers; it was subjected to overall state control, to a totalitarian power which deeply affected even private life. It restricted the free expression of opinion, imposed censorship on the press, cut it off from all communication with foreign countries, and made it entirely dependent on the official information office, which accustomed the people to official communiqués which only very rarely divulged the whole truth, and in many cases suppressed, mutilated, or falsified it. More or less compulsory state or war loans swallowed up private incomes, later annihilated by inflation, which practically led to ruin and the end of fiduciary currency. Those possessing real estate (*Sachwerthesitzer*) had a monopoly, all the educated middle classes were impoverished, and large sections of society became solely dependent on state salaries and pensions or on private business; innumerable people who had been independent were so no longer.

As a result of such general changes, the party system on which the liberal state was founded was modified. Under the influence of uni-

---

[1] Hitler half-admitted this himself. *Hitler's Table Talk*, No. 25.

versal suffrage, the parties were no longer composed of groups of notables, of clubs whose members were men who were socially and financially independent, who knew something about politics and were interested in them. They became mass organisations, directed by the electoral machine formed by a more or less highly organised party bureaucracy. The political agent took the place of the political idealist, and planned propaganda took the place of personal conviction and persuasion.

At the same time, the style and content of publications were changed. Political education, real discussion, individual thought ceased to be important; instead, what was required was mass appeal. In order to interest the masses, they must be attracted by sensationalism. He who is best at sensationalism is also the most popular. The most effective method is always the sermon of hatred, the least effective the voice of peaceable reason, since it makes the reader think, and even requires a certain wish to learn, and some knowledge.

(2) Similarly, *political intentions* changed: In the nineteenth century the struggle (particularly in Central Europe) was for national unity and for liberty guaranteed by a constitution—that is to say, for the participation of the governed in state affairs, for an assured, liberal legal system, and for protection against arbitrary acts. These were ideal ends, which had sprung mostly from spiritual impulses. By the end of the century they had been achieved in Italy and in Germany (with two exceptions).[1]

In their place the economic preoccupations of modern industrial society came to the fore. The struggle for a higher standard of living became the main cause of internal political differences; the idea of liberty was eclipsed by the idea of 'social justice'; Liberalism was attacked and discarded in favour of Socialism. Political thought became more and more materialistic. Instead of being preoccupied by unity and liberty, it was interested in class conflicts, material interests, and the struggle for daily bread; in foreign policy the questions of the hour were *Lebensraum*, the great outlets and sources of raw materials, trading profits, and the rate of exchange.

So in general, politics stopped striving towards an ideal, and the prestige of parliaments declined. Since it had now become a matter of the interests of groups of people, the personal integrity of the representatives of these people is doubted. The details of their debates on economic subjects become more abstruse and uninteresting;

---

[1] In Italy the aspirations of the Irredenta must be borne in mind; in Germany the desire for Greater Germany, which had sprung up so strongly in 1918–19, which aimed at union with German-speaking Austria, and political propaganda to make the *Volksdeutschen* (foreigners of German origin) in other countries more German-minded—a procedure which was to be encouraged by the cession of German territory under the Treaty of Versailles. But the question of Greater Germany was not taken up in Hitler's propaganda before 1933.

the great complexity of modern economy partly controlled by the state, and the large number of opposing interests represented in parliament, make definite solutions, understood and approved by all, extremely rare. Therefore there is a great deal of discontent, and discontent breeds the summoning of a 'strong man'. The great groups of interests take 'direct', extra-parliamentary action; there are strikes, the big workers' and employers' unions exert pressure on public opinion, there are processions, demonstrations, and mass meetings. The place of real debates is taken by announcements. Political struggles become more violent—he who has armed or semi-military partisans, ready to strike, at his call has the best chance of success.

Here, too, the World War accelerated and exaggerated this evolution. Like all great wars, it left behind it many adventurous spirits who were unable to settle down again to a *bourgeois* existence. They were nationalists, ready to serve any political adventurer who could use them for his 'patriotic' activities. In *Mein Kampf* Hitler severely criticised the indiscipline of these eternal soldiers, without political aims, grouped together in bands (*Freikorps*), secret societies, and armed associations of all kinds, who sometimes supported and sometimes threatened republican governments. To him the fact that these armed bands and *Freikorps* had at times protected the republic from Communism showed nothing but unpardonable stupidity. He disapproved strongly of their Vehme murders, too, because they liquidated minor traitors without daring to deal with the 'great November criminals'.

In fact, however, many of these toughs became members of the *Sturmtruppen*, and the *Führerkorps* was mostly made up of them. There is a close connection between the SA and SS terrorists and these adventurous stragglers from the First World War. The inflation which took place in 1923, as a result of the war, left many people without money and with nothing to lose, so that they were ready to become political agents.

(3) *The changes in religious life* produced the same results. Christian teaching scarcely reached the populations of industrial towns; European civilisation became more and more secular as a result of the technical progress which took place in this rationalised and 'unsupernatural' world. In Germany idealist philosophy, which had been a substitute for religion in *bourgeois* society for many years, began to be rejected, not in favour of philosophical materialism but of the modern 'philosophy of life' which was spreading throughout Europe. This 'philosophy of life' influenced large sections of society, and there was much talk of the supremacy of will, of biological explanations of mankind and of society, the glorification of physical strength, and of pure vitality, instead of a higher spirituality; the in-

tellect and the rational were despised, while strong 'instincts' (*Triebe*) and the vital impulse (the *élan vital* of H. Bergson) were admired. Nietzsche's doctrine of the superman and of the will to power as the prime force in the world, envisaged at first as an aristocratic ethical system, became in popular literature the deification of brutal mankind, of will to domination, of the eternal struggle for existence, of brute strength—though not without the complicity of that philosopher who unhesitatingly set the most daring aphorisms before the world. Darwinian ideas of the 'survival of the fittest', of the eternal struggle for existence of all creatures, influenced all political thought. In all countries, including those of Western Europe, the age of imperialism brought with it books extolling the doctrine of might; with no knowledge of life, wars were no longer thought to be disasters for civilisation, but rather creative crises without which there could be no historical evolution.

Marxist theories were even more widespread, although not always recognised as such—the only political reality was the conflict of material interests, and political ideals were only ideological camouflage. (That this was a serious mistake is proved by all history, including that of National-Socialism.)

The example of the romanticism of the younger generation at the beginning of the twentieth century, with its scorn of *bourgeois* security and of reason and its call for 'a dangerous life' and for exciting experience (*Erlebnis*), might lead one to believe that European countries were tired of the long period of peacefulness which had brought them their material well-being. Well-being and security were both destroyed by the First World War, which reduced society to a uniformity which could be touched only by mass violence and brutality.

This complete change of the political climate gave a new and troubling reality to the theories of Wilfredo Pareto about the eternal circular movement of activist *élites*, about the deceit of middle-class morality, and about the propelling force of deep feeling. The same was true of Georges Sorel's theories about 'violence' and the 'myth' which moves the masses, without the truth of its content having any importance. During their first phase, French syndicalists wished to replace old-style parliamentary groups by the ideal leader's party and militant *élite* which would pursue the aims of combat rather than the ideals of the *bourgeois* middle classes, and thus showed the young Mussolini his first and most pressing plan of action. The large-scale destruction of the war showed the way for futurist policies (in the meaning given to them by men like Gentile, Papini, and Marinetti) which refuse all connection with the authorities of the past.

(4) *New technical facilities for political propaganda* made the mobilisation of the masses much easier than it had been in the age of

bourgeoisies; facilities such as loud-speakers, radio, a daily press rapidly printed in thousands of copies, lorries and motor-coaches which made possible the speedy deployment of political shock troops, almost limitless mass transport by railway, road, and air, so that it was possible to go proselytising from one end of the country to the other and to address a different mammoth meeting each evening. In 1922 40,000 Blackshirts formed ranks for the march on Rome, and caused a political panic simply on account of their numbers. At each of his national party congresses Hitler assembled and addressed some half a million men.

Thus did it become possible to make a reality of the theory of the sovereignty of the people, in a radical manner that was completely new. The masses could now be activated directly to become the political sovereign, and the roundabout method of the election of people's representatives to Parliament was no longer the only one.

It is clear that from the start the direct control of the 'will of the people' was fundamental to democratic radicalism, unlike the Anglo-Saxon liberalism. The latter was originally founded not on the political rights of the many, but on the political privileges possessed by the various estates under feudalism, and which were perpetuated in the party groupings in modern parliaments. Groups of important people 'represented' the people; in England these groups slowly became parties of the many during the nineteenth century.

The principle of direct sovereignty of the people, on the other hand, was in existence in the primitive democracy of the free American states in the seventeenth and eighteenth centuries. It was manifest in the town meetings of the settlers which constituted the first germs of American democracy; this principle is still in existence today, as shown by the President's position as a man on whom the nation, on whom every voter, but not Congress, can rely; before Congress his position is that of the executor of the will of the people.

Political compromise reached by discussion, the just balancing of the opposing desires and interests of different classes, groups, and individuals, belongs to the liberal parliamentary system. The nation is not regarded as a uniform mass of men, but as a collection of different individuals. The individual is important not only as a comrade of the people (*Volksgenosse*), but also as a person with claims on life and independent action.

Democratic radicalism, on the other hand, with terrible consistency, requires definite decisions instead of compromise. Sovereignty means deciding and not compromising. The best example of this rational principle is the idea, invented by Jean-Jacques Rousseau, of the 'general will', an absolute idea which does not recognise any minority rights; if one opposes the general will it is because one has mistaken the general good (*Social Contract*, Book IV, chapter 2). The general will is the sworn enemy of individual intellect, of groups of individuals, because such groups are unaware of, or opposed to, the real public good; the more the individual intellect is overcome, the more probable it is that the real general will, the true interests of the people, will operate (*Social Contract*, Book II, chapter 3). Direct sovereignty of the people is infinitely preferable to any form of parliamentary government, for parliaments are the legacy of feudalism, and therefore the place in which private interests, and not the public good, struggle for supremacy (*Social Contract*, Book III, chapter 15).

Jean-Jacques Rousseau's general will became a myth at the time of the great revolution; aided by groups of individuals, it dominated parliamentary discussion and became increasingly intolerant. The people, now sovereign, is united in a popular political community (this was the most important innovation), a community of which each individual is part, although his particular rights are not protected (as Rousseau required). No appeal to higher authority is possible, because the people is sovereign, and there can be no appeal to ancient rights or privileges of the kind that was possible under the monarchy. Any one who opposes the will of the people is considered dangerously selfish, and therefore excludes himself from the community (this exclusion may then be made certain by banishment, imprisonment, or the guillotine).

How can the absolute and indivisible will of the people best be expressed? The best and simplest way, as Rousseau saw it, was the convocation of the sovereign people to a citizens' meeting, as in the classical city-state, the Swiss canton, or the American town meeting. But this form of direct democracy is of necessity limited to a very small community.

In large states there is the plebiscite which may be employed to show support for, and to be complementary to, the legislative machinery of parliament; for especially important laws, administrative decisions, and questions of foreign policy there would be a referendum. This system is cumbersome, costly, and difficult to operate, however, and does not really make possible a radical popular government.

A third method may be employed in large countries, however. The will of the people may be transferred to one man in whom confidence is reposed, who thus becomes an embodiment of the people, tangible and visible to all. Such a transference is made directly by the votes of the people, without passing through Parliament.

This can be done in two ways: either by the legal procedure of the plebiscite, or by gathering as large a following as possible throughout the land, preferably including armed elements, and by holding a great many popular meetings designed to encourage support.

These two methods can, however, be combined. For the first one the man seeking power must be certain of a large majority beforehand—either as a result of impressive political and military successes (such as Napoleon I contrived, and Napoleon III desired), or by bureaucratic pressure, or both. If only the second method is to be employed (the method of the state as one single party made up of a personal following), then terrorism, the control of men (*Gleichschaltung*) by violence, in order that one single will of the people may be established, is indispensable. Since the total unity of the will of the people is always mythical, on account of the multiplicity of interests of which it is composed, violent measures of control are essential before a complete popular community (*Volksgemeinschaft*) can be attained. Therefore, with the help of a group of activists ready for anything, a minority must be brought to power, and all opposition prevented. The minority must be respected, must be a model of patriotic virtue, and seem to be the true liberator of the people from the domination of dark reactionary forces. Such was the method employed by Robespierre, Danton, and Lenin.

The safest method is to combine a legal plebiscite with illegal violence carried out by a following of activists. This technique was employed by Mussolini and Hitler for their seizure of power. Both combined popular votes with some sort of latent civil war. But genuine parliamentary debates and real opposition cannot be tolerated. When they exist and continue to operate, there may be popular leaders, like the Prime Minister in England and the President in America, who can claim to represent the will of the people while they are in power; but in such circumstances absolute and durable overall power of the kind possessed by the Caesar of the Napoleonic system and the modern dictator in the one-party totalitarian state does not exist.

The success of the twentieth-century dictatorships is conceivable only against this broad canvas of history. Of course they should not be considered in any way as the belated result of the French Revolution, or as having been influenced in any way by the works of Jean-Jacques Rousseau—this would be a very false interpretation of these historical remarks. Each of these dictatorships found its opportunity and its particular modern form in an extremely recent past.[1]

Yet the latent possibility of a sudden change from radical democratic liberty to totalitarian tyranny is not modern. It grows where

---

[1] I do not believe that either Italy in 1922 or Germany in 1933 were consciously influenced by the French Revolution; this was certainly the case however with Marxist doctrine, or with Lenin in 1917. In this instance memories of the Paris Commune in 1871 may have had an even more immediate effect.

the great, socially disorganised, intellectually uniform masses in the modern city awaken to political consciousness, and where the former public authorities with their roots in the dim past (monarchy or parliamentary government) are destroyed or discredited. In such circumstances success seems assured if the distrust of a system of domination, already smouldering, is inflamed and a compact front is formed with a solid following. The masses are more ready to trust a living man than an anonymous institution.

Should a leader appear who is able to pass himself off as the representative of the most pure will of the people and as a real leader, then he will gain the support of the people, especially if he has a good few hard-hitting adherents.

Nowadays, when there are so many technical ways in which the masses can be dominated, the majority no longer decides; instead political 'activities', the mass shock tactics of a brutal minority rule are decisive. Such minorities regard themselves as an *élite*, the true representatives of the will of the people. The community, consisting of men in the mass (*Massenmensch*), must be uniform; the will of the people is the same thing as complete unity. Anyone who opposes it is morally discredited, a danger to the people (*Volksschädling*), and is eliminated by violence, placed in concentration camps, or liquidated. The constitution of the Russian Soviet Republic states that the essential 'human right' of the liberated proletariat is to 'pitilessly suppress employers' and to 'abolish the parasitic layers of society'.[1]

The collapse of the monarchy in Germany happened much more unexpectedly than in Russia, where the nihilists had been preparing the ground since 1860. Considering that there was no conspiracy of anarchists, it is difficult to understand how the Hohenzollern dynasty would have collapsed so quickly without foreign intervention (Wilson!), in spite of the serious moral uncertainty caused by the Wilhelmian régime and the disastrous result of the war. The political shock produced by this catastrophe was all the more violent because of this.

The appearance of a man, using like Lenin the general confusion and disintegration of every authority in order to bring a minority of resolute activists to power under the guise of the 'general will of the people', was quite possible in the political chaos then reigning. Karl Liebknecht made an attempt, but failed.   The pass-word, absolute defeatism, with which Lenin won over the mutinied soldiers at Leningrad, did not appeal to the German army, which had

[1] Article III of the constitution of the Soviets, 10 Jul. 1918. It seems that in Russia, unlike Italy and Germany, the dictatorship of one man only emerged slowly from a dictatorship by a group of powerful activists. But, from the first Lenin's was the strongest personality, and his corpse was embalmed as soon as he died, a people's saint.

not staggered from defeat to defeat, like the Russian one; Lieb-knecht's relations with foreign countries (bolshevist dictators) com-promised him, and German socialists had gone through a long period of parliamentary education, which made them anxious for a parliamentary form of constitution.

The fact that monarchist *milieux* offered no resistance during the first years of revolution makes the affair even more surprising. Events seemed to have paralysed them; the Hohenzollern dynasty, abandoned by all its protectors, even the High Command of the army (*Oberste Heeresleitung*), thought that all was lost, and did not endeavour to make a fight; the Emperor fled abroad, and all the German princes also faded quietly away. Had the brilliance of the princely régime been nothing but a splendid façade, a ghost of the past, without real power or popularity? Or was its popularity sud-denly swallowed up in the abyss made by the disastrous war? This was a question that troubled many people at the time, and to which no one found an answer.

This uncertainty explains, too, why attempts to restore the monarchy, or even serious hope of a restoration, were not important in the Weimar republic. The speedy failure of the Kapp *putsch*, a typical Free Corps undertaking, made it evident that such attempts had no chance of success. In spite of the definitely strong mon-archist feeling in the army, none of the generals, nor Hindenburg himself (at first supported by all monarchists as a candidate for the presidency), even considered the restoration of the monarchy.[1] Why was this? The answer to this question takes us to the heart of the question examined here, the specific *foundations in German history which led to the rise of National-Socialism.*

Hitler himself never sought a restoration; he sought its opposite. He thought that the patriotism of conservative *milieux* looked to-wards the past, was out of date, and absurdly inefficient as regards mass propaganda. In *Mein Kampf* (Book 2, chapter 7) he described the boredom of the meetings held by the national Germans and other *bourgeois* nationalists with scornful irony. The national slogans of the day before yesterday accomplished only one thing—they

---

[1] It is, I think, a mistake to maintain as François-Poncet does in his book *De Ver-sailles à Potsdam* that Hindenburg's, or rather Brüning's, emergency ordinances were a sort of transition to monarchic or dictatorial government, and that Hinden-burg secretly wished to rule the *Reichstag* with the support of the army. Hinden-burg's influence was sinister and questionable from the first, even during the war, but not for these reasons. The emergency ordinances were intended to save, and not to paralyse, the parliamentary democracy under extremely difficult conditions (the increase of left-wing and right-wing extremism), in which the parliaments could no longer function. Hitler, on his part, issued no emergency ordinance under Article 48 of the Constitution. Instead of employing this method, he persuaded the *Reichstag* to grant him full powers, formally and legally, under an emergency law so that parliament could be completely passed over.

drove the man in the street away from these meetings. Hitler's propaganda was based not on the memory of 'our forefathers' deeds', but on an indomitable will for the future. His state was to be completely new, something that had never before been seen, contemporary and modern, a state that could be created only once. He poured criticism and scorn on the institutions which existed under a hereditary monarchy under which the ultimate orders were made not by the most able, but by those in power on account of an accident of birth and of heredity, as he said in private.[1] But in public, in his propaganda, for as long as he needed the support of conservative groups (national Germans), he expressed no such views. In fact, the only thing which he had in common with the monarchists was his opposition to the Weimar system, and only such fanatical, blind, and single-minded people as the German conservatives (Hügenberg's followers) could be unaware of, or ignore, how far his attitude was revolutionary and anti-monarchist. The fact that a few German princes wished to support him is explicable only because Court circles, in which the opinions of the people were unknown, left them completely devoid of instinct. Hitler did not regard himself as a member of the upper classes, but as a common man, a people's leader (*Volksführer*) in the most radical democratic manner—the direct representative of democratic principles, the representative of the will of the people, the 'only delegate of the nation' as he often described himself in his 'leader's speeches' (*Führerreden*).

It is a very great mistake to believe that the modern function of leader of the people is in any way the heritage and continuation of the old, monarchic power of the princes. Neither Frederick the Great, Bismarck, nor Wilhelm II were the historical precursors of Adolf Hitler. His precursors were the demagogues and Caesars of modern history, from Danton to Lenin and Mussolini. It is also erroneous to see in the fanatical enthusiasm which millions of men felt for Hitler between 1930 and 1933 a continuation of the traditional veneration of Germans for their ancient princely houses. Our people's old attachment to its dynasties was, where it existed, the result of a traditional feeling; it was primarily caused by respect for a very ancient custom.

Hitler's party was, on the contrary, composed of numerous uprooted individuals whose mentality was revolutionary, who all consciously desired a new order, and who were convinced that their *Führer* was superior to any earlier leader. The characteristic of the Hitlerian movement which most strongly attracted the masses was its modernity, the fact that it was contemporary (facts which were

[1] See *Hitler's Table Talk*, particularly No. 177. His distrust of monarchist reactionaries never diminished, and led him to dismiss all members of ancient princely families from the army during the war.

brought out by the very far-flung technical apparatus used to gain support for the Party). Hitler's obscure, popular origins added to this attraction, and seemed an assurance that he could have nothing in common with the hated right-wing reactionaries—the great Junker landowners, the officer class, and the great capitalists—even if he was sometimes obliged by force of circumstances to co-operate with people like Ludendorff and Hugenberg. Ludendorff himself declared himself opposed to Junker and capitalist prejudice, and a public-spirited friend of the people.[1] Hitler and his supporters always contended that the electoral alliance established between the National-Socialists, the Stahlhelm group, and Hügenberg's party— the 'Harzburg front' of 1931—was nothing more than a tactical agreement, for Hitler detested 'all reaction'.[2] And when he opened negotiations with the big industrialists once more, being short of money and desirous of rapid success, Otto Strasser and the Schwarze Front, the most convinced revolutionary elements in the Party, deserted the cause and started an open rebellion. Later he was to seize every opportunity of condemning the 'selfishness' of the capitalist class and stating how much his policy favoured the workers.

In any case, he did not wish to be a conservative, either socially or politically; he wished to be a revolutionary. But what did this revolution imply? What was the difference between his dictatorship and that of other modern dictators? What was specifically German in it, what could be only explained by specifically German historical events?

If the situation is simplified somewhat, one can answer that *Volksführer* Hitler's mission in history was to accomplish that which the Emperor and his Government had been unable to accomplish in the First World War: to weld the nation into a closed, warlike community under the leadership of a really popular *Führer*, respected by all.

The total failure of the German monarchy in providing leadership was one of the most surprising results of the war. Before 1914 no one doubted (abroad military writers were convinced of it) that the German military monarchy was, as far as organisation was concerned, well in advance of Western parliamentary democracies— through the fact that the supreme civil and military commands were fused in the person of the monarch himself, a born military leader, who was supreme war-lord above all rivalry between politicians and soldiers. It was thought that this system made the elimination and

[1] See Otto Strasser: *Hitler and I* (1940), p. 23.
[2] Th. Düsterberg's Memoirs, *Der Stahlhelm und Hitler* (1949), clearly illustrate the fragility of this alliance and Hitler's total lack of respect for his allies, as well as his complete superiority as a political propagandist and tactician.

smoothing over of the inevitable disagreements between civilians and soldiers who considered war only from the technical point of view, more easy than any other. There were memories of the absolute authority with which the king of Prussia, Wilhelm I, had always resolved conflicts arising between Bismarck and Moltke. In fact, as *roi-connétable* (king and high constable), according to the Frederickian tradition of ancient Prussia, the King was still 'the supreme lord of war', on whom all the glory of victorious campaigns and battles shone.

In the 1914–18 war, however, Emperor Wilhelm II passed quite unexpectedly out of the limelight in which his generals stood, gathered no glory in spite of the initial successes of the German army; he was completely unable to resolve the serious conflicts which arose between the chiefs of staff and the chancellors; and when Hindenburg and Ludendorff were made supreme commanders of the army he became almost a stand-in called in only in an emergency. He was even not sufficiently well informed, and when collapse threatened he was left in the lurch politically. Why was he such a failure? It could not be explained solely by Wilhelm II's personal faults; there were reasons greater than the sovereign— the completely changed character of modern war.

Twentieth-century totalitarian war employs the whole people to an extent never before known; the people must work itself to the bone, sacrifice all well-being, reduce its consumption of even the most essential necessities to a degree sometimes exceeding tolerable limits. In a socially advanced country this can be done only by systematically and intensively working on public opinion all the time, so as to convince the people that these sacrifices are essential. The masses must have unquestioning faith in their leaders if internal tensions are to be avoided. It is extremely difficult for the political controllers of the war to keep this confidence; for if war brings political successes, the victorious general puts the statesman in the shade; if it brings setbacks and crises, there is the question of responsibility, and the politician finds it difficult to avoid being blamed for not having supported the military leaders or for having interfered unreasonably; these dangers were particularly intense in Germany, a country which placed its faith in armies.

In France and England, too, public opinion swung between confidence in and distrust of the generals and the political control of the war. But these two countries came through such trials because their democracy placed at their heads popular and gifted leaders who were also experienced parliamentarians, able to make themselves personally represent their country's will to fight and win, and thus gaining considerable popular confidence. Both Lloyd George and Clemenceau could guide their people through waves of hope and despair, through attacks of pessimism and failures, and inspire them with courage to continue—to continue until the end of the crisis, when American aid began to make itself felt.

In order to accomplish this, modern propaganda methods such as no monarch can employ were necessary—direct appeals to the masses and to their passions, the unceasing declaration of the will to fight and destroy, indeed to hate; these propaganda methods are useless unless they insult and slander the enemy.

The German Confederation's system of constitutional monarchy did not bring to the head of the Government men gifted for such tasks; its chancellors, ministers, and secretaries of state had all come to politics from liberal professions, mostly from the diplomatic corps or from senior positions in the Civil Service. They felt themselves to be officials serving the monarchy and the empire, and had nothing in common with modern leaders of the people. Prior to 1918 they would have thought themselves to be violating their dignity as ministers if they were seen at popular meetings or wished to speak to the crowd.

The majesty of the Crown was, of course, even more inaccessible to the common people. The search for supporters among the masses could not therefore be seriously considered. Further, the Emperor no longer carried out his former task as supreme war lord of resolving conflicts and giving clear-cut orders. Wilhelm I had had great difficulty in carrying out these tasks. The enormously increased scale of modern war in the twentieth century, with its technical evolution involving innumerable matters of economic organisation, made its control impossible for a king. The unity of politics and of the control of the war could be assured only by institutions such as that of Great Britain, where a national defence council, composed of commissions of experts, advised its president, an energetic, subtle, and extremely popular politician, with precise technical information, without, however, preventing his liberty of decision. In Germany the Emperor was surrounded by numerous military and political authorities whose disputes he was unable to resolve even with the aid of occasional 'meetings of the Council of the Crown', since he lacked both the necessary training and certainty of political instinct.

Wilhelm II only once succeeded in getting near the heart of the nation as a whole, on 4th August 1914, when he said to the *Reichstag* assembled in the Berlin castle: 'I know parties no more, I only know Germans'. These words had a tremendous effect. The idea of a popular, unified political community struck the people with the same effect that the French had experienced at the festival of the Federation on 14th July 1790. Yet this was an isolated incident; the new-found community broke up in conflicts about the aims of the war and its methods, and the Emperor's rule failed so completely that the German monarchy received a death-blow.

The Germans experienced a bitter disappointment when not only was the war lost in spite of tremendous efforts, terrible economic privation, and millions of deaths, but also when the popular community broke up instead of becoming stronger. The Right, bellicose nationalists out for conquest, and the Socialist leaders, who were opposed to imperialism and desirous of peace, no longer saw eye to eye. They attacked one another so violently, supporters of 'victorious peace' (*Siegfrieden*) and 'peace by agreement' (*Verstandigungsfrieden*) the 'prolongers of war' (*Kriegsverlangerer*) and 'defeatists', as they described each other, that the nation was split into two halves.

This bitter conflict was the decisive and perhaps fundamental occurrence which led to the rise of National-Socialism. In comparison with this, all other considerations seem to me to be of secondary importance. Hitler's party was brought to power primarily by his efforts to overcome the old and fatal conflict between the nationalist *bourgeois* parties of the right and the masses of the left, the working and lower middle classes. It was not called the 'German workers' National-Socialist Party' (*National-sozialistische deutsche Arbeiterpartei*) in vain. The name was a programme in itself.

The class struggle between the middle classes and the proletariat had been intensified and embittered by the conflict on national policy of power—the old, fatal relic of Bismarck's Reich. It originated in the Social-Democratic Party's opposition to the Prussian military monarchy and its rejection of the Prussian military organisation. This opposition had been increased by Bismarck's efforts to suppress, by police methods, the Social-Democratic Party. Right-wing *bourgeois* circles thought the socialist plans for a militia impractical, and almost considered the declaration of the 'international solidarity of the working class' to be high treason. Before 1914 every military budget was carried by the 'national *bourgeois*' parties, while the radical left voted against them. During the last decades before the First World War, Friedrich Naumann and his National-Social (*national-sozial*) followers did not succeed in overcoming this division and in winning the working class over to his power- and world-policy (*Macht- und Weltpolitik*) in which he incorporated the sociological theories of Max Weber. After Bismarck's departure and the end of measures against the Socialists, the German Social-Democracy continued to grow within the national state. But it remained extremely suspicious of the imperialist aspirations of the German middle class, a feeling which was reciprocated by the latter's suspicion of the Socialists' 'trustworthiness' from a national point of view.

During the war this mutual distrust took the form of violent accusations based on the question of the aims of the war, while the

Bethmann-Hollweg Government, whose existence was threatened by the hostility of the war High Command (that is Hindenburg and Ludendorff), did not dare to make its position clear.

After the war these accusations continued to pollute the atmosphere of the Weimar Republic. The right-wing nationalists were accused, not without reason, of having uselessly prolonged the war, of not having realised, in their blind fanaticism, that all hope of success had vanished, of preventing a new policy from being formulated. In reply, the 1918 revolutionaries were accused of having sabotaged victory by stabbing the army in the back—an absurd allegation, but none the less effective and dangerous, for it was undeniable that the radical propaganda of Socialists and Communists had weakened or destroyed the will to fight of many sections of the army, particularly the depots, and had thus affected the front line; also, a civil war to preserve the monarchy and the old régime had lost all chance of success, as a result of the demobilisation of the army.

Hitler's party promised the nation that it would bridge over the abyss which had been created—this was his great promise which won him most of his idealist supporters.

It is, of course, true that the great electoral success of 1930, when the Party suddenly received six million votes, and that of 1932, with almost fourteen million, was the direct result of the poverty implied by mass unemployment. Yet it was not the Party's economic promises (which were not very definite) but National-Socialist political propaganda that was the decisive element in this success.

Hitler did not refrain from making economic promises on occasion, particularly to the peasants. The old Munich programme contained, too, a number of remarks about economic reform. But the leader of the Party left the work of unceasingly reiterating material pledges to his subordinates. He himself had too much political instinct (and was not himself sufficiently well-informed about economics) to stick to a definite economic programme, whose possibility and effectiveness might be questioned. Instead, he stressed all the more the need for an energetic *political* reform.

Typical in this respect was his Düsseldorf speech to the *Industrie Klub*, on 27th January 1932, though this is only one example chosen from many others. The German economic crisis, he said, is not simply the result of the world economic crisis about which we can do nothing; it is not even the result of the abortive peace of Versailles. It is, above all, the result of Germany's mistaken politics. If this were not the case, we should despair of the future. But German politics can be changed. The economic distress cannot be averted by emergency ordinances, and by economic measures in general, but only by the total regeneration of the body of the German people.

Politics, not economics, are at the bottom of this situation.[1] A healthy economy can exist only in a strong and powerful state. To create such a state, the first need is a select popular community which can surmount all opposition. The most dangerous and important opposition is that separating the section of the people which is ready for the struggle and has nationalist sentiments, and the Marxists, the 1918 revolutionaries who have internationalist sentiments. The most serious threat to our future and to that of Europe is Bolshevism. The National-Socialist Party is the only one which can stamp out this danger. Against the religion of Bolshevism it sets a stronger and healthier world creed; at the same time it sweeps away —in its own ranks first of all—the old class conflict between the middle class and the proletariat. If it succeeds in regenerating the body of the German people, Germany will be cured not only as regards economics, but she will achieve a new height in the eyes of the world. It is not true that the political and economic situation of the world necessarily decides our future. For, in the last analysis, everything depends on internal renewal.

Hitler was careful not to make even the smallest reference to an economic programme before these economic experts.[2] He relied solely on the effect of his political ideal of a united and renewed nation. At first, he said, we cannot do much about the unemployment situation; but the nation must go forward with serried ranks, and then the main peril will be past; the people's great ideals must be restored to them, so that they are not stifled by material cares.

The effectiveness of this propaganda was fully confirmed by success. Material interests are not the prime motive force of historical movements, as the Marxists believe; everywhere and always the wish to show one's worth is stronger for peoples as well as for individuals. In order to show one's political and social worth, great material sacrifices are made; sometimes even life itself is not considered too high a price to pay. The German people's wish to show its worth was as great as its vitality. The big defeat of 1918 had deeply wounded her self-esteem. But her physical and intellectual vitality were unbroken. The chief misfortune of the Weimar Republic was that it was unable to satisfy the nation's need to show its worth politically.

[1] See the section on 'State and Economy' in the 'Munich' chapter (I. 4) of *Mein Kampf* (28th ed., 1933), p. 167.
[2] One sentence alone, which might easily be overlooked, mentions in a very muddled manner, the long-term future end which a new and powerful State would pursue: 'Either new *lebensraum* and the development of a great home market, or the external protection of German economy by using the massed might of Germany' (p. 31 in the official text of the pamphlet published by Eher. Complete English translation in *The Speeches of Adolf Hitler, April 1922 to August 1939*, edited by Norman H. Baynes, 1942, Vol. I, pp. 777–829). This speech decisively gained for Hitler the confidence of the heads of the Rhineland economy.

O

A peaceful national consciousness, without aggressive tendencies, can develop in modern civilised states only if their people is satisfied that it has the place and the rank which it deserves. In Germany this feeling had predominated in the first decades following the foundation of the Reich, when Bismarck continually declared that the empire was 'saturated'. Later the rivalry with England, the ambition to become a people of the world (*Weltvolk*) and a sea-power began. In this forced atmosphere, composed of the national consciousness of strength, of inferiority complex, and the fear of being cut off from other countries, was born the radical nationalism of the Pangermanists, whose writings contained many characteristics of National-Socialist propaganda.

Although before the war its influence was not very wide, during the war the Pangerman League helped to bolster up nationalist propaganda and the supporters of annexation, and thus increased its activities; it was therefore all the more seriously affected by the catastrophe which put an end to its public activities. At first the militarists and the supporters of annexation were seriously compromised; the electoral successes of the parties of the right, their associates, were very modest.[1] But in general the result of the war and the Treaty of Versailles were regarded as unjust; France's new lead in Europe as unnatural; the defeat seemed the result of overwhelming material superiority and not of military inadequacy; the treaty seemed brutally violent, and not a true peace arrangement in relation to the real distribution of forces, and also as the violation of America's solemn promises.

There is no point in discussing once more to what extent this conception was correct or incorrect; for nothing is more problematical than the peace settlement after totalitarian wars involving whole peoples. In fact, all German parties and groups, including most of those of the left, violently criticised the Treaty of Versailles. Yet their unity in this criticism did not lessen the differences between parties; on the contrary, it aggravated them, since right and left each placed the responsibility for the disaster at the door of the other.

The violent arguments about the responsibility for the war and the 'stabbing-in-the-back' legend might perhaps have caused civil war between right and left if the Communist peril had not been so great and urgent as to oblige the non-communist parties to establish a common front against the extreme left.

Following the example of Hindenburg, even the national right-

[1] 1919 elections: National Germans (Conservatives) 10 per cent of the votes, popular party (*Volkspartei*) (National Liberals) 4 per cent; 1920 elections: 15 and 14 per cent. Hügenberg was the main and most sinister representative of Pangerman traditions. It is noteworthy that the German nationalists' feeling ran mostly against France after 1919, whereas before 1914 it had been against England.

wing cadres of the army took up arms in the service of the Weimar Republic against Bolshevism. But 1923 brought even more serious dangers; the dispute with France about the Ruhr aggravated the inflation of the currency and made it extremely severe; separatists were endeavouring to separate the left bank of the Rhine; Communist insurrections took place in Saxony, Thuringia, and Hamburg, while Bavaria was becoming increasingly independent of the Reich. The Republic was saved only with the help of the *Reichswehr*. But this success, which was brought about by governments more tinged with *bourgeois* nationalism than Socialism, in no way increased their moral authority; on the contrary, in the fight against Communism, nationalist opposition to 'the Marxist system of Weimar' became more vigorous and obdurate than before.

No government could survive without injury such serious and humiliating failures in foreign policy as did that of the Weimar Republic at that time.[1] In addition, there were the devastating effects of the financial catastrophe, both from the material and moral aspects. Have not these republican governments deceived the people (such were the sentiments of the majority of people who were ruined by the inflation) by devaluing their money, by seizing the painfully gained savings of those with small unearned incomes, and by allowing the big traders and industrialists to make fabulous profits by shady currency deals? Were not the members of the Government in league with all the big business men? And was not this financial chaos indicative of unbelievable corruption as compared with the excellent, economical, and inspired financial administration of the old Prussian system?

Yet this first serious crisis was overcome. The 'miracle of the *Renten-mark*' took place, the stabilisation of German currency as a result of the salvation-bringing American loans, and surprising economic prosperity which occurred very rapidly, too rapidly (1924–28). Stresemann's extremely skilful policy of reconciliation with France had a success which impressed the Germans, and nationalist resentment diminished. In 1928 the national Germans gained only 14 per cent of the total number of votes cast. The plebiscite organised by the extreme right to protest against the Young Plan for the payment of reparations was a lamentable failure (only 13·8 per cent of the electorate participated), and a left wing which was prepared to come to terms broke away from the national German Party, which had been, since 1928, led by the Pangerman Hügenberg.

If the prosperity of these years had continued, if the republic had

---

[1] I will not enumerate them here once more, but refer the reader to Viscount d'Abernon's Memoirs, in which their consequences are described with great vividness.

had new successes in internal and foreign policy and thus reestablished the public's confidence in it, the Weimar Republic might have slowly become stronger, and the internal divisions which had seemed irreconcilable might slowly have been reduced. In 1928 only 2·6 per cent of the electorate voted for the extreme right (National-Socialists) and only 10·6 per cent for the extreme left (Communists); the centre groups, from the Social-Democrats to Stresemann's party, received 58 per cent of the votes.

The repercussions of the international economic crisis on Germany's cheap-credit policy were disastrous to parliamentary democracy because the electors' confidence was once more destroyed. An impression of disaster became widespread—this republic is doomed to failure; and the efforts of the nationalists who recalled with gusto 'the good old days' strengthened this impression. For much of the electorate the economic prosperity and the political brilliance of the former Empire were closely connected with all the symbols of Prussian military monarchy. The new republic had heaped humiliation upon humiliation, and it was now adding to this the horrors of mass unemployment.

This general sentimental impression dominated reflection and reason. Stresemann's death on 30th October 1929 meant that the republic had lost its foremost leader, the only one in whom the confidence of the self-styled 'national' *bourgeoisie* reposed. His greatest success—Germany's membership of the League of Nations—lost its *éclat* beside the failure of his successor at the Ministry for Foreign Affairs (Curtius) to establish at least an economic union with Austria. This failure once again shook people's confidence in democracy, and earned the parliamentary government its reputation for irremediable weakness.

Furthermore, as unemployment increased, the Communist peril quickly became more serious. This manifested itself mainly in the big towns, especially in Berlin, where Communist votes in the *Reichstag* elections increased by 38 per cent between 1928 and 1932; there the Communist Party was the most powerful of all the parties, while in the Reich as a whole it gained 17 per cent of the total number of votes and sent some hundred representatives to the *Reichstag*. Everywhere people wondered if the republic could deal with this threat from the left without a civil war. The middle classes were still imbued with the terror of the 1922 and 1923 Communist insurrections. Then the right-wing armed bands had helped to save the situation.

Later, Hindenburg was elected President of the Reich, and a strong government under a popular figure was hoped for—his popularity in the First World War had not been forgotten. This was, of course, an illusion; no one could seriously believe that this quiet old gentleman possessed the intellectual ability and the independent energy necessary to deal with serious economic problems and grave political crises.

The emergency ordinances (*Notverordnungen*) of Brüning were inadequate to deal with them, too, and he, a conscientious and honest politician who was worthy of confidence, lacked the gift of arousing popular enthusiasm. Could a doctrine of peaceable reason, the rigorous reduction of public expenditure, and the carrying out of certain economic reforms be a popular success, and prevent the water from flowing to the mill of an agitator who was ready to insult everyone and exaggerate anything in order to shake the authority of the 'system of Weimar'? The extreme right and left cut away the ground from beneath the feet of Brüning's Government.

The result of the presidential election showed what a desperate situation had been reached by 1932—the left could put forward as a candidate against the leader of the National-Socialists no one other than the aged Hindenburg once more. Formerly the hope of the armed national associations and of the national Germans, the latter now were opposed to him, and put up their own candidate against him, Düsterberg, chief of the *Stahlhelm*. A grotesque change of sides! It was no longer a question of defending parliamentary freedom with armed associations, as it had been in 1919–23, and the Social-Democrats vainly endeavoured to dam the flow advancing from left and right with its own militant associations.

The crisis which took place in 1929–32 was above all a crisis of *confidence*. The German people would have required great patience and steadfast hope to have overcome it without a revolution of the parliamentary system. They should have told themselves that in spite of all the disappointments of the League of Nations, Germany's position in foreign affairs had definitely improved since Locarno; the 1929 Young Plan did, after all, mark considerable progress; other facilities for payment had followed the Young Plan, and even, in the summer of 1932, the ending of reparations payments by a final settlement was imminent. Further, if the economic *rapprochement* with Austria had failed, this was perhaps not irremediable; Germany's position abroad had become easier in some respects since the settling of the former Austro-Hungarian question and the establishment of various medium-sized new states from the Baltic to the Balkans situated between Germany and the great might of Russia. These states, even if hostile to Germany, needed her on account of her economy and as a support against Bolshevism; for their alliances with France could bring them only small or negligible assistance from that quarter. In any case, these alliances, which had at first seemed so threatening, were more of a burden than an advantage for France, who was no longer strong enough to maintain her role as the most influential country in Europe for any length of time.

The 'chains of Versailles' had for some time been becoming less binding, although rather reluctantly. And, more important, the Russian frontier had now moved much further east; the old pressure on two fronts which in various forms had been exerted on Central Europe for centuries, and which had such disastrous results in the First World War, had now been removed, or at any rate very much reduced. (Since Rapallo, Bismarck's famous 'line to St Petersburg' even seemed to have been re-established!)

They ought also to have told themselves that the 1929 economic crisis was international, and that it would one day die out or be overcome by the regeneration of world economy; the rest of the world was, in the long run, anxious, for its own good, that Germany should have large and healthy outlets. The productive apparatus of German economy, which had been much enlarged and modernised between 1924 and 1928 and now represented by far the greatest economic potential on the Continent, should attract more capital, and once again play a leading part in world trade. Finally, the deflationary policy could be relaxed, and the recovery of economic life could be aided by public works, both policies which Brüning had planned in detail.

But the people would have needed a great deal more perspicacity and patience than it possessed in order to consider matters in this light. It was practically impossible to make of these very reasonable considerations and hopes a wide popular programme which would have any effect. There were a large number of people who had decided to remain calm at all costs, even among the right (one group was formed by the young Conservative Party (*jung-conservative Partei*), which broke away from the national German Party). But the majority of electors who supported Hitler lacked the patience and perspicacity necessary to do so. They were moved by feelings, as the masses usually are, and not by intellectual considerations— mainly by feelings of hatred, which Hitler, the popular orator, whipped up with such skill.

Lacking any kind of critical ability, the masses saw in Hitler a saviour and a prophet, as he described in a voice hoarse with passion the violent brutalities committed by the victorious Powers on a defenceless Germany, as he promised that the criminals of November 1918 would be punished ('Some tens of thousands', he wrote in *Mein Kampf*, 'shall one day expiate this crime against the state'); as he poured ridicule on the bungling of the 'Marxist fumblers', as he pilloried the internal corruption of the 'system of Weimar', or invoked the satanism of Bolshevism, or the grotesque spectre of an international conspiracy of Jews. No one asked how much this deluge of accusations contained of truth, exaggeration or slander, of wild invention or of lies. We can still remember the horror with which we saw this preaching of boundless hatred echoed in the newspapers of the period, and its effect on a public opinion which was both worried and contaminated.

It is extraordinary that these speeches filled with hatred were interpreted as the preparation for a new and more fundamental popular community (*Volksgemeinschaft*). Yet they were interpreted in this way. Many people were aware of the eccentric side of Hitler's visions of the future and of the fanaticism and furious passion of his movement. His *confrères*, shadows of demagogy, partly corrupt, partly suspect, and partly plebeian, were much more strongly criticised. It was realised that the minor leaders of the new movement were the men who had created disturbances at public meetings, and were therefore not worthy of confidence; the National-Socialist press was unreliable, its intellectual level very low, and its writings peculiar and of miserable quality. Nevertheless, the new popular community, the political and moral regeneration of the whole nation which was extolled in it, was regarded as an imposing doctrine, full of possibilities for the future.

How was such blindness possible? Was it the result of general decadence, of the disappearance of the tenets of religious morality? Did the German people lack moral instinct, and were they therefore unable to sense when a thing came from below? This lack of political and moral flair seems to be the most serious guilt with which the Germans who supported Hitler in these years can be reproached, and this reproach is not diminished by the fact that Germany was certainly not the only country to lack political and moral instinct where Hitler was concerned.

However, three factors must be taken into consideration. In the first place, calumnies, insults, and the moral abasement of the opposition are part of the normal equipment of every political struggle, and the violence with which this deplorable method is used varies only in degree. He who preaches distrust in a tottering government will always have great success in a modern mass democracy (as we have already remarked). And in Germany the political discussion was developing into a latent civil war; in a civil war strong fists are superior to all speeches and convictions. Of course, the peaceable *bourgeois* is inferior in such a sort of combat.

Secondly, it needed a high degree of moral and intellectual superiority to rest quiet and patient in such a situation as the Germans experienced in 1931–32, in the face of steadily growing millions of unemployed and of continual failures of foreign policy.

Thirdly, and more important, Hitler's demagogy was not restricted to negation alone. It gave the masses an admittedly indefinite conception of the future, but one which impressed them and aroused their enthusiasm. Hitler's criticism of existing Powers was not designed to cause despair, but to prepare the way for what he named the regeneration of the state and the people.

The 'chains of Versailles', he said, will be cast off as soon as Germany is regenerated from within, as soon as the will of the people really becomes assured, and thus permits a strong and definite leadership. The German people must put an end to the reign of numerous parties, must seize power from the November criminals, and place it in the hands of a national leadership; then Germany will be so great that the victorious Powers of Versailles will be obliged to give her her 'right to life' (*Lebensrecht*) without a struggle. Germany must be strong, so as to be indispensable to other countries; then she will not lack allies.[1]

First of all, Germany must be set in order. A definite plan of action in the field of economics was hardly mentioned. But Hitler's hearers, dazzled by the vision of a new and more glorious Germany, scarcely noticed this omission. The appeal to instincts of hatred was covered up by declarations of idealist and patriotic sentiments—virile courage, discipline, selfless readiness to serve the community, the tendency of all forces towards one great end: spontaneous devotion to the whole, the social brotherhood of all classes.

As in Mussolini's Italy, the ideal of brotherhood at the front, where in the World War there were no party or class differences, was extremely important. Hitler also adopted the ideal of military leadership and discipline as the best means of creating an orderly state. For the people, however, to be led was to co-operate voluntarily and not to be commanded; his followers (*Gefolgschaft*) were governed by fidelity to the *Führer*, himself an official carrying out the will of the people, who undertook on his side to be faithful to his followers.

Thus was born the false image of a moral community, which concealed the future dictator's lust for power. He was able to appeal simultaneously to the highest and lowest instincts. This mixture is always the most effective in politics—good and evil, noble and vile, truth, lies, and half-truths.

The essential, and in the last analysis decisive, factors which explain Hitler's swift rise to power have been given. In my opinion all that remains to be said is of secondary importance.

Above all, great care should be exercised in making use of literary

---

[1] In *Mein Kampf* (I, 4 and II, 13) the possibility of an alliance with England was raised—an alliance in which Germany would be protected by 'the greatest Power in the world', and would overthrow France and acquire a great colonial empire in Russia for German settlers. Hitler stuck to his *idées fixes* with almost unbelievable tenacity, as illustrated in *Hitler's Table Talk*. Naturally, in his electoral campaign in 1933 these 'distant ends' were veiled or not mentioned; for many years after the National-Socialist seizure of power the slogan 'Vote for Hitler and vote for peace' was still to be seen on posters.

evidence in order to show that the German mind had propensities which made it particularly accessible to *National-Socialist doctrines*.

These doctrines, tirelessly hawked round by Hitler, were based on the racial superiority of the German people, thanks to its Nordic-Germanic elements, over all non-Germanic peoples, and hence the German claim to dominate others. This doctrine of a 'people of German lords', which was transformed into incredible methods of violence during the Second World War, made the National-Socialist régime (and also the name of Germany) detested by the whole world. It is thought to be Hitler's distinctive (and very evil) mark on the one-party state, as opposed to the one-party states of Italy and Russia.

Whence came this doctrine? Was it widespread in Germany before Hitler's day, or did he himself develop it? Up to the present time precise scientific research on Hitler's intellectual origins has scarcely begun.[1] But it is clear that his theory of a 'people of lords' is not based either on the general racial theories of biologists and ethnologists, or on that branch of the biological theory of races which is applied to history (Gobineau, Schemann, or Chamberlain), with, moreover, the unanimous contradiction of German historians. Similarly German and Austrian anti-Semitism, which changed its character in these two countries as in others from a purely denominational movement to a purely racial one, cannot be regarded as being the basis of the 'people of lords' doctrine.

It is true that such theories were to be found in small, isolated groups of people, composed of fanatical germanophile racial theorists with occultist tendencies, whose writings were regarded in pre-1914 Germany as wildly eccentric, and that the young Hitler apparently studied them with enthusiasm. Apparently a group of his friends and future adherents belonged to a group of this kind in Munich after 1919 (among them Hess and Rosenberg)—the 'Thule Society' (*Thule Gesellschaft*), which was connected with an older 'Germanic order', violently anti-semite, founded in 1912. The obscure writings of this racialist society, which partly followed in the wake of the Pangerman movement, contained by 1914 numerous ideas which are similar to the later National-Socialist racial writings. Up to the present time the way in which these writings, anti-semite pamphlets and books of all kinds, Nietzsche's works and the cult of Wagner may have influenced Hitler's thought has not been sufficiently examined. He read a great deal, and had had no formal intellectual education. Innumerable combinations were therefore possible. The history of

[1] See especially Joachim Besser's informative, but still provisional, essay: 'Die Vorgeschichte des National-sozialismus in neuem Licht' in *Die Pforte*, second year, numbers 21, 22, November 1952. The German institute for the study of the Nationalist-Socialist period at Munich is engaged in preparing a detailed study of Hitler's beginnings.

Hitler's intellectual background certainly bears little relation to the general intellectual history of Germany.

It is more related to the history of his own country, Austria. The domestic history of the Habsburg state is surely one of the decisive factors, not of Hitler's rapid rise to power, but of his political theories. The unusual situation of the Danubian state, with its numerous peoples, made the national consciousness of the Germans there particularly excitable and assertive. For many centuries they had really been 'a people of lords', and were now deposed by non-Germanic peoples. The nationalist struggle embraced all classes of people, including the working classes, so that a connection between nationalism and Socialism was possible in Austria, and National-Socialist parties sprang up well before Hitler's arrival. Here lay the roots not only of the partisan spirit of Hitlerian nationalism, but also of his racial pride as regards the Slavonic peoples—the unceasing and ever more acrid disputes between Austrian Germans and Czechs and Poles, the constant fear of Pan-Slavs and Russian imperialism. The 'cultural superiority' of Germanism in the face of the Slavonic races was a battle-cry which was continually raised. There were, no doubt, similar conflicts in the German states which bordered on Poland; but a nationalist born in the Reich would never turn his energies to these, instead of to the traditional rivalry with the West, with the 'hereditary enemy', France, nor dream of a great campaign against Russia in alliance with England, so that a large German colony might be established on Russian soil—a dream which Hitler tried desperately to make a reality in 1941–42.[1]

In this respect, therefore, the historical origins of Hitlerism are to be found outside the Reich. It is impossible to state that there was in Germany a traditional hatred for the Slavs which was the basis of an anti-Russian policy. Only the Poles were hated, not the Russians, and that only after Germany's bitter post-war experiences.

Hitler's racial doctrines had much less scope in Germany than in Austria, as a result of natural and historical circumstances. The German people were, indeed, flattered to hear themselves continually declared a people of born lords, and that the Germanic–Nordic race was superior to all others. But when the causes of Hitler's great electoral successes are examined, his racial doctrines cannot be regarded as very important. In any case, the most profound secrets of this doctrine, as expounded by Rosenberg in the form of a muddled mystique, were incomprehensible to the masses. What was the race, and 'racial patrimony'? Was it a physical or an intellectual phenomenon? What is the difference between race and nationality? Throughout the reign of National-Socialism most Germans never knew the answers to these questions. Mass sentiment

[1] See *Hitler's Table Talk*, No. 1.

saw no difference between the nationalists' praise of the German people and praise of the race of Germanic lords.

The appeal to instincts of hatred for the Jews had much more practical effect. These instincts were stronger in Germany than in Western European countries, but less strong than in the countries of Eastern Europe. These instincts had, by 1914, already been made use of in politics, but anti-semite groups had not been able to last for long. In the period after the war, hatred of the Jews had been aroused once again by numerous disagreeable incidents, principally the migration of Jews from the East—a circumstance which favoured National-Socialism. Most educated people continued to regard politically active anti-Semitism as a plebeian affair; but Hitler's anti-semite agitation at first had a powerful effect on the lower middle class. When, under the Third Reich, he passed from words to action on a huge scale, it is true to say that his popularity diminished rather than increased.

The most effective of all National-Socialist theories was undoubtedly the doctrine of the struggle for *Lebensraum*, of all creatures' eternal struggle for existence, and of the natural law of the strongest. This was not invented by Hitler, but came from Darwinian theories which had been influencing the political literature of Europe for many years, and which caused disturbing symptoms in the writings of other countries too.

Why did the theory of a people without room (*Volk ohne Raum*) have so great a success in Germany? There is no point in discussing this at length. The geographical situation, the natural vitality of the nation, and the strong pressure of an expanding population are sufficient to explain it. But it is certain that Hitler would never have dared make his warlike plans for conquest known to the public earlier than 1933, for fear of destroying all the electoral success of his party. A war of conquest was certainly not a slogan for elections.

All this raises serious doubts as to whether the National-Socialist racial doctrines, their *Weltanschauung*, won the masses over to Hitler's side. This conception of the world remained until the collapse of the Third Reich, an idea which was much talked of and little understood, which innumerable lessons were to instil into the German people, but which never became really popular (as the fate of most of the party's publications shows). The masses did not hail Hitler as the prophet of a new conception of the world, but as a man in whom they could put their trust, and they expected him to bring about a new unity within the nation through which deliverance from the internal and external troubles of the post-war period would be attained.

The most powerful element in his advent (which continued to act even during the Second World War) was his gift of radiating

confidence in the future—an indomitable confidence in the principle
'where there's a will there's a way'. This confidence was due to his
fanatical faith in himself and in his mission, a faith that doubts and
self-criticism scarcely touched. This was what assured him political
superiority over so many highly cultured politicians in the Weimar
Republic, who were, however, tormented by doubts and problems.
The sentimental feeling that the victory of this man would put an
end to these gnawing problems and that speedy action would then
begin certainly won him a great many supporters.

His indomitable confidence in himself was closely connected with
his belief that he represented the true will of the people. Therein lay
his strength, but also the danger which was to be fatal to him.
Since his confidence in himself laid low all criticism, it became
idolatry. If one rises up as a superman, one becomes inhuman. By
challenging all the world to take up arms against him, he became
the victim of his own inhumanity.

It may perhaps be legitimate to point out that the danger which
became visible in Hitler did not end with his fall; not because his
supporters have not entirely disappeared, and nationalists even less
so; but mainly because it seems as if there is today a dangerous want
of proportion between the indomitable self-confidence of the heads
of totalitarian states whose instinct for power goes straight to the
point, and the mentality of the free Western world, which is tormented by innumerable doubts and even by outbursts of nihilism.

10

AN EXPLANATION OF THE ECONOMIC CONDITIONS WHICH CONTRIBUTED TO THE VICTORY OF NATIONAL-SOCIALISM

Friedrich Lütge

THERE can be no doubt that the successful advent of National-Socialism in Germany was brought about by a great number of interrelated causes. This essay, however, is specifically concerned with the relevant economic factors: so that a class of data which in fact should be considered only in the light of their interdependence with other intellectual, sociological, and political factors are here treated separately. This essay is not an attempt to give one single explanation of causes, but to deal separately with this class of facts. It is true that the field of economics has increased in every way during the last century, and that economic factors especially played an important part in the victory of National-Socialism; but economic conditions could not have caused this victory had they not acted in connection with other factors.

The economic evolution of Germany after the First World War was characterised by three disastrous events which must be mentioned at the outset.

1. The direct economic effects of the First World War and the costs of the reparations associated with it.
2. The great inflation between 1918 and 1923.
3. The great world economic crisis between 1930 and 1932.

These three factors did not contribute equally to the development of National-Socialism. In particular it is worth noting that the damage caused by the first two events seemed to have been overcome during the years 1924–29; for during these years the German economy experienced a boom which seems to indicate this. Well-being increased, and even the standard of living of the public in general improved. Germany's economic relations with foreign countries seemed secure, and her currency was at that time one of the strongest in the world. It can be said that the National-Socialists would never have attained power if this favourable development had continued and not been suddenly and disastrously

417

interrupted by the world economic crisis. So it might appear that this world economic crisis was the decisive economic factor leading to the victory of National-Socialism. Such a supposition, however, is false. For this crisis awakened memories of past disasters which exerted a profound influence on the communal psychology of the German people. Certain economic consequences of the earlier disasters only now began to make themselves felt: e.g., the complete eradication of the classes with small and medium-sized personal estates, and hence the destruction of economic reserves whose exist-ence would have enabled Germany to get through the depression more easily. The people were again reminded of the great losses suffered in the previous war and of the burden of the reparations—so that many Germans were led to believe that salvation and help were to be found only through the policy advocated by the prophets of the National-Socialist ideology.

It is for this reason that economic developments before the world economic crisis must be examined as well as those of the subsequent depression.

1. The Effects of the First World War

The collapse of Germany in 1918 had widespread consequences for both her internal and external economy. Basically, German economy had been spared the direct effects of the war; however, four and a half years of war had forced Germany to exploit her economic strength unmercifully, and these excesses had serious results. In addition to the 165 billion marks which the war had cost her, her productive equipment was completely worn out. It had been im-possible to replace machinery, even the most essential repairs had not been carried out, the yield of cultivable land had decreased con-siderably as a result of the shortage of labour and of fertilisers, and communication facilities were in an extremely bad state. The popu-lation, which had been unable to acquire sufficient consumer goods for years, had accumulated an extraordinary demand for goods, which had still to be satisfied.

These were the economic ills inevitably caused by so great a war even in the victorious countries, though certainly in France to a greater extent than in England.

Furthermore, the health and capacity for work of the German people, which had suffered severely as a result of the long blockade and of famine, could only recover slowly. For many years hundreds of thousands of prisoners were detained abroad as labourers, and this also reduced the German labour potential.

The cession of important territories caused additional losses to an already weakened economy: Alsace-Lorraine, the Saar territory (until 1935), parts of Poznan and West Prussia, the eastern part of Upper Silesia, Danzig and the Memel territory, as well as all the German colonies, whose economic development had made considerable progress in the years before the First World War. The ceded territories (including the Saar) occupied 13·1 per cent of the area of the Reich; but this amounted to 14·6 per cent of the cultivable land, 75 per cent of the iron ore deposits, 68 per cent of the zinc deposits, and 26 per cent of the output of coal.

To these losses must be added reparations in money and in kind. According to the official figures, Germany paid a total of 51·7 billion marks (gold marks) as reparations up to 31st August 1924. Even though the Reparations Commission registered only about 8 billion marks out of this total in its accounts, the fact remains that the German economy was depleted of these assets, while the countries to which they were destined were correspondingly enriched. The 51·7 billion marks included the following items:

	Million marks
Liquidation of private German assets (except in the United States, Russia, Brazil, and Cuba)	10,080
Renunciation of claims on former allies	8,600
Cession of assets belonging to the Reich or to the Länder .	9,670
Coal and coke	2,334
Ships handed over or confiscated	4,542
Railway equipment surrendered	1,106
Army goods of non-military character left in occupied territories	5,041
Payments in specie on the basis of the London stipulations .	1,700

To this figure of 51·7 billion marks must be added loans totalling about 8 billion on the basis of the London Protocol of 1924, and of about 3·1 billion on the 'Dawes Plan' until 31st July 1931.

Comparison of these loans—without taking into account the assets lost in the colonies—with the 4 billion marks indemnities paid by France after the war of 1871—a useful comparison—shows that Germany was obliged to pay twelve times as much per head of population as France at that time. The indemnity imposed on France in 1871 amounted to 3·2 per cent of her national wealth in the immediately preceding peace year; Germany paid 38 per cent, or twelve times as much. In comparison with France in 1871, Germany's payments expressed as a proportion of national income were nine times as high. As a proportion of her monetary reserves, Germany even paid twenty-two times as much. And these sums were regarded then as a beginning only. Other demands, always excessively high, were made which had their effect on the economic and psychological situation. In 1921 J. M. Keynes declared that the reparations demanded of Germany were three times as great as the German economic potential.

One particularly important fact was Germany's loss of all foreign investments. Since about 1890 Germany had become a creditor, instead of a debtor country; her balance of trade, becoming more and more passive, was counterbalanced by invisible items (services, interest, etc.), and in fact considerable capital investment had taken place abroad. In one stroke this situation was completely changed. Germany had lost all her foreign investments, her fleet, etc., and had again become a debtor country. She was suddenly compelled to activate her balance of trade not only to meet her accumulated requirements of raw materials and foodstuffs, but also in order to make the cash payments which had been imposed upon her. The truth which the English philosopher David Hume had once tried to impress on his compatriots—viz. that the prosperity of a country depends on that of its neighbour—seemed to have been forgotten.

That simple truth applied even more after the great progress which the international division of labour had made in the 150 years which had elapsed since David Hume. Only in this way—the way of international co-operation—could general prosperity be re-established and the general distress left by the war be remedied. Foreign countries should therefore have adapted themselves to the expansion of German exports. However, just the opposite happened. The Peace Treaty imposed numerous conditions intended—and with success—to create a one-sided handicap for German trade. Thus, the most-favoured-nation clause acting unilaterally in favour of France and of other countries: imports free of import duty, and a 26 per cent duty on exports, etc.

It is impossible, and pointless, to pursue the development of the reparations question here. In general, this development took the form of a slow, very slow, return to political and economic good sense, with a fatal interruption in 1923, when the industrial basin of Western Germany was occupied by force and cut off from the Reich. This deprived the German economy of about 1,370 million marks of services in kind and in money, and, in addition, caused the total collapse of the currency. These services, like those already mentioned, had to be financed from what remained of Germany's economic substance, with a corresponding lowering of her economic potential. It was only slowly that Germany's former enemies adopted a more reasonable economic policy. In 1918, at the time of the parliamentary elections in Great Britain, the annual sum to be paid by Germany was fixed at 28·8 billion marks; in 1919 the French Minister for Finance laid down a figure of 18 billion marks per annum; in such circumstances the 'Dawes Plan', which fixed a figure of 2·5 billion marks (although with the condition that this sum would increase as German prosperity increased), was a change which indicated a more intelligent approach to the whole problem, and events in the next few years seemed to show that this arrangement was feasible. Yet, even so, it must be realised that Germany was unable easily to effect the annual transfer of such sums without the help of considerable foreign loans, principally American, which from September 1924 until the Hoover moratorium in July 1931 totalled 10·821 billion marks. German reparations paid before 1924 came from her assets, those paid after 1924 from credit only. The disastrous nature of such a method was to become clear as soon as the great world economic crisis caused the withdrawal of credits. But this will be discussed in greater detail later.

In general, it is true to say that the victorious Powers' treatment of the reparations question gave rise to inflammable sentiments inevitably reinforcing the nationalist tendencies which are always a danger in a conquered people wishing to regain its former position. Memories of the generous peace settlement made with France in 1815, after her wars of conquest had ravaged the whole of Europe, were awakened, a settlement which, above all, left intact the economic strength of France, and which testified to a wisdom greater than following generations could attain. It is true that as soon as von Papen's Government came into power all further claims to reparations were definitely cancelled; but owing to the troubled circumstances which prevailed at the end of 1932 the National-Socialist Government, which came into power in January 1933, succeeded in concealing this fact and pretended that the release from all reparations commitments was the work of the National-Socialists.

II. THE GREAT INFLATION

In conjunction with the direct and indirect effects of the First World War, the great German inflation added other serious consequences which affected the social and economic structure of Germany.

Like other countries, Germany had been compelled to abandon the gold standard at the beginning of the war, i.e., to suspend the convertibility into gold of the notes issued by the *Reichsbank*. Had this not been done, the *Reichsbank*'s gold reserves would have been exhausted in a few weeks or months. And since this gold would have been hoarded principally by the public, currency in circulation would have been reduced to such an extent as to cause the collapse of economic life. Considered as an economic measure, the abandonment of the gold standard was therefore completely justified. In itself, this step was not a sign of inflation.

Nor was the increasing amount of paper money in itself an evil. This increase was caused by a larger issue of bank-notes on the basis of Reich Treasury bills (*Reichsschatzwechsel*), and by the establishment of loan banks (*Darlehenskassen*), which gave credit to *Länder* and municipalities. These lent on securities which the *Reichsbank* did not itself accept, and paid out a new paper money—loan banks' certificates (*Darlehenskassenscheine*). All wars necessitate an increase in fiduciary currency because new accounts are opened (for military supplies, military units, etc.) which have to be provided with means of payment. All the other countries did the same thing.

Similarly, it is a fact that any modern war (together with the necessary production of armaments) must inevitably entail a certain inflationary increase of the volume of money. For the individual's income cannot immediately be limited sufficiently (either by reducing wages and salaries or by increasing taxation) to reduce the flow of money as much as the output of consumer goods, which is diminished because of those goods which have been produced for purposes of destruction and which are not available for exchange against any part of the national income. All that can be done is to keep the inflationary tendency within reasonable limits. And, in this respect, much depends on the way in which the war is financed.

It must be admitted that the way in which the war was financed in Germany was altogether wrong, and that this gave the great inflation a decisive impetus.

Instead of a great reduction of spending power by reducing incomes or by increasing taxation, resort was had to printing money to finance the war. This must be principally explained by the fact that those in power in Germany had not reckoned with the war, and that even when hostilities began, they expected them to last only a short time. This at any rate is the only explanation which can be found for the German method of financing the war. The number of banknotes in circulation and of the loan banks' certificates was steadily increased. The sums of money which had been brought into circulation were subsequently absorbed by war loans; they were transformed into long-term loans, in fact. Furthermore, no special war taxes, such as had been immediately imposed in England, were imposed in Germany. Fiscal measures were decided upon only relatively late, and in a completely inadequate manner—the introduction of a war profits tax (*Kriegsgewinnsteuer*), of a tax on turnover (*Umsatzsteuer*), later a tax on coal (*Kohlensteuer*) and on transport (*Beförderungssteuer*). War loans yielded a total of nearly 100 billion marks, which covered only about 60 per cent of the war expenditure. In all, during the war the circulation of notes increased sixfold, and the amount of cash deposits (*Buchgeld*) fivefold. As regards the budget, the war was financed not from the ordinary budget (taxation, etc.) but almost entirely from extraordinary budgetary items (war loans), as from the sale of Treasury bills to the *Reichsbank*. As a comparison: in 1913 the Reich's debts amounted to 5·4 billion marks and the servicing of the National Debt cost 230 million marks; in 1920 the National Debt of the Reich totalled 200 billion marks, and the servicing of the debt cost 12·4 billion marks, or 45 per cent of the ordinary budget.

With a few exceptions neither the population nor those in power in Germany realised the implications of such measures. They had no experience of such situations and remained faithful to the nominalist theory of money, excellent in itself, as propounded by G. F. Knapp, even when this theory had become absurd ('one mark is worth one mark'). Finally the closing of the Stock Exchange had removed any possibility of accurately estimating values. At the end of the war phase of inflation the exchange value of the German mark with neutral countries was still 50 per cent of its former level. If a sensible economic and financial policy had been carried out in Germany and abroad, the situation could have been re-established quite satisfactorily. Foreign countries, by their policy on reparations and trade relations, and Germany, by her monetary and financial policy, prevented such a re-establishment from taking place. The development of foreign policy is clearly reflected in the rate of exchange of the dollar. In the spring of 1922 the dollar rate in Berlin was 290 marks to the dollar—still a fairly stable exchange. When, from the middle of that year onwards, Poincaré's Government in France resorted to ever more violent political threats, the dollar rate rose rapidly, and reached a record height of 9,150 marks on 8th November 1922. The occupation of the Ruhr in January 1923 set the last disastrous development into motion, which was rendered more serious by the fact that the whole of the German people had resorted to 'passive resistance', so that the Reich was compelled to support the millions of workers and civil servants in the Ruhr, as well as their families, and this could be done only by printing money, since the revenue from taxation was insufficient. On 19th October 1923 one dollar was worth 12 billion marks, on 1st November, 120 billion marks, and finally, on 20th November, 4,200 billion marks, which was the equivalent of 2·3 trillion paper marks for one gold mark. History had never seen so great a depreciation of currency. Even the famous *assignats* of the French Revolution had kept one four-thousandth of their original value!

It has already been observed that the financial policy followed by Germany at that time is open to severe criticism. She did not balance the budgets of the Reich, the *Länder*, and the municipalities in time by rigorously increasing taxation. Of course the speed with which the currency depreciated in 1923 could not have been dealt with by any administration, for in the time which must inevitably elapse between the imposition and the yield of taxes a new and considerable rise in the dollar rate took place. But the surpluses of the Reich's budget in 1922 soon gave place to enormous deficits 'covered' by printed money. The stabilisation of the German currency, first through the provisional *Rentenmark* and then through the *Reichsmark*, could succeed only because the monetary policy was supported by a really energetic financial policy, which removed deficits from the budget and, after some fluctuation, ensured the stability of the exchange rates of German currency even abroad.

The economic consequences of inflation should not be judged by purely quantitative criteria. One of the consequences has already been mentioned—the eradication of the classes with small and medium-sized estates. This wealth consisted mainly of deposits in savings banks, mortgages, and securities, particularly among the upper middle classes, who, actuated by patriotic considerations, chose to convert a great deal of their holdings into war loans. And since the nominal value of these war loans was never raised, they represented a total loss.

It is sometimes remarked that inflation freed the German Reich from debt. This argument is entirely false; for it ignores the fact that the public debt represented a source of income for the creditors who were citizens of the Reich. These sources of income were abolished by inflation. Thus the whole middle class lost the economic reserves which it had formerly possessed, and was obliged to rely entirely or almost entirely on income from labour.

This factor was later very skilfully exploited by the National-Socialists: those who refused to submit to them were liable to the imposition of sanctions which would damage their reputations or cause dismissal—at least as far as officials were concerned—and heads of families were often faced with the alternative of either complying or else jeopardising the economic support on which their families depended. This process of 'proletarianisation' accomplished by inflation, and which to a large extent caused the economic uprooting of the middle classes, was certainly one of the most important factors responsible for the victory of National-Socialism, independently of the political feeling engendered by the reparations policy of other countries, in particular that of France.

However, the serious errors made at that time by the economic leaders of Germany must also be stressed; small and medium incomes were not re-established as quickly as was possible. From that time onwards the great masses without property were confronted with a small group of extremely rich persons. And the abyss which separated them was made deeper by a distinctly unhealthy distribution of income. Then, too, the millions of people with small or tiny incomes, the comparatively small group with medium incomes, and an extremely small, but economically extremely powerful, group of persons with large or very large incomes found themselves face to face. In such conditions it is not surprising that a hatred of 'capitalism' developed and that people began to gravitate towards a movement 'which described itself as socialist but was definitely anti-Marxist, and which joined with its socialism the password of nationalism'. The rejection of 'capitalism' was transformed into a rejection of a free economy, and the marriage of this type of socialism with nationalism seemed able to accomplish the task ordained by fate. Two additional factors strengthened these tendencies. The first was the great invasion of German economic life by foreigners. For a few dollars foreigners could acquire not only scarce consumer goods, but also real estate, shares, stock, and other types of assets.

In addition to this there was the large influx of nationals of Eastern European countries or races, chiefly Jews from the East, who were frequently able to amass large fortunes without doing productive work, simply by deals on the Stock Exchange and by acting as middle-men in commercial activities, while the poverty of the masses became daily more acute. The families of German Jews who had lived for many years in Germany often themselves denounced this unfortunate development, and warned people of its inherent dangers, fearing, quite correctly, that a wave of anti-Semitism would arise which, like all mass psychoses, would not differentiate between 'the just and the unjust'. Indeed, the anti-semite movement in Germany, which until 1914 had never been very important, received an impetus which was exploited by National-Socialist propaganda. It is not now necessary to make excuses, but simply to give the psychological explanation of events which, without this explanation, would remain completely incomprehensible.

III. INTERLUDE: THE ECONOMIC UPSWING (1924–1930)

After 1924 Germany recovered from her earlier economic troubles with a speed and to an extent which seemed scarcely credible, and was able to pay off the reparations loans without undue difficulty. It has been said that there is no comparable feat to be found in European history. In the place of dilapidated industrial plant a completely new equipment sprang up, fulfilling every requirement of modern methods. In spite of the numerous obstacles in the way of exports, German industry began to recapture her former position in world markets with surprising rapidity, especially as regards the electrical, chemical, and optical industries, and also partly in the textile and machine industries. The merchant fleet was re-equipped with completely modern ships and soon provided more efficient services than the fleets of other countries which generally consisted of older ships. By 1930 the tonnage of the German merchant fleet almost equalled that of the year 1914. Exports increased rapidly, reached the pre-war level by 1926, and continued to increase until 1929. Heavy investments were made in housing, as well as in cultural and social activities.

This whole development appears almost inexplicable, and has indeed been described as a 'miracle'. It is, however, quite comprehensible if only the core of the question is understood: the powerful influx of foreign capital, especially from America. In all, from 1924 to July 1931 Germany received 20 billion *Reichsmarks* in public or private loans, and also about 5 billion *Reichsmarks* in direct capital investment. As has already been stated, these loans provided the funds with which the reparations were paid during these years; but enough was left to compensate the inadequate formation of capital at the beginning of this period, and to make possible the enormous capital investment which, added to the reawakening of the energy of the German people, set a powerful economic upswing in motion. It is true that this capital meant a heavy burden in interest and amortisation for the future, and it is important to realise that the high rates of interest in Germany were the result of political, and not of economic considerations. The optimism of that period saw no dangers in the high rates of interest nor in the size of the foreign debt, for it was thought that the recent increase in German exports would make it possible to meet these obligations without difficulty, and this optimism was shared by foreign countries; if this had not been the case, it is unlikely that they would have agreed to grant so much credit.

Furthermore, German investments abroad had reached the considerable sum of 10 billion *Reichsmarks* in these years, which meant that there were corresponding sums on the credit side of the balance of payments.

A few critics declared that the entire edifice was nothing more than a house of cards destined to collapse if the development did not continue in a straight line; but the majority of politicians and economists believed in a long-lasting upswing, or at any rate in stability, and considered these warnings to be groundless. The impact of the great world economic crisis of 1931 gave rise to a situation which surpassed the fears of even the most pessimistic critics.

IV. THE WORLD ECONOMIC CRISIS (1930–1932)

The great crisis, whose first signs appeared in 1929, when the New York Stock Exchange collapsed, and which reached its height in 1931, must be described as a *world* economic crisis, even from the point of view of German economy. For this disastrous crisis caused the collapse of international economic relations.

The reparations problem was solved only superficially. The 'Young Plan', which had replaced the 'Dawes Plan' on 30th January 1930—so named after Owen D. Young, Chairman of the Commission of Experts, Director of the General Electric Company—had indeed brought further progress, but no solution. Although it removed the controlling organisations which humiliated Germany, it also set up a payments plan which would not be terminated until 1988. The Plan recognised, no doubt, that Germany's ability to pay depended on her future potentialities, and that her ability to transfer sums of money depended on her exports; but the truth of the axiom formulated by Keynes in 1921, that an increase in German exports of this nature would have a strong adverse effect on the British economy, and that in general the carrying out of a reparations programme did nobody any good, had not yet been recognised. In particular, the fundamental element of the Young Plan was ignored—it did not merely force Germany to undertake unilateral obligations, but also compelled the other contracting parties to create, on their side, those conditions which were necessary if Germany were to fulfil her part of the agreement. This meant that other countries must be prepared to accept German imports, or, in other words, that they must abandon a protectionist commercial policy. But at the very moment when the crisis occurred protectionism was strengthened, and that at a time when new markets should have been made available.

One other factor played a disastrous role; German reparations payments and the payments which the Allies had undertaken to make to the United States were interconnected. Arrangements made in various places for the abolition of reparations always came to nothing because the United States was unable to decide to abolish or substantially reduce payments due to her as a result of the war, and, conversely, other countries did not consider that they could abolish reparations. The equilibrium of the American balance of payments was clearly dependent on the Allied payments.

There was thus an obvious contradiction between the granting of enormous loans to Germany and the refusal to take into account her pressing need to develop her exports; for how could she meet the payments of reparations governed by political reasons as well as pay interest and amortisation on large private loans except by exporting products and services.

One particular trouble was due to the fact that most of the foreign loans were given for a short term only, but that they had of necessity been invested in fixed assets. Apart from the possibility of transferring these sums, the short-term recall of these loans inevitably caused collapse and crisis.

In order to make this situation of interdependence clearer, let us consider the position of the German banks. Banks in Germany, particularly the large ones, combined the functions of deposit banks and investment banks, a combination which made them much more sensitive to crises than purely commercial or investment banks. Their credit structure depended to only a small extent on their own capital, but mainly on the influx of foreign money (deposits). The great inflation had accentuated this situation, so that as soon as this structure began to totter the crisis might be expected to become more serious.

The banks had lost most of their own capital as a result of the inflation. After the currency had been stabilised in 1924 they were unable to increase their capital partly through lack of time and opportunity, partly through an inconceivable error. In their active transactions, therefore, they invested not their own capital, but the money of their depositors. Before the First World War the ratio of their own capital to deposited money was 1 to 3 or 4; when the great crisis occurred this ratio was 1 to 15 or 20. A loss of 5 or 10 per cent of their investments was therefore enough to absorb the banks' own capital. The fact that a large proportion of their deposits was in foreign money—40 or 50 per cent in the big Berlin banks—meant that they were to an extraordinarily great extent dependent on economic developments abroad. There was no lack of well-informed men who recognised the dangers of such a situation and who advised against it, but those responsible for the German banks, and also foreigners, who saw none of these dangers, dismissed the warnings with an optimism which was incomprehensible to later observers. The *Reichsbank*, led by men with considerable insight, lacked sufficient power to intervene. For reasons which were valid in themselves, the *Reichsbank* had been made autonomous, independent of the authority of the Reich, as a guarantee against inflationary measures; but no provisions had been made in the law (*Bankgesetz*) to allow the *Reichsbank* genuinely to dominate the banks.

Similarly, there were no regulations for private banks laying down a healthy proportion between the total of paid-up capital and the volume of transactions, for example, or the total of liquid reserves, etc. It was for this reason that the municipalities could be prevented from incurring foreign debts only by the establishment of a new consultative bureau. As a whole, the battle against incurring short-term debts with foreign countries and against the size of these debts, waged principally by Dr Schacht, had few results.

All these abuses, for which not only those who controlled German economic policy were responsible, but perhaps even more the political leaders of Germany and of foreign countries, gave National-Socialist propaganda a good opportunity of severely criticising German economic policy as a whole. And when the great crisis occurred, the National-Socialists pointed out how right they had been, and how essential it was to avoid too great a dependence on foreign countries and to turn towards a policy of autarky. This, too, is an extremely important factor in explaining the National-Socialist victory.

In fairness it must be added that the labour leaders, too (in the unions as well as in the Social Democratic Party), did not seem endowed with much perspicacity. Foreign loans were welcomed, since they made it possible to finance the social advances promised to the electorate. This also explains why the working classes allowed the National-Socialists to abolish workers' unions and political parties without resistance, and why they perhaps felt a certain malignant joy when this happened.

The middle classes also felt themselves forsaken. The burdens of war and inflation had weighed most heavily on them, as has been stated. Many of them had derived no profits from the great boom period of 1924–30. Rationalisation strengthened the tendency which had been apparent for a considerable time to favour unilaterally large undertakings, cartels, chain stores, and large banks. Besides such men, who, although one may criticise their attitude, were certainly economic leaders of great personal integrity, there were others who, by making use of too easily acquired credit, were able to undertake dubious speculations, and whose personal integrity is less easy to decide. Names such as Ivar Kreuger, Lahusen, etc., are significant in this respect. Many middle-class people who worked in business, industry, or banks were ruined, and joined the ranks of subordinate employees. A comparatively small number of 'leaders of the economy'—the 'captains of industry' (*Industriekapitäne*)—controlled industry, commerce, banks, insurance, and other branches of economic activity. The distribution of property and income caused by inflation, which was already socially dangerous, as has been noted elsewhere, did not improve during this period, but rather became worse. The situation was rendered intolerable by the feeling of the majority of the people that they personally had been completely deprived of the benefits of the economic uplift. This was the point at which the National-Socialists could take up the cudgels, while their attacks on large undertakings, 'capitalism', the 'slavery of profits', and their passwords supporting the middle classes won them many supporters from this section of the population, which was at the time extraordinarily unstable.

Even more unfortunate was the fact that a number of great industrialists decided to get into contact with the National-Socialist movement, or even to provide it with funds. These men believed that, with the help of Adolf Hitler and his party, they would be able to check those tendencies of the socialists and of the middle classes which seemed likely to prove troublesome, and that they would then themselves be in a position to control Hitler. A serious mistake, showing a culpable lack of insight, but a fact which explains a great deal of the National-Socialists' success.

Finally, a pronounced feeling of discontent was rife among German farmers, among the great landowners of Eastern Germany, as well as among large numbers of the peasants. Inflation had, it is true, removed many long-standing debts; but soon heavy new debts were contracted with the aim or re-establishing and increasing the yield of property and farms. The slump, especially in the price of rye, which hit Eastern and Northern German agriculture so hard, did indeed occasion measures to alleviate indebtedness, but to an extent which those concerned judged inadequate. Small landowners in Western Germany, in particular the wine-growers, also met with considerable difficulties. These conditions offered tremendous opportunities to National-Socialist propaganda.

But all these were only latent danger spots; the National-Socialists laid them open and used them, but such conditions would never have led to the 'seizure of power' (*Machtübernahme*) had not the great world economic crisis broken out in 1930 and thrown into the open arms of National-Socialism those millions of unemployed and discontented people who did not go over to Communism. To these malcontents were soon added millions of other Germans who no longer believed parliament and the '*bourgeois* parties' capable of handling the situation, and thought that Communism could be defeated only with the help of the National-Socialists. Faced with the choice between these two rival and radical parties, they preferred National-Socialism.

The world economic crisis began with the collapse of the New York Stock Exchange in October 1929. The general optimism had not only brought about a dangerous rise in prices on the Stock Exchange, it had also attracted to the United States a large volume of capital from all over the world in order to share in the profits obtained by speculation in Wall Street, and which did in fact share in them for a short time. This super-speculation had to come to an end. At the beginning of October 1929 large numbers of shares were offered on the New York Stock Exchange. The banks' endeavours to bolster prices were unavailing; the amount of stock offered for sale continued to increase, and before long caused panic and tremendous losses, which were felt not only by professional speculators, but also by a great many small shareholders or holders of other securities. After a short time the banks were no longer able to give credit, and so, despite good harvests, high production figures, and abundant man-power, a collapse took place which was terminated only many years later by the 'New Deal' policy.

This crisis, whose origin was solely in America, soon spread throughout almost the whole world. Foreign capitalists withdrew their money from the United States, and the United States began to withdraw hers from Europe, especially from Germany; Germany's other creditors followed suit. The National-Socialists' astonishing victory in the September 1930 elections to the *Reichstag* caused alarm, and increased the withdrawal of credits. 1931 and the first half of 1932 were spent in vigorous but ultimately sterile attempts to overcome the crisis, particularly the German one. The Hoover moratorium of 19th July 1931 ended German reparations payments (except for the service of the Dawes and Young loans) and all payment of inter-Allied debts. In addition, on 25th June 1931 the International Payments Bank and the central banks of Great Britain, France, and the United States awarded the *Reichsbank* a credit of 420 million *Reichsmarks*, which it needed because the withdrawal of foreign credits had exhausted its gold and currency reserves. But none of these measures sufficed to free Germany from the crisis.

This crisis began as a *banking crisis*. The collapse of a well-known bank—the Austrian *Kreditanstalt*—in May 1931 was the first sign. On 13th July 1931 one of Germany's great banks, the *Darmstädte-und-Nationalbank* (Danat Bank), was forced to suspend payments; other banks soon found themselves in the same position. Finally the German Government intervened: it decreed a bank-holiday (*Bankfeiertag*) in order that the rush on the vaults might be stopped, and also had recourse to means of bolstering prices, not in order to save shareholders from losses, but to prevent the collapse of the entire payments system and to protect the public against useless losses engendered merely by panic.

The German Government can indeed be blamed for not having prevented the collapse of the *Darmstädte Bank*. But the extremely difficult situation with which the government (Chancellor Brüning) was faced must be taken into account. There is only one effective way of avoiding such panics: to pay out and go on doing so until confidence has been restored. But to do this the banks must be able to obtain the means of payment from the central bank, in this case the *Reichsbank*. The *Reichsbank* was required to cover 40 per cent of its issued notes with gold or gold-standard assets, and this gold it was (and not paper money) that was claimed by foreign creditors, so that, despite the credit aid given by foreign countries, it would have been possible to provide the threatened banks with means of payment only if the condition concerning this coverage was removed or avoided (by the issuing of paper money under special conditions, for example). The government was unwilling to make this decision—to some extent its hands were tied, since the memory of the great inflation was still vivid in the people's minds, and this revived their fears. The government feared, therefore, to take steps which might contain concealed dangers of inflation or merely provoke fear of inflation. Neither the government of the Reich nor the *Reichsbank* dared do what England did a few months later, i.e., to untie the pound sterling from gold and to effect a monetary depreciation. Today, when it is possible to see these things in perspective, this policy may be severely criticised; but the dilemma of the German Government at the time must not be under-rated. Germany therefore maintained the value of her money at the cost of a terrible economic crisis which greatly helped the National-Socialists to attain power.

At the last minute, when all the reserves were exhausted, a moratorium (*Stillhalteabkommen*) was declared, and by this means the remaining gold and assets (there were still loans totalling about 10 billion *Reichsmarks*) were prevented from leaving the country, an occurrence which might have endangered the currency, and exchange control was introduced. Furthermore, by maintaining the old reserve regulations, the government forced the banks to cut down and withdraw credit.

This was what transformed the banking crisis into a general economic crisis. The banks withdrew their loans from industry, for example, and the latter immediately became involved in difficulties; for industry, too, relied to a large extent on short-term credit for long-term investments, and soon had difficulty in paying; it could not get rid of its stocks fast enough to obtain ready money. The German market was unable and unwilling to absorb sufficient goods to make such rapid sales possible. As a result, production was reduced, and a large number of workers were dismissed or put on part-time work in order to cut costs and thereby enable obligations to the banks to be met. The reduction of wages reduced purchasing power for agricultural and industrial products still further.

The crisis soon affected Germany's external trade, and it was then that many symptoms of depression became evident. Before the crisis about a third of Germany's industrial production went abroad. The crisis reduced the number of possible outlets, and the situation was made worse by the increased rigidity of the protectionist policies of countries like the United States. Other countries, such as England, achieved favourable conditions for exports by monetary depreciation, and thus forced back German exports. Germany, which in 1929 had exported goods worth 13·5 billions, exported goods worth only 4·8 billions in 1933, and imports fell even more.

The government had bound itself to parity. Unless it was to trust in the long-term 'self-regeneration of the economic forces', only one course was open to it: deflation. By exerting strong pressure on the level of wages and prices, a deflationary policy should offset the lower prices of the other great countries with which Germany competed, and to which she wished to export. To this end, energetic political measures were necessary; these were provided by Article 48 of the constitution of the Reich, an emergency article authorising the President of the Reich to issue emergency ordinances if necessary. No doubt the *Reichstag* was immediately informed of these ordinances, and it had the right to demand their suspension. But the *Reichstag* did not make use of this opportunity, and was therefore as fully responsible for these measures as were the President of the Reich and the Chancellor.

The policy of Brüning's emergency ordinances—called after the Chancellor—had become practically inevitable on account of the parliamentary and the domestic political situations; the political parties seemed incapable of framing decisive measures upon their own initiative or of agreeing on what was necessary. Since this question is one of political history, it will not be discussed in detail here. But it is important to note that in this way the tendency, already stronger among Germans than in many other countries, to expect the government to provide salvation was strengthened. Later the National-Socialists exploited this situation with great skill.

In this connection the fact that political considerations played an important part in Germany's economic structure must be emphasised, since the wage rates and the level of most prices had been conditioned by politics for a considerable time. The arbitration procedure which had been established for wage disputes had given official, or semi-official, bodies immense power, so much so that there was not, in fact, a free market. A number of other prices were similarly fixed. Many prices were fixed by cartels which had a virtual monopoly, or by other marketing organisations on which the Reich was able to exert considerable pressure after the passing of the 1923 'cartel law'. Thus not only was there a means of political intervention in economic matters, but more, public opinion was accustomed to such methods. In this way salaries, prices, and interest rates were reduced by decree.

Deflationary policies are always unpopular; when a deflationary process takes place in free economies, no one knows who is responsible for it, as Stolper so rightly observed; but if a government consciously followed a policy of deflation, all those who are discontented blame the government for it. As the deflationary policy continued apparently without results, general dissatisfaction with the government and with the democratic parliamentary system in general increased. Grasping the situation, the National-Socialists and Communists addressed their propaganda to the discontented and despairing people, employing all methods of modern demagogy.

The problem of the unemployed became the central issue. The number of unemployed had increased rapidly in the crisis, and the policy of deflation had almost doubled it. At the end of March 1931 the percentage of unemployed in relation to the total number of employed persons was 14·2 per cent in Germany—higher than in the United States (12·5 per cent) and England (12·8 per cent). Before the National-Socialist seizure of power, the number of unemployed in Germany amounted to 20–25 per cent of the employed persons. To give some figures: at the end of 1932 the number of officially registered unemployed was over 6 million, and non-registered unemployed probably totalled another million. In addition to these unemployed were their families, equally hard hit, and also the numerous partially unemployed, whose purchasing power had decreased correspondingly.

Experience has often shown that men faced with economic disaster are the most prone to revolutionary upheavals. The National-Socialist Party adroitly exploited the situation through its propaganda, and also made practical capital out of it; for example, every member of the SA (*Sturmabteilungen*, assault detachments) received a daily bowl of hot soup and other tangible benefits, as well as a mass of promises for the future, for the time which would follow the seizure of power; such measures constituted very real economic inducements, and in the circumstances very effective ones, for joining the Party. In this way the German Workers' National Socialist party (NSDAP) gained many followers from among the ranks of the unemployed, who could see no other prospect of hope.

The situation became worse, particularly for German agriculture. Prices fell so much that the government, which otherwise was engaged in trying to reduce industrial prices, was obliged to carry out a policy of maintenance of agricultural prices, by means of widespread measures of debt cancellation, and the imposition of numerous controls, such as graduated import duties, the fixing of import quotas, and even the prohibition of imports, state purchasing, etc. But none of these measures sufficed to guarantee a healthy basis for German agriculture, and many farmers went over to the National-Socialist camp.

In fact, the whole deflationary policy tended to encourage exports, and thus to surmount the crisis; and it is a fact that in this respect it met with some success. An export surplus, and hence a favourable balance of trade, was reconstituted, although the latter was arrived at only by a rigorous restriction of imports, and on account of the reduction in the price of raw materials on the world market. Raw materials, one of Germany's most vital imports, fell in price more than the finished products which could and had to be exported from Germany.

It is unquestionable that the effectiveness of this policy of deflation was retarded by various factors: the depreciations of the currency which gave the economy of Great Britain and of the other countries concerned considerable headway with which it was not easy to catch up, and also the protectionist policy of the United States, which made exports to that country so difficult. In addition, it may be mentioned that at that time Russia was offering large quantities of cereals, minerals, and wood on the world market at a low price— a factor which greatly hindered the economic recovery of many countries.

Nevertheless, the conclusion must be reached that Brüning's policy of deflation was aimed too unilaterally towards the recovery of German exports alone, and was too little concerned with the strengthening of the internal market. It is true that some steps were taken to provide work. Papen's Government made a definite and intentional change in this respect, and Brüning, too, in the last days of his government, had drawn up plans intended to prepare the termination of his policy of deflation by increasing credit facilities.

V. Conclusion

It was, however, too late. Hitler's nomination as Chancellor created an entirely new political situation and led to the 'seizure of power'. The initial success of National-Socialism was based on an almost inextricably confused mixture of correct views on political economy, which saw in the development of the domestic market the point from which a new upswing should start, and an adroit demagogy which promised each social and economic group the fulfilment of its own particular desires.

In conclusion, it can be seen that a series of different economic factors contributed to the victory of the National-Socialists, but that neither individually nor as a whole can these factors be regarded as the sole cause of that victory. They were closely and reciprocally connected with social, sociological, intellectual, and political factors.

One group of economic factors dates back to the days after the First World War—the very unfortunate reparations policy and the great inflation. Although they remained in the background during the boom period of 1924–30, they still constituted a constant, if latent, source of danger—a danger which became very real at the time of the great depression—when the policy of deflation which aimed at countering the effects of the crisis destroyed so much of what had been rebuilt.

Two other groups of factors must be emphasised. One is the economic constitution of Germany at that time, which from the first gave the Government wide opportunities for intervention in economic affairs, and of which the new rulers were at once able to make use. The other is the unfortunate way in which international economic relations had developed, with the particular result that

Germany was peculiarly vulnerable to any international crisis, not least on account of the vast amount of short-term debts which she had incurred.

Only thus can one understand why the National-Socialist programme was judged and accepted by millions of men as being the only way of escape from the sorry plight in which they found themselves.

NOTE BY THE PUBLISHING COMMITTEE

Since the total amount paid in reparations has been discussed at great length, the Publishing Committee has decided to print, in addition to Professor Lütge's essay, some observations made by Professor Etienne Weill-Rayal, who was for many years a member of the Reparations Commission, and who is the author of an important book on this subject (*Les Réparations allemandes et le franc*, Paris, 1947, 3 vols.).

The Wolff agency's *communiqué* of 29th January 1932 gives the figure of 56·6 billion gold marks paid in reparations, comprising 42 billion as reparations and 14·6 billion in various accounts some of which were not paid to the Allies. The Reparations Commission's estimates are: for the first figure 9·7 billion gold marks; for the second, the Commission took only occupation costs, amounting to 811 million gold marks.

Liquidation of private German assets (by Powers other than the United States, Russia, Brazil, and Cuba): 10 billion gold marks. Most of these assets were not accounted for by the Reparations Commission; the purpose of the liquidation of sequestrated German assets was to compensate Allied nationals for the confiscation during the war of assets which they possessed in Germany, or to pay their pre-war trade debts. This did not therefore constitute reparations, but the paying off of the debts of German individuals or of the Reich.

Waiving of claims on former allies of Germany: 8·6 billion.

Surrender of state assets in territories ceded by Germany: 9·7 billion. The estimates of the inter-Allied service of the Reparations Commission make this account 2·7 billion.

Coal and coke: 2·3 billion. Reparations Commission estimate: 954 million. The difference between these two estimates is mainly due to the fact that the German figures estimated coal and coke at world prices, which, especially in 1920, were much higher than domestic German prices (overestimate of transportation costs). In 1920, however, most of the coal handed over by Germany was the equivalent of the reduction in the production of the French mines in the North and in the Pas-de-Calais, destroyed upon the order of the German authorities; hence the means of valuing laid down by the Treaty of Versailles.

Shipping handed over and confiscated: 4·5 billion. The inter-Allied Service estimated their value at 1 billion.

Railway equipment handed over: 1·1 billion. In 1926 the German Government accepted the Reparations Commission valuation; in any case, the latter does not differ very greatly from the German estimates: 827 million.

Non-military booty left by the German armies in occupied territory (left during the war): 5 billion. Reparations Commission's estimate: 140 million. The enormous divergency between these two estimates can be explained in part by the fact that the German figures relate to all fronts (including the Russian front), while the allied figure relates only to the Western front.

Loans made on the basis of the London protocol in 1924 (implementing the Dawes Plan): 8 billion. Reparations Commission estimate: 7·6 billion. The difference is caused by the fact that the Wolff Agency included a loan of 800 million gold marks made to Germany in 1924 for payment to the Allies, and the five first annual payments for servicing the interest and amortisation of this loan.

For the *Ruhr loans* the Wolff Agency's communique gives 1,370 million gold marks, comprising 550 million in bullion and 820 million in kind. The Reparations Commission's estimate is 426 million for payments in bullion and 504 million in kind, a total of 930 million, to which must be added 26 million for the value of paper marks and services requisitioned for the occupation troops stationed in the Ruhr.

P

THE NATIONAL-SOCIALIST USE OF MORAL TENDENCIES IN GERMANY
Theodor Litt

THE rapid rise of National-Socialism in the third decade of this century is one of those events which not only are calculated to astonish contemporaries, but have still something enigmatic about them when one looks back and considers them. The movement led by Hitler had in it so much that was revolting, the men whom it brought to the fore were so little apt to awaken sympathy, the methods which it introduced into political life were so contrary both to humanity and to good taste, that one might have expected a complete fiasco rather than so sweeping a success. And in fact, it should be remembered, there were moments when it looked as if the danger of the rise of National-Socialism was averted. The Party did not attain victory without some notable setbacks. The fact that it did nevertheless manage to gain control of the state was the consequence of a highly complicated interlocking of general conditions and of constellations of personalities. Any attempts to reduce the course of events to any single series of causal connections is doomed to failure. We must try to uncover the interaction of causes and effects in its whole extent.

If one does this, one remarks how much certain general currents of thought have contributed towards bringing about the final result: without wishing to serve National-Socialism directly, they have helped to prepare the ground for the Nazi theses and inclined people's minds to receive and follow them. The effects of these movements of thought confirmed the old experience that a German is prone to let himself be won over to any cause for which he finds a point of departure in his own *weltanschaulich* convictions. Where he is asked to give his agreement, he is unwilling to forego his 'metaphysical need'.

Since we are here concerned with the efficacity of 'ideas', we shall do well to trace the process principally in the so-called 'cultivated' classes. For naturally these were the classes at which National-Socialism principally aimed in the ideological part of its programme. To enrol the mass of the working-class population other methods had to be employed.

This is indeed a chapter which a German can only write with a heavy heart. For the representatives of so-called 'culture' ought to have been the first to show up the emptiness of the National-Socialist ideology, to unmask the errors of the racial doctrine, and expose the brutality of the consequences drawn from it. That this should not have happened as much as might have been expected is the humiliating fact, which the analysis of the intellectual situation must take as its starting point.

I

In the Germany of those years were many places where the intellectual development to be dealt with here could be studied. An especially good observation post was to be found in that cultural institution where the present author spent these decisive years: the university. Experience demonstrates time and again that certain changes in thought manifest themselves early and distinctly where thousands of young people intellectually more awakened and more mobile than the average are gathered together by the need for professional training and are at the same time moved to the formation of common opinions and aims. In times of unrest and change the universities are always the places where one can discern most surely the signs of approaching storm.

In this case especially it could not be otherwise, because National-Socialism had set itself, from the beginning, to win over the youth of the universities by systematic recruitment. From very early on it was among the university students that recruits were sought; it was from their ranks that the Party drew its most devoted, ingenious, and resolute champions.

Looked at from the other side, the university provided also the equally instructive opportunity of studying how the teaching staff met the challenge of National-Socialism both in theory and in practice.

This is not the place to recall the social and economic conditions which were bound to dispose the students of those years to lend an ear to the blandishments of Hitler and his henchmen. All we are concerned with is to lay bare the intellectual, or spiritual, points of departure which the Hitler movement found for its recruiting activities. In indicating these points of departure we shall be helping considerably to illuminate the general question which is before us.

Consciously or unconsciously, the youth which National-Socialism was trying to win over was under the influence of the tradition which stemmed from the beginnings of the so-called *Jugendbewegung*. This movement which, at the turn of the century, had begun to spread among the young of the *bourgeois* middle class, had produced in the younger generation a new self-consciousness, a programme of aims for the young, a way of life peculiar to the young. Youth began to feel, and to behave, as a special group, self-contained and with a value of its own, within the life of the nation. The more consciously it upheld the youth principle, however, the more it was obliged to stake out this determination and give it a conceptual basis. In true German fashion, it went in search of a *Weltanschauung* which would allow it to bear witness on its own behalf. And it found this in that multiform philosophical tendency known as the 'Philosophy of Life' (Nietzsche, Bergson, Klages, etc.). The ambiguous and strongly emotional concept of 'Life' thus became the centre of this agitated youthful thinking. It became a battle-cry against everything that youth, in its will for renewal, found to condemn in actual conditions: the mechanisation of labour, the hardening of public regulations by organisation ; the intellectualist devastation of spiritual life ; the dying-out of creative energies. Over against these symptoms of decline the idea of 'Life' appealed to the deep-seated forces of primitive existence and expressed the certainty that these forces were still present in youth, unexhausted and constructive.

On the origin of this 'Philosophy of Life'—to which youth attached itself even when it did not expressly formulate its aims—there can be no doubt: it is the heir and renewer of *romanticism*. That is where it gets its confidence in the creative richness of the primitive forces which reign and rise in the dark depths of the Unconscious; its admiration for the stormy dynamism of the life-force breaking out from these depths; its aversion to the rationalist stiffness of abstract thought and the utilitarian ordering of life.

The danger and temptation in this idea of 'Life' is that, with its indeterminate and ambiguous character, it can take on and transfigure the most diverse contrasts. It can go so far as to view the irresistible impetuosity with which a movement fights its way through as its sufficient justification—the proof that in it 'Life' is breaking through. 'Life' is invoked equally by the philosophy of power of a Nietzsche and the clarified historical world-picture of a Dilthey. Where is it to end if in the last resort the will to expansion of an aspiration is recognised as the perfect justification of its right to life, if all other criteria but strength are set aside?

It would be unjust to the *Jugendbewegung*, in the pure form it had at the beginning, to pretend that it succumbed to the temptations inherent in this 'Life' concept. This is clear from the way in which it understood and developed the 'Life' concept in a certain definite form. Romanticism had already looked for the creative forces of life by preference in the 'organic' ensemble of the *Community*, and had found the particular embodiment of this community in the *People*. To romantics the People was the womb out of which are born all the great creations of spiritual life, beginning with language, myth, art, and religion.

In this respect likewise, the *Jugendbewegung* followed Romanticism faithfully. All its longings and aims united in the idea of the popular community (*Volksgemeinschaft*). In its origin, this watchword—it must be stressed—was in no way directed against other peoples, and had no spearhead of aggressiveness. The People was sought and found exclusively in those expressions of life in which it gives its nature plastic representation: in popular customs and speech, folk-poetry, folk-music, folk-dancing. And the conviction was felt that, by loving care of these riches of common life, not only was the brotherly union of all men not excluded, but it was called for by way of completion. It was the spirit of Herder's *Stimmen der Völker* that animated this generation of the *Jugendbewegung*. The idea of the *Volksgemeinschaft* was seized upon with an especial fervour when, after defeat in the First World War, the German people was torn by party strife of an unusual fierceness. This idea of what youth could be seemed then the releasing message which alone could protect our people from the fate of self-destruction. Its task was to be a guiding star to the people's inner life, not to direct its forces outwards.

But although the idea of the 'People' cultivated by these young generations was at first free from any nationalistic tang, it is easy to understand, given its indeterminateness, how easily it could be transformed and aimed in the direction of nationalist intolerance. To gain this result it was only necessary to give it a stronger turn towards the sphere of *political* life and a more decided echo of the oppositions prevailing in that sphere. The original *Jugendbewegung* had escaped this danger because, being a self-proclaimed movement of secession, it was outside political reality. Only, among the passionate divisions brought by the experience of the First World War and its sequel, this non-political attitude could not be kept up. The harsh discussions of internal and foreign policy which arose after the war made it no longer possible to stand aside. When the young felt themselves thus more and more drawn into the whirlpool of political strife, the idea to which they had rallied revealed its highly dangerous ambiguity. Henceforward 'Life' no longer meant a peaceful organic growth from inborn creative instincts. It was now understood in the way in which certain tendencies of thought in the nineteenth century had wished to interpret it. Living, they said, is first and foremost striving. Darwin's doctrine of the struggle for existence—which had already given Nietzsche's philosophy of life some of its essential points—was invoked in order to bring into the limelight the 'warrior' character of the true, strong life, and Nietzsche himself with his doctrine of the 'will to power' must be enrolled as a fellow-conspirator.

How gladly a people tormented by the results of a lost war and feeling itself harshly treated by the victors received such a message as this: 'A People in the ascendant looks on the world abroad, the unknown world, as its enemy'! Such considerations made the bridge by which many young people could cross to the political battlefield and join up with politically aggressive doctrine and groups. In the course of this evolution the idea of the *Volksgemeinschaft* also became more and more a battle-cry: both in internal politics, against those groups which were considered guilty of having destroyed the *Volksgemeinschaft*, and in foreign policy, against those peoples and states which were accused of oppressing the German people and curtailing Germany's living space.

It was thus that the *Weltanschauung* which had 'Life' as its directing idea was able to take on biological, voluntarist features, and finally those of an extreme nationalism, without making the representatives of this evolution conscious that they were turning away from the original spirit of the *Jugendbewegung*. The Romantic faith in the inexhaustible dynamism of 'Life' finds room for some very diverse ideas. The fervour of devotion, issuing in love, and the fervour of revolt, manifested in strife, can both of them come into being and fruition as the supreme fulfilment of this dynamism.

For these possibilities to become realities only one thing was necessary: the appearance of a movement aiming at capturing these tendencies and aspirations for its own political ends. There appeared at the same time the virtuosi of demagogy, who with unscrupulous refinement set themselves, by inflamed words and resounding imperatives, to lay hold of this youthful enthusiasm and use it as a propellant force in the political struggle. National-Socialism knew what it was doing when it founded its party programme on the construction of a *Weltanschauung*. It knew that there is no better way of mastering a German than by the lofty formulae of a metaphysical system conferring on any and every political action the consecration of eternity. And it knew how to get at youth by giving it the assurance that it was itself nothing other than the uprising of the youthful elements of the nation, whose optimism and strength of will were taking their stand against the sated self-satisfaction and futile laziness of age ripe for abdication.

In the campaign waged to conquer the soul of this young generation and that of the German people, the Party developed a propaganda equipment which owed its success, above all, to one thing: no concern for truth, but limitless devices for falsifying facts to suit its interests and its tendencies. Even with minds in disarray as they were, it could not have gone so far if it had not had to do with a collectivity in which the sense of honesty and truth had already suffered a considerable weakening.

Here, too, we come up against an essential feature of the intellectual situation which certain influential doctrines had largely helped to form. Once again the 'Philosophy of Life' had a symptomatic significance. Anyone who puts the dynamism of ever-changing life above everything can very easily reach the point where he relegates what we mean by 'truth' to the ups and downs of this movement of life. In this way truth loses its claim to an independent value and turns into the expression of the conditions of life at the moment, the indicator of the momentary needs of life. It changes its shape with every change in the events of life, and can only be judged according to whether it represents the contemporary life-situation appropriately; if it does, it is sanctified in the name of life.

From this it is only a step to the assertion to which the widespread voluntarism was already tending: 'truth' is no more than one of the weapons by which life wins through in its concentration on enlarging the space at its disposal. Here again it is Nietzsche who draws the ultimate conclusion. What, for him, is truth? 'An apparent world, chosen . . . from the standpoint of utility with a view to the maintenance and strengthening of a certain species of animal.' And this interpretation of 'truth' was bound to suit a Party which in any case was determined to bend truth according to its own sweet will. For it, truth became an 'apparent world chosen from the standpoint of utility, with a view to the strengthening of a certain Party'. In the end it went so far as to make of this pragmatic version of 'truth' the very programme for the scientific investigation of truth. It did so by proclaiming a 'political science'—that is, a 'science' directed by the political will. The logical consequence of its enthronement was that any effort to obtain 'objective' truth, that is to say a truth not coloured by any of the interests of life, was bound to be condemned as the symptom of a life weakened and gone astray.

With this the struggle against truth had been carried right into the citadel of scientific research, into the university. It is no use pretending that the demand for a complete politicising of science did not find an enthusiastic welcome among a great part of the young generation of students—striking evidence of how the idea of pure and disinterested truth had lost ground.

Among the many 'truths' which the will-to-live of the National-Socialist Party thought fit to hammer into the general consciousness, by far the most effective, the most rich in consequences, and the most fateful was the doctrine of Race, which it endeavoured to spread with all the arts of unscrupulous seduction. Once more the idea of life in its biological formulation made it simpler for it to hang this

on to earlier currents of thought. It was child's play to reduce the
dynamism of 'life' to 'blood'. In this 'blood' all the subterranean,
darkly fertile, demoniac, and instinctive elements after which the
Romantics had already yearned, could easily be recognised. And
recourse could also be had to this same blood to rouse the warlike instincts. The myth of blood once arrived at, the transition was
easy to the apotheosis of blood as defined by race—that is, of the
blood of *one's own* race. Certain pronouncements of Nietzsche's,
dealing very vaguely with 'race', provided the desired support.
Above all, certain statements and doctrines, which till then had been
reckoned merely as ideas of scientific cranks and had won only a very
limited following, were now raised to a truly canonical authority.
The racial theory of Count Gobineau now experienced a resurrection. Paul de Lagarde's condemnations of Judaism were zealously
collected, studied, and arranged for practical use. Houston Stewart
Chamberlain's *Grundlagen des XIX. Jährhunderts,* which subordinated the whole world of history to the leading idea of race, was
hailed as the supreme scientific revelation. It is not difficult to understand that the National-Socialist efforts to win over the intellectuals
and, above all, intellectual youth to the racial principle were greatly
favoured by being able to appeal to such 'scientific' authorities.

The exact aim of all this deployment of metaphysics and philosophy of history is as clear as daylight. In reality, only two races
were in question, one of which was to be raised to primacy in the
history of the world, and the other must disappear from it. The
weltanschaulich basis for the German People's claim to domination
and for the struggle against the Jewish race had to be made visible.
And, first and foremost, the already existing anti-semitic moods and
tendencies, stemming as they did from some highly robust interests
and antipathies, had to be harnessed to the needs of the Party.
What could have been more welcome to minds already prejudiced
against Jewry than a political confession of faith which provided,
for a hatred of the Jews which was only waiting for such an invitation, a basis in principle? The German is so made that he feels he
can only yield to a passion with a good conscience if he has had it
sanctioned by a hard and fast doctrine. And so National-Socialism's
racial dogma found open ears in many quarters.

Here what concerns us most is to know how far youth was ready
to welcome and carry into practice, along with the National-
Socialist message, the myth of race and the consequences which
were drawn from it with regard to the Jewish race. The original
Jugendbewegung had shown its peaceful character in this among other
things—that it asked no questions about racial origin and freely
received Jews into its ranks. Unfortunately it did not stick to this.
It cannot be denied that already during the First World War, and

certainly after its end, the anti-semitic tendencies which had existed for a long time found a strong echo in an important section of the younger generation—and precisely among the students. Even during the war it was common to accuse the German Jews of seeking the 'cushy jobs', of being nationally unreliable, and of unscrupulous profiteering, and afterwards many of the students back from the front adopted these accusations wholeheartedly. In these circles it became usual to make Jewry largely responsible for the German catastrophe, and sweepingly to wipe out all that the Jews had done, at home and abroad, in the struggle for Germany. One of the most depressing facts of these fateful years is that there are few places where racial hatred found such favourable ground as in Germany's high schools, and that National-Socialism there swept all before it, especially in the anti-semitic part of its programme. And so the aiders and abetters of racial dogma whom we mentioned above were diligently read and quoted.

We have briefly indicated the basic factors which made it possible for National-Socialism, when it came before German youth with its message, to meet with moods, tendencies, and traditions which were of extraordinary assistance to its work of recruitment. By adaptation and interpretation it was able, almost unperceived, to entice these young people on to the ground of its *Weltanschauung*. And it was sufficiently unscrupulous to make full use of the opportunities which lay to hand.

Thus it is understandable that not a few of the then leaders of the *Jugendbewegung* passed into the camp of a Party whose spirit was so opposed to the original tendencies of this movement. We must of course bear in mind that the young people who swam into the Nazi net were not the same as those who had given the *Jugendbewegung* its initial direction. (To that extent the change cannot be described as a self-betrayal.) But in spite of this distinction the tradition of life and behaviour in youth, handed down by the *Jugendbewegung*'s first generation to its successors, did contain for National-Socialism certain points where it could gain a hold and break in, just as also its youth organisations took care to preserve certain of the outward forms of the old *Jugendbewegung*. Only examination after the event can measure the size of the gap which separates the flock of the *Wandervögel* sweeping through forest and field from the regimented, marching formations of *Jungvolk* and *Hitlerjugend*. All that was left of the romanticism of the beginning were certain flowers of rhetoric and outward signs.

The intellectual fate undergone by the student youth in its encounter with National-Socialism has given us a particularly pregnant example of the general process which is the subject of our inquiry: the penetration by National-Socialist assertions and tendencies into those sections of the German people which had been, as it were, ripened for the Party's message by their inner make-up, and afterwards failed to develop the power of resistance and the critical judgment which might have immunised them against the arts of blandishment of the Party propaganda. National-Socialism was up against certain sympathies and antipathies, certain dispositions and aspirations, which it confidently confronted with its programme. It was up against opinions, values, ideas, and doctrines which could, with a little adroitness, be so transformed and reshaped that they seemed to represent the first steps and preparation for the Party's official *Weltanschauung.* It had only to blend these ingredients cunningly and add a strong dose of an all-heating and all-melting fanaticism, to be able to appear as the realiser of Germany's longings and the executant of Germany's mission, with no need to recoil before the opposition of the informed. That so large a part of German youth, and this, truly, not the worst part, should have rallied to the banner of National-Socialism, was due to the fact that National-Socialism knew how to play this Messianic part with such skill.

But what, above all, opened people's hearts to the *Weltanschauung* was the diabolical virtuosity with which its advocates managed to kindle into bright flame all the instincts of hatred latent in the German people—class hatred, race hatred, party hatred, hatred of the foreigner—while conjuring these negative sentiments into the most highly prized virtues. How good it was, for *Volksgenossen* labouring under many resentments, to have their passionate enmities sanctified by a full-bodied *Weltanschauung!* It was only by such a manufacture of false currency that a movement like the *Jugendbewegung,* initially disposed to tolerance, forgiveness, and harmony, could be won over to a gospel of raging hatred. 'Ideas', thanks to their ambivalence, can be only too easily changed into the opposite of what they originally meant. And a people which takes ideas as seriously as the German people does is particularly open to their inherent dangers.

II

Let us now turn to the question of how National-Socialism mastered the *older generation.*

We must first remember that this generation included those from whom the first generation of the *Jugenbewegung* had been recruited. But it cannot be said that this had a serious influence on the behaviour of the older generation as a whole. This was so because, as experience shows, the impulses that a man derives from membership of a youth movement lose their force in later life, or are even repudiated altogether. People learn to adapt themselves to a life on which, as young revolutionaries, they had declared war. So it was by other tendencies, experiences, and trains of thought that National-Socialism prepared the older generation for capture. It is not indeed impossible that the same doctrines in which the *Jugendbewegung* found ideological expression for its longing helped the maturer generation to attain its self-assurance. But it was in different, or differently interpreted, ideological motifs that it found the confirmation it sought.

Once again we have the essential facts before us in outstanding clarity if we examine what happened to the older generation in the high schools of Germany, to the *teaching profession*. It by no means passed into the National-Socialist camp with banners flying. Even when the Party had come into power, those who subscribed to it heart and soul formed only a minority within the whole. But those were also only a small minority who, in obedience to tradition and to the spiritual mission of the university, felt it their duty to offer resistance to the rise of the Party when it menaced the essence of scientific research and education, and to refuse to follow the Party at its zenith, when it attacked the spirit of the educational institutions by brutal interventions.

What was decisive in determining the attitude of the universities was the large section who, whether from opportunism or from fear, wanted to avoid any clash with the men in power or even, without actually identifying themselves with the Party, believed they could find in it so much good that they were prepared to be patient with certain undeniable defects of its qualities (*Schönheitsfehlern*). This malleability is typical of the way in which the *bourgeois* class resigned itself to the new situation.

One has to go back a long way in history to be able to trace this readiness to submit to the commands of new masters to its ultimate motives. And there events and political developments interlace in an almost indissoluble whole with the thoughts, ideas, and theories of the same period. The German citizen, habituated since the century of the Reformation to a patriarchal régime which excluded him from all participation in political training, and scarcely affected by the political movements and disturbances in which Western Europe acquired its political shape, had, even in his reflections about the state, in his theories about the nature of the state, forbidden himself all temerity of the sort which had made political thinkers in England and France into the creators of a new world of political ideas. Both in theory and in practice he was unreservedly 'state-contented' (*staatsfromm*). And when, very late in the day, as a result of the wars of liberation, the idea of political freedom gained a footing in Germany too, and out of the depths of the people there arose an endeavour to lead Germany upwards to freedom as well as unity, he experienced, after a hopeful start, the defeat of these aspirations, and this left behind it a profound discouragement and the most painful disappointment. One must picture to oneself the dark background of this national experience in order to understand the part played in the formation of German political consciousness by the fact that what the popular movement of 1848 had striven for in vain was realised in a few years through the determined energy of the Prussian State. In the exaltation of unity won at last, people were glad to forget the criticisms which a friend of liberty might make against the new state of affairs. Inevitably the centuries-old disposition to say yes to anything commanded by the government was powerfully reinforced during the Bismarck period.

And it was the 'cultivated' class that was foremost in this confident devotion. No doubt union with the new state was rendered much easier for it by the fact that the 'culture' of which it felt itself to be the bearer and director was, from its origin, too far removed from the political sphere for any political demands to come from it. It was essentially the legacy of that generation which, unconditionally loyal to the state but also unconditionally excluded from the state, had sought and found its field of creative activity in the realm of 'ideas'.

Its heirs and successors were now fated to go through that turning-point of history, which, overnight as it were, transported the 'People of Poets and Thinkers' into the raw climate of politics—and indeed high politics. It had now to find its bearings on the unaccustomed horizon of changing world politics, to come to terms with the totally unfamiliar experience of political power. Is it to be wondered at that, in the suddenness of this change, this introduction to politics was felt and prized as an ecstasy, and that those who fell under the spell of this ecstasy subscribed to a version of politics which, in its uncompromising hardness, was the exact opposite of the world-embracing 'humanity' to which the non-political generation of the classical period had dedicated itself?

Then it was that there began to shine in the *bourgeois* world that ideal of so-called *Realpolitik*, to which people felt obliged to rally in order to show beyond doubt their freedom from cosmopolitan confusion. Then it was that there developed in the German soul that dualism which the succeeding generation vainly sought to resolve: the dualism of an idea of culture which clung to the classical heritage and an urge for power and success which concentrated on politics, economics, and technique.

Here, as always, the need was quickly felt to see the newly won political self-consciousness founded and justified in an ideology. The latest political experiences had to be brought within the general picture of life, the newly dominant political demands had to be referred to values and principles. In the pursuit of this need people caught hold, on the one hand, of what traditions they found to hand, while on the other hand new conceptions came to the fore, in answer to the changed situation.

It was in this way that a certain doctrine of Hegel's—who was then in general almost forgotten—began to exert a fresh and more or less subterranean influence: this was the doctrine of the role played by peoples and states in world history, that each, at the historical moment reserved for it, receives from the spirit of the age (*Weltgeist*) the word which calls it to make its special contribution to the solution of the problem set by world history. This teaching naturally tended to fortify people in their faith in the historical mission of their own nation.

It was the historians of the new Reich who above all spoke out, foremost among them Heinrich von Treitschke. For them it was not merely a matter of explaining to the German people the development which had at last led to the accomplishment of the national desires. They wished also to make clear to it the lessons it ought to learn from its painful history, and so to contribute as best they could to forming in it a will turned towards the future. And Treitschke finally gave the quintessence of these doctrines the most compact expression when he declared that the essence of the state is 'in the first place power, in the second place power, and in the third place, again, power '. This was the profession of faith of *Realpolitik* in its purest form.

To support this profession of faith Darwin's doctrine of the 'struggle for existence' and Nietzsche's glorification of the 'will to power' were joyfully and unrestrainedly called into service. Thus the German people, so far as the classes responsible for spiritual leadership were concerned, threw itself head over heels into the struggle for political power, from which for centuries historical ill-fortune had excluded it. The gulf separating a culture which resided in the realm of 'ideas' and was therefore non-political, and the newly awakened political will, was to be closed all at once.

This, then, was the attitude with which the German *bourgeoisie* crossed the threshold of the twentieth century; ready, by and large, to submit without a murmur to the orders of the government, convinced that in the struggle between nations nothing but the most determined will to power and aggrandisement can bring salvation, and full of mistrust towards all ideas and aspirations whose aim was to mitigate international conflicts by a studied moderation on both sides or even to prevent the outbreak of hostilities.

The average political thought of the German teaching profession contained itself within this same framework. History shows that fundamental attitudes of this sort remain firm through the gravest historical crises and can even outlast a total overthrow of the state. It is no wonder, then, that the National-Socialist propagandists, when they accused the policy of the Weimar Republic of having weakly abandoned the national interests, and set up *Realpolitik* as watchword against its alleged desire for fraternisation, were able to attach themselves to moods and opinions which had long been traditional, and that their claim to be the exclusive representatives of the nation's true interests found widespread credence.

And here, once more, what filled people's heads and hearts as a living conviction sought and found confirmation in the realm of formulated thinking. There was, first of all, the widely circulated literature whose object was to hold fast and express the front-line experience of the First World War and which, by so doing, willingly or unwillingly re-kindled enthusiasm for heroic struggle. But there was one thinker and writer above all who built up his version of the essence and tasks of the period by means of an all-embracing theory of history and answered directly the German need for a universal basis and justification. The 'morphology of world history'—the subtitle which Oswald Spengler gave to his *Decline of the West*—had on its side not only the fact that it provided a metaphysical basis for the mood of decline which so easily came to fill men's hearts after a lost war: it also won agreement more particularly by those arguments with which it attempted to define the attitude of will imposed on the German people as a duty by that moment in history. In his exposition of this attitude Spengler moved on, step by step, to graver and graver conclusions and demands. What was demanded, first of all, in view of the civilising character of the late period into which we were born, was a cold, clear will, keeping free of romantic pretensions and of unrealisable longings and purely concentrated on its purpose. What was demanded of the people as a whole was to be 'in form', that is to say, to be ready to play its part without fail in the pitiless struggle between the world's peoples which forms the content of this late period. In face of this hard but ineluctable necessity any idea of reconciliation between the nations is ridiculed and rejected as the humanitarian day-dreaming of fanciful people remote from the world. To put it in an epigram: 'Ideals are lies'.

Then this glorification of the instincts directed towards self-protection and expansion of power reaches its high point in the thesis—connected with Nietzsche's amoralism—that Man should take pride in the fact that he is a 'beast of prey', and should cultivate, out of all the expressions of his nature, chiefly the one which most clearly reveals his character as beast of prey—hate!

If one realises that the man who preached to men such an evaluation of themselves was one of the most widely read and highly esteemed writers, one is no longer astonished that a movement like the National-Socialist movement, whose best allies were the instincts of hatred which lay to hand, did not provoke in 'cultivated' circles the loathing that might have been expected from its sermons of hate. It makes no difference, in this respect, that, once Hitler had come to power and given the first examples of his political methods, Spengler openly drew away from him and his Party. It was not the first time that an idea, which caused no scruples either in its author or in its readers as long as it existed only on paper, aroused terror of itself as soon as it took tangible shape in practice.

It was exactly the same with another author, also much read and admired. Ernst Jünger, too, from the beginning and once for all repudiated all connection with National-Socialism. And yet a book like his *Arbeiter* is among those writings which helped to habituate men to that 'realistic' way of looking at things and to that ice-cold, heartless attitude of will, which so signally aided recruitment to the National-Socialist *Weltanschauung*. Once a mentality, which believes that intellectual honesty is in duty bound to treat as 'swindles' all aspirations that tend towards considerateness and conciliation, has come to occupy a place of honour in the 'cultivated' world, bestiality has little trouble in referring even its worst crimes to the authority of what is claimed to be 'necessity'.

When it is seen how irresistibly the tendencies of thought here described spread through the world of the 'cultivated' from the founding of the Reich onwards, the conclusion is unavoidable that the 'culture', whose guardians and advocates these circles still felt themselves to be, though it continued to exist in the phrases which were on people's lips and in the hobbies of their leisure hours, had very largely ceased to be a power capable of determining their lives and giving them their shape. Had it been otherwise, the many forms of degeneracy by which National-Socialism offended good taste, contradicted all sober ways of thinking and struck at all morality must not only have rendered any alliance with it out of the question but made resistance to it the self-evident course. The absence of this obvious reaction is the proof that those circles whose spiritual make-up is under discussion did not abandon the cultural gospel of our classical period just at the moment when National-Socialism made its bid for them, but had already fallen when the hour of trial came. Painful as it is to admit this, truthfulness compels us to recognise the fact without reserve. The admission is made less difficult by the consideration that, in this case as always, unconditional honesty with oneself is the indispensable means to recovery. This requirement would be in no way less binding if it should be found that other peoples had not escaped, or not entirely escaped, the same self-undoing.

III

Although the class of the 'cultured' *bourgeoisie* represents, in terms of percentage, a small minority in the nation as a whole, particular attention should be paid to what goes on in it, because naturally it reveals the fate of 'ideas' with especial clarity.

If now we turn to the majority of Germans, whose professional training and activity do not allow them to enjoy this culture to the full, we must first and foremost remember how great a success and how many followers National-Socialism won in those circles whose intellectual or spiritual make-up is best designated by the phrase 'semi-culture'. Modern society is so formed that it contains an intermediary stratum of men who are in the position to glance from time to time at the spiritual world of culture but are prevented from taking part in it fully. From this intermediary position there results, for those who find themselves in it, a spiritual make-up which renders them particularly sensible to spiritual influences of a certain kind. As experience shows, they come only too easily under the spell of phrases whose bombast impresses the heart and whose confusion paralyses the critical judgment. The speeches which the Party's propaganda machine indefatigably hammered into them were of this kind. They appealed with stubborn insistence to the patriotic, heroic, 'racist' sentiments of those whom they addressed; they held out to them the prospect of happy participation in a higher life; and they filled them with the hope that by joining the Party they would enjoy a wonderful expansion of their personal life. To intensify this hope to the utmost was not only the job of the legion of 'storm-troop orators' (*Stosstruppredner*) who poured the stream of their eloquence over innumerable party meetings; a whole literature arose, which adapted itself by its standard and tone to the demands of whatever stratum of readers it was meant to reach. What is noteworthy about this literature is that it often used expressions and ideas which were familiar in the field of serious literature and which were now made to undergo a brutal coarsening and vulgarisation.

In this respect the maltreatment suffered by the word *Weltanschauung* in the mouths and from the pens of these propagandists was symptomatic. Born in the realm of philosophy and rendered current in the scientific world by a certain tendency of the so-called 'Philosophy of Life', it was now misused in order to give the Party dogma a more distinguished appearance and endow it with the dignity of metaphysics. This transplantation and cheapening were facilitated by the servile aid which certain all too easy-going representatives of science gave to the Party's doctrine.

As the ideas and ways of thinking of the cultivated mind were thus adapted to the needs of the average man, there was formed an atmosphere of sentimental uplift and phrase-mongering vanity in which many members of the lower middle class felt themselves wonderfully at home, because the illusion of participating in that spiritual world agreeably enhanced their sense of their own import-ance. Certain average judgments on the state and history, on art and poetry, science and religion were suggested to them, and by adopting them they came to feel themselves connoisseurs and judges by vocation. The arrogant sufficiency of many small people pro-moted by the Party to the position of *Amtswalter* was the visible sign of this artificial rise.

IV

The conditions with which National-Socialism was faced when it addressed itself to the broad mass of the *working-class population* were not at all favourable. In their ranks there were few traditions and ways of looking at things that could easily be amalgamated with the leading phrases of the *Weltanschauung*.

Nonetheless, so far as the *peasant* class was concerned, there was already a picture of the essential nature of peasant life which could be used as a starting-point. Unfortunately it did not spring from the peasantry itself but had a literary origin. It its desire for a primitive life based on the soil and in its quest for an *organically* developed morality and way of life, Romanticism had discovered the peasantry afresh and pushed it out into the bright light of its poetical version of existence. The *Jugendbewegung* had followed it in this, as we have seen, and had unearthed and held up to admiration many a country usage (*Brauchtum*). A Party which had the words 'blood and soil' ceaselessly in its mouth could revive this romanticised picture of the peasant and set to work imposing on the German peasant with the help of the press, the cinema, and meetings properly controlled by propaganda technique, his fairy-tale version of its nature. The peasant was to be admired and taken as a model as being the original human being, the human being grounded in the soil, the man of the community, ready for sacrifices. Only, as was to be expected, the attempt at literary glorification brought only the smallest returns in the way of love from the peasantry. This picture lived only on paper and on the screen. Peasant life went on undisturbed, clinging to its elementary customs.

If the Party everywhere tried to transform already existing traditions and lines of thought into its own message, it had its work cut out to do this when it began recruitment among the German *working-class*. For the most influential ideas about men, history, and public affairs prevalent among the working class stemmed precisely

from the doctrine against which National-Socialism claimed to have
taken its stand with a view to annihilating it. The greater part of
this class believed in the social and historical theories of Karl Marx.
Against these National-Socialism had sworn war to the death. It
repudiated them, if for no other reason, on account of their author:
he was a Jew. It repudiated them because, with their programme
of an international fraternisation of the proletariat, they denied the
principle of the nation. It repudiated them because they allotted
the position as historically determinant factor, which belonged to
'Race' according to the *Weltanschauung*, to 'Society' (*Gesellschaft*),
that is, to the direction of the economico-social structure. Above all,
if it was not to contradict itself, it was bound to condemn the gospel
of the historically necessary class-war as the worst menace to the
unity of the *Volksgemeinschaft*. Thus, to all appeareances, the working
class with its Marxist mentality offered none of those possibilities
of contact which National-Socialism had been so ingenious in dis-
covering elsewhere.

But the agility of its propaganda was too great to allow it to resign
itself to failure, even in this case: rather it set out to find ways of gaining a hold on the German worker. First of all, it took over from
Marxism those ideas which flattered the working masses with a sense
of their importance. That the working class is that part of the people
in which the destiny of the nation is decided and the shaping of the
future prepared: this was the form in which the Marxist thesis of the
world mission of the proletariat was taken over and assimilated.
Certainly no one could deny that the majority of this class was inclined towards the Marxist doctrine; but the attempt was made to
lessen this dangerous deviation by giving the worker the assurance
that only infection with the poison of Jewish deception had made
it possible for him to fall, temporarily, victim to this doctrine. But
in reality it was he who had always been the truest son of his people,
and it would suffice to clean off the coating of Jewish 'foreignising'
(*Überfremdung*) to bring out in all its brightness his *völkisch* sentiment.

A second trick, however, was even more effective. While condemning the class-war theory as an un-German, a Jewish invention,
care was taken to provide the tendencies to class warfare with the
nourishment they required. And how could this be better done than
by opposing to the picture of the worker still at heart German and
loyal to the people, the picture of the do-nothing, selfish *bourgeois*,
ready for no sacrifice, and, above all, of the greedy and exploiting
industrialist? This was the cliché which governed the speeches of the
propagandists, and especially those of Hitler. It was possible in this
way in one breath to make war on the class struggle as a Marxist
tenet and to support it as a social reality. There is no disputing

the fact that a not inconsiderable part of the working class fell victim to this refined method of capturing men's minds.

Over the whole expanse of German life we come across the same picture: everywhere National-Socialism contrives to find dispositions, opinions, ideas which, if properly arranged, will allow themselves to be harnessed to its carriage. If in their original form they come half-way to meet it, they can simply be taken over and incorporated. If they resist annexation, they are interpreted, twisted, deformed until they allow themselves to be melted into the *Weltanschauung*.

The success which these summary proceedings never failed to gain provided a shattering demonstration of how vulnerable the 'people of poets and thinkers' was to such methods of recruitment as contrive, by their outward disguise, to give themselves the appearance of metaphysical depth or, at any rate, of a basis in principle.

Naturally the seductive power of big words is especially effective where people have in any case an inclination to abandon sane human understanding in favour of obscurely felt meanings that lurk behind and below. It is beyond question that this reveals a specific weakness of our people. Whoever is severe on this weakness should at least not forget what the recognition of it can do to excuse those charged with it. For the false appearance of profundity to have the effect aimed at, it was necessary for those who were being courted to possess a great deal of readiness to take seriously in all good faith what they were being told—that is to say, to be to a great extent unsuspicious of the real purposes of those who were playing these tricks on them.

There is also a second misunderstanding against which the exposure of this chain of consequences can put us on our guard. Let us beware of summarily labelling as 'pioneers' of National-Socialism every spiritual or intellectual movement of the past which National-Socialism with its usual brazenness claimed for its own, and so sanctioning after the event the Party's arts of falsification. In every case we must be careful to examine whether, and in what degree, the affinities of which so much was made really existed, or were only part of the make-believe of those virtuosi of the lie. As always, it should be remembered that there is no idea, no tenet, no message which cannot be twisted by senseless or ill-intentioned minds into the opposite of its original meaning.

12

THE ROLE OF FOREIGN POLICY IN THE SUCCESS OF THE NATIONAL-SOCIALIST PARTY

Maurice Baumont

THE treaties of Versailles and Saint-Germain, the reparations, and the occupation of the Ruhr, provided excellent material for a nationalism which condemned the humiliations and the injustice of which Germany was regarded as the victim. The condition of international affairs, exploited to the limit by National-Socialism, explains to a great extent the success of Hitler, the demagogue, who, as the mouthpiece of a Germany determined to avenge her defeat, claimed to lead the fight for the liberation of the German people.

The embryo of Hitlerism is an inexorable nationalism, and by what might be called an historical law of proportion, the advances of National-Socialism follow upon a general surge of nationalism. Indeed, many of the elements of Hitlerism existed before Hitler, particularly the Pangermanist and ultra-nationalist aspirations of which his propaganda made the utmost use. It is not necessary to examine here this problem, which always arises, as soon as one considers the causes of the rapid growth of National-Socialism.

As Julien Benda puts it: 'The case of Adolf Hitler raises the eternal question of History. Are the great actors of the world the creators of the movements which bear their names, or are they chiefly their interpreters?' And Julien Benda replies: 'Hitler certainly seems to be the expression of movements existing before him, whose origins lie deeper than the circumstances of the day'. With certain differences, the accounts of Professor Ritter and Professor Litt throw light on this fundamental question.

I

In the present account we will merely give a critical analysis of the superficial arguments used by National-Socialist propaganda. Edmond Vermeil has rightly observed that these superficial arguments were just as important as the fundamental reasons. As he declares, 'It is up to the one who will give the most violent expression to the claims of nationalism'. And he even wonders if there was, in their foreign policy, such a very real difference between the Weimar régime and National-Socialism. There did in fact exist among the Weimar parties, however divided their opinions on home affairs may have been, an almost complete unanimity when it was a question of protesting against the new European order created at Versailles or against its application to Germany.

In a recent book, *Visage de l'Allemagne actuelle* (Paris, 1950), Comte Robert d'Harcourt published the moving letter of a Württemberg pastor.

'You forget one word, sir, in your enumeration of the factors that contributed to Hitler's rise to power, and that word is: Versailles. If the German spirit has become sick, it is because it was poisoned by the rage which the extravagances and the evils of the *diktat* aroused in it, namely the rape of our colonies, the theft of our private bank accounts and of our merchant navy. Our National-Socialism was only the normal rise in temperature which always accompanies suffering.

'An incalculable responsibility in the growth of this phenomenon of National-Socialism weighs on the Allies' shoulders, and particularly on the French, who were inspired solely by a desire for revenge. It was not our Pangermanists who barred our road towards democracy, for until 1919 the average German merely smiled at them; it was the policy of the Allies, the shackles of the *diktat*. And this is the reason why one day the road lay open to the ambitions of a semi-lunatic.

'You write that the great majority of Germans applauded Hitler, and on this point I do not contradict you. What people loving their country and their honour do not applaud the man who breaks their chains?'

While the Allies boasted of having fought to establish democracy throughout the world, Germany accused them of imposing on her a degrading peace, a Carthaginian peace. She was suffering cruel trials. The privations resulting from a blockade which was only finally lifted after the peace treaty had been signed, added to the sufferings of starving children.

As Edmond Vermeil has written:

'Who was responsible for the war and the defeat, if not the Prussian military and bureaucratic aristocracy? And who had signed the peace treaty in 1919, except the representatives of the parties who were going to lead the democratic and republican cause, and who formed the centre of social democracy? From then on fatal discredit was to come upon the Weimar régime.'

The most conciliatory Germans condemned the Versailles

Treaty and have never ceased to demand its revision and a redress of the injustices for which it was responsible.

Could concessions on the part of the Allies have in any way mitigated this discontent? From a strictly historical point of view it is not easy to undertake any serious discussion on this subject. We will merely observe that most Germans have been and still are convinced of it.

Sir Lewis Namier, however, thought otherwise. In a recent study (26th April 1951) entitled *Were Chances Missed by the Allies?* he writes:

> 'Undoubtedly, if after the First World War the Western Powers had promptly evacuated the occupied zones of Germany, written off reparations, and admitted Germany to equality in armament, the Germans would have felt that a measure of atonement had been made for the crime of defeating them—or for their having been, according to Hitler, fooled into throwing away their arms by chatter about President Wilson's fourteen points.'

Could one be sure that the Germans would in the long run acknowledge that concessions, even moderate ones, had been made to them? It was said in 1919 that if they did not feel the weight of the defeat, they would take back at the first opportunity that which they had had to give up.

The 'German demands', presented by the Reich delegation to the Allies, were for a plebiscite in Alsace-Lorraine, which was largely a former German possession. But the organisation of a plebiscite in Alsace-Lorraine would have caused all kinds of troubles; even—and this seemed likely—if it were to have turned out in favour of France, Germany could still have refused afterwards to recognise the validity of a vote held so soon after her own collapse.

In any case, the Treaty of Versailles gave rise to almost unanimous German protest.

In his *Grenzen der Naturwissenschaftlichen Begriffsbildung*, the Heidelberg philosopher Heinrich Rickert observed:

> 'Had a German, the day after the end of the war, expressed satisfaction concerning the Treaty of Versailles, we would have understood what he meant, but could never have sympathised with his attitude. We cannot imagine the state of mind of the German satisfied by the Versailles Treaty.'

There was in this revolt against Versailles something more than indignation against various clauses of the treaty which will be discussed later. There was something more general, something more elementary—and that was Germany's vitality.

II

It was Hitler who made the most violent protest against Versailles, and National-Socialism was notable for its outbursts of fury against the 'slave'régime, as it was called, imposed on Germany. As Gerhard Ritter has written, until 1930 the Nazis were considered as super-patriots without any great practical importance. Theodor Litt likewise has stated that the National-Socialists who accused the Weimar Republic of abandoning through its weakness the national interests, found a great hearing when they claimed to be the only ones who really represented these interests.

Even Hitler's enemies had to acknowledge this. In February 1924 General von Lossow recognised that there was a 'healthy centre' in Hitler's movement: for this movement could convert workers to nationalism.

Hindenburg and his followers had a secret sympathy for the nationalism which lies at the heart of the Hitler movement. And nationalism was indeed the starting point of National-Socialism.

Hitler pushed to the point of fanaticism the cult of Germany, and with him patriotic ardour reached hysteria. In *Mein Kampf* he explained, in an apparently very reasonable way, how he intended to judge all questions of foreign affairs : 'Will such a solution be to our people's advantage now or in the future?' His extreme nationalism prevented him from giving an intelligent answer to this question. For Hitler was a passionate nationalist who proclaimed in *Mein Kampf* that Germany possessed forces which no one in the world could overcome. Stirring up the violence secretly at work in a Germany shaken by the inflation, he gave utterance to the most violent claims of continental Pangermanism.

On 24 February 1920 the twenty-four points of the 'programme of the German workers' party', of which Gottfried Feder was the chief editor, were made known to the public.

1. 'We demand the union of all Germans (according to the law allowing all nations to govern themselves) under one great Germany.
2. 'We demand that Germany should enjoy the same rights as other nations. The Treaties of Versailles and Saint-Germain must be abolished.'

Thus Hitler's catechism proclaims the ideal of a great Germany and, for the German people, their right of free government, as well as absolute equality between Germany and other nations, principles which would involve the abolition of the Versailles and Saint-Germain Treaties.

But if Hitler had inherited the vocabulary of the Pangermanists, he gave to his words an Austrian colour, for he dreamt particularly of an expansion in eastern Europe. This prodigious demagogue was an Austrian Pangermanist. And the ideas of Austrian Pangermanism were reflected in *Mein Kampf*; Hitler, claiming that Germanism is being 'more and more oppressed from year to year' in the 'impossible state of the Habsburgs', violently attacked what he called 'a vile system of slavifying and de-Germanising', which meant that in this 'babel of languages' Austria has ceased to be a German state 'in order to become a mixture of Czechs, Poles, Hungarians, Ruthenians, Serbs, and Croats, not to forget the dissolving bacilli of humanity, Jews, Jews, and more Jews.'

Hitler did not only want Germany to become once more the powerful national state which Bismarck had built up: he went much further, following the ideologists who extended the Reich beyond Bismarck's frontiers. The place a nation held in the world depended only on its strength. In the eyes of history, acquired rights did not exist. Germany as such only represented the nucleus from which could be expanded a Reich that would enforce its hegemony on Europe.

Hitler rejected not only the frontiers of 1919, but also those of 1914, which, being 'provisional and haphazard', had never corresponded with economic necessities. The intention merely to re-establish the frontiers of 1914 was 'madness'.

Mein Kampf raged against 'unctuous windbags' who attempted to indicate to the German people that the aim of their foreign policy was to obtain the correction of the injustice of 1918, when what was really required was to 'secure for the German nation the territories due to her'. Germany had too little space for her needs and aspirations, the German people must conquer their *Lebensraum*.

'Between the size and growth of the population on the one hand, and the extent and quality of the soil or territory on the other, a lasting and natural relationship must be established.'

It was necessary both to occupy the area which was at that time essential to the deployment of German energies, and to ensure for them further territories for subsequent expansion. 'Political frontiers are created by men and modified by men.'

Today there are 80 million Germans in Europe: according to Hitler, in less than a hundred years there must be 250 million, 'not living on top of each other like factory coolies working for the rest of the world. To begin with, we must regain our independence, recover our lost territories, shake off the yoke of slavery, and force our enemies and conquerors to come to terms.' For, as *Mein Kampf* puts it, 'The oppressed territories will be reincorporated in the fatherland, not by violent speech, but by blows delivered by the conquering sword'.

Now, the people can be led only by their feelings. Hitler knew just to what extent these simple minds could be indoctrinated. He aimed at choosing only those ideas which primitive intelligences could grasp, and he appealed directly to the very heart of the masses. In spite of the 'unheard-of stupidity shown by the German *petit bourgeois* when he talks politics', National-Socialism wanted to arouse again in this nation, 'a spirit of national pride, of haughty virility, of hate, the daughter of anger'; and, as one finds in *Mein Kampf* all the near future predicted by the man who had the boldness necessary for shaping this future over a period of a thousand years, one also finds in it these lines (Book 11, chapter 13):

"We need a government which will be the herald of national consciousness. Once our people have a government which realises that that is its mission, six years will not pass before a fearless leadership in the Reich's foreign policy will find itself supported by the equally fearless determination of a nation athirst for liberty.'

After the seizure of power in 1933, six years did in fact mark the beginning of the Second World War.

The armistice, the Treaty of Versailles, and its strict enforcement had closely involved the life of the German people in the difficulties of international affairs. Hitler guessed what the crowd wanted. He kept intuitively in touch with the desires and the anger, the regrets and the passionate hopes of the populace. He understood its confused aspirations and knew how to put them into lapidary terms in the fanatical propaganda of an excessive Germanism. 'A great fire has been lit: in its ardent flame will be forged . . . the sword which will give back life and freedom to the German nation.' Monster meetings drew panting crowds, and, indefatigable and histrionic, he succeeded in convincing them, in rousing their enthusiasm by his calculated brutalities, and in fascinating them by his personal magnetism.

The technique of using short, commanding, emphatic slogans, whose meaning mattered little, worked wonders on the crowds. His hoarse voice broke into curses, very occasionally into lamentations. For, if Thomas Mann in his *Reflections* of 1917 had already defined Germany as the country of protestations *par excellence*, Hitler did not forget Moeller van den Bruck's saying: 'We are destined never to leave others in peace'.

The noisy mysticism of National-Socialism awakened and excited the collective spirit of the helpless masses, object of the humiliations of the Versailles *diktat*. Hate rose in a Germany haunted by the memory of its power and still deprived of the means of reviving it; a Germany, however, who felt herself full of unused powers of expansion. 'The oppression which our enemies make us suffer', observes *Mein Kampf*, 'is no longer accepted as in former times with bursts of laughter, but arouses bitterness and anger.'

III

To found a policy in this way on indignation and enthusiasm was certainly a great risk, for these are assuredly not political states of mind. But National-Socialist propaganda made constant use of these methods of action.

To be convinced of this, one need only analyse Hitler's attitude towards events which led to the armistice and peace. To a great extent National-Socialism was, and aimed to be, a revolt against the defeat of 1918.

Above all, the armistice of 11th November was a crime. The Jews were chiefly responsible for the fatal issue of the war, the Jew being the symbol of all that is essentially non-German. The tortuous manœuvres of international Jewry had got the better of Germany. *Mein Kampf* clearly advocated the sanguinary projects which Hitler was not to be afraid of carrying out in full after 1942 against the Jews.

'If in the course of the war, twelve or fifteen thousand of these Jewish corruptors of the people, had been subjected to the poison gas which hundreds of thousands of Germans had to endure at the front . . . the sacrifice of millions of men would not have been in vain.'

It was the presence in Germany of this alien element, the Jews, which explained the defeat of 1918; and this simple piece of reasoning was to become a very important factor in the growth of anti-Semitism. The nation's anger at having been betrayed by the treachery of fate would seek to prove and punish a real act of treachery.

Hitler never ceased to incite the crowds against the 'November criminals': by which he meant the Jews, above all, but also the Marxists. Germany, which could never have been defeated by force of arms, found her strength wasted by the undermining work of the revolutionaries. She would not have lost the war if she had not been 'stabbed in the back' by the Marxists and the Jews. 'The men of November' betrayed the glorious armies, who returned from the battlefields 'undefeated', heads held high, still bearing arms, without their native soil having been invaded.

'The November crimes will be punished, and heads will fall.' How many times, before his rise to power, did Hitler repeat these famous words, often adding, 'Heads will fall; either ours or theirs. Let us see to it that it be theirs'. No one took Hitler's terrible threats quite seriously.

IV

It goes without saying that National-Socialism proudly ignored the concessions admitted by the Allies. In spite of all Lloyd-George's endeavours in the spring of 1919 to secure, against the opinion of the Foreign Office, an 'equitable peace', the National-Socialists were convinced that the Allies wanted systematically to create a permanent discord between Germany and Poland.

Certainly, Germany's protests against East Prussia's separation from the Reich were unanimous. Had not this country in the course of history flowed with German blood? Moreover, the plebiscites of 1920 had turned decisively against the Poles. Even the most moderate German did not accept either the 'corridor' or the surrender of a large part of Posnania, or of a part of Upper Silesia. Sir Lewis Namier points out that a very great part of German opinion considered, as the memorandum addressed in July 1922 by General von Seeckt to the Chancellor Wirth declares, that Poland's very existence was 'incompatible with the vital needs of Germany'. Namier observes: 'Although at least 80 per cent of the population in the territories ceded by the Germans to Poland were Polish, not one responsible statesman or general of the Weimar period would have accepted these frontiers as final'.

While he protested loudly against 'the oppression of German territories', Hitler had only sarcasm for the rights of nations to self-determination, and for Wilson's scheme which, when put into effect, 'balkanises Europe'.

The outcome of 1848, the principle of nationalities, which extended the democratic idea into the international field, had been loudly invoked during the war in each belligerent camp: against the Empire of the Tsars the German's upheld the Poles and the Balts, just as the Allies appealed to the Slavs against Austria-Hungary, and to the Arabs against the Ottoman Empire. If the application of the principle of nationality was carried far enough in 1919, no one even dreamt of carrying it to the extreme solution which later met with the approval of the all-powerful *Führer*: the displacment of populations.

But, with the 'Balkanising' of Europe, with Austria reduced to the state of a deformed dwarf, with the Polish Corridor and the muddle of Danzig, the reconstruction of Europe was compromised by strange malformations.

The whole of the peace, however, was vitiated, because of the conditions on which the armistice was conceded to the Germans.

Generally considered very severe, this armistice was not a capitulation. Wilson's 'Fourteen Points' were accepted by all the belligerents, including Germany, as the basis of future peace settlements. Now, this basis was ambiguous, as the 'Fourteen Points' were general principles which had been given no agreed interpretation. The vanquished were resentful, claiming that the 'Fourteen Points' accepted as the basis of the peace, were not respected, either in the letter or the spirit, by the treaty.

The refusal to allow the defeated to take part in the negotiations round the conference table completed that mental isolation to which Germany was condemned. Peace was 'imposed' on her. Germany was notified by the conquerors of the conditions, when she herself had taken no part in the framing of the treaty. She felt herself deceived, betrayed, subjected to a forcibly imposed peace, treacherously substituted for the equitable peace promised to her when she had laid down arms. It was a *diktat* that was being imposed on her, contrary to the 'Fourteen Points', and it sealed the oppression of the German people.

Hitler maintained that this *diktat*, made by a 'pitiless conqueror', had 'reduced Germany to slavery', forcing her to drag out her life under the 'threat of perpetual wretchedness'. Versailles signified 'limitless oppression', corresponding to 'perpetual slavery', and an unprecedented plundering of the German people, victims of 'unbounded extortions' and of a 'shameful degradation'.

Infinitely more subtle than Hitler, a future National-Socialist such as Friedrich Sieburg admitted that the conquerors did not want to wipe out the German people: they were satisfied to weaken them, imagining and hoping that in this way they would consolidate their preponderant position. The liberal and humanitarian ideology proclaimed by the 'crusade' against Germany prevented the killing of the German people. They were not being killed, but they were being deprived of means of existence. 'The most cruel and the most refined method of attrition that has even been applied to a nation in modern times.' Civil war, famine, inflation leading to a general pathological crisis were the immediate consequences of the exhaustion resulting from this policy.

The union of Austria and Germany corresponded, according to Lansing, Secretary of State under Wilson, to the 'almost unanimous wishes' of the Austrian people. In 1919 the Weimar constitution expressly made room for the absorption of Austria. It was not surprising that Hitler, the Austrian, should have been one of the most ardent adherents of the idea of the greater Germany.

The Germans, deprived in Europe of the 'rights of self-determination' which had been solemnly granted to the Poles, the Czechs, the Slovenes, the Yugoslavs, and the Romanians, found themselves also debarred from all expansion outside Europe. The war had seen the disappearance one after another of the German colonies. The Treaty of Versailles removed them all at once. Such a settlement of the colonial question appeared an act of brigandage, of plunder, at the expense of a Germany declared incapable of fulfilling the sacred mission of all colonising nations. The colonies in Africa, Asia, and Oceania, were all snatched from Germany, and handed over to the conquerors, although Germany having 'a population without living space', needed colonies, and in the history of colonisation had produced its pioneers, its explorers, its missionaries. In the institution of mandates, the Germans saw and denounced a bogus internationalism and an unctuous hypocrisy which ill concealed old imperialism. The 'hunt for mandates' exasperated a country which had been declared unworthy of governing coloured nations.

Point 3 in the programme of the 'German Workers' Party', published on 24th February 1920, claimed the restitution of the colonies taken away from Germany: 'We demand territories and land to nourish our people, and the opportunity of emigration for our surplus population'.

This demand for the restitution of the colonies sprang from feelings of resentment. They must put to right an injustice, and protest against an act of violence.

But the Germans were far less preoccupied by the colonial problem than by the question of Poland or reparations. Certainly, the colonially-minded did not give up their hopes. However, their demonstrations of loyalty to the colonial idea were not on any very large scale and there even existed a fairly pronounced hostility to this idea. Before the rising tide of the coloured races, in China, in India, in Egypt, before the success which greeted such works as Oswald Spengler's *Decline of the West*, some people congratulated themselves that Germany had the fortunate privilege of being spared a great and imminent conflict. Not having, thank Heaven, any colonies to defend, she ought to renounce a 'colonial plaything'. Free from the strain which marked all colonial powers, she gained, particularly from China, sympathy and confidence, because she had had to renounce the privileges of the white races. As the Chancellor Hermann Mueller declared in 1928, 'She enjoys great prestige with the colonial peoples striving to free themselves, precisely because she does not take part in colonial activities'.

Bearing in mind this train of thought, Germany had since then directed her colonial aspirations exclusively towards Africa. Rather than widen her activities, in a new *Weltpolitik*, she limited the colonial question to the 'dark continent'. Besides, was not Africa the theatre of her first colonial ventures? The Reich fairly soon ceased to claim all its old colonies. It limited its demands to black Africa, pointing out the need for colonial development by European nations and claiming that Germany should play an important part in this common task. *Mittel Africa* was the only thought of colonially-minded Germans.

Being little disposed in favour of the colonial policy, the National-Socialist Party remained 'completely cold' as far as the colonies were concerned. *Mein Kampf* criticises the 'inept colonial policy' of Wilhelm II. Hitler abandons colonial aspirations, in order to extend the territory of the Reich in the east.

In the Party itself, however, such former colonial officers as General von Epp continued to advocate a policy of acquiring colonies. Moreover, the policy of the *Gleichberichtigung*—of equality of rights—automatically brought up the claim to colonies. The acquisition of colonial territories was a 'question of honour', since all great nations possess colonial territories.

However unjust the territorial clauses had seemed to the embittered Germans, they were not the section of the treaty which roused the greatest indignation in that country. Other clauses inflicted a feeling of humiliation upon her. More than at the prospects of economic and financial burdens, or even at the territorial losses, German opinion, almost unanimously, revolted against those 'ignominious articles' of the treaty in which provision was made for the trial of persons accused of having committed actions contrary to the laws and customs of war. Penal sanctions were decreed against Germans, headed by Wilhelm II, accused of having violated 'the laws and practice of warfare and the laws of humanity'.

Fierce manifestations denounced this 'blot on the honour' of Germany. In face of the agitation's violence, the Allies quickly gave up extradition in favour of an investigation entrusted to a special tribunal in Leipzig, which in turn was abandoned after various incidents and the passing of conciliatory, mild sentences. In the obscure fermentations of a Germany reduced in Europe, deprived of her colonies, and shrinking into herself, Hitler's 'ideas' developed.

In order to justify the demand for 'reparations', the vanquished were forced to admit themselves 'responsible, through having caused them, for all the losses, for all the damages sustained by the Allied and Associate Governments and their subjects, as a result of the war, initiated by the aggression of Germany and her allies'. This article (231) of the Versailles Treaty had not, originally, the significance universally attributed to it, of a judgment, of a verdict against a guilty party. It established the responsibility of the Germans in civil law for all material damage and pronounced only financial responsibility, in no way arising out of criminal law. Elaborated from a plan put forward by American financiers and from a memorandum presented by Lloyd George, it had been drawn up by American and British experts.

By the partisan protestations which it aroused, Article 231 was to become 'the rock on which the whole treaty was ultimately shipwrecked'. It rendered a whole nation guilty. The victors, as sole judges, pronounced a moral condemnation against the publicly defiled loser, and demanded that he acknowledge his guilt. For the vanquished, who was not prepared to admit it, such an avowal, forced out of him, was worthless. Added to the material sacrifices, here was a clause which appeared to contain an unnecessary or insulting declaration of guilt. The passing of judgment on a people is not compatible with a peace treaty.

Obstinate in their tenacity, which was to them 'a point of honour', the Germans would not rest until they had overthrown this system of incrimination. They demanded moral rehabilitation and founded their desire for revenge on the premise that the treaty was 'built upon a lie'. They protested against the accusation which rendered their country responsible for the war, they made it a pretext for arguing over the principle of reparations, for militating against the confiscation of their colonies, against the interdiction of union with Austria, and against the eastern frontiers imposed upon them. The German people had been insulted.

Germany rebelled passionately against the military restrictions imposed at Versailles. It was considered as a mutilation of German sovereignty, wounding national feeling. Armament was limited, all heavy artillery prohibited, light artillery was reduced to two hundred and eighty-eight pieces, and aircraft forbidden. Vast quantities of war materials were destroyed. An inter-allied Control Commission watched over the disarmament in Germany and checked the production of authorised material. The navy was confined to coastguard duty, and submarines were prohibited. The left bank of the Rhine was demilitarised, as was a fifty-kilometre strip east of the river.

Naturally Hitler was in the forefront of the fight against military restrictions, which for a number of years were to render Germany incapable of sustaining a war, even against Poland. This attitude of protest had the effect of ranging military sympathies on the side of National-Socialism, and as the struggle for equal rights in the field of armaments was popular, the whole country lent its support.

Any régime of foreign occupation tends to inflame national feeling. The presence of foreign troops on German soil was a humiliating expression of defeat. Germany suffered and was irritated by it. Seven million Germans, wrote Hitler, languish under foreign domination. It goes without saying that he denounced 'the black dishonour' (die schwarze Schmach) which Germany claimed to be enduring. He was indignant to see black troops installed in the Rhineland; even though they only put in a short appearance, the days following the armistice, the North-African contingents added to 'the black dishonour'. *Mein Kampf* noted that the Rhine, 'the life artery of the German people', flows through 'a land where negro hordes disport themselves'.

National-Socialist fury at the injustice of Versailles did not spare the League of Nations. It was regarded simply as an extension of the group of 'Allied and Associate Powers' joined by neutrals, and merely a conservative body called upon to preserve the *status quo* established in the victors' favour.

Resentment against France was general. She was saddled with the responsibility of the peace that had failed, and the 1914 war was ascribed to her. It was said that one of her greatest deceits was her unwillingness to realise the causes of that war until the effects asserted themselves. However, as soon as one examined the deeper sources, her guilt became evident. She had violated Wilson's 'Fourteen Points', holding that they had not come into force, although their moral postulates had dominated the armistice negotiations. Not content with a cruel peace, she wanted to keep what she called her 'natural frontiers'. Her armies would never leave the Rhine.

In Hitler's view France was 'the century-old enemy', whose avidity hovered over the Rhine, 'that most German of all rivers'. It was her burning desire to destroy Germany, whom she wanted to see 'disunited and partitioned'. She must be 'brought to reason'; all the forces of the Reich would have to be 'gathered and thrown against her. There would have to be 'an active show-down with France'. Hitler never doubted the irreducible enmity of the two countries; he was convinced of the fierce hatred of the French people for the German people. 'If I were French myself', he wrote, 'I could not and would not act otherwise than Clemenceau.'

After signing the 'shameful armistice', the Reich was assailed by 'new demands' which France was ceaselessly formulating. She increased her 'plundering raids', she repeatedly demanded 'more pieces of flesh from the body of our people'. She never ceased disturbing the peace. She was vehemently blamed for everything—for the delivery of livestock and material exacted for the populations of the countries invaded by the Reich, for the ceding of merchant-ships to replace torpedoed tonnage, for the coal intended to take the place of that which the northern French mines would have supplied had they not been systematically destroyed during the war, for the smuggling which poured through 'the western breach' opened on the Reich's flanks by the military occupation.

In 1923 she occupied the Ruhr, 'the land where forges glow and' high furnaces smoke'. *Mein Kampf* states, quite correctly, that this occupation of 1923 was of 'great importance' in the development of National-Socialism.

Enough of the enemy's one-sided and arbitrary decisions! The devil take the unworthy rulers who have 'humbly sought the favour of France' and who insist on 'bowing and scraping' before 'the great nation'. Hitler proclaimed 'the burning desire to put an end to incessant humiliations'.

Much has been written about the strange use made of certain funds by a French military intelligence service. Just as the Farnese Palace had effectively supported Mussolini at the outset, so Hitler was supposed to have received French money. But, according to Konrad Heiden, one of Hitler's biographers, and one not over-tolerant with his hero, 'a little of the French money, which in the early post-war years, flowed into Bavaria, may have gone to Hitler. That it should have influenced the *Führer* in France's favour is out of the question.'

For him France was enemy number one, the 'mortal foe' who brought negroes to the Rhine, who was the slave of Jewish finance, and who intended to annihilate Germany.

When the Franco–German *rapprochement* was at its closest, thanks to Aristide Briand and Stresemann, the Germans reproached France for evacuating by driblets, despite 'the spirit of Locarno'. The National-Socialists described as buffoonery the tiny alleviations to which the Quay d'Orsay consented under pressure from London. Any reduction in the number of French troops in the Rhineland was, in the Germans' opinion, delayed too long to be of any value when it finally took place.

Although National-Socialist policy was based upon hostility and even hatred towards France, it sometimes forgot its passionate ill-feelings. Though the pages in *Mein Kampf* relating to France have never been retracted and no modification has ever been made to them, there has been no lack of officious commentators to point out that they were written when passions ran high owing to the invasion of the Ruhr.

Following the great National-Socialist victory in September, on 24th October 1930, in the *Völkischer Beobachter*, Hitler replied to Gustave Hervé's open letter putting forward suggestions for a Franco–German *entente*, by saying that he was desirous of improving relations with France and that he wished for friendly relations among all civilised nations. Similarly, Rosenberg gave an assurance that National-Socialism did not seek war with France.

When in power, Hitler emphasised this mode of appeasement, evidently for tactical reasons. On 20th August 1934, before the Saar plebiscite, he declared in Koblenz: 'Once the question of the

Q

Saar is resolved, there will remain no reasonable . . . grounds for the two great nations to continue quarrelling until the end of time'. After the Saar plebiscite, on 1st March 1935, he declared in Saar-brücken: 'We hope that by this act of justice . . . relations between Germany and France will definitely improve. . . . It must be possible for two great peoples to shake hands, in order to face, by a common effort, the evils ·that threaten to engulf Europe.'

At times he hoped, and was to hope, that under the direction of National-Socialist Germany, France would enroll in the anti-Bolshevik and anti-semitic Europe, of which he dreamed, for he envisaged the universal spread of National-Socialism, 'in France as elsewhere'.

When he decided on the military reoccupation of the Rhineland, he pointed out on 7th March 1936 in the *Reichstag*: 'I have removed from the German press all hatred of the French people', and he accused France of having 'replied to Germany's friendly offers and repeated peaceful assurances by concluding an alliance exclusively directed against Germany': the Franco–Soviet pact.

In general, there is no doubt that for Hitler and according to his own words 'the mortal enemy of the German people' was and remained France with 'her aspirations of European leadership'. She would have to be isolated. England and Italy were the possible allies against her, and he wished fervently for such an alliance.

At the time he wrote *Mein Kampf* he lived, like many of his countrymen, in the belief and even in the hope of a Franco–British conflict. For him England was 'the enemy of France'. Therefore political expediency demanded an agreement with England, although England was torturing the Irish people and had swindled India. *Mein Kampf* (Part II, chapter 13) explains to what extent France, through her geographical position, was threatening England, and the *Führer* certainly had the same ideas in his mind again in the summer of 1940:

> 'France along much of her coast is encamped opposite the vital centres of the British Empire. Not only do these offer an easy target to planes and long-range guns, but the communication lines of British commerce would be exposed with no defence from the attacks of submarines. The Anglo–German alliance is all the more desirable since an alliance can rest on no other basis than a good bargain for both sides.'

Now, Germany had to acquire territories at the expense of Russia, which was England's traditional rival. If not an ally, England's selfish motives could at least make her the accomplice of Germany.

The natural ally was Fascist Italy. The Italian alliance, which would ideally complement the English alliance, was to be sought actively. Southern Tyrol, dear to the Germans and even more so to the Austrians, must be abandoned. Considering the vast scale of the struggle in which the Powers would face each other, one should not shrink before 'this sacrifice, after all a limited one', particularly since Italy, the home of Fascism, had as its leader a dictator of genius: Mussolini.

If Hitler was 'convinced of the need to settle accounts with France', it was because Germany had 'to protect her rear' in order to advance in Eastern Europe. A dynamic Germany had to overcome two obstacles: France in the west and Russia in the east. The defeat of France would give the German people an opportunity to spread eastwards, in accordance with the exhortations of *Mein Kampf* about German territorial policy in the future. The colossal eastern state was ready to crumble, which would allow the acquisition of the soil necessary to the German people. The march 'on the path of the ancient Teutonic Knights' was to begin again, and the German sword was to win the land needed by the German plough.

Hitler's anti-French leanings were certainly not a novelty to Germany. His anglophile tendency coincided with feelings that had made themselves felt in the Reich since 1919. The anti-British suspicions of the end of the nineteenth and the beginning of the twentieth century, the anti-English fury of 1914 with the *Gott strafe England* were all forgotten. It was said of ambassador d'Abernon that he was 'Lord Protector' of the Reich.

Whereas Francophobia and pro-British feelings conformed to the emotional currents stirred by a nationalism which since 1919 was again in full swing, Hitler's systematic hatred of Russia constituted a novelty for Germany; it was something specifically Austrian. For Austria Russia was the adversary, the traditional enemy. The same was not true in the Empire of Bismarck and Wilhelm II, where the conservative elements were generally more or less pro-Russian; it was the Social-Democrats who indulged in Russophobia.

However, in 1917 Russia had ceased to be the Empire of the Tsars. As the sworn enemy of Bolshevism, Hitler had no intention of joining with revolutionary Russia. If Russia's example were followed, the revolution would certainly spread to Europe. Yet Hitler gave his utmost support to the military men who had crushed Spartacus.

Like Rosenberg, he incessantly maintained that the Bolshevik régime was shaking. His future quarrels with Gregor Strasser were foreshadowed in 1926. Gregor Strasser was unwilling to allow a blind anti-Bolshevism to disturb the emotions of German youth, who would unwittingly become the bulwark of the capitalist system of exploitation. Hitler countered: whoever misunderstands Russia to such a degree, does not realise that a Russo–German alliance would mean the immediate Bolshevisation of Germany.

Although Count Reventlow, who in January 1927 came under Hitler's 'orders', declared himself against a foreign policy 'susceptible of serving capitalist interests', he was far from endorsing the pro-Russian trend, laid down by Strasser.

Also, at the monetary conference in London of July 1933, the German nationalist Hügenberg, for a few months Hitler's minister, presented a memorandum which demanded 'space in the East' for Germany.

VI

We are not concerned here with a discussion of the very serious faults of the Treaty of Versailles. We shall merely indicate that these faults, immeasurably exaggerated by strong feeling, raised such criticism, not only in Germany but in almost every country, that international opinion generally sided violently against the treaty which had rapidly become unpopular. This semi-Wilsonian treaty, which was neither a peace of total victory nor of moderate compromise, was furiously attacked by its principal English and Italian authors, and as early as 1920 it was disowned by the Americans. Born mainly of American inspiration, it was henceforward vitiated at its very source. It was rejected by the United States, and Russia had not been present at Versailles. It was branded in 'the neutral countries' as the principal cause of growing economic and political difficulties. Under the title 'The Slandered Peace'— rightly or wrongly—Etienne Mantoux showed that the Treaty of Versailles was not as badly drawn up, or as disastrous in its 'economic consequences' as had been maintained by Keynes, the famous British economist; it had become the butt of general criticism which was hindering its execution. It came to be generally believed that Germany could not live under the Treaty of Versailles.

Instinctively and in a frenzy of national passion, Germany confronted the irreducible differences of the Allies with her opposition to a hard treaty, in which she claimed to see a systematic programme of pillage for the benefit of inhuman masters, ingeniously concealed under a pretext of moral guilt.

Criticism of the Treaty of Versailles provided an admirable element of agitation, from which Hitler resolved to draw the maximum advantage. All the arguments tirelessly and methodically used to build a case against the great injustice of Versailles were used and amplified in Hitler's speeches. He had not invented them; he only took them up again with passionate violence, and repeated them unceasingly. Tirelessly he would return to the same topics.

As early as 1923, in Munich, General von Lossow observed that 'Hitler's long speeches contained almost always the same things'. Hitler raged against 'the infamous treaties of Versailles and Saint-Germain', and in a general way against what he called the treaties signed 'in the suburbs of Paris'. For he was not one to allow 'German children to be deprived of their daily bread for love of peace'.

During the years of bitter humiliation experienced by Germany, criticism of Versailles was one of his most efficient means of popular agitation. He, who had already described the Austro–Hungarian ultimatum of July 1914 as 'far too moderate', did not hesitate to contrast the 'humaneness' of Brest-Litovsk and the 'cruelty' of Versailles. In October 1919, when first speaking in public before some hundred people, the theme of his harangue was 'Brest-Litovsk and Versailles'. His first declarations therefore related to foreign policy. He would not have it said that 'the shame of opprobrium' of Versailles was a punishment for Brest-Litovsk.

The Weimar diplomacy was invariably accused of complying with all Allied demands. Hitler scourged its 'contemptible cowardice'. He was determined to bring to a halt the policy of boundless compliance by 'a Germany ready to accept anything imposed upon her'. He condemned the 'criminal', 'senseless', 'catastrophic' policy, which abandoned national interests, and the 'cringing servility' to foreign countries. 'Irresponsibility and incompetence' had until then guided German policy.

Hitler mercilessly attacked the German pacifists: the 'foolishness of incorrigible dreamers'. The German pacifist would be 'silent about the most outrageous violence committed against the nation. . . . He does not think of vengeance or even of defence.' Every time the people were threatened he would consider on which side objective justice lay. This 'cursed objectivity' poisoned the heart, and the 'lulling chatter of the whining cowards' would have to come to an end.

It was time to recover outward independence in a spirit of decisiveness and purpose. An independent, vigorous and dynamic German state would have to come into being again.

Every instance of 'foreign pressure' on Germany gave Hitler the opportunity to increase his prestige as agitator. The furious exaltation of patrotic exuberance discredited the rulers, accused of stupid and criminal weakness. Hitler recalled Clausewitz with the words, 'an honour stained by cowardly submission can never be wiped clean'. He derided the Weimar Government's patient efforts methodically to take advantage of the lengthy prevarications over disarmament, as it had been conceived at Versailles, the victors having to submit to the same disarmament obligations as the vanquished and being bound to follow Germany's example later.

Disarmament, it was said in Geneva, was above all the disarmament of others.

On the question of reparations, Germany confronted her conquerors, in particular France, in an implacable duel. It was not desired to impose 'war indemnities' on Germany, therefore 'reparations' were demanded of her. The very word 'reparations' seemed to Hitler a 'term as monstrous as it is insolent'. He simply rejected every kind of 'reparation'; he wanted no 'tribute' to be paid to foreign countries. With all his propagandist violence he stiffened the resistance of a Germany encouraged by dissensions among the Allies, and wounded in her material interests by the reparations. Not only the extent of the latter, but their very principle, was contested by a nation which, disclaiming any responsibility for the war, considered it had nothing to pay. The thought that in order to meet the victor's tribute, Germany proposed the payment of one hundred milliard gold marks, 'an insane amount', aroused Hitler's indignant protests. In April 1920 he demanded that politicians such as Erzberger and Simons should be hanged. In 1921, at the time of the London ultimatum, he was raging against 'the shameful tutelage in which we are placed by that band of brigands', the Allies, and he preached fierce resistance to bring about a German renaissance. Not only the Allies' proposals, but also the counter-proposals of the Foreign Minister Simons, provoked nationalist indignation. The announcement of payments spread over half a century caused 'national passions to reach boiling-point'. Many Germans only saw in the losses to be made good a pretext to have their country despoiled. Why work and save if the 'French Shylock' would come and seize the product of German labour? The noisy protestations which in 1919 had accompanied the publication of the Treaty of Versailles were again resounding in an outburst of maledictions.

National passions were growing, encouraged by anxiety over the plebiscite in Upper Silesia; they flourished in those circles which were determined to give the 'criminals of Versailles' an example of German obstinacy. The drama of Upper Silesia inflamed nationalist resentment against France, who was siding with Poland.

The 'policy of compliance' was branded as a policy of treason. Daily protests were the occasion of new outbursts of an opinion over-excited by betrayal of the peace. With the growing depression of her finances, Germany refused to abide by the conditions of the London ultimatum. With the collapse of the mark, she was in no position to provide what was demanded of her. The chains of Versailles were responsible for Germany's plight.

In 1923, the 'thunderbolt' of the occupation of the Ruhr produced a warlike tension. In the name of 'the Fatherland, the Fatherland alone', a violent rhetorical offensive was unleashed against the

Treaty of Versailles, which had let loose 'the rage of the international spoilers of peoples'. The two rallying and challenging cries rang out: *Deutschland, erwache! Heil Hitler!*

The National-Socialists wanted to replace the 'passive resistance' ordered in the Ruhr, by an active resistance, in the hope of crushing France under the various burdens produced by the antagonism of a whole people. The Hitlerian ideology thrived in the bitterness of the new defeat, in the misery of the dreadful monetary crisis. The occupation of the Ruhr lent a soul to National-Socialism. In face of the tragedy that had stricken Germany, Hitler, dreaming of the successful Fascist march on Rome, on 8th November 1922, thought the moment had come to deal the great blow.

Recalling the extraordinary energy born in Prussia under the impulse of the shock of Jena, Arnold J. Toynbee points out that 'the cycle has recurred in our times in a manner too painfully known to warrant any comment. The German defeat in the 1914–18 war and the exacerbation of that defeat by the French occupation of the Ruhr basin from 1923 to 1924 resulted in Nazi revenge.'

When the storm had passed, Hitler denounced the state of mind which believed the Dawes Plan—'a second Versailles'—to be a piece of 'good fortune' and the Treaty of Locarno to be a 'success'. The point had been reached when the German Republic was nothing more than 'a colony of slaves in the service of foreigners', the German people 'sinking to the level of a slave-people' and pouring out millions to their enemies.

The National-Socialists were careful not to mention that in Germany the 'bleeding' caused by the reparations was more than compensated by an American 'blood-transfusion', i.e., by the foreign loans which attempted to redress the balance.

Like the German nationalists, the National-Socialists refused to follow Stresemann's supple diplomacy, which, according to Count Westarp, went 'from illusion to deception, and from deception to a new illusion'. In a spirit of defiance they would not agree that Germany should proclaim herself averse to regaining 'German lands' by force. They would not accept the surrender of Alsace-Lorraine. The National-Socialists accused Stresemann of leading Germany from one disaster to another by his policy of negotiation.

After suffering a serious setback in the 1928 elections, which only gave him twelve seats in parliament, Hitler began to act the part of a political personality, and not only a propaganda mouthpiece. For, early in 1929, he contracted an alliance with Hügenberg in order to wage a campaign against the Young Plan, which was to replace the Dawes Plan. A violent campaign was started against the 'tribute' imposed on Germany by the Young Plan, which would 'condemn the German people to slavery for the remainder of the

twentieth century'. At the end of 1929 a plebiscite was held 'against
the Young Plan and against the lie of the war debts'. This great idea
of Hügenberg allowed Hitler to use to his own advantage the formidable propaganda instrument which that press and film magnate
controlled. Hügenberg's machine gave the National-Socialist orators
a wide hearing.

The plebiscite collected only four million votes during the first
round, and 5,600,000 during the second—figures below those polled
by the right wing in the 1928 election. The serious and genuinely
active elements of the right-wing opposition seemed at that time to
be formed not by the brown militia of Nazism, but by the impressive
association of the *Stahlhelm*.

When Hindenburg signed the Young Plan on 13th March 1930,
Rosenberg declared that 'Hindenburg having taken leave of Germany, Germany equally takes leave of him'. Strasser called for
'the heads of those who signed the Young Plan'.

Although the last French soldiers withdrew from the left bank of
the Rhine on 30th June 1930, nationalist manifestations, certainly
not unconnected with Nazism, followed the evacuation.

After the elections in September 1930, Arnold Toynbee wrote:
'It is already apparent that the blows which have fallen upon Germany since the armistice of 1918, have had the same stimulating
effect as those that were inflicted upon Prussia a century before, in
1806–1807'.

At the end of 1930, during the Leipzig trial, Hitler described
Germany as 'bound by the peace treaties. German legislation today
has no other result than to anchor the peace treaties in the German
nation. National-Socialists do not consider these treaties as law, but
as something imposed by force. We cannot admit that future,
absolutely innocent generations, should have to carry their burden.
. . . We shall fight against the treaties with all means, even those
which in the opinion of the world seem illegal.'

Like almost all German rulers, Brüning thought he would defeat
the National-Socialists by adopting their theme, in order to 'take the
wind out of their sails'. The customs and financial union which
Foreign Minister Curtius suddenly tried to effect with Austria, in
March 1931, was seemingly inspired from similar tactics. Impatient
to apply the 'active' foreign policy, for which the nationalists were
eagerly clamouring, Stresemann's successor raised the question of
the *Anschluss*. The protests of France, Italy, and the Little *Entente*
caused it to be shelved. It has been said that this setback also
helped to increase the chances of National-Socialism against a weak
and discredited government.

In order to block the advance of a growing National-Socialism,
those in power attempted to wrest from it its nationalist propaganda

arguments. Their efforts to bring reparations to a halt succeeded; they were practically stopped. After the Hoover moratorium (20th June 1931), the Lausanne agreement, on which Papen prided himself, was concluded on 9th July 1932. The burden of reparations was almost entirely abolished.

Once the question of reparations was settled, German foreign policy made great forward strides towards equal rights in the matter of armaments. This equality of rights, demanded in the form of the reconstitution of a large German army, was discussed in principle on 11th December 1932 at the disarmament conference, France being prepared to follow the lead of the United States, Great Britain, and Italy in this matter.

Already considerations of foreign policy had ceased to be serious factors in the advance of National-Socialism. The masses no longer thought of the Versailles Treaty, now that foreign soldiers no longer trod on German soil, and the burden of reparations had come to an end.

The eyes of the masses were now fixed upon home affairs, and 'work and bread' took the first place in their demands. In this respect, there is no doubt that Hitler's decisive success had its source in the economic and social crisis of 1930–32, with its disastrous unemployment. It was not on an issue of foreign policy that the number of National-Socialist votes rose from 2·6 per cent in 1928 to 18·3 per cent in 1930. At any rate it was not the determining factor.

The financial collapse which had ruined the middle-classes and led to unprecedented impoverishment had assured Hitler's first successes, but financial stabilisation and economic recovery had brought about a retreat. The economic crisis drove the movement on with passionate violence. National-Socialism was an answer to the crisis. Hitler emphasised the socialist elements of his National-Socialism; he talked less of the 'disgrace of Versailles' which had turned the German people into proletarians, and more about 'the work and the bread' which he promised loudly to the eager though enraged crowds.

These tactics constituted one of the principal elements in his success. For they reassured influential circles, inside and outside Germany, which were much concerned at Hitler's violence with regard to foreign policy. It is noticeable that, as his power increased, violence was first relegated to the background (the dominating theme being the economic crisis and not foreign policy) and later it was almost entirely passed over.

The moderate language which Hitler used as Chancellor, for several years, except as regards the rulers in Moscow, was agreeably received and seemed comforting. He was not so mad as not to agree with Bismarck that politics was 'an art of the possible'. It was possible to doubt whether he would maintain in power the ultra-nationalist policy which had undoubtedly very much helped him in winning over the masses.

The latter were convinced that since the National-Socialists waged the most violent campaign against the Versailles Treaty, they were in a better position to demand and obtain from Germany's adversaries the maximum concessions. Nevertheless, many optimists supposed that, when confronted with realities and responsibilities, Hitler would limit his ambitions. Germany could, without a war, so guide the course of events, as to dominate the Continent. For there is no doubt that, as always, only a minority desired revenge by force of arms. Even the pessimists would not believe that the *Führer* would allow his 'intuition' to carry him further than was reasonably possible.

Yet Hitler was at great pains to dispel these illusions. Recalling the speech made on 14th March 1936 by 'the most infamous politician of our era' who claimed that he 'pursued his mission with the assurance of a sleep-walker, a mission which Providence had assigned to him', Arnold Toynbee adds that these words caused millions to shiver, whose nerves were still affected by the shock received seven days previously by the military reoccupation of the Rhineland. It was clear that a new pre-war era had begun.

13
NAZISM'S WAY TO SUCCESS
J. J. Schokking

THE techniques and practices employed by Nazism to win over supporters to its cause, and those which it applied in order to transform
the German Republic, were complementary to each other. In the
first period, from the early beginnings immediately after World War
I until January 1933, when Hitler acceded to power, enlarging the
Party's ranks was the primary concern of the Nazis. Nevertheless,
efforts to undermine the Weimar Republic began long before the
Nazi Party commanded any substantial influence. Conversely, after
having seized all the key posts in the Republic, the Nazi Party continued its endeavours to increase the number of its adherents and
sympathisers.

The two types of techniques present, however, different problems.
They appear in a different setting.

How did Nazism succeed in assembling large sections of the German population under its banner? This question can be discon-
nected neither from the special features of the Nazi movement nor
from the general cultural, social, and political conditions prevailing
in the Weimar Republic.

What methods enabled the Nazi Party to change the Weimar
Republic without a *coup d'état*, without an overt revolution, indeed
with the maintenance of a show of legality, into a highly centralised,
totalitarian state, submitted to the control of one single party? In
this case the skill shown by the Nazis in exploiting the weaknesses of
the Weimar system and in profiting from the semi-dictatorial
methods which the Governments immediately preceding them had
already introduced, mainly determined the course of events.

This essay will deal only with the problems that are related to the
expansion of the Nazi movement, to the factors which made for the
slow but steady development of Nazism up to the economic crisis of
1930 and for its rapid expansion in the ensuing three years. This
survey may not fully explain the further growth of Nazism in the
following period, when circumstances were no longer the same and
other potent factors had come into play. It throws nevertheless
some light upon them, because victorious Nazism kept faith with the
experiences it had undergone during the time it had to fight on the

threshold of power, and repeated, almost monomaniacally, the methods it had then used.

II

Here a preliminary question must be inserted. Is it permissible to speak of 'methods' in this context? The answer may be given by raising a counter-question. Would it ever occur to anybody to ask by what techniques and practices the Anabaptists were able to stir up, within an amazingly short space of time, the German principalities and bishoprics of the early sixteenth century?

It seems unlikely. The historian will focus his attention on the social unrest, the economic hardships, the religious dissensions and uncertainties prevailing at the time. The theologian is likely to be inclined to analyse Thomas Münzer's teachings concerning the immediacy of divine inspiration and the election of those who chose to follow him. Possibly the theologian will also ask why these doctrines appealed so strongly to a people in distress. The sociologist in his turn will concentrate his interest on the social changes which took place during the period of the Reformation. Likewise he will want to understand the connections, if any, between those shifts and the Anabaptist belief in the early advent of a kingdom in which all things would be held in common. The social psychologist will wish to investigate whether the panicky situation created by the confessional split and other social disruptions engendered by themselves the disturbing movements of Anabaptism, or whether it must be assumed that this situation was merely provoked by a general disposition of the period which gave the movement and its fanatical leaders an exceptional chance. None of these disciplines will worry about the techniques, practices, and methods by which Anabaptism succeeded in impressing itself on the masses of its day. The question would appear to have no meaning, as obviously the overwhelming zealotry displayed by the Anabaptist upheaval has left no room for a clear distinction to be made between ends and means.

When referring to Nazism in his book on the German General Staff, Walter Görlitz uses, incidentally, the expression, 'Hitler's nationalistic Anabaptism'.[1] The comparison is both illuminating and dangerous.

Indeed, National-Socialism, like Anabaptism, arose in a society which was passing through a process of disintegration, though neither society was—and this very fact led to unbearable tensions in

---

[1] 'At that time (1931) it had gone so far that the last aged Chief of the once great General Staff had also become the last defence against Hitler's new nationalistic Anabaptism; there was no other choice but to cling fast to Hindenburg.'—Walter Görlitz, Der Deutsche Generalstab. Geschichte und Gestalt 1657–1943 (Verlag der Frankfurter Hefte, Frankfurt am Main, 1950), p. 384.

the sixteenth century as well as in the twentieth—in a state of decay. Again, similarly to the Anabaptist pattern, National-Socialism seemed to offer a way out from personal and social miseries and to replace material and spiritual despondency by a new hope. In the third place, Nazism may be said to have repeated, on a gigantic scale, Jan van Leyden's reign of terror, to which in 1534 the citizens of Münster enthusiastically submitted.

In another respect, however, it may be misleading to bring Anabaptism and National-Socialism under one heading. A false picture is certainly drawn when National-Socialism is presented as 'a socio-religious doctrine of salvation', an expression that slipped from Walter Görlitz's pen a few pages later.[1] Anabaptism did contain such a doctrine—at least a seedling of it, from which a theology and social philosophy could spring. Proof of this may be found in the subsequent development of the Mennonite fraternity, into whose quiet waters the gushing stream of Anabaptism was finally canalised.

Viewed from this angle, National-Socialism and Anabaptism widely diverge. Anabaptism's outbursts were the spontaneous reactions of a disorientated people to the preachings of Thomas Münzer. In these preachings an attempt was made to theologise, to take a doctrinal stand. The tendencies to get hold of the reins of power were merely an unavoidable sequence of the movement's swift spread. Neither organisational calculations nor considerations regarding the most effective ways to expand its influence had any part in Anabaptism. Rather it leaned towards anarchism. Lacking all kinds of preconceived 'instrumentality', it did not apply means that were not at the same time its ends, and it pursued no ends that did not work immediately as means. Running amok, Nazism was not inspired by a special doctrine of its own; it was from the very outset exclusively dominated by the will to conquer power. Though Nazi zealotry was not less intense than that of Anabaptism, the organisation of the Party machine and the question of how to extend the Party's grip on men and matters stood in the forefront of its activities from the time it was but a small group of conspirators until the heyday of its might. Preoccupation with the instrumentalities of power was the essence of Nazism, while the zealotry of the Nazis performed but a special function within the framework of their organisation. The Nazi leaders were possessed of the uncanny faculty to make a strategic and, in case of need, a tactical use of their own passions. They knew how to direct those of their disciples accordingly. Whilst Anabaptist and Nazi fanaticism both involved an identity of ends and means, the Nazi species does not exclude the

[1] 'The new political army' (i.e. the S.A.) 'serving not the state but an idea, a socio-religious doctrine of salvation, numbered some 400,000 men under arms, composing 24 S.A. Groups, comparable to Army Corps.' ibid., p. 402.

question of techniques. In a way the zeal which Hitlerism exhibited was in itself one of its most effective techniques.

III

However, on what incentives did the Nazis act? From what sources did their will to power originate? Where did the energy by which the machine of their instrumentality was kept in continuous motion come from?

No answer can be given to these questions unless an attempt has been made to see the social significance of militarism in general, and of the militarist tendencies in Germany after the defeat of the Wilhelmian armies in particular.

Where militarism reigns, two attitudes are predominant. The army considers itself, and is treated by the rest of the nation, as a 'community' in and of itself, solely integrated by man-to-man contacts of its own makings, and not as an organisational set-up providing an effective collaboration of armed citizens for the national purpose of security. Secondly, the very existence of the socio-political order is assumed to depend on the strength of this self-contained force, not to be merely shielded by it.

Under a system of standing armies militarism has other implications than under a system of conscription.

The professional soldiers of standing armies in non-democratic states are indifferent to the political community. They only know their allegiance to the man who personifies their own 'community' —their supreme commander. Beyond that they do not go. As their community consciousness is narrowed down to the confines of the army, there is nothing which induces them to be concerned with the motives of their chief whenever he is acting in his capacity as political leader, or to concern themselves with the interests of the political community—that is, the nation as a whole. That the army is not only a fighting machine, but possesses also the quality of being valued in its own right as a constitutive element of the socio-political order, is the supreme commander's affair, not theirs.

Now, conscription changes these relationships fundamentally. At the origin of conscription stands Rousseau's democratic view, that to serve as a soldier is every citizen's duty, but that no citizen ought to take up this service as a profession.[1] Nevertheless conscription may be applied as a method of recruitment in states which otherwise remain as militarist as they were before. Under such conditions conscription tends to make participation in the army the exclusive form of community participation, not merely for professional soldiers, but

[1] 'Tout citoyen doit être soldat par devoir, nul ne doit l'être par métier.' J.J. Rousseau, *Gouvernement de Pologne*, Chap. XII.

for all men who by the dispositions of the conscription laws are compelled to serve with the colours. The barracks will often enough get the meaning of a home for the conscript soldier, the regiment will be his family, the army emblems his religious symbols, the army regulations the overriding rules of human conduct. On the other hand the army becomes susceptible of losing its special feature of forming a separate 'community'.

Moreover, though militarism continues to determine the character of political and social life, the introduction of conscription will certainly transform the substance of the state. The army's unique position in the state is no longer taken for granted. After being conscripted into the service, the sons of the people will not follow in a docile fashion the tradition established by the standing armies of the militarist type. They will not be inclined to acknowledge that the supreme commander, on the sole ground of being their warlord, is entitled to dispose of their lives. Yet, as long as militarism continues to shape the socio-political order, they are prevented from exercising the democratic notion according to which the supreme commander is not more than an outstanding expert, charged by the community of all citizens—i.e., the nation—with the responsibility for defence. There is only one way out of this dilemma. It is feasible that the political institutions and the link-up between military and political leadership be so framed as to make the supreme commander the embodiment of the nation. He would then become the absolute head not only, as he has hitherto been, of the army and the Government, but also of the nation—a kind of military, political, and social autocrat, whose decisions determine how the nation will be structured and what ends it should aspire to attain—in short, a man without whom there would be no nation at all.

Obviously a transformation of this kind involves the people at large. It cannot be brought about unless all layers of society absorb militarism and are ready to think in militarist terms. This means that they have to be imbued with the idea that war is the inevitable destiny of mankind, that victory in war alone gives the fittest a chance to survive, and that the waging of war is man's most natural occupation. The people who want to constitute themselves as a nation must envisage the army as the nation's core and the supreme commander as the incarnation of its collective will.

Germany has passed through all these stages of militarism. Eighteenth-century Prussia exemplified in the most perfect way the militarist state based upon a standing army. The army came first; but as far as Prussia's domestic affairs were concerned, her rulers were always careful to heed the wants of the population and the regulations of the law, and in foreign relations they had an eye for diplomatic no less than for military exigencies. If the prince himself was not an enlightened ruler—as happened, e.g., in the case of Frederick II—a dutiful, law-abiding, and capable bureaucracy were unfalteringly ready to keep the army within its limits. They were, of course, aware of the army's essential significance in politics. However, this was not the soldier's business, certainly not directly. For them, their concern had to be limited to the army, their task being a restricted one: the army has to fight, or to be prepared to fight. Intent on maintaining the army's so-called ' non-political ' character, the generals would never be inclined to ignore the outspoken wishes of the bureaucracy. At the same time, generals and bureaucrats were both commanded by the prince, the supreme commander and chief of state.

This Prussian type of militarism became a tradition, deeply rooted in and effecting all social relationships. With the introduction of conscription, new forces were released that were incompatible with it; yet the tradition was not at first weakened. During the greater part of the nineteenth century it continued to shape policies and attitudes. Even in a later period, and up to World War II, it remained quite strong.

It began to lose its impact when, prior to World War I, the military legislation of the Wilhelmian era extended the size of the imperial armed forces at an ever-increasing pace. Then the significance of the combination of militarism with conscription revealed itself fully.

It became apparent that it was necessary to 'generalise' militarism—that is, to extend it ever farther. The 'old' Prussian militarism was no more than a maxim of statecraft; it was therefore not capable of being spread among the broad masses of the people. In order to inculcate militarism into the popular mind it had to be metamorphosed into a general and all-pervading attitude towards life, towards history, and towards contemporary socio-political conditions. In short, it had to be made into an 'ideology'.

When propaganda for militarism as an ideology began to be set into motion, by no means all responsible Germans were happy about this development. Even those who took an active part in it sometimes felt ill at ease. They were not always blind to the contradictions between the Prussian tradition and Kantian ethics in which they had been reared, and their new actions. Nor did it wholly escape them that they were supporting a pseudo-democracy, and thereby raising appetites which one day might lead to demands for a genuine democracy, a system they abhorred.

All this, however, did not prevent them from using every means of psychological conditioning at their disposal. The misgivings they felt when doing so explain at least partly the strange mixture of rigidity and puffed-up enthusiasm which, under the influence of their forced efforts to propagate militarism as an ideology, became more and more one of the most striking features of German social life.

Special emphasis was laid on education by the new militarism. In the face of strong opposition, indoctrination in militarism was gradually made a foremost objective of teaching in German schools and universities.

The question may now be asked: did the attempts to imprint the militarist ideology on the whole of the German people really succeed? Was this people made thoroughly familiar with the idea that nationhood was a matter dependent in all its aspects on the will of the emperor as war-lord, head of the state, and embodiment of the nation in arms? This is often contended, though the arguments which are usually invoked in support of this view are not convincing. Wilhelmian Germany was a highly complicated country, the battlefield of many tendencies. This much may be said. The deliberate effort to impart militarist sentiments to the German people and to marry the Prussian tradition with a popular militarist ideology produced three characteristic features, each of profound significance. The army retained its character of a closed and exclusive community, and consequently, more than in democratic countries, moulded the personalities of the boys who were enlisted. Secondly, the ties which joined the army to the socio-political order remained; in fact, the two became even more strongly allied in the minds of the soldiers and people than they were before. Democracy could therefore not be established in Wilhelmian Germany without both defeat in war and revolution from within. Thirdly, in the event of defeat innumerable young men were in danger of losing their sole community attachments, while state and society would lose their cohesion.

Such was the picture of the situation at the end of World War I. Defeat was not envisaged. But the unexpected happened indeed. After a strenuous war, which in its first stages had raised popular militarism to a high pitch of intensity, defeat came.

With the fall of the army in 1918, the whole structure of Wilhelmian Germany broke asunder. There was no alternative to replace it—at least not immediately. The mere act of founding the Republic—a rather external, a purely constitutional change—was not enough. In order to establish a stable democracy Germany would have had to be reorganised from top to bottom. It required a new social integration, on the basis of democratic principles and usages. The remnants of the Prussian tradition, as well as the effects of the queer, ambivalent propaganda for popular militarism, which had supplemented this tradition in the preceding decades, had to be wiped out. Intentions to do so were not absent, nor was there a lack of men who had the will and the capacity to reframe Germany along democratic lines. In order to succeed, however, they needed freedom from foreign pressures, the immediate prospect of economic recovery and of increasing prosperity, and, most of all, they needed time. None of these conditions was granted to them.

One of the most pernicious effects of the sudden collapse of Germany was that all groups and individuals for whom militarism had become the guiding ideology and the only possible way of life, felt themselves deprived of their beliefs, their community, their nation. They rejected the Republic, not so much because they were against the replacement of monarchical institutions by republican ones, as because it represented in their eyes a society which was strange to them and in which they could have no share—a victory of forces which had thrown them back on their own mental and material resources, to manage as best as they could as scattered and isolated individuals. In the great majority of cases these resources were very small or did not exist at all.

Now that the social fabric which had satisfied their wants of sociability had fallen to pieces, many ex-officers and soldiers, hoping to escape the loneliness they were unable to face and somehow to gain a substitute for the lost footholds in life, and also thereby to find an occupation and material support, sought refuge in the several Free Corps, which at the end of the war and in the first post-war years were formed all over Germany. These were fighting units, operating haphazardly under self-appointed leaders. Marching against the Reds in Germany and on Germany's eastern border, resisting the Poles, stimulating local revolts in the Ruhr and elsewhere, they were inspired by the social and political aspirations of the past that had disappeared, and were ever animated by an outright hostility towards the Republic. Otherwise they followed the precepts of their militarist training, which somehow forbade soldiers to intervene constructively in politics or to pursue a positive policy of their own. The inner contradiction of this mental situation was a cause of utter frustration. Despite their tenacity, audacity, and ruthlessness, the Free Corps came to nothing.

National-Socialism was a different movement from the outset. Though born of the same deceptions and urges which led to the creation of the Free Corps, National-Socialism chose another approach.

It did not confine its appeal to demobilised officers and soldiers, but extended it to all militaristically-minded Germans, whatever they were or had been. In the course of time, after the Free Corps had disbanded, many of their former members were to become Nazism's fiercest enemies, while others took the opposite course and found a lasting home under the Nazi roof. In any case among the high echelons of the Nazi hierarchy the proportion of Free Corps veterans was gradually to become very numerous. From their side, however, the Nazis undertook nothing to continue the Free Corps tradition of segregation, but consistently tried to penetrate into all sections of German society.

Moreover, Nazism understood that under the changed conditions a revival of militarism could not be brought about by copying the Wilhelmian methods. It sensed that the spell of the Prussian tradition had to be broken and that a new, more radical, and more exclusively popular orientation was wanted. Nazism realised that the militarism prevalent before World War I had been closely connected with the social and political texture of Imperial Germany. Being aware of the fact that this had been destroyed beyond repair, Nazism foresaw the possibilities of socialising militarism and of creating a powerful nation-in-arms, an armed society, a people living by war and for war. As slogans these notions had already been used by militarist propaganda under the Kaiser, but the will to accept the full consequences of them was absent then. Such a will implied the necessity of throwing overboard all technical inhibitions, all endeavours to direct the socio-political institutions in consonance with the dictates of justice and rationality, and indeed all other doctrines and theories. Instead, the demands of expediency, resulting from total mobilisation for total war, had alone to prevail.

To National-Socialism politics meant the struggle for 'naked power' by all means promising rapid success.

The Nazis viewed themselves as the nucleus of the militarised people in the process of becoming, as the military 'counter-society' that had one day to take the place of the Weimar Republic and of all other states in which Germans lived. They thought that they had only to increase their numbers and strength in order to reach their political aims. The movement was instrumental to the new German militarism and its quest for power. That in this development the Weimar Republic had to disappear was taken for granted. To reach their ends, however, it was not necessary, in the first instance, to fight it with physical means. For the Nazis a private army had its advantages; it was in a way indispensable, but it could be really effective only if the movement gave priority to the political aim and in pursuit of that knew how to profit from the opportunities which were offered by the Weimar democracy. In contradistinction to the Free Corps, the Nazis discovered that democracy could be wrecked by constant abuse of its liberties. By instinct, rather than by calculation, they knew that once militarist tendencies were developed to the utmost in German society their movement would automatically sweep away the Weimar Republic, and eventually the other European States within whose frontiers Germans were living.

IV

In order to be capable of acting politically in this sense the Nazis had to build up a special organisation. In other words, the Nazi movement needed an organisation adapted to its unusual character; its conduct, purely adventitious at first, could not be permanently left to chance alone.

It so happened that the kind of organisation Nazism was bound to evolve worked as a powerful magnet on many circles, but particularly on circles who, far from having any liking for popularised and ideological militarism, were rather fearing its increasing hold on the masses. Likewise, when the Nazis did not hesitate to make their pursuit of naked power the sole norm of their behaviour, they impressed and attracted not only kindred souls, but also numerous other Germans by whose standards Nazi actions and atittudes were utterly contemptible. Therefore the quick expansion which the movement was to gain in the decisive few years before they acceded to power must not be too readily ascribed to an exceptional capacity of the Nazis in devising outstandingly effective propaganda techniques. Their organisational and operational methods found deep responses in several quarters, responses either of hope or fear, both often evolving from erroneous assumptions. This accounts undoubtedly for much of the results they were to obtain.

Every political party foreshadows in its own organisation the general state of things it wants to bring about. The Nazis were no exception to this rule. Militarism demands a hierarchy. Thus, at the time when the Party was still in its infancy, and its organisation therefore very primitive and simple, the hierarchical principle already began to be strictly observed. As early as 1920 Adolf Hitler became the Party's supreme head, its inspirer and organisational chief, when membership hardly exceeded a few hundred and sympathisers probably amounted to no more than 2,000.

Since Mussolini's victorious march on Rome in 1922 the Nazis felt induced to follow as closely as possible the example set by Fascism, with the result that the hierarchical distinctions were given a sharper edge and Adolf Hitler's position embellished with more glamour. Nevertheless the Party's organisation remained embryonic for a long time. Only in 1925, when Nazism re-emerged after the withdrawal of the proscription which was inflicted on the Party as a sequel to the unsuccessful Munich Beer-Hall *putsch* of 1923, the organisation made some modest attempts at rationalisation. Having learned the lesson of its hitherto not too happy experiences, Nazism wanted to follow henceforth a more systematic course of action.

However, the movement was unable—or unwilling—to depart

radically from its cherished empiricism. To be sure, the hierarchy was somehow formalised, but, on the other hand, the new organisation enhanced rather than reduced its highly personal traits. Special tasks were confided to special departments. In addition to the creation of these functional bodies whose heads were responsible for particular Party matters falling within any field allotted to them and applying even to Germans outside of Germany, a further territorial sub-division of general Party activities was made.

As time went on the number of departments increased rapidly; as a rule they tended to become shadow-ministries for the new military empire to which the Nazi aspired, showing, moreover, a marked inclination towards extreme centralisation. In the course of time the territorial party districts—the *Gaue*, *Kreise*, *Orgsgruppen*, and, in the case of larger cities, *Zellen* and *Blöcke*, all passed through a similar process; gradually they achieved the character and usurped the competences of shadow local government authorities. Unavoidably this double-track organisation of the Party—partly centralised, and partly functionally and territorially decentralised—led to overlapping, to sterile competition, and to continuous tensions. The embarrassments occasioned all round thereby, sometimes most baffling and disconcerting, did not, as might have been assumed, and as was not seldom predicted by outside observers at the time, weaken the Party. For, as the leaders of the functional party departments and the territorial party organisations were equally dependent on the decisions taken at the top—i.e., ultimately—by Hitler himself, the muddle on the lower levels gave the *Führer* every time a new opportunity to cut a Gordian knot, thus practically strengthening Hitler's personal position and consolidating the hierarchical character of the organisational structure. So long as Hitler succeeded in maintaining the hold he wielded over the Party, the conflicts between the various services and levels of command did not become really dangerous. By keeping the Party busy, by centring the attention of Party members on Party affairs, their zeal was not lessened, but stimulated. Even more was achieved by these internal conflicts. In retrospect it is difficult not to be bemused by the pompousness with which the Nazis went about their affairs, irrespective of whether their business was measured by the rational standards of their environment, to say the least of it, not very material. Simple letters on the arrangement of meetings would be treated *as if* they were state papers of the highest importance. As the years went on, this 'as if' attitude became steadily more compulsive. The confusion caused by the imprecise delimitation of organisational capacities attributed to the several Party levels created a score of opportunities to organise further bodies which would give the 'as if' action a further, more captivating semblance of the real thing. This intentional self-deceit of the Nazis did not fail to deceive others as well. Ultimately the 'as if' behaviour ceased being a make-believe, it was reality itself.

Thus, though expediency was their idol, the Nazis hardly gave proof of being particularly efficient organisers. They knew, however, how to establish a hierarchy. For them the hierarchical pyramid of the Party's organisation was an object inspiring passion and pride; it was the fulfilment of a deep-felt want.

This want was shared by a large number of their followers in and outside Germany who, though strongly opposed to the disarmament clauses of the treaties by which World War I was concluded, were unwilling to accept the tenets of a popularised militarism as their guiding ideology. On the contrary, these Germans were saturated with romantic notions regarding the necessity of unifying the German people on a so-called spiritual ('*geistig*' and '*seelisch*') basis. They were vaguely longing for the emergence of a common national will which would spring from an intimate spiritualised community embracing man and man, a profoundly shared participation of all Germans in the ideal of nationhood, free from internal dissensions, unpolluted by opposition, class, rank, denominations, interests, or loyalties to different political entities: a common devotion to the general weal and the greatness of that German nation which so far had never been fully realised, and was now to be realised. Liberalism, so they thought, could not bring about this purified nationhood. Liberal and parliamentary institutions would rather prevent it from taking shape. Political parties and party strife, with its selfish ambitions, unending divisions among the component parts that had to be unified, were the inevitable outcome. True democracy demanded, therefore, at least as far as the German people were concerned, divided socially and dispersed over many European States as they were, a personal form of leadership, and from above. The leader would not necessarily have to be a monarch, except that he had to symbolise the nation with the full weight of his personality and to hold out in behaviour and by his prestige the forthcoming completion of the community of all Germans in its spiritual sense and of national unity in the political sphere.

The multifarious German conventicles indulging in these ideas, playing, so to say, with them, and haggling with each other on their doctrinal platforms, were all impotent to undertake steps for the practical implementation of their philosophies. As long as they stayed away from reality, the dreamers and the doctrinaires composing these groups could consider their conceptions about nation and nationhood as the last word of political wisdom. Being mostly men with a heavy sense of responsibility as far as their daily actions were concerned—though showing scant regard for the practical implications of their higher thoughts—they wavered as soon as they were confronted with the material consequences of their wishes. Very prone to flirt with the theoretical notion of revolution, they did not dare to make the great revolution of Germanism.

These coteries observed with awe the rise of the Nazi hierarchy. They listened eagerly to the Nazi speeches. The rhetoricians of the Party, thoroughly familiar with the attitudes of their various audiences as they regularly were, took every care to sound on the appropriate occasions the tunes of a romantic, spiritualised nationalism. When the preferences of the circles addressed demanded it, Nazi propaganda was sagacious enough to give only a veiled expression to the Party's desire for conquest and suppression. However strongly the originators of this propaganda may have despised the sentimental idealism which was based on philosophies concerning the historical calling of the German people rather than on concrete and material ambitions, Nazi orators were frequently very prone to use its vocabulary. They knew how effective this could be with these audiences. As a consequence, the adepts of this idealism were easily bemused. Inconspicuously they allowed themselves to be drawn into the magic circle of those endowed with the will to win. Adolf Hitler and his crooked paladin Goebbels might not even remotely resemble the pure Siegfried figure of their imaginings—nevertheless he acted where they only talked and wrote. The Nazi hierarchy progressed apace before their eyes. This hierarchy was created in the image and exerted its pressure in the name of what was venerated above everything else: the community of all Germans, their unity beyond all considerations of social status and political frontiers. Hitler condemned what they had condemned—liberalism, parliaments, political parties, the freedom of churches to lay a greater emphasis on confessional differences than on national coherence, the trade unions with their international connections, above all, the Versailles Treaty and the Weimar Republic. The Nazi Party organisation gave evidence that another road existed. So why not take it?

Yet the romanticists of the German revolution could be under no illusion. Hitler never hid his determination to terrorise, to kill, and to slaughter. Besides, the monotonous rhythm of the SA boots marching along the streets was telling enough. Could civil war really be an improvement on the disputes of parliaments and of parties? Could a Nazi reign of violence really promise an era of German community life and unity?

In many cases the portents were heeded. In others they were not, for the indoctrination among those circles that Nazism was the only possible and practical answer to their longings was often so strong that many romanticists did not even try to overhear Hitler's threats, but reassured their uneasy conscience by the cheap subterfuge that all great historical changes of the past had been accompanied by periods of oppression and the shedding of some blood.

In this way the movement was propagated, almost automatically, by the mere existence of the Nazi hierarchy and the dynamism it displayed. No special techniques had to be contrived. To boast of the results obtained, to make crude speeches about the organisation and its doings in a language with which German romantic nationalism was familiar, and to use mystical terms of its own invention, was enough to induce many people to apply for membership, or at least to adopt an attitude of deferential expectation.

Nazism had no philosophy. Driven by the will to socialise and popularise militarism and to establish in that way a mighty German empire, it was, with regard to its Weimar setting and its wider European environment, nothing more than a movement of blind and indiscriminate protest, of sheer action, an outburst of ill-repressed dissatisfaction, provoked by men in whom this feeling had reached the most extreme degree of dynamic intensity. Nazism repudiated everything that had been accomplished or was being striven for in the world which surrounded it: western parliamentary democracy and Bolshevism; Capitalism and Socialism as professed by the existing socialist parties of every shade; it was as strongly opposed to the restoration of the monarchy as to continuance of the Weimar Republic; it condemned as ardently the social effects of modern technology and mechanisation as it denounced technological backwardness and moral objections to the demand for efficiency as the decisive rule for human conduct. This incongruous negativism was at the same time a blunt and primitive refusal to accept guidance from any sort of rational thought, or, expressed in the Nazi slang, a direct reaction of 'blood' against 'spirit'. Neither Hegel nor Fichte, neither Nietzsche nor Spengler, neither Keyserling nor Moeller van den Bruck occupy in National-Socialism a place comparable with that held by Rousseau in connection with Jacobinism or of Marx, Engels, and Lenin in connection with Communism. National-Socialism never recognised the authority of any philosopher or theorist. Its bible was Hitler's *Mein Kampf*, an extensive pamphlet dealing with a variety of subjects, written without any concern for clean thinking and directed exclusively to the question of how the Nazi Party could be brought to power, and how the German people in the Weimar Republic and living as German-speaking minorities in other countries could be united and, once unified, attain command over the European continent and the Western Russian plains.

In the Germany of the 'twenties, countless philosophies and pseudo-philosophies were fighting each other. On both sides of the main dividing line separating rationalism and irrationalism, around each school of philosophy or of pseudo-philosophy, groups were formed, each exclusively bent on the continuation, the refinement, and the propagation of its own doctrinal system. In the great majority of cases the theories and speculations, however abstract they usually were, involved very definite social and political tenets. In a society disrupted by war and defeat, by armed conflicts between the various segments of the population, clashes between doctrinal groups must of necessity become exceptionally vehement and cause mutual hostility. The embarrassing multitude of competing philosophies and pseudo-philosophies, the fierceness of their clashes, and the contents of some of the most important doctrines contributed each in its own way to the growth of a state mind which it was not difficult for Nazism to make use of.

The absence of all intellectual bonds permitted National-Socialism to adapt its spoken and written propaganda to the widely divergent views—divergent even on fundamental issues—held by the competing groups and parties into which the German population was split up. As hardly any one of these groups was homogeneous in its composition, the same technique, which widened the gaps between the groups intentionally, could be applied to play out minorities against majorities. It was always possible to sharpen the desires, to absolutise the ideals, to deepen the doubts and the aversions of each group and sub-group. The contradictions and inconsistencies, which thus became rather the rule than the exception, gave no room for any hesitations. The Nazis were too keenly aware that the brutal emphasis with which they put their power purposes into the forefront, the unvarying determination with which they identified themselves with the German nation—the German people as such—would before long spread the belief in the masses that after all only Nazism held out the promise of a regenerated Germany.

In this connection Nazism had carefully seen to it that the force of its proselytising campaigns was not weakened by any rigid specification of purposes.

It is true that in the early days—it was on 24th February 1920—the Party adopted a programme, the famous twenty-five articles. But Nazism was not tied to it. Though Hitler, during his detention in the Landsberg fortress, gave some care to a revision of the programme, he was filled with contempt for written formulas. To bother about them was, as he stressed in *Mein Kampf*, the futile pastime of *bourgeois* parliamentarians. Instead, he pointed out, the National-Socialist programme intended only to give the man in the street a rough picture of the Party's will. As such it had to win support—it had to serve, as a critical commentator on Hitler's expositions might say, as an advertisement, a poster, a signboard. Hitler himself added that the programme was also indispensable as a symbol under which the separate will of the Party members could be welded together into one indivisible common will. But that was all it was really good for. Therefore it had to be unalterable too. Discussions on its wording were a danger. Thereby the attention might easily deviate from the main effort, which ought to remain unflinchingly directed to the strengthening of the character of the movement as a concentrated force of will-power and determination.

In conformity with Hitler's views a decision was taken on 22nd May 1926 officially forbidding anyone to alter the programme. In *Mein Kampf,* Hitler had shown full understanding of the fact that, as he put it, a programme drafted under the influence of a momentary psychological constellation may soon be out-of-date. This was, he thought, not harmful. The leader, standing at the top of the Party's hierarchy, could be trusted to take care of that. If subsequent psychological constellations should demand a different outlook the fitting interpretation could be duly given by him. In this matter the leader must be given complete freedom of decision. Otherwise the movement might be defeated in the political struggle, its supreme *raison d'être.* Hence, too, the preference of Nazism for the spoken word above any written expositions of policy, for the mass-meeting above small gatherings with their propensity to discussions, for exhortations instead of explanations, and for the use of symbols above all.

The Weimar Republic was poor in symbols. Besides, whatever symbols it had, reminded numerous Germans merely of a defeat they were refusing to accept as an unchangeable historical fact. An exception may be made for the hymn '*Deutschland, Deutschland über alles*', which, at the instigation of the Republic's first President, Friedrich Ebert, was adopted as the national anthem, and as such appealed to all Germans alike.

Why was the Republic so unresourceful in the matter of symbols? Did the rational conceptions underlying the constitutional fabric of the Republic prevent its leaders from developing a creative imagination in this respect? Did the undeniable connection between the birth of the Republic and Germany's defeat stultify the few abortive attempts that were made? The reasons were manifold. Anyhow, the lack of symbols revealed Germany's incapacity for coping with the sudden interruption of social continuity caused by defeat and the simultaneous change of régime. It was the unmistakable proof that the Weimar Republic had no firm social roots.

Being exclusively bent on clustering its adherents together, on bequeathing to them the faculty of developing an all overpowering common will, Nazism had no other adequate means of expressing its intentions than the symbolic ones. Being determined to efface the memory of defeat, to distort history, and to call into existence a national consciousness for which not defeat and everything it implied, but rather German superiority, was to have the value of unshakable

reality, Nazism aimed at bewitching its followers so that they would
henceforth, as it were, accept as the manifestation of the genuine
truth feelings enlivened or evoked by the Party symbols, and no
longer those which the Republic tried to spread with its declarations,
expositions, and deliberations. Nazism had to replace the world of
reality by a world of symbols. Being unrestrained by rational considerations, and, *a fortiori*, not subjected to rationalist dogmas, the
Party could give free play to the forces of imagination.

The result is well known. Nazism borrowed the swastika symbol
from the Free Corps; the red colour from revolutionary socialism, and
indeed from the European revolutionary tradition in general; the
Roman, now called 'German' salute, from the Italian Fascists;
certain rituals observed at the initiation of new Party members from
Freemasonry; the habit it imposed on its members of addressing each
other as 'comrade' from early Socialism and Bolshevism; from older
German usages the cry 'Heil', by which the common enthusiasm of
Party gatherings unloaded itself, and by which, after it had been reduced to a formula, the stereotypes of *bourgeois* etiquette were replaced in the correspondence of Party members even with outsiders;
it used community singing and similar techniques for fixing the
attention of large crowds and borrowed them from the example of
the organisation of great events in the world of sport; it invented
its own uniforms, though mostly their designs were kept very closely
to traditional patterns; in the military make-up of its meetings and
demonstrations it copied, at a distance, the modes of the Wilhelmian
army.

In its first period, which came to an end in 1923, the Nazi movement had not yet fully developed this extreme symbolism. It is also
important to note that at that time the character of the movement
was still somewhat ambiguous. Hitler, Röhm, Göring, and others
who were orientated in the same direction had still to give attention to
the wishes cherished by the honest representatives of a mild, nationalistic, and, it must be added, rather confused middle-class socialism.
In spite of the Party's hierarchical structure, these middle-class persons retained a great influence. In the beginning Party members
were mainly recruited among the old and new middle classes, both
weakened and embittered by defeat and inflation. For the Feders
and the Strassers the concrete social and economic aims the Party
had proclaimed were more than propaganda slogans. The value of
the Party depended in their eyes on the contribution it would be able
to make to the realisation of these aims. Moreover, the lower middle-
class elements did not share the revolutionary mood by which the
Party's top leaders distinguished themselves. In this respect their
attitude was very similar to that of the romantic conventicles, which
have been described. Though always inflating their indignation by

making ample use of the word 'revolution' in their meetings and pamphlets, they were fundamentally not rebellious. Obviously they had reasons enough for being sometimes suspicious of the symbolism that in the name of the Party was evolved by its chiefs. This symbolism was thoroughly revolutionary and had nothing to do with the feeble grumblings of middle-class people playing in their free hours with vague notions of Socialism and Nationalism.

Meanwhile the chiefs had their way. The symbolism of the Party grew. It grew also in the following period, which lasted from 1924 to 1929, though for the time being without producing impressive effects. During those years the Republic was able to some extent to justify its existence. Economic conditions improved; internationally the exactions of the Versailles Treaty were substantially mitigated; Germany was recognised again as a great Power and enabled to throw its weight into the political scales; internally German society seemed to be progressing rapidly on the road towards a new stabilisation.

The economic depression and the social unrest which it entailed put an end to all this. Then the extreme symbolism of the Nazis was bound, by its very contrast to the barren, matter-of-fact procedures of the Republic, to move many of the dissatisfied circles in Germany. The few years of redress had some reconciling effects on those who after the war were economically weakened and had originally blamed the Republic for the wounds inflicted on them by defeat and inflation. Now, being driven back into the mood of despair, they imputed their miseries with increased insistence to the Republic's internal structure and its alleged subservience to foreign Powers. As the figures of unemployment rose and bankruptcies became the order of the day, the Nazi symbolism was deployed more fully, and was soon to reach the final stage. The movement expanded simultaneously; the numbers of its adherents began to run from hundreds of thousands into millions.

Nazi symbolism made use, however, not only of signs and songs, greetings and uniforms, rituals and processions as media to convey to its members and outsiders its will towards unity and community building. The conceptions and slogans that were repeated in its addresses and harangues were not chosen on account of their rational contents, but for their symbolic appeal. As has been shown, the function of the Party's programme was in the first place symbolic. The same may now be remarked with regard to all assertions bearing the Party stamp.

The objection might be made that racism, as reflected by the oft-repeated word 'blood' and 'soil' had at least a doctrinal, a theoretical meaning. This view is very common. That it is held so widely, however, proves only how effective Nazi propaganda has been.

In fact, the word 'blood', when used by the Nazis, did not refer to a biological reality—racial, tribal, or familial. It served as a symbol. As such it gave expression to the urge inherent in Nazism to constitute the body of its membership as an 'ingroup', which recognised that, in order to succeed in the quest for power, they had to form a compact and cohesive unit of men who were bound personally to each other. Sheer inability to envisage human community under any other aspect than the biological one induced Nazism to make in this connection a symbolic use of the word which usually signifies biological relationships of all kinds. This word 'blood' thrust itself upon Nazism for a second reason. Possessing a strange mystical value, it needed only to be pronounced to evoke sensations of universality. Owing to this quality, 'blood' provided Nazism with a powerful symbolic substitute for rational universalism, and thus with a sharply edged weapon in its propaganda campaigns against the dogmas, doctrines, and theories of its opponents.

The same may be said regarding the word 'soil'. This word symbolised the Nazi promise that no power could ever be effective unless it had a territorial foundation, and, consequently, that whoever wanted power had to get hold of territory. At the same time, once elevated to the rank of symbols, the words 'soil' and 'earth' inevitably stirred up hidden forces in the souls of those who were attracted by them or were beginning to give way. Used metaphorically, these words are always certain to arouse a mysterious sense of unity or the craving for it, if real unity is lacking.

The common view is that National-Socialism had committed itself to racism as a theory. As evidence, the way in which it applied the terms 'blood' and 'soil' is referred to. However, this is wrong. Those who make this error are judging National-Socialism by their own rational standards. The racist terms used by the Nazis are not an endorsement of racism as a theory. Indeed, to be sure, the racial theory—whatever may be understood by this doubtful qualification —was neither a Nazi invention nor was it ever adopted by Nazism as a true explanation of human conditions. The close connections that unquestionably existed between Nazi activities and attempts to 'purify' the German people in accordance with the precepts of the so-called race theories were far more complicated. This question, however, does not fall within the scope of this article.

Nor did the measures taken against the Jews emanate from theoretical convictions. The instinctive, but highly personal hatred of the Jews, by which most of the Nazi leaders, among them Hitler in the first place, were animated, suited perfectly the National-Socialist book. The Nazis knew all too well that, given the very widespread anti-semitic disposition of Germany, their propaganda would be extremely effective if it played on this hatred and tried to generalise it. Directing its propaganda against the Jews, Nazism let loose passions the fury of which was, in a later phase, to become boundless. The prospects by no means upset the Nazis; on the contrary, they never ceased to stimulate those passions, to drum them up from one excess to the other. This was not done, however, for reasons to be inferred from any racial theory, but because the pleasure of Jew-baiting symbolised submission to the Party's collective will. Participation in the persecution of Jews meant participation in the Nazi community.

National-Socialism did not depart from its essential opportunism even in its relations to Jews. Göring's bold statement: 'I decide who is a Jew or not a Jew' (*wer Jüde ist, bestime ich*) was as truly National-Socialist as Goebbel's accusations that Jewish influence was at the root of all social evils, or Ley's depraved tales about sexual misdeeds which he stated to have been misdeeds of Jews. Düsterberg, the vice-president of the veterans' organisation '*Stahl-helm*', recommended his followers of the traditional Right wing, who in the first ballot of the presidential elections of March 1932 had voted for him, to vote in the second ballot not for Hitler, but for Hindenburg, then the candidate of the Centre and the democratic Left. Thereupon, he was most ignominiously besmirched by the Nazi Press for having a Jewish grandfather. This did not prevent Hitler from urging Düsterberg to accept, on 30th January 1933, the post in the coalition Cabinet which von Papen offered, nor did he blench at apologising on this occasion for the calumnies of the Nazis papers. When Düsterberg refused to comply with Hitler's wishes his Jewish grandfather promptly reappeared, to be used as a token of racial disgrace—in other words, as a symbol of unpermissible opposition to the Party's command.

In fact, the same is true of other points about which the Nazis seemed to be particularly concerned. They spoke incessantly about the need for stronger cohesion among the German people, for economic security, and for a unifying national purpose. Actually, however, Nazism never expected anything from an approach that would merely open up the perspective of a stronger cohesion among the German people, more social security, or a unifying national purpose. The Nazis were familiar enough with the German situation to recognise that these demands would have a great appeal. Under the Weimar Republic too many people were hungering for social reintegration. But the Nazis realised that, if they limited themselves to the intensification of these longings, the Party would not be essentially different from other parties; their own Party would perhaps ultimately be brought to adjust itself to the prevailing social conditions and the parliamentary methods of the Republic. From the beginning to the day of its decisive victory—the acquisition of power

—the Party was on the alert that this should not happen. The Party had to be a movement, a driving force, a constant action. It should never forget that it wanted to destroy the Republic, that it was in itself forging the iron unity of a new militarised German people. The followers had to be kept impassioned; they had to be kept fanatical. If the Party were to continue acting up to the urges from which it had sprung, its dynamism had to grow more impetuous every day. This dynamism must not be allowed to run the danger of ebbing away imperceptibly. No better means, so Nazism thought malignantly, to sustain the favour of the Party than to cause it to be fiercely hated by the outside world and to incite its members to hate their opponents, directly and personally. Making the Party a centre of uncompromising hatred, erecting between it and the outside world insurmountable barriers of mutual bitterness and rancour, became for the Nazi leaders almost an end in itself, and certainly one of the practices they most consistently applied.

Their expectations in taking this course were well defined. In the first place, the Party members would be irrevocably bound to the organisation and have no other choice but to obey blindly the will of its hierarchy, when they were cemented together both by being the common object of the same hostility and by being compelled to meet this with a collective retort. Secondly, as, in consequence of this, all possibilities of escape were cut off, the personal fate of each Party member would become so inextricably intertwined with the fate of the Party as a whole that the impetus to add more weight to its dynamism—i.e., to increase its chances of winning—would never be lacking. Thirdly, this process within the Party would of necessity create reactions among the public outside. It would inspire them with fear. Questions regarding the implications of an eventual Nazi victory would begin to be asked. These would have a bearing on individual and social attitudes, as the absolute severance of the Party from its environment meant that the prizes for its members would be high and the penalties to be paid by its opponents extremely severe. Fourthly, the Party's power would increase immensely, if, while being hated, it would be able to over-trump its enemies by evolving a more violent hatred against them. Once a power, the Party would be taken seriously by other power groups in Germany that were hostile to the Republic. Though these groups might reject Nazism and its ways of behaviour, they would not be in a position to neglect it. After the inevitable link-up Nazism would go on and finally prevail.

Accordingly Nazi symbolism was carefully calculated so as to strengthen or to originate generous emotions and evil passions at the same time. Particularly where it was intended to express hatred and envy, and to advertise the Party's inflexible will to get the upper hand, every manifestation of the Party life was given a symbolic value. Very real actions, some of them of momentous importance, were often undertaken mainly because they exemplified the thoroughness of the Party, its desire to be hated and to hate. On the other hand, actions either belonging to the normal business of any political party or constituting a merely tactical move of specific Nazi policy were always extravagantly boasted of, and thereby given a symbolic meaning, which was seldom, if ever, in exact conformity with their real significance, and which in any case transcended this.

When in 1930, in consequence of the economic setbacks, the power of the Party began to expand rapidly, the peculiar party organisation, the absence of rational directives and limitations, their essential opportunism, and the singularities of their symbolism enabled the Nazis to evolve a great variety of operational techniques, and thereby to achieve a noticeably accelerated further expansion of their influence. To these techniques Nazism's ultimate success was largely due. After they had become the rulers of Germany the Nazis improved their operational procedures and, being supported by the agencies of the state, now at their disposal, they made them more effective. In a still later stage the efficiency thus reached diminished, partly as a result of over-organisation and the loss of the indispensable adaptability, partly because the forces of opposition became more active and also more capable of frustrating the Nazi concepts.

The techniques and methods concerned may be divided into three categories, though each single operation may have shown features appertaining to two or even all three of these categories alike.

The Nazis have in fact demonstrated what a determined political movement may achieve in a modern industrial society by means of systematic provocation, constant intimidation, and cautiously schemed infiltration in social and economic relationships of all kinds.

Nazism's collective demeanour was deliberately provocative from the beginning. As time went on, the Party demanded from its members that they should always behave provocatively in their intercourse with their non-Nazi environment. The SA, the Party's private army, was originally called into being on the argument that the police gave insufficient protection to Nazi meetings, and that therefore the Party had to take its own measures in order to prevent aggressive opponents from causing disturbances and riots. This argument was already provocative in itself. Later, the SA, which also symbolised the militarist spirit of the Party, became an instrument of organised and premeditated provocation, ever ready to make its appearance to this effect when circumstances offered a favourable opportunity. Also the 'German salute' was frequently used for purposes of provocation. As the Party grew in strength the habit developed for Party members to raise their arms and outstretched hands when they were present at funerals or other solemn occasions, the meaning of which had either no connection at all with Nazi aims, or was even interwoven with the values Nazism wanted to extirpate. Many more examples could be quoted. In all the cases of public provocation the general picture would, however, be the same. What happened openly, happened likewise in private. The Nazis knew how to be subtle. Thus, at a meeting of a public committee or of the managing board of a Corporation which included two or more Nazis whose party membership was not known to the others, one Nazi would propose to appoint a Jew to a vacancy, and, if the appointment was made, the other Nazi would uncover himself and make a row over it.

Successful provocation had, of course, an intimidating effect. But not all Nazi endeavours to propagate their movement by making it feared began with a provocation. In the Munich Beer-Hall, where the overthrow of the régime was planned to be completed, Hitler told his audience the lie that the regular army and the county police had taken his side and somewhat later in the same meeting, lying again, he told them that a compromise with the rebels of the traditional Right—Kahr, Geisser, and von Lossow—had been reached. What was done in 1923 was repeated many times. The pattern did not change. In the decisive years between 1929 and 1933, when the Nazis were steadily gaining more influence, when their power was already a force which had to be reckoned with, lies of this type, either pronounced in public speeches or spread as rumours, were bound to make a deep impression on a people suffering under the uncertainties of the economic and social situation. The Nazis had no objections against utilising the miseries of their countrymen for the strengthening of their hold on them.

They had realised that particularly in times of economic adversity the masses could be easily intimidated, but that in order to get a more permanent grip on the course of events, intimidation had to go along with infiltration. For this the hierarchical organisation, with its '*Zellen*' and '*Blöcke*', and also with its functional divisions and sub-divisions, provided excellent means. Besides, as Party members, who by joining the Party had entered a community which had advisedly alienated itself from the outside world, were of necessity in the hands of their superiors, there was no lack of personnel. In this way the Party planted its posts of observation, which were at the same time agencies of pressure and intimidation, in every factory, workshop, office, and school—indeed in many households as well.

Provocation, intimidation, and infiltration together furnished the Party with many thousands of new members. Having been brought into the Party under the impact of fear, these new members often experienced a sort of deliverance, once they felt themselves a part

R

.of its community. Being henceforth in the same position with regard to the outside world as the older partisans, they were willing to behave as these had done. So the individual process started all over again. The Party did not cease to expand.

V

All the same, it must not be forgotten that so long as free elections were held, the Nazis never succeeded in attaining more than 36·9 per cent of the votes. Their ups and downs under the Weimar Republic appear in their rough outlines from the following figures: [1]

Date of Election for the National Parliament (*Reichstag*)	Total number of votes	Seats	Votes for Nazis	Nazi seats
4 May 1924 . . .	29,388,577	472	1,924,018	32
7 Dec. 1924 . .	60,565,994	493	908,087	14
20 May 1928 . .	28,633,009	475	809,541	12
14 Sep. 1930 . . .	34,552,302	577	6,401,210	107
31 Jul. 1932 . . .	36,319,998	603	13,732,779	230
6 Nov. 1932 . . .	34,689,133	575	11,705,256	196

Therefore, as far as numbers are concerned, in January 1933— the month in which the Chancellorship of the Reich was confided to Hitler—the movement was already on the decline. It had passed the peak, which could be reached by the application of the techniques described in this article.

January 1933 was, however, the beginning of Nazism as a ruling power, capable of controlling the fate of Germany and, with it, the fate of Europe as a whole. In its later struggles the Party did not change its methods. It applied them more systematically; it had more opportunities and was met with less resistance. The tasks hitherto undertaken by Party organs now became the task of the state, of its police, secret or non-secret, of the civil administration and the judiciary. Whenever civil officers or judges did not comply with the Party orders, the Party was in possession of effective means for breaking their firmness. Often blackmail and unfounded accusations, even physical violence, imprisonment, detention in concentration camps, were added to provocation, intimidation, and infiltration.

The tactics used by the Nazis in the parliamentary bodies and in the Government agencies must equally be explained in this light. To analyse them in detail would demand a separate study. Such analysis should give attention also to the many constitutional issues involved.

In conclusion, a reference may be made to a statement of General Halder. At the end of a pamphlet on Hitler's military capacities, this

[1] Source: Friedrich Stampfer, *Die Vierzehn Jahre der ersten Deutschen Republik*, *Graphia* (Karlsbad, 1935).

military expert quotes a thought expressed by Hitler during the Russian campaign: 'A Germany', Hitler said, 'that would be unable to win, should be destroyed, not by the violence of the victorious nations, but by his own will, the will of the Supreme commander and the Dictator.' [1]

'For Hitler,' Halder added, 'as he stood at the top of his power, Germany did not exist at all, however often the word may have been on his lips; for Hitler, only his ego existed, which in the literal sense of the phrase was put by him, as their Incarnation, in the place of the people he once promised to serve.' [2]

Hitler—on this point Halder is silent—was in his turn the outcome of a socialised and popularised militarism, that understood nothing but naked power within the scope of a soulless hierarchic order and, having no specified ends, made everything instrumental to the demands of its dark, subconscious urges.

[1] Franz Halder, *Hitler als Feldherr* (Munich, 1949), p. 62.
[2] ibid.

14

THE GERMAN COMMUNISTS AND THE RISE OF HITLER

Alan Bullock

THE fortunes of the German Communist Party between the end of the War in 1918 and Hitler's Chancellorship followed a chequered and erratic course. Four times between 1918 and 1923 the Communists made a bid for power and four times suffered overwhelming defeat: in November 1918; in January 1919 (when Rosa Luxembourg and Karl Liebknecht were murdered); in March 1921 (the 'March Action'); and in October 1923. Even after these defeats the Communists, however, could still win 3·69 million votes at the *Reichstag* elections of May 1924. Between 1924 and 1929, it is true, the Communists, like the Nazis, went through a period of decline. But they had already begun to recover by the 1928 elections, and in the three remaining elections before Hitler came to power—aided no doubt by the severe economic depression—they steadily increased their vote to just short of 6 millions in November 1932 and their representation in the *Reichstag* to 100 deputies.

On the eve of Hitler's Chancellorship, therefore, the German movement was the most powerful Communist Party in Europe outside the Soviet Union. Molotov had sung its praises at the 16th Congress of the Soviet Communist Party in July 1930. It was well-organised and disciplined, uncompromising in its revolutionary programme, free of all taint of reformism or opportunism, and convinced that it was within sight of its goal: the establishment of a Soviet Germany by revolutionary means. Six months later, by the summer of 1933, this powerful revolutionary party had been dissolved, its leaders and many of its rank and file imprisoned, its funds confiscated, its press silenced, its name and organisation erased. And all this without a fight, with far less effective resistance than the Communists had shown to the police under the Weimar régime.

How is this to be accounted for? To provide an answer to this question is to open up the further question with which this paper is principally concerned: what was the part played by the German Communist Party in Hitler's accession to power?

II

The reasons for the double failure of the Communist Party to prevent Hitler coming to power, and to use the circumstances of 1932–3 for carrying out their own revolution, are not to be found in any weakness of the Party's rank and file, or of its discipline. On the contrary, at the elections held in March 1933, after Hitler had come to power, after the *Reichstag* Fire, and after all the resources of the Nazis in intimidation and obstruction had been directed against the Communist movement, the Party was still able to poll 4,848,100 votes—a remarkable testimony to the loyalty of its supporters. The plain truth is that the Communist failure was due to gross misjudgment by the Communist leaders—in Moscow as well as Berlin—of the situation in Germany and of the character of the Nazi movement.

This conclusion is precisely what the previous history of the Communist Party before 1930 would lead anyone to expect. For the failures of the period 1918–23, and especially the failure of October 1923, had all been marked by similar errors of political judgment. Thus, in March 1921, the Party had tried to seize power at a time when the situation was entirely unfavourable to such an attempt; while if there was a revolutionary situation in 1923, the moment chosen by the Communists to exploit it was too late. The opportunity had passed while they were still arguing about its analysis. A major part in formulating these mistaken judgments had been played by the leaders of the Comintern, sitting in Moscow, remote from any contact with what was happening in Germany. If the Party's ideas were erratic, swinging from a Right-wing policy of co-operation with the Social Democrats and the trade unions to the extreme of Left-wing intransigeance, these zig-zag changes of course rarely, if ever, originated in Germany; they were dictated from Moscow by the Executive Committee of the Communist International. The German leaders were summoned to Moscow, but the Comintern's decisions came increasingly to reflect the needs of Russia's own national interests or of one or other party in the struggle for power inside Russia. This was concealed by finding scapegoats for failure inside the K.P.D.[1] Each change was followed by the proscription of those who had become identified with the discarded policy, or who showed independence and opposition towards the new ruling handed down from Moscow. Thus Paul Levi after the failure of the March Action (1921); Brandler after the failure of 1923; Maslow and Ruth Fischer after the swing to the Right in 1925, were each in turn faced with the alternatives of being hunted out of the Party or of making an unconditional submission to those who, by definition,

---

[1] *Kommunistische Partei Deutschlands*, a convenient abbreviation which will be used for the rest of this paper. S.P.D.: *Sozialdemokratische Partei Deutschlands*.

never erred: the Mandarins of the Kremlin. This process of sapping the independence of the German Communist Party and rendering its leadership responsive to orders from Moscow may be followed in the account of Ruth Fischer, who had been General Secretary of the K.P.D. and a member of the Comintern Presidium before her expulsion from the Party for opposition in 1926.[1] Its history lies outside the scope of the present article, but its results were of importance for the period after 1928. For by that year any tendency to independence on the part of the K.P.D. had been stamped out and the conduct of the Party was in the hands of men—Ernst Thälmann, Hermann Remmele, Heinz Neumann, Fritz Heckert, Wilhelm Pieck—on whom Stalin and the Comintern leaders believed they could rely to do as they were told.

III

Since 1925 the policy pursued by the K.P.D. on orders from Moscow had been one of conciliation and co-operation with the Social Democrats and the trade unions. At the elections of 1928 this policy seemed to have borne fruit: the K.P.D. recovered much of the ground lost in 1924 and 1925 and the two working-class parties, Communist and Social Democrat, together polled 40 per cent of the votes cast. There were strong arguments for continuing the policy of co-operation between them and forming a united front. But these arguments, based upon conditions in Germany, were brushed aside as irrelevant. At the 6th World Congress of the Communist International (*Comintern*) held in Moscow in the summer of 1928 a new policy was laid down which was dutifully echoed by the 5th Congress of the Red Trade Union International (*Profintern*) in 1930. The new policy was to meet a changed situation, but, as Arthur Rosenberg points out,[2] it was the situation in Soviet Russia, and not in the world at large, which had changed. The policy of compromise in Russia represented by the New Economic Policy and the concessions to the *Kulaks* was at an end; the policy of the United Front which was its counterpart in Comintern directives must also come to an end. Russia was about to make an abrupt swerve towards the Left in the so-called Stalinist Revolution, represented by the adoption of the first Five-Year Plan. The Communist Parties outside the Soviet Union, irrespective of the situation in their own countries, must follow suit.

The new Comintern policy was formulated as that of the 'third

[1] Ruth Fischer, *Stalin and German Communism* (Harvard Univ. Press, Cambridge, Mass., 1948). cf. also Franz Borkenau, *The Communist International* (London, 1938); Ossip K. Flechtheim, *Die K.P.D. in der Weimarer Republik* (Offenbach, 1948), and A. Rosenberg, *A History of Bolshevism* (Oxford, 1934).

[2] Arthur Rosenberg, *A History of Bolshevism* (Oxford, 1934), pp. 231-3.

period' which was now discovered to be beginning in the international Labour movement. The first period had lasted from 1917 to 1923 and had been one of direct revolutionary struggle; the second covered the years 1923–8, the years of stabilisation. The third period would be one of intensified class struggle in which the Communist Parties must refuse to co-operate with the Social-Democratic parties and trade unions of the 2nd International. These had now become the allies of World Capitalism, the forerunners of Fascism. All attempts to create a United Front of working-class parties—the policy followed since 1925—must therefore be rejected.

The K.P.D. at once turned about and came into line. The new directive was set in an Open Letter from the Central Committee of the Party and the Comintern Executive, published on 19th December. Those who hesitated or doubted were expelled, and the policy of a swing to the Left (for advocating which Arkadi Maslow and Ruth Fischer had been proscribed in 1925) was now elevated into orthodoxy. The K.P.D. ostentatiously dissociated itself from the Social Democrats. On 1st May 1929 the Communists proposed to organise a separate May Day demonstration of their own in Berlin, and not to join with the Social Democrats and trade unionists in the traditional common procession. When the Social-Democratic Police President of Berlin, Zoergiebel, banned all demonstrations for 1st May, to avoid a clash between the two and preserve public order, the Socialists submitted, but the Communists resisted. As a result there was street-fighting in the Berlin working-class districts of Neukölln and Wedding, in which twenty-five people were killed and thirty-six badly hurt. The Communist Press at once raised a howl of outrage, called for a general strike (which, according to Franz Borkenau, was observed in a single factory), and denounced the Prussian State Government, in which the Social Democrats were strongly represented, as the accomplices of Fascism. Herr Zoergiebel became the symbol of the Social Democrats' treacherous betrayal of the working-classes, and the Communists again saw their theory confirmed when in the same month Karl Severing, the Prussian Minister of the Interior and one of the members of the Social-Democratic Party, banned the *Rote Frontkämpferbund* (the K.P.D.'s fighting organisation, the Red Front) throughout Prussia.

It was in this inflamed atmosphere that the 12th *Parteitag* of the K.P.D. was held in Wedding, scene of the recent street-fighting, in June 1929. Echoing the decisions of the 6th Comintern World Congress, Thälmann proclaimed the opening of the 'third period'. He advanced the thesis that the German democratic parties taking part in the governments of the Reich and Prussia—notably the Social Democrats, who provided both the Reich Chancellor (Hermann Mueller) and the Prussian Minister President (Otto Braun)—were openly acting in the interests of Capitalism and as the accomplices of Fascism against the working-classes. Bitner declared: 'Social Democracy is the forerunner of Fascism,' and Thälmann spoke of 'a particularly dangerous form of fascist development, that of Social Fascism.' Social Fascism was now the officially adopted Communist view of the Social-Democratic Party and of the Weimar régime it supported.

It is easy to be misled by the term 'Social Fascism' and to dismiss it as no more than a phrase of political abuse. On the contrary, the Communist theoreticians were only too serious in their identification of the Weimar régime with the role of preparing for a Fascist dictatorship. In December 1930 Heinz Neumann, referring to the Brüning Government (which the S.P.D. tacitly supported), declared: 'Fascism is with us!' This was too categorical, and in the spring of 1931 the Comintern Executive corrected this description of the Brüning Government to 'a government seeking to establish fascist dictatorship'. In a pamphlet published in February 1932, *Der revolutionäre Ausweg und die K.P.D.*, Thälmann wrote:

'The process of establishing a fascist dictatorship by means of the Brüning Government, as analysed by us a year ago at the January 1931 plenary meeting, has assumed alarming proportions within the last twelve months. No one will doubt any longer today that the course followed by the Brüning–Groener Government in the Reich and by its associate Braun–Severing Government in Prussia is that of Fascism, and that we were right when in December 1930 we spoke of a developing fascist dictatorship not yet fully matured.' [1]

'Democracy and fascist dictatorship not only draw their support from the same classes . . . but they also employ similar external methods . . . thus becoming associated with one another.' [2]

This argument, as applied to the Brüning Government which governed Germany from 1930 to 1932 without a stable majority in the *Reichstag* and by virtue of the President's emergency powers, was not without some point. Brüning was no Nazi, but his use of emergency decrees helped to prepare the way for Hitler's dictatorship. The Communists were not wrong to sound a warning of the dangers of the political course on which Germany had been launched with the tacit, if reluctant, support of the Social-Democratic Party. But if there is this much to be said for the Communists' argument, despite its exaggerations, the consequences which they drew from it were unexpected. For, instead of concluding that therefore everything possible should be done to strengthen the Brüning Government in the Reich and the Braun–Severing Government in Prussia against

[1] *Der Revolutionäre Ausweg und die K.P.D.*, p. 23.
[2] *Die Internationale*, XV, 213.

the danger of a Nazi dictatorship, they proceeded to do everything they could to weaken their resistance and to hasten this development. While they criticised the Social Democrats' argument of the lesser evil in their support of the Brüning Government and participation in the State Government of Prussia, they themselves embraced the argument of the greater evil, declaring it to be better that the Nazis should come openly into power. Thus in a speech which he made in the *Reichstag* on 14th October 1931, the Communist deputy Remmele argued that, if the Nazis came into power, then the United Front of the Proletariat would at once spring into being under resolute Communist leadership and the revolution be more easily and quickly accomplished. Rarely has the distorting effect of a determinist philosophy of history on the political judgment of a party been more clearly demonstrated. The proletarian revolution and the triumph of the Communist cause were inevitable. The only question, therefore, was how best the K.P.D. could intervene to speed up the pre-determined course of events. Answer: by shortening the transitional phase and by pushing forward the open transference of power to the Nazis which was the inevitable—but of course temporary—prelude to the Communist Revolution itself.

It followed, therefore, that the first duty of the K.P.D. was to strip away the democratic pretence with which impostors like the Social Democrats deluded the working classes. This applied, of course, to all the democratic parties under the Weimar Republic, but the K.P.D. was especially concerned with the Social Democrats. They were by far the biggest and best-organised of the Weimar parties, they claimed—not without some justification—to be a working-class party and, not least, they were the greatest obstacle to the Communist leadership of a united proletariat which was the K.P.D.'s dream.

Ever since the days of 1914–18, when the Spartacists had denounced the S.P.D. as Social Patriots for their support of the War, there had been bad blood between the S.P.D. and the K.P.D. After the war the S.P.D. openly took up the position of a reformist Labour party, linked with a powerful but conservative trade-union movement, prepared to support the Weimar régime, without worrying about its *bourgeois* character, and ready on occasion to join in a coalition government. Nothing could have more bitterly stirred the contempt of the Communists, still faithful to their belief in the inevitability of proletarian revolution. For tactical reasons it might be necessary temporarily to combine with the Social Democrats, but relations between the two working-class parties were never easy nor their suspicions of each other stilled for long. It was impossible to disguise the fact that they were rivals for the support of the working class. What added to Communist bitterness was the greater success which the Social Democrats persistently secured in attracting the votes of the unregenerate proletarians. At no *Reichstag* election up to 1933 was the Social Democratic vote less than one and a quarter millions above the Communist; and most of the time the S.P.D. polled two to three times as many votes as the Communists. The new policy which now permitted and encouraged attacks on the 'Social Fascists' of the S.P.D. was therefore welcome to many Communists, irritated and frustrated by years of unsuccessful struggle to capture working-class leadership from the Social Democrats.

The new policy also fitted in well with Russia's national interests. The Russians had long shown great hostility to the Weimar Republic's foreign policy—the main object of which was to re-establish good relations between Germany and the Western Powers, France and Great Britain. The Russians suspected that such good relations were likely to be developed at the expense of the U.S.S.R., and were eager to keep a wedge driven between Germany and her ex-enemies. Here was further ground for Communist criticism of the democratic Republic and of the Social-Democratic Party, which (for example, during the chancellorship of the Social Democrat, Hermann Mueller) had steadily supported the 'Western' policy Streseman had followed. At the 12th *Parteitag* (June 1929) Thälmann spoke of the danger of an imperialist war of the Western Powers against the U.S.S.R. and denounced the German Government (still led by Hermann Mueller) for joining the anti-Soviet Front by signing the Young Plan. 'Social Democracy is no longer playing a passive part . . . but is the most active champion of German Imperialism and its policy of war against the U.S.S.R.' Thälmann added : 'The defence of the Soviet Union must be made the main thesis of the revolutionary policy of workers of all nations. . . .' Heckert echoed his words: 'We see in the Soviet Union our fatherland, to which we dedicate ourselves to the last breath in our bodies and the last drop of our blood.' He proceeded to sum up the K.P.D.'s double characterisation of Social Democracy: 'The establishment of the policy of war and of Social Fascism is the platform on which Social Democracy has placed itself.' In line with this new directive, during the autumn and winter of 1929–30 the K.P.D. joined the Nazis and the Nationalists in their denunciation of the Young Plan, which marked an important stage in that *rapprochement* between Germany and the Western Powers they had been instructed to prevent.

IV

Communist policy in Germany, therefore, during the years before Hitler's Chancellorship was dominated by a number of theses:

There was nothing to chose from the working-class point of view between *bourgeois* democracy and the Fascist dictatorship the Nazis wanted to set up.

The Social-Democratic Party, despite the fact that it represented millions of working-class votes, had in fact betrayed the workers' interests and had become a pillar of that *bourgeois* democracy, which was the façade used by the big capitalist interests to disguise their exploitation of the workers.

The end of the democratic republic and the open establishment of the Nazis in power would in fact be a gain from the Communist point of view, since it would end the democratic camouflage which still deceived large numbers of the working class.

Once the Nazis had come to power, the end would be in sight. The masses, no longer confused by the fraudulent reformism of the S.P.D., would rise united and irresistible behind the leadership of the revolutionary K.P.D. and would establish the dictatorship of the proletariat.

The practical tasks, therefore, were clear: by every means possible to undermine the strength of those republican institutions and parties —above all, the S.P.D.—which were holding up the necessary transition from the disguised Fascism of the Weimar régime to the open Fascist dictatorship of the National-Socialists.

This programme the K.P.D. proceeded methodically to put into practice between 1929 and the end of 1932. Circumstances favoured them. These were precisely the years of the depression, of falling production and rising unemployment. The depression presented the German Government with problems so vexed and controversial that it became impossible either to maintain the coalition of parties in Mueller's ministry or to find a successor to it which could command a stable majority in the *Reichstag*. An answer was found in Brüning and in the use of the President's emergency powers under Article 48 of the Weimar Constitution. But the need to resort to such an expedient underlined the failure of German democracy and the democratic parties to provide a government capable of meeting a major crisis, while the methods of emergency legislation used by Brüning and his successor, von Papen, inevitably made easier the transition to Hitler's open dictatorship.

At the same time the bad trade and rising unemployment [1] placed the S.P.D. leaders in a difficult position. They were convinced that they must support Brüning's efforts to prevent a total collapse in Germany, but to call for restraint and sacrifices on the part of the working classes at a time of rising discontent inevitably laid them open to the charge, which the Communists were not slow to make, of betraying the workers. At all three of the *Reichstag* elections between

---

[1] Number of unemployed registered in Germany:

Jun. 1929	. 1,260,044	Dec. 1930	. 4,383,843	Jan. 1932	. 5,475,778
Dec. 1929	. 2,850,849	Jan. 1931	. 3,953,946	Dec. 1932	. 5,772,984
Jan. 1930	. 2,640,681	Dec. 1931	. 5,615,187		

1929 and 1932 the K.P.D. put the attack on the S.P.D. in the fore-front of their campaign, exploiting to the full the difficulties of the Social Democrats, without any scruples about responsibility, dema-gogy, or the truth. The one thing that mattered was to smash the S.P.D., and they were not without some success, although it fell far short of their hopes. At every one of these elections the S.P.D. vote fell while the Communist vote rose.[1] It scored particularly among the unemployed workers. Franz Borkenau, after attempting an analysis of the character of the K.P.D.[2] membership, concludes that in 1932 the German Communist Party must have consisted of about three-fifths unemployed; it had become 'a party leading the un-employed against the employed workers'.

These undermining tactics were extended from the S.P.D. itself to the trade unions, which were the basis of German Social-Democracy's strength. In 1929 the Communists for the first time for some years put up independent lists for the shop-steward elec-tions. They constantly tried to call 'wild-cat' strikes in defiance of union discipline, invariably with little success, but with the result that the weapon of the strike became discredited. Finally, they tried to set up their own rival unions (*Revolutionäre Gewerkschaftsopposition* —R.G.O.), again with little success.

A third field for Communist wrecking activity was in Prussia. The Prussian State Government, which ruled over three-fifths of the Reich's sixty-odd million citizens and two-thirds of the country's area, had long been in the hands of a coalition government of Social Democrats and the Catholic Centre Party. This coalition had proved more stable than the succession of Reich ministries, and it was uni-versally regarded as the main bulwark of German democracy, especially after the breakdown of parliamentary democracy and the introduction of Brüning's 'presidial' Cabinet in the Reich. The over-throw of the Prussian Government, in which one Social Democrat (Otto Braun) was Minister President, and another (Karl Severing) Minister of the Interior with control of the Police, was a main objective of the anti-democratic Nationalist and Nazi Parties. The Communists now put their shoulders to the wheel to help them.

In the summer of 1931 the Nazis and Nationalists secured and organised a referendum in Prussia to demand the removal of the Coalition Government. At first the K.P.D. opposed this move with

---

[1]	May 1928	Sep. 1930	Jul. 1932	Nov. 1932
S.P.D.	9,153,000	8,577,700	7,959,700	7,248,000
K.P.D.	3,264,800	4,592,100	5,282,600	5,980,200
N.S.D.A.P.	810,100	6,409,600	13,745,800	11,737,000

[2] Franz Borkenau, *The Communist International* (1938), c. xxi. The main sources he uses are the periodic analyses of Communist Party membership published in the Comintern International Press Correspondence (*Imprecorr*) by Ossip Piatnitzki, the head of the Comintern's Organisation Bureau.

the slogan 'Down with the fascist fraud against the people'. But under the lead of Heinz Neumann and Remmele, once the Nazis had got the 10 per cent support necessary for a plebiscite and moved on to hold the actual referendum, the K.P.D. turned round and joined them, helping to push the vote up to 9,800,000 (37 per cent). 'The struggle against the Prussian government is a decisive part of our general mass struggle against capitalist dictatorship and Fascism.'[1]

Next year, on 24th April 1932, the State elections gave the K.P.D. another chance. Again they campaigned against the Prussian Government and won fifty-six seats in the Prussian *Landtag*. The Nazis won 162. Together they possessed a clear majority and the K.P.D. proceeded to use it. On 25th May 1932 the Communist fraction in the *Landtag* introduced a motion of no confidence. In the course of introducing the notion Wilhelm Pieck attacked not only the Prussian Government, but also the National-Socialists, with whose co-operation the K.P.D. were proposing to overthrow the Government. When Pieck called them a party of murderers, the Nazis set on the Communists and beat them up in the Chamber, injuring quite a number of them. But the Communists were not to be deterred. They still stuck to their motion, and with the help of the Nazis who had beaten them up passed their vote of no confidence on 3rd June.

Although the Braun Government had been defeated, no alternative combination of parties proved feasible, and the old ministers stayed on as caretakers. At this point, Wilhelm Abegg, the Prussian State Secretary, asked two of the Communist *Reichstag* deputies, Torgler and Kasper, to see him and tried to persuade them to change their tactics in Prussia and join the S.P.D. and the Centre in preserving a democratic form of government there. The addition of the K.P.D. block of votes would have made this possible, but the Communist representatives gave no definite answer. While they remained silent, the new Reich Chancellor, von Papen, acted. On 20th July 1932 he turned out the Prussian Government by force and appointed himself as Reich Commissioner. Now the K.P.D. swung round and demanded a general strike to support the Government they had themselves overthrown. This was universally regarded as a face-saving manœuvre. In any case, the S.P.D. leaders had had enough of the Communists, and no one followed their call. Shortly before this, on 8th July 1932, a number of S.P.D. leaders had met Thälmann, Pieck, and Schehr to discuss the possibility of Social-Democratic participation in *Antifa (Antifaschistische Aktion)*, a new 'Unity' organisation set up by the K.P.D. But this manœuvre, too, which could have only had the effect of splitting the S.P.D., was too blatant and led to nothing.

Meanwhile the K.P.D. could congratulate itself on the course

[1] *Die Internationale*, XIV, p. 507.

events were taking. Brüning had gone, and been replaced as Reich Chancellor by von Papen, the man who six months later was to bring Hitler into power; the Prussian Government of Social-Democrats and the Centre Party had been ousted, and at the Reich elections of 31st July the National-Socialists won the greatest victory achieved by any party during the years of the Weimar Republic, 13,745,000 votes, 37 per cent of the total, more than the K.P.D. and S.P.D. combined.

Throughout 1932 street clashes between the Nazi SA and the Communist Red Front were frequent. Between 1st June and 20th July 1932 there were 461 political riots in Prussia, in which eighty-two people were killed and over 400 seriously injured.[1] A particularly violent clash between Communists and Nazis took place at Altona on 17th July, in which fifteen people were killed and 200 injured. Despite all this, despite the staggering rise in the Nazi vote from 800,000 in May 1928 to 13,745,000 in July 1932, despite the menacing growth of the brown-shirt SA (which now heavily out-numbered the Red Front) the Communists stuck to their beliefs, summed up by Trotsky in a criticism of their tactics as the view 'that the task of struggle against fascism is a task of the second order; that it can wait, that it will solve itself; that fascism is essentially already in power; that Hitler will bring nothing new; that Hitler does not have to be feared; that Hitler will only break a path for the Communists'.[2]

This view the Communists did not change throughout the remaining few months before Hitler's Chancellorship. When, in the November elections to the *Reichstag*, the Nazis for the first time lost votes—two million less than in July—the Communists concluded that the Nazi danger was fading, and that they could now concentrate with renewed vigour on smashing the Social Democrats. This same month, November 1932, when the Berlin transport workers went on strike, the Communists worked side by side with the Nazis to encourage and speed the strike as one more blow at the Trade Union leadership, which refused to recognise it. By the end of January 1933 the K.P.D. at last got its wish: on 30th January Adolf Hitler became Reich Chancellor, the Nazis were openly in power. The revolutionary movement had come, the moment so long prepared for—and nothing happened. The Communists suggested a general strike in co-operation with the Social Democrats, but as this was the sixth time they had called for it since 1929, as the number of men looking for jobs in Germany was nearing seven millions, and as the Social Democrats and the trade unions—the 'Social Fascists'—had had too much bitter experience of K.P.D. tactics in the last three

[1] Figures given by Albert Grzesinski, at that time President of Police in Berlin, in his memoirs, *Inside Germany* (New York, 1939), c. X.
[2] Quoted by Konrad Heiden, *Der Führer* (London, 1944), p. 364.

years, no one listened. That was all. In the next few weeks, especially after the *Reichstag* Fire of 27th February, the Communists began
to feel the revolutionary terror on their own backs. At the elections on
5th March 1933 the Party was still able to muster 4,848,100 votes, a
loss of only one-fifth since November. But the leadership was quite
unable to turn this support to advantage. The Party which for
fifteen years had talked of nothing but revolution failed when the
crisis it had itself prescribed as the revolutionary moment came.
The opportunity did not stay for them. The eighty-one K.P.D.
deputies were never allowed to take their seats in the *Reichstag*. Together with the key men in the party organisation throughout the
country, they were swept into the concentration camps, the organisation broken up, and the Party suppressed.

Even this did not shake the confidence of the Comintern leadership
or of the German party members who had escaped. The Communist
Imprecorr, now transferred to Basel under the name of *Rundschau*,
declared on 1st April:

'The momentary calm after the victory of Fascism is only a
passing phenomenon. The rise of the revolutionary tide in
Germany will inevitably continue. The resistance of the masses
against Fascism will inevitably increase. The open dictatorship of
Fascism destroys all democratic illusions, frees the masses from the
influence of the Social-Democratic Party and thus accelerates the
speed of Germany's march towards the proletarian revolution.' [1]

Heckert, one of the leaders of the K.P.D. added:

'The talk about the German Communists being defeated and
dead is the gossip of philistines, of idiotic and ignorant people. . . .
The jailing of a few thousand communists cannot kill a party with
a following of five millions. Instead of those who have been
arrested the politically and culturally highly trained German
proletariat develops new forces and will always develop them.' [2]

When a group of dissident Communists blurted out 'that the proletariat has lost a battle and been defeated, and that Comrade Thälmann and the Central Committee are responsible for the realisation
of a Fascist dictatorship,' the official Communist *Rundschau* described
such views as 'a crass mixture of naked opportunism, insidious
Trotskyism, and downright Putschism'. Worse, they were 'an open
attack not only upon Comrade Thälmann and the leaders of the
party, but upon the Comintern Comrades Stalin and Manuilski,
the decisions of the 11th and 12th Plenums of the Comintern'.[3]
Three years later the authors of these outrageous views are said to
have been shot in Moscow.

[1] Quoted by Franz Borkenau, op. cit., pp. 376–7.
[2] ibid., p. 377.
[3] Quoted from *Rundschau*, No. 17, 1933, by Franz Borkenau, op. cit., pp. 378–9.

In Moscow the apologists of the Comintern echoed the assurance of *Rundschau*. In *Bolshevik* of 15th February, Karl Radek wrote:

'Hitler may be able to destroy the legal organisation of the Communist Party. But every blow against it will help to rally the working masses to its support. A Party that receives six million votes, deeply linked with the entire history of the German working class, cannot be dismissed from the balance sheet of history.' [1]

On 1st April the following resolution was recorded:

'The President of the Executive Committee of the Communist International, having heard the report of Comrade Heckert on the situation in Germany, declares that the policy carried out by the Executive Committee of the Communist Party of Germany with Comrade Thälmann at its head, up to and during the time of the Hitlerite coup, was absolutely correct.' [2]

The infallibility of authority had to be preserved immaculate.

VI

In fact, even from their own point of view, the Communists had made a series of disastrous mistakes. The first was to believe that there was nothing to choose between the democratic Weimar régime, even in the attenuated form which existed under Brüning, and the open dictatorship of the Nazis. This may have been a good line of attack on the democratic parties, but the Communists were very unwise to be confused by their own propaganda. For, however much contempt and hostility they may have felt towards the Republican system, it was undeniably different from the régime the Nazis proposed to establish. It was, for instance, a fact that under the Weimar system for fifteen years the K.P.D. had enjoyed a very considerable degree of freedom to organise and agitate for its overthrow, while within a few weeks of Hitler's chancellorship the Party was to be deprived of all rights, and silenced. There was a very great difference in the meaning of what the Communists called 'intolerable oppression' when it was a question of the Social-Democratic Police President Zoergiebel banning a May Day demonstration, and when it was a question of Göring using all the resources of the Prussian State and police to smash the Party's organisation for good. Not to have been able to see the likelihood of such a difference in advance, when the Nazis were advertising it all the time, suggests blindness on the part of the K.P.D. leaders.

Their second mistake—again, even from their own point of view —was to put the fight against the Social Democrats before the need to fight the Nazis. Even if all that the K.P.D. said about the role of the Social-Democratic Party as the betrayer of the working

[1] Quoted by Max Beloff, *The Foreign Policy of Soviet Russia*, Vol. I, p. 67.
[2] ibid., p. 68.

classes, the agent of capitalism, the precursors of Fascism, etc., had been true, it was still more important to recognise the big new fact about German politics, the sensational rise of the National-Socialist Party, and to grasp that while the S.P.D. lost support, the Nazis were leaping into first place. In 1928 the Nazis polled under a million votes, in 1930 six and a half million votes, in July 1932 thirteen and three-quarters. In the same period the S.P.D. vote fell from over nine millions to under eight. But the K.P.D. leaders stubbornly refused to see the real characteristics of the N.S.D.A.P., or to recognise that they themselves—leave alone the Social Democrats—were outclassed by the Nazis both as a party attracting mass support and as a party of revolution. Judged by the tests of either the ballot-box or street-fighting, the Nazis looked much more like a revolutionary party about to sweep into power than the K.P.D. But this was precisely what the Communists could not admit.

This led to their third mistake—the belief that, once the Nazis had come to power and the situation had become one of undisguised class war, the masses would rally behind the K.P.D. To go on saying this when the Nazis polled between two and two and a half times as many votes as the K.P.D. required a childlike faith in Marxist prophecy. For every unemployed man the K.P.D. won for its ranks, the Nazis won two. The real mass party of Germany in the early 1930s was the N.S.D.A.P., and once they had come into power their mass support went up, not down. In the elections of March 1933, after Hitler had become Chancellor, they polled seventeen and a quarter million votes, three and a half million more than they had got at the peak of their success before 1933. It is true that the combined support of the S.P.D. and the K.P.D. approached that of the Nazis (in the November 1932 elections their combined poll actually exceeded that of the Nazis), and that between them they got far more working-class support than the Nazis. But the whole policy of the Communists since 1928 had been directed to making such a combination impossible, and the unscrupulous tactics the K.P.D. had followed in its attacks on the Social Democrats and the trade unions had not only alienated their leaders, but had also disgusted and confused their rank and file. For most of the workers in the ranks of the S.P.D. who were despondent at the passive policy of their own party leaders and anxious to do something to prevent Hitler coming to power, the last party they were likely to turn to was the K.P.D. As late as November 1932 the K.P.D. co-operated with the Nazis in the Berlin transport strike against the trade unions and the S.P.D., and had discredited itself as leader of any anti-Nazi front by its steadily pursued policy of attacking the S.P.D. as the more important enemy, even to the extent of taking the same side as the Nazis and the Nationalists.

The last mistake is the most surprising of all. After talking about revolution and civil war for fifteen years, it emerged in 1933 that the K.P.D. had made virtually no preparations to provide itself with the first essentials of such a policy—arms and a military organisation. The K.P.D. had certainly enough strength—especially in areas like Hamburg, the Ruhr, and the working-class quarters of Berlin—to have put up a hard fight, if anybody had ever worked out carefully what was to be done and seen to the provision of arms and organisation. Such open resistance would have faced Hitler—whose whole policy rested on coming to power legally—with a difficult problem. Could he have relied on the *Reichswehr* to intervene, when one of the most important arguments in favour of bringing him into power had been that thereby the Army could avoid being drawn into civil war? Is it not possible that by making a fight—and in this way alone—the K.P.D. would have overcome both the defeatism and the distrust of the Social Democrats and rallied a large section of the working class to resist the Nazis? No sure answer can be given to these questions, but at least there was a sufficient chance of success to have made the risk worth taking, if the K.P.D. leaders had been prepared to make good their pretensions to be a party of professional revolutionaries. But the K.P.D. never found a Röhm or a Göring. Instead they fell back on the theory of historical determinism. Max Brauer, the Social-Democratic mayor of Altona, met Ernst Torgler, chairman of the Communist *Reichstag* fraction in Berlin on 23rd February 1933 and begged him to give up the fight against the S.P.D. and form a united front to fight the Nazis. As late as that—three weeks *after* Hitler had come to power—Torgler could answer: 'It doesn't enter our heads. The Nazis must take power. Then in four weeks the whole working class will be united under the leadership of the K.P.D.' When Brauer repeated the same question to the Soviet Ambassador a few days later in Hamburg, he got the same reply: 'No, the Nazis must come to power now, and then at last the old fight will come to an end. In four weeks the Communists will have the leadership of the whole working class.' [1] Four weeks later the German Communist Party—the most powerful Communist Party outside the Soviet Union, the party of revolution and no compromise, the party dedicated to the seizure of power by force—had ceased to exist, and had disappeared without a fight.

VII

How far did these mistakes of the German Communist Party contribute to Hitler's success? From the beginning the Nazis had been as much an anti-Marxist as an anti-semitic party. The simple

[1] This incident is recounted by Konrad Heiden, *Der Führer*, p. 432.

existence of a powerful Communist movement in Germany openly proclaiming its intention of carrying out a revolution on the Bolshevik model and setting up a Soviet state gave substance to Hitler's doubtful claim to be the saviour of Germany from Bolshevism. It is, of course, impossible to say how much support fear of the Communists won for Hitler, but that it was a considerable factor in reinforcing the Nazi appeal on other grounds (particularly the Nationalist appeal) is not open to doubt. With the growth of the K.P.D. vote to a figure just short of six millions in 1932, it was not implausible to believe in the threat of a Communist seizure of power in Germany. To vote for the Nazis as a preferable alternative may well have been jumping into the fire, but there were many in Germany who believed that the Nazis, pinned down by the responsibilities of power and by their Nationalist partners in the coalition of January 1933, represented a better choice than the dictatorship of the proletariat in Russian leading strings.

Whatever the policy pursued by the K.P.D., therefore, the very existence of a strong movement in Germany aiming openly at a Communist revolution was a factor which helped the Nazis. The tactics adopted by the Communists only heightened the importance of this. Apart from a period in the middle of the 1920s, Communist hostility to the Republican régime was unrelenting. This meant that for the greater part of its life the Weimar Republic had to face the attacks of a party (latterly the third party in the *Reichstag*) which openly made the overthrow of the régime the object of its policy, and set itself without scruple to discredit and destroy the German people's faith in democratic institutions. The K.P.D. was not alone in this: the Nazis and the Nationalists played exactly the same game—the Nationalists with the least justification of all, since they were by profession conservative, while the K.P.D. was avowedly a revolutionary party. In fact the extreme Left and the extreme Right acted as pacemakers for each other's political agitation and violence, whether in the *Reichstag*, at elections, or on the streets. The Communist Red Front and the Nazi SA were even more interested in weakening the authority of the State and the police than they were in beating in each others' heads. Major Röhm, the creator of the SA, spoke with admiration of the Communist spirit, and transference of allegiance between the two extremes was not uncommon. The K.P.D. shared with the extreme Right the responsibility for debasing the currency of politics to the point where party intolerance, the defamation of political opponents, violence, gangsterism, even murder, became an accepted part of German political life.

This is particularly true of the period after 1928, when the K.P.D., under orders from the Comintern, followed an extreme policy, with the intention of undermining the Republican régime and the parties loyal to it, notably the S.P.D. The German Social-Democratic Party had long since ceased to be a revolutionary party, and its leadership lacked those qualities of boldness and toughness which were needed to make any effective resistance to the Nazis. Its virtues were mediocre, its mood one of caution, its tactics those of compromise. It is unlikely, even without the wrecking activities of the K.P.D., that the Social Democrats would have been able to prevent Hitler coming to power. But the Communists, far from helping to remedy these defects, far from supporting the efforts of the S.P.D. and the trade unions to preserve the Republic, deliberately set out to break up the only organisations which, whatever their shortcomings, offered a possible basis for the defeat of the Nazis. Hitler at any rate did not underrate the potentialities of the organised working-class movement. He gave its destruction the first priority after he came to power. His accomplices in this were the German Communists, who, up till and even after their own Party had been destroyed, continued to believe that it was more important to destroy the S.P.D., the trade unions, and the democratic system they supported than to join in common action to stop the Nazis. Convinced that they alone would be the heirs of the collapse of the Weimar Republic, unable to conceive of a revolution that was not theirs, they conscientiously sought to split and weaken the opposition to Hitler, and could only congratulate themselves on the removal of the democratic shams of the Republic and reformist Social Democracy. Such were the results of the Communist tactics in the years between 1928 and 1933.

VIII

But, while the existence of a strong Communist Party in Germany and the course it followed without doubt contributed to Hitler's successful rise to power, they were not the decisive factor. It is not convincing to argue that, but for the Communists, the Nazis would never have come to power. To maintain such a view would be not only to exaggerate the Communists' success, but to ignore the weakness of the democratic parties (including the S.P.D.), to underestimate the attractiveness of Hitler's nationalist and authoritarian appeal to millions of Germans, and above all to neglect the part played by those who put Hitler into power, the group of men round the President, right-wing politicians like von Papen and Hügenberg, the generals, the industrialists, the bankers, and the Junkers. The mistakes made by Hügenberg's Nationalist Party, the miscalculations of von Papen and the *Reichswehr* leaders were as great as those of the K.P.D., and, since they had greater power to influence events, more decisive. Even without the Communists to harass them, it is

unlikely that the leaders of the Social Democrats—or the Centre—
would have kept the Nazis out. Finally, if it be true that a majority
of the German people never voted for Hitler in a free election, it is
also true that the Nazis—in the free elections of July 1932—polled
more votes and got nearer to a majority than any other party since
the elections to the National Assembly in January 1919.

Later Communist pretensions to have led the fight against Nazism
will not bear examination in the light of the facts set out in this
article. They did all they could to weaken the opposition to Hitler
and to help the Nazis into power. Their contribution was considerable, but they were far from being the only people who contributed,
and the analysis of the political conditions favouring Hitler's rise to
power—while it must include the part played by the K.P.D. and the
Comintern—must also include the part played by a lot of other
people in the Germany of the early 1930s.

NOTE ON SOURCES

A. CONTEMPORARY SOURCES. The most important of these are
the publications of the K.P.D. and of the Comintern:

Imprecorr (International Press Correspondence), the German edition of which
was published in Berlin until 1933, after that in Basel under the title
of *Rundschau*.

The Communist International, the German edition of which was also published
in Berlin up to 1933, *Die Internationale, Zeitschrift für Theorie und Praxis
des Marxismus*.

Besides these two Comintern periodicals and the contemporary K.P.D.
press (e.g., *Die Rote Fahne*), there is important material in a number of party
reports:

Protokoll des 6 Weltkongresses der kommunistischen Internationale (Hamburg,
1929).
Bericht ueber die Verhandlungen des 12 Parteitages der K.P.D. (Berlin, 1929).

The official K.P.D. policy was put by Ernst Thälmann in a series of
pamphlets:

Was ist Sozialfaschismus? (Berlin, 1930).
Der Revolutionäre Ausweg und die K.P.D. (Berlin, 1932).
Wie schaffen wir die rote Einheitsfront? (Berlin, 1932).
In Kampf gegen die faschistische Diktatur (Berlin, 1932).
Kampfreden und Aufsätze (Berlin).

B. MEMOIRS. The most important account by an ex-Communist is
that of Ruth Fischer: *Stalin and German Communism* (Harvard University
Press, 1948). Although this deals with the period 1918–28, it throws considerable light on the period after 1928.

Among Social Democrats' memoirs may be mentioned:

Otto Braun, *Von Weimar zu Hitler* (New York, 1940).
Albrecht Grzesinski, *Inside Germany* (New York, 1939).
Friedrich Stampfer, *Die vierzehn Jahre der ersten Deutschen Republik*
(Offenbach a.M. 1947).
Carl Severing, *Mein Lebensweg*, Vol. 2 (Cologne, 1950).

C. SECONDARY WORKS. A careful and scholarly, but short, account of the K.P.D. has been published by Ossip K. Flechtheim, *Die Kommunistische Partei Deutschlands in der Weimarer Republik* (Offenbach a.M., 1948). A brief account of the German working-class movement is given by Evelyn Anderson, *Hammer or Anvil?* (London, 1945). The best discussion of Comintern Policy is Franz Borkenau's *The Communist International* (London, 1938) which devotes several chapters to the K.P.D. This can be supplemented by Arthur Rosenberg, *A History of Bolshevism* (Oxford, 1934) and by the few pages of chapter 5 of Max Beloff, *The Foreign Policy of Soviet Russia*, Vol. 1 (Oxford, 1947).

The fullest accounts of the events of 1930–33 in Germany are:

R. T. Clark, *The Fall of the German Republic* (London, 1935).
Konrad Heiden, *Der Führer, Hitler's Rise to Power* (London, 1944).
J. W. Wheeler-Bennett, *Hindenburg, The Wooden Titan* (London, 1936).
Alan Bullock, *Hitler, A Study in Tyranny* (London, 1952).

15

THE SEIZURE OF POWER

A. J. P. Taylor

NATIONAL-SOCIALISM was based on fraud; and no fraud was greater than the legend of the seizure of power, which was supposed to have taken place on 30th January 1933. Certainly this day, on which Hitler became Chancellor, was the most important moment in his life and a turning-point in German history. But there was no seizure of power. That had been tried by Hitler at Munich in November 1923. It had failed; and he was determined never to repeat the attempt. There was an alternative path to power which he sometimes contemplated: that the Nazi Party should actually win a majority of the popular vote and thus impose Hitler as Chancellor by strict democratic choice. But this alternative, too, proved beyond him. The Nazis never received more than 37 per cent of votes at a free election for the *Reichstag*. The third path, and that which Hitler followed, was the way of intrigue; he would become Chancellor as the leader of a minority and would then use the power of the State to establish his dictatorship. The answer to the question how Hitler came to power is therefore to be found more in the actions of those German politicians who were not National-Socialists than in those of Hitler himself. He waited; they decided.

The Weimar Republic always suffered from a multiplicity of parties. No single party ever possessed a majority in the *Reichstag*; and every German government after 1918 rested on a coalition. This would have mattered less if there had been at least a majority in favour of the Republic; but this, too, was lacking after the first elections in 1919. The middle-class Liberal parties faded and disappeared. Only the Social Democrats remained a genuine Weimar party. The Nationalists welcomed anything that weakened the Republic; the Communists welcomed anything that discredited the Social Democrats. The Roman Catholic Centre Party certainly took part in republican governments along with the Social Democrats; but it had no republican principles. It was a sectarian party, ready to work with any system that would protect Roman Catholic interests; and in the last days of the Republic it stretched out its hand to the forces of destruction, just as in the last days of the Empire it had turned to the republicans. Every party contributed to the fall of the

Weimar Republic—the Social Democrats from timidity, the others with conscious ill-will. But none contributed with such cynicism as the Centre—indifferent to the Republic or even to Germany, so long as the Roman Catholic schools enjoyed their favoured position.

The failure to establish strong stable governments brought unexpected power to the President. The makers of the constitution in 1919 had intended to give him the position of monarch in a parliamentary State choosing the Chancellor, but without independent authority in himself. The Chancellor was to be the heir of Bismarck, the true wielder of power. But the short-lived Chancellors never held this position. They were little more than parliamentary managers for the President. Even Ebert drew on his reserve of authority. Hindenburg, who became President in 1925, possessed it in greater measure and believed that his duty was to use it. Moreover, as the military leader of the World War, Hindenburg both commanded the allegiance of the army and voiced its demands. The army was the one stable point of order in an unstable society. It is a mistake to suggest, as some have done, that the army chiefs were bent on overthrowing the Republic. They would have attempted this only if the republican politicians had accepted permanently and sincerely the disarmament imposed upon Germany by the Treaty of Versailles; and none did so. The generals were willing to work with the Republic if it provided stable government. But this it failed to do; and the generals were obsessed with anxiety lest Germany's limited army, the *Reichswehr*, be called upon to intervene in civil strife. They did not make this civil strife, nor even welcome it. They were insistent that a civil solution should be found for it. That solution, they supposed, could only be strong government; and, since this was beyond the Republic, it must come in some other form. They were indifferent whether this form should be a presidial government (i.e., one resting on the authority of the President), monarchy, or dictatorship. Their overriding concern was to keep the army out of politics.

There was another impulse making for strong government between 1929 and 1933. These were the years of the great depression, which —starting in the United States—carried unemployment and financial collapse across the world. Keynesian economics were unknown, at least among public men; and it was universally supposed that, when men lacked the money to buy goods, the answer to the crisis was to deprive them even of the little money that they had. When, in the autumn of 1931, the British National Government unwillingly abandoned the gold standard, and so stumbled on the path to recovery, a former Labour minister exclaimed plaintively: 'No one told us we could do this!' His ignorance was universally shared. The only solution proposed was the reduction of wages and unemployment benefit; and for this a strong government was needed. Moreover, in times of bewilderment and distress, men demand authority for its own sake. They have no idea what should be done, but they long for a commanding voice which will resolve their doubts. Here again it is a mistake to suppose that Germany's economic leaders were consciously set on overthrowing the Republic or destroying the trade unions. They would have accepted a republican leader if one had appeared with unquestioned authority and self-confidence, just as Franklin D. Roosevelt was accepted by the business leaders of the U.S.A. But they demanded strong government from somebody; and they were rightly convinced that the Republic could not provide it.

This, then, is the background of Hitler's rise to power. Far from his hammering at a door which was long kept closed against him, he was constantly being invited to enter by those within; and he held back in order to increase his market value. Everyone assumed that he would end up as Chancellor sooner or later. The real problem in German history is why so few of the educated, civilised classes recognised Hitler as the embodiment of evil. University professors; army officers; business-men and bankers—these had a background of culture, and even of respect for law. Yet virtually none of them exclaimed: 'This is anti-Christ'. Later, they were to make out that Hitler had deceived them and that the bestial nature of National-Socialism could not have been foreseen. This is not true. The real character of National-Socialism was exposed by many foreign, and even by some German, observers long before Hitler came to power. It could be judged from Hitler's writings and his speeches; it was displayed in every street brawl that the Nazi Brown Shirts organised. Hitler did not deceive the responsible classes in Germany: they deceived themselves. Their self-deception had a simple cause: they were engaged in fighting the wrong battle and in saving Germany from the wrong enemy. Hitler's hostility to Communism was his strongest asset. The Bolshevik peril in Germany had once perhaps been real; therefore anyone who was anti-Communist seemed to be on the side of civilisation, and the Communists themselves fed this illusion by treating Hitler as their only serious enemy. 'Better Hitler than Communism' was the phrase which opened the way for Hitler first within Germany and then on a wider scale in Europe.

Further, the directors of German policy were obsessed with the struggle against the Treaty of Versailles. They regarded the disarmament clauses as a personal humiliation; and they genuinely believed, though without justification, that reparations were the cause of Germany's economic difficulties. They could not repudiate wholeheartedly a movement which raged against the Versailles system. Rather they welcomed it as an ally. Every advance of National-Socialism strengthened the argument that Germany should receive concessions in foreign affairs—otherwise the National-Socialists would get stronger still. And the argument was not without force. Can any English or French observer honestly maintain that reparations would have been ended or the Rhineland evacuated without the mounting shadow of Hitler? Even apart from questions of foreign policy, respectable Germans—especially army officers—were bound to look with favour on a movement equipped with uniforms and acting under military discipline. More than one general remarked: 'It would be a shame to have to fire on these splendid young men in their brown shirts'. Experience in other countries has repeatedly shown that the only answer to a Fascist Party, with an organised private army, is to suppress it by force of law. The Red peril and the system of Versailles made it impossible to give this answer in Germany.

Even so, the lack of alarm among civilised Germans remains a strange puzzle. The explanation may perhaps be found in the taste which so many of them had for political intrigue. A country with a long constitutional history develops a political class. The politicians look after government. The generals and bankers and professors mind their own business. This has always been true in England; and it was largely true in the third French republic, despite an occasional political general. In Germany men were always coming in from outside; a political class never had a chance to develop. Even Bismarck was a gifted amateur, who knew nothing of politics until he started at the top. Of his successors as Imperial Chancellor, one was a general, one a diplomatist, one a civil servant. In the reign of Wilhelm II generals like Waldersee and Ludendorff pushed into politics on one side; and business-men like Ballin or Rathenau pushed in on the other. The practice was maintained in the Weimar Republic. There was no true statesman in Germany after the death of Stresemann in 1929. Her fate was in the hands of amateurs, who mistook intrigue for political activity. Hindenburg, the President, was a retired professional soldier, a Field-Marshal over eighty years old. Brüning, who became Chancellor in 1930, was half scholar, half army captain, but never strictly a party leader. Papen, his successor, was a dashing cavalry-man of great wealth, with no political standing. Schleicher, the most influential of all, lived for intrigue and nothing else: claiming to represent army opinion with the President and the President's authority to the army, but in fact playing off one against the other. All four thought that they were a great deal cleverer than Hitler and that they would take him prisoner in no time. They never feared Hitler or took precautions against him. Indeed, the fact that he was a politician and the leader of a political party made them despise him, as they despised the other politicians. The Austrian generals of the old régime made much the same mistake when they came up against Bonaparte.

Intrigue took the place of politics when Brüning became Chancellor in March 1930. The previous republican governments claimed to rest on a majority of the *Reichstag*, even though the claim was not always justified. Brüning did not attempt to construct a parliamentary Cabinet. He relied on the authority of the President and ordered the *Reichstag* to vote for him, much as Bismarck had done in his great days. The *Reichstag* had not always responded to Bismarck's commands; it was even less likely to be overawed by Brüning. In July 1930 his measures were defeated; and the *Reichstag* was dissolved. Political theorists in other countries with a multiplicity of parties often lament that the executive cannot threaten parliament with dissolution. The German example shows that the remedy can be worse than the disease. General elections may provide a solution when they are contested by two strong parties. But the voter cannot be expected to solve the riddle that has baffled his leaders. A dissolution could have only one effect in the existing circumstances. The voters were told by Brüning, the Chancellor, that all the parties were equally factious and difficult. Many voters therefore turned to the political leader who said exactly the same. And this leader was Hitler. The National-Socialist Party had been an insignificant group in the previous *Reichstag*. It was inflated and artificially fostered by the repeated electoral campaigns of the two years that followed. How otherwise could the voters respond to Brüning's demand and return a *Reichstag* of a different character? If there had been no 'Brüning experiment', and hence no general election in September 1930; if Germany had struggled on with weak coalition governments throughout the great depression, the National-Socialist party would never have won at the polls and Hitler would never have triumphed.

The election of September 1930 brought great gains to the National-Socialists, and only slightly smaller gains to the Communists. It lessened Brüning's chance of achieving a parliamentary majority. Even now there was plenty of time for the forces of order and decency to unite against National-Socialist barbarism. But Hitler's victory elated the political jugglers, instead of frightening them. They imagined that they could use the threat of National-Socialism against the other parties in the *Reichstag* without ever being endangered themselves; and they even hoped that Hitler would be obliging enough to act as their agent. Brüning depended on the authority of President Hindenburg; but the President's term ran out in 1932. At the beginning of the year Brüning proposed a bargain to Hitler: Hindenburg's term should be prolonged for one or two years; then Brüning would resign, and the way would be clear for Hitler. Brüning's calculation was clear. Hitler was to perform a service now in exchange for a reward that might never have to be paid. Hitler's answer was equally clear: Brüning must be dismissed and a new *Reichstag* elected (with, no doubt, a larger Nazi representation); then he would support a prolongation of Hindenburg's term. In other words, he must have his price before he would perform his service. The negotiations broke down. A presidential election was held, with Hitler as candidate of the Nazis and the Nationalists, Hindenburg—absurdly enough—as the candidate of the Left, including the Social Democrats. Hindenburg was elected. The voters had rejected National-Socialism; but they had not supported anything, except a figure-head of eighty-five. The problem of finding a strong government, based on a *Reichstag* majority, remained.

Brüning did not recognise this problem. He proposed to remain in office and to continue to govern with the support of the President and the *Reichswehr*. But this programme was rejected by the generals and, above all, by Schleicher, their political spokesman; they were determined not to be drawn into the conflict of parties. Brüning and Gröner, his Minister of Defence, thought that they could now act against Hitler. On 14th April 1932 the Nazi armed forces were dissolved by decree. On 12th May Schleicher told Gröner that the *Reichswehr* had no confidence in him; and the following day he resigned. A fortnight later, on 30th May, Brüning also resigned, on Hindenburg's order. The old man had been persuaded that Brüning was the sole obstacle to a deal with Hitler and so to a government with a democratic majority. The instrument chosen for this deal was Franz von Papen, a wealthy aristocrat of no sense, though much courage. Schleicher said of him: 'People sometimes say that Herr von Papen is frivolous. But that is what we need.' And Papen characterised himself when he asked an economist for a programme: 'I know nothing of economics, but I'll do what you suggest. I'm a gentleman-rider; and I'll jump, I'll jump.'

Papen, like Brüning, was a member of the Centre Party, though, unlike Brüning, he carried no weight in it. Schleicher did not understand this. He supposed that the Centre would support Papen and, with Hitler supporting him as well, the 'functioning *Reichstag*' would be made. This scheme at once broke down. The Centre insisted that Hitler must take real responsibility, not exercise influence behind the scenes; failing this, they opposed Papen's Government. Hitler, on his side, demanded power; and he, too, continued in opposition when this was refused. Papen's was perhaps the weakest government that has ever ruled a great country—a Cabinet of elderly 'Barons' and no support at all in the *Reichstag*. This did not worry Papen. He was content to wait until Hitler came to heel. And Hitler also waited until Papen's difficulties swept him away. Both gambled on Germany's distress—the one a vain intriguer, the other the greatest demagogue of modern times. In June, Papen dissolved the *Reichstag*, not with any hope of getting support for himself, but solely as a demonstration to Hitler that he could wear him down. The Nazi election funds would not last for ever; and, besides, the voters might turn elsewhere if Hitler failed to achieve anything.

The election of 31st July gave Hitler his greatest success: 37·3 per cent of the votes cast. But he was still far from an independent majority, and the Nazi rate of increase was slowing down. In fact, as the next election showed, the tide had already turned. The bargaining of May was renewed. Hitler demanded full power; himself as Chancellor, other Nazis in all the key posts. It is true that he was prepared to include also some non-Nazis and asked only 'as much power as Mussolini got in 1922'. Papen and Schleicher were not well-grounded in current history. They only knew that Mussolini was dictator of Italy, and forgot the slow process by which he had reached that position. In any case, the analogy was revealing enough: however Hitler began, he, too, would end as dictator, and they were only prepared to employ him as their parliamentary agent. They offered Hitler the post of Vice-Chancellor, safely under Papen's control. On 13th August Hitler was summoned to appear before Hindenburg. The President rated him for the violence and illegality of the Nazi Party. 'He was ready to accept Hitler in a coalition government . . . but he could not take responsibility for giving exclusive power to Hitler alone'. Hitler tried to repeat that he wanted 'only as much as Mussolini'. The fatal analogy roused Hindenburg's anger.

The interview of 13th August was the sharpest set-back that National-Socialism ever received. Until then its prestige and the votes cast for it had been growing steadily. Hitler had spoken openly of the seizure of power and of the 'St Bartholomew's night' that would follow. Now it was clearly established that the so-called national revolution could take place only with the permission of the President. And that permission had been refused. Papen's gamble seemed to be working. Many of the lesser Nazis lost heart. Some worried over their security as deputies; a few over the future of the party. Hitler's great triumph lay in the iron control over his party which he managed to maintain during the next few months. If it had once begun to crumble, he would have been left isolated in a very short time. It is in this sense that Hitler was brought to power by his gifts for leadership. The National-Socialist party was never strong enough to force Hitler into power; but he never needed to look over his shoulder. The other politicians worried about their followers and their voters; and worry breaks a politician's nerve sooner or later. Hitler always assumed that his control of the Party was unshakable—rather as Napoleon always assumed that he would win a battle, and therefore never wasted men in securing a line of retreat.

But for the moment it was Papen who went over to the offensive. On 12th September the *Reichstag* was again dissolved; and Germany was involved in yet another general election, in order to wear down the National-Socialists. The results, which came in on 6th November, seemed to confirm Papen's calculation. The Nazis lost two million votes; their share of the total fell to 33 per cent and their deputies from 230 to 196. It was less encouraging that most of these votes were transferred to the Communists, who increased their representation to 100. Still, Papen hoped to repeat his manœuvre of August under more favourable conditions: Hitler should be offered office without power, under strict control, in order to save himself from further decline. On 16th November Hitler again refused. Papen then swung over to his alternative line: he would show that no one was capable of producing a parliamentary majority, and would then transform his temporary dictatorship into a permanent one. Instead of again dissolving the *Reichstag*, he would govern without it. On 17th November Papen resigned, ostensibly to give Hitler his chance. The step was meant as a pretence; for Hitler could obviously not produce a *Reichstag* majority. He came again to Hindenburg, this time in a rather more friendly atmosphere. But the deadlock remained. Hindenburg would make Hitler Chancellor if he could offer 'a secure workable majority in the *Reichstag* with a coherent programme'. Hitler demanded to be made Chancellor on the same terms as Papen—governing, that is, on the President's authority. Hindenburg refused. With Hitler as Chancellor, the cabinet would not be a presidential government, but a party dictatorship. The future was to prove him right.

Papen seemed to have played his cards correctly. He could now resume office without being open to the reproach of barring the way against a majority cabinet. On 1st December he went to Hindenburg with his plan: he would prorogue the *Reichstag*, proclaim a state of emergency, and govern by decree. If there was opposition from Nazis or Communists, he would crush it by force. But this was the very proposal for involving the *Reichswehr* in civil strife which the generals had always rejected. Schleicher opposed Papen's scheme, both as Hindenburg's military adviser and as spokesman of the army. Besides, he claimed, he could succeed where Brüning and Papen had failed: he could provide a parliamentary majority. He had been negotiating with Nazi leaders, such as Gregor Strasser, who were dissatisfied with Hitler's rigid line; and he believed, as well, that he could win the support of the trade unions. The Social-Democrats, the Centre, and the dissident Nazis would give him a workable coalition. Hindenburg preferred Papen to Schleicher; and he authorised him to form a government.

But Schleicher soon carried the day. On 2nd December the new cabinet met. Schleicher produced a report from Major Ott of the General Staff, which asserted that the *Reichswehr* could not do what Papen wanted. The Poles might seize the chance of internal disturbance in Germany to attack her eastern frontier; and 'defence of the frontiers and the maintenance of order against both Nazis and Communists was beyond the strength of the forces at the disposal of the Federal and State Governments'. The *Reichswehr* was, no doubt, a limited force; yet it had managed to maintain internal order in 1920 and 1923, when the chance of Polish intervention had been much greater. Even now there is little doubt that the *Reichswehr* would have been prepared to act if it had been agains the Communists alone. But the Nazis, whatever their violence, were a 'national' element. This was the underlying sentiment of Ott's memorandum. Papen was still ready to face the risk, but his colleagues were reluctant, and Hindenburg still more so. He said to Papen: 'I am too old and have been through too much to accept the responsibility for a civil war. Our only hope is to let Schleicher try his luck.' Schleicher became Chancellor the same day.

His luck turned out to be a poor resource. He offered to make Strasser Vice-Chancellor; and Strasser was willing to accept. But he could not carry the Nazi Party with him. Hitler forbade any bargaining with Schleicher; and Strasser lost his nerve. On 8th December he went off to Italy for a holiday. Hitler reasserted his domination over the party and determined once more to 'throw the whole party into the struggle'. Strasser's abortive revolt and failure actually strengthened Hitler's appeal to the propertied classes; for he could claim to have shaken off the extreme, Socialist wing of his party. Nazi finances were in a bad state. Even Goebbels had a feeling of 'dark hopelessness'. But Hitler's resolution was strong as ever; and this time he was justified. Schleicher's feeble attempts at coalition had broken down. What is more, Papen—though out of office—continued to live next door to Hindenburg and continued to busy himself in political intrigue. He would have been less than human it he had not wanted his revenge on Schleicher; and while the latter had failed with Strasser, himself hoped to succeed with Hitler. On a more elevated plane, he could make out to be still pursuing the bargain with Hitler which had been everyone's object for the last two years. Papen and Hitler met, more or less secretly, on 4th January 1933. Papen, according to his own account, merely urged—in the most disinterested way—that Hitler should become Vice-Chancellor in Schleicher's Government. Schroeder, the Cologne banker in whose house the meeting was held, gives a different and more likely story. Hitler insisted on becoming Chancellor, though with Papen and his friends as ministers; in particular he did not ask for control of either the army or foreign affairs. Papen thought that he had performed the miracle: he had taken Hitler prisoner, figurehead of a respectable non-Nazi Cabinet. Wealthy Germans drew the same conclusion. Subscriptions began to flow into the Nazi funds. Goebbels noted: 'The financial situation has improved very suddenly'.

Schleicher did not realise that the position had changed. Once in office, he thought, like Brüning and Papen before him, that he had only to issue orders for the crisis to disappear. It soon ceased to worry him that his political combinations collapsed. Gregor Strasser turned out to be a broken reed: he could not carry a single National-Socialist with him. The Social Democrats and the trade unions were not won over. Like everyone else, they seem to have come round to the view that office was the best means of taming Hitler; and they still imagined that they could resist him if he attempted anything illegal. On the other hand, the extreme Right, though they distrusted Hitler, were alienated by the steps Schleicher had taken to conciliate the Social Democrats. The *Reichstag* was due to meet on 31st January. Its first subject for discussion was the *Osthilfe*—the subsidies to landowners in eastern Germany, which had involved many scandals reaching even to Hindenburg himself. On 28th January Schleicher had to confess to Hindenburg that he could not control the *Reichstag*; and he asked, as his two predecessors had done, for a decree dissolving it. This was the very policy of governing Germany by force which Schleicher had rejected when it had been put forward by Papen in December. Hindenburg liked Papen and, by now, disliked Schleicher. He refused the decree of dissolution. Schleicher then claimed that he could produce a parliamentary majority by negotiating with the National-Socialists. But this was exactly what he had failed to do during the last six weeks. Moreover, Hindenburg knew, as Schleicher did not, that Papen could do it more successfully. Schleicher was dismissed; and Papen was entrusted with the formation of a new government.

A single pattern ran through all the negotiations from the fall of Brüning, or even before, to the accession of Hitler. The President and his confidential advisers worked persistently for a coalition government, in which Hitler would provide the votes and would yet be held in check by his associates. There was never any attempt to build a coalition government which would exclude Hitler or the National-Socialist party; and the delay came from Hitler, not from the side of the respectable classes. Now Hitler agreed to come in. It is impossible to say what led him to compromise. Perhaps he recognized that the Nazi tide was ebbing; perhaps he felt that the old order was now sufficiently weakened and would crumble of itself; perhaps the position of Chancellor, even under Papen's control, made the difference. More probably, his decision sprang from his unconscious sense of timing, just as a great general might find it difficult to explain why he flung in his reserves at the critical moment.

On 30th January Hitler became Chancellor. This was far from a seizure of power. Indeed, the forces of the old order imagined that they had seized Hitler. Though he was Chancellor, there were only three Nazis in a Cabinet of eleven; the two key posts of Foreign Minister and Minister of Defence were in the hands of non-political agents of the President; and Hitler could not see Hindenburg except in the presence of Papen, who was Vice-Chancellor. No arrangement could have been neater or more cynical. Yet it broke down within the first few days. What Hitler appreciated and his conservative associates did not was that, while the Nazi Party was not strong enough to seize power when the forces of the State were hostile, it was strong enough to do so once these forces were neutral or on its side. Papen remarks regretfully that 'existing institutions and parties gave up without a fight'. What else could they do? They might have resisted the Nazis if the police and the courts were there to maintain order. They could no longer do so when the police were under Nazi control and when, therefore, the defence of democracy took on a revolutionary character. Again, Hitler had been crippled by the fact that he did not possess a majority in the *Reichstag*; this had driven him to accept Papen's terms. But once in office he could argue that a further general election would give him a majority; and, since this had been the object of all the negotiations, his demand for a dissolution could not be refused. This time Hitler supposed that he could indeed deliver the parliamentary majority which had hitherto evaded everybody. Once the National-Socialists dominated the *Reichstag*, he could shake off Papen and the other elderly gentlemen who controlled him, and establish a Nazi dictatorship by law.

Hitler's calculation did not succeed. The election campaign was conducted with every weapon of Nazi terror; and the burning of the *Reichstag* building on 27th February enabled Hitler to declare the Communist Party illegal. Nevertheless on 5th March the National-Socialists secured only 43·9 per cent of the votes. Even with the co-operation of the right-wing Nationalists they had only a bare majority—enough to control the *Reichstag* from day to day, but not enough to carry through any fundamental change in the constitution. Hitler, however, was set on an Enabling Law which would give him all the powers of a dictator. If the so-called democratic parties had held together, Hitler would have been driven to illegal action— or would have remained powerless. The Communists had been driven underground. The Social Democrats, though feeble in action, held nobly to their principles and voted against the Enabling Law, despite the threats of terror against them. The decision rested on the Centre, with its 102 votes. The leaders of the Centre were

s

men of personal courage. But their Party cared little for democracy; it was concerned only to secure the position of the Roman Catholic schools. It had a long tradition of doing this by intriguing with successive parties and governments; it had long lost the tradition of resistance which had once enabled it to defeat Bismarck. The Centre leaders were fobbed off with promises from Hitler in which they only half believed; and on 23rd March the Centre votes were cast in favour of the Enabling Law. These votes alone gave Hitler's dictatorship its legal character.

One barrier remained: Hindenburg's veto, and Hitler's promise that he would do nothing to override it. But Hitler, who had wooed millions of voters, did not find it difficult to cajole an old man, never mentally acute and now senile. Papen soon found that he was not needed when Hitler had his interviews with the President. He went on dreaming that some day Hindenburg would reassert his independence and that the Nazis would be overthrown—again under Papen's direction. He waited patiently, as he had waited before. And fifteen months later he thought that his chance had come. On 17th June 1934 Papen delivered at Marburg the only public speech against the Nazi dictatorship ever made in Germany after Hitler's seizure of power. Even now his line was equivocal. His appeal was to Hitler to behave better, rather than to Hindenburg and the generals to overthrow him. In any case, Hitler was soon able to outbid Papen's feeble gesture. He, too, had his difficulties with the Nazi extremists—the leaders of the Brown Shirts who wanted to carry through a real social revolution now that their Party was in power. He broke them in the blood-bath of 30th June. This seemed a guarantee to the generals that there would be no demagogic interference with the army. Hitler was already promising them rearmament on a great scale. Why, then, should they resist him for the sake of democracy or the constitution? This would be the very interference in politics which they had always rejected.

On 2nd August 1934, Hindenburg died. The army leaders were content that Hitler should take his place. Within an hour of Hindenburg's death, the office of President was merged with that of Chancellor; and Hitler became undisputed Head of the State. He kept his bargain with the army. For three and a half years it remained autonomous, standing outside politics and repudiating all responsibility for the Nazi terror. Early in 1938 Hitler overthrew this balance. He was now moving towards an aggressive war in Europe; and he could tolerate no independent authority. The army leaders were discredited by a series of personal scandals, some of them without foundation. Hitler dismissed those who stood out against him; made himself head of the armed forces, the *Wehrmacht*; and at the same time put his agent, Ribbentrop, in the Foreign Office in place of Neurath. The seizure of power was complete in February 1938. It had taken Hitler four years to destroy legality in Germany by legal means.

If we look back over this wretched story, we see a man bent on success on the one side, and a group of politicians without ideas or principles on the other. Hitler was resolved to gain power. He did not know how he would do it, and he tried many means which failed; but he had an unbreakable purpose. The others were only concerned to strike a bargain with him. If there had been a strong democratic sentiment in Germany, Hitler would never have come to power—or even to prominence. He would have failed even if the weak democratic parties had held together. He had two great weapons. He could promise the generals a great army, if they let him in; he could threaten civil disturbance, if they kept him out. The promise was more potent than the threat. One can blame all the parties in turn. The Communists started the habit of violence and disrupted the working-class front. The Social Democrats had lost all ability to act and faith in their strength. The Centre would bargain with anybody, even with Hitler. But the greatest responsibility lay with those who let Hitler in and established him as Chancellor. Hitler recognised it himself. In 1938 Papen, then German ambassador at Vienna, accompanied Schuschnigg to the fateful interview at Berchtesgaden which ended Austrian independence. In the course of the argument, Hitler turned to Papen and said: 'By making me Chancellor, Herr von Papen, you made possible the National-Socialist revolution in Germany. I shall never forget it.' And Papen answered with soldierly pride: 'Certainly, my *Führer*.'

NOTE ON SOURCES

THE political events preceding 30th January 1933 are now well-documented, though there are still some disputed points. Konrad Heiden gives a detailed account in *Der Führer* (1944), which is substantially accurate, despite some ingenious guess-work. The most recent scholarly account is in Alan Bullock, *Hitler* (1952). This has also an excellent bibliography. It is therefore no longer necessary to use earlier, more sensational studies, which attributed Hitler's victory to a capitalist conspiracy.

Brüning gave his version of events to J. W. Wheeler-Bennett soon after his fall; and this is reproduced in *Hindenburg, The Wooden Titan* (1936), which also deals with Hindenburg's death and testament. A rather different version appears in 'Ein Brief' which Brüning published after the war in *Deutsche Rundschau* for July 1947. There is also some admirable material in an article on 'The *Reichswehr* and National Socialism', which Gordon Craig published in *Political Science Quarterly*, lxiii.

G. Castellan, 'Von Schleicher, von Papen et l'avènement de Hitler' in *Cahiers d'Histoire de la Guerre*, No. 1, uses French and German material. Papen wrote an elaborate defence on his conduct in his *Memoirs* (1952). His story is not always confirmed by other accounts. Schleicher was killed before he could go on record, and his motives have to be guessed from his actions and from the accounts of others. A great deal of material was brought out at the trials of the war-criminals at Nuremberg, but it has not yet been put into a form useful for historians. The most important testimony was by Papen, Schacht, Schroeder, and Meissner, Hindenburg's secretary. Oskar von Hindenburg, the President's son, also gave evidence at a later trial. But of course the principal object of witnesses was to exculpate themselves, not to provide historical material.

It was not Hitler's habit to explain his policy or course of action. But he gave an account in conversation of what happened just before 30 January. It is reproduced in *Hitler's Table Talk* (1953).

PART THREE

16

AN ECONOMIC AND SOCIAL DIAGNOSIS OF NATIONAL-SOCIALISM

Louis R. Franck

THE present study is concerned with the techniques which the German National-Socialist movement used to exploit the economic and social environment from which it sprang, in which it had evolved and which, for a moment, it dominated. Modern dictatorships did not grow up in a vacuum. They had to take the strictest account of the strength, the psychology, the methods, and the tactics of the determined adversaries whom they had to overcome, as well as of those of the hesitant or doubtful sections of the population which they had to reassure and carry along with them; i.e., the principal social groups of their time, among which the labour unions of every colour and their political spokesmen were the most important. As a diagnosis of National-Socialism in its period of growth before its seizure of power the present study will analyse its offensive tactics against the traditional economic and social groups, and will also consider the defensive tactics of these groups. We will study their deficiencies and confusions which were to facilitate, if not entirely account for the rise of totalitarianism. National-Socialism was strongly influenced by the instability of the world in which it grew up, and the attitude of the traditional social groups towards National-Socialism was to exert a considerable influence on it. Our diagnosis, therefore, will recall many of National-Socialism's criticisms and destructive practices, but it will also deal with the many promises or pseudo-promises of constructive action which it made. To what extent were these promises honoured? If this diagnosis is to help the detection of comparable movements, perhaps a rapid analysis of previous results might serve as a useful warning for those who might be attracted by similar promises in the future. In any case this analysis will be succinct, and our diagnosis will be the most important part of this contribution.

The outstanding factors which explain or surround the rise of National-Socialism would appear to be:

1. The German social structure.
2. The economic crisis and its political consequences.

3. Unemployment.

4. The fight against Socialism and traditional liberalism and the personification of this fight in the Prussian spirit.

5. The violent opposition between Communists and Socialists.

6. The profound impact made by Hitler himself.

1. In the first place the social structure. The great landlords played a determining role in Hitler's rise to power, as did also the large industrial cartels and the great basic industries. Around 1925 the agricultural population in Germany was only 23 per cent of the total population. The agrarian scene was characterised both by a considerable proletariat and by a system of large private properties; there were about 2,607,000 agricultural workers, as opposed to 2,202,000 private owners. Farms of more than 100 hectares accounted for 20 per cent of all the cultivated land, but these *latifundia* were roughly grouped in a small number of large regions: East Prussia, Pomerania, Brandenburg, southern Silesia, Mecklenburg-Schwerin, and Saxony. [1]

When confronted with this large rural proletariat, the defensive reaction of the medium and large proprietors was fairly similar and easily understandable. The pressure they exerted first on the pre-totalitarian governments and later on the dictatorial régime was the result of necessity—the result equally of psychological, social, and economic anxieties.

But, above all, Germany is a country of great industrial cartels. In 1925 more than 40 per cent of the working German population was in industry and the crafts. At that time less than 2 per cent of all the industrial units employed more than fifty people and accounted for about 55 per cent of all wage-earners. In 1932, at the eve of Hitler's rise to power, 192 corporations, each with a capital of over 20,000,000 R.M., were able on their own account to capitalise more than 13 milliards, or 54 per cent of the total capital employed in all public and private companies. During the period of inflation from 1922 to 1923 and in that of rationalisation from 1926 to 1928, and later in the years of crisis and unemployment from 1929 to 1932, the influence of heavy industry was all-important.

2. The German totalitarian régime expanded in a climate of economic crises; in fact the gestation of Hitlerism was accompanied by a mounting crescendo of crises: inflation, rationalisation, and the depression itself, all inflicted appalling blows on the social structure of the country. The inflation which started in 1919 as a trivial economic and monetary phenomenon rapidly became a moral

---

[1] *Statistisches Jahrbuch für das deutsche Reich*, 1932, pp. 20, 51, and following. 0·37 per cent of all the holdings of more than 100 hectares accounted for 20·1 of the total area. Thus 58 per cent of the holdings in Mecklenburg were of more than 100 hectares, in Pomerania 50 per cent, and in East Prussia 40 per cent.

disaster. If, on the one hand, it freed industry from its debts and seemed to facilitate the illusory conquest of the great world markets, it equally ruined the traditional middle classes and reduced them to the status of the proletariat. The rationalisation which followed was based on two movements—an uninterrupted expansion and growth of international outlets and an uninterrupted injection of foreign credit, mostly from America. During the five years from 1924 to 1928 we can estimate that 39 milliards of German R.M. were invested in the German economy, which became rapidly over-equipped. In January 1929 the number of unemployed was 3 millions, and by January 1932 it had mounted progressively to the frightening figure of 6·1 millions. The index of production fell from 100 in 1928 to 61 in the first quarter of 1931. The German crisis was on the same scale as the American crisis, just as the German rationalisation also had been on an American scale. One of the foremost students of Germany thus described the birth of National-Socialism:

'It is generally admitted that Hitlerian National-Socialism rose from the middle classes which had been reduced to working-class status by the inflation of 1923 and the crisis of 1929–32 which followed on four years of false economic recovery; and that it spread on the one hand to the oligarchy of the right which needed it to fight Marxism and the proletarian organisations, and on the other hand to the proletariat itself which had been hit by unemployment and partially reduced to the status of a "fifth estate" and which turned in its despair to a nationalism which described itself as both socialist and German. There is much truth in this outline.' [1]

3. Up to a certain point the unemployment which was the most pathetic manifestation of the crisis, confirmed the theory of German over-population or, if one prefers, of the proletarian nation. A quotation from Moeller van den Bruck's famous book *Das Dritte Reich* underlines the point:

'Socialism has never given a moment's thought to the problem of over-population. It seems never to have noticed this most serious of all social problems which became important in Germany in the eighties, when it was evident, even if only from our large-scale immigration, that we had become what Hans Grimm was to call "A people without *Lebensraum*".'

[1] Edmond Vermeil, *L'Allemagne. Essai d'explication* (Gallimard, Paris, 1940), p. 301. In the same way: 'the German people of that time was nothing else but an extremely impoverished feudal oligarchy, an aristocratic and *bourgeois*, agrarian and industrial oligarchy confronted with two immense camps, each of which represented about one half of the population: the middle classes on the one hand and the proletariat on the other.'

'German Social-Democracy dodged all the demographic difficulties of an over-populated nation with the help of Malthusian
prescriptions and the evasions of free-thinkers and free-traders,
and when non-Socialists from time to time stressed the difficulties,
they enunciated liberal but absolutely non-Socialist points of view.'

4. On a more philosophical level it was equally a period of
repudiation: repudiation of democratic liberalism and humanitarian
socialism, which, despite their apparent antagonism, were seen as
the two sides of a materialism which was hedonistic, individualist,
and anthroprocentric: repudiation of free trade unionism, of the right
to strike, and of the Marxist class struggle: repudiation of inter-
nationalisms, both capitalist and proletarian.

As against these great repudiations was opposed a private
economy dedicated to the service of the state and the directives of
the dictatorial power; the pseudo-social function of property, the
famous distinction between productive capital (*'schaffendes Kapital'*)
and exploiting capital (*'raffendes Kapital'*); the voluntary identification of the individual's ends with those of the government; the
compulsory fusion—or at least it was claimed as such—between
capital and labour within a corporative organization subservient to
the totalitarian régime and dedicated to the pursuit of autarchy and
the building up of a war economy. All this, according to a Spengler
or to a Moeller van den Bruck, was to be found in Prussia and their
theories were desperate affirmations of the universality of the Prussian
spirit. In German thought the Prussian example furnishes the model
of an autonomous, national, spontaneous socialism. Whether it was
a question of Werner Sombart's *Deutscher Sozialismus*,[1] of Oswald
Spengler's *Preussentum und Sozialismus*,[2] of Ernst Rudolph Huber's
Die Gestalt des deutschen Sozialismus,[3] of Moeller van den Bruck's
Socialismus und Aussenpolitik,[4] and so many others, the fundamental
idea was the same: each nation had the socialism proper to it;
Germany's was neither proletarian nor internationalist, nor egalitarian, nor materialist: it had to be national, hierarchic, and
military. Its ultimate aim was the aggrandisement of the German
people, as defined and attained by the German state. But was not
that precisely the ideal of Prussian civilisation? Spengler would
say that the 'freedom to obey' characterised the best Prussians; and
so this line of thought resulted in the Prussian army, the Prussian
administration, the Socialism of Bebel as opposed to that of Marx, and
as Moeller van den Bruck said:[5]

'Even today we still have Prussian Socialism which is based on
labour and which Spengler teaches is the essence of Socialism.'

[1] Buchholz und Weisswange Verlag, 1934.   [2] First published 1922.
[3] Hanseatische Verlagsanstalt, Hamburg, 1934.
[4] Wilhelm Gattl, Korn, Breslau ed., 1933.
[5] *Socialismus und Aussenpolitik*, p. 59.

5. The attitude of the two large workers' parties, Socialist and Communist, towards each other was no small contribution towards the final totalitarian victory, and is an important element in our diagnosis. It is now admitted that whether in power or opposition the Socialist Party failed to take advantage of the truly revolutionary moment which occurred at the end of the First World War, and failed to give the people who believed in it the dynamic action they had expected; and so through ineptitude the Socialists paved the way for the success of the demagogic gambits, both social and economic, of their opponents. The economic situation in Germany between 1930 and 1932, the unemployment and the fall in prices, however serious they were, were nevertheless probably amenable to a programme of reform of the New Deal type. German Social-Democracy could have effected such a programme rather than accept, in a spirit of bitter resignation, Chancellor Brüning's dangerous deflationary programme.

For their part the Communists, as faithful interpreters of dialectical materialism and convinced of the ultimate success of their cause, patiently waited for the proletarian revolution to emerge from the rising tide of totalitarian triumphs. As the Socialists competed with the Communists on their own ground and forced them, from 1920 to 1933, into various manœuvres, the Communists looked upon the Socialist-Democrats as their primary opponents and maintained that the downfall of the Socialists was the surest way of stopping dictatorship. Through its concern for legality (a reflection of its own instinct for self-preservation), the Communist Party discouraged armed resistance to the first totalitarian manifestations, and through its proletarian scruples firmly opposed any move towards a national union of workers, peasants, and middle-class which could have exalted the feeling of national solidarity of which the dictators claimed to have a monopoly.

The German Communists spoke out with a striking brutality. In this connection the programme put forward by their leader, Ernst Thälmann, in February 1932 to the Central Committee of the German Communist Party, is most significant. Speaking of the Brüning–Socialist coalition he writes:

'From now on, nobody can doubt that with the Brüning–Gröner régime in the Reich and its step-child Braun-Severing in Prussia, we are dealing with the evolution of a fascist movement; we were right, therefore, when in December 1930 we spoke of a fascist dictatorship which was ripening if not already ripe.'

He added:

'It is only by waging the most stringent battle now against the Brüning–Socialist policy, against, that is to say, the policy of a dictatorship of the *bourgeoisie*, that we can simultaneously wage a serious mass war against Hitler and Hügenberg.'

And as a final touch:

'The practical application of our strategy in Germany means a death-blow to social-democracy . . . for that represents the most active factor in the fascisisation of our country.' [1]

And this a year before Hitler came to power. . . .

6. Hitler's personal experience was that of a *declassé*. We know that there are all kinds of *declassés* in different countries, but this does not necessarily imply that these countries are threatened with imminent tyranny by this group: when, however, social and economic unrest reach a certain point, together with psychological and spiritual trouble which follow the calling in doubt of those principles which are the essential basis of national life, then the way is open for such *declassés* to assert themselves. Their experience is therefore an integral part of our economic and social diagnosis.

Hitler was not an ex-Socialist who turned against his party but a *petit bourgeois* who, in the economic and psychological instability of his adolescent years, conceived a neurotic repulsion for the trades union movement. From this point of view certain pages of *Mein Kampf* form a remarkable autobiographical document.

'I was brought up among the *petite bourgeoisie* which had little contact with real manual labourers. Strange as it may seem, the gulf which separates this under-privileged class from the world of the workers is bigger than one could believe. . . . They almost hate each other because those who have recently risen above the manual workers are frightened of falling back into a class they despise, or even of appearing still to belong to it. And then, let us remember all that is repugnant about these lower classes and their total lack of culture. If people, however modest, have once been saved from this lowest of social strata there is a shame about falling back into it even for a moment.'

In Vienna as a worker, although he was often unemployed and generally badly treated, he refused to become a union member.

'What most disgusted me about Social-Democracy was its hostility to any fight for the conservation of Germanism—its banal flirtation with our "Slav comrades". Having once come into contact with the practical results of their ideas, it took me only a few months . . . to understand what disease was concealed beneath the mask of social virtue and love of one's neighbour, and how important it was for mankind to get rid of such people if it was to survive at all. I was twenty when I was first able to distinguish

[1] Ernst Thälmann, *Der revolutionäre Ausweg*, Feb. 1932.

between the trade unions as the organs for the defence of the social rights of the workers and for better living conditions, and the unions as party tools in class warfare. . . . The free union will soon become one of the most appalling instruments of terror directed at the security and independence of national economy, the equilibrium of the state and individual liberty.'

It is not only his attachment to the middle-class party, so characteristic of Hitler, which had its origins in his first Viennese experience. At the same time the famous Dr Lüger, Mayor of Vienna and leader of the Social Christians, became an object of his admiration by openly adopting 'in the first instance, and as the basis of his new party, the threatened middle classes in order to assure himself of a solid following, ready for any sacrifice and full of enthusiasm for the fight. . . . He would devote the greater part of his political activity to gaining the adherence of these classes whose very existence was menaced.'

It is hard to imagine a more radical antagonism than that between Marxist Socialism, which considers the middle classes as a transitory social phenomenon, and Hitler's point of departure, which, on the contrary, makes them the basis of his future offensive.

I. Economic and Social Evolution (1918–33)

The three principal stages of the economic and social evolution of Germany between the Armistice of 1918 and Hitler's coming to power in January 1933 are: the inflation of the years 1921–3; the industrial rationalisation of 1926–8; and the crisis and unemployment of 1929–33. They gave rise to events which were on the scale of German industry, and they ran their course in a violent and brutal political and social climate which was in some sort characteristic of Germany at that time. Unemployment, the fall in production, the collapse of agricultural prices in the 'thirties were not particularly more severe in the Reich than they were in the America of Hoover: it is striking to observe the difference in the methods pursued, almost simultaneously, by Hitler's Germany and Roosevelt's United States with a view to solving problems whose strictly economic content was not essentially different.

1. INFLATION

The first post-war years are characterised, in Germany, by a strong resistance to the Left-wing constructive movements and the rapid failure of these movements; by the re-establishment of the socially privileged owners of big industry and large landed property; and, still more, by the inflation, which was destined to ruin the middle classes and consolidate the omnipotence of industry.

Following the Armistice, the Spartacist movements, making their bid for power on behalf of the Workers' and Soldiers' Councils, were rapidly destroyed; the Socialist administration in control of Berlin suppressed the attempts at revolution. 'Bolshevism', declared Noske on 13th January 1919, 'means the death of liberty, the death of peace, the death of Socialism, which intends to accomplish its task by constructive work and liberate the workers from all economic exploitation.' The strikes in the Ruhr in February and March failed; Spartacism was extinguished in Bavaria after May 1919.

Various Socialisation Commissions succeeded one another, but without being very effective: whether they were concerned with coal production or with industrial planning organised by evenly balanced commissions, as provided for, indeed, by Article 165 of the Weimar Constitution and desired by the great Walther Rathenau, nothing was destined to remain of them but empty phraseology. Towards the end of the year 1922, although the mass of the members of the various trade unions, free and Christian, was over 10 millions, the structural reforms had been definitely shelved, while numerous modifications of the eight-hour day were being made in practice.

The resistance to the revolutionary movements was accompanied by unprecedented acts of violence and brutality. According to E. J. Gumbel,[1] between the beginning of 1919 and June 1922 (the murder of Walther Rathenau took place on the 24th), 376 political crimes were committed in Germany, 354 of them by the Right-wing organisations and twenty-two by those of the Left; these crimes, more often than not, went unpunished or were dismissed with light penalties.

Karl Liebknecht and Rosa Luxemburg were assassinated on 15th January 1919, by Pflugk-Hartung, Runge, and Krull: the war tribunal responsible for the trial of the murderers did everything to save them. The first attempt on the life of the Catholic leader Mathias Erzberger took place in January 1920; he was assassinated on 26th August 1921 by Heinrich Schulz and Heinrich Tillesen: the head of the organisation to which these men belonged, Manfred von Killinger, was acquitted in February 1923 and was later, in 1929, to become National-Socialist deputy for Saxony. The Socialist leader Scheidemann and the famous journalist Maximilian Harden were also, in 1922, the victims of political or 'racist' outrages. Walther Rathenau was murdered on 24th June 1922 by Erwin Kern and Hermann Fischer, who attacked him with a machine-gun from a car belonging to a big industrialist of Saxony, Johann Küchenmeister, who was connected with the organisation *Schutz und Trutz*. The moving spirit of so many outrages, the

[1] E. J. Gumbel, *Les Crimes Politiques en Allemagne de 1919 à 1929* (Gallimard, Paris, 1931).

notorious Ehrhardt, was arrested at Munich in the spring of 1923, but escaped from prison and managed, not long afterwards, to invade Communist Thuringia with detachments of Bavarian police.

The murder of Kurt Eisner in Bavaria had already taken place, in February 1919;[1] in the following spring bands from North Germany penetrated into Bavaria, and their leaders, after having shot some fifteen Communists in the *Hofbrau*, were acquitted; the Bavarian Civic Guard, set up in the spring of 1920 by the Escherich and Kanzler organisations (*Orgesch und Orka*), was to be responsible for the assassination of the Independent Socialist Gareis.

The military *putsch* of Kapp and Luttwitz, in March 1920, failed, thanks to the general strike of the Berlin workers. But certain efforts to improve labour conditions, fomented by the agricultural workers of Mecklenburg, were ruthlessly punished by the bands of the Rossbach organisation, which lent their support to General von Lettow-Vorbeck and Baron von Brandenstein. In 1928 the Stettin tribunal legalised the repressive actions carried out by the Rossbach bands. These actions took the form of self-defence, self-protection against working-class aggression, in Mecklenburg, Pomerania, and the Ruhr. They attest, from the very start, the virulence of the class war in pre-Hitler Germany, and how far the ground was already prepared for the coming of the dictator.

The setting up, in April 1919, of the *Reichsverband der deutschen Industrie*, later united with the *Vereinigung der deutschen Arbeitgeberverbände*, bears witness to the vitality of the German industrialists' organisations on the morrow of the defeat. These organisations were firmly resolved not to accept any workers' control over industry and to whittle down considerably the eight-hour day. The conservative circles under the leadership of Hellferich carried on a furious campaign against Erzberger's fiscal schemes: a progressive tax on global income, taxes on industrial and commercial profits, taxes on income from capital, and death duties. It is striking to notice how, in Germany, opposition to increased taxation crystallised the opposition to liberal régimes. In the course of the years 1921 and 1922, spokesmen of heavy industry addressed a regular series of ultimata to the Governments and to Chancellor Wirth. Moreover, the elections in June 1920 constituted a real triumph for the conservative forces—the German National and Populist parties. According to M. Edmond Vermeil, close relations were established between the National-Socialists and the *Herrenhaus*, Count Behr and Count von Wartenburg in 1921; they were extended in 1922 to the North

---

[1] The murderer, Count Arco-Valley, was condemned to death on 20 Jan. 1920, had his sentence commuted, and was then set free, in 1924, to become director of the *Süddeutsche Lufthansa*.

German nationalists (von Gräfe) and to the industrialists of the West, such as von Borsig.

But it was above all the inflation of the years 1922–3 that was to exercise a decisive influence on the development of National-Socialism. In fact, German industry from 1920 onwards (and, indeed, did not statesmen as clear-sighted as Rathenau accept it?) desired inflation as a means of increasing its export trade. Between April and November 1922 the value of the dollar rose from 65 to 775 marks. The *Reichsbank*, directed by Rudolf Havenstein, was at that time at the beck and call of industry and pursuing a policy of cheap money; between the beginning and the end of 1922 the average market price of German securities was multiplied by fifteen, that of international loans by fifty-five; any attempt at a healthy financial policy, such as the establishment of a gold coverage, was rejected by the spokesmen of heavy industry.

These are the conditions in which the battle of the Ruhr was to begin. During the nine months it lasted, the collapse of the currency was made unavoidable but the prestige of the *Schwerindustrie* remained practically unaltered. Civil servants, people with savings, people with pensions, and workers were pitilessly ruined by the rise of prices and the inflation, while the consortiums, the cartels, and the masterpieces in vertical concentration of a Stinnes were being built up.

2. RATIONALISATION

The battle of the Ruhr, and the crises and reconstructions which followed, consolidated still further the social power of large-scale industry. During the weeks covered by the capitulation of the Reich in the Ruhr, industry had treated with the Government on equal terms. On 7th October 1923, Hugo Stinnes had insisted on a promise of full indemnification for the losses undergone in the Ruhr and of an increase in hours of work: this ultimatum, which followed the withdrawal of the Socialist ministers, was practically accepted by Stresemann. On 15th October the order setting up the *Rentenbank* consolidated the ruin of the victims of the inflation; a few months later, on 14th February 1924, the Government decided to exclude from all revalorisation the bearers of public bonds and to suspend the payment of interest on the Debt, thus consummating its open bankruptcy. Industry, having been enabled by the inflation to amortise its debts, was left the major beneficiary of the whole operation.

The years which followed were those of industrial rationalisation. In the reconstituted cartels the influence of the big firms increased; their directors did not conceal their aversion to democracy; on 5th February 1924, Thyssen declared: 'In Germany, democracy represents nothing,' and Albert Vögler called for the end of socialisation, of state control, and for encouragement to private enterprise. The Government's policy with regard to taxation and tariffs became entirely favourable to industry; and under colour of the limited crises of 1925–6 industry demanded retrenchment of public expenditure and an easier credit policy.

Rationalisation on American lines was introduced in Germany; the era of great business magnates began. 'It is', said Albert Vögler in September 1926, 'personalities that lead peoples, and masses are never the source of progress.' Herren Duisberg and Bosch for the chemical industry, Vögler, Flick, Thyssen, and Poensnagen for the steel industry, Simson and Koettgen for electricity, became the leaders of the renewed Germany.

'In three years [Max Hermant was to write] the output of the mines has doubled. That of the blast-furnaces has almost trebled. The Reich has beaten England and even the United States as an exporter of finished products. German savings have shown a clear improvement. The merchant navy has been reconstituted, the dividends paid by industrial firms are well above the 1913 level. Taking the position as a whole, Mr Parker Gilbert, writing in 1930, remarks that the increase in the means of production achieved by Germany since 1924 exceeds in value, several times, the amount of the external debt she has contracted.'[1]

The 1928 elections brought Social-Democracy back into power, and a coalition Cabinet, headed by the Socialist Chancellor Herman Müller, governed Germany until 1930.

3. THE CRISIS

From the autumn of 1929 onwards the first signs of the economic crisis began to appear. In its agricultural, industrial, banking, and social aspects it was destined to overthrow the very data of German political life.

The agricultural crisis was first and foremost a reflection of the world over-production of grain. The fall in grain prices had necessitated the imposition of higher and higher protective duties; this was the 'hothouse policy' (*Treibhauspolitik*) which maintained corn prices at a level far above world prices. Agricultural indebtedness (it was estimated at 13·8 thousand millions at the end of 1930, of which 4·8 were short-term) involved Government assistance, especially to help the farmers in East Germany: it was the *Osthilfgesetz* of 31st May 1931 that determined the distribution of considerable subsidies and whose administration was to provoke in

[1] Max Hermant, *Les Paradoxes Economiques de l'Allemagne Moderne, 1918–1931* (Colin, Paris, 1931), p. 154.

1932, under the Schleicher Government, keen polemics leading to the latter's fall.

The agrarians had, it seems, cleverly enlisted the interest of the aged Marshal von Hindenburg in their affairs by offering him, as early as 1927, the estate of Neudeck, the purchase of which had been financed with money from the industrialists by a friend of the Marshal's, von Oldenburg-Januschau. Their complaints therefore always found in him an attentive ear, every time a proposal for breaking up the big mortgaged properties and re-distributing them among the peasants came up. Januschau worked for the fall of Brüning in 1932. A few months later, the *Landbund*, formed of powerful agrarians, was to denounce Schleicher's policy in the same way: Count Kalkenreuth reproached him with ruining rural economy for the benefit of the 'exploiters of international export industries'.[1]

From the end of 1927 unemployment increased steadily: it reached 1·3 millions in July 1929, 2·8 millions a year later, 4 millions in July 1931, and 5·4 millions in July 1932. These figures apply to the totally unemployed and a large number of partially unemployed must be added. During the second half of 1930 industrial equipment was idle up to more than half its capacity; the enormous concentration of industry had naturally facilitated over-production and brought with it a bad use of the available savings. During the whole of this period the prices of the cartelised products were to fall little if at all—this was the case with the steel industry and coal—while those of goods for consumption and farm products were to collapse. Wages themselves showed great rigidity up to the beginning of 1931.

The crash of the principal Austrian credit house, the *Kredit Anstalt*, in July 1931, caused numerous withdrawals of capital. On 13th July the *Darmstädter und National Bank* closed its doors. The Government was compelled to refloat the *Dresdner Bank* and decided to raise the discount rate stiffly and to limit the repayment of advances. In 1931, of the global capital of the six big banks, amounting to 531 million *Reichmarks*, the Reich held 201 millions and the *Golddiskonto Bank*, attached to the *Reichsbank*, 153 millions.

In face of the crisis and of the budgetary difficulties, the Brüning Government reacted with orthodox measures of general deflation.

Civil servants' salaries were reduced by 12·5 to 16 per cent by three successive decisions in July and December 1930 and June 1931. Unemployment assistance was severely cut in amount and duration in July 1931 and June 1932. The burden of agricultural indebtedness was also modified in November 1931. The order promulgated

[1] Konrad Heiden, *Histoire du National-Socialisme, 1919-1934* (Stock, Paris, 1934) pp. 46 and 106,

on 8th December 1931 was by far the most important: it brought about the reduction of wages to the level they had reached on 1st January 1927, the limitation of interest on bonds to 6 per cent, a cut of 10 per cent in rents, and a lowering by 10 per cent of the price levels established by producers' associations.

All these measures engendered an immense discouragement throughout the Reich, and the 160 million *Reichmarks* allotted to public works for combating unemployment were not sufficient to make up for it. A Commissariat on the cost of living was also to create great discontent among the small traders. As the well-known journalist Georg Bernhard wrote:

> 'While preaching renunciation, Brüning gave the masses no hope of any improvement in the near future. On the contrary, he gave the people to understand that times would get harder and harder, and that the difficulties would only be overcome by even greater economies and by renunciation of every pleasure in life. It is not surprising that the National-Socialist movement, re-floated by the hardships of the period, felt that this atmosphere of despair and hardship was preparing the ground admirably for an unscrupulous agitation.'[1]

Two intermediary Governments, that of von Papen and that of von Schleicher, still separate us from the arrival in power of the National-Socialists on 30th January 1933. Schleicher was to attempt the creation of a social order based on the free trade unions and the sincere elements of the Hitlerian Left wing, grouped around Gregor Strasser. He announced plans for the agrarian colonisation of the Eastern provinces, the organisation of a voluntary labour service and a vast programme of public works. The *Osthilfe* scandal, however, brought about the fall of von Schleicher. The way was now open for the advent of National-Socialism.

II. POLITICAL ATTITUDES

It was during these three years of crisis that the various political attitudes reached their highest temperature and manifested themselves at their maximum intensity. Our examination must trace them as they were in the parties of the Left and among the National-Socialists themselves.

The Left-wing parties remained, or claimed to remain, to the end convinced that Hitlerism would eventually fail; they believed in legality; they showed themselves incapable of understanding the psychological and social upheaval which had resulted from inflation

[1] Georg Bernhard, *Le Suicide de la République Allemande* (Rieder, Paris, 1933), p. 396.

followed by crisis; they wore out their forces in strife among themselves.

As far as Hitlerism is concerned, examples are legion, both among the Socialists and among the Communists.

Take the Communist *Rote Fahne*: '14th September 1930 was the culminating point of the National-Socialist movement. What will follow can only be weakening and decline.' At the end of January 1932 the Communist leader Thälmann thought he discerned 'the veering of the class forces in favour of the proletarian revolution'; on 6th November of the same year the *Rote Fahne* declared that 'everywhere we see SA men deserting the ranks of Hitlerism and coming to place themselves under the Communist flag. Hitler is beginning to be denounced within his own movement.'

The Socialists exhibit the same blindness. 'It is ten years ago', writes the *Vorwärts* on 6th November 1932, 'that we foretold the bankruptcy of National-Socialism; it is there in black and white in our paper'; and the *Leipziger Volkszeitung* of 21st January 1933: 'We cannot escape from the smell of the rotting carcase. Fascism is definitely beaten: it will not rise again.'

Respect for legality was professed just as much among the Communists as among the Socialists: at the moment when the von Papen Government dismissed the Socialist administration of Prussia, German Social-Democracy contented itself with appealing, in a platonic protest, to the Supreme Tribunal at Leipzig; nothing must be done to irritate the National-Socialists; although, at the end of 1931, Karl Holtermann had tried to revive the *Reichsbanner* under the new form of Eiserne Front and to arm the free trade unions, the labour leaders met at the Trade Union building in Berlin and allowed the anti-Socialist *Diktat* to be accomplished. On 30th January 1933, the *Vorwärts* wrote:

'Brought face to face with government by a threatened *coup d'état*, Social-Democracy stands firm with both feet on the ground of the Constitution and of legality.'

The Communists reasoned no differently. 'Above all,' they said on 7th February 1933, 'do not let yourselves be provoked. The life and well-being of the workers of Berlin are too dear to us for us to risk them lightly: they must be kept for the day of struggle.' A few days later Wilhelm Pieck added: 'Let the workers remain prudent so as not to provide pretexts for fresh measures against the Communist Party.' And Torgler, at the Leipzig trial:

'The Communist Party had nothing to hope for from an armed insurrection and looked forward to one thing only: to last undamaged till the elections, at which it was confident of a clear success.'

As Konrad Heiden says:

'Up to 1932 the Communists obeyed the remarkable principle, that Hitler must be allowed to take power, because it was only after domination by Fascism and its collapse that the way would be open to Communism.'

Thus the energies of the two Left-wing parties were employed chiefly in settling their internal struggles, a point on which we have already laid great stress in our introduction.

Neither the Socialists, bogged down in the policy of supporting the Brüning Cabinet, nor the Communists, bogged down in their violent campaigns against the Socialists, understood the new social alignment resulting from the crisis, superimposed upon the inflation which had preceded it by six years. The proletarisation of the middle classes, the ruin of many agricultural producers, the appalling unemployment of the 'thirties, had built up in Germany a mass of desperate people whose interests Socialism might have solidarised, cemented with its own. The elections in the spring and summer of 1932 were held under the banner of unemployment: the creation of supplementary jobs (*Arbeitsbeschaffung*), of the labour service (*Arbeitsdienst*), housing and the repair of housing—such were the clear and simple rallying-points around which National-Socialism was to galvanise the masses and whose appeal the working-class parties failed to exploit.

In complete contrast, National-Socialism set to work to use the economic and social situation with an extraordinary tactical skill and an opportunism facilitated by the divergent shades of opinion which existed within the Party itself.

From the beginning—this is beyond doubt—Hitler's sympathies were on the side of large-scale capitalism, and as the very essence of the movement was that it was political and considered the economic difficulties as susceptible of a primarily political solution, the attitudes taken by Hitler were profoundly affected by this. But the movement had a left wing, a pro-labour wing—that of Gregor Strasser; and it had troops, brutal troops which must not be discouraged: all this was also to condition his tactics.

Points 10 to 17 of the National-Socialist programme of 24th February 1920 define the movement's initial economic policy:

'10. The first duty of every citizen must be to exercise some intellectual or physical activity. The activity of the individual must not go against the interests of the community, but must be carried out within the framework of the whole and for the benefit of all.

'11. We demand the suppression of all income acquired without labour and trouble, the abolition of any domination by gold and money.

'12. We demand the uncompromising recovery of all war profits.

'13. We demand the state ownership of all businesses hitherto carried on in the form of trusts and cartels.

'14. We demand the workers' share in the profits of big business.

'15. We demand a wide extension of old age insurance. . . .

'16. We demand the creation of a healthy middle class and its maintenance, in contrast with Marxism which lays down the annihilation of the middle class as a "law of nature". We demand the immediate communalisation of the big stores and their renting at low rates to the small artisans.

'17. We demand an agrarian reform appropriate to our national needs, the passing of a law providing for the expropriation of the land for purposes of common utility without compensation, the suppressing of landed interests and the prohibition of all speculation in land.'

This essentially *petit bourgeois* programme is as vague as it could be about actual wages. If Article 17 reveals, at the start, a genuine antipathy to the landed interests, Hitler was, in the comments he made on it on 13th April 1928, soon to reduce its scope considerably. This is one of those oscillations characteristic of the Hitlerian technique:

'Our enemies having published malicious interpretations of Point 17 of the NSDAP Programme, the following declaration is necessary: Since the National-Socialist Party admits the principle of private property, it is evident that the words "Expropriation without compensation" refer only to the creation of legal means of expropriating, where necessary, lands which have been wrongfully acquired or which are not administered in accordance with considerations of the People's well-being. This concerns, therefore, first and foremost the Jewish companies for speculation in land values.'[1]

It is striking to observe National-Socialism's absence of trade-union policy during the period of its rise. Hitler, indeed, expressed himself clearly on this in *Mein Kampf*. He devotes the whole of Chapter 12 of the second volume to the problem; his attitude is entirely dominated by the conviction that it is dangerous to associate economic preoccupations prematurely with a great political movement: this would in practice give rise to the danger of exhausting the energies of the movement in a sterile rivalry.

Certainly the trade unions are necessary as members of the

---

[1] See also the comments, highly reassuring for the landed proprietors, published by Alfred Rosenberg in *Wesen, Grundsätze und Ziele der N.S.D.A.P.*, 1937 edition.

future National-Socialist corporations. Nonetheless, those corporations will not be organs of class strife, but only of professional representation. The Nazi state knows no class but, from the political point of view, only citizens with equal rights and likewise general duties, and, side by side with them, 'persons under the jurisdiction of' the state who, from the political point of view, enjoy no rights. For it, the strike will not be a means of destroying or upsetting national production, but a way of augmenting and canalising it, through the struggle against all the obstacles which, on account of their anti-social character, have been preventing the economic betterment of the masses. The Nazi worker will know that the prosperity of the national economy means his own material happiness; the Nazi employer, that the happiness and contentment of his workers are the first condition of the existence and progress of his own economic prosperity. Above them, the state will exercise sovereign arbitration; employers and wage-earners will find the solution of their disagreements in the professional chambers and a central economic parliament. Till then, Hitler recommends the Nazi workers to remain in the existing trade unions in order to carry on subversive action there.

This position in no way prevented National-Socialism, in point of fact, from adopting the most disconcerting attitudes up to its final victory.[1]

During the whole period of the rise of Hitlerism the Party was to exploit both anti-capitalist and anti-Marxist phraseology.

On 1st February 1927, Hellmuth Brückner, *Gauleiter* of Silesia, wrote:

'Let the victims of exploitation overthrow their tyrants! Let our comrades unite in an oath to the Country: then socialism and nationalism will be united as Adolf Hitler demands. No reform will rebuild the house in which they must live united for life. Only the German revolution, which Fate calls for, will make the Third Reich a reality.'

[1] A characteristic example of this double game is to be found in a small work called *Entwicklung der N.S. Bauernbewegung in Hessen* by one of the Nazi organisers, Wilhelm Seipel. It demonstrates perfectly the local application of the orders from above:

'We opposed the thesis, so often put forward by our enemies, that we National-Socialists were national indeed but also socialist. We declared that we were distinguished from the Marxists not only because we were nationalist and they internationalist, but also because our position was the very opposite of Socialism: the Marxists in fact see in property a theft, but we have a point in our programme according to which "National-Socialism recognises property fundamentally and places it under the protection of the State". The Marxists demand "the same for all", and we, on the contrary, "To each what is his." We were also accused of being opponents of protective tariff. It is a subject on which the peasant is not easily taken in. But there too we succeeded in convincing people that we were just the opposite.' (op. cit., p. 158.)

And in October 1929 Teckshon, likewise a *Gauleiter*, speaking at Neuhaus on the Elbe, said:

'The Party is striving against the present system and against the "three hundred" international capitalists who govern the world. . . . Our young brown-shirts will, if need be, risk their lives in this struggle and will carry it on by every means.'

On his side Gregor Strasser wrote, in April 1926:

'This party [the Social-Democratic] once made so great by the burning brain of a Bebel and by the sacrifice and renunciation of thousands and thousands of ardent hearts, has now become the party of Bauer, of Heilmann, of Richter and of Leinert—narrow *petits bourgeois*, ambitious intriguers. . . . From Bebel to Bauer, there is the way you are going! And just look at that fat Galician Jewess, Ruth Fischer, *alias* Madame Gohlke, that miserable Jewish specimen of the intellectual "Scholem", and the whole of that band of rootless ghetto people.'

The Communists, he said, like the cowards they are, send their comrades into the fight but do not expose themselves:

'Nice and safe in their central office, they urge the workers forward, they give them orders: the poor devils are arrested, imprisoned, condemned, and they are left to fall, and out of the dead the material for a fresh agitation is made.'[1]

In the middle of October 1930 Hitler gave his approval to a strike of the Berlin metal-workers, and his lieutenants justified his action as a brake which it was necessary to apply to Socialist propaganda. Otto Strasser, in Saxony, supported some tumultuous strikes and provoked lively reactions on the part of the employers.[2] As late as the beginning of November 1932 the Party even supported a transport strike inspired by the Communists. But, in the opposite direction, on the morrow of the publication of von Papen's order of 9th August 1932, on the suppression of terrorism, one of the Potempa workers, Pietrzuch, was assassinated by the Nazis: the five murderers having been condemned to death by the Beuthen tribunal, Hitler defended them with extreme violence and demanded the dismissal of the von Papen Government.

The decisive *rapprochement* between National-Socialism and business circles goes back to 1928–29. At that period Hitler had practically eliminated the quasi-Socialist organisations of Strasser in the Ruhr, and had approached the notorious coal and steel magnate Emil Kirdorf through the intermediary of Dr Otto Dietrich. In 1929 Kirdorf was the Party's guest of honour at the Nuremberg

[1] Gregor Strasser, *Kampf um Deutschland* (Franz Eher Verlag, Munich, 1932), pp. 121 ff.
[2] See Otto Strasser, *Hitler and I.*

Congress; from that moment the financial contributions of heavy industry to Hitler's funds never ceased, and it was fully reassured as to the pseudo-Socialism of the future dictator.

On 14th October 1930, Gregor Strasser, head of the Left wing, nevertheless laid before the *Reichstag* a proposition which caused some stir:

> 'The entire fortune of the banks and of the princes of the Stock Exchange, acquired by the Jews from the East who came in after 1st August 1914, and other foreigners, by their next of kin and other relatives, as the result of war, revolution, inflation or deflation, shall be expropriated without indemnity, in accordance with the desire of the majority of the German people. The big banks shall be entirely transferred to State ownership.'

But this proposal for expropriation was supremely displeasing to Hitler and was quickly withdrawn.

In October 1931 Hitler confirmed these ties by associating himself, in the Harzburg Front, with the magnate Hugenberg and with the Stahlhelm, led by Dusterberg and Seldte; the resignation of Chancellor Brüning was demanded; at this period neither Socialists nor Communists knew how to meet the crisis. As Konrad Heiden says:

> 'The deepest reason for the unfruitfulness of the German Socialist parties was, however, the collapse of their very basis. The proletarian class collapsed; a new class consciousness penetrated it from various directions and split it. This process, which was by no means limited to Germany, put an end to the Weimar Republic, whose maxim had been to educate a class of workers to a consciousness of national responsibilities, whereas the very object of this education was already disappearing.'[1]

At the beginning of the year 1932, the economic crisis had reached its highest point: heavy industry itself was at its last gasp: the steel magnate, Friedrich Flick, who had become master of the *Vereinigte Stahlwerke*, found himself obliged to give up his interest to the Government of the Reich—a memorable example of that socialisation of losses, that *Konkurssozialismus*, which had become the panacea for the ills from which large-scale production was suffering; at the same moment the members of the National-Socialist Storm Troopers were also going through a social crisis of the gravest order; the Party coffers were empty and many of its members were reduced to begging! Thyssen had already financed Hitler during the struggle carried on in Germany against the adoption of the Young Plan;[2] he became officially a member of the Party in December 1931; and

[1] Konrad Heiden, op. cit., pp. 32 ff.
[2] Franz Thyssen, *I Paid Hitler* (Farrar and Rinehart, New York, 1941).

was not Rudolf Hess also an intimate friend of Kirdorf's, the Director-General of the *Kohlensyndikat*?

On 27th January 1932, Hitler went, at Thyssen's invitation, and spoke for two hours and a half before a meeting of big business representatives at Düsseldorf. But his reception was still ambiguous; Krupp, who had replaced Duisberg at the head of the *Reichsverband der deutschen Industrie*, was far from being convinced.

On 10th April 1932, Hindenburg was finally elected President of the Reich. Meanwhile Gregor Strasser had not given up stressing the socialist character of 'National-Socialism'. He it was who edited and distributed the famous *Wirtschaftliches Sofortprogramm der NSDAP*. The pamphlet had an irresistible persuasiveness increased by some well-coined slogans:

> '*Arbeitslosigkeit bringt Not. Arbeit schafft Brot.*'
> (Unemployment means misery. Work creates bread.)
> '*Nicht Kapital schafft Arbeit. Arbeit schafft Kapital.*'
> (Capital does not make labour. Labour makes capital.)

It is certainly centred on the struggle against unemployment, but goes beyond it by demanding the control of exchange rates and of foreign exchange and the repatriation of exported capital. Artisans and small traders are not forgotten:

> 'The middle class is attacked, from above, by finance capital. . . .
> From below, it is attacked by Marxism, directly with the help of the red co-operatives, and indirectly through legislation.'

The opening of new chain stores and cheap stores will therefore be forbidden, the fiscal concessions to the co-operatives will be abolished. But the prices charged by the cartels will also be controlled; new taxes will make possible the financing of big schemes of public works to combat unemployment. Agricultural prices will be raised thanks to prohibitions of exports, and improved conditions for the peasantry will be guaranteed by a reduction in rates of interest, in the price of manures, etc. . . .

On 10th May 1932, Gregor Strasser made a speech in the *Reichstag* full of socialist yearnings, a speech with which many Marxists, in their heart of hearts, had little fault to find.

> 'If the distributive machinery of the present economic system is not up to the task of distributing our natural resources equitably, this is because this system is wrong and must be modified. . . . The essence of the present trend is the tremendous anti-capitalist feeling which is sweeping through our people, and which has seized hold, consciously or unconsciously, of some 95 per cent of our fellow-citizens. This anti-capitalist feeling is not in the slightest degree aimed against property acquired decently by work and thrift. It has, in particular, nothing to do with the senseless

and destructive tendencies of Internationalism. . . . It is a proof that we are on the threshold of a great change: the surmounting of Liberalism and the rise of a new economic doctrine and a new way of organising the state.'[1]

Strasser got into touch with the free trade unions and with Leipart and fought side by side with them against the growing influence of Ley. But it was certainly too late to modify the deep-seated tendencies of the Movement. Gregor Strasser resigned on 8th December 1932 and was to be, along with Schleicher, the most memorable victim of the massacres of June 1934.

In any case, at the moment when they were spoken, these words, even if condemned by Hitler himself, whether openly or in his own mind, discountenanced Socialists and Communists and facilitated, in the same way as the *Wirtschaftliches Sofortprogramm*, the work of rallying opinion.

III. NATIONAL-SOCIALISM'S ECONOMIC AND SOCIAL DOCTRINE

Like all great movements, National-Socialism crystallised many previously existing ideological tendencies into a whole. *Mein Kampf* provided its *Summa*. But it would be absurd to look for a coherent, dogmatic whole in its doctrine: on the contrary, the necessities of Hitler's tactics imposed on it an essentially empirical and pragmatic character, susceptible of unexpected compromises and disconcerting *volte-faces*. One of the theoreticians of the régime, Hans Tesche-macher,[2] could write that 'Das nazional-sozialistische Wirtschaft-system ist eine sehr undogmatische Bildung' ('the National-Socialist economic system is a highly undogmatic creation'), just as Mussolini liked to repeat that Fascism was neither a museum of dogmas nor a museum of principles. And the following phrase of Teschemacher's proves it:

'The new state has the power and creative force necessary for establishing the plan and pursuing the realisation of effective reforms: on the one hand certain socialistic innovations aimed towards the future and based on large-scale capitalism, which is for us a datum to be preserved carefully; on the other, the restoration of forms of economic life inherited from a very remote past, which find their natural foundation in Soil and Blood.'

Socialism, large-scale capitalism, Blood-and-Soil emotionalism—there is something there to please everyone, all within a confusion which is in no way unintentional.

---

[1] Konrad Heiden, op. cit.
[2] Hans Teschemacher, *Der deutsche Staat und der deutsche Kapitalismus* (Stuttgart, 1934), pp. 41, 42. Quoted by François Perroux in *Les Mythes Hitlériens* (Spes, Lausanne, 1935).

There are to be found, however, in this fabric as a whole, certain permanent ideas, certain unshakeable convictions which are characteristic of it: the aversion to Marxist Socialism and to *bourgeois* Liberalism, both of them internationalist; the belief in a specifically German Socialism, authoritarian, hierarchical—in a word, Prussian; and the idea that a corporative state, kept under close discipline by the governmental bureaucracy, and watchful over the interests of the middle classes may become the instrument of the new policy.

I. THE PRECURSORS [1]

1. *Critique of Mechanical Civilisation, and Appeal to the State.* From the end of the war many German thinkers and sociologists criticised, often with nostalgic romanticism, the new industrial civilisation, with its excessive mechanisation depersonalising and despiritualising the producers, both employers and wage-earners. In so far as this criticism, being directed both against large-scale capitalism and against proletarian trade unionism, indirectly exalted the middle classes, the artisans, small-scale industry, and the peasant living in close association with the land, it could only help the confused ideology of National-Socialism. As, at the same time, those who put it forward saw, for the most part, the remedy for every economic ill in a strong, arbitrating state, sustained by a new *élite* whose expression it would be, the cure might easily suit Nazism quite as well as the diagnosis.

The great Walther Rathenau is to some extent the father of this line of thought: although the crisis and unemployment were a good deal less violent when he was writing than at the moment when the sociologists of *Die Tat* attacked the problem, he eloquently deplored the defects of the capitalist society of which, for a decade, he had been an illustrious representative—a representative, nevertheless, who had a bad conscience, and said so. To achieve the new economic society with a spiritual basis, classless and without unemployment, a controlled economy must be created, whose instrument is to be the corporative state, the *Volksstaat* which will 'make of all Germans workers, with equal rights and duties, classed by professional categories in accordance with the great idea of "Stand", which is the only one capable of restoring to the People its pride and its discipline'.[2] The new pluralist state, regulating banking, production, prices, and wages, will be the expression of a new *élite* formed of

---

[1] See Moeller van den Bruck, *Das Dritte Reich* (Hanseatische Verlaganstalt, Hamburg).

[2] On all this and on the *Die Tat* group, see the excellent book by Edmond Vermeil, *Doctrinaires de la Révolution allemande* (Nouvelles Editions, Latines, Paris, 2nd ed., 1946), pp. 66 and 155.

producers who will have in some sort 'passed beyond' their original class, whether employer or worker.

Ten or a dozen years later the suggestions made by the *Die Tat* writers, Ferdinand Fried and Hans Zeher, were to recall those of Rathenau.[1] But the crisis was raging, unemployment was reaching the proportions of a national disaster, and political decomposition was at its height. The appeal to the lost *élites*, to the new *Obrigkeit*, became more desperate, the denunciation of an American-style régime, through which Germany was betraying her real mission, more imperious. In Fried's view money and credit have despiritualised man; the competitive liberal régime has resulted in the ending of competition itself, in the apotheosis of the trusts and cartels and the ruin of the middle classes; it is finally condemned; it is time to have done with the obligations imposed by world competition and the law of comparative costs; Germany must, to begin with, think of her own organisation, and of dissociating herself from a chaotic world. An autarkic, independent control of her own economy is essential to her, and there again only a strong state will be able to impose it. For Zeher, too, salvation lies only in an interventionist state, capable of defending the rights of the peasantry and middle classes against the trusts and cartels in their solidarity with the Marxist proletariat. This state must be directed by a new *élite*, the expression of a professional corporatism imbued with religious and romantic sentiments, in which the youth organisations would have the important place which is their due.[2]

2. *Critique of the Double International, and Proposals for a German Form of Socialism.* Among the thinkers who contributed most, in post-war Germany, to the criticism of the double International (capitalist and socialist) and to the working-out of a German form of Socialism, Moeller van den Bruck, Oswald Spengler, Werner Sombart, and Ernst Rudolph Huber deserve mention.

Moeller van den Bruck was the one who insisted most on the specifically national character which Socialism must have: 'Each people has its own socialism' was, in *Das Dritte Reich*, a dominant theme. 'Marx has destroyed German Socialism. He would by no means allow it to grow, but stifled the germs that existed in Wilhelm

[1] Vermeil, op. cit., pp. 163–75.

Ferdinand Fried's book, *Das Ende des Kapitalismus* (Diederich, Jena, 1931), had its moment of celebrity, and Mussolini made use of it in one of his speeches to the Italian Chamber of Corporations.

[2] As is also well known, Othmar Spann, professor at Vienna University, may be considered as one of the great forerunners of the system. See, especially, in his *Fundament der Volkswirtschaftslehre* (Gustav Fischer, Jena, 1921), by way of appendix, his apologia for the romanticism and anti-capitalism of Adam Müller. To Müller, liberal capitalism means the disintegration, the dismemberment of any community and any true responsibility to the state—'*Zersetzung und Dismembration alles Gemeinsamen und aller wahren Staatlichkeit*'.

Weitling and, of a different kind, in Rodbertus.' For Moeller van den Bruck, German Socialism has to be understood as a corporative conception of the state ('eine korperschaftliche Auffassung von Staat und Wirtschaft') and of economy, which may have to be realised by revolutionary means but must then recover its conservative character.

'The ideas which have issued from the oldest tradition, allied to the most recent conception of the aim to be attained: that is German Socialism.' And here is a crucial passage:

'Socialism is for us an organic growth; it is hierarchy, membership. Marxism alone professes an international socialism. . . . It is the liberalism in socialism that has exerted, here as elsewhere, this disintegrating action—a stiff, logic-chopping, rationalistic liberalism which through sheer reasoning has failed to see reality. . . . Where Marxism ends, socialism begins: a German socialism, whose vocation it is to dissolve all liberalism in the spiritual history of mankind.'

It is where the proletariat awakens to the idea of nationalism that it becomes truly socialist: the proletariat then becomes conscious of the values it has inherited: its understanding becomes more supple and its outlook wider: it is ready to fall in behind leaders who will be able to bring Germany's interrupted evolution to a fruitful outcome for the nation. Moeller van den Bruck is one of the first to have drawn attention to the process of proletarianisation which had made whole social strata, respected professions, sink to the level of the proletariat in spite of the desperate resistance put up by individuals against their fate.[1]

It was in *Preussentum und Sozialismus*, published in 1922, that Oswald Spengler developed ideas that were close to those of Moeller van den Bruck, on Socialism and the Prussian ideal and way of life. To him, it was Friedrich Wilhelm I, and not Karl Marx, who was the first conscious Socialist; it was Prussia—the Prussia of Stein and his councillors, the Prussia of hierarchy, duty and work well done—that was the chosen land of Teutonic Socialism as opposed to the English materialistic Liberalism of the Vikings. When Marx wrote his Manifesto he was under the influence of an England where manual labour was considered a bad thing and poverty a sign of divine reprobation; Marx envies the parasites who do no work (Fichte would have despised them), he had his place in England, he

---

[1] In a work less well known than *Das Dritte Reich, Sozialismus und Aussenpolitik*, published between 1919 and 1923 in the form of articles, Moeller van den Bruck praised Russian Bolshevism for its national character and wondered whether, when all was said and done, it was not in a close alliance between a national German Socialism and Russian Bolshevism, with its respect for this national Socialism, that the future of Germany lay. He added: 'Sozialismus ist die Anglegenheit einer ganzen Nation die leben will.'

has none in Prussia, for Prussia is the whole people, beyond the capitalist 'good' and the proletarian 'evil'. Socialism is at bottom no more than Prussian bureaucratic organisation, which determines for everyone his place and task in accordance with a plan laid down by the state (or the monarchy), that supreme arbiter of economic life, wages, and social disputes: it is therefore not a conception of property but a technique of administration. The socialist state of the future is essentially a state of civil servants.

Werner Sombart likewise devoted a book to Socialism, 'German style'. It is called *Deutscher Sozialismus* and dates from 1934.[1] German Socialism, in his view, cannot be either proletarian or *petit bourgeois*, for it cannot be a partial Socialism. It can only be a general, universal Socialism of the whole population—in a word, totalitarian (*totalistisch*). Nor can it be the advent of a classless society, 'the kingdom of God on earth': German ideology must liberate itself from the 'disgusting faith in progress which dominates proletarian Socialism and, still more, liberalism'. German Socialism will be a 'social normativism' (*ein sozialer Normativismus*), a hierarchised order tending towards the total organisation of life. Being national, its realisation can only take place within the framework of the national community: the powers which are to make possible this achievement can only be state powers, and it is incumbent on the statesman to determine and guide the reciprocal play of ideas and interests which go to make up history.

Ernst Rudolph Huber's book, *Die Gestalt des deutschen Sozialismus*,[2] takes up again, with, indeed, an outstanding forcefulness, the complex of arguments which have just been set out.

'Democratic socialism and bolshevism differ profoundly in their methods, but the content of their conception of history and the aim of their political will are identical. The Marxist interpretation of history is at bottom nothing but a liberalism pushed to its final limits and going beyond itself. Liberalism has reduced the individual destiny of the human being to the predominant pursuit of the satisfaction of material needs; Marxism has erected this materialism into a principle of political action. . . . German Socialism is a true socialism, because it issues from the reaffirmed unity of the nation, because by transcending the notions of property and non-property, enterprise and labour, town and country, it expands into the popular community. . . . This socialism is, first and foremost, a new spiritual attitude towards economic life, a new economic ethics. . . . While the centre of the

---

[1] Werner Sombart, *Deutscher Sozialismus* (Buchholz und Weisswange, 1934). French translation *Le Socialisme Allemand—une nouvelle théorie de la société* (Payot, Paris, 1938).
[2] (Hanseatische Verlaganstalt, Hamburg.) Published in the collection *Der deutsche Staat der Gegenwart*; editor, Carl Schmitt.

materialist programme was socialisation, expropriation, that is to say the transfer of the ownership of the means of production to the collectivity, German Socialism is built on the basis of the traditional ownership of property by the individual. . . . But this property must henceforward be administered with full responsibility towards the community. . . .'

With regard to the Catholic solidarism laid down in the encyclical *Quadragesimo Anno*, the new German Socialism does not proceed from an awakening spiritual consciousness foreign to political power: it proceeds, on the contrary, from the political consciousness of the nation, which is realised in the Government of the state.[1]

2. HITLER'S SOCIAL AND ECONOMIC DOCTRINE AND ITS EVOLUTION

Independently of the motives provided by the psychological uprooting to which we have already alluded, Hitler has insisted so much in *Mein Kampf* on the origins of his double aversion to international capitalism and to Marxist Socialism, that he himself traces out the paths for our analysis.

1. *Opposition to Marxist International Trade Unionism, whether Socialist or Communist.* International trade unionism, whether Social-Democratic or Communist, is, under the orders of international Jewry, 'one of the most formidable instruments of terrorisation against the security and independence of the national economy, against the equilibrium of the state, and against individual liberty'. It was towards the end of the last century that, 'led astray in the accursed circle of social democracy', it tended to become no more than a means of pressure in the class struggle. Doubtless, as the organ for the defence of the social rights of the workers and for the struggle towards better living conditions, trade unionism is justified and, within the national framework, perfectly admissible; but in so far as it is the expression of the desire of the masses on the economic and social plane it becomes in some sort anti-natural; the Jewish doctrine, Marxism, rejects the aristocratic principle which is observed by Nature and, in place of the eternal privilege of strength and energy, establishes that of number and its dead weight. Marxism denies man's individual value, contests the importance of the ethnic entity and of race, and so deprives humanity of the preliminary condition of its existence and progress.

The class struggle is therefore criminal and anti-national. 'At the moment when the final orders were being given to the German

---

[1] Between this thought and the social nationalism of a Rocco or a Corradini in Italy the identity seems complete: the same sources, the same expressions, the same conclusions.

divisions for the great offensive of 1918, the general strike broke out in Germany.' It is therefore responsible for the defeat of the Reich. For the necessities of mere tactics, the movement could not dispense with an appeal to the masses: his experience in Austria and, more particularly, the Pangermanist policy of von Schönerer had revealed its importance to Hitler. Such is the essential reason for the choice of the movement's first name, 'Social Revolutionary Party'. During the long period of the rise to power, Hitler took care to avoid recommending the creation of Nazi trade unions. It would have been a breach of the formal rule about the primacy of politics. What he does recommend to his companions is either to leave free trade unions to which they may belong, or, preferably, to remain in them with a view to dissolving them from within.

2. *Opposition to Financial and International Capitalism*. The national importance of capital results from the fact that it is intimately bound up with the greatness, liberty and power of the state—that is to say, of the nation. The duty of the state is therefore to see that capital remains its servant and does not claim to dominate the nation; and so he lays down an essential distinction between productive capital, the result of work which is itself productive, and the capital of speculation and exploitation, between *schaffendes* or *schöpferisches* capital and *raffendes* or *räuberisches* capital. It is well known that this distinction, due to Gottfried Feder and for a time famous, was Hitler's road to Damascus; indeed, in *Mein Kampf*, with a perhaps involuntarily naïve mingling of tactical preoccupations with his recent doctrinal illumination, he adds:

'The separation made between stock exchange capital and the national economy offered the possibility of going into battle against the internationalisation of German economy, without at the same time threatening the foundations of an independent national economy by a fight against capital. . . . In Feder's teaching I foresaw a powerful watchword for the struggles to come.'

This condemnation of finance capitalism extends to limited companies, to the depersonalisation of capital itself, to all loans financed by bonds. The burden of these latter on German economy is fifteen times heavier than the dividends paid to shareholders in industry; it is the cornerstone of German indebtedness. One can see immediately how easily this theory will be used to justify and legitimate the inflationism of the big industrialists in the years 1922–23. 'Interest', that index of a good investment which finance capitalism insists on, has got to disappear; to free German society from the tyranny of interest is to be, from the first, one of the watchwords of growing National-Socialism; it implies, naturally, the end

T

of any payment of reparations to the Allies, and especially to France; it implies denunciation of the Dawes and Young Plans.

3. *Protection of the Middle Classes.* The middle classes carried National-Socialism to power. Naturally its programme takes the fullest possible account of them and opposes Marxism all the more by striving to prevent their annihilation. Small traders must be protected against the big stores' competition by the communalisation of the latter; the artisans will benefit by preferential orders from public institutions; finally, the peasants will be helped by an agrarian reform, somewhat vaguely defined, which would involve land expropriation without compensation, suppression of landed interests, and the banning of real-estate speculators.

4. *The Proletarian State.* Rich in its surplus population, Hitler's Reich will lay claim to the territories necessary to the feeding of its people and, through colonisation, an outlet for its excess of population. The right to work and life for all citizens in the Reich involves, for the state, corresponding obligations; if it should prove impossible to feed the whole population, the members of foreign nations who are not German citizens will have to be expelled; any fresh immigration will be forbidden, and the non-Germans who have immigrated into Germany since 2nd August 1914 must be compelled to leave the Reich.

5. *Labour and Property: the Future Corporation.* Since the activity of the individual should be exercised for the benefit of all, property becomes a sort of social service. All income acquired without labour must be suppressed, together with dividends and interest; the large-scale cartelised enterprises will be taken over by the state, and the workers admitted to a share in the profits.

The strike will no longer be a means of destroying or upsetting national production, but a factor making for the expansion of this production, by allowing it to overcome those obstacles which, by reason of their anti-social character, prevented the economic improvement of the masses. The new worker will become conscious of the fact that a prosperous national economy means his own material well-being; the new employer, of the fact that the well-being and contentment of his staff become the essential condition of his own prosperity.

Workers and employers, grouped together, will form the Nazi Corporation, an organ of professional representation opposed to the old trade unions of class warfare and subordinated to the trusteeship of the state; professional chambers and a Central Economic Parliament will allow *entrepreneurs* and workers to solve, in harmony, their common problems for the good of the popular community and of the state, 'the idea of which must appear in shining letters above everything else'.

IV. ECONOMIC AND SOCIAL RESULTS OF NATIONAL-SOCIALISM

1. THE WAGE-EARNERS

1. *The Destruction of the Trade Unions.* The first cells of National-Socialist enterprises had been founded in 1928 by a Berlin Nazi, Reinhold Muchow; their beginnings had been slow and difficult: as is indeed well known, Hitler did not particularly desire their formation. In March 1933 they obtained only 3 per cent of the votes in the special elections to the Business Councils: they numbered no doubt at that moment between 300,000 and 500,000 members, as against the 3 to 4 million subscribers to the various free trade unions, and these members were mainly unemployed, or workers in public organisations. The destruction of free trade-unionism by violence thus became a necessity for National-Socialism; meanwhile the leaders of the free trade unions multiplied their overtures to Hitler; they declared themselves ready to leave the World Federation of Trade Unions and submit to the authority of the state.

'The trade-union organisations are the expression of an irrefutable social necessity, an indispensable part of the social order itself.[1] They have been created by the working class in its effort to help itself, and in the course of their history, according to the natural order of things, they have become more and more integrated in the state. The social function of the trade unions must be fulfilled whatever the nature of the régime of the state. Having recognised the arbitration of the state and availed themselves of it, the trade-union organisations have shown that they recognise the state's right of intervention in discussions between the organised workers and the employers, when the general interest requires it.'

And the *Metallarbeiter Zeitung*, organ of the metalworkers' federation, for 1st April 1933, adds:

'The Hitler–Hügenberg–Seldte Government is resolved to free the German peasants and workers from their intolerable economic misery. It has said so in its first appeal and repeated it many times, and on 23rd March, in the Chancellor's speech to the *Reichstag*, this task and the determination to accomplish it were given an important place. After all this, it is not permissible to doubt that the necessity of freeing the mass of the German people from economic distress is recognised, in all its harshness, by the

[1] Quoted in *Vingt Ans d'Histoire Allemande (1914–1934)* (Institut Supérieur Ouvrier, Paris, 1936), pp. 97–8.

present Government. Neither can it be doubted that the Government has in its hands all the means to this end.

'If economic misery is now really to be combated, and energetically, no one will greet this action more warmly than the trade unions. Nothing will be lacking to make their co-operation zealous and resolute. . . . The preceding German Governments had in fact accomplished nothing towards putting an end to the economic misery of the masses. Perhaps they lacked the necessary decision and forcefulness. But both are certainly not lacking in the present Government. Its *legal* and full powers allow it unquestionably to limit, and even to suppress, economic misery. And it can rest, for sure, on the loyal co-operation of the trade unions of all tendencies.'

These humble overtures left the triumphant leaders unmoved. On the morrow of the *Reichstag* fire, the right to strike was virtually suppressed and any encouragement to strike severely punished. Hitler's troops occupied many trade-union offices. Then the free trade unions lost their monopoly of representing the workers at the *Reichswirtschaftsrat* and in the Labour Courts. The Joint-Production Committees had their competence restricted; their members were often suspended and replaced by safe men. Employers from now on might dismiss their employees for opposition to the state. Simultaneously, the Nazi cells made efforts to enrol the members of the free trade unions.

Hitler decided to make the First of May 1933, a day of incomparable splendour; after military and athletic displays and symbolic manifestations of loyalty to the régime, Hitler said:

'We shall bring the Germans closer together even against their will. What used to separate them shall henceforth unite them. What is the meaning of the festivity we are celebrating today? It is to honour labour and respect the worker. German people! You are not a second-class people. Remember your past achievements, the achievements of your fathers. Forget fourteen years of decadence, and remember three thousand years of history. The compulsory labour service will be an expression of the unity of the people, which today is recovered.'

Next day all the trade-union leaders were arrested and their offices occupied by Hitler's militia-men. While the Christian trade unions made haste to submit, the mass of the working-class organisations, from now on completely emasculated, were melted together on 10th May into the 'Labour Front', with Dr Robert Ley at its head. It was to be one of the pillars of the future corporative state.

The Communist Party was outlawed immediately after the *Reichstag* fire; its property was confiscated and it was forbidden all activity after 26th May 1933. In spite of the protestations of loyalty made by many of the Socialist leaders, these were dismissed; on 22nd June all activity was likewise forbidden to the Socialist Party and all its property was confiscated. On 16th May the right to strike was finally abolished; on 19th May the trade unions lost their right of collective bargaining. Throughout the year 1934 the various working-class professional federations were dissolved, one after another.

2. *The Front and the Labour Charter.* The Labour Front was supposed, in theory, to group together wage-earners and employers; it was in no sense a body for the defence of the interests of the labour world; it was much more a body designed to impregnate the working-class world with a National-Socialist consciousness. As Dr Ley was to declare, on 27th November 1933:

> 'The lofty aim of the Labour Front is the education of all those men who are working for the National-Socialist state. It is the school of those men who will be called upon to co-operate in a decisive fashion in the business firms and organs of our social constitution, the labour tribunals and social insurance. It will see to it that the social honour of the leader of a business firm and of the worker may become an active force for the construction of the new economic and social organisation.'

The Labour Front had thus essentially a politically educative function, carried into practice by works meetings or *Betriebsappelle* of labour groups and the specialised press.

The whole social philosophy of National-Socialism is epitomised by the Labour Charter which was promulgated on 16th January 1934, and entered into force on 1st May of the same year. Its entire tendency is to glorify the function of business leader or *Führer*, whose staff forms the following or *Gefolgschaft*. The only rights now left to the wage-earner are that of being elected, or electing others to the Council of Confidence or *Vertrauensrat*, that of drawing the attention of the Labour Commissary to any offences against social honour of which any member of the Labour Community may be guilty—including the employer—and finally, that of being protected against an unjustified dismissal.[1]

The *Vertrauensrat* is elected by the members of the firm from a list drawn up by its head and the representatives of the enterprise cell —that is to say, of the Party. The various conditions of eligibility include an undertaking 'to be ready to work at any moment without reserve on behalf of the national state'. The Council considers all questions of a social nature, including the management of the firm;

---

[1] In case of dismissal the worker is able to have recourse to the Labour Tribunal in case of 'undue harshness' or 'if the situation of the enterprise did not make it necessary'. These are extremely elastic and vague guarantees.

but its head is in no way bound to follow these recommendations. When the Council appeals against a decision of the employers before the Labour Commissary, this appeal has no power to suspend action. In fact (Article 2) the business leader takes the decisions, as opposed to the working-class collectivity, in all matters of interest to the enterprise in so far as they come under the Labour Charter. He must 'take care' of the staff. The staff, in return, owes him loyalty —a loyalty founded on the Labour Community or *Werkgemeinschaft*.

The new system of social law was inspired by a phobia for collective bargaining; for this technique, which makes it possible, in free countries, to regroup the mass of the workers in similar firms over against the employers, National-Socialism rejected irrevocably.

'Go back to work! How many times [said Dr Ley] have we not given that order. We National-Socialists have attacked the fortresses of trade unionism with a dash, a courage, an endurance, a doggedness which will be, for future generations, the proof of the formidable, painful and exhausting work of the Party. . . . At the doors of the factory a new world begins, a new community. A new spirit appears there. Woe to him who would oppose it.'[1]

The regulations governing enterprises, regulations which, once again, no collective bargaining was to unify, involved, in particular, compulsory clauses relating to hours of work, to the way in which wages should be paid, to fines, etc. The amount of wages might be included in the regulations—but need not be: nothing, in this matter, would bind the employer, except the fear, more often than not hypothetical, of Tribunals of Honour chosen jointly by the Government and the Labour Front.

3. *Income from Labour and the Fight against Unemployment.* From 1929 to 1936 the proportion of labour to miscellaneous income in the national budget changed as follows:

	Labour.	Miscellaneous.
1929	59·5	14·8
1932	54·1	11·8
1933	53·6	13·6
1934	55	14·3
1935	56·4	14·5
1936	56·3	16·1

But out of the nominal income, the fiscal and social contributions increased beyond comparison, and this explains, if not the deterioration of all real wages, at least certain huge transfers of income—from

[1] A. Dauplin-Meunier, *L'Economie Allemande Contemporaine* (Fernand Sorlot, 1942), p. 132.

workers formerly employed to those at one time unemployed, from workers in general to beneficiaries of social security, aid for the newly-married and the Party organisations.[1]

The struggle against unemployment is, on the other hand, one of the assets of National-Socialism. Unemployment reached its peak in February 1932 with 6·1 millions totally unemployed; every year 350,000 more individuals over eighteen years old were being poured on to the labour market. The various programmes set in motion by Brüning (160 millions), Papen (540 millions), and Schleicher-Gereke (500 millions) had only a very limited effectiveness and barely got into motion; unemployment still stood at 5·4 millions in June 1933. It fell to 3·7 millions in January 1934, 2·9 millions in January 1935, 2·5 millions in January 1936, 1·8 millions in January 1937—to fall below the million mark in the spring of that year. The re-absorption of the unemployed resulted from an increase in the demand for labour (railways, roads, and, above all, rearmament) and from the fact that fewer workers were seeking employment, itself the result of various devices. Emergency works (*Notstandarbeiten*) organised by Unemployment Officies (reafforestation, land reclamation, dams and barrages); the Labour Service (*Arbeitsdienst*) which was rendered compulsory at the beginning of 1935 and enrolled the young people of eighteen to twenty-five; the re-establishment of compulsory military service; Rural Aid (*Landhilfe*): all this was to absorb, according to the period, from half a million to a million young labourers.

2. ECONOMIC ORGANISATION

Following Hitler's arrival in power, the *Führer*'s economic advisers who had socialist leanings dreamed of taking measures of *Gleichschaltung* with regard to major industry similar to those which had fallen upon the labour world. Thus on 1st April 1933 Dr Wagener envisaged the dissolution of the *Reichsverband der deutschen Industrie* and the elimination of Herren Krupp and Kastl, who had up to then shown a certain aloofness towards the movement. He failed completely: Krupp, who had rallied to Hitler's side after his victory, became in the middle of June 1933 president of the *Reichsverband der deutschen Industrie*; Dr Wagener was replaced by Wilhelm Keppler, a man extremely favourable to heavy industry. In the Ruhr and among great steel producers, numerous intrigues ended by bringing Franz Thyssen into power; the Hitlerian leaders recognised his economic dictatorship by writing to him as follows:

[1] The tax on wages; contributions to sickness insurance, to unemployment insurance, to disability insurance; contributions to the Labour Front, to the *Winterhilfe*; aid for married persons; and civic taxes: absorbed at that time 15–35 per cent of gross wages.

'You have become, for our economic district, the highest economic authority of the state. Accordingly we have given orders to all our services to refer to you invariably all questons of economic policy excepting questions of agrarian policy, and to regard your decisions as binding.'

Thyssen himself, in his amusing and cynical book, *I Paid Hitler*, writes quite openly:

'Dr Klein, the friend of Othmar Spann and Social Secretary of the I.G., had interested Hitler in the corporative system; the Party had chosen Thyssen to direct an Institute of Studies relating to the establishment of this system, but this choice aroused the opposition both of Dr Ley and of certain industrialists. Finally Hitler solemnly declared that everything would be done according to my plans and those of my friends: in eight days we were to establish a corporative system for Germany. Hitler thus decided that, if our political movement had had its origin at Munich, our economic reform would have its origin at Düsseldorf.'

Thyssen adds, not without malice:

'One of the reasons why Hitler favoured a corporative system was his opposition to the fusion in a single organism of the three general labour federations which then existed in Germany. What he wanted was to divide the Labour Front, and he was quite right.' [1]

1. *The New Régime for Agriculture.* Blood and soil—*Blut und Boden*—were to refashion Germany, and so agriculture was to be in the foreground of the preoccupations of the new Reich. The régime owed too much to the big landowners, who had given it financial support and had caused the successive falls of the Brüning and Schleicher Governments, it owed too much to the small and medium farmers of the West who had joined the movement in large numbers, to afford to forget it. There was no longer any question of expropriating the large estates or of colonisation at home; as early as July 1933 Walther Darré, Hügenberg's successor, promised, with Hitler's agreement, that, whatever might be their extent, the big estates capable of subsisting on their own should not be touched, nor should those debt-ridden properties whose owners would freely decide their development.

The essential innovation of the policy was the law of 29th September 1933, on the hereditary estate or *Erbhof*. Hereditary farms are to be unalterable and inviolable, and to be worked by the owner himself and his family; their area varies according to the regions

[1] The kinship with Mussolini's attitude to Rossoni is obvious. Thyssen says, again: 'National-Socialism never had a real economic plan. Some were wholly reactionary; others wanted a corporative system; others again had extreme Left-wing opinions. Hitler thought it very intelligent to agree with everybody.'

and the crops cultivated, but cannot exceed 125 hectares. The owner may not dispose of them, whether by gift or by sale; the estate is immune from any action by creditors, and its harvest cannot be seized. The estate must be bequeathed undivided—in principle to the oldest son if there is one. In certain cases the peasant may be assisted by a right-hand man or *Vertrauensmann*, and by a syndic or *Treuhänder*.

The problem of rural debts (they amounted to about 8 milliards at the time), which had already been dealt with by a moratorium combined with control by an agricultural association, received a permanent solution on 1st June 1933: the interest on these debts was limited by authority to 4·5 per cent, of which 1 per cent was taken over by the Reich, and their amortisation, after conversion into bonds, was graded at from 0·5–5 per cent per annum.

But it was chiefly through the price policy devised and decided by National-Socialism and carried through by the Foodstuffs Corporation or *Reichsnährstand* of 13th September 1933, that German agriculture received substantial encouragement and saw its total income greatly increased in the following years.

Under Walther Darré, Leader of the Reich's Peasantry, the *Reichsnährstand* grouped together all the agricultural producers, all the agricultural co-operatives, the processing industries, and the distributing trades. The Foodstuffs Corporation was itself empowered to settle markets and prices for the various products; the Government could use its authority to group together producers, processors, and distributors: these groups forming the market organisation, or *Zusammenschlüsse*, were themselves endowed with powers of decision which were binding upon their members.

All this showed its results in a marked rise in the price of farm products; Herr Darré was able to declare, on 21st January 1934:

'The peasant is now withdrawn from the capitalist framework; the social price replaces the free price.'

This meant simply the development of autarchy and its natural consequence, the sacrifice of the consumer; between the beginning of 1933 and the end of 1934, agricultural wholesale prices rose by some 25 per cent. By comparison with world prices c.i.f. Hamburg,[1] the prices of the various German grains were to reach, in October 1933, about 200 per cent—three times as much; meat, butter, and eggs were two to three times dearer than in Denmark; an official increase in the price of margarine and fresh duties on butter were to bring about a rise in the price of butter, and with it, that of milk and cheese; these simple manipulations were to increase by 500

[1] See *Revue d'Economie Politique* (1934), p. 1431; *L'Agriculture Allemande*, by C. von Dietze.

millions the income of dairy producers. From 1932 to 1936 the total income of farmers rose by 50 per cent, and passed from 8·2 to 9·6 per cent of the national income.

2. *Industrial and Financial Organisation.* The laws of 15th July 1933 allowed the formation of compulsory cartels to include all firms in the same sphere of production, and the banning of new firms except under special licence. But the law of 20th January 1934 deprived the Cartels Tribunal, which had been set up on 2nd November 1923, of its previous rights concerning the relations between cartelised industries and between cartels and consumers; these powers were transferred to the Ministry of National Economy—that is to say, to the Government itself.

The laws of 27th February and 27th November 1934 laid the foundations of the new economic organisation.

All firms were thenceforward grouped within a double organisation: the vertical groups and the horizontal chambers.

(a) The seven *Reichsgruppen* were: Industry, the Artisans, Commerce, Banking, Insurance, Power, and Transport; each of them included principal groups (*Hauptgruppen*), divided into economic groups (*Wirtschaftsgruppen*) and professional groups (*Fachgruppen*). Membership of these groups became *compulsory*, and the choice of the directors of groups was subject to purely governmental decision: any form of election was carefully excluded.

(b) The Economic Chambers. Each territorial division, or *Gau*, had now an Economic Chamber, to which were affiliated all industrial, commercial, and artisan enterprises. The head of each of these chambers was at the same time an active business man, and the Gauleiter's adviser. Close ties existed between these Chambers and the Party.

Groups and Chambers together formed the *Organisation der gewerblichen Wirtschaft.* They had educational—that is to say, police— duties; they were the 'long arm of the state'; they were supposed to supervise the rallying to the Party of all the co-ordinated enterprises and to see that they received the general directives of the Government; they were supposed to direct these members, and they had over them the widest disciplinary powers: under cover of autarchy and war economy, the allocation of raw materials was by itself enough to give the economic leaders formidable weapons for keeping their charges in order.

The Government and large-scale industry naturally took great care to prevent any meddling by the labour world in this totalitarian organisation of economy. A genuine corporative system would have required that *elected* representatives of employers and employed should participate voluntarily and on an equal footing in the free discussion of measures to be taken in common. Here there was nothing of the kind; at most, the Leipzig Convention of 21st March 1935 provided for the setting-up, in each *Gau*, of a Labour and Economy Council, representing the Labour Front and the Economic Chamber.

The law of 12th November 1936 gave these Groups and Economic Chambers a power of control over the Cartels and a veto power over the measures taken by them; rather than rigid price-fixing and production quotas, there was now to be persuasive action, effected above all in the fields of standardisation of accounting systems and of conditioning. Organisation, regulation of the markets, *Marktordnung, Marktregelung,* were now essentially controlled with a view to the achievement of economic autonomy, to the establishment of a war economy; the 'Commissariat for Price Formation'—for prices shaped to this end—became the instrument of this organisation.

This close harnessing of the economy to state and Party crops up again in certain regulations governing limited companies—features in which some people have tried to see an element of Socialism. Doubtless the dividends which may be distributed are now limited, by a text dated 29th March 1934, to 6 per cent as a general rule; doubtless the shareholders of limited companies lose most of their rights after the law of 30th January 1937:[1] but this dispossession confirms the dictatorial and totalitarian character of the economic system; it in no way indicates a socialist orientation. In point of fact industrial concentration became more burdensome and extensive year by year.

All the vacillations of this policy are evidence of clashes of personalities and prestige, but cannot for an instant conceal the fundamental agreement and substantial unity of the Hitlerian dictatorship and big business. This agreement remains the clue to the whole German economic organisation from the spring of 1933 onwards.[2]

[1] The shareholders may 'ask questions', to which the director of the company is in no way bound to reply; the general meeting no longer nominates the director, and no longer supervises his conduct of the business; it loses its right to examine and approve the balance-sheet. The director being essentially the delegate of the Party or of the Government for the carrying-on of the business, any conflict between the shareholders and him is fundamentally unthinkable.

[2] The war economy, and then the war itself, naturally consolidated this tendency. Here, according to Jurgen Kuczinsky, is the extent to which big business was represented in the Armaments Council in 1942:

Wilhelm Zange	Director, Mannesmann Rohrenwerke
Hermann Bücher	Krupp; electrical construction
Hermann Röchling	Röchlingwerke, Saar
Albert Vögler	Vereinigte Stahlwerke
Ernst Poensgen	Vereinigte Stahlwerke
Philip Kessler	Bergmann Elektrowk and Siemens
Paul Pleiger	Hermann Göring Wk.
Helmuth Röhnert	Hermann Göring Wk.
Quandt	Close friend of the Goebbels family

17

THE NAZIFICATION OF THE LOWER
MIDDLE CLASS AND PEASANTS

Arthur Schweitzer

PEOPLE in democratic countries often ask curiously how and why anyone should like to give up his democratic rights in favour of dictatorial oppression. Two explanations are usually offered in answer to this question. Insufficient training in democratic methods and understanding of democratic ideas or the aggressive character of the nations concerned and their worship of might are said to lead to fascist dictatorships. Actually, these explanations give, at best, merely a picture of the general background of countries inflicted with fascist régimes. They do not tell us specifically why the Nazi movement rose to predominance in the early 1930s and why a dictatorial party received such energetic support from the masses that it was able to obtain power. A most significant cause of the rise of a fascist party lies in the evolution of a counter-revolutionary movement of the middle class.

The present essay describes briefly the role of the middle class in the Nazi Party and régime, examines the causes of the Nazification of the German middle class, and, by implication, points to the specific conditions that must be avoided in order to prevent the rise of a fascist mass movement.

I

Revolutionary and counter-revolutionary movements spring from specific social classes. In industrial societies, labour provides the social basis for revolutionary movements, whereas the lower middle class has constituted the social basis for the counter-revolutionary movements of Nazism and Fascism. The majority of its supporters came from the peasants, artisans and small merchants and shop-keepers, from the sales clerks, bank and insurance employees, and other office workers, from the school teachers and also from members of the free professions.[1] Most of the Nazi leaders came

[1] It is in terms of these groups that we speak of the 'lower middle class' in this essay. Manufacturers, industrialists, bankers, and large-scale merchants are specifically excluded from this definition of the middle class.

from these groups. Nazi ideology derived many of its ideas from the aspirations of the various segments of the urban and rural middle class. From 1930 to 1933 the Nazi movement constituted a genuine counter-revolutionary mass movement, led by a dictatorial party. A process of mutual penetration took place during these years. The middle class became Nazified; the Nazis absorbed the economic and social demands of the middle groups. This mutual penetration led to the formation of a new branch of Nazi ideology called 'middle-class socialism'. 'Artisan socialism' became the ideal of Nazified artisans; 'peasant socialism' presented the aspirations of the Nazified peasants. Nazi ruralism was devised to attract the foodless labourers in cities and the landless labourers in the villages. The middle class thus contributed one of the most significant features of Nazi ideology, at least up to the time of the establishment and consolidation of the Hitler régime.

When the Nazi Party had usurped the power and instruments of the State, the Nazified middle class transformed its ideology into an economic and political programme of action. The programme for the peasants is best known. They wanted a stable system of markets, a larger share of the national income, and a Nazified form of entailed rural estates (*Erbhöfe*), as well as a plan to increase the proportion of peasants in the population and to attain self-sufficiency in foodstuffs by settling labourers in the villages. The programme for the artisans was no less extensive. It included the elimination of the private banking system in order to destroy the 'thraldom of interests'. It called for a new economic organisation of enterprises in the form of closed corporations or guilds. It insisted upon an extensive programme of vocational training leading to the selection of masters who alone should be allowed to open and operate shops and stores. Finally, artisans should be granted the right to fix prices and enjoy ordered markets similar to those for the peasants. The programme for the white-collar group was less extensive and specific. The Nazified leaders of this group fought for a separate economic organisation within the 'Labour Front'. They obtained the recognition of the Labour Front for their comprehensive vocational training programme, which culminated in annual vocational competitions for prizes on a local, regional, and national scale. The Nazified white-collar group strongly supported the idea of promoting salaried employees to managerial positions and strongly favoured the Nazi slogan of 'a house for every family'. Intensive efforts to realise these economic programmes of the middle class took place from 1933 to the end of 1936. In this period the three segments of the lower middle class acted as organised interest groups, tried strenuously to obtain party recognition and support for their ideas, and worked feverishly to make 'middle-class socialism' a reality.

The programmes and policies of the Nazified middle class could be put into effect only to a very limited extent. Proponents of 'middle-class socialism' ran into a fourfold opposition. Ideologically, 'middle-class socialism' was only one strand in the set of ideals sponsored by the Nazis. The five other features of the original Nazi ideology can be designated as racialism, imperialism, autocratic rule of the leaders, social harmony, and Nordic religion. Many of these ideals, especially imperialism and social harmony, would have had to be discarded if the ideal of 'middle-class socialism' had been given full recognition by the Nazi rulers. The unlimited power of the leaders within the Party, and of the Party over all middle-class and labour organisations, would have had to be significantly reduced. This was exactly what the more intransigent supporters of 'middle-class socialism' demanded. They claimed priority for their goal over all other Nazi targets.

This demand for priority created an ideological conflict within the Party. It was not resolved by discussion and persuasion. The resolution came as a by-product of the purge of the SA leaders in June 1934. Some of the demoted or beheaded leaders had fought for a 'second revolution'.[1] 'Middle-class socialism' was destined to be the economic programme for the 'second revolution'. In demoting the SA and killing its leaders, Hitler, in one stroke, placed 'middle-class socialism', Nordic religion and social harmony into the category of ideals which, in the main, were to be used for propaganda only. Especially after 1936, imperialistic and racialist tendencies alone inspired the oligarchic rulers of the régime who had obtained full acceptance of the leadership principle from the Nazified middle class and its leaders.[2]

Politically, Nazified middle-class organisations tried to obtain organisational autonomy from the Party and the State. This violated the Nazi principle of organisational uniformity, whereby all mass organisations had to be led by Party members designated from above, and had to be organisationally supervised by the treasurer of the Nazi Party. As early as the summer of 1933, the Nazified leaders of the white-collar workers were thrown out of their positions; the separate organisations of white-collar workers were dissolved; all salaried employees became compulsory members of the Labour Front; and were organised along industrial lines without distinction

---

[1] The 'first revolution', according to Nazi terminology, was Hitler's advent to power on 30 Jan. 1933.

[2] When these leaders still insisted upon realising their original artisan or rural programmes, they were condemned to a political death. Gottfried Feder was the best known but by no means the only one of those who disappeared from the political scene. Walther Darré experienced the same fate a few years later, when he insisted upon promoting the programme of entailed estates in spite of the requirements for war.

of occupational skill or social status. Their attempt to build up an economic policy for the enterprises under their control, would have severely limited the power of the Government over economic affairs. The State would have retained only the function of legislator for corporatives, guilds, and similar bodies, and as an umpire to settle disputes among them. Nazi rulers did not enjoy the vision of a State which would be powerless in the economic sphere. Hence, Rudolf Hess, Hitler's deputy, directed all Party members to cease agitating for corporatives (guilds). The middle-class leaders were instructed to integrate all middle-class organisations into two comprehensive organisations which were called 'estates'—one 'estate' for handicraft, and one 'estate' for agriculture. Despite the elaborate structure given to these 'estates', they were to refrain from political activity and were merely 'to represent' the artisans and the peasants, without determining economic policy, which privilege was reserved for the State. Corporativism (guild system) was thus a still-born child that was said to be incompatible with the Aryan ideal of the Third Reich.

Militarily, Nazi rulers and generals were interested in a mass army to be fed with food supplied from domestic agriculture. The rural resettlement programme would have led to a dismemberment of the feudal estates in Eastern Germany and to the distribution of that land among the new farmers. Realisation of the artisan programme would have given preference to artisan shops. Industrial enterprises at one time were ordered by the 'estate of handicrafts', either to close their repair shops or to designate them as artisan shops to be managed by certified masters of the respective craft. There was also a prohibition upon new investments, a measure by which the more intransigent Nazis intended to limit the growth of industrial enterprises. According to Feder, who, during a certain period, held the title of Commissioner for Resettlement, land should be used only according to an extensive plan worked out by his agency. Industries should be decentralised; they would no longer be located near coal deposits; canals instead of railways should become the preferred means of freight transportation; and labourers should work in semi-peasant villages close to decentralized factories.[1] This programme of resettlement in all its aspects aroused the generals to action. They successfully limited the programme of settling farmhands to those estates that were voluntarily sold by their owners. The generals thwarted all efforts at decentralisation and relocation of industry. Together with the *Junkers*, the generals succeeded in placing emphasis upon grain production. Together with the leading bankers, they spoiled the extensive programme to build semi-rural

[1] For details on resettlement, rurification of labourers, and decentralisation of industry, see Arthur Schweitzer, 'Depression and War: Nazi Phase', in *Political Science Quarterly*, Sep. 1947, pp. 321–53.

communities, depopulate the cities, and make not rearmament but housing construction the backbone of the governmentally initiated policy of full employment. All these actions, the generals asserted, would be detrimental to the extensive programme of economic mobilisation. In adopting the rearmament programme of the generals, the leading Nazis administered the death-blow to the programme of transforming Germany into a state of social harmony where everyone should in some way be attached to the soil and derive only a fraction of his income from industrial pursuits. An artisan economy, ruralism, and 'peasant socialism' were incompatible with an economy capable of effective economic mobilisation.[1] Hence, the aspirations of the Nazified middle class had to be, and were successfully frustrated by the ruling Nazi clique as well as the generals.

Economically, a conflict of interest developed between big and small business. The Nazification of the latter had a threefold effect. First, the organised artisans and merchants saw in themselves the leading economic class. They regarded artisan production as being superior to industrial production. Small business thus fought for the leadership of the economy. Secondly, small business developed a principle of economic organisation that deliberately limited the opportunities for industrial growth. The artisan guilds tried to preserve certain areas of economic activity for themselves, excluding the methods of industrial production and large-scale distribution. Within these areas, guilds applied the principles of a closed association and of a horizontal structure of organisation. Masters only were permitted to join the guilds; masters alone were permitted to operate enterprises after they had worked successfully as apprentices and journeymen. Certified masters should thus replace industrial managers; artisan shops should take the place of modern factories. Thirdly, a clash arose between the organisations of big and small business about price and sales policies. Both accepted the idea of prices being fixed by producers. But who should fix that price, industrial cartels or artisan guilds? Both types of organisations were against 'unfair competition', but each defined this concept quite differently. The guilds promoted the idea of each artisan shop having its established customers who would place their orders in advance of production; goods would be produced according to their specific instructions and tastes. Any attempt to disturb this relationship be-

[1] How peasant socialism failed has been well described by Frieda Wunderlich, 'The National Socialist Agrarian Program', in *Social Research*, Mar. 1946. Recent information reveals the full impact of the measures taken by German authorities during the early stages of World War II, to change the rural landscape in Lorraine and Western Poland. These were among the territories which were to be incorporated into 'Greater Germany'. Small farms were replaced by entailed rural estates. The houses of the small owners were torn down. This created an extreme housing shortage which still continues at the time of writing.

tween customer and artisan was regarded as 'unfair competition'. Large-scale advertising was regarded as undesirable. The extensive control of advertising, and the compulsory organisation of advertising agencies under the direction of the Ministry of Propaganda, originated in part from the determination of the guilds to establish a system of closed markets. There was a cleavage between big and small business over leadership, economic organisation, and economic policies.

It is well known today that big business won this struggle during the years from 1933 to 1936. The factory system won over the artisan shop; sales to open markets prevailed over those of closed markets. Economic leadership remained with big business, which, at that time, became concentrated on the national level in the hands of Schacht. A relatively large portion of his time as Minister of Economics was devoted to resisting and defeating the demands of the organised guilds of small business. However, victory was not complete, especially in the field of economic organisation. All firms, large or small, were pressed into the compulsory business organisations (*Wirtschaftsgruppen*). Small business succeeded in retaining its guild organisation which it had secured two weeks prior to the purge of 1934. Artisans were able to establish a system of vocational training and compulsory examinations. Shops and stores of 'incompetents' were closed under pressure and direction of the guilds. The result was a closed economic organisation for artisans and merchants, and a partially open organisation for big business.

This very summary statement on the role of the middle class in the Nazi régime suggests three lessons. In the first place, there was an intimate relationship between the middle class and the Nazi movement. Labour was the enemy, capital in its three forms of big business, owners of estates, and generals, was at the same time the collaborator and active opponent of the Nazi movement and Party. The middle class, however, was a part of the Nazi movement. It was the social class from which the overwhelming majority of its original supporters as well as many of its leaders came, and from which were derived some of its original ideals. A part of the economic programme of the Nazis was identical with the economic demands of the various segments of the middle class. It thus seems possible to say of one aspect of the Nazi movement: in the years 1930–36 it was the movement of the German middle class which had become *the* counter-revolutionary force in Europe.

In the second place, the Nazi movement and Party was more than merely the organised expression of the middle class, trying to represent honestly and adequately the aspirations and interests of the middle groups. 'Middle-class socialism' was only one feature of Nazi ideology. The top leaders of the Nazis felt little psychological or political attachment to the middle class, its aspirations, interests, and well-being. The Party tried to control the existing middle-class groups, and succeeded in establishing a form of organisation that led first to the direction and then to the domination of the middle class. Direction changed into domination during the years 1936–8 when there was the great change in the Nazi régime from rearmament boom to war economy, from the promotion of all Nazi ideals to the exclusive concentration upon imperialism and racialism, from the equal partnership between capital and the Nazi hierarchy, to the reduction of the capitalist groups to the minor holder of power in the régime. After the great divide had been crossed, the middle class lost its privileged position as the social basis of the Nazi movement and was dominated by the ruling Party hierarchy, as was labour.

In the third place, different methods of propaganda, of techniques of control, were employed by the Nazis in the three periods of the relationship between the Nazi Party and the middle class. In the first phase there was mutual penetration of ideas and sentiments. In the following phase, which began after the purge of 1934, there was a concentrated effort by Nazi leaders to mould the middle-class groups into a controlled mass which could be directed successfully without being suppressed outright. It took two years for the direction of the middle class to become complete. In 1937 began the phase of successful domination in which collective self-determination as a group and self-expression of genuine ideas by the various segments of the middle class was suppressed by the Nazis. It was in 1937–8 that the last vestige of middle-class ideological influence disappeared, when the pattern of domination—first developed for and imposed upon labour —was inflicted also upon the middle class.

II

What specifically were the ideas and instruments through which the middle class became the social basis of the Nazi Party? Which conditions facilitated the transformation of the diverse groups between labour and capital into a politically strong, ideologically uniform, counter-revolutionary movement?

Let us begin with the causes of the transformation of the middle class into a bulwark of fascism. Germany in the formative period of the Nazi movement experienced three combined forms of social disintegration. The severity of the economic depression produced a general disorder in the economy and the State. This destroyed the economic foundation for most occupations or professions of the middle class. The threat to the economic existence of entire groups created a widespread emotional insecurity, which resulted in a loss of faith in the values and symbols of the prevailing social order. Economic disorder and emotional insecurity generated, or contributed to, the personal disintegration of many members of the middle class. This was especially true of young men, in business or in the professions, who saw not only their present jobs, but also their expectations of a successful career vanish under the impact of the general disintegration. Many of these men grew very intolerant of others and accepted violence as a means to overcome their personal crises as well as their fear for the continued existence of the middle class. The result of these forms of disintegration was a situation of unrest and increasing radicalism that lent itself to exploitation by political parties.

Why was the overwhelming majority of the middle class receptive to Nazi ideals and why did they accept the principle of political dictatorship? Why, under the impact of the depression, did the resentment of the middle class, which had smouldered before, now bring about an outright counter-revolutionary situation? [1] The answer to this question hinges upon some specific economic, political, and ideological factors that moulded the thinking and directed the actions of middle-class people in the situation of disintegration.

The severe depression had an especially disastrous effect on the middle class. The withdrawal of foreign capital developed into a dangerous flight of capital in 1931. This threatened the currency as well as the banking system and created an extreme situation of external and internal deflation.[2] This deflation was superimposed upon the 'regular' depression, leading to a severe monetary and banking crisis. The banking holidays interrupted money circulation. Banks refused loans or charged a high rate of interest, thereby drying up credit, especially for small business. Deflation thus exerted an extreme downward pressure upon the level of employment of the urban middle class. The crisis was intensified by the Brüning Government, whose efforts to overcome the depression through deflationary measures aggravated the decline of income felt by small business.

Agricultural prices fell severely during the depression, while the prices of many industrial products remained fairly high through the concerted efforts of cartels and combines. Farm prices declined because the demand for agricultural produce decreased as a result of the decline of labour income in the cities. Restriction of agricultural imports was of little avail, since German demand for food was increasingly satisfied by home production. To increase this production, as many farmers did, only had the effect of reducing further the prices of agricultural products. The drastic decline in farm income

---

[1] For the essential data on the depression in Germany, see J. A. Schumpeter, *Business Cycles* (New York, 1939), Vol. II, Chapter XV.

[2] See the penetrating analysis of the deflation and its relation to the depression by Hans Neisser, *Some International Aspects of the Business Cycle* (Philadelphia), Chapters III and IV.

could not be mitigated through loans. On the contrary, the credit crisis induced banks to insist upon payment of debts by farmers. Default in payment, which was an inevitable result of the decline in farm income, was answered by banks with attempts to foreclose farms. Auctions of farms incensed farmers into actions of violence. Resistance to foreclosure became the slogan and practice of the peasants in many regions of Northern Germany. It was the sharp increase in the number of foreclosures that caused the peasant vote to shift from the two conservative parties to the Nazi Party.[1]

The combined impact of price and income decline plus credit crisis was especially felt by the urban middle class, because not many of them were able to rely upon past savings, most of which had been destroyed during the previous hyper-inflation. Nor were the owners of stores or shops, whose net income fell often to almost zero, able to secure unemployment compensation, since they were not covered by the social insurance scheme. On the other hand, white-collar people who lost their jobs tried their hand in retailing, if they had some funds. Thus, the number of retail stores increased greatly while the total volume sold and the turnover per store, diminished severely. The urban middle class had no cushion whatsoever to soften the shock of depression and deflation.

Democratic governments were very willing to subsidise peasants. However, they adopted inadequate methods. High tariffs ceased to be an adequate protection when home production exceeded domestic demand for farm produce. A heavy duty on grain merely increased the costs of the livestock industry, which had to pay higher prices for domestically produced animal food. An adequate programme of supported prices and Government storage did not become effective during the period of the Weimar Republic.[2] The greatest share of the subsidies paid went to the owners of the large estates in East Prussia, upon the personal insistence of President von Hindenburg.[3] The preference given to Junkers thus stood in the way of an effective programme of agricultural price or income support, as did the opposition of big business and some liberal economists who rejected the principle of price support by the Government. The funds spent for agriculture thus did little to soften the impact of depression and deflation upon the peasants.

Depression and deflation created misery and thereby caused a

[1] Compare the conclusive study of the economic status and political affiliation of peasants in North Germany by Rudolf Heberle, 'The Political Movements among the Rural People of Schleswig Holstein, 1919 to 1932', in *Journal of Politics*, Feb. 1943.

[2] See Fritz Baade, *Schicksalsjahre der Deutschen Landwirtschaft* (1933). This book was privately printed and illegally distributed in Nazi Germany. It seems that copies are available only at the libraries of Harvard University and Kiel University.

[3] Brüning and Schleicher were dismissed as Chancellors by Hindenburg when they became reluctant to continue paying the subsidies to the landed estates.

NAZIFICATION OF THE LOWER MIDDLE CLASS AND PEASANTS 585

shift in the mentality and outlook of the middle class. A fundamental protest arose against private capitalism and democracy. Both were held responsible for depression and deflation; the middle class insisted that capitalists and democrats had to be held responsible for the misdeeds they had inflicted upon small business.

Prior to the Great Depression, various groups of the German middle class exhibited simultaneously pre-capitalist, pro-capitalist, and anti-capitalist sentiments. Sentiments favouring capitalism were especially pronounced in urban small business; pre-capitalist sentiments were favoured especially by the rural section of the middle class. Anti-capitalist ideas and sentiments were limited to some segments of the white-collar group. In the 'twenties, union leaders of non-socialist salaried employees strongly believed in solidarity among social classes, in the common interest of employers and employees in enterprises. Studies made by these unions of the economic conditions of salaried employees from 1928 to 1930 revealed widespread discrimination against white-collar workers; salaries below the rates fixed by collective agreements; closed lines of promotion within large concerns. Promotion to the higher managerial positions had almost ceased.[1] As the economic situation for salaried personnel got worse, pro-capitalist sentiments declined rapidly.

The anti-capitalist mentality spread first among the white-collar workers, then among the peasants, and finally among the artisans. An intense hatred pervaded them all. They were looking for an enemy, and found it in some features of private capitalism. Peasants hated, especially, the bankers and wholesalers buying or speculating in farm products. Artisans were incensed by the competition of chain stores, department houses, and consumer co-operatives, as well as by the low prices of industrially manufactured consumer goods which replaced hand-made products. Many white-collar workers hated industrial capitalists and their personnel policies, especially those of dropping older workers on principle or of replacing office staff by machines. All these policies threatened not only the economic position of salaried employees; they also hurt their feelings of class distinction, so typical of Germany. In all, four features of private capitalism came under increasing attack. They were the prevailing credit and banking system, the methods and organisations of monopolistic pricing and buying, the capitalist markets that created such great fluctuations in demand and prices for the products of small urban and rural business, and the large-scale methods of production and distribution of goods by modern combines. Although

---

[1] Among the studies dealing with the situation of salaried employees before and during the Great Depression, see especially Carl Dreyfuss, *Beruf und Ideologie der Angestellten* (Munich, 1933) and Svend Riemer, *Upward Mobility and Social Stratification*, translated by Howard Lissance (New York, 1937).

these institutions were hardly attacked by any one group simultaneously, they incurred the wrath of the various segments of the middle
class. Anti-capitalist sentiments made all sections of the middle class
receptive to radical ideas.

Why did the Nazis succeed in obtaining the loyalty and political
support of these traditionally conservative groups? Three historical
factors, typical of the German middle class, favoured the Nazis.
First, the intense animosity that many peasants or artisans felt
towards the labour movement. Secondly, the lack of democratic
ideals and the indifference of many groups, located between
capital and labour, to the Weimar Republic. And, finally,
the peculiar attachment of strong sections of the middle class to
romantic ideas and their preference for a pre-industrial way of
life. These three factors gave the growing radicalism of the middle
class a counter-revolutionary direction that was beneficial to the
Nazis.

It was an established tradition for the governments of Imperial
Germany, ever since the days of Bismarck, to influence the public
against socialism, as well as against organised labour. This line of
policy was continued in the Weimar Republic by most of the right-
wing political parties and newspapers. It resulted in an increasing
social distance, if not animosity, between organised labour and other
groups. The middle classes had three complaints against organised
labour during the 1920s. The increasing power of the trade unions
had led to a rise of real wages after the hyper-inflation. The power of
unions penetrated into small shops; higher wages raised the cost of
production for their owners and frequently reduced their net profits.
Organised labour was able to get the whole social insurance programme upon the statute books. These laws demanded contributions from smaller employers, yet they were not able to obtain coverage for themselves and their families against the risks most labourers
had secured protection against. Increase in income, protection
against social risks, and greater political influence gradually raised
the standard of living for workers, and gave to the skilled worker a
social status that was higher than that enjoyed by most white-collar
workers and many poor peasants. Relative to many workers, the
middle and upper groups of the middle class experienced a decline
in their social status. The resultant animosity and envy were transformed into outright hatred when the trade unions succeeded in
slowing down the wage decline during the depression, and provided
insurance payments for jobless workers. There was, thus, a conflict
of economic interests affecting both wages and prices. There
was mutual animosity and distruct that developed into a pronounced antagonism during the depression. There was an ideological aversion to working-class socialism of whatever shade, which

many small owners had come to fear as a threat to their business and way of life. Hence, all efforts of trade unions and Social Democrats to change their own policies towards a recognition of some of the economic interests of the small business groups and towards a political alliance between labour and the middle class bore no fruit whatsoever.[1]

Ideals of liberalism and democracy had permeated many sections of the German people after the revolution of 1848. Two events had terminated the peasant support of liberal economic policies: the long agrarian depression of the 1870s which put an end to the peasants' preference for free trade, and German industrialisation in earlier decades, which undermined the predominant position of artisans in the urban economy. Both circumstances were utilised by Bismarck to introduce a policy of protection; this split the democratic parties, one of which supported his measures. The effect of Bismarck's successful policy of agrarian and industrial protection was to divorce economic liberalism from political democracy. Living in the Bismarckian tradition, German small business never fully accepted the principle of free trade in domestic or foreign exchange. Being against *laissez faire* and for artisanship in all its forms, small business could not be satisfied by an anti-trust policy. Nor did its leaders favour the abstinence of the State from interference in economic affairs. For the majority of the German upper and middle classes, democracy was merely one political credo, one mode of government among many, to be chosen according to its practical usefulness in a specific situation. As a result of the breakdown of the monarchy and the defeat in the First World War the majority of the urban and rural middle class voted for democratic parties. When the hyper-inflation of the early 1920s had largely destroyed the savings of the urban middle class and undermined the economic and political order, the middle-class vote went mainly to the two conservative parties, one of which was antagonistic to the Weimar Republic. The disintegrating effect of the inflation thus destroyed the mild beginnings of democratic sentiments and ideals among those groups. The middle class merely tolerated the Weimar Republic. The small political parties, which increased in number prior to the depression, tried merely to represent and to protect the special interest of segments of the middle class. The rise of many splinter parties attests to the fact that a significant portion of the middle class had become ideologically detached from democracy even before the rise of the Nazi

---

[1] The change in policy of the Social Democrats came in 1927–8. It led, for instance, to the adoption of the agrarian tariff programme by the Social Democrats in 1930. This concession proved to be a wrong choice of method, since tariffs ceased to be an effective means of protection for agriculture because of the fall in aggregate demand for food and a rise of domestic agricultural production. Promotion of price supports by the Social Democrats would have been much more effective.

movement. The experiences they had during the depression some eight or ten years after the inflation destroyed their confidence in conservative parties and further undermined their tolerance of the Weimar Republic.

Anti-capitalist feelings, animosity to democratic institutions, antagonism towards labour, united the middle class in opposition to other groups. The depression thus had the effect of overcoming the differences in sentiments among the various segments of the middle class and uniting them into one group that hated capital and labour simultaneously. Both were regarded as the arch enemies of the middle class. The will to destroy the power of both multiplied with the increase in economic misery. This situation confronted the peasant and artisan leaders with the question: What shall replace the prevailing economic order?

The ideal of 'middle-class socialism' was the result of the animosities felt and ideas cherished by many segments of the middle class. The most hated institutions of capitalism had to be replaced first of all. The primary target was the capitalist market, which meant instability of prices and incomes for peasants and owners of shops or stores. Instead of concentrating upon the insufficiency of aggregate demand as the cause of the decline of their incomes and prices, leaders of the urban and rural middle class saw the decisive deficiency in the institution of an unregulated market.[1] The organisations of the producers in city and country should fix prices, determine the entry of firms into the industry, formulate the rules for production and marketing, and set the quality standards of goods. Production and distribution of goods were, as in the old times, to be regulated and directed by the guilds of the producers. Equally, bankers should no longer be allowed to foreclose on farms or shops, nor should they be able to charge excessive interest rates, thus putting the producer in bondage to the bank. The capitalist banking system, dominated by a few large-scale banks, should be abolished. A series of savings banks and credit co-operatives should provide for the credit needs of producers, supported by an effective system of governmental clearing institutions for short-term loans. Similarly monopolies should be replaced by guilds, modern corporations transformed into partnerships, and large mechanised plants into artisan workshops.

The radicalised middle class thus formulated the essentials of a new ideal society. A careful reading of the resolutions of various economic organisations, of their newspapers, periodicals, and pamphlets pub-

---

[1] Economists distinguish between a price deficiency for agricultural goods, and insufficient aggregate demand for the economy as a whole. Yet many try to overcome this deficiency, not through extensive regulations of markets, but through the device of support prices or 'forward pricing'. See especially Theodore W. Schultz, *Agriculture in an Unstable Economy* (New York, 1945).

lished during the depression, suggests two inferences. The contemplated economic reforms suggested themselves to the old leaders of the middle class under the impact of the depression. In other words, their proposals for new institutions were not inferred from a theoretical analysis of capitalism, nor from a critique of the prevailing economic or political philosophy.[1] The ideas propagated by these leaders derived from the romantic nostalgia of artisans for the guilds of the Middle Ages, from a vague preference for a pre-industrial society.

III

How did the Nazis exploit the situation of a middle class that had become united through anti-capitalist, anti-labour, and anti-democratic sentiments and ideas? What was the Nazi attitude towards the romantic ideals of the middle class? The Nazis seized the unique chance to lead and represent the middle class, to rise to power on the wave of resentment and energy of the radicalised middle class. Nazi policies with respect to these groups can be summarised readily under four headings: (a) glorification of the romantic ideals of the middle class, (b) political redirection of its anti-democratic sentiments, (c) identification with its new economic programme, (d) efforts to obtain a Nazified leadership of the middle-class organisations.

The Nazis captured the minds and hearts of the majority of peasants and small business-men through a glorification of the pre-capitalist ideology of the middle class. The desire of peasants for security of land tenure, for protection against creditors, for the stability and continuity of the family farm were glorified by the Nazis into two ideals. The peasantry should be the wealth-giving and value-creating class of the 'new Germany'. Said the leading Nazi agricultural expert, 'The Third Reich will be a peasant Reich or it will not be at all'.[2] Peasants should be enabled to live the best possible lives on model farms, cultivate the land in the most effective manner, produce the healthiest children, and be able to own and utilise their land perpetually. The vision of a society, built upon blood and soil, in which the peasants were to be honoured as the most important social class that lived the most beneficial life, pro-

---

[1] It was Werner Sombart, not the leaders of the middle class, who came to the ideal of a pre-industrial life through an economic and philosophical analysis. See his *Deutscher Sozialismus* (Berlin, 1934). The book was published after the purge of 1934. It was thus rejected by the Nazi leaders instead of being hailed as the 'bible of middle-class socialism'. But Sombart was an ideologist of 'middle-class socialism'; he was a Nazi only in the sense of fully supporting this particular aspect of Nazi ideology.

[2] Herbert Backe, *Das Ende des Liberalismus in der Wirtschaft* (Berlin, 1936), p. 16.

duced a great enthusiasm for the Nazis in all segments of the rural population.

Similar versions were presented to small business-men and to the uprooted and unemployed labourers in cities. The slogan of 'a house for every family', to be built in the countryside or in small communities, satisfied the longing for independence of many workers who did not know how to pay the next rent if the welfare office should withdraw its monthly subsidy. Keepers of stores and shops were heartened by the picture of an artisan economy in which all small owners would have to be thoroughly trained before exercising a trade, where all would produce first-rate products with their own hands, in which everyone would deal honestly with the other masters of his trade or guild, and in which these organisations were to be governed by an ethical code that was enforceable by special courts of honour. Glorification of craftsmanship, recognition of the guild system, and establishment of autonomous 'courts of honour' appeared to many members of the urban middle class as heralding the beginning of a new epoch in which industrialism and ruthless competition would be banned forever.

The Nazis became masters in exploiting the wounded pride of the middle class, and their hatred against other groups. These aversions were transformed into active antagonism towards labo ur, capital, and foreign Powers. Labour was identified with Communism, the arch enemy of Germany. Liberals, democrats, and socialists were all called 'communists'. A fear of an immediate communist revolution was created that became an obsession with many of the new followers of the Nazis. A few of them became zealots in the cause of saving the fatherland from the 'red menace'. Identification of the whole labour movement with Communism enabled the Nazis to present labour leaders as subhuman beings who should be physically eliminated at the first opportunity. Marxism should be eradicated from the minds of every man and woman in the nation; the designation of Communism as the arch enemy, the debasement of its ideology, and the vilification of its leaders, were very powerful devices to mould the middle class into a counter-revolutionary mass movement.

The aversion of the German middle class to the Treaty of Versailles was transformed into intense hatred of the Powers who had been victorious in the First World War. The treaty was represented by the Nazis as the main cause of German economic and political misery. Territorial losses and payment of reparations, it was asserted, had reduced Germany to a proletarian nation. Although payment of reparations was mitigated greatly by the extensive foreign loans, reparations were said to be the major cause of the severe depression. Then came the master trick: the Republic of Weimar was pictured as the tool of the victorious Powers. Democracy was said to be alien to the German national character. Democratic government was claimed to be instigated and imposed by the victors in order to suppress Germany. Hence, democracy had to be destroyed so that Germany could live again; national freedom had to be regained so as to put an end to the depression.

The stage was set for a unilateral destruction of the Treaty of Versailles: nationalism became chauvinism. In placing responsibility for the economic crises upon foreign Powers, and in accusing the German republic of being their tool, the Nazis created a link between depression and democracy, between economic misery and the Treaty of Versailles. The fight against democracy was thus effectively disguised. There was no frank discussion, no careful weighing of the advantages or disadvantages of either democracy or dictatorship. The democratic form of government was simply declared to be responsible for the depression, and this accusation was linked with the promise that a new Reich, its dictatorial character undescribed, would remove democracy, and thereby create national freedom and full employment for all. The preference of the middle class for dictatorship was thus created through the illegitimate identification of democracy with internal depression and external oppression, of dictatorship with full employment and 'national freedom'. No fascist party or régime has ever been able to win middle-class support solely on the merits of dictatorship as a form of government. Dictatorship was presented and accepted as the great saviour of the country from internal and external enemies that threatened its very existence.

The Nazis identified themselves with the specific economic interests of the various middle-class groups. They fought against the forced sale of land or farms by private bankers. They opposed the industrial monopolies or cartels that charged high prices for machines, tools, and other supplies bought by the small business-man or the peasant. They attacked ferociously the chain and department stores as well as consumer co-operatives for their competition against the small merchants. They accused large concerns of paying too low salaries to white-collar workers, and demanded continued employment of older salaried employees. Almost all the immediate economic complaints of the various segments of the middle class were thus accepted by the Nazis and incorporated into their programme for immediate action, once they would come into power.

In interpreting this economic policy, however, the Nazis modified the anti-capitalist sentiment of the middle class. A distinction was made between German and Jewish capital. The latter had to be destroyed or driven from German soil. German capital was declared desirable and necessary. Only two branches of German capital that had misused their power were attacked. Banking capital had exploited peasants and small business-men through excessive interest charges and through foreclosure on encumbered farms. Hence, the banking system had to be reorganised in order to protect the small borrowers from exploitation by financial capital.[1] Equally, trusts and combines were accused of successfully maintaining their prices almost at the pre-depression level, whereas the prices paid by these concerns for the products of peasants or suppliers had been drastically reduced. Hence, the Nazi newspapers in one phase called for the abolition of trusts and for the control of cartels. Misuse of power by large banks and cartels should be eliminated, whereas these organisations themselves should be granted protection.

This interpretation of the role played by large banks and combines had two consequences. Violent anti-Semitism became accepted by various segments of the middle class as a policy of economic reform. Not capitalism itself, but only the association of some capitalists with Jewry, should be terminated; Jewish property should be expropriated by the State. In supporting 'German capitalism', the Party had to revise its 'eternally valid' programme. 'German socialism', they said, was not against the system of private property. Hence, they deleted from their programme the demand for expropriating land without compensation. The proposal to nationalise trusts was struck from the programme. The demand that workers should share the profits of the firms at which they were employed was to be limited to giant enterprises. Private savers should receive the full prevailing market rate of interest for their capital invested; the fight against the 'thraldom of interest' was to apply exclusively to large-scale banks![2] This revision practically eliminated the economic demands of the original Party programme. At the same time, those factions of the Party which favoured public ownership of the means of production were excluded from leading positions. The revised programme incorporated some of the demands of the middle class which facilitated the mutual penetration of the Party and these groups. Finally, recognition of 'German capital' allayed the suspicions felt by some industrial leaders who were now willing to finance the Party more freely. Acceptance of the private enterprise system was a necessary step towards Hitler's appointment as Chancellor, towards a coalition government with Hügenberg, the Conservative leader, in 1933. As the middle class became more Nazified, the Party leaders became more property-minded and friendlier towards a 'German' capitalism. This foreshadowed the resistance of the Party leaders to 'middle-class

---

[1] An investigating commission was appointed in April 1933 which proposed the new Banking Act of 1935. It gave the State the power to fix rates of interest, restricted somewhat the activities of commercial banks, but left the branch banking system of the five large banking concerns undisturbed.

[2] See H. Reupke, *Der Nationalsozialismus und die Wirtschaft* (Berlin, 1931); Hans Aron in *Die Arbeit*, 1931, pp. 137 ff.

socialism'. In the formative period, however, property-mindedness made the Nazi Party more acceptable to capitalists as well as to peasants and artisans.

A similar process of interpenetration can be observed on the level of organisational activities. On the one hand, the Nazis built up their own organisations for the middle class. Many of the younger elements in these groups became active Nazis. Mass meetings, parades, organised violence against members of opposite political organisations, increased the self-esteem of these young men and transformed them into experienced workers for the Party. On the other hand, these Party members were given the assignment to penetrate into the existing middle-class organisations, to become their leaders and to spread Nazi ideas. The Nazified leaders familiarised themselves with the economic problems of the members of those groups and organised campaigns against foreclosure of farms, sales of goods by department stores or by consumer co-operatives, and the like. They even engaged in tax strikes, and organised a collective refusal of farmers to pay interest on their loans to banks. Such actions established the Nazis as the genuine and effective leaders of many economic organisations of the middle class. In other cases, where the old leaders remained at the helm, the rank and file were induced to adopt resolutions supporting the Nazis. In this manner, the membership of these organisations entered politics on the Nazi side and steadily increased the influence of this Party within the middle class.

Ideological penetration, political direction, economic 'actions', and organisational infiltration exerted a profound effect on the middle class. For the first time in many decades, there existed one genuinely accepted ideology that united all sections of the middle groups—namely, 'middle-class socialism.' There was now uniformity in political beliefs and action. The traditional middle-class parties were almost swept from the scene. The Nazis had become the main Party of the middle class.[1] Organisational multiplicity and economic conflicts among the various organisations had come to an end. The economic identification of the Party with these organisations gave their interest a rapidly rising significance that could no longer be overlooked by governments. In consequence, the middle class became the social basis of the Nazis, who had established themselves as the recognized leaders of a counter-revolutionary mass movement.[2]

[1] This is especially true in rural areas. In two districts of Schleswig-Holstein, for instance, the Nazis received 92 and 87 votes out of 100 rural middle-class electors in the November election of 1932. See Rudolf Heberle, 'Ecology of Political Parties', in *American Sociological Review*, Aug. 1944.

[2] On the typology of mass movements, dominated by ideologies, see Arthur Schweitzer, 'Ideological Groups', ibid., Aug. 1944.

IV

What are the circumstances that favour the rise of fascist mass movements?

An analysis of the formative periods of Nazism in Germany and Fascism in Italy seems to support four propositions. First, counter-revolutionary movements spring from a fundamental disorganisation of society which seems to, or actually does, threaten the very existence of the middle classes, economically and politically, socially and psychologically. Secondly, the middle class, before or during a period of disintegration, loses confidence in the system of democratic values, becomes estranged from the leading capitalist groups, develops a gradually increasing antagonism against democratic government, and favours a fundamental change in the prevailing order that points in the direction of a past but idealised phase of the nation's history.[1] Thirdly, a fascist party is able to secure leadership over the diverse middle-class groups only if it succeeds in convincing them that without a fascist dictatorship, the 'arch enemy' cannot be defeated, and if it is able to identify itself with the ideals, sentiments, and interest of all these groups. Fourthly, the fascist party, supported by a radicalised middle class, can usurp political power only if the democratic State is weak, if the armed forces take an attitude of benevolent neutrality towards the fascist private army, and if the capitalist class grants financial support and enters into a political alliance with the fascist party. It is only when the conditions implicit in these four propositions are coexistent, or succeed each other, that disorganisation leads necessarily to a fascist régime.

[1] Compare Theodore Abel, 'The Pattern of a Successful Political Movement', in *American Sociological Review*, Jun. 1937; Louis Wirth, 'Ideological Aspects of Social Disorganisation', ibid., Aug. 1940; Herbert Blumer, 'Collective Behaviour', *An Outline of the Principles of Sociology* (Barnes & Noble, New York, 1939).

18

THE INFLUENCE OF NATIONAL-SOCIALISM ON THE COURTS OF JUSTICE AND THE POLICE

Gerhard F. Kramer

A POLITICAL conspiracy which aims at seizing power and making use of it, is likely to tackle first of all those state institutions which, wielding public authority, can be used for the immediate control of the citizen's conduct. In the modern state such institutions are the judicial power, represented by the courts, and the executive power, principally represented by the police. These are the authorities which claim to compel the individual citizen and the community as a whole to adopt certain standards of conduct, and which lay down penalties in cases of digression from these standards. In democratic countries these standards of conduct are laid down by law, and especially by the constitution within whose terms all laws are made, since their nature must clearly conform to the spirit of the constitution. In a democracy not only is the citizen obliged to conform to the standards of conduct laid down by the law, but the dual nature of the law's force also obliges those institutions whose function it is to enforce the law to act in accordance with the law and with the constitution, both in theory and in practice (the principle of the legality of the administration, the judge subject to law). Those who desire to abolish constitutional order and to replace it with a system laid down by themselves are confronted by the resistance of the authorities whose function is to preserve the constitutional foundations of the nation's life, the law courts, and the executive power.

It is a mistake to believe that the assumption of power can simply be the result of seizing the legislative power. When an opposition movement, having gained a majority as a result of parliamentary elections, has the power to make laws, it is still far from being able to overthrow constitutional order, unless it also controls the executive and judicial powers. This is a consequence of the complicated balance of the three powers in a modern democracy, although fortunately they are not separated from each other in so absolute, and consequently sterile, a manner as Montesquieu advocated. Let us illustrate the effects and relationship of these

595

reciprocal restrictions by a concrete example: the destruction of the Weimar Republic by Hitler and the conspiracy [1] of which he was the head. The German democracy lacked neither a well-defined basic legal constitution, nor a parliamentary majority of parties which respected the constitution. What it did lack, however, was an executive, an executive capable of opposing the conspirators' subversive attacks with adequate strength. The democracy lacked, too, a judicial power able and willing to protect the established constitution from its assailants by a strong enough application of the law. Furthermore, when Hilter secured parliamentary power by 'legal channels', he simultaneously acquired without difficulty sufficient power to discard the constitution *de facto* and to set up his dictatorship.

The Enabling Act of the 24th March 1933 was nothing but a shameful parliamentary screen hiding the modification of the very structure of public life, a change which had already been made, and which was officially justified only after it had occurred.[2] The main reason why the Nazi conspiracy was able to secure effective power so easily was the disintegration of the executive and judicial powers which the conspirators had managed to engineer during their fourteen years' struggle for power. How and in what conditions and circumstances these influences were exerted on public institutions, and how they created disorder, will be described in the first part of this study. In the second part we shall see how, thanks to the use of effective measures, the power which had been acquired was used to control the conspirators and to establish the dictatorship until the completion of the whole system.

I. The Conquest of Power

In order to make the situation quite clear, a general description must be given of the judicial and police systems in Germany from 1918 to 1933.

[1] There is no point in showing here that the movement entitled 'National-Socialist' was in fact a veritable political conspiracy. The fact that the nature of this movement was that of a conspiracy against peace was established in the reasons adduced in judgment at the International Court at Nuremberg, at the trial of the major war criminals. The fact that it constituted from the first a conspiracy against law and order in the Republic of Germany is evident from Hitler's own declarations. In *Mein Kampf* (p. 414), for example, he writes of 'the attack on established order', and of 'brutal attack'. On p. 418 he states that 'the tenets of the party form the new basic laws governing the State'; on p. 507 he writes: 'With the rise of Christianity arose the first spiritual terror (sic) . . . and since that time the world has been dominated by that compulsion . . . compulsion can only be broken down by compulsion and terror by terror,' etc.

[2] See also *Judgment of the International Military Tribunal*, Vol. I, p. 197: 'Hitler then submitted the Enabling Bill to the *Reichstag*. After he had made it clear that if this law was rejected other violent measures would be taken, the law was passed on 24 Mar. 1933.'

The German judicial system was based on the 'laws of justice of the Empire' (*Reichsjustizgesetze*),[1] which had all come into force on the 1st October 1879. Under these laws, jurisdiction was exercised by the independent State courts (*Länder*), and in the highest instance by the High Court of the Empire (*Reichsgericht*). The courts were administered by independent judges holding life appointments, who could not be transferred against their wishes. The judges were bound only by law and by conscience. They were not elected, but nominated through administrative channels by the supreme judicial authorities. The qualifications required for a magistrate were acquired after at least three years' study of law at a university, followed by a preparatory period of three years in the courts, with the public prosecutor, an advocate or notary. At the end of the period at a university there was an examination called the referendary examination (first state examination), and after the preparatory period another examination entitled the assessor's examination. The whole German system of jurisdiction was (and still is in the Federal Republic) in the hands of jurists trained in this way. The system of justices of the peace who deal with minor cases was, and still is, unknown in German law. Juries elected by the people were, and are, only to be found as assessors to qualified judges in collegiate courts. One exception, however, were the Assize Courts (*Schwurgericht*), which existed for the trial of serious crimes and had a separate bench of jurymen (since 1849 in Prussia, and for the rest of the Empire from 1879 until 1924).[2]

The apprehension and prosecution of criminals was the responsibility of the Public Prosecutor (*Staatsanwaltschaft*). The Public Prosecutor's authority was distinct from that of the courts. Appointments were made in accordance with the laws of Justice of the Empire already mentioned. They had to be qualified jurists. Unlike judges,

[1] The law relating to the constitution of Courts (*Gerichtsverfassungsgesetz*) of 27 Jan. 1877, the Code of Criminal Procedure (*Strafprozessordnung*) of 1 Feb. 1877, and the Code of Civil Procedure (*Zivilprozessordnung*) of 30 Jan. 1877.

[2] Emminger's judicial reform law (named after the Minister of Justice then in office) caused the disappearance of the Assize Court. In its place was set up a court consisting of three qualified jurists and six jurymen assessors who sat together, in secret, and with the right to speak and vote on fact as well as law. The name Assize Court (*Schwurgericht*) was, however, kept. This measure complied with an old demand of the reactionary magistrature who considered the Assize Court to be a running sore, mainly because the judges had no direct influence over the jury. In the German magistrates' journal, for example, one author (De Niem) expresses his dislike of it in the following terms (*Deutsche Richterzeitung*, 1922, p. 1): 'The proposed municipal magistrates court (*Schöffengericht*) is nevertheless preferable to the total failure constituted by the Assize Court (*Schwurgericht*), of which the only thing of any use is its name. It would be admirable if the name and all its responsibilities were transferred to the new court. The public would then be satisfied, as would the street-corner politicians. The Assize Court would thus be conserved (!) and liberty preserved. The new court is at any rate acceptable in that its judges, that is the judge-civil servants of the old school, retain its direction, and in that the large juries will willingly allow themselves to be ruled by them.'

U

however, they were subject to instructions from higher authority (Ministry of Justice), and could be transferred or retired at any time.

Finally, the profession of advocate, practised by independent advocates who are also qualified jurists and are grouped in Chambers of Advocates, was also subject to a certain degree of discipline and jurisdiction of a professional nature.

The organisation of the German police, in the form which it had in the years 1918–33, was appreciably younger than the judicial organisation. The Empire had been satisfied with a comparatively small police force. A large army supported the public powers in the maintenance of internal order, an army which, as it was said at the time, could be used at any moment against 'the internal enemy'.

After 1918, in accordance with the terms of the Treaty of Versailles, the Republic maintained an army of 100,000 men, the *Reichswehr*. This army could not, however, be called upon by the *Länder*, although they alone were responsible for maintaining internal order and peace under the constitution. The *Reichswehr* was primarily, as its name shows, envisaged as representing the Reich's strength, although in practice it was soon transformed into a sort of state within the state.[1] The President of the Reich could only use the country's forces in accordance with Article 48 of the Weimar constitution—that is, when order and peace were seriously endangered throughout or in part of the Reich and when local forces were too few to restore order. The Treaty of Versailles had established that the governments of the *Länder* should have at their disposal police forces in sufficient strength to provide effective protection: the *Schutzpolizei* (protective police), who wore first green, then blue uniforms.

This police was entirely new. Unlike the judicial system, it was not a system inaugurated by the Empire and adopted by the Republic, nor was it a natural descendant of the Wilhelmian army or of its illegitimate and abandoned by-product, the 'Free Corps', as was largely the case of the *Reichswehr*. The *Schutzpolizei* was rather a true child of the Republic. The political desires of the Republican ministers fashioned its external appearance as well as the type of officers and men in its ranks. The biggest and most powerful formation of the *Schutzpolizei* was that belonging to the state of Prussia. Prussia, the largest and most powerful of the German states, had

---

[1] cf. for the role of the *Reichswehr* in the Kapp *Putsch* of 1920: Olden, *Hindenburg*, p. 169, etc. For the relations between the army and the SA: Hitler, *Mein Kampf*, p. 619 (a somewhat reticent account by Hitler himself). For the 'fixed-period volunteers' of the *Reichswehr* troops and their connection with the Vehme murders: Grimm, 'Legal study of the proceedings against Fuhrmann and others' (Lieutenant Paul Schulz); also the judgment of the *Landgericht* III of Berlin of 26 Mar. 1927 (Ref. F.5.J.892/25); for the influence of the *Reichswehr* on government policy: Olden, quoted above, p. 234, etc., 'The army rules'.

under the Empire always been considered the cradle of reaction, militarism, and the 'Junker' spirit. Under the government of the old prime minister Otto Braun, Prussia became the first standard-bearer of republican freedom. The main executive prop of this state was its police, set up by the Minister of the Interior, Carl Severing. The first chief of the Gestapo [1] had this to say of its members: 'The vigilant activity of these men had made of each one of them a considerable personage, and, aided by their *savoir-faire*, their political instinct and their dignity, they gained the respect of the Communists and of the National Socialists themselves, as the symbol of a *raison d'état*. Ruled personally by the Minister of the interior with a rod of iron, under the care of Abbeg [2] and Klausener, [3] the *Schutzpolizei* was the only really solid institution among the short-lived improvisations of the Weimar Republic.'

Although the most important facts concerning the organisation and strength of the police authorities can be given in a few lines, a study of the judicial organisation of the period is of necessity a great deal longer.

The following point, the most important, must be considered first:

In 1918 the Republic took over all the employees and all the laws of the Wilhelmian judicial system. In the opinion of the author, too much importance should not be attached to the fact that the laws concerning the judicial system remained intact. Apart from the unfortunate and insignificant role played by the 'lay' judges (*Laienrichter*), the German judicial system was certainly not one of the most imperfect in an imperfect world. The truth of Plato's observation that the best institutions of the state are useless if the 'inspired men' whose function is to represent the 'reason of the whole' are lacking [4] is illustrated in this case. The phrase 'men, not measures', with the brevity of a proverb, means the same thing. But the employees of the state, especially the magistrates of the monarchy, were all without exception taken over by the Republic. The 1918 revolution did not alter the irremovability of the judges installed by the *Länder* monarchies and sworn in by them—a further reason for doubting whether the upheaval of the 9th November 1918 was in fact a true revolution or whether it was not merely the consequence of the military disasters and of the flight of the princes. [5]

[1] Diels, *Lucifer ante portas*, p. 163.
[2] Secretary of State to the Minister for the Interior of Prussia.
[3] First secretary to this ministry, later to the Ministry of Transport, assassinated on 30 Jun. 1934.
[4] Quoted by Wilamowitz-Moellendorf, *Plato*, p. 542.
[5] Anschütz, an eminent authority on the Weimar Republic states (note 5, p. 32): 'Between the new and the old Reich the judicial relationship is not one of succession, but of identity.' Warnegger, in *Die Justiz*, Vol. 5, p. 5, accepts the continuity in the evolution of law from the Empire to the Republic, via the Revolution.

In any case, it was astonishing that the independence of the judges was respected. Even at the congress of German magistrates at Augsburg on the 14th and 15th September 1925 the chairman [1] himself admitted that he considered it 'peculiar' that the judicial position of judges in the state had remained positively the same as in 1911.

One of the principal causes of the failure of the public authorities in the face of the Nazi conspiracy lay in the sociological structure and the spirit of the body of magistrates, accepted by the Republic as a legacy from the Monarchy. This cause was active within the Weimar system itself; for this reason I have named it the internal cause of the collapse, as opposed to National-Socialist attacks which came from without, and were therefore external causes. The two types of cause, internal and external, worked together, each reinforcing the effects of the other, and together prepared the ground for the ruin of democracy and the victory of dictatorship.

The body of magistrates, in its social structure, belonged to the middle classes. These were the strata of society which, inheriting the great spiritual traditions of classical German humanism from the age of Goethe, had led the nation to that hope-filled spring of 1848.[2] The autumn of reaction which followed this democratic spring allowed a new kind of *bourgeoisie* to arise. Bismarck's 'blood-and-iron' policy produced the external lustre of power and plenty. The consolidation of the Empire and the increased well-being which were the result of booming industrialisation created a new kind of German middle class: profit-seeking, centred on material pleasures and on life, proud of the power and greatness of its country and obedient to that authority which it judged legitimate. It was the type of middle class of the Wilhelmian period described by Heinrich Mann in *Untertan*, which, apart from the limitations essential in novels, is so extraordinarily near the truth. The German judge came from this class. He had grown up in the atmosphere of confidence with which the Empire favoured the *bourgeoisie* as 'props of the state'. The magistrature was legitimist; it considered the country's monarchic constitution as an historic evolution willed by God. It was positivist; the idea of a spiritual, moral, and human

---

[1] Wunderlich, 'The Situation of the German Judge' in *Deutsche Richterzeitung*, 1925, pp. 19 seq.: 'On approaching the first question, that of the situation of the judge, I must personally state that the details given by our president in 1911 about our judicial position in the state are still very largely true today. Few changes have been made compared with the past, notwithstanding the great change in the régime which occurred in 1918–19. Professor Errera, in his *Droit public du Royaume de Belgique*, speaking of the 1830 Revolution, quotes as particularly rare the fact that this revolution did not abolish the irremovability of the office of judge. . . . We may make the same remark.'

[2] See Ricarda Huch's description of political and social currents in *The Nineteenth-Century Revolution in Germany*.

class of natural law, a law superior to formal law and to the manifestations of the state, was foreign to it. Furthermore, this body of magistrates came into existence at a time when the masses were making a violent irruption into the established order. This historic happening, whose characteristic mark is branded upon our time, also allowed an unfortunate type of small *bourgeois* to become important within the magistrature, a type of *bourgeois* for whom power signifies 'moral grandeur', success 'moral justification', and science 'a sum of acquired experience'.[1]

Such were the magistrates whose task it was to defend the Republic from the attacks of the Nazi conspiracy; their views, fundamentally legitimist in the monarchic sense, naturally led them to detest that republic which seemed to them the result of high treason against the nation. The fact that the republican constitution was the work of a national assembly formed by free elections meant nothing to them; in fact they were unfamiliar with the idea of the sovereignty of the people. They considered themselves members of an exclusive caste endowed with many privileges. Their pretence of administering a justice free from and uncontaminated by any political influence was as invalid as the *Reichswehr*'s claim to be non-political. With very few exceptions, the magistrature as a whole was a high-class political mouthpiece. This was clear from the way in which the judges gave justice in political cases. As to the extent to which their repeated professions of political neutrality, this a-political attitude of the German judges of that period, is to be believed, a glance at a few numbers of the *Deutsche Richterzeitung*, the official organ of the association of German jurists, with 12,000 members, including the majority of the magistrates, is sufficiently enlightening. In innumerable articles, appeals, and orations it is continually stated that German judges are a-political, and that politics must be outlawed from jurisprudence.[2] In fact, reading between the lines, a strong political attitude, opposed to the republic and to democratic government, can clearly be discerned. Under the guise of defending the independence of magistrates, the intrusion of laymen into justice is opposed by bitter attacks upon democratic institutions.[3]

[1] cf. Ortega y Gasset, *The Revolt of the Masses*, pp. 72 seq.; 116 seq.

[2] Two examples are given although there are many others: *Deutsche Richterzeitung*, 1922, p. 258: 'The Song of Songs of German Judges,' Wunderlich, *Deutsche Richterzeitung*, 1925, suppl., p. 34: 'It is for me a banal truth that the judge should disregard all political influence in the exercise of his duties.'

[3] de Niem (op. cit. 1922, p. 1 seq.) writes of 'street-corner politicians', of 'the brawler in popular meetings, the man high-placed in the party, the secretary in the union, the politician in the street'; Unhold, op. cit. 1922, pp. 34 seq.: 'We declare that we live in a democracy, in a free people's state, but we are advancing towards ever more brutal domination by the masses and by the plebs'... 'the fathers of the Weimar Constitution ... are unaware that they ... have constructed a democracy for the inevitable reign of the masses or of the plebs (Ochlocracy)'.

There are attacks upon the First article of the Constitution of the Reich.[1] This definition of a fundamental law was not considered applicable to their practice of the legal profession.[2] It was not even thought that the judge's oath bound him to the republican state.[3]

Friedrich Ebert, first President of the German Republic, died on the 28th February 1925. It was to him that the judges of the monarchy owed their independence under the Republic. He it was who had put a stop to the revolution of 1918. His remark, 'I hate revolution as I hate sin', is well known. The *Journal of the German Magistrature* devoted precisely five sentences to his memory; and, on account of the a-political nature of this journal, the fact that it was not possible to do justice to this leader of the state was stressed.[4]

On the other hand, on the 9th November 1923 von der Pfordten, Judge of Appeal of the Supreme Court of Bavaria, died. He met his death before the famous *Feldherrnhalle* in Munich while taking part in the Hitler–Ludendorff *Putsch*. One of his colleagues, Counsellor Pöhner, who was also involved in the *Putsch*, was tried and sentenced to five years imprisonment for high treason. Before the court Pöhner rejoiced in the fact that he had been a traitor for five years, ever since he had sworn allegiance to the constitution of the Reich.[5] The *Deutsche Richterzeitung* published an obituary notice expressing its regard for von der Pfordten and also extending its sympathy to the convicted traitor.[6]

[1] 'The German Reich is a republic. The authority of the state emanates from the people.'

[2] Richard Fränkel, *Deutsche Richterzeitung*, 1923, pp. 65 seq.: 'The judge must refuse a republicanism which makes him the door-keeper of the republican state of the moment.'

[3] Reichert, president of the association of German jurists and editor of the *Deutsche Richterzeitung* at the time of the congress of magistrates at Hamburg 1925 (*Deutsche Richterzeitung*, 1925, appendix, p. 17): 'German judges honour and respect the Constitution; they have sworn allegiance to the Constitution and a German judge keeps his word. But the interpretation which we judges give to the Constitution is not primarily the form of the State.'

[4] *Deutsche Richterzeitung*, 1925, p. 133: 'The professional association of German judges whose members are of all parties has always rigorously forbidden any political activity or demonstration. Therefore the true value of the political work of the late President cannot be fully described in these pages. But, without compromising our non-political aims, we can express our great regard for him and our gratitude to him for his efforts to guide the ship of state through so troublous times and over the reefs of such painful political contrasts, efforts which led him to the most exalted post in the Reich.'

[5] From the verbatim report of the proceedings quoted in V. Kursell: *The Trial of Hitler*, p. 40; Pöhner: 'If what you accuse me of is high treason, then I have been a traitor for five years.'

[6] *Deutsche Richterzeitung*, 1924, p. 121: 'The names of two of the most eminent Bavarian judges were associated with Hitler's venture. Von der Pfordten fell in the fighting of the 9th November; it is difficult to decide to what extent he was involved in the affair. The Minister of Justice was present at his funeral which shows that he was not regarded as a traitor. He was an idealist whose eyes were fixed on the highest pinnacles, and who pursued with unshakeable determination those ends

Let us consider next the jurisprudence of the magistrature of the German Republic. Goethe wrote in *Faust*: 'A judge who is unable to punish becomes ultimately the criminal's partner!' The order of this sentence could almost be reversed. How could those who were in sympathy with the enemies of the Republic punish those who infringed republican laws? How even could they distinguish between justice and injustice, between good and evil, when they themselves were deeply involved in a conflict of opposing opinions, and had long ago taken up sides?

I now propose to select a few typical examples from numerous judicial rulings in order to throw light on the opinions of the courts, and therefore on the internal causes of the collapse of the Republic, without, for the moment, dealing with external causes.

The Hitler–Ludendorff trial, which took place before the Munich *Volksgericht* [1] (Extraordinary People's Tribunal) from the 26th February to the 1st April 1924 [2] is significant both from the political and from the legal point of view. Part of the main hearing took place in camera, and public opinion will doubtless never know what took place in secret. What took place during the public hearings was so monstrous that it can only be described as a legal catastrophe. [3] The principal public prosecutor, Dr Stenglein, thought it advisable to mention in his indictment that the revolution of the 9th November 1918 had constituted 'a crime of high treason'. In his outline of the circumstances of Hitler's *putsch* of the 9th November 1923 he could not gloss over the fact that the accused's crime, from the latter's own sincere confession, constituted a case of high treason. But this did not deter him from furnishing political explanations in favour of the

---

which seemed to him to be right. Pöhner is a man of the same calibre, except perhaps that his view of life is less sure and less optimistic. He is entitled to say of himself: Patriae in serviendo consumor! (I die in the service of my country).'

[1] The atmosphere of Munich was much more favourable to Hitler and to the others who were accused than that of Berlin (seat of the High Court) or that of Leipzig (seat of the Supreme Court of the Empire). However, the competence of the Munich *Volksgerichtshof* to try the criminals of the 1923 affair was very widely discussed; from a purely legal point of view it undoubtedly was not competent. The prosecution was based on the second paragraph of Article 81 of the penal code, which lays down penalties varying from five years' detention to life imprisonment for any person found guilty of high treason. Under Article 134 of the law on the constitution of courts, the *Reichtsgericht* was normally the competent body to try such offences. But as a result of the promulgation of the law on the protection of the Republic on 21 Jul. 1922, the highest authority competent to try the crime of high treason was the *Staatsgerichtshof* (Article 13 of this law). A struggle for powers of jurisdiction took place between the central judicial authorities and those of Bavaria. The authority of the Reich was at that time so weak that the powerful state of Bavaria succeeded in winning the day (cf. Breuer, *Der Hitler–Ludendorff-Prozess*, p. 12).

[2] cf. for the account of the proceedings: Bremer and v. Kursell, *The Hitler–Ludendorff Trial*, p. 12; Heiden, pp. 172, seq.

[3] Högner, *Deutsche Justiz*, Vol. III, p. 323.

accused, explanations which amounted to the glorification and in fact the justification of his deeds.[1] The prosecution also glorified the acts of the other defendants, in particular those of Ludendorff. Hitler, Weber, Kriebel, and Pöhner were each sentenced to five years imprisonment and a fine of 200 gold marks, but with the remission of the period they had already spent in custody. Brückner, Röhm, Pernet, Wagner, and Frick were each sentenced to fifteen months imprisonment for aiding and abetting high treason. In the reasons adduced in judgment the court found the means of glorifying the defendants.[2] The verdict shows that the court was unwilling to apply the terms of the law on the protection of the Republic (art. 9, para. 2) in the case of Hitler. The terms of this law are as follows: 'Extradition from the territories of the Reich shall be declared in the case of foreigners.' This is a legal and obligatory injunction to judges. Hitler was Austrian, and therefore a foreigner, and his extradition from the territories of the Reich should have been declared. The court refused to apply the terms of this law in Hitler's case on the grounds that the paragraph in question could not be made to apply 'to a man who thought and felt so like a German'. It was a veritable denial of the law, and at this point the judge becomes the criminal's accomplice.[3]

This was not the only anomaly, however; five of those sentenced, among whom were Röhm, the future chief of the SA, and Frick, were given a stay of execution of sentence valid from that moment until the 1st April 1928, and were set free. The other sentenced men, like Hitler and Pöhner, were given to understand that a similar stay would be granted them after they had been in prison for six months. This whole proceeding was nothing but a subtle comedy performed in favour of Adolf Hitler, the leader of the conspiracy. The leading part in this detestable comedy whose *dénouement* had tragic consequences for the German people and for the world was none other than the Bavarian Minister of Justice, Dr Gürtner.[4] This fellow conspirator of the Nazi criminals, ignoring his duty, made use of his position as head of the Bavarian administration of

[1] About Hitler (Kursell, pp. 223 seq.), 'Adolf Hitler, of modest origins, fought in the Great War as a volunteer and distinguished himself by exceptional bravery. In spite of the revolution his views remained constant, and, after a very modest beginning, he founded the National-Socialist movement whose aims were to combat Marxism and the Jewish race, and to punish the November criminals (1918). . . . His claim to glory remains, that of having propagated belief in the Great German Cause by his efforts.'

[2] Kursell, p. 224: '. . . but against this deed must be set Ludendorff's selfless devotion to the cause of the people to whom he dedicated his life, the purity of his intentions and aims, and the debt of gratitude owed by the people of Germany to a great military leader.'

[3] Heiden, p. 198: 'Hitler appeared before judges who were in reality his accomplices.'

[4] Heiden, pp. 202 seq.: 'Gürtner saves Hitler.'

justice to protect Hitler from punishment and to set him loose as quickly as possible on the people of Germany. Gürtner was rewarded for his splendid action after the seizure of power when he became Minister of Justice, a post he held, to the greater misfortune of the German people, until his death on the 29th January 1941.

Gürtner's actions in assisting Hitler caused a commission of inquiry to be held at the Bavarian *Landtag*.[1] The results of this inquiry were as follows. In 1922 Hitler had been sentenced to three months' imprisonment for breaking the peace. He served one month in prison and the other two were remitted. On the 1st May 1923 he committed another crime by having weapons and ammunition seized from a *Reichswehr* barracks so as to arm his partisans and to 'shoot down like mad dogs' the workers on the holiday of the 1st May. He was unable to carry out this criminal project because General von Lossow foiled it by recovering the arms and weapons from the barracks—it was for this reason that Hitler accused him at the *Volksgericht* hearing of having broken his promise.[2] In any case the preparations already made for this project constituted a crime provided for by the criminal code. It is a curious fact that both the sub-committee and its critics Högner and Sinzheimer only mention the crime of setting up an armed band.[3] There can be no doubt that what Hitler planned for the 1st May 1923 involved much more serious criminal actions; first, incitement to breaking the peace inasmuch as the leaders of the conspiracy were concerned (Art. 49 (*a*) and Art. 125 (para. 2) of the Penal Code); and secondly, preparation for the crime of murder (Art. 49 (*b*) of the Penal Code under Art. 25 of the law on the protection of the Republic, in force in Bavaria since 24.8.22). When the Public Prosecutor, who had been responsible for the preparatory investigation of the crime, desired to place the matter before the *Volksgericht*, Gürtner instructed him first of all and 'before taking any further steps' to draw up a list of the persons who, in his opinion, should be accused, and to send him this list with his views on the advisability of opening criminal proceedings. He was later instructed not to demand the fixing of a date for the hearing until he received an order to do so from the Minister of Justice. This order never came. The possibility of combining the proceedings concerning the happenings of the 1st May 1923 with a high treason charge on the Hitler–Ludendorff *putsch* of the 9th November 1923 was examined. But this proposal was also rejected. On the 22nd May 1924, the Public Prosecutor, in agreement with

---

[1] Sinzheimer, *German Justice III*, p. 196, and Högner, op cit., pp. 315 seq.
[2] Kursell, p. 181.
[3] Art. 127 of the Penal Code: 'Any man who without authorisation sets up an armed band . . . or assembles a company of men without legal authorisation and provides it with arms or equipment of war shall be punished by a prison sentence not exceeding two years.'

Gürtner, suspended the proceedings under the new Article 154 of the code of criminal procedure which had been in force since the 22nd March 1924. Here it must be mentioned that in German law (Art. 152 of this code) the Public Prosecutor is under the obligation of taking action on all illegal activities when grounds for such action exist. There are few exceptions to this established legal principle. Article 154 of this code did, however, lay down that the Public Prosecutor could suspend proceedings if the penalty for the crime in question was not consistent with the penalty already announced for another crime. As a result of the legal reform brought about by the Minister of Justice for the Reich, Emminger, the Public Prosecutor had had the right, since the 22nd March 1924, to suspend proceedings on minor offences conflicting with some other crime, under Article 154 of the code of criminal procedure. Apparently Gürtner did not wait for this legal reform before finally quashing the proceedings against Hitler concerning the affair of the 1st May 1923. Furthermore, the effect of the offence of the 1st May 1923 should have been to suspend the two months' remission of sentence granted Hitler after his crime of breaking the peace in 1922. But, under Gürtner's orders, the Public Prosecutor never thought of demanding the revocation of this remission of sentence and of making Hitler serve his full term. This, too, constituted a flagrant breach of law. Before the sub-committee of inquiry Gürtner made the excuse that this was done for reasons of political expediency. Schweyer, Minister for the Interior, who had also been a member of the Bavarian Government in 1923, demolished this defence before the committee. Schweyer even stated that if Hitler had been sentenced for his activities of the 1st May 1923 and if his remission of sentence had been cancelled, the leaders of the *putsch* of the 9th November 1923 would almost certainly have been unable to carry out their plans. From a purely legal point of view, they should at that moment have been behind bars. Thus Gürtner was morally, and also perhaps legally, responsible for the events of the 8th and 9th November 1923.

Yet Gürtner did a great deal more than this for Hitler and his adherents. The Department of the Public Prosecutor appealed against the *Volksgericht*'s verdict of the 1st April 1924 on the question of the 1923 *putsch*, which granted Hitler and his associates a remission of sentence after six months. On the 24th April 1924 the Public Prosecutor withdrew his appeal on the orders of the Bavarian Minister of Justice. On the 26th September 1924 the Third Penal Chamber of the *Landgericht* (Court of Appeal) at Munich granted the remission of sentence. The Public Prosecutor appealed once more. But the Supreme Court of Bavaria gave the following decision: the decision of the *Volksgericht* on the 1st April 1924 constituted a valid recognition of the law on the remission of sentence. And since, on the instructions of the Minister of Justice, the Public Prosecutor had withdrawn his appeal, this verdict became enforceable. So that, the Supreme Court continued, the question of whether the remission decreed by the *Volksgericht* was valid in law no longer arose.

Hitler and his accomplices were released on the 11th December 1924. The commission of inquiry set up by the Bavarian *Landtag* agreed unanimously that Gürtner had not been guilty of partiality in the exercise of his duty.[1] But the Commission was unable to reach agreement on the question of whether he had violated the Bavarian constitution.

These events show how completely one man can control the machinery of law, and therefore how he can be responsible for events profoundly affecting the evolution of history.

In any case, consciously or unconsciously, the jurisprudence of German courts was so actively at work to destroy the Republic, and therefore to prepare the way for Nazism, that these few officials who were in fact accomplices of the conspirators needed to do little. In accordance with Article 12 of the law on the protection of the Republic, a kind of High Court (*Staatsgerichtshof*) had been established within the Supreme Court of the Reich (*Reichsgericht*); this court, composed of three members of the *Reichsgericht* and of six others who were not necessarily qualified jurists, also indulged in an extremely odd kind of jurisprudence. In any case it was dissolved in 1926. The *Reichsgericht* once more became competent to deal with cases of high treason, and the criminal senates of the regional courts dealt with less serious offences. Infractions of the law on the protection of the Republic which did not constitute high treason[2] were from the first dealt with by the ordinary courts.

These are a few examples taken from the proceedings of the High Court (*Staatsgerichtshof*) and of the ordinary courts:

The hearings of actions against members of secret para-military organisations accused of the murder of other members who were supposed to have betrayed their organisation (known as *Vehme* murders on account of the axiom 'traitors shall be punished by *Vehme*') almost always took place in camera, apparently because of the fear that preparations for German rearmament might be disclosed.

---

[1] Art. 346 of the Penal Code: 'Any official, who in the exercise of his duty to punish or to carry out the sentence of the law as required by his position, refrains from instituting proceedings against any person guilty of a punishable action with the intention of illegally protecting that person from the penalty laid down by law, shall be liable to a penalty not exceeding five years' imprisonment.'

[2] Arts. 7 and 8: Outrages and defamation committed against members of the Government of the Republic, whether they be dead or alive, glorification of the murder of members of the government, taking part in secret meetings, public outrages against the republic or its colours.

This was regarded as prejudicial to the interests of the Reich, unlike the fact of the existence of secret organisations, which was not regarded as a danger. The conviction of the pacifist author Carl von Ossietzki by the *Reichsgericht* in 1932 for 'literary treason' is also a case in point. Von Ossietzki had published in his paper the *Weltbühne* [1] articles by Berthold Jacob on the clandestine army (*Reichswehr*). This simple example indicates with terrifying clarity the extent to which jurisprudence under the Republic logically tended towards the Nazi dictatorship. After Hitler's assumption of power, Jacob was kidnapped by the SS in Switzerland in 1933, but after an action at the arbitration court at the Hague, the Nazis were obliged to return him to Switzerland. Later Ossietzki was imprisoned in a concentration camp and was only released when he was awarded the Nobel Prize for Peace. He died as a result of his captivity, and Germans living under the authority of the Nazis were forbidden to accept a Nobel Prize for Peace.

The verdict of the *Staatsgerichtshof* at the second Rathenau trial is typical. A man named Küchenmeister, who had provided the car used by the murderers, was extradited from Austria, tried by the *Staatsgerichtshof*, and acquitted. And this in spite of the fact that it had been definitely established at the first trial of the murderer's accomplices that Küchenmeister had a store of arms in his house. [2] The public only learnt incidentally, during the hearing of one of the men who had been convicted at the first trial, that this man had been reprieved. [3] In this manner, too, an actor was sentenced for having given a public recital of works by the contemporary poet Ernst Toller and by the *bourgeois* revolutionary of 1848, Georg Herwegh. [4]

Leaving the *Staatsgerichtshof*, that select body whose special function was to protect the Republic, in order to consider the ordinary courts, the picture becomes even more lamentable. The main characteristic of their jurisprudence was to consider the hostility to the Republic of defendants as an extenuating circumstance. One defendant, with a very bad record, was merely fined for seriously slandering Hörsing, head of the Republican *Reichsbanner* association, and an important Prussian official. The fact that his intention was to describe 'the system which he hated fanatically' rather than the person himself was considered a reason for special clemency. [5] The practice of the courts in the judgment of political

---

[1] This paper was the organ of the German liberal left, middle-class and radical-pacifist.
[2] Brammer, *The Political Consequences of the Rathenau Trial*, p. 47.
[3] cf. *Deutsche Justiz*, Vol. I, p. 74. The circumstances legally necessary for obtaining a reprieve were poverty or mental debility.
[4] ibid., p. 75.
[5] ibid., p. 518.

torts was such that Wilhelm Marx, Chancellor of the Reich, was led to state in a public speech to the *Reichstag* on the 12th March 1926 that in future he would bring no more actions for political torts, since the state of jurisprudence at that time left him in no doubt as to their outcome. Shortly before, a Nazi who had declared that Ebert, President of the Reich, made business deals for his own advantage—a slander that attracted a great deal of publicity—had been sentenced to a fine of fifty marks.

The great danger which this jurisprudence was to public morality only became really clear when hatred of the Republic became as strong as hatred of the Jews. Anti-Semitism had a place in the programme of the popular precursors of Nazism from the start. Hitler later made of it a racial doctrine that was the focal point of the Nazi faith.[1] The Nuremberg laws of the 15th September 1935 [2] constituted the formal consecration of this doctrine of the Third Reich, a doctrine which was to reach its highest degree of intensity and its terrible conclusion with the massacre of six million Jews in the gas chambers of the Eastern countries occupied by Germany.

Here are a few examples of how this phase, racial madness in the Republic, is reflected in the jurisprudence of 'republican' courts. In 1925 the Helling–Haas–Schröder affair aroused public opinion with a violence comparable to that aroused in the French people a quarter of a century earlier by the Dreyfus case. But alas, in Germany there was no Zola to awaken the people's conscience, and no Clemenceau to transpose the demands of awakened conscience to the level of political reality. There was much noise and shouting, but nothing was changed. These are the essential facts of this affair, which took place in Saxony. A man named Helling had been murdered, and all the clues pointed to Schröder; however, the examining magistrate, Kölling, and the criminal commissioner, Tenholt, suspected the industrialist Haas. Haas was a Jew and supported the pro-republican *Reichsbanner* Association. He was arrested on suspicion. Although evidence against Schröder was building up, the examining magistrate was unwilling to abandon his first theory of Haas' guilt. At this stage Hörsing, first President of Saxony, entrusted the inquiry to the Berlin Criminal Commissioner, Busdorf; the latter made nonsense of the preliminary investigation of Kölling and his minions. The story now became even more fantastic; instead of listening to the voice of reason, Kölling stuck ever more rigidly to his position of suspecting Haas; he was supported by his superior, *Landgerichtsdirektor* Hoffman. Both regarded Hörsing's efforts to get to the bottom of the affair as interfering

[1] cf. 'Peoples and Races' in *Mein Kampf*, pp. 311 seq.
[2] See for example 'the glorification of the anti-semitic racial policy' in Stuckart-Globke, *Commentary on German racial legislation*, pp. 3, 7, 9 seq.

with the independence of justice. The reactionary, anti-semitic judges entered into a struggle with the republican administration of the state, at the expense of Haas, who had had nothing to do with the matter. At last Schröder was completely unnerved, and confessed. Haas was set free. As the result of a disciplinary inquiry, Kölling got off with a warning, and Hoffman was removed from his post. In fairness it must be admitted that neither of the two magistrates had consciously denied the law. Both were convinced of the guilt of Haas and that the independence of justice had been infringed. The affair was symptomatic. That such states of mind could have existed at that time throws a most revealing light on the jurisprudence of the period.[1]

The expression 'republic of Jews' was an insult much prized by the enemies of the Republic; it was also used in songs, like the chorus of Ehrhard's famous song 'We don't want a republic of Jews; oh, a republic of Jews'. Two of the senates of the *Reichsgericht*, the first and the fourth, did not see in this an offence against the Republic. The first Senate did indeed make its anti-semitic attitude quite clear in its findings of the 22nd June 1923 (I.D. 459/23), but went to the trouble of disguising this attitude under a pretence of mystical profundity,[2] while the fourth Senate, giving judgment on the 18th January 1924 (4.D 747/23), unreservedly approved the findings of the Penal Chamber which had tried the matter in the first instance; these findings were that the expression 'Republic of Jews' did not constitute an insult to the Republic, since it was to the Jews, and not to the Republic, that it referred.

Yet this state of mind was not the only attribute of the repressive courts. The Borkum affair was a striking example of how the efforts of the executive to make democracy a reality were foiled by the courts. At the summer resort of Borkum, on the North Sea, the band at the Casino usually played a nationalist song. Summer visitors sang this song, named the Borkum song, to words which made fun of the Jews and demanded their expulsion. On these occasions acts of violence against Jews or people who were thought to be Jews took place. The responsible administrative authorities published an order forbidding the playing of this song, and the

---

[1] Hoffman showed strength of character. He resigned from the service of the state, renounced his pension rights, and became an advocate. The Nazis made him president of the Berlin *Landgericht* in 1933, the most important *Landgericht* in Germany. However, they did not take much interest in the old reactionary bore. He therefore retired with a pension, having found that the Nazis did not respect the independence of justice either.

[2] '. . . the new legislative and social order which was established thanks to the prominent participation of German Jews.' This unwarrantable sentence used in giving judgment by the highest court in Germany is nothing but anti-semitic propaganda. It might equally well have been pronounced by Hitler or by the propagandists of racial persecution.

police enforced this order. At this point the commune of Borkum obtained a provisional ruling from the Emden court (*Amtsgericht*), on the 27th June 1924 (4 G 37/24), forbidding the state of Prussia, under penalty of a fine of 100,000 gold marks, to prevent the band in the Casino at Borkum from playing this song. This judgment was illegal, since Prussian law laid down that actions against administrative decisions made by the authorities should not be examined by civil courts but by administrative tribunals, and in accordance with a special procedure. But the commune of Borkum also took this course. By its order of the 12th July 1925 [1] the high administrative tribunal of Prussia suspended the police order as being illegal. Neither of these courts gave any consideration to the fact that the singing of an anti-Jewish song constituted the crime of causing a class struggle [2] or a grave disorder.[3]

Finally, let us take an example from the rent tribunals. The owner of an apartment house named Nordheimer, a German of the Jewish faith, filed a request for expulsion against a foreign tenant who had several times called him a 'German pig'.[4] The *Berlin-Mitte Amtsgericht* gave the following reply to this request: 'Without prejudice to his German nationality, the plaintiff is not a person who can be regarded as German in the popular sense of the word.' The President of the *Amtsgericht* refused to take action on a request that this judge be reprimanded.[5] Thus in 1925 a German judge anticipated Hitler's 1935 nationality legislation, by which Jews became German nationals but not German citizens. But this judge had sworn allegiance to the German constitution, a thing which the promoters of the Nuremberg laws had not done. And Article 109 of the constitution laid down that 'All Germans are equal before the law'.

How did the Nazi conspiracy conduct its struggle with state institutions? Before describing Nazi methods in detail, one point must be made clear: the deep roots of Nazism, both as regards the ideas and the person of its highest representative, lay in the underworld of society. The distinction must be made, at least for this period of struggle, between the older so-called national characteristics which worked with, but were soon outdistanced by, Nazi propaganda, and Nazism itself. The fact that the German nation, a highly cultured people, should have contracted the disease of mass psychosis is one of the most sinister examples in history of popular madness and human aberration.

---

[1] cf. *Deutsche Justiz*, Vol. I, pp. 79 seq.
[2] Article 110 of the Penal Code.
[3] Article 360, para. II, of the Penal Code.
[4] cf. Radbruch, *Deutsche Justiz*, Vol. I, p. 196.
[5] Report of the German League for the Rights of Man, p. 131.

National-Socialism was, above all else, Adolf Hitler. His personality and background explain the movement which he founded. The most significant fact about Hitler is that, professionally and socially, he was a failure.[1] At Vienna all his artistic efforts did not gain him admittance to the school of art either as a painter or as an architect, and at that moment, without means or friends, he fell into the most terrible social, physical, and moral poverty. One day he even tried to beg from a drunkard, who threatened him with a stick. The workhouse became his home. When he moved to a 'bachelors' hostel' in one of the poorest districts he regarded this as an improvement. Hitler himself described his early days very differently.[2] He asserts that in Vienna he learnt to know 'the worker'—an understandable embellishment. What he did in fact learn to know was not the worker, the active and productive representative of the fourth estate, but rather the fifth estate, the low proletariat of rogues, unemployed drunkards, penniless aristocrats, filthy pedlars (whom he regarded as typical Jews), and down-and-outs—those, in short, in the same situation as himself: a *declassé* fallen from a higher stratum of society. This ruined period of his youth must have caused, in this son of a *petit bourgeois* family whose childhood had been contented, an accumulation of virulent hatred and pathological resentment. What he learnt during that time was the law of the lawless in which might is right, in which the only possible way of asserting oneself is brute strength, or, if that is unsuccessful, deceit and guile. It was the law of the jungle, learnt in the jungle of a great city and applied to a political struggle for the conquest of Germany and of the world.

The principal weapon used in that struggle was brutal terror. Hitler mentions it quite openly in his propaganda writings;[3] he mentioned it with even fewer scruples to his friends and supporters. For example, he told one of his friends of the hard years in Vienna, a man named Hanisch, that one of the happiest days of his childhood was when he was allowed to admire a museum collection of lethal weapons taken from the peasants of Upper Austria during disturbances.[4] Later, when he had come to power, Hitler was even more explicit before his circle of collaborators. Cruelty, brute strength, salutary terror—these were the methods which he openly adopted in politics.[5] From the first the activities of the SA were designed to inspire terror. Teams of toughs roamed the streets of Munich at night and beat up passers-by whom they recognised as,

---

[1] For his biography cf. Heiden, Vol. I, pp. 1 seq.   [2] *Mein Kampf*, pp. 39 seq.
[3] ibid., pp. 414, 418, 423, 507.
[4] Heiden, Vol. I, p. 47.
[5] Rauschning, p. 22: 'We must be cruel. We must win good consciences over to cruelty,' p. 78: 'Yes, we are the barbarians, we desire to be so,' p. 81: 'Cruelty nspires respect. Cruelty and brute strength . . . people need salutary terror.'

or thought might be Jews.[1] The dark period through which Germany was then living encouraged such horrors. Political murder, whether of someone in the other camp or of someone who had betrayed his own, became a normal weapon in this struggle.[2] Professor Ruge, an extremist nationalist, invented a cynical term for these murders, '*umlegen*' [3] (remove). (Later the Nazis were to adopt the word 'liquidate' for the assassination of political enemies such as Jews, religious opponents, Communists, and the peoples of the East, in concentration camps.) In fights at meetings flying columns attacked those taking the part of the opposition and 'removed' them with chairs, beer tankards, rubber clubs, or steel bars. It was rather more difficult to oppose the police. When the courage to use force was lacking guile was often employed. When the state forbade the wearing of uniforms, the brown shirts were left at home, and companies marched by in respectable white shirts, or, with great effect, stripped to the waist. Guile was also employed when violence was not enough to deal with meetings. Gustav Stresemann, Minister for Foreign Affairs, was speaking one day at a meeting of the German People's Party; Hitler's supporters were unable to cause a disturbance because adequate precautions had been taken. Heckling interruptions were skilfully countered by Stresemann. In despair, the flying columns started to sing 'Deutschland, Deutschland über alles'. Stresemann's supporters took up the song, the speaker was unable to continue his speech, and the meeting broke up in chaos. White with rage, Stresemann reproached members of his party for behaving like this; they replied that they had had to sing with the others for fear of being described as less patriotic than the Nazis. This was one of the traps in which honest citizens were caught.

While the Nazis were still enacting before the authorities their comedy of legality, they exploited the *bourgeois*' susceptibility to the theme of love for the Fatherland. When, in March 1927, Hitler was permitted to speak in public in Bavaria for the first time since the *putsch* of the 9th November 1923, his speech was particularly pacific and conciliatory, packed with solemn assurances about the supposed nature of his Party—no illegal aims, no illegal methods.[4] The Party was beginning to take part in the parliamentary struggle, and to establish itself in the *Reichstag* and in the parliaments of the *Länder* with an ever-increasing number of votes; and more and more the man in the street thought that it had withdrawn its revolutionary horns. This gave Hitler an undreamed-of opportunity of declaring solemnly and publicly before the *Reichstag* that his movement and the ambitions of his Party and of the SA were legal. This opportunity occurred in the autumn of 1930, thanks to the

---

[1] Heiden, Vol. I, pp. 148 seq.   [2] cf. Gumbel, *Four Years of Political Murders*.
[3] Heiden, Vol. I, p. 151.   [4] ibid., p. 239.

trial for high treason before the *Reichsgericht* of some officers of the Ulm garrison of the *Reichswehr*, Lieutenants Scheringer, Ludin, and Wendt. Why Hitler was called as a witness is a question frequently asked.[1] In the reasons adduced for judgment on the 4th October 1930 (12 J 10/30 XII H 41/30), by which the accused were sentenced, the judges explained why they had allowed the request of the defence to call Hitler as a witness.[2] They wanted Hitler to make his position as regards the *coup d'état* quite clear, and they also wished to find out whether Hitler had been aware of the actions of the accused officers.[3] The record of the case states that Hitler declared that 'he rejects categorically and on oath' and 'in unequivocal terms' the idea of a *coup d'état*, and that 'he only pursues his ends by strictly legal methods, and that he was only involved in the Munich affair in November 1923 under compulsion'. The findings also state that Zweigert, Secretary of State at the Ministry of the Interior of the Reich, another witness, gave evidence that there were in his ministry documents which had been condensed into a memorandum proving that the National-Socialist Party was preparing to carry out a *coup d'état*. The findings continue: 'The Senate refused to examine evidence concerning this matter, since the question had no decisive bearing on the passing of judgment on this case.' So then, in a trial of considerable historical importance, in which the fate of the nation was at stake, the highest court in the Reich thought it wise to question the leader of the powerful opposition party, which rejected the nature of the state and fought against it, in order to find out whether the state was to be opposed legally or illegally and whether three men were guilty of preparing for a *coup d'état* which was to benefit the NSDAP. The court heard the witness Hitler; but when the prosecution wished the witness Zweigert to refute Hitler's evidence, this refutation was covered up and was not mentioned again. Zweigert, a Secretary of State, was insulted before a crowded court by an advocate, Frank, future Commissioner of the Reich for Justice and Governor-General of Poland, who accused him of being 'the hired tool of a moribund régime'.[4] Zweigert also tried to bring up Hitler's failures to keep his word, recognised at the Munich trial in 1923, in regard to the *putsch* affair;[5] but neither the court nor the Advocate-General saw any necessity to blame the witness Hitler

---

[1] *Deutsche Justiz*, Vol. VI, p. 63.   [2] ibid., Vol. IV, pp. 212 seq.
[3] 'What was the position of the head of the NSDAP if such a *coup d'état* was intended by the party?'
[4] *Vossische Zeitung*, 26.9.30; *Deutsche Justiz*, Vol. VI, p. 65.
[5] *Deutsche Justiz*, p. 62: Hitler, speaking to the Minister of the Interior, Schweyer, in November 1923, 'Mr. Minister, I give you my word of honour that I will never undertake a *putsch* as long as I live'.—Colonel Seisser to Hitler on the 8.11.23, 'You did not keep your promise never to undertake a *putsch*'. Hitler, 'That is so, forgive me, but I did it in the interests of the Fatherland' (extract from the records of the Munich *Volksgericht*, I.XIX, 421/23).

for this. No allusion to these contradictions is made, no explanation is given of how Hitler was acting under compulsion on the 9th November 1923 when the promise which he had given should have compelled him not to undertake this *putsch*. None of this is held against the witness Hitler. The court decided to make him take the oath. . . . Hitler swore that he had said nothing but the whole truth, that he had falsified nothing and added nothing.

It is possible that the court was not aware of what it was doing, but the conspirators were very well aware of it. Hitler's hearing had been preceded by conversations lasting several days between the advocates for the defence, Frank and Kamecke.[1] Those concerned had expected the court and prosecution to show more intelligence, courage, and sense of responsibility than they did during the trial. Two things were important for them—to give the leader of the NSDAP a chance of declaring the legality of his movement on the witness stand of this court on which the eyes of the whole world were fixed, and to declare the revolutionary intentions of the Party for the time which would follow the legal assumption of power. And these two declarations needed to be made, if possible, on oath. In fact Hitler was ready to swear to anything which could not immediately be interpreted as perjury. Yet no one had seriously planned for him to speak on oath.[2] The content of Hitler's statements had been carefully decided upon, although it was realised that they raised rather a problem—since on the one hand they had to affirm the legality of the movement, and on the other to glorify its revolutionary intentions. The first was necessary to protect the Party's activities from state intervention, and the other essential in order to attract supporters or persuade those who might become supporters to join the Party. They realised that the effect of a straightforward declaration of legality would be damaging from the propaganda angle, for the masses' conception of the Party led them to expect it to bring about a revolution. So it was decided that Hitler should declare the legality of the Party's intentions as well as its revolutionary nature. Hitler made this declaration before the *Reichsgericht* in a two-hour speech, in which he employed all the wiles of his art of demagogy. Here is a dramatic extract from this so-called evidence:[3]

The Chairman: 'In *National Socialist Letters* there is the following

---

[1] This description of events at the trial is based on information made available to the author in 1938 by the advocate Otto Kamecke, defending advocate for Ludin, after he had renounced National-Socialism. Kamecke died in 1948.

[2] Article 57, para. 3, of the Code of Criminal Procedure: 'Persons suspected of taking part in, helping, or receiving in the matter being investigated shall be heard without taking the oath.'

[3] cf. *Vossische Zeitung* of the 26th Sep. 1930, and reasons adduced in judgment number II, 7.

passage: "Hitler said one day 'In this struggle, heads will roll on the ground, our heads or theirs. So let us make sure that it is theirs.'" These words are attributed to you.'

Hitler: 'If our movement wins the day a new High Court (*Staatsgerichtshof*) will be set up before which the crime of November 1918 will be expiated. Then, in any case, heads will fall.' (These words were spoken extremely passionately, and emphasised by public applause.)

The Chairman (reprovingly): 'We are in a court room, not in a theatre or a political meeting. And I repeat again that any demonstration or applause is strictly forbidden; should anything of this nature occur again, I shall be obliged to take action.'

Hitler continues: 'If there are two or three more elections to the *Reichstag*, a National-Socialist rising will have to occur. Then we shall recognise no more the agreements which are imposed on us. We will take up our stand, and all methods leading to the annihilation of these agreements will be permitted. Then we will be in the midst of Revolution.'

The Chairman: 'Is that to be done illegally?'

Hitler: 'Only if the events of 1807, 1808, and 1809 are considered illegal, too.'

While this exchange was taking place, thousands of people gathered outside the *Reichsgericht* were enthusiastically cheering Hitler. These legal proceedings, under the auspices of the German Republic, gave the signal for a revolution which was to destroy this same Republic. Times had changed—the overture to the great French Revolution of 1789 had been Beaumarchais' graceful play *The Marriage of Figaro.* . . . The funeral dirge of the German republic was a rustling of legal documents and writs.

As far as the fate of the three defendants was concerned, the tragedy soon became a farce. From the description of the case someone not familiar with the workings of the law might have thought that the defendants would have been found not guilty of the crime of high treason. A grave mistake! They were found guilty. A knowledge of the procedures of jurisprudence is required to make this verdict comprehensible. The NSDAP desired, above all, legality. The heads of the Party had assured the defendants at Party headquarters in Munich that a *coup d'état* was not envisaged. Yet these rogues, 'Notwithstanding the instructions they had received at Munich, refused to believe that the National-Socialist Party did not have illegal intentions. They were even convinced that a National-Socialist *putsch* was to be expected in the near future'.[1]

[1] Reasons adduced in judgment II, number 8.

The next part of the judges' report is incredibly naïve: 'It is not surprising that they had come to be convinced of this.' The court even goes so far as to blame the defendants for not having arrived at the conclusion that Hitler was a traitor after he had been found guilty by the Munich *Volksgericht* on the 1st April 1924. They should have realised, from reading the papers and National-Socialist writings, that the Party would employ force in order to arrive at power. But the judges could not really blame Hitler for the inconsistency of his actions and his evidence because they were making use of these same facts in order to establish the guilt of the defendants. This was too deep for the *Reichsgericht*; only the accused officers were guilty of high treason. 'The fact that the National-Socialists' plans for a *coup d'état* only existed in the minds of the accused did not affect the factual nature of their offence.' This point of view can be explained by the *Reichsgericht*'s constant application of the 'subjective theory'.[1] 'Subjective' traitors were found guilty. Hitler, who respected the law and was objective, left the court in triumph.

Hitler's evidence was in itself an offence—it broke the law on the protection of the Republic, and constituted threats of violence.[2] He also committed the offence of preparation for high treason, for it cannot seriously be admitted that the legal assumption of power authorises a political party to carry out a *coup d'état* by revolutionary means.[3] Yet no one was prepared to start proceedings against Hitler, and the slogan 'legal seizure of power' became a normal weapon in the armoury of National-Socialist propaganda. In 1931 the famous Boxheim document,[4] that 'first proclamation made by our commander after the existing high authorities have been removed and after victory over the Commune', was discovered in the possession of Dr Best, deputy judge and later Chief of Criminal Police and of the SD in occupied Denmark; the authors of this document quite unconcernedly took into account the fact that the proclamation would become valid only after the expected Communist uprising and the resultant collapse of the Republic. Hitler's promise of legality was bearing fruit.

While the chief conspirator skilfully distorted the scales of justice, his subordinates tried to imitate him to the best of their ability. The law on the protection of the Republic was used by the National-

---

[1] Reasons adduced in judgment II, number 9a, para. 3.

[2] Article 241 of the Penal Code: 'Any person who criminally threatens a third party . . . shall be punished.'

[3] Chancellor Brüning: 'If one declares (once one has attained power by legal means) that one will overthrow the barriers of the law, then there is no more law.' (Quoted by Radbruch, *Deutsche Justiz*, Vol. VII, p. 197.)

[4] cf. Heine in *Deutsche Justiz*, Vol. VII, p. 154, and Radbruch (see note 68), p. 195.

Socialists. Frick, who took part in Hitler's *putsch* on the 9th November 1923, had become Minister for the Police in Thuringia. Under this law he issued a number of orders banning publications of the democratic press.[1]

Whenever the courts ventured to try National-Socialists, the latter were increasingly insolent to the judges. Those advocates who were made available by the Party for its members reported the attitude of the judges and public prosecutors to the Party or to the SA. The law was systematically spied on so that the necessary steps[2] might be taken when the Third Reich was established.

The next step was to assert the incompetence of those judges who were politically troublesome, under the pretext of their partiality. The Appeals Court (*Landgericht*) of Chemnitz had allowed a complaint of this kind.[3] The two judges concerned were found incompetent because they were members of a democratic party and of the republican association of magistrates, and further because one of them was a Jew. The request that they be found incompetent was granted because, in the opinion of the court, there was a danger of partiality affecting the 'subjective opinion' of defendants. After this decision the Party instructed all Nazi organisations to demand systematically that every judge known for his republican opinions be found incompetent.[4]

The National-Socialists successfully repeated their Borkum song tactics in another case, in which disagreements between civil courts and administrative authorities were exploited as described above. A court issued a provisional order restraining the first President of Hanover (the supreme administrative authority in Hanover) from banning a particularly extremist National-Socialist newspaper which, in the first president's opinion, contravened an order issued by the President of the Reich, the 'Easter peace order'. Such a decision by a civil court was completely contrary to Prussian administrative law. The administrative actions of the President could only be contested before administrative courts and not before civil courts. Furthermore, the civil court came to this decision without oral proceedings. Its decision was based solely on the sworn statement of a single private individual—a statement which the President was unable to dispute—and found the state guilty of 'arbitrary actions and overriding the law' (Hanover, *Landgericht*, 9 April 1932, 2 IX, Qu 149/32). This decision was of course reversed by the high court at Celle, but the affair provided a great deal of favourable propaganda for the NSDAP.

[1] cf. *Deutsche Justiz*, Vol. VI, pp. 353 seq.
[2] cf. ibid., pp. 396 seq.
[3] Motion on 23 Jan. 1932, quoted in *Deutsche Justiz*, Vol. VIII, pp. 259 seq.
[4] cf. *Deutsche Justiz*, Vol. VI, p. 313.

Goebbels' scorn for republican justice was made clear with brutal cynicism. On the 23rd January 1932 he gave evidence before the Penal Chamber of the Berlin–Moabit court and refused to reply to a question put to him by the court. When he was told that he was under a legal obligation to answer, he declared: [1] 'The Code of Criminal Procedure does not concern me. I am here on behalf of cleanness. The only thing that matters to me is public health. If National-Socialist principles dictate that in the circumstances I must not make a statement, the Code of Criminal Procedure will not make me do so.' Under German law a penalty (fine or imprisonment) can be imposed on witnesses who are guilty of contempt of court. Similarly, a witness who refuses without legal justification to make a statement is liable to a fine or imprisonment. But Goebbels was exempt from these penalties because of his immunity as a member of the *Reichstag*. Since this immunity made it impossible to take action against Goebbels in any way, he could only be 'provisionally excused' from making a statement. He left the court with his head held high, without being troubled and with no intention of returning. Exactly one year before the formal seizure of power, this was the typically overbearing National-Socialist attitude towards a defenceless judicial system.

It is ironical that at this very moment the second volume of *Justice in Chains* appeared. A certain Ewald Moritz, who understandably enough wrote under a pseudonym (Gottfried Zarnow), tried to show in this book, whose first volume had appeared in 1931, that the courts received instructions from the political authorities of the Republic. To prove this, the author referred to the Haas affair,[2] the trial of the *Vehme* murders,[3] the trial for high treason of the officers of the Ulm *Reichswehr*,[4] the trial of the Holstein peasants who blew up the Treasury buildings,[5] etc. This diatribe is written in the usual virulent and partisan manner of the Nazi press, and its substance is completely false, as has been shown not only by Dr Schmidt, then Prussian Minister of Justice, but also by Dr Deerberg, German National Party deputy to the *Landtag*, President of the Senate of the *Kammergericht*, vice-president of the Barmat Commission of the Prussian *Landtag*, and therefore a knowledgeable lawyer who was also a resolute but objective opponent of the Republic.[6] Moritz's book was of course widely used in National-Socialist propaganda directed against the law.

---

[1] Ernst Fraenkel in *Deutsche Justiz*, Vol. VII, p. 275.
[2] *Gefesselte Justiz*, Vol. I, pp. 70 seq.   [3] ibid., pp. 153 seq.
[4] ibid., pp. 166 seq.   [5] ibid., Vol. II, pp. 1 seq.
[6] Deerberg, who in spite of his anti-republican views often found himself at odds with the National-Socialists in the legal Commission of the Prussian *Landtag* before the collapse of the Republic, became President of the criminal Senate at the *Kammergericht* for cases of high treason after Hitler's rise to power. After this he lost

The National-Socialist attitude towards the law soon became true terrorist propaganda. At the meetings of the Prussian *Landtag* in May and June 1932 the NSDAP deputies, Dr Freisler,[1] and Kube,[2] provoked a turmoil. They made incredibly insulting remarks about the judicial system, called the judges profaners of law, told a Public Prosecutor that he was a crook and a despicable *provocateur*, referred to the presidents of the Chambers of advocates as 'sons of Jews' and 'brats',[3] etc.

Hitler himself directed this campaign of terror. During the summer of 1932 a horde of SA brutally murdered a worker in Potempa in Upper Silesia by dragging him from his bed in the middle of the night and beating him up. They finished him off as he writhed on the ground by kicking him in the throat. A *Sondergericht* (extraordinary court) was set up by the Chancellor, von Papen, and five of the SA were condemned to death for murder. Every detail of the affair was made known to the German public, yet Hitler, who had testified on oath to the legality of his movement, was not deterred from sending the sentenced men a telegram expressing his sympathy. He described the murderers as 'my comrades' and demanded their release 'as a point of National-Socialist honour'. Von Papen declared 'a man who calls murderers his comrades cannot have any claim to govern'.[4]

Five months later Adolf Hitler became Chancellor of the German Reich. Von Papen was vice-chancellor in Hitler's Government.

II. THE USE OF POWER

How the Nazi rulers abused the power which they had legally obtained to control the police, justice, and every other state institution as best suited them is a question which can easily appear unreal. One is tempted to reply that the conspirators were in a position to do whatever they pleased, and that they did in fact do whatever they pleased.

But so simple a solution cannot be applied to every factual situation. After the seizure of power Hitler held practically all powers; but a considerable amount of 'dross' survived from the era of the republican constitution and adhered to the steel of true

---

his objectivity and became a cruel judge, violent and prejudiced. Morally a victim of the dictatorship, he apparently thought that he had to act in this way in order that his former attitude might be forgotten.

[1] Later President of the famous *Volksgerichtshof*, and the man who sentenced the conspirators of the 20th July 1944 and many others to death.

[2] Later First President of the province of Brandenburg; he was disgraced by a sordid divorce action in which he was in collusion with the witnesses concerning his wife.

[3] *Deutsche Justiz*, Vol. VII, p. 457.

[4] Heiden, Vol. I, p. 311.

dictatorship. This dross had to be removed before the sword of dictatorship could be effectively wielded. Every political party other than the NSDAP was dross. The government was no longer a parliamentary coalition when these parties were dissolved. Hügenberg, leader of the German National Party, left the government at the end of June 1933. The other so-called 'bourgeois' ministers remained, not as ministers in the political coalition, but as Fachminister (specialist ministers). Among these was Gürtner, Minister of Justice; as early as 1923 and 1924 he had shown his attachment to the Nazi cause. In the Länder, which lost their status as members of the federal German empire and became nothing more than administrative areas, governors named by Hitler, and the Gauleiters (district chiefs) of the NSDAP, made certain that political activity should not conflict with the central will of the Führer. Every sphere of public activity was similarly redirected towards a central government. Workers' unions and trade associations became part of the German Working Front and of other National-Socialist organisations; artists were enrolled in the Cultural Chamber of the Reich, with its specialised Chambers for the theatre, cinema, literature, etc. Naturally the executive and legislative powers were similarly reorganised to make them subject to the will of the dictatorship.

During the first months of the 'National-Socialist revolution', as those in power named the political upheaval engineered by them after the seizure of power, the police remained the responsibility of the Länder. The state secret police (Geheime Staatspolizei—Gestapo) was itself the creation of the prime minister of Prussia, Göring, who in 1933 made of it the police authority in Prussia. The first concentration camps (Sachsenhausen near Oranienburg and Lichtenburg) were also Prussian institutions established by local SA units with the agreement or on the suggestion of Göring. Similar institutions were later set up in other Länder on the instructions of the regional authorities or of local SS and SA organisations (e.g., Dachau in Bavaria, Fuhlsbüttel near Hamburg). SA formations were often used as an auxiliary police force when the regional police was inadequate or untrustworthy. It is not to be wondered at that this use of the SA soon brought about the greatest excesses—extortion, arbitrary imprisonment, and murders; [1] indeed, given the composition and commanders of this organisation, this was only to be expected. The establishment of one police organisation dependent on the central authorities of the Reich was possible only after the creation of the Gestapo, under the commander of the SS, Himmler, and his deputy, Heydrich, on about the 1st April 1935, [2]

---

[1] cf. Diels, pp. 222 seq.
[2] cf. ibid., pp. 229 seq.

and after the power of the SA had been destroyed by the mass murders on the 30th June 1934.

From that time the SA lost their position as executors of the power behind the National-Socialist state, and their importance as an organization for educating people in National-Socialist ideology was also considerably diminished. Responsibility for the police was withdrawn from the *Länder*, and the police and the SS were unified. Himmler was made a minister of the Reich, and *Reichsführer* of the SS and of the German police at the Ministry of the Interior. Dr Frick, a product of the Bavarian school of administrators who was Minister of the Interior, was not considered worthy to command the police, although he was an old party member and had taken part in the *putsch* of the 9th November 1923. The fact that the chief of the SS was considered more suitable was a sign of the extremist tendencies of the time.

Under Himmler's control the Central Criminal Investigation Department and criminal police became the strongest elements in the police system. The system of concentration camps was also centralised. These camps were both the government's most important method of inspiring terror and a source of income for the SS. Under Himmler the SS organisation finally became a sort of state within the state. The permanent members of the SS were selected from the *Allgemeine SS*, a volunteer organisation for which recruiting was carried out according to special principles of selection; the professionals, Death's head units and assault guards (*SS-Totenkopfverbände and Wachsturmbanne*) guarded the concentration camps, and were the real internal SS defence troops. The *Waffen-SS*, a kind of armed SS force corresponding to the ordinary *Wehrmacht*, were only formed later. The financial administration of the SS was carried out by the DEST (initials of the 'German earth and rock undertakings'), and other concerns which made certain that the slave workers in the concentration camps were used in accordance with established principles.

This SS state also wielded its own justice, although justice is not perhaps the best word for such proceedings. For SS members there were 'SS and police courts' [1] administered by lawyers holding the rank of officers in the SS. For ordinary people there was the warrant for arrest on suspicion which led to the concentration camps, followed by extermination through work, beating to death, hanging, and finally the gas chamber. There is no need to describe such proceedings in detail, for it is evident that they constituted criminal actions. But it is a curious fact that this SS justice in the Hitlerian state was not the only judicial system in existence; there was also a

---

[1] In the war these courts were often given authority to try the population of occupied countries.

system of civil law. This latter could not always ignore the mass crimes of the SS and of the police state, but equally it was not in a position to take action and punish the offenders even if the wish to do so had been there. The courts could no longer call on the police, since this authority had been taken from them and given to the SS state. German lawyers were almost daily made aware that the executive of the SS state was taking the place of their juris-prudence. In the Gestapo's records there was usually a note of 'restitution'. This meant that the defendant should not be set free if a writ for his arrest was not issued, but handed over to the Gestapo. This was valid for political prisoners, for victims of racial persecu-tion and for the so-called anti-social criminals (absentees from work, abortionists, and common law offenders, etc.). As a general rule a writ was issued for the arrest on suspicion of those whose 'restitution' was demanded, and the prisoners were sent to a con-centration camp. The same procedure was employed when the SS authorities were of the opinion that an offender convicted by the courts, and who had served his sentence, should be imprisoned in a concentration camp.

It may well be asked why the dictatorship, which was able to make use of that very convenient executive, took the trouble to maintain a judicial organisation as well. That it was done to put people on the wrong scent is not sufficient explanation. It is true that the Hitlerian state was anxious to keep up a good reputation in the civilised world, and the international treaties which it managed to make were proof of its success. It is possible that the maintenance of religious institutions and the existence of a judicial system were thought indispensable for keeping up international prestige.

But this one motive was certainly not decisive. The true nature of the Hitlerian state cannot be understood if it is thought to have been nothing but the 'regiment of terror' which it became during the last phase of its desperate struggle for existence. Like the statue of the god Janus, the Hitlerian state had two heads—one the savage and bloodthirsty head of terror, the other the peaceful, gentle head of lawfulness. To what extent this lawfulness could and was intended to be genuine in the constitutional state must be established in a study of the development of justice under the Third Reich. It is a mistake to think that the Hitlerian state wished to dispense with the resolution of human conflicts by means of the law. That this state should be voluntarily supported by the people within it was of the greatest importance to it. It was for this reason that Hitler un-ceasingly endeavoured to grip the imagination of the people by repeated speeches on the wireless and articles in the press. It was for this reason, too, that Goebbels built up the enormous propaganda machine. It is wrong to think that a modern dictator, in the age of popular movements, could or should have wished merely to dominate his subjects. At all events, Hitler demanded at least the external approval of the masses. He wished to be popular, and, if possible, loved. But such a result of propaganda could certainly not be attained through concentration camps, warrants for arrest on suspicion, corporal punishment, and mass liquidations, all things which were notorious. But it could be attained through organisations such as 'strength through joy', and the German Front of Labour, which gave the great majority of the population an opportunity of rest and relaxation. An efficient health service and a proper judicial system were also in this category. A judicial organisation, at least as a constitutional institution, was all the more necessary because the people as a whole had no idea of the true nature of the dictatorial state and of its ultimate intentions, and had no intention of supporting it. So, as a first step, it must be stated that Nazism conserved the judicial organisation in its traditional form.

Materially, of course, justice could not be the same in a dictatorship as in a constitutional state. The dual obligation of law— obligation of the citizen and obligation of the state—and the resultant necessity for the state to seek justice before its own courts, found no place in a totalitarian system. The idea of the independence of the courts, too, was swept overboard. As law lost its status as the autonomous rule of law of the community and became an order issued by an absolute *Führer*, so the judges lost their status as independent law-makers and became agents who merely carried out the orders of the *Führer*. The judge was no longer the impartial representative of the concept of justice, but a servant of the machinery of government, just as much an official carrying out orders as any member of the executive. And such a state of affairs means the end of jurisprudence. There can be no doubt that this was the ultimate aim of the Nazi dictatorship.[1] What methods did it employ to attain this end, and to what extent did it succeed?

The methods were clearly the same as those employed at the time of the seizure of power—organisation, propaganda, and terror.

In theory the judicial organisation, as set up by the laws of justice of the Reich, was little changed by dictatorship; in practice it was greatly changed. All the courts retained their former constitution. However, on the 21st March 1933, an order had been issued creating the *Sondergerichte* (special courts), which were

[1] For details see the Nuremberg decision on jurists, German edition, pp. 90 seq., and English edition, pp. 76 seq. (*Trials of War Criminals before the Nuremberg Military Tribunals* (Washington, Government Printing Office), Vol. III, p. 954.)

composed of three qualified judges without a jury, and were competent to try political offences, especially offences under the law 'against anti-national activities' (*Heimtückegesetz*) (Ordinance of the 28th February 1933, later replaced by the law of the 20th December 1934). The powers of these courts were greatly increased after the war had begun and they were made competent to deal with crimes against the war economy, crimes covered by the ordinance 'against individuals dangerous to the nation' (*Volksschädlingsverordnung*), and offences against the regulations governing listening to the wireless. They could impose all penalties, including the death penalty, and their verdicts could be put into force immediately. The *Volksgerichtshof* in Berlin took the place of the *Reichsgericht* for the trial of high treason cases; unlike the *Reichsgericht*, which was composed only of professional judges, a jury was present at the sessions of the *Volksgerichtshof*. This jury, however, was chosen solely from among important party members—highly placed officials in the SA, SS, the Labour service of the Reich, etc. Less important cases of high treason were still tried by special senates of the supreme regional courts. During the war, juries took no part in the proceedings of ordinary courts; there were no more municipal magistrates' courts and no more Assize Courts of the '*Emminger*' type. Appeals against executory sentences and definitive acquittals which before had not existed in German justice were established by law on the 16th September 1939.[1]

As a result of various decrees issued by Hitler and by the Minister of Justice, judicial procedure was steadily simplified and a large number of legal safeguards were removed. The final culmination of these actions was the establishment of courts-martial (*Standgerichte*) to try the Poles and Jews in the occupied lands to the east of Germany;[2] Hitler's 'Night and Mist' (*Nacht und Nebel*) decree on the 7th December 1941, aimed at resistance movements in the occupied countries, became particularly notorious. This decree ordered that persons guilty of attacks on the security of the Reich or of German military forces in occupied territory should be secretly sent to Germany and handed over to the criminal police and SD. Relatives of arrested persons were not to be info.med where they were being held. It would take too much space to describe every step taken by the dictatorship to degrade, or rather to pervert, the course of justice. The Nuremberg verdict on the most notorious

---

[1] Article II, para. 3 of this law is as follows: 'The advocate general of the *Reichsgericht* may, within one year of the execution of sentence (or in the case of an acquittal within one year of the acquittal becoming final), appeal against such sentences or acquittals if he is of opinion that through a miscarriage of justice the proceedings should be re-opened and a different verdict brought in.'

[2] Ordinance of the 14th December 1941. For most crimes the only penalty laid down by this ordinance was the death penalty.

lawyers (3rd and 4th December 1947) gives an objective appreciation of these measures. One may note, however, that courts-
martial for trying German nationals were only set up in the last
months of the war.[1]

As regards the officials in the judicial administration, the Nazis
found themselves face to face with the same men who had administered the laws of the Republic. The judges were for the most
part similar to those described above, men who had, whether
consciously or not, prepared the way for Nazism. Among them, too,
were judges and public prosecutors who had brought the law into
operation against the conspirators, and who were therefore detested
by the Nazis. It was to be expected that the dictatorship would
not make the same mistake as the Republic in 1918, by retaining all
judges without exception in their posts. The irremovability of
judges was abolished. The law on the re-organisation of the permanent Civil Service (7th April 1933) ordained the dismissal of all
public servants, including judges who were not regarded favourably
by the new régime. Advocates were treated similarly. Officials
and judges included in this description were expected by their
general attitude 'to guarantee that at all times and unreservedly
they will take up the cudgels for the National State'.

After the political and racial purge came National-Socialist
integration (*Gleichschaltung*) in all walks of public life. The Associa-
tion of German Judges was merged with the association of National-
Socialist lawyers under a convinced National-Socialist, the former
Munich advocate Frank II, Commissioner of Justice for the Reich.
In the spring of 1935 the law was 'centralised'. The ministries of
Justice in the *Länder* were dissolved. Thus Gürtner, Minister of
Justice for the Reich, became the head of all officers of law through-
out the Reich, and they were controlled directly by the Ministry of
Justice at Berlin. Judges and public prosecutors were appointed
and sworn in by the *Führer* after nomination by the Minister of
Justice.

The control of jurisprudence which the Nazis desired was far
harder to achieve than the control of the legal profession which they
had attained. They regarded the law with distrust as long as the
régime lasted. Many judges, public prosecutors, and advocates
proved by their courageous attitude that they were worthy of this
distrust. For those who had been educated in the legal tradition
of the liberal *bourgeois* period the doctrines of the new régime seemed
a terrible anomaly. And indeed many reactionary judges, too blind

---

[1] Ordinance issued by the Minister of Justice of the Reich on 15 Feb. 1945.
These bloodthirsty courts required that the death sentence be carried out immediately it had been pronounced. Their nature bore no relation to justice.

to have opposed the conspirators against the Weimar Republic with all the force of the law, now discovered with terror what it was that they had themselves prepared. From among the ranks of these men the true representatives of resistance against the transformation of a constitutional state into a despotism often came.

Resistance of this kind cannot, however, prevent a revolution. As usual the general public accepted and helped. Professional ambition, careerism, the wish to improve one's standard of living, were all extremely important factors. A Civil Servant can only hope for promotion if his political attitude is irreproachable. In the files of the Ministry of Justice, which have almost all been preserved, there are many generous tributes of this kind: 'This official has shown that at all times and unreservedly he will promote the interests of the National-Socialist cause.' Such tributes are even to be found in the personnel files relating to officials who resisted National-Socialism. Yet these things were not sufficient to bring about promotion; before the name of an official was put forward for promotion, the department of the *Führer*'s deputy was consulted. This department provided an official party statement on the political attitude of the candidate. No one in the Third Reich could become an official or be promoted against the wishes of the Party.

In order that legal circles might acquire the desired political attitude, it was necessary to influence them in the right direction. Such influence was generally exerted by means of propaganda, at which the National-Socialists were particularly skilled. In the case of officials this propaganda was called 'special education'. Students of law at universities became members of the National-Socialist association of students. If they wished to get on in their career, they were obliged to join the SA. Later, they had to attend camp, where there was instruction on their professional outlook, or rather on National-Socialist ideology with emphasis on racial doctrines. And as soon as they became judges or public prosecutors they were sent to a camp for officials who were members of the NSDAP. Finally, to complete their instruction with practical details concerning the exercise of the legal profession, there were the 'National-Socialist letters to judges' issued by the Minister of Justice, Thierack; these letters were issued from the 1st October 1942 onward.

Despite organisation, propaganda, and controlled education, the law did not become the powerful stay of the dictatorship that was intended. The state was continually obliged to interfere with the law. In the early years following the seizure of power, such intervention took place in individual cases only, and consisted of isolated acts of terrorism; later it became more methodical, at first under the guise of new laws, then as orders issued by the *Führer*.

In cases being tried by the *Sondergericht* (special courts), the defendants would show their scarred backs to the advocates for the defence; the latter would then attack the Gestapo's statement, which contained the so-called 'confession' of the defendant. In these cases the courts would decide to rule the Gestapo's evidence out of court. The author himself saw the president of the First Berlin *Sondergericht* [1] close the dossier and throw it into a corner of the room in a similar case. But this did not do the defendants any good, for they knew very well that if they were acquitted the Gestapo would arrest them again, extract new confessions from them, and that the next time they would be sentenced, and, having completed their sentence, would be sent to concentration camps.

Later on no such incidents occurred; 'intensive interrogation', which meant torture until a confession was made, became the Gestapo's official method. No one accused of a crime dared to withdraw his confession. 'Intensive interrogation' was of course authorised by Hitler. The author was informed at that time by a reliable informant that Gürtner, then Minister of Justice, had endeavoured to get this practice suppressed; Hitler had agreed with Himmler, however, that 'intensive interrogations' were essential.

The advocates for the defence as well as the defendants suffered from these illegal machinations. In 1934 and 1935 there were innumerable occasions on which advocates were threatened by the Gestapo if they did not conduct the defence in the way desired by the Gestapo. The author himself was threatened in this way by the Public Prosecutor, in a case in which he was defending a man who had called the Nazi hero Horst Wessel a pimp. The author had found out the address of a girl with whom Wessel had been living before he died, and who was the cause of the brawl in which Wessel was killed by a certain Höhler, who lived off immoral earnings. The Nazis, for reasons which are easy to understand, never mentioned this girl in their propaganda; apparently she was being watched by the police. Before the author had requested to be allowed to call this girl as a witness, he was approached by the Public Prosecutor who brusquely told him that the Gestapo had decided to use any means to prevent this girl from appearing as a witness. The removal of the defendant and of his counsel were among these means. The author must admit that, with the defendant's approval, he decided not to use this witness. The defendant was dismissed with an unusually lenient sentence and was not handed over to the Gestapo.

A further example of this travesty of law, which almost had a tragic ending, was caused by the deceased composer of the national anthem, *Horst Wessel*, in 1934. Those responsible for the murder

[1] Dr Rehn, who died in 1934.

(there was a woman as well as Höhler) had been sentenced prior to 1933 to a term of imprisonment; some members of the SA removed them from prison and killed them.[1] But, at the same time, three members of the 'association of combatants for the Red front' were arrested and brought before the Assize Court. Although the real author of the crime had been sentenced to prison prior to 1933 for manslaughter, in 1934 the Assize Court managed to sentence two of the accused to death for aiding and abetting murder, and the third to twelve years imprisonment. These sentences were passed as a result of the evidence given by members of the SA. This legal crime was completed by the execution of the two victims, Epstein and Ziegler, on the 10th April 1935.[2] The SA terrorists had succeeded in removing two innocent men by using false witnesses and by exploiting the virulent prejudice of the court.

When the widow of Herr Klausener, a high official who was murdered on the 30th June 1934, brought an action against the state for damages, her advocates were sent to the Sachsenhausen concentration camp. They were not released until they had formally withdrawn the action.

Sauckel, the governor of Thuringia, had the legal adviser to the Jewish owner of a large industrial firm imprisoned until the factory had been handed over to the state.

Later the Bar was also controlled more systematically. Before defending Jewish clients, advocates required the permission of the legal department of the NSDAP, whether they were Party members or not. Later still, only Jewish 'consultants' were allowed to represent or defend Jews. (This rule was broken when the interests of the state required the presence of a defending counsel 'of German blood', as for example at the *Volksgerichtshof*.) All advocates were not permitted to plead before the *Volksgericht*; only a certain number of specially chosen official advocates for the defence were permitted to do so, while advocates chosen separately by defendants were allowed to plead only if a special request had been made.[3] Furthermore, those advocates who were allowed to plead before this court were subject to certain restrictions, advocates for the defence were obliged to surrender the record of the charges after proceedings

---

[1] cf. Diels, p. 307.

[2] The author was personally connected with this affair. He undertook the defence of Epstein—a Jewish house painter with serious tuberculosis, who was also feeble-minded, and who was completely innocent of the murder of Horst Wessel—in an appeal before the *Reichsgericht*, after the Assize Court had condemned him to death at the first instance. His defence before the Assize Court was conducted by an official defending counsel.

[3] Such requests were not usually granted. The author was only permitted to undertake the defence of one client before the *Volksgerichtshof*; on his second request he was informed that he would not be allowed to plead again before this court under any circumstances.

X

had been closed. Very frequently, too, the whole list of charges was not given to the advocate, but only an extract with notes about his particular client.

The rights of the defence became increasingly restricted even in the ordinary courts. The censorship of the letters of the accused, including their correspondence with the lawyers defending them, was no longer carried out by the judges, but by the Public Prosecutor. Similarly, authorisations to visit prisoners were now given by the Public Prosecutor and not by the responsible judge. The Prosecutor's position was in general considerably strengthened. As has been stated earlier, the Public Prosecutor is, in German law, a political authority bound by rules; but in the liberal conception of law, the dependence of the Public Prosecutor existed only as regards duties which, in the public interest, had to be exercised where the penal laws and the code of criminal procedure were concerned. The Public Prosecutor could, for example, be asked to make or withdraw an appeal against a verdict, or to state whether an action was in the public interest; but in no circumstances could he be required to request a definite penalty or an acquittal at the first hearing of a trial. On the contrary, the Public Prosecutor was entirely free to decide the penalty for which he would ask after proving his case. The higher authorities' right of intervention did not extend into the court-house.[1] But under the Hitlerian régime the Public Prosecutor was usually instructed what penalties he should request. In political trials the Public Prosecutor was obliged to inform the Minister of Justice what penalties he proposed to demand. He often received instructions concerning the nature and extent of the demands which he was to make.

On the 30 June 1934 Hitler himself seriously offended against the law in a revolutionary manner. In a declaration issued on the 13th July 1934 he formally claimed responsibility for the murders which had been committed, and appointed himself the highest judge in the land. The *Reichstag* approved a law introduced by Gürtner which definitely legalised the murders of the 30th June 1934.

Interventions also took place in favour of defendants. In April 1934 Göring, Prime Minister of Prussia, put a stop to proceedings which were being taken against a well-known industrialist. It must be mentioned that Göring made the industrialist pay the sum of 3,000,000 *Reichsmarks* to be used as Göring thought fit. It has proved impossible to establish whether Göring blackmailed the industrialist, or whether the industrialist bribed the Prime Minister.

The question of quashing criminal proceedings was later settled in such a way that the *Führer* alone had the right to stop proceed-

[1] Feisenberger in *Deutsche Richterzeitung* (1925), p. 385. 'La plume est serve—la parole est libre.'

ings. He established a department of the Ministry of Justice which he called 'movement'. This department examined all penal proceedings against important Party members; its files were then sent to Hitler with a report. Hitler himself decided in each case whether the matter should be stopped or brought to court.

There is one point which must be made, Despite this despotism, there were a few judges of integrity. Let us give some examples.

Superintendent-General Dibelius, who is now senior bishop in the Protestant Church, was acquitted by the Berlin *Sondergericht* I on a charge of attacks on the government of a treasonable nature. The court's decision caused great agitation among those in power. Hitler himself asked for a copy of the reasons adduced in judgment, but did not interfere. A few months later Martin Niemöller, a fearless protestant minister, was acquitted by the Berlin *Sondergericht* II on a similar charge; although he was sentenced to a short term of imprisonment for a formal offence, he was released immediately, having served his sentence before trial. A large crowd gathered outside the prison from which Niemöller was to be released in order to give him an enthusiastic welcome. But the Gestapo had already arrested him again and taken him away through a concealed door.

In both these cases the judges were not molested. They were merely transferred to other divisions of the court in the normal course of the allocation of duties.

Cases of this nature became more and more frequent as the reign of terror became more savage and more intense. The Lüneburg *Landgericht* dismissed a Polish day labourer on account of extenuating circumstances. The Hamburg *Landgericht* refused to enforce the 'penal ordinance against the Poles' in the case of a Polish defendant. These are only a few examples, for it is impossible to list in detail every case of a similar nature in this essay. Finally a judgment was pronounced which reduced the dictator to frenzy. A *Landgericht* sentenced a man named Schlitt to ten years imprisonment for manslaughter. Schlitt, having served another sentence, had been released, and in the course of a quarrel with his wife who had been unfaithful to him on many occasions, killed her. Hitler made an example of this judgment, for the affair gave him a splendid chance of setting the people against the courts. On the 26th April 1942 he made a violent attack on the law before the *Reichstag*; he asked the *Reichstag* formally to grant him the right to intervene in all legal matters, and to dismiss 'those judges who patently ignore the imperative law of the present time'. The *Reichstag* took the steps he required; Hitler was formally made the highest judge in the land. The judgment in the Schlitt affair was annulled. On the 6th May 1942 Schlegelberger, secretary of

State at the Ministry of Justice, reported to Hitler that Schlitt had been condemned to death and executed. Thus was all organised law suppressed. The dictator became the sole representative of supreme governmental authority and of law. The courts were able to exercise a certain degree of independence, however, during the short remaining period of the régime's existence—in questions of civil law and in minor penal cases which were too unimportant to concern the *Führer*. But in all the important spheres of law, as in the whole life of the nation, the arbitrary rule of the dictatorship reigned supreme.

BIBLIOGRAPHY

Anschütz, Gerhard, *Die Verfassung des Deutschen Reiches*, 12th Imp. (Georg Stilke, Berlin, 1930).

Brammer, Karl, *Das politische Ergebnis des Rathenau-Prozesses* (Verlag für Sozialwissenschaft, Berlin, 1922).

Breuer, Robert, *Der Hitler–Ludendorff-Prozess vor dem Münchener Volksgericht* (Verlag für Sozialwissenschaft, Berlin, 1924).

Das Nürnberger Juristenurteil (Rechts- und Staatswissenschaftlicher Verlag, Hamburg, 1948).

Der Prozess gegen die Hauptkriegsverbrecher (Nuremberg, 1947).

Deutsche Liga für Menschenrechte, '*Das Zuchthaus als politische Waffe*' (Hänsel & Co., 1927).

Deutsche Richterzeitung, Organ des Deutschen Richterbundes (Verlag Hermann Sack, Berlin, Jahrgänge 1922/1933).

Die Justiz, Organ des Republikanischen Richterbundes (Dr Walther Rothschild, Berlin, Bd. I, III, IV, V, VI, VII).

Diels, Rudolf, *Lucifer ante portas* (Deutsche Verlags-Anstalt, Stuttgart, 1950).

Grimme, Friedrich, *Rechtsgutachten in der Strafsache des Oberleutnants a.D. Paul Schulz* (J. F. Lehmanns Verlag, Munich, 1928).

Gumbel, E. J., *Vier Jahre politischer Mord* (Neue Gesellschaft, Berlin, 1922).

Heiden, Konrad, *Adolf Hitler* (Europa-Verlag, Zurich, 1936).

Hirschberg, Max, und Thimme, Friedrich, *Der Fall Fechenbach* (H. C. B. Mohr, Tübingen, 1924).

Hitler, Adolf, *Mein Kampf* (Franz Eher, Munich, 1933).

Huch, Ricarda, *Die Revolution des Neunzehnten Jahrhunderts in Deutschland* (Gustav Kiepenheuer, Berlin, 1948).

Kiesow, Wilhelm, und Zweigert, Erich, *Das Gesetz zum Schutze der Republik* (Bensheimer, Mannheim, 1923).

Kursell, Otto von, *Der Hitler-Prozess* (Deutscher Volksverlag, Dr E. Böpple, Munich, 1924).

Löwe-Rosenberg, *Die Strafprozessordnung für das Deutsche Reich* (de Gruyter & Co., Berlin and Leipzig, 1929).

Olden, Rudolf, *Hindenburg oder der Geist der Preussischen Armee* (Nestverlag, Nuremberg, 1948).

Ortega y Gasset, Jose, *Der Aufstand der Massen* (Deutsche Verlagsanstalt, Stuttgart, 1950).

Rauschning, *Gespräche mit Hitler* (Europa-Verlag, Zurich, 1940).

Stuckart, Wilhelm, und Globke, Hans, *Kommentar zur deutschen Rassengesetzgebung* (C. H. Beck, Munich and Berlin, 1936).

Vossische Zeitung vom 25.–30.9.30 (Ullstein-Verlag, Berlin).

Wilamowitz-Möllendorff, Ulrich v., *Platon, Sein Leben und seine Werke* (Weidmannsche Verlagsbuchhandlung, Berlin and Frankfurt/Main, 1948).

Zarnow, Gottfried, *Gefesselte Justiz*, 2 Vols. (J. F. Lehmanns Verlag, Munich, 1931 and 1932).

19
THE REIGN OF THE BLACK ORDER.
THE FINAL PHASE OF NATIONAL-SOCIALISM:
THE SS COUNTER-STATE
Karl O. Paetel

THE writing of history involves a constant preoccupation with facts. Interpretation only becomes necessary if events no longer speak for themselves, analysis only if, for lack of material, the facts can only be accounted for by putting forward hypotheses like so many bridges.

If one considers the history of the last twenty years, the political part played by the German SS becomes clear. It is enough to remove a few weeds from the garden of National-Socialism. If one considers the SS in the framework of the movement as a whole, one realises how it comes to shape and condition the Third Reich, and finally, for a relatively short time, to dominate it almost entirely. The peculiar thing about this process is that, in neutralising the other organisations, which like itself had their origin in National-Socialism, in giving an ideology, whatever it may be, a purely relative value, an *élite*, which had made itself autonomous, set out deliberately to place at the disposal of the Idea and the *Führer* a human type that was increasingly hard and increasingly aware of its strength.

The peculiar features of the SS are reflected in its acts. The rare political and technical instructions issued by the SS High Command throw only a certain light on them.

There is little one can add, apart from the evidence given by a few of their victims who survived, and some intelligent and penetrating observations by their adversaries. In this way we shall get a clear picture of the Order, of the technique it employed to seize power, and the principles on which it based its education.

It is not my intention to philosophise about the SS state, but to use as few quotations as possible to establish what path it followed and what was its goal.

The non-German reader, on opening Hitler's *Mein Kampf*, is quite likely to exclaim with surprise: 'But he told us all we ever needed to

633

know about himself and his aims!' No one believed him. And that is probably the only thing one cannot reproach him for.[1]

I. THREE STAGES OF NATIONAL-SOCIALISM IN GERMANY

To explain National-Socialism and throw light upon the inner laws of its development, a parallel is frequently drawn between the Nazi slogans and the words they borrowed from previous German writers. These writers were labelled 'forerunners' of the movement. The general conclusion has invariably been drawn that the Hitler Movement confined itself to translating into action ideas which represented, historically and inherently, the outward expression of the German mind as a whole, ideas which belonged intrinsically to the very character of the German people, whether innate or acquired by education.[2]

It must be admitted that on the young Hitler, as on anyone, certain books exercised as strong an influence as certain people. But the one thing that is not a matter of chance is the kind of reading matter to which, in a given situation, we react positively.

The characteristic features of National-Socialism—those which distinguish it, for example, from pre-Weimar anti-Semitism in Germany [3]—depend to a large extent on the given facts and the given situation with which its spokesmen and interpreters found themselves confronted at a specific moment in history. This is confirmed by the obvious fact that National-Socialism, more than any other contemporary political movement, at various successive stages of its evolution produced successive types of National-Socialism, each of which in its turn was conditioned, more by instinct than volition, by the changing demands of the political situation. The type of representative National-Socialist also changed. The layer of race-conscious and anti-semitic *petit bourgeois*, which, immediately after 1919, moved over *en masse* from the '*Deutschvölkischer Schutz- und Trutzbund*' to NSDAP organisations, the Brownshirt battalions of the 'unknown SA' which demanded 'the freedom of the streets' and came mostly

---

[1] The material on which this study is based comes almost exclusively from German and American sources. In a few cases I found it impossible to obtain the German original and had to rely on quotations at second hand. That is why occasionally I have not been able to give exact page-references and have been compelled to take certain quotations not from the original text but from a translation. Though anxious not to overburden my text with notes and references, I have considered it essential to back up my own personal views as far as possible with quotations and references.

[2] I shall only quote a few examples of this view of history: Paul Winkler, *The Thousand-year Conspiracy, Secret Germany behind the Mask* (New York, 1943); Derwent Wittlesey, *German Strategy of World Conquest* (New York, 1942); Stephen Raushenbush, *The March of Fascism* (New Haven, 1939); Rohan d'O. Butler, *The Roots of National Socialism* (New York, 1942).

[3] Paul W. Massing, *Rehearsal for Destruction, a Study of Political Antisemitism in Imperial Germany* (New York, 1949).

from the unemployment bureaux of the big towns, the members of the 'Death's Head' SS formations, and finally the soldiers in the armoured divisions of the *Waffen-SS*, all of these have little in common. What unites them is the all-embracing National-Socialist conception of the world and the oath of loyalty that binds them to the *Führer*. Any literary research that attempts to draw a parallel between Hitler's slogans and the ideas of his alleged predecessors becomes futile, as soon as one fails to find a parallel quotation for this evolution of type, which, in reality, was the most characteristic feature of the National-Socialist movement.

It would be equally erroneous to regard German National-Socialism as a separate entity that was born in the beerhalls and ended when the *Führer* issued illusory decrees from his bunker in Berlin. There is no definition or concept that can embrace both the period in which National-Socialism appeared as a '*völkische*' movement and the period when it was the vanguard of a social revolution, when the Party was taking the big towns of Germany by storm. And still less can one include the later evolution from the One-Party State to the SS Counter-State.

In 1923, 1933, 1939, and 1945, National-Socialism in Germany maintains a certain continuity, but its face is constantly changing.

When Hitler decided to enter politics, it was under the impulse of the Pangerman and racial ideology, with which he had come in contact in Vienna and to which he added his own bitter resentment against Imperial Germany, a sort of blind hatred for the 'November criminals'. His most deep-rooted feeling was one of disgust that the war had been lost not by the German Empire but by all that the name 'German' stood for. Ideas of this kind were indistinguishable from those of countless nationalist, racial, and anti-semitic groups all over Germany and the German-speaking frontier areas.

He soon realised—with all his profound personal faith in the two pillars on which his whole conception of the world was based: the struggle against the '*Diktat*' of Versailles and the struggle against Judaism, in whatever disguise he thought to find it—he soon realised that the arsenal of the old-fashioned nationalism was no longer effective. With the enthusiasts in the racial camp, who dreamt of an esoteric Germanism, he never had the slightest sympathy. In *Mein Kampf* he makes several sarcastic references to them. The *Ariosophy* and other such eccentricities left him quite cold.

His real discovery—for Germany, of course—was the exploitation, by means of an enormous propaganda machine, of the slogan 'national socialism'. It came from Austria, or more precisely from the Sudeten Germans, and bore the hallmark of an ideology adapted to the exigencies of the moment. There were many who, disillusioned both by the collapse of the *bourgeois* system and by the November revolution, pricked up their ears. It was not only the social derelicts who felt drawn to Hitler.

Up to the time when the two 'Strasser crises'—the apostasy of Otto and the alliance of Gregor with Schleicher—forced Hitler's hand, he had been steering his 'German National-Socialist Workers' Party' irresolutely between restoration and revolution. On 9th November 1923 he declared that his aim was 'to repair the injustice of the November 1918 revolution', but, on the other hand, he toyed for some time with the idea of committing his party to a social revolution. For many years the National-Socialist Party was a mixture of anti-socialist nationalists, or pro-Russian socialists, of priests and pagans, of monarchists and republicans. Even the Party's basic anti-Semitism was a subject of dispute. The left wing of the Party demanded times without number the expulsion of Julius Streicher and his faction.

Around 1923 the Hitler Party represented the racialist and anti-semitic wing of the great national movement, and the SA was no more than a rather undisciplined group, useful for breaking up the public meetings of political opponents and for supplying the Party's speakers with bodyguards.

After the abortive *putsch* of 8th November 1923, after the unsuccessful fusion with Wulle-Gräfe's '*Deutschvölkische Freiheits-Bewegung*' (Race Movement of German Freedom), after the period of imprisonment in the fortress at Landsberg, a slow, and at first almost imperceptible change came over the new NSDAP which, as soon as the ban on its activities was lifted, revived the tradition of the old movement. The most diverse ideologies were combined with the old, original formulæ.

Hitler knew how to make full use of propaganda and he understood all too well the technique of marrying divergent ideas. The '*völkichse*' note became markedly subdued and gave way to a militant socialism, to the unknown SA's call to arms. It was not always easy for the headquarters in Bavaria to keep the peripheral forces under control. When, in 1930, after his famous meeting with Adolf Hitler, Otto Strasser issued the statement: 'The Socialists will leave the Party', only a few of the rank and file followed him. The rebellion of Captain Stennes, the second in the SA ranks in northern Germany, seemed for a few days to have shaken the Party to its foundations, but it, too, proved to have no serious effect on the NSDAP, which had become a party of the masses and was about to gain its first parliamentary victories. The National-Socialist Party had a much greater drawing power than had at first been thought possible.

If one looks back today on the later phases of the Nazi régime, it seems quite logical that sound conservatives like Hermann Rauschning,[1] or self-avowed reactionaries like Fritz Thyssen [2] should, in the years after 1933, have seen in the 'national revival' a movement of *bourgeois* restoration, which would soon lose its first flush of subversive enthusiasm and whose excesses would be corrected by the state—so long as these excesses, directed against dangerous left-wing elements, did not appear 'to some extent justified'.

When Hitler, in the presidential box at Potsdam, bowed before Wilhelm II's Marshal, the 'November treason' seemed wiped out and the times of glorious ancestors restored. Among the old-time dress uniforms, still redolent of mothballs, the brown shirts of the 'guards' ready for civil war passed unnoticed. The aim, quite clearly, was counter-revolution. And there were many indications that the counter-revolution was beginning.

At the same time, too, revolution was being contemplated and gained momentum.

In its struggle 'against the Red Front and reaction' the SA had seen its list of dead increasing; motivated much more by a revolutionary urge than by any revolutionary theory, when the SA sang of the barricades of the German revolution, its real, fundamental object was a social upheaval.

Petit bourgeois and unemployed assembled in the Storm Troops with students-turned-proletarians and former officers, and they marched through the towns of Germany towards a new state, a state that would right each man's wrongs and end the general misery. The *bourgeois* classes in power, who like a single entity with a thousand faces, embodied the Weimar régime, would be swept out of power, dispossessed, and annihilated. This was a very different thing from what Konrad Heiden [3] has in mind when he speaks of a revolt of 'Bohemia in arms'.

To begin with, they wanted a revolution, a genuine revolution. In North Germany the Strasser brothers with the '*Kampf Verlag*' programme were the leaders of one wing which, from the social point of view, was clearly revolutionary, as was apparent in the discussion with Hitler and the Munich group on the indemnification of the Princes. In its internal policy, this kind of 'national socialism' undoubtedly wished to be regarded as a movement of the left.

Neither the left-wing of the NSDAP nor the Young Conservatives who preached a 'revolution of the right'—a revolution which would permeate the state to its foundations and whose programme Hans Freyer had elaborated [4]—realised that, from the moment the Third

[1] Hermann Rauschning, *Konservative Revolution, Versuch und Bruch mit Hitler* (New York, 1941).
[2] Fritz Thyssen, *I Paid Hitler* (New York, 1941).
[3] Konrad Heiden, *Der Führer, Hitler's Rise to Power* (Boston, 1944).
[4] Hans Freyer, *Revolution von Rechts* (Jena, 1931).

Reich came into being, the leader of the National-Socialist movement in his famous talk with the banker Schröder and the opportunist von Papen had abandoned the anti-capitalist aspirations of his Storm Troops, just as he abandoned illusions of an authentic Conservatism. The Storm Troopers and the bankers never lived to see their hopes and aspirations realised. As time went on, their mood worsened. Hitler no longer felt sure of them. The 30th June 1934 seemed finally to provide proof that the Nazi Party intended to eliminate the radical elements from its ranks, to intimidate its reactionary partner, and to adopt a new line.

This process cost the morally disqualified head of the Brownshirts his life, together with that of two generals, one of whom had been Chancellor; in addition, several highly respectable right-wing politicians had been assassinated 'by mistake'. It was an ugly incident, but for the 'realists' on the right it did not, in the long run, serve as an effective warning. Very few conservatives realised clearly that the firing-squads of Stadlheim and Lichterfelde had liquidated not only the claims to power of the 'old fighters' in the SA, but also the ideal of a state based on law and the hope of a real conservative revolution. The significance of the 30th June 1934 was not understood, and quite a number, who in fact were victims of it, gave cries of victory.

In his capacity as 'Oberster Gerichtsherr' (supreme judicial head), Hitler had just mapped out the road National-Socialism was to follow. If it was to survive, as a political power in a new form, it had to deal ruthlessly with two adversaries: Socialism on the left and true Conservatism on the right. And action had to be taken before either or both of these tendencies got hold of its own ranks. In every case, in the assassination of the SA leaders, and particularly of Gregor Strasser, and, on the same 30th of June, in the murder of General Schleicher and personalities from conservative and religious circles, in the ruthless struggle against 'Marxist illegality' and in the scandalous rumours spread about Blomberg and Fritsch, right up to the 20th July 1944, when the flower of the Prussian nobility and ringleaders of the working-class movement were executed, the same motive is behind everything: if the Third Reich is to survive, Socialists and patriots with conservative ideas must be eliminated as dangerous. The NSDAP, composed of civilians, could not have waged this battle on two fronts. The entire state administration was riddled with people who could not be relied upon. Once it was purged, the SA, which had gained power on behalf of the dictator, was a mere shadow of its former self.

The SS stepped, almost unnoticed by outside observers in Germany and abroad, into the place of the National-Socialist Movement.

It is correct to say that the 30th of June 1934 marked the end of the period in which German National-Socialism believed in a social revolution. (It is interesting to see, as Ignazio Silone points out, with documentary evidence to support him, how Italian Fascism was compelled to go through the same difficulties with its 'old fighters'.[1]) But it is wrong to believe that the same date marked a victory for the army, representing order, law, and security of the citizen. The victor was Heinrich Himmler, and with him a new form of National-Socialism. Heinrich Himmler, Gregor Strasser's friend, Himmler who had been a member of Röhm's immediate entourage, Himmler, the double traitor, was the man who came out on top.[2]

H. G. Gisevius [3] gives an illuminating description of how Hitler, returning from his 'punitive expedition' to Wiessee and Munich, was met by Himmler at the Tempelhof airport, and the following passage throws a revealing light on the situation after the 30th of June:

'. . . And now Himmler produces from the cuff of his overcoat a long list of names on a crumpled piece of paper. Hitler reads it, while Göring and Himmler keep talking to him in a low voice. Hitler's fingers can be clearly seen moving down the list. Now and then he stops at a name. The other two continue talking to him in undertones but with more urgency. Suddenly Hitler throws his head back. A gesture of anger—not to say refusal—so violent that everyone present could not fail to see it . . .'

What was happening? Gisevius continues:

'Nebe and I exchange glances. The same thought has crossed both our minds like an electric shock. "They have just made him swallow the alleged suicide of Strasser." ' [4]

Hitler contented himself with this violent gesture. He never called Gregor Strasser's murderers to account. He never found occasion to utter one word of regret concerning this act of murder.

From that moment, Heinrich Himmler had his hands free. Hitler approved the *fait accompli*: the SS leader had not only fulfilled the

[1] Ignazio Silone, *Der Faschismus, seine Entstehung und seine Entwicklung* (Zürich, 1934).
[2] We have only a fragmentary knowledge of the events on 30 Jun. 1934. Gisevius tells only a part of it, from what he knew; Heiden brilliantly places himself in other people's position, but tends to exaggerate the truth. Otto Strasser, who was well versed in the situation within the Party, tells what he knows with great passion in *Die deutsche Bartholomäusnacht* (Zürich, 1935). He gives us as facts many things which have since proved mere figments of his imagination. The best analysis until now is to be found in *Vierteljahrshefte für Zeitgeschichte*, Stuttgart, I, 2, 1953: *Die 'Zweite Revolution'—Der 30. Juni 1934*, by Hermann Mau.
[3] Hans Bernd Gisevius, *Bis zum bitteren Ende* (Zürich, 1946), Vol. I.
[4] ibid., p. 248.

mission entrusted to him, but like Göring, had taken it upon himself to 'enlarge it'. From now on, the representative of the 'Socialists' in the ranks of the NSDAP would no longer ridicule 'Pince-Nez' (Riri-les-Binocles) Himmler in good Bavarian dialect and would no longer head a faction within the party.

The socialist revolution, which in the SA's scheme of things was to follow on the national revolution, the 'second wave' of National-Socialism, that Röhm had ominously foretold without ever making the slightest attempt to prepare the way for a *coup*, had been drowned in blood before it had become more than a slogan.

The way was open for the National-Socialism of the third period, that of the 'Black Order'. Himmler was taking the ascendancy. Slowly and gradually, Hitler had decided: against the movement and for the SS.

If a religious note may be introduced without any apparent inconsistency, Joachim Günther was substantially correct when he wrote in a German review that appeared after the fall of Hitler: 'The basic idea that inspired the SA was defeated on the 30th of June, 1934 by a purely satanic idea, that of the SS.' [1]

II. The Order Advances Towards Seizure of Power

When, on 30th January 1933, the *Führer* of the National-Socialist Party became Chancellor of the German Reich, it was as the representative of the national movement, which had achieved unity. The civil war army of Brownshirts was, for a time, diverted from its aim and used to hunt down enemies of the state. On the periphery of the *'nationale Bewegung'*, whose ranks had been swollen by opportunists of every imaginable brand, the SA awaited the final decision, which was slow in coming: the implementation of 'German Socialism'.

It is at this point in the Third Reich that the rule of the 'authoritarian' Party began. 'It is the Party that gives orders to the state.' [2] But this does not mean that Party and state automatically became one. The Party itself was far from being one. This was all too apparent on 30th June 1934. When the small racialist group, with all its bits and pieces, had been transformed into the mass-movement of National-Socialism, endless quarrels had arisen with dissidents of every kind. The transition from the National-Socialist One-Party State to the rule of the SS involved much shedding of blood. The period of SS domination reached its climax when, after the 20th

[1] Joachim Günther, 'Die Stufen zum Satanismus, Umrisse einer Genealogie der KL-Ideologie,' in *Deutsche Rundschau* (Gelsenkirchen), LXXVI, 3 Mar. 1950, pp. 174–83.
[2] Adolf Hitler, 7 Sep. 1943, at a Party Rally, in Nuremberg: 'It is not the State which gives orders to us, but we who give orders to the State.'

July 1944, scaffolds were erected. This period was to end with Germany in ruins.

By the middle of 1934 two chapters of National-Socialist history were already written: that of the '*völkische*' Movement and that of 'national socialism'.

The old-time racialists were no longer taken seriously. With the death of Gregor Strasser, the Socialists had lost their spokesman, and they were either leaving the Party, keeping quiet, or even howling with the wolves. Idealists of every kind, people who, following Gesell or Feder, dreamt of monetary reform (Hitler had realised at a very early stage that he would gain nothing by trying to break the power of the banks, by making the struggle against money the backbone of his programme), people who wanted to establish a new way of life on 'Nordic' principles, apostles of neo-paganism, all of them had talked their way into dissident groups before the Party came to power, or continued to vegetate inside the Party. They were treated with contemptuous smiles and remained without any influence.

The day the SA became a spent force the third period began, the period in which the SS set out to seize power.

On 3rd July 1934 the Reich Cabinet promulgated a law on measures to be taken for the legitimate defence of the state. Its only article ran as follows: 'The measures taken and implemented on June 30 and July 1 1934 to frustrate attempts at high treason directed against the country were taken as measures of legitimate defence and are legal'. On 13th July Hitler himself, speaking before the *Reichstag*, confirmed the legality of the terror measures taken on the German night of St Bartholomew and, on 20th July the SS, which until then were subordinate to the Chief of Staff of the SA, were made autonomous and completely independent of the Storm Troops. The decree ran as follows:

'By virtue of the outstanding services rendered by the SS, particularly during the events of June 30 1934, I raise them to the rank of an autonomous organisation within the NSDAP. The Commander-in-Chief of the SS for the Reich will, therefore, together with the Chief of Staff of the SA, be directly subordinate to the supreme head of the SA. The Commander-in-Chief of the SS for the Reich and the Chief-of-Staff will both hold the Party rank of *Reichsleiter*.' [1]

This decree, as was subsequently realised, set the scene for the final period, the decisive period in the history of National-Socialism. Heinrich Himmler, the renegade secretary of the Socialist Gregor

[1] Fritz Maier Hartmann, *Dokumente des Dritten Reiches* (Munich, 1939), Vol. II, pp. 159–60.

Strasser, the watchdog who kept guard over the Party internally, had just taken a decisive step forward. More intelligent than most of the Party's propagandists, he had, at a very early stage, expressed the view to Hermann Rauschning that

> ' "when power had been attained there was not only no unity in regard to future policy but no united group of leaders." The party included a sort of sample collection of all political outlooks in Germany, from crass reactionaries to doctrinaire pacifists and the extremist Left-Wing Socialists.—"The splitting up of the party into various camps, involving the collapse of the whole German revolution," continued Himmler, "was inevitable if stern measures were not adopted. Thus an impressive terroristic act was indispensable." ' [1]

These acts of terrorism had been committed. Himmler was becoming the head of an independent organisation and was obliged to give an account to no one, short of Hitler himself.

The effect was soon felt inside the Party. It had never included a large number of theorists in its ranks. A small handful who had tried to base Party action on a '*Weltanschauung*' and whose writings had for some time made them appear the most representative group in the Party, came into conflict with the SS in the next few years and were almost all thrown overboard. I do not mean that there were no intellectuals in the ranks of the SS. The medical services of the SS acquired considerable fame, though of an unenviable kind.[2] The *Reichsführer SS* was no scholar when it came to German pre-history and Germanic racial ethnology. He soon grew tired of summoning ethnologists who had not the slightest intention of harnessing their research on race to his political ambitions. So he surrounded himself with a bevy of hand-picked experts, whose function it was to supply him with the necessary material to back up his assertions. This select group also included specialists in administration. The sole condition was that they had no ideas of their own. When *SS Obergruppenführer* Werner Best proposed a new administration for Greater Germany [3] and revealed that he still clung to some of the ideas of Friedrich Naumann, which were not in keeping with absolute domination, pure and simple, he was packed off to Denmark out of harm's way.

Heinrich Himmler mistrusted people with ideas of their own. And, while the '*Mythus des 20. Jahrhunderts*' was readily accepted, on the whole, Alfred Rosenberg was made fully aware of it.

---

[1] Hermann Rauschning, *Men of Chaos* (New York, 1942), p. 26.
[2] Mitscherlich and Mielke, *Das Diktat der Menschenverachtung, Dokumenation zum Nürnberger Ärzteprozess* (Heidelberg, 1947).
[3] Werner Best, *Grundfragen einer deutschen Grossraumverwaltung. Festgabe für Heinrich Himmler* (Darmstadt, 1941).

Rosenberg, who had the responsibility of supervising National-Socialist literature, had made all preparations to force the other ideologists out of business and push thought in the Party into the background. He had, for example, taken the most jealous care to prevent Oswald Spengler, Moeller van den Bruck or Othmar Spann from gaining any hold on the Party with their ideas and from influencing the Party's work. But he had forgotten that a high-ranking position is no guarantee of real power, unless one has force on one's side. When Rosenberg became Minister for the Eastern Territories, Himmler, addressing the leaders of the SS and the police, told them openly that, in the occupied territories, it was they who had the whip-hand, that they were subordinate to him and him alone, and that Mr Rosenberg need only continue writing his books in peace without meddling in anything else. As was quite understandable, Alfred Rosenberg, after a time, had completely lost touch with events. The whole edifice of his conception of the world suddenly ceased to play any part at all. Even in the death-cell he still complains.[1] He writes indignantly:

'While he was pretending to fight for Germanic values, Himmler introduced into the brave SS committed to his care a trait that is anything but Germanic and that left a terrible stain on this fair name. He was charged with the internal security of the Reich, but by his actions he inevitably roused feelings of indignation against the government of the Reich. . . . As time went on, in all regional branches of the party, Himmler's police-system built up an enormous bitterness against us. Against "the Order of the SS" the Party took an increasingly clear stand, in spite of precautions which, in public service, it could not avoid taking.'

He adds bitterly: 'It was too late. The sectarian triumphed over the Idea.' Here Rosenberg is wrong. The technicians of absolute power —who were by no means sectarians—after years of systematic work, and by treating the Party as a closed community, had succeeded in removing all those who, in the first stages of the National-Socialist Movement's evolution, had represented it and spoken for it.

In the Nazi Party, the dogmatists and the believers had outlived themselves. The men of action, the opponents of any ideology, had begun to concentrate in their own hands the apparatus of the state, the army, and even the economic organisations, to remove the civil elements in the Party from all positions of power, and to create, at the centre of the state, a zone which belonged to them and in which they were omnipotent.

[1] Serge Lang and Ernst von Schenck, *Portrait eines Menschheitsverbrechers, nach den hinterlassenen Memoiren des ehemaligen Reichsministers Alfred Rosenberg* (St Gallen, 1947), pp. 205, 208.

David Rousset, describing the enormous power wielded by the SS who controlled the concentration camps, makes this remark: [1]

'At the centre of this empire forever invisible, a brain unifies and controls all the police resources of the Reich—and Europe—and dominates with absolute will every aspect of the camps—the brain of Himmler and his intimates . . .'

Reichsleiter Rosenberg and the prisoner Rousset have the same experience: Germany, and indeed Europe, was governed from the barrack-rooms of the SS.

Himmler and his Order kept watch over the National-Socialist movement. He also had complete control of the police of Greater Germany, while the senior officers of the SS and the police, in effect, controlled the occupied territories.[2]

Everywhere on his path, however, he came up against the army. More than one suspect 'emigrated' into the army to escape from Himmler's jurisdiction. Party police and state police were both indispensable to the man in power. But 'the arrogance' of the army could only be broken if the Order—assuming that every attempt to conquer it from within had failed—made itself indispensable to the *Führer* as his sword-bearer too.[3] Proof had to be given that Germany's military power and her sway over a whole Empire depended on the SS, the state police who had proved themselves at the front, and not on the army, which consisted of civilians mobilised under a compulsory service.

Parallel with the 'General SS' and the SD (Security Service of the SS), fighting units must be created and developed, the *Waffen-SS*, which, side by side with the army, played a more and more important part.

Up to the outbreak of war, the '*Standarten*', the regiments of the '*SS-Verfügungstruppen*' (SS Troops on active service) had hardly competed with the army. Subsequently they grew, under the name *Waffen-SS*, to brigade, then to division strength. They comprised all arms, were mechanised, and for the most part turned into picked armoured divisions. Very soon they were recruited also from territories outside the Reich, particularly to form the so-called

---

[1] David Rousset, *The Other Kingdom* (New York, 1947). The original title is *L'Univers concentrationaire* (Paris, 1946).

[2] We cannot follow in detail the means by which the SS came to control the key positions in the state, whether in Germany or in occupied Europe. The chapter 'Police' in Raphael Lemkin's *Axis Rule in Occupied Europe, Laws of Occupation, Analysis of Government, Proposals for Redress* (Washington, 1944) gives a picture of the basic laws of the SS police state, with all the necessary data and sources indicated.

[3] cf. the note of 13 Apr. 1935, by the U.S. ambassador in Berlin, in *Ambassador Dodd's Diary*, ed. William E. Dodd, Jnr, and Martha Dodd (New York, 1941), p. 233.

'Germanic' divisions, then finally recruiting spread to non-Teutonic territories.

In mid-1940, in a secret order addressed to the regular army chiefs, Hitler defined the specific functions of the *Waffen-SS*. These troops, which were later to carry out police duties in the framework of the New Order in Europe, were first of all to see action at the front. The principle of voluntary recruitment was abandoned. Members of the army who had proved themselves, were transferred *ex-officio* to the *Waffen-SS*, then members of the Hitler Youth were enrolled. Towards the end of the war the *Waffen-SS* comprised thirty-seven divisions, among them extremely well-equipped armoured units. Before the Inter-Allied War Council at Nuremberg Jodl estimated the total strength at 700,000 men.[1]

The general order I have just mentioned, which was signed by Hitler himself, represents, after the decree of 30th June 1934, the second decisive step towards establishing the Order as all-powerful and assuring its autonomy in Germany. It shows to what an extent, at that time, Hitler had accepted the ideology of the SS.

The seed sown by Himmler was bearing fruit.

Hitler had little confidence in the former *bourgeois* and conservative leaders and still less in the army. On the other hand, it seemed clear to him that he could not count on the whole-hearted loyalty of the 'old comrades' of the Party. With a few restrictions meant to allay suspicion, he gave his categorical approval when it came to increasing the praetorian guard.

In an appendix to a communication reserved exclusively for army commanders,[2] the Commander-in-Chief expresses the wish that the widest publicity should be given in the army to the following considerations:

'Secret. Subject: *Waffen-SS.*

'On August 6 1940, when he issued orders for the inclusion in the Army of the regiment of his personal bodyguard, *"Leibstandarte Adolf Hitler"*, the *Führer* elaborated the principles, summarised below, which prove the necessity of establishing the *Waffen-SS.*

[1] Erich Kordt, *Wahn und Wirklichkeit* (Stuttgart, 1948).
[2] The following message was sent in a circular note to several members of the Wehrmacht: 'Transcript, strictly secret. Army chief of command, H. QU. OKH. 21.3.1941. Section no. 137/3 41 c. (1) Object. Orders from the *Führer* concerning the future militarised police. Cf. Army chief of command, Sect. no. 24/9 40 C.V, 11.9.40. There was some doubt at the time that the *Führer*'s views of the subject of the Waffen-SS were published, whether these were really intended to be made public. The army commander-in-chief has decided it could be nothing but desirable for these views to be given the widest possible publicity. The above-mentioned circular treated only of the general military command. Also there are added the intentions of the *Führer* concerning the Waffen-SS. Signed by the Lieutenant-Colonel I.C. An enclosure herewith.'

'The Greater German Reich, in its definitive form, will not only comprise within its frontiers ethnic groups which have always, on principle, shown good will towards the Reich. It is, therefore, essential to provide, outside the old provinces of the Reich, a military State police, which will be in a position, in all circumstances, to represent and impose the authority of the Reich within our frontiers.

'This task can only be carried out by a military State police which only includes in its ranks men of the best German blood and which, without any restriction, embraces completely the *"Weltanschauung"* on which the Greater German Reich is founded.

'Only a troop so constituted will be capable, in moments of crisis, of opposing the action of disruptive influences.

'Proud of its impeccable purity, such a body will never fraternise with the proletariat and with the underworld world that would like to undermine the Idea inspiring us. In the future Greater German Reich, a police troop will only have authority over other citizens if it has been educated in a soldierly spirit.

'Our people, thanks to the glorious achievements of this war and by virtue of the education given to it by the National-Socialist Party, has adopted such a soldierly attitude that a police force fit only to knit socks (1848) or corrupted by a spirit of officialdom (1918) would not earn any respect. It is further necessary that this State police should prove itself on the field of battle, as part of regular units, and should sacrifice its blood in the same way as any unit of our armed forces.

'Once they have been tested and have returned from the frontline, the units of the *Waffen-SS* will have the necessary authority to carry out all their duties as State police. This use of the *Waffen-SS* in the interior will be of advantage even to the regular Army.

'In future it will no longer be tolerated that the Regular Army, recruited by compulsory military service, should at critical moments be employed against its own fellow-citizens. If it came to that, it would be the beginning of the end. A State that finds it necessary to resort to such measures is no longer in a position to engage its Army against the external enemy and, that being so, ceases to exist. Our history has a number of tragic examples of this. In future, the Regular Army will be exclusively employed against external enemies.

'In order to ensure that the quality of the men in the *Waffen-SS* units always remains high, the number of units to be formed will be limited. The *Führer* considers that the units of the *Waffen-SS* should not exceed 5 to 10 per cent of the strength of the peace-time Army.'

Thus spoke the *Führer*. Leaving out of account the fact that the last provision, which was made to pacify the army chiefs, was never adhered to, the tenor of this long speech is abundantly clear: even in the event of a victorious outcome to the war, the future was giving the *Führer* of the Greater German Reich much food for anxiety. 'The underworld', the proletariat and the oppressed peoples 'which show no goodwill', were all potential enemies. If the situation became critical, no confidence could be placed either in the ordinary citizen or in the Party or, still less, in the army if it emerged victorious.[1] The measure of this is that Himmler remains not only *Reichsleiter* in the Party with decisive powers, not only head of the entire German police forces in the whole of Europe, but also the military head of a second army, which comes directly under the *Führer*.

The SS High Command very soon made it clear, with a remarkable frankness that leaves no room for doubt, that it expected to meet with increasing difficulties in the theatre of operations inside Germany (this is later extended, without causing any grave ideological difficulties, to cover the New Order in Europe) and that those difficulties could be overcome only if no holds were barred. The day Heydrich, *SS-Obergruppenführer*, proposes in 1935 [2] to enlist the support of civilians enrolled in the Party has passed. The *Reichsführer SS*, in a jeering voice, takes cognisance of the fact that his organisation is not exactly looked upon with favour by the public. In 1936 Himmler declares:[3] 'I know that in Germany there are a considerable number of people who hate the sight of a black uniform. We understand them very well and, besides, we do not expect too many people to like us.' In 1936, in his New Year Message, he had clearly indicated the way that lay ahead: 'One of the most pressing duties confronting us is to seek out all the enemies, open or hidden, of the *Führer* and the National-Socialist movement, to fight them and to destroy them.'

As the years pass, the tone of the public declarations issued by the Black Order [4]—they are, incidentally, not frequent—becomes more and more authoritarian, more threatening and more hysterical, up till the day when the *Reichsführer SS*—on 9th June 1942—stands before the coffin of Heydrich, who had been assassinated, and cries: 'It is the law of the SS that, if the nation demands it, we shall spare neither our blood nor that of others.'

[1] See the comments of the American paper *Nation* (Argus, 'Behind the Enemy Line,') 12 Dec. 1942, p. 649, and Himmler's speech as *Reichsführer SS* and commander of the Army in Reserve, before the officers' corps of an infantry division, in *Stoffsammlung, Herausgeber Nationalsozialistischer Führungsstab der Wehrmacht, Führungsunterlagen Folge III, Nur für den Gebrauch innerhalb der Wehrmacht, Teil der Sammelmappen 'Der Nationalsozialistische Führungsoffizier'*, p. 160.
[2] R. Heydrich, Chief of the *Sicherheitshauptamt des Reichsführers SS, Wandlungen unseres Kampfes* (Munich, 1935).
[3] Heinrich Himmler, *Die Schutzstaffel als antibolchewistische Kampforganisation* (Munich, 1936), p. 29.
[4] Gunther d'Alquen, *Die SS, Geschichte, Aufgabe und Organisation der Schutzstaffeln der NSDAP, bearbeitet im Auftrage des Reichsführers SS* (Berlin, 1939).

Dr Best once attempted to limit the relative functions and juris-diction of the various SS and police formations, in order to give them a legal status:[1] he achieved no practical results.

The role of Triarians which the SS played in the Third Reich was particularly noticeable, even from outside, at the time of the abortive *coup d'état* of 20th July 1944.

All the evidence goes to show that the *Reichs-Sicherheitshauptamt* (Security Headquarters of the Reich), which came under Himmler, knew which people were preparing the *coup* and knew their back-ground, but—and this is an astonishing fact—Himmler's entourage was taken unawares by the *coup* itself.[2] It was not the SS but, para-doxically enough, the '*Gross-Deutschland*' Division (Hagen-Remer) that was chosen to take reprisals, once Stauffenberg's attempt had failed. Yet the abortive *coup d'état* had a boomerang effect that re-bounded, at first, to Himmler's advantage.

Goebbels, who, as on 30th June 1934, had clung to the SS—again thanks to the presence of mind with which he brought in Remer against the Bendlerstrasse—obtained full powers, not without justification, 'for the complete mobilisation of the Reich' and found himself promoted over the heads of men like Speer, Sauckel, and Ley. Nominally, Göring lost none of his functions, in fact he was theoretically confirmed in all of them, but in practice he had to dele-gate to Goebbels the dictatorship he exercised in the economic sphere and, furthermore, place formally at Himmler's disposal an Air Force Division under the Command of Colonel-General Stumpf.

The real victor, that day, was the Black Order.

When an SS official reorganised the administration of northern France and Belgium, the latter, which was subject to military ad-ministration and not to a Commissar specially appointed by the National-Socialist Party, came under Himmler's jurisdiction. In the fighting forces senior SS officers were appointed directly to very high commands. *SS-Obergruppenführer* Hausser, until then in charge of the Second Armoured Corps, took over the Command of a group of armies of the *Wehrmacht*, which were playing a decisive part in France. *SS-Gruppenführer* Jungclaus was appointed Commander-in-Chief of all the troops in northern France and Belgium. On the Eastern Front the same procedure was being adopted: the SS chief responsible for Warsaw was given command of a Regular Army.

Where the SS were unable to take over functions directly which gave them an effective command, these functions were entrusted to one or other of the 'young' Nazi generals on Colonel-General

[1] Werner Best, *Schutzstaffeln der NSDAP und die Polizei* (Berlin, 1939) in *Deutsches Recht*, p. 47.
[2] '*SS-Bericht über den 20. Juli*', *Aus den Papieren des SS-Obersturmbannführers Dr Georg Kiesel* in *Nordwestdeutsche Hefte*, II, 2 (Hamburg, 1947), pp. 5–34.

Guderian's staff, the specialists in tank warfare who had established themselves as a separate school ever since the resurrection of the German Army. Guderian was made the responsible Chief of General Staff. He combined the functions which Keitel and Zeitzler had hitherto fulfilled, and those of Jodl were very much restricted. For the moment the picture of the redistribution of powers was very clear: the *Führer*'s Headquarters, with the support of the *Waffen-SS* and the 'young' Party-trained generals, had at last liquidated all potential trouble-makers.

The main effect of the reorganisation that followed 20th July was to leave the SS in effective control of the entire organisation of the Army Reserve. For close on two years Colonel-General Fritz Fromm had succeeded in defending the *Stellvertretende Generalkommando* against all attempts at infiltration by the *Waffen-SS*. Himmler had tried in vain (at a given point, it was one of the demands he made of Marshal von Reichenau) to have Fromm replaced either by the Command Service Head of the *Waffen-SS*, *SS-Obergruppenführer* Jüttner, or by the Head of the Recruiting Service of the *Waffen-SS*, *SS-Obergruppenführer* Juers. Resistance had been too strong.

The events of the 20th July removed the last obstacles in Himmler's way.

It was Himmler himself who took command of the army reserves. He already had control of the national territory—for he was Reich Minister of the Interior, Commissar-General for the administration of the Reich, and Head of the German police forces, he had also, as *Reichsführer SS*, supreme control over all SS organisations and the *Waffen-SS*, and now he managed to bring under the control of the Black Order the very effective link between the Fatherland and the front-line troops.[1] In German strategy the Army Reserve played a much more important part than its modest title would seem to indicate. Its function was not only to muster replacements and prepare them for front-line action in accordance with the instructions of the 'Head of Establishment and Supply', but also to control the entire rolling-stock of military transport by rail, road, and river; it was responsible for military censorship, information, counter-espionage, clothing and food supplies, pay-master duties and first-aid—to quote only a few of the more important services.

It is hardly necessary to stress how important it was for the SS

---

[1] The organisation of the SS as a whole falls into four main departments: (i) *Reichsführung SS* (12 principal officials); (ii) *Allgemeine SS*; (iii) *Waffen-SS*; (iv) *SS Totenkopfverbände*. Each of these organisations carried its influence into practically every branch of public life thanks to the *personal union* which ensured that the control of other organisations was given to the leaders of the SS, so as to form 'according to inviolable laws a military National-Socialist State . . . a brotherhood whose various *sippen* were bound together by the same oath'. cf. *Ergänzender Begleittext zur Übersicht verbrecherischer Nazi-Organisationen* edited by the *Länderrat* of the American zone.

to control military transport, education, and, above all, information in all its forms.

It is by no means unlikely that certain reports published abroad, to the effect that the 'moderate elements' in the Party had tried to prevent Himmler from acquiring complete power, were well founded. A telegram that passed almost unnoticed and which was dated 19th July 1944 said that 'somewhere in Thuringia a conference had been held at which, with reference to the removal of General von Falkenhausen, G.o.C. Belgium, Göring had tried to mediate between the representatives of the General Staff and the dominant clique at the *Führer*'s Headquarters'. Without success, however, as was apparent the following day. But there remained, as was seen later, considerable mistrust of Göring and of his hundred per cent loyalty to the Party.

A second attempt to strike a compromise between the Party and the army was undoubtedly made by certain people in the SA and the *Luftwaffe*. It failed, but it achieved one result: the rumour went round that *Gruppenführer* of the SA Lohse would be appointed a member of the General Staff as a political adviser representing the Party.

But the time for compromises had passed. Himmler was destined to take complete power and the pendulum would stop swinging. Ten months before the final collapse, the SS had Germany completely under its thumb. And, as on 30th June 1934, Himmler did not do things by halves. All those who might in any way hamper his domination were removed. With or without a trial. On 10th April 1945, Fabian von Schlabrendorff wrote in prison: [1]

'An adjutant of the SS, who has had a drop too much, tells me that yesterday they had to send members of the "*Abwehr*" to the gallows. These hangings were not carried out as a result of a verdict, but Himmler had ordered the liquidation of these people by virtue of his absolute powers. Also, the warders, who had lent a hand, had received an extra ration of sausage and schnaps.'

Once again the *Reichsführer SS* had done 'more than his duty'.

In the most important of his books,[2] Hermann Rauschning has done more than anyone else to explain the change that had taken place in the structure of National-Socialism. With remarkable penetration and an astonishing flair for typological changes, especially at such an early stage, he shows how the young generation of Nazi leaders, shortly after the advent to power, and particularly among the SS and, still more, the leaders of the Hitler Youth under SS in-

[1] Fabian von Schlabrendorff, *Offiziere gegen Hitler* (Zürich, 1946), cf. p. 188.
[2] Hermann Rauschning, *Die Revolution des Nihilismus* (Revised edition, Zürich, 1938).

fluence, began to be amused by both Ley's 'Strength through Joy' propaganda and Rosenberg's Nordic theses. Whenever a decision was taken that involved politics, they contrasted these theses with perspectives that transcended the old postulates. In this they saw proof that these theses were unreal and mere museum-pieces. If National-Socialism was to become a genuinely imperial force, thought these young leaders, whose ambition had grown under the influence of the SS, then all this talk was futile.

Propaganda could still serve a purpose, but in fact preparations had to be made for one central, totalitarian organisation to become the sole means of gaining power, of wielding it and adding to it. The task that lay ahead consisted in organising Europe in such a way as to remove all national boundaries, both political and economic, with the Black Order in the background. For all practical purposes this new Europe could conveniently be called 'Great Germania', although, in reality, the term derived from ideas which had lost their topicality. An SS of all the nations would see to it, if necessary by force of arms, that 'progress' was not held up by any rebellion on the part of the masses under the impetus of international Marxism or of a national tradition that had had its day.[1]

'This youth [declared Rauschning] [2] sees today that great revolutionary events have one characteristic feature in common: they destroy, they undermine. This youth has ceased to attach any value to divergence of doctrines and ideas. It has gone beyond the narrow frontiers of national or imperialistic aspirations, and over the dogmatic theories that base worldly happiness on justice in an ordered society. For this youth, the purpose of life is to live dangerously, and one's duty is to seize power; the means, violence; the final goal, an *Imperium* that will embrace the entire Globe.'

At one time the Brownshirts marched through German cities towards the 'German revolution'. From now on, the SS aims at overturning the world. Not that it has a doctrine of salvation, but so

---

[1] One can see in a germinal form the atrocities of the following years in the aggressive tone with which Himmler in 1937 announced 'a definitive statement towards the internal enemy'. This famous speech was delivered in secret before officers of the *Wehrmacht*, but the *Neue Vorwärts*, which appeared at Karlsbad, published on 26 Sep. of that year, four closely printed pages containing in a simplified form the programme of the SS, 'In the coming conflict, we will not only have an Army front on land, a Naval front on the sea, and an air front over Germany; we will also have a fourth front, the interior of Germany'. The civil army will be mobilised immediately before the *Wehrmacht* 'And if this is used, it will act without any scruples of pity, there is no other possible way'. An abridged version in English appeared under the title: *Once in 2000 Years, Secret Speech delivered by Heinrich Himmler, chief of the German Secret Police (Gestapo) to the German Army General Staff, published by the American Committee for Anti-Nazi Literature* (New York, 1938).

[2] Hermann Rauschning, *Die Revolution des Nihilismus*, op. cit., p. 90.

that a new *élite*, devoid of all doctrine, may take over power, the 'revolution of nihilism' uses national and social conflicts as driving-belts, in order to further its aim of absolute domination.

It is strange, in all this, that Heinrich Himmler, as far as he personally was concerned, had none of the ambitions of a great leader. In his behaviour he was a typical *petit bourgeois*, and it seems clear that it was almost by accident that, in transforming his SS into an independent army, parallel to the *Wehrmacht*, and in expanding it till it became a European male fraternity, he automatically unleashed ambitions and demands, as is natural with the creation of an Order of this kind. Reinhardt Heydrich, who came immediately below him in the SS hierarchy, was, on the evidence of those who knew him, much more ambitious and much more intelligent. While he maintained a very shrewd outward reserve, he undoubtedly did everything in his power to rid the *Reichsführer SS* and the functions of the SS of a certain element of provincialism, which still remained from the time when they were inspired by an ideology. Himmler himself, right up to the last, always hesitated before taking any step which might harm his relations with Hitler. There is no doubt that, through a personal friend, Dr Langbehn, he maintained contact for some time with the former Minister Popitz, who belonged to the 20th July group. There is no doubt that, when *SS-Obergruppenführer* Karl Wolff, on his own initiative, put out the first feelers for a surrender in Italy,[1] Himmler no more thought of putting him up against the wall than he did *SS-Brigadeführer* Schellenberg, who, during his negotiations with Count Bernadotte, quite bluntly proposed the removal of the *Führer*. But, on the other hand, he never yielded to any of the temptations to which he was subjected personally, even to that of taking absolute power.[2] The SS was and remained a National-Socialist formation.[3]

---

[1] Forrest Davis, 'The Secret History of a Surrender', in *The Saturday Evening Post* (New York, 22 and 29 Sep., 1945) pp. 9–11, 107–8, 111; 117, 105–6.

[2] The publication entitled *Who killed Hitler? The complete story of how Death came to Der Führer and Eva Braun, together with the first Intelligence Report on the Mystery of Adolf Hitler's death—as developed by Private Intelligence—from never-before-published facts and documents—at variance with the official British and Russian Intelligence Reports*, edited by Herbert Moore and James W. Barrett, Foreword by W. F. Heimlich, Former Chief Intelligence Officer for the U.S. Army in Berlin (New York, 1947) has no force in its arguments, and may be passed over in silence. At no point does it succeed in sustaining a plausible argument. On the question of Hitler's death, Gerhardt Boldt, *Die letzten Tage*, edited by Ernst A. Hepp (Hamburg, 1947), is always reliable, and especially H. R. Trevor-Roper, *The Last Days of Hitler* (London, 1947), to which should be added as complementary the same author's remarks in *Wer weiss von Hitlers Tod?* which appeared in *Der Monat* (Berlin) III, 26, pp. 126–8. Moore and Barrett contend that Himmler murdered Hitler. Trevor-Roper never mentions this at all.

[3] Himmler remained steadfast to his own words. In his speech on 12 Nov. 1935 at Goslar, he said of the SS: 'We teach the members of the SS that many things in this world may be forgiven, but one thing never: disobedience to orders.' Repro-

The cruel demands made by a fight that would lead to world domination had to be met. The 'civil sector' of the National-Socialist Movement and the so-called 'reactionary' army were eliminated in that order, after each had been pronounced unfit. Ideology after ideology was jettisoned. Of the original ideology there remained, at bottom, only the struggle against Judaism, the struggle against Bolshevism and, in defiance of the Treaty of Versailles, Germany's right to dominate the world. Some sort of secularised replica of the Jesuit Order was being sought and a new form being given to the National-Socialist ideas by applying the principles of austerity and intransigence and confining the ideology to essentials. Yet one principle remained, that of a single *Führer*, a principle raised to the level of a charismatic symbol and personified by Adolf Hitler.

Ignatius Loyola had never questioned the position of the Pope. Similarly, the SS never drew away from the *Führer*. Its very structure, of course, made such a thing impossible. As R. Heydrich has aptly pointed out in his *Wandlungen unseres Kampfes*, in reality and by virtue of its internal law it could not be anything else but 'the shock-troops of a certain *Weltanschauung*, the Guards of the *Führer* Idea, and, at the same time, while fulfilling its duties as a State Police force, the political police for the protection of the National-Socialist State'.[1] Himmler never lost sight of that, even when, on occasion, he was tempted to rebel. He did not even dare, shortly before the end of the war, personally to defend the Black Order that day when Hitler, in a fit of blind rage, subjected the 6th Armoured Corps under *SS-Obergruppenführer* Sepp Dietrich to the most dreadful insult imaginable, that was directed at the *Führer's* personal bodyguard. Against Hitler's orders, this army had fallen back on Vienna before vastly superior Russian forces. Hitler telegraphed orders that the SS Divisions 'Adolf Hitler', 'Death's Head', 'Das Reich', and 'Hohenstauffen' were no longer to wear on their sleeves the armband bearing their name, 'in view of the fact that they had not fought as the situation demanded'. Sepp Dietrich was on the verge of mutiny. He refused to carry out the order and sent back all his decorations to Hitler. The *Reichsführer SS* Himmler, said not a word.[2]

In fact, such quarrels were no longer important. A few days more and Hitler was dead. Himmler followed him shortly after. But more than one member of the *Waffen-SS* never forgave them for their conduct. Even in the internment camp.

It is very natural. The supreme heads did not live up to the image

---

duced in *Dokumente der deutschen Politik* (Berlin, 1937), vol. III, pp. 33–49 and especially p. 45.
[1] R. Heydrich, *Wandlungen unseres Kampfes*, op. cit., p. 20.
[2] Milton Shulman, *Defeat in the West* (New York, 1948), p. 316 seq.

people had conjured up of the SS and its bearing. They did not behave like an *élite* which feels bound by an oath.

The SS never conceived or developed a single idea of their own. They tried to knock into shape the ideas round which the National-Socialist Movement had been built up. It is a long way from the uproar of the beerhalls to the armoured divisions of the SS, but at an early stage the general direction was clear: 'The German nation is at last on the point of finding a mode of life. . . . It is the mode of a column of soldiers, marching no matter where or to what goal.' [1]

Himmler and his entourage well knew the virtual impossibility of training a whole nation to adopt such a mode of life unanimously, but they knew that it was possible to recruit an *élite* out of the mass which, in its turn, would create organisations with the help of which, 'no matter where or to what goal', leaders who know what they want could act with force.

There can be no doubt that the SS leaders took as their model a sort of synthesis of the Teutonic Order and the Society of Jesus. More than once, in the *Schwarze Korps*, the organ of the SS, reference is made to the Teutonic Order.[2] According to reports from people who were 'in it', both Hitler and Himmler quite frequently, in private conversation, expressed their wholehearted admiration for the psychology of a command such as was practised, in their view, in the Jesuit Order.

Conditions of entry—which became less and less strict (the recruit had to be of a certain height, give proof of his forbears, be of Nordic descent etc.), the permission to marry which every SS-man had to obtain from his formation, the establishment of special SS villages or settlements, the plans for veterans on the pattern of the colonies of Roman legionaries, and the introduction of a special jurisdiction— all these measures and many others, designed with the same ends in view, proved the desire to segregate the Black Order more and more from the world and the immediate social environment, to make it autonomous in relation to Party and state organs, while, at the same time, endeavouring to establish its control—with the help of 'emissaries' chosen from its members—over the state, the Party, society, cultural works, rural and industrial organisations.

Grotesque as it may seem on the surface, we even have a record kept by Heinrich Himmler's doctor of a conversation in which, in all seriousness, the *Reichsführer SS* declares that, after the victory, Hitler intended to detach Burgundy from France and turn it into a sovereign Stage devoted to the propagation of the SS. This report contains the following passage: [3]

[1] Alfred Rosenberg, *Gestaltung der Idee, Blut und Ehre*, Vol. II (Munich, 1936).
[2] cf. Himmler's Goslar speech, op. cit., p. 41.
[3] *The Memoirs of Dr Felix Kersten* (New York, 1947) with an introduction by

'The founding of the new State of Burgundy was much discussed by Himmler, following an address which Hitler made in
March 1943 at Berchtesgaden. "At the peace conference," said
Himmler, on March 5 of that year, "the world will learn that the
old Burgundy will be resurrected, that land which was once the
seat of learning and art, and which has become but an appendage
to modern France, known only as a wine-producing province.
The old culture will be revived in the new Burgundy, which will
include French Switzerland, Picardy, with Amiens, the Cham-
pagne district with Reims and Troyes, the Franche-Comte, with
Dijon, Chalons and Nevers, the Hainaut and Luxemburg. Burgundy will have access to the Mediterranean, as well as an outlet
on the English Channel.

"The capital has not yet been decided upon. Hitler is hesitating
at the moment between Ghent and Dijon. The official language
of Burgundy will be German. But in the beginning the people will
be allowed to continue to speak French." '

If we quote these details, it is because they prove that, to all appearances, the plan in question had been studied in great detail and
that, in consequence, the arrangements made to complete the project—arrangements that leave one gasping with astonishment—are
not without a certain logic. Kersten continues his report as follows:

' "The State of Burgundy will be governed by a Chancellor,
who will be responsible to a high official of the German Reich
bearing the title of *Reichsverweser*. It is expected that whoever is
the *Reichsführer* of the SS will occupy that position. Leo Dégrelle,
the leader of the Belgian Rexists, will be the first Chancellor of
Burgundy, it is expected.

' "Burgundy will have her own army, her own government, her
own laws, her own currency, her own postal services. The State
will, of course, be a National-Socialist State. The officials will be
drawn from the local population, but the Chancellor will summon
aides and experts from the German SS.

' "Burgundy will be a model state, admired and copied by the
whole world." ' At this point I observed that the future of Burgundy
did not sound to me one which would attract Burgundians, as it
did not sound as though it would be an autonomous state, but
rather a dependency, a subjective (sic) state of Germany.

' "You are mistaken," cried Himmler. "Hitler has formally declared that the German National-Socialist Party would not have

---

Konrad Heiden. This book, though it records many astonishing facts about the
immediate surroundings of Himmler, leaves at first a confused impression. What
he tells is in places quite amazing. But the facsimiles of letters of the SS Commander to his personal doctor, the photo showing them side by side, the quotations of
living witnesses, many of them foreigners, even Jews, and finally the fact that
Konrad Heiden wrote the preface, all these things show, on closer inspection, that
this book deserves our confidence, even if the author sometimes goes out of his way
to create an effect.

the right to meddle in Burgundy's administration. It will have its own foreign policy. There will be a Burgundian Embassy in Berlin and a German Embassy in Burgundy." Himmler went so far as to say that, since he, as *Reichsführer SS*, would be the first *Reichsverweser* in Burgundy, he would use all his authority to implement there all the "Weltanschauung" of the SS.'

It is of little consequence, when all is said and done, if Hitler took the trouble to map out in detail his plan for a sovereign SS State. But one cannot doubt Kersten's sincerity when he relates dreams that emerged directly from Himmler's secret ambitions.

One can well imagine Himmler visualising himself as a new Dietrich of Verona, the powerful vassal of Attila and almost his peer, who, in the hour of crisis, protected his sovereign lord, master of the world, with his lance and shield.

But he needed liege-men. Dr Ley formulated the following requirement:

'We must know for certain whether these men have in them the will to be leaders and masters, the will to dominate. The National-Socialist Party and its leaders must have this will to dominate. The man whose desire for totalitarianism stops short of the will to lead the people, who wishes to share with others this function of guide, is incapable of playing a leading part in the NSDAP. We have the will to dominate, we feel joy in commanding, not for the pleasure of playing the despot or paying homage to the sadism of tyranny but because we have the firm, rock-like belief that in all spheres only one man is capable of being the leader and that only one man is capable of bearing the responsibility.'

Statements of this kind—Dr Ley uttered the words we have just quoted at the opening of the first of the '*Ordensburgen*' (Castles of the Order), which were placed under his control—were like the carillons that heralded the SS period of National-Socialism. And the Black Order translated into action the threats that Dr Ley then issued:

'The man whom the Party deprives of the right to the brown shirt—each of us must realise it—will not only lose his functions but he will be destroyed, in his person, in that of his family, of his wife and children. Such are the immutable, the ruthless laws of our Order.' [1]

It is in this same spirit that the SS established its schools for SS Cadets. It is in this spirit that, particularly during the last six or seven years, the SS exercised an increasing influence on the formation of Hitler Youth leaders and succeeded in exercising an immediate influence on public education. *SS-Obergruppenführer* Heissmeyer,

---

[1] Quoted by Lang and Schenck, *Portrait eines Menschheitsverbrechers*, op. cit., pp. 167–8.

on 23rd April 1941, when he opened a *Napola* (Centre of National and Political Education) produced this crystal-clear formula, which, so to speak, reduces the entire doctrine to the lowest common denominator: 'Believe, obey, fight; full stop. That's all'.

Reference is no longer made to eternal Germany or even to the National-Socialist State. Ideas and philosophies have either been thrown overboard or are regarded as having no more than a relative value. The sole aim now is: to dominate. Of men who had undergone such a régime it could rightly be said:

'In many ways, indeed, the SS represents a new German nobility, privileged, terroristic. It is willing to face death for its interest and ideas. Seen in even broader terms of universal military history, the SS-in-Arms embodies once more a military fanaticism such as the world has hardly seen since the days of the Mahdi and Omdurman.'[1]

An SS leader whom Eugen Kogon describes as 'well-educated, of superior intelligence and no fool though completely fanatical'[2] at the end of autumn 1937—before he himself had occasion to observe this training and to feel its effects—defined clearly and unequivocally the aims of the SS education:

'We, who must mould these young people into leaders, are aiming at a modern state which finds its inspiration in the city of the ancient Greeks. It is to these democracies led by an aristocracy and resting on the economic foundation of a large class of helots that antiquity owes the finest masterpieces of its civilisation. Five to ten per cent of the population, the flower of its *élite* must have the command, the remainder have only to work and obey. Only by this means will we succeed in achieving those supreme values that we must demand of ourselves and of the German people. The choice of the new class of leaders will be made by the SS. It will be made, in the positive sense, in the *Napolas* at the preparatory stage, then in the Castles of the Order which will be the centres of Higher Education of the future National-Socialist aristocracy, and finally in a period of practical experience which will follow immediately with the stress on active politics. It will also be made by eradicating all inferior elements from a racial and biological point of view, by eliminating such of our political opponents as are incapable of conversion or refuse on principle to recognise our "*Weltanschauung*", which is the basis of the National-Socialist State, and the vital institutions of that State.

'Within ten years at most we will in this way be in a position to dictate to Europe the law of Adolf Hitler and thus to put an end to the otherwise inevitable decadence of our Continent and to create

[1] Alfred Vagts, *Hitler's Second Army* (Washington, 1943), p. 73.
[2] Eugen Kogon, *Der SS-Staat, Das System der deutschen Konzentrationslager* (Munich, 1946), pp. 1–2.

a true community of peoples with Germany at its head to guide it and to maintain order.'

The official pronouncements in *Das Schwarze Korps* and the publications designed for the education of the new leaders were not always so explicit [1] but they never failed to underline the *élite* character of the SS formations. The ideal was domination of the Order over helots whose sole function was to obey and work. Such was the vision of 'aristocratic democracy' which the innermost circles of the Order never lost sight of.

The SS Counter-State, by slowly setting up cells, through its emissaries, in the National-Socialist State, which was essentially a One-Party-State, was becoming the obvious source of supply of the new *élite*. While it took pains to maintain quietly, in some respects, the appearance of the old order, and employed more than one of its slogans and ideas, it was, nevertheless, not a system of terror and concentration-camps only.

These camps were symbols and not essential features of what was happening.[2] The decisive task the Order had allotted itself—Germany and with her the whole of Europe may consider themselves fortunate that the project was barely under way when those in whose brains it had been hatched met their fate—was, in effect, to transform the peoples of the European Continent into nomadic populations, to transform whole nations and countries into one empire of warriors, which would lose all traces of nationality and would be founded on colonisation, systematic planning, normalisation.

To achieve such an aim, it was absolutely essential that all natural roots should be severed, that all systems of values should be destroyed. In the closed circles of the initiated certain plans were under discussion at a given moment, one to abolish legal monogamy, another to introduce a regulation specifying exactly which profession could be practised by individuals 'of races and nationalities of different values', and yet another to make German the sole language in Europe after a sufficient time had passed for habits to change. Although these plans apply only to a fairly remote future and seem to be the product of pure imagination and not of a knowledge of reality, they all point in the same direction.

The supplanting of Christianity, abolition of the obsolete bonds of the family, a direct or indirect division of citizens into free men and non-free men, special rights for members of the Order—all this was in the first stage of execution.

---

[1] *Schriftenreihe des Reichsführers SS und Chefs der deutschen Polizei* and *Mitteilungen des Reichsführers SS und Chefs der deutschen Polizei* (Munich).

[2] Eugen Kogon, in the preface to the revised edition of his book *Der SS-Staat* (Berlin, 1947), p. 5, uses the following formula: 'In fact, the plans were prepared for an SS State, and the concentration camps were their terrible model in microcosm.'

It was, of course, only a very limited circle of highly-placed or leading SS men to whom these theories and aspirations were known or who set themselves voluntarily to implement them. Members of the formations were only slightly aware of them when they were obliged to declare that they no longer belonged to any Church, or when they were compelled, before marriage, to ask the consent of their leaders, or when they were brought within the special jurisdiction of the SS, which, incidentally, was extremely severe, but which had the effect of placing them beyond the jurisdiction of the civil authorities. Then they saw that, apart from the laws of the Order, they had no other obligation and that they had ceased to have any 'private' existence.

A totalitarian state, as such, does not exist.

The modern state, however authoritarian it may be or might have been in its various manifestations, rests, ever since Frederick II organised in Sicily the beginnings of a state run by career officials, following the example set by Charlemagne with his Counts to counterbalance the forces which pulled the various provinces in different directions—the modern state, as I was saying, rests on separation of powers, a balance of forces, on a harmonious interplay of the elements that command and those below. Though often enough corrupted and frequently reigning by terror, the modern state has never possessed omnipotence. Compromise is the rule of the game, when one is not strong enough to compel one's adversary to follow to the same goal. There have also constantly been social forces which made compromise necessary when the risk of chaos was too great.

Chaos cannot be reconciled with the general conception of the state, which, for Europe, has its organic origin, in the last resort, in the tradition of a central power dispensing grace. The basic idea of domination is the maintenance of order, of that order which is a gift from God, or order whose aim is the well-being of peoples.

The idea of domination for the pleasure of dominating was always introduced in the state by organisations which placed themselves apart from the other citizens in order to acquire power: they were minority parties which aimed at dominating by terror, conspiracies, secret societies and 'orders'.

The National-Socialist State, when it began, was not a 'total state'. It was undoubtedly based on absolutism and terrorism, but it proved incapable of existing without making a compromise with the economic forces,[1] with the demands of those who considered

---

[1] Franz Neumann was one of the first, in his book *Behemoth, The Structure and Practice of National-Socialism* (New York, 1942), to emphasise the 'anti-state' character of the Nazi system. He did not see, however, that this character drew its strength from the absolute domination of the SS order. He thought moreover that the Third Reich was dominated by economic motives.

themselves socially underprivileged,[1] and with the intransigence of its own supporters.[2] So long as these forces continued to exist side by side, it was impossible to talk of omnipotence.

Totality only became possible the moment the idea was abandoned of a state conceived as a juridical force that in the last resort holds a balance between opposing forces.

The Third Reich became a 'total state'—though this is a contradiction in terms—when the ministers of the Reich and the Cabinet ceased to make any important decisions and these were made by the spokesmen of the militant party minority. In Russia, where the CPUSSR and the NKVD had more time to develop, the phenomenon was much clearer and may serve as an example. In Germany it was, in the last resort, the SS, though only for a relatively short time, that dominated the state, because the counter-state it represented, by virtue of the fact that it had the ear and the confidence of the *Führer* up to, or almost up to, the end, always kept the upper hand in the confusion and conflicts between various state bodies and the Party, and because, being in control of all police forces, it was able to repress immediately any potential opposition before it could take action.

In the years 1944 and 1945 there was not a single body in the national economy, the state or the Party that could parry the action of the SS. The key positions everywhere were occupied by SS chiefs, if only as seconds-in-command.

The state had become the embodiment of the 'Order'. As long as the *Führer* said 'yes'. He alone could say 'no'. He doubtless said it, on occasion. But no one else had the power to say 'no' to the counter-state of the Black Order.

There was nothing in the way of check between the nerves of Hitler, whose decisions were always quite unpredictable, and the advice given to him by Himmler. In fact, if one takes the word state seriously, there never was an SS state, although here we have been adopting Kogon's interpretation and using the word. There was a dictatorship of the National-Socialist Order, which stifled all real life in the state and gave the *Führer* a guarantee that it could carry out forthwith any measures he cared to take against the army, the Party, the administration, the economic world, the Ministries of the Reich

---

[1] Frequently, after the seizure of power, Goebbels repeated, in sense, at least, his threat cast in the face of 'Reaction': 'The National-Socialist struggle has been a socialist revolution; it has been the revolution of a workers' movement, and those who made it must today also be its spokesmen'. Quoted from K. Heiden, *Der Führer*, p. 738.

[2] In *Die verfassungsrechtliche Gestaltung der Ein-Partei*, in *Zeitschrift für die gesamte Staatswissenschaft* (1938), p. 688, Gottfried Neese, one of the most perceptive jurists among the younger generation of National-Socialism, admits that by retaining the name *party* which by definition and according to all logic can only mean a *part*, the Nazi State has made a concession to tradition.

or Justice. Only the SS Counter-State existed. There was not a single state official whom the Order, on Hitler's instructions, could not have stripped of his office and brought up for trial, or, more simply, liquidated. The Order had taken possession, sometimes openly, sometimes more discreetly, of all power. All that was not a part of it was, in its view, no more than an instrument.

At the end of 1944 there were only two men who mattered in Germany: Adolf Hitler and Heinrich Himmler.[1] It was a considerable time since the German *Reichstag*, in March 1933, had passed a law giving Hitler full power, in a way that Walter Frank describes ironically:[2]

'. . . The Centre party votes for the adoption of the law. [Applause.] This monotonous phrase marks the end of an era. Chancellor Hitler is given dictatorial powers for four years. Parliamentarianism is shown the door. . . . Within a few hours the revolution has been legalised.'

Then came the time when it was hard to remember that dictatorship had been 'given' to anyone. There came the time of the 'cold SS revolution', in which the National-Socialist Order, 'which was on the point of becoming a state',[3] took into its hands all the many state, Party, and army services that could be utilised, and all this in order to pave the way for the march of the 'new Goths', who advanced with hubris:

'But what the Goths, the Varangians and all the migrators of Germanic blood failed to do we shall achieve now, we, the new Germanic migration and our *Führer*, the *Führer* of all the Teutons. Now that the assault from the steppes has been repulsed, now that the Eastern frontier of Europe has been made secure for all time, now we shall see accomplished what the Teuton warriors dreamed of in their forests and the vast expanses of the West. A chapter in history, a chapter that began three thousand years ago, reaches its glorious conclusion today. The Gothic horsemen have been in the saddle again since 22 June 1941 and each one of us is conscious of being a Germanic warrior.'[4]

One wonders if the average German worker, peasant or *petit-bourgeois*, was at any time during the Second World War conscious of

[1] In order to see this fact in its true light one must above all be careful to avoid accepting at their face value the many anecdotes about Himmler which make him out to be a sort of Hollywood villain. For instance this is the case in the book *Himmler, Nazi Spider Man, The Man After Hitler*, by George Hamilton Combs, Jnr, (New York, 1942). On no account should such sensational trash as *Heydrich, the Murderer* by X, a former Gestapo officer, rendered into English by Richard Baxter, London 1942, be taken seriously. Hardly a single one of the facts stated here are verifiable with documentation.

[2] Walter Frank, *Zur Geschichte des Nationalsozialismus* (Hamburg, 1934), p. 34.

[3] Alfred Rosenberg, *Der deutsche Ordensstaat, Ein neuer Abschnitt in der Entwicklung des nationalsozialistischen Staatsgedankens* (Munich, 1939), p. 17.

[4] *SS-Leitheft*, published by *Reichsführer SS*, SS H.Q., Berlin 796, p. 2.

Y

being a Gothic horseman. But in the *Waffen-SS* Himmler was not unsuccessful in evoking images of this kind, romantic and romanticised. The frontiers of the Greater German Reich had been conquered in fierce fighting. A good start had been made towards becoming the masters of Europe or rather of 'Greater Germania'. Their hands were already outstretched to seize the mastery of the world. With a vehemence that lacked all sense of reality, with a blind intransigence they falsified the struggle for national independence and sang the challenging air: 'Today Germany is ours, tomorrow the whole world!' [1]

The lack of proportion with which the Black Order made use of any and every means to acquire or retain power took a form, in the middle of the twentieth century, in the midst of the Christian and humanist civilisation of the 'people of poets and thinkers', which was, in effect, a revival of barbaric atavism. One might almost have imagined that the fifth century, the expedition of Genseric and his Vandals across Africa and Italy, had come to life again in modern times: this unshakeable will to destroy that found expression in the gas-chambers, in the SD Commandos behind the Russian lines, had no relation to the salvation of the Fatherland or to military necessity.

No satisfactory explanation has yet been found for the psychological motives behind Auschwitz and all that the word stands for. The Nuremberg trials also did not really throw much light on the subject, and the many psycho-analytical explanations, which declared that entire nations could lose its mental balance in the same way as isolated individuals, only served to obscure the problem.

No one knows what passed through the minds of those in Himmler's immediate entourage when he issued extermination orders. But how could such orders be obeyed? Hannah Arendt offers the following explanation: [2]

> 'The same average German, who, despite years of mad Nazi propaganda, could not take it upon himself to kill a Jew . . . will set the death-machine in motion without a word of protest. By contrast with the early SS and Gestapo formations, Himmler's organisation does not rely on the support of fanatics or sadists who find a voluptuous pleasure in murder: it relies quite simply on 'normal' men, of the same species as Heinrich Himmler.'

The explanation is only half-true, for recruitment to the Death's Head SS, which provided the guards for the concentration camps, was not always left to chance.

---

[1] The original printed text was called 'For today Germany hears us . . . '.
[1] Hannah Arendt, *Organisiente Schuld* in *Die Wandlung* I, 4 (Heidelberg, 1945–6), pp. 333–4.

III. A Typology of the SS Man

From the beginning a new type of National-Socialist emerged in the ranks of the SS. In the early phase of the movement it was mainly muddle-heads, monomaniacs, and 'toughs' who had formed the basis of the organisation. But gradually another type emerged. He was the member of a political and military Order, to which he was bound by oath, and for him the Party member was no more, in the last resort, than a lay brother placed at his service. The German SS and later the European SS became the rallying-point of all those who neither could nor would adapt themselves to a peaceful and quiet 'civil' life. The SS became the fraternity of those who could not conceive of life otherwise than as the intoxication of power, the sense of living dangerously, a perpetual protest against the modest desire of their contemporaries to be allowed to enjoy a little happiness and a little peace.

Above all, it was essential to despise life, one's own and that of others. 'Give death and accept it' was the principle taught in the SS cadet training-schools.[1] The result was that moral conscience, as we usually understand it, had only a relative value. The ethical code that makes us respect our fellow-men, even those unknown to us, was abandoned and was replaced by absolute loyalty to the formation. The oath of the Black Order was, in essence, the final and absolutely logical consequence of the total abandonment of one's own personality to a community, such as is demanded—for National-Socialism is not alone in this—by the various forms of anti-humanist activism in the twentieth century.

This does not mean that these group-formations have no morality. But their morality is limited: it applies only to a certain part of society—that part to which one belongs. The individual as such has no value. He only achieves stature and value as a member of the community, as a fighter who follows his leader. Fidelity, courage, and honour are not defined according to any universal, objective standard of values, nor are they founded on the personal moral conscience, but are determined by the law of the Order.

This National-Socialist order, with its black uniform bearing the insignia of the Death's Head and swastika, brought nothing new, in its structure, to what one already associated with earlier examples of such fraternal Orders. It merely added certain modern, technical variations, peculiar to the twentieth century.[2]

---

[1] The *Schwarze Korps*, 26 Nov. 1942, about the Junker Schools of the *Waffen SS*. 'Those who enter through the immense doors of these schools for soldiers and leaders where one learns to give and to get death, will always be held by these pictures.'

[2] Eugen Lennhoff, *Politische Geheimbünde* (Zürich, 1931). René Fülöp-Miller, *Macht und Geheimnis der Jesuiten* (Leipzig, 1929).

It is always the same features that distinguish this Order, which is self-sufficient, autonomous, and omnipotent, from all the diversions that occupied the leisure of the Freemasons or from the purely literary plans which, around 1900, were put on paper by so many German intellectuals, enamoured of racial or popular revival, of abstruse secret leagues, of Germanic Orders, and of imitations of Druidical colleges. This time the absolute obligation to break with the world, with society, caste, class, and family, was taken very seriously. From this absolute obligation, from the sense of being 'one of them', came a communal sense, and a special law was promulgated. The ceremony of handing over the SS Rune must have resembled fairly closely what Reinhold Schneider tells us [1] when he describes how, in the great hall, the Refectory of Marienburg, the members of the Teutonic Order bowed low under the vows that made of them 'the Church militant'.

'They came from countries of divers kinds, from a restless life, they entered into the closed austerity of this château and abandoned their personal shields, whose coats of arms had been borne by at least four ancestors. Now their symbol would be the Cross which commands the most severe of combats and which promises eternal life.'

Although not every member of the SS, in his innermost heart, did go so far as to make a 100 per cent break, yet individuals could be removed from their natural surroundings, trained against the Cross, and bound to an 'anti-Church militant'. Himmler and his men had just such a goal in view. The obligations imposed, at least theoretically, were exactly the same. The words of Walter Flex: 'If you swear on oath to the Prussian flag, you have nothing left to call your own' have never been so frequently quoted as in the SS training-camps, and more than one idealist in the SS took them seriously. Here perhaps lies the explanation of the fact—at a first glance an astonishing fact when one remembers the cases of corruption among senior SS officers, which were reported by almost all former inmates of concentration camps—that the *Reichsführer SS*, on occasions, descended on his own formations with fire and sword and 'put up against the wall' whole rows of black uniforms.

On 4th October 1943, Heinrich Himmler addressed a meeting of *SS-Gruppenführer*.[2] After calling upon his men, with inconceivable cynicism, to massacre all the Jews, he issued a warning which, in fact, may have been quite sincere:

'The riches they had we have taken. I have given formal orders, which were carried out by *SS-Obergruppenführer* Pohl, that these

---

[1] Reinhold Schneider, *Die Hohenzollern Tragik und Königtum* (Leipzig, 1933), p. 16.
[2] *Die Masken fallen, Aus den Geheimpapieren des Dritten Reiches*, edited by Hermann Hassbargen (Hamburg, 1949), p. 99.

riches should be transferred, as is fitting, in their entirety to the Reich. We have retained nothing. If, in isolated cases, SS men failed to obey this order, they will be punished in accordance with the law, which I laid down from the beginning and which said: any man who keeps for himself so much as one Mark is a dead man. A certain number of members of the SS—they are not many —infringed my order. They will die, without mercy. We had the moral right and indeed a duty towards our people to kill this people that wanted to destroy us. But we have not the right to grow rich on the spoils, even by so much as a fur-coat, a watch, a Mark, a cigarette, or anything however small. After all, because we are exterminating a germ, we have no desire to catch the disease and die of it. I will not tolerate the slightest stain of corruption among us and still less will I allow corruption to set in. Wherever it appears, we shall attack it, all together, with a red-hot iron. . . .'

Did Himmler always take his threat seriously? That is another question. But there is only a superficial contradiction in commanding a massacre in one and the same phrase as one demands absolute loyalty towards the Order. In fact, these two injunctions merely reflect the basic rule of the Order: You are nothing, the Order is everything.

Clearly in the SS hierarchy, and in its troops which were growing in numbers from one day to the next, there was not just one type of man. The SS central command never really succeeded in creating a *ne varietur* model of SS man.

In the SS there were criminals and idealists, fools and others who deserved to be called intellectuals. There were some—like Skorzeny —who did nothing but obey and fight. There were others who drew up plans and great visions of the future, who gave orders knowing precisely what they involved. Some had joined the SS more or less by chance; others were opportunists who joined a particular formation because it promised them power and prominence; others again wanted to loot, to lead a life outside the law. Some were mere tools, others were violent and cynical. And others again had been forced into the SS. The Order could impose its will on thousands and hundreds of thousands; it could not change the individuals. But it used whoever entered its ranks, the sadists as well as the dreamers.[1]

It would be wrong—for the problem would be over-simplified— to take as the typical SS-men the Death's Head SS, who, from an early stage, were mainly employed guarding the concentration camps. The latter had been selected from the ranks of the *Allgemeine SS*, after the police, on 30th June 1934, had taken over from

[1] Like the 999 Division in the Army the notorious Dirlewanger SS-Division consisted mainly of those 'declared unfit for military service', not to speak of poachers. It was a punishment for demoted SS servicemen and an opportunity for volunteers from the KZ's, above all for professional criminals.

the SA and its various police formations, which, it was felt, could no longer be relied upon. In the ranks of the *Waffen-SS*—not only at the end of the war in the so-called Germanic units—there was undoubtedly another type of SS-man, whose outstanding feature was a sense of sacrifice and who believed sincerely that a sort of international brotherhood could be established, which would create a new European order.

This type barely made himself felt inside the SS hierarchy, although he is said to have existed in appreciable numbers among the leaders. The 'most respectable' were certainly the 'fine soldiers' of the *Waffen-SS*, who remained apart, as individuals, from all the crimes, but frequently declared that it was not their business to intervene.[1] The *Waffen-SS*, however, remained a case by itself.

The first declarations made by General Eisenhower took this into account, as did the Nuremberg verdict, for the same sentence that condemned the SD-SS (Security Services) and the Security Office of the Reich as criminal organisations made some exceptions concerning the *Waffen-SS*.[2] The events that took place at Eupen and Malmedy, the accusations of the French, particularly against the *Das Reich* and *Hitlerjugend* divisions of the SS, are a chapter by themselves. One is bound to admit that the *Waffen-SS* though commanded by the Order, were for the most part composed of soldiers with a certain personal integrity. But there can be no doubt about the SS 'Death's Head' formation: they were mere executioners for the concentration camps, troops designed to terrorise their own fellow-citizens. Those who still corresponded to the type of the old '*SS Verfügungstruppen*' were transferred, when war broke out, into the 'Death's Head' division of the *Waffen-SS*, which was practically wiped out in Russia. The remainder—and one must not forget that in the concentration camps formations that were Ukrainian, Galician, Polish, Russian, Lithuanian, Lettish auxiliaries, together with anti-aircraft troops of the *Luftwaffe*, SA-men from the reserve, the police, and units of every kind from time to time relieved the SS and proved no more tolerable than the Death's Head; the remainder represents the SS type who, in all accounts of the unparalleled

---

[1] Heinrich Orb explicitly states from personal knowledge in his book *National-sozialismus, 13 Jahre Machtrausch*, that high-ranking SS leaders of this category existed. The book contains a scrupulously detailed account of the organisational and personal network of the SS apparatus in Party, Police, Army and Economic positions.
The author's burning hatred of National-Socialism is beyond doubt.

[2] It is impossible to go into the many branches partly conflicting among themselves of the various central and special Himmler Organisations further. Kogon has a survey that is by no means complete. A collection of documents going deeper into the subject is that published by the U.S. Zone Control Commission *Survey of Criminal Nazi Organisational Structure*, and the accompanying text that completes it.

brutalities in the concentration camps, the reprisal and extermination camps, became, with good reason, the symbol of the terror practised by the Gestapo and the SD.[1]

Even this type is not very clearly defined. It was not merely a-social or primitive elements that served in the camps. Schenck[2] rightly draws our attention to the following point:

'Amongst the murderers who killed men *en masse* in the concentration camps, there were men of university education, and many of the leaders of these SS ruffians were definitely cultured men. What is still worse is not so much that men of university education should have been captivated by the Nazi theories but that they were able, without inhibition, to become interested in nauseating experiments, which went as far as to include vivisection and which were practised on people deprived of their rights, and that they were able to derive certain positive scientific results from these experiments.'

It was, however, not the 'initiates' who, shortly after Hitler came to power, left the fairly thin ranks of the personal bodyguard known as the *Allgemeine SS*, which Heinrich Himmler had formed by drawing upon the SA troops for special duties to form the new 'Death's Head' formations. Like the SS *'Verfügungstruppen'*, which was set up shortly afterwards, they were a regular Praetorian Guard, whereas the other SA or SS remained ordinary civilians in uniform. In general, when this *élite* was selected, the particularly vigorous, courageous, and unscrupulous types in the SA were picked out.

When they spoke of living under their own laws, they meant little more than: 'We want no more interference from the police'. And the few political courses they attended were designed merely to make them loathe the Jews, the Bolsheviks, and 'those pigs who had grown fat under the Weimar régime'.

They became masters of the concentration camps after Röhm's SA was relieved of its functions in the 'lightning-swift' coups of 30th June 1934, and the subsequent days. They were brutal; their hate, like their sympathy, was subject to strange whims; one never knew what they would devise. The route they follow is strewn with corpses. But, on the whole, they did not massacre either on principle or in a spirit of sadism, but because they were revolutionaries.[3] The

[1] See the brochure, *Der Prozess gegen Mitglieder verbrecherischer Organisationen* (Berlin, OMGUS.). In Volume I, pp. 27 ff. of the German edition of the minutes of the Nuremberg trials and in the verdict Volume XXII, pp. 570 ff. of the German edition there is an index of the organisations declared to be criminal together with an exact summary of their branches.
[2] Ernst von Schenck, *Europa vor der deutschen Frage, Briefe eines Schweizers nach Deutschland* (Bern), p. 36.
[3] Thierry Maulnier certainly indicates something which really existed. He does not rationalise when he considers it the driving force in his essay *The Epoch of Terrorism* in *Merkur*, III, 2 (Baden-Baden, 1949), pp. 105–15: 'Terrorism is linked

unshakeable scientific will to kill only came later after the character of the camps changed from detention or re-education camps from which quite a number of political opponents emerged still in the years immediately following 1933 to slave-labour and extermination camp. They had been detained for varying periods; they came out intimidated or embittered, but still alive. Subsequent accounts tell us of the perverted pleasures in which the guards used to indulge; I am thinking particularly of Langhoff's description of their vulgar amusements.[1]

A few years later the inmates of the concentration camps would have been grateful if the SS had retained the type of humour Langhoff describes. Unfortunately, games of a very different kind were being played then.

We cannot possibly deal with the German concentration camps in all their various aspects: German culpability, the crime of silence, tacit complicity; still less the question of the relationship between SS ideals and SS terrorism. Yet the concentration camps are worth considering in this investigation, if only because they show what was not only possible in the SS State but was sanctioned by law, where opponents and 'inferior' people were concerned. Himmler himself had declared once:

'If we neglect this theatre of operations, the interior of Germany—and we must be clear about this whatever happens and for all time—we are bound to lose the war.' [2]

To turn out gross louts with a barrack-square humour and, above all, new recruits for the SS into such automatic, insensible, and cynical murderers as appeared at Auschwitz, time was needed and, still more, a detailed plan: it was also essential that the Order should systematically indoctrinate the individual and that he should be able to gain practical experience. More than one SS-man committed suicide because he could no longer bear what was imposed on him in the camps or in the SD's 'interception' commandos in Poland and in Russia. More than one exchanged the SS uniform for the striped uniform of a camp inmate, because he had 'fraternised with the underground', which means, because he had shown signs of human re-

---

with revolution by a rather irrational and rather fundamental bond. It is not the tool of Revolution, it is its exorcising and cleansing ritual, its liturgy, its Mass and mystery . . . no revolution can be let loose without murderous forces also being unleashed and they can only be unleashed on the condition that they are given a goal.' This has only any value during the short time that the combatants of the National-Socialist Revolution terrorise the political opponents of their party. Where the doctrinal Party line of terrorism was directed towards final solutions (The Jewish Question) and towards the exploitation of those arrested (Slave Labour), no room remained for myths of self-purification through revolution.

[1] Wolfgang Langhoff, *Die Moorsoldaten* (Zürich, 1935).
[2] *Geheimvertrag Himmlers*, 26 Sep. 1937.

flexes and a pale flicker of pity. The great majority accepted what they were taught. Just as the front line produced a special type of SS-man in the *Waffen-SS*, so the camps produced another. The result was frequently as Benedikt Kautsky describes it: [1]

'Lazy and stupid, brutal and cowardly, undisciplined and corrupt, these are the main qualities that the SS Command look for when they set out to create an average SS type. A standard product, who is the result of special moral and physical training and carries out his duties irreproachably.'

One may doubt whether the SS Command did, in fact, accept this type as perfectly satisfactory. He was much more a product of the day-to-day education in the camps than of the Order's ideology.

'But we come to the very core of the problem [says Gerhart Hermann Mostar rightly],[2] when intelligent, extremely cautious witnesses, admirably devoid of passion, tell us that such and such a young boy or such and such an old SS-man, when he first arrived at the camp, behaved in a completely inoffensive manner, and that, as soon as he became accustomed to the camp, without any possibility of steeling himself inwardly or in his behaviour against such outrages, he was trained to the point of becoming a bloodthirsty watchdog.'

The ideal image, in fact, is subject to demands of reality. Its salient features were laid down by a group of leaders.[3] Before it becomes even an approximate reality in the organisations that are being created, time passes; and the expansion of the SS—an expansion that was dictated by organic requirements—slowed up the process still further and even, to some extent, reversed it. And one must also take into account hundreds of variations and deviations of this process. One can state with some degree of accuracy, however, that in the two main SS formations, the *Waffen-SS* and the *Menkopf* units, there was a marked divergence between those who quite seriously accepted it as law that they should be prepared to give their lives and those who interpreted the same law as meaning: 'Be prepared to give death'. SD, Gestapo, and other 'special groups' which, under pressure of circumstances, had to be interlarded with elements from the old judicial police, from the political police or Army counter-

[1] Benedikt Kautsky, *Teufel und Verdammte, Erfahrungen und Erkenntnisse aus sieben Jahren in deutschen Konzentrationslagern* (Zürich, 1946), p. 98.
[2] Gerhart Hermann Mostar, *Portrait eines Weibsteufels, Die Dolchstosslegende der Ilse Koch* in *Aufbau*, 5 Jan. (New York, 1951), p. 3 ff.
[3] Thus for instance the SS H.Q. published a training manual for the SS entitled *The Soldier's Friend* with the following message: 'The task of the SS-HA is to establish a severely closed Order. It is therefore responsible for selecting men suited for Guards Echelons and for taking charge of SS members and their families as to what concerns their outlook and politics and to educate and train the whole of the SS, Police and Military.'

espionage, and from the various intelligence services, acquired, in the end, a structure that was no less contradictory.

But however apparent the variations, particularly of behaviour, may have been in the SS, there is nonetheless a sort of common denominator that makes it possible to discern a well-defined type.

The first to join the Order were rebels against their own environment: ex-soldiers, former members of the Free Corps who could not settle down to a life of inaction when, returning from the shell-holes of the world war, they were systematically ignored in their own country. They were offered no work, and found themselves driven straight into the arms of the conspirators.

Coming from the pitched battles in the Ruhr or Upper Silesia, or from the black *Reichswehr*, they almost automatically took the road that led to the SS. Then came a whole category of young people, who had missed the great adventure of the war because they were children at the time but who, their hearts fired with enthusiasm and filled with an admiration that blinded all judgment, listened to their elders relating their experiences. They believed the great chance of their lives had come when they were asked to cooperate in the 'actions' proposed by a semi-illegal Right.[1] They flocked to the SS behind those whom they longed to emulate.

These men were militant, not criminal, elements, even when they were prepared, on behalf of the Idea, to commit murder. Yet, although they succeeded for a time in joining the SA of the National-Socialist Party, they were a very different type from the 'unknown SA' recruited from the Labour Bureaux of the big towns.

The events of 30th June 1934, in which the egoism of rival organisations undoubtedly played its part, as did the class interests, served to cover up a violent clash between two types of National-Socialists, between two very different forms of life and thought.

The SA had brought together unemployed, men who wanted some occupation, *petit-bourgeois* who, thanks to the Movement with its readily comprehensible slogans, hoped to revive their professional activities, before they went under altogether, and to regain their social standing. The battle that was beginning would lead, they hoped, to a new era of security. Thanks to the *Führer*, thanks also to the contribution each of his men was making to the work of liberation, a new order would be established, in which it would no longer be necessary to come to blows with one's adversaries at every public meeting and every street corner, an order in which one could enjoy a quiet, peaceful life with one's wife and children.

---

[1] Ernst von Salomons' book *Die Geächteten* (Berlin, 1931) and his later works give the best insight into the world of these law-breaking conspirators. Salomons himself never became a National-Socialist but held himself apart from them.

Even when more than that was visualised, when the desire for a real social upheaval, for a true revolution, was in evidence, even when National-Socialism as one understood it—that the big-shots, the wealthy, the bankers and the capitalists, 'the nobles, the Jews and the war-profiteers' would all be chased out of power—even when this National-Socialism carried explosive charges, it was still the revolutionary aims that gave the movement its direction, and not fighting for the joy of fighting.

The new order they dreamed of was, in the last resort, a *bourgeois* order which they and their children would enjoy. This type of National-Socialist, while he aimed at social harmony, was capable at times of bouts of fury, and he gave vent to them. But he was no supporter of action for action's sake. He had not donned the brown shirt because he dreamt that, with his fellows, he would one day hold the reins in a new world-empire and, with his comrades, would form a race of overlords. The SA-man remained a rebel within the framework of the *bourgeois* order. That was true of those who joined the shock battalions. But among the ten per cent who had already got beyond the *bourgeois* dream, who, in mind and soul, had burnt their boats behind them, there were some who, having reached the summit of the SA, tried in their ambition for power to speak in terms of the revolutionary trends, which, though rather nebulous, animated the rank and file of the brown army; these were liquidated on 30th June. Those who did not insist on keeping the SA marching in the same direction were gradually absorbed into the SS. The SS was the rallying-point for the discontented, those who could not keep step, the mercenaries from every hole and corner who were at loggerheads with their environment and with all social order, for whom education and origin meant nothing, and for whom ideas often were the 'rationalisation of history'. A fair part of what had once been the structure of the Free Corps was revived in the SS. Unhampered by any social conventions, units were formed which were ready to stake their lives in order to gain power. In the Free Corps during the first months after 1918 quite young second lieutenants, commissioned in action, were commanding companies that consisted of officers, all of whom had been senior to them. Similarly in the SS the ranking of the *bourgeois* world had no validity. What counted was complete lack of reserve, courage, and blind obedience.

The SS is not alone in having demanded such virtues of its members. The shock-troop 'Commandos' of every nation made the same demands of their *élites*. Today many of those who were in them tell us that the first essential for success was to ignore systematically every *bourgeois* prejudice. Men were ready to ignore these prejudices for Adolf Hitler's Reich. Neither National-Socialism nor the SS ever carried the word 'crime' on their banners. When the call came, it was answered in order to help the Fatherland recover its freedom and independence, its greatness and its prosperity. But no one ever told those who had answered the call that, to achieve these ends—which, among the supreme leaders of the Order, had become a dream of world-domination—one would stop at nothing. A well-known Englishwoman, writing during the war, stressed this point:

'What gives all this an alarming and even sinister character is that some of the things that Hitler says to them are in themselves true. It amazes me that some people in our own countries seem to imagine that Hitler stands up and describes all the beastly sadistic orgies he can imagine and thereby attracts the wholehearted enthusiasm of youth. Were he to do so, he would be far less dangerous and certainly far less powerful, because he would then only attract the criminal or the pathological types, whereas now he gets the energy, the enthusiasm and the generous response of the best elements in the youth of the country.' [1]

Alongside men from the 'underworld', some of the best types of German fought for Hitler, Germany's symbol, right into the ranks of the SS, because they were in no position to distinguish what was truth from what was falsehood amongst the aims for which they had been called to the colours. What was diabolical in National-Socialism, particularly in the final period in which the SS was predominant, was this twilight that was neither lie nor truth, this amalgam of 'noble' slogans and executioner's work. In this way hundreds of thousands of men died for an idea which meant ruin for Germany, without their realising it. Do the survivors realise it even today? [2]

IV. The End

It came as a surprise to all those outside Germany who, during the Second World War, had devoted some time to studying the structural change in German National-Socialism, to observe that the *Waffen-SS*, in the last few days of German resistance, did not fight against the Allies 'to the last ditch', as the *Werwolf* transmitter had announced, and that, with a few exceptions, the Order, after suffer-

[1] E. Almy Buller, *Darkness over Germany* (London, 1944), s.p. 137. It is interesting to note in this connection, that the SS itself while seeking wider publicity in no way devoted itself to a philosophy of terrorism but rather acted on a natural basis in a sort of juvenile spirit of competition with the advocates of other types of popular societies e.g., the collection of essays from the 'Black Corps' by Gunther d'Alquen, *Auf Hieb und Stich, Stimmen zur Zeit am Wege einer deutshen Zeitung* (Munich, 1937).

[2] It is not quite clear whether elements of the old SS spirit are making themselves apparent in the neo-Nazi movement which is slowly stirring again. There are only a few indications of this. Apart from the book *Nürnberg oder das gelobte Land* by Maurice Bardèche (translated from the French by Hans Rudolf, Zürich), there are few expressed opinions confirming this; the journal *Nation Europa* appearing in Coburg whose moving spirit is Hans Grimm the writer, seems to give space to tendencies of this kind.

ing losses during the preceding years which far exceeded the average losses of the *Wehrmacht*, behaved exactly like any other troop of civilians in uniform and accepted the argument that the struggle had now become a hopeless one.[1] In any case, it was an anticlimax to see men bearing the armband '*Leibstandarte Adolf Hitler*' surrender quite happily four-deep in the prisoner-of-war camps of the American Army. It was far from being a handful of the 'Faithful of the Faithful' that calmly survived their *Führer* and also their *Reichsführer SS*.

What could have rendered the law of the Order inoperative at the peak of the struggle?

Undoubtedly the main reason was that the fighting troops of the SS had lost faith in their leaders. I have mentioned Hitler's demented message to Sepp Dietrich degrading his best front-line divisions: it was the last straw, the final drop that made the brimming vessel overflow. In day-to-day fighting side by side with the soldiers of the *Wehrmacht*, a spirit of comradeship had sprung up which was accepted more or less readily, but the reactions of the soldiers in the *Waffen-SS* divisions to the 'satraps behind the lines' were just as scornful as those of the *Wehrmacht* towards the Army General Staff. The various Command posts of the SS were no nearer the front than those of the *Wehrmacht*. After all, it was two *SS-Führer* who, considerably before Army Generals had the idea—especially since the 20th July 1944 had shown with unmistakable clarity that the gallows was the only reward one could expect for having ideas of one's own —it was two *SS*-commanders who made contact with the enemy and, in the last resort, helped no little to carry to the point of absurdity the 'final battle of the Nibelungen'.

It was not merely 'reactionary' *Junker* but also SS officials Wolff and Schellenberg who sought some way of ending the fighting. One may well wonder how much patriotism and how much opportunism was behind their action, but there is no doubt that their initiative saved thousands of lives.

It was not merely 'German patriots' endowed—up to a point— with reason (let us leave aside, for the moment, their motives), it was not merely SS leaders who, at the critical moment—the moment of the Nibelungen massacre—broke with the Order and its now bloodless myths. It seems fairly well established that Himmler himself, during the last weeks, was confident that, as the man who could have organised a mass rising against the Allies, in which the Party would have played no part, he would be allowed to discuss terms with the enemy and take the floor again. Here we have an incredible example of a man deceiving himself.[2] More than that, Skorzeny, the

---

[1] Karl O. Paetel, 'Himmler's Janitscharenarmee' in *Deutsche Blätter* (Santiago, Chile, 1944, pp. 9–10, 18–20).

[2] Count Folke Bernadotte, *The Curtain Falls* (New York, 1945).

activist *par excellence*, the prototype of those who fought without asking why, ceased to issue orders when the end came. Nothing reveals more clearly the grotesque form of education given by the Order: life and its meaning were reduced artificially to the relations between a superior who commands and a subordinate who obeys, and this training defeated its own ends, as is clear if one glances at the autobiography of this same SS Colonel Skorzeny.[1] 'The most feared man in Europe,' as his shrewd editors call him, 'the liberator of Mussolini', as he likes to describe himself, the prototype of the SS overlords, behaves like any common gangster as soon as he is cornered: he surrenders to the police—in this case the American Army—instead of fighting to the last bullet. His book closes with these simple words: 'And now, whatever happened, I was merely a prisoner'. Not a word of regret for his country's defeat, the death of his *Führer*, or the end of National-Socialism.

A combatant simply finds himself exposed to a professional risk: he succumbs, and that is all.

For the man who really had had faith in the SS the solution was not so easy. The day he became aware of the lamentable conduct of his supreme leaders, not only the Order but a whole world—his world—tumbled about his ears. We have not many first hand accounts from the rank and file of the SS among the many that appeared in the years following the capitulation. One of them, however, is extremely representative,[2] and confirms this disillusionment. In these 'Daily Notes taken during a visit to the Headquarters of the *Waffen-SS* in Berlin' we read the following:

'Everyone knows, officially, that it is five minutes to zero hour but acts as if nothing had changed. Every one still displays, with ostentation, his fine faith, a Sunday faith, in the SS conception of the world and repeats: "We must have confidence in the *Führer;* he will find a solution; but, whatever happens, do trust the *Reichsführer-SS*".'

The writer of these Notes subsequently met the *SS-Brigadiergeneral* whom he had come to see and who listened, dispiritedly, to the re-

[1] *Skorzeny's Secret Missions, War Memoirs of the most dangerous man in Europe* (New York, 1950). This book is also extremely rich in information for the understanding of this special SS type: that is of the *Landsknecht* completely devoid of any ideology. The author is anything but a National-Socialist if under this heading is understood a militant adhering to any sort of idea or ideology, be it perverted or false even. Not a single word about National-Socialism is found in the whole book—no word of hatred either against any 'enemy'.

A robot has put himself at the disposal of a master and obeys. A 'pro' is unnecessary in the matter. The 'against' is indicated by the man who gives the orders.

[2] 'Das Ende einer Illusion', H.Q. *Reichsführer SS*, 1945, in *Christ und Welt* (Stuttgart, 1950), III, 33, p. 6.

port of this young *Waffen-SS* man fresh from the front. The Notes continue shortly after:

'I was sorry not to have seen the *Obergruppenführer* in order to dot all the i's. The *Obergruppenführer*. . . . Suddenly he appeared in the ante-room, where we had all been waiting for him for hours. Everyone jumped to his feet and saluted. . . . I reported what I had come to say, more calmly and in fewer words than to his Chief of Staff. Yet what I had just told him seemed to make a profound impression on him, for, before several others there, he burst out: "Yes, and to whom do we owe all this? To whom do we owe it, I say?" Then he howled: "To our bloody High Command that landed us in ——!" Instinctively I glanced round. I had expected anything but this. Then, stammering and stuttering, I ventured a question, and the very fact that I was asking it made me feel I was committing treason: "General, are Hitler and Himmler part of this bloody High Command that has landed us in the ——?" He bellowed into my face: "One is a criminal and the other a fool!" ' [1]

The poor SS-man fresh from the front thought the bottom had fallen out of the world. He asked his chief why he, an *Obergruppenführer*, was taking no action. Reply: 'The *Reichsführer SS* has a long arm!' That was early April 1945. At the end of the month the writer of these notes meets the same *SS-Obergruppenführer* at the SS Cadet Training School at Tölz. He makes this entry in his diary:

'He was there. . . . Everything had become meaningless. . . . He poured out a stream of hollow, mushy phrases over us. He adopted a superior air when dealing with the realities of the situation and spoke in a tone of awkward familiarity. What do we have in common with these fat senior officers, who began their service in the Q.M., went from there to the SA police then the civilian SS and now strut about before us in field-uniform with general's flashes, when they have no more military knowledge than a corporal? I know people say that it is among the corporals that you find the best strategists. . . . "And long live our beloved Adolf Hitler!" My ears are still ringing with it. That was how he

[1] A book by a member of the *Waffen-SS* has appeared in Switzerland and needs mention: Erich Kern, *Der Grosse Rausch, Russlandfeldzug 1941–45*. If one has surmounted the gross language of the front-line soldier, this description gives interesting sidelights which have some bearing on our work. This sentence occurs towards the end—the author is not fundamentally without political bias since he considers *émigrés* and Resistance members merely left-overs and is in no way friendly towards the victors, yet has an honest self-understanding: 'Were we ourselves not really guilty in the great national disaster which burst upon us and on the whole world? Did we say "No" deep in our hearts, when our troops marched into the Protectorate after Munich? We strayed from the paths of National-Socialism already then—quite blatantly, comrades. We already then broke our word as a people, which he had given in our name: a people of Germans, the Czechs are not and never were Germans . . . etc.' A National-Socialist recognises, rather late however, what Fascism meant, p. 187.

closed his lecture, with tears in his eyes. I would have been moved by it, if I had not stood in front of him exactly a fortnight before and heard him shout: "And we owe all this to our bloody High Command that has landed us in the ——!" '

In this diary, which is an interesting psychological document, one can read the tragedy of the German *Waffen-SS*, the drama that thousands and thousands of honest and morally sound young Germans lived through.

Fine words, oaths, duty, all that had been taken seriously.[1] And then their eyes were opened: 'My God! That's what they really are, our leaders?' And the next stage was the prisoner-of-war camp instead of the heroic last stand in the Alps.

As for those who, for some time past, had been arbitrarily transferred from the Army or the Air Force into the ranks of the *Waffen-SS*, those who had been compulsorily enlisted when they left the Hitler Youth or the Labour Service, all those who knew practically nothing of the SS ideal, they just waited, and it is not surprising, to follow the example of the others when the red light appeared and they were glad the war was over. The SS High Command lacked homogeneity; most of its members, as human specimens, were not equal to their task. The 'idealists' in the Order lost all confidence in leaders who were found wanting; a mass of people who, in the circumstances, had escaped fanaticism had invaded the ranks of the SS by virtue of the exigencies of war. The SS edifice crumbled, and what remained was a mere epilogue.

On 20th May 1945, British soldiers, at the Bremervörde Bridge twenty-five miles west of Lüneburg, arrested a man carrying papers in the name of Hitzinger.[2] Together with two men accompanying him, he was taken to the military police. He wore civilian clothes, was clean-shaven, and had a bandage over one eye. For three days British officers attempted to establish his real identity. Finally he removed his bandage and said: 'My name is Heinrich Himmler'. He was subjected to a further thorough search, then was given the choice of putting on American clothes or wrapping himself in a blanket. He chose the blanket.

When, in the course of a very thorough medical examination, he was told to open his mouth, the prisoner crushed between his teeth an ampoule of poison, which he had been carrying in his mouth, and collapsed. Every effort was made to revive him, but in vain.

[1] *Aufbruch, Briefe germanischer Kriegsfreiwilliger*, Der Reichsführer SS, SS H.Q., 1942.
[2] The details reported by those who witnessed the last hours of the National leader of the SS vary slightly. E.g. John C. Schwarzwalder's *The Strange Death of Heinrich Himmler* contains the eye-witness account of an American officer of the Information Service who was taking part in the investigation (*Coronet*, N.Y., Jan. 1947).

Twenty-five minutes later, the *Reichsführer SS* was dead. His death was officially recorded as having taken place at four minutes past eleven on the morning of 23rd May 1945.

Three days later a British Major and three N.C.O.s took charge of the body in the same villa at Lüneburg where the interrogation had taken place. The party adjourned to a nearby wood not far from the town. A grave was dug and the body buried.

No cross or tombstone marks the grave. The earth was carefully levelled over it. No one knows exactly where Heinrich Himmler lies.

Thus ended the man who, for more than ten years, made Germany, Europe, the whole world gasp with his cold-blooded, scientific terror. Thus ended the man who, in more than one respect and more so than even the *Führer* himself, had given the final, decisive period of National-Socialism a stamp of its own.

In the *Führer*'s concrete bunker in Berlin the illusion of a Greater German Reich that was to last a thousand years, the Reich that the early National-Socialists dreamt of, this illusion was finally shattered. At Lüneburg the Counter-State of the SS met its end.

20

THE USE AND MISUSE OF
PHILOSOPHY AND PHILOSOPHERS

F. Grégoire

THE National-Socialist movement did not issue from a philosophy and, strictly speaking, no philosophy is at its source. It was born of what may be called traditional reflexes of the German people, powerfully intensified by the defeat of 1918 and by the situation of 'national distress' which followed from it. A few words must be devoted to recalling this, in order to make intelligible the part philosophy consented to play in the National-Socialist movement and the forms it took.

In face of the division of Germany into a mosaic of states, a pleiad of parties, inimical social classes, and opposed religious sects, we get the aspiration to unity and unanimity. In face of penetration by foreign ideologies, cultures, and ways of life, we find the will to national originality. In face of the banality of economic preoccupations and selfish interests and the flatness of everyday life there comes the aspiration to give a new value to existence. By way of compensation for the obsession of the country's political encirclement and economic subjection, the will to absolute independence and the will to power; and, finally, the conviction of a historic mission to be fulfilled in all fields. These aspirations formed a bundle firmly tied together: national individuation was desired with a view to national unity; unity with a view to power, and vice versa; unity, individuation, and power with a view to putting a halo round existence, to feeling that all were working together to realise a grandiose enterprise borne onward by destiny.

After the defeat these aspirations became obsessions in most Germans and sought a focal point.[1] National-Socialism seized on the

---

[1] On the subject of individuation, here are some typical statements taken from National-Socialist philosophers. As the result of the national circumstances, wrote E. Krieck,' no other people has had to expend so much trouble and tenacity to reach self-knowledge and self-consciousness'. Under a thousand different forms this response is to be heard in German history: 'We are those who are eternally becoming, forever tending towards a distant achievement, those restless beings who could never find appeasement in any condition' (E. Krieck, *Grundlagen, Aufbau und Wirtschaftsordnung des Nationalsozialistischen Staates* (Berlin–Vienna), Vol. IX, 1936–9, p. 10). Another brings out 'the thousand-year-old effort and aspiration of our blood towards a Reich of its own, a law of its own, its own art, science and economy—in a word, towards the fashioning of everything around us and in us in accordance with

idea of race. Not content with using as rallying-point the memories and traditions of their ancestors, the definition and accentuation of their original contribution, the restoration of their virtues, and the rediscovery of their strength, they saw—more deeply, as they believed—in their uniqueness their virtues, power, and their whole heritage, the fruits of a single biological substratum, which they declared—more deeply still—to have issued straight from the Divinity by special privilege, and to be marked by the Divinity with a grandiose and mysterious destiny. Thenceforth the idea of race was to make all the fundamental aspirations converge upon it. To achieve individuation—the higher individuation—would be to restore and develop the physical and moral characteristics considered to belong to the preponderating race in Germany, the Nordic race; unity would be obtained by common participation in the Nordic qualities and by concord between blood-brothers who know themselves for such; power would be born of the virtues of pride, courage, and fidelity which mark that race and are to be developed with fervour; the supreme value would reside in the people, the community founded upon the race, 'affirming itself' in the form of a model Reich, and master of the other peoples in conformity with the call of the Divinity. The idea of the race and of its destiny becomes thus, for the movement for political renovation, its fundamental motive image. But that is not all. Partly to make it more surely the pole of attraction of the political movement, National-Socialism tried to find in the idea of race the principle of a total renewal extending to all fields of national life. This is why the idea of race and the ideas supposed to be bound up with it were proclaimed as a *Weltanschauung*, a 'total' and exclusive *Weltanschauung*,[1] a complete interpretation of the world and of life, an integral vision of the meaning of the cosmos and the meaning of human existence, a vision reached by a sure 'instinct', an infallible 'vital sentiment' (*Lebensgefühl*), a profound conviction, a 'faith'.[2] The racist *Weltanschauung*, with the scale of values it implies, was declared the only *Weltanschauung* in conformity with the Nordic race, necessarily, by virtue both of its Nordicity and its superiority, since the Nordic race, when not bastardised, possesses a sure instinct for what is fitting for it and for what suits a superior race—for what is, at the same time, in conformity with the divine order of things.

The constellation of ideas and images known as a *Weltanschauung*

its individual nature, our individual nature' (W. Stuckart, ibid., Vol. XV, p. 13). It is towards satisfaction in the at last rediscovered Germanic uniqueness that the National-Socialist philosophers are bent on leading philosophy too.

[1] 'Allein, ganz allein und kompromisslos' (A. Rosenberg, *Der Mythus des 20. Jahrhunderts* (Munich, 1936), p. 699).

[2] For the general notion of *Weltanschauung* according to the National-Socialist philosophers, see for example E. Krieck, *Nationalpolitische Erziehung* (Leipzig, 1937), p. 89; *Völkisch-politische Anthropologie*, Vol. I, 2nd Imp. (Leipzig, 1938), p. 42.

is not a philosophy, and National-Socialism does not consider it as a philosophy. It lacks for that purpose the required degree of intellectual elaboration. It is composed of primary, pre-philosophic convictions. Since the task of philosophy is to furnish the simple *Weltanschauung* with a justification and development, it will be useful to recall the themes of the *Weltanschauung*, of what National-Socialism, after Rosenberg, calls the National-Socialist 'myth'—'myth' in the laudatory sense of great motive dream, dynamic image.[1]

There is first of all the race, which must be preserved and restored by a rigorous catharsis, in its blood and in its soul, and must be educated in accordance with its native qualities. Its soul—that is to say, its innate moral *traits*: the sense of honour, of liberty, of loyalty, of courage. By this means to achieve the racial type, the Nordic man, heroic man.

Next comes the soil, which has nourished the race, has fashioned it by selection, and whose configuration—landscape—is in harmony with the soul of the race.

The vital space necessary for the support and proliferation of the race and for its absolute independence.

The popular community (*Volksgemeinschaft*), a national society with a racial basis, a society of which all racial brothers are members by nature, and to whose service they owe themselves, without any reserve in any field.

National-Socialism means in the first place precisely this absolute dominance of the common interest over private interest, and consists also in the right of all racial brothers to work, in the honour accorded to everyone's work as soon as it serves the community, and in the comradeship (*Kameradschaft*) which renders possible this sharing of honour.

Art, letters, science, and technique must make the race and the community conscious of themselves and unreservedly help them to fulfil their mission.

The popular state (*Volksstaat*) is an organisation and an exercise of authority, placing the state at the service of the racial community, thanks to the presence, at the head of the state, of a *Führer* in whom are expressed the deep-set purposes of the community, and who is endowed with a totalitarian power; thanks also to a strong hierarchical organisation in all fields. Subordinates are united to their chief by a companionship relation (*Gefolgschaft*). Their honour is their loyalty. Each member of the community is, in his rank and field, a 'political soldier'.

---

[1] See A. Rosenberg, *Mythus*, 453; E. Krieck, p. 94; *Nationalpolitische Erziehung*, p. 94: 'wegeweisendes Schaubild'.
Needless to say, the elaboration of a simple ideology progresses by degrees, and it is not possible to draw a clear line between simple *Weltanschauung* and philosophy.

The Party groups together the members of the people who devote themselves wholly to the ideal of the race and keep watch to maintain it alive within the community.

Amidst the other nations, the popular state, in pursuit of its honour and its liberty, affirms itself as Reich. The Reich is the *Volksstaat* in its aspect of independence, power, and prestige. Each of its members places his own liberty and his own honour in the liberty and honour of the Reich. For the Reich, everyone is ready for the supreme sacrifice, is ready to become a hero.

This myth-complex is the object of a 'faith', in the religious sense. The *Weltanschauung* does in fact proscribe materialism categorically. It implies belief in the Divinity, the Nordic spirit being considered as essentially religious.[1] A great liberty is indeed allowed as regards the way of conceiving the Divinity. What is essential is to believe that the National-Socialist order is 'willed by God', that is to say, that there exists a non-sensible and mysterious Foundation of the cosmos from which emanates the destiny of the race. The attempts to transpose the ancient German paganism or to found a new cult are admitted just as much as the constitution of a 'positive' Christianity and as the maintenance of the traditional confessions themselves, on condition that the latter do not obstruct but, on the contrary, support the political renewal and, more fully, the biological and moral renewal. In relation to the particular religious ideologies, the *Weltanschauung* thus aims at playing the part of a general framework or, better still, general foundation, normative and dynamic.

In face of this *Weltanschauung*, which National-Socialism calls *the Weltanschauung*, it paints with hasty strokes the enemy ideology, the family of enemy ideologies, which it often does not deign to name *Weltanschauungen*. These ideologies have in common political and cultural internationalism, which implies a total misunderstanding of race as a historical factor and as a value to be realised. Under that head are grouped liberal democracy, Marxism, and 'political Christianity', as pursuing respectively the world domination of a caste of capitalists and freemasons, of a class, and of a clergy. In the democratic conception, internationalism or universalism is linked with economic, moral, and cultural individualism. Capitalist and Marxist democracy have in common the primacy they accord to material interests—a moral materialism which, in the Marxists

---

[1] Sometimes it is explicitly stated that the *Weltanschauung* does not, strictly speaking, include religious belief, that it limits itself to giving a view of this world without extending to the Divinity; but never without adding immediately that it presupposes a religious belief which furnishes it with its 'justification' (*Rechtfertigung*) (E. Krieck, op. cit., p. 96). From the moment when it is thus asserted that religious belief must be such as to provide the *Weltanschauung* with a foundation, the nuance just indicated is scarcely important.

and often in the *bourgeois* too, is accompanied by ideological material-ism, irreligion. As for 'political Christianity', religion there appears contaminated by temporal ambitions.

By these various qualities the ideologies in question sap the unity, originality, independence, and power of the German nation.

In the last analysis, they all show the perverse influence of that enemy race *par excellence*, the Jewish race, whether through the action of the Jews themselves, or through that of other men infested by the Judaic spirit.[1]

Given the character of instinctive, indisputable self-evidence which is granted to the *Weltanschauung*, given also the part attributed by this same *Weltanschauung* to intellectual life in the community, it was to be expected that the National-Socialist philosophy would assign to itself, as its one and only task, the justification of the *Weltan-schauung* and the polemics against the opposed ideologies and the philosophies which support them. And this even at the cost, for National-Socialist philosophy, of finding a philosophical basis also for this way of conceiving its task. This is in fact how the National-Socialist philosophers understood their function.

And first of all, to the National-Socialist intellectuals, the elabora-tion of a philosophy seemed an indispensable and urgent business.[2] It could not be otherwise in a people so traditionally enamoured of philosophy as the German people.[3] This being so, the National-Socialist philosophers vie with each other in repeating that philo-sophy must attach itself exclusively to the 'justification in terms of thought' of the *Weltanschauung*, and thus place itself, in spite of its inclination to rebel, 'at the service of the *Weltanschauung*';[4]

[1] There is no need to indicate here the documents which—with *Mein Kampf* at their base—justify the outline just traced of the *Weltanschauung* in its positive and in its polemical aspect. Let us merely recall that a sort of codification of the *Weltan-schauung* is to be found in the National-Socialist Party's official encyclopædia: *Grundlagen, Aufbau und Wirtschaftsordnung des Nationalsozialistischen Staates* (Berlin–Vienna, 1936–9) which appeared in separate instalments. The instalments most important for a knowledge of the elements of which National-Socialist philosophy was to make use are: I, II, VI, VIII, IX, XV, XVI, XVIII. Succinct summaries of the *Weltanschauung* may be found, for instance, in Vol. IX (pp. 5–6) and Vol. XV (p. 13).

[2] See O. Dietrich, *Die philosophischen Grundlagen des Nationalsozialismus* (Breslau, 1935), pp. 5–7 (a pamphlet reproducing a lecture by the author, who was Party Press Chief, at the University of Cologne in 1934 and given great prominence by National-Socialist propaganda).

The constitution of a National-Socialist philosophy is 'the greatest scientific task ever required by German intellectual history', writes H. Härtle in the *National-sozialistische Monatshefte* (Sept. 1939), No. 114, p. 779. Whence this slogan: 'From the political programme to the *Weltanschauung*, and from the *Weltanschauung* to science and philosophy' (ibid., p. 773).

[3] Dietrich himself notes this (op. cit., p. 41). The elaboration of a National-Socialist philosophy is also necessary, according to him, in order to make the *Weltanschauung* understood by foreigners (p. 5).

[4] F. Böhm, *Anti-Cartesianismus. Deutsche Philosophie im Widerstand* (Leipzig, 1938), pp. 155, 15, 19, 20.

that speculation must express in its fashion the fundamental tendencies of the racial community;[1] that it is in no way an end in itself, but in truth a mere means to the service of the life of the people.[2]

Had the National-Socialist philosophy, by 1945, achieved its self-assigned programme as regards degree of definition and systematisation? Half-way, at most. The National-Socialist philosophers themselves recognised how imperfect their work still was, and this while expressing their full confidence in the future of National-Socialist philosophy.[3] That did not prevent them from putting everything into action to assure their thought a widespread influence in Germany, above all upon the young at the universities—nor from succeeding, up to a point.

Among the philosophers or thinkers with philosophical pretensions who rallied to the National-Socialist Party, aspired to form its philosophy, and had acquired authority within the Party (although it was officially admitted that their writings committed none but themselves, and not the Party),[4] one may place, after A. Rosenberg;[5] A. Bäumler (professor at Berlin);[6] E. Krieck (rector at Heidelberg)[7] and his school, which includes F. Böhm[8] and W. Classen;[9] H. Schwartz;[10] then two philosophers attempting to bend existentialist philosophy in the direction of racism, H. Heyse[11] and Fr. A. Beck;[12]

---

[1] A. Rosenberg, *Mythus*, pp. 343–4, 684–8; E. Krieck, *Völk.-pol. Anthr.*, Vol. I, p. 42; H. Härtle in *Nat.-soz. Monatshefte* (Sept. 1939), pp. 775, 778.
[2] A. Rosenberg, *Mythus*, p. 684; *Blut und Ehre*, 22nd Imp. (Munich, 1939), p. 203.
[3] A. Rosenberg, *Mythus*, p. 3; E. Krieck, *Völk.-pol. Anthr.*, Vol. I, p. vii; Vol. III, p. 13.
[4] A. Rosenberg, *Mythus*, p. 3.
[5] *Der Mythus des 20 Jahrhunderts* (Munich, 1930), (we quote for example 103–4th Imp. (Munich, 1936)).
Blut und Ehre (Munich, 1939), (22nd Imp. (Munich, 1939)).
[6] *Politik und Erziehung* (Berlin, 1937).
Studien zur deutschen Geistesgeschichte (Berlin, 1937).
Bildung und Gemeinschaft (Berlin, 1942).
[7] *Nationalpolitische Erziehung* (Leipzig, 1932).
Leben als Prinzip der Weltanschauung und Problem der Wissenschaft (Leipzig, 1938).
Völkisch-politische Anthropologie.
   I. *Die Wirklichkeit* (Leipzig, 1935) (2nd Imp., Leipzig, 1938).
   II. *Das Handeln und die Ordnungen* (Leipzig, 1937).
   III. *Das Erkennen und die Wissenschaft* (Leipzig, 1938).
'Nationalsozialistisch Erziehung', in *Grundl., Aufb. u. Wirtsch. des N.-s. Staates*, Vol. IX.
E. Krieck published a magazine: *Volk im Werden.*
[8] *Anti-Cartesianismus. Deutsche Philosophie im Widerstand* (Leipzig, 1938).
[9] *Thomistische Anthropologie in völkisch-politischer Sicht* (Karlsruhe, 1937).
[10] *National-Sozialistische Weltanschauung* (Berlin, 1933).
Zur philosophischen Grundlegung des Nationalsozialismus (Berlin, 1936).
[11] *Idee und Existenz* (Hamburg, 1935).
[12] *Im Kampf um die Philosophie des lebendigen Geistes* (Breslau, 1936).
Idee und Wirklichkeit (Würzburg, 1936).

next, H. Härtle,[1] who was, with the above-mentioned A. Baümler, the great promoter of a return to Nietzsche; lastly, E. Bergmann (professor at Leipzig).[2] O. Dietrich must also be mentioned, because of his official role in the Party.[3] As regards the philosophy of the state more specifically, we may content ourselves with adding to the preceding names certain collaborators in the Party encyclopædia, above all W. Stuckart[4] and O. Köllreutter.[5] Such are the authors on whom we shall mainly base our *exposé*.[6]

In a fuller study than ours it would obviously have been right to begin by summarising the doctrine of each of them in order, then to bring out the points they have in common, and finally to plot out the traces of each philosopher's respective influence. We shall content ourselves with indicating the common orientations and noting, besides, certain individual variants. The task is made easier by the kinship between the authors. Krieck's group is the most influential centre. Between the panvitalism professed by him and the doctrine of certain other philosophers drawing their inspiration from existentialism the resemblances are numerous, the differences often merely of vocabulary. This general kinship makes it possible to presume what would have been the direction of the National-Socialist philosophy of the future.

We shall show the use which National-Socialist philosophers make of certain philosophical doctrines to support racist conclusions, and likewise the use made of certain philosophical authorities, whether traditionally recognised in Germany or set up for the needs of the cause (as is the case with Meister Eckhart, 'launched' by Rosenberg). As for misuse, it consists first of all (as all our readers will agree) in the attempt to found on generally invoked philosophical positions and authorities such inadmissible positions as (1) recourse to the nation's aspirations and interest as the one and only criterion of value, (2) the integral subordination of personal destiny to the

---

[1] *Nietzsche und der Nationalsozialismus* (Munich, 1937).

[2] *Die natürliche Geistlehre* (Stuttgart, 1937).

[3] *Die philosophischen Grundlagen des Nationalsozialismus* (Breslau, 1936). 'Der Nationalsozialismus als Weltanschauung und Staatsgedanke', in *Grundl. Aufb. u. Wirtsch. des N.-s. Staates*, Vol. II.

[4] 'Nationalsozialismus und Staatsrecht', in *Grundl. Aufb. u. Wirtsch.*, Vol. XV.

[5] 'Der nationalsozialistische Rechtsstaat', ibid., Vol. XVI; 'Der Aufbau des deutschen Führerstaates', ibid., Vol. XVIII.

[6] Neither Heidegger, nor O. Spann, nor L. Klages can very well be grouped among the philosophers of National-Socialism. Whatever the ambitions of those thinkers, their direct influence has been too little marked, or even their ideas too violently disputed (this is so in the case of Klages, who has been reproached for his extreme anti-intellectualism, and of Spann, attacked among other things for his universalism).

Philosophical *aperçus* are to be found in some authors whose concern is the science of races, such as L. F. Clauss and H. F. K. Günther; and also in those who, like E. Bergmann, whose name was mentioned above, tie up with the *Deutsche Glaubensbewegung*, such as J. W. Hauer, E. von Reventlow, and H. Wirth.

national community, (3) competition, without any juridical norm between nations, with the refusal to exclude war, (4) the autocratic and totalitarian character of the political state, and finally (5) the racist aspect of the whole philosophy, including the four theses just indicated. Another form of misuse is the attempt to found racism on general doctrines in themselves false. On this point we shall let the reader judge for himself according to his own general positions in philosophy. There remains, finally, the misuse in giving a manifestly tendentious interpretation either of philosophies considered to be opponents or of those whose patronage is invoked. We shall point to cases of both kinds of this last abuse.

In favour of a renewal of German philosophy, the National-Socialist philosophers draw attention to the state of anarchy and of separation from human life and national life characteristic of European thought, including German thought, at present.[1] At all costs there must be found for philosophy a principle drawing German minds closer together, a principle which will at the same time draw philosophy closer to life, German life. Where is this to be found? Examination of the various systems and tendencies in which the history of philosophic thought in Europe and in Germany has been concerned reveals, we are told, two fundamental currents. Certain philosophies have in common general positions which are false in themselves and have led to a moral and political ideology likewise manifestly erroneous, the ideology opposed to the *Weltanschauung*: internationalism and individualism. These general positions boil down to intellectualism, rationalism, to the idea that, by his abstract and reasoning intelligence, man and, in principle, anything in the shape of man, is capable of arriving at one and the same truth—in other words, that there exist universal and eternal verities; and that, in addition, man is fundamentally characterised by intelligence, which, being alike in all men, as has just been remarked, makes them all beings equal in value and dignity, both across all frontiers and within all frontiers. From this follow many consequences. To begin with, equality between citizens, the conception of the state as a merely contractual society, the abandonment of authority to the vote—in a word, the programme of the Declaration of the Rights of Man; next, the idea of a culture valid for all men, 'humanism', the pursuit of the true, the beautiful, and the good (Von Humboldt), defined in a universal and eternal fashion;[2] and equality between the nations, all composed of men similar because of intelligence and called to a

[1] O. Dietrich, *Philos. Grundl.*, pp. 11–12. (These capital defects of contemporary philosophy, notes the author, manifested themselves plainly at the Prague international congress of philosophy in 1934.) E. Krieck, *Völk.-pol. Anthr.*, Vol. III. p. 13.
[2] E. Krieck, *Völk.-pol. Anthr.*, Vol. II, pp. 20–1.

single culture, and, in consequence, the maxim of peace at any price, an equal having no right to use force against an equal. The consequences extend also to the metaphysical field. In fact, the abstract, deterministic intelligence cannot conceive of the cosmos except as a vast mechanism, either as a mechanism existing and functioning on its own in the materialist way, or as a mechanism constructed and set in motion by a God who is 'architect of the universe', or, yet again, as a mechanism in which an absolute Mind, conceived on idealist lines, expresses itself. If pure intelligence arrives at such images, this is because, from the start, it is inevitably inclined to establish a radical distinction between 'mind', pure, suprasensible mind, and pure sensible matter; that done, either it refuses to admit the existence of pure mind and tends in consequence to reduce everything to mere matter, or else it maintains both mind and matter but is content to place them side by side, to join them from outside. At the same time it conceives both of them statically, as forms of 'being'. When, however, intelligence speaks of a becoming, as happens in particular in human history, it conceives this becoming as subject to a well-defined law of infallible general progress, the 'progress of enlightenment', whose plan has been laid down by an 'architect' God, or else emanates, all determined, from an absolute Mind, or else, yet again, results automatically from the universal mechanism.

Who are responsible for this intellectualist, static, dualist, and mechanistic ideology? A. Rosenberg points to Socrates as the founder of the logical method, considered to be universally human but really contrary to life, which has spread in Europe to its harm. After Socrates this method was schematised by Aristotle, whose last great disciple was Hegel—Hegel who dared to write: 'Logic is the science of God'.[1] The Greeks, pronounces E. Krieck, have left us the double and deplorable heritage of rationalism and atomism.[2] Others, with F. Böhm, bitterly attack Descartes as the prototype of all modern intellectualist ideology in the West, and so as the philosophic enemy *par excellence* of German thought.[3] To the pernicious Cartesian spirit the greatest German thinkers have paid their tribute, often a very generous one. This is the case with Kant, with Hegel,[4] and—although to a lesser degree—with Fichte himself. As

---

[1] *Mythus*, p. 287; on Socrates, see pp. 283–7. Same opposition to Socrates in A. Baümler, who on this rallies to the side of Nietzsche (*Stud. zur deutschen Geistesgesch.*, p. 287).

[2] *Völk.-pol. Anthr.*, Vol. I, p. 37.

[3] Whence the title of F. Böhm's work: *Anti-Cartesianismus. Deutsche Philosophie im Widerstand*. In it Descartes and his influence are studied, pp. 37–108.

[4] Contrary to what is often believed, Hegel was not in favour with National-Socialism. Apart from the intellectualist character of his metaphysics, Rosenberg reproaches him bitterly with having defined the 'people' as 'the part of the State which does not know what it wants', a point of view which, like democracy, is at

for A. Baümler, without neglecting Descartes he addresses himself specially to the form taken by the primacy of 'mind' in German idealism[1] and, obviously still afraid of the prestige exerted by idealism on the thought of his fellow-citizens, he writes that between National-Socialism and idealism there is no compromise possible.[2]

But there is perceptible, above all in Germany and nourished by authentic Germans, a quite different current. It claims, principally, Albertus Magnus (Albert 'the German'), Meister Eckart (considered not only as a great mystic but as a profound philosophic mind);[3] Bruno, Paracelsus, Leibniz, Goethe, Hamann (according to some, Pascal);[4] next, Kant, Schelling, Fichte, and Schopenhauer in virtue of a part of their thought; P. de Lagarde and, of course, Nietzsche.[5]

---

the origin of the idea of the state as mere authority (*Mythus*, p. 527). Others stress how his intellectualism led him to the dualism of sensible matter against suprasensible mind—a dualism which the 'dialectic' does not succeed in surmounting and which can be resolved only by the idea of a single life that is in becoming and takes diverse forms (A. Baümler, *Bild. und Gem.*, pp. 88–93). Or again, Hegel is accused of having allowed, in conformity with the intellectualist tradition, the idea of an absolute and universal verity; of having made 'mind' the motive force of history ('world mind' diversified into 'minds of peoples'; with, at the root of everything, the 'absolute idea'), of having in consequence represented history as a struggle between 'minds', the 'minds of peoples', rather than as a *real* struggle, and of having imagined that, led by a *universal* Mind, it tended towards a *universal* harmony; of having considered intellectual contemplation as the highest value there is and as the final aim of history ('absolute Mind'); finally, of having believed that history stopped with him, Hegel (F. Böhm, *Anti-Cartesianismus*, pp. 24–36, and elsewhere). This is why (so runs the conclusion) it is an urgent duty for German thought to 'liberate itself from Hegel' (ibid., p. 35). This position with reference to one of the traditional patrons of Germanic nationalism is in the highest degree revealing as regards the vitalist and radically particularist orientation adopted by National-Socialist philosophy.

[1] *Bild. und Gem.*, pp. 87–95.
[2] ibid., p. 197.
[3] A. Rosenberg, *Mythus*, pp. 223–4; A. Baümler calls Eckart 'the first German philosopher' (*Bild. und Gem.*, p. 188).
[4] F. Böhm, *Anti-Cartesianismus*, p. 111.
[5] A. Baümler, who edited works of Nietzsche and extracts from them, advocates forcefully the rallying of German thought and German youth around Nietzsche, in whom he salutes the only thinker to have really broken with the intellectualist tradition (*Bild. und Gem.*, pp. 196–202), a man of genius defending life both against Socrates and against Christianity (*Stud. zur deutschen Geistesgesch.*, p. 257), the bard of heroism (ibid., pp. 235, 237). This is why Baümler sees the author of *Wille zur Macht* surrounded, in spite of the unfinished character of his thought, by the great light of the future for National-Socialist philosophy (*Bild. und Gem.*, pp. 186–97, 202).
    The same exhortations and same hopes are to be found in H. Härtle, the author of a Nietzsche anthology with commentaries for the use of National-Socialists (*Nietzsche und der Nationalsozialismus* (Munich, 1937)), which brought him a wide welcome. Once allowance is made, in Nietzsche, for the errors due to the ideas of his time (for instance, the European ideal and the false estimate of the work of Bismarck), Härtle welcomes in him, among other themes, the exaltation of life, anti-egalitarianism, the importance of the racial factor (though regretting that Nietzsche should have considered irremediable the hybridisation of Europe), the 'ethics of

This current is characterised by an inclination towards intuition, vital experience (*Erlebnis*), and by the primacy given in man to will and action. Neither man nor the Whole are any longer decomposed into two motionless elements, radically different and merely juxtaposed—pure mind and mere matter; the human being is the expansion of a single 'life', and the same is true for the Cosmos. And life is essentially becoming, dynamism, growth. The Absolute is 'Life' and the source of 'life'. And in the same way society is all a 'living', 'organic' whole. Man is conceived not on 'egalitarian' but on 'aristocratic' lines. This is why life in society obeys not the democratic but the hierarchic principle. No automatic 'progress', but a mysterious destiny leaving play to will, to responsibility, and issuing from the divine 'Life'. In short, specifically German thought takes, as Rosenberg says, the form of a 'mystic and cosmic vitalism'.[1]

The supposedly manifest presence of this current of ideas in Germany above all already constitutes, in the eyes of the National-Socialist philosophers, a presumption in its favour. Finding, in the philosophic field as in all the others, Germany divided[2] and largely invaded by foreign influence,[3] National-Socialism shows itself strongly animated, here, also, by the will to unity and the will to individuation. German thought will find unity again precisely through individuation, by rallying to a specifically German current of ideas.

Of course, that is not all. Given, on the one hand, that the general philosophic themes which inspire the current of thought in question are considered as true and that, on the other hand, they harmonise quite

---

combat', the affirmation of Germanic values and the rejection of Jewish values (pp. 162–3).

Härtle (ibid., p. 164) like Baümler (*Stud. zur deutschen Geistesgesch.*, p. 284) sees in Adolf Hitler, thinker and man of action, the realisation of what Nietzsche had announced to the world. That is why, concludes Baümler (ibid.), 'if we cry out to German youth "Heil Hitler!", we are also greeting: "Friedrich Nietzsche!".'

Besides numerous references to this or that philosopher singly, we find in our authors dynastic lists; for example, A. Rosenberg, *Mythus*, pp. 630, 690–1; E. Krieck, *Völk.-pol. Anthr.*, Vol. I, pp. 2, 13, 46–7; E. Böhm, *Anti-Cartesianismus*, p. 111.

[1] *Mythus*, p. 142.

General pictures of the two great ideologies in conflict are to be found, for instance, in E. Krieck, *Völk.-pol. Anthr.*, Vol. I, pp. 43–4; Vol. II, pp. 8–9, 45–7. The whole of the already mentioned work by F. Böhm is aimed at separating them. In addition, within specifically German thought, Böhm distinguishes two complementary currents characterised respectively by amplitude and by intensity—by a tendency to a profound apprehension of the Cosmos in all its immensity (Albertus Magnus, Paracelsus, Böhme, Goethe, Hölderlin, Schelling, Schleiermacher, and Nietzsche), and by a tendency to live with intensity the personal life, a personal life directed indeed towards action (Meister Eckart, Nicolas of Cusa, Luther, Leibniz, Kant, Hamann, Fichte, Jacobi, de Lagarde) (*Anti-Cartesianismus*, p. 187, and see pp. 174–87).

[2] O. Dietrich, *Philos. Grundl. des Nationalsoz.*, pp. 11–12.

[3] Quantitatively speaking, F. Böhm notes, European philosophy outdoes German philosophy in Germany (*Anti-Cartesianismus*, p. 120).

naturally—so it is reckoned—with the specific claims of the *Weltanschauung*, lead up to them and have sometimes even appeared in connection with the presentiment or already lively consciousness of the importance of the idea of race,[1] these themes appear, in relation to the *Weltanschauung*, as a foundation which only needs reinforcing and developing. Reciprocally, indeed, the racist *Weltanschauung*, considered as true in anterior to all philosophy in the strict sense, confers its own value upon these philosophical themes, the only ones to show themselves in harmony with it.[2]

We must now set forth the way in which National-Socialist philosophy attempts to exploit the themes in question to support the *Weltanschauung* and, above all, to support the idea of race. For, as A. Baümler writes, 'the discovery of race is the Copernican idea of modern times'.[3] We shall insist rather on the positive side of National-Socialist philosophy than on its polemical side.

To provide a basis for the *Weltanschauung*, will National-Socialist philosophy exalt the scientific knowledge of races or the strictly historical study of the racial factor? Without neglecting the contribution of the sciences and of history,[4] it appeals much more fundamentally to a cognition of a philosophical type. Not, it is true, resembling rational philosophy—the understanding is incapable of attaining reality—but of an intuitive type. Everything rests on deep intuitions (*Anschauungen*), on vital experiences (*Erlebnisse*) of a metaphysical order.[5]

[1] This is what, at the price of a glaring misinterpretation, A. Rosenberg finds even in Meister Eckart (*Mythus*, pp. 257–8).
[2] We shall deal below, *ex professo*, with this pragmatist aspect of National-Socialist philosophy.
[3] *Politik und Erziehung*, p. 40. Same reflection in A. Rosenberg, in *Nationalsozialistische Monatshefte*, n. 103, 1938, p. 85.
[4] This is why A. Rosenberg gives, as a slogan: '*Wissen und glauben*' (*Mythus*, p. 115). By *wissen* he means partly scientific knowledge (the other part being philosophical elaboration). See also *Blut und Ehre*, p. 242, and E. Krieck, *Völk.-pol. Anthr.*, Vol. I, p. 52.
[5] 'The decisive question is not how far science has already managed to approach races—their reality and significance. . . . Race reveals itself to instinct (*Instinckt*), to vital sentiment (*Lebensgefühl*), to intuition (*Schau*), to immediate vital perception (*unmittelbare Lebenserfahrung*) and through this rises from being a datum to being a duty' (E. Krieck, *Nationalsoz. Erziehung*, p. 27). It is not, in this case, a matter of explanation (*Erklärung*), analysis or intellectual synthesis, but of 'comprehension' (*Verstehung*) by 'intuition' (*Anschauung*) (see *Völk.-pol. Anthr.*, Vol. I, pp. 28–9, 46; Vol. III, p. 12). The most frequent expressions with a technical air occur in E. Krieck, especially *Anschauung*, and next *Erleben*.
    On *Anschauung* see also A. Rosenberg, *Blut und Ehre*, pp. 135–46, 202; A. Baümler, *Bild. und Gem.*, p. 91; F. Böhm, *Anti-Cartesianismus*, pp. 123, 244. Fr. A. Beck speaks of 'unmittelbare Offenbarungen' (*Kampf um die Philos. des leb. Geistes*, pp. 31 ff.); H. Heyse says, for his part, that what is needed is 'die Wahrheit . . . durch Einsatz und Tun als existenzielles Wissen erfaren', and declares himself a partisan of a 'Metaphysik der Erfahung der Wahrheit und Unwahrheit des Lebens' (*Idee und Existenz*, p. 251–2); O. Dietrich advocates an 'irrationale Erfassung im Erlebnis,

Intuition has no need of previous justification. All preliminary criticism of knowledge is an enterprise as useless as it is impossible.[1] Subject and object once separated, the intellectualist tradition has always shown itself incapable of reuniting them. This is why criticism of knowledge can only result in destroying everything. Idealism leads to nihilism.[2] Besides, criticism of knowledge, by shutting mind in upon itself, is akin to egoism.[3] Intuition plunges at one swoop into reality, and reality reveals itself to it in a manner indissoluble from the intuition which seizes it. This does not mean that reality can be known exhaustively—contrary to shallow intellectualism, true philosophy has the sense of mystery;[4] but what is known of reality is known exactly.[5]

How is this possible? Because there is no consciousness that is not a consciousness of something;[6] subject and object are in a 'polar' relation with each other.[7] Also because man, who knows, is reality, as the thing known is reality; whence the possibility of a 'feeling of reality' (*Wirklichkeitsgefühl*).[8] More precisely, the man who knows is life as everything else is life;[9] man has therefore merely to re-live (*erleben*) life.[10] This is why, in general, National-Socialist philosophy declares itself resolutely 'realist'.[11]

Instinckt, und Intuition' (*Philos. Grundl. des Nationalsoz.*, p. 21). Dietrich adds that 'if recent philosophy says that the intuition of essences (*intuitive Wesensschau*) is the immediate intuition of what is in conformity with the law of things (*die unmittelbare Anschauung des Gesetzmässigen*), in that case this aptitude is exemplified in the highest degree in the personality of Adolf Hitler' (p. 36).

[1] Especially E. Krieck (*Völk.-pol. Anthr.*, Vol. III, pp. 18–19). According to A. Rosenberg there is indeed a criticism of knowledge, but it is aimed only at theoretical knowledge (*Erkenntnis*), and not at the grasping of values, and it constitutes only a very limited part of the task of philosophy. Philosophy is, in fact, essentially '*Bekenntnis*' and not '*Erkenntnis*' (*Mythus*, pp. 115–8).

[2] E. Krieck, ibid.; see also E. Bergmann, *Natürel. Geistl.*, p. 47.

[3] E. Krieck, *Völk.-pol. Anthr.*, Vol. I, p. 34.

[4] F. Böhm, *Anti-Cartesianismus*, p. 93.   [5] E. Krieck, *Leben*, p. 184.

[6] F. Böhm, *Anti-Cartesianismus*, p. 170.

[7] E. Krieck, *Völk.-pol. Anthr.*, Vol. I, p. 32; F. Böhm, *Anti-Cartesianismus*, p. 174; E. Bergmann, *Naturel. Geistl.*, p. 72.

[8] F. Böhm, *Anti-Cartesianismus*, pp. 135, 160.

[9] O. Dietrich, in *Grundl. Aufb. u. Wirtsch. des Nationalsoz. Staates*, Vol. II, p. 1; *Philos. Grundl. des Nationalsoz.*, p. 37.

[10] E. Krieck, *Völk.-pol. Anthr.*, Vol. I, pp. 28–9. F. Böhm speaks of the 'enveloping Whole in which and by which I live, act and know' (*Anti-Cartesianismus*, p. 228). The man of the age of myth, the same author writes, enjoys a fusion with the reality which surrounds him—'he *is* still what his world is'—before all distinction between subject and object, before that pernicious gash invented by Descartes. The true task of philosophy, that 'knowledge of knowledge', is to give us back that first experience (ibid., pp. 248–9, 252–3).

[11] A. Baümler, *Bild. und Gem.*, p. 86. National-Socialist philosophy is idealist, notes A. Baümler, only in the practical sense of the term, meaning attachment to the higher values (ibid.) E. Bergmann calls himself a 'critical realist' (*Die Nat. Geistl.*, p. 5).

A. Rosenberg is nearer to Kant, being idealist as regards space, time, and causality. In this idealism, which he traces already in Meister Eckart (!), Rosenberg sees a position favourable to mystical experience (*Mythus*, pp. 223–4).

It is also made clear that the Reality reached by intuition—whether it concerns the individual, the racial community or the universal Life—is not a mere 'factualness' (*Tatsächlichkeit*) on which its sense and value are conferred from outside by man (a conception to which we might give the name 'idealism of value'). The Real possesses in itself a sense and value which the vital experience is content to discover.[1]

It is thus a mutilation of man to reduce all the forms of knowledge, by which he is distinguished from the animal, to abstract logic and the sciences of observation. Not that abstraction has not an indispensable part to play in philosophy: there must be formation of concepts, reasoning, deduction, but on the basis of vital primary experiences and inspired by them.[2] There is no science—not even positive sciences—'without presupposition'.[3] If, then, by philosophy, in a restricted sense, is meant precisely a product of abstract thought, it must be said that philosophy is in a 'polar' relation with intuition—and therefore, to put it concretely, in a 'polar' relation with the *Weltanschauung*.[4] This is what is manifested to intuition itself.

Besides, in order to express the primary intuitions, preference should be given to symbolic images, which are active and subtle, over abstract concepts which necessarily tend to join together in an inert, narrow, and fixed system.[5] The expression of fundamental intuitions—and, concretely, of fundamental intuitions belonging to the race—should be discerned already in a people's primitive mythology.[6]

If intuition, imagination, and understanding can and should cooperate in this way, it is because they emanate, within the individual, from a single and unique impulse of life, a single radical, preconscious 'will', the centre of all our forces,[7] the 'pre-rational root' from which one cannot cut oneself off.[8] This profound 'life', this fundamental 'will', are marked with the characteristics of the race; and for this reason to become really conscious of this 'life' and this 'will' is the same thing as to become conscious of the aspirations proper to the racial type, its scale of values, which the imagination

---

[1] A. Baümler, *Bild. und Gem.*, pp. 90–1; E. Krieck, *Völk.-pol. Anthr.*, Vol. I, p. 45; F. Böhm, *Anti-Cartesianismus*, pp. 113, 225, 241.

[2] A. Rosenberg, *Mythus*, p. 137; F. Böhm, *Anti-Cartesianismus*, p. 123, n. 3, etc. There is sometimes insistence on the relative importance of the understanding in opposition to those who utterly disdain it (A. Rosenberg, *Blut und Ehre*, pp. 140–1).

[3] F. Böhm, *Anti-Cartesianismus*, p. 240.

[4] ibid., p. 126. As examples of such symbols Böhm quotes, among others, 'the spark' of the soul in Meister Eckart, and man as microcosm in Paracelsus. See also A. Rosenberg, *Mythus*, p. 135.

[5] F. Böhm, *Anti-Cartesianismus*, p. 19.

[6] ibid., p. 133. A. Rosenberg cites, among other examples, the Greek myth of Eros generator of life, and the German myth of the Paradise of Honour and Duty.

[7] F. Böhm, *Anti-Cartesianismus*, pp. 241, 266.

[8] ibid., p. 241.

and intellect will later have to translate, each in its own way. That the values in question are in fact specifically racial is made plain intuitively by the contact with men of the same ancestry.[1] The National-Socialist philosophy often appeals to the fruitfulness of action as criterion of truth. One frequently comes across a quotation of Goethe's saying: '*Was fruchtbar ist, allein ist wahr*',[2] and he is made to mean not merely that truth is fruitful and fruitfulness is therefore *one* criterion of truth, but that fruitfulness is the sole criterion of truth, and even—at least this seems to be the sense of certain texts—that truth resides formally in fruitfulness.[3] By fruitfulness is meant the fact of contributing to the development of life; that is to say, it is at once added to the development of the race. In the last analysis, do the National-Socialist philosophers mean to say that truth is purely and simply identical with fruitfulness, to the exclusion of any idea of a correspondence of knowledge with the object, and also of any question as to what authorises us to take fruitfulness as criterion of truth? In reality this criterion is granted an independent foundation, namely the existence of the race as reality *par excellence* and as in itself marked with the meaning of human existence. And this foundation, this *Urphänomenon*, is perceived by intuition.[4]

But it is not only by the roundabout way of its fruitfulness, registered afterwards or meanwhile, that action is the source of truth; it is so through itself, in itself. There is in the will to gain results, placed intensively at the service of the race, a light which makes visible the truth of the race and of the *Weltanschauung*. Will and intuition, it is strongly insisted, penetrate each other intimately.[5]

[1] A. Rosenberg, *Mythus*, pp. 116, 251, 459; *Blut und Ehre*, pp. 139, 143, etc. Rosenberg calls '*Dasein*' the deep-seated will directed towards the values proper to a race, and '*Sosein*' all its expressions: symbols, art, sciences, religion, philosophy, style of living.
According to F. Böhm, it is in the first layer of his being, the one where 'he *is* still what his world is', that a man is marked with the eternal racial tendencies (*Anti-Cartesianismus*, pp. 253, cf. 244). The deep source is 'something which we are not, but is only *through* us and acts out of us, something which is not in *our power* but is *power in us*'. 'It is the anonymous in us, out of which everything can and still must become.' We become a *Selbst* in consequence of the demands of history, which force us to 'choose between our value and our non-value' (p. 245).
From all that we have just said about intuition according to the National-Socialist philosophers it follows that, in them, the expression '*Weltanschauung*' takes on more firmly and more precisely the meaning of *intuition* (*Anschauung*) of the world —a meaning which it already tends in itself to suggest.
[2] A. Rosenberg, *Mythus*, pp. 386 ff.; E. Krieck, *Völk.-pol. Anthr.*, Vol. I, pp. 35–6; O. Dietrich, *Philos. Grundl. des Nationalsoz.*, pp. 37–8.
[3] Thus A. Rosenberg writes that a theory which one day appears as erroneous was 'true' as long as, in fact, it proved fruitful (*Mythus*, p. 386).
[4] With reference to the divine and eternal character of the person, Rosenberg, as we shall see below, makes use, side by side with the fruitfulness criterion, of a more speculative reason, which is indeed declared to be secondary, and appeals at the same time to intuitive experience.
[5] A. Rosenberg, *Mythus*, pp. 229–31, 262–7; F. Böhm, *Anti-Cartesianismus*, pp.

Side by side with this pragmatic aspect of National-Socialist philosophy another aspect, akin to it, likewise causes a certain perplexity in the mind. This is its strong relativist tendency. It is said repeatedly that the idea of some 'one and eternal truth', of a pure objectivity, is a chimera.[1] There is no 'universal human intelligence'[2] in any form, and therefore, in particular, there is no transcendental absolute 'I'.[3] Man is the measure of all things.[4] Not that the individual can choose his truth according to his own sweet will, nor even that there is a truth naturally in harmony with each individual, but there is a truth for each race. Each race has by nature its own scale of values and its way of representing the Whole, which are 'true' for it, with a 'truth' which necessarily escapes every other race. This is what causes the *Weltanschauung* to be 'true' for the Nordic race and for it alone.[5] 'True' for it, and for it only, is all that expresses its essential tendencies, its authentic values, and assures them their accomplishment, all that causes the race, according to an expression borrowed by Rosenberg from Meister Eckart, to become 'one with itself'.[6] The measure of all things, including our thoughts, is the racial soul of the people.[7] This is what, as opposed to 'absolute' truth, Rosenberg calls 'organic' truth (for, he notes, an organism tends by an immanent law to realise a determined form).[8] The true philosophy will therefore be an 'organic philosophy'.[9] Must we see in this an extreme relativism, that is to say a neutral relativism, refusing to raise from any absolute point of view the question of the respective value of the 'myths' of each race, each 'myth' that authentically expresses a race being 'true' for it, beyond any possibility of comparison? In spite of certain appearances, this is not the position

---

277, 279; H. Heyse, *Idee und Existenz*, pp. 251–2, 305, 342. (Other references will be found below, *a propos* of religion.)

The close relationship established between the grasping of the *Weltanschauung* and action makes the meaning of the word '*Weltanschauung*' easily overflow the domain of knowledge, so as no longer to designate merely a way of seeing the universe, the life of man and human action, but also the very exercise of that action, the putting of the vision into practice. In this way to possess the *Weltanschauung* comes to signify adopting a total attitude (*Gesittung*) embracing knowledge, will and action, an attitude which, in the individual, issues from a single life of racial type directed towards a single value—the primary racial value, honour—and a single end—the popular community.

[1] A. Rosenberg, *Mythus*, p. 119 *et al.*; F. Böhm, *Anti-Cartesianismus*, p. 131; H. Heyse, *Idee und Existenz*, p. 251.

[2] A. Rosenberg, *Mythus*, pp. 119, 681, 689, 692. E. Krieck, *Völk.-pol. Anthr.*, Vol. I, p. 33; Vol. III, pp. 123–7.

[3] E. Krieck, *Völk.-pol. Anthr.*, Vol. I, pp. 32, 41; Vol. III, pp. 8 ff.

[4] ibid., Vol. I, p. 32.

[5] A. Rosenberg, *Mythus*, pp. 119–20.

[6] ibid., pp. 689–93.

[7] ibid., p. 697.

[8] ibid., pp. 681–5, 690.

[9] ibid., p. 697. See also O. Dietrich, *Philos. Grundl. des Nationalsoz.*, p. 17. For the same idea in other words see H. Heyse, *Idee und Existenz*, p. 251.

z

adopted; for it would mean refusing to judge from any absolute point of view the value of the races themselves—which is certainly a long way from the thought of our authors. The Nordic race being in reality superior to any other, the *Weltanschauung* is not only 'true' for it, it is in many respects true absolutely, even if other races are not capable of perceiving its truth. And for example it is true, speaking absolutely, that the Nordic scale of values, with honour at the peak, is more noble, more in conformity with the loftiest impulses of cosmic life, than the 'myth' of profit and of perverse destruction which polarises the Jewish mind or the myth of washed-out love of which Christianity dreams. It is true, speaking absolutely, that the cosmos derives from a First Cause of which the races of men, unequal among themselves, are the essential manifestation. In one way, doubtless, knowledge of the divine principle of the cosmos is relative, not in the sense that the ways in which the different races manage to represent it to themselves would be of equal value, or would bear the question of their respective value being even raised, but in the sense that the loftiest way of representing it, that of the Nordic race, itself remains inevitably marked by a certain anthropomorphism, even in the philosophers.[1]

Such are the oscillations of National-Socialist philosophy with regard to the relative or absolute character of truth. In short, when it is desired to fight the intellectualist philosophies, with all their moral and political consequences, insistence is placed on the inevitably and legitimately relative nature of truth, specifying that the relativism in question is racial, since truth cannot present individual variants except within the limits of the racial norm.[2] And our authors go so far as to extend this racial relativism to all the sciences without exception, including the physical and mathematical sciences.[3] That done, and passing from the negative and polemical

---

[1] E. Krieck expressly points out the anthropomorphism of the representation of the cosmos as a universal Life. But he does so only to add immediately that this anthropomorphism is superior to that which consists, according to the cast of mind, in representing the Absolute to oneself as the constructor of a universal mechanism (*Völk.-pol. Anthr.*, Vol. I, p. 14). A. Rosenberg seems to adopt an analogous position (*Mythus*, pp. 222–4; see also 391, 398 n.).

[2] E. Krieck, *Völk.-pol. Anthr.*, Vol. I, p. 33; Vol. III, p. 126; A. Baümler, *Polit. und Erz.*, p. 101.

[3] E. Krieck, *Völk.-pol. Anthr.*, Vol. III, pp. 128–30.

Others are less absolute. Thus E. Bergmann professes racial relativism in metaphysics, ethics, and religion, but without extending it to the theory of knowledge, to logic, and to the sciences (*Nat. Geistl.*, p. 9). O. Dietrich also excludes from it the sciences (*Philos. Grundl. des Nationalsoz.*, p. 35) as well as the principle itself, which proclaims the racially relative character of the other fields (p. 25). Distinctions of this kind are obviously necessary. From omitting to make them, and from having treated things globally, National-Socialist philosophy often fell into confusion. E. Krieck does, indeed, claim to overcome the opposition between absolute truth and relative truth (*Völk.-pol. Anthr.*, Vol. I, p. 34), but without one's seeing exactly how. As for F. Böhm, he holds that the 'systems' may differ from the moment when they

task to the positive task of inculcating the *Weltanschauung*, they present this, fundamentally, as something absolutely valid *by right* in many of its aspects, its relative character consisting most often merely in being *in fact* perceptible only by the Nordic race, whether it be a matter of adequate representation or, as is the case in the purely metaphysical domain, of the highest form of representation humanly possible.[1]

The same oscillation is found again when, passing on to the relation of truth to time, the question of universal truths becomes more precisely the question of eternal truths. In the polemics against those who, in the name of the permanence of truth, would like to remain attached to ideologies which existed before National-Socialism, all idea of eternal verities is condemned energetically, and the 'historic' character of truth is asserted: not only has each race its truth, but the truth varies for it in the course of its history; every turning point of history has its own truth.[2] But to push this idea to its extreme would be to recognise that National-Socialism is a phase like the others in the long existence of the Nordic race. Now of course it is not at all a phase like the others, and the 'historic' truth enjoyed by the *Weltanschauung* which expresses and directs this phase is not just any 'historic' truth. Its 'historic' truth consists precisely in the fact that, at the present moment of history, the Nordic race, whose 'essence is eternal', has at last attained its own truth, which is in consequence eternal like it. This is, indeed, said with vehemence when, after the polemics, attention is devoted to the positive justification of the *Weltanschauung*.[3]

It is thus clear how, at the price of many confusions, the National-Socialist philosophy has it, at need, both ways—that of relative truth and that of absolute truth.

Before leaving the question of knowledge, let us list what may be

---

express, each in its own way, the immutable essence of the race (*Anti-Cartesianismus*, pp. 136–8)—which does not tell us, either, how far the nucleus of truth corresponding to that essence may be absolute or simply relative to the Nordic race.

[1] For H. Heyse there is only one metaphysics (*Idee und Existenz*, p. 341), but the Nordic race alone possesses the capacity to penetrate to it (p. 267).

[2] E. Bergmann, *Die Nat. Geistl.*, p. 6; F. Beck, *Kampf um die philos. des leb. Geistes*, pp. 27–8.

[3] The two poles of this oscillation—purely 'historical' and transitory truth, and 'eternal truth, eternal values', manifesting 'the eternal essence of the race'—are to be found in A. Rosenberg (*Mythus*, pp. 681, 689 and pp. 396, 636, 684 respectively), in H. Schwartz (*Zur philos. Grundl. des Nationalsoz.*, p. 14, on the one hand and, on the other, p. 7, where it is a question of the 'eternal meaning' perceived by the members of the people and of an 'experience of eternity' (*Ewigkeitserleben*) bearing on the values of the race), and in Fr. A. Beck (on the one hand *Idee und Wirklichkeit*, pp. 38 ff., and, on the other, *Kampf um die philos. des leb. Geistes*, p. 55).

On the eternal truth see also E. Krieck, *Völk.-pol. Anthr.*, Vol. I, p. 45; Vol. III, p. 28: there is truth, one and eternal, where there is life one and eternal—that is to say, in the racial community; O. Dietrich, *Philos. Grundl. des Nationalsoz.*, p. 37; H. Heyse, *Idee und Existenz*, p. 350; F. Böhm, *Anti-Cartesianismus*, p. 244.

called the fundamental 'categories' of National-Socialist philosophy, it being understood that these categories are, in its eyes, so many general aspects of Reality itself manifesting itself to intuition—to an intuition which is not, indeed, purely receptive, but active, and active in itself (not merely united to an active will).[1]

First there is 'becoming'—'active', 'dynamic' becoming, as opposed to the 'being' of rationalist thought; then there is 'continuity' and especially 'polarity' (the relation of reciprocal dependence in which there is radical penetration), as opposed to 'atomism', separation, juxtaposition, purely external relation; then 'totality'—'organic totality', a whole of which all the elements are united by highly penetrating relations of reciprocal dependence, as opposed to 'mechanism', a whole of which the elements are united by merely external relationships; the 'organic totality' is also 'life',[2] and within it there is diffused (through *Ausgliederung*) an active and indefinable principle of unity, a 'life' which animates it and penetrates it altogether;[3] there is membership (*Gliedschaft*), the integration of an element in a living totality; and finally, the reconciliation of contraries (*Aufhebung*) which is implied in any 'organic totality'.[4]

Now let us come to the idea of man, which has already been set forth in part in dealing with knowledge.

There is strong insistence on the very close unity prevailing between the human being's different elements—generally speaking between the physical and the psychic. And this idea is at once used to extend the idea of race to the whole of the individual. Thus Krieck, after having set forth how a man is a unique 'life' developing in those elements joined together 'polarwise'—the body, the soul, and the mind (a division taken from Goethe)—adds that the racial type marks all three of them indissolubly.[5] Race, the racial type, is the immanent law governing the development of the whole of the individual. This internal law—which the word 'blood' designates symbolically—makes individuals of the same ancestry members both of one and the same line of generations and of one and the same

---

[1] E. Krieck, *Völk.-pol. Anthr.*, Vol. I, pp. 28–9; Vol. III, p. 20.

[2] All 'Ganzheit' is 'Lebensganzheit', says E. Krieck, *Völk.-pol. Anthr.*, Vol. I, p. 10.

[3] E. Krieck often designates the principle of a 'totality' by the name '*entelechy*' (borrowed from Aristotle), which he sometimes gives as synonym for internal 'law' (ibid., Vol. II, p. 13).

[4] See especially the lists given by E. Krieck, *Völk.-pol. Anthr.*, Vol. I, p. 28; Vol. III, pp. 12, 73–4. (On 'polarity' see also A. Rosenberg, *Mythus*, pp. 125–6.)
In the lists in question, E. Krieck calls the idea mentioned last by us *coincidentia oppositorum*. In the course of his works one realises that what is meant is an overcoming of contraries by higher transposition, akin to the *Aufhebung* of Hegel and called by Krieck as well *Aufhebung*.

[5] *Nationalpol. Erziehung*, p. 24; *Völk.-pol. Anthr.*, Vol. I, pp. 3–4, 7, 9 (with an attempt at systematisation), *et al.*

community.[1] We are neither angel nor beast, writes A. Baümler for his part, nor some more or less fortunate mixture of the two. In man the aspect 'nature' and the aspect 'mind' are both of them specifically human. And it is this human whole, this ensemble of unconscious forces and tendencies, all of them essentially human, that is—likewise essentially—racial, similar in all men of common ancestry.[2] Thus race defines the concrete man, the only kind of man that exists; race is the *Urphänomenon*. It is the 'eternal essence' of which all individuals are the transitory and partial realisations.[3]

Among the functions of man, the undisputed primacy is given to the will. National-Socialist philosophy declares itself 'voluntarist'.[4] Fichte and sometimes Schopenhauer are invoked on this subject, but above all Nietzsche.[5] By the word 'will' is meant sometimes the faculty which makes decisions and dominates their execution, sometimes the strength of this faculty ('character'), sometimes the whole of the higher spontaneous tendencies and profound aspirations towards the values, as opposed to the mere instincts.[6] Between these tendencies towards the values—which are, of course, the values considered proper to the race: honour, liberty, discipline, courage, sacrifice—and the mere instincts, the faculty of decision is capable of choosing (free will).[7] Which amounts to saying that the will to decision is capable of either conforming to or resisting the deeper 'will'. But, it is added, inside the general domain of values itself, it is not capable of willing any but the values proper to the race. One of the philosophical aspects of the idea of race, it is pointed out, is precisely that of thus circumscribing the field open to the power of decision.[8] By this remark, National-Socialist philosophy evidently desires to deflect Nordic human beings (and those who, at need, are assimilated to the Nordic) from the pursuit of values foreign to the racial type (for instance, Christian charity or world peace), these being considered as psychologically impossible for Nordic people, while at the same time reassuring them by the implication that the values of their racial type are the higher values.[9]

[1] *Völk.-pol. Anthr.*, Vol. I, p. 74; *Grundl. Aufb. u. Wirtsch. des Nationalsoz. Staates*, Vol. IX, p. 11.
[2] *Bild. und Gem.*, pp. 64–5.
[3] A. Rosenberg, *Mythus*, p. 23.
On the question of a survival of the psychic element of man, the declarations of the National-Socialist philosophers are not in agreement, but the general tendency is markedly unfavourable to that belief; see *infra*.
[4] A. Baümler, *Bild. und Gem.*, pp. 188–9.
[5] Sometimes also J. Böhme, for instance, in H. A. Grunsky (professor at Munich), *Jakob Böhme als Schöpfer einer germanischen Philosophie des Willens* (Munich, 1940).
[6] See A. Rosenberg, *Mythus*, p. 343.
[7] ibid., p. 396, A. Baümler, *Bild. und Gem.*, pp. 62–5; E. Bergmann, *Natürl. Geistl.*, p. 218.
[8] A. Baümler, *Bild. und Gem.*, pp. 62–5; cf. A. Rosenberg, *Mythus*, p. 396.
[9] It would remain to be explained how it is that, in the course of their history, the Germans have often let themselves be carried away by foreign values, and in

At the point we have reached, we have been told concerning intuition that, joined to action in the midst of one's race brothers, and diving down into the history of the race, it leads the individual to perceive, deep down in himself and within his race brothers, the deep-seated will of the race, the aspiration to the values proper to the race.

All the National-Socialist philosophers are in agreement with Rosenberg in placing honour at the top of the Nordic scale of values, the other values being considered to emanate from honour (by *Ausgliederung*).[1] They have not shown themselves very anxious to describe with precision the relations between the various values in the scale.[2] We shall have occasion to return to these values in detail below.

But intuition has not finished yielding up to us its riches.

The individual who, as we have said, is a 'totality', is, however, a 'totality' only from a partial and subordinate point of view. In reality, man is a social, essentially a social, being, and not only in the sense of being social through one part or one aspect of his essence, but indeed through his whole essence. On this subject recourse is had not only to social psychology but, first of all and more profoundly, to metaphysical experience. This reveals that man is, in the deepest depths of his being, a member of society. O. Spann is here invoked (though with the important correction we shall mention in a moment).[3] But what sort of society, exactly, is meant? Society in general, indeterminately, even though one's accidental circumstances determine the group or groups of which one forms part?[4] Or else, more precisely, might the society already inscribed in the very essence of man mean the nation—but can this mean the nation considered in any fashion, including a national group in which the individual has been born by chance and which he might leave for

---

particular by the 'Judaic' aspects of Christianity: love, pity, humility, penitence. Might it be that the non-Nordic but still Aryan elements present in Germany in fairly considerable proportion have led, through a more or less widespread hybridisation, to a lowering of the German qualities? That is what is no doubt in the mind of, for instance, E. Krieck (*Völk.-pol. Anthr.*, p. 127); he mentions hybridisation without saying exactly what sort of hybridisation he means. Must one add a certain amount of hybridisation with Jewish elements? This we are not told. Or must it also be admitted that the Aryan elements, including the Nordic, have often, in the course of history, lacked intuition for the perception of the racial values and character for their pursuit. This hypothesis is not stated, and it would indeed not fit in well with those qualities which are attributed to the race. In any case it is apparent that the Christian aspect of German history constitutes a phenomenon embarrassing to our philosophers.

[1] A. Rosenberg, in *Grundl. Aufb. u. Wirtsch. des Nationalsoz. Staates*, Vol. I, p. 1.

[2] Essay on the systematisation of the values, in E. Krieck, *Völk.-pol. Anthr.*, Vol. II, pp. 46–7.

[3] A. Rosenberg, *Mythus*, pp. 695–6; O. Dietrich also mentions Auguste Comte (ibid.). W. Classen quotes certain statements of St Thomas Aquinas (*Thomist. Anthrop. in völk.-pol. Sicht*, pp. 39 ff.).

[4] As is the case in St Thomas Aquinas, according to W. Classen (ibid., pp. 36–7).

another? Or else, again, might it mean in the last analysis, as Spann thought, an all-embracing human society, humanity as a whole? Not at all. The society to which the essence of the individual refers itself, that of which he is member through the whole of himself, is his people, the people in the sense of a group of men of the same blood, having its own political and cultured history.[1] Whether he likes it or no, whether he behaves as the friend or enemy of his people, the individual is fundamentally and totally an element of his people. His people and he are in a relationship of 'polarity'. The individual is only a 'relative organic totality', which only exists subsumed under a higher 'organic totality'.[2] The popular community is that Whole which precedes and exceeds the individuals among which it is distributed (*sich ausgliedert*) and which emanate from it in everything they are—their body, their soul and their mind.[3] The people is the 'living substance',[4] the 'substantial life-unity',[5] 'the primary all-embracing Reality'.[6] Separated from his people, the individual has only a 'pseudo-existence'.[7]

In support of this 'organic' conception of national society, appeal is made to the Romantic thinkers, though with regret that they should have sought the unity of the people in the direction of 'mind' (cf. *Volksgeist*) and not fundamentally in that of race, and also that, despairing of ever seeing the people recover its native purity, they should have sunk into the nostalgia for the Golden Age.[8] Use is often made—sometimes with mention of Tonnies, who made it classic[9]—of the distinction between natural society, community (*Gemeinschaft*), and purely contractual and institutional society (*Gesellschaft*), making it clear, of course, that the true community has race for its basis.

As for humanity as a whole, that is an 'idea without essence'[10] which belongs only to the schematic intellect and can find no place in an 'organic' philosophy.[11] This notion is as artificial as the kindred

[1] If a nation composed of several races is in question, it in any case always includes one race which is biologically preponderant and which, for this reason, should have the preponderant influence (E. Kreick, *Völk.-pol. Anthr.*, Vol. I, p. 76; Vol. II, p. 21; *Grundl. Aufb. u. Wirtsch. des Nationalsoz. Staates*, Vol. IX, pp. 11–12; W. Stuckart, ibid., Vol. XV, p. 20). One thinks here of how the Nordic race is represented in Germany according to the National-Socialist *Rassenforschung*, in a proportion of more than 50 per cent.
[2] W. Classen, *Thomist. Anthrop. in völk.-pol. Sicht*, p. 44.
[3] ibid., pp. 38, 50; W. Stuckart, in *Grundl. Aufb. u. Wirtsch des Nationalsoz. Staates*, Vol. XV, p. 13.
[4] W. Stuckart, ibid., p. 15.
[5] W. Classen, *Thomist. Anthr. in völk.-pol. Sicht*, p. 50.
[6] W. Stuckart, in *Grundl. Aufb. u. Wirtsch. des Nationalsoz. Staates*, Vol. XV, p. 15.
[7] E. Krieck, *Völk.-pol. Anthr.*, Vol. I, pp. 44 ff.
[8] A. Rosenberg, *Mythus*, p. 140; F. Bhöm, *Anti-Cartesianismus*, p. 265.
[9] For example, O. Dietrich, *Philos. Grundl. des Nationalsoz.*, p. 19.
[10] Fr. A. Beck, *Kampf um die Philos. des leb. Geistes*, p. 34.
[11] A. Rosenberg, *Mythus*, p. 697.

notion of the individual as a reality in itself and an end in itself. Hence the humanitarianism patronised by Freemasonry (the idea of *universal* liberty, equality, and fraternity), and the *universal* love which the Roman Catholic theocracy desires to impose by converting the whole world to Christianity, and which international Marxism also, in its fashion, tries to enthrone, are so many forms of one and the same anti-natural and corrosive dream.[1] The same is true of the project of a 'world culture', of a 'world economy' and of a 'world peace'.[2] In reality, humanity is a thing 'devoid of structure',[3] a mere conglomeration of races competing for life, in a state of 'engagement' with one another in all fields.[4] In humanity, the supreme totality, the 'only real totality with an organic growth . . . that life knows', is the people.[5] Above the people there is only the telluric and cosmic totality (we shall deal with this below).

Such are the capital discoveries of intuition. But that is still not all. Along with his essence as member, intuition reveals to the individual his duty as member. The two are but one, since to be intrinsically and wholly a member is to be made in order to act only as a member. In other words, if the people is the only reality, it is in virtue of that, the only end.[6] Since the individual is, in the depths of his being, a member and moment of his people, it is by his people that, in the depths of his being, he is called. The true realisation of the person, the true quality of personality, thus consists in solely and integrally serving the people. There can be no such thing as 'private life'.[7] The authentic personality is 'personality as member'[8] (*Gliedpersönlichkeit*). In this way, National-Socialist philosophy places 'at the centre of German thought and German action the unity of race and personality'.[9] That is the only way, in its view, of surmounting (*aufheben*) the contradiction between individual and society.[10] If this is the true notion of moral personality, evil consists essentially in preferring the individual self to the popular community. This egoism, it is added, this capacity for separation, is like every break in the continuity of life, the price of the intellect.[11]

True personality is also true liberty. In fact, to obey the duty of

---

[1] A. Rosenberg, *Mythus*, pp. 21, 22, 161, 200, 201, 204, 321, 387, 495, 682, 698; E. Kreick, *Völk.-pol. Anthr.*, Vol. I, 2, p. 55.

[2] A. Rosenberg, Nuremberg Congress, 1938.

[3] idem, *Nationalsozialistische Monatshefte*, n. 105 (Oct. 1938), p. 851.

[4] idem, *Mythus*, p. 1.

[5] O. Dietrich, in *Grundl. Aufb. u. Wirtsch. des Nationalsoz. Staates*, Vol. II, p. 6.

[6] W. Stuckart, ibid., Vol. XV, p. 15.

[7] E. Krieck, in *Grundl. Aufb. u. Wirtsch. des Nationalsoz. Staates*, Vol. IX, p. 16: W. Stuckart, ibid., Vol. XV, p. 19.

[8] E. Krieck, *Völk.-pol. Anthr.*, Vol. II, p. 26.

[9] A. Baümler, *Bild. und Gem.*, p. 188.

[10] E. Krieck, *Völk.-pol. Anthr.*, Vol. I, p. 52; Vol. II, pp. 18–19.

[11] ibid., Vol. I, pp. 78–9; A. Rosenberg, *Mythus*, p. 137, which on this point refers back to L. Klages.

serving the community without reserve is for a man, as has been said above, to obey his deep self, his immanent law (and here appeal is made to Kant), which demands that he realise in himself the race type in the service of the race. That is what it is for the individual to obey himself, to be 'one with himself', to be free. This form of liberty is indeed accompanied by another, which consists in ridding oneself of the tyranny of selfish interests. And it leads, in addition, to that supreme liberty which there is in being member of a free people and assuring its liberty.[1]

Personality is a matter of degree: it is a function both of how far an individual places himself at the service of the people and of the quality of the services he renders it. This is proved in practice, and very clearly, in the leaders of the people in all domains—sciences, arts, organisation, etc.—but above all in the political leaders. The *Führer* is the first among personalities.[2]

The man who dedicates himself entirely to the race by being ready for the supreme sacrifice is the Hero. The true personality is the 'heroic personality'.[3] To discover in sacrifice the hidden and divine law of the world is a peculiar characteristic of the Nordic race.[4] And so it is to heroism that the *Weltanschauung* calls every Nordic man. It strains towards the 'heroic vital affirmation of the nation'. The *Weltanschauung* is a 'heroic *Weltanschauung*'.[5] It is in the appeal to heroism that A. Baümler sees the essence of Fichte's message,[6] and, still more, of Nietzsche's message.[7]

Being entirely integrated to the community by his being and his duty, the individual possesses no rights as man. The quality of man is an abstraction, there is no 'natural right'. Every right derives from the community, the individual has no rights except as a member. It is therefore only as such that the community owes him protection, and only with a view to its own good.[8]

The political state, with the *Führer* at its head, is not an end in

---

[1] On all this, see A. Rosenberg, *Mythus*, pp. 343, 396, 529–37, 697 (sketch of a systematisation of the race-people-personality relations); F. Böhm, *Anti-Cartesianismus*, pp. 206–19; W. Classen, *Thomist. Anthr. in völk.-pol. Sicht*, pp. 52–4; O. Dietrich, *Philos. Grundl. des Nationalsoz.*, pp. 30–1.

[2] E. Krieck, *Völk.-pol. Anthr.*, Vol. II, p. 35.

[3] A. Rosenberg, *Mythus*, p. 138, etc.

[4] H. Heyse, *Idee und Existenz*, pp. 306–7, 342.

[5] O. Dietrich, in *Grundl. Aufb. u. Wirtsch. des Nationalsoz. Staates*, p. 2.

[6] A. Baümler, *Bild. und Gem.*, p. 190.

[7] idem, *Stud. zur deutschen Geistesgesch.*, pp. 235–7. The key to Nietzsche's thought, that heritage from the Greeks, is not the Dionysic spirit, but the heroic spirit (ibid.).

[8] O. Dietrich, *Philos. Grundl. des Nationalsoz.*, p. 21. Dietrich here quotes with warm approval a passage from P. Krannhals: 'The individual as such has neither the right nor the duty to exist, for every right and every duty derives in the first place from the community' (*Das organische Weltbild*, 1928); E. Krieck, *Völk.-pol. Anthr.*, Vol. II, p. 37; W. Stuckart, in *Grundl. Aufb. u. Wirtsch. des Nationalsoz. Staates*, Vol. XV, pp. 19, 20.

itself but, according to the formula taken from Adolf Hitler, a 'means' to the service of the popular community.[1] E. Krieck, who, in the field of life, abominates the expression 'means' (to which he gives only the meaning of means extrinsic to end, a mechanistic category),[2] prefers to speak here of a relation of 'polarity' between the state and the people (he means, no doubt, reciprocal purpose and reciprocal causality).[3]

This function of the state is, precisely, the basis of the state's absolute authority. Exercised by a political state taking itself as an end, absolute authority would be despotism, but a state placed at the service of the community as the absolute end of individuals possesses, by this very fact, in virtue of a 'law of life',[4] a power without reserve in all fields. The state will therefore be 'totalitarian'. To be precise: since the individual emanates from the community in all that he is—his body, his soul, and his mind—the state has full power over the individual in his body, his soul, and his mind,[5] in order to shape him wholly as a member of the community and place him wholly at the service of the community.

The *Führer* is 'also a member of the community'. He is the 'purest and strongest human embodiment of the community'. He leads it because it is what expresses itself in him. And 'he is not irresponsible towards it'. *Führer* and community are thus in a 'polar' relationship. Hence the *Führer* directs the community 'not with the aid of external means of compulsion, but by his power of persuasion'.[6]

The Party is composed of the '*Weltanschauliche élite*',[7] that is to say, all those who wish to realise fully in themselves the *Weltanschauung* of the dominant race and to model the community upon it in accordance with the views of the *Führer*. In the Party the *Führer* is linked with the members by the companionship relation (*Gefolgschaft*), which implies that the will of the companions is embodied and takes form in the leader and binds itself spontaneously to him through loyalty. Companionship achieves a unique union (*Aufhebung*) of the democratic principle and the aristocratic principle.[8]

This idea of 'companionship' is extended to the relations between the *Führer* and the whole of the people. From which it follows that the political régime of the nation considered as a whole realises the unique union of democracy and authority just mentioned.[9]

[1] W. Classen, *Thomist. Anthr. in völk.-pol. Sicht*, pp. 45–6; W. Stuckart, in *Grundl. Aufb. u. Wirtsch. des Nationalsoz. Staates*, Vol. XV, p. 18; O. Köllreutter, ibid., Vol. XVIII, p. 5. Reference is made to *Mein Kampf* (281–5th Imp., Munich, 1938), pp. 433 *et al.*
[2] E. Krieck, *Völk.-pol. Anthr.*, Vol. I, p. 15.   [3] ibid., pp. 98–9.
[4] W. Classen, *Thomist. Anthr. in völk.-pol. Sicht*, p. 46.   [5] ibid., pp. 46–9.
[6] W. Stuckart, in *Grundl. Aufb. u. Wirtsch. des Nationalsoz. Staates*, Vol. XV, p. 29.
[7] ibid., p. 16.   [8] E. Krieck, ibid., Vol. IX, p. 9 *et al.*
[9] W. Stuckart, in *Grundl. Aufb. u. Wirtsch. des Nationalsoz. Staates*, Vol. XV, p. 29; O. Köllreutter, ibid., Vol. XVIII, p. 29.

Once the will of the race has been grasped by intuition, together with the community as reality and 'all-embracing' end, it is evident that all forms of culture—arts, sciences, religion—must set themselves to express the racial community to itself, and to contribute, each in its fashion, as simple 'means' to its conservation and to its growth.[1] Science for science's sake, art for art's sake, speculation for its own sake and private religion are revealed as aberrations.[2] This is confirmed by the feeling of emptiness they leave behind them.[3] This being the case, 'soldierly-heroic' aspirations and way of life should find their response in a 'soldierly-heroic' poetry, music and art.[4] Science and philosophy must be 'militant'.[5] (And here we have the justification, on the basis of the primary intuitions, of the function National-Socialist philosophy has attributed to itself.) All the education given to the young should be inspired by these principles.[6] And the state must watch over the whole of the national culture and the whole of the national education. It is called a *Weltanschauungsstaat*,[7] not only because it takes its inspiration from a *Weltanschauung*, but also because, in exchange, it must constitute itself its guardian.

Between the race and the soil, more particularly the landscape and, above all, the Germanic forest, E. Krieck sees a deep-seated 'polarity' relationship. Through this the race attaches itself indeed to an organic totality greater than itself: the earth, mother earth, living and sacred.[8] It in its turn is subsumed under the universal organic Totality, the living and divine Cosmos, life as a whole. Intuition is what unveils these different living unities together with their living framework, the whole hierarchy of 'entelechies' which rises from individuals—in the animal, and vegetable worlds as in the human—up to the universal 'entelechy' which embraces them all.[9]

In this way, 'all is life'.[10] 'Life is the beginning, the middle and the end of everything.' It is the *Urphänomenon*.[11] The mechanical aspect of the universe, which is studied by the experimental sciences, is real, but partial and subordinate; it must be regarded as embraced, as integrated (*aufgehoben*) in the general life.[11]

[1] A. Rosenberg, *Mythus*, pp. 343–4 (with an attempt at arranging in a system the various elements of culture), 684, 688; *Blut und Ehre*, p. 203: 'Mittel'.
[2] F. Böhm, *Anti-Cartesianismus*, pp. 8, 10, 140–1. [3] ibid., p. 242.
[4] E. Krieck, in *Grundl. Aufb. u. Wirtsch. des Nationalsoz. Staates*, Vol. IX, p. 13.
[5] ibid., p. 18.
[6] Here appeal is made to Plato's *Republic*, with an attempt to bring it back into esteem (ibid., p. 23).
[7] W. Stuckart, in *Grundl. Aufb. u. Wirtsch. des Nationalsoz. Staates*, Vol. XV, p. 18.
[8] E. Krieck, *Völk.-pol. Anthr.*, Vol. I, pp. 24, 77 ff.
[9] ibid., Vol. I, pp. 28–9. On individual organisms E. Krieck points out that the existence in them of a principle of living unity should not be demonstrated by rational procedures in the manner of H. Driesch, but rather perceived by intuition (ibid., Vol. I, pp. 11, 28). [10] ibid., Vol. I, p. 26. [11] ibid., Vol. I, p. 19.

Thus we come to metaphysics in the strictest sense and to the philosophy of religion.

All the National-Socialist philosophers admit one single, supra-sensible source of the universe, of life, of races and individuals. They also all call this universal source 'God'. To our knowledge it is no-where affirmed by them that this 'God' is conscious and personal. On the contrary, its unconscious nature is sometimes to be found clearly asserted.[1] The impression, on the whole, is that National-Socialist philosophy hesitates, on this point, between agnosticism[2] and pure and simple denial. In any case there is unanimity in pre-senting 'God' not as a 'Being', but as a 'Becoming' (for all is be-coming), as a 'Life', one and mysterious, developing by itself naturally in the form of universal life and animating this from within.[3] This conception is upheld energetically against the idea of a God creating the world out of nothing. The idea of creation im-plies an artificial opposition both between being and nothing[4] and between mind and nature, or matter;[5] it also constitutes an ille-gitimate extension of the category of causality to the relations be-tween the Absolute and the world; and is in the last analysis only a survival of magic conceptions which made their appearance in primitive Asia.[6] In reality, the Absolute and the cosmos imply each other, they are in a 'polar' relation—such is the Nordic conception of things.[7] Similarly the Nordic mind goes beyond and reconciles being and not-being in the experience and idea of becoming.[8] The idea of becoming is indeed also the only one that brings together 'mind' and 'matter' by making them appear as two forms taken by

[1] E. Bergmann, Natürl. Geistl., p. 305.

[2] See for instance, E. Krieck, Völk.-pol. Anthr., Vol. I, p. 206; A. Rosenberg, Mythus, pp. 222–4. Rosenberg allows that the Absolute may be referred to as 'Father', but this by a highly symbolical kind of expression (ibid., pp. 391, 398 n.), and he does not specify how far, actually, the symbolism goes.

[3] For the idea that God is 'Becoming', see A. Rosenberg, Mythus, p. 689, cf. p. 134; E. Krieck, Völk.-pol. Anthr., Vol. I, pp. 19, 38–9; Leben, pp. 39, 168; H. Schwartz, Nationalsoz. Weltansch., p. 12.

When the unconscious nature of God is clearly stated, it is held that the 'un-conscious God', 'God-Nature', becomes 'conscious God', 'God-Mind', in man. (Thus E. Bergmann, Die 25 Thesen des Deutschen Religion (Breslau, 1942), p. 84.) Man is thus, in the strongest sense of the expression, the 'birthplace of God' (idem, Natuerl. Geistl., p. 152). More explicitly still: 'Man is really and truly God' (idem, Die Deutsche Nationalkirche (Breslau, 1934), p. 112). An analogous idea is found in H. Schwartz, according to whom the soul can offer unconscious God the possibility of 'becoming himself in it' (Nationalsoz. Weltansch., p. 7).

For the idea that the Divinity is 'life', see also A. Rosenberg, Mythus, p. 689; H. Schwartz, Nationalsoz. Weltansch., p. 111; H. Heyse, Idee und Existenz, pp. 352–3.

[4] E. Krieck, Völk.-pol. Anthr., Vol. I, pp. 38–9.

[5] A. Baümler, Bild. und Gem., pp. 88–9.

[6] A. Rosenberg, Mythus, pp. 248–50, 395–6; cf. E. Bergmann, Natuerl. Geistl., p. 152; H. Härtle, in Nationalsoz. Montathefte (Aug. 1938), p. 693.

[7] A. Rosenberg, Mythus, p. 231.

[8] E. Krieck, Völk.-pol. Anthr., Vol. I, pp. 38–9.

one and the same growing 'Life'.[1] And therefore, in reality, 'God' and the universe form a single and supreme 'organic totality', the 'universal Life' (*All-Leben*).[2]

Agreement is also general among the National-Socialist philosophers to allow that from the divine ground of things, the principle of races and of their members, there emanates a mysterious destiny for the races and for each of their members. This destiny is neither a plan ready-made in advance and to be realised without a setback, nor a merciful Providence, nor—either—a crushing and senseless fate. It is a 'call' (*Anruf*), a 'vocation' (*Berufung*), a 'demand' (*Forderung*) which, rising from the divine ground of things, invites peoples and individuals to a great task defined only in its main lines, and leads them to it while leaving them a wide margin for initiative and responsibility.[3] Destiny is the eternal essence of the people, facing towards time, towards history or, concretely, towards the present, to which it gives as law: 'the future at all costs!'[4] To each 'chosen' people 'God' proclaims by the voice of its leaders: 'We are the elect, in us a destiny accomplishes itself'. This is what is happening in the present German Revolution, in which the German people perceives the vocation of which the *Führer* is the 'bearer'.[5] In this way the course of history—for the people that is 'called' and for the other peoples [6]—is suspended between the divine call and the response of man.[7] In the *Führer* this response is inseparably

---

[1] A. Baümler, *Bild. und Gem.*, pp. 88–9. Fichte is the first philosopher to have 'dynamised' the idea of the universe. But if in so doing he gave a new meaning to the mind–matter opposition, he nonetheless failed to surmount it really. It is necessary to wait for Nietzsche to see all life appear at last as the forms of one and the same Life (ibid., pp. 191, 196).

[2] E. Krieck, *Völk.-pol. Anthr.*, Vol. I, pp. 28–9.

[3] A. Rosenberg, *Mythus*, pp. 395–404; E. Krieck, *Leben*, p. 206; *Völk.-pol. Anthr.*, Vol. I, pp. 58–9; 'Das Schicksal' in *Volk im Werden*, Vol. VII (June 1937), pp. 265–71; F. Böhm, *Anti-Cartesianismus*, pp. 277–82; H. Heyse, *Idee und Existenz*, pp. 252, 292, 352.

[4] F. Böhm, *Anti-Cartesianismus*, pp. 266–7, 264. The idea of destiny, Krieck notes, is 'irrational'. Up to the present the intellect has not yet succeeded in rendering into its language a satisfying expression of the eternal destiny and its relation with time ('Das Schicksal', art. cit., p. 263). A. Rosenberg makes the same remark (*Mythus*, pp. 395–7). There is to be found here once more, notes Rosenberg, a replica of the theological problem of the reconciliation of Predestination with freedom (ibid.).

[5] E. Krieck, *Völk.-pol. Anthr.*, Vol. I, p. 60.

[6] ibid., p. 82. Krieck does not here specify the incidence of the destiny of the people on the fate of other peoples. Elsewhere he writes that the German people must serve as model to the other peoples (ibid., Vol. II, p. 10). On the whole, explicit mention of the other peoples makes its appearance very rarely, but the allusions to the 'living space' and the continual call to heroism, sacrifice, combat in all fields, are not exactly reassuring. The word '*Kampf*' occurs—and this is the case with all the National-Socialist philosophers—like an obsession. E. Krieck is on occasion more definite: '*Kampf um die Hegemonie*' by political, economic, and cultural means (*Leben*, p. 190). And Rosenberg invites the National-Socialists to be the 'bearers of a *Weltanschauung* of combat' in *Grundl. Aufb. u. Wirtsch. des Nationalsoz. Staates*, Vol. I, p. 1.   [7] ibid., p. 87.

a religious decision and a political decision,[1] a political leadership rooted in a religious act of will grounded in destiny.[2] This is the basis of the primacy, in the people, of the political element over all the rest—economy, art, science, education, and culture.[3]

Religion consists, for every member of the people, in perceiving the destiny, the call, and responding to it. It is indeed in so far as one responds practically to the call that one perceives it truly and experiences the divine source from which it emanates—with, as counter-proof, the feeling of emptiness left by disloyalty.[4] It is thus, and thus only, that one can know 'God', for it is impossible to know him 'as he is in himself'.[5] 'God can grasp us, we cannot grasp him or understand him.'[6] The call of destiny is the only divine 'revelation'.[7]

By reason of his closeness to the destiny the *Führer* is, through his personal religious feeling, the norm of the religious feeling of the people.[8]

Without insisting on the possibility, for the people, of a complete disloyalty to the destiny, and therefore of a decisive setback, stress is sometimes laid on the possibility of individual disloyalty, following on a powerful inclination towards evil, towards selfishness, contrary to the life of the race. This is the 'original evil' (*Urböse*), the 'hereditary sin' (*Erbschuld*), the '*Schweinshund*' present in all men, including the Germans.[9]

Religious experience takes on a more solid content in the writings of those who, like Rosenberg, allow the individual soul a certain form of eternity. According to the author of the *Myth*, each soul, in its depths, is at the same time unique in its kind (*Leibniz*)[10] and situated beyond space, time, and causality, beyond the 'world as representation'.[11] What is more, each soul is with 'God' in a relation of 'polarity'[12] such that without it, without its peculiar originality and its eternity, God would not be God and that, in addition, the soul is not merely like God but equal to him.[13]

---

[1] E. Krieck, *Völk.-pol. Anthr.*, Vol. I, p. 76.   [2] ibid., p. 57.
[3] ibid., pp. 57, 87.   [4] ibid., p. 58.   [5] ibid., p. 57.   [6] ibid., p. 67.
[7] ibid., pp. 63–7. 'He who has never reached an activity full of decision', writes F. Böhm for his part, 'does not know, either, that God exists' (*Anti-Cartesianismus*, p. 277). The will to obey destiny is 'in polar tension with the primitive Reality of the mythic forces' (ibid., p. 279). (The author calls the deep-seated Will 'mythic forces'.)
[8] ibid., Vol. I, pp. 232–3. The *Führer's* religion, with the views on the world, man, and history which it implies, 'is not a norm for us because he is the political Chief, but because the things he knows, springing from his mission, contain the most profound truth, the greatest power of shaping things and the greatest amplitude. Here, he does not command, but understands and persuades. In that is revealed his vocation, which no-one shares with him' (E. Krieck, *Völk.-pol. Anthr.*, Vol. II, p. 15, n. 1).
[9] ibid., Vol. I, pp. 102–5.   [10] *Mythus*, pp. 389, 689, 692.
[11] ibid., pp. 218, 222, 223–4, 388–92.   [12] ibid., p. 248.
[13] ibid., pp. 232–3. What exactly is 'God' for A. Rosenberg? By the idea of 'God' religion represents to itself positively what philosophy defines by the purely

The immortality of the soul is a Nordic idea which, mysterious though it is, must be admitted ·because of its fruitfulness and also, subordinately, because it answers to an intrinsic finality in man.[1] Equality with God is also an essential theme of Nordic religious feeling.[2] In this religious feeling the 'nobility' of a soul is self-sufficient and is seen as what is highest; this is the deepest metaphysical root of the idea of honour, a value which subordinates itself to no other. Hence the soul, equal to God, does good without any reference to God and in complete disengagement from everything.[3] Such is, in religion, the 'aristocratic ideal' of the Nordic race.[4]

Rosenberg holds that one can have a certain profound experience of transcendence from the bottom of the soul in relation to the 'world as representation', as well as to the equality of the soul with God.[5] But this experience of the centre of the soul united to God is not obtained by withdrawal from the world and from action; on the contrary, in Nordic religious feeling it is precisely by turning towards action that the soul enters into communion with God. It is in combat, victory, and mastery over the world.[6] Concretely speaking, this means the combat and victory of the race. Hence that statement with which the *Myth* ends: 'the God we honour would not exist if our soul and our blood did not exist'.[7] From all of which it follows that to defend the 'new faith', the 'myth of the blood', is to defend 'with the blood, too, the divine essence of mankind as a whole'. According to this faith, which incorporates itself in the clearest knowledge, 'the Nordic blood represents that mystery which has replaced and overcome the ancient sacraments'.[8]

---

negative, limitative idea of 'thing in itself' (p. 224). When the soul desires to become conscious of the depths of its being, it realises that a certain zone escapes it. Into this non-representable beyond it projects a content similar to that of the zone which is perceived (p. 222). We suppose Rosenberg means that into this indefinable Reality we project the will to honour, to liberty, etc., which reveals itself in those depths of the soul which are accessible to ordinary consciousness.

[1] *Mythus*, pp. 389 (cf. p. 394), 692. But on the exact nature of the eternity of the soul, all vain speculation must be set aside (p. 611).
[2] ibid., p. 246.   [3] ibid., p. 238–9.
[4] ibid., p. 252.   [5] ibid., pp. 223–4, 248, 389, 391.
[6] ibid., pp. 229–31, 262–3 (an analogous remark occurs in E. Krieck, *Völk.-pol. Anthr.*, Vol. III, p. 79).   [7] ibid., p. 701.
A. Rosenberg believes he finds the type of religious feeling just described (with, as regards the blood, at least one very clear allusion) in Meister Eckart, whom he calls the 'creator of a religion, our religion' (*Mythus*, p. 239) and whom he hopes to see become the inspirer of the German religion of the future (pp. 259, 611). Following Rosenberg, all the National-Socialist philosophers accord great authority to Meister Eckart, who is viewed as a religious genius (see for instance A. Baümler, *Politik und Erziehung*, pp. 18–19; *Bild. und Gem.*, p. 18; H. Schwartz, *Nationalsoz. Weltansch.*, pp. 13 ff.).
In reality the recension given by Rosenberg to Meister Eckart's thought is based on questionable texts erratically interpreted (see, on this subject, 'Zum Eckart-Problem' in *Kirchlicher Anzeiger für die Erzdiocese Köln* (October 1934), pp. 95–126).
[8] ibid., p. 114.

According to others, such as E. Krieck, the individual as individual disappears entirely at death. After having given himself to his race, he returns to mother earth, the living and divine, from which he had issued. "From earth art thou taken, and to earth thou shalt return. The individual life has its origin and its end in the people, and the people has its roots in the earth through the blood and through the soil; the earth is the unity and totality of the life of the terrestrial globe, the earth is life, life's source, the mother of its creatures. . . .' [1] To become earth once more is not exactly to die. 'There exists nothing dead in itself. . . . Death is in its nature the same as birth: the one is the positive pole, the other the negative pole of one and the same change in the form of life.' [2]

In general the National-Socialist philosophers expressly aspire to see a specifically German religion arise, with its own system of symbolic beliefs and its own rites.[3] While waiting, they subject tradition and Christianity to a radical purge, and to transpositions [4] aimed at making it conform to the type of religious feeling we have just described.

To A. Rosenberg the true predestination is the destiny of the people and of each of its members,[5] the genuine redemption is the sacrifice of the heroes who have shed their blood for the people, especially the two million dead of the 1914–18 war.[6] And so on. The true shape of Jesus was 'Nordic': that of a powerful preacher, driving out the money-changers from the Temple, and training the people.[7]

According to E. Krieck, 'the people—in the unity of nature and mind—is the son of God; this son of God is the Way, the Truth, and the Life, it is the vine of which we are the branches; with the birth of each one of us members of the people is repeated the rebirth of eternal life from the common ground of life; in the popular community and the chosen members of the people, God the Son is born anew ceaselessly; the people is, for each of us, the common treasure of life and of grace from which each one lives and comes to redemption; God dies in us when with our ego we desert the community and fall into separation and sin.' [8] Such is the creed of the 'renewed' [9] Christianity.

The racial community thus takes the shape of a religious com-

[1] E. Krieck, *Völk.-pol. Anthr.*, Vol. I, p. 81.   [2] ibid., p. 23.
[3] Some, like Bergmann, try to trace the features of the future religion.
[4] '*Nicht radikal abreissen, sondern radikal umbilden*' (E. Krieck, ibid., p. 68).
[5] *Mythus*, pp. 395 ff.   [6] ibid., pp. 698–701.   [7] ibid., p. 604.
[8] E. Krieck, *Völk.-pol. Anthr.*, Vol. I, p. 68.
[9] ibid., Vol. I, 69.
There is to be found no attempt at a reconciling, an *Aufhebung*, of the values thought of as Nordic and the specifically Christian values. These latter, considered as 'judaic', are categorically eliminated. Such is the imperative given by the primary intuitions and the deep-seated will.

munity, a Church, and the Reich appears as the real Kingdom of God. Hence this form of Lord's Prayer:

> *Dein Reiche komme,*
> *dein Wille geschehe.*
> *Und erlöse uns vom Übel,*
> *damit wir werden,*
> *wozu wir berufen sind.'* [1]

A thought of the vitalist type (tinged in some way by existentialism) and taking a racial, mystical, and imperialist form: such, then, is the shape which National-Socialist philosophy gave itself in the service of the National-Socialist Revolution. Along with a *Rassenforschung* of dubious quality, this philosophy has recourse to a certain number of general philosophical ideas, sometimes sound, picked up here and there [2] and, more often than not, reproduced in a summary form, as well as to a muddy naturalistic mysticism—all this with a view to expressing and keeping up, in drunken orgies of abstract terms, an intense and deplorably concrete offensive of pride.

In short, this philosophy, and above all that of E. Krieck and his group, appears as a sort of violent abortion of Bergsonism. A Bergsonism that has portioned out the *élan vital* for ever among races spinning round upon themselves; that has stopped dead at the 'closed morality'; and caught the 'echo', not of St John of the Cross and of the Christ of the Gospels, but of a falsified Meister Eckart and of a caricatured Jesus; making the life-force out to be derived not from a God of love and generosity calling men to generosity, but from a God of battles driving the chosen race to the honour of hegemony by force. A Bergsonism, what is more, as summary as it is dictatorial, the Bergsonism of autocracy and imperialism—a 'soldierly' Bergsonism which ran great risks of becoming, for the universities and the intellectual youth, a police Bergsonism.

All this as the result of a frantic refusal of the indispensable *Aufhebungen* as well as of the true 'Totalities', which are *universal*.

---

[1] A prayer which E. Krieck allowed to be printed in his review *Volk im Werden*, Vol. VII (April 1939), p. 148.

[2] And sometimes from the works of the philosophers who are out of favour and who are made use of without being mentioned, such as Hegel and, doubtless, Husserl, who was a Jew, and Bergson, likewise a Jew.

21

NATIONAL-SOCIALIST AND FASCIST PROPAGANDA FOR THE CONQUEST OF POWER

Henry M. Pachter

I. PROPAGANDA AND VIOLENCE

TOTALITARIAN[1] propaganda is a form of violence. To the faithful it promises a share in the exercise of power. The bewildered, the wavering, and the hesitant it browbeats to induce them to join in the pleasures of 'conquest'. The recalcitrant it warns not to obstruct the 'wave of the future'. Enemies it threatens with 'annihilation'. Its argument is imposition; its counter-argument, intimidation.

'The masses do not understand unless they are made aware of their master. The cruder and more brutal your language, the larger the crowd who will be ready to listen to you.'—Hitler.

Hitler's method was not persuasion; nor, incidentally, was it deception, as so many of his adversaries have charged. His aim was to subject the audience to his will—to do violence to their minds.

'It is wonderful to exert power over guns. But it is still more wonderful to exert power over the hearts and minds of men.' —Goebbels.

What in this confession seems to be a figurative use of the word 'power' has, if taken literally, a sinister meaning. The Nazi specialist of propaganda understood that it was his business to wield power and to conquer. When he boasted that 'propaganda made the Third Reich', he hardly thought of well-phrased arguments, but remembered the beer-hall battles in which he 'conquered Berlin'. For example, he and his storm troopers would go to a meeting of the 'Red Veterans' League' in Wedding, the most outspokenly Communist suburb, and break it up with clubs and a judicious use of panic. On the following day, Goebbels gleefully reports in his account of his stewardship, applications for membership began to swamp his office.

Communist militia-men frequently went over to the Nazis after their Party decided to avoid armed encounters. Republican defence-squad leaders always complained that the loyalist press gave too little publicity to the heroic resistance which they organised.

[1] The term is used here to cover both Nazis and Fascists.

Hitler, on the contrary, openly sanctioned the terror which his troopers exercised in the streets, and in court he proudly declared that he 'stood by the boys' who had perpetrated cold-blooded murder in the village of Potempa. The assassins of the German statesmen Rathenau and Erzberger were glorified as heroes by the Nazi movement.

'Individual terror', abhorred by Marxism, was sanctioned by the Fascists—provided, of course, that no risk was involved. 'Punitive expeditions' must always be successful to be good propaganda. The Fascist Party and its shock troops, the *Squadri d'Assalto* or *Arditti* ('the keen ones'), trembled when workers occupied factories in northern Italy. But as soon as that movement broke down (for reasons that will not be discussed here), the Fascists organised their rise to power through systematic terrorism. The famous 'March on Rome' could hardly have taken place—much less succeeded—had the military been willing to oppose it; but it was excellent propaganda in the Fascist sense. And terror propaganda reached its apex when Mussolini assumed responsibility for the murder of his widely respected antagonist, the member of Parliament, Matteotti. Then the Aventinian coalition collapsed.

Terror and propaganda not only alternate in the fascist method of conquering power. Terror, for them, is propaganda at its highest pitch. The Nazi professor of political science, Eugen Hadamovsky, candidly disclosed the essence of psychological civil warfare in his book *Propaganda und Nationale Macht*.

'The ordinary person, and even more so the masses, infallibly succumb to the power of the spoken word, no matter whether it is true or false. Propaganda, if applied with the proper tactics, will influence the human will; hence it is more thorough, deeper, and more powerful than the open force of suppression.

'However, propaganda and violence are never absolutely opposed to each other. The use of force can be part of propaganda. Between them lie different grades of influence that can be exerted on the masses—sudden excitement, attention, friendly persuasion of individuals and incessant mass propaganda [a precious differentiation!—H.P.]; from loose organisation of devoted people to the cause, to the creation of semi-official institutions; from individual terror to mass terror; from the authorised use of force by the stronger to the military enforcement of obedience and discipline through the death penalty.

'The most effective form of mass demonstration is the visible exhibition of power; the numbers, the size of the meeting and the display of power through weapons, uniforms, military organisation etc. . . .' [1]

[1] Quoted in *The Axis Grand Stategy* (Farrar & Rinehardt, New York, 1942), from Hadamovsky, *Propaganda und Nationale Macht* (Stalling, Oldenburg, 1934) abbreviated version.

II. The 'Crowd'

Hadamovsky belonged to that circle of German army psychologists who, in the First World War, developed the concept and practice of *Menschenführung*—the leadership of men. When they sent Hitler to preach against the Republic, they gave him their manual as a guide, and in *Mein Kampf* he expounded their theories which originally applied to the subjection of recruits to command.

The Nazi mass meeting imitated the conditions of army discipline, placing people under the spell of its power display. Insignia and flags, brass bands marching in front of armed formations, men in uniform, the Party anthem intoned *unisono*—all was designed to impress and over-awe the onlooker, or rather to make him into a participant. Other movements that have used similar devices did so to provide the public with a spectacle; for the Nazis the pageant is the movement itself, with the theatrical devices integrated into the performance of a ritual which expresses its spirit.

In the Nazi meeting the speaker is a 'drummer', not an advocate. He marches in front of the audience; he does not confront them. He does not plead and argue; rather, his speech is a mock performance of the fight into which he is going to lead them. The oration is not a discourse, open to debate; it is a ceremony of exorcising the enemy before giving battle—one is tempted to say: a propitiatory rite. It culminates in another ritual, the mass chorus vowing obedience to the Leader: 'Command, *Führer*, we shall follow thee', or, '*Duce*, at your bidding we shall attack', with the hands extended toward the leader in the Roman salute, symbolising surrender to his will.

After that, a question period would naturally be an anticlimax. Debate is definitely discouraged; even the occasional heckler, whom a democratic speaker would welcome as a counterfoil, is ruthlessly silenced by the SA. The very idea that anybody can debate with the Leader is vicious. Hitler spoke sarcastically of the 'philistine' speakers who enjoy criticism. Successful propagandists, he insisted, do not argue: they manipulate or command.[1] They deliberately cater to the submissive traits in human nature and may, on occasion, go out of their way to tell the crowd how much they despise it and how low they rate its intelligence.

In the mass meeting the speaker has authority over the crowd, and conditions for manipulation are ideal. The audience is inert, inarticulate, and shapeless, abandoned to the superior will-power of anyone who has the courage to mould it into his image. It is swayed

[1] cf. *Mein Kampf*, pp. 531–2, 548–9.

by hope and fear, easy to lead and to deceive, ready to be whipped into frenzy and shape; moreover, it tends to forget the natural bonds of family, class, religion; business interests and other social determinants, which under ordinary conditions keep the critical abilities on the alert, are relegated below the threshold of consciousness.

'The mass meeting is necessary, if only for the reason that in it the individual who, by adhering to a new (small) movement feels isolated and is easily seized with the fear of being alone, receives for the first time the picture of a greater community, something that has a strengthening and encouraging effect on most people. . . . If he steps for the first time out of his small workshop or out of the big enterprise in which he feels pretty small into the mass meeting and is now surrounded by thousands and thousands of people with a like conviction—he himself succumbs to the magic influence of what we call mass suggestion.' [1]

The 'magic' which Hitler praises is the technique of severing each individual from the covenant of civilisation and of reducing all collectively to the dehumanised status of the herd, ready to follow the primitive tribal instincts which, psychologists assert, emerge when the bars of personal integrity are lowered and the ties of social responsibility are loosened.

The German army psychologists who were Hitler's tutors found this theory in the writings of Gustave LeBon, a Frenchman who had undertaken to 'debunk' the propaganda success of labour and other democratic mass movements. Mussolini, too, was familiar with LeBon's analysis of 'crowd psychology', and he deliberately used the methods which his teacher said the Social Democrats were using by instinct.

LeBon's bias is too obvious to deserve discussion here. He gave the name of inarticulate 'crowd' to the socially articulate, democratically organised group or class which, at the end of the nineteenth century, was striving for recognition of its interests. He chose to misinterpret their show of strength, originally intended to impress the authorities with the groups' power and to extort concessions from them, as if this had been a method of obfuscating the minds of the demonstrators. Hitler took this *quid pro quo* at its face value; he never used the mass meeting as an instrument of policy, but he found it propitious in creating a mental state of exaltation and of low critical resistance in which suggestion may result in submission. Contemptuously he called the crowd 'feminine', and he lusted after subduing it.

'If I approach the masses with reasoned arguments, they will not understand me. But if I awaken in them the appropriate emotions,

[1] *Mein Kampf*, pp. 535–6.

then they will follow the simple slogans I give them. In the mass
meeting, the reasoning power is paralysed. . . . The larger the
crowd, and the more there is a mingling of different kinds of
people, such as farmers, workers, and public employees, the sooner
will the typical character of the "crowd" become apparent. Never
try to speak to meetings of the intelligentsia, or to trade associations.
Whatever you may be able to teach them by reasoned enlight-
ment will be eradicated the next day by opposite information.
But whatever you tell a crowd when it is in that receptive state of
fanatical abandonment, that will remain like an order given
under hypnosis; it is ineradicable and will withstand any reasoned
argument.' [1]

Hitler gave much thought to the means of creating this 'crowd
mentality'. He went into such details as the advantage of calling a
mass meeting in the late hours of the evening rather than in day-
time, because resistance is lowered when people are tired after a
day's work, or because the night is traditionally the time for spiritual
experiences. (Mussolini, for the same reasons, would often call
meetings with high party functionaries at midnight, or even in the
small hours of the morning.) Hitler advised his propagandists to
avoid close reasoning, which invites questions and sharpens the
wit; instead, he preferred to talk in images and symbols. Of particular interest is his shrewd remark about special interests. His
adversaries have often wondered how he managed to reconcile
rural and urban crowds, employers and employees, producers',
sellers', and consumers' interests. It was the essence of his propaganda that he did not even attempt to reconcile them; he endeavoured not to mention group interests at all, but to sever the
individual from his social group. In the 'amorphous crowd' of the
mass meeting, the particular and concrete ties of family, business,
and class are dissolved, and group consciousness is superseded by,
and submerged in, the revelling in tribal emotions, as LeBon has
taught.

After the conquest of power, the fascist leaders were, of course,
able to force every citizen to participate in the rituals which made
him an unconscious member of the crowd. The whole nation now
joined in the metric conjurations, such as the joyful *Eia Eia Alala*,
the rhythmic idiocy of the *Ce-du-Ce-du-Ce-du*, the thundering evocation of the Fatherland in the '*Deutschland erwache*', or the breath-
taking *mazdaznan* exercise of the *Heil—Heil—Heil*. The nation became an extension of the mass meeting. Even with complete
domination of the radio, Hitler and Mussolini never rose to the
reasoned intimacy of the 'fireside chat', but had to address real
crowds—for only in that situation can the magic ritual be per-

[1] Rauschning, *Gespräche mit Hitler*, p. 199.

formed, and the whole nation, listening in, participates vicariously in the experience of those present.

In these mass meetings the communication is not one of thought or discourse; it is a 'performance'—the symbols of power dominate the audience; words of command are heard; the chorus greets the leader; the names of the Party's martyrs are called out, and to each name the crowd shouts, 'Present'. The leader consecrates a new flag by touching it with one hand, while with the other he 'draws' the spirit of the old Party combatants from the famous 'blood flag' he had used in the abortive *putsch* in Munich. His charisma creates the crowd.

Words here are spells rather than message: they are not supposed to challenge, but to bind. Judiciously employing the 'archcraft of rhythm' (Ernst Krieck), the leader drowns the private thoughts of each listener, makes his own words sound as the sole and true voice that rings in each heart, until all individual will has been transferred on to him and he truly speaks in the name of those who listen, or rather, participate.

To call this 'mass suggestion' is misleading, it is an artfully contrived 'mass regression' into the age of tribal magic, an extinction of personal identity such as today, among civilised nations, is achieved only under combat conditions. To the 'lonely individual' whom—as Hitler (unknowingly quoting Dürckheim) says—society has reduced to a 'dust-particle', Nazi propaganda offers an escape from his anxiety, thus offering him a means of enjoying the amputation of his humanity. The *Erlebnis* of the mass meeting, of singing and marching in community, of identifying himself with the leader (or even with the *corpus mysticum* of a movement or with destiny), affords him the delusion of a harmony which is otherwise inaccessible to his dissonant mind. In fact, the SA attracted many unemployed and uprooted 'philistines' with an almost irresistible magnetism because it gave them a sense of 'belonging' and offered them a place in society—a place of sorts, though.

III. The Sham Revolution

The 'little man', however, was interested not in social adjustment, but in revenge. The leader promised him not a job, but a share in power, an opportunity to get even with the 'bosses'. LeBon taught that crowds thrive on hostile feelings and destructiveness. Using this negative approach, the Nazis were able to pose as more revolutionary than any other critics of capitalism; when their speakers incited the masses to hatred and violence against individual 'plutocrats', Jews, and 'bosses', and promised that not one of them would survive, they sounded more radical than any party that would reform society, but they let the gluttons and racketeers live.

Moral indignation was substituted for politically relevant action; the hate feelings on which agitation thrives were shored up, but had to remain impotent. This self-perpetuating cycle of frustration and rebellion gave the little man no chance to come to grips with his enemy or with his problem. Instead, the imagery of the 'night of long knives' supplied him with the day-dream of vicarious gratification. Any 'acting out' of the pent-up hate feelings was channelled to suit the Nazi design: sadism took the place of revolution.

'Heads will roll in the sand', Hitler prophesied, and Göring added sarcasm when he promised the leaders of the democratic Republic that the Nazis would be 'polite when conducting them to the gallows'. On a different plane, the Fascists exploited to the hilt President Roosevelt's disability; their constant reference to '*Il Paralitico*' was in character: infirmity proved him the proper target for their cruelty. By the same token, the Nazis had their fun with defenceless prisoners, and castor oil humiliated the victim as much as it seemed to justify the humiliation. In cartoons the Jews were shown as 'vermin' inviting extermination: salacious anecdotes characterised them as morally depraved, emasculated or to be emasculated, dangerous only as long as their tricks were not exposed. Thus, the verbal sadism was self-righteous, and its decidedly subversive ring, moreover, gratified secret desires. It afforded, or at least promised, revenge for all resentment and frustration. Its theme was, in a nutshell: 'We may not be smart, but we are not yellow'.

Hitler considered sadism to be a morale-builder:

'You can win the soul of a people only . . . by annihilating the enemy. . . . The masses do not understand handshakes. . . . They want to see . . . the destruction of the weaker or his unconditional subjection.' [1]

Sadism thus became socially significant, even ennobled. It was particularly attractive to the decadent intelligentsia who took so much pride in the 'shattering of *bourgeois* values', glorified vice, and craved to give expression to the 'wisdom of the blood'. Depraved students became notorious for thinking up refinements of cruelty, and Heinrich Himmler, a school teacher, organised the most terrible system of mass torture and execution ever invented.

Yet it is not sufficient merely to denounce the Nazi appeal to sadism. We must also try to understand why at this particular juncture of history such an appeal could be successful. We cannot

[1] *Mein Kampf*, pp. 371–2.

explain the effectiveness of Nazi propaganda unless we recognise the rebellious, insurgent elements in it.

The 'animal protest' against humanist 'culture' had been smouldering in European philosophy for a long time. Irrationalism, vitalism, and existentialism rebelled against the High Court of Reason; years before Fascism and National-Socialism appeared in the political arena, futurism in Italy and the romantic Youth Movement in Germany gave expression to ideas about the new way of life which were brewing in a new generation of anti-Victorians and anti-Wilhelmians. Some saw the allegedly carefree existence of the soldier as a salvation from philistine moralism; but mostly it was the rebellion of the 'open collars' against the 'stuffed shirts', striving to gain recognition for the senses, the instincts, and the emotions. These movements, which at first conceived their programmes as attempts to expand the sphere of human experience, soon degenerated into a violent attack on all intellectual values. Nietzsche's 're-valuation of values' became a 'devaluation'. Wagner's and d'Annunzio's sensuousness was transformed into a negation of civilisation. Thomas Mann clothed it all in the noble armour of 'Culture's' fight against the '*literati*'.

The Nazis were able to identify the rigours of social and intellectual rationality with 'democracy', and the nihilism of young hoodlums with a manly 'will to power'. Plebeian resentment against highbrow culture was cross-bred with the guilt-feeling of the little man who failed to succeed in a world that apparently others had planned to suit the 'fine people' and their higher abilities. The common denominator of all these undercurrents of European civilisation was the new feeling that 'life' had been slighted. It expressed itself in a vitalistic philosophy which the Nazis bowdlerised into a murderous Racism, the Fascists into a swaggering Nationalism. Transposed by them to the political scene—where it did not belong—this pseudo-rebellion appeared as sadism, clothed in the glitter of heroism. The rebellion of the instincts condemned a world where 'sissy altruism' could succeed. 'Whenever I hear the word culture I uncock my gun', says the storm-trooper in Hanns Johst's play. The whole spook will disappear if one bangs one's fist on the table; only weakness is wicked.

Strange to say, therefore, the Nazis and Fascists were convinced that they were fighting for 'freedom'. The authoritarian record of their régimes after they had come to power has overshadowed these rebellious and revolutionary sources of their strength which distinguished them from ordinary reactionaries. In contrast to the latter, the Nazis and Fascists did everything possible to give the impression that they, and only they, spoke the down-to-earth language of the plain people and knew their grievances. Italy was systematically depicted as a 'proletarian nation', Germany a 'have-not'; many a storm-trooper honestly believed that he was fighting for a social revolution (and he consequently had to be liquidated after the conquest of power). The Nazis not only dwelt on all the social evils that the Republic had failed to cope with; they articulated the anti-'philistine', anti-*bourgeois*, or anti-capitalist resentments of the frustrated masses, and moreover supplied a complete imagery of rebellion: abolition of the parliamentary constitution, 'banging the door' of the League of Nations, 'tearing up' of written treaties, 'bursting the fetters' of the 'thraldom of interest', 'hanging' of the traitors, and 'liquidation' of the Jews. No wonder, then, that an analysis of their propaganda themes is a catalogue of what they were 'against'; they were anti-republican and anti-monarchist, anti-capitalist and anti-labour; anti-*bourgeois* and anti-libertine; anti-semitic and anti-clerical—in short, anti-everything at the same time. They could even pose as anti-militarists.

IV. The Great Deception

Since the Nazis and Fascists were so effectively 'against' everything, it mattered little what they were for. Their critics have vainly attacked their conflicting promises: to the farmers higher prices and to the consumers a lower cost of living, higher profits to the capitalists and 'socialism' to the workers; to the big corporations free enterprise and to the small business 'guilds' or 'the corporate state'. They were for the 'strong state', of course, but also for the 'freedom of the individual'. Looking backward, some may be amazed to find Hitler polemising against 'omnipotent government' in *Mein Kampf*; Mussolini, like his predecessor Louis Bonaparte, who glorified in the honorary title of 'liberal emperor', asserted in 1920: 'I start out from the individual and I strike out at the state'. Just as the manipulator tries simultaneously to arouse the subversive and the submissive inclinations of the audience, so he promises them freedom and dictatorship at the same time. Those critics missed their aim because ambiguity was an asset, not a fault.

Observing the rise of Bonapartism a hundred years before the rise of Fascism, the German poet Heinrich Heine remarked that it attracted 'malcontent people . . . who do not know exactly what to think or what they want (the Republic or the Monarchy). . . . '

> 'The Napoleonic Empire was neutral soil for people of the most heterogeneous views. It was a useful bridge for those who had saved themselves from the turmoil of the Revolution and who for twenty years wavered between the right and the left bank of the mainstream of contemporary opinion'.[1]

[1] *Works of Heine* (Cotta ed.), Vol. II, p. 219.

Likewise, Fascists and Nazis were consistently sitting on the fence on the issue of capitalism, and its abolition; always in advance and at the same time lagging behind progress, they successfully avoided taking sides in the burning issues of the day. While exploiting the social malaise to the hilt, they refused to relate its causes to the shortcomings of society; while stimulating discontent to glowing hate, they eschewed the responsibility of relevant action towards social change. In their verbal orgies of hate and violence, they shifted the focus of aggression from the scene of the present society, where concrete reforms were needed, to the abstractions of the heroic-sadistic day-dreams, to the vices of the out-group and the viciousness of the enemies across the border. Incidentally in its vagueness, as well as in its false 'determination', the Nazi language was an adaptable vehicle of this duplicity.

Nazi and Fascist propagandists expressed general indignation at the state of the world, but maintained a ready duplicity and lack of seriousness whenever they were asked what they intended to do about it. They never expected their followers to discover the ambiguities or to mind any of their glaring inconsistencies. And their judgment was correct: democratic counter-propagandists who endeavoured to exploit these contradictions only reaped laughter. Pounding on the irresponsibility of Nazi propaganda, they overlooked the fact that it was successful exactly because it was irresponsible; trying to give the Nazis the lie, they failed to see that the Nazis never told a lie which their followers did not like to hear. Debunking such lies was like taking a dangerous toy away from a child: it only made the debunker more hateable, the more so as Nazi minds are usually devoid of any sense of humour.

With the emotional core of their challenge to the powers that be well anchored in the minds of their followers, the Nazis could afford to be eclectic in their methods and ideas. They might take part in a strike, but that did not alienate their middle-class faithful; they might use the legal mechanism of the courts or the parliamentary procedures of elections, but the followers understood that they did so only to pervert the institutions of democracy or to make a mockery out of them. 'We shall be within the law until the noose is around the neck,' Göring jeered.

Two random examples will show that the followers never expected responsible action from the Nazis. Alleged Polish atrocities had always been a show-piece of Nazi propaganda, which accused the Government of 'selling out to the Pollacks'. Chancellor Brüning, hoping to put the Nazis on the spot, asked them to rally behind him in a protest action. Hitler, of course, refused. To the applause of his adherents, he denied the Republic the right to come to the rescue of oppressed Germans. Anti-Nazi propaganda was unable to draw any benefit from such 'outrageous betrayal of German nationalism'.

Nor did the unemployed storm-troopers blame Hitler when, during his 'struggle for power', he refused to divulge his mythical 'make-work' plan. They understood better than the democratic counter-propagandists that Hitler was not supposed to increase anybody's well-being and that he could not be expected to fight for the realisation of ideas or to formulate any.

In both cases Hitler irresponsibly refused to make any constructive contribution towards the solution of burning questions. Instead, he told his followers to wait for the 'total change' to upset 'the whole cursed system' which was rotten beyond remedy and reform. Dealing in discontent and thriving on frustration, he deliberately widened the gap between the ugly 'now' and the blissful 'then'. He was apt to go to ridiculous lengths in the use of this device; once he told a delegation of women that in the Third Reich each of them would have a husband—thus dodging the issue of women's rights. The Nazis never said *what* should be done: for them, *who* should do it was the all-important question of the day. Contrariwise, their propagandists made ample use of the devices which Whitehead has called 'the fallacy of misplaced concreteness' and 'the fallacy of misplaced abstraction'. They pointed to a particular 'boss' or 'Jew' and commented: 'There you have the whole "system" '; vice versa, when they had to deal with a concrete situation requiring action, they shrugged their shoulders: 'Nothing can be done while "they" are in power'. This pseudo-revolutionary radicalism is typical of the 'little man' who despairs of his ability either to fit into the world or to change it. Projecting his sado-masochistic day-dream into the image of Destiny, he expects the general cataclysm any minute. Though he is unable to relate the now and the then, he trusts that the Party and the *Führer* will somehow scurry out of the general doom, and that he will then be among the 'we'. For the tenseness of this situation the Nazis had the word 'fanaticism'. Hitler praised this as a virtue in a significant context:

'The conviction that it is right to employ the most brutal weapons is always associate dwith (always depends on) the fanatical belief in the necessity of a new and revolutionary transformation of the world. A movement that does not strive for such high aims will never be capable of using such extreme methods.' [1]

---

[1] Synthesising the political outlook of an ideal type of agitator, Lowenthal and Gutermann in *Prophets of Deceit* (Harper, New York, 1950), p. 142, write: 'Oppression and injustice, as war and famine, are eternal; idealists who claim otherwise are fooling themselves. . . . I offer no peace or security. . . . If you follow me you will ally yourself with force, might and power—weapons which ultimately will decide. . . .'

V. Propaganda for War and by War

Even without deep psychological insight, nobody can doubt that the 'extreme means' really are the aim, and that the ideals are a mere adornment, with fanaticism recognised as a prerequisite for the Night of Long Knives. It is the 'fanaticism' of the means (turned aims), and not any specific contents, which makes this propaganda 'fascist'. No transition negotiates between total doom and total salvation.

The Wagnerian setting was an essential prerequisite of Nazi propaganda. No other movement has capitalised on its martyrs as much as the Nazis—while actually it had fewer than its opponents. Only the Nazis could conceive of the idea that all Germany should perish with them. Goebbels basked in the pageant of funeral rites after the destruction of a German army at Stalingrad, and he instituted what has come to be known as the 'propaganda strategy of gloom'.[1] Unlike Churchill's now famous phrase of 'blood, sweat, and tears', it implied more than a supreme appeal to sacrifice in the face of extreme danger: it climaxed two decades of Nazi complaints that Germany was always slighted and frustrated, that traitors and arch-enemies were constantly scheming to bring the *Führer*'s grand designs to naught, and that the world at large was full of horror and damnation. Even a few months before Hitler acceded to power he was full of ill forebodings for himself and his movement:

'I am fighting against this system today, as I fought thirteen years ago, just as I shall fight the fight today and ten years hence. I have chosen to fight, and I shall remain faithful to the fight until the earth covers me. They may kill my friends, they may kill me, but we shall never desist.'

'When I shall be dead, this our flag shall cover me, and my epitaph shall read, Here lies a man who has fought all his life, who was hated by many who failed to understand him.'[2]

Destructiveness, self-destruction, and the desire to be destroyed met in the term, 'tragic realism', coined by Ernst Jünger, one of the fathers of Nazi philosophy.

In this gloomy philosophy, which was sometimes passed off as 'heroic', the alternative is not between a poorly organised and an improved world, but between 'them' and 'us', underdogs and top dogs. The fascist propagandist assumes that the masses will join his gang because its more ruthless methods promise greater assurance of victory. And in adversity he expects them to stick with him because,

---

[1] Ernst Kris and Hans Speier, *German Radio Propaganda* (New York, 1943).
[2] Quoted in Heinrich Hoffmann and Josef Berchtold, *Hitler über Deutschland* (Franz Eher Verlag, Munich, 1932), p. 7, 17.

like criminal conspirators, they will fear that they might all perish together. When Germany was on the verge of defeat, Goebbels conjured up before the eyes of his fellow Germans the picture of a vengeful mankind (symbolised as 'international Jewry'), holding them collectively responsible for the crime against humanity which, he thought, united them in a community of guilt.

'No German can escape by saying, "I have always been a democrat, only the Nazis prevented me from showing my true feelings". In the eyes of international Jewry, every German will be guilty. The Jews will never forgive us for it.' [1]

But the same phrase, 'The Jews will never forgive us', had appeared in a broadcast even at the height of victory in Russia, in the winter of 1941. In fact, the habit of reminding the listeners of the 'Covenant of the Gangsters' which tied them to their leaders (as Ernest Kris appropriately called the device),[2] was more than a mere device of propaganda. It had appeared in the earliest Nazi documents as a central concept of the fascist war-myth. Its reek pervaded the novelistic interpretations of the First World War, from which the young shock-troop leaders came home with the appalling notion: What we have done there is irremediable; we cannot readjust to civilian life; war has become the eternal state of things.

Jünger developed his concept of 'total mobilisation'; his fellow Schramm criticised the conduct of the First World War on the grounds that it had not been a war 'for the sake of the profound idea of warriordom'. Mussolini rejoiced that 'war alone can carry human energies to the maximum of tension', and asserted that 'war is for man what motherhood is for woman'. D'Annunzio and the futurist Marinetti raved about the beauty and virtuousness of war; young officers jeered at the 'desk generals' whom they despised as 'philistines'. Hitler rejected the humdrum nationalism which never could elevate its spirit above such ancient patriotic instructions as '*dulce et decorum est pro patria mori*'. The totalitarians thought higher and deeper of war; it was not to be degraded to some purpose, but vice versa, all civilian activities had to be imbued with war-like purposes and attitudes.

So the SA began 'marching' in 'closed ranks'; as Mussolini was 'one who marches'. The organisation of the movement, its symbols and rituals, its language became propaganda of war, for war, and by war. They constantly referred to 'struggling', 'fighting', and 'dying'. Later, they had their 'battle of employment', battle of the grain, battle against mice, battle of the cradle (*Geburtenschlacht*— literally: 'battle of births'!); there was exaltation of 'blood-sacrifices'

[1] *Rheinische Zeitung*, Mar. 1943. This article was broadcast.
[2] *Journal of Criminal Psychology*, Vol. IV, pp. 445 ff.

until their final self-annihilation. Folk wisdom was right when it dubbed Hitler's peace offers 'peace offensive'. A Fascist is always 'at war', 'living dangerously'; diplomacy, for him is 'war conducted by different methods' (reversing Clausewitz's famous dictum).

Fascist war propaganda is, therefore, more than glorification of a patriotic sacrifice: it denies civilisation. It does not preach war, but assumes war as the natural condition of man. Its effectiveness resides in the ability of the manipulator to shape all forms of everyday life in the image of war.

VI. SHAM DYNAMISM AND 'DESTINY'

A war-like philosophy, war-like attitudes in civilian and political matters, a war-like organisation and war-like phraseology gave the Nazi and Fascist 'movements' their revolutionary flavour. Any political move had to be executed '*schlagartig*' (with lightning speed): war itself became 'lightning war', and even Hitler's greatest diplomatic victory was spoilt for him because he was not allowed to overrun Czechoslovakia. His interpreter Schmidt reports how bitterly Hitler fought at Munich during the decisive conferences with British and French leaders in September 1938, to save at least the propagandist appearance of a military action. Thinking it undignified to declare war formally, he accustomed the world to regarding formal peace as an abnormal state of affairs, war as normalcy.

'The heroic mind', says Jünger, 'does not look upon war as an act of man. Total mobilisation was not made; it happens. Modern integration can neither be chosen nor declined. It is unavoidable. Freedom and obedience are identical. Domination and subservience are all the same.'

This passage makes it perfectly clear what the war myth does for Nazi propaganda. While appearing to be extraordinarily 'dynamic', in reality the soldier propagandist accepts the powers that be and teaches his audience not to bow before them, as a mere reactionary would do, but to recognise them as their own 'Fate'. The freedom which it promises is that of the mad railway engine, or of the tank on the battlefield. In fact, Hitler once asked his Finance Minister, von Schwerin-Krosigk, who was plagued by doubts and qualms over the direction of Nazi policy: 'Did you ever try to leave an express train in motion?' [1]

In the Nazi universe people are lined up behind the leader in a prearranged order, and things are so laid out that no one can escape his 'destiny'—a word which had never before been used so often and in so many contexts as during the Nazi régime. It was the

[1] Rauschning, op. cit., p. 104.

destiny of the German race to dominate others, just as later it was its destiny to go down in defeat. The 'wave of the future' took over where human beings might have rebelled against that very fate; man himself became a mere cog-wheel of that 'dynamic machine racing towards its destiny'.

'War has a beauty of its own because it brings forth the mechanical man who is perfected by the gas-mask, the terrorising loud-speaker and the flame-thrower, or is enshrined in the armoured car which stabilises man's mastery over the machine. War has a beauty of its own because it starts the metalisation of the human body.' [1]

What matters are not the mad contents of the message, but the pseudo-revolutionary dynamism of its tenor—that particular blend of motion where nobody moves, with freedom where everybody is obedient. Reactionaries tell the people that they must submit to unalterable facts or expect to be pushed around by them; revolutionaries either debunk the claim of unavoidability, or rebel against it; fascist propaganda—in its most effective specimens, at least—achieves the mystical identification of man and material. It denies change and development; but it substitutes the pseudo-revolutionary dynamism of abstract 'movements', races, nations, or whatever is suitable at the moment, for concrete actions of people. Geopolitics, which in proper hands may be a subject of military instruction, became an effective doctrine for propaganda where 'power lines', triangles, and pressure centres went conquering each other all on their own account, with the humans 'sucked into the stream' or 'seized by the spirit of the *matériel*' (quotations from Ernst Jünger).

The relations between man, society, and nature are perverted. Even the grammar and language of the fascist propagandist reflect his confused state of mind. We mentioned '*Geburtenschlacht*'—'*Opfer an der Idee*'—'*battaglia del grano*' and similar high-pressure slogans. In these terms, and in many sentences written in 'Nazi German', subject and complement are interchangeable.[2] Very frequently, the meaning of statements is completely vague. For example, in a passage by Hitler to which we have to refer again later on he speaks of 'the annihilation of an idea and of its dissemination', leaving the audience guessing whether he wants to 'annihilate' or to 'disseminate' the idea. Again, it is typical of this language that nouns take the place of verbs, as if human action were contained in a bureaucratic ukase. This emasculation of the language, however, is not a deliberate device; it happens along with

[1] Marinetti, *Il Poema Africano*, p. 27.
[2] See the essay by Professor Betz on 'The National-Socialist Vocabulary', p. 784.

the world-wide trend towards the dehumanising of man. Thus, in a country which is not under discussion here, a war-time appeal to students to breed rabbits was telescoped into the 'rabbitisation of youth'. Such perversions of speech tend to establish a totalitarian outlook on life in the minds of the speakers.[1]

Worse still is the stylistic confusion in literature. Who is acting and what is being acted upon never become clear. Redundant, high-sounding verbs hardly conceal the absence of actions. Duplication of words covers up where concreteness would betray a lack of meaning. It is amazing to find how little ever happens in Nazi novels; even when they are full of 'action', the characters never develop, and in each case the implicit lesson is to deny history. The race doctrine states this philosophy in explicit terms, and carries it to the ultimate extremes. The author of *Das Dritte Reich*, Moeller van den Bruck, who did not believe in racism, nevertheless said: 'There is, no evolution, only creation.'

The world is rigidly structured. 'Germany' is always strong and beautiful, though at times she may be asleep and needs to be 'awakened'. The enemy, on the contrary, is consistently vicious and weak; though he may assume different shapes at different times, he is always the same identical enemy; appearances to the contrary are the work of traitors and treacherous magicians working through underhand juggling—a very strong propaganda device. Particularly 'the Jew' (consistently used in the singular, as though there was no room for individualisation) is always evil; a specimen of the race that seems to be fair-haired or fair-minded is only that much proof of Jewish deceptiveness. No Jew can deny his base origin, just as no German can renounce his share of the German blood, be he ever so alienated from the homeland. An irrevocable fate bound the German–Americans to Germany's Germans; nor could citizenship in a foreign country release the Japanese from their obligations towards their Emperor.

The uncanny dynamism of the 'movement', of the war machine or of the geopolitical symbols has its counterpart in the immobility of the individual. Not only evolution is denied, the propaganda arrangements are so laid out that the individual no longer sees any choice. Where everybody is 'marching', those who are out of step will be trodden under by the collective foot. It is not by accident that a philosophy which emphasised the freedom of choice gained great popularity in the underground movements of resistance.

[1] More examples in H. Pachter, *Nazi Deutsch* (Unger, New York, 1943) and G. Klemperer, *L.T.I.* (Leipzig, 1946).

VII. DEVALUATION OF IDEAS

The 'mystique' of the movement, the cult of dynamism for its own sake, had still another function. 'Vitality' relieved the propagandist from the embarrassing obligation to make specific contributions towards the solution of current problems. Instead of ideas, and propaganda for programmes, he had flags and marching columns. Instead of social content, his imagery offered 'fronts'. The names of most totalitarian parties betray nothing—'Fasci', 'Falange', 'Arrows', 'Frontism', or (in England, where imagery is least successful) simply 'New Party', in Mexico 'Silver Shirts'—all these suggest dynamism without any specific direction. Mussolini's reluctance to give his party any idea of what it was fighting for is well known; he even made a point of it.

'A doctrine must be a vital entity, not a verbal exercise. Hence the pragmatic trend of Fascism, its urge for power, its will to live, its emphasis on violence'.

Or, bowdlerising a famous dictum of Mazzini's:

"Like every sound political conception, Fascism is practice and thought, action in which a doctrine is immanent and doctrine which, arising from a given set of historic forces, is inscribed therein and works from within.'

(*The Doctrine of Fascism*, first sentence.)

Hitler's approach to programmatic ideas is even more startling; his twenty-five 'points' are incoherent and of different relevance, but, once announced, he declared them to be the 'unalterable foundation of the movement':

'The task of today's and tomorrow's members of our movement must not be to revise these theses critically (from time to time); they must, on the contrary, be pledged to defend them. Otherwise the next generation might think it equally right to waste their own energy on another spell of such purely formalistic work within the Party instead of winning new members and, thereby, new strength for our movement. The majority of our followers will anyway see the essence of our movement, not in the letter of our theses, but in the meaning which we shall give them.' [1]

' "And what about the land reform, the abolition of the 'thraldom of interest', and the nationalisation of the banks (which our platform promises)," I (Rauschning) objected.

' "Now you, too, bring up the platform," Hitler replied with impatience. "Do I have to tell you what the platform means? Simpletons may interpret it literally. . . . I shall not alter the platform, and it is meant for the masses. . . . It is like the dogma of the

[1] *Mein Kampf*, p. 514.

Church. Is the significance of the Church contained only in its dogma, or does it not rather lie in its activities and its rites? The masses need something for their imagination and also firm doctrines which cannot be altered. The initiated know that nothing is unalterable." ' [1]

He claimed that he had learned this principle from the Catholic Church, which also will not sacrifice one iota of its dogma, although it may be dated:

'Its survival (the Church's) is not due to its . . . ability to adjust itself to the days' scientific findings . . . but to its rigid adherence to the once-established dogma.' [2]

In contrast to practically all other political parties and mass organisations of history (including the Churches), fascist parties do not claim that their ideas are better, but appeal to people who distrust ideas in general and intellectuals in particular. Mussolini called the intellectuals 'babblers', and Hitler poured biting irony on them because they thought that people can be moved by arguments.

'To be a leader means to know how to move the masses. The ability to form ideas has nothing whatsoever to do with ability for leadership.' [3]

The Nazi revolt against the foundations of Western civilisation started when they first rejected reasoned argument in propaganda. Declining to meet them on their own grounds, they undermined the values of their opponents. They refused to match ideas against ideas and facts against facts, but proposed to exterminate both with clubs.

'The use of violence alone, without the impulse (which comes) from a basic mental concept as its prerequisite, can never lead to the annihilation of an idea and of its dissemination, unless even (its) very last supporter is absolutely extirpated and the last trace of (its) tradition is destroyed.' [4]

In the characteristic jumble of grammar which usually betrays Hitler's effort to impute his own ideas to his enemies, he here confirms that he would not fight ideas with ideas; all he ever tried to do was to suppress them, to eliminate such ideological contests. The symbol of civilised debate was the place where argument had been institutionalised—Parliament. The Nazis referred to the German Parliament as 'Quasselbude' (literally chatterbox); they did their best to make it unworkable and then accused it of inefficiency; they fanned hatred against this institution to blazing heat until, finally, the building itself went up in flames. The device was effective; it

[1] Rauschning, Gespräche mit Hitler, p. 177.
[2] Mein Kampf, pp. 512–13.
[3] ibid., p. 650.   [4] ibid., p. 187.

attracted all those who did not believe in compromise and reasoning —just as the propaganda against the League of Nations attracted the isolationist rabble which does not believe in diplomacy.

After the conquest of power, neither Nazis nor Fascists, with all the powerful propaganda apparatus of the state at their disposal, ever took any chances with the freedom of debate. They established a tight monopoly of publicity and information, which was never relaxed, but was constantly perfected. Not that Goebbels or Mussolini lacked confidence in the technique and devices which their adversaries admired so much and to which they attributed their success— erroneously, we suppose; but there would have been much less to admire had the Nazis not refused to meet argument with argument.

All democratic propaganda is essentially discussion. Even the most ruthless demagogue who shuns no calumny and appeals to all prejudices, at least pretends to respect the reasoning power of his audience. Even the professional liar thinks that he must deceive people by twisting his arguments. We are far from saying that the Nazis did not lie and deceive, but we contend that their lies were neither more skilful nor more effective than any propaganda of their opponents, be it truthful or false. On the contrary, the Nazis were most effectual when they bluntly told the truth—that they did not think people were capable of judgment and understanding. They wanted them to believe in the *Führer*, and their arguments were words of command. Their appeal. was directed neither to interest nor to insight, but to duty and faith. For this reason, they also appeared to cut across all the other parties, each of which represented a group interest.

Again, democratic propaganda implicitly assumes that the audience understands its own interests or those of the country. Its arguments rest on the belief that people want to help themselves, and the listeners are supposed to believe that man, eventually at least, can be perfected. Fascist propaganda, on the contrary, tells its propagees that the leader knows best, that he will fight for them, and that people generally are not smart enough to learn from experience. It is based on the proposition, however, that man can be manipulated.

Manipulation can, of course, best be achieved through a monopoly of information. When he still has to compete with others for the voters' attention and allegiance, this propagandist must disrupt and negate the mechanism by which public opinion is forming in free discussion. His second-best chance of success, next to the 'complete annihilation' of his competitors, therefore, is to deny that he is debating with an enemy. He does not appeal to the audience as to a jury which hears his case as well as the opponent's; he addresses the whole nation as though it was already lined up behind him, ready to follow his call to 'action', though often benumbed by enemy deception or mentally imprisoned by vicious conspiracy. The nation as a whole, not each individual, is supposed to hear the master's voice of command—'*a noi*' or 'awake', 'march', and 'close the ranks'.

VIII. THE CAPTIVE AUDIENCE

Fascist propaganda, therefore, has only one problem and uses only one basic device—to place the unconquered minds under the spell of its symbols of power as though their choice was already a foregone conclusion. In terms of professional publicity techniques: this propaganda sought to place the entire nation in the position of a 'captive audience'.

An audience is 'captive' if it cannot avoid seeing or hearing the full content of an advertisement—e.g., the public in a motion-picture theatre, or, better still for our simile, the passengers on a bus: while the mad tank is taking the Nazis to their destiny, they are fed the Nazi slogans. The problem for Goebbels was not what to tell people, but how to get them on the band-wagon. The first task of the Nazi propagandist was to become conspicuous, then to arouse constant and ever-increasing curiosity, and finally, to be omnipresent in the minds of the public at large. He achieved these aims by representing the Nazi movement as the great threat, and he succeeded in keeping this threat constantly in the public mind. When all nations finally expected their daily Nazi surprise, he had won.

It was incidental to this policy of 'keeping the world's nerves on tenterhooks' that the Nazis tried to be seen and heard as much as possible, through demonstrations, mass meetings, by plastering the town with their posters, by inducing news-dealers to display their papers prominently, but above all by the eccentricities of their policy. What will they do next? was the question everybody had to ask himself every day, first in Germany, then in all countries of the world.

Here again the basic propaganda device is terror. The Nazi antics, however inconsistent they might seem to outsiders, were always converging on this double aim: to disrupt the social-political pattern of the existing régime and to sever the Nazi followers from its mechanism. Opposition against the Government and its policy was to be wrought into absolute negation; there was to be no salvation outside the Nazi movement. For good reasons, therefore, organisation and propaganda are treated together in the same chapter of *Mein Kampf*:

> 'The first task of the (Party) propaganda is to win people over for the coming (Party) organisation (that is, as potential Party

workers); the first task of the (Party) organisation is to win people over who would carry the (Party) propaganda forward. The second task of the (Party) propaganda is to disintegrate the present state of affairs and to infiltrate it with the new doctrine; whereas the second task of the (Party) organisation must be the fight for the conquest of power (to become the governing Party) in order to secure the definitive success of the doctrine.' [1]

Here, the specious meaning of the term 'doctrine' in fascist propaganda is clearly stated—the doctrine consists in propaganda to 'disintegrate the existing state of affairs', and the immediate object and principal device of this propaganda is 'organisation'. To be sure, all political movements make propaganda to strengthen their own ranks. This is so obvious that we must suspect a more specific thought in the passage just quoted. Indeed, we find the relation between 'propaganda' and 'organisation' much closer in fascist parties than anywhere else. Loyalty is not built up on behalf of an idea, but for the leader and his hierarchy. Hate is being preached not so much against doctrines and institutions but against certain 'types' of people and against their organisations. The conflict of programmes is reduced to the level of a conflict between persons— on the positive side, the leader, who 'is always right'; on the other the vermin, who are always incapable, immoral and degenerate.

Quite generally, even all fascistoides concentrate their propaganda on this pseudo-moral aspect of politics. The 'system' is always characterised by its abuses; its standard-bearers are all profiteers or knaves; their corruption is matched by their infernal designs alone. The Nazis managed to conduct a year's campaign on the basis of a fur coat the possession of which the wife of Berlin's mayor allegedly could not account for; the pornography of Streicher's weekly acquired world notoriety.

Of course, scandals have always made good copy for any opposition party, but content analysis shows that fascist propagandists rely on them to a far greater extent and use very much more exaggeration and vituperation than do their opponents, and that references to scandal not only abound in quantity, but also occupy a central place in their imagery. They are not examples of the mismanagement of the attacked régime, but are somehow represented as defining its essence. A closer view shows that this technique exposes the enemy as morally and physically depraved, disintegrating, and doomed. The device fells several pillars of the enemy's castle at one stroke, without committing the agitator to any positive policy or programme.

At the other pole of the value scale, the propagandist consistently exalts the moral and physical strength of his own organisation and,

[1] *Mein Kampf*, p. 654. Hitler's style is hard to translate.

in particular, of the leader. No fascist movement has ever been successful without a leader cult. (A numerous mass audience is far from equivalent to an organisation which is built on obedience to the command of its leader.)

The tightly knit machines of totalitarian hierarchies and the iron discipline of the followers argue the strength and virtue of the leader. Vice versa, the leader-myth of omnipotence, infallibility, and incorruptibility is the supreme argument of any totalitarian party. Faith in the movement's future might be fickle at times, but faith in the leader and his mission could never fail. 'Loyalty is my honour,' says the motto of the SS.[1]

The leader cult also made it possible for propaganda to operate on very different levels with very different approaches and promises at the same time. The intelligentsia, who are always sensitive to points of doctrine, could be silenced by the appeal to their ability to believe: the man in the street, who might like to 'see results', could be prevailed upon to prove his loyalty to the leader. 'Give me four years,' Hitler asked his followers when he took power, and they gladly consented to wait that long for the coming of the kingdom. From the *Führer*'s deputy down to the last SA man, and further on to the simple block warden and private soldier, everyone finally accepted his place within the society of the régime. 'Command from above, obedience from below', said Göring. But this was not a mere result of Nazi education, it was the essence of the movement from its inception. In *Mein Kampf* Hitler had already asserted that the movement must anticipate the new society in its structure and intent.

'Organisation', then, is hardly differentiated from propaganda. It expresses the spirit of the movement better than words could do. It is the living denial of debate and of intellectual values. The strength of the machine, its hierarchy, a man's rank in the movement, his loyalty to the leader—these are the values which determine the personal success of the agitator and the success of propaganda. The scale of values does not run from 'right' to 'wrong', or from 'correct' to 'incorrect', or from 'right side' to 'left side'; it only knows 'weak' and 'strong', 'soft' and 'ruthless', 'analytical' and 'integrated'. Its criterion is faith, not reason. Hence, the leader can do no wrong. Pacifism, for instance, might be either good or bad; but those who nourished pacifist ideals certainly were displaying softness, if not moral depravity. The Nazis therefore disdained to

---

[1] Although the Nazis frequently borrowed vocabulary and imagery from religious institutions of all times, I cannot agree with those who speak of a 'Nazi religion'. The psychological mechanism the Nazis manipulated to build up faith in one man, is different from the one that satisfies a metaphysical craving. Not that Goebbels had not tried—but Hitlerism as such died with Hitler and could be revived only by another Hitler—whereas religions thrive on dead founders.

prove anti-militaristic ideas wrong; they simply denounced them as despicable, or treasonable. However, when the *Führer* made one of his ominous peace manoeuvres, he did so 'from strength' or wisdom.

Finally, organisation was entwined with propaganda not only in this intimate, quasi-metaphysical way. It also had a direct technical aspect. The Nazi organisers had a very shrewd judgment of strategic procedure in propaganda. They did not wait for their mass appeals to reach a scattering of people and then for these converts to form cells; they pinpointed their propaganda in locations where they could hope to achieve the greatest immediate results in building up machines and forming nuclei for the further spreading of organisation and propaganda. In advancing from village to village they tried to win first the doctors, apothecaries, and teachers, if possible the pastor, and they did so not through methods of mass persuasion, but through a personal approach, involving the victim in their organisation even before they found it necessary to discuss their doctrine with him. In the cities they selected strategically situated 'pubs' or poolrooms, where they installed their headquarters, organised a certain to-do and coming and going, with guards visible from the street and occasional sallies into 'enemy' territory conducted under propitious auspices. Thus they were able to 'conquer' street by street, somewhat as trade union organisers will concentrate on one plant after the other.

IX. The Big Lie and the Big Truth

Propaganda must constantly work on three levels: to indoctrinate and fortify the followers; to paralyse, split, irritate, or mislead the adversaries; and to win ascendancy over the undecided. In democratic countries and in democratic parties it is also the task of propaganda to galvanise people into action. Fascist leaders are less interested in that aspect; they rather use fake calls to 'action' as a means to win ascendancy. The annual 'Winter Help' campaign for charitable donations (which donations had to be given anyway as compulsory contributions) was actually designed to rally the population behind the Nazi chariot, rather than to bring aid to those who had been crushed under its wheels. 'I fanaticised the masses in order to make them into a tool of my policy,' Hitler confided.[1]

These words really summarised all there is to fascist propaganda. Neither Hitler nor Goebbels nor Mussolini had at their disposal any special powers of persuasion which their opponents could not have used had they been equally unscrupulous. A careful examination of the pronouncements of the top Nazi and Fascist propagandists on

[1] Rauschning, op. cit., p. 198.

the subject, and of their techniques, does not reveal any invention nor any of the 'startling insights into human weaknesses' with which some pundits of the Left have credited them. The myth of the irresistible spell-binders suited the losers well enough: it implied that they had been beaten by blows below the belt, and it somehow seemed to cover up their own failure to offer, at decisive moments, a positive programme for reconstruction, a way out of the political and social crisis. Actually, it came to pass that they tried some pitiful imitations of Nazi methods and slogans (in which game they were bound to lose) instead of putting forth new and forceful ideas. They were beaten, not because they lacked the strength or the personal courage to fight the ever bolder Nazis, but because they lacked what it takes to fight bewilderment and despair—and the Nazis frankly played on just that.

There was never any 'secret doctrine' or any magic formula for fascist propaganda. Hitler, for example, openly proclaimed his techniques in the wordy and clumsy tirades of *Mein Kampf* as early as in 1925. Moreover, they are simple enough. He insisted, first, that propaganda must appeal to the emotions, not to reasoning. Its intellectual level must be adapted to the understanding of the morons.

'Its effect (that is, the effect of propaganda) must always be directed rather to the emotions and only under very special conditions to the so-called intelligence ... and its intellectual level must be adapted to the capacities of the stupidest.' [1]

Also, according to *Mein Kampf*, propaganda must pick out a few striking points and hammer a few slogans into unforgettable images:

'... (It is necessary) to limit (propaganda) to a very few points, and to use these, in sloganised form, so long until certainly even the last person will be able to associate with the word what we want.' [2]

Again, propaganda must not be subtle, for instance, by ridiculing the adversary. (Making fun of somebody still leaves a certain tie of friendliness with him.) On the contrary, it must represent the adversary as brutal and inhuman. It must not be 'fair' to the opponent, and must never concede that there may be two sides to a question in dispute. 'Would anyone advertise his soap by admitting that other soaps might be good, too?'

'... The task of propaganda is not to weigh who is right in this and that respect, but the exclusive emphasis on the one side. It is not to search objectively for the truth which then would be put before the masses with doctrinaire sincerity, but must uninterruptedly serve its own cause.' [3]

Hitler goes on to berate the '*Objektivitätsfimmel*' (the idolatry of

---

[1] *Mein Kampf*, p. 197. [2] ibid., p. 190. [3] ibid., p. 200.

objectivity), which deprives the German people of the ability to stand on their rights, and he condemns all '*Halbheit*' (half-measures). Even a lie will be believed if told over and over again with brazen impudence.

'. . . a lie which only by the unconditional, impertinent, one-sided obstinacy with which it was presented, took account of the attitude of the people at large which (attitude) is emotional and always extreme, and therefore (the lie) was believed.' [1]

And the bigger the lie, the better:

'The bigness of the lie is always a certain factor for its acceptance, because the people at large . . . in their primitive simplicity are more easily taken in by a big lie then by a small one, since while they themselves use petty lies they would be too much ashamed of lies which are too big. An untruth of that magnitude will not even occur to them, and they will be incapable of believing that it is possible that others would be so brazenly impudent as to distort with such extreme infamy; nay, even when disproved, the lie will linger on as doubt and indetermination and they will at least still assume that there was some sort of truth behind it; that is why even of the boldest lie, something will remain and stick.' [2]

Yet, notorious and utterly unscrupulous as especially the Nazis were in the use of the technique of 'the big lie', it must be added that they scored many a propaganda success by using the technique of 'the big truth'—and, in particular, in *combining* the big lie with the big truth.

By the technique of the big truth we mean two things: the blunt and merciless exposure of weaknesses of the system and the political parties they intended to eradicate; and the intentionally crude 'frankness' with which they announced their own ultimate aims. Before the Nazis and Fascists came into power, their agitators never tired of telling the people how badly off they were, and that the others had no policy and offered no leadership. On the other hand, they never made a secret of their own nostrum against all evils—foreign conquests. Were not Italy and Germany 'late-comers' in the distribution of the world's territories and riches, while others had done the grabbing before? Italy and Germany, too, would gain in might and prestige by acquiring more of the world's natural resources. The middle classes whom Marxist propaganda clumsily threatened with 'proletarisation', were to receive commissions in the armed forces or in the administration of dependencies. 'One cannot deprive a nation of its wealth unless one gives it glory and honour instead,' said Mussolini.

Much of that had a ring of truth or seemed obvious, especially as the moderate and left parties often offered no alternative to

---

[1] *Mein Kampf*, p. 202. [2] ibid., p. 253.

such suggestions. In fact, they often believed that the best defence against fascist chauvinism and militarism lay in attempts to out-do them in nationalism. The behaviour of the Italian delegation at the Paris Peace Conference, even in 1919, intensified the impression ceaselessly propagandised by the Fascists that Italy was being nationally humiliated by the fellow-victors. Another example: surrendering to the Nazi ideology, the German Communists joined the Nazis in a referendum against the Young Reparations Plan.

A district-by-district analysis of subsequent election returns showed that Nazi progress was fastest wherever this Communist stratagem had succeeded. The traditionally nationalistic and militaristic parties anyway had no defence against the fascist demands. Mussolini and Hitler merely had to state that they stood for the same aims, only more so, and that they were ready to use more ruthless methods. Again, everybody from the moderate Left to the extreme Right was, of course, against 'Bolshevism', but the Fascists and Nazis could show blood on their hands as proof that their hatred was more genuine; and once middle-of-the-roaders were no longer prepared to protect the civil rights of a Communist, even many non-Fascists concluded that fascist methods were the most effective in dealing with the Communist scale. This weakness of the moderate parties confronted with a revolutionary bogey has been exploited by virtually every counter-revolutionary dictator-to-be during the last four hundred years. It was Mussolini's and Hitler's pet device, too.

Whether lie or truth, fascist agitation made it a rule that propagandists must always stick to their guns, avoid any change, repeat the 'great outlines' (*die grosse Linie*) over and over and, if forced to digress, in the end return to the original slogans.

'You will be amazed what gigantic, almost incomprehensible success is the reward of such perseverance. Any publicity, whether in business or in politics, succeeds by its continuation and through uniform repetition.'[1]

On the basis of this insight into the effectiveness of repetition, he concentrated his fire on one outstanding adversary at a time. This not only afforded him the chance of channelling all pent-up aggression in one direction, and to combine all real and alleged evils into one personification. It also made repetition more versatile; for example, President Roosevelt would be used as standing for Bolshevism as well as for Plutocracy; 'Jewry' for suppression as well as for subversion. This leads us to the question why eventually all totalitarian propaganda must find its proper vehicle in anti-Semitism. Even Mussolini, who personally did not hate Jews, ended by denouncing the alleged 'Jewish World Conspiracy'.

[1] *Mein Kampf*, p. 203.

X. Polarisation

In propaganda analysis the device of building up an arch-enemy is called 'polarisation'; it has, of old, been a stand-by of sectarian and, particularly, of political agitation. The Nazis perfected it by making their counter-images as 'total' as they were themselves—the arch-enemy was universal, he was everywhere, he was the intangible and world-wide evil, ever-present in a thousand disguises.

Once the picture of an arch-enemy has been firmly established in the minds, it can be used like a clothes' rack, to be endowed with any hostile symbols and emotions. The imagery which populates the agitators' universe is very stable. As in a serialised cartoon, the 'types' never change; they are stereotypes. This is true of all propaganda, but it went to extremes in the symbolic thinking of these publicists. This can be explained by the very nature of fascist propaganda aims. Whereas other publicists, however demagogically they may deal with their audiences, must eventually invite discussion, give explanations, exhibit principles, and, above all, must propose specific remedies for specific ills, their fascist counterparts must avoid all this and deal in images of positive and negative characters, the 'we' and the 'they'. 'We' and 'they' must, of necessity, be immutable. For example, such matters as the various phases of the business cycle, or problems of taxation, or wage calculations with which 'they' deal in their discussions and speeches, are rather complicated matters; and the solutions 'they' offer are often difficult to grasp and not unequivocal. 'The Jew', on the contrary, is always equally hateable in the pseudo-palpability of his abstract 'essence'. Likewise, the image of 'the plutocrat' may or may not fit any number of individual millionaires, but everyone knows the 'type', and all bankers, bosses, racketeers, and schemers are instinctively rolled into one composite big master mind which commands an international network conspiring to make the people poorer and the rich richer. Again, the sinister and mysterious conspiracy may be the work of 'the freemasons', or 'the Jesuits', or 'communism', as well as of 'international finance capital'; at the height of the battle of Stalingrad, when the tide of military successes changed and the population, numbed, felt the beginning of the end, Goebbels produced the pyramidical 'Jewish bolsho-pluto-democratic International'.

However, for Nazi propaganda, the real arch-enemy was 'the Jew'. The other arch-enemies were either allied, or identical with him. In this connection a word might be said on political anti-Semitism as distinguished from mere Jew-hating and Jew-baiting; it is a technique of mass domination designed to divert hate away from the ruling class and to shift it on to a mythical symbol of 'otherness' (Devil). Such a dark power is handily provided by the image of a 'Jewish World Power' which allegedly (according to the notorious falsification, 'Protocols of the Elders of Zion') directs the destinies of all nations, organising revolutions as well as counter-revolutions, pulling the strings of the Stock Exchange just as it commands the labour movement, surreptitiously dictating the course of history for some unavowedly sinister purpose, conspiring to frustrate the hopes of all decent men, but using them for a deceptive shadow-play; at all times, this myth has given food to the imagination of the lunatic fringe of the disinherited. But the Nazis made it a cornerstone of their propaganda. They noticed that it is simple and striking; it satisfied simultaneously the need to 'explain' the common man's frustrations, and the desire to attribute them to some irrational cause. It is the perfect mystery, just imperfectly enough demystified to leave it mysterious. Hitler's great mystifier, Alfred Rosenberg, went as far as to detect the symbols of the secret world government in the design on German coins.

The concept had two outstanding advantages. In the first place, it 'explained everything'. Anything which apparently shows the absurdity of the idea is, on the contrary, proof of a clever Jewish deception, contrived to mislead the 'Aryan simpleton, who is much too good-natured', and to conceal the great conspiracy. The poor Jew whose ragged clothes aroused the sympathy of a decent German, Dr Goebbels wrathfully warned, had been placed in that position by his wealthy cousin in Wall Street for no other purpose but to divert attention from the Jewish World Conspiracy—against which an 'anti-Jewish uprising' was justified and timely: a world revolution which made it possible for the Nazi strategists to pose as the friends of all peoples while subverting all nations. Hence their 'internationalism'.

Secondly, the notion of the Jewish World Government provided a rationalisation for Nazi conquest of world power. The conclusion was obvious: if the world had to be run by a conclave, then why not by one that was virtuous and of purer blood? The conspiracy could be overcome only by a counter-conspiracy. The battle then was joined on the very simple terms: The Jews or We?

' "My Jews are a precious pawn, left in my keeping by the democracies. In all countries a propagandising anti-Semitism is the all but indispensable means of disseminating our political fight. You will see in what short time we shall overthrow the whole world's concepts and standards, simply and solely by our fight against Jewry. For that matter, the Jews themselves are our best helpers in this struggle. In spite of their dangerous situation, they always mix with the foes of order and subversives' ranks insofar as they are poor, and they are far and wide conspicuous as owners of huge riches which everybody envies them. Hence, it is easy everywhere to furnish down-to-earth evidence for our claims by pointing out popular and concrete instances occurring right next door. As soon as, by specific exposure of the Jews, the race principle has made its entry, everything else will take care of itself promptly. People will be forced, then, to dismantle, step by step, their political and economic order and to absorb the new ideas of biological politics.'

'He said that anti-Semitism was doubtless the most significant part of his propaganda arsenal and almost everywhere was dead sure to succeed. That was why he had given Streicher *carte blanche* in his job. Moreover, Streicher had an amusing and very clever way of doing this job, and it made him wonder where in the world Streicher got that new material all the time. He looked forward eagerly to each new issue of the *Stürmer*, and it was the only paper he liked to read and did read from the first to the last line. . . .

'I asked him if he meant to say that the Jew should be annihilated altogether.

' "No", Hitler replied. "We would have to invent him. You need a visible foe, not merely an invisible one." The Catholic Church, he said, found the Devil insufficient; it needed visible foes in order not to slacken in its fight. "The Jew always sits inside us. But it is easier to fight him in a living shape than as an invisible demon. . . ." ' [1]

Any word of comment would be an anti-climax. The point here is not to show Hitler's cynicism, but his insight into his cynicism. He well knew how explosive was the scheme he let loose and how best it could be exploited. By depicting the poor Jew as the enemy of law and order he would subvert the domestic and international order. By inveighing against the wealth of Jews he would so undermine other nations the better to capture their own wealth. The last part of the quotation shows his awareness of the psychological mechanism which made polarisation so powerful a propaganda weapon. The evil must be shown to the people as being 'outside' themselves, in order to paralyse the spirit of compromise 'inside' (within) themselves; liberation from all evil 'inside' themselves was promised to those who would recognise the need for the unconditional victory of the movement against the evil 'outside'.

Sooner or later all totalitarian movements will avail themselves of the tremendous propaganda opportunities which reside in anti-Semitism or equivalent polarisation devices. The visible existence of total evil, the arch-enemy, can best justify the extremist claim of the movement to achieve a 'total' purge. If the national tradition fails to provide such an arch-foe, propaganda must create one or build

[1] Rauschning, *Gespräche mit Hitler*, pp. 222–3.

up an existing enmity into total rejection. It is for this reason that totalitarian policy against the arch-enemy cannot stop at administrative measures however harsh (just as Nazi anti-Semitism could not stop at administrative measures to 'curb Jewish influence') but must aim at 'total annihilation'.

XI. Victims of Their Own Cunning

After the conquest of power, the same psychological mechanism continues to operate, and calls for a continuously growing radicalism in the propaganda. Since the 'evil', the 'arch-enemy' exists not only in its original form, the Movement-State must fight it also in its other forms. The dynamism of its own demagogy thus drives the fascist state to find new enemies at home, and to destroy the last vestiges of possible resistance. Not that the fascist régime, with all its police power and its monopoly of propaganda, need fear these remnants of opposition. On the contrary, it could not exist without constantly proving that opposition still exists; how necessary, therefore, is its own cruelty against the 'traitors', and how mistaken is the simple-minded follower who thinks that the sinister 'conspiracy' has long since been stamped out. Hence, if the police destroys the opposition, propaganda must re-invent it.[1]

In order to export their ideas abroad, the Nazis did not even have to 'invent' the Jewish danger. Their own prosecutions at home produced a 'Jewish question' in countries whereto the destitute and homeless endeavoured to emigrate—often, in fact, being driven to violating some of the immigration laws of those countries. Gleefully, the organ of the SS, the 'Schwarze Korps', could point to the 'scum of the earth, the wanderers without citizenship, without means of livelihood, without passports, and therefore without rights, who, wherever they went, became the living proof that their persecutors had been right after all.' With satisfaction the Foreign Ministry noted in a circular letter 'to all senior Reich authorities and the NSDAP Bureau for Foreign Affairs', shortly after the government-directed pogroms of November 1938:

---

[1] Thriller-writers like Koestler answer the question: 'Why do accused traitors confess?' instead of asking: 'Why are such confessions believed?'. American would-be Fascists have successfully used the Yalta Conference as a symbol of 'world-wide conspiracy' against the traditions of their country, and are forever hunting 'traitors' whom they would rather hold responsible for a reality which they refuse to recognise. However, our discussion suggests that, despite some terroristic traits, this propaganda will never achieve the herostratic dignity of 'Fascist'. On the other hand, anti-American propaganda in Europe and Asia recently has assumed some weird features of the polarised sham universe. Comparison of Continental reactions to British wealth in the nineteenth century, with Continental resentment of American power today, reveals the fascistoid components which paralyse significant action.

'The emigration movement of only about 100,000 Jews has already sufficed to awaken the interest if not the understanding of many countries in the Jewish danger. . . . Germany is very interested in maintaining the dispersal of Jewry. The assumption that as a consequence (of Nazi persecution of the Jews) boycott groups and anti-German centres would be formed all over the world, disregards the following fact which is already apparent: the influx of Jews in all parts of the world invokes the opposition of the native population and thereby forms the best propaganda for the German Jewish policy. . . . The poorer and therefore the more burdensome the immigrant Jew is to the country absorbing him, the more strongly the country will react and the more desirable is this effect in the interests of German propaganda. . . .' [1]

Once a movement of this type is in power it can cause things to happen according to its own predictions. It is able to create propaganda facts at home and even abroad. Since it is ever ready to attack the *status quo* anywhere in the world, it can freely choose the field where it wishes to go of its own choosing at a time of its own convenience. Since it is not bothered by considerations of principle its fifth-column organisations can execute peace manœuvres or war threats; they can co-operate with friendly governments or try to disrupt hostile ones as the need arises. In doing this, propaganda often not only precedes the event on which it is built, but actually determines the course of events. It was for reasons of propaganda, or morale-building, that Hitler wanted Italy to join the war, although his military advisers cautioned him that she would be a liability rather than an asset. Mussolini in turn, somewhat put to shame in the eyes of his more fervent and reliable followers by his belated rush to join the winner, then had to start a war all of his own—against the advice of his generals, he attacked Greece. Likewise, Hitler's war against the Soviet Union might have brought him less disaster had he conducted it with less regard for the requirements of propaganda—trying to take Moscow, to advance to the Caucasus, and to the Volga, to hold on to untenable lines, etc. [2]

[1] Circular of the Ministry of Foreign Affairs, 83–26 19/1 Ang. II, dated Berlin, 31 Jan. 1939, on the subject of 'The Jewish Question as a factor in German foreign policy in the year 1938'. (Nuremberg Document 3358-PS, reproduced in German in *Trial of the Major War Criminals before the International Military Tribunal*, Nuremberg, 1948), Vol. XXXII, pp. 234–45; reproduced in English translation in: Office of U.S. Chief of Counsel, *Nazi Conspiracy and Aggression* (U.S. Government Printing Office, Washington, D.C., 1946, Vol. VI, pp. 87–95).

[2] Amplifications on other aspects of the totalitarian sham reality will be found in: Franz Neumann, *Behemoth* (New York, 1942); Ernst Kris, Hans Speier and others, *German Radio Propaganda* (Oxford University Press, New York, 1943); Theodor W. Adorno, Marie Jahuda and others, *The Authoritarian Personality* (Harpers, New York, 1951); Hannah Arendt, *Origins of Totalitarianism* (Harcourt, Brace and Co., New York, 1951); Harold D. Lasswell and Abraham Kaplan, *Power and Society* (Yale Univ. Press, New Haven, 1950); Daniel Lerner and others, *Propaganda in War and Crisis* (George W. Stewart, New York, 1951).

Propaganda thus becomes responsible for the weird aspect of reality in the fascist world. Facts can no longer be evaluated in their own terms. Decisions are made according to the way in which events fit into the pattern of the ideological propaganda, rather than in relation to other events. Reality becomes a front, a shadow-play, an affirmation of power. Not only the propagandist, but even the allegedly all-powerful leader and policy-maker, loses his grip on the real world, and ends by chasing his own fantasies.

The fascist propagandist who started out by falsifying and distorting reality, is finally caught at his own game. He has to precipitate the *Götterdämmerung* which he predicted.

Long before the final holocaust, however, the spell of propaganda has lost its magic. Its symbols worn thin, its slogans emptied of meaning, its language grown trite, its devices now become self-defeating, its rituals mockingly performed in the face of belying reality, its images evoked in ironical quotation marks: 'Of course, we all follow the *Fuhrer*—into death', quoth the Berlin worker. The winking of the eye now accompanies every communication as the mirage of sham reality falls apart.

What is true of the totalitarian party in power also applies to the totalitarian movement on the rise to power. Unless the leader can provide the daily miracle or delusion, his charisma wears off. Unlike other parties which are founded upon more permanent interests, totalitarian movements rarely survive defeat. Unless they proceed to quick conquest, they falter; their membership is fickle, their vote-gathering appeal subject to wide fluctuations. Experience has shown that they thrive on appeasement, notably if their adversaries make ideological concessions giving nourishment to their dreams; it has also shown that, confronted with determined opposition and firmly forced to face realistic problems, the leader loses his power and his magic dissolves.

22

FASCIST MILITARISATION AND EDUCATION FOR WAR

John H. E. Fried

THE foremost aim of the fascist movements in Italy and Germany was to create, in Harold Lasswell's apt phrase, 'the Garrison State'. Their totalitarianism consisted in establishing the supremacy of their own military type over the nation, and in reshaping all aspects (the 'totality') of the nation's life in the image and for the purposes of this military type. Characteristic of the 'Garrison State', as Lasswell pointed out, is the 'supremacy of the specialist on violence, the soldier'. Immediately upon Hitler's coming into power, Sir (then Mr) Winston Churchill warned of the 'tumultuous insurgence of ferocity and war spirit' in Germany. Joseph Goebbels, Hitler's Propaganda Minister, said admiringly that Mussolini's Party 'has become, I would almost say, the kneading machine (*die Knetmaschine*) of the fascist nation. After the raw material has gone through this machine, a coherent mass comes out of it, which then can be utilised and manipulated for political aims of the State . . .' [1] The 'raw material' for the 'kneading machine' were the people.

In modern non-fascist society the military profession forms a respected sector, but does not dominate it. Fascism, in turn, aims at 'militarising' the entire nation in its own image, and at structuring the state and society in a hierarchy which is carefully conditioned by and for its special brand of militarism. The extent to which this militarism differs from normal standards can be exactly measured, in peace-time by the extent of its disregard of the law of the land, and in war-time by the extent of its violations of the laws and customs of war.

That fascism was 'militaristic' was immediately realised. Not, or insufficiently, recognised were the *complexities* of this militarism; the *differences* between it and other types of militarism; the *debasement* of military concepts it necessarily created; the *degree of disaster* to which it would potentially lead. Thus it was able to grow, to gain power, and to fulfil its circle.

For Fascism, violence—but not always physical violence, otherwise fascists would not have been experts in violence!—was the essence of

[1] Joseph Goebbels, *Der Fascismus und seine Politischen Ergebnisse*, p. 21.

political action. The amount and intensity of violence it used were a reliable barometer of its stages of development.

At the same time, it renounces none of the traditional methods of politics, from the election promise to material favours, and from the Party newspapers to the astute use of parliamentary procedure. But everything it undertakes is permeated by garrulousness and aggressiveness. Fascism does not argue disputes in a violent and aggressive manner; rather, violence and aggressiveness, in multiple forms (of which more later), constitute its main arguments.

Its leaders possessed a peculiar mastery in the different forms of violence, their direction and timing. In this sense, and even when the brutality of the National-Socialists hit the bottom of infamy, they were *not* brutes in the choice and scheming of their policies. They used brutality pitilessly, as a matter of principle; but the very systematisation and inventiveness of their brutality revealed careful and, it must be said, masterful calculation. Seen in isolation, an attack by some black-shirted men looked like an uncomplicated act of brigandry. But the strategy of these attacks, considered as a whole, constituted an extremely skilful campaign, aiming at, and achieving, the undermining of a major European country. While the others waited for the 'excesses' of storm-troopers to subside, their leaders perfected the methods of those excesses and applied them on an ever larger scale, and for ever bigger targets. Between the methods of a gangster and Himmler's machinery of concentration camps the distance is immense, not only in the magnitude of the results, but also in the manner of cleverness involved. Yet the gigantic inhumanity of those camps, organised at the height of power, was but the ultimate fulfilment of the same mentality which dictated the strategy of a handful of 'rowdies' only a few years earlier.

Actually, the outward appearances of the violence of the first phases were deceptive. Because they looked like deeds of hoodlums (and so they were), the astuteness of their planning and, first of all, the stakes for which the game was played, were not fully understood. They perfected the art of destroying civil liberties and the art of the half-concealed and unilateral civil war, and must also be credited with having adopted and combined old, and invented new, forms of physical, intellectual, and mental attack and subversion.

These specialists of violence built their Garrison State on a complex militarism all their own. They understood—much better than did their opponents and victims—the various forms which militarism can assume, and in how many different ways and for how many different purposes in how many widely separated fields these different forms of militarism can be used—if no scruples stand in the way. One of the main secrets of their success was the skill with which they used and blended different types of militarism.

The paradox was that they were able to do this in an era of deep *aversion* against militarism and, first of all, against war. In order to trace their methods and techniques in this respect, we must therefore endeavour to break the complex militarism which was fascist militarism into its component parts, into the several forms or types of militarism of which it was composed. For lack of more convenient or generally accepted terms, we shall call these different types, merely for identification, 'party militarism', 'army militarism', 'civil militarism', and 'education for war'. Each was, in turn, composed of several ingredients. For example, as we shall see, education for war did not consist only in glorification of war, but included, among other things, even the exploitation of the aversion against war.

PARTY MILITARISM

'It is good always to think of fight.'—Joseph Goebbels.

One of the major inventions of Fascism was to conceive of politics, literally, as military action, to conduct political campaigns as military campaigns, to incapacitate opponents physically, to 'occupy' strategic buildings or even towns. This transfer of military techniques into the political and civilian life is an easily discernible trait of incipient Fascism. It consists in the establishment of para-military formations, the display of physical force, the use of violence even to the point of applying actual battle tactics, the spreading of intimidation and terror by the use of non-physical violence.

The core of the early activists consisted of demobilised officers and soldiers who had learned the shock-troop techniques in World War I, and now applied these techniques to the political scene at home. They were joined by other disgruntled men who were easily indoctrinated with the same spirit.

This fact remained important throughout the ascendancy period —which in Germany lasted very much longer than in Italy—and equally after the accession to power. The most militant members were uniformed, were trained by the Party in military techniques and the use of weapons. The Party troops developed a quasi-military hierarchy, organised into battalions, regiments, divisions, and corps, and closely paralleling the organisation of the regular army; they eventually had their own arms depots, their own intelligence system, their own quartermaster departments, etc. Much thought and care were given to the design of Party uniforms, insignia, emblems, ribbons, flags, and other paraphernalia of military display, such as the martial and awe-inspiring appearance of their marching columns.

Marching songs, set to popular tunes, were systematically used to spread defiance and the war spirit.[1]

[1] Here are some examples of songs of the Hitler Youth and SA troops:

Unfurl the Blood-Soaked Banners

1. Unfurl the blood-soaked banners,
   And redden the sky with glow.
   A coward who of himself still thinks
   When enemies threat all around us.
   We never shall shrink from the enemy,
   We of Adolf Hitler's fifth company.

2. While cowardice and treason reign
   We shout our combat songs,
   We're marching toward buoyant deeds,
   Last guardians of German freedom.
   For Germany's grandeur any time
   To die we are always ready.

3. And if, one time, the days of vengeance nears
   And the *Führer* to war does call us,
   Then we shall carry from woe and shame
   The swastika to victory.
   Then we shall march in morning's dawn
   For Hitler's banner unto death.

We're Marching through the Street

1. We're marching through the street
   In heavy step and step,
   The banner, high above us,
   It flows and furls along.

   Trum, trum, trum, trum,
   di-ri-di-ri-trum.

   . . . . .

2. Perhaps by next tomorrow,
   I must die in my own blood—
   The boy knows not what love means,
   Nor what to die may mean.

   Trum, trum, trum, trum,
   di-ri-di-ri-trum.

Seest Thou the Dawn of Morning in the East?
   . . . . .

4. The young and old, and man for man,
   Hold strongly the swastika banner.
   Burgher or peasant or working man,
   They swing the sword and the hammer
   For Hitler, for freedom, for work and for bread.
   Germany awake! Death to the Jews! Nation, to arms!

They Tremble in their Weakly Bones

1. They tremble in their weakly bones,
   Great War makes the world all jitter.

The use of uniforms proved to be a particularly successful technique. Its significance was six-fold. Firstly, the Party uniforms distinguished its bearers from the rest of the population. One had only to observe a column of *squadristi* marching down a village road, or a group of SA men noisily boarding a street-car, to realise how the uniform inflated their sense of self-importance and induced them to display the provocative behaviour so ardently desired by the leaders. Secondly, the uniform created cohesion among these unruly and motley men, and a sort of *esprit de corps*, with a distinct group mentality where the normal commands of 'civilian' decency no longer prevailed. Thirdly, the 'common garb' helped the leaders to make the claim that, contrary to the inimical society 'outside', the Party had within its own ranks done away with class distinctions.[1] Fourthly, the public appearance of even a few, or a single person in any of the conspicuous Party uniforms, in a small village, in a town, on a train, at a public gathering, or anywhere else, was a constant visible reminder of the Party's strength and ubiquitousness.[2] On the other

---

For us, War lost its dreadfulness,
For us, 't spells victory.

We shall march on, just as before
When everything falls to smithers,
For today we master Germany
And tomorrow the whole wide world.

2. And if the world in debris lies
From battle, piled in mountains,
We do not give a devil's damn,
We'll build the world anew.

We shall march on, just as before, etc.

3. And if the oldsters grumble,
Let them whine and complain,
And if whole worlds oppose us
Still we shall victors be.

We shall march on, just as before, etc.

(From the Hitler Youth Song Book, *Uns Geht die Sonne Nicht Unter*, compiled by Hugo W. Schmidt for the use by schools and by the Hitler Youth for the Western territories of the Hitler Youth (1931?).

[1] To give another example of the Hitler Youth. Its leader, Baldur von Schirach, always emphasised that its uniform did away with differences in dress between rich and poor. 'The uniform [of the Hitler Youth] does not express a war mentality but is the garb of comradeship. It extinguishes class differences. . . . For these young people, socialism has been achieved.' (*Wille und Macht. Führerorgan der National-sozialistischen Jugend*. Year 5, Berlin 1937, No. 1.)

[2] The ubiquitousness was, in fact, not seldom pretended. For example, while in 1939 Mussolini's Fascist Militia had close on 500,000 members, hardly more than 30,000 officers and men were on regular full-time service, including the special Frontier Militia, Roads Militia, Railways Militia, and Ports Militia. The overwhelming majority of the members had only two functions: to don their uniforms at parades and other official occasions; and to act, when required, as informers to the OVRA (Party Secret Police). However the population was not aware of the

hand, the uniforms most visibly indicated the differences of rank and power within the Party formations. They thus facilitated the maintenance of internal discipline and the strict application of the *Führer* principle. Finally, again because the uniforms and the entire quasi-military organisation made differences in rank so conspicuous, they at the same time stirred the ambition for promotion, and thereby made the members more pliable in the hands of their superiors. The careful gradation of ranks and insignia permitted the leadership to play shrewdly on the vanities and jealousies of the members.

The existence of various militarily organised Party formations was of extraordinary assistance to the movements. They were instruments of organised provocation, intimidation, and terror, but also instruments of persuasion (namely, through their sheer existence and public appearances, persuasion by visual means, and not by rational arguments). The Party formations were a vehicle for indoctrinating the activists and, at the same time, for controlling them. They trained a reservoir of Party leaders on all levels. They permitted the granting of posts, ranks, 'prestige', to thousands of followers to whom the Party, before it was in power, could not have given such gratifications. In the case of Germany, the well-trained para-military formations of the Party increased the war potential of the country, in circumvention of domestic and international regulations.[1] Also, in these formations National-Socialism was able to train and select the most unscrupulous and ruthless elements for 'special assignments' in the future. Once the Party had gained power they would join the special police, which brutalised, at first, their own fellow-citizens and during the war, also, and even more, the inhabitants of victimised countries.

In Germany the build-up of the strongly militarised Party formations gave the Party from the beginning an opportunity to gain the support of influential circles among the active and the demobilised regular military officers. The leaders realised that this support was vital, especially in the incipient stages of the movement; and however violent they may have been in their attacks against all sorts of opponents, including the rival nationalistic groups, they hardly ever directed their attacks against the Armed Forces, even during the

---

comparatively small number of the full-time members of the Militia, nor of the distribution of work between the Militia, the OVRA, and the regular police. So much secrecy surrounded the OVRA that people were not even sure of the meaning of those ominous initials (*Opera Volontaria per la Repressione Antifascista*, or *Organizzazione di Vigilanza per la Repressione Antifascista*).

[1] Interestingly, not only in Germany (where at first the régime did not feel strong enough openly to repudiate the restrictions of the Peace Treaty), but also in Italy (where such restrictions did not exist), the build-up of the Air Force was in the hands of a trusted Party man, Balbo in Italy, and Göring in Germany. Although by 1935 these secret activities of Göring's were '*enttarnt*' ('de-secretised'), he tended to the end to consider the *Luftwaffe* as 'his' domain. In Italy the General Staff maintained strong opposition against the domination of the Air Force by the Party.

intermediary half-decade or so of relative stabilisation in Germany (between the turbulent years of the incipient movement and the crisis years preceding their ascension to power), when the support from the military decreased very considerably.

ARMY MILITARISM

'What the German people owe to the Army can be briefly summarised in a single word, namely: everything.'—Adolf Hitler, *Mein Kampf.*
'An Army is the best training school for National-Socialist leaders. At the same time, it is an indispensable basis of power for a ruler who is not going to head the opinion of the masses.'—Konstantin Hierl, Leader of Hitler's Labour Service.

'Army militarism' can most simply be described as an exaltation of the Armed Forces for their own sake. It begins when the Armed Forces start to play a role which goes beyond their strictly professional tasks. A definite sign of army militarism is the tendency to measure the prestige or the worth of the nation by the number of soldiers and guns, and to consider the military as the most important group in society. It is fully grown when the demands of the military overrule, or are carried out independently of, the will of the civilian authorities and when, especially, a disproportionate part of the economic production of the country is being devoted to military purposes, although the international situation does not warrant this. It must be emphasised that army militarism is not, in and of itself, identical with 'war militarism'. Even the extreme form of army militarism—namely, military dictatorship—does not necessarily imply that the military who rule the country are preparing for war. On the other hand, the more powerful the military forces, the easier it will be to prepare for war, economically, militarily, psychologically, and diplomatically.

Neither the Hitler nor the Mussolini régime was a military dictatorship. In Italy the question of 'classic' military dictatorship (a dictatorship established by military *putsch* and kept in power by the military) did not arise. In the Germany of the immediate post-World War I period the possibilities of such a *putsch* were variously and earnestly discussed by high military personalities, and a *putsch* was actually carried out only one and a half years after the disappearance of the régime of the Kaiser. It must be realised that its failure greatly increased Hitler's chances.

THE FAILURE OF THE PURELY MILITARY *PUTSCH* (THE KAPP *PUTSCH* OF 1920)

This *putsch* has been named after Herr Kapp, a high-ranking official of the Prussian administration, who was the main conspirator. An inveterate Pangermanist, Kapp was not a National-Socialist.

He acted in March 1920, with the help of various Free Corps[1] and some generals of the regular army, as well as of Ludendorff, the famous Quartermaster-General of the Kaiser, of a former Berlin Police President, and of others. The plan was to occupy Berlin by a lightning stroke, arrest the Government, and proclaim a 'National Dictatorship'. At first the plan worked surprisingly well. The troops occupied Berlin without meeting any resistance. General von Seeckt, the highest-ranking officer on the Government side, refused to fight the rebels. The Cabinet fled the city. But the Social-Democratic members of the Government called for a general strike against the 'bloody freebooter elements', in order to 'strangle this military dictatorship'. After four days, the rebellion collapsed.

Thus it was made apparent that in a country of Germany's social and political structure a military dictatorship could have been established only through a deliberate decision of the head of State, and even then its chances would have been small. In the ensuing years the proclamation of a military dictatorship was again variously contemplated, by General von Seeckt and others,[2] but they finally decided against it because they felt that a military régime would lack the necessary mass basis in the country. The point is highly relevant for our present discussion; for this essential element for establishing a new militarism—mass support—was eventually contributed by the National-Socialists. The expectation that they would be able to do so, however repugnant their methods and unrespectable their leadership, increased their significance and chances immensely beyond their, as yet, small following.

The abortive military *putsch* of 1920 taught those military leaders who desired a radical re-militarisation of Germany that no such scheme could succeed without a strong mass movement to back it. After Hitler's accession to power no effort was made to conceal this. It was, for example, typically expressed by Colonel (General Staff)

---

[1] The most important among these troops was Captain Ehrhardt's Volunteer Marine Brigade, one of the worst of the terrorist armed groups of the period. Its spirit was expressed in the 'Ehrhardt Song':

> The Swastika on the helmet of steel,
> Black-white-red band,
> The Brigade of Ehrhardt
> Is known around the land.
> Workman, workman, what will become of you
> When the Ehrhardt Brigade stands ready for the fight?
> The Brigade of Ehrhardt knocks everything to bits,
> Woe to you, woe to you, workman, son of a bitch!

[2] See, e.g., Walter Görlitz, *Der Deutsche Generalstab* (The German General Staff) Frankfurt-a/M. (1952?). In fact, Seeckt, Ludendorff, and Stresemann discussed a strong-man régime or a military dictatorship as early as in 1916, two years before the end of World War I. The younger Staff officers thought even at that time that any dictatorship needed a mass basis (Görlitz, p. 261).

von Wedel, of the Supreme Command of the Armed Forces, in an official publication in the following words:

'The unbroken military spirit (*das ungebrochene Kriegertum*) [of Germany's Army at the period of the Kapp *putsch*] survived the lost war and the political upheaval, and was not willing to abdicate in the face of weakness and pacifist theories. Yet, the miscarriage of the Kapp *putsch* of 1920 proved that recovery required time and had to ripen slowly. The Kapp *putsch* also taught that bayonets may be able to conquer power for a moment but that without approval and consent from at least a large portion of the mass of the people, power cannot be maintained.' [1]

The lesson was, first of all, not lost on Hitler himself. He saw that many of the pro-Kapp forces marched into Berlin wearing the swastika on their steel helmets, but that they were not helped at all by the civilian population. (The National-Socialist movement started in Berlin only several years later.) He saw the ambiguous attitude of the official army. He noted that after the *coup* had collapsed, von Seeckt guaranteed an unconditional pardon to the high military personalities involved. Hitler was convinced that his Party alone could provide the missing political idea and the missing mass movement.

'The historical development has shown that our nation never lacked great soldiers but always lacked strong political *führers* and—this is particularly decisive—a healthy political idea. Hence, if a new State was to emerge, the German people had to be given a political idea, and had to be united under that idea. The Germans possessed soldierly qualities. . . . Now, the point was to lay a political basis [for those soldierly qualities]. Political strength was bound, by necessity, to develop into military prowess. It was in accordance with this principle that Adolf Hitler surrounded himself with real men, and trained them to be flag-bearers of his ideas.' [2]

THE FAILURE OF THE INSUFFICIENTLY PREPARED FASCIST *PUTSCH* (THE HITLER *PUTSCH* OF 1923)

In the years following the Kapp *putsch*, Hitler's movement grew, thanks largely to open and concealed support from influential military circles, and became increasingly violent and self-assured. How-

---

[1] Oberstltnt. des Generalstabes von Wedel, Oberkommando der Wehrmacht, 'Von der Reichswehr zur Wehrmacht des Dritten Reiches', in Donnevert, ed., *Wehrmacht und Partei*, 3rd ed. (Leipzig, 1941), p. 34. See also, e.g., Görlitz, op. cit., p. 322: 'The new fiasco of the purely military dictatorship without mass basis was a new lesson for the General Staff. Seeckt had correctly foreseen this fiasco.' (Officially, no General Staff existed in Germany at that time. Seeckt was head of the *Truppenamt*—'Troop agency'—the inconspicuous name for the camouflaged General Staff.)

[2] Chief of Staff of the Berlin SA, Lutze, 'SA und Wehrmacht' in: *Donnevert*, ed., op. cit., pp. 72–3.

ever, this growth was in the main limited to Bavaria, in the south of Germany, and the support from the military came, not from the central authorities in Berlin, but from the local Army Command in Munich—as whose undercover agent Hitler had started his political career. Then, one day in March 1923 (eight months before Hitler attempted his own *putsch*), he received the visit of the Commander-in-Chief, von Seeckt, who had come from Berlin on an information tour. Among other things, the General was interested in the possibility of co-ordinating Hitler's private army—the SA troopers—with the regular army in case of a showdown with France. Seeckt, usually quite sarcastic, was 'extraordinarily impressed' by Hitler, although the obsessiveness with which that ex-corporal demanded the leadership of the nationalist movement for himself and his small party 'caused some misgivings to Seeckt'.[1]

While in Munich, von Seeckt also visited one of the leading representatives of the old school, the Kaiser's retired Quartermaster-General Ludendorff, who declared his willingness to lend his 'historic name' to the war against France if he were made Commander-in-Chief—a demand which von Seeckt neither accepted nor rejected.

It appears that during the summer of that year several plans for a military dictatorship were prepared and that von Seeckt himself drafted a secret sixteen-page memorandum for such a project. Then he again dropped the plan, deciding instead to look for a man able to provide popular support for a régime which would carry out the wishes of the military. But Hitler had got wind of the project, and his Munich paper, the *Völkischer Beobachter*, publicly attacked von Seeckt for planning a 'reactionary dictatorship'. The attack, coming from the arch-plotter, was as impertinent as it was logical. Had he not told Seeckt that he, Hitler, was to head the nationalist movement? If there was to be such a régime, the leadership was not to go to the professional military, but to the National-Socialist experts in demagogic manipulation.

Seeckt was angered by the attack. (Incidentally, the *Völkischer Beobachter* added for good measure that Frau von Seeckt was Jewish.) He asked the military commander of Munich, General von Lossow, to use his emergency powers and to prohibit Hitler's paper. But Hitler's influence among the Munich officers was then so strong that von Lossow refused to obey. Thereupon von Seeckt deprived von Lossow of his post as military commander of Munich. Von Lossow defied this order, too. He was backed by the Prime Minister of Bavaria, Kahr, who in turn caused General von Lossow and Lossow's troops to switch their oath of allegiance from the German Reich to the State of Bavaria alone. Kahr had his own plans, with the aim of separating Bavaria from the rest of Germany and of establishing an

[1]Görlitz, p. 347.

ultra-conservative royalist régime. There are strong indications that Hitler staged his Munich Beerhall *putsch* of 8th November 1923 precipitately, for fear lest Kahr should strike immediately and proclaim a Bavarian kingdom.

The events show in miniature the law of fascist gravity—namely, that if schemes of this type compete with each other the advantage lies with the most extreme and most unscrupulous competitor—in that case, Hitler. At the famous Beerhall meeting on the evening of 8th November, the Kaiser's old Quartermaster-General (whom Hitler had promised to make Commander-in-Chief—the condition Ludendorff had made to von Seeckt), publicly pledged support to Hitler, as did General von Lossow and Prime Minister Kahr.

But why did Kahr and von Lossow, literally overnight, change their minds? The very next morning Hitler and a column of his followers (still including Ludendorff) marched with swastika flags towards the centre of Munich to take over power, but they were dispersed by a single salvo from a detachment of Bavarian police. This was the end of Hitler's *putsch*. He did not have the mass support which would have induced a sufficient number of military leaders on the one hand, and a sufficient number of reactionary leaders, like Kahr, on the other, to back him. The Federal Government declared martial law, and von Seeckt prohibited the National-Socialist as well as the Communist Parties. He observed to his adjutant that the officers who had sided with Hitler had broken discipline, which was inadmissible—but had those young men not participated, one would have to despair. In a confidential letter a few days later he stated that he saw no way without 'a certain dictatorship' (*eine gewisse Diktatur*). 'I would be glad if a man could be found. I myself do not desire to rule, but to see the aim realised.' [1]

Hitler had acted with consummate skill. If only for a few hours, he succeeded in fusing the military and the monarchist conspiracies, which were much stronger and more respectable than his own movement, and in having his own leadership accepted by both. From his failure he learned that his Party, possessing as it did only local strength, was not yet big enough, and that if the army so desired it could block him. He also saw that he got away with a ridiculously light sentence. He concluded that next time powerful groups whose backing he needed for coming into power would not withdraw their support if he were able to convince them that his movement had the vitality, dynamism, and radicalism which they themselves lacked.

After his early release from prison it took Hitler and the Party only about eight years to accomplish this. The National-Socialist methods

[1] Letter by von Seeckt to his sister, Countess von Rotkirch und Trach, dated 18 Nov. 1923, quoted by Görlitz, p. 353.

of terror and brutality were often repugnant to the groups Hitler was determined to outshout, to cajole, and to seduce. But it soon became clear that they were not capable of waging a whole-hearted campaign against him. (This is speaking of them as a group; individual rank-and-file members and also some leaders, and some splinter groups, did make a fight, but eventually they either acquiesced or were pushed aside.)

The method used by the National-Socialists to accomplish this gradual paralysation and eventual conquest and absorption of rival groups and parties was both simple and effective. It consisted in being always twice and three times as extremist and fanatical as the others: when others were against socialist-controlled trade unions, the Nazis were against all trade unions, including Right-wing ones; when others endeavoured to make gains in the international field by propagandistic and diplomatic means, however daring, the Nazis were aggressively provocative; if others were 'traditionally' anti-semitic, the Nazis revelled in bloodthirstiness; and so on.

First of all, the others did not push resolutely enough the interests of the military forces. Here the National-Socialist equation of patriotism with militarism paid the best dividends. Armaments, a bigger military establishment, more military prowess in every respect—only he who worked ceaselessly for these aims, with complete disregard of considerations and consequences, was a patriot. No other party clamoured for these things as they did: they were the true patriots. Their young 'activists' did not hesitate to beat up old women who had lost their sons in the war, and who now had the insolence to demonstrate for disarmament. They set themselves up as arbiters and jealous guardians of the national good, and by putting the target always a few degrees beyond the attainable, were always able to show that their rivals fell short of the goal.

They soon found out that any rivalling group which did not squarely oppose the basic Nazi aims was, in the long run, caught and that therefore they were able largely to call the tune even before they were in power. They set the pace, and the more the others tried to 'take the wind out of the sails of the Nazis' by showing that they actually had the same aims, the more did the competitors become prisoners of the National-Socialists and lost votes and influence to them. It was a race in which the National-Socialists could not lose— as long, that was, as the others tried to live up to, instead of opposing, the cynical demagogy of the National-Socialists.

This technique of the spiral paid off in geometric proportion. It led of necessity to an ever-increasing temperature in the domestic and international policy of the rival non-fascist parties in power, and also to an ever-increasing radicalisation of the National-Socialists themselves. The Party had relentlessly to heighten its pitch, and the others had to heighten theirs because they mistakenly hoped to beat the National-Socialists at their own game.

For all this to succeed, the National-Socialists had constantly to whip up emotions, fears, and prejudices; to maintain, foster, and intensify tension; and to create and intensify an atmosphere of anxiety and crisis, of the feeling that 'something big is bound to happen, "this way" it cannot go on much longer'. Words became effective, not by the amount of reason they contained, but by the amount of foam at the mouth. As in an individual, the fever created at the same time restlessness and apathetic exhaustion in the body politic, and both these reactions helped the swastika.

Yet another essential aspect of their methods and techniques was that they kept within such boundaries as would just still be tolerated by the head of the State. Mussolini and Hitler were completely contemptuous of constitutional niceties, but realised that ultimately they needed the decisive formality of being invested with the premiership by one individual—the King of Italy, and the President in Germany. Because they were keenly aware of this need, they insisted, before coming into power, on their own 'legality'. Stripped of all details, their emphasis on 'legality'[1] meant their determination to have the door which would lead them into power opened to them by the constitutional authority—that is, the head of the State. The only alternative was an attempt to open the door themselves, by direct military means—civil war. They were realists enough to know that the outcome of a civil war was by no means certain. Hence they never permitted an irreparable break to occur with the head of the State and his most influential advisers. Historically speaking, it is correct to say that the heads of State helped them decisively, and to this extent their advent to power was favoured by specific circumstances and what chanced to be the character of identifiable individuals. To this extent the gambler's instinct of Mussolini and Hitler was decisive. While even many of their own followers feared that they overplayed their hands, the *Duce* and the *Führer* proved to be better judges of the foibles of the men on whose eventual surrender they had to stake their success.

For Mussolini the step into the premiership was comparatively easy. His King was so bewildered by a confusing situation that he made him the head of a coalition government, although this was wholly unwarranted by the actual strength of the Party. Badoglio

---

[1] 'The consolidation, however transitory, of the internal situation [in Germany] destroyed all chances for any illegal *putsch*, and left only the way of legality as promising success. That this turn toward parliamentary tactics had nothing whatsoever to do with the basic attitude [of National-Socialism] was self-evident,' Otto Dietrich, Hitler's Press Chief, in his analysis of Hitler's tactics, *Mit Hitler in die Macht, Persönliche Erlebnisse mit meinem Führer*. (Munich, 1934), 11th ed., pp. 26–7.

urged the King to declare martial law, whereupon the army would easily do away with the *Fascisti*, but Vittorio Emanuele refused; he may have been mindful of the fact that four generals were among the leaders of the 'march on Rome'.

The developments in Germany throw even more light on the methods of ascending Fascism because there the road to power was much slower. President von Hindenburg, the former Imperial Field-Marshal, considered to be the very incarnation of traditional military attitudes, was reluctant to assign to an upstart the position which Bismarck had once held. His contemptuous reference to Hitler as the '*Gefreiter*' (corporal) has become famous. He had gradually to be persuaded that the political crisis—which the Nazis did everything to inflate, just as the *Fascisti* had done in Italy a decade before—could not be solved otherwise, and that the National-Socialists would re-militarise the country.

On the latter point the officer whose views we have already quoted as typical of the way men like him saw the developments stated, 'It must have overjoyed the aged Field-Marshal of the World War [President von Hindenburg] that before his death he was able to see the dawn of military-political freedom.' [1] The fateful event is regarded as the intrinsically logical culmination of the relations between army and Party which had existed throughout the preceding years:

'On the thorny road of those years [the Armed Forces] had to struggle against weakness, ignorance and malice [with respect to military matters] at home, against control commissions [established to prevent Germany's clandestine remilitarisation] of the allied enemies, and against traitors within the nation itself. On the one side, there was the open struggle against the enemy abroad and against the marxistically and pacifistically infected part of our own people, on the other side a hidden struggle against misunderstandings and distrust that prevailed among large groups of even nationalistic Germans. . . .

'Except for the propaganda battle of the National Socialist Party, there was certainly no school and no organisation which gave as penetrating an education on the dictate of Versailles as did the *Reichswehr* (Armed Forces) of the pre-Hitler Weimar Republic.

'. . . Thus, *the Armed Forces kept open all the roads toward a better future*. It kept *the house ready and in shape for the entry of a new spirit* which, *outside* the Armed Forces under Adolf Hitler's leadership, *slowly created the prerequisites for the ascendancy to power* [of the National-Socialists].

'On that 30th of January 1933 [when Hitler became the head of the Government] the Armed Forces and the Party coalesced—both

[1] Lt.-Col. von Wedel, p. 40.

inspired by the community of the trenches, both based on a soldierly ideology, and both, albeit each according to its own respective tasks, and although they were separated from each other in their development by the Versailles Dictate and the Weimar Constitution, had *for years marched towards the identical goal.*

'When on the 30th of January 1933 the *Führer* took Germany's leadership into his strong hands . . . the German Armed Forces were also at his disposal, in firm discipline. What the union (*Vereinigung*) of the two factors, National-Socialist movement and Armed Forces meant for the nation, was expressed by the *Führer* himself: "The best hope which we so long nourished has been fulfilled: National-Socialism and Armed Forces have fused into one, have merged into a single unit." '

It is recognised that there was some friction between Armed Forces and Party, but it subsided as Hitler remilitarised:

'It is true that at first there was some scepticism in the ranks of the Armed Forces. This was in connection with the special position of the Armed Forces within the State.[1] . . . But very soon the soldier recognised in National-Socialism a soldierly mentality which was altogether akin to his own, and therefore familiar to him and his own aim. . . . And when the National-Socialist revolution broke the chains of Versailles [that is, the provisions on military restrictions] the last ice melted in the heart of even the last sceptic. . . .

'Indeed, how could it be otherwise? National-Socialism is the political incarnation of true soldierdom; . . . Soldierly mentality was elevated by Adolf Hitler to the basic law of the nation.' [2]

In June 1934, Hitler, after the first period of stabilisation of his régime (having been in power for seventeen months), and with Hindenburg still President, had several high-ranking military officers assassinated, among them General of Infantry Kurt von Schleicher, who had been his predecessor as Reich Chancellor. This evidenced Hitler's feeling of strength, but it infuriated the army. A petition, addressed to Hindenburg by fellow officers of Schleicher's regiment and signed by about thirty active and retired generals, described how von Schleicher and his wife were murdered by SS men 'who belonged to the personal guard of Herr Prime Minister [of the State of Prussia] Göring'.

'Your Excellency, as the glorious representative of German soldierly honour and military genius, are most respectfully requested to protect the honour of the Army which is being threatened by criminals. . . . How can we continue to wear with pride the

---

[1] The author alludes to Hitler's concentration of power, which tended to limit the high degree of independence the Armed Forces enjoyed under the Republic.
[2] Col. von Wedel, pp. 34–7. (Italics added.)

honourable garb of the soldier if one of our best . . . can be murdered and the murderers remain unpunished?'

The memorandum of discontented military officers to the Field-marshal-President of 18th July 1934 again shows the dilemma of those who criticised the methods but not the essential aims of the régime. They urged Hindenburg to form a new government but, interestingly, under Hitler:

'. . . National-Socialism was supposed to unite the disunited nation, and to *prepare it for the inevitably approaching encounter with the exterior enemy.* After one and a half years of [Hitler's] National Government we must state with deepest regret that the task has not been fulfilled . . . A large part of the working population still stands sulkingly aside and is hostile to the new State. The nation is divided by an unfortunate cleavage among the Churches. As long as the political and religious cleavage is not overcome, as long as the masses at large do not unreservedly back the State, we shall not be able to meet the *great military tasks of the future.* Those strata of society who are steeped in the traditions that have made our nation great, are excluded from power [by the National-Socialists] . . . The Reich Minister for Economic Affairs has not succeeded in organising the raw materials basis which is indispensable in case of conflagration by war.'

Likewise, 'the foreign policy of the National Government has not established the prerequisites which, as the [first] World War showed, are indispensable for a victorious outcome.'

The memorandum counsels 'to change the policy toward the East and to seek a rapprochement with Russia' since 'only in this manner can the war-on-two-fronts be avoided'. In order to *'create the prerequisites for a victorious war'* a 'Directorate' must be established with Hitler at the helm, 'to carry out all internal and external preparations for the inevitable encounter of the future . . . The only and exclusive task of the new government would be, within the period of one and a half to two years which we need, to *establish the interior peace by all means,* and to create the necessary conditions in the field of foreign policy. It would have the task of organising the economy to fulfill the war task confronting it.' [1]

Hindenburg died soon afterwards. But it is doubtful whether he could have followed such advice [2] and, if he had, whether events would have taken a different course. Hitler knew that much was

---

[1] Quoted in *Weissbuch über die Erschiessungen des 30 Juni* (1934). 3rd ed. (Paris, 1935), pp. 148–52. (Italics added.)
[2] He died on 2 Aug. 1934. The executions took place on 30 June. On 2 July he had sent the following telegram to 'The Prime Minister (of Prussia), Infantry General Göring. For your energetic and successful proceeding of smashing treason I express to you my thanks and recognition. With comradely thanks and regards von Hindenburg.'—Quoted in Erich Gritzbach's biography of Göring, *Hermann Göring: Werk und Mensch* (Munich, 1938), p. 253.

B B

still to be done. He was himself out 'to establish the interior peace by all means'—that is, to make the great majority of the people confirmatively support, or at least quietly accept, the grandiose militarisation, and to prevent the indigestible rest from interfering with it. As to the 'inevitably approaching encounter', the best method was outwardly to present the whole endeavour only as 'army militarism'—pretending that the feverish armament was for the sake of national pride and equality, and not for the sake of war.

For example, one of the most important steps (March 1935) was the re-introduction of general compulsory military service. This was heralded as re-establishing the country's self-esteem and designed for the vigour of its youth. The citizen who listened to the countless official and inspired declarations was to gain the impression that the general conscription was somewhat of a mixture between an (expensive, to be sure!) ritual for the nation's prestige and a (tough, to be sure!) physical exercise for the nation's health. As a by-product, this line fanned resentment against foreign countries, which begrudged them the newly-won freedom. While the policy aimed, of course, at German *superiority*, the official propaganda skilfully played upon the very standards which the régime rejected—it appealed to international *equality*, condemned 'discrimination' against any country, and, first of all, denied to the victor in war any right over the defeated.

The enormous armament manufacturing programme which was pushed with disregard for everything else (guns instead of butter) was more difficult to explain as merely another requirement for obtaining military prowess commensurate to the nation's position and defensive needs. The true magnitude of the programme was carefully hidden. Also it was depicted as the harbinger of economic prosperity and full employment.

Throughout those years, in innumerable articles, books, lectures, and meetings, the régime claimed and received credit for its main achievement—namely, to have built a record military might and to have united the nation for this task, and through this task.

All means were used for this purpose. On the negative side, literally every organisation and institution was suppressed which could even remotely be suspected of lack of sympathy—from the non-party press and the labour unions, for example, to the sport organisations, and from the most innocent chess club to the influential associations of manufacturers. The ubiquitous police and well-controlled penal courts did their share to extinguish every flickering of opposition. Positively, the skilful operation of huge, compulsory, or monopolistic Party organisations such as the Hitler Youth, the National-Socialist Students' Association, the Labour Service, and so on, were all designed to underpin and strengthen the military potential. For example, the aims of the Hitler Youth organisation were described as follows by a high-ranking official:

'There has to be a clear-cut decision whether one wants to live a soldier's life or a civilian life. Either the one way of life is correct, or the other. If we in Germany have to make this decision, we can in our era choose but one way of life, namely, the soldierly way of life. . . .'

This is not entirely easy to achieve because 'we have to admit that the way of life in the youth organisation differs from the way of life in the Armed Forces. Our time, however, allows us to draw a single and straight line all the way from the tenth year of life [when the boy joins the Hitler Youth] up to the time of discharge from the Armed Forces. This line goes from para-military education (*Wehrerziehung*) through military education (*militärische Erziehung*). It is of immense educational importance, not only for becoming a soldier but quite in general. The boy must feel that here he is going through a natural progression, and must experience this as a continuous, unrestrained upward-trend of his life. The young scout gradually grows into becoming the nation's arms-bearer. This re-establishes the natural progression well-known to every unsophisticated warrior class which always has made the boy first a scout, later has provided him with training-arms, and ultimately has deservedly handed him the deadly weapon of the grown-up man. . . . The programme for the future will not only mean an education for becoming a soldier but, inseparably, for becoming a German man, whose decisive final casting occurs while he serves in the Armed Forces. . . .'

'Militarily speaking, everything the boy learns up to the time [he reaches the age of conscription] serves but to make him get at the enemy and to have him give an account of himself with arms (*an den Feind heran and zur Wirkung mit der Waffe zu kommen*). . . . It is a strange mentality for a nation to apportion several years during which hours are spent every day on penmanship and spelling but not a single hour on shooting. Liberalism inscribed over the school doors, "Knowledge is Power". But we have learned in the war and post-war era that the power of a nation ultimately rests on its weapons solely, and on those who know how to use them.' [1]

At the same time, the militarisation policy was always described as *protection against war*. Hitler's deputy, Rudolf Hess, in a typical appeal for sacrifices in the interest of rearmament, gave this formulation of a theme repeated in many variations:

'The *Führer* is not given to doing things half-way. Every additional gun, every additional tank, every additional airplane gives

[1] *National Political Study Course for the Armed Forces*, 15–23 Jan. 1937, reproduced only for official use by the Armed Forces. *Obergebiets-Führer* Dr Hellmuth Stellrecht, '*Die Wehrerziehung der Deutschen Jugend*' (The Military Education of German Youth), pp. 165–76.—On the methods of absorbing the non-Party youth associations, see below in this essay, p. 774.

additional security to the German mother, that her children will not be slaughtered in a cursed war—that they will not be tortured to death by bolshevist bands. We are seeing to it that any desire to attack us will disappear forever.' (Speech at Hof, Bavaria, 11th October 1936.)

The policy strengthened the grip of the régime over the military. Their demands were now eagerly fulfilled; nay, they were prodded to ask for more. Gone were the press attacks on military expenditures and the inquiries of parsimonious budget committees.

'In Germany today, nobody would even think of asking questions, let alone of casting 'doubts on, the behaviour of the Armed Forces. Not to speak of the "distrust" [against the military] which used to be the habit of many a parliamentarian and which today strikes us simply as tragi-comical. Today, nobody knows anything anymore of all those woeful political worries. They are simply inconceivable. . . .'[1]

The schools, the radio, the newspapers, and the Party organisations vied with each other to speak of the need and value of military strength. Until 1938, when Hitler actually began marching into other countries, he respected the prerogative of the officers' corps to do their own selecting and promoting of officers, although many were not Party members. He preferred to have tradition-bound officers 'grow into' the new order.[2]

There is no gainsaying the fact that some military leaders foresaw the ruinous ultimate consequences, and shuddered at them. But the din of praise muted the voices of criticism. For example, in October 1935 the War Academy was established, 'to carry out its activity openly, restricted by nothing'. As on similar occasions, Hitler received unreserved homage. At the elaborate opening ceremony the Commander of the new War Academy, Lieut.-General Liebmann, told him in the presence of a galaxy of military leaders: 'We are convinced in our deepest soul that we have to thank only your determined will and your infallible leadership for our freedom' (in military matters). War Minister General von Blomberg, in his *Sieg-Heil* to Hitler, added that 'the military recognised that they had the good fortune of working at a task never before presented so handsomely and honourably to German soldiers'.[3]

But the régime exacted a price: it was the very fact that they served a régime of the moral qualities of Hitlerism, imbued with lust for

---

[1] Major of the Luftwaffe, Cohrs, 'Der Offizier als Erzieher im Dritten Reich' in: *Donnevert*, ed., p. 112.
[2] See, e.g., Friedrich Hossbach, *Zwischen Wehrmacht und Hitler* (Hanover, 1949), pp. 46, 179, 184.
[3] *Berliner Börsenzeitung*, 16 Oct. 1935.

aggression and subjugation. Time-honoured standards of military respectability fatefully degenerated when they were tinged and infected by the standards of Hitlerism. The trend began even before the Party were in power, and revealed its final catastrophic results in their conduct of the war. Many, especially the products of the Free Corps era and of the Party, had lost the capacity to understand what was wrong; many among the officers disliked it, but gradually became somehow reconciled that these were the new ways of militarism; some closed their eyes and considered themselves 'only soldiers', even while giving indispensable professional co-operation; there were those who took it with mental reservations and grumbled privately; some resigned, and some rebelled even to the point of plotting against Hitler.[1] What counted was that the régime was able to receive co-operation from so large a portion that the misgivings of the rest was irrelevant.[2] This crucial success was obtained by making the military profession stronger than they had ever been before; by

[1] A plot to overthrow the régime began to take shape among a small group of top-ranking officers before the summer of 1938, but led nowhere, largely because of Hitler's gain in prestige as a result of the Munich Agreement. In fact, some of the plotters subsequently played leading roles in World War II.—An attempt on Hitler's life was made in Jul. 1944, at a time when experts realised that the war was lost and should be ended quickly. Some of the conspirators were animated by true revulsion against the crimes of the régime. But conspiracy and assassination were part of the game in the Third Reich—no other way was open to replace the demoniac Führer. Participation in the conspiracy showed realisation of this fact, and great daring, but not necessarily the moral value of the decision.

[2] A famous case was the resignation of General Beck, Chief of the General Staff of the Army, at the height of the crisis over Hitler's 'unalterable decision' to attack Czechoslovakia by 1 Oct. 1938. The deadline had been tentatively set in the top secret 'Directive for the Uniform Preparation of War (einheitliche Kriegsvorbereitung) by the Armed Forces' of 24 Jun. 1937. The directive asked for case 'Deployment Green' ('Two-front war with gravity South-east'), 'to enable the great mass of all forces to invade Czechoslovakia rapidly, with surprise and with fullest impact, and to provide for the West only a minimum of forces as rear cover for this aggressive operation. . . .'

Beck was opposed to the plan. A deep cleavage developed between the Chief of Staff and the Commander-in-Chief of the Army, General von Brauchitsch. After the war, an officer with intimate knowledge of the events published, e.g., this memorandum from Beck to von Brauchitsch, dated 16 Jul. 1937:

'With reference to the responsibility which, according to instructions, I shall have to bear for the preparation and execution of a war, I beg to express the urgent request to induce the Supreme Commander of the Armed Forces [Hitler] to stop the war preparations which have been ordered by him, and to postpone (solange zurückzustellen) the intention of settling the Czech question by force until the military preconditions for it have changed fundamentally. At present, I consider them hopeless. . . .'

Beck's repeated request to von Brauchitsch to pursue a policy of restraint were in vain. 'By the summer of 1938 the tension between the two men increased so much that Beck repeatedly thought of resigning, and actually did so in Aug. 1938.' But even before Beck's resignation, von Brauchitsch 'increasingly asked Lieut.-General Halder, then Quartermaster I at the General Staff of the Army, to deal with tasks of the General Staff' (Hossbach, p. 418). Halder succeeded Beck on 1 Sep. 1938. Incidentally, Beck's own predecessor as Chief of the General Staff of the Army, General Adam, had also resigned.

removing all obstacles from the path of the military; by putting a
larger portion of the country's resources at their disposal than any
other government had done. It was like the case of the shady character who suddenly showers bounty on his family, but with the
understanding that no questions be asked about the origin of those
riches.

THE DEGENERATION OF MILITARY VIRTUES

Discipline and correctness are among the indispensable military
qualities. They are the barriers which prevent the improper use of
organised violence. Once these barriers weaken, the forces which
possess the instruments of death and destruction get out of hand, and
there is no end to danger. The holders of weapons must be disciplined, just as gasoline dumps must be protected against fire; if the
gasoline dumps catch fire they are apt to destroy the very community
they are intended to serve.

Interestingly enough, the National-Socialists attached enormous
importance to what may be called the paraphernalia and trimmings
of military correctness and discipline. They were meticulous about
such things as the polishing of brass knuckles, the heel-clicking, the
Hitler salute, the ribbons and emblems, the correct marching. In
fact, they heaped ridicule on the 'weaklings' and 'degenerates' who
did not share their concern about these attributes of manliness. But
they systematically and deliberately corrupted and violated the
essential of military correctness and discipline. That is, in plainest
words, they boldly and defiantly did things which true military correctness and discipline would absolutely have forbidden them to do.
They kicked their—correctly polished—boots without scruple into
the groins of defenceless women.

It would be ridiculous, of course, to maintain that the indignities,
humiliations, and brutalities they systematically administered to
their victims had anything to do with military matters. Yet it is
characteristic, for example, that the Supreme SS Leader Himmler,
lecturing to military officers, assured his listeners that in his concentration camps there was 'order, strict order and cleanliness, strict
discipline'. The way the inmates had to stand at attention, to march,
to sing, he said, 'all of these things must be done in absolute, strict
soldierly discipline and order'.[1] One of the tortures customary in the
concentration camps, which was applied in many studied varieties
and with great gusto, was the 'punitive drill'. The emaciated and
groaning victims had to do excruciating mock 'military exercises',

---

[1] Himmler's lecture was reproduced, 'only for the use by the Armed Forces',
in *National Political Study Course for the Armed Forces*, 15–23 Jan. 1937, op. cit.,
p. 149.

often to the point of death—for example, to run in circles with stone-filled bags on their backs, or to hop around in crouching positions ('frog-hop'), and the like, with the guards, whip in hand and bloodhound on leash, shouting 'military' commands.

Such methods were possible only after the Party had come into power. But long before, beating of persons and destruction of property were carried out with 'military' precision under 'military' formation. 'Military' techniques were used to make brutality more efficient. It goes without saying that this was a parody of military behaviour. The methods of the concentration camps within Germany before World War II, later on the even multiplied horrors of the Gestapo cells and the Security Police in the occupied lands, and finally the techniques of the extermination camps and gas chambers were the ultimate flowering of the carefully organised methods of brutality in the formative period of the movement.

Since brutality (called 'ruthlessness') was calculated and of the essence, it was a key quality of the Party leaders and activists. 'Soft' personalities who still somehow adhered to democratic principles had no place among them, and the most ruthless had the best chances. Without this negative principle of selection the régime could not have carried out its far-reaching plans.

Two illustrations from two different periods may be given. In Berlin, the key city, the Party was for years unable to gain a real foothold. In October 1926 Hitler sent one of his top men, Goebbels. to Berlin 'with special full powers' to remedy the situation. Writing in retrospect eight years later, Goebbels stated:

'I was fully determined to use these full powers ruthlessly (*in rücksichtsloser Weise*). What at that time called itself the Party in Berlin . . . was a checkered conglomeration of a few hundred people who thought in a National-Socialist way, each of whom had formed his own private idea on what National-Socialism was. . . . This Party was not manœuvrable. Quite apart from its numbers, one could not deploy it for the decisive political battle even in view of its quality. One had first to give it cohesive form and inspire it with a new *hot impulse*. . . . One had to *hammer* its name and its aim into the public consciousness and *through fight obtain for the movement, if not love and respect, at least hatred and passionate rejection.* . . . Some sub-groups behaved completely like a patriotic bowling club, rather than like a revolutionary fighting movement. In such cases, ruthless (*rücksichtslos*) action had to be taken. In the political organisation [of the Berlin Party] a sort of parliamentary democracy had emerged, and some people thought the new leadership [Goebbels] could be made the spineless play-ball of majority decisions of the various cliques. This was done away with, at once. To be sure, we thereby lost a number of *unusable elements* who had fostered themselves on the Party. But *essentially they did not belong to us at all.* . . . Unruffled by all too many [party members] we hoisted the flag of our idea and *set fanatical people in march for it who were fighting without giving quarter.*'

He was satisfied with the eventual success:

'I still remember with deep emotion how one evening I, completely unknown, rode through Berlin to a meeting, seated on the upper deck of a bus with a few old-timer comrades. On the streets and squares, the ant-like hustle of the big city. . . . Above, the scintillating light-glow of that city-monster. Then one of us anxiously queried if we would ever be able to *force upon and hammer into* (*aufzuzwingen und einzuhämmern*) this city our own names, irrespective of whether Berlin wanted it or not. Much sooner than we could believe and hope at that hour, the facts unmistakably answered that fearful question.' [1]

In 1940, Hans Frank, President of the Academy of German Law and Governor-General of part of occupied Poland, told his collaborators:

'What counts for us is to build up German authority in this region. For such work we cannot use the criteria of governments of past centuries as to the happiness of the individual Pole, but we judge our measures only by the extent to which they make it more and more impossible for Poland ever to get on her feet again. This may sound harsh and cruel, but in the struggle of nations for centuries and millennia there can be no different decision. It is completely clear that only utterly strong and hard characters are fit for this task. Those who are not fit for this task have long since gone from our midst or have otherwise left us. We think here imperially in the grandest style of all times. The imperialism which we develop cannot even stand comparison to those miserable efforts which former, weak German governments undertook in Africa . . . This territory [of Poland] is fated to be the labour reservoir on a huge scale. We have here nothing but a gigantic work camp where everything that means power and independence, is in the hands of Germans. . . . ' (Meeting of section heads of the Government-General, 6th November 1940.) 'The Pole here must feel that we are not building for him a State with a rule of law (*Rechtsstast*), but that he has one single duty—namely, to work and to be meek. Evidently this sometimes leads to difficulties, but in your own interest you must see to it that all measures be taken ruthlessly, in order to master all this. You can absolutely rely on me. . . .' (Meeting of section heads, 19th December 1940.) [2]

Organised brutality had to be fertilised by fanaticism. The miasmatic hatred could be sensed almost physically. It spread as the

---

[1] Joseph Goebbels, *Kampf um Berlin* (Munich, 1934), pp. 23, 30–4.
[2] Reproduced in Vol. 2 of the Diary of Governor-General Hans Frank (Nbg Doc. 2233-PS, *Trial of the Major War Criminals before the International Military Tribunal, Nuremberg*, 1948, Vol. 29, pp. 380–1.

movement spread. Newspapers, speeches, books, parades, and manifestations of all kind fostered it deliberately. To the mind of the Fascist all those who were against him, or who in his own opinion could possibly be against him at some unknown future date, or whom by fiat he put beyond the pale—all of them, individuals as well as entire categories of people, were despicable, unworthy, traitorous. They were stamped not only as enemies, but also as scum. Hence 'all measures' might be taken against them. The emotions which were thus whipped up were so bitter that they became impenetrable by rational argument, and made the people more and more insensitive to the wrongs committed. Feelings of hatred and contempt were to be kept so inflamed that facts and explanation could not reach them. This was another barometer of the advance of Nazism—namely, the degree to which the elementary sense of justice, the instinct for fair play, was blurred among the people at large. Much has been said about the lying techniques of the National-Socialists. But it can be asserted that Nazism was fully successful to the extent to which it could afford *not* to lie. Its success was complete when it dared to tell the stark *truth*, when it was able to *display* its trespasses, instead of having to hide or to deny them.[1]

This education started long before the Party came into power— at a time when, in spite of the creeping corrosion of fundamental rights, the opponents still had ample opportunity to expose it. In those earlier stages benevolent critics would admonish the National-

---

[1] To quote, for example, two utterances by Governor-General Hans Frank. On 6 Feb. 1940 Governor-General Hans Frank told a reporter who interviewed him, for publication in the German Press: 'If for every seven executed Poles I wanted to hang out public announcements, then the forests of Poland would not suffice to produce the paper for such announcements.' On 1 Aug. 1942, he said in a Party mass meeting at the Opera-House of Lwow (Lemberg):

'Men and Women Party Comrades! Soldiers! . . . We cannot thank the *Führer* enough that he decided to give this old Jew-haunt, this dilapidated castle of high-road and low-road robbers, this polackish settlement, at long last to German fists which, with shovel in hand, with insecticides and other required utensils, have taken care that Lemberg is again fit for a German person to live in. [Thunderous applause.] I must say, Party Comrade Wächter, you have done a fine job; within one year you have made us forget what kind of a filthy place (*Drecknest*) this was. Lemberg is again a proud German city, under German leaders, German in its buildings, German in the ideology of its leaders. That's what is so handsome in this war, that what we once have got we shall never give up. [Hilarity and applause.] . . . Evidently, we in the Government-General are so to speak the oldest battle troop as far as experience in the set-up of a conquered land is concerned, and we know what the *Führer* has done in giving us this district of Galicia. I am not speaking of the Jews whom we still have here; with those Jews we shall also know how to deal. Incidentally, today I did not notice anything of them. What has happened? Allegedly, once upon a time there used to be thousands and thousands of those flatfoot-Indians (*Plattfussindianern*) in this city—not a single one was to be seen today. For heaven's sake, you have not perhaps been mean to them? [Great hilarity.]'

At that time the mass extermination of the Jews was in full swing. (*Diary of Governor-General Hans Frank*, pp. 461, 540–1.)

Socialists 'to behave', and thereby to win over many people who were repulsed by their methods. Such admonitions underrated the ulterior ambitions of the National-Socialists and the central role of this pugnacity. Their eventual intentions required *ever greater* violence, and to reach the goals, their followers had to be as shock-proof as possible. Many could not be numbed in their own conscience, but in the end only those counted who could.

Disregard for the rights of the adversary led, in turn, to perversion of another cardinal military virtue—namely, courage. They never tired of extolling courage. They knew that praise for courage was good propaganda, as was, particularly, deriding the opponent for lack of courage. Actually—and with exceptions which existed but did not change the pattern—their tactics conspicuously *lacked* courage. This was true both with respect to physical danger as well as to risks of being arrested and the like. Ever since the early 'swift' administration of castor oil by *Fascisti*, much ingenuity was spent in devising techniques which would at the same time be offensive and safe. Illustrations abound. It may suffice here to cite one stratagem used by National-Socialists during their growing period in cities where the police was likely to be energetic. A group of SA troopers would inconspicuously enter the university grounds in civilian clothes, change into their brown uniforms in the well-protected rooms of friendly student organisations, and then create a fracas by beating up opponents, including girls, with sticks and clubs. They knew that under the autonomy enjoyed by universities the police would be unable to intervene.

Characteristically, the other side was never conceded the right of defence or counter-attack in a figurative or in a real sense. Efforts to strike back were denounced as new evidence of the depravity and insolence of the adversary. This was contrary to the military code, but useful as propagandist strategy. If they met no obstacles, the opponent was ridiculed;[1] if they did, further hatred was created through denunciation of the opponent's vileness and furious complaints of being persecuted.

The tendency to consider every difficulty as ignominy, every setback as the result of sinister, treacherous conspiracy, every opposition to themselves as somehow subversive against the nation, made them pretend that, on the contrary, they were justified in using subterfuge, intrigue, and violence without compunction and even with pride. It must be realised that also in this respect their mentality gave them a head start *vis-à-vis* other political movements which were restricted by the civilian rules of democratic procedure. They

---

[1] ' If the other side has arms, we have what the other side does not have: the lust for violence.'—Joseph Goebbels, *Diktatur und Ständestaat* (chapter 'Der Wille zur Macht'), p. 18.

despised these rules. They were committed to the basic proposition that in internal and international affairs the method to be used was the method of violence (which includes, of course, the threat of violence also other than physical). And are ruses and stratagems not elements of the clever conduct of war?

Yet, just as an honourable soldier even in war will not illegitimately kill an enemy, there is a crucial demarcation line for the military profession between the permitted and the not-permitted trickery. (We are dealing here no longer with the basic point, which is that, of course, the use of '*military*' methods in domestic *political* affairs is in itself inadmissible even with adherence to the military code, just as in international affairs aggressive war is inadmissible even if the aggressor obeys the rules of warfare. We are discussing the point that not only did fascism 'militarise' everything, but, in addition, it cast aside the proprieties of military conduct, which are the only protection against nihilisation and the law of the jungle.) For very compelling reasons, the concept of 'honour' is central to military conduct. In fact, conscious of the appeal of the concept, the National-Socialists always spoke of honour. The Party's official ideologist, Alfred Rosenberg, wrote in his *Der Mythus des 20. Jahrhunderts*—which ranked immediately after Hitler's *Mein Kampf*—that 'the idea of honour, of national honour, becomes for us the alpha and omega of all our thinking and acting'. But they usurped the right to define honour as it suited them. 'Outside of honour, there must be no other guiding principle, of whatever character, neither Christian love, nor the humanitarianism of free-masonry . . .' 'Our interpretation of honour will determine our whole future, in Germany as well as in Europe.' [1] In this respect the Party in its formative period profited from the peculiar atmosphere of deception and conspiracy which resulted from clandestine circumvention of military limitations.[2]

---

[1] Alfred Rosenberg, *Der Mythus des 20. Jahrhunderts*, 87th–90th ed. (Munich, 1935), p. 543, 514, 153. In World War II, Rosenberg organised and directed the 'Staff Rosenberg', which plundered museums, libraries, art collections, and private houses, mainly in occupied Western Europe. It took 26,984 railroad cars to transport to Germany only the furnishings confiscated in Western Europe, more than half of it in Paris. As Reich Minister for the Occupied Eastern Territories, Rosenberg ordered, e.g., 50,000 boys and girls between ten and fourteen years of age to be shipped to Germany for forced labour.

[2] According to a German military expert, around 1925 Field-marshal von Blomberg (who in 1933 became Hitler's War Minister) coined the word that previously the honour of the Prussian officer had been to be correct but now the honour of the German officer was to be '*verschlagen*' (sly) (Görlitz, p. 348). The atmosphere at the time was described as follows by the same authority: In 1925 the camouflaged General Staff 'began to consider how the Army could be increased beyond the permitted limit. A project for the mobilisation of 21 divisions emerged . . . secret inventory of available armaments . . . hiding of arms on East Prussian estates. . . . The Parliament (*Reichstag*) had, of course, always to be fooled. Much of this was naturally covered by [President] Hindenburg. . . . Secret preparations for the production of war material, first of all by Krupp. . . . Organisations for the advancement

The reasoning was that the movement *had* to gain power in order to save the country from weaklings and traitors, and therefore any means, fair or foul, were permitted, and in a higher sense honourable, to achieve this end. Conspiracies and intrigues were carried out in an atmosphere of over-secrecy. For example, writers reporting about illegal military preparations were liable to prison sentences for divulging state secrets, or for treason. But at times the secrecy surrounding the military preparations was deliberately broken by the leadership itself, as a gesture of defiance, or as a test of the reactions at home and abroad.

For the man in the street all these things were bewildering and frightening. This was intended. The main purpose was to create a mixed atmosphere of feverishness and apathy—feverishness, to keep up the pitch of militarisation; apathy, to dull the sense of opposition, to habituate the people to the enormous tasks which lay ahead.

Yet the description would be incomplete without emphasising another point. Despite its repugnant features, and although it was apparently obvious that a Frankenstein was being nurtured here, the unparalleled militarisation also generated a great deal of enthusiasm and much true patriotism and idealism—without which, in fact, the Third Reich could not have succeeded to the point it did. This is perhaps the most serious lesson to be drawn from that fateful interlude in history.

CIVILIAN MILITARISM

'For me, all who participate in the economic process, are soldiers.'—Robert Ley, head of the 'Labour Front', the compulsory organisation replacing all former trade unions.

We said that one of the main secrets of Fascism was its skill in using and blending different types of militarism. So far we have briefly

of military sciences, "sport clubs" of all sorts, the veterans' association "*Stahlhelm*" played a big role. . . . The most fateful consequence was that all the important officers in the War Ministry and the General Staff became used to conspiratorial methods. They got into the habit of keeping constant contact with organisations which basically were inimical to the State, such as the "*Stahlhelm*" . . .' (Görlitz, pp. 360–6).

For example, a detailed secret history, written by a naval officer, of the activities of the Navy between 1919 and 1935, carries the following revealing chapter heads:

I. Early Protective Actions against the Execution of the Versailles Treaty.

II. Independent Armament Measures [by the Navy] behind the Back of the Reich Government and of the Legislative Bodies.

III. Systematic Armament Efforts Tolerated by the Reich Cabinet but Behind the Back of the Legislative Bodies (from 1928 to [Hitler's] Seizure of Power).

IV. Rearmament under the Leadership of [Hitler's] Reich Cabinet in Camouflaged Form from 1933 until the Liberation from Armament Restrictions in 1935.

(Secret Navy Memorandum, No. 15, M.Dv.Bo.352, *Der Kampf der Marine gegen Versailles* (The Fight of the Navy against Versailles), published in 1937 for restricted circulation by the Supreme Command of the Navy.)

discussed two brands of its militarism—which we called party militarism (the device of organising party activists and activities in quasi-military manner) and army militarism (emphasis on military prowess). Alone, neither would have sufficed, nor both combined. The whole nation was to be appropriately moulded. The magnitude of the task was always emphasised. Hitler gave a characteristic formulation in 1932 (before he was in power) in the magazine *The SA-Man*:

'In the future, Armies even if militarily excellent, will be worthless unless the peoples who stand behind them think like soldiers [*soldatisch*], and therefore are dedicated to the same deeds and the same sacrifices. Hence, the task of the truly responsible politician and statesman is no longer to put up an Army, more or less well trained, but to transpose a whole nation into a mental state of unconditional military willingness and military readiness.'

The brand of militarism which was used for this purpose can be called civilian militarism. It directly enveloped more people than either party militarism or army militarism—namely, potentially the entire civilian population.

While it was, of course, in various ways blended with army militarism, civilian militarism, considered by itself, had nothing directly to do with the armed forces. It means militarisation of the civilian life.

After Hitler's downfall, his former adjutant, Colonel Hossbach, criticised this type of militarism in the following words:

'Militarism must not be confounded with the justified endeavour to make a nation militarily strong and to enable it to defend its country. It is an *unhealthy offspring of military mentality and mode of life*. It represents an *unjustified encroachment* into the realm of *politics*, of *cultural pursuits* and of the *economy*. It has *nothing to do with the profession of the soldier as such*. Proponents and adherents of [this] militaristic mentality can be found among all occupations and all strata of a nation.'[1]

Being 'total' militarists, the Party leaders had to militarise the civil life of the nation. They traced the ills of society to lack of discipline, lack of unified leadership and direction. They preached against the amount of discussion, of arguing, of the play of interests against interests which was going on before they came into power. They spoke of the advantages of strictness and severity, of clear command and clear obedience, over absurd and unending debates. If the country was to be strong and the individual secure, uniformity had to replace diversity, authoritarian methods the cumbersome procedures of negotiation.

---

[1] Hossbach, p. 39. (Italics added.)

The aim behind these demands was clear. The nation had to be severely regimented, for two purposes: in order to destroy all opposition and in order to assure the smoothest possible execution of the rearmament programme and the military build-up. It was an iron police state, to be sure, but more than that: the aim was to instill the mentality of the iron policeman into the entire body politic.

The most significant illustration of this militarisation of civilian life was the new relation between employer and worker, and the position of labour in general. The relation between employer and worker was to be that between a war-lord and his fief (these were their actual designations in the Nazi Labour Code). Just as there must be officers who command and soldiers who obey, there must be persons who are responsible for production, and others who loyally carry out their commands.

'To work means to have discipline. . . . The worker has discipline, and so has the soldier. Thus, both worker and soldier are the clearest incarnation of a nation and its race. . . . From the hardest thing there is, iron, shall we humans learn what discipline is. . . . The best social order, for all times, is the soldierly social order.'

Differences in income and living standards are really irrelevant. It was customary to describe this order as Socialism:

'It does not matter whether the worker is a manual labourer or a professor, both deserve the same respect. . . . Consider how small are the differences between the consumption of human beings. . . . Even the rich can only sit in a single room, sit on a single chair, eat only a single piece of meat.' [1]

After the outbreak of the war the advantages of the strictly authoritarian employer–employee relations for the war-production programme were openly acknowledged. Göring said of the huge compulsory workers' organisation which took the place (and the money) of the trade unions—the Labour Front—that it 'guaranteed even in peace time what was to reveal its full significance in war. Now [in war] we can unreservedly make use of this asset.' [2]

The Labour Front was also in charge of organising a large and diversified programme of sports, recreational activities, theatre, movie and musical performances, vacation journeys, and the like. This fulfilled several aims. Firstly, it was to give the workers the feeling that the régime really cared for them; and it was true that the 'Kraft durch Freude' (Strength through Joy) organisation, which carried out these activities, and its model, Mussolini's 'Dopolavoro' (After

[1] From the programmatic speech by Dr Ley, Berlin, 13 Oct. 1934, reprinted in: Robert Ley, *Durchbruch der Sozialen Ehre. Reden und Gedanken für das Schaffende Deutschland* (Berlin, 1938), pp. 188–94.
[2] Preface by Göring to a collection of Ley's speeches, *Schmiede des Schwertes. Der Grossdeutsche Arbeiter im Grossdeutschen Freiheitskampf* (Munich, 1942), p. 11.

Work) organisation, offered much to workers and their families which they did not previously enjoy. (However, everything was paid for from workers' contributions.) The second aim was to have an additional means of keeping the workers under control and Party surveillance, even when they went fishing. Thirdly, it helped their indoctrination, not only because on those occasions there was an ample display of Party flags and emblems and a great number of exhortatory speeches, but more directly because the Party was able to select the workers' cultural fare—for example, of plays, movies, exhibitions, and the like. Furthermore, an essential aspect was the emphasis on sport activities which were militarily useful, analogous to the para-military sport activities of the youth organisation. This emphasis on military sports opened another avenue for para-military training. Strength through Joy was even used for espionage. For example, it was revealed later that among the crowds of vacationists who came on pleasure-boats of Strength through Joy, to do sight-seeing in Norwegian towns, there was a good contingent of military and SS personnel to carry out reconnaissance and espionage.

Analogous steps to regiment the civilian population along authoritarian lines were taken in virtually all fields. This affected the personal and professional life, and the group organisation of all strata of society, the associations of manufacturers as well as the artisans, the teachers and the physicians, the lawyers and the actors, etc. The associations were either dissolved and replaced by new ones along party lines, or changed in leadership and by-laws. The result was abrogation of free intra-group activity, and instead authoritarian control over the rank and file by reliable leaders imposed from above.

THE IMPORTANCE OF THE *FÜHRERS*

Among the techniques which enabled Fascism to streamline the nation in its own image, the *Führer* principle holds first rank. It means rule by authoritarian leaders, and is essential to the system, following logically from its basic tenets: Fascism wishes to be a mass movement, but fundamentally despises, or at best mistrusts, 'the masses'. Discipline, obedience, authority of command must replace the 'civilian' methods of elections, negotiation, compromise ('horse-trading'). It teaches the inefficiency of democracy because it desires a guarantee that all power be concentrated and kept in the hands of leaders of its own type. Hence the *Führer* principle is identical with their '*élite*' principle. Only their own, self-styled *élite* may lead. The power of the *Führer élite* must be arbitrary and authoritarian because it must be independent of the will of the 'followers'.

At first this sounded ridiculous. People who decreed themselves to be 'leaders', and even boasted of their ruthlessness, should decide the destiny of the nation? To the opponents the scheme appeared absurd, and they erroneously considered the Constitution an impregnable barrier. To undermine that barrier, one of the strongest weapons was the carefully propagandised demand for the 'strong man' and the 'strong movement'. But it was not the strong man who 'made' Fascism. It was Fascism that 'made' him—mainly because it gave tens of thousands of *other* ambitious and 'energetic' men the big chance of becoming part of the leader *élite* themselves. Even before the Party gained power every village 'leader' of the Party had his sense of self-importance boosted in various ways, and expected, once the Party were in control, to become mayor of the village without having to be elected by the villagers.

It was implicit that there had to be, so to speak, many *duces* and *führers*, of many different grades and types.[1] Eventually, the number of the high leaders alone was so large that they were spoken of in Germany as the Leaders' Corps (*Führer Korps*, in analogy to 'officers' corps') and in Italy as the Hierarchy (*Gerarchia*).

Even the low-ranking leader profited from being neither dependent on nor responsible to the rank and file. His appointment in the first place, the extent of his power, the length of his tenure, all depended primarily on his superiors in the *führer* hierarchy. The higher the position of a leader, the greater was his power of making and unmaking lower leaders, in addition to his power over the followers. Yet every petty Party functionary, every *unterführer* (subleader) had his own minuscule satrapy, and the simple SS trooper still 'was more' than a civilian.

Just as such a system is a parody of the military principle of command hierarchy, so does it open a whole new field for promotions. This fact accounts for the peculiar social mobility which is characteristic of Fascism. Since the régime controlled so many institutions and groups which formerly enjoyed self-rule, and since every police-state requires a large network of overseers, there were many more official positions than before. And even the holder of small functions wielded much more power than did his counterpart in any democratic system, and not seldom over people who in social rank, education, and income definitely surpassed him.

The *führer-élite* principle made it possible to freeze the social struc-

---

[1] For example, the head of the Hitler Youth described the leadership principle among the young people as follows:

'A *single* will leads the Hitler Youth. The commanding power of *every* Hitler Youth *führer*, whether of the *smallest* or the *biggest* of its units, is absolute—that is, he has the unlimited right to issue orders, because he bears the unrestricted responsibility. . . . An organisation of young people, too, can only be successful if it unreservedly accepts the authority of the *leaders*. The success of National-Socialism is based on discipline . . .' Baldur von Schirach, *Die Hitler Jugend. Idee und Gestalt* (Leipzig, 1934) (?), p. 68. (Italics added.)

ture *as a whole*—that is, it prevented any alteration in the relative political and economic situation of the various strata of society (except, of course, the military). But at the same time the *führer-élite* principle created considerable social mobility for many *individuals* of *all* strata. Thus, the counter-revolution of Fascism took on certain *aspects* of a revolution because it drastically changed the position, influence, and economic circumstances of large numbers of individuals, both upwards and (for those in disfavour) downwards. That many who were riding the wave were upstarts and worse merely underscored the fact. One has only to think, as illustration, of the numerous confidential agents, informers, and denouncers who were planted in shops, factories, schools, etc., and who now saw themselves rewarded and feared and 'playing a role'. The standards of merit changed. Many who under normal standards were notoriously disreputable rose to prominence. The claim of the system that it gave 'the lowest' an opportunity to advance was only too correct. But the régime could not have survived had the entire leadership been of such calibre. Respectable people were also being tempted by the temptation of increased power. They did not have to do the ugly things, or so they thought, as long as they gave their particular professional skill. Thus chances were opened not only to the disreputable but, at a price, also to the respectable of all classes. Careers were now possible which previously had not been possible. To this extent a social upheaval took place.

Contrary to the widespread belief that Fascism means *only* oppression, the ambitious adherents realised quickly that they themselves were to gain, and not to lose—or, anyway, to gain more than they would lose—from this authoritarianism. Of course, the régime made havoc of rights and liberties. But at the same time and, it could be said, in inverse geometric proportion, it *increased* the 'liberty of action' —and often the income—of all who were *themselves* the authority within the authoritarianism. They accumulated, so to speak, the sum total of the rights taken away from the others. Those who joined, or accepted an official position, did so not because they were attracted by the idea of sacrificing their liberty. Quite the contrary. Whoever was in the saddle had 'freedom' from even the most elementary restriction. They were relatively many.

Still larger was the number of those who hoped they would make it. As the régime suppressed the independence and self-rule of more and more associations, groups, and institutions—which also meant, of course, that their assets were taken over [1]—it increased by the same token its own ability to dispense more and more posts, favours,

[1] e.g., the dissolution of the trade unions alone brought the Party hundreds of millions—namely, all funds and bank accounts of the unions, their office buildings, schools, rest homes, printing establishments, and other assets.

prestige, and money. It cleverly manipulated the ambitions of the seekers for them. Behind the granite façade of strict order there was a scramble for positions and all that went with them, which was more brutal than under any normal system, because the atmosphere was so brutalised, because the ruffians had the upper hand, and because the régime was, insofar as personnel were concerned, in flux. Yet it appears that these very aspects of competition and intrigue made for more, and not less, cohesion among the 'leaders'.

Since political reliability was a prerequisite for success, and not infrequently even for the permission of exercising certain professions and activities at all, the régime knew that it had the people on the hook. Once this stage was reached, once civil liberties and democratic process were abolished, the alternatives for the isolated individual were economic difficulties and social ostracism, and a great deal of conviction was needed for not falling in line.

While the absorption of some mass organisations, such as the trade unions, was accomplished immediately by single, sweeping blows, in other cases it took place in stages. The fate of the German youth organisations is a good example. Early in February 1933 (Hitler became Chancellor on 30th January), Baldur von Schirach, the head of the Hitler Youth, by a surprise raid of fifty of his boys, physically occupied the offices of the National Central Committee (*Reichsausschuss*) of Youth Organisations, confiscated the records, and dismissed its head, a General Vogt. Simultaneously he dissolved all workers' youth associations. Through a raid on the central youth hostel office, he took over all youth hostels. He then concentrated on the associations, including the Boy and Girl Scouts, whose political shade went from middle-of-the-road to the nationalist right. These associations had founded, as a common roof, the Greater German Youth League, which was headed by Navy Chief of Staff (ret.) Admiral von Trotha. Although Schirach called Trotha 'an admirable man' who 'wanted to accomplish with his League essentially the same as I with the Hitler Youth', much friction developed because the Admiral was only willing to have the League join the Hitler Youth as an entity, to save some independence for his organisations. Dissatisfied, von Schirach in June 1933 had himself appointed by Hitler as 'Reich Leader of the German Youth'. Thus armed with unlimited power (leadership principle), 'the first thing I did was to dissolve the Greater German Youth League. . . . I did not hesitate for a moment to take this step'.[1] (Schirach also mentions in his description of the events that General Vogt was co-opted into the Reich Youth Leadership and Admiral von Trotha, 'after his own organisation had been smashed', became Honorary Leader of the Navy Hitler Youth.) When the war veterans' association Steel Helmet was absorbed into

[1] Baldur von Schirach, *The Hitler Youth*, pp. 32–7.

the Nazi war veterans' organisation, the deposed head of the Steel Helmet voluntarily put the youth groups of the association under the Hitler Youth. By then the Hitler Youth had increased its membership from 1 million on 30th January 1933 to 3 million. Now came the turn of the religiously orientated youth groups. The Protestant groups, despite a valiant fight by the president of the Protestant Young Men's Association (*Evangelisches Jungmännerwerk*), were absorbed in December 1933. The Catholic groups held out longer, but the Hitler Youth finally achieved its complete monopoly with the Hitler Youth Act of 1st December 1936, which tersely stated that 'all German youth in the Reich is organised within the Hitler Youth'.

There was a fateful overflow of military concepts, in fact of a war mentality, into the civilian life. In war there can be little tolerance for the enemy, but in peace-time a normal society does not look on the non-conformist as an outlaw. Fascism did this characteristically. With people who have different opinions one can shake hands, but not if they are stamped as enemies or traitors. Disapproval was sharpened into ostracism. The result was much fear, denunciation. and mutual distrust. There was a constant trend away from diversity, towards an ever sharper polarisation into either ally or enemy. The trusted friend, the famous book, once suspected of some deviation, belonged to the enemy camp.

Often under a borrowed, allegedly military language, sternness and severity permeated many aspects of the society. Not only were military war games now more often realistic through the use of live ammunition. Softness had no longer a place in the teaching methods of school-children or for example in the treatment of offenders. A long chapter could be written on the 'disciplination' of the law courts, especially the penal courts.[1] Laws were overhauled and newly enacted, better to reach the non-conformists. Crooked interpretations were used to impose more severe penalties than even these laws permitted (or, in turn, to let the crimes of Party people go unpunished). Unco-operative judges and prosecutors were dismissed. Special courts were established, largely manned with reliable

[1] 'It is self-evident', wrote the Chief of the Criminal Law Section in the Reich Ministry of Justice in 1936, 'that we had to turn our back to the effeminating idea of forgiveness (*Abkehr von dem verweichlichenden Verzeihungsprinzip*).' For example, 'the right to deal with petitions for clemency was taken away from the judges and given to the public prosecutors, with the basic instruction that penalties had, as a matter of principle, to be carried out unmercifully and completely (*unnachsichtlich und rückhaltslos*), with pardon to be limited to exceptional cases. This radical change of policy revealed itself with special sharpness in the case of death sentences. . . . Since 1928, pardon (commutation into jail term) had been the rule but now the execution of the death sentence has become the rule and commutation into jail terms the rare exception. Similarly, prisons cease to be "boarding houses" for the inmates.' (Dr Wilhelm Crohne, in: *Das Neue Strafrecht*, prefaced by Reich Minister of Justice, Dr Franz Gürtner (Berlin, 1936), p. 153.)

military and Party men. The reasons for, and the frequency with which dissenters were prosecuted as traitors, enemies of the State, subversives, corroders of the nation's military prowess, and similar technical accusations under police and courts laws, clearly indicated the upward trend of Fascism.

In his speech to army officers in January 1937, the Supreme SS Leader Heinrich Himmler stated that his intelligence 'Security Service' (*Sicherheits-Dienst* or *SD*) had to find out '*was mit dem Gegner los ist*' (what goes on among the enemy). 'Hence the Security Service deals, above all, with Communism, Jewry, Freemasonry, Ultramontanism [the Catholic Church], the activity of [other] politically minded religions, and reaction.' [1] In other words, the head of the intelligence police considered the large majority of the population as enemies—the communists (who for him included many socialists), the Jews (who for him included everybody with some Jewish blood, irrespective of religious affiliation), the Freemasons, the active groups of every religious denomination, and the reactionaries (who for him included many conservatives).

Except for the Jews, even a Himmler could not possibly deal with all of them. Apart from the hard core of irreconcilables, and the 'grumblers' and 'traitors' who were taken care of by police, law courts, concentration camps, deprivation of jobs, etc., the large masses of *potential* opponents had to have their attention taken away from the many things which could have awakened them to articulate dissatisfaction. With the help of an—admittedly large—mass of convinced adherents, they had to be given an *over-riding, unifying goal*, so that they would, if possible, forget their grievances. This unifying goal was the building of a military nation. Much drive and many energies were mobilised in this way. The Third Reich was able, even in peace-time, by focusing attention on matters directly or indirectly military, to create a climate of urgency and of that suspension of the normal political issues which is typical of a nation at war. How could anybody complain about taxes or inadequate school buildings, or any of the other philistine concerns of times less crucial and dangerous—at a time when the country was in the pangs of its national rebirth, and when destiny called it to become the leader among the nations, stronger than the others, and champion of the race?

This climate put 'civilian pursuits' into second line. A new, common yardstick was now available, to decide on the usefulness or not of most activities of the citizen. There was disdain, sometimes subtle, sometimes gross, for the arts of peace. Everything pertaining to military matters in the widest sense had priority, from investment programmes to college curricula. Just as the manufacturer had to

[1] Reprinted in *Study Course . . .*, p. 151.

reckon with the scarcity of certain raw materials because they had to be stockpiled, so had the mother to cook a prescribed one-dish menu for her family because this facilitated the military programme. To disturb the effort was unpatriotic and just 'not done'. The emphasis on the urgent national task permeated the entire country, and was made to silence controversies and to disregard matters which now were irrelevant. In fact, the policy was helped by the misled patriotism of those who genuinely believed that they had to submit to everything, and to do their own best to assist in making their country bigger and stronger.

This militarisation of the civilian life did by no means make everybody a soldier in uniform. The business man, the worker, the scientist continued in their interests and pursuits, but each with a change. Workers became habituated to the idea that armament meant full employment. Their employers were trained to acquire a vested interest in the continuation of war orders. The scientist had to use his speciality for military research. And so on. The common denominator made for the artificial 'unity' which the régime required.

It was this constant and obsessive reference to military matters and nationalist considerations which coloured the work of the clerk who haggled over import licences for non-strategic goods, and the professor who cleansed textbooks of 'anti-national' authors; the sportsman whose defeat would have brought shame to the flag, and the driller who had to increase his hourly output; the typist who had to organise Party cell evenings to keep face with her colleagues, the janitor who doubled as informer, the accountant who learned glider flying as preparation for a better-paying job, the judge who pronounced harsh sentences in order to be promoted, and the school-boy who went on a night hike with a 30-pound knapsack on his back to advance in his Hitler Youth outfit. A drop of the same tint coloured everything. A swastika was woven into the housewife's apron and the worker's overall.

EDUCATION FOR WAR (WAR MILITARISM)

'The average person is inclined to disregard the laws, to pay no taxes, and not to go to war.'—Mussolini.

'As I see it, to fight is the fate of all beings. . . . My decision is unalterable. . . . Violation of the neutrality of Belgium and Holland is irrelevant . . .'—From Hitler's speech to the Commanders-in-Chief, 23rd November 1939.

Fascism was fascinated by war. 'Fight', 'struggle', 'battle', 'sacrifice', 'victory', 'heroism', and the like were its key words. The difficulty was that in the twentieth century aggressive war is hard to sell —very much harder than a militarised Party, or a big military build-up, or even the militarisation of the nation. While it was true that preoccupation with war was at the core of the system, those other ingredients brought them more support than did their emphasis on war, both before and after their accession to power.

The situation of Fascism with respect to war was therefore somewhat complex. On the one hand, the minority who were emotionally inclined towards war had to be educated and steeled. On the other hand, the majority of the people who were, in different degrees of intensity, against war, had to be conditioned for it. The latter was the much more difficult task.

Open glorification of war, the exaltation of war as the noblest, the most manly undertaking, the father and promoter of history, was emphasised for those—mainly intellectuals and professional or semi-professional military—who were favourably disposed to receive such messages, and for the youth. For the readers of the *Enciclopedia Italiana*, Mussolini stated as 'the first article of fascist faith' in his famous essay, 'The Doctrine of Fascism': 'Perpetual peace is neither possible, nor useful to the human race. War alone brings all human energies to their highest state of tension and stamps the seal of nobility upon the people that dare to face it.' For youth he had the slogan, '*Meglio vivere un giorno da leone che cento anni da pecora*' (Better to live one single day as a lion than a hundred years as sheep).

The theme of heroism was expressed in innumerable variations. For example, Hitler's Propaganda Minister once used this formulation:

> 'Fascism is by its essence anti-liberal, not only in its results but in its spiritual principle. Fascism is not only anti-liberal but anti-pacifist. . . . It destroys the false humanitarian ideal of liberal democracy to its roots, and replaces it by manly heroism.'[1]

No evidence was given to show why the humanitarian ideal of liberal democracy was false; and the need of replacing that ideal by manly heroism was posited axiomatically. The reasoning behind the espousal of war was extremely rudimentary. The fact that war, if it were to come, would be an enormous holocaust was not denied. Yet the official exhortators did not find it necessary to prove why, then, war would be desirable or necessary. It was evidently considered a better tactic to surround war with an aura of metaphysical irrationality.

The conditioning of the basically anti-war majority had to be done with a much greater variety of arguments, even if they were mutually contradictory.

1. There was, first of all, the straight anti-war line. The Party statute which was adapted after the first meeting of the *Fascio di Combattimento* on 23 March 1919 (the famous meeting of the Piazza

---

[1] Joseph Goebbels, *Der Faszismus und seine politischen Ergebnissse*, p. 13.

di San Sepolcro in Milan) states as Point 5: 'Abolition of general military conscription, general disarmament, and prohibition for all nations to produce arms for war.' And Point 14 demanded: 'Open conduct of international politics, which must be inspired by the solidarity of the peoples and their independence within the Confederation of States.' [1] (The League of Nations did not yet exist. 'Confederation of States' implied a demand for such an institution.) Similarly, Hitler in his early days frequently told his audiences that World War I broke out only as a result of a 'Jewish–Masonic–Marxist–Capitalist conspiracy'. In this respect the tenacious fight against the clause in the 1919 Peace Treaty which declared that Imperial Germany had caused the World War of 1914–18 was very revealing. It was to show indignation against any State which would unleash a war.[2] After having unleashed World War II, Hitler often blamed the same conspiracy for it. The argument was of course inconsistent with his own assertion that he had the perfect right, and indeed the historical duty, to start that war in the interest of his country. He said so privately to his inner circle. But he knew that to say so publicly would have been the wrong propaganda.

To disclaim any intention of making war was useful not only for foreign consumption. Paradoxically enough, it helped in causing the people to accept the military build-up ('army militarism') and the militarisation of the civilian life ('civilian militarism'), because it assuaged the anxiety as to where all this would lead.

2. On the other hand, everything was done to suppress organised peace groups and peace propaganda, and to deride and discredit the League of Nations, as well as any other instruments for the peaceful co-ordination and conciliation of the international policies of nations.

3. Instead, the notion was spread that the conduct of international affairs was by its nature of a special crookedness, and was therefore not to be measured by normal morality and decency. Their own pre-fascist governments—the people were told—had, out of treachery or stupidity, not been up to the sly game of the other countries, and had therefore always been deceived and taken for a ride. These things were hard to understand for the ordinary, honest person, and hence had to be left to the new men who understood that foreign affairs had their own rules. Hitler reached the zenith of popularity at home in 1938 when he obtained foreign territories by blackmail and military threat (but without actual warfare). Foreign policy, said Mussolini in the Senate after the Corfu incident of 1923, is

---

[1] Quoted in Dorso, *Mussolini alla Conquista del Potere* (1949), pp. 139–40. (The programme had fourteen points, in imitation of President Woodrow Wilson's Fourteen Points.)
[2] At the same time, university students were taught that a distinction between prohibited aggressive war and permitted defensive war was legally and politically wrong (see e.g., Professor Karl Schmitt's treatise, *Der Diskriminierende Kriegsbegriff*).

something for which the nation has to pay with blood and treasure, adding that these matters had to be decided by him alone, the people's duty being to bear the consequences in discipline.

4. Another argument, very frequently used, was that foreign nations actually threatened the country with encirclement, or were preparing themselves for an attack on it. Sometimes it would be conceded that there was no danger 'at the moment'—but since powerful nations were jealous and hostile, and while perhaps no attack would come in the foreseeable future, who could guarantee that it would never come or, again, might not come any moment? This obliquely suggested a 'preventive' war, although preventive war was hardly ever openly advocated. What the people were not permitted to see was the fact that the fear of attack, if genuine, should have been an additional reason to work for general disarmament and real collective security. Nor were they permitted to understand that an absolute assurance of security could least of all be achieved by war, which always creates more problems than its settles.

(The leaders knew this. They realised that even their own complete victory and their most ruthless extermination measures would not make the Third Reich secure. For example, in July 1941 Hitler explained to some of his most trusted collaborators that the war in Russia would have to be waged, if necessary, for a hundred years— 'all successors of the *Führer* must know this'—until no military force other than German would exist west of the Urals.[1] Heinrich Himmler told his higher SS leaders in a programmatic speech in 1943:

'You must never forget that our fortunate situation of keeping many parts of Europe occupied, also involves the disadvantage of having millions of people and dozens of alien nationalities under us and, therefore, against us. Automatically, we have everybody against us who is a convinced communist, we have every freemason against us, every democrat, every convinced Christian. These are the ideological opponents who are against us all over Europe and who are all on the enemy's side. But we also have against us the nationalists for good or bad reasons, for example in France, Norway, Denmark, the Netherlands or Serbia.'

He warned his listeners that after the victory in the war, and for generations to come, every SS trooper would have the duty to produce many sons, so that two or three of them could always be killed on the battlefield and the continued propagation of the SS be nevertheless guaranteed. He also predicted that the Germanic nation of, he hoped, 250–300 million which by then would rule over

[1] Memorandum on Hitler's conference with Rosenberg, Lammers, Keitel and Göring of 16 Jul. 1941, Nbg. Doc. 221-L.

350–400 million Europeans, would one day have to fight a life-and-death war against a resurgent Asia with her 1,000–1,500 million mass-men (*Masse Mensch*). That enormous conflagration would again last for generations.[1])

5. At times class-struggle language was transposed into the international field. Just as the poor had to fight for every concession because of the selfishness of the rich, so were the 'have-not' nations prevented by the greed of the over-saturated 'have' nations from occupying their rightful place. If one day there would be an explosion, it was hinted, the arrogant have-nations would be responsible. The reasoning was, of course, particularly strange in the mouth of people who simultaneously boasted of the power and might of the same 'have-not' nation. In fact, the real meaning of the complaint became more transparent when it was formulated, as it often was, in concrete form—namely, that other nations possessed or controlled more natural resources. For in peace time foreign raw materials were freely accessible through international trade. If certain raw materials were scarce, this was mainly caused by import restrictions which were self-imposed in order to achieve 'autarky'—that is, economic self-dependence in the event of war.

6. Probably more influential than such quasi-rational arguments in conditioning the population for war, was the general assertion that 'wars are inevitable'. This assertion was spread axiomatically, as a law of nature which it would be futile to try to alter, despite the peaceful intentions of one's government. Since this argument did, by definition, not permit of being contested by counter-arguments, it created much of the awe and fatalism which the leaders desired. They spread the mysterious notion of the inevitable fatality of war while they skilfully manipulated that fatality themselves.[2]

[1] From Himmler's speech at the meeting of SS Leaders, Posen, 4 Oct. 1943, pp. 59, 73, 115 (Nbg. Doc. 1919-PS, Exh. USA-170).
[2] For example, the people did not know that on 4 Nov. 1937, almost two years before the first bombs fell, Hitler had told his intimate collaborators that he not only intended to take over two neighbouring states, Austria and Czechoslovakia, but also that this was to be in preparation for further aggressions—namely, to obtain strategic protection and twelve additional divisions for 'a possible advance westward', i.e., against Western Europe. After further military preparations, he declared in his directive to the Commanders-in-Chief of 30 May 1938 his 'unalterable decision to smash (*zu zerschlagen*) Czechoslovakia by military action' (Top Secret Directives, OKW 42/38, Nbg. Doc. 388-PS, Exh. USA-26). When he received part of Czechoslovakia without war through the Munich Agreement of 30 Sept. 1938 he issued another order for the preparation of the 'liquidiaton of the remainder of Czechoslovakia' on 21 Oct. 1938 (Nbg. Doc. C-105, Exh. USA-105). In fact, Hermann Rauschning reported in his book *Hitler Speaks* (p. 46) that as early as in the summer of 1932, half a year before becoming Reich Chancellor, Hitler told him and others that 'the Bohemian-Moravian Basin . . . will be colonised by German peasants. We shall transport the Czechs to Siberia or the Volhenian district.' That this statement of Rauschning's 'roughly coincided' with what had been 'decided in Party circles' was after the war confirmed by Hitler's erstwhile Governor in Prague, Karl Hermann Frank.—On 25 May 1939 Hitler announced at a military

We see that the arguments used to condition the basically anti-war majority for aggressive war were of considerable variety. Some of them were mutually contradictory. This, however, was intentional. Any argument had to be used with utmost cynicism which could be expected to impress and confuse. It will be noted also that all of the arguments for mass consumption (as distinct from those for the pre-war minority) had one thing in common. They did not depict war as something noble and exhilarating.

In order to condition the country for aggressive war, it was not necessary to create a war spirit in the literal sense of widespread desire for war. It sufficed to habituate the people to the general climate of truculence and bellicosity which permeated the atmosphere long before the war was started. The Party, even before it was in power and afterwards all the more, engendered a large fund of rambling hostility, and directed it in chosen doses against variously chosen targets. Venom and malice were in the air.

This was very important as psychological preparation for actual war. For, measured by normal peace-time standards, war is the great paradox and paroxysm. Especially as the National-Socialists conceived it, it is the most complete denial of humane behaviour, reason, respect for the lives, dignity, and property of others. By corroding these normal standards even in peace-time, the transition to war was less of a sudden change.

Yet, in spite of all this and of the most complete machinery of indoctrination, they did not arouse any large-scale enthusiasm for aggressive war. The leaders realised that they would be unable to accomplish this in a modern industrial society. What they achieved was to anaesthetise, to lull, to paralyse the moral and mental resistance against aggressive war. Resistance against aggressive war would have had to come long before the war was actually unleashed. By the time this had been done by the anaesthetisers, the anaesthetised knew that the knife was cutting into their own flesh. By that time they were unable to resist. They were not glad. There was a noteworthy absence of popular enthusiasm over victories in battles. But for the régime it was sufficient to have the people conditioned to the extent of doing their duty, as decreed by the *Führers*.

There comes a point in this complicated process of paralysing the capacity of mental and moral resistance at which the paralyser can

---

conference his decision to attack Poland. 'Circumstances must be adapted to needs. This is impossible without invasion of foreign States or attacks upon foreign property. . . . There is no question of sparing Poland. . . . There will be war.' War preparations were feverishly intensified, and on 22 Aug. 1939 he stated to the assembled military leaders, 'Everybody shall have to make a point of it that we were determined from the beginning to fight the Western Powers. Struggle for life or death.'

know that the paralysation has succeeded. That moment has come when it is no longer necessary for him to lie. The people can now be told the naked, ignominious truth—that everything had been done for the purpose of attacking and subjugating other peoples—because too many have by now forgotten to recognise the ignominy of that truth. They have lost their sense of revulsion, or learned to repress it so completely as not even to become aware of it—until they woke up among the debris of their own cities, bequeathed to them by their infallible war lords.

23

THE NATIONAL-SOCIALIST VOCABULARY

Werner Betz

ACCORDING to Hitlerian theory the two most important elements in the preparation of the success of a movement are propaganda and organisation. It is for this reason that language is, for National-Socialism, primarily a weapon of propaganda. Adolf Hitler expressed his views on propaganda in the following terms:

'All propaganda should be popular and its intellectual level should be established according to the powers of assimilation of the most narrow-minded person amongst those to whom it is addressed. The purely spiritual content of propaganda should be increasingly less in proportion to the number of men to be won. When however an entire people is to be drawn under one's dominion, as is the case with propaganda designed to sustain a war, one cannot take too many precautions to avoid intellectual postulations which are too deep.

'The more modest the scientific apparatus of propaganda, and the more exclusively preoccupied it is with the sentiments of the masses, the more complete will be its success. For success, and not the contentment of a few scholars or young aesthetes, is the best yardstick by which to measure the rightness or wrongness of propaganda.

'The art of propaganda is precisely that, having won over the masses' universe of emotional conceptions, it finds through the correct psychological approach the surest way to the attention, and even more to the heart, of the greatest masses. If it does not touch the "high-brows" only their own intellectual idleness and vanity are to blame!

'If however one realises the necessity of directing this art of mobilizing minds, propaganda, towards the great masses, the following lesson can be drawn from it: It is a mistake to make propaganda as complex as a scientific treatise. The powers of assimilation of the masses are extremely restricted, their intelligence weak and their memory very short. Therefore all effective propaganda should be restricted to a few essential points which should be exploited in the form of slogans, until even the simplest person can seize the intended meaning.' [1]

[1] *Mein Kampf* (Munich, 1933), p. 197.

Goebbels clearly stated the same views on many occasions. Thus, for example, in a speech at Berlin on 18th May 1933 he said:

'But propaganda is of such a nature as to win men over to an idea in so profound and vivid a way that finally they are ensnared so that they can never again set themselves free of it. This is why it is wrong to believe that the good wins the day because it is good, and also why it is naïve to debar propaganda because of its methods, for propaganda is not an end in itself but only a means to an end. If propaganda attains its end it is good, if not it is bad.' [1]

The National-Socialist treatment of language follows fairly closely the guiding principles indicated above. It endeavours to work on the most narrow-minded, and does so by means of formulae continually repeated in the form of slogans. For this reason it turns to men's feelings above all, it endeavours to stimulate and control by corresponding metaphors, by verbal images. Examination of the images of National-Socialist language will illustrate the fundamental elements of National-Socialist linguistic technique.

The images of National-Socialist language are borrowed from just those fields which make the greatest appeal to the feelings and which are the most expressive. Thus for example the sphere of religious feelings is incessantly drawn upon. A definite effect is also to be expected from working on the emotions in the narrowest sense. Poverty and popular morality, biology, battle, and sport are all among the emotional themes continually exploited by National-Socialism. A brief examination of the work of Goebbels published in 1926, Die Zweite Revolution, Briefe an Zeitgenossen, shows that the same principles were equally valid at the beginning of National-Socialism. This book is an excellent introduction to the imagery and technique of metaphor of National-Socialism. It begins with a statement of the function of the Führer written in the form of a letter to Hitler, and which starts 'Most honoured Mr Hitler'. On the first page Goebbels assures the reader that he sees in Hitler the man 'who guides our steps in our fanatical will for liberty'. It is clear that Goebbels' language gave at a very early stage a completely new meaning to the pejorative term 'fanatic', which in this context has an eulogistic meaning which was to become general in National-Socialist language. To 'fanatical will' are later added 'fanatical belief', 'fanatical confession', 'fanatical love', and many other fanaticisms. Two ends are sought by such usage; on the one hand an emotionally effective word is chosen so that its effect will be the greater on the hearer; on the other, a manifestly non-bourgeois pejorative word is re-valued so that it becomes a positive term incorporated in

[1] Quoted in Rudolf Strauch, Das Weltbild des Nationalsozialismus (Leipzig, 1934), pp. 12–13.

normal language as a constant element of exhortation, as a perpetual stimulant embedded in the flesh of peaceable people. But beyond certain limits the effectiveness of the term is lost, as for example in Gritzbach's biography in which Göring is described as 'a fanatical friend of animals'. Through its wide currency, the word has practically compromised its power to act successfully as a re-valued foreign stimulant. This first phrase has already made clear two factors to be noted in our study of the language of National-Socialism: choice of emotional orbit and semantic re-valuation of a current expression (pejorative term in the present case).

In the next sentence is mentioned the 'deepest mire of parliamentary democracy' and the 'single principle of German authoritarian leadership' (*Prinzip des deutschen Führertums*). These formulae indicate another field of metaphor and another stylistic procedure which both later became constituent elements of National-Socialist language, the image of mud applied to one's adversary—connected in this case with the dangers of mires in general—and the extensive, often complete substitutions of positives by superlatives. To this may be added the appeal to the nationalist and militarist sentiments of the masses by the evocation of 'German leadership'. In the next sentence Hitler is described as 'Symbol and sentinel of the new spirit of national and socialist solidarity'. 'Symbol' belongs to the high-sounding style of foreign words in National-Socialist language, as do 'guarantor' (*Garant*) 'paladin' (*Paladin*), etc. By 'sentinel' (*Schildwächter*) the warlike field of ideas is once more evoked, and is also transposed to a misty past which is particularly susceptible to sentiment. Just as in the formula 'National-Socialist' two ideas which had formerly been considered contradictory are united, National-Socialist language employs in other fields sentiments as numerous and contradictory as possible. To the return to the past implied in the word 'sentinel' (*Schildwächter*) is opposed the accentuation of the 'new', of the 'new spirit' in this particular case. In the sentence immediately following there is 'the greatest shame' and the 'delivering word'. The first of these phrases brings us once more into the narrowest emotional sphere and at the same time into the sphere of moral preoccupations, of a popular morality inevitably described in the superlative, while the image of deliverance belonging to the next phrase is borrowed from one of the fields which was later to be the most exploited in National-Socialist language: the religious. The next sentence mentions the 'miracle of belief' before passing on to 'belief in the new Reich'. The image of 'unveiling' was to be in its turn much appreciated in later National-Socialist language. In its very frequent form of 'tearing off the mask' this image is contained in the following sentence, though not without bringing in a series of other weighty images of emotional content; he 'ruthlessly tore off the mask hiding a face twisted by greed for money'. 'Greed for money' arouses the emotions of popular morality, and the twisted grimacing face belongs to those images of squalor and ugliness which the National-Socialist confers upon his enemies; furthermore, it awakes the biological instincts of the people which are confused with popular morality. The words 'shamefully depraved and infamous' in the same sentence also belong to popular morality, as does the word 'system' (of democracy), which, by associations of a vague foreign character, by romantic antithesis, and by having the value of a slogan became one of the most effective formulae of National-Socialist language.

This brief analysis of a single half-page of the speech made by Goebbels in 1926, and the references to images contained in only seven sentences may suffice as an introduction. But before proceeding to more general conclusions with a wider bearing on National-Socialist language, I quote in its entirety the analysed paragraph so that the reader may have an opportunity of examining it and may have a more correct idea of the whole text:

'Most honoured Mr Hitler,
'If I address this letter concerning authoritarian leadership to you personally, it is because I see in you the man who guides our steps in our fanatical will for liberty. Bogged down as we were in the deepest mire of parliamentary democracy, you were the first to set free the clear and single principle of German leadership. You became for us young Germans the symbol and sentinel of the new spirit of national and socialist solidarity. At that time of the greatest shame and the greatest division, you found the delivering word for an entire generation, and thus you have become the pioneer and the achiever of the still confused desires of post-war German youth.
'You arose like a meteor before our astonished eyes, and you have worked a miracle of enlightenment and belief in a world of scepticism and despair. Filled with faith and sure of the future, you rose above the masses with a will to liberate them, with infinite love for the fervour of those who believe in the new Reich. For the first time our shining eyes perceived a man who ruthlessly tore off the mask, hiding a face twisted by greed for money, of those mediocre creatures who belong to parliamentary business; a man who showed us the extent to which the system was depraved, a system by which the leader (*Führer*) is elected by the party and by gossip'.[1]

To obtain rather more general and comprehensive information about the early language of National-Socialism let us examine the language used in Goebbels' book *Die zweite Revolution*.

[1] Jos. Goebbels, *Die zweite Revolution*, 1926, p.

This examination shows the great number of terms and expressions taken from the vocabulary of religion which Goebbels used. Here again, both in form and spirit, 'sacrifice' appears most frequently. Goebbels speaks of a 'total sacrifice to the Idea,' of the 'urge to fulfil the mission which burns like a sacred fire', of sacrifice on the same level as battle and desire. The national community is achieved by a few rare personalities endowed with the absolute courage to sacrifice their own existence. The chapter 'Idea and Sacrifice' assures fighters for the Idea of the joy and gallantry of sacrifice. They are 'ready for the sacrifice', they are 'ready to sacrifice themselves to the last man for the Idea'. Whereas at first it was a question of 'sacrifice to the Idea', it now becomes 'sacrifice of the Idea', in both cases the 'sacrifice for the Idea' probably being meant. In the second chapter there is 'the Idea for which we sacrifice ourselves' and the verbs 'to sacrifice' and 'to act' are almost interdependent. Goebbels calls on the 'Director General' to be prepared for the last sacrifice: 'Sacrifice before it is too late'. The lack of a national spirit of sacrifice is responsible for poverty, sacrifices must be made and the New State must be fought for. In the other letters appear the phrases 'will to sacrifice', 'the fighters and sacrificers' (associated with German idealists and activists), and 'the spirit of sacrifice'. In all, Goebbels uses the term or the concept of sacrifice some thirty times in fifty-eight pages, which makes an average of once every two pages.

It is significant that the next most frequent religious word in Goebbels' vocabulary is 'deliverance'. Not only are the simple forms 'to deliver' and 'deliverance' used very often, but also they are associated with extremely characteristic phrases and expressions such as 'socialist deliverance' and 'National-Socialist deliverance' and, more exalted, 'deliverance through oneself', and finally sentences like: 'Then shall we be heroes, Saviours'. Deliverance is often connected with an idea of 'marching', 'deliverance is on the march'. In all, the word or idea of 'deliverance' appears some twenty times, or an average of once every three pages.

The words 'miracle' and 'faith' are close runners-up in the vocabulary of the young Goebbels, where religious metaphors are concerned. The two words are used together in the phrase 'the miracle of faith', but this does not prevent their use in 'the miracle of a liberty which delivers' and 'the miracle of the impossible' as he describes politics. But also there is the 'national miracle', the 'approaching miracle' and the 'miracle which took place among the hearers'. One miracle after another! The same is true of 'faith'. Hitler accomplished the 'miracle of enlightenment and faith'. There is, too, a 'catechism of the new political faith'. Goebbels frequently stresses the fact that it is a '*new* faith'; this faith is 'unshakeable'. And true adepts of National-Socialism always have 'faith'; they are the 'faithful' believers. Faith and miracle appear some fifteen times, or an average of once every four pages.

The relative frequency of 'sermon', 'to preach', and 'preacher' (used eight times) brings us to the theme of the last chapter, 'Thinkers and Preachers', but also brings us back again to the conscious exploitation of religious images and terms.

The term 'apostle' was also seized by the National-Socialists: 'apostle of the new idea', 'apostle and orator in battle', and, on the other hand, 'apostle of slavery'. National-Socialist language adopts Christian expressions in so automatic a way that it was never aware of those occasions when such language had the opposite effect from that intended.

The word 'mission', adopted in its turn by the National-Socialists, shows religion being biologised (or biology becoming religious), and is used in oft-repeated phrases like 'the impulse of mission'. In this kind of language they liked to rise to monumental and historical realms: 'Mission of historic importance' (*weltgeschichtliche Mission*). The word 'soul' is always used in its national or social meaning: 'German soul', 'soul of the proletariat', 'soul of the German worker'. The sacred is 'biologised' by Goebbels: 'thrice-sacred life'. The term 'messenger', which acquired its biblical tone through St John, is associated by the chief of National-Socialist propaganda with a word taken from sport: 'messenger and pace-maker' (*Wegbereiter und Schrittmacher*). 'Sin' appears in the guise of '*bourgeois* sin', 'historical sin' or 'atrocious sin against the people'. 'The work of revenge for liberty and bread' is described as 'Gospel'. National-Socialist secular appropriation of the eschatological idea of 'empire' (of God) is already evident in this work of Goebbels: 'The new Reich', 'the third Reich', 'the approaching Reich'. The eternal 'song of work' and the 'prayer of hammers and axes' is part of the usual toilers' lyricism.

In order to understand the word 'Idea' (*Idee*), which appears about once every five pages, it is important to remember the intoxicating obscurity of every foreign word. Here is an example of one of the idealist and biological short circuits of which National-Socialist oratorical technique was so enamoured: 'We manure (*düngen*) with our whole being and with our whole life for the Idea'.

Next to the vocabulary of religion, Goebbels exploited the vocabulary of morals and moralising most frequently in order to obtain the desired effects. If words of religious origin appear twice on every page, words taken from the vocabulary of morals and moralising appear on an average once a page. Most important are attacks against the middle class (*Bürger*), who are described as *bourgeois* (*Bourgeois*) and Philistine (*Spiesser*); even here in the

C C

beginnings of National-Socialism the normal term *Bürger* has acquired a distinctly pejorative meaning. Goebbels speaks of 'obese *bourgeois* parties', of 'lying and ignorant *bourgeois*', of '*bourgeois* selfishness' and of '*bourgeois* stupidity'. 'Well-fed *bourgeois*' is an alternative to 'obese *bourgeois* parties' in Goebbels' vocabulary. Later, the middle classes are accused of 'small-minded surfeited *bourgeois* calm' and 'Philistine middle-class order and calm'.

'Cowardice' also belongs to the vocabulary designed to liquidate enemies, particularly the middle classes. The term is usually associated with other verbal abuse: stupid, lazy, lukewarm, cowardly; stupidity, cowardice, meanness; stupidity, meanness, cowardice, verbiage, and lying; political loafers and cowards. The ridicule poured on the enemy by accusations of stupidity is very often associated with the 'cowardice' of the victim. Opinions differing from National-Socialist ones become 'verbiage', 'silly prattle'; the *Reichstag* is a gossip circle and the adversary consists of 'gossips and pen-pushers'.

'Lying' is one of the favourite National-Socialist moral labels attached to opponents: 'lying ignorant *bourgeois*'. 'Lying Jews foreign to the race', 'system completely corrupted from within by lies'. This sentence is extremely illustrative: 'From the poverty and lies of a perverted and slimy pacifism; from the misery and lies of a chattering, bloated internationalism, national instinct raises its victorious banner above the crumbling systems of Europe.'

Also in this vocabulary are the terms 'shameless', associated with 'corrupt and abject' and 'disgrace', especially in the phrase 'the greatest disgrace'; 'without honour', 'without land', 'big-wigs', and 'revolt'. The pejorative suffix *-aster* is also employed 'dirty politician' (*Politikaster*). Inevitably, a hand is stretched out to those who are on the other side of the fence: 'The lost German worker must once more become part of the great front of national unity.'

Goebbels makes use of the language of emotion, of sentimental terms and images, almost as frequently as of moral terms. Most frequent is the conception 'fanatic', used in phrases like 'fanatical will', 'fanatical follower', 'fanatical zeal', 'fanatical energy', or 'fanatical desire', 'proclaimers of truth' or 'fanatic of truth' are used synonymously. A 'fanatic' or a 'fanaticism' appears almost once every four pages. This term exemplifies the greatest praise and the highest example of hope and of the ideal. Complete determination is required of the National-Socialist man. Goebbels makes a note that one of his companions seems only 'partially fanatical in lying as in truth'. So, by 1926, 'fanatic' had become a term of unequivocal praise in Goebbels' mouth. Victor Klemperer, in his book *LTI* (Berlin, 1947), devoted a special chapter to this word.

The next most frequent terms in Goebbels' vocabulary of sentiments are 'passion', 'ardent desire', and 'fervour'. Passion appears as 'the greatest passion', as the 'last passion' and as 'national passion'. Fervour, too, appears as 'national fervour'. Fervour is also used in the phrases 'the greatest fervour', 'holy fervour', and, occasionally, in the plural 'the deepest fervours'.

Goebbels very often uses the image of fire, of ardour, on account of the violent feelings which it evokes: 'burning consuming ardour', 'blazing flame', 'the ardent pulsations of the heart', 'ardent fanaticism', 'the liquid fire of national and social revolution which burns in our soul', 'the idea of German liberty burns ardently in this search'.

On occasion, however, Goebbels employs more tender emotional themes of almost *bourgeois* sentimentality; he speaks of the benevolent power of new ideas in places where one would have expected him in his usual language to have spoken of 'fanatical and passionate forces'. He speaks also of the 'kind and powerful *Führer* inured to storms' in contexts where one would have expected 'the greatest' or 'the most sublime'.

The influence of the biological character of National-Socialism upon Goebbels' vocabulary is so strong that a word connected with blood or the soil is to be found almost once every two pages. The most frequent is of course 'instinct', which appears every five pages. 'Instinct and not knowledge', Goebbels insists. National or popular instinct is mentioned on several occasions. One's opponent also possesses instincts, of course negative instincts: 'commercial instincts'. The literal terminology of blood and of the soil is better represented here than later: 'national, that is to say bound to the earth', 'deep rooted', 'the tang of the soil', 'our country's soil'. Life, the vigour of life, is emphasised; 'the national will to live', 'the will for national assertion'; 'will to life', 'life, battle, passion'; life is encircled by a ceremonious religious dignity: 'thrice-sacred life'. Race is strongly stressed: 'good racial mixture', 'of the same mind and blood', 'lying Jews foreign to the race', and 'near Hitler the best human stock is to be found'. We have already had occasion to refer to the image, in doubtful taste, 'that which manures the idea'. The slogan 'community of need, bread and fate' (*Not-Brot- und Schicksalsgemeinschaft*), combines three fields of ideas whose effectiveness Goebbels was fond of exploiting: bread represents the biological and material world, needs are explicitly described, and fate provides that element of pathos essential to the secularised religion.

Expressions denoting misery and bondage appear almost as frequently as expressions of blood and the soil in the vocabulary of the young Goebbels, on an average of almost once every two pages, in fact. First comes the word 'misery', on an average once every six pages, and about as often 'bondage' and 'slavery'. Other words connected with the sphere of misery which Goebbels exploits are 'torture', 'suffering', 'despair', and 'terror'. The adjective 'socialist' still retains its primitive meaning, which suggests primarily 'misery' and 'struggle'.

The terminology of war is almost as well represented as that of blood, the soil, and misery. 'Fight' and 'to fight' are of course most frequent. But warlike images are transposed into other fields; indeed, the 'national idea' is not the only thing which is 'on the march'; 'liberation is on the march' too, in Goebbels' language. 'The passionate will for liberty is on the march', also 'intellectual perception is on the march'. And later Goebbels adds: 'We shall accomplish all if we get hunger, despair and sacrifice to march together to attain our ends.' Goebbels liked to employ certain rather archaic warlike terms whose historical appeal is emotional: 'Lansquenets of the future', 'haranguer in battle', 'sentinels', 'pioneers', and 'battle-song'. This did not, however, deter him from mentioning immediately afterwards the brutal aspects of war: 'Here chimney stacks and towers preach brutality and the battle-song.'

Just as—surprisingly—warlike terminology is certainly not the most favoured in the language of Goebbels' first writings, nationalist and racial terminology did not play a part of the first importance, either. The latter does, however, find a place on an average of once every three pages in the guise of: 'national community', 'national idea advancing', 'national instinct', 'national miracle', 'national will for life and assertion', 'national passion', 'national fanaticism for liberty', 'flame of national despair and of the instinct of the race'.

Images taken from popular medicine appear once every four pages in the same work; often in the form of the image of 'decomposition', represented by the verb 'to decompose', by the noun 'decomposition', or by 'agent of decomposition'. Words like 'plague', 'contaminate', 'mind suffering from sclerosis', 'squint', 'infection', 'spiritual poison', and 'gory peoples', etc., are employed.

Terms taken from the imagery of motion, motion in sport, and dynamics in general are relatively rare (appearing once every six pages), in comparison with the groups of ideas already considered. This is all the more surprising since National-Socialists always stress the dynamic character of their movement. 'Movement' is in fact the term which is most frequent, with various associations: 'movement for freedom', 'workers' movement', and 'movement' on its own. Work is dignified by the expression 'Supra-movement'. 'Action' and 'activists' are of course among these terms. 'Pace-maker' in its meaning, connected with sport, curiously associated with the biblical 'messenger' has already been mentioned. The revaluation of values and the will to power can be attributed to reminiscences of Nietzsche. The 'new' is mentioned every seven pages: 'the new Reich', 'the new idea', 'the new political faith', 'the new Third Reich', 'the new man', 'the new State', 'old and new'.

Terms and images connected with work occur about as frequently, that is, relatively rarely: 'the eternal song of work which delivers the earth', 'creative men', 'active national community', 'man with hammer and anvil', 'gigantic German work', 'the prayer of thousands of hammers and axes', 'the soul of the German worker'.

The young Goebbels used the image of the filthiness of his adversaries about as often: 'the mire of parliamentary democracy', 'the mire of parliament', 'stupid and filthy thing', 'democratic slime', 'slimy pacifism', 'slimy mass of property and culture'.

This study has shown that the language which the young Goebbels preferred to employ was composed of images and metaphors of an expressive character; that words with strong associations, pregnant with emotional content, were often employed, and that a well-defined sequence of frequency exists between the various groups of words and images. Religious terms are twice as numerous as words belonging to the next most frequent group of ideas, morality (which shows a distinct tendency towards popular morality). From religious vocabulary the term whose popularity is most typical is that expressing the concept of 'sacrifice'. This term was to become even more common in later National-Socialist language. Next to terms belonging to religious and moral spheres, terms of emotion are the most frequent. Next, in that order, terms and images from biology, misery, battle, the idea of the nation, popular medicine, movement, the 'new', work, and filthiness. The range of words, emotions, and associations which Goebbels used is clearly distinguishable, as is the method employed in order to extract from the available facilities of the language powerful, far-reaching effects. This method corresponds exactly with the principles of mass propaganda formulated by Hitler and by Goebbels himself.

A more detailed examination would be necessary in order to decide the extent to which the language of the young Goebbels is representative of early National-Socialist language. It is, however, true that the language of Goebbels is in general similar to that of early National-Socialism, since Goebbels was the most active creator of the language of National-Socialism, even in its early days. Much work is still to be done in order to reconstitute the language of National-Socialism in time and in history; with special regard to the ends sought and the methods employed to attain them. To accomplish this, much more preparatory work, more time, and more space would be necessary than are available in this brief essay. In the following paragraphs some specimens of the language of Hitler will be given, followed by an attempt to show some specific characteristics of the National-Socialist treatment of language.

The specimens of Hitler's language given here are taken from those chapters of *Mein Kampf*[1] which deal with the author's life. As regards religious terms, there is 'those witnesses of the blood who fell on 19th November 1923', and the 'sacred mission of the preparation of arms which will seize definitive liberty'. Among moralising terms, 'the majority of men are idle and cowardly', 'good-for-nothings', 'breakers of the November movement', 'profiteers', 'abominable propaganda', 'low politicians', 'mania for objectivity'. From the field of biological concepts and metaphors: 'one single blood in one Reich', 'of Bavarian blood', 'the human material to be shaped'. Amongst terms of battle: 'fencing-room', 'citadel', and the numerous words composed with 'leader' (*Führer*): 'leading brains', 'quality of a leader', 'efficiency of a leader', 'genius of a leader', and 'impulse of a leader'. From the vocabulary of misery: 'the most profound suffering', 'the lowest degradation'. The vocabulary of motion provides: 'fencing-room' and 'movement'. Nationalist vocabulary: 'national importance' and 'national enthusiasm'. A few terms taken from popular medicine: 'charlatan', 'decomposition', and 'parasites on the state'. These few examples show that in general Hitler's conception of language is much the same as that of Goebbels. More detailed examination would be necessary in order to decide the extent to which they differ on points of detail.

As time went on those religious images typical of the beginnings of National-Socialism whose effect was, through various associations of ideas, to awaken religious sentiments were increasingly directed towards National-Socialist institutions. An 'eternal sentinel' was set up at the *Felderrnhalle*, and on the 9th November 1935 Hitler described the fallen of the party as 'my apostles'; later he spoke of them in the following terms: 'In the Third Reich you have risen from the dead.'[2] The role of Providence becomes increasingly great in Hitler's speeches, and when the 'Ordensburgen' were established, the design of chivalric religious orders was adopted in its entirety by the National-Socialist party. *Mein Kampf* is described as 'the sacred book of National-Socialism and of the new Germany', and, in some verse edited by Baldur von Schirach, Hitler is named 'the Saviour'. The world of Christian conceptions is also used by Hitler as when, in a speech broadcast on the 10th November 1933, he declared: 'At the thirteenth hour, Adolf Hitler comes to the workers.'[3]

Non-native words, whose effect was both confusing and stimulating in early National-Socialist language, became increasingly lofty and high-flown: 'the guarantors (*Garanten*) of the future', 'the most faithful paladin (*paladin*) of the *Führer*'; and privates (*Schützen*) are once again dignified with the title 'Grenadier' (*Grenadiere*).

---

[1] *Mein Kampf*, 19th Ed. (Munich, 1933), pp. 1–17, 193–204, 649–69, 684–700.
[2] Klemperer, *LTI*, p. 118.   [3] ibid., p. 45.

Superlatives, already in full bloom in the early stages of National-Socialism, become more and more superlative; 'the greatest general' is no longer linguistically strong enough, and must become 'the greatest general of all time'. As before, Hitler's speeches are constantly designed to 'provoke endless ovations'. Of course, the super-superlative character of National-Socialist language tended to work against its own authors and become ridiculous. Yet the remarkable results which the National-Socialists obtained from steadfast repetition must not be forgotten: 'The curse of the superlative is not always self-destruction; quite frequently it is the destruction of the opposing intellect.' [1]

As the military situation became increasingly serious, coarse, belittling images began to make their appearance in order to meet it. Goebbels now takes his metaphors from the sport ordained by Hitler as providing a rule of conduct for the higher German classes: boxing. After Stalingrad the situation is described by Goebbels: 'Now we're wiping the blood from our eyes, so that we can see clearly, and in the next round we shall again be standing firm.' The destruction of German towns in the bombing causes Goebbels to make this remark: 'A boxer who has gained the world title is no less strong than before even if his opponent has broken his nose.' [2]

Some of the neologisms taken into National-Socialist language for propaganda purposes met with great success. Passages relating to sacrifice and misery were frequently used by the young Goebbels. But later, when sacrifices involving real privation had left their mark on German minds, the warmth and friendliness of the 'Winter Help Campaign' (*Winterhilfe*) marked the true success of linguistic propaganda. This was also true of phrases like 'coal thief' (*Kohlenklau*), 'Farthings' grave' (*Groschengrab*), 'one pot' (*Eintopf*), etc.

The use of inverted commas to convey irony was a typical stylistic procedure in National-Socialist language. A word whose meaning is generally accepted, and whose value is positive, is branded with inverted commas, or, if spoken, by the tone of voice, and thus acquires a grotesque, pejorative meaning. Even in his early works Goebbels put 'objective judgment' in inverted commas, and in *Mein Kampf* Hitler wrote: 'Let not the hearts of our children be infected too with the curse of "objectivity".' So that objectivity became a term of abuse in National-Socialist language: 'Mania for objectivity.' In some cases the word 'Gentleman', or 'Mister' (*Herr*) has retained a reinforced pejorative meaning in present-day German as a result of Hitler's attacks upon 'Herr' Churchill.

The National-Socialists also invented a kind of conventional language of camouflage. Those who had to be discarded from public activity were 'taken into protection', for example. The war with

[1] Klemperer, *LTI*, p. 246.   [2] ibid., p. 246.

Poland began with 'police action' (a phrase which was later to be imitated elsewhere). As the military situation became more serious, language was obliged to become more and more inventive: retreats were 'movements carried out according to pre-arranged plans', 'shortenings of the front line', or 'straightening of the front' (*Frontbegradigung*). Such expressions reached their height, I think, with this sentence from a newspaper in 1944: 'The enemy was unable to hinder the withdrawal of our troops.' In this way any failure could be interpreted as a success. And the power of the word, which could so completely misrepresent fact, was certainly not the most inconsiderable factor in maintaining for so long the hopes of so many people in a total reversal of the situation, even amongst the ruins of a reality which was falling about their heads.

The word cannot change the world so much, but mankind . . .

24

NATIONAL-SOCIALISM AND THE CATHOLIC CHURCH IN GERMANY

Robert d'Harcourt

BEFORE describing the tactical methods used by National-Socialism in its struggle with the Catholic Church, it is useful to note briefly its theoretical position as regards Roman Catholicism.

This position is indicated by the principal authorities in the Party, above all by Hitler. In *Mein Kampf* Hitler reproaches the Catholic Church on two main counts: it failed to recognise racial duty; and it failed to recognise national duty.

Its attitude of steadfast opposition to eugenic theories and its stubborn condemnation of sterilisation rendered it guilty of a serious wrong against the race. In doing so it illustrated of itself the fact that it did not understand the law which makes biology the postulate of the spiritual and the moral. How could it refuse to recognise the self-evident truth that no moral progress can be expected of a humanity ravaged by physical defects, of a humanity in which 'the syphilitic, the tuberculous, the hereditarily tainted, the legless cripples, and the cretins' are allowed to reproduce themselves indefinitely as they wish? Beneath the eyes of the Church, and with no protest from it, marriage had become 'a permanent stain on the race'. Too often today it is not 'beings in God's image' that come into the world, but 'wretched creatures half-way between man and ape'. 'The Churches have committed a veritable crime against the image of the Lord . . . by speaking only one word, Spirit, and allowing the representative of the Spirit, man, to degenerate into a rotten proletarian.' The state must fill the gap left by the Churches by 'placing the most modern facilities of medical technique at the disposal of racial eugenics'.

This was the offence against the race. Complementary to it was an offence against the nation. How had the Catholic Church overlooked the fact that its first field of activity was Germany, and that before setting out to evangelise Zulus and Kaffirs it should have looked to the ills and sores of its own country. The very idea of missions abroad, which is connected with the principle of the universality of the Church, is a sin against the nation. Whilst our European peoples disintegrate in the most terrible of physical and moral leprosies, our devout missionaries think that they have nothing better to do than to go to Central Africa to found missions among the blacks, and to await the fruition of our great culture in those parts by making of a primitive but healthy race a race of rotted degenerates.

One of the points which Hitler brings out most strongly in his book is the danger of using religious ideals for political ends. 'Political Catholicism' (*politischer Katholicismus*), 'Church talking politics' (*politisierende Kirche*)—this is the grievance which was to become the weapon with which the Catholic Church in Germany was battered in the Nazis' campaign against it. The Church has overstepped its rights and betrayed its mission by descending into the political arena. The Catholic becomes an enemy from the moment he exploits his religious position in politics. The vital text in this context is the following passage from *Mein Kampf*:

'One can never be ruthless enough with the wretched profiteers who see in religion only a means of doing better deals *politically*. These shameless people with lying mouths (*freche Lügenmäuler*) make their profession of faith in stentorian voices heard throughout the world, not with the intention of dying for their faith, but with the definite intention of using it to improve their lot in this world. They would betray their faith for any worthwhile political gain. They would sign an alliance with the Marxists, the deadly enemies of religion, for ten seats in parliament. They would wed the devil for a minister's portfolio.'

The history of the dispute between National-Socialism and the Catholic Church shows how these lines were enthusiastically adhered to, and how they made the Party take up a firm stand in the struggle.

Electoral considerations infiltrating among spiritual ones, the Church abandoning its mission to become 'an ally of Marxism'— these are the principal grounds of the indictment. The passage quoted above was a call to battle as well as a verdict.

The accusation was made even more detailed by Alfred Rosenberg (*Der Mythus des 20. Jahrhunderts*), and the political party described but not named by Hitler is now plainly named:

The Centre has constantly set the interests of religion against the interests of the nation. If politics and religious beliefs are mixed, then the living body of the people is cut in two. The setting up of a political party to defend the interests of the Church constituted a crime whose results were felt by our whole country on the 9th November. It was all the more a crime because in fact religious belief was no more than a label, a sign in the shop window (*Aushängeschild*) behind which was sheltered unadulterated political intrigue or material profits of the vilest kind. We must act in such a way that the rising generation will call these attempts to disrupt the nation by their true name, high treason (*Hochverrat*).

The difference in tone is very apparent. *Mein Kampf* as a whole, and even in its complaints about the Catholic Church, was discreet. *Der Mythus* in its attacks on Roman Catholicism was a violent indictment. The man of letters is free to express himself in a way that is denied the politician by the very nature of his profession. Rosenberg, editor of the *Völkischer Beobachter*, the principal journal of the Party, was from the start the real and authentic doctrinaire of the Party, although his position as a journalist writing on his own authority made it possible for the heads of the régime to make convenient denials whenever he went too far. 'Rosenberg does not commit the party' was the facile reply to all attacks on their racial ideology.

Rosenberg's basic grievances are the same as those of Hitler: the Catholic Church fails to recognise both racial and national duty, which are in any case interconnected. By having its focal point beyond the frontiers of Germany, it places itself on the fringe of the nation. Greedy for temporal domination under cover of the Gospel's lying vocabulary of gentleness and humility, it does not hesitate to associate with the most bitter adversaries of Christianity, the Marxists and Jews. Its entire ideology constitutes an attitude of impassioned opposition to the creed of Germanic values. Its servile obedience to the orders of Rome is a denial of the pride and the religion of honour of the German (are not the words 'flock' and 'shepherd' a challenge to the Germanic mind?). Its cosmopolitan universality is incompatible with racial consciousness. By placing religious values above national values, the Catholic Church shows no hesitation in formally making high treason legitimate. The 'German man' will not comply with the commands of a power 'whose central point is outside Germany'. The German's gospel is within himself.

'The dogma of the papacy representing the temporal delegation of God on earth is today violently rejected and victoriously combated by the German's faith in his own values of soul and race.'

Rosenberg violently attacks the Vatican and the Pope. 'It is to Pius IX that Europe owes the most disgraceful memorial of all time' (papal infallibility). The vulgar belief in infallibility enthroned on the seat of Peter brings the Catholic nations of modern times near to the mental simplicity of negro tribes—the Pope is a big witch-doctor (*Medizinmann*). The pure teachings of Jesus have been forgotten a long time ago. 'The Christianity of Rome is the progressive elimination of the person of Christ, beneath which the edifice of the Church and the domination of the priests is inserted.' The 'league of priests' (Rosenberg ritually describes the Church of Rome as *Priesterbund* or *Männerbund*, terms which were to become incorporated in the basic racial vocabulary) knows 'no other god than itself'; it 'exploits' belief in Jesus and calls 'patristic dialectics' to the rescue of its power politics (*Machtpolitik*) with as much cynicism as did 'the politician-priests of Babylon and Etruria' of old.

This was the outline of the National-Socialist position as regards the Roman Catholic Church. Its ideology of violence was to be turned to positive action and foster the Party's strategy in its struggle with the German Church, a struggle whose premises were, from the start, contained in its nature.

The first clash between the Catholic Church in Germany and National-Socialism occurred in September 1930. The vicar of a Catholic parish in the province of Hesse asked his bishop for definite instructions on the attitude he should take towards the believers in National-Socialist racial doctrines. A reply was soon forthcoming. The Bishop of Mainz laid down the practical ways in which one should behave towards National Socialists. There were perhaps a few passages in *Mein Kampf* in which Hitler mentioned the Christian religion and Catholic institutions with respect. But these passages could not deceive us as to the incompatibility of the cultural policy of National-Socialism and Catholic Christianity. Three questions were put to us:

1. Can a Catholic be a registered member of the Hitlerian Party?
2. Has a Catholic priest the right to allow members of the Hitlerian Party to take part collectively in the services of his Church?
3. Can a Catholic who adheres to the principles of the party be allowed to receive the sacrament?

We are forced to answer 'no' to these three questions.

The attitude of the Catholic Church was laid down even more clearly by the declaration of the Bavarian bishops in February 1931. After forcefully making known their decision to remain on purely religious ground and stressing 'the non-political purely pastoral nature' (*den apolitischen rein seelsorglichen Charakter*) of their position, the Bavarian bishops condemned the five major errors of Hitlerian racialism:

1. Racialism places race above religion.
2. It rejects the revelations of the Old Testament, and even the ten comandments of Moses.
3. It does not recognise the primacy of the Pope in Rome because his is an authority 'situated outside Germany'.

4. It fosters the project of a 'dogma-less German national Church'.

5. Under Article 24 of its programme it proposes to set up the 'moral feeling' (*Moralgefühl*) of the Germanic race as a criterion for Christian moral laws, which are essentially universal.

The various statements which had been unequivocally made by the heads of the Party during their demonstrations gave the bishops good reason to conclude: 'What National-Socialism describes as Christianity is not the Christianity of Christ.'

This solemn declaration of the attitude of the Church is followed by practical instructions which are in general similar to those issued by the Bishop of Mainz.

Eighteen months later the position of the Church was once more defined by the declaration of the Bishops of Bavaria, who had met at Freising on the 7th September 1932:

> 'In the struggle against what are called supranational powers (*überstaatliche Mächte*) is concealed a new *Kulturkampf*, a new effort to strike at the heart of the Catholic Church by founding a national Church. In this struggle we will do no less either in moral strength or in fidelity than did our predecessors and ancestors in the Bismarckian *Kulturkampf*.'

Both sides had taken up their stand in a blaze of public interest which precluded any withdrawal. We have seen the attitude of the German Church. The attitude of racialism is equally intransigent: 'We refuse to recognise any right of existence of a doctrine which replaces the national and moral discipline of the race by what it calls universality' (*Völkischer Beobachter*, 29th November 1929).

After the bishops' condemnation of them, what was the reply of the National-Socialists? It was the reply which could be foreseen from the declarations in *Mein Kampf* and *Der Mythus des 20. Jahrhunderts*. The Church, declared the leaders of the movement in speeches or in the press, does not pursue spiritual aims. The spiritual is only a screen for the temporal; ambition for completely earthly power is concealed beneath the alleged care of souls. 'Political Catholisicm' and 'Church talking politics' are the terms continually repeated in the speeches and writings of the Party leaders. They maintained that the bishops had not condemned the errors of National-Socialism; what they condemned was a party, a party which was in their way. They themselves acted as members of a party. '*Zentrumsbischof, Zentrumskardinal*' (bishop of the Centre, cardinal of the Centre), cried the *Völkischer Beobachter* to the Bishop of Munich. The intrusion of the spiritual into the temporal serves a political purpose. All action taken by the Catholics is based on the deliberate fusion and confusion of religion and politics.

However, all Catholics did not unhesitatingly obey their bishops. For some the dispute involved a most difficult moral choice—between the Church and Germany, between the spiritual and the temporal fatherland. Some of them settled the question in a 'national' sense. The Catholic Baron de Schorlemer, whose name was one of the most famous in the history of the Centre, a name which gained renown in the struggle against the Bismarckian *Kulturkampf*, made the following statement of his position with regard to pastoral letters:

'The Catholic Church, through its clergy (that is the cardinals and bishops of Germany), thinks it right to attack the German Hitlerian movement with great violence. But we German Catholics have a feeling of moral liberation when we see a Catholic priest take up sides with our movement and with the German cause. All the power of the Church, all its methods of intimidation will be powerless to stop us. Neither the Church nor any of its dignitaries has the right to stop the mouth of a German Catholic who courageously confesses his belief in a Christian *Deutschtum*.'

Here the question was brought on to its own ground, or at least on to the ground which Hitler intended for it. National-Socialism is not a party, it is interconnected with the nation, and identical to *Deutschtum*. To attack it is to attack Germany. The Church demands that the Fatherland be denied. Fidelity to the Church is apostasy to the nation.

The attitude of the bishops in condemning the movement is not only a crime against the nation, the Nazis said, it also shows extraordinary blindness to the true interests of the Church, of that Church which they claim to be defending. We have already noted this argument in *Mein Kampf*. It was reintroduced by Hitlerian propaganda in typical terms:

How could the bishops be unaware of the fact that by associating with the Centre, which associated with Social-Democracy, they were finally working against themselves? How were they unable to realise that all these unhealthy alliances would ultimately open the flood-gates holding back the devastating current of atheist Marxism which would carry away the nation and the Church with it? The Church was clearly unable to realise on what side its defenders lay. It was the theme of National-Socialism as the only defender of the Church against Marxist godlessness, and its corollary, the blindness of the Church, which attacked its saviour instead of its enemy, and thus itself sawed away the branch on which it stood, which is given classic expression in an article in *Völkischer Beobachter* of the 10th March 1931:

'High dignitaries of the Church have, in this latest statement (a pastoral letter issued by the bishopric of the Rhine), delivered a new and overt attack on the only movement which is today in a position to undertake the defençe of the Christian Church against the world-wide assault of godless forces. The hope that, in the chaos common to all nations, the bishops of Germany would retain sufficient clearsightedness to be able to reveal the mortal peril to the Church of the lunatic policies of the Centre, has proved false. We are faced with this staggering sight: German priests who are too far removed from the realities of this world to realise where the common, the mortal, danger lies.'

A very definite tendency is shown by these different texts—the bishops are behind the Centre, the Centre is itself behind the Marxists and the Jews. The series of elements bent on achieving 'the decomposition of the Reich' (Rosenberg) is complete.

National-Socialism possessed an admirable weapon which it was to use widely against the Catholics. It had become the sole proprietor of patriotism, had appropriated it for its own use alone, had made of it its servant and its chattel. The Catholics were unable to claim it, for they were in the shameful situation of allies of the Marxists. The slogans were already fixed: *nationale Unzuverlässigkeit, nationale Minderwertigkeit*. The Catholic is 'inferior' and also 'unreliable' in the nation. Brave members of the Catholic camp at the front of the battle were daily reviled by their adversaries. Professor Schmittmann (Cologne), Father Moenius (Munich), Reverend Father Stratmann, O.P., a few names selected almost at random, were called by the racialist press names like 'Germans without dignity', 'pacifist traitors' (*landesverräterische Pazifisten*), 'stateless rogues' (*vaterlandslose Gesellen*), 'birds that defile their own nests' (*Vögel, die das eigene Nest beschmutzen*).

The Jew, the Marxist, and the Roman Catholic (*Römling*—in the scornful terminology of the Party) are all considered by the National-Socialist as being associates in the task of bringing about the disintegration of the living forces in the Fatherland. They are bound by the same fetters of national unworthiness (*nationale Würdelosigkeit*). And, inevitably, Versailles is brought up against the Catholics.

The Catholic, like the Marxist, is a man who, his head held low, accepts Versailles, and approves the *Erfüllungspolitik* and 'national shame'. The racialists composed a carol for Christmas 1930, in which the Catholics are shown in their true character of legal traitors, German renegades hiding behind the mask of submission to international agreements. Here are a few lines from this racial carol, which was printed in the *Illustrierter Beobachter*, the illustrated supplement of the *Völkischer Beobachter*:

Wir hassen fort, unter den Weihnachtskerzen,
Aus heisser Brust und brennendem Herzen
In der hohen heutigen Weihenacht,
Alle, die uns ins deutsche Elend gebracht,

Wir hassen die roten und schwarzen Halunken,
Die als Wilsons blindgläubige Dolchstossunken
Nach Frieden schrieen und von Freiheit unkten
Und in jede Pakttinte die Feder tunkten.

(Beneath the Christmas candles, on this holy Christmas night, we detest with our heated breasts and our burning hearts all those who led us into Germany's woe. We hate the bandits, red and black, Wilson's blind traitorous slaves, who hoot for peace and screech for liberty and dip their pens in the ink of every pact.)

This attitude of hostility towards Catholicism became confirmed when Adolf Hitler rose to power. It is stated in detail in the speech made by Hermann Göring at Essen on 11th March 1933. It is now an official, and not a journalist, who expresses these opinions. Since 30th January, a vital date in the history of the movement and in German history, Hitler had been Chancellor, and National-Socialism had stopped being a party and become the Government. In his speech announcing the programme of the Party, Göring stated that he saw in the black, red, and gold flag of Weimar the symbol of everything that must be overthrown—the symbol of union, of the 'system of three internationals, the black international (Roman Catholicism), the red international (Socialism), and the yellow international (Jewish finance)'. In this speech he described the role of the Catholics during the fourteen years of Weimar: 'The black man stood guard (*der Schwarze hat Schmiere gestanden*) while the Marxist robbed the house of Germany.'

The Party press, with the unison of a well-drilled orchestra, took up the same themes with expression. The alliance of Marxism with Catholicism remained one of the basic *leitmotifs* of racialist propaganda:

'We must', wrote the *Völkischer Beobachter* after the burning of the *Reichstag*, 'pillory the system, the alliance of the old parties for the ruin and death of Germany, Catholicism, Social-democracy, Communism. The offenders are giving themselves away. All the better, we shall be able to finish the job' (*dann kann gleich ganze Arbeit gemacht werden*).

Also in March 1933 Hitler made a vital speech before the *Reichstag*. This speech, made by the Chancellor of the Reich, appears formally to contradict the spirit of Göring's Essen speech. This contradiction is only one of appearances, however. Hitler's views on the German Catholics and their alliance with the parties of the left were similar to Göring's. But the Chancellor had a practical end in view—to obtain from the parliament resulting from the elections of the 5th March 1933 [1] the passing of a 'law of full powers' (*Ermächtigungs Gesetz*) which would give him a free hand.

---

[1] The results of the poll were: National-Socialists 17,269,000 votes; Social Democrats 7,177,000; Communists 4,845,000; Centre 4,423,000; Nationalist Germans 3,133,000. Popular Bavarian Party 1,073,000.

For this decisive motion he needed the votes of the Catholics in order to gain the substantial majority necessary to him if he was to be regarded as the representative of the nation. He therefore adapted his speech to the needs of the moment. The fact that the two speeches, Göring's on the 11th March and Hitler's on the 23rd March, were made so near together in time, and were so completely opposed in tone and spirit is a sign of the essential opportunism of the Party's leaders. The whole history of the National-Socialist dispute with the German Catholic Church is marked by their policy of alternating intimidation and *détente*. Göring played on the theme of violence. This is how, a few days later, Hitler played on the theme of appeasement:

'The National Government sees in the two Christian faiths essential elements for safeguarding the soul of the German people. It will respect the agreements made between the Churches and the *Länder* [an allusion to the concordats made under the Weimar government between the Vatican and Prussia, Bavaria and the state of Baden]. It declares its resolution not to tamper with their rights. In schools and in the Ministry of Education the Government has decided to ensure that the two Christian Churches shall have the influence which is their due. Its ambition is peaceful accord between Church and State. We consider the spiritual forces of Christianity to be essential to the moral recovery of the German people: We hope to improve our friendly relations with the Holy See.'

These assurances acted as they were intended to do—Hitler obtained the desired votes. The Centre granted him full powers through their President, Mgr Kaas.

The National-Socialist success surpassed all hopes. The Catholic bishops, carried away by the new atmosphere of peace and concord of which Hitler's declaration before the *Reichstag* on the 23rd March bore witness, decided to retract their former harsh verdict. On the 28th March they made a statement declaring that they thought that 'they could confidently state that the warnings and interdictions of a general nature issued recently need not be considered necessary in the future'. Shortly afterwards their conciliatory attitude was made even more definite by the Archbishop of Cologne, who allowed men in uniform to receive the Sacrament, even in military units, removed all opposition to religious burials, and permitted banners to be brought into places of worship.

The spring and summer of the first year of the Third Reich showed many vivid examples of the double game: intimidation and *détente*. Scarcely a few weeks had passed since Hitler's solemn declaration of intended good relations with the Catholics, and particularly the Vatican, when he gave his troops leave to act with a free hand in the streets.

20–23rd June. Arrests of Catholic priests increase and become increasingly widespread. The clergy are prosecuted for 'activities hostile to the state' or for having behaved in a way destined to 'pour scorn on the national movement and its symbols'. In what did this endeavour to 'pour scorn on' National-Socialism (*Verächtlichmachung*) consist? What exactly were the 'symbols of the national movement'? The vagueness and the conveniently wide scope of the charges are obvious. With a little imagination a government desirous of using intimidation can make anything come under the head of 'efforts to pour scorn' on the régime.

Berlin, 21st June. At the Lustgarten Dr Robert Ley states that it is essential for the new state to 'fight with a brutality that knows no mercy' all its former enemies, and particularly 'the reds and the blacks':

'We respect the Churches, but we tell them frankly: "Make your task the salvation of German souls". The salvation of souls in no way requires the existence of Catholic gymnasiums or of Protestant or Catholic workers' hostels. These institutions are the duty of the State. We will take steps against all reactionary movements, including black reaction.'

Berlin, 22nd June. Statement issued by Dr Ley:

'All other associations including workers' associations which call themselves (sic!) Catholic or Protestant shall be regarded as enemies of the state. They stand in the way of our great task of reconstructing the new régime. We must smite them, for it is time that they were made to vanish.'

28th June. Mass arrests of priests throughout the Reich. Assaults and violence to private individuals. The assaults on priests are particularly brutal. Some priests attached at night in their rooms after the windows have been broken; others attacked in the streets by masked men.

Berlin, 1st July. An official statement by the command of the state secret police (*geheimes Staatspolizeiamt*) announces the banning of a great many Catholic youth organisations (among them the *Jugenbund deutscher Katholiken*, the *Windhorstbund*, the *Kreuzschar*, *Sturmschar*, the *Volksverein für das katholische Deutschland*, and the *Katholischer Jungmännerbund*), and also the closing of the premises used by them as meeting-places. The Gestapo is anxious to leave no one in doubt about the 'national' motives responsible for this measure: the 'organisations claiming to be religious', masked satellites of the Centre, are guilty of 'activities against the state' (*staatsfeindliche Betätigung*). Their 'systematic campaigns of unrest and hatred' have tainted the nation by 'endeavouring to disrupt the Catholic people's natural support for national Germany'.

Munich, early July. The correspondent of *The Times* estimates the number of Catholics imprisoned in a few days as about 3,000.

The assaults in the streets, which occurred only with the consent and encouragement of the central authorities, had one advantage—official sources could always disclaim any responsibility for them and say that they were due to 'inflamed popular sentiment' (*die kochende Volksseele*). Deliberately concerted and progressively increased, these assaults were to come to a sudden stop at the desired time. Hitler made use of the same tactics in his domestic policy against the Catholics as he was later to use in his foreign policy—he used with great mastery the psychological shock treatment of a sudden *détente* following intimidation.

It should not be thought that the calculated outrages against the Catholics which took place in the summer of 1933 made Hitler forget the intention he had announced on the 24th March to create 'friendly relations' (*freundschaftliche Beziehungen*) with the Vatican. As well as a policy for the streets, he had a policy for chancellories. He wished to consolidate his power, and for some time had had the idea of an agreement with the Vatican, which would, he thought, ensure the respect of foreign countries by making him appear to be the head of a respectable state. This design progressed, and on the 8th July 1933 a concordat with the Holy See was signed. As soon as the first signatures had been exchanged by the Secretary of State, Mgr Pacelli, and the Vice-Chancellor of the Reich, Franz von Papen, Hitler issued a cleverly worded statement. In it he announced that the Catholics would be treated leniently, and also required of them submission to the new régime:

> 'The signing of the Concordat seems to me to be sufficient guarantee of the loyalty of citizens of the Catholic faith. It is to be hoped that in future they will unreservedly (*rückhaltlos*) serve the National Socialist State. I therefore decree: (1) The immediate lifting of the ban on all Catholic associations recognised by this agreement. (2) The ending of all measures of restraint of which the clergy may have been the victim.'

Hitler faithfully carried out his tactics of intimidation followed by *détente*. How faithful he remained to his essential spirit of opportunism and realism which made him delay an action on which he had decided until he was sure of possessing all the means of carrying it out! He made up to the Catholics as long as he needed them to vote for him on the law giving him full powers. He was friendly towards the Vatican for as long as he thought necessary to bring about the signing of a concordat which he thought would be politically profitable. Hardly was the ink of the signatures dry when he laid his cards on the table. He had for some time intended to bring in the sterilisation law, which enforced one of the theories nearest to his heart, but had realised that he could not simultaneously carry out two so completely irreconcilable projects as the sterilisation law and the concordat with the Holy See. Patience was necessary. The sterilisation law was approved in Hitlerian Council on the 14th July. It was not announced until the 25th. The official ratification of the Concordat took place between these two dates, on the 20th. Hitler's calculations are obvious; they are quite clear from the dates alone. The men of the Third Reich decided that the interests involved were worth more than a few hours' delay in the execution of their favourite plan. They wished to settle the Concordat before making public a law that was an affront to the Church. The objective study of the course of events makes it unlikely that the Third Reich ever sincerely intended to honour the agreement to which they put their signature. They hypocritically respected the container and destroyed the content. The spirit of the agreement was violated without the signatures upon it being affected. This intention of the Third Reich, which was never admitted but is none the less real, can be clearly read from the facts and from the official statements of the Party's leaders.

One of the most vital fields of activity in the eyes of the Church is indisputably the education of the young. It was very soon apparent that the Third Reich had resolved to abolish all religious youth organisations. The very fact of the choice of Baldur von Schirach, a disciple of Alfred Rosenberg, as official leader of German youth left little doubt as to the way in which Article 31 of the Concordat was to be interpreted.

The desire to bring about the complete unity of German youth within the organisation of the *Hitler-Jugend* became quite clear towards the end of 1933. At Frankfurt, Hitler declared himself resolved to 'remove all the obstacles presented by religion', at Brunswick (9th December), that he had decided not to tolerate 'opposition groups of a religious nature within the *Hitler-Jugend*':

'We claim and proclaim that all German youth organisations other than ourselves have lost every reason for their existence. These organisations must vanish and leave Hitler Youth a clear field. That youth associations should continue to exist on the fringe, protected by I know not what private concerns of the Churches, is in itself a situation that we cannot tolerate.'

Mr Hartmann-Lauterbacher, youth leader in Western Germany, sounded the same note in a speech at Coblenz:

'The remaining youth associations still in existence must be unwaveringly suppressed. . . . The spirit of totalitarianism requires the utter dissolution of religious associations.'

Thus, a few months after signing the Concordat, the intrinsic aims and the real policy of the National-Socialists became clear: to box in the Church, immure it behind darkness and silence, cut off its communications with the life of the nation, especially as regards the future—the young. By banning religiously inspired clubs, the Church's main channel of communication with the young was cut. Young people, and especially the youth of Germany, cannot do without public manifestations, externalisation. It would lose all contact, those in power in the Third Reich rightly thought, with a Church which is allowed its chasubles, but whose flags are forbidden it.

The principle of strict unification was not applied to youth organisations alone. It also extended to the press. In the Germany of tomorrow no religious press was to exist. Any citizen of Hitlerian Germany who has the audacity to demand a Catholic press is a 'corrupter of the people, a traitor destroying the unity of the nation, that unity which was so laboriously achieved. Any German who, under the pretence of spiritual concerns, desires to recreate the old spiritual divisions is a grave-digger of the national mind; he is worthy of the term (which was often applied to him) of *Volksverderber*'.

After the promulgation of the sterilisation law immediately following the signing of the Concordat, another action was to illuminate the intentions of the Third Reich towards the Catholic Church—Alfred Rosenberg's appointment as director of the cultural and educational department of Germany (24th January 1934). By making the most violent enemy of the Church and Christianity director of culture, or the nation's director of conscience, Hitler abandoned all pretence. He felt that he had become strong enough to be able to dispense with guile, and his true intentions were revealed.

From this moment on the war against the Catholic Church was to become increasingly intense. More and more the Catholic was to be thrust to one side and defrauded of his rights. He can best be robbed if he is dishonoured. And it was to this end that the double-headed offensive of scandal, currency trials, and immorality trials was launched against him. Currency actions were brought against travelling members of the Church for infraction of the law on the exportation of currency. Actions for immorality were brought against members of the clergy for assaulting children in their care. In both cases the defendants were, thanks to Dr Goebbels' many-mouthed propaganda, exhibited to the nation as common law criminals.

The scope of this essay does not permit us to pursue further the course of the attacks on the Catholic Church under the Third Reich. We have seen the general outline of Nazi tactics. The first grievance against the Catholic Church in Germany was that it was a Church which talked politics (*politisierende Kirche*). The Catholics, repeat all the organs of Hitlerian propaganda, use their faith as a cloak; they exploit the spiritual so as to be more sure of their temporal power. Priests do not serve the Church, they serve politics (*Zentrumprälaten, Zentrümler!*).

But the Catholics incur an even graver reproach—their obedience to the orders of Rome makes them suspect from the national point of view. Fidelity towards Rome becomes treason towards Germany. The connection between *Römling* (man of Rome) and *Volkschädling* (man who harms the people) is a close one. So as to make certain of power, the Catholics did not hold back from taking the hands of the worst enemies of Germany—the Jews and the Marxists. In the eyes of the Nazi a trilogy has been set up—Rome, Judah, and Moscow.

We have seen the methodical and cunning advance of the offensive, the steady forcing back of the Catholics to the position of second-class Germans from whom all rights are methodically withdrawn. But at no moment did Nazism entirely abandon prudence: the Concordat would be violated and destroyed little by little, but it was never denounced.

The history of the struggle of the Third Reich against the Catholic Church is a story of a conflict which was more painful than surprising. The differences were contained in the irreconcilability of the gospel of blood and the Gospel of Christ. The time always comes when the opposition of ideas engenders blows between men.

25

NATIONAL-SOCIALISM AND THE
PROTESTANT CHURCHES IN GERMANY

Birger Forell

I. THE TWO FRONTS

THE few passages of *Mein Kampf* which give evidence of the position of National-Socialism with regard to the Christian Churches are presented as if the author was a Christian loyal to the Church. Wilhelm Stapel, a Protestant writer who has made a very thorough study of National-Socialism and its attitude to Christianity, asserts: 'The fact that Hitler takes his Catholicism seriously is well known from his book *Mein Kampf* and from numerous other declarations'. (*Six Chapters on Christianity and National Socialism*, p. 2). Hitler himself attests it in his book, which is generally taken as the 'Bible of National-Socialism':

> 'The movement resolutely refuses to take up any position with regard to problems that are outside its political work or do not present a fundamental interest for this work. The mission of the movement is not in the nature of a religious reform, but in the nature of a political reorganisation of our people.'

If, however, one is willing to take the trouble to read the *whole* of Hitler's book with its statements on 'race, blood, and soil', its monstrous and hate-breathing attacks on the Jews, its contemptuous revelations of the man's views on propaganda, etc., one will have difficulty in understanding nowadays how so many good Christians have managed so completely to misunderstand the National-Socialist movement and its chief. This might be explained in part by the ambiguity of the ideas put forward by Hitler in *Mein Kampf* and elaborated in the movement's later declarations. In fact, National-Socialist propaganda was glad to invoke ancient traditions, but only after giving them surreptitiously a new content. This begins with terms like 'conception of the world', 'religion', 'faith', 'love', etc., which are precisely the most significant ones for any attempt to describe the position of National-Socialism with regard to the Christian Churches. What Hitler means by 'conception of the world' has very little to do with the traditional meaning of this term:

'The conception of the world is not passive, it cannot be content with the role of one party among others, but claims imperiously its own total and exclusive recognition together with the total revaluing of public life as a whole in accordance with its own conceptions. This is why it could never endure, side by side with it, a representation of an "anterior" state. This applies also to religions.'

There, in a few lines, it is stated that National-Socialism places its own conception of the world on the same plane as a religion. Many Christians, who had viewed early National-Socialism with sympathy, only realised very late in the day that the totalitarian demands of the new movement could not be reconciled with the demands of Christ.

The position of National-Socialism with regard to the Christian Churches is formulated in a similarly ambiguous way in the 24th paragraph of the Party programme:

'We envisage the liberty of all religious confessions within the State, in so far as they do not threaten its integrity and in so far as they do not shock German customs and the morality of the Germanic race. The Party as such represents the point of view of a positive Christianity, without binding itself on the confessional plane to a particular church.'

By the formula 'positive Christianity' the movement attracted many Protestants. Many foreigners also let themselves be led astray by this way of presenting things. Few were those who perceived from the beginning that this formula concealed a quite different meaning from that generally attributed to it by Christians loyal to the Church. Many Christians never thought that, in the paragraph under review, Christianity was being subordinated to the customs and moral sense of the Germanic race. In his book *Mythus des 20. Jahrhunderts* Alfred Rosenberg, supervisor of culture and director of education for the National-Socialist movement, defined the meaning of the passage in question more closely:

'We realise nowadays that, belonging as they do to a negative Christianity, the central values of the Roman and Protestant churches do not correspond to our soul, that they prevent the full expansion of the organic forces of the peoples of nordic race, and that they must let themselves be reinterpreted in the direction of *Germanic* Christianity. It is in this that the religious efforts of today consist.'

The various phases of the war waged by National-Socialism against the Protestant Churches—a war which began in 1933 and was to last till the defeat in 1945—showed clearly that the elimination of the Church from the life of the people envisaged by Rosenberg was, from early on, an objective necessary in the eyes of the chiefs of the Party, even though, for tactical reasons, they muted this hostility and covered it with ambiguous ideas until the situation was judged ripe for them to come out into the open. Martin Bormann, the *Führer*'s representative, indeed, threw off the mask in 1941:

'The National-Socialist and Christian conceptions are irreconcilable. It follows from this incompatibility that we must prevent the reinforcement of the existing confessions and refuse all protection to newly created confessions. On this plane no difference should be made between the various Christian confessions. This is the reason why the idea of organising a Reich Protestant Church by uniting the various Protestant churches has been abandoned, for the Protestant Church stands in our way with as much hostility as the Catholic Church. Any reinforcement of the Protestant Church will infallibly turn against us.'

No one could be more explicit. It must be added, too, that such frankness was only used at the moment when the Church war had at last shown that the Protestant Church would not let itself be 'assimilated' as easily as had been believed at the start.

If the war waged by National-Socialism against the Protestant Church only came into prominence after the war waged against the Catholic Church, this was due to the fact that the new movement developed, as a Party, in an essentially Catholic *milieu*—at Munich and in Bavaria. Up to 1929 the membership of the Party was rather small. In 1929, at the Nuremberg Party Congress, the *Völkischer Beobachter*, the Party's chief organ, reported only 150,000 regular members. The number of supporters was certainly greater, but it must not be forgotten that the Party was not yet 'recognised' in certain *bourgeois* circles. It was at the *Reichstag* elections of 14th September 1930, when so many National-Socialists got into the House, that the responsible circles of the Protestant Church saw themselves obliged to pay more attention to the new movement.

The economic crisis of 1930–3 having caused an extraordinary increase in the rank and file of the National-Socialist Party, the Protestant Church found itself, on its side, undermined by an internal crisis which was to weaken noticeably its capacity of resistance to the totalitarian demands of National-Socialism. The disaffection of the masses made itself felt in the ranks of Protestantism much more than in those of Catholicism. Out of the 45,000,000 or so Protestants in Germany in 1939, only about 150,000 were divided amongst the various Free Churches—Baptist, Methodist, etc. The rest belonged to the twenty-eight Churches, of which some were Lutheran, others Reformed, and to the largest provincial Church of Prussia, the so-called 'Church of the Old Prussian Union' of 1817, which, with its 18,000,000 faithful, Lutheran and Reformed, was the real touchstone in the eyes of conscientious Lutheran bishops and theologians. Thus the Protestants did not possess so firm a leadership as the Catholics, and the influence of sectarian disagreements conditioned by historical factors (as, for example, the conflict between Prussia and Bavaria) was destined to prove more harmful to the Protestant Church in its struggle with National-Socialism. No less harmful were the consequences of the animosity and bitterness lodged in German hearts by the internal disputes between the various theological and ecclesiastical tendencies. National-Socialist propaganda was able to exploit these dissensions and misfortunes cleverly, and one of its favourite slogans was that of 'parsons' quarrels' (*Pfaffengezenk*), applied to the Church war. With the same cleverness, this propaganda exploited the not very important Free Churches by setting them up against the provincial churches.

II. The Struggle Against the Provincial Churches

It was against this divided Protestantism that National-Socialism was soon to undertake a long war. The most varied methods that can characterise a totalitarian régime were to manifest themselves in this war. It started under the cover of that ambiguity of terms which National-Socialist propaganda had arranged for itself as camouflage, and it took, naturally, the form of a whispering campaign. Among the legends spread all over the country by this silent propaganda should be noted the tale of the pious *Führer* reading his New Testament every day. In this technique of camouflage the 'fifth column' was to play a most important part. When this method did not give the expected results, recourse was had to 'legal means', to the laws and regulations, in order to neutralise the adversary. Where this method failed in its turn, terror intervened, exercised in its most varied forms by its controlling organ, the 'Secret State Police' (*Geheime Staatspolizei*), the famous Gestapo. In his book *Mythus des 20. Jahrhunderts* Alfred Rosenberg at least suggested these various methods:

> 'A man . . . or a movement wishing to help these (Germanic) values to seize total victory has the moral right not to spare the adversary. Man or movement find themselves obliged to conquer the enemy on the spiritual plane, to harry him on the organisational plane and to render him politically impotent.'

It was precisely the formula 'harry him on the organisational plane' that played so important a part in the struggle in which the Protestant Church and National-Socialism were opposed.

The small minority party which National-Socialism was before 1933 had not the means of employing terror in the struggle against the Churches. Before that date the Party could not afford to prejudice whole groups of the population against it by excessively provocative declarations. Given that it was presenting itself as a party of malcontents *par excellence*, National-Socialism tried to carry with it the agreement of the Protestant groups, which were indeed very numerous. Among the millions of men who were only nominally Christian, there were many elements, especially in the big towns, who no longer 'believed' and had no longer any contact with the Church. On the average, each pastor had about 2,600 faithful to look after, while only 1,100 faithful fell to the responsibility of each Catholic priest. These averages were decidedly higher in the big towns. In these conditions it is hardly surprising to find that the number of unbelievers was so great in the ranks of the Protestant Church, and that National-Socialism, with its idea of a new and totalitarian life, managed to recruit many supporters in these circles. Where there is no spiritual substance, a conception of the world that presents totalitarian claims may easily gain ground. In his book, quoted above, Wilhelm Stapel states:

'The Church is face to face not with a "spiritual" movement but with an elementary movement whose nature is instinctive; a movement which does not allow itself to be drawn into argument but tries to crush its adversary; a movement which uses words not for discussion but for haranguing, for stimulating, for exciting and for commanding.'

This description of National-Socialism is pregnant with meaning, and helps us to understand a great many things about the attitude of the Party to the Christian Churches. In an embryonic state this character was imprinted on National-Socialism from the start, but it was only later, after 1930, when the most isolated villages suddenly returned votes for National-Socialism, that public opinion understood that it must reckon with the new movement.

In the provincial Churches, here and there, some National-Socialists became members of the parochial councils and the synods. But they saw that little was heard of them before 1932. Some of them had become National-Socialists because they really believed that the so long awaited and so necessary reform of the Church 'from top to bottom' was going to be realised with the aid of this 'dynamic movement'. They had not yet perceived that the formula 'positive Christianity', written into the Party programme, was only a bait. The propaganda carried on in the Party press, the speeches and declarations of the *Führer*, gave sufficient assurances to the faithful on the desire of the movement to be 'positively Christian'. The official commentator on the Party programme, Gottfried Feder, wrote in 1931 in a widely circulated pamphlet: 'It can never be

stressed enough that nothing is further from the spirit of the
NSDAP than the intention to attack the Christian religion and its
worthy servants.' In the light of later events, such affirmations must
be suspected of having been an integral part of the Party's tactics of
camouflage. More thorough studies of Hitler's book *Mein Kampf*
and of Rosenberg's book *Mythus* could have shed the necessary
light on the true nature of the 'positive Christianity' put forward by
National-Socialism. But the majority of Christians—as indeed of
non-Christians—behaved like that Protestant bishop who, when
asked if he had read *Mein Kampf*, gave (this is no exaggeration) this
reply: 'I only managed to read one page in three.' The great
propagandist Hitler was well served by knowing that it is never
unsafe to bet on the indolence, stupidity, and chimerical dreams of
men.

It was at the parochial elections at the beginning of 1932 that the
National-Socialist candidates presented themselves for the first time
in large numbers. In the majority of cases they were camouflaged
under such labels as 'National Union of Confessing Christians'
(*Christlich-Nationaler Bekennerbund*), 'Association for Positive Christianity and for the German People' (*Vereinigung für positives Christentum und deutscher Volkstum*), or something similar.

It was in March 1932 that the shock troops, through which the
Party, and later the régime, were to try to realise the integration of
the Protestant Churches into National-Socialism, entered the Protestant Churches. This group of militant National-Socialists called
itself 'The German Christians Faith Movement' (*Glaubensbewegung
Deutscher Christen*). It envisaged a 'Reich Church as the Church of
German Christians, that is to say, of Christians of Aryan race' (the
famous 'Aryan paragraph' applied to the conception of a church!)
and declared itself thus in favour of racial anti-Semitism. It envisaged also the 'leader principle' (*Führerprinzip*) in the Church, and
wished to grant to a 'Reich bishop' the powers of which no Pope had
ever disposed in the Catholic Church. By the adoption of this
position, conflict became inevitable with the circles of the Protestant
Church that were unwilling to let themselves be integrated and, for
reasons of faith, could not admit the 'Aryan paragraph'.

Not long after the seizure of power on 30th January 1933 the
Church war broke out with all the passion which characterises wars
of religion. For it was one in fact, in so far as it concerned the whole
of the Protestant Church. In the foreground of this war were the
problems of the Reich Church, the Reich Bishop, and the Aryan
paragraph.

It was in the interests of the National-Socialist régime to present
this war, abroad, as a 'purely internal ecclesiastical affair'. The
'German Christians' lent themselves only too willingly to the part of

'fifth column' in these camouflage tactics, even though the majority of them, in their credulity and the unlimited admiration they had for their *Führer*, did not at all realise the job they were being made to do. To gain the necessary control, Hitler had appointed in 1933 the Pastor to the *Wehrmacht*, Ludwig Müller, as his 'right-hand man in the affairs of the Protestant Church'. The German Christians had made him their candidate for the post of Bishop of the Reich. The great mass of the faithful had proposed, as opposition candidate, the well-known director of the Betheler Institute, Pastor Friedrich von Bodelschwingh. And the leaders of the provincial Churches raised Bodelschwingh to the dignity of Reich Bishop. Then it was that the Government intervened, designating a fanatical National-Socialist, Dr Jäger, to the post of State Commissary for the most important provincial Church, the Protestant Church of the Prussian Union. The bodies representing the provincial Churches were dissolved and the leaders of the Protestant Church, the superintendents-general, deprived of their offices. Among these was Dr Dibelius, who bravely riposted to this act of violence by replying to Dr Jäger that he was unable to submit to the control of the state in the exercise of his spiritual and pastoral functions. The reaction of the other leaders was much less firm, and for the most part they bowed before 'higher authority'. Pastor von Bodelschwingh had to renounce his office because the leaders of Churches, whose duty was to support him in this trial, were not ready to react against the intrusion of the totalitarian state. Ludwig Müller became Reich Bishop, but he was only able to exercise his functions up to the middle of the year 1935, because the opposition of the faithful and the pastors became stronger week by week, in spite of the measures of coercion imposed by the régime.

The ecclesiastical circles united around Pastor von Bodelschwingh were under the direction of a group of young theologians and pastors, known by the name of 'The Young Reform Movement', which had taken up position in favour of a Reich Church. Later there intervened on its side the 'Union of Pastors' (*Pfarrernot Bund*) led by Pastor Niemöller, who was to assume a capital part in the opposition movement up to his arrest in 1937. On 11th July 1933, under the pressure of events, the new ecclesiastical régime with a view to a Reich Church was set up by decree. The faithful were to take their stand on 23rd July by a plebiscite. The elections organised for this purpose were a perfect example of 'free elections', that is to say, elections of the same kind as those with which we were to become so familiar later on in the totalitarian states. With the aid of the SA, the Police, the Gestapo, and volunteers recruited from among the 'German Christians', the National-Socialist régime let loose a wave of terror against the ecclesiastical opposition movement in its stand against the subjection of the Church. On the eve of the elections Hitler attacked in person: in a broadcast speech addressed to the Protestant faithful, he summoned them to vote for the 'German Christians'. The opposition was too little used to such methods to be able to oppose them adroitly and with any chances of success. Two-thirds of the votes went to the 'German Christians', and this decided the Church war provisionally in favour of the régime. The German Christians' candidate, Ludwig Müller, thus became Reich Bishop.

The National Synod at Wittenberg, held in September 1933, was a confirmation of this success: some 2,000 pastors led by Niemoeller raised none the less an energetic protest, and gave a warning against the methods of oppression, the 'Aryan paragraph' and the 'violation of the confession' by the measures taken by the 'German Christians'. It was from this point that the words 'confession' and 'heresy' were inserted regularly in the protests of the opposition. It was on the occasion of a great meeting which took place at the Sportpalast in Berlin in November 1933 that the extremist groups of the German Christians declared war openly on the Old Testament 'with its tales of cattle merchants and pimps'. They demanded that 'the pure teaching of Jesus' should become once more the foundation of the Church, a teaching of Jesus 'corresponding entirely with the demands of National-Socialism'. 'It is with this in view that we should mistrust too great an apologia for the crucified. We cannot have as our leader a God enthroned somewhere in the distance, but only the combatant without fear. . . . The adoration of the heroes should merge into the adoration of God,' said the principal orator, among other things. Stormy altercations took place between the German Christians and the opposition, and also between the various tendencies among the German Christians. The most extremist elements of the German Christians formed part of an independent group called the 'German Christians of Thuringia'. In time the German Christians of Thuringia claimed an even more vigorous integration, insofar as they took up position in favour of a Church which should unite both the Protestants and the Catholics under the protection of Adolf Hitler. After this declaration a split was inevitable. Not long afterwards the first movements became evident towards a consolidation of all the forces of the opposition in the 'Confessing Church' (*Bekennende Kirche*), which was later to become known throughout the world.

In its opposition to National-Socialism's policy of integration, the Protestant Church chose a platform of purely ecclesiastical principles. By no means all the confessing Christians, indeed, had understood from the beginning that the abyss which separated off the Church of the Third Reich, as it had been defined by Rosenberg, was irreducible. They were only to perceive this later, when the methods of oppression had become more and more severe. It was part of the methods of the 'Third Reich' to dissimulate its real intentions by a cunning camouflage. In the first years of the Church war, few of the faithful were convinced that it was the National-Socialist State that was behind the control levers of the German Christians. The high personalities of the National-Socialist movement were, indeed, not greatly approved of by the German Christians and their representatives, but the fact remains that these latter played the part of a fifth column to 'harry on the organisational plane' a troublesome adversary.

In any case, the Reich Bishop was a docile instrument in the policy of integration of the Protestant Church by the new state. Hardly had the storm raised by the Sportpalast meeting calmed down a little, than a new blow was aimed at the Confessing Church. In December 1933—it should be noted that all these events took place in the first year of the National-Socialist régime—the Reich Bishop informed his *Führer* of the 'spontaneous' adhesion of the Protestant youth organisations, with a strength of some 800,000 members, to the Hitler Youth. The totalitarian demands of National-Socialism, bearing as they did on the whole of a man, could not admit that a great section of the coming generations should receive a Christian education—as indeed Hitler made clear in *Mein Kampf* and Rosenberg in the *Mythus*. At the beginning of 1934 the (to Hitler) faithful Reich Bishop tried to gain a lead over the ecclesiastical opposition by dictatorial decrees which aimed at forbidding all criticism directed against the directing organisations of the Church, on pain of suspension of the offenders. Some pastors were indeed suspended immediately afterwards. But the disturbance caused in the country was so great that the Reich Bishop was obliged to call the Protestant Church leaders to a meeting in Berlin. In the discussions which ensued, the opposition demanded the resignation of the Reich Bishop and brought the matter before the *Führer*, who again intervened personally in the debate. On 25th January 1934 the Protestant ecclesiastics of the Confessing Church were summoned, together with the Reich Bishop, before Hitler. Hermann Göring was present also, in his capacity as president of the Prussian Council. He gave information on certain telephone conversations of Martin Niemöller's, who seems to have expressed himself somewhat rudely about the President of the Reich, von Hindenburg, and about his Chancellor, Hitler. Impressed by one of the celebrated fits of fury which used to seize Hitler in such circumstances, the opposition Protestant bishops were caught unawares and declared themselves ready to submit to the Reich Bishop and 'make peace'. This attitude was considered by the radical opposition, led by Niemöller, as an act of treachery. The Reich Bishop was able to exacerbate the disagreements between Niemöller's group and the moderate elements of the Confessing Church, led by the provincial bishops of Bavaria and Hannover and by the Bishop Wurm (of Württemberg). To tell the truth, this disagreement was never settled definitively, and it was to play a pernicious part during the ensuing years. The National-Socialist state and its instrument, Ludwig Müller, were well able to exploit this difference in the interests of their own cause.

The opposition movement of the Confessing Church sought, from that time on, a more subtle form of resistance and, in 1934, began to hold 'Confessing Synods' (*Bekenntnis Synoden*) so as to reinforce co-operation with laymen.

Meanwhile Dr Jäger, whom we mentioned above, was charged by the régime, in his capacity as administrator of the Protestant Church, with incorporating the independent provincial Churches into the Reich Church. To attain this aim, he had to carry on desperate struggles, especially when he tried to incorporate the openly Lutheran Churches of Bavaria and Hannover. In spite of measures of oppression comprising, among others, the suspension and arrest of the bishops by the Gestapo, Jäger and the Reich Bishop did not succeed in breaking the opposition. In Württemberg, where the same methods were employed, the faithful reacted with such energy that the state commissory and the administrator, Jäger, were obliged to beat a retreat. Some of the twenty-eight provincial Churches did, nonetheless, allow themselves to be 'integrated' and, in consequence, were placed under the well-nigh dictatorial direction of the Reich Bishop.

The opposition of the Confessing Church was, however, not broken by the repeated persecutions. The opposition was organised and reinforced in the Confessing Synods. At the General Synod of the Confessing Church (held at Barmen in May 1934), which the representatives of the Lutheran, Reformed, and united provincial Churches attended, the Synod declared itself the representative of the *legal* Protestant Church of Germany; another Synod, which met in November 1934, designated a 'temporary' directing body for the Confessing Church. So that the Protestant Church now had two directing bodies, each claiming to represent the legal Church.

At the beginning of 1935 the conflict aroused by the person of the Reich Bishop took second place as the result of a new attack let loose against the Churches by a group of fanatical National-Socialists. The 'neo-paganism' represented by Rosenberg had found a slightly modified form in the 'German Faith Movement' (*Deutsche Glaubenbewegung*) led by Professor Wilhelm Hauer, a well-known historian of religions and an ex-missionary. By this new 'Germano-nordic' faith, it was sought to construct a sort of 'third confession in a third Reich'. There was talk of an 'orthodox religion', and there were attempts to show that Christianity represented a deviation from this 'German faith' which was in conformity with the race. Exactly like the doctrine of Rosenberg, this new movement rejected the values of Christianity and envisaged a 'heroic piety', to be based on 'blood and soil'. This 'neo-paganism' had obtained the official support of the *Führer* when, at the beginning of the year 1934, Rosenberg had been nominated 'cultural director of education with reference to conceptions of the world' for all National-Socialist organisations. The 'German Faith Movement' had found a protector in the Minister of the Interior, Frick, and as, at the same time, all its leaders were eminent National-Socialists, it could be sure of the support of the Party.

The Confessing Church declared war on this movement and at the same time concentrated its attacks on Rosenberg's *Mythus*. In a circular of the chancellery may be found these words:

'We see our German People menaced by a mortal danger. This danger consists in a new religion . . . The new religion signifies the abolition of the First Commandment. In this new religion the social and national conception of the world becomes a myth. Blood, race, nationality, honour and liberty are represented in it as idols. . . . Such idolatry has nothing to do with Christianity. It is a negation of Christianity.'

The German Christians dropped, for some time, to the second place, as did Ludwig Müller, who was obliged purely and simply to retire at the end of the year 1935, because in the campaign to integrate the Protestant Church his methods had failed.

In July 1935 Hitler appointed a personal friend of Göring's, a certain Dr Kerrl, to the post of 'Reich Minister for Ecclesiastical Affairs' (*Reichsminister für die kirchliche Angelegenheiten*). In his capacity of Minister of the Church he was to try to achieve what the Reich Bishop had failed to achieve: the assimilation of the Protestant Church. From the start, Kerrl had at his disposition an appreciable asset in the discord which prevailed between the 'radical' wing of the Confessing Church, led by Niemöller, and the moderate elements, led by the very prudent Lutheran bishops Mahrarens and Meiser. There were also in the country a great number of communities and pastors who preferred to hold aside from the Church war. For it can often be dangerous, in a totalitarian state, to pass for a genuine 'confessing Christian'. Many are those who try to remain 'neutral' as long as possible and that is how things happened in Hitlerian Germany. People wanted, as far as possible, 'to live in peace'. To justify such an attitude they were glad to invoke the Martin Luther of the declaration of submission to the higher authorities, but they too

D D

easily forgot the reformer who, at Worms, had arisen *alone* against the emperor and the powerful of this world, in spite of the many threats that were weighing upon him. It was out of this ill-understood Lutheranism and its attitude to the state that the pre-war period managed to create the legend of Martin Luther as precursor of Hitler. One should not be too astonished at it.

The new Church Minister, Kerrl, appealed especially to these Lutherans of 'neutralist' mentality, to gain their collaboration for the policy of appeasement in the Church War. The neutralists were indeed entirely disposed to aid him. The superintendent-general, the aged Dr Zöllner, was invited to preside over a committee of the Churches of the Reich whose aim was to find a solution for the Church War in agreement with the representatives of the German Christians, of the Confessing Church, and of the 'neutral' elements. Niemöller and the 'radical' wing of the Confessing Church refused their co-operation with the work of the Committee. Up to February 1937 the Committee tried to re-establish order in the Protestant Church by acting as an instrument of the National-Socialist State. It was once more an instance of an attempt to camouflage the integration policy pursued by the régime. The venerable Dr Zöllner who, in his good faith (which indeed he shared with many of his fellows who thought as he did), had accepted the mandate entrusted to him by the state, was obliged to renounce his efforts in February 1937, because the authorities and Kerrl were making his task impossible. All sorts of measures of coercion were put into effect during this time by the National-Socialist authorities. This new attempt by the state to reach appeasement failed in its turn, and naturally Kerrl put the responsibility on the Committee of the Churches.

The Confessing Lutherans had, however, profited by this respite to find means of reinforcing the opposition front. The Lutheran Council gradually gained in authority. Apart from the so-called 'intact' provincial Churches of Hannover and Bavaria, numerous communities belonging to other provincial Churches, as well as to isolated groups, succeeded in realising a certain unity of organisation. The Lutheran Council had been able to co-operate on many points with the actual leaders of the Confessing Church, but, on the other hand, there were many other problems it had been impossible to approach. The attitude of the Church to the state was what constituted the kernel of the problem. While the Confessing Lutherans were obviously trying to adopt a 'loyal' attitude to the Hitlerian State, the radical wing was under the influence of the theological position which may be rendered in the formula: 'the first duty of a Christian towards the state is to keep his distance'.

It is through this attitude that one must try to understand the memorandum addressed by the provisional leaders of the Church to the *Führer* in May 1936. Courteous in its terms but uncompromising in its spirit, it protested against the many anti-Christian tendencies which were manifesting themselves in the Third Reich. Among other things, the memorandum protested against anti-Semitism, against the oppression of men's consciences by the too frequent obligation to take an oath, against the attacks aimed by the state at the Church, against the concentration camps, and against the excesses of the Gestapo. This memorandum cost one of the collaborators of the V.K.L., Dr Weissler, his life: accused of having given the text of it to the foreign press, he was murdered in 1937 in the concentration camp of Sachsenhausen. Among the signatories of the memorandum were Niemöller, von Thadden, Dr Bohm, Vicar Müller-Dahlem, and Pastor Asmussen, all of whom were arrested afterwards. The Olympic Games were going on in July–August 1936, and this saved them from immediate arrest, for in accordance with directives given by Hitler there were to be no arrests of pastors during that period.

At the beginning of the year 1937, Frick, the Minister of the Interior, intervened also in the Church War, by forbidding, among other things, the making public of the suspensions within the Churches. The collections of the Confessing Church were forbidden, and this measure aimed at paralysing the organisation financially. The same objectives were allotted to the so-called 'Financial Committees', which, from 1935 onwards, were supposed to begin a forced administration of the Churches' revenue.

In September 1937 the *Reichsführer S.S.* and head of the Gestapo, Himmler, intervened in his turn in the Church war, by trying to prevent, by forbidding it, the formation of cadres of theologians by the independent organisations of the Confessing Church. The formation of these cadres was nonetheless carried on clandestinely till the beginning of the war. Many collaborators in this work were imprisoned for months, and a young 'docent', Dietrich Bonhoeffer, was murdered in 1945 in a concentration camp. After Himmler's personal intervention, the number of arrests increased, and the police restrictions became still more rigorous. On 1st July 1937 Martin Niemöller, the most dogged adversary of Hitler, was arrested in his turn. The sentence did not come till eight months later: a fine of 1,500 marks and seven months in prison (already served) for 'illegal collection'. That was all that could be found against him. The Gestapo then intervened and shut Niemöller up for eight years, first in the Sachsenhausen concentration camp, later at Dachau. The year 1937 alone saw 804 arrests in the circles of the Confessing Church. No passports were granted to the representatives appointed by the Confessing Church to the Oxford Congress of World Churches in 1937, and none of them was able to take part. A whole series of other measures of oppression were taken against the Protestant Church, but the opposition could not be broken.

A last attempt to 'harry the adversary on the organisational plane' was made at the end of 1937. A National-Socialist jurist, Dr Werner, was appointed president of the Reich Church and of the Old-Prussian provincial Church, his mission being to liquidate the opposition by administrative means. Dr Werner had at his side a 'Council of spiritual confidence', with, as members, the Lutheran bishop Mahrarens and the German Christian bishop Schulz. The name of Mahrarens was there to furnish the state with a new means of camouflage in its integration manoeuvres. The provincial bishop went so far in his 'loyalty' that—under menace from Dr Kerrl, it is true—he read the following declaration: 'The National-Socialist conception of life is the national and political teaching which determines and characterises German manhood. As such, it is obligatory upon German Christians also.' This declaration was made after the incorporation of Austria into the Third Reich (11th March 1938). Many Protestant Christians rejoiced at this great victory of the Hitlerian régime which made a reality of the 'Greater Germany', and it rendered them better disposed towards the National-Socialist régime. This was the moment the National-Socialists chose for exacting from the pastors an oath of fidelity to the *Führer*. The discussions lated for months and months. The Confessing Church made it clear that a Christian ought to take such an oath only if it were formally exacted by the state. On the other hand, if all that was in question were a mere suggestion emanating from Dr Werner in his capacity as a civil servant, it could not be accepted. Dr Werner succeeded, nonetheless, in inducing the majority of the pastors to take the oath, although in certain cases it was taken with a mental reservation. That 'dynamic' movement, National-Socialism, had thus gained a great victory over the Church opposition. The combatants were rather tired, after five years of struggle.

The great political events of the year 1938—the *Anschluss* in March and the Czech crisis in September—coming at a moment when the whole world was trembling for peace, did much to stifle the echoes of the Church War. It was little talked of in the world at large. Here and there the disagreements were smoothed out. Not long after Chamberlain's visit to Munich, the provisional leaders of the Confessing Church obtained permission to hold religious services devoted to peace. The appropriate liturgy contained terms more violent than any the Protestant Church had ever dared to pronounce in the Third Reich. Several pastors and several laymen who had particularly insisted in favour of Masses dedicated to peace had to pay for their rashness with long months of prison.

The war between National-Socialism and the Protestant Church went on essentially upon the 'internal' plane. Many foreign Christians wondered why the opposition concentrated so exclusively on purely ecclesiastical problems. To understand this situation it is necessary to bear in mind the internal divisions which separated the members of the Protestant Church, especially concerning the attitude to be adopted towards the state and the social order. Confusion of mind on this point contributed towards prolonging the life of the Third Reich. Fear in face of the 'higher authorities' was so widespread in the ranks of the Confessing Church that criticism of the measures taken by the state in the 'secular' field was not thought to be necessarily a Christian duty. According to this conception, only the measures taken by the state in a specifically 'ecclesiastical' domain could be criticised and could involve a stand being taken by the individual as a Christian. This way of looking at things rests on a false interpretation of Martin Luther on the 'two governments'. It contributed towards establishing a dissociation in human life, which is precisely what Martin Luther had tried to surmount. This explains for us the hesitations of the Protestant Church in face of the violations of right by the National-Socialist régime, and in face of the measures of oppression exercised against those who did not share the opinions of National-Socialism and against the Jews. National-Socialism cleverly exploited this weakness.

If National-Socialism was able to draw such profit from its engagements with the Protestant Church, the reason is that it was able to present a well-defined programme in the social and public field. In contrast, the profound doctrinal division, the confusion and disagreements which prevailed within the Church about the attitude to be taken towards the Church–State–People problem turned out to be unfortunate for Protestantism.

III. The Attitude of National-Socialism towards Free Churches and other Christian Organisations

When, in August 1934, the Baptists of all sovereign countries met in Berlin to hold their world conference, many Confessing Christians learned the news with consternation, even in Germany. Scarcely two months had gone by since the 'Röhm rebellion', the 'St Bartholomew's Night' of the Third Reich. In spite of the clever propaganda deployed inside the country as well as abroad by the National-Socialist propagandists, what had happened on 30th June 1934 was still sufficiently understood for it to be possible to see that the Third Reich was not a state where justice reigned. Eminent foreign Baptists were warned not to accept the invitation to Berlin. But they did not follow this advice.

The conference was a great success, above all for National-Socialist propaganda, which was well able to exploit the situation adroitly, both during the conference and after, by setting the Free Churches against the Confessing Church. The Church War was represented to the foreign Baptists as if it were principally a question of the preservation of the 'principle of the Church in the state'. This way of presenting things was able to find a favourable echo because the members of the Congress who belonged to the Free Churches of Germany—almost all of whom, indeed, were National-Socialists—themselves believed in it. In fact they had been spared the ferocity of the authorities. Doubtless they were attacked in their turn later on, but as they had been morally 'integrated', they could bear these attacks much more easily. It cost Hitler nothing—on the contrary—to keep outside the Church War what was only a handful of people (about 100,000 to 150,000) out of the 40,000,000 Protestant Christians. All the more since he knew that this handful of people had, among the Methodists and Baptists all over the world, millions of brother-sectarians who were naturally disposed to judge the situation in Germany in accordance with the idea which the Baptists and Methodists of the Reich had of it. World public opinion needed several years in order to grasp this trick of German propaganda. Many people were in the end enlightened at the time of the World Conference of Churches, held at Oxford. No representative of the Confessing Church was able to take part, whereas the representatives of the German Free Churches, armed with recommendations from the Berlin Minister of Propaganda, defended the Third Reich with vehemence. But what they put forward could no longer deceive anybody. The information in the world press and the accounts given by visitors to the Third Reich contradicted the statements of the representatives of the German Free Churches. Back from Oxford, many of these gradually changed their attitude and even sought an understanding with the Confessing Church. For them too the journey to Oxford had served some purpose. The attitude they had adopted at Oxford was determined by political pressure rather than by any intimate convictions, and their position at the Congress had not been exactly an easy one. But involuntarily they had given the representatives of the other Churches a useful lesson on the methods of propaganda in a totalitarian state and on the harmful consequences of internal and external isolation under a régime of dictatorship.

The four most important Free Churches—the Baptists, the Methodists, the 'Evangelical Community in Germany' (*Evangelische Gemeinschaft in Deutschland*), and the 'Union of Free Evangelical Communities' (*Bund Freier Evangelischen Gemeinden*)—had set up, before 1933, a body to represent them jointly—the 'Association of Evangelical Free Churches' (*Vereinigung evangelischen Freikirchen*).

This representative body was persecuted from the start of the Church War. In fact, National-Socialism would have been glad to incorporate the Free Churches into the Reich Church. But thanks to the support of their brother-sectarians abroad, 'integration' could be avoided.

The 'Oxford Group' enjoyed at the beginning a certain benevolence on the part of the authorities of the Third Reich. Dr Frank Buchman was able to visit Germany in person several times, and so were several of his collaborators. But this friendly treatment on the part of the National-Socialist authorities was due to the hope of obtaining in exchange good reports on the Third Reich, rather than to the desire really to adopt the message of this movement. The zealous propagandists of National-Socialism avoided discussing the Church War with the representatives of this movement, in order to concentrate the debate upon some eventual arrangement between the State Church and the Free Church. It suited them to present the Church War as the result of a regrettable misunderstanding by the Confessing Church. 'Old-fashioned' and extremist in its 'confessionalism', this Church had not, they said, managed to gather round it 'modern men', as the Oxford Group had done. Many foreign visitors found this version plausible, and the propagandists took advantage of them to raise one Christian group against the other.

Among the small sects, it was the *Bibelforscher* who had the most to suffer. Their pacifist attitude seemed very dangerous in the eyes of National-Socialism. Many of them were executed, and they bore the persecutions with a courage that was often admirable.

IV. The Struggle for the Control of Youth

The 'Church War' in the narrow sense of the term was the sharpest manifestation of the disagreement which opposed National-Socialism to the Protestant Church. It was not merely a question of persons (as in the case of the Reich Bishop, for example), or a question of organisation or form (as, for example, in the case of the Reich Church). What was at stake above all was the problem of youth and of its attitude to National-Socialism and to Christianity.

Not long after the integration of the youth organisations, which were placed under the direction of Baldur von Schirach, the war for the control of youth broke out with violence. When, in February 1934, Alfred Rosenberg was entrusted with the post of 'cultural director for the education of youth as regards their conception of the world', covering all the youth organisations, this nomination was bound to have unfortunate consequences for the Protestant youth. Having realised the gravity of the situation, certain Protestant circles tried to contact the Catholic Church, in order to take certain measures in common. But the hesitation of Protestant circles was still too great for it to be yet possible to carry such an enterprise to success. And so each Church was reduced to continuing the struggle separately. The 'letters for education', of which Rosenberg had 750,000 copies printed, and which were meant for the youth organisations, were feverishly studied by the Hitler Youth. Cleverly drawn up, these letters played the part of a regular 'catechism', and they were well adapted to inculcate the new 'conception of the world' in a form that might pass as natural in the eyes of the younger generations. The *élite* of the young leaders was educated in special organisations, the *Ordensburgen*, isolated from all Christian influence. At the time of the integration of the Protestant youth organisations into the Hitler Youth, Baldur von Schirach had promised to reserve two days a week for religious education. But soon this spiritual education was sabotaged by every imaginable means: if not always by formal bans, at least by various manoeuvres, for instance, by fixing exercises and courses at the times set aside for the religious services or for the study of the Bible. It must be admitted that the National-Socialist régime displayed a great deal of skill in its attempts to 'harry the enemy on the organisational plane'.

German youth was fond of parades, music, and uniforms, which exalt adolescent feelings. Certainly there were processions and singing in the Protestant organisations too. But a decision taken in the month of July 1935 forbade the Protestant youth organisations to parade in public as independent troops, to have their own bands and to wear badges. The pretext invoked to justify this ban was the 'de-confessionalisation' of the New Germany. From the month of August 1935 onwards, prayers ceased to be obligatory in German schools. The war against Protestant literature and against the educational centres of the Confessing Church was carried on by bans and acts of sabotage; the SS, SA, and Gestapo also intervened on occasion. In November 1935 the training centre for Protestant youth leaders, the house of Burchardt in Berlin, was occupied by a hundred SS, and sundry property was seized.

The war waged against religious instruction in the schools was particularly violent. On this terrain the local authorities, when they had got into the hands of fanatical National-Socialists, were able to indulge in experiments of all sorts: substituting the 'Sources of the German divine revelation' for the Old Testament; eliminating certain particularly dangerous 'judaic elements' from the New Testament; introducing the reading of the nordic legends in place of the reading of the Bible, etc. If the opposition of the population became too great, the central authorities could always pretend that these excessive measures were due to over-zealous local elements.

In the name of the watchword 'deconfessionalisation' the régime was always trying to reduce religious education in schools to the minimum. Lively incidents broke out in Württemberg (1937), where the confessing schools were very strongly represented. The régime tried to replace the confessing schools by a 'uniform' state school. But the opposition of the population, under the influence, as it was, of a long-standing ecclesiastical and religious education, was very lively. To break the opposition, the régime reacted with various measures of oppression directed against the pastors who gave religious teaching, or with the suppression of the subsidies to the Church, etc. Thanks to his quiet tenacity, the aged provincial Bishop Wurm, who led the opposition, managed to inflict a check, here as elsewhere, on certain actions of the extremist elements of the National-Socialist Party.

It is not easy to determine how far National-Socialism succeeded in winning to its cause that part of German youth which had had the benefit of a Christian education. Of course the propaganda of Baldur von Schirach, Alfred Rosenberg, and the representatives of the 'Germano-Nordic' conception of the world cannot have been entirely sterile. But it must be remembered that the period of twelve years during which the National-Socialist régime held power was much too short for it to have been able to infect a whole generation. It is certain that, after its fall, National-Socialism has left behind it many young people who are morally broken. It will be part of the Christian Church's duty to stand at the side of these young people, to see that at least the post-war generations have the benefit of the spiritual resources of which the preceding generation was deprived. This is, indeed, not only the duty of the German Protestant Church, but the duty of the whole of Christendom.

V. Anti-Semitism and the Protestant Church

In the war of religion waged against the Protestant Church, the anti-Semitism of the National-Socialist movement played a decisive part. A remarkable fact about the situation in 1933 as a whole is that it was impossible to get trustworthy information on the total number of German Jews at that period (end of 1933–beginning of 1934). Even in the chancelleries of the Church nothing precise was known. This is the reason why National-Socialist propaganda was able for months to present, both in Germany and abroad, the wildest over-estimates and this—what is more—with success. On this terrain the Protestant Church was as ill-equipped as elsewhere.

There were, certainly, some attempts to take up a position on the Jewish problem before 1933. But there was lacking any formal condemnation of anti-Semitism by the Church. On the contrary, some very eminent personalities, such as the Court chaplain to Wilhelm II, had been supporters of anti-Semitism. Thus the attitude of the Confessing Church with regard to anti-Semitism remained somewhat hesitant.

In addition, anti-semitic propaganda was busy in ecclesiastical circles. Few were those who really knew how many Jews there were in Germany. In 1933 the number of practising Jews was about 500,000, without counting the 50,000 or so 'non-Aryan Christians'. Such figures were often presented by the National-Socialists as valid for the town of Berlin alone, and there were many who in their good faith let themselves be taken in by these dishonest calculations. Statistics were produced after 1935 to establish the number of 'half-castes' (*Mischlinge*)—about 200,000–300,000.

The Protestant Church took a stand especially against the 'Aryan paragraph', that is to say, against the decision according to which any member of the Church who could not prove his ancestry to be Aryan up to two or three generations back must be excluded from the Church. (These persons were known in National-Socialist Germany as 'Jew-Christians'—*Juden-Christen*.) But even on this point opinions differed. The Confessing Church was frankly opposed to the 'Aryan paragraph', and Karl Barth declared: 'A Protestant Church that would exclude the Jew-Christians or would regard them as second-class Christians would cease to be a Christian Church.' The Faculty of Theology at Marburg shared the same opinions—which did not, however, prevent it from declaring: 'The German people today considers the Jews of Germany as a foreign population. The Church must recognise this fundamental right of the state to take such administrative measures' (meaning the 'Aryan paragraph'). The 'Aryan paragraph' was adopted by the Church of the German Christians, in spite of the protests of the Confessing Church.

The attacks of the National-Socialists against the Jews were intensified after 1937 until they reached the large-scale racial persecutions which broke out after November 1938. The Jewish shops were pillaged and the synagogues set on fire. Almost all male Jews were arrested and shut up in concentration camps, and in this way forced into self-expatriation. Many Jews lost their lives.

Some Protestants courageously hid Jews. Through its leaders the Protestant Church raised its voice in favour of the victims of persecution, and prayers were said for them in the churches. But the Protestant Church as such never found the appropriate words to protest against the very principle of anti-Semitism.

The assistance to non-Aryans organised by Pastor H. Grüber of Berlin and his fellow-workers will always remain an honourable page in the history of the Jewish people's sufferings. The Berlin office was closed in December 1940, and Pastor Grüber had to pay for his work in aid of the Jews with three years in a concentration camp. His closest collaborator, Pastor W. Sylten, who tried to continue Grüber's work, was arrested in 1941 and died in 1942 at Dachau. The two of them had tried every means to prevent the mass deportations which began in 1940. Nothing was any good, and the extermination of the Jews went on.

Among the important figures in the Protestant Church the old Bishop Wurm was the one who, above all, most often raised his voice in violent protest against the persecutions of Jews. During the war Bishop Wurm was the real spokesman of the Christian conscience of the Protestant Church.

The number of Protestants, lay or ecclesiastical, who courageously put up a firm resistance to the National-Socialist régime before and during the war is not so small as is usually thought abroad. For the eminent ecclesiastical figures (of whom the foreign press did make mention at the time) are not the only ones to have taken the risks of a personal stand. In many communities violent incidents took place, and obscure Protestants took great risks and made great sacrifices to uphold their Christian ideas.

But the majority of those who felt called upon to make a stand were caught unawares; people were not well enough equipped for the struggle. All the elements that render modern war so hard, including partisans and the fifth column, were engaged in the religious war of the Third Reich. It must be hoped that in the next stage of the show-down between the Christian world and the totalitarian forces, the Christians will be better able to recognise their real enemy and will not let themselves be made fools of by big words. As for the spiritual leaders of the Christians, it must be hoped that they will perceive, before it is too late, that war with the forces of totalitarianism is a question of life or death. In such a war there can be no question of remaining 'neutral'.

26

THE WEAPON OF ANTI-SEMITISM

L. Poliakov

It is a notorious fact that a virulent, ruthless anti-Semitism formed an integral part both of the ideology and of the practice of German National-Socialism, and did much, in fact, to give it its peculiar stamp. The outrageous form it took, as well as its far-reaching and dramatic consequences, tend to make it seem an end in itself ('extermination of the Jews'), whereas a closer analysis, such as we invite the reader to embark on now, shows that it was essentially a means towards the general ends envisaged by National-Socialism. And two points should be established at the outset:

1. From the ideological viewpoint, the Nazi doctrine was almost entirely devoid of originality; it confined itself to systematising, codifying, and spreading certain views and conceptions, which were in existence long before the Third Reich.

2. From the practical viewpoint, on the other hand, when National-Socialism came to apply these ideas, it introduced certain fateful and disconcerting innovations, employing methods and techniques which were both characteristic and novel.

But at this point we must look at the historical background.

I

When Hitler came to power in January 1933 he was at the head of Germany's most powerful Party, which, in the elections in July 1932, had gained more than 37 per cent of the total votes; in the 1933 elections he gained 44 per cent of the votes. All the other national and jingoistic parties and groups had already, some time before, given ground to National-Socialism and were virtually eliminated from the political stage. The hold National-Socialism had gained over the mass of the German population was due to the unrivalled effectiveness of Nazi propaganda, which worked in depth and had been in operation without a break for thirteen years. The basic principles of this propaganda were outlined with remarkable frankness by the *Führer* himself in *Mein Kampf*.

'The receptive capacity of the mass of the people is very limited, their intelligence is small, but their faculty for forgetfulness is very great. In the light of these facts, any effective propaganda must confine itself to a small number of important points and use them as slogans (*"schlagerartig"*), till everyone understands the intended meaning. . . . The great majority of people have feminine traits and reactions, and it is not sober reflection but sensations and feelings that determine thoughts and actions. Feelings which, far from being complex, are concise and simple. They contain few nuances but a positive (side) or a negative (side), love or hate, justice or injustice, truth or lie. . . . No propaganda can be successful unless it takes into account a basic principle: to confine itself to a few things and repeat them incessantly. . . . Then one is amazed by the tremendous, inconceivable results such consistency achieves. . . .' [1]

Mein Kampf was written by Hitler during his detention in Landsberg prison in 1923–24. A few months later, in one of the first speeches he made after his release, he returned to the same theme with particular emphasis:

'To make the great mass of the population understand a campaign, it must be directed against two objectives: against a person and against a thing.

'Against whom was England fighting? Against the German Kaiser as person and against militarism as a thing.

'Against whom are the Jews fighting with the help of their Marxist power? Against the *bourgeoisie* as a person and against capitalism as a thing.

'Against whom must we therefore fight? Against the Jew as a person and against Marxism as a thing.'

And Hitler added:

'For a people like the German people, it is particularly necessary to indicate one sole enemy, to march against one sole enemy.' [2]

According to this doctrine, then, the support of the masses could be gained only by confronting them with a single enemy, who, on the one hand, is absolutely bad and hateful, but, on the other hand, is tangible and accessible. This is an elementary principle of all demagogic propaganda. But it fell to Hitler to push it to its ultimate conclusion with an astonishing sequence of ideas. It is not important for this study (nor is it relevant) to know at what point the *Führer* and his lieutenants added faith to the both simple and intoxicating ideas which they took upon themselves to blazon abroad. On the other hand, once the principle is established that an incarnation of

[1] *Mein Kampf* (42nd Imp., 1939), pp. 198 ff.
[2] Speech delivered at Munich, 27 Feb. 1925.

Evil must be chosen, it is important to show why this particular choice was made and why it had to be the Jew in preference to any other objective.

Let us first recall the peculiar situation of the Jews in European history. In medieval Christian society they were the only non-Christian confession: and mass antagonism to them found expression all the more readily in a violent, aggressive hostility because, in accordance with the teachings of the Church, they were also, traditionally, the deicides: a people, so to speak, that was criminally defective, condemned by its own transgression to perpetual servitude.[1] In the period of the Crusades, in particular, a period of great mass exaltation and warlike fervour, popular agitators, adding to this standard accusation a series of circumstantial grievances (plague-spreading, well-poisoning, ritual murders, etc.), launched massacres and large-scale exterminations. In this way the Jews came to play, in history, the dreadful role of scapegoat on whom every form of social hatred was concentrated (and it is this very relentless hostility which, by a reverse reaction, forced Judaism to draw still more closely together, a fact which undoubtedly explains how they managed to survive throughout the ages and to maintain their religious and national identity). The gradual secularisation of European societies from the eighteenth century onwards, the apparent triumph of the Age of Reason, seemed, for one brief moment, to change the problem completely and to pave the way—this, at least, was what Christians and Jews hoped in all good faith—for the adjustment or assimilation of the Jews to the society around them, and thus put an end to the traditional hatred. But this hatred appears to have been too deep-rooted in the minds of the European peoples, for anti-Jewish passions flared up again in the twentieth century in a new form, the main difference being that, in keeping with the prevailing trends of the period, they fell back this time on science, in the shape of anthropological and racial doctrines, to provide them with ideological arguments and proofs. Such was the birth of modern anti-Semitism, a social plague that left few countries untouched, and that took a particularly virulent form in time of crisis.

It is not our task to investigate why the phenomenon in this form was at its most intense in Germany. Suffice it to say that if, in countries like Czarist Russia, it was, to a large extent, an instrument of government policy, artificially cultivated by the régime, and finding expression in a special legislation, in Imperial Germany, where the Jews benefited in principle from the equality of rights, it affected large masses of the population, but above all the *élites*. It was in

[1] From the dogmatic point of view, the position of the Catholic Church was defined by St Thomas Aquinas in his *Summa Theologia* (11, 11a, question 10) and by several Papal Bulls and Decretals, especially by Innocent III and Gregory IX.

Germany, around 1873, that the term 'anti-Semitism' was coined; [1] it was in Germany that race theories (first evolved in the main by Count Gobineau, a French aristocrat) were most laboriously interpreted and commented upon and most enthusiastically embraced, radiating beyond national frontiers and, in particular, towards that 'brilliant satellite' Austria.[2] Before the 1914–18 war Germany was the only European country in which *social discrimination*, that characteristic form of modern anti-Semitism, was systematically and openly practised in the army, and in state service in particular. And the picture of the Jew as a source of unrest and evil-doing, a ferment of decomposition and a poisoner of peoples, the opposite of this parasite being the frank, honest Aryan, a noble warrior or productive worker—a picture such as Hitler is to paint—is already becoming crystallised in people's minds with the works of H. S. Chamberlain (*The Foundations of the Nineteenth Century*) or the propaganda of Stöcker, chaplain of the Imperial Court: in this respect the *Führer* had invented nothing new.

One of the after-effects of the shock caused by the First World War was a marked revival of anti-Semitism in many countries. It is characteristic that the fable of 'The Elders of Zion', first circulated fifteen years before by agents of the Czarist *Okhrana*, was seriously discussed at this time for several months in the columns of the British Press, including *The Times*. But Germany, defeated and disrupted, was infected in a special way, in proportion, one might say, to the extent of the disaster, of the traumatism inflicted on this proud nation. What a relief for many an embittered soul to be able to ascribe the cruel reality to the systematic activity of hidden forces, of a mysterious factor, of a secret, maleficent power! As early as 1919 a pornographic pamphlet by a certain Dinter entitled *The Sin against the Blood* (it appeared in 1911, but for a time remained almost unnoticed) reached a circulation of 600,000 copies. The former *élites* in particular, ruling circles and officers without pay, adopted the anti-semitic line all the more easily because the Weimar Republic, which they hated so much, provided the unusual and shocking spectacle of Jews occupying high positions in administration and political

---

[1] It seems to have appeared first in Wilhelm Marr's pamphlet: *The Victory Judaism over Germanism*.

[2] Adolf Hitler's native country displays special characteristics, the picture there being complicated by numerous particular tensions (between Slavs, Germans, Hungarians, etc.) forming the basic pattern in the mosaic of nationalities which made up the Danubian monarchy. But the German-speaking Austrians, the leading race, were an integral part of the German cultural group. Perhaps the most important single factor in the growth of Hitler's personal ideology was the violent anti-semitic propaganda launched at the beginning of this century by the Christian-Socialist party of Lüger, mayor of Vienna. The author of *Mein Kampf* speaks of it at length in his autobiography, and on this point for once, one need not question his sincerity!

life. Symbolic of this state of affairs is Ludendorff, the fallen marshal who became the exponent of a curious demonological doctrine, according to which mysterious 'supra-state' powers (Jews, Jesuits, Freemasons) were responsible for Germany's misfortunes (and for the misfortunes of humanity as a whole). Out of this arose the '*Bund für deutsche Gotterkenntnis*' of the Ludendorffs; there were, of course, many other similar small groups, each expounding its own particular version of the original.

Such, then, was the ground on which the seeds of Hitler's propaganda fell, and it explains why his extreme anti-Semitism had every chance of success. Once certain vague, latent preconceptions had been stirred up by methods prescribed in *Mein Kampf*, they promised to become unusually dynamic. In the circumstances then prevailing there seems to have been no other objective in Germany so appropriate as an incarnation of the enemy as the Jew.

But while Adolf Hitler, as we have pointed out, had nothing new to offer in the way of ideas and concepts, when it came to implementing and applying them, he immediately produced some revolutionary innovations, a study of which will enable us to look more closely at certain important characteristics of totalitarianism. And let it be recognised at once that these innovations, which in the early days of National-Socialism met with a certain amount of criticism and resistance even from nationalistic and anti-semitic circles, were ultimately responsible for much of its success. As one German author, M. Müller-Claudius, puts it, the *Führer*'s main task is to transform 'static hate' into 'dynamic hate'.[1]

The means employed can be enumerated under five headings:

1. In the first place—and it is implicit in the word 'totalitarianism'—the *Führer* always pursued implacably whatever argument or line he adopted to its ultimate conclusion. As far as medieval anti-Semitism in particular is concerned, conversion was, in the eyes of Christian society, an easy means of rehabilitation and salvation for the Jew. In modern anti-Semitism this escape-hatch no longer functioned (although the tendency to assimilate the Jew to the Devil, to the incarnation of Evil, was always present). On the other hand, the spokesmen of modern anti-Semitism usually made a number of reservations, drawing subtle distinctions between Judaism in general ('the Jewish spirit') and the individual Jew. There are many examples. Ludendorff, for instance, admitted that there existed 'noble Jews'.[2] Other authors excepted their personal friends. H. S. Chamberlain, for example: 'I myself have had Jewish friends whom I re-

---

[1] Michael Müller-Claudius, *Der Antisemitismus und das deutsche Verhängnis* (Frankfurt, 1948), pp. 76–9.
[2] cf. W. Martin, *Die Legende von Hause Ludendorff* (Rosenheim, 1948).

spected and loved, and I find it very pleasant to do business with honest and shrewd Jews'.[1] And in fact, such reservations are invariably based on personal, living contact with Jews, which breaks through clouds of abstraction. One glimpses something of the inner conflict between paranoiac tendencies, hare-brained views projected on a convenient, classical backcloth, and genuine personal experience based on reality. The extent to which the latter can persist is strikingly illustrated in a speech by Himmler, delivered before literally hundreds of thousands of Jewish corpses in the autumn of 1943:

'. . . I want to talk to you about the evacuation of the Jews, about the extermination of the Jewish people. This is something it is very easy to talk about: "The Jewish people will be exterminated," says each member of the Party, "that is clear; it is in our programme: elimination of the Jews, extermination, we shall do it", and then they come, 80 million, good Germans, and every one of them has his "good" Jew. Of course the other Jews are swine, but this one is a first-class Jew. Not one of the people who talk like this has seen the corpses, not one of them has seen the corpses, not one of them was on the spot,' etc., etc.[2]

It is on mental reservations of this kind that the *Führer* declares uncompromising war: and doubtless, knowing how persistent such reservations can be, with consummate cunning he quotes himself as an example in a passage of *Mein Kampf* in which he describes the 'inner conflicts' he had to wage before he became a convinced anti-Semite and how he emerged victorious:

'. . . slowly my views on anti-Semitism changed with time. It gave rise to the most violent of all the struggles in my inner soul, and it was only after a long conflict between reason and emotion that the victory fell to reason. Two years later, emotion came round to the side of reason and from then on acted as its watchful guardian and counsellor.'[3]

So, no individual exceptions, no extenuation or pardon: following this absolute principle, the Nazi doctrine prescribes certain 'subhuman' categories, relegating the Jew to the category of anthropoid apes, etc.,[4] while more popular propagandists prefer to place the Jew among the traditionally vilified insects.[5]

[1] H. S. Chamberlain, *Briefe, 1882–1924* (Munich, 1928). Letter to von Schröder, 26 Dec. 1907.
[2] Speech at Poznan, on 4 Oct. 1943.
[3] *Mein Kampf*, ed. cit., pp. 59 ff.
[4] Thus for example, H. Gauch: '. . . there is no essential quality which distinguishes man from other animals, only a distinction between Nordic Man, on the one side, and animals on the other; non-nordic man being considered in a stage of transition' (H. Gauch, *Neue Grundlagen zur Rassenforschung* (1933)).
[5] Thus, for example, Goebbels: '. . . it is true that the Jew is a human being, but in the same way the flea is a living creature, none the more agreeable for that. . . .

2. No less complete and no less fundamental is deformation of the truth as prescribed in *Mein Kampf*: it is not the task of propaganda 'to seek objective truth. . . . If propaganda concedes even a vestige of right to the opposing party, it is paving the way for doubts on its own right.'[1] The procedure adopted is a two-fold one, the sword has two edges: for, if the Jew is the incarnation of all that is negative, once he is treated as a principle of evil, all that is bad (or, in other words, all the obstacles in the way of the Nazi movement) is stigmatised as essentially Jewish. It is an easy, classic procedure, which has been adopted instinctively by all demagogues since time immemorial, but the Nazis gave it a fresh twist and perfected it by giving it a much wider application than ever before, without flinching before even the most flagrant falsehoods. Indeed, if one is considering 'techniques and methods', one can speak of an original contribution: for example, not only the Weimar Republic is Jewish, but Lord North-cliffe and, later, Roosevelt (Rosenfeld!; Stalin is only a half-Jew); capitalism and Communism may appear to be mutually opposed, but that is mere camouflage, for both are instruments employed by the Jews to mystify the masses and pave the way for Jewish world domination; and, if the 'Jewish' press denies the authenticity of the 'Protocols of the Elders of Zion', these denials in themselves are the best proof of their authenticity.[2] Examples could be quoted *ad infinitum* and *ad nauseam*;[3] equally classic, on the other hand, are the misquotations and bowdlerisations of Jewish authors, and particularly of the Talmud, a field in which the morbid imagination of the Nazis roamed with unbelievable results. . . . What is important is to realise the ambivalence of the procedure: the more terrible, omnipresent, and insidious the enemy, the more easily can the opposing forces, movements, trends, or influences be identified with him and combated with equal fury. Let us glance rapidly at the main parties or groups to which the label 'Jew' was most persistently attached. In Germany, the two main left-wing political parties (Social Democrats and Communists), but also the 'Zentrum'—the Catholic Party —together with the press in general ('Jewish press'); abroad, the USSR in particular, together with France (negrified but also Juda-

---

Our Duty towards ourselves and towards our conscience, is to make it inoffensive, it is the same with the Jews'. (Goebbels, *Questions and answers for the National-Socialist* (1932), p. 12.)

[1] *Mein Kampf,* ed. cit., p. 200.

[2] ibid., p. 337. 'They (the Protocols of Zion) are a forgery', is the constant complaint of the *Frankfurter Zeitung,* 'which proves beyond question their authenticity.' With regard to the other accusations, we will refrain from burdening the text with references to a subject so universally familiar.

[3] The reverse process should also be remembered, in which the most glorious names of world history are identified with germanism, and attributed to 'nordic' origins. Thus Dante Alighieri ('Aliger'), Michelangelo, etc., become naturalised Germans; even Jesus Christ is shown to be of Aryan origin.

ised), the English aristocracy, the American financier, and finally the Catholic Church. The labels were, of course, attached at various times, depending upon the political situation and the tactical requirements of any given moment.

3. If what we have just considered reveals the complete contempt which Nazi anti-semitic propaganda had for the intellectual capacity of the masses, it does not follow that it showed the same contempt for the powerful appeal to the same masses of the modern achievements of human reason in the form of the popular and semi-magical slogan of 'science'. In fact, the race doctrines are based on a popular form of pseudo-Darwinism; it was important to increase the violence of anti-semitic passions by proving that they are borne out by the findings of scientists in different fields. The stock formula was: 'It has been scientifically established that . . .'; in the essay on 'racialism' the tremendous effort made by German anthropologists in this direction is discussed.[1] History was also used as evidence, and other fields that were exploited were the history of music, æsthetics, and even phonetics. Vast collections, encyclopædic dictionaries were produced: *Lexicon of the Jews in Music*,[2] etc.; *Galician Nicknames (Galizische Ekelnamen)*[3] etc. The countless theses that were produced in this way were subsequently circulated and abbreviated in popular brochures: to quote only one example, *The Biblical Moses, a Leader of Brigands and an Arch-Bolshevik according to Biblical Evidence*[4] was a pamphlet designed to 'explain' the miracles of the Old Testament, and its Chapter II proves on the evidence of chemical formulæ (alternating with Biblical quotations) that Moses knew the secret of the manufacture of gunpowder and dynamite and used it to bring about his 'miracles'.

This point seems to me important. For, whatever the peculiar characteristics of a totalitarian ideology, the misuse of scientific hypotheses, presented in dogmatic form and blown up into laborious compilations for the use of all classes and adapted to all levels of society, seems inevitably to play its part.

4. The fourth characteristic feature of Nazi methods is their exploitation of the entire gamut of human emotions, with each individual element called into play. Throughout the ages the favourite weapon of anti-semitic agitators has been the appeal to feelings of envy and hate—and the Nazis applied this weapon with even greater force—but it seems to me that a new element comes in with the systematic appeal to the sexual passions. *Mein Kampf*, that political

[1] See the essay by Professor Klineberg, pp. 858–9.
[2] *Lexicon der Juden in der Musik* (Berlin, 1941).
[3] Galicia was a province of central Poland.
[4] *Der Biblische Moses ein Räuberhauptman und Erzbolchevist, nach dem Zeugnis der Bibel* (Wissenberg in Bayern, 1936).

Gospel of Nazism, is full of passages that are typical in their violence:
'The young dark-haired Jew lies in wait for hours, with a look of
satanic joy on his face, for the simple girl, whom he soils with his
blood and so ravishes from her people . . .'[1] 'The black parasites are
systematically sullying our inexperienced blonde maidens and are
thus destroying something that is irreplacable in this world . . .'.[1]
And so on. The object is somehow to stimulate anti-semitic feeling
by linking it with a threat to the most sacred of human conceptions:
the wife and mother. But this form of stimulus was employed particularly by Julius Streicher, the *Gauleiter* of Franconia, a sex-para-
noiac, whose publication, *Der Stürmer*, was lavishly illustrated and
reached a considerable circulation by constantly offering its readers,
under striking headlines, stories of rape, race violation, and sadistic
murders. . . . Even more virulent than this pornographic weekly,
however, were the books for children published under the auspices of
the '*Stürmer*' and containing variations on the same themes. I shall
merely quote one example, taken from the collection *The Poisonous
Toadstool (der Giftpilz)* and entitled 'Inge at the Jewish Doctor's'.

'Inge has been waiting for an hour. Once more she opens a book
and tries to read. Then the door suddenly opens. Inge looks up.
The Jew appears. Inge utters a cry. Overcome by fear, she drops
the book. She jumps to her feet in terror. Her eyes are fixed on the
Jewish doctor's face. It is the face of the Devil. In the middle of
this diabolical face is a huge hooked nose. Two criminal eyes
gleam behind the spectacles. "At last I have you, little German
girl!" And the Jew flings himself on her. His fat fingers lay hold
on her . . .'[2]

The story from which this extract is taken, like many other stories
of the same calibre, was written for children between ten and
fourteen.

I believe the blatantly sexual appeal may be regarded as quite
peculiar to Hitlerism. A more detailed study might bring out even
more the pathological features of the particular 'terrain' on which
German National-Socialism flourished.

5. By contrast the physical excesses and tortures, the 'object
lessons', which were taught by the most active supporters of National-
Socialism, especially by the 'SA', were less specifically original. Just
as Mussolini's Blackshirts, for example, distinguished themselves by
administering castor oil to their political opponents, the Brownshirts excelled themselves with an interminable series of brutalities,
which were highly praised by the leaders of the movement, and of

[1] *Mein Kampf*, ed. cit., pp. 357 and 630 respectively.
[2] *Der Giftpilz* (*The Poisonous Toadstool*) stories by Ernst Himmer (Nuremberg,
1938).

which the Jews were the main victims. Such outbreaks of violence, by giving free rein to obscure, perverse instincts, served to stimulate the dynamism of the movement. I shall have occasion to point out later how alive certain Nazi leaders were to the collective psychological effect produced. The streets were the main scenes of the riots: the large Party demonstrations often ended with more or less serious incidents. In May 1926, for example, when the SA held its first big demonstration in Berlin, Goebbels wrote: 'Late that evening a few presumptuous Hebrews, who could not keep their dirty mouths shut, were dealt some hearty blows.' [1] A year later, after the Party had been temporarily banned in Berlin: '. . . One inevitable result of the ban was political outrages in the street. Many a Berlin Jew got knocked about on that occasion.' [2]

Apart from public incidents of this kind, it was the educational establishments that were singled out for acts of systematic and 'educative' brutality: attacks on Jewish students, expulsions, free fights between students in colleges and schools. Admittedly, such incidents had always been linked with anti-semitic agitation, and were sometimes even cunningly inspired from above; what is new is the public, open approval of them expressed by those in power and by the ideologists.

So throughout the whole of Germany squads of extremists and ex-convicts were trained and tested, who, as soon as the great economic crisis of 1929-30 broke, served as rallying and focal points for millions of embittered, disillusioned, and discontented people.

II

If ever contemporary observers were fundamentally mistaken about the political significance of a phenomenon, this was certainly true of the accession to power of National-Socialism. Quite a number of influential circles in Germany and abroad, which were very far from accepting his doctrine, hailed Hitler, the agitator, as a useful bulwark against Communism; in fact, the enormous majority of observers considered that the trials of office were bound to exert a moderating influence on the movement. The German Jews, on the whole, shared this illusion: in certain Jewish circles there was even a tendency to support the new régime, a tendency which took concrete, though ephemeral, form in the 'Union of German National Jews'. Underlying it was the idea that, given certain reductions of rights and certain sacrifices, by means partly of emigration and partly of some kind of new 'statute', an 'elimination of the Jewish influence' could be brought about by 'peaceful' methods; whatever might have been the disadvantages and terrible injustice of such a

[1] Goebbels, *Kampf um Berlin* (1934), p. 102.　　　　[2] ibid., p. 180.

solution, it would have been in line with other compromises reached in this imperfect world of ours.

But, to paraphrase Goethe's famous saying: it was not injustice but disorder that Hitler was aiming at. Subsequent events show to what an extent, far from solving the 'Jewish problem', he sought to make it more acute, and how the anti-Jewish campaign, far from being for the *Führer* an end in itself, was, above all, a convenient means of exciting the passions, of mobilising to the extreme the energies and aggressive dynamism of the German people.

No sooner are the Nazis in control of the vast legislative, administrative, and police machine of a modern state than they make use of it to consolidate their power and to condition the German population to the pursuit of a policy of imperialism and domination. And the meaning of their anti-Jewish measures, as of the entire anti-semitic propaganda apparatus, becomes clear when examined from this particular point of view.

What is the aim? To establish for centuries to come the world hegemony of the German nation. What must be done to achieve this aim? Stir the masses to fanaticism, inculcate in them both a blind discipline and a blind obedience, instil in them a fury and cruelty that know no bounds, and mould the new youth, whom, according to Rauschning,[1] the visionary *Führer* described as 'hard, violent and cruel . . . with the force and beauty of young beasts.' 'Eradicate conscience, this invention of the Jews,' is another of Rauschning's quotations: we cannot know if these were Hitler's exact words, but we do know that the brilliant manipulations of this empirical psycho-technician tended to give to his people's conscience a new and completely different content.

The government's anti-semitic policy was an instrument in the hands of the Nazis for fulfilling these aims. Both the aims pursued—discipline and obedience on the one hand, cruelty and fanaticism on the other—were pursued, as we shall see, simultaneously and by the same methods.

1. To begin with, there was an avalanche of laws and decrees to enforce, rigidly, the race doctrines, backing the propagandist's work with all the authority of the legislator. As soon as the Party came to power in 1933, a series of edicts appeared specifying countless disqualifications, discriminations, and bans where the Jews were concerned, in particular barring them from most professions and, in the end, condemning them to rapid impoverishment. But here again it is the use of sexual taboos that illustrates my thesis most strikingly. The Nuremberg Laws (1935), which, incidentally, deprived all Jews of German citizenship (transforming them into second-class 'subjects'), introduced severe penalties not only for Jews but also for

[1] H. Rauschning, *Gespräche mit Hitler*.

Germans who were found guilty of 'race-violation':[1] the Party organs, for their part, heightened the intimidation by organising (the legislator had not foreseen this) public processions and pillorying of delinquents. But from then on the entire existence of the Germans, right down to the simplest daily tasks, was controlled in such a way as to guarantee permanent observance of the new, ruthless law: in the streets, in shops and public transport, and even in the squares where benches were 'forbidden for Jews', placards acted as a constant reminder. There was a veritable flood of edicts, of legislative and administrative orders, from municipalities and from the Party, which covered every sphere of life, applying the legal ban even to Jewish property, even to animals owned by Jews: rural authorities, for example, decreed that cows and goats belonging to Jews could not be touched by the communal bull or ram. The penalties were always heavy: if the wife of a Nazi bought a post-card from a Jewish shop, her husband was expelled from the Party, etc., etc. The only factors that limited this plague of decrees were the economic situation and the international situation, as well as the vague resistance of public opinion, which quickly broke down (and which, in fact, proved extremely malleable).

An important point is that these decrees were aimed against Jews 'by race', and therefore applied to Jewish converts to Christianity, even if the conversion took place a generation before, a fact which, as one can well imagine, involved adherents of the two Christian confessions in severe internal conflicts.[2] Behind the scenes, however, the system of concentration camps was emerging and developing, a mysterious world of punishment surrounded by sacred terror, which was mostly to be peopled by Jews but also by opponents of the régime

---

[1] That is to say, sexual relations between Jews and Germans. Here is the text of one of the Nuremberg laws.

'Acting in the knowledge that purity of German blood is essential to the perpetuation of the German race, and moved by the unshakeable will to assure the future of the German nation, the *Reichstag* has unanimously adopted the following law, in the following clauses:

(1) Marriages between Jews and subjects of German birth or extraction are forbidden.

(2) Extra-marital relations between Jews and subjects of German birth or extraction are forbidden.

(3) No Jew may employ in his household, servants of German blood or extraction under the age of forty-five years.

(4) It is forbidden for Jews to use the German national colours. They may on the contrary, use their own Jewish colours: this right is guaranteed by the State.

(5) Breakers of Art. 1 of this law are liable to imprisonment with hard labour. Breakers of Art. 2, will be punished with up to a year's imprisonment and a fine, or one of these penalties.

[2] On the contrary, a German 'by race' converted to Judaism was exempt from these provisions if he could prove his Christian descent. It would be vain to describe the endless genealogical researches which this involved.

whom it endeavoured, in a way now familiar to all of us, to identify with Judaism.

2. The countless edicts and decrees also had the effect of stimulating a feeling of hatred and contempt for the untouchable Jews—whether converts or not—and of instilling in the Germans a habitual and complete lack of scruple towards the 'sub-humans'. The anti-Jewish mud-slinging campaign, which we examined in the last chapter, was markedly reinforced by the legal measures taken, of which the most characteristic, perhaps, were the imposition in 1938 of an obligatory Christian name—in the circumstances they had a ludicrous tinge: Israel for men, Sarah for women [1]—and later, in 1941, the wearing of a yellow star. But, above all, the gradual intensification of Jewish persecution—that is, the systematisation of the sporadic excesses we considered in the last chapter—provided an opportunity for submitting the members of the *élite* which the régime had created, the SA and SS, to a practical course of training that toughened them for the tasks lying ahead. Let us glance at a concrete case, which arose during the first large-scale pogrom launched by the Nazis after they came to power, and which shows to what extent the Nazi chiefs were concerned with systematic, conscious 're-education'.

In November 1938, ostensibly to avenge the assassination in Paris of the German diplomat, Ernst von Rath, by the young Polish Jew, Grynspan, the Party organised the pillaging of Jewish shops and the burning of synagogues in every German town, while more than 20,000 Jews were rounded up and interned in concentration camps. But a certain number of SA and SS men engaged on the operation exceeded the instructions given to them and committed theft, murder, and rape. The civil police opened an inquiry, which the Party cut short by referring back all incidents of this kind to its special jurisdiction. And, in February 1939, Major Walter Buch, the Party's Chief Justice, submitted his findings to Göring. These findings have since been recovered intact.[2]

As an illustration, Buch analysed in his report sixteen concrete cases. Thirteen of these cases—cases four to sixteen—were murders, which he proposed to investigate no further, on the grounds, explicitly stated in his report, that the culprits were entitled to believe they were carrying out the wishes of the Party, which were 'clearly realised though obscurely expressed', and that 'they were com-

---

[1] It should be mentioned that the names Israel and Sarah (together with Biblical names in general) had, since the time of their assimilation, fallen into disuse among German Jews. They had, indeed, come to be used as symbols in anti-semitic propaganda, through the spoken word, writing or illustration, in the course of the preceding decades.

[2] Secret report on the events, and on the organisation of the party tribunal, concerning the anti-semitic demonstrations of 9 Nov. 1938 (Munich, 13 Feb. 1939).

pelled, moreover, to overcome the gravest psychic inhibitions in order to do what they did'. They were therefore all exonerated, including even those who acted in obvious defiance of the orders given, since in this case 'impure motives' (*unlautere Motive*) could not be imputed.

On the other hand, there was a strong case for excluding from the Party 'those who have derived profit from the struggle for liberation organised by the Party against Jewry for ignoble personal ends or who had been actuated by criminal motives'. These are cases 1, 2, and 3—two rapes and one theft—concerning which Judge Buch decided on the arrest of the culprits, whom he demanded should be handed over to the civil courts, which were competent to deal with cases of 'race violation'.

So it is clear that the Party leaders were not prepared to grant their followers complete licence with regard to the Jews to be destroyed; but still less was there any lingering sense of public order, in the sense in which we understand it, that led to their protection. As I have said, the Nazi methods in the Jewish question were designed to accustom the uniformed organisations of the régime to cruelty and at the same time to discipline; and it was with this in mind that Himmler cried in the Poznan speech we have already quoted: '. . . most of you know that it is a heap of 100 or 500 or 1,000 corpses. To have passed by it and, at the same time, with the exception of those who suffer from human weakness, to have remained honest, that is what *has hardened us.*'[1]

3. While this seems to be the main thread, the essential feature of the Jewish persecution in Nazi Germany, there are also certain secondary aspects and results which must be mentioned. It is purely for the record that we recall the part anti-semitic circles in various European countries played in forming what was generally known as the 'Fifth Column', and the benefits German National-Socialism derived from it in the international sphere. Later, when the Nazi occupation spread to a large part of Europe, the pro-Nazi focal points played an extremely important part in the phenomenon of 'collaboration'. Just how skilfully the Nazi administrators wielded this instrument emerges clearly, for example, from a report to Berlin in January 1941 by Knochen, the German Police Chief in France, who prognosticated the mass arrest of the Jews in Paris:

'. . . it has appeared virtually impossible to cultivate in the French an anti-semitic feeling based on ideological considerations, whereas the prospect of economic advantages would be more likely to arouse sympathy for an anti-Jewish drive (the internment of some 100,000 foreign Jews living in Paris would give many

---

[1] Author's italics.

Frenchmen the opportunity to rise from the lower to the middle classes).'

This brings us back to the part played by economic jealousy, by the struggle for a higher status, in modern anti-Semitism. It is self-evident that in Germany itself the complete elimination of Jews from economic life and from the liberal professions allowed the régime to consolidate its position by providing it with avenues of advancement and reward. But, at the same time, the impoverishment of the German Jews and their emigration provided Hitler's complex strategy with further scoring points, some of which are enumerated in a German diplomatic report,[1] which I shall quote in conclusion:

'. . . experience will teach the population (of foreign countries) what the Jewish danger really means to them. The poorer the Jewish emigrant, the heavier will be the burden he represents to the country of immigration and the more forcefully that country will react . . . in a sense entirely favourable to German interests. . . . A wave of anti-Semitism is already becoming apparent in all the countries towards which the stream of Jewish emigration is flowing. One of the duties of German foreign policy is to increase this wave.'

And this report, which is dated January 1939, complacently enumerates the results already achieved in France, the Low Countries, Norway, USA, Uruguay. . . .

III

On 30th January 1939, the anniversary of his accession to power, Hitler spoke thus in his annual speech of commemoration:

'. . . On this day, which perhaps will remain a memorable one not only for the Germans, I should like to say this: in my life during the struggle for power, I have frequently been a prophet and I have frequently been held up to ridicule—chiefly by the Jewish people. I think the hearty laughter of the German Jews has meanwhile stuck in their throats. Once again, today, I am going to be a prophet. If international Jewry were to succeed, in Europe or elsewhere, in hurling the nations into a world war, the result would not be a bolshevisation of Europe and a victory for Judaism but the *extermination* of the Jewish race in Europe.'

We know today that at that moment Hitler had already definitely decided to make war; and subsequent events have shown all too clearly how much of that cruel prophecy was to be realised. In the years that followed, Homo Sapiens was made richer by a new experience: the elaboration of a technique of wholesale murder, the

---

[1] *The Jewish question, as a factor in foreign policy in the year 1938*. A report signed by Schaumburg, dated 25 Jan. 1939.

appearance, in eastern Germany and in occupied Poland, of those vast industrial plants of death called Auschwitz, Treblinka, and Belsen. Those symbols of pure destruction, into which the Nazi régime poured a great deal of energy and resources, strike one immediately by their senselessness, their absurdity, as much as by their horror.

It only remains for us to consider whether the vast undertaking called by the Nazis 'the final solution of the Jewish question' must be regarded as an infernal end in itself, motivated by a desire for vengeance, by an insatiable hatred of the Jews, or whether one can regard it in the same light as the anti-Jewish policy in general which we have already discussed; in other words, can it be interpreted as one of the means, one of the techniques employed by the Nazis in their effort to gain world supremacy for the 'master race'? The problem is all the more delicate because the factors and documents on which we could form a judgment are remarkably rare. The 'final solution' operation was by way of being the *Führer*'s private preserve: the history of its conception is (and will doubtless remain) largely shrouded in mystery; the relevant discussions and decisions were almost always in verbal form. But it would be a mistake to interpret as the mere caprice of a satrap or as a problem of individual psychology such a crucial decision by a man who gave every sign of being extremely sensitive to the impulses and the conscious and unconscious reactions of the masses he manipulated.

Let us examine the few data known to us. The first thing we notice is that the campaign of total extermination was launched in the second half of 1941, the period when, as a result of the extension of the war, first Russia, then to the USA, the last prospects of a negotiated peace disappeared, and when the war really became a total war (more precisely, the launching of the 'final solution' took place in two stages: wholesale massacres of Jews in Russia immediately following the invasion of the USSR; creation of the 'death camps' with their colossal crematoriums, for the extermination of the Jews from other countries, following immediately on America's entry into the war). If we now consider the men who operated in the immediate entourage of the *Führer*, there are certain indications that Goebbels, the régime's chief propagandist, put his shoulder to the wheel, whereas Himmler, his chief executioner, seems to have played a passive, if not a reserved role.[1] And as far as Goebbels' reasons and motives are concerned, his diary contains the following curious entry:

'We are, in particular, so involved in the Jewish question, that it is no longer possible for us to turn back. So much the better. A

---

[1] We refer, in what concerns this highly complex question, to our own work *The Breviary of Hate* (Paris, 1951).

movement and a people that have burned their boats behind them fight with much greater energy—as experience proves—than do those who can still retreat.' [1]

As regards the benefit that a Nazi leader hoped to derive from the 'final solution', this is an interesting pointer: 'burning one's boats', widening the gulf that separated Nazi Germany from the rest of humanity, in order to make return impossible or terribly difficult, and in this way to stimulate his men to the maximum of fury. That this was an argument familiar to the·psycho-technicians of the Third Reich is borne out by another document which, in this case, came from the General Staff of the *Wehrmacht* and was signed by General Jodl. This report, dated February 1945, considers the relative advantages or disadvantages of a formal denunciation of international agreements on the conduct of war. As is well known, Hitler at that time was considering, as a reply to the Allied bombardments, mass reprisals against Western prisoners of war. And among the advantages Jodl stresses this: 'The resolute elements among the German people will be stimulated, if we burn our boats, to a still higher degree of fighting fervour.' [2]

The rapid collapse of Nazi Germany and the fear of counter-reprisals prevented this plan from being carried out, whereas the extermination of the Jews had unfortunately proved much easier to realise. One cannot help comparing such an intellectual approach with the classic method employed quite instinctively by leaders of criminal gangs, when they seek to implicate their subordinates in their crimes, to let them become seriously involved, in order to make doubly sure of their loyalty and devotion. It is one of the oldest truths, borne out by experience, that nothing is more binding than a common crime. Seen from this angle as a psycho-technical criminal operation carried out on a colossal scale, the 'final solution' certainly deserves to be counted among the specific methods and techniques of the Nazis. And if demagogues and agitators have always been masters at the art of exploiting the enormous fomentation of collective hatred, one cannot deny that the Nazi had the macabre originality to try to make the maximum possible use of this weapon, to pursue the method to its bitter end.

Was it effective? Although it may appear to be somewhat outside the range of my subject, I think it might be worth our while to devote

---

[1] *The Journal of Dr Goebbels* (Paris, 1949), p. 246. The authenticity of this document, the original of which is in the Hoover War Library, USA, is beyond question.

[2] Report by Jodl to Hitler, dated 21 Feb. 1945. The report concludes 'that in the present situation, the disadvantages outweigh the advantages', since the Allies would then be able to have resource to gas or bacteriological warfare, in which they are superior, since the number of German prisoners in the hands of the Allies is greater than the number of American and British, etc., etc.

a few moments to the evidence of certain highly placed German observers and even to the reports and confessions of some who were actively engaged.

General Johannes Blaskowitz, Commander-in-Chief of the German armies in Poland (*Oberbefehlshaber Ost*), had this to say in a report to the Supreme General Staff of the *Wehrmacht* in February 1940.

'The greatest possible damage is done to the German people by the present situation, considering the unrestrained brutality and moral depravation that will rapidly spread like an epidemic through the finest of Germany's manpower. If the senior officials of the Police and the SS demand violence and brutality and praise them publicly, then convicts will soon be ruling us. It is astonishing the rapidity with which people of the same calibre, people of low character, meet their like, in order, as in Poland, to satisfy their bestial, pathological instincts. It is almost impossible to keep them much longer in check: not without justice they feel they are authorised and encouraged to commit the most arrant acts of cruelty.' [1]

From the Ukraine, General Thomas, Inspector-General of Munitions, summarised his observations in the following six points (December 1941):

'Summing up, one can say that the method adopted of solving the Jewish problem in the Ukraine, obviously in accordance with ideological principles, has had the following consequences:

(*a*) Elimination of some of the superfluous mouths in the towns;
(*b*) Elimination of some of the population who could not but hate us;
(*c*) Elimination of workers who were absolutely indispensable for the needs of the *Wehrmacht*;
(*d*) Obvious effects in the spheres of propaganda and foreign policy;
(*e*) Unfortunate repercussions for the troops who take part, even indirectly, in these executions;
(*f*) A degrading influence on the police units charged with these executions.'

From White Russia, a senior officer on a tour of inspection gave the following details in a report dated 23rd October 1941:

'Following instructions, the Jews are "transferred". It is done in this way: they receive an order to report the next night at a specific place and to bring with them their best clothes and their

[1] The quotations that follow are extracted from the files of the International Tribunal of Nuremberg.

jewels. No consideration is taken either of social position or of sex or of age. They are then taken to an out-of-the-way spot and liquidated. Some of the incidents that take place are so heart-rending as to be indescribable. They have their inevitable effect on the German Commandos. In general, an execution can only be carried out in a state of alcoholic stupor. One officer, who had been detailed to act as observer, reports that the following night he had the most terrifying nightmares.'

The massacres in question here were of the kind perpetrated in Russia with the co-operation of special units of the Military Police, the '*Einsatzgruppen*'. Some of the reports that were sent regularly to Berlin by these units have been found, and in one of them the following appreciation is made:

'Our men stood up well to the physical strain. The extreme psychical effort demanded of them can only be properly appreciated if one considers the large quantity of liquidations. It was only by constantly reminding them of the political requirements that their spirits and bearing could be maintained unimpaired.'

Astonishing statements in the same style were made at the Nuremberg Trials by certain killers in the '*Einsatzgruppen*', whose very cynicism seems revealing. Any pity they could muster was reserved for themselves. Not a word, not a thought for their victims. 'Our men who took part in the executions suffered more nervous exhaustion than those who were to be shot' (Colonel SS Paul Blödel). 'Many men suffered terribly and, for a variety of reasons, had to be sent home; either their nervous system went to pieces or the moral strain was too much for them' (General SS Otto Ohlendorff). 'The men of the *Waffen-SS* said that they would rather have fought in the front line than remained here. I asked why, and they replied: "We would prefer not to say." ' (Sergeant SS Graf).

Few of the *Waffen-SS* men in question were volunteers. The '*Einsatzgruppen*' consisted, for the most part, of former members of the police corps and the gendarmerie, who had been conscripted for these special duties. So it was chance that governed their selection, and they comprised only a very small proportion of 'idealists' in the sense in which this word is used by an eye-witness of the massacres, whose report contains this revealing phrase: 'The operation (of Novgorodek) was the work of a special SS Commando, which, out of idealism, conducted the entire exterminations without recourse to schnaps.' These men, in consequence, during their bloody orgies, imposed upon themselves 'out of idealism' an additional psychical burden.

All these observations are only valid for men to whom, cruel and aggressive as they were, normal criteria, in the clinical sense of the term, can be applied. The very special stratum of the concentration camp and the death-factory, which was the result of long years of rigorous selection (the SS 'Death's Head' division had been formed in 1934) and which was riddled with sadists and perverts, must be considered entirely apart. At the same time, even in this world of concentration, a human factor continued to operate on a variety of pretexts; as Professor Abel rightly observes,[1] complete automatisation can never be achieved on such a large scale, neither in the gaolers nor in the prisoners, and this fact should be borne in mind when one considers any prediction of a human robot society of the future.

So, cautious as one must be in such cases, the conclusion still seems justified that the gigantic Nazi operation appears, to a large extent, to have failed. The 'psychic inhibitions', of which Walter Buch spoke, still persisted, even among the select of the SS, after ten years of National-Socialist re-education, and while, unfortunately, their persistence was powerless to prevent massacres being perpetrated on an enormous scale, at least they seem to have imposed certain limits beyond which the reconditioning of inhibitions and the recasting of values, in a society moving towards complete perversion, could not be pushed too far. Had the outcome of the 1939–45 conflict been a different one—had Nazi world domination been assured for some time to come—it seems unlikely that the ruthless, apocalytic society the Nazi leaders had in mind would have been practicable or viable.

[1] Professor Theodore Abel, *The Sociology of Concentration Camps*. A report delivered to the conference on the history of the Second World War, Amsterdam, September 1950.

27
RACIALISM IN NAZI GERMANY
Otto Klineberg

It is, of course, a commonplace that the race theories adopted and developed by the Nazis did not entirely originate with them. There was a preceding history of racial thinking in Germany which prepared the way for later developments, and which served as a fruitful soil in which racialism could grow. Hitler himself acknowledges his debt to at least some of his predecessors, and the racial philosophy which finally emerged represents an amalgam of points of view, theory, fiction, and occasional fact, which were together restructured for Nazi purposes.

It is not easy to put one's finger on the origins of Nazi racialism, nor is it necessary for our purposes to go farther back than the writings of the Frenchman Gobineau, who is usually considered the spiritual father of Nazi race thinking. Count Arthur Joseph de Gobineau, 1816–82, author of the four-volume *Essai sur L'inegalité des Races Humaines* (Paris, 1853–55), states that he wrote this work in part to prove the superiority of his own racial ancestry, and in part as a consequence of an investigation which he had begun on his own family tree. Briefly stated, he preached the superiority of the white race over all others, and among the Whites he regarded the group whom he called the Aryans as representing the summit of civilisation. Civilisation in his view sprang from the Aryans, declining when Aryan blood became diluted. The civilisation of India was due to the Aryans; that of Egypt was created by an Aryan colony from India; that of Greece was due to Aryans with some Semitic intermixtures. Civilisation without an Aryan creator is unthinkable; and among the Aryans the Teutons may be regarded as the purest modern representatives.

Not everything that Gobineau said was helpful to the position that the Nazis later adopted. For example, he regarded race mixture as having high value for the development of civilisation; it is only when two races mix, in his opinion, that civilisation can develop. He saw race mixture as inevitable, and rejected the hope that a 'pure race' might preserve itself intact. This aspect of Gobineau's position was neglected by the Nazis, as is well known, in favour of the cult of racial purity and the belief that the Germans could be kept 'pure'. The other aspects of Gobineau's position, especially his emphasis on the superiority of the Aryans and the Teutons, became the cornerstones of Nazi racial philosophy. Even before Nazism, Gobineau was hailed by many Germans as their intellectual leader, and Gobineau societies sprang up all over the country.

Gobineau's most important follower was Houston Stewart Chamberlain, who published his *Grundlagen des 19. Jahrhunderts* in 1899. Although an Englishman by birth, he lived most of his life in Germany, was an influential member of the Gobineau Society, and his writings were so popular with the ruling class in Germany that he was known as the Kaiser's anthropologist. Chamberlain, too, classified the Teutons as the most important representatives of the Aryan people. The Teuton is everywhere triumphant; the Renaissance was due to the Teutons in Italy; all the great minds of western Europe were Teutons; Paul and Jesus were Aryans, not Jews.

With Chamberlain we find an attempt to give some kind of physical anthropological basis for racial theorising. He describes the Teutons as being for the most part tall, fair, and dolichocephalic —the characteristics regarded by physical anthropologists as typical of the Nordic peoples of Europe. There were obvious difficulties which arose from the fact that so many Germans did not conform to this 'ideal' physical type, and Chamberlain was forced to admit that in many cases a Teuton or Aryan cannot easily be recognised; in such cases it may be necessary to use intuition or 'spiritual divination', which Chamberlain dignifies with the name of rational anthropology. Even the Jews, whom he regards as an alien people, cannot always be distinguished, on the basis of their physical characteristics alone, from the Germans among whom they live. There are, in fact, Chamberlain confesses, many Jews who are not recognisable as such and who could usually be mistaken for Germans; but, he maintains, it often happens that even when a Jew of this type enters a room, a German child, usually a little girl, will unaccountably begin to cry. This is the 'rational' anthropology on which Chamberlain relied. The difficulty of reconciling 'racial purity' with the wide range of physical characteristics found among Germans, and the impossibility of distinguishing Germans from non-Germans with any certainty, had to be faced directly by the German racial theorists of a later date.

These two, Gobineau and Chamberlain, are credited by Hitler with developing the racial philosophy and creating the climate which he later found so useful. There were others who made their contribution. For example, Ludwig Woltmann (*Politische Antropologie*, 1903) 'proved' that all the great Italians were Germans, and

E E

that even their names had originally been German. Giordano Bruno was Braun; Leonardo da Vinci was Wincke; Giotto was Jothe. The same was true of the great Frenchmen—Gounod was Gundiwald; Diderot was Tietroh; and so with many others.

There were other more serious scholars who helped to prepare the way. Among them may be mentioned Baur, Fischer and Lenz, who, in their *Menschliche Vererblichkeitslehre* (1929), united the presentation of much scientific material from the fields of biology and anthropology with a completely unscientific psychological characterisation of the various 'races' of mankind. Negroes are described as lacking in foresight, poor in imagination, childish, devoid of the power of mental creation. Mongols are regarded as having quick apprehension and excellent memory, but lacking in imagination, critical faculty, or abstraction. Among the European groups there was the usual subdivision into the three major physical types. The Alpines are considered to possess marked tenacity and intelligence but little imagination; the Mediterraneans to have a taste for gesture and oratory but little sense of truth and honour; the Nordics march in the van of mankind because of their high intellectual endowments, their courage, imagination, foresight, and constancy of will. Eugen Fischer, the senior author of this treatise, later occupied an important academic position under the Nazi régime.

One other man who contributed to this background of racialism was H. F. K. Günther, who, in a series of publications (*Rassenkunde des Deutschen Volkes*, 1924; *Adel und Rasse*, 1927; *Rasse und Stil*, 1927), which received enormous circulation in pre-Hitler Germany, glorified the Nordics even further; they are the bearers of all conceivable virtues and the leaders in civilisation everywhere. Günther recognised the racial diversity of the German people—there were at least six racial types that he described as constituting the German population—but this difficulty tended to be lost sight of in his glorification of the Nordics.

In the pre-Hitler era, perhaps the most effective 'solution' to the paradox that the evident physical variations among Germans had to be acknowledged, while also emphasising the notion of German race purity, is represented in the statement of Kossima, who, in his *Ursprung der Germanen*, published in 1928, stated that, 'Nordic souls may frequently be combined with non-Nordic bodies, and similarly a soul which is decidedly non-Nordic may be found in a perfect Nordic body'. This doctrine, which was further developed in later writings by him and various others, made it a little easier to present an extremely discriminatory racialism to a heterogeneous population.

These are only a few of the instances that might be given of writers who prepared the way for Nazi racialism. It would be doing an injustice to German philosophy and science, however, not to point out at the same time that there were many voices which were raised in a different key, emphasising the unity rather than the lines of demarcation among human groups. For example, Herder, in his *Ideen zur Philosophie der Geschichte der Menschheit*, wrote:

'I could wish that distinctions between the human species, that have been made from a laudable zeal for scientific classification, be not carried beyond the due bounds. . . . Race refers to a difference of origin, which in this case does not exist. . . . In short, there are neither four nor five races, nor exclusive varieties on this earth . . . all are at least but shades of the same great picture, extending through all ages and over all parts of the earth.'

Even before Herder, the German scientist who is usually credited with developing one of the most common of all classifications of human races—that which divides mankind into five races according to skin colour—protested that no sharp distinctions could be made between peoples. This was Blumenbach, who, in his *De Generis Humani Varietate*, published in 1775, wrote,

'Although there seems to be a great difference between widely separate nations . . . yet when the matter is thoroughly considered, you see that all do so run into one another, and that one variety of mankind does sensibly pass into the other, that you cannot mark out the limits between them.'

Twenty years later Blumenbach wrote:

'No variety of mankind exists, whether of colour, countenance or stature, etc., so singular as not to be connected with others of the same kind by such an imperceptible transition, that it is very clear they are all related, or only differ from each other in degree.'

To take only one more example, the great German explorer, Alexander von Humboldt (*Cosmos*, 1849), specifically repudiates what he calls 'the depressing assumption of superior and inferior races of men'. He insists that all groups 'are in like degree designed for freedom', and that no one group has the right to oppress, dominate, or enslave any other.

This contrast in the writing of two different groups of Germans could make one paraphrase the famous word of Goethe to the effect that there are 'two souls' within the German nation. In recent writing this notion of a fundamental dichotomy within German thinking has been revived by a number of writers; in connection with German attitudes to racialism we see it once again. Arrogant racialism had its antecedents, but also its opponents. Up to the time when Hitler came to power there were influential voices of protest against the extremes of racialism which were so assiduously spread by the Nazis. Ernst Kretschmer, for example, stated it as his conclusion that most men of genius, far from being racially pure, were of mixed ethnic ancestry. He goes on to suggest,

'One may assume, with some propriety, that the rise of lofty civilisations, blossoming with genius, at other times and in other races and nations, was caused by a similar biological process of cross-breeding.' [1]

Kretschmer also insisted that the Germans of Nordic ancestry had been unduly glorified at the expense of the Alpine type, which he regarded as equally valuable in the German national structure.

It is difficult, therefore, to assume that there was something specifically German in the development of racialism. Similar views have certainly been held by people in other countries, and are now still found in some regions. It seems more reasonable to suppose that Hitler and the theorists who aided him in developing his philosophy looked back into the stream of earlier German thinking, and selected that which they found of value to them. The voices raised in protest were simply neglected. It may be that it was easier to find examples of racialist thinking in Germany than elsewhere, but it is certainly incorrect to regard this as in any sense exclusively German. There were two trends, one of which Hitler found palatable. When he came to power, that became the only position which could be expressed, and many Germans, scientists as well as laymen, helped him to make this philosophy felt throughout Germany, and later in other countries as well.

II. Racialism under National-Socialism

In the period before Hitler actually assumed power, the two books which undoubtedly paved the way for the all-pervasive racialism which was to follow were Hitler's *Mein Kampf* and Rosenberg's *Der Mythus des 20. Jahrhunderts*. Hitler's attitude towards race in general may perhaps best be summed up in his own statement that:

'The total educational and training work of the folk-state must find its crowning-point in that it burns instinctively and rationally the sense of race and feeling of race into the hearts and minds of the youth entrusted to it.'

Alfred Rosenberg, who was regarded as the philosopher of the Nazi movement and, in particular, the philosopher of race, expressed

[1] *The Psychology of Men of Genius* (1931).

his idea even more mystically in terms of the eternal virtues found in a particular blood. He wrote as follows:

'A nation is constituted by the predominance of a definite character formed by its blood, also by language, geographical environment, and the sense of a united political destiny. These last constituents are not, however, definitive; the decisive element in a nation is its blood. In the first awakening of a people, great poets and heroes disclose themselves to us as the incorporation of the eternal values of a particular blood soul. I believe that this recognition of the profound significance of blood is now mysteriously encircling our planet, irresistibly gripping one nation after another.'

Although it would be difficult to find any continuing thread of logic or systematic presentation in the racialist theories developed by Nazi spokesmen, it is possible to separate for purposes of convenience a number of interrelated, though distinguishable factors, which played a part in the development of this whole theory.

I. THE ANTI-JEWISH ASPECT

This characteristic of Nazi racialism is the subject of treatment in another part of this volume, and it is not necessary to enter into a discussion of its implications at this point. It is mentioned here only because it brought the Nazis into some conflict with other groups as a result of the implications of their anti-Jewish position with regard to the wider problem of racialism generally. The term anti-*Semitism*, for example, which has been traditionally used for anti-Jewish attitudes, was regarded by the Nazis as potentially alienating many of the Semitic-speaking peoples of the Near East, whom the Nazis were trying to gain as allies. One Nazi spokesman, Dr Walter Gross, resolved the problem by making a distinction between the Jews, whom he considered a 'race mixture', and the Oriental race or the peoples of the Near East, against whom the Nazi race theories were emphatically not directed. Referring to the peoples of the Near East, Gross writes:

'. . . it turns out that these races too, where they have appeared as relatively pure, strike the European, it is true, as alien and different in species (*andersartig*) but in their own living space and within the cultural patterns created by them they present quite esteemable and agreeable traits. Let me mention only the Arab tribes and peoples whose racial foundation is fairly purely Oriental . . . *And it would be well for the sake of clarity if the European world in its struggle against the Jews always remained aware of this context and did not call the struggle, as hitherto, anti-Semitism.* Because it is directed not against peoples of Semitic tongue but against the unharmonious Near Eastern–Oriental–Mediterranean Jew-people which is being so passionately rejected also by the purely or preponderantly Oriental, Semitic tribes and peoples.'[1]

As a matter of fact, the so-called Oriental race had been rather badly handled, so far as its psychological characteristics were concerned, by Günther and others of similar viewpoint, but this was conveniently disregarded, and the peoples of the Near East were assured of a warm welcome as allies in spite of the difficulties placed by racial theories in the way of such an alliance.

2. THE APPEAL TO 'SCIENCE'

It is striking that in the attempts to win over the mass of people to the racial viewpoint consonant with Nazi philosophy, a concerted attempt was made to call in the aid of scientists. Germany's scientific tradition was still sufficiently alive, and the standing of German scientists still sufficiently great, for the appeal to science to constitute a powerful propaganda weapon. Many scientists responded; there were others who held out. In those cases in which there was some disagreement regarding the scientific facts, it was a fairly simple matter to remove the recalcitrant professors from their Chairs, or deny them the opportunity to speak or to publish. In other cases, people who had been attacked by the scientists for the extreme, unsubstantiated views which they held were elevated by the Nazis to positions of influence and authority. One such case was that of Günther, to whom reference was made above, who had previously occupied a position which might be regarded as on the fringe of the scientific world, and who was later rewarded by being made Professor of Anthropology at Jena.

In some cases outstanding scientists came to the support of the Nazi position. A distinguished psychologist, Vice-president of the German Society of Psychology, suggested that *Mein Kampf* be used as a textbook in the teaching of political psychology. Another well-known psychologist described a personality type which he called anti-Nordic—disintegrated, dissolute, egocentric, a product of race mixture.

As indicated above, difficulties quickly arose from the attempt to use the approach of respectable science as a means of supporting the Nazi doctrine. The glorification of the Nordic—the tall, blond, dolichocephalic type—was not of much use. Hitler, Goebbels, and a host of other Nazi leaders fell far short of the Nordic standard. The attempt to use a physical or anatomical basis to describe the Aryans or the Teutons was similarly doomed to failure. This was recognised

[1] Quoted by Weinreich, *Hitler's Professors* (1946), p. 111.

by many of the scientists who had supported theories of racialism. Eugen Fischer, for example, acknowledged that:

'The racial extraction (of a person) is really not always easy to establish . . . and in some parts of the population (one finds) a very strong crossing of Northern, Eastern-Baltic, Alpine, Dinaric (elements) . . . and one sees a tremendously variegated picture of single individuals.' [1]

Perhaps as a result of difficulties of this kind, caution was thrown to the winds by those who attempted to find a factual support for the racial position. The most extreme case is perhaps that of Hermann Gauch, who in his *Neue Grundlagen zur Rassenforschung*, published in 1935, described the differences between Nordics and non-Nordics in such ridiculous terms that any resemblance to the facts of anthropological science is no longer discernible. As examples may be cited the following statements from his book:

'The non-Nordic man occupies an intermediate position between the Nordics and the animals, just about next to the anthropoid ape. He is therefore not a complete man. He is really not a man at all in true contradistinction to animals, but a transition, an intermediate stage. Better and more apt, therefore, is the designation "Subhuman" (*Untermensch*).'

And again:

'If non-Nordics are more closely allied to monkeys and apes than to Nordics, why is it possible for them to mate with Nordics and not with apes? The answer is this. It has not been proved that non-Nordics cannot mate with apes.'

Still another difficulty which arose in making use of any kind of science in defence of racialism was the problem of what to do with the Japanese. The earlier writers on race whom the Nazis utilised were by no means flattering to the peoples of the Far East. Again resort was made to subterfuges in an attempt to overcome this difficulty. As Benedict points out (*Race, Science, and Politics*, 1943) Hitler excepted the Japanese when he struck out against non-Aryans; Japanese residents of Germany were not subject to the racial laws of the Third Reich. They were permitted to intermarry with German Aryans, and this was not regarded as an example of race mixture. Perhaps nowhere did the race theory fall down more seriously than here, but this was only one example of the impossibility of carrying through a consistent racial philosophy. It was easier to forget about physical type and speak of 'blood' or 'soul'.

[1] Quoted in Weinreich, op. cit., p. 32.

3. THE ALL-PERVASIVENESS OF RACE

This point hardly requires documentation. The writings of Günther and others prepared the way for the view that all behaviour, and all culture, were related to race. Art, philosophy, science (including natural science), politics, family life—all of these were dependent on racial origins; those of 'alien race' could imitate, but they could not really incorporate into themselves what had originated in the blood of a different people. This aspect of racialism was particularly convenient as a means of eliminating Jews from the Universities, and from all other public positions throughout Germany, but it was also used to distinguish the life and culture of the Germans from those of the British, the French, the Americans, the Russians, etc.

4. RACE HYGIENE

It is, of course, true that the field of eugenics had been cultivated outside Germany; its origins, as a matter of fact, lie in England. In Germany, however, it took an altogether different form. It was no longer eugenics, but race hygiene, and became an integral part of Nazi theory. One of the Nazi leaders, Hans Schemm, stated that 'National-Socialism is applied biology'. Professor Martin Stämmler expressed the goal in the following terms:

> 'Let us, therefore, free the Nordic soul from the fetters of materialism; then it will again attain its former bloom. Then we will again recognise it as what we should like to set before our people as the breeding aim.
> 'Extinction and selection are the two poles around which the whole race cultivation (*Rassenpflege*) rotates, the two methods with which it has to work. . . . Extinction is the biological destruction of the hereditary inferior through sterilisation, the quantitative repression of the unhealthy and the undesirable. . . . The . . . task consists of safeguarding the people from an overgrowth of the weeds. . . .' [1]

In practical terms this meant, of course, that sterilisation could be introduced wherever those in power regarded it as expedient, and compulsorily enforced against those who were 'unhealthy' and 'undesirable' according to this race doctrine. It meant further that the sexual mores of the people could be oriented to the point of permitting the breeding of children out of wedlock, so long as they represented the superior, desirable stock. It meant again a complete neglect of social and environmental factors which determine behaviour in favour of a narrowly defined biological principle. It also

[1] Quoted in Weinreich, op. cit., p. 34.

gave to the Germans—at least to those who were left unsterilised—
a feeling of their own biological fitness and even superiority.

5. THE RACIAL HIERARCHY

Implicit in all that has been said is the notion, according to Nazi
racialism, that there is a hierarchy of races; that it is not sufficient
to divide them into superior and inferior, but that there are all
degrees and variations. In a summary of the views which were
current in Germany concerning this hierarchy, Weinreich, in his
Hitler's Professors, writes as follows:

> 'In Nazi definition, a *folk* consists of several *race* components.
> The German folk, for example, is said to be predominantly
> Nordic but also to contain strains of Faelic, Dinaric, Mediter-
> ranean, Baltic, and other race blood. The Norwegian folk possesses
> more Nordic components and therefore ranks even higher than the
> German in hierarchy. The English folk is said to consist of prac-
> tically the same components as the Germans, only in different
> proportions. Consequently, both Norwegians and the English are
> cognate (*artverwandt*) to the German folk. If they deviate from
> their right way in history it is because miscegenation has led to
> deterioration of the stock. As to the Eastern European peoples,
> the noble elements are represented among them to a much lesser
> degree; for that reason they are less valuable folks or, in common
> parlance, lower races. Finally, the Jews are essentially a counter-
> race (*Gegenrasse*); they are alien in species (*artfremd*), since they
> are a mixture of the Near-Eastern (*vorderasiatisch*) and Oriental
> races, with some other minor admixtures.'

This had obviously certain important practical consequences.
When the Germans conquered a good deal of Europe, the measures
which they imposed in the areas which they dominated varied
tremendously, and were pretty definitely in line with the hierarchical scheme outlined above. The treatment of the Norwegians
and the Danes was different from that accorded the French, but these
in turn were treated better than the Poles, and the Jews of all
nationalities were, in turn, treated still worse than the Poles. There
is a dramatic expression of this hierarchy or gradation in racial
discrimination in the book by Odd Nansen (*Day by Day*, 1948).
Nansen tells of his experiences in a concentration camp and of the
manner in which the Nazi guards differentiated in their treatment
of the prisoners, with Nansen and other Norwegians at one extreme
of favourable treatment, and the Jewish prisoners at the other. The
racial hierarchy was not just a theoretical structure for the Nazis;
it had very practical and very real implications.

III. Racialism as a Technique

In what has already been said the function of racialism as a technique used by the Nazis for their own purposes emerges clearly. It is obvious that the various facets of racialism, frequently self-contradictory, presented a pattern which could be used by the Nazis to gain adherents, and therefore power, to keep that power, and to direct it into the required channels. The purposes which the racialism served may be briefly summarised as follows.

Firstly, it helped to unify the Germans, or at least a substantial proportion of them, around the banner of Nazism. The American sociologist, Sumner, long ago pointed out that the feeling of 'ingroup' is greatly enhanced if there is an 'outgroup' which constitutes an apparent threat, and serves as a clear means of self-identification. If there were an 'enemy' which could be presented to the Germans—and this enemy was identified not only as the Jews but as other 'racial groups' as well—the strong feeling of ethnocentricism among Germans could be made even stronger. We are not suggesting that the ingroup feeling can come only as a result of the identification of an outgroup, but it seems clearly to develop more easily under such conditions.

Secondly, together with this there developed a strong feeling of ego-enhancement, of increased status and self-confidence. The Germans were not only different, they were racially superior. They were assured, over and over again, that all the great contributions to civilisation had been made by men who were similar to them, who were related to them. No matter how much they as individuals may have failed, they could take comfort from the fact that they were one with the great of the world, and that they, or their kin, were destined by the laws of biology to prevail over the others. This must have been particularly palatable to a people who had lost a war and who had gone through a great economic crisis, and who were now assured over and over again that the fault could not be their own, since they were part of the world's *élite*. There can be little doubt that the rallying around National-Socialism was facilitated by this kind of flattery.

In the third place, there were obvious economic gains that resulted from the racialist philosophy. Through the exploitation and elimination of the Jews, as has been pointed out many times, jobs and property became available as rewards to those who joined the Nazi movement. Later on, racialism could be used as a justification of slave labour. Since other ethnic groups were inferior, they could justifiably be forced to do the bidding of the *Herrenvolk*. It might be argued that the Nazis might have carried out their huge slave-labour programme in any case, but the fact remains that racialism facilitated this process and was apt to numb the consciences of those Germans who arrested or exploited or maltreated the foreign deportees and who might otherwise have protested.

Lastly, racialism prepared the way for aggressive war, and justified the extension of the war. As one example of the manner in which racialism and the conduct of the war were integrated, we cite the statements of Dr Friedrich Lange in *Deutsche Volksgeschichte, Deutsches Raumdenken* (1943):

> 'We are entitled to leadership in the new spaces by virtue of our large number (we are the largest people of Europe proper), by virtue of our position (we are placed in the heart of our continent, we are the "country between countries" and the "country between seas"), by virtue of the creative ability of German blood (who counts and names the great Germans!) and, finally, by virtue of our greatest sacrifices for saving the European space from bolshevism in the East and plutocracy in the West.'

Lange reinterprets history in terms of the Nordic defence against the attacks of inferior peoples:

> 'Again and again, ever since the times when the Huns invaded the Reich of our Goths, real swarms of peoples rose from the wide plains near the Black Sea and the Caspian which invaded and sacked the fields and gardens of the civilised peoples of the middle. . . . Against this formlessness, against this quicksand and human flood of the steppes of the East again and again rose the Nordically defined Teutonic person. . . .'

The present writer had the occasion, immediately after the war, to interview a number of Germans who had occupied positions of varying prominence in the Nazi Party. He put to them the question: 'Why did the Germans keep on fighting when the war was so obviously lost to them?' Many reasons were given, but one reason which recurred was the belief, bolstered by Goebbels and his propaganda ministry, that the Germans were superior, that they could not be conquered by people who were far below them in ability, far inferior in 'blood'; that somehow the Germans would come up with something extraordinary, something miraculous, which in spite of everything would yield them the final victory.

These are only some of the ways in which racialism functioned, but even this brief listing furnishes considerable evidence to show its power as a weapon in the hands of the Nazi propagandists. It clearly must be listed among the most powerful weapons at their disposal in achieving and maintaining power.

28

THE ORGANISATION AND EFFICIENCY OF THE GERMAN FIFTH COLUMN

Louis de Jong

IN the middle of October 1936, nearly three weeks after the outbreak of the Civil War in Spain, the President of the Spanish Republic and some of the ministers left Madrid. A few weeks later, on 6th November, they were followed by the other ministers. Madrid, abandoned by the Government, was to be defended by General Miaja. By that time four columns of General Franco's army were converging on the Spanish capital. General Franco was confident that its fall would not be long delayed. His four columns consisted of seasoned troops and, as one of his principal lieutenants, General Mola, had boasted, a 'fifth column' was already in existence in Madrid itself, eager to help the approaching insurgents.

General Mola's phrase 'has had the fortune of becoming familiar in every language of the world'.[1] It is impossible to say precisely how and why this occurred. Perhaps it was because the struggle for Madrid was followed everywhere with passionate intensity. General Mola's boast raised the hopes of German Nazis and Italian Fascists. At the same time his phrase caught the imagination of all those who were alarmed at the undermining activities conducted in many countries by the Italian and German Governments. Mola's words, carelessly uttered, became overnight an effective symbol of increasing international tensions, charged with fear. Out of his 'fifth column', one of a series of military factors, the 'Fifth Column' was born as a general concept.

This general concept has never been clearly defined. Nowadays nearly every political ideology labels some of its opponents as 'Fifth Columnists'. Before and during World War II the term was mainly used to indicate and stigmatise the representatives and sympathisers of Fascism and National-Socialism in the countries which is was believed Italy and Germany intended to conquer. They were seen as belonging to a secret league, preparing foul deeds in the darkness of conspiracy. These representatives and sympathisers were, of course, never seen as an entirely homogeneous group. A distinction was made between several sorts of 'Fifth Columnists', between a

[1] Salvador de Madariaga, *Spain* (London, 1942), pp. 382–3.

German 'Fifth Column', consisting of Germans who did possess German nationality and of other 'Germans' who did not, and a native 'Fifth Column', consisting of movements, parties, groups, sects, all of which were more or less pro-Nazi or pro-Fascist.

The German 'Fifth Column' and the native ones cannot be entirely separated, although we know that in many cases, generally speaking, contacts between the two were less frequent and intimate than was believed before and during the war. The 'native' Fifth Columns form a most interesting but at the same time very difficult subject, as each of them can be understood only in its own national context. The present study deals almost exclusively with the German Fifth Column.

Did this German Fifth Column really exist? That after 1935 many Germans abroad tried, by order of their Government, to undermine from within potential opponents of the Third Reich is an indisputable fact. It can be proved with hundreds of documents. On the other hand it should be acknowledged that the ideas which in the course of the years developed among Germany's opponents regarding the ubiquity and the dangerous effectiveness of this Fifth Column are not entirely in accordance with facts. Fear has played a major part in developing those ideas.

The growth of this fear was by no means accidental. After 1933 ever-increasing sections of the population in countries surrounding Germany began to feel threatened. Germany was obviously rearming at a fast tempo. She was breaking one international agreement after another, Hitler being allowed to go his own way, unchecked, and although certain groups of the populations in the Western democracies consoled themselves with the thought that he was a perfect defender against bolshevism, there is no doubt that the hidden fear of German aggression, the extent of which one had experienced in World War I, was increasing yearly among the peoples as a whole. Many of Germany's neighbours instinctively felt that the Third Reich was trying to gain world domination, and that to this end energetic attempts were being made to turn all Germans living abroad into grim soldiers of the *Führer*. That was what one saw happening. In all parts of the globe, in nearby Luxembourg as well as in far-off Patagonia—everywhere in the German colonies, centrally organised groups were set up which professed their faith in Hitler as their highest faith and prided themselves on receiving and obeying instructions from Berlin.

These secret intrigues were not known in detail, but the fact that the atmosphere was one of suspicion and half-knowledge was conducive to the growth of a fear which also fed upon the development of events. In July 1934—only eighteen months after Hitler had come into power in neighbouring Germany—the Austrian Premier

Dollfuss was murdered as part of a rebellion which had obviously been organised with the knowledge of German authorities. Fear of National-Socialist aggression was stimulated by Franco's war. Again eighteen months after the outbreak of disturbances in Spain, the Austrian *Anschluss* was carried out with a speed which by itself seemed to offer convincing proof of treason from within. In appointing Seyss-Inquart Minister of the Interior, the unfortunate Schuschnigg seemed to have drawn in the Trojan Horse. The usurpation of Austria was followed, in two stages, by that of another adjacent country, Czechoslovakia; there the unity of the State had been undermined by a National-Socialist movement of German-speaking Czechoslovak citizens ('Sudeten Germans') under the leadership of Konrad Henlein, who evidently acted on German instructions. The occupation of Prague was followed by the annexation of Memel, where a National-Socialist movement had been built up, too. The particularly militant Nazis in the Free City of Danzig created an atmosphere in that region which Hitler used as pretext for occupying it on the first day of the war. Whether after the outbreak of World War II the German troops invading Poland had received assistance from the Germans living there, seemed not quite clear. Public opinion in the Western Countries, however, believed that the surprisingly quick success of the German occupation of Denmark and Norway could be explained only by the assumption that in both countries all vital points of defence had been treacherously occupied by Fifth Columnists, both native and German.

Then, as people saw it, the true and final danger of the German Fifth Column became apparent. Everywhere National-Socialist Germany had politically mobilised its citizens abroad in order to use them militarily. When, on 10th May 1940, the German armies started their general attack on the Western front, fear of the German Fifth Column developed into a veritable panic. Although all German citizens living in the Netherlands, Belgium, and France had been arrested and interned, people thought they saw signs everywhere clearly indicating that important assistance was given to the invading Germans by Fifth Columnists. Rumours were spread, roads obstructed, troops misdirected, secret lights shown, detachments shot at, wells poisoned—all manifestations of the activity of a mysterious, ubiquitous German Fifth Column which acted in every sort of disguise, as workmen and travellers, 'as pedlars, postmen, bricklayers, and at times women'; one was told that Fifth Columnists had been discovered 'disguised as priests and even nuns'.[1] The co-operation between Fifth Columnists and German aircraft was reported to have taken 'the form of signalling by setting haystacks on

[1] Marie Bonaparte, *Myths of War* (London, 1947), pp. 84-7.

fire or spreading charts or even newspapers on the ground'.[1] Former German maid servants were said to have landed in the neighbourhood of homes that had once employed them and to have made themselves useful as guides for other parachutists. In Amsterdam 'the traitors were carefully organised' :

'At one moment they succeeded in issuing a warning against people who were selling poisoned chocolates to soldiers and children. This warning which was broadcast . . . succeeded in making people feel very uneasy. For if the Fifth Columnists were selling poisoned chocolates, was there then anything which they might not do? Perhaps the milk was poisoned too, or the drinking-water. . . .' [2]

It would lead us too far from our main theme to describe in detail the consequences of the panic which originated in Western Europe in the dark year of 1940. It is, however, a fact that the ideas which have been formed in Western countries as regards the German Fifth Column are still largely determined by conceptions which have grown up under the influence of fear which was activated by military aggression. Next to the real Fifth Column an imaginary one has developed.

No doubt there have been instances when during their offensive in Western Europe cunning deceit was used by the Germans; in the southern part of the Netherlands, for example, they attempted to capture by surprise all important bridges, by having Dutch Nazis, trained in Germany, operate in faked uniforms under German military leadership. So far, however, no satisfactory proof has been found for the accusation that in 1940 in Northern and Western Europe a considerable Fifth Column was operating which made an important contribution to German victories. In many places German citizens assisted German troops after their entry. This, however, is vastly different from the many forms of secret and preparatory intrigues which many thought had been detected in 1940. It would be difficult to refute all contentions dating from that period. But it might be of some value to point out that on 9th April 1940, when the Germans suddenly occupied Oslo and the other principal towns of Norway, eighty German Nazis were living in the Norwegian capital and that serious post-war research has shown that they had no knowledge of the coming German attack and were not occupied in any special activities which might be termed Fifth-Column action.

The exaggerated lengths to which most ideas concerning this imaginary Fifth Column went, has resulted in those Germans who were considered to be the leaders of this Fifth Column denying the

[1] *The Times*, London, 20 May 1940.
[2] L. de Jong, *Holland Fights the Nazis* (London, 1941), p. 16.

entire concept of the Fifth Column. These tactics were pursued in particular by the leaders of the *Auslands-Organisation der NSDAP*, in which the members of the German Nazi Party living abroad had been organised together with German seamen. E. W. Bohle, the leader of this organisation, which will presently be described in greater detail, repeatedly stressed before the war 'that not in a single case has it been found possible to prove that even one single party comrade has come into conflict with the law of his host country anywhere in the world'.[1] Bohle maintained at Nuremberg, both before the International Military Tribunal as a witness, and before the American Military Tribunal, where he himself was one of the defendants (Case XI, the trial against Weiszäcker *c.s.*), that the *Auslands-Organisation* had no connection whatsoever with any Fifth Column:

> 'Neither from the former Deputy of the *Führer*, Rudolf Hess, nor from myself as the leader of the *Auslands-Organisation* has this organisation in any way received orders the execution of which might be considered as Fifth Column activity. Not even Hitler himself gave me any directive in that respect. Summarising I can say that the *Auslands-Organisation* did at no time, as long as I was its leader, display any activity in the sense of the Fifth Column. . . . Of course, it is known that just as citizens of the then enemy countries, Germans also were employed in the espionage and intelligence service abroad. This activity had, however, nothing at all to do with membership in the *Auslands-Organisation* groups which worked legally and entirely in the open'.[2]

Several factors make it not so simple to approach historical truth on the subject of the German Fifth Column.

Firstly, Fifth Column activity was secret activity *per se*. Not all activity was secret. A movement like the *Sudetendeutsche Partei* of Konrad Henlein in Czechoslovakia was active in public, but was, of course, very careful to hide its connections with Berlin. These connections form the crux of the matter. The *Auslands-Organisation*, already referred to, took many special measures to guarantee the secrecy of its correspondence. Its *Mitteilungsblätter* (Information Bulletins), a confidential periodical distributed to its staff all over the world, were unknown even to high officials of the *Auswärtiges Amt*.

Secondly, in the last phase of the war many collections of records which might have thrown light on the secret links of German governmental and party offices with German or other groups abroad disappeared or were destroyed. Other collections became inaccessible. No doubt it was possible at the Nuremberg trials to watch an 'awe-

---

[1] *7th Reichstagung der Auslandsdeutschen (AO) in Graz* (1939), pp. 35–6.
[2] *Trial of the Major War Criminals before the International Military Tribunal, Nuremberg 1947–1950*, Vol. X, p. 15 (in further quotations will be indicated as IMT).

inspiring march of documents',[1] but the fact that there were large gaps should not be lost sight of. The central archives of the *Auslands-Organisation* have not been discovered; the records of the Reich Security Main Office (*Reichssicherheitshauptamt*) were destroyed. No documents were used in Nuremberg from the records of the Intelligence (*Abwehr*) department of the *Oberkommando der Wehrmacht*, the principal German military institution in the field of intelligence and sabotage, nor from the records of the Party Chancellery (*Parteikanzlei*) of the NSDAP. As a result our knowledge of many subjects which might be considered to come under the German Fifth Column has remained fragmentary. This is all the more regrettable since detailed data based on indisputable documents are desirable on this theme, which, like that of espionage and secret intrigues in general, stimulates the imagination and easily leads to all sorts of stories which are as sensational as they are uncontrollable.

Thirdly, the Fifth Column is a subject which is difficult to approach, because, especially at top level, the Third Reich has shown so many elements of administrative chaos. Matters were not seen in that light before 1945. One used to consider Nazi Germany as being effectively centralised; of course, it was possible to discern a multitude of institutions taking part in undermining activities abroad, but the impression prevailed that all of them had been built into one single consistent plan and one centralised system of organisation, in which all wires were pulled by one man: the *Führer*. There was a feeling of being face to face with a devilishly organised, gigantic conspiracy. This conception is to be found in many pre-war publications on the Fifth Column. It is too simple. It is largely due to an over-estimation of the National-Socialists' power of organisation and to the general human tendency to reduce a multitude of events which are not completely clear, to one single active factor. We know better now, and we are able to discern the violent inner struggles that were hidden behind the apparent external unity of the Nazi régime. Hitler and his principal followers were without doubt linked by a similarity of goal and spirit; their aggressiveness towards the external world was, however, reflected by uncontrolled individual aggressiveness towards each other, which was prompted by the atrophy of all bodies which might have led to forms of collective action. This atrophy was entirely to Hitler's liking. After power had been taken over by the Nazis, serious discussions ceased in the German Cabinet; after February 1938 the Cabinet was no longer convened. The *Geheimer Kabinettsrat* (Secret Cabinet Council), set up in that month, existed only on paper; the *Reichsverteidigungsrat* (Reich Defence Council) was only twice in session. Hitler was repeatedly giving contradictory instructions and powers, partly from laziness, partly

[1] *Final Argument of the Prosecution*, Case XI, p. 26,920.

from calculation. He enjoyed confusing his closest Berlin collaborators no less than his foreign opponents. To General Halder he once said that he expressed his innermost thoughts to no one and added somewhat sarcastically: 'not even to those in my closest surroundings, who seem to know for sure what I am thinking'.[1] Weizsäcker's impression was 'that he enjoyed mixing up jurisdictional spheres' which led to 'a grandiose state of muddle in the order of business'.[2]

Owing to this muddle, Hitler's foreign policy, although easy to follow in its main lines, is not so easily analysed in its realisation. The German Fifth-Column activities of central German agencies developed into a combination of factors partly overlapping, partly even opposing each other. The citizens of the Reich who lived abroad, and the 'German *Volksgruppen*' (groups of ethnic Germans who were citizens of their respective countries of residence) were influenced by all those factors in differing degrees. It must also be remembered that these persons carried out their undermining activities in a bewildering variety of historical surroundings. The historical background of the German Fifth Column in the former German colony of South-west Africa is entirely different from that of the German Fifth Column in Austria; the German Fifth Column in the United States is different from the one which was active in Poland. In this study we have to restrict ourselves to the indication of a few main patterns.

First of all it should be pointed out that use and misuse of Germans living abroad or of foreign citizens who were considered by Berlin to be 'ethnically' Germans completely fitted into Hitler's plans of world conquest. These people were seen by him as outposts to be used effectively at the right moment. In his fantasies of the future, which bore eloquent testimony to his destructive inventiveness, he was completely frank on this score. Shortly after coming to power he told the *Gauleiter* of Danzig, Forster, in the presence of Hermann Rauschning:

'When I conduct a war, Forster, I will one day in the middle of peace have my troops appear for example in Paris. They will be dressed in French uniforms. They will march through the streets in full daylight. Nobody will stop them. Everything will have been prepared down to the smallest detail. They will march to the building of the General Staff. They will occupy the ministries and the building of Parliament. Within a few minutes France, Poland, Austria, Czechoslovakia, will be robbed of their leading men. The army will be without a General Staff. All political leaders will be finished. There will be unparallelled confusion. I, however, will

[1] *Proceedings of the Trial against Ernst von Weizsäcker et al. before US Military Tribunal at Nuremberg, 1947–9*, p. 20,722.
[2] ibid., p. 8,086.

have my connections with men who will set up a new government. A government to my liking. We will be able to find such men, we will find them in every country. There is no need for us to buy them. They will come out of themselves. They will be driven by ambition and blindness, party squabbles and pride. Peace will be concluded before the war has started. I guarantee you, gentlemen, that the impossible will always succeed. What is most unlikely is safest to do. We will have sufficient volunteers, men like our SA, silent and ready to sacrifice themselves. In the middle of peace we will bring them across the frontier. This must be done gradually. Nobody will believe them to be anything but peaceful travellers. Today maybe, gentlemen, you will not believe this, but I will carry it out, step by step. . . . Our strategy, Forster, is to destroy the enemy from within, to allow him to defeat himself.' [1]

The German Fifth Column was the result of this strategy. It should, however, be realised that on this, as on many other points, Hitler was unable to realise completely his most ambitious plans both as a result of actively opposing factors and of the normal inertia of man and society.

In addition to the 'native' opponents of foreign régimes whose ranks had to be penetrated and undermined, all Germans living abroad were considered by Hitler as useful participants in this Fifth-Column action. In doing so he was not only considering the so-called *Auslandsdeutsche*, persons of German nationality, but also the descendants of Germans who had emigrated abroad, particularly to the United States and to Latin-American countries, and German-speaking groups in Europe, consisting of people who were of foreign nationality: the so-called *Volksdeutsche*. There are no exact figures as to the strength of these groups. Apart from German political refugees, many Germans who lived abroad in 1933 were not keen on keeping in contact with National-Socialist Germany. The German consul in Milan complained in September 1937 that there was 'an unlimited multitude of Germans in Italy of whom nobody had had any idea' [2]—that is, who disregarded the consul's invitation to register and to keep contacts with them. It was only in March 1938 that every German citizen who stayed abroad for a period exceeding three months was forced to report to the nearest German consul. In 1933 the number of those *Auslandsdeutsche* was estimated by the Germans themselves at two to three million.

[1] Hermann Rauschning, *Gespräche mit Hitler* (Zürich, 1940), pp. 13–4. Rauschning reports on the basis of notes made at the time of his talks with Hitler. His quotations cannot be taken literally. I agree, however, with Trevor-Roper that 'the vast mass of intimate matter since available has shown Rauschning to be completely reliable' (H. R. Trevor-Roper, *The Last Days of Hitler* (London, 1947), p. 4).
[2] Letter from Otto Bene to the Head of the *Auslands-Organisation*, 11 Nov. 1937. Nuremberg document NG-072, pp. 2–4.

As regards the *Volksdeutsche*, estimates are even more vague. Chauvinistic Germans prided themselves on the fact that the German people was '*ein Hundertmillionen Volk*': a people of one hundred million. To arrive at this figure, the German-speaking Swiss were included, as well as over six million Austrians, three and a half million 'Sudeten Germans' who were citizens of the Czechoslovak Republic, and other groups of Germans extraction, including ten million persons of German descent in the United States of America. As early as in 1914 the dangerous principle of double nationality had been incorporated into the German citizenship law. Foreign nationality was not respected by the Nazis. The members of, for example, Addo Schwarzenberg's *Deutsche Jugendbund* (German Youth Association) in Chile, many of them citizens of this Latin-American Republic, were considered by Hitler to be just as much subject to his orders as were the members of the *Gau* Berlin of the NSDAP. The Party members in Austria, Danzig, and Memel were even officially and publicly subject to the party leadership in Munich.

Furthermore, all members of the NSDAP living abroad had been grouped into a separate organisation which refrained from interfering with the various local associations of *Volksdeutsche*, both in deference to foreign susceptibilities and because it was Hitler's tactics to have every organisation work in isolation and concentrate on its own task. This organisation was the *Auslands-Organisation der NSDAP* (Foreign Countries Organisation of the Party), many references to which will be found in every publication on the German Fifth Column.

It seems worth while to have a closer look at this organisation. In the 'twenties Hitler's name was almost completely unknown to Germans living abroad. In 1928–9 in some foreign countries small National-Socialist groups were set up, mostly by German soldier emigrants who were in contact with the aggressively nationalist German movements which were fighting the Weimar Republic in Germany itself. Secret connections with the Nazi Party in Germany were established and kept up mostly by German seamen, 800 of whom had joined the NSDAP by 1931. As a result it became necessary for the officials of Hitler's movement to set up an office which would maintain all contacts with groups of the NSDAP in foreign countries. The Party's organiser, Gregor Strasser, said he 'needed someone to answer the letters from abroad which were threatening to swamp my own desk'.[1] A separate office was set up, headed by a prominent member of the NSDAP who was at the same time a member of Parliament, Dr Hans Nieland. This happened in 1931. When, in January 1933, Hitler came to power, the *Auslands-Organisation* of the NSDAP had approximately 3,300 members. Nie-

---

[1] Kurt G. W. Lüdecke, *I Knew Hitler* (London, 1938), p. 372.

land's leadership led to many complaints, and in May 1933 he was succeeded by Ernst Wilhelm Bohle.

Bohle was born in Bradford, England, in 1903. He had spent his youth in England and South Africa. After World War I he studied for some time at German universities. Afterwards he entered on a business career. From December 1931 he worked as an unpaid assistant in Dr Nieland's office, out of a desire, as he put it, to instil into the Germans abroad that same degree of national solidarity which he had seen among the British and for which he envied them. On 1st March 1932 he was admitted into the NSDAP. When Dr Nieland disappeared he was appointed Head of the *Auslands-Organisation*. It was Hitler's deputy, Rudolf Hess, born in Egypt, himself an *Auslandsdeutsche* (just as Hitler was), who gave his protection to the *Auslands-Organisation*. In 1934 German seamen who were members of the NSDAP were told to join the *Auslands-Organisation*, and as from 1st April 1935 the organisation, usually referred to as the 'AO', was being administered as a separate *Gau* of the NSDAP.

Organisational development of the AO was very rapid. In nearly all colonies of '*Auslandsdeutsche*', Hitler's advent to power led to considerable tension. In general, these groups had been characterised by the same political dissents and social differentiations as the Germany of the Weimar Republic. As a result of the forced disappearance of all anti- or non-national socialist organisations in the Third Reich the position of their adherents abroad was gravely undermined. This confusion was used by members of the AO to occupy most of the important positions in these German colonies. Their own '*Ortsgruppe*' (local branch of the Berlin *Auslands-Organisation*) regularly usurped the political leadership in those groups. Most of the other non-political organisations—many of a social character—were grouped in Associations which in turn were organised into the *Verband Deutscher Vereine im Ausland*, an organisation in which effective power was again exerted by a few prominent members of the AO.

In many countries the complete organisational *Gleichschaltung* ('falling into step') of these colonies of Germans took a few years. This *Gleichschaltung* did not always take place in the same way. Let us consider Egypt, the country of origin of Rudolf Hess. His brother, Alfred Hess, was the first leader of the NSDAP for the whole of Egypt (*Landesgruppenleiter*).[1] In 1934 he left Egypt to go to Hamburg,

---

[1] Apart from the 'local branches' of the Party in foreign cities (*Ortsgruppen*), the Party had, in each country where such organisation could be built up, a *Landesgruppe*—that is, a branch comprising all Party members of the respective country. Both *Ortsgruppen* (local branches of the Party) and *Landesgruppen* (Country branches of the Party) were organised under the leadership principles: therefore, their leaders were not elected by the members, but appointed by or at least with the approval of the central AO in Berlin.

where he became Bohle's right-hand man. His successor, Hans Schröder (and now we are going to quote a German source):

'believed in the autumn of 1934 that the moment had come to take all German associations of Egypt organically into the body politic of the German people. Members of the NSDAP (in Egypt) who were at the same time members of the *Deutsche Verein* (German Club) proposed a motion aiming at a thorough change of regulations of the *Verein* in accordance with the *Führer* principle which was proposed by the *Landesgruppenleiter* and accepted unanimously —a wonderful sign of appreciation for the new national-socialist Germany. According to the new regulations which were issued by the *Landesgruppenleiter*, the leader of the *Deutsche Verein* at Cairo was appointed by the *Landesgruppenleiter* and might be deposed by him. The *Landesgruppenleiter* was solely authorised to change, eliminate, or add to the regulations of the *Deutsche Verein*. As all other groups of the *Verein*, in particular the educational association, the sport association, the women's association, the youth organization and the relief association, were subordinated to the *Deutsche Verein*, Cairo, the entire association system of (the Germans in) Cairo formed an indivisible unity. This unity aimed at bringing together all *Reichsdeutsche* and people of German origin and at gaining their cooperation in every respect.' [1]

As a second example we might take the development of the organisation in the Spanish harbour town of Malaga. Here in 1929 a retired German army officer was the first to join the NSDAP. His attempts to convert other members of the German colony failed. Not until 1932 did the NSDAP in Malaga enlist its second member. At the end of February 1933, one month after Hitler came into power in Germany, a Party member from Barcelona paid a visit to Malaga, where he made a speech about the Party programme of the NSDAP. Three Germans asked to be admitted into the NSDAP. A fortnight later the local German consul declared his readiness to join the movement. In October the first meeting took place of the *Ortsgruppe* Malaga. In December the group was visited by the German Consul-General at Barcelona, who was a member of the NSDAP, and by the leader of the German Nazis in Spain. The third meeting of the *Ortsgruppe* took place on 18th January 1934. Its leaders felt sufficiently strong to invite the entire German colony to be present at a celebration on the occasion of the first anniversary of the Nazi régime, 30th January 1934. The invitation was accepted by 'many people'.[2]

Nearly all citizens of Germany living abroad felt intimidated by the AO. There was little active resistance against the presumptions

---

[1] Otto Krahn, 'Die Deutschen Kolonien in Egypten', in *Wir Deutschen in der Welt*, 1936, p. 84.
[2] 'Chronik der Ortsgruppe Malaga der NSDAP', in *Schwarz Rotbuch, Dokumente über den Hitler-imperalismus* (Barcelona, 1937), p. 42.

of this organisation. It is, however, a significant fact that from all those who might have joined the AO as members, only a small minority did so. Membership figures were kept strictly secret, but in 1935 the percentage of members compared to the total number of German citizens living in foreign countries was called 'extraordinarily low'[1] by Bohle himself. In fact, statistics kept by the treasurer of the NSDAP, Schwarz, show that on 31st December 1937, total membership of all foreign groups was only 30,000, which is a low figure indeed compared to the two to three million German citizens domiciled abroad. Clearly the AO was a movement of an active minority. This minority has done much evil.

Of course, there was also another side to it. Undiluted evil does not exist. Through the AO, many poor Germans received financial or other assistance, many thousands of German women and children were enabled to regain their health in special rest-homes in Germany, and owing to the efforts of the AO after 1933 German seamen, who had been rather neglected by German communities abroad, were enabled to visit their own centres in foreign ports; no doubt the AO aimed at the strengthening of normal feelings of national solidarity among Germans living abroad. These and similar activities, however, should not be isolated from the context in which they took place. It was Bohle who acknowledged that 'the AO as such was a political organization'.[2] Therefore there was always a political slant to activities of the AO, which on the surface were totally unpolitical. Poor Germans who were opponents of National-Socialism received no financial or other assistance; their women and children were not allowed to visit the German rest-homes of the AO; the club-houses of German seamen in the foreign ports were centres of National-Socialist propaganda for the more than 20,000 men of the merchant marine who had joined the AO; and the feeling of national solidarity which was fostered by the AO had at the same time the ideological content of National-Socialism.

The AO's work was by no means restricted to the general and social activities which have been referred to. The AO was, also, an organisation for the political supervision of all German citizens living or sent abroad. Its authorities were instructed, for example, to gather material on the attitude of German journalists abroad as well as on the reporting of foreign journalists working in Germany. They sent secret reports on the political attitudes of people who returned to Germany, German business-men who wanted to travel abroad were required to have a declaration from the AO to the effect that there were no political objections against them. The AO's 'press controllers' (*Presswarte*) had to make out long reports on the political

[1] *Mitteilungsblatt der AO der NSDAP*, No. 33, Dec. 1935, p. 2.
[2] *Proceedings of the trial against Ernst von Weizsäcker*, et al., p. 13,486.

attitude of every paper in every country. The 'radio-controllers' (*Funk-warte*) had to report on the reception of German broadcasts. In many cases information was gathered by the AO on anti-Nazi Germans, who were then subjected to all sorts of insidious pressure from Germany; in December 1933, for example, the head of the Legal Department of the AO received information that eleven Germans in South-west Africa were agitating against National-Socialism; he wrote to the local AO organisation:

'Kindly inform me whether material, i.e. proofs, against the above-mentioned can be obtained. If this is the case, I intend to effect the withdrawal of the rights of citizenship from them.' [1]

No doubt, 'the threat of expatriation, initiated and executed by the state authorities, was one of the strongest threats wielded by the Nazis in order to keep Germans abroad obedient to their will'.[2]

Germans travelling abroad who made critical remarks on the Third Reich had to be reported by the AO. From records found in the Netherlands several cases could be quoted where representatives of the AO performed duties similar to those of the *Sicherheitspolizei* in Germany, both with regard to Dutch citizens and to German political refugees and other Germans. Worse still, in many cases political opponents of National-Socialism were arrested abroad with the assistance of the AO, smuggled aboard German ships and brought to Hamburg or other German ports where they were handed over to the *Sicherheitspolizei*. In this and in other respects, especially as regards the smuggling of propaganda, the so-called Harbour Service (*Hafendienst*), which was organised by the AO in every harbour frequented by German ships, acted as an indispensable link between the groups abroad and the AO's central agencies. Its leader, Kurt Wermke, boasted in May 1935 that 'an excellent warning service was maintained by several *Landesgruppen* and *Ortsgruppen* thanks to which we have been able to identify, to remove or to arrest a major percentage of co-nationals who were tramping, or who were inflicting damage, upon German communities abroad.' [3] Two months later he warned all foreign groups against six anti-Nazi German students, adding: 'Their transport home should be safely prepared with the assistance of the competent representatives of the Reich.' [4]

When in 1937 the Harbour Service's Central Office (*Hafendienstamt*, Hamburg) was liquidated, probably as a result of the publication of compromising documents found in Spain, its duties were taken over

[1] Quoted by Benjamin Bennett, *Hitler over Africa* (London, 1939), pp. 157–8.
[2] *National Socialism: Basic Principles, their Application by the Nazi Party's Foreign Organisation and the Use of Germans Abroad for Nazi Aims* (Washington, 1943), p. 86.
[3] *Mitteilungsblatt der AO*, No. 27, Jun. 1935, p. 5.
[4] ibid., No. 29, Aug. 1935, p. 4.

by another of the AO's many Central Offices (*Inspektionsamt*). Wermke remained in office. It is impossible to estimate the number of cases in which police functions were carried out by the AO outside Germany's frontiers contrary to all rules of international law. There may have been hundreds.

Special attention was paid by the AO to eliminating the influence of German emigrants, in particular Jewish emigrants. As part of the anti-semitic policy characterising the régime, heavy pressure was exerted by the AO on German business firms lest they should maintain connections with Jewish representatives or with Jewish firms in other countries. Bohle had sufficient understanding of foreign susceptibilities to realise that Streicher's paper *Der Stürmer* did not enhance the régime's popularity abroad. Personally he was not a rabid anti-Semite. The AO's pressure was not immediately effective in all cases. Much depended on the business firms concerned. Even in the second half of the war there were many complaints in the correspondence of the AO against German business firms which were keeping Jewish personnel in their service abroad despite all threats and forms of intimidation. Information as regards this personnel was carefully collected and kept up to date in innumerable files compiled by the Office for Foreign Trade of the AO (*Aussenhandelsamt*).

Of course, the leaders of the AO were conscious of the fact that they were infringing upon the national laws of many countries in spite of the 'Ten Commandments' printed on all membership cards ('Observe the laws of the country whose guest you are', said Commandment No. 1)—all most reasonable, and completely irrelevant, except as a form of camouflage. If a foreign government protested against the activity of the organisation and urged that it be dissolved, usually after the exchange of numerous diplomatic notes the demand was complied with and a new organisation was set up which continued the work of the former under a different name. This happened, for example, in the Netherlands. In emergencies the AO was always able to fall back upon the immunity of diplomatic or consular posts. In some cases members of the German diplomatic or consular service were at the same time authorities of the AO; in others such authorities were given diplomatic status at the last moment. The publication of incriminating German documents found in Spain, which has already been mentioned, resulted in the *Auswärtiges Amt* issuing an order to German diplomatic posts in which they were asked to investigate immediately whether it would be possible to keep all records of the AO in one of the rooms of the buildings of the legations, a matter which had 'to be handled with the utmost secrecy'.[1] In another typical case the German minister in Sofia

[1] Telegram from Dieckhoff to the German Minister, Reval, 26 Sep. 1938. Nuremberg document NG–3804, p. 1–2.

reported to Bohle that he had decided 'in view of the tense international situation to list the Party's deputy-leader of the "country group Bulgaria" with the Bulgarian Foreign Department as an official of the (German) Legation in order to safeguard the Party's interest under all circumstances.'[1] Many similar examples might be quoted.

Lastly, it is of importance that in some cases the AO functioned as a channel for the collection of political, economic, and military intelligence. The *Abwehr* (Intelligence) department of the OKW had its own liaison office in the Central Office of the AO, which was headed by one Heinz Cohrs. In one case—the Netherlands—it can be proved in detail that a military intelligence organisation was set up by the AO's principal representative, Otto Butting, in which a dozen local leaders of German groups were active. This happened immediately prior to the invasion of the Netherlands by Germany.

Small wonder that the details which in the course of the years became known regarding the activities of the AO led to considerable uneasiness on the part of many foreign governments. Before the war so many warnings were issued against the AO that one might easily be led to over-estimate the importance of the organisation in the framing of German foreign policy. Bohle maintained good relations with Hitler's deputy, Rudolf Hess. Not once, however, was Bohle personally received by Hitler. The powerful *Gauleiter* (leaders of the *Gaue*) of the Party considered him as an outsider who was 'too soft'; 'he did not seem to be dogmatic enough. He was considered as an anglophile and in a derogatory sense he was regarded as a type of intellectual'.[2]

In the beginning of 1937 Bohle was at the height of his power. The German Minister for Foreign Affairs, Baron von Neurath, took him into the *Auswärtiges Amt* as a State Secretary in charge of all matters pertaining to *Auslandsdeutsche*. But this promotion was not too important; and Bohle's small influence as a State Secretary totally disappeared when von Neurath was succeeded by Joachim von Ribbentrop, who considered Bohle merely an annoying rival. During the war Bohle's star descended together with that of Hess. He assisted Hess in writing the letter which Hess took to England. This fact remained unknown, but in the same year (1941) Ribbentrop tried to incorporate the entire AO into the *Auswärtiges Amt*. His proposals, however, were not accepted by Hitler. He only succeeded in having Bohle deprived of his function as State Secretary. When Germany capitulated, Bohle was a disillusioned man. His plea of

---

[1] Letter from the German Minister Sofia to the Head of the AO, 28 Sep. 1938. Nuremberg document NG-2561, p. 1.
[2] Witness Alfred Leitgen, *Proceedings of the trial against Ernst von Weizsäcker*, et al., pp. 13,942-3.

guilty to the charge of membership, after 1st September 1939, in the criminal organisation of the SS was 'the only plea of guilty ever entered in any of the Nuremberg trials'.[1]

Let us look back on the AO for one moment. We can consider as the dominating feature of this organisation the strengthening of politcal cohesion among the *Auslandsdeutsche* in order to foster German imperialist aims; as a result the AO exerted a disruptive influence on the countries in which these *Auslandsdeutsche* were living.

If we maintain the distinction between, on the one hand, the strengthening of political cohesion among German citizens abroad and foreign supporters of National-Socialism and, on the other hand, the promotion of the political disruption of real and potential opponents of the Third Reich, one can discern that the other organisations which were engaged in Fifth-Column activities put their main accent either on the one or on the other of these two aspects, although there was hardly any institution of the Third Reich that kept strictly within the limits set for it.

Apart from the AO, political cohesion among the *Auslandsdeutsche* was also promoted by the *Auswärtiges Amt*, which, for example, financed the sending abroad of hundreds of Party orators for the celebration of national holidays, and by the Department of Joseph Goebbels, the *Ministerium für Volksaufklärung und Propaganda* (Ministry for Popular Enlightenment and Propaganda), which saw to it that in the German Press and radio much attention was paid to the position of the *Auslandsdeutsche*. The *Auslandsdeutsche* were also the object of scientific study on the part of the *Deutsches Auslands Institut*. This had been founded in Stuttgart in 1917. In 1933 it was nazified. In that year a *Volksdeutscher* from Rumania, Prof. Dr Richard Csaki, was nominated director. Just as kindred scientific institutes—for example, the *Ibero-Amerikanisches Institut*—the *Deutsches Auslands-Institut* closely co-operated with the *Akademischer Austauschdienst* (Academic Exchange Service), which was supervised by Party circles and saw to it that the interests of National-Socialism were served in the exchange of students and professors.

We have already indicated that in a few cases *Auslandsdeutsche* were used for activities aimed directly at the undermining of the security of other States. This brings us to the tricky terrain of espionage. Direct espionage was largely carried out by the organisation of Admiral Canaris, the *Abwehr*. In some cases the *Abwehr* made use of connections built up by the AO. Apart from the *Abwehr*, agents were also sent abroad by the *Hauptamt Sicherheitspolizei*, the *Sicherheitshauptamt des Reichsführers SS* (Heinrich Himmler) and the *Geheimes Staatspolizeiamt*, which, together with the *Reichskriminalpolizeiamt*,

[1] Telford Taylor, *Final Report to the Secretary of the Army on the Nuremberg War Crimes Trials under Control Council Law*, No. 10 (Washington, D.C., 1949), p. 214.

were combined into the notorious *Reichssicherheitshauptamt* in September 1939. In 1937, 40,000,000 RM were spent by the *Geheimes Staatspolizeiamt* alone. Hundreds of agents must have been active abroad, many of them German citizens. It should, however, be remembered that British, French, American, and other citizens performed similar tasks for their own secret services, although probably of a less reprehensible character and on a much smaller scale. The typical feature of National-Socialist policy with regard to German citizens abroad is not the fact that some were used for intelligence services, but the attempt to secure a tight grip on all of them and to transform an unorganised mass into organised shock troops of the Third Reich.

Similar attempts were carried out by the Nazi leaders with regard to the so-called *Volksdeutsche*—that is, citizens of foreign countries who considered themselves, or who were considered by the Nazis, as 'ethnic Germans'.

In the United States and in many Latin-American republics the National-Socialists made systematic efforts to amalgamate the *Auslandsdeutsche* and the *Volksdeutsche* into one dynamic entity. In those States, however, the governments were anxious to develop among immigrants and their descendants a feeling of cohesion with and loyalty to their new homeland, thus counteracting their consciousness of their original nationality. Had National-Socialist strategy been successful, it would have caused the dissolution of those States into their originally multi-national composite parts. Such dissolution was in fact promoted by the Nazis. They greatly overestimated their chances of success. In contrast to most representatives of the *Auswärtiges Amt*, they overlooked the fact that nothing would lead to more violent reactions than those very attempts to turn both *Auslandsdeutsche*—that is, German citizens residing in those countries—and *Volksdeutsche*—that is, citizens of those countries who were of German descent—into a single National-Socialist phalanx. It was of importance that Hitler's conception of a country like the United States had little connection with reality. The strongest Power on earth was believed by him to be a loose and corrupt conglomeration in which power might easily be won by the independent German element. In fact, little effective influence was exerted by organisations like the German–American Bund, which were set up with the assistance or sympathy of National-Socialist Germany.

National-Socialist attempts to penetrate and dominate German *Volksgruppen* (ethnic groups) and to use them for Germany's aims had most success where these *Volksgruppen* were living as strong and coherent units in political and economic conditions which they believed to be unsatisfactory. The two most striking examples are offered by Austria and Czechoslovakia. It is moreover a significant fact that fully-fledged National-Socialist parties were in existence in these (which both border on Germany) partly before, partly immediately after World War I, at a time when Hitler had not yet found any important response for his action in Germany itself. Hitler knew exactly how the feelings of dissatisfaction on the part of these *Volksgruppen* should be stimulated and played off in propaganda which was directed both against the governments of the countries where they lived and against the big European Powers. In reality their lot did not interest him. To him they were only pawns. He was just as ready to shed crocodile tears on the 'persecutions' against the Sudeten Germans and the *Volksdeutsche* in Poland, as to sacrifice the cruelly oppressed German minority in Southern Tyrol which had been annexed by Italy, on the altar of his alliance with Mussolini.

As the *Auslandsdeutsche*, the *Volksdeutsche* ('ethnic Germans', i.e. foreign citizens of German extraction) were the object of energetic action on the part of numerous central German agencies, official and unofficial. Their political cohesion was promoted by the *Auswärtiges Amt* and the *Ministerium für Volksaufklärung und Propaganda* by which from 1933 to 1938 more than 4,000 domestic broadcast programmes were devoted to the position of the *Volksdeutsche* in other countries. Much attention was paid to the *Volksdeutsche* by the *Deutsche Auslands-Institut*. Political work among them was greatly assisted by a League dating from before World War I, the *Verein für das Deutschtum im Ausland* (Association for Germanism Abroad), commonly called the VDA, which had started as an organisation to assist German schools abroad. In 1933 the VDA was led by an aggressive Nazi from Carinthia (Austria), Dr Hans Steinacher, who allowed himself to be called *Reichsführer*, a privilege which he was soon to drop, as it seriously annoyed the *Reichsführer-SS*, Heinrich Himmler, that he was not the only one who could claim this magnificent title. Relations between the VDA and the AO were far from satisfactory; Bohle and Steinacher were jealous of each other's influence. This unequal struggle was lost by Steinacher, who lacked the protection of influential men like Rudolf Hess. In particular he was powerless against the growing influence of the SS. When in July 1938 the *Volksdeutsche Mittelstelle* (Co-ordination Agency for Ethnic Germans) was set up, later to become one of the *Hauptämter* (Main Offices) of the SS, which was charged with the co-ordination of all activities amongst the *Grenzdeutschen* (German-speaking people, who lived close beyond the German borders) and *Volksdeutschen*, Steinacher was forced to disappear. In the beginning of 1939 he had to drop the leadership of the VDA. There is adequate evidence that political organisations of the *Volksgruppen* (compact groups in other countries who spoke German or, anyway, considered themselves or were considered by the National-Socialists to be of German extraction)

F F

abroad received important financial support through the VDA. In many cases the money was provided by German official agencies. In general, the VDA closely co-operated with organisations of Germans who had emigrated from areas which Germany had been forced to cede after World War I, as the *Bund der Elsass-Lothringer im Reich*, the *Schleswig-Holsteiner Bund*, the *Deutsche Memelland Bund*, and others. Through these organisations cultural and political influence was exerted among the respective German *Volksgruppen* abroad; sometimes they also received economic assistance. An important device was to advance money to pro-National-Socialist German-speaking farmers abroad in order to enable them to buy the land they cultivated. It is an obvious supposition that agencies like the *Abwehr* (military intelligence) made good use of the connections of the VDA and its subsidiaries in foreign countries in which the most aggressive representatives of the ethnically German minority groups (*Volksgruppen*) had been organised.

We have been able to indicate here only a few themes. Basically the case of the *Volksdeutsche*—the minority groups in other countries who either because they spoke German or because they were, or were claimed to be, of German descent—is even more involved than that of the *Auslandsdeutsche*—German citizens residing abroad. The more one tries to analyse the factors which have conditioned the success of National-Socialist propaganda among many of these *Volksdeutsche* groups, the more one realises how deeply this success was rooted in history. In many cases during Hitler's régime only a new chapter was added to the age-old struggle between the Germans and their neighbours, especially the Slavs. Hitler was unable to create entirely new opportunities. He made destructive use of opportunities, both manifest and hidden, presented to him as a result of this struggle, and which he was confident he would decide once and for all in Germany's favour.

And, of course, in studying the way in which National-Socialist Germany was able to strengthen and, in turn, to profit from, the nationalistic efforts of *Auslandsdeutsche* and *Volksdeutsche*, it must be remembered that to a considerable degree Hitler's chances of success depended on the development of international relations. On the part of the Western-European democracies, lack of insight into the true nature of the Nazi régime played an important role. The annexation of Austria and the break-up of Czechoslovakia can never be explained in the terms of *Auslandsdeutsche* and *Volksdeutsche* alone.

We now approach a new field of activity of the German Fifth Column. The promotion of political cohesion and of an aggressive spirit amongst the *Auslandsdeutsche* and *Volksdeutsche* meant that all States which Hitler considered to be his opponents were being indirectly weakened. This weakening, however, was also directly fostered from Berlin—the Government, and Munich—the Party Headquarters. Disruption was the aim of all German propaganda abroad. To create and stimulate anti-Semitism was one of the sharpest and most dangerous weapons in Goebbels' inexhaustible armoury. This propaganda was served by virtually all organisations which we have mentioned so far. We ought to add a few others. The *Aufklärungsausschuss* ('Committee for Enlightenment'), which had its office in Hamburg, is of particular interest on account of the extremely cunning methods of camouflage followed by this Institute. It specialised in the publication of articles in foreign papers which had seemingly been written by foreigners, in reality, however, by the Institute's staff in Hamburg. The so-called *Fichtebund* (Fichte Association) and the violently anti-Semitic *Weltdienst*, Erfurt (World Service) have also been of importance. Both organisations must have disposed of considerable financial means. The aggressively Pan-germanist *Fichtebund*, which was directed by one Heinrich Kessemeyer, had been set up in 1914; after 1919 it was one of the principal centres of the world-wide propaganda against the Versailles Treaty; in 1935 alone seventy-five pamphlets, eleven in German and sixty-four in other languages, were distributed by the *Fichtebund*, totalling more than five million copies. It co-operated with the *Verband der Deutschen Vereine im Ausland* (Association of German Organisations in Foreign Countries) and with the *Auslands-Organisation der NSDAP*, although in some cases the work of the *Fichtebund* was stopped or curtailed as being too offensive. Its Spanish representatives had built up a file with the names of 100,000 Spaniards who were believed to be interested in its publications. In fact, the *Fichtebund* had its relations in almost every country.

The *Weltdienst* (World Service) was the creation of a German retired officer, Ulrich Fleischhauer. Once a fortnight he published a vehemently anti-semitic periodical which in 1935 was appearing in six different languages. The publications of the *Weltdienst* were sent to many *Auslandsdeutsche* for their own enjoyment and for distribution among their friends and associates.

The disruption of opposing states was also promoted by the National-Socialist régime by means of giving support to political or non-German national minorities. The idea was to use such minorities as a crowbar to prise the States concerned out of their joints. Relations were therefore established with numerous National-Socialist parties in other countries and also with organisations of dissatisfied, non-German national minorities. On this terrain Alfred Rosenberg was especially active. He was born a Russian subject in Reval and educated in St Petersburg, and he is therefore another *Volksdeutscher* who became prominent in the Nazi movement. To the honours of being the editor-in-chief of the *Völkischer Beobachter* and the author of many books which were as authoritative as they were little read, he hoped to add that of Minister for Foreign Affairs. In 1933, however, Hitler reassured and flattered von Neurath by pointing out that he himself 'really did not understand foreign policy'.[1] He preferred von Neurath's continuation in office; his stolid features would lend the régime an air of respectability. The impatient Rosenberg was consoled and fobbed off with permission to set up the *Aussenpolitisches Amt der NSDAP* (Foreign Policy Office of the Party), the official task of which was:

'1. To observe the foreign political situation from the point of view of National-Socialist faith and to take up and carry out all ensuing tasks.

2. To propagate the aims and efforts of the National-Socialist State in the field of foreign policy into all offices and formations of the Party.

3. To inform the world abroad, especially foreigners who are visiting Germany or who are staying there as representatives of the Press, about the true nature and aims of National-Socialism in order to create a better understanding of the vital necessities of the German people in the midst of foreign nations.'[2]

Every single one of these tasks could not fail to bring Rosenberg repeatedly into conflict with numerous other German agencies. In fact, he was soon considered a nuisance by many other high authorities of the régime, especially by Baron von Neurath and by Goebbels. Ribbentrop was furious at his constant interference. On paper the organisation of the *Aussenpolitisches Amt* seemed to be perfect, in reality its activities were of an erratic character. Little systematic work was done. Nevertheless Rosenberg was able to establish contacts in certain countries which helped Hitler's aggressive policy. This holds particularly true for Rumania and Norway. It was Rosenberg who in December 1939, on the basis of former contacts, introduced Vidkun Quisling to Admiral Raeder and to Hitler, thus stimulating Hitler to prepare the sudden occupation of Norway and the resulting occupation of Denmark.

It was Rosenberg who also made every effort to incite national minorities in other countries to action aimed at greater independence. In 1934 an *Internationale Arbeitsgemeinschaft der Nationalisten* (International Working Party of Nationalities) was set up under the auspices of the *Aussenpolitisches Amt der NSDAP*. In France, Rosenberg was in contact with small groups who wanted autonomy for Brittany, Alsace, and Corsica. With his assistance a *Verband Erwachender Kelten* (Association of Awakening Celts) was founded in

---

[1] Rudolf Rahn, *Ruheloses Leben* (Duesseldorf, 1949), p. 118.
[2] *Organisationsbuch der NSDAP* (Munich, 1943), p. 310. Point 1 does not occur in some earlier editions of the *Organisationsbuch*, at least in the 1937 one which I was able to consult.

Munich, which it would be difficult to describe as a centre of Celtic civilisation. Close relations were also maintained by Rosenberg with Ukrainian and White Russian refugees. Generally, however, his high expectations—that he would be able to mobilise these and sundry national minorities against their respective governments— were not fulfilled. The small movement for autonomy for Brittany, for example, received much German support after the German occupation of France. In July 1940 a conference was called at which the 'national independence of Brittany' was to be proclaimed. The conference ended in total failure amid the jeers of the population; and when in November 1940 Hitler was told by Admiral Raeder that the question of Brittany was still being pursued 'in certain quarters' and led to many difficulties with the French, he curtly issued instructions 'that the Brittany question is to be dropped'.[1]

In many cases not only the victims of the German Fifth Column but also the Fifth Columnists themselves did not fully realise to what extent they were being used and abused by the *Führer*. To him they were like tools, easy to handle, easy to put away.

Activities partly similar to those of the *Aussenpolitisches Amt der NSDAP* were also pursued by a separate office which Joachim von Ribbentrop was allowed to set up in 1934, the *Büro Ribbentrop*. Driven by unbridled ambition, Ribbentrop had found his way to Hitler in the early 'thirties. He had given him important support among influential sections of Berlin society. In 1934—while not yet Foreign Minister—he was able to gain permission to set up this separate 'Bureau Ribbentrop', which came very close to being a rival Foreign Office. Its staff was soon totalling 300 people. With this big apparatus at his disposal he was able to have his eager fingers in every pie. A description of Ribbentrop's policy, both as head of his *Büro* and, after February 1938, as Foreign Minister succeeding von Neurath, falls outside the scope of this study; but we ought to add that Ribbentrop, who had his full share of responsibility for the reign of Nazi terror in the occupied countries, was, at the same time, particularly keen to set up associations of foreigners and Germans in those countries under the pretence of 'promoting goodwill'. Their most important task was to sap the will to resistance of the Western democracies. A striking example is offered by the *Comité France-Allemagne* (founded as early as 1935), in which an important part was played by Ribbentrop's protégé Abetz.

In this connection it should also be pointed out that all international organisations, set up by National-Socialist Germany were really used as vehicles of explicit or implicit Nazi propaganda. Pacifist tendencies abroad were carefully fostered by the Nazi organisation of German ex-servicemen. Robert Ley's international organ

[1] *Führer Conferences on Naval Affairs* (London, 1947), Vol. II (1940), p. 125.

Freude und Arbeit (Joy and Work) aimed at undermining the influence of free trade unions and at creating interest in the 'new', 'social'-minded Germany. The Hitler Youth, which made every attempt to educate the young *Auslandsdeutsche* and the young *Volksdeutsche* in the spirit of National-Socialism, also took the initiative to set up an *Internationale Arbeitsgemeinschaft für Jugendherberge* (International Working Party for Youth Hostels). Here we see the same phenomenon which struck us in describing the *Auslands-Organisation der NSDAP*: activities, which in themselves were certainly not evil, and in different circumstances would have been entirely innocent, but which became dangerous because they were carried out by National-Socialists. They formed part of an entity which, however, one should not picture as a carefully thought-out conspiracy. It was rather an aggressive pattern which revealed itself as the years progressed; its general direction had been indicated by Hitler, from whom it also received continuous new impulses.

Again we should like to stress that these impulses were adopted by no more than a minority of the German citizens residing abroad (*Auslandsdeutsche*). Within Germany the approach and the outbreak of World War II were watched by many with deep concern. Even greater concern was felt by a large proportion of the Germans abroad—if for no other reason than for their better understanding of the ultimate superiority of the coalition which Hitler had created against himself. The fact that a more sober judgment prevailed in many of those circles may easily remain hidden behind the feverish activity which ever after 1933 so many official and unofficial German agencies were displaying abroad.

Of necessity the preceding part of this study has largely consisted of a summary of certain data, policies and institutions; this contribution would exceed its proper length if we tried to prove in detail every fact and every connection we have mentioned. We are confident, however, that we have shown it to be likely that the 'German Fifth Column' was anything but a cheap propaganda phrase invented by Germany's diabolical enemies. Most of the sensational stories regarding the Fifth Column dating from 1940 may, it is true, be disregarded; it seems, however, that behind the phantom of an imaginary Fifth Column a real and solid National-Socialist Fifth Column was in existence. Its picture is very complicated; it was, by its nature, devious instead of simple and straightforward.

This Fifth Column was an instrument of aggression, both direct aggression and aggression 'by proxy', which was wielded by Hitler with amazing dexterity. In the period preceding Germany's military attacks a host of offices, organisations and movements were active in the service of his aggressive intentions. In the different countries these offices, organisations and movements, which we have met so far in this study, come to the fore in ever new combinations. The German minority in Poland was influenced in the same spirit, but certainly not in the same way or with the same methods, as the German minority in Alsace. Much depended on the action which originated from this minority itself. And, as we have already said, this action was dependent on the historical development and the position of the minority concerned in the state in which it lived. In each case these varieties of combining and opposing factors must be analysed and evaluated against the background of the development of the international situation. This would mean too great a digression, but it might be as well to have here a closer look at one specific case of German Fifth-Column aggression which seems a convenient example because it shows so many of the tendencies which have been indicated: the case of the Sudeten Germans.

We cannot, even for this particular example of aggression by proxy, pay adequate attention to the international aspects, but the international developments leading up to the Munich Agreement will be known to our readers in their main outline. One word of warning should be added. Comparatively speaking, the German Fifth Column in Czechoslovakia was particularly efficient. Impressions derived from this case should not be generalised.

The historical background of the role played by the Sudeten Germans,[1] three and a half million citizens of Czechoslovakia (most of them inhabiting Czechoslovakia's frontier districts), is of singular importance. Czechs and Germans have quarrelled since the Middle Ages, until a state of feeling was created where, as one authority put it:

'The Sudeten German regards the Czech as a half educated creature, to some extent saved by German influence, who is politically intolerable and unreliable, socially never satisfied, and always pushing for his nation, while the Czech sees in the Sudeten German the invader, the remorseless conqueror; the apostle of world hegemony, the economic tyrant, who only lives in the land in order to subject the Czech people socially, politically and in every other way.'[2]

In setting up an independent Czechoslovakia in 1918–19 the Allied Powers realised that the future of the new state was by no means assured. Their experts stated 'that the prosperity and perhaps

---

[1] It must be pointed out that, while these people were German-speaking, they were not German citizens even before the establishment of the independent State of Czechoslovakia in Nov. 1918, but until that time the territory where they lived was for centuries part of the lands governed by the Habsburgs; they were, therefore, Austrian citizens.

[2] Dr Gustav Peters, quoted by Elizabeth Wiskemann, *Czechs and Germans* (London, 1938), p. 118.

also the existence of the new state will depend on the success with which it incorporates the Germans as willing citizens.' [1]

From the very beginning there was a hard core among the German-speaking population who were decidedly unwilling citizens of President Masaryk's republic. Until after Germany's acceptance of the Treaty of Versailles in the summer of 1919, Sudeten German volunteers who clandestinely crossed the frontier into Germany were armed and trained in bases all around Czechoslovakia. They were not many, but what they lacked in numbers they made up in fanaticism. Thus there existed a German National-Socialist workers party in Czechoslovakia before the NSDAP was properly organised in Munich. At a Pangerman conference held in Salzburg, Austria, in 1920, the Sudeten Nazis met their like-minded friends from Austria and from Germany (Adolf Hitler and Anton Drexler). There an 'Interstate Bureau of the National-Socialist party of the German people' was set up with a Viennese Nazi lawyer, Dr Walther Riehl, acting as chairman. After the failure of Hitler's *putsch* in Munich in November 1923, another such conference was held in Vienna in December 1923, where the Nazi deputies from Prague, Jung and Knirsch, 'were splendid, contributing all their Party could spare'.[2] These Sudeten Nazis had the same programme, the same banners, the same uniform, the same battle-songs as the German ones.

In the 'twenties the vast majority of the Sudeten Germans were not keen on supporting National-Socialism. In 1929, for example, out of seventy-three German deputies elected to the Czechoslovak Parliament fifty-one belonged to the parties supporting the Coalition Government. On that occasion only eight seats were won by the Sudeten Nazis. They gained considerably in strength, however, when after 1929 the Sudeten districts were badly hit by the world economic crisis. Mass unemployment formed one of the principal bases of National-Socialist success. The Sudeten Germans were made to believe that their economic distress was due to a deliberate policy on the part of the Prague Government. Old resentments were stimulated and the atmosphere became heavy with dissatisfaction. Gradually the Sudeten Nazis who had maintained their connections with the Reich were able to increase their hold on the German-speaking minority of Czechoslovakia.

In January 1933 Hitler came into power.

Among the German citizens living in Czechoslovakia—their number was substantial—all influential positions were quickly occu-

---

[1] *Report on Czechoslovakia*, adopted 16 Jun. 1919, at the twenty-second meeting of the Committee on New States of the Peace conference, quoted by Wiskemann, *Czechs and Germans*, pp. 91–2.
[2] Lüdecke, *I Knew Hitler*, pp. 175–6.

pied by German Nazis who were members of the *Auslands-Organisation*. They were not allowed to set up an openly National-Socialist organisation. An existing relief society, the *Hilfsverein* (Assistance Association), was turned into 'an instrument of the NSDAP'.[1] Anticipating the course of events, we should like to point out here that it is very likely that the political movement among Sudeten Germans received considerable assistance from this *Hilfsverein*, which had its connections throughout Czechoslovakia. This cannot be proved in detail. The principal factor, at any rate, in the process of disruption which manifested itself in Czechoslovakia, were not the German citizens residing in Czechoslovakia, the *Auslandsdeutsche*, but the Sudeten German group, the *Volksdeutsche*, themselves.

It was among these *Volksdeutsche* that a new political movement came to the fore shortly after 1933. The original Sudeten Nazi Party, of which Jung was one of the leaders, had organised *Sport-Abteilungen* which were closely modelled on the SA troops of the NSDAP.[2] When it was revealed before the courts that these paramilitary formations had been guilty of intrigues against the Republic of Czechoslovakia, the Nazi Party was forbidden there, and its foremost leaders, among them Jung and another member of Parliament, Krebs, fled to Germany. This happened in the autumn of 1933.

A substitute movement had been set up in time. Krebs had approached one Konrad Henlein and had requested him 'to found a new movement before the Party was officially dissolved'. This occurred on 4 October. Three days earlier, however, Henlein 'issued an appeal to the Sudeten Germans to form a Sudeten German Home Front'.[3]

Konrad Henlein, who was born in the Sudeten area in 1898, had been a bank employee until in 1925 he had changed his uneventful job for that of instructor of the German Gymnastic Association in the small Bohemian town of Asch, the most important of the Pangerman sport organisations among the Sudeten Germans. He educated its members in a truly National-Socialist spirit. His speeches were perfect examples of Nazi ideology. It was therefore by no means accidental that it was he who was asked to continue the work of Jung and Krebs. Henlein called his new movement the *Sudeten Heimatfront* (Sudeten Home Front). In 1935 the name was changed to *Sudetendeutsche Partei* (Sudeten-German Party) or SDP. When in October 1934 the Party held its first mass meeting, 20,000 people were present.

---

[1] *Jahrbuch der Auslands-Organisation der NSDAP*, Vol. I, 1942, pp. 32–3.
[2] It will be noted that the abbreviation of '*Sport-Abteilungen*' is also 'SA', just as that of their German parallel organisation; but they were able to claim that their initials stood for 'Sport Groups' and not for 'Storm Troops'.
[3] Article by Krebs in the *Neue Zeitung*, Innsbruck, 1 Oct. 1943, quoted by B. Bilek, *Fifth Column at Work* (London, 1945), p. 26.

From the very beginning financial support was forthcoming from Germany. In 1933 the Party's organ received 120,000 Czech crowns from the Reich to pay its debts. It is claimed that in the same year the VDA, acting on instructions given by Hitler's deputy, Hess, granted Henlein a subsidy of eight million crowns.[1] After the Czechoslovak elections of 1935, when Henlein's Party succeeded in obtaining forty-four deputies, or over 60 per cent of all elected representatives of the German-speaking population in Czechoslovakia, the *Auswärtiges Amt* started to pay a fixed subsidy to Henlein. Every month 12,000 RM were paid out to him by the German Legation at Prague, and another 3,000 RM were put at the disposal of his Berlin liaison Office, the *'Büro Bürger'*, which was also a centre for the distribution of propaganda material. These arrangements did not prevent Henlein from sending a telegram of loyalty to President Masaryk when in 1935 the election results were made known. There is adequate evidence that apart from these subsidies other and much larger sums were made available to Henlein, at least in 1937, by various agencies of the German NSDAP. In those cases the *Auswärtiges Amt* 'was only the postman'.[2]

As Hitler's régime grew stronger its interest in Czechoslovakia increased. This was pointedly stressed by the nomination, in 1936, of Krebs and Jung as members of the German *Reichstag*. Konrad Henlein, however, was not fully trusted in all Nazi circles. In the eyes of the SS especially there had been too many contacts between him and members of the aristocracy. Furthermore, in some of his speeches Henlein had underlined the value of parliamentary democracy. But Hitler was far too clever a politician not to understand that it would be difficult to make the Sudeten Germans rally behind another leader. He realised that Henlein had solid reasons for camouflage and that the very criticisms levelled against him were proof of Henlein's tactical skill.

In November 1937 Hitler was clear in his mind that in the near future he would have to 'eliminate' (*'niederzuwerfen'*)[3] not only Austria, but also Czechoslovakia. Shortly afterwards, on 19th November 1937, Henlein wrote a secret report to Hitler of which a copy was sent to Hitler's Foreign Minister, von Neurath, from which the following passages deserve special attention:

> 'The Sudeten Germans are conscious of their particular political duty towards the anti-German mission and the policy of Czechoslovakia as ordained by the West and the Bolshevist East, and are resolved to be a factor in the National-Socialist policy of the Reich.

[1] Bilek, *Fifth Column*, p. 28.
[2] Witness Altenburg, *Proceedings of Weizsäcker Trial*, p. 17,607.
[3] Hossbach protocol, Nuremburg document PS–386, IMT, Vol. XXV, p. 408.

'The policy hitherto pursued by the Sudeten-German Party has made the following contribution to *the new order in Europe in the spirit of National-Socialism and of the policy of the Reich:*

(*a*) The Sudeten-German Party . . . has become in its struggles the unequivocal proof of the injustice of the Versailles Treaty structure.

(*b*) By the mere fact of coming forward as the strongest party in Czechoslovakia, and at the same time as a party of opposition to the system of government the Party has destroyed the fiction of the Czech national state to be politically consolidated on national, social and economic foundations and has materially weakened the political and military value of Czechoslovakia as an ally. . . ..

'The Sudeten-German Party must camouflage its profession of National-Socialism as an ideology of life and as a political principle. As a party in the democratic parliamentary system of Czechoslovakia it must, outwardly, alike in its own structure, and in the organisation of the Sudeten-German element, employ democratic parliamentary methods. In consequence, it may appear to uninitiated German circles of the Reich to be disunited and unreliable. This disunion, however, cannot be avoided so long as there still exists the necessity of a legal party, and the existence of such a party in Czechoslovakia presupposes the profession of democratic principles.

'The apparent lack of unity of the Sudeten-German Party is intensified by the circumstance that at heart it desires nothing more ardently than the incorporation of Sudeten-German territories, nay the whole of the Bohemian, Moravian, and Silesian area, within the Reich, but that outwardly it must stand for the preservation of Czechoslovakia and for the integrity of its frontiers, and must try to display some apparently genuine aim in the sphere of internal politics to justify its political struggle.

'Although the leaders of the Sudeten-German Party were from the outset clear as a result of their profound political experience, that an understanding between Germans and Czechs in Czechoslovakia was not possible, it was necessary at the first great political demonstration of the Party at Böhmisch Leipa in 1934 to put forward *understanding* as the aim of practical politics and to introduce in 1937 the so-called "bills for the protection of ethnic minorities" to satisfy the demand for Sudeten German *autonomy*. Only thus was it possible to put the Czechs in the wrong before the world and to undertake the presentation by means of propaganda of the Sudeten-German question before the Powers which guaranteed the Minority Protection clauses of the Treaty of St Germain (Peace Treaty with Austria of 1919), but above all in the eyes of the British. . . .

'Today, however, the Sudeten-German Party knows that . . . it will become increasingly difficult to put forward an aim in internal politics which can be represented as a *practical political* aim even with the bare resemblance of a possibility of achievement in the eyes of serious foreign observers, to say nothing of the Sudeten-German following. *From the standpoint of practical politics it has become senseless to advocate autonomy of the Sudeten-German territory, since it is this very region that has been made the concrete wall and fortified belt of the Czechoslovak state.'*

Henlein believed that there was 'an urgent need for a discussion of fundamental principles between the leaders of the Reich and the leaders of the German *Volksgruppen* in regard to the further conduct of the policy of the Sudeten-German Party'.[1] Apparently such discussions had not yet taken place at the highest level.

Even before events in Austria moved to the dramatic climax of the *Anschluss*, 11th to 12th March 1938, Henlein had established close personal connections with the German Minister in Prague, Eisenlohr. On 4th February 1938, Eisenlohr reported to Berlin that Henlein had

'promised to come to Prague every week and, apart from the contacts already existing between the Legation and his deputy, K. H. Frank, and the fraction of the Sudeten-German Party, also to maintain regular personal contact with me. For his part he expressed the wish that I should inform the Reich Government of the present situation and of the possibilities which might sooner or later arise from it, so as to prepare and facilitate attitudes and decisions which might become necessary.' [2]

Barely six weeks later the 'possibilities' to which Henlein had alluded began to be outlined. After the annexation of Austria Czechoslovakia was clearly next on the list of Hitler's victims. Henlein's followers were told to beware of precipitate action. Hitler's policy needed careful preparation. Every grievance of the Sudeten Germans had to be exploited to the utmost, every chance of a reasonable agreement between the Sudeten Germans and the Prague Government had to be sabotaged. It was in the interest of German policy to establish close co-ordination between Henlein's policy and that of Hitler. Timing and synchronisation ought to be perfect. Again Eisenlohr took up the problem with the leader of the Sudeten Germans. In the week following the *Anschluss* he held 'exhaustive discussions' with Henlein and his deputy K. H. Frank, in the course of which the German Minister received the 'following assurances':

1. Course of German foreign policy as communicated by Legation is to be sole determining factor for policy and practical procedure of Sudeten-German Party. My instructions are to be strictly observed.

---

[1] *Documents on German Foreign Policy, 1918–45*, Series D, Vol. II (Washington 1949), pp. 56–62.
[2] ibid., p. 123.

2. Public speeches and Press will be passed in agreement with me. . . .
3. Party leadership is abandoning former intransigent course, which might eventually lead to political complications, and will adopt policy of gradual furthering of Sudeten-German interests. Aims are to be determined always jointly with me and supported by parallel diplomatic action. . . .
4. If consultation with Berlin offices is necessary or desirable before any of Henlein's important propaganda declarations this would be proposed and arranged through Legation.
5. All communications from Sudeten Germans to German offices are to pass through hand of Legation.
6. Henlein will have weekly contact with me, and, if requested, come to Prague at any time.'

Eisenlohr hoped 'to keep Sudeten-German Party under close control which is more than ever necessary for coming developments in foreign policy'.[1]

One day after this interview Henlein wrote a letter to Ribbentrop, whom he complimented 'upon the happy turn of events in Austria'. 'Our gratitude to the *Führer* will be shown in redoubled efforts in the service of Greater German policy', Henlein stated. He asked to be granted an audience in Berlin with two of his closest collaborators.[2]

On 28 March 1938 Henlein had his first meeting with Hitler. Rudolf Hess, Ribbentrop and *SS Gruppenführer* Lorenz, head of Himmler's *Volksdeutsche Mittelstelle*, were also present. Conversations lasted for almost three hours.

'The *Führer* stated that he intended to settle the Sudeten-German problem in the not too distant future. He could no longer tolerate Germans being oppressed and fired upon. He told Henlein that he knew how popular he (Henlein) was and that he was the rightful leader of the Sudeten-German element.'

Henlein objected that he could only be a substitute, but Hitler magnanimously replied: 'I will stand by you, tomorrow too you will be my viceroy [*Sie sind auch morgen mein Statthalter*].[3] I will not tolerate difficulties being made for you by any department whatsoever within the Reich.'

The report of this significant meeting ended:

'The purport of the instructions which the *Führer* has given to Henlein is that demands should be made by the Sudeten-German

---

[1] *Documents on German Foreign Policy, 1918–45*, Series D. Vol. II (Washington, 1949), pp. 169–70. German text, IMT, Vol. XXXII, p. 4.
[2] Letter from Henlein to Ribbentrop, 17 Mar. 1938, Nuremberg document PS–2789, IMT, Vol. XXXI, p. 117.
[3] Actually, when Germany occupied the Sudeten territory a few months later, Henlein was dropped.

Party which are unacceptable to the Czech Government. . . . Henlein himself would be responsible for events for the time being. However, there would have to be close co-operation. Henlein summarised his view to the *Führer* as follows: "We must always demand so much that we can never be satisfied." The *Führer* approved this view.' [1]

In April 1938 Henlein announced his so-called eight Karlsbad demands, asking virtually complete autonomy for the Sudeten Germans. It is interesting to point out that in the middle of May he had a conversation in London with Winston Churchill and Sir Archibald Sinclair in the course of which 'he offered to give his word of honour that he had never received orders or even recommendations (*Weisungen*) from Berlin'.[2] It is equally noteworthy that when on 7th September 1938 the Karlsbad demands were accepted in their entirety by the Czech Government, this and any other agreement were turned down by Henlein and his followers, 'although one of the Party leaders when he read the plan cried out in amazement: "Good Heavens, they have given us everything!" '.[3]

As the summer of 1938 progressed, the pressure which Hitler exerted on Prague by means of the docile Henlein, and also in other ways, was increased. He played for very high stakes, but he was confident that victory would be his. He had made up his mind: 'Czechoslovakia had to be eliminated'. His 'unalterable decision', expressed in a top secret order of 30 May 1938, was that Czechoslovakia 'had to be smashed by military action in the near future'. In preparation for this action the 'war of propaganda had to intimidate Czechoslovakia by means of threats and to wear down her power of resistance on the one hand, on the other it had to give instructions to the national groups in order to enable them to assist military action'.

The moment the attack started, German armoured columns would as soon as possible have to break through the Czech defence fortifications. 'Success would be dependent on co-operation with the population of the Sudeten-German frontier districts, deserters from the Czechoslovak army, parachutists or airborne troops and the organs of the sabotage service.' All preparations for sabotage and insurrection had to be carried out by the *Oberkommando der Wehrmacht* (Supreme Command of the Armed Forces) 'in agreement with and according to the requirements of the branches of the *Wehrmacht* (Armed Forces) so that their effects in both time and place will harmonise with operations by the army and air force'.[4]

---

[1] *Documents on German Foreign Policy, 1918–45*, Series D, Vol. II, pp. 197–8.
[2] cf. Note of a Conversation with Mr Churchill and Sir Archibald Sinclair (sent to the Foreign Office, 15 May 1938), *Documents on British Foreign Policy, 1919–39*, Third Series, Vol. I, p. 633.
[3] Bilek, *Fifth Column*, p. 39.
[4] Nuremberg document PS–388, IMT, Vol. XXV, pp. 34–9.

The order of 30th May clearly shows that Henlein's movement would not only be used as a political crowbar against Czechoslovakia; in this case Hitler was determined to make full use of the military possibilities offered by the German Fifth Column. It is a pity that on this subject no documents have been published so far from the records of the *Abwehr*, which had been charged with all preparations. The Czech counter-espionage, however, had been able to penetrate the *Abwehr* networks, and it was very well aware of the intrigues prepared and carried out by Admiral Canaris and his staff.

On Czechoslovak territory a wide network of agents was organised. Special recruiting agents were dispatched who enlisted Sudeten-German terrorists. Next:

'In Germany special courses were arranged in the use of firearms and for carrying out acts of terrorism, lasting for a week-end or longer. There were weekly courses, where participants received both theoretical and practical training in the use of the revolver, the automatic pistol and the Mauser rifle, in grenade throwing, in dealing with explosives etc. Training was given both to individuals and groups in attacking observers and sentries in trenches, sentries guarding objectives such as warehouses, barracks, small fortifications, etc. The assaults were made with real weapons. Even exact replicas of Czechoslovak fortifications were set up so that N.C.O.'s could demonstrate the model destruction of such obstacles and concrete defences. Further the syllabus included night training.

'At the end of the course Czechoslovak citizens swore an oath on a drawn sword, pledging loyalty to the Supreme Commander of the German Army, the Chancellor of the Reich, Adolf Hitler. By placing their right hand on the sword or by raising their right arm, the men swearing this oath pledged themselves to lay down their lives for the cause of Greater Germany.' [1]

These intrigues would have been unthinkable unless a considerable part of the Sudeten-German minority was ready to take certain risks. This readiness was present. By that time many Sudeten-German opponents of National-Socialism had been cowed by the drumfire of Henlein's propaganda. After the *Anschluss* of Austria, Hitler seemed invincible. In fact, at the municipal elections of 22nd May 1938 Henlein's party gained a resounding victory. It polled no less than 91 per cent of all Sudeten-German votes. This was only a stimulus to intensify an atmosphere in which Henlein was receiving adoration, if not as the Deity Hitler himself, then at any rate as his Prophet. It repeatedly happened that when he was passing through a village women fell on their knees at the roadside and raised their

---

[1] Bilek, *Fifth Column*, pp. 10–11, cf. Document 10, pp. 93–6, and document 17, pp. 105–6.

clasped hands towards him as their saviour, 'while he raises his hand as if in blessing calling out: "The day will come!"' [1]

The active National-Socialist minority—by 31st March 1939, out of three and a half million Sudeten Germans barely 120,000 had joined the NSDAP—had succeeded in creating a chauvinist ecstacy in the entire Sudeten area which daily led to incidents with the Czech population—incidents which in their turn were used by the Sudeten-German Press and the radio in Germany to intensify the ecstacy. The German 'war of propaganda' which Hitler had ordered grew in ferocity from month to month. In the middle of May 1938 German papers were instructed to appoint a special editor for Sudeten-German questions. His articles had to be violent in tone. What had been written so far was qualified by the Ministry of Propaganda as 'weak lemonade'.[2] In the next months, however, the mixture was continually made stronger, until in September 1938 a stage had been reached which was bordering on the pathological.

During the summer of that year the number of secret German military training courses was increased. Some of them started operating at the end of July. Militant young Sudeten Germans, all of them potential saboteurs and guerillas, were organised in small groups of three and four members. In some villages there were as many as ten such groups. Members were for the most part recruited from the ranks of Henlein's storm-trooper organisation, the *Freiwilliger Schutzdienst* (Voluntary Protection Service), or FS. At the same time arms were poured into the country in considerable quantities. By the middle of August (18th August 1938) Henlein issued a secret circular to his storm-troop commanders instructing them 'to observe every movement of Czechoslovak troops and State Police'. Changes of residence of 'Czechs, social democrats, communists and Jews' should be reported, and 'elements putting up resistance should be dispatched across the frontier (into Germany) as quickly as possible'. Henlein also ordered:

'(a) The men included in the FS must be severely examined as to reliability with a view to serious tasks. As far as possible, people without family obligations should be accepted.

(b) Everything necessary for the rebellion should be secured from the appropriate district leader, who will approach the appropriate provincial leader.'[3]

The Czech authorities were very much alive to the dangers threatening them. They were not prepared to have their state

---

[1] Anonymous report quoted by Bilek, *Fifth Column*, p. 220.
[2] Quoted by Walter Hagemann, *Publizistik im Dritten Reich* (Hamburg, 1948), p. 351.
[3] Bilek, *Fifth Column*, pp. 43-4, document 34 p. 116.

sustain mortal injury from Henlein and his followers. In the middle of September a climax was reached. On the fifteenth of that eventful month the *Sudetendeutsche Partei* was forbidden and Henlein's storm troops were disbanded. Martial law was declared in the frontier districts. Sporadic fighting took place. The rebellion of the Sudeten Germans quickly collapsed. Their leaders fled to Germany, where a *Sudetendeutsches Freikorps* (Sudeten-German Free Corps) was organised under the command of Konrad Henlein. In the first nine days after it had been set up this *Freikorps*, which was partly financed by German big business, was involved in over 300 engagements with Czech units.

When matters reached this point decisions as to the future of the Sudeten-German districts were no longer taken by Henlein or Benes. The drama had been finally transferred to a larger stage. Even if military use of the Sudeten-German Fifth Column had failed, the political use to which Hitler had been able to put its activities abroad had proved effective. It was one of the factors leading to the Munich Agreement as a result of which the territories inhabited by the Sudeten Germans were incorporated into Germany. This made Czechoslovakia's fall inevitable.

Of course we do not claim to have given here a full explanation of this fall. The weakness of the Western Powers, the sharp distrust between the Soviet Union and the West, the vacillations of many Czech elements—they all influenced a fatal development. These, however, were secondary factors. The primary factor was Hitler. He was the only one who took action according to his own desires and ideas, using Konrad Henlein as his principal tool and ally, incorporating most institutions of aggression, both open and hidden, which we have met in this study, playing with perfect virtuosity on the grand piano of world policy evoking both the darkest sounds of ferocious threats and the shrillest notes of faked moral indignation.

To be sure, the case of the Sudeten Germans cannot be considered to be typical, in the sense of providing a yardstick against which all other cases of German Fifth-Column action could be measured. We have already pointed out that impressions derived from this case of *Volksdeutsche* aggression (that is, with the help of a compact German-speaking minority) may not be extended to other cases, and even less to the *Auslandsdeutsche* groups (that is, to German citizens living in other countries). Circumstances were different in every single case. It is, however, clear that Fifth-Column action on the part of German *Volksgruppen*, finally leading to military assistance to the German invaders, was most intense in such cases where these *Volksgruppen* were subjected to the highest pressure. Here again this pressure should usually be seen as a reaction to the even heavier pressure exerted previously by the 'ethnic Germans' in those areas on the remaining population. This was particularly so in the case of Poland and Yugoslavia. In the Western democracies it is possible to discern a German political Fifth Column. It is also true that individual Germans carried out intelligence and sabotage activities, mainly in connection with the *Abwehr*, which have led to prominent trials, for example, in Britain and the United States. A mass Fifth Column in a military sense did not, however, exist in Norway, Denmark, the Netherlands, Belgium (there has been more activity in Luxemburg) and France, and has never been organised for Britain and the United States. Moreover, in these two countries all Germans who were considered to be dangerous were interned soon after the outbreak of war. In Britain during the panic of 1940 this measure was even extended to all Germans (and Austrians), political refugees included. As regards the Soviet Union, there is no evidence that the Third Reich succeeded in building up connections with the groups of *Volksdeutschen* who were living mainly in the Ukraine and near the Volga. In the autumn of 1941, when the Ukraine was being over-run, the Volga Germans were transferred to Siberia by order of the Soviet Government.

We are now dealing with World War II and it does not seem necessary to describe in detail the experiences of *Auslandsdeutsche* and *Volksdeutsche* during the war. The *Auslandsdeutsche* were interned in many countries which were at war with Germany. Some tens of thousands of them served in the German armed forces after their return or escape to Germany. The *Volksdeutsche* groups suffered the misfortune of Heinrich Himmler's special attention. As *Reichskommissar für die Festigung deutschen Volkstums* (Reich Commissar for the strengthening of Germanism), a function which he assumed in the autumn of 1939, he induced or forced many hundreds of thousands of them to leave their homes and to settle in districts where they were often considered as intruders. One of Himmler's closest collaborators, Gottlob Berger, the head of the *SS-Hauptamt* (SS Main Office) exerted merciless pressure on the *Volksdeutsche* lest they should fail to provide sufficient recruits for the *Waffen-SS*. It is interesting to observe that, as Germany's military position deteriorated, all exclusiveness was abandoned in those circles of the SS which used to be especially keen to 'keep the blood pure'. Himmler's racial fanaticism triumphed in meting out harsh punishment to people of 'Germanic race' who refused to become Germans. It did not matter to Himmler that in the conglomeration of peoples in Eastern Europe the application of any yardstick would lead to the most arbitrary interpretations. A nice illustration was given by the Reich Finance Minister, Schwerin von Krosigk, who in 1939 paid a visit to a finance office in Posen, in occupied Poland, where thirty Poles and eighteen *Volksdeutsche* were employed:

'They were assembled in a long room. I went there and addressed the various *Volksdeutsche*. The first ones I talked to had Polish names and spoke only broken German. I then turned to the Poles. The first Poles I talked to were called Luther and Müller and spoke German fluently. When I told the supervisor that obviously he had placed them the wrong way round, he said "No, it is actually like that. People with German names call themselves Poles here and vice versa. Nobody knows what's what around here. . . . !" ' [1]

In practice only little materialised of Himmler's ambitious plans for re-Germanisation. During the last phase of the war in Central and Eastern Europe everybody was considered to be German by the SS who stood on Germany's side, whatever the composition of his blood mixture. The wheel had turned full circle.

It should also be mentioned that, of course, *Auslandsdeutsche*—German citizens who lived abroad or who knew foreign countries from having lived there previously—were used as administrators of German-occupied countries or for purposes of intelligence and sabotage. The latter activities were organised, at first by the *Abwehr* and later in the war by the *Reichssicherheitshauptamt* (Reich Security Main Office). I have not the impression that this happened on an exceptionally large scale, but that is another chapter where, however, one might find most curious and glaring examples of the growing disorganisation and muddle of the *Führer* State.

We have come to the end. It remains, however, to point out that the chapter of the Fifth Column has had a tragic aftermath for most of the 'ethnic Germans' and Reich Germans concerned. In several countries they lost all their possessions after the war. Millions of them were moved to Germany under conditions which led to much suffering, especially in Eastern and Central Europe. Many factors, no doubt, contributed to the desire 'to be rid of the Germans', but one of them, which was particularly effective because it was born out of experience of the recent past and of fear for the future, was the desire to remove the German Fifth Column. The *Auslandsdeutsche* were believed to have intrigued against the nations which had given them a home, to have infringed upon the sacred right of hospitality, thus wounding many host-countries in their most sensitive spots. The *Volksdeutsche* were considered to have lacked even the most basic loyalty towards the countries they inhabited and of which they had been citizens.

As regards many of these persons, the accusations levelled against them as a group were perfectly justified. Particularly in view, however, of the low percentage of members of the *Auslands-Organisation* (Foreign Countries Organisation of the German Nazi Party), it

[1] *Proceedings of Weizsäcker Trial*, p. 23, 361.

might not be out of place to ask whether in this whirlpool of misery numerous families have not been engulfed which, just as practically all non-Germans, ought to be seen as victims rather than as enthusiastic supporters of the most cruel and backward régime known to recorded history.[1]

[1] Since writing this brief survey the author has more fully dealt with the problems indicated in a book called *De Duitse Vijfde Colonne in de tweede wereldoorlog* (The German Fifth Column in World War II) (Amsterdam, 1953). An American edition is due to be published by the University of Chicago Press in the spring of 1955.

INDEX